Langenscheidt's Pocket Japanese Dictionary

Japanese-English
English-Japanese

Edited by the
Langenscheidt Editorial Staff

LANGENSCHEIDT

NEW YORK · BERLIN · MUNICH

compiled by LEXUS with

秋山真有子 (*Mayuko Akiyama*)
八幡尚子 (*Takako Y Hyland*)
Anthony P Newell

General editor: Peter Terrell

© *Langenscheidt KG, Berlin and Munich*
Printed in Germany

01
02
03
04
05
*
5
4
3
2
1

Preface

Here is a new dictionary of English and Japanese, a tool with some 40,000 references for those who work with the English and Japanese languages at beginner's or intermediate level.

Focusing on modern usage, the dictionary offers coverage of everyday language, including vocabulary from areas such as computers and business.

The Japanese in this dictionary is written both in Japanese characters and in a romanized pronunciation system – a modified version of the standard Hepburn.

The two sides of this dictionary, the English-Japanese and the Japanese-English, are quite different in structure and purpose. The English-Japanese is designed for productive usage, for self-expression in Japanese. The Japanese-English, which can also be accessed through the Jōyō Kanji index, is a decoding dictionary, a dictionary to enable the native speaker of English to understand Japanese.

Clarity of presentation has been a major objective. The editors of this book have set out to provide the means to enable you, the user of the dictionary, to get straight to the translation that fits a particular context of use. Is the *mouse* you need for your computer, for example, the same in Japanese as the *mouse* you don't want in the house? Is *flimsy* referring to furniture the same in Japanese as *flimsy* referring to an excuse? The English-Japanese dictionary is rich in sense distinctions like this – and in translation options tied to specific, identified senses.

Grammatical or function words are treated in some detail, on both the English-Japanese and the Japanese-English sides. And a large number of idiomatic phrases are given to show how the two languages correspond in context.

All in all, this is a book full of information, which will, we hope, become a valuable part of your language toolkit.

Contents

How to use the dictionary

To get the most out of your dictionary you should understand how and where to find the information you need. Whether you are yourself writing a text in Japanese or wanting to understand a text written in Japanese, the following pages should help.

1. How and where do I find a word?

1.1 English headwords. The English word list is arranged in alphabetical order.

Sometimes you might want to look up terms made up of two separate words, for example **antivirus program**, or hyphenated words, for example **absent-minded**. These words are treated as though they were a single word and their alphabetical ordering reflects this. Compound words like **bookseller**, **bookstall**, **bookstore** are also listed in alphabetical order.

The only exception to this strict alphabetical ordering is made for English phrasal verbs - words like **♦ go off**, **♦ go out**, **♦ go up**. These are positioned directly after their main verb (in this case go), rather than being scattered around in alphabetical positions.

1.2 Japanese headwords. The Japanese word list is arranged in English alphabetical order by being sorted on the romanization system or romaji. So if you know how a word is pronounced, or how it is written in romaji, you can look it up straightforwardly.

If, however, you are decoding a Japanese character, and have no idea how it is pronounced or written in romaji, then you can make use of one of the three indexes of Japanese characters. These indexes are on pages 11-32.

1.3 Running heads

If you are looking for an English or a Japanese word you can use the **running heads** printed in bold in the top corner of each page. The running head on the left tells you the *first* headword on the left-hand page and the one on the right tells you the *last* headword on the right-hand page.

2. Swung dashes

2.1 A swung dash (~) replaces the entire headword when the headword is repeated within an entry:

sly zurui ずるい; *on the* ~ kossori to こっそりと

Here *on the* ~ means *on the sly*.

2.2 When a headword changes form in an entry, for example if it is put in the past tense or in the plural, then the past tense or plural ending is added to the swung dash - but only if the rest of the word doesn't change:

fluster *v/t* menkurawaseru めんくらわせる; *get ~ed* urotaeru うろたえる

But:

horrify: *I was horrified* zotto shimashita ぞっとしました

2.3 Headwords made up of two, or sometimes three, words are replaced by a single swung dash:

> ♦ **hold on** *v/i* (*wait*) matsu 待つ; TELEC kiranaide matsu 切らないで待つ; *now ~ a minute!* chotto matte ちょっと待って

> ♦ **come in on**:~ *a deal* keiyaku ni sanka suru 契約に参加する

3. What do the different typefaces mean?

3.1 All Japanese and English headwords and the Arabic numerals differentiating English parts of speech appear in **bold**:

> **alcoholic 1** *n* arukōru-chūdoku-kanja アルコール中毒患者 **2** *adj* arukōru-iri (no) アルコール入り(の)

3.2 *italics* are used for :

a) abbreviated grammatical labels: *adj, adv, v/i, v/t* etc

b) all the indicating words which are the signposts pointing to the correct translation for your needs

c) explanations

> **mailbox** (*in street*) posuto ポスト; (*of house*) yūbin'uke 郵便受け; COMPUT mērubokkusu メールボックス

> **Thai 1** *adj* Tai (no) タイ(の) **2** *n* (*person*) Tai-jin タイ人; (*language*) Tai-go タイ語

> **serve 1** *n* (*in tennis*) sābu サーブ **2** *v/t food, meal* dasu 出す; *customer in shop* ... no yō o ukagau ...の用をうかがう; *one's country, the people* ... ni tsukaeru ...に仕える

> 脚 **ashi** leg (*of table etc*)

> あたし **atashi** I (*used mainly by women*)

> な **na** (*forms adjectives*): 憶病(な) **okubyō** (*na*) cowardly

3.3 All phrases (examples and idioms) are given in ***secondary bold italics***:

> 損失 **sonshitsu** loss; 損失を出す ***sonshitsu o dasu*** make a loss

> **linguist** (*professional*) gengo-gakusha 言語学者; ***she's a good ~*** kanojo wa gaikokugo ga jōzu da 彼女は外国語が上手だ

3.4 The normal typeface is used for the translations.

3.5 If a translation is given in italics, and not in the normal typeface, this means that the translation is more of an *explanation* in the other language and that an explanation has to be given because there is no real equivalent:

> **banker's card** chekku kādo, kogitte o tsukau toki ni hitsuyō na kādo チェックカード、小切手を使うときに必要なカード

> 単身赴任 **tanshinfunin** *living away from one's family after a job transfer*

4. What do the various symbols and abbreviations tell you?

4.1 A solid black lozenge is used to identify a phrasal verb:

♦ **auction off** ... o kyōbai ni kakete shobun suru ...を競売にかけて処分する

4.2 A white lozenge is used to divide up longer entries into more easily digested chunks of related bits of text:

a, an ◊ (*no translation*): *a cat* neko 猫; *an apple* ringo りんご ◊ (*with countword*): *a pencil and an eraser* enpitsu ippon to keshigomu ikko 鉛筆一本と消しゴム一個; *five men and a woman* go-nin no otoko to hitori no onna 五人の男と一人の女 ◊ (*per*): *$50 a ride* ikkai gojū doru 一回五十ドル; *once a week* isshūkan ni ikkai 一週間に一回

It is also used, in the Japanese-English dictionary, to split different translations when the part of speech of each translation is different:

いらいらする **iraira suru** frustrating; nerve-racking ◊ get worked up

海抜 **kaibatsu** altitude; elevation ◊ above sea level

4.3 The abbreviation F tells you that the word or phrase is used colloquially rather than in formal contexts. The abbreviation V warns you that a word or phrase is vulgar or taboo. Be careful how you use these words. The abbreviation H means that the word is used to make yourself humble before the person you are speaking to.

4.4 A colon before an English or Japanese word or phrase means that usage is restricted to this specific example (at least as far as this dictionary's choice of vocabulary is concerned):

accord: *of one's own* ~ jihatsuteki ni 自発的に

次第 **shidai**: あなた次第です *anata shidai desu* it's up to you

4.5 The letters X and Y are used to indicate insertion points for other words if you are building a complete sentence in Japanese, for example:

♦ **get away 1** *v/i* (*leave*) tachisaru 立ち去る **2** *v/t*: *get X away from Y* Y kara X o toriageru YからXを取り上げる

shoestring: *do X on a* ~ shōgaku-shikin de X suru 小額資金でXする

Suspension points (...) are used in a similar way:

below 1 *prep* ... no shita ni ...の下に; (*in amount, rate, level*) ... ika ni ...以下に

5. Does the dictionary deal with grammar too?

5.1 All English headwords are given a part of speech label, unless, in normal modern English, the headword is only used as one part of speech and so no confusion or ambiguity is possible. In these cases no part of speech label is needed.

abolish haishi suru 廃止する

lastly saigo ni 最後に

But:

glory *n* eikō 栄光 (*n* given because 'glory' could be a verb)

own[1] *v/t* shoyū suru 所有する (*v/t* given because 'own' is also an adjective)

5.2 Japanese headwords are not given part of speech labels. Where their English translations can be of more than one part of speech, then these are separated by a white lozenge. For example:

異なる **kotonaru** differ ◊ dissimilar

前 **mae** front ◊ before; ago

5.3 Where a Japanese word has a grammatical function, this is illustrated:

な **-na** ◊ (*forms negative imperative*): 忘れるな **wasureru-na** don't forget ◊ (*for emphasis*): きれいだな **kirei da na** it's beautiful, isn't it!

か **ka** ◊ (*question particle*) いいですか **ii desu ka** is it OK? ◊: ...か...か **... ka ... ka** either ... or...

5.4 Object particles

Object particles such as 'no' and 'ni' are included with translations of transitive verbs in the English-Japanese half of the dictionary. If an object particle is not given, then you can assume that the correct particle to use is 'o'.

win 2 *v/t* ... ni katsu ...に勝つ; *lottery, money, prize* ateru 当てる

In phrasal verbs the object particle is always given.

♦ **live on 1** *v/t rice, bread* ... o tabete ikiru ...を食べて生きる

6. (no) and (na):

Where the Japanese translation of an adjective is given with (no) or (na) the general rule is that the 'no' or 'na' is only used if the adjective is placed before its noun:

quiet shizuka (na) 静か(な)

a quiet room shizuka na heya 静かな部屋

the room was quiet heya wa shizuka deshita 部屋は静かでした

flowery *pattern* hanamoyō (no) 花模様(の)

flowery dress hanamoyō no doresu 花模様のドレス

the dress is flowery doresu wa hanamoyō desu ドレスは花模様です

7. Verbs of activity and verbs of being

The translation of some basic prepositions (or postpositions in Japanese) depends on the type of verb used with the preposition. Verbs of activity are verbs like: work, run, eat, verbs of being are verbs like: live, be.

I used to work in Tokyo watashi wa Tōkyō de hataraite imashita 私は東京で働いていました

does he still live in Tokyo? kare wa mada Tōkyō ni sunde imasu ka 彼はまだ東京に住んでいますか

The pronunciation of Japanese

All Japanese characters in this dictionary are accompanied by a romanized script known as romaji. Not all romaji letters are pronounced as you would normally expect on the basis of English. The following is a guide to the pronunciation of romaji.

Vowels

There are only five vowel sounds in Japanese:

a	as in f*a*ther	o	as in p*o*rt (but shorter)
e	as in g*e*t or b*e*d	u	as in p*u*t
i	as in h*ea*t (but shorter)		

Remember that there are no silent letters. So when 'e', for example, comes at the end of a word it must be pronounced: 'are' is ah-reh' (not as in 'are' in English).

A bar, or macron, over a vowel means that it has twice the length of a vowel without a bar. Distinguish carefully between obasan (aunt) and obāsan (grandmother) or koji (orphan) and kōji (construction).

When two vowels are adjacent they should not be made into a single sound (as in English), but each should be pronounced separately:

ai	like Thai	ie	pronounced ee-eh
ae	pronounced ah-eh	oh	pronounced o-oo
ee	pronounced eh-eh	ue	pronounced oo-eh
ei	like the ay of pay		

Consonants

g	as in *g*o or *g*irl	s	always as in ma*s*s (never z)
j	as in *j*ar	y	as in *y*et

Note that 'y' is never a long 'i' sound. For example, the Kyū of Kyūshū is like the 'cu' of cute and never like the 'ki' of kite.

The letter 'r' sounds more like an 'l'.

Double consonants are an important feature of Japanese. Each part of a double consonant should be pronounced separately: anna is pronounced an-na; kippu is kip-pu; gakkō is gak-kō.

An apostrophe is used to indicate a slight pause when speaking.

Stress

To all intents and purposes there is no stress in Japanese. So give the same value to all syllables: say Yo-ko-ha-ma not Yo-ko-HA-ma.

Abbreviations

adj	adjective	MUS	music
adv	adverb	*n*	noun
ANAT	anatomy	NAUT	nautical
BIO	biology	*neg*	negative
BOT	botany	*pej*	pejorative
Br	British English	PHOT	photography
CHEM	chemistry	PHYS	physics
COM	commerce, business	POL	politics
COMPUT	computers, IT term	*prep*	preposition
conj	conjunction	*pron*	pronoun
EDU	education	PSYCH	psychology
ELEC	electricity,	RAD	radio
	electronics	RAIL	railroad
F	familiar, colloquial	REL	religion
fig	figurative	s.o.	someone
FIN	financial	SP	sports
fml	formal usage	sth	something
GRAM	grammar	TECH	technology
H	humble, showing	TELEC	telecommunications
	humility to the	THEA	theatre
	listener	TV	television
interj	interjection	V	vulgar
LAW	law	*v/i*	intransitive verb
MATH	mathematics	*v/t*	transitive verb
MED	medicine	→	see
MIL	military	®	registered
MOT	motoring		trademark

Jōyō Kanji

Although Japanese uses more kanji than those listed here, this table, known as the Jōyō Kanji List, is the full listing of the 1,945 characters that the Japanese government recommends as a guideline for the Japanese press and for the general writing of Japanese by both native and non-native speakers.

1 stroke

一 ichi, itsu, hito(tsu)
乙 otsu

2 strokes

七 shichi, nana(tsu)
丁 tei, chō
九 kyū, ku, kokono(tsu)
二 ni, futa(tsu)
人 jin, nin, hito
入 nyū, i(ru), hai(ru)
八 hachi, ya(tsu), yat(tsu)
刀 tō, katana
力 ryoku, riki, chikara
十 jū, jit(tsu), tō,
又 mata
了 ryō

3 strokes

下 ka, ge, shita, shimo, moto, sa(geru), sa(garu), kuda(ru), kuda(su), kuda(saru), o(rosu), o(riru)
才 sai
三 san, mi(tsu), mit(tsu)
上 jō, shō, ue, uwa, kami, a(garu), a(geru), nobo(ru), nobo(seru), nobo(su)
丈 jō, take
万 man, ban
与 yo, ata(eru)
丸 gan, maru(i)
及 kyū, oyo(bu), sen, chi
亡 bō, mō, na(i)
凡 bon, han
刃 jin, ha
勺 shaku
久 kyū, ku, hisa(shii)
口 kō, ku, kuchi
土 do, to, tsuchi
士 shi
夕 seki, yū
大 dai, tai, ō(kii), ō(ini)
女 jo, nyo, onna, me

子 shi, su, ko
寸 sun
小 shō, chii(sai), ko, o
山 san, yama
川 sen, kawa
工 kō, ku
己 ko, ki, onore
干 kan, ho(su), hi(ru)
弓 kyū, yumi

4 strokes

不 fu, bu
中 chū, naka
丹 tan
午 go
升 shō, masu
屯 ton
乏 bō, tobo(shii)
五 go, itsu(tsu)
互 go, taga(i)
井 sei, shō, i
介 kai
今 kon, kin, ima
化 ka, ke, ba(keru)
仁 jin, ni
仏 butsu, hotoke
元 gen, gan, moto
公 kō, ōyake
分 bun, fun, bu,

	wa(keru), wa(karu)	月 getsu, gatsu, tsuki	収 shū, osa(maru)
六	roku, mu(tsu), mut(tsu)	木 moku, boku, ki, ko	本 hon, moto
円	en, maru(i)	欠 ketsu, ka(keru), ka(ku)	末 matsu, batsu, sue
内	nai, dai, uchi		未 mi
冗	jō	止 shi, to(maru)	失 shitsu, ushina(u)
凶	kyō	比 hi, kura(beru)	生 sei, shō, i(kiru), i(kasu), i(keru), u(mareru), u(mu), o(u), ha(eru), ha(yasu), ki, nama
切	setsu, sai, ki(ru)	毛 mō, ke	
刈	ka(ru)	氏 shi, uji	
匁	monme	水 sui, mizu	
区	ku	火 ka, ko, hi, ho	
匹	hitsu, hiki	父 fu, chichi	
反	han, hon, tan, so(ru)	片 hen, kata	
厄	yaku	牛 gyū, ushi	弁 ben
双	sō, futa	犬 ken, inu	甘 kan, ama(i)
友	yū, tomo	王 ō, kimi	央 ō
予	yo		甲 kō, kan
太	tai, ta, futo(i), futo(ru)	**5 strokes**	由 yū, yu, yui, yoshi
天	ten, ame, ama	以 i	母 bo, haha
夫	fu, fū, otto	北 hoku, kita	世 se, sei, yo
孔	kō	矛 mu, hoko	史 shi
少	shō, suku(nai)	玉 gyoku, tama	申 shin, mō(su)
尺	shaku, seki	巧 kō, taku(mi)	冊 satsu, saku
幻	gen, maboroshi	包 hō, tsutsu(mu)	仙 sen
引	in, hi(ku), hi(keru)	丘 kyū, oka	仕 shi, ji, tsuka(eru)
弔	chō, tomura(u)	凸 totsu	代 dai, tai, ka(waru), yo, shiro
心	shin, kokoro	凹 ō	
戸	ko, to	且 ka(tsu)	
手	shu, te, ta	必 hitsu, kanara(zu)	他 ta
支	shi, sasa(eru)	斥 seki	付 fu, tsu(ku)
文	bun, mon, fumi	矢 shi, ya	令 rei
斗	to	左 sa, hidari	刊 kan
斤	kin	丙 hei	召 shō, me(su)
方	hō, kata	出 shutsu, sui, de(ru), da(su)	加 ka, kuwa(eru)
日	nichi, jitsu, hi, ka	民 min, tami	功 kō, ku
		半 han, naka(ba)	幼 yō, osana(i)
			皮 hi, kawa

写	sha, utsu(su)	巨	kyo	任	nin,
市	shi, ichi	旧	kyū		maka(seru)
玄	gen	白	haku, byaku,	仰	gyō, kō, ao(gu),
古	ko, furu(i)		shiro(i), shira		ō(se)
平	hei, hyō,	示	ji, shi,	伝	den, tsuta(eru)
	tai(ra), hira		shime(su)	仮	ka, ke, kari
外	gai, ge, soto,	永	ei, naga(i)	全	zen, matta(ku)
	hoka, hazu(su)	氷	hyō, kōri, hi	企	ki,
占	sen, shi(meru),	礼	rei, rai		kuwada(teru)
	urana(u)	主	shu, su, omo,	合	gō, ga', ka',
正	sei, shō,		nushi		a(u)
	tada(shii), masa	石	seki, shaku,	会	kai, e, a(u)
圧	atsu		koku, ishi	肉	niku
用	yō, mochi(iru)	立	ritsu, ryū,	次	ji, shi, tsugi,
冬	tō, fuyu		ta(tsu)		tsu(gu)
処	sho	目	moku, boku,	壮	sō
汁	jū, shiru		me, ma	兆	chō, kiza(shi)
去	kyo, ko, sa(ru)	田	den, ta	羽	u, ha, hane
払	futsu, hara(u)	皿	sara	印	in, shirushi
打	da, u(tsu)			州	shū, su
兄	kei, kyō, ani	**6 strokes**		刑	kei
号	gō			列	retsu
台	dai, tai	多	ta, ō(i)	交	kō, maji(waru),
可	ka	死	shi, shi(nu)		maji(eru),
句	ku	気	ki, ke		ma(jiru),
司	shi	両	ryō		ma(zaru),
右	u, yū, migi	朱	shu		ma(zeru),
好	kō, kono(mu) ,	年	nen, toshi		ka(u),
	su(ku)	西	sei, sai, nishi		ka(wasu)
奴	do	衣	i, koromo	充	jū, a(teru)
布	fu, nuno	吏	ri	妄	mō, bō
犯	han, oka(su)	毎	mai	考	kō,
穴	ketsu, ana	再	sai, sa,		kanga(eru)
広	kō, hiro(i)		futata(bi)	老	rō, o(iru),
庁	chō	曲	kyoku,		fu(keru)
尼	ni, ama		ma(garu)	缶	kan
囚	shū	伏	fuku, fu(seru)	色	shiki, shoku,
四	shi, yon,	休	kyū, yasu(mu)		iro
	yo(tsu),	件	ken	争	sō, araso(u)
	yot(tsu)	伐	batsu	危	ki, abuna(i),
札	satsu, fuda	仲	chū, naka		aya(ui),

	aya(bumu)	
羊	yō, hitsuji	
灰	kai, hai	
辺	hen, ata(ri), be	
込	ko(mu), ko(meru)	
巡	jun, megu(ru)	
迅	jin	
同	dō, ona(ji)	
匠	shō	
式	shiki	
弐	ni	
池	chi, ike	
汚	o, kitana(i) , kega(su), kega(rawashii), yogo(su)	
汗	kan, ase	
江	kō, e	
忙	bō, isoga(shii)	
各	kaku, onoono	
地	chi, ji	
寺	ji, tera	
至	shi, ita(ru)	
先	sen, saki	
存	son, zon	
在	zai, a(ru)	
扱	atsuka(u)	
吐	to, ha(ku)	
叫	kyō, sake(bu)	
吸	kyū, su(u)	
舌	zetsu, shita	
向	kō, mu(ku)	
后	kō	
名	mei, myō, na	
如	nyo, jo	
妃	hi	
帆	han, ho	
行	kō, gyō, an, i(ku), yu(ku), okona(u)	

芋	imo
芝	shiba
共	kyō, tomo
安	an, yasu(i)
守	shu, su, mamo(ru), mori
宇	u
字	ji, aza
宅	taku
光	kō, hika(ru), hikari
当	tō, a(taru)
劣	retsu, oto(ru)
吉	kichi, kitsu
尽	jin, tsu(kiru)
回	kai, e, mawa(ru)
因	in, yo(ru)
団	dan, ton
朴	boku
机	ki, tsukue
朽	kyū, ku(chiru)
肌	hada
有	yū, u, a(ru)
早	sō, sa', haya(i)
旨	shi, mune
百	hyaku
旬	shun
灯	tō, hi
成	sei, jō, na(ru)
自	ji, shi, mizuka(ra)
血	ketsu, chi
糸	shi, ito
米	bei, mai, kome
舟	shū, fune, funa
虫	chū, mushi
耳	ji, mimi
竹	chiku, take

良	ryō, yo(i)
身	shin, mi
来	rai, ku(ru), kita(ru), kita(su)
束	soku, taba
里	ri, sato
我	ga, ware, wa
更	kō, sara(ni), fu(keru)
亜	a
寿	ju, kotobuki
位	i, kurai
伸	shin, no(basu)
伴	han, ban, tomona(u)
体	tai, tei, karada
伯	haku
佐	sa
作	saku, sa, tsuku(ru)
似	ji, ni(ru)
但	tada(shi)
低	tei, hiku(i)
住	jū, su(mu)
何	ka, nani, nan
伺	shi, ukaga(u)
余	yo, ama(ru)
含	gan, fuku(mu)
状	jō
冷	rei, tsume(tai), hi(eru), hi(yasu), sa(meru), sa(masu)
求	kyū, moto(meru)
防	bō, fuse(gu)
邦	hō

即	soku	
卵	ran, tamago	
却	kyaku	
判	han, ban	
別	betsu, waka(reru)	
助	jo, tasu(keru), suke	
励	rei, hage(masu)	
努	do, tsuto(meru)	
忘	bō, wasu(reru)	
対	tai, tsui	
克	koku	
角	kaku, kado, tsuno	
弟	dai, tei, de, otōto	
谷	koku, tani	
兵	hei, hyō	
呉	go	
医	i	
沖	chū, oki	
決	ketsu, ki(maru)	
沈	chin, shizu(mu)	
没	botsu	
汽	ki	
沢	taku, sawa	
坊	bō, bo'	
坑	kō	
坂	han, saka	
均	kin	
走	sō, hashi(ru)	
赤	seki, shaku, aka(i)	
扶	fu	
把	ha	
折	setsu, o(ru)	
抜	batsu, nu(ku)	
抄	shō	
抑	yoku, osa(eru)	
批	hi	

抗	kō	
技	gi, waza	
投	tō, na(geru)	
択	taku	
快	kai, kokoroyo(i)	
吹	sui, fu(ku)	
吟	gin	
呈	tei	
告	koku, tsu(geru)	
否	hi, ina	
乱	ran, mida(reru)	
豆	tō, zu, mame	
君	kun, kimi	
妨	bō, samata(geru)	
妊	nin	
妙	myō	
妥	da	
希	ki	
狂	kyō, kuru(u)	
役	yaku, eki	
形	kei, gyō, kata, katachi	
芳	hō, kanba(shii)	
花	ka, hana	
芸	gei	
孝	kō	
究	kyū, kiwa(meru)	
完	kan	
肖	shō	
労	rō	
岐	ki	
志	shi, kokorozashi, kokoroza(su)	
壱	ichi	
売	bai, u(ru)	
声	sei, shō, koe, kowa	

床	shō, yuka, toko	
応	ō	
序	jo	
近	kin, chika(i)	
迎	gei, muka(eru)	
返	hen, kae(su)	
廷	tei	
尿	nyō	
尾	bi, o	
局	kyoku	
困	kon, koma(ru)	
囲	i, kako(mu)	
図	zu, to, haka(ru)	
杉	sugi	
材	zai	
村	son, mura	
条	jō	
肝	kan, kimo	
児	ji, ni	
災	sai, wazawa(i)	
社	sha, yashiro	
改	kai, arata(meru)	
攻	kō, se(meru)	
忍	nin, shino(bu)	
忌	ki, i(mawashii)	
戻	rei, modo(ru)	
戒	kai, imashi(meru)	
辛	shin, kara(i)	
見	ken, mi(ru)	
臣	jin, shin	
利	ri, ki(ku)	
私	shi, watakushi	
秀	shū, hii(deru)	
初	sho, haji(me), hatsu, ui, so(meru)	
町	chō, machi	
男	dan, nan, otoko	

系	kei	阻	so, haba(mu)	泳	ei, oyo(gu)
言	gen, gon, i(u), koto	附	fu	泊	haku, to(maru)
		邪	ja	注	chū, soso(gu)
貝	kai	邸	tei	泡	hō, awa
車	sha, kuruma	制	sei	法	hō, ha', ho'
足	soku, ashi, ta(riru), ta(ru), ta(su)	刺	shi, sa(su)	況	kyō
		到	tō	沿	en, so(u)
麦	baku, mugi	刻	koku, kiza(mu)	沼	shō, numa
		刷	satsu, su(ru)	治	chi, ji, osa(meru), nao(ru)

8 strokes

		券	ken		
		劾	gai		
非	hi	効	kō, ki(ku)	泥	dei, doro
長	chō, naga(i)	叔	shuku	河	ka, kawa
表	hyō, omote, arawa(su)	受	ju, u(keru)	坪	tsubo
		夜	ya, yo, yoru	幸	ou, saiwa(i), sachi, shiawa(se)
画	ga, kaku	卒	sotsu		
果	ka, ha(tasu)	京	kei, kyō	拓	taku
東	tō, higashi	享	kyō	拝	hai, oga(mu)
垂	sui, ta(reru)	育	iku, soda(tsu)	押	ō, o(su)
奉	hō, tatematsu(ru)	斉	sei	抽	chū
		盲	mō	抹	matsu
毒	doku	版	han	拙	setsu
事	ji, zu, koto	協	kyō	披	hi
乳	nyū, chichi, chi	直	choku, jiki, tada(chini), nao(su)	拍	haku, hyō
承	shō, uketamawa(ru)			抱	hō, da(ku), ida(ku), kaka(eru)
		奔	hon		
依	i, e	卓	taku		
使	shi, tsuka(u)	免	men, manuka(reru)	抵	tei
価	ka, atai			担	tan, katsu(gu), nina(u)
例	rei, tato(eru)	並	hei, nara(bu), nami		
佳	ka			拐	kai
侍	ji, samurai	典	ten	招	shō, mane(ku)
供	kyō, ku, tomo, sona(eru)	延	en, no(biru)	拡	kaku
		周	shū, mawa(ri)	拠	kyo, ko
併	hei, awa(seru)	殴	ō, nagu(ru)	拘	kō
侮	bu, anado(ru)	泣	kyū, na(ku)	拒	kyo, koba(mu)
舎	sha	沸	futsu, wa(ku)	性	sei, shō
念	nen	油	yu, abura	怖	fu, kowa(i)
命	mei, myō, inochi	波	ha, nami	怪	kai, aya(shii)
		泌	hitsu, hi	味	mi, aji(wau)

呼	ko, yo(bu)	尚	shō	昇	shō, nobo(ru)

呼 ko, yo(bu)
知 chi, shi(ru)
奇 ki
姓 sei, shō
妹 mai, imōto
姉 shi, ane
始 shi, haji(maru)
妻 sai, tsuma
学 gaku, mana(bu)
弦 gen, tsuru
彼 hi, kare, kano
征 sei
径 kei
往 ō
参 san, mai(ru)
苗 byō, nae, nawa
英 ei
茂 mo, shige(ru)
芽 ga, me
若 jaku, nyaku, waka(i), mo(shikuwa)
茎 kei, kuki
苦 ku, kuru(shii), niga(i), niga(ru)
昔 seki, shaku, mukashi
宗 sō, shū
宝 hō, takara
実 jitsu, mi, mino(ru)
宙 chū
官 kan
宜 gi
定 tei, jō, sada(maru)
突 totsu, tsu(ku)
空 kū, a(ku), sora, kara

尚 shō
歩 ho, fu, bu, aru(ku), ayu(mu)
武 bu, mu
岬 misaki
岩 gan, iwa
岸 gan, kishi
岳 gaku, take
府 fu
底 tei, soko
店 ten, mise
届 todo(ku), todo(keru)
屈 kutsu
居 kyo, i(ru)
国 koku, kuni
固 ko, kata(i)
林 rin, hayashi
枚 mai
杯 hai, sakazuki
析 seki
松 shō, matsu
枝 shi, eda
枠 waku
板 han, ban, ita
枢 sū
肪 bō
肥 hi, ko(eru), koe
服 fuku
肢 shi
青 sei, shō, ao(i)
肯 kō
明 mei, myō, a(kasu), a(ku), a(keru), a(kari), aka(rui), aka(ramu), aki(raka)

昇 shō, nobo(ru)
易 eki, i, yasa(shii)
昆 kon
的 teki, mato
者 sha, mono
炊 sui, ta(ku)
炉 ro
炎 en, honō
祉 shi
祈 ki, ino(ru)
牧 boku, maki
物 butsu, motsu, mono
放 hō, hana(su)
欧 ō
忠 chū
肩 ken, kata
房 bō, fusa
所 sho, tokoro
具 gu
和 wa, o, yawa(ragu), nago(mu), nago(yaka)
委 i
季 ki
取 shu, to(ru)
金 kin, kon, kane, kana
雨 u, ame, ama
門 mon, kado

9 strokes

食 shoku, jiki, ta(beru), ku(u), ku(rau)
飛 hi, to(bu)
発 hatsu, hotsu
衷 chū
甚 jin,

	hanaha(dashii)		o(u)	赴	fu, omomu(ku)
巻	kan, ma(ku), maki	急	kyū, iso(gu)	挟	kyō, hasa(mu)
専	sen, moppa(ra)	首	shu, kubi	拷	gō
奏	sō, kana(deru)	前	zen, mae	挑	chō, ido(mu)
重	jū, chō, omo(i), kasa(naru), e	美	bi, utsuku(shii)	持	ji, mo(tsu)
乗	jō, no(ru)	盆	bon	括	katsu
信	shin	厘	rin	拾	shū, jū, hiro(u)
促	soku, unaga(su)	厚	kō, atsu(i)	指	shi, sa(su), yubi
便	ben, bin, tayo(ri)	迷	mei, mayo(u)	咲	sa(ku)
係	kei, kaka(ru), kakari	退	tai, shirizo(ku)	品	hin, shina
俊	shun	追	tsui, o(u)	姻	in
保	ho, tamo(tsu)	逃	tō, ni(geru), ni(gasu), noga(su), noga(reru)	姿	shi, sugata
侵	shin, oka(su)	逆	gyaku, saka(rau)	要	yō, i(ru)
俗	zoku	送	sō, oku(ru)	帥	sui
侯	kō	迭	tetsu	独	doku, hito(ri)
限	gen, kagi(ru)	述	jutsu, no(beru)	狭	kyō, sema(i), seba(maru)
郎	rō	迫	haku, sema(ru)	狩	shu, ka(ru)
郊	kō	建	ken, kon, ta(teru)	弧	ko
卸	oroshi, oro(su)	耐	tai, ta(eru)	律	ritsu, richi
削	saku, kezu(ru)	風	fū, fu, kaze, kaza	待	tai, ma(tsu)
契	kei, chigi(ru)	段	dan	後	kō, go, oku(reru), ato, nochi, ushi(ro)
勅	choku	津	tsu, shin	革	kaku, kawa
勇	yū, isa(mu)	浅	sen, asa(i)	荘	sō
叙	jo	洗	sen, ara(u)	草	sō, kusa
軍	gun	洪	kō	荒	kō, a(reru), ara(i)
冠	kan, kanmuri	活	katsu	茶	cha, sa
帝	tei	浄	jō	宣	sen
変	hen, ka(waru)	洋	yō	客	kyaku, kaku
哀	ai, awa(remu)	海	kai, umi	室	shitsu, muro
亭	tei	派	ha	窃	setsu
南	nan, na, minami	洞	dō, hora	栄	ei, saka(eru), ha(eru)
貞	tei, sada	城	jō, shiro	単	tan
虐	gyaku, shiita(geru)	垣	kaki, kai	孤	ko
負	fu, ma(keru),	型	kei, kata	県	ken
		封	fū, hō	峡	kyō
				峠	tōge

炭	tan, sumi	神	shin, jin, kami,	卑	hi, iya(shii)
幽	yū		kan, kō	疫	eki, yaku
度	do, to, taku,	祖	so	級	kyū
	tabi	祝	shuku, shū,	糾	kyū
庭	tei, niwa		iwa(u)	紀	ki
屋	oku, ya	珍	chin,	紅	kō, ku, beni,
面	men, omo,		mezura(shii)		kurenai
	omote, tsura	皇	kō, ō	約	yaku
相	sō, shō, ai	性	sei	計	kei, haka(ru)
柄	hei, e, gara	施	shi, se,	訂	tei
柱	chū, hashira		hodoko(su)	則	soku
柳	ryū, yanagi	政	sei, shō,	軌	ki
枯	ko, ka(reru)		matsurigoto		
査	sa	恨	kon, ura(mu)	**10 strokes**	
某	bō	恒	kō		
柔	jū, nyū,	悔	bu, anado(ru)	既	ki, sude(ni)
	yawa(rakai)	故	ko, yue	殊	shu, koto
染	sen, so(maru),	怒	do, oko(ru),	射	sha, i(ru)
	shi(miru)		ika(ru)	残	zan, noko(ru)
架	ka, ka(keru)	怠	tai,	耗	mō, kō
胞	hō		namake(ru),	耕	kō, tagaya(su)
胆	tan		okota(ru)	倒	tō, tao(reru)
肺	hai	威	i	倣	hō, nara(u)
胎	tai	研	ken, to(gu)	俳	hai
背	hai, somu(ku),	砂	sa, sha, suna	候	kō, sōrō
	se, sei	砕	saku, kuda(ku)	修	shū, shu,
映	ei, utsu(ru),	音	on, in, oto, ne		osa(maru)
	utsu(su),	臭	shū, kusa(i)	倍	bai
	ha(eru)	看	kan	俸	hō
昨	saku	省	shō, sei,	俵	hyō, tawara
昭	shō		habu(ku),	借	shaku, ka(riru)
冒	bō, oka(su)		kaeri(miru)	倹	ken
星	sei, shō, hoshi	盾	jun, tate	倫	rin
是	ze	秋	shū, aki	値	chi, ne, atai
春	shun, haru	秒	byō	個	ko
皆	kai, mina	科	ka	倉	sō, kura
泉	sen, izumi	香	kō, kyō,	准	jun
昼	chū, hiru		kao(ru), ka,	凍	tō, kō(ru),
畑	hatake, hata	胃	i		kogo(eru)
点	ten	思	shi, omo(u)	将	shō
為	i	界	kai	陣	jin

陛	hei	逝	sei, yu(ku), i(ku)	弱	jaku, yowa(i)
降	kō, fu(ru), o(riru), o(rosu)	透	tō, su(ku)	徒	to
院	in	造	zō, tsuku(ru)	徐	jo
除	jo, ji, nozo(ku)	途	to	従	jū, shō, shitaga(u)
陥	kan, ochii(ru), otoshii(reru)	通	tsū, tsu, tō(ru), tō(su), kayo(u)	華	ka, ke, hana
郡	gun	匿	toku	荷	ni, ka
剖	bō	酒	shu, sake, saka	恭	kyō, uyauya(shii)
剣	ken, tsurugi	浦	ho, ura	家	ka, ke, ie, ya
剤	zai	浪	rō	宰	sai
剛	gō	浜	hin, hama	宴	en
帰	ki, kae(ru)	流	ryū, ru, naga(reru)	害	gai
脅	kyō, obiya(kasu), odo(su), odo(kasu)	消	shō, ke(su), ki(eru)	宮	kyū, gū, ku, miya
桑	sō, kuwa	浸	shin, hita(ru)	案	an
衰	sui, otoro(eru)	浴	yoku, a(biru)	宵	yoi, shō
恋	ren, ko(u), koi(shii)	涙	rui, namida	容	yō
高	kō, taka(i)	浮	fu, u(ku)	挙	kyō, a(garu)
畜	chiku	埋	mai, u(maru)	党	tō
真	shin, ma	起	ki, o(kiru), o(koru)	峰	hō, mine
索	saku	挿	sō, sa(su)	島	tō, shima
勉	ben	捕	ho, to(ru), tora(eru), tsuka(maru)	庫	ko, ku
兼	ken, ka(neru)	捜	sō, saga(su)	座	za, suwa(ru)
差	sa, sa(su)	振	shin, fu(ru)	唐	tō, kara
益	eki, yaku	唆	sa, sosonoka(su)	席	seki
翁	ō	員	in	展	ten
原	gen, hara	唇	shin, kuchibiru	桟	san
辱	joku, hazukashi(meru)	哲	tetsu	株	kabu
連	ren, tsura(naru), tsu(reru)	娘	musume	根	kon, ne
		娯	go	桃	tō, momo
速	soku, haya(i), haya(meru), sumi(yaka)	娠	shin	桜	ō, sakura
		姫	hime	格	kō, kaku
		孫	son, mago	核	kaku
逓	tei	帯	tai, o(biru)	校	kō
逐	chiku	師	shi	栓	sen
				梅	bai, ume
				殺	satsu, sai, setsu, koro(su)
				朕	chin
				脂	shi, abura

脈	myaku	留	ryū, ru,	隻	seki
胸	kyō, mune,		to(maru)	夏	ka, ge, natsu
	muna	畝	se, une	馬	ba, uma, ma
胴	dō	鬼	ki, oni		
朗	rō, hoga(raka)	疲	hi, tsuka(reru)	**11 strokes**	
骨	kotsu, hone	病	byō, hei,		
能	nō		ya(mu), yamai	野	ya, no
時	ji, toki	症	shō	粛	shuku
書	sho, ka(ku)	疾	shitsu	偶	gū
殉	jun	紡	bō, tsumu(gu)	偽	gi, itsuwa(ru),
烈	retsu	純	jun		nise
祥	shō	紙	shi, kami	側	soku, gawa
珠	shu	納	nō, na', na,	停	tei
班	han		nan, tō,	偵	tei
特	toku		osa(maru)	偏	hen, katayo(ru)
泰	tai	紛	fun, magi(reru)	斜	sha, nana(me)
旅	ryo, tabi	紋	mon	陳	chin
致	chi, ita(su)	素	so, moto	陪	bai
敏	bin	料	ryō	陸	riku
悟	go, sato(ru)	粋	sui	陵	ryō, misasagi
悩	nō, naya(mu)	粉	fun, ko, kona	隆	ryū
悦	etsu	航	kō	陰	in, kage(ru)
恵	kei, e,	般	han	険	ken, kewa(shii)
	megu(mu)	蚊	ka	陶	tō
息	soku, iki	蚕	san, kaiko	郵	yū
恐	kyō, oso(reru),	恥	chi, ha(jiru),	都	to, tsu, miyako
	osoro(shii)		haji	郷	gō, kyō
恩	on	笑	shō, wara(u),	部	bu
扇	sen, ōgi		e(mu)	郭	kaku
栽	sai	託	taku	剰	jō
破	ha, yabu(ru)	討	tō, u(tsu)	副	fuku
砲	hō	記	ki, shiru(su)	動	dō, ugo(ku)
竜	ryū, tatsu	訓	kun	勘	kan
眠	min, nemu(ru)	財	zai, sai	率	ritsu, sotsu,
秩	chitsu	貢	kō, ku,		hiki(iru)
秘	hi, hi(meri)		mitsu(gu)	斎	sai
租	so	軒	ken, noki	商	shō, akina(u)
称	shō	配	hai, kuba(ru)	虚	kyo, ko
被	hi, kōmu(ru)	酌	shaku, ku(mu)	貧	hin, bin,
票	hyō	針	shin, hari		mazu(shii)
畔	han	飢	ki, u(eru)	瓶	bin

進	shin, susu(mu)	据 su(eru)	寄 ki, yo(ru)
逮	tai	惨 san, zan,	窒 chitsu
逸	itsu	miji(me)	袋 tai, fukuro
週	shū	情 jō, sei, nasa(ke)	巣 sō, su
淑	shuku	惜 seki, o(shimu)	蛍 kei, hotaru
渇	katsu,	悼 tō, ita(mu)	常 jō, tsune, toko
	kawa(ku)	唯 yui, i	堂 dō
混	kon, ma(zaru)	喝 katsu	崎 saki
淡	tan, awa(i)	唱 shō, tona(eru)	崩 hō, kuzu(reru)
渓	kei	啓 kei	崇 sū
清	sei, shō, kiyo(i)	婚 kon	殻 kaku, kara
渋	jū, shibu(i)	婦 fu	康 kō
渉	shō	婆 ba	庸 yō
深	shin, fuka(i)	帳 chō	麻 ma, asa
添	ten, so(u)	猫 byō, neko	庶 sho
液	eki	猛 mō	械 kai
済	sai, su(mu)	猟 ryō	豚 ton, buta
涼	ryō, suzu(shii)	張 chō, ha(ru)	脚 kyaku, kya,
涯	gai	強 kyō, gō,	ashi
域	iki	tsuyo(i),	脳 nō
培	bai, tsuchika(u)	tsuyo(maru),	脱 datsu, nu(gu)
堀	hori	shi(iru)	曹 sō
基	ki, moto, motoi	術 jutsu	習 shū, nara(u)
執	shitsu, shū,	得 toku, e(ru),	乾 kan, kawa(ku)
	to(ru)	u(ru)	黒 koku, kuro(i)
推	sui, o(su)	彩 sai, irodo(ru)	視 shi
掛	ka(karu),	彫 chō, ho(ru)	理 ri
	kakari,	尉 i	球 kyū, tama
排	hai	菓 ka	現 gen,
接	setsu, tsu(gu)	著 cho, arawa(su),	arawa(reru)
控	kō, hika(eru)	ichijiru(shii)	望 bō, mō,
掲	kei, kaka(geru)	黄 ō, kō, ki, ko	nozo(mu)
採	sai, to(ru)	菜 sai, na	旋 sen
授	ju, sazu(keru)	菊 kiku	族 zoku
探	tan, sagu(ru),	菌 kin	救 kyū, suku(u)
	saga(su)	寂 seki, jaku,	教 kyō, oshi(eru),
措	so	sabi(shii)	oso(waru),
描	byō, ega(ku)	宿 shuku,	赦 sha
掃	sō, ha(ku)	yado(ru)	務 mu,
捨	sha, su(teru)	密 mitsu	tsuto(meru)
掘	kutsu, ho(ru)	窓 sō, mado	欲 yoku, ho(shii),

	hos(suru)	笛 teki, fue	陽 yō
悪	aku, o, waru(i)	符 fu	階 kai
患	kan, wazura(u)	訪 hō,	隊 tai
悠	yū		otozu(reru),	割 katsu, wa(ru),
章	shō		tazu(neru)		wa(reru), wari,
産	san, u(mu),	許 kyo, yuru(su)		sa(ku)
	ubu	訟 shō	創 sō, tsuku(ru)
翌	yoku	設 setsu, mō(keru)	勤 kin, gon,
眼	gan, gen,	訳 yaku, wake		tsuto(meru)
	manako	敗 hai, yabu(reru)	蛮 ban
眺	chō, naga(me)	販 han	博 haku, baku
規	ki	貫 kan,	象 zō, shō
祭	sai, matsu(ru)		tsuranu(ku)	着 chaku, jaku,
移	i, utsu(ru)	責 seki, se(meru)		tsu(ku),
略	ryaku	貨 ka		tsu(keru),
累	rui	軟 nan,		ki(ru), ki(seru)
異	i, koto(naru)		yawara(kai)	善 zen, yo(i)
盛	sei, jō, mo(ru),	転 ten, koro(bu)	尊 son, tōto(i),
	saka(ru),	酔 sui, yo(u)		tōto(bu),
	saka(n)	釣 chō, tsu(ru)		tatto(i),
盗	tō, nusu(mu)	雪 setsu, yuki		tatto(bu)
細	sai, hoso(i),	問 mon, to(u), ton	普 fu
	hoso(ru),	閉 hei, to(jiru),	遇 gū
	koma(kai)		to(zasu),	達 tatsu
紳	shin		shi(meru),	運 un, hako(bu)
紺	kon		shi(maru)	遂 sui, to(geru)
組	so, ku(mu),	頂 chō,	道 dō, tō, michi
	kumi		itadak(ku),	遍 hen
終	shū, o(waru)		itadaki	遅 chi, oso(i),
紹	shō	魚 gyo, uo, sakana		oku(reru)
経	kei, kyō, he(ru)	鳥 chō, tori	過 ka, ayama(tsu),
粒	ryū, tsubu			su(giru),
粗	so, ara(i)	**12 strokes**		su(gosu)
粘	nen, neba(ru)		遊 yū, yu, aso(bu)
釈	shaku	健 ken,	測 soku, haka(ru)
断	dan, ta(tsu),		suko(yaka)	湖 ko, mizūmi
	kotowa(ru)	備 bi, sona(eru)	港 kō, minato
舶	haku	偉 i, era(i)	湾 wan
船	sen, fune, funa	傍 bō, katawa(ra)	温 on, atata(kai)
蛇	ja, da, hebi	傘 san, kasa	湿 shitsu,
第	dai	隅 gū, sumi		shime(ru)

湯 tō, yu	循 jun	晩 ban
満 man, mi(chiru)	裂 retsu, sa(ku)	暑 sho, atsu(i)
滋 ji	装 sō, shō,	晶 shō
渡 to, wata(ru)	yosō(u)	景 kei
渦 ka, uzu	裁 sai, saba(ku),	量 ryō, haka(ru)
減 gen, he(ru)	ta(tsu)	最 sai, motto(mo)
堪 kan, ta(eru)	落 raku, o(chiru)	替 tai, ka(waru)
場 jō, ba	葬 sō, hōmu(ru)	焼 shō, ya(ku)
堤 tei, tsutsumi	葉 yō, ha	無 mu, bu, na(i)
塔 tō	募 bo, tsuno(ru)	煮 sha, ni(ru)
塚 tsuka	寒 kan, samu(i)	然 zen, nen
塀 hei	富 fu, fū, to(mu),	琴 kin, koto
堅 ken, kata(i)	tomi	散 san, chi(ru)
堕 da	営 ei, itona(mu)	敬 kei, uyama(u)
報 hō, muku(iru)	覚 kaku,	敢 kan
超 chō, ko(eru)	obo(eru),	欺 gi, azamu(ku)
喪 sō, mo	sa(masu)	款 kan
揚 yō, a(geru)	掌 shō	惰 da
提 tei, sa(geru)	喜 ki, yoroko(bu)	慌 kō, awa(teru)
援 en	廃 hai, suta(reru)	愉 yu
揺 yō, yu(reru)	廊 rō	惑 waku, mado(u)
搭 tō	属 zoku	悲 hi,
揮 ki	圏 ken	kana(shimu)
換 kan, ka(waru)	棟 tō, mune, muna	雇 ko, yato(u)
握 aku, nigi(ru)	棚 tana	扉 hi, tobira
喫 kitsu	極 kyoku, goku,	越 etsu, ko(su)
喚 kan	kiwa(meru)	幾 ki, iku
就 shū, ju, tsu(ku)	棋 ki	硬 kō, kata(i)
登 tō, to, nobo(ru)	棒 bō	硫 ryū
短 tan, mijika(i)	棺 kan	硝 shō
尋 jin, tazu(neru)	検 ken	童 dō, warabe
媒 bai	植 shoku, u(eru)	殖 shoku, fu(eru)
婿 sei, muko	森 shin, mori	程 tei, hodo
帽 bō	脹 chō	税 zei
幅 fuku, haba	勝 shō, ka(tsu),	補 ho, ogina(u)
猶 yū	masa(ru)	裕 yū
弾 dan, hi(ku),	腕 wan, ude	塁 rui
hazu(mu), tama	期 ki, go	畳 jō, tata(mu),
御 go, gyo, on	朝 chō, asa	tatami
街 gai, kai, machi	暁 gyō, akatsuki	番 ban
復 fuku	晴 sei, ha(reru)	買 bai, ka(u)

衆	shū, shu	
疎	so, uto(i)	
痢	ri	
痛	tsū, ita(mu)	
痘	tō	
結	ketsu, musu(bu), yu(u), yu(waeru)	
絡	raku	
給	kyū	
絵	kai, e	
絞	kō, shibo(ru), shi(meru), shi(maru)	
統	tō, su(beru)	
絶	zetsu, ta(eru)	
紫	shi, murasaki	
粧	shō	
奥	ō, oku	
歯	shi, ha	
筆	hitsu, fude	
策	saku	
筋	kin, suji	
等	tō, hito(shii)	
答	tō, kota(eru)	
筒	tō, tsutsu	
訴	so, utta(eru)	
評	hyō	
証	shō	
詐	sa	
診	shin, mi(ru)	
詔	shō, mikotonori	
詠	ei, yo(mu)	
詞	shi	
貯	cho	
費	hi, tsui(yasu)	
貴	ki, tatto(i), tatto(bu), tōto(i),	

	tōto(bu)	
貿	bō	
貸	tai, ka(su)	
賀	ga	
軸	jiku	
軽	kei, karu(i), karo(yaka)	
距	kyo	
酢	saku, su	
鈍	don, nibu(i)	
飲	in, no(mu)	
飯	han, meshi	
雄	yū, osu, o	
集	shū, tsudo(u), atsu(maru)	
焦	sho, ko(geru), ase(ru)	
雲	un, kumo	
雰	fun	
閑	kan	
間	kan, ken, ma, aida	
開	kai, a(keru), a(ku), hira(ku), hira(keru)	
項	kō	
順	jun	

13 strokes

業	gyō, gō, waza	
働	dō, hatara(ku)	
傾	kei, katamu(ku)	
傑	ketsu	
僧	sō	
傷	shō, ita(mu), kizu	
債	sai	
催	sai, moyō(su)	
随	zui	

隔	kaku, heda(teru)	
勧	kan, susu(meru)	
勢	sei, ikio(i)	
裏	ri, ura	
棄	ki	
準	jun	
艇	tei	
虞	osore	
虜	ryo	
慈	ji, itsuku(shimu)	
義	gi	
農	nō	
滑	katsu, sube(ru), name(raka)	
滝	taki	
溝	kō, mizo	
滞	tai, todokō(ru)	
溶	yō, to(keru)	
漢	kan	
漠	baku	
源	gen, minamoto	
滅	metsu, horo(biru)	
塊	kai, katamari	
塩	en, shio	
塑	so	
塗	to, nu(ru)	
搬	han	
携	kei, tazusa(eru)	
摂	setsu, to(ru)	
搾	saku, shibo(ru)	
損	son, soko(nau)	
嘆	tan, nage(ku)	
嗣	shi	
群	gun, mu(reru), mura	
豊	hō, yuta(ka)	
嫁	ka, totsu(gu),	

	yome	聖	sei	詩	shi
嫌	ken, gen, kira(u), iya	解	kai, ge, to(ku)	詰	kitsu, tsu(maru)
猿	en, saru	数	sū, su, kazo(eru), kazu	話	wa, hana(su), hanashi
微	bi	慨	gai	誇	ko, hoko(ru)
夢	yume, mu	慎	shin, tsutsushi(mu)	該	gai
愛	ai	愚	gu, oro(ka)	詳	shō, kuwa(shii)
蓄	chiku, takuwa(eru)	愁	shū, ure(eru)	試	shi, tame(su), kokoro(miru)
蒸	jō, mu(su)	想	sō, so	賄	wai, makana(u)
墓	bo, haka	感	kan, kan(jiru)	賊	zoku
幕	baku, maku	戦	sen, tataka(u), ikusa	賃	chin
靴	ka, kutsu	歳	sai, sei	資	shi
寝	shin, ne(ru)	碁	go	較	kaku
寛	kan	意	i	載	sai, no(seru)
誉	yo, homa(re)	新	shin, atara(shii), ara(ta), nii	践	sen
奨	shō	辞	ji, ya(meru)	跳	chō, ha(neru), to(bu)
鼓	ko, tsuzumi	睡	sui	路	ro, ji
廉	ren	督	toku	跡	seki, ato
殿	den, ten, tono, dono	禁	kin	酪	raku
園	en, sono	稚	chi	酬	shū
楼	rō	裸	ra, hadaka	鉢	hachi, hatsu
楽	raku, gaku, tano(shii)	褐	katsu	鉄	tetsu
腰	yō, koshi	署	sho	鈴	rei, rin, suzu
腹	fuku, hara	罪	zai, tsumi	鉛	en, namari
腸	chō	置	chi, o(ku)	鉱	kō
暇	ka, hima	盟	mei	飽	hō, a(kiru)
暗	an, kura(i)	痴	chi	飾	shoku, kaza(ru)
暖	dan, atata(kai)	絹	ken, kinu	飼	shi, ka(u)
幹	kan, miki	続	zoku, tsuzu(ku)	雅	ga
煩	han, bon, wazura(washii)	継	kei, tsu(gu)	雷	rai, kaminari
煙	en, kemu(ru), kemuri	触	shoku, sawa(ru), fu(reru)	電	den
照	shō, te(ru)	節	setsu, sechi, fushi	零	rei
献	ken, kon	誠	sei, makoto	頒	han
福	fuku			預	yo, azu(keru)
禅	zen			頑	gan
禍	ka				

14 strokes	彰 shō	綱 kō, tsuna
	髪 hatsu, kami	網 mō, ami
僕 boku	慕 bo, shita(u)	精 sei, shō
僚 ryō	暮 bo, ku(reru)	製 sei
像 zō	寡 ka	算 san
豪 gō	察 satsu	管 kan, kuda
疑 gi, utaga(u)	寧 nei	箇 ka
暦 reki, koyomi	腐 fu, kusa(ru)	誤 go, ayama(ru)
歴 reki	層 sō	誘 yū, saso(u)
遭 sō, a(u)	概 gai	語 go, kata(ru)
適 teki	構 kō, kama(u)	誌 shi
遮 sha, saegi(ru)	模 mo, bo	読 doku, toku, tō,
際 sai, kiwa	様 yō, sama	yo(mu)
障 shō, sawa(ru)	膜 maku	認 min,
隠 in, kaku(su)	静 sei, jō,	mito(meru)
遣 ken, tsuka(u)	shizu(maru),	説 setsu, zei,
遠 en, on, tō(i)	shizu(ka)	to(ku)
違 i, chiga(i)	旗 ki, hata	誓 sei, chika(u)
漁 ryō	歌 ka, uta(u)	踊 yō, odo(ru)
漸 zen	憎 zō, niku(mu)	酷 koku
漂 hyō, tadayo(u)	慢 man	酸 san, su(i)
漆 shitsu, urushi	慣 kan, na(reru)	酵 kō
漫 man	態 tai	銭 sen, zeni
漬 tsu(karu)	碑 hi	銀 gin
演 en	磁 ji	銘 mei
滴 teki,	端 tan, hashi, ha,	銑 sen
shitata(ru),	hata	銃 jū
shizuku	種 shu, tane	銅 dō
漏 rō, mo(ru)	稲 tō, ine, ina	雌 shi, mesu, me
境 kyō, kei, sakai	穀 koku	雑 zatsu, zō
増 zō, ma(su),	複 fuku	奪 datsu, uba(u)
fu(eru),	魂 kon, tamashii	需 ju
fu(yasu)	鼻 bi, hana	聞 bun, mon,
塾 juku	罰 batsu, bachi	ki(ku)
墨 boku, sumi	維 i	閥 batsu
摘 teki, tsu(mu)	練 ren, ne(ru)	閣 kaku
鳴 mei, na(ru)	緒 sho, cho, o	関 kan, seki
嫡 chaku	綿 men, wata	領 ryō, rei
獄 goku	緑 ryoku, roku,	駄 da
徴 chō	midori	駅 eki
徳 toku	総 so	駆 ku, ka(keru)

28

15 strokes

舞	bu, ma(u), mai	
儀	gi	
億	oku	
劇	geki	
褒	hō, ho(meru)	
膚	fu	
慮	ryō, omonbaka(ru)	
養	yō, yashina(u)	
遷	sen	
選	sen, era(bu)	
遺	i, yui	
遵	jun	
潮	chō, shio	
潜	sen, mogu(ru), hiso(mu)	
潟	kata	
潔	ketsu, isagiyo(i)	
澄	chō, su(mu)	
潤	jun, uruo(u)	
墜	tsui	
墳	fun	
舗	ho	
撲	boku	
撤	tetsu	
撮	satsu, to(ru)	
噴	fun, fu(ku)	
嘱	shoku	
器	ki, utsuwa	
幣	hei	
衝	shō, tsu(ku)	
徹	tetsu	
影	ei, kage	
蔵	zō, kura	
審	shin	
寮	ryō	
賓	hin	
窮	kyū, kiwa(maru)	

窯	yō, kama
導	dō, michibi(ku)
賞	shō
撃	geki, u(tsu)
摩	ma
慶	kei
憂	yū, ure(eru), u(i)
履	ri, ha(ku)
槽	sō
標	hyō
横	ō, yoko
権	ken, gon
暴	bō, baku, aba(ku)
暫	zan, shibara(ku)
熟	juku, u(reru)
勲	kun
熱	netsu, atsu(i)
黙	moku, dama(ru)
敷	shi(ku), fu
敵	teki, kataki
弊	hei
歓	kan
慰	i, nagusa(meru)
戯	gi, ge, tawamu(reru)
確	kaku, tashi(ka)
穂	sui, ho
稼	ka, kase(gu)
稿	kō
魅	mi
罷	hi
監	kan
盤	ban
縄	jō, nawa

線	sen
緩	kan, yuru(i)
縁	en, fuchi
締	tei, shi(maru)
編	hen, a(mu)
緊	kin
趣	shu, omomuki
範	han
箱	hako
課	ka
諸	sho
謁	etsu
談	dan
請	sei, shin, ko(u), u(keru)
諾	daku
論	ron
調	chō, shira(beru), totono(u), totono(eru)
誕	tan
賠	bai
賜	shi, tamawa(ru)
賦	fu
賛	san
質	shitsu, shichi, chi
輪	rin, wa
輩	hai
輝	ki, kagaya(ku)
踏	to, fu(mu)
鋳	chū, i(ru)
鋭	ei, surudo(i)
餓	ga
霊	rei, ryō, tama
震	shin, furu(eru)
閲	etsu
駐	chū

16 strokes

儒 ju
凝 gyō, ko(ru)
興 kyō, kō, oko(ru)
激 geki, hage(shii)
濃 nō, ko(i)
濁 daku, nigo(ru)
壊 kai, kowa(su)
壌 jō
壇 dan, tan
墾 kon
壁 heki, kabe
操 sō, ayatsu(ru), misao
擁 yō
撼 kan
嬢 jō
獲 kaku, e(ru)
衡 kō
衛 ei
薪 shin, takigi
薄 haku, usu(i)
薬 yaku, kusuri
薫 kun, kao(ru)
薦 sen, susu(meru)
憲 ken
磨 ma, miga(ku)
機 ki, hata
樹 ju
橋 kyō, hashi
膨 bō, fuku(ramu)
曇 don, kumo(ru)
燃 nen, mo(eru)
獣 jū, kemono
整 sei, totono(eru)
憤 fun, ikidō(ru)
憶 oku
懐 kai,

natsuka(shimu),
natsu(ku),
futokoro
隣 rin, tona(ru),
tonari
避 hi, sa(keru)
還 kan, kae(ru)
憩 kei, iko(u)
親 shin,
shita(shii), oya
穏 on, oda(yaka)
積 seki, tsu(mu)
奮 fun, furu(u)
縦 jū, tate
縛 baku, shiba(ru)
緯 i
縫 hō, nu(u)
繁 han
糖 tō
融 yū
篤 toku
築 chiku, kizu(ku)
諮 shi, haka(ru)
謀 bō, mu,
haka(ru)
謡 yō, uta(u), utai
諭 yu, sato(su)
賢 ken, kashiko(i)
輸 yu
錘 sui
錬 ren
錯 saku
錠 jō
録 roku
鋼 kō, hagane
館 kan
隷 rei
頼 rai, tano(mu),
tayo(ru)
頭 tō, zu, to,
atama, kashira

17 strokes

優 yū, yasa(shii),
sugu(reru)
償 shō, tsuguna(u)
翼 yoku, tsubasa
濯 taku
擬 gi
擦 satsu, su(ru)
嚇 kaku
矯 kyō, ta(meru)
厳 gen, gon,
kibi(shii),
ogoso(ka)
膽 tō
燥 sō
環 kan
犠 gi
懇 kon, nengo(ro)
礁 shō
覧 ran
爵 shaku
療 ryō
繊 sen
績 seki
縮 shuku,
chiji(mu)
齢 rei
聴 chō, ki(ku)
謝 sha, ayama(ru)
講 kō
謹 kin,
tsutsushi(mu)
謙 ken
購 kō
轄 katsu
醜 shū, miniku(i)
鍛 tan, kita(eru)
霜 sō, shimo
頻 hin
鮮 sen, aza(yaka)

18 strokes

濫 ran
藩 han
繭 ken, mayu
曜 yō
覆 fuku, ō(u),
　　kutsugae(su)
懲 chō, ko(riru)
礎 so, ishizue
瞬 shun,
　　matata(ku)
臨 rin, nozo(mu)
観 kan
穫 kaku
襟 kin, eri
癖 heki, kuse
癒 yu
繕 zen, tsukuro(u)
織 shoku, shiki,
　　o(ru)
糧 ryō, rō, kate
翻 hon,
　　hirugae(ru)
職 shoku
簡 kan
贈 zō, sō, oku(ru)
鎖 sa, kusari
鎮 chin,
　　shizu(meru)
難 nan,
　　muzuka(shii),
　　kata(i)
闘 tō, tataka(u)
類 rui
顔 gan, kao
顕 ken
額 gaku, hitai
題 dai
騎 ki
験 ken, gen

騒 sō, sawa(gu)

19 strokes

瀬 se
藻 sō, mo
麗 rei, uruwa(shii)
臓 zō
覇 ha
爆 baku
璽 ji
羅 ra
繰 ku(ru)
簿 bo
譜 fu
識 shiki
警 kei
韻 in
鏡 kyō, kagami
離 ri, hana(reru)
霧 mu, kiri
髄 zui
願 gan, nega(u)
鯨 gei, kujira
鶏 kei, niwatori

20 strokes

懸 ken, ke,
　　ka(karu)
欄 ran
騰 tō
競 kyō, kei,
　　kiso(u), se(ru)
籍 seki
譲 jō, yuzu(ru)
護 go
議 gi
醸 jō, kamo(su)
鐘 shō, kane
響 kyō, hibi(ku)

21 strokes

魔 ma
艦 kan
躍 yaku, odo(ru)
露 ro, rō, tsuyu
顧 ko, kaeri(miru)

22 strokes

襲 shū, oso(u)
驚 kyō, odoro(ku)

23 strokes

鑑 kan

Hiragana and Katakana Table

In addition to the *kanji*, or Chinese characters, Japanese uses two sets of characters known as *hiragana* and *katakana*. Unlike *kanji*, each *hiragana* or *katakana* character has a single reading and represents a sound rather than a meaning. Loan words are usually written in *katakana*.

ひらがな **hiragana**	カタカナ **katakana**	ローマ字 **rōmaji**	ひらがな **hiragana**	カタカナ **katakana**	ローマ字 **rōmaji**
あ	ア	a	ふ	フ	fu
い	イ	i	へ	ヘ	he/e
う	ウ	u	ほ	ホ	ho
え	エ	e			
お	オ	o	ま	マ	ma
			み	ミ	mi
か	カ	ka	む	ム	mu
き	キ	ki	め	メ	me
く	ク	ku	も	モ	mo
け	ケ	ke			
こ	コ	ko	や	ヤ	ya
			ゆ	ユ	yu
さ	サ	sa	よ	ヨ	yo
し	シ	shi			
す	ス	su	ら	ラ	ra
せ	セ	se	り	リ	ri
そ	ソ	so	る	ル	ru
			れ	レ	re
た	タ	ta	ろ	ロ	ro
ち	チ	chi			
つ	ツ	tsu	わ	ワ	wa
て	テ	te		ウィ	wi
と	ト	to		ウェ	we
				ウォ	wo
な	ナ	na	を	ヲ	o
に	ニ	ni			
ぬ	ヌ	nu	ん	ン	n
ね	ネ	ne			
の	ノ	no		アー	ā
				イー	ī
は	ハ	ha/wa		ウー	ū
ひ	ヒ	hi		エー	ē

ひらがな hiragana	カタカナ katakana	ローマ字 rōmaji	ひらがな hiragana	カタカナ katakana	ローマ字 rōmaji
おお/おう	オー	ō	ちゃ	チャ	cha
が	ガ	ga	ちゅ	チュ	chu
ぎ	ギ	gi	ちぇ	チェ	che
ぐ	グ	gu	ちょ	チョ	cho
げ	ゲ	ge	にゃ	ニャ	nya
ご	ゴ	go	にゅ	ニュ	nyu
ざ	ザ	za	にょ	ニョ	nyo
じ	ジ	ji	ひゃ	ヒャ	hya
ず	ズ	zu	ひゅ	ヒュ	hyu
ぜ	ゼ	ze	ひょ	ヒョ	hyo
ぞ	ゾ	zo	みゃ	ミャ	mya
だ	ダ	da	みゅ	ミュ	myu
ぢ	ヂ	ji	みょ	ミョ	myo
づ	ヅ	zu	りゃ	リャ	rya
で	デ	de	りゅ	リュ	ryu
ど	ド	do	りょ	リョ	ryo
ば	バ	ba	ぎゃ	ギャ	gya
び	ビ	bi	ぎゅ	ギュ	gyu
ぶ	ブ	bu	ぎょ	ギョ	gyo
べ	ベ	be	じゃ	ジャ	ja
ぼ	ボ	bo	じゅ	ジュ	ju
ぱ	パ	pa	じぇ	ジェ	je
ぴ	ピ	pi	じょ	ジョ	jo
ぷ	プ	pu	びゃ	ビャ	bya
ぺ	ペ	pe	びゅ	ビュ	byu
ぽ	ポ	po	びょ	ビョ	byo
きゃ	キャ	kya	ぴゃ	ピャ	pya
きゅ	キュ	kyu	ぴゅ	ピュ	pyu
きょ	キョ	kyo	ぴょ	ピョ	pyo
しゃ	シャ	sha			
しゅ	シュ	shu			
しぇ	シェ	she			
しょ	ショ	sho			

A

あーあ **āa** oh God!; ah!; aha!; oh!

暴く **abaku** disclose; expose; show up

あばら屋 **abaraya** hovel

暴れまわる **abaremawaru** rampage

暴れる **abareru** become violent; act violently

浴びる **abiru** take *shower*

浴びせる **abiseru** throw *water*; shower (*with questions*)

あぶ **abu** horsefly

危ない **abunai** dangerous

脂 **abura** grease; fat

油 **abura** oil; 油をさす **abura o sasu** oil

油絵 **aburae** oil painting

脂っこい **aburakkoi** fatty; greasy

脂身 **aburami** fat

脂っぽい **aburappoi** greasy; oily

アーチ **āchi** arch

あちこち **achikochi** here and there; あちこち旅行する **achikochi ryokō suru** travel around

あちら **achira** over there

アダプター **adaputā** adapter

アダルトチルドレン **adaruto-chirudoren** screwed-up adult (*brought up in a dysfunctional family*); weirdo

アドバイス **adobaisu** advice

アドレス帳 **adoresuchō** address book

あえぐ **aegu** gasp; pant

亜鉛 **aen** zinc

アフガニスタン **Afuganisutan** Afghanistan

アフガニスタン(の) **Afuganisutan (no)** Afghan

あふれる **afureru** overflow

アフリカ **Afurika** Africa

アフリカ(の) **Afurika (no)** African

アフターサービス **afutā sābisu** after sales service

あがる **agaru** get nervous

上がる **agaru** go up, increase, rise; be up

揚がる **agaru** fly (*of flag*)

上がってくる **agatte kuru** come up

あげる **ageru** give; let out *groan, yell*

上げる **ageru** increase, raise; hold up *hand*; turn up *volume*

揚げる **ageru** deep-fry, fry; hoist

上げ相場 **agesōba** bull market

あご **ago** chin; jaw

あぐらをかく **agura o kaku** sit cross-legged

あひる **ahiru** duck

愛 **ai** love

愛着 **aichaku** love

間 **aida** through, during ◊ interval

アイデア **aidea** idea

アイドル **aidoru** idol

相いれない **aiirenai** incompatible

愛人 **aijin** lover; mistress

愛情 **aijō** affection; love; 愛情の深い **aijō no fukai** loving

合い鍵 **aikagi** duplicate key

相変わらず **aikawarazu** the same as ever

合気道 **aikidō** aikido

あいこだ **aiko da** be quits with

愛国者 **aikoku-sha** patriot

愛国心 **aikoku-shin** patriotism

愛国的(な) **aikokuteki (na)** patriotic

アイコン **aikon** icon

愛くるしい **aikurushii** adorable

IQ **ai-kyū** IQ

合間 **aima** interlude

あいまい(な) **aimai (na)** ambiguous; vague

あいにく **ainiku** unfortunately

アイヌ **Ainu** ethnic group based in *Hokkaido*

アイライナー **airainā** eyeliner

アイロン **airon** iron; アイロンをかける **airon o kakeru** iron

アイロン台 **airon-dai** ironing board

アイロンがけ **airon-gake** ironing

アイルランド **Airurando** Ireland

アイルランド(の) **Airurando (no)** Irish

あいさつ **aisatsu** greeting

あいさつする **aisatsu suru** greet; salute

アイシャドウ **aishadō** eye shadow

ICU **ai-shī-yū** intensive care (unit)

相性 **aishō** chemistry *fig*; affinity

愛称 **aishō** pet name; shortened form

愛想のいい **aisō no ii** amiable

愛想の悪い **aisō no warui** unfriendly

愛すべき **aisubeki** darling; lovable

アイスホッケー **aisuhokkē** (ice) hockey

アイスコーヒー **aisukōhī** iced coffee

アイスクリーム **aisukurīmu** ice cream

愛する **ai suru** love

(アイス)スケートリンク **(aisu)sukēto-rinku** ice rink

アイスティー **aisutī** iced tea

開いた **aita** open

相手 **aite** companion; opponent

空いている **aite iru** free; vacant

あいつ **aitsu** so-and-so; that guy

相次いで **aitsuide** successively

合図 **aizu** signal

合図する **aizu suru** signal

味 **aji** taste; savor

アジア **Ajia** Asia

アジア人 **Ajia-jin** Asian

アジア(の) **Ajia (no)** Asian

味気ない **ajikenai** bland

味index **ajimi suru** taste

あじさい **ajisai** hydrangea

味付けする **ajitsuke suru** flavor

味わう **ajiwau** taste; savor

あか **aka** grime

赤 **aka** red

赤ちゃん **akachan** baby

赤い **akai** red; rosy

赤字 **akaji** deficit; 赤字である *akaji de aru* be in the red

赤味 **akami** glow; tinge of red

赤身(の) **akami (no)** lean *meat*

赤ん坊 **akanbō** baby

あからさま(な) **akarasama (na)** frank; open; stark *reminder, contrast*

etc; obvious

明り **akari** light

明るい **akarui** bright; light; cheerful; rosy *future*

明るく **akaruku** brightly

明るくする **akaruku suru** brighten up; lighten

明るさ **akaru-sa** brightness

赤線地区 **akasen-chiku** red light district

赤信号 **akashingō** red light

明かす **akasu** unveil

明けましておめでとうございます **akemashite omedetō gozaimasu** Happy New Year!

開ける **akeru** open; undo; unwrap; make *hole*

空ける **akeru** vacate; empty

明ける **akeru**: 梅雨が明ける *tsuyu ga aketa* the rainy season is over; 夜が明ける *yo ga akeru* dawn is breaking

秋 **aki** fall

空き **aki** opening

空き部屋 **akibeya** unoccupied room

明らか(な) **akiraka (na)** apparent, obvious, evident; visible *difference*

明らかにする **akiraka ni suru** specify; identify; manifest; disclose, reveal ◊ revealing; 明らかにされていない *akiraka ni sarete inai* untold

あきらめ **akirame** resignation

あきらめる **akirameru** give up; despair of

あきらめた **akirameta** resigned

あきれる **akireru** be shocked; be astonished

あきれた **akireta** outrageous; horrifying

飽きる **akiru** tire of

悪化させる **akka saseru** aggravate

悪化する **akka suru** degenerate; deteriorate, worsen

あこがれ **akogare** yearning

あこがれの的 **akogare no mato** heart throb

あこがれる **akogareru** worship; admire; yearn for

空く **aku** be empty

開く **aku** open

悪 **aku** evil

アクアラング **akuarangu** air tank, aqualung

あくび **akubi** yawn

悪意 **akui** malice; spite; 悪意のある *akui no aru* malicious, malevolent

飽くことのない **aku koto no nai** insatiable

悪魔 **akuma** devil; demon; fiend

あくまで守る **aku made mamoru** stick up for

悪名の高い **akumei no takai** infamous, notorious

悪夢 **akumu** nightmare

悪人 **akunin** villain

アクロバット **akurobatto** acrobat; acrobatics

悪性(の) **akusei (no)** malignant; virulent

アクセル **akuseru** accelerator, gas pedal

アクセサリー **akusesarī** accessory

アクセスコード **akusesu kōdo** access code

アクション **akushon** action

握手する **akushu o suru** handshake; 握手をする *akushu o suru* shake hands with

悪臭 **akushū** stench, stink

悪態 **akutai** verbal abuse, cursing; swear word; 悪態をつく *akutai o tsuku* swear

悪党 **akutō** crook; rogue

悪徳 **akutoku** vice

悪用 **akuyō** misuse

悪用する **akuyō suru** misuse

あま **ama** bitch

尼 **ama** nun

アマチュア **amachua** amateur

雨垂れ **amadare** raindrop

甘える **amaeru** act like a spoilt child; …に甘える *… ni amaeru* depend on the good will of

甘い **amai** sweet; indulgent; permissive; luscious

あま皮 **amakawa** cuticle

甘口(の) **amakuchi (no)** mild

甘くする **amaku suru** sweeten

あまり **amari** not so much; あまり…で ない *amari … de nai* not overly, not very

余る **amaru** be left over

余った **amatta** to spare

余っている **amatte iru** be left over

雨宿りの場所 **amayadori no basho** cover; shelter (from the rain)

甘やかされた **amayaka sareta** spoilt

甘やかし **amayakashi** indulgence

甘やかす **amayakasu** pamper; spoil

甘酒 **amazake** sweet sake

甘酸っぱい **amazuppai** sweet and sour

あめ **ame** candy

雨 **ame** rain; 雨が降る *ame ga furu* rain

雨模様 **amemoyō** rainy

アメリカ **Amerika** America

アメリカ合衆国 **Amerika-gasshūkoku** USA, United States of America

アメリカ合衆国(の) **Amerika-gasshūkoku (no)** American

アメリカ人 **Amerika-jin** American

アメリカ国防総省 **Amerika-kokubō-sōshō** the Pentagon

アメリカンフットボール **Amerikan-futtobōru** football

アメリカンフットボール競技場 **Amerikan-futtobōru-kyōgijō** gridiron

網 **ami** net

編み出す **amidasu** formulate

編み物 **amimono** knitting

編み物する **amimono suru** knit

アーモンド **āmondo** almond

編む **amu** knit; plait; weave

穴 **ana** hole; pit; puncture; leak; 穴の ある *ana no aru* leaky

アナボリックステロイド **anaborikku-suteroido** anabolic steroid

あなご **anago** eel

アナログ式(の) **anarogu-shiki (no)** analog

あなた **anata** you (*singular polite form*); darling, honey

あなたの **anata no** your (*singular polite*)

あなたたち **anatatachi** you (*plural polite*)

あなたたちの **anatatachi no** your (*plural polite*)

アナウンサー **anaunsā** announcer

アナウンス **anaunsu** announcement

アンダーシャツ **andāshatsu** undershirt

安ど **ando** relief

姉 **ane** big sister

案外 **angai** unexpectedly

暗号 **angō** code

兄 **ani** big brother

アニメ **anime** cartoon

アニメ映画 **anime-eiga** animation

暗示 **anji** hint ; 暗示にかける **anji ni kakeru** influence by suggestion

アンケート **ankēto** questionnaire

暗記 **anki** memorizing

暗記している **anki shite iru** know by heart

暗記する **anki suru** memorize

あんこ **anko** sweet bean paste

あんこう **ankō** monkfish

暗黒 **ankoku** blackness

暗黒街 **ankokugai** underworld

暗黒(の) **ankoku (no)** black *fig*

アンコール **ankōru** encore

あんま **anma** massage

あんまり **anmari** not a lot, not really

暗黙(の) **anmoku (no)** implicit; tacit

あんな **anna** such a; that sort of

案内 **annai** information; guidance

案内係 **annaigakari** usher; attendant; guide

案内標識 **annai-hyōshiki** signpost

案内人 **annai-nin** guide

案内する **annai suru** guide; lead

案の定 **an no jō** sure enough

あの **ano** that; those

あのう **anō** well

あのね **anone** well; hey!

アノラック **anorakku** parka

あの世 **ano yo** the afterlife

あのよう(な) **ano yō (na)** such

アンプ **anpu** amplifier

安楽いす **anraku-isu** easy chair

安楽死 **anraku-shi** euthanasia

暗殺 **ansatsu** assassination

暗殺者 **ansatsu-sha** assassin

暗殺する **ansatsu suru** assassinate

安静 **ansei** rest cure

安心 **anshin** peace of mind

安心させる **anshin saseru** reassure

◊ reassuring

安心する **anshin suru** feel relieved

暗礁 **anshō** reef

暗証番号 **anshō-bangō** PIN, personal identification number

暗唱する **anshō suru** recite

安定 **antei** stability

安定させる **antei saseru** stabilize; steady

安定した **antei shita** firm; secure; stable; steady

安定する **antei suru** stabilize

アンテナ **antena** antenna

暗算 **anzan** mental arithmetic

安全 **anzen** safety

安全地帯 **anzen-chitai** (traffic) island

安全第一(の) **anzen-daiichi (no)** safety first

安全でない **anzen de nai** insecure

安全(な) **anzen (na)** safe; invulnerable

安全ピン **anzen-pin** safety pin

安全性 **anzensei** safety

安全対策 **anzen-taisaku** safeguard

あんず **anzu** apricot

青 **ao** blue

あおぐ **aogu** fan oneself

青い **aoi** blue

青写真 **aojashin** blueprint

青白い **aojiroi** pale, white; pasty; sickly; ghastly

青二才 **aonisai** greenhorn

あおりたてる **aoritateru** incite; inflame

あおる **aoru** whip up

アオサギ **aosagi** heron

青信号 **aoshingō** green light

青ざめる **aozameru** go pale

青ざめた **aozameta** wan

アパート **apāto** apartment; apartment block

アピール **apīru** appeal

アポストロフィー **aposutorofī** apostrophe

アップルパイ **appurupai** apple pie

アプローチ **apurōchi** approach

アラビア語 **Arabia-go** Arabic

アラビア(の) **Arabia (no)** Arabic

アラビア数字 **Arabia-sūji** Arabic numeral

アラブ(の) **Arabu (no)** Arab

荒い **arai** rough

粗い **arai** coarse

洗い流す **arainagasu** flush away

あらかじめ **arakajime** in advance

あらかじめ備えさせる **arakajime sonae saseru** forearm

あらまし **aramashi** outline

あら探しをする **arasagashi o suru** find fault with

あられ **arare** hail

あらし **arashi** storm

争い **arasoi** conflict; contest; struggle, fight; …を争っている **… o arasotte iru** be in contention for …; …と争っている **… to arasotte iru** be at odds with

争う **arasou** struggle; dispute; contest

荒す **arasu** damage; ruin

洗う **arau** clean; wash

あらわにする **arawa ni suru** reveal

現れる **arawareru** appear, show up

表れる **arawareru** manifest itself

表す **arawasu** embody; register *emotion*; show *interest, emotion*

あらゆる **arayuru** all kinds of

あれ **are** that one; that

荒れ地 **arechi** wasteland; wilderness

荒れ果てた **arehateta** dilapidated; godforsaken *place, town*

あれから **are kara** after that

あれこれ **are kore** this and that

荒れ狂う **arekuruu** rage

荒れ模様(の) **aremoyō (no)** stormy; inclement

荒れる **areru** get stormy; get worked up; get violent

アレルギー **arerugī** allergy; …にアレルギーがある **… ni arerugi ga aru** be allergic to …

荒れた **areta** rough; wild

あり **ari** ant

アリバイ **aribai** alibi

ありえる **arieru** probable

ありふれた **arifureta** common; everyday; trite; nondescript

ありがたい **arigatai** grateful

ありがたく思う **arigataku omou** appreciate

ありがとう **arigatō** thank you, thanks

アリゲーター **arigētā** alligator

あります **arimasu** there is; there are

ありそうもない **arisō mo nai** unlikely

ありそう(な) **arisō (na)** likely

ある **aru** be; be located, lie (*of place, building, object*); measure ◊ certain, particular; …がある **… ga aru** have…; there is / are; ある日 **aru hi** one day; ある意味では **aru imi de wa** in a sense; ある程度は **aru teido wa** to a certain extent

アルバイト **arubaito** part-time job; part-time work

アルバム **arubamu** album

アルファベット **arufabetto** alphabet

アルファベット順(の) **arufabetto-jun (no)** alphabetical

歩いて **aruite** on foot

歩いていく **aruite iku** walk

あるいは **arui wa** or; perhaps

歩き **aruki** walking

アルコール **arukōru** alcohol

アルコール中毒患者 **arukōru-chūdoku-kanja** alcoholic

歩く **aruku** pace; tread; walk

アルミニウム **aruminiumu** aluminum

アルゼンチン **Aruzenchin** Argentina

アルゼンチン(の) **Aruzenchin (no)** Argentinian

麻 **asa** hemp; linen

朝 **asa** morning

朝ごはん **asagohan** breakfast

浅黒い **asaguroi** swarthy

浅薄(な) **asahaka (na)** shallow *person*; unwise

朝日 **asahi** morning sun; rising sun

浅い **asai** shallow; superficial

朝飯 **asameshi** breakfast (*not a polite word*); 朝飯前です **asameshi-mae desu** be a piece of cake

朝寝坊 **asanebō** late riser

あさり **asari** short-neck clam

浅瀬 **asase** ford

あさって **asatte** the day after tomorrow

汗 **ase** sweat; 汗をかく **ase o kaku** sweat

あせる **aseru** get impatient; fade

汗ばんだ **asebanda** sweaty

汗びっしょりになる **asebisshori ni naru** covered in sweat

あせた **aseta** faded

あし **ashi** reed

足 **ashi** foot; paw; leg

脚 **ashi** leg (*of table etc*)

足跡 **ashiato** footprint

足場 **ashiba** scaffold(ing)

足留めされる **ashidome sareru** be stranded; be forced to stay in *hotel*

足取り **ashidori** way of walking; gait; tracks

足掛り **ashigakari** foothold; stepping stone

足ひれ **ashihire** flipper

足首 **ashikubi** ankle

足元に気をつけて **ashimoto ni ki o tsukete** mind the step!

足の裏 **ashi no ura** sole

足音 **ashioto** footstep; tread

アシスタント **ashisutanto** assistant

明日 **ashita** tomorrow

あそび **asobi** play TECH

遊び **asobi** game; play; pleasure

遊び回る **asobimawaru** play around

遊び人 **asobi-nin** playboy

遊び友達 **asobitomodachi** playmate

遊ぶ **asobu** play; enjoy oneself

あそこ **asoko** over there ◊ that place

阿蘇山 **Aso-san** Mt Aso

あっさり **assari** simply; plainly; *assari shita tabemono* plain food

圧縮する **asshuku suru** compress

明日 **asu** tomorrow

アース **āsu** ground ELEC

アスパラガス **asuparagasu** asparagus

アスピリン **asupirin** aspirin

与える **ataeru** give; award; provide; spare

値する **atai suru** deserve ◊ worthy

頭 **atama** head

頭でっかち(の) **atamadekkachi (no)** top heavy

頭がいい **atama ga ii** smart; brainy; academic

頭が悪い **atama ga warui** dense; unintelligent

頭金 **atamakin** down payment

新しい **atarashii** fresh, new

新しくする **atarashiku suru** freshen

新しさ **atarashi-sa** freshness

あたり前 **atarimae** natural; reasonable

あたる **ataru** take it out on

当たる **ataru** strike; be right; win

あたし **atashi** I (*used mainly by women*)

温かい、暖かい **atatakai** cordial; hot; warm

温かく、暖かく **atatakaku** warmly

温かみ、暖かみ **atatakami** warmth

温かさ、暖かさ **atataka-sa** warmth

温まる、暖まる **atatamaru** warm up

温める、暖める **atatameru** warm up, heat up

当たった **atatta** winning

宛て **-ate** addressed to

宛て名 **atena** address

当てにならない **ate ni naranai** unreliable

当てにする **ate ni suru** bank on, count on

当てる **ateru** win

充てる **ateru** devote; set aside

あてずっぽう **atezuppō** guesswork

跡 **ato** mark; trace; trail

後味 **atoaji** aftertaste

後で **ato de** afterward; later, later on

後へ引かない **ato e hikanai** stand one's ground

あと片付け **atokatazuke** clearing away

後回しにする **atomawashi ni suru** put on the back burner

後戻り(の) **atomodori (no)** retrograde

後に **ato ni** after; behind

アトラクション **atorakushon** attraction

アトリエ **atorie** studio

後始末 **atoshimatsu** ordering

後ずさりする **atozusari suru** back away

熱々(の) **atsuatsu (no)** piping hot

厚切り(の) **atsugiri (no)** thickly-sliced

厚着する **atsugi suru** bundle up

厚い **atsui** heavy; thick

暑い **atsui** hot *weather, day*

熱い **atsui** hot *object, food, water*

扱い **atsukai** handling; treatment

扱いにくくなる **atsukainikuku naru** play up; be difficult to handle

扱いやすい **atsukaiyasui** manageable

厚かましい **atsukamashii** impudent

熱かん **atsukan** hot sake

扱う **atsukau** handle; treat; trade

集まり **atsumari** gathering; reunion

集まる **atsumaru** assemble; collect; congregate; rally around

集める **atsumeru** collect, gather; pick up *information*; raise *money*

圧力 **atsuryoku** pressure; 圧力をかける **atsuryoku o kakeru** pressure

圧力団体 **atsuryoku-dantai** lobby

厚さ **atsu-sa** thickness

暑さ **atsu-sa** heat (*weather*)

熱さ **atsu-sa** heat (*water*)

あっという間に **atto iu ma ni** in a flash

圧倒する **attō suru** overwhelm; …に圧倒される **... ni attō sareru** be overawed by

圧倒的（な）**attōteki (na)** overpowering; predominant; 圧倒的な勝利 **attōteki na shōri** landslide victory

あう **au** meet with *sth unfavorable*; get involved in; suit

合う **au** fit; go; match

会う **au** meet

アウトである **auto de aru** be out SP

アウトプット **autoputto** output

泡 **awa** bubble; froth; head (*on beer*); foam; lather

あわび **awabi** abalone

泡立て器 **awadateki** mixer; whisk

泡立てる **awadateru** whip; whisk

泡立つ **awadatsu** effervescent

淡い **awai** pale; faint

合わない **awanai** clash

阿波踊り **awa-odori** *festival dance in Tokushima*

哀れみ **awaremi** pity

哀れ（な）**aware (na)** miserable; pitiful; unfortunate; pathetic

合わせる **awaseru** join; set *alarm clock, broken limb*; チャンネルをあわせる **channeru o awaseru** tune in

あわただしい **awatadashii** hurried

あわただしさ **awatadashi-sa** scramble

あわてる **awateru** be flustered; panic

あわてている **awatete iru** be in a hurry

誤り（の）**ayamari (no)** false

謝る **ayamaru** apologize

誤る **ayamaru** make a mistake

誤った **ayamatta** misguided; mistaken

あやめ **ayame** iris

怪しげ（な）**ayashige (na)** sinister

怪しい **ayashii** shaky; fishy, suspicious

あやす **ayasu** rock; dandle; caress

操り人形 **ayatsuri-ningyō** puppet

操る **ayatsuru** manipulate

危うくする **ayauku suru** compromise; endanger

あゆ **ayu** sweetfish

あざ **aza** bruise; birthmark

あざけり **azakeri** derision; mockery; ridicule; taunt

あざける **azakeru** ridicule

あざらし **azarashi** seal

あざ笑う **azawarau** scoff; sneer

鮮やか（な）**azayaka (na)** vivid

鮮やかさ **azayaka-sa** brilliance

預ける **azukeru** leave

B

ば **-ba** if; when; whenever; 雨が降れ
ば *ame ga fureba ...* if it rains ...;
その音楽を聞けば *sono ongaku o
kikeba ...* whenever I hear that
music ...

場 **ba** scene; place

バー **bā** (cross)bar (*in high jump*);
saloon (bar)

ばばシャツ **babashatsu** long-
sleeved thermal undershirt

バーベキュー **bābekyū** barbecue

バーボン **bābon** bourbon

バブル経済 **baburu-keizai** bubble
economy

ばち **bachi** drumstick

罰 **bachi** punishment

場違い(の) **bachigai (no)**
unsuitable

バッジ **badji** badge; button

バドミントン **badominton**
badminton

バーゲン **bāgen** sale (*at reduced
prices*)

倍 **bai** double

場合 **bāi** occasion; case; situation

バイバイ **baibai** bye-bye

売買 **baibai** buying and selling

梅毒 **baidoku** syphilis

ばい菌 **baikin** bug, germ

バイク便 **baiku-bin** motorcycle
courier

バインダー **baindā** binder

倍(の) **bai (no)** double

バイオリン **baiorin** violin

バイオリン奏者 **baiorin-sōsha**
violinist

バイオテクノロジー **baiotekunorojī**
biotechnology

バイパス **baipasu** bypass

バイリンガル(の) **bairingaru (no)**
bilingual

バイセクシャル **baisekusharu**
bisexual

陪審 **baishin** jury

陪審員 **baishin'in** juror

賠償 **baishō** recompense

売春 **baishun** prostitution

売春婦 **baishunfu** prostitute

売春宿 **baishun'yado** brothel

買収 **baishū** purchase; bribe

買収する **baishū suru** bribe; buy,
take over COM

バイスプレジデント **baisu-
purejidento** vice president

媒体 **baitai** medium; vehicle

売店 **baiten** booth

バイト **baito** byte; part-time job;
part-time work

バイヤー **baiyā** buyer

ばか... **baka...** very; too;
ridiculously

ばか **baka** idiot; fool, imbecile; jerk

ばかばかしいほど **bakabakashii-
hodo** ridiculously

ばかばかしさ **bakabakashi-sa**
absurdity

ばかげた **bakageta** absurd,
ridiculous

ばか(な) **baka (na)** idiotic, silly,
stupid

ばかにする **baka ni suru** deride;
mock; 人をばかにした *hito o baka
ni shita* contemptuous

ばからしい **bakarashii** ridiculous;
silly

ばかり **-bakari** approximately; only;
just; just because; 五人ばかり
gonin-bakari approximately five
people; 大人ばかり *otona-bakari*
adults only; 着いたばかりだ *tsuita-
bakari da* I've just arrived

ばかさわぎする **bakasawagi suru**
go (out) on a spree; fool around

ばか笑い **bakawarai** guffaw

ばか笑いする **bakawarai suru**
guffaw

馬券屋 **baken'ya** bookmaker

化ける **bakeru** disguise oneself as

バケツ **baketsu** bucket

罰金 **bakkin** fine, penalty

バック **bakku** back; backhand; reverse MOT

バックアップ **bakku-appu** backup, support

バックミラー **bakkumirā** mirror; rear-view mirror

バックパッカー **bakku-pakkā** backpacker

バックパック **bakku-pakku** backpack

バックル **bakkuru** buckle

バックさせる **bakku saseru** back, reverse

バックスペース(キー) **bakkusupēsu (kī)** backspace (key)

バックする **bakku suru** back, back up, reverse

バーコード **bākōdo** bar code

ばくち **bakuchi** gambling

ばくち打ち **bakuchiuchi** gambler

ばく大(な) **bakudai (na)** great; huge; vast; enormous; infinite

爆弾 **bakudan** bomb

爆弾騒ぎ **bakudan-sawagi** bomb scare

幕府 **bakufu** *government under the shogunate*

爆撃 **bakugeki** bomb attack

爆撃機 **bakugekiki** bomber

爆撃する **bakugeki suru** bomb

爆破する **bakuha suru** blast; blow up, bomb

爆発 **bakuhatsu** blast, explosion; outburst

爆発物 **bakuhatsu-butsu** shell

爆発させる **bakuhatsu saseru** detonate, explode

爆発する **bakuhatsu suru** detonate, blow up; explode, go off

暴露 **bakuro** exposure; revelation

暴露する **bakuro suru** expose, uncover

爆薬 **bakuyaku** explosive

漠然と **bakuzen to** indefinitely; vaguely

漠然とした **bakuzen to shita** indefinable; indeterminate

バン **ban** van

晩 **ban** evening

番 **ban** move; turn

バナナ **banana** banana

バンド **bando** band; vocal group; strap

バンドエイド **bando-eido** Band-Aid®

ばね **bane** spring

番号 **bangō** number

番号間違い **bangō-machigai** wrong number

晩ごはん **bangohan** evening meal

番組 **bangumi** program

バニラ **banira** vanilla

万事 **banji** everything

万能 **bannō** versatility

万能(の) **bannō (no)** all-purpose; all-round

バンパー **banpā** bumper

伴奏 **bansō** accompaniment; backing; 伴奏をする **bansō o suru** accompany

ばんそうこう **bansōkō** adhesive plaster, sticking plaster

万歳 **banzai** hurray!, hurrah!

番付 **banzuke** sumo rankings

抜本的(な) **bapponteki (na)** drastic

ばら **bara** rose

ばらばらに **barabara ni** out of sequence

ばらばらになる **barabara ni naru** come apart; disintegrate; be scattered

ばらばらにする **barabara ni suru** take to pieces

ばらばら(の) **barabara (no)** sporadic; in pieces

バラエティーショー **baraetī-shō** vaudeville

ばら色(の) **bairairo (no)** rosy

ばらまく **baramaku** scatter

バランス **baransu** balance; coordination

バランスのとれた **baransu no toreta** balanced

バランスの悪い **baransu no warui** unbalanced

ばらす **barasu** take to pieces; reveal *secret*; kill

バレーボール **barēbōru** volleyball

バレエ **baree** ballet

バレエダンサー **baree dansā** ballet dancer

バレリーナ **barerīna** ballerina

ばれる **bareru** be out (*of secret*)

バリカン **barikan** hair clippers

バリケード **barikēdo** barricade

馬力 **bariki** horsepower; 馬力のある **bariki no aru** powerful

バロメーター **baromētā** barometer

バルブ **barubu** valve

場所 **basho** locality; place; location; site; spot; room, space

抜歯 **basshi** tooth extraction

抜糸をする **basshi o suru** take the stitches out

抜粋 **bassui** excerpt, extract

罰する **bassuru** discipline; punish

バス **basu** bass; bus

バスケット **basuketto** basket

バスケットボール **basukettobōru** basketball

バスマット **basu-matto** bath mat

バス(の) **basu (no)** bass

バスローブ **basu-rōbu** bathrobe

バスターミナル **basu-tāminaru** bus station; bus terminal

バスタオル **basu-taoru** bath towel

バス停 **basutei** bus stop

バスト **basuto** bust

バター **batā** butter

ばたんと閉まる **batan to shimaru** bang, slam

ばたんと閉める **batan to shimeru** bang, slam

バーテン **bāten** bartender

罰 **batsu** penalty; punishment

抜群 **batsugun** outstanding, excellent

ばつ(印) **batsu(jirushi)** cross

ばった **batta** grasshopper

バッター **battā** batter

バッテリー **batterī** battery

バット **batto** bat

バウンド **baundo** bound

バウンドさせる **baundo saseru** bounce

バウンドする **baundo suru** bounce

ベアリング **bearingu** bearing

ベビーベッド **bebī-beddo** crib

ベビーいす **bebī-isu** highchair

ベビーシッター **bebīshittā** baby-

sitter; ベビーシッターをする *bebīshittā o suru* baby-sit

ベッド **beddo** bed

ベッドカバー **beddokabā** bedspread

ベッドメーキングする **beddo-mēkingu suru** make the bed

べき **-beki** should, ought to; 驚くべき *odoroku-beki* surprising

別館 **bekkan** annex

別居 **bekkyo** separation

別居中(の) **bekkyochū (no)** estranged

別居した **bekkyo shita** separated

別居している **bekkyo shite iru** live apart

別居する **bekkyo suru** separate

ベーコン **bēkon** bacon

弁 **-ben** dialect

弁 **ben** speech; valve

便 **ben** convenience; feces

ベンチャー事業 **benchā-jigyō** venture

ベンチ **benchi** bench

弁護 **bengo** defense

弁護人 **bengo-nin** defense lawyer

弁護士 **bengo-shi** lawyer, attorney; counsel

弁護する **bengo suru** defend

ベニヤ板 **beniya-ita** plywood

便所 **benjo** toilet

弁解 **benkai** excuse

弁解がましい **benkai-gamashii** defensive

便器 **benki** lavatory

勉強 **benkyō** study

勉強家(の) **benkyōka (no)** hard-working

勉強させる **benkyō saseru** work

勉強する **benkyō suru** study; do *subject at school*; work

便秘 **benpi** constipation

便秘している **benpi shite iru** constipated

便利 **benri** convenience

便利(な) **benri (na)** convenient, handy

弁償 **benshō** recompense

弁償する **benshō suru** reimburse

弁当 **bentō** packed lunch; lunch box

ベランダ **beranda** balcony; porch; veranda

ベル **beru** bell

ベール **bēru** veil

ベルベット **berubetto** velvet

ベルギー **Berugī** Belgium

ベルギー(の) **Berugī (no)** Belgian

ベルト **beruto** belt

ベルトコンベヤー **beruto-konbeyā** conveyor belt

ベース **bēsu** bass

ベスト **besuto** vest; the best

ベストをつくす **besuto o tsukusu** do one's best

ベストセラー **besuto-serā** best-seller

ベテラン **beteran** veteran

ベテラン(の) **beteran (no)** veteran

べとべとした **betobeto shita** soggy; sticky; tacky

べとべとする **betobeto suru** gooey

ベトナム **Betonamu** Vietnam

ベトナム(の) **Betonamu (no)** Vietnamese

別 **betsu** difference; distinction

別々に **betsubetsu ni** independently of; separately

別(の) **betsu (no)** another; different; separate

備蓄 **bichiku** reserve; stockpile

備蓄する **bichiku suru** stockpile

ビデオ **bideo** video

ビデオカメラ **bideo-kamera** video camera

ビデオテープ **bideo-tēpu** video cassette

美人 **bijin** beautiful woman

ビジネスクラス **bijinesu-kurasu** business class

美人(の) **bijin (no)** beautiful

美術館 **bijutsukan** art gallery; gallery, museum

ビーカー **bīkā** beaker

ビキニ **bikini** bikini

びっくり仰天させる **bikkuri-gyōten saseru** shock

びっくりさせられる **bikkuri saserareru** be shocked by

びっくりさせる **bikkuri saseru** shock, astonish; scare ◊ shocking; stunning

びっくりする **bikkuri suru** shock, amaze

びくびくしている **bikubiku shite iru** jumpy

微妙(な) **bimyō (na)** delicate; subtle

びん **bin** bottle; jar

便 **bin** flight

貧乏 **binbō** poverty

ビニール袋 **binīru-bukuro** plastic bag

便乗する **binjō suru** get a ride; jump on the bandwagon

敏感(な) **binkan (na)** reponsive; sensitive

敏感さ **binkan-sa** sensitivity

便名 **binmei** flight number

便せん **binsen** notepaper; writing paper

ビラ **bira** bill, poster; handout

ビリヤード **biriyādo** billiards; snooker

ビール **bīru** beer

ビル **biru** building

ビルディング **birudingu** building

ビルマ **Biruma** Burma

ビルマ(の) **Biruma (no)** Burmese

微笑 **bishō** smile

微小(の) **bishō (no)** microscopic

びしょぬれになる **bishonure ni naru** be wet through

ビスケット **bisuketto** biscuit

ビタミン **bitamin** vitamin

ビタミン剤 **bitamin-zai** vitamin pill

美的(な) **biteki (na)** esthetic

ビート **bīto** beat

美徳 **bitoku** virtue

ビット **bitto** bit

琵琶湖 **Biwako** Lake Biwa

美容院 **biyōin** beauty parlor

美容(の) **biyō (no)** cosmetic

美容整形 **biyō-seikei** cosmetic surgery

美容師 **biyōshi** beautician; hairdresser

ビザ **biza** visa

微罪 **bizai** misdemeanor

棒 **bō** bar; pole; rod

防備なし(の) **bōbi nashi (no)** unprotected

ボブ **bobu** bob

墓地 **bochi** cemetery, graveyard

膨張 **bōchō** expansion

膨張する **bōchō suru** expand

膨大(な) **bōdai (na)** vast

防弾(の) **bōdan (no)** bullet-proof

ボディーチェック **bodīchekku** body search; ...のボディーチェックをする *... no bodīchekku o suru* frisk

ボディーガード **bodīgādo** bodyguard

ボディーランゲージ **bodīrangēji** body language

ボディースーツ **bodīsūtsu** bodice; body (suit)

暴動 **bōdō** disorder; disturbances; riot; 暴動を起こす *bōdō o okosu* riot

防衛 **bōei** defense

防衛庁 **Bōeichō** Japan Defense Agency

防衛予算 **bōei-yosan** defense budget

貿易 **bōeki** trade

貿易収支 **bōeki-shūshi** balance of trade

望遠鏡 **bōenkyō** telescope

望遠レンズ **bōen-renzu** telephoto lens

防腐処理を施す **bōfu-shori o hodokosu** preserve; embalm

暴風雨 **bōfū** hurricane; rainstorm

妨害 **bōgai** interference; disruption

妨害する **bōgai suru** disrupt; jam

墓碑銘 **bohimei** epitaph

ボーイ **bōi** bellhop

ボーイフレンド **bōifurendo** boyfriend

ボイコット **boikotto** boycott

ボイコットする **boikotto suru** boycott

母音 **boin** vowel

ボイラー **boirā** boiler; furnace

ボーイソプラノ **bōi-sopurano** treble

ボーイスカウト **bōi-sukauto** (boy)scout

傍受する **bōju suru** intercept

傍観する **bōkan suru** look on; stand by

ボーカル **bōkaru** vocalist

ぼかす **bokasu** blur; obscure

冒険 **bōken** adventure

簿記 **boki** bookkeeping

簿記係 **boki-gakari** bookkeeper

募金 **bokin** collection; fundraising

勃起 **bokki** erection

暴行 **bōkō** assault; beating

膀胱 **bōkō** bladder

母国 **bokoku** native country

母国語 **bokokugo** mother tongue

暴行する **bōkō suru** assault

牧場経営者 **bokujō-keiei-sha** rancher

撲滅 **bokumetsu** elimination

暴君 **bōkun** despot; tyrant

暴君(の) **bōkun (no)** tyrannical

ぼく **boku I** (*used mostly by males*)

ボクサー **bokusā** boxer

牧師 **bokushi** clergyman; minister

ボクシング **bokushingu** boxing

牧草地 **bokusōchi** meadow

忘却 **bōkyaku** oblivion

亡命 **bōmei** exile

亡命者 **bōmei-sha** exile

亡命する **bōmei suru** go into exile

盆 **bon** tray

ボーナス **bōnasu** bonus

凡人 **bonjin** ordinary person; mediocrity

ボンネット **bonnetto** hood

盆踊り **bon'odori** festival dance

盆栽 **bonsai** bonsai

ぼんやりした **bon'yari shita** absentminded; blank; vacant; dim; hazy; misty; dazed

母乳 **bonyū** milk (*woman's*)

防音(の) **bōon (no)** soundproof

ぼっ発 **boppatsu** outbreak

ぼっ発する **boppatsu suru** flare up

暴落する **bōraku suru** crash; slump

ボランティア **borantia** volunteer

ボランティア(の) **borantia (no)** voluntary

ボレー **borē** volley

ボーリング **bōringu** bowling; ボーリングをする *bōringu o suru* bowl

ボーリング場 **bōringu-jō** bowling alley

ぼろ **boro** rag

ぼろぼろになる **boroboro ni naru** perish (*of material*)

ぼろぼろになった **boroboro ni natta** worn-out

ぼろぼろ(の) **boroboro (no)** ragged

ぼろ負け **boromake** massacre (*in

game)

ぼろ負けする **boromake suru** be massacred, get a licking

ボール **bōru** ball; football; bowl (*for cooking, salad*)

ボール紙 **bōrugami** cardboard

ボールペン **bōrupen** ballpoint pen

ボルト **boruto** bolt; volt

暴力 **bōryoku** brute force; violence

暴力団員 **bōryokudan'in** mobster

暴力的(な) **bōryokuteki (na)** violent

ボリューム **boryūmu** volume

防災訓練 **bōsai-kunren** emergency drill

母性 **bosei** maternity

母性的(な) **boseiteki (na)** maternal, motherly

紡績工場 **bōseki-kōjō** mill

帽子 **bōshi** cap; hat

防止 **bōshi** prevention

母子家庭 **boshi katei** single parent family (*mother only*)

防止する **bōshi suru** prevent

募集 **boshū** recruitment

募集人員 **boshū-jin'in** intake

募集活動 **boshū-katsudō** recruitment drive

募集する **boshū suru** recruit

防臭剤 **bōshūzai** deodorant

没収する **bosshū suru** confiscate

防水(の) **bōsui (no)** showerproof; waterproof

防水シート **bōsui-shīto** tarpaulin

棒高跳び **bōtakatobi** polevault

ぼたん **botan** peony

ボタン **botan** button

ボート **bōto** rowboat; boat

冒頭 **bōtō** opening

冒とく **bōtoku** blasphemy; impudence; violation

冒とくする **bōtoku suru** blaspheme

没落 **botsuraku** downfall

ぼーっとさせる **bōtto saseru** stupefy

没頭する **bottō suru** be absorbed in; be devoted to; 仕事に没頭する *shigoto ni bottō suru* bury oneself in work

ぼやけた **boyaketa** fuzzy; hazy

ぼう然とした **bōzen to shita** dazed

ぼう然として **bōzen to shite** in a daze

坊主 **bōzu** Buddhist monk

部 **bu** department, division; part, section

歩合 **buai** commission; percentage

無愛想(な) **buaisō (na)** inhospitable; surly; unsociable

部分 **bubun** bit; part; component; piece

部分的(な) **bubunteki (na)** incomplete, partial

部分的に **bubunteki ni** partially, partly

ぶちまける **buchimakeru** pour out; disclose

部長 **buchō** head

仏陀 **Budda** Buddha

ぶどう **budō** grape

ぶどう園 **budōen** vineyard

ぶどうの木 **budō no ki** vine

部外者 **bugai-sha** outsider

舞楽 **bugaku** court dance

部品 **buhin** part; unit

ブイ **bui** buoy

ブーイング **būingu** booing

無事である **buji de aru** be safe

無事(な) **buji (na)** safe

無事に **buji ni** safely

侮辱 **bujoku** humiliation; insult, slight; snub

侮辱する **bujoku suru** insult; snub

武術 **bujutsu** martial arts

部下 **buka** subordinate

不格好(な) **bukakkō (na)** misshapen; crude

不格好にする **bukakkō ni suru** deform

武器 **buki** weapon; arms

無気味(な)、不気味(な) **bukimi (na)** ghostly; eerie; uncanny

ぶきっちょ **bukitcho** clumsy person

不器用 **bukiyō** clumsiness

不器用(な) **bukiyō (na)** clumsy

物価 **bukka** commodity prices

ぶっきらぼう(な) **bukkirabō (na)** abrupt; blunt; curt; gruff

ぶっきらぼうに **bukkirabō ni** bluntly

仏教 **Bukkyō** Buddhism

仏教(の) **Bukkyō (no)** Buddhist

仏教徒 **Bukkyōto** Buddhist

部門 **bumon** sector

ブーム **būmu** boom; craze; ブーム (の) **būmu (no)** all the rage

文 **bun** sentence

分 **bun** portion

ぶな **buna** beech

分べん **bunben** labor (*in pregnancy*)

分べん室 **bunben-shitsu** labor ward

文房具 **bunbōgu** stationery

文房具店 **bunbōgu-ten** stationery store

分断された **bundan sareta** segmented

文学 **bungaku** literature

文学修士 **bungaku-shūshi** MA, Master of Arts (*person*)

文学修士号 **bungaku-shūshigō** MA, Master of Arts (*degree*)

分譲マンション **bunjō-manshon** condo

文化 **bunka** culture

文化の日 **Bunka no hi** Culture Day

分解する **bunkai suru** break up (*into component parts*); cannibalize; dismantle

文化的(な) **bunkateki (na)** cultural

分割 **bunkatsu** division; partition

分割払い **bunkatsu-barai** paying by installments

分割できない **bunkatsu dekinai** indivisible

分割する **bunkatsu suru** divide; partition

文系の学位 **bunkei no gakui** arts degree

文献目録 **bunken-mokuroku** bibliography

分岐する **bunki suru** branch off, diverge

分岐点 **bunkiten** fork

文庫本 **bunkobon** pocket-sized book

文明 **bunmei** civilization

文脈 **bunmyaku** context

分配 **bunpai** distribution; split, division

分配する **bunpai suru** distribute

分泌 **bunpitsu** secretion (*activity*)

分泌物 **bunpitsu-butsu** secretion (*product*)

分泌する **bunpitsu suru** secrete

文法 **bunpō** grammar

文法(の) **bunpō (no)** grammatical

文楽 **bunraku** *traditional Japanese puppet play*

分裂 **bunretsu** division; fission; split; disagreement

分裂させる **bunretsu saseru** divide; split

分裂する **bunretsu suru** split; disagree

分離 **bunri** separation

分離できない **bunri dekinai** inseparable

分離する **bunri suru** separate; isolate

分類 **bunrui** classification

分類する **bunrui suru** break down; classify, sort

分量 **bunryō** amount

分析 **bunseki** analysis

分析する **bunseki suru** analyze

分子 **bunshi** molecule

分子(の) **bunshi (no)** molecular

文書 **bunsho** document

文章 **bunshō** writing; composition

分数 **bunsū** fraction

文体 **buntai** style of writing

分担 **buntan** my/his/her etc share

分担する **buntan suru** share

文通 **buntsū** correspondence

文通相手 **buntsū-aite** correspondent

文通する **buntsū suru** correspond

分野 **bun'ya** area, field, sphere

物品 **buppin** article, item

ぶらぶらする **burabura suru** lounge around; mess around; take a stroll; wander around

ブラインド **buraindo** blind; shade

ブラジャー **burajā** brassiere

ブラジル **Burajiru** Brazil

ブラジル人 **Burajiru-jin** Brazilian

ブラジル(の) **Burajiru (no)** Brazilian

ブラックボックス **burakku-bokkusu** black box

ブラック(の) **burakku (no)** black *coffee*

ブラックリスト **burakku-risuto** blacklist

ブラックユーモア **burakku yūmoa** black mood, black humor

ブランチ **buranchi** brunch

ブランデー **burandē** brandy

ブランド **burando** brand

ブランド志向 **burando-shikō** brand loyalty

ブランコ **buranko** swing; trapeze

ぶら下がる **burasagaru** dangle

ぶら下げる **burasageru** dangle

ブラシ **burashi** brush; scrubbing brush; ブラシをかける **burashi o kakeru** brush

ブラスバンド **burasu-bando** brass band

ぶらつく **buratsuku** wander; stroll

ブラウニー **buraunī** brownie

ブラウス **burausu** blouse

ブラウザー **burauzā** browser

無礼 **burei** rudeness

無礼(な) **burei (na)** rude

ブレーカー **burēkā** circuit breaker

ブレーキ **burēki** brake; ブレーキをかける **burēki o kakeru** brake

ブレンド **burendo** blend

ブレンドする **burendo suru** blend

ブレスレット **buresuretto** bracelet

ブレザー **burezā** blazer

ぶり **buri** yellowtail

ブリーチ **burīchi** bleach

ブリーダー **burīdā** breeder

ブリーフ **burīfu** briefs

ブリーフケース **burīfukēsu** briefcase

ブローチ **burōchi** brooch; pin

ブロードライ **burō-dorai** blow-dry

ブロッコリ **burokkori** broccoli

ブロック **burokku** block

ブロークン(な) **burōkun (na)** broken

ブロンズ **buronzu** bronze

ぶる **-buru**: いい子ぶる **ii ko-buru** pretend to be behaving well; 学者ぶる **gakusha-buru** pose as a scholar; 上品ぶる人 **jōhin-buru hito** person who puts on airs; prude

ブルドーザー **burudōzā** bulldozer

部類 **burui** category, class

ブルース **burūsu** blues

不作法 **busahō** misbehavior; bad manners; 不作法にふるまう **busahō**

ni furumau misbehave

不作法(な) **busahō (na)** ill-mannered

物色する **busshoku suru** browse; hunt for

部署 **busho** post; place of duty

不精ひげ, 無精ひげ **bushōhige** bristles, stubble

無精ひげ(の) **bushōhige (no)** unshaven

無精(な) **bushō (na)** lazy

部首 **bushu** radical (*in Chinese character*)

武装解除 **busō-kaijo** disarmament

武装解除する **busō-kaijo suru** disarm

不足 **-busoku** shortage of; 水不足 **mizu-busoku** shortage of water; 睡眠不足 **suimin-busoku** lack of sleep

武装させる **busō saseru** arm

武装した **busō shita** armed

武装していない **busō shite inai** unarmed

物質 **busshitsu** material, substance; matter

物質主義 **busshitsu-shugi** materialism

物質主義者 **busshitsu-shugisha** materialist

物質主義的(な) **busshitsu-shugiteki (na)** materialistic

物質的(な) **busshitsuteki (na)** material

豚 **buta** hog; pig

豚皮 **buta-gawa** pigskin

豚小屋 **buta-goya** (pig)sty, pigpen *also fig*

舞台 **butai** scene; stage THEA

部隊 **butai** unit; corps

舞台げいこ **butai-geiko** dress rehearsal

舞台装置 **butai-sōchi** stage scenery

舞台裏で **butaiura de** behind the scenes

ブータン **Būtan** Bhutan

豚肉 **butaniku** pork

ブータン(の) **Būtan (no)** Bhutanese

豚野郎 **butayarō** pig

ブティック **butikku** boutique

ぶつ **butsu** beat; smack

ブーツ **būtsu** boot

ぶつぶつができる **butsubutsu ga dekiru** break out in a rash; blister

ぶつぶつ言う **butsubutsu iu** mumble; grumble

物々交換 **butsubutsu-kōkan** barter

物々交換する **butsubutsu-kōkan suru** barter

仏壇 **butsudan** Buddhist altar

ぶつかる **butsukaru** bump into; knock, hit

ぶつける **butsukeru** bang; bump

物理学 **butsuri-gaku** physics

物理学者 **butsuri-gakusha** physicist

物理療法 **butsuri-ryōhō** physiotherapy

物理療法士 **butsuri-ryōhōshi** physiotherapist

仏塔 **buttō** pagoda

ぶよ **buyo** gnat

ブザー **buzā** buzzer; doorbell; ブザーを鳴らす *buzā o narasu* buzz

びょう **byō** tack

秒 **byō** second (*of time*)

屏風 **byōbu** screen

平等 **byōdō** equality

平等(な) **byōdō (na)** even

平等に **byōdō ni** equally

平等(の) **byōdō (no)** equal

平等主義(の) **byōdō-shugi (no)** egalitarian

病院 **byōin** hospital; infirmary

病弱(な) **byōjaku (na)** sickly

病気 **byōki** illness, disease; infirmity; sickness

病気になる **byōki ni naru** fall ill, be taken ill; sicken

病気(の) **byōki (no)** ailing; ill; sick

病人 **byōnin** invalid

病歴 **byōreki** case history, medical history

病理学 **byōrigaku** pathology

病理学者 **byōrigaku-sha** pathologist

描写 **byōsha** description; portrait; portrayal

描写する **byōsha suru** describe

秒針 **byōshin** second hand

病室 **byōshitsu** sickroom

病的(な) **byōteki (na)** compulsive; morbid; pathological

病棟 **byōtō** ward

秒読み **byōyomi** countdown

C

茶 **cha** tea

茶番劇 **chabangeki** farce

ちゃち(な) **chachi (na)** flimsy; cheap

チャイム **chaimu** chime

茶色 **chairo** brown

茶色(の) **chairo (no)** brown

チャイルドシート **chairudo-shīto** car seat

着-**chaku** order of arrival; マラソンで二着になった *marason de nichaku ni natta* I came second in the marathon ◊ *countword for clothes*

着々と **chakuchaku to** steadily

着服する **chakufuku suru** pocket, embezzle

着実(な) **chakujitsu (na)** steady, reliable

着陸 **chakuriku** landing, touchdown

着陸させる **chakuriku saseru** land

着陸装置 **chakuriku-sōchi** landing gear, undercarriage

着陸する **chakuriku suru** land, touch down

着席する **chakuseki suru** take a seat

着色する **chakushoku suru** stain;

色剤 **chakushokuzai** coloring agent; stain

着水する **chakusui suru** splash down

ちゃん **-chan** *affectionate suffix added to names*

チャンネル **channeru** channel; station

チャンピオン **chanpion** champion

チャンス **chansu** chance; …にチャンスを与える *... ni chansu o ataeru* give a break

ちゃんと **chanto** straight; clearly; properly

ちゃんとした **chanto shita** proper

ちゃりんこ **charinko** bicycle

チャリティー **charitī** charity

チャーター便 **chātā-bin** charter flight

チャーターする **chātā suru** charter

茶わん **chawan** bowl

ちぇっ **che'** blast; damn

チェック **chekku** check

チェックアウトする **chekku-auto suru** check out; チェックアウトの時間 *chekkuauto no jikan* checkout time

チェックイン(カウンター) **chekku-in (kauntā)** check-in (counter)

チェックインする **chekku-in suru** check in; チェックインの時間 *chekku-in no jikan* check-in time

チェック(の) **chekku (no)** check, checked, checkered

チェックリスト **chekku-risuto** checklist

チェコ共和国 **Cheko-kyōwakoku** the Czech Republic

チェコ(の) **Cheko (no)** Czech

チェーン **chēn** chain; snow chain

チェーンストア **chēn-sutoa** chain store

チェロ **chero** cello

血 **chi** blood

治安 **chian** law and order; 治安のいい *chian no ii* safe ; 治安の悪い *chian no warui* dangerous; rough

チアリーダー **chiarīdā** cheerleader

血走った **chibashitta** bloodshot

チベット **Chibetto** Tibet

チベット(の) **Chibetto (no)** Tibetan

乳房 **chibusa** breast; tit, boob

父 **chichi** father

乳 **chichi** milk; boob, tit

父方(の) **chichikata (no)** paternal

父親 **chichioya** father

父親(の) **chichioya (no)** paternal

父親のよう(な) **chichioya no yō (na)** fatherly

血だらけ(の) **chidarake (no)** bloody, covered in blood

知恵 **chie** wisdom; 知恵を絞る *chie o shiboru* rack one's brains

知恵遅れ(の) **chieokure (no)** backward, retarded

チフス **chifusu** typhus

違い **chigai** contrast; difference

違いない **-chigai nai** surely; 彼らはもう着いたに違いない *karera wa mō tsuita ni chigainai* they must have arrived by now

違いのわかる **chigai no wakaru** discerning; discriminating

違う **chigau** different

違う風に **chigau fū ni** differently, otherwise

ちぎる **chigiru** tear into small pieces

地平線 **chiheisen** horizon

地方 **chihō** district; region

地方分権にする **chihō-bunken ni suru** decentralize

地方自治体 **chihō-jichitai** local government

地方自治体(の) **chihō-jichitai (no)** municipal

地方検事 **chihō-kenji** DA, district attorney

地方(の) **chihō (no)** provincial; rural; regional

地位 **chii** level; position; rank; status

地域 **chiiki** area; neighborhood; terrain

小さい **chiisai** small, little; petty; low

小さくする **chiisaku suru** reduce; turn down

小さ(な) **chiisa (na)** small, little; petty; low

知事 **chiji** governor

縮こまる **chijikomaru** cower

縮み上がる **chijimiagaru** cower

縮む **chijimu** shrink

知人 **chijin** acquaintance

縮れた **chijireta** frizzy; curly

地上 **chijō** above ground

地上管制室 **chijō-kanseishitsu** ground control

地上整備員 **chijō-seibiin** ground crew, ground staff

地下 **chika** basement

地下貯蔵室 **chika-chozōshitsu** underground vaults (*for wine*)

地下で **chika de** underground

地階 **chikai** basement

近い **chikai** near; ...に近い *... ni chikai* border on

誓い **chikai** vow

知覚 **chikaku** perception

近くに **chikaku ni** around; close by, near

知覚する **chikaku suru** perceive

近道 **chikamichi** short cut

地下(の) **chika (no)** underground

ちかん **chikan** groper

ちかんする **chikan suru** molest; feel up

力 **chikara** strength; force; power; might

力こぶ **chikarakobu** biceps

力ずく(の) **chikarazuku (no)** forcible

力強い **chikarazuyoi** strong; powerful; forceful

地下鉄 **chikatetsu** subway

誓う **chikau** pledge; swear; vow

近寄る **chikayoru** approach; ...に近寄らない *... ni chikayoranai* keep away from ...

近づける **chikazukeru** have access to

近づきにくい **chikazukinikui** unapproachable

近づく **chikazuku** draw near, draw on, approach; 近づかない *chikazukanai* keep away

遅刻する **chikoku suru** arrive late

遅刻した **chikoku shita** late

地区 **chiku** district; precinct; quarter

乳首 **chikubi** nipple; teat

チクチクする **chikuchiku suru** prickly; tickle

チクる **chikuru** inform on, snitch on

蓄積 **chikuseki** build-up, accumulation

蓄積する **chikuseki suru** accumulate

畜生 **chikushō** damn it!

地球 **chikyū** the earth; globe

地球儀 **chikyūgi** globe (*model*)

地球(の) **chikyū (no)** global; 地球の温暖化 *chikyū no ondanka* global warming

血まみれ(の) **chimamire (no)** bloodstained

致命傷を受けた **chimeishō o uketa** fatally injured

致命的(な) **chimeiteki (na)** deadly, fatal; mortal

チーム **chīmu** side; team

チームワーク **chīmuwāku** teamwork

鎮圧 **chin'atsu** suppression

鎮圧する **chin'atsu suru** suppress; put down

沈没 **chinbotsu** sinking

沈殿物 **chindenbutsu** sediment

賃金 **chingin** wages

賃金労働者 **chingin-rōdō-sha** wage earner

陳述 **chinjutsu** statement (*to police*)

沈下 **chinka** settlement; subsidence

沈下する **chinka suru** subside

珍味 **chinmi** delicacy

沈黙 **chinmoku** hush, silence

知能 **chinō** intelligence

血の気 **chi no ke** blood; 血の気を失う *chi no ke o ushinau* turn pale

知能(の) **chinō (no)** mental

知能指数 **chinō-shisū** IQ

チンパンジー **chinpanjī** chimpanzee

チンピラ **chinpira** hood, hoodlum

陳列している **chinretsu shite iru** be on display

陳列する **chinretsu suru** display; lay out

鎮静剤 **chinseizai** sedative

賃借契約 **chinshaku-keiyaku** lease

賃借する **chinshaku suru** lease

賃貸契約 **chintai-keiyaku** lease

賃貸契約書 **chintai-keiyakusho** rental agreement

賃貸料 **chintai-ryō** rental; rent

賃貸する **chintai suru** lease; rent

out

チップ **chippu** chip (*in gambling*); tip (*money*)

ちらちら光る **chirachira hikaru** shimmer

ちらちらする **chirachira suru** flicker

散らかった **chirakatta** untidy

散らかっている **chirakatte iru** be a mess

散らかす **chirakasu** scatter; make a mess

ちらりとひと目見る **chirari to hitome miru** catch a glimpse of

ちらし **chirashi** circular; leaflet

散らす **chirasu** disperse

ちらつく **chiratsuku** flicker; fall lightly (*of rain, snow*)

ちらっと見る **chiratto miru** glance at, give a quick look

ちり **chiri** litter; dust

地理 **chiri** geography (*of area*)

地理学 **chirigaku** geography (*subject*)

ちり紙 **chirigami** tissue paper

ちりぢりになる **chirijiri ni naru** be scattered

地理的(な) **chiriteki (na)** geographical

ちりとり **chiritori** dustpan

散る **chiru** scatter; disperse

治療 **chiryō** treatment

治療不可能(な) **chiryō-fukanō (na)** incurable

治療法 **chiryōhō** cure, remedy

治療法(の) **chiryōhō (no)** therapeutic

治療可能(な) **chiryō-kanō (na)** curable

治療過程 **chiryō-katei** course of treatment

治療する **chiryō suru** cure; treat

知性 **chisei** intellect, mind; mentality

治世 **chisei** reign

知識 **chishiki** familiarity; knowledge

知識人 **chishiki-jin** intellectual

知識のある **chishiki no aru** knowledgeable

致死(の) **chishi (no)** lethal

致死量 **chishiryō** overdose

地質 **chishitsu** geology (*of area*)

地質学 **chishitsugaku** geology (*subject*)

地質学(の) **chishitsugaku (no)** geological

地質学者 **chishitsugaku-sha** geologist

窒素 **chisso** nitrogen

窒息 **chissoku** suffocation

窒息させる **chissoku saseru** choke; smother; suffocate

窒息する **chissoku suru** suffocate

血筋 **chisuji** bloodline; lineage

地帯 **chitai** zone

知的(な) **chiteki (na)** intellectual; cerebral

膣 **chitsu** vagina

秩序 **chitsujo** order

散っていく **chitte iku** disperse

ちやほやする **chiyahoya suru** make a fuss of; pamper

地図 **chizu** map

チーズ **chīzu** cheese

地図帳 **chizuchō** atlas

チーズケーキ **chīzukēki** cheesecake

著 **-cho** written by

ちょう **chō** butterfly

腸 **chō** bowels; gut, intestine

長 **chō** head; 店長 **tenchō** store manager; 部長 **buchō** department chief

超 ... **chō...** extremely

兆 **chō** trillion

町 **chō** administrative division of city; area; block

庁 **chō** government agency

跳馬 **chōba** vault

帳簿 **chōbo** accounts book

腸チフス **chō-chifusu** typhoid (fever)

貯蓄 **chochiku** saving

貯蓄する **chochiku suru** save up

ちょうど **chōdo** exactly, just; on the dot; now, immediately; just about; ちょうどその本 **chōdo sono hon** the very book

ちょうだい **chōdai** please

重複 **chōfuku** repetition

重複する **chōfuku suru** repeat; overlap

調合物 **chōgōbutsu** concoction

長波 **chōha** long wave

挑発 **chōhatsu** provocation

挑発的(な) **chōhatsuteki (na)** provocative

徴兵 **chōhei** draft, conscription

徴兵忌避者 **chōhei-kihisha** draft dodger

徴兵する **chōhei suru** draft

長編映画 **chōhen-eiga** feature movie

長方形 **chōhōkei** rectangle

長方形(の) **chōhōkei (no)** oblong, rectangular

超人的(な) **chōjinteki (na)** superhuman

帳尻が合う **chōjiri ga au** balance

長女 **chōjo** first daughter

頂上 **chōjō** summit; tip; crest

著述業 **chojutsugyō** writing

超過 **chōka** excess

懲戒(の) **chōkai (no)** disciplinary

聴覚 **chōkaku** hearing

朝刊 **chōkan** morning paper

超過料金 **chōka-ryōkin** excess fare

超過する **chōka suru** overrun

帳消しにする **chōkeshi ni suru** write off

貯金 **chokin** savings

貯金箱 **chokinbako** piggybank

長期(の) **chōki (no)** long-range; long-term

貯金する **chokin suru** save, put away

ちょっかい **chokkai** …にちょっかいを出す … **ni chokkai o dasu** interfere with, mess with

直角 **chokkaku** right-angle

直感 **chokkan** intuition

直径 **chokkei** diameter

直行便 **chokkō-bin** nonstop flight

直行で **chokkō de** nonstop

直行(の) **chokkō (no)** direct, nonstop

直行列車 **chokkō-ressha** through train

徴候, 兆候 **chōkō** indication, sign

ちょこ **choko** sake cup

彫刻 **chōkoku** sculpture

彫刻家 **chōkoku-ka** sculptor

彫刻する **chōkoku suru** carve

チョコレート **chokorēto** chocolate

チョコレートケーキ **chokorēto-kēki** chocolate cake

超高層ビル **chōkōsō-biru** skyscraper

聴講する **chōkō suru** audit

チョーク **chōku** chalk

直面する **chokumen suru** confront; encounter

直立した **chokuritsu shita** erect; upright

直流 **chokuryū** direct current

直線 **chokusen** straight line

直接(の) **chokusetsu (no)** direct; firsthand; *family*

直通バス **chokutsū-basu** through bus

直通(の) **chokutsū (no)** direct

長距離(の) **chōkyori (no)** long-distance; long-range

長距離通話料 **chōkyori-tsūwaryō** long-distance phone toll

調教師 **chōkyō-shi** trainer

超満員(の) **chōman'in (no)** overcrowded

著名(な) **chomei (na)** eminent

調味料 **chōmiryō** flavoring; seasoning

聴聞会 **chōmonkai** hearing LAW

弔問客 **chōmonkyaku** mourner

蝶結び **chōmusubi** bow (*in hair etc*)

長男 **chōnan** eldest son

蝶ネクタイ **chōnekutai** bow tie

ちょんまげ **chonmage** topknot

超能力(の) **chōnōryoku (no)** psychic

超能力者 **chōnōryoku-sha** psychic (*person*)

超音波 **chōonpa** ultrasound

超音速(の) **chōonsoku (no)** supersonic

調理師 **chōrishi** cook, chef

調理室 **chōrishitsu** galley

調律する **chōritsu suru** tune

鳥類保護区 **chōrui-hogoku** bird sanctuary

調査 **chōsa** examination; investigation; inquest; probe; search; survey

著作権 **chosaku-ken** copyright

調査する **chōsa suru** examine; probe; check out, investigate

調整 **chōsei** coordination; adjustment

調整する **chōsei suru** coordinate; set, adjust; tune up

朝鮮 **Chōsen** Korea

挑戦 **chōsen** challenge

朝鮮語 **Chōsen-go** Korean

朝鮮人 **Chōsen-jin** Korean

朝鮮民主主義人民共和国 **Chōsen-minshu-shugi-jinmin-kyōwakoku** Democratic People's Republic of Korea, North Korea

朝鮮(の) **Chōsen (no)** Korean

挑戦者 **chōsen-sha** challenger; contender

挑戦する **chōsen suru** challenge; attempt

調節 **chōsetsu** regulation; adjustment

調節できる **chōsetsu dekiru** adjustable

調節する **chōsetsu suru** adjust; readjust; regulate

著者 **chosha** author

調子 **chōshi** pitch; tone MUS; 調子が合っている **chōshi ga atte iru** be in tune; 調子がはずれている **chōshi ga hazurete iru** be out of tune; 調子が悪くなる **chōshi ga waruku naru** play up; 調子がよい **chōshi ga yoi** fit; 調子を合わせる **chōshi o awaseru** tune up; 調子を悪くする **chōshi o waruku suru** trouble; 調子はどうですか **chōshi wa dō desu ka** how are you?, how are things?

聴診器 **chōshinki** stethoscope

聴診する **chōshin suru** sound *chest*

超自然(の) **chōshizen (no)** supernatural

超自然的(な) **chōshizenteki (na)** transcendental

長所 **chōsho** merit; strong point

調書 **chōsho** record; report; 調書をとる **chōsho o toru** put on record; book (*for speeding*)

朝食 **chōshoku** breakfast

聴衆 **chōshū** audience

徴収する **chōshū suru** levy

貯水池 **chosuichi** reservoir

超大国 **chōtaikoku** superpower

調停 **chōtei** arbitration, mediation

調停人 **chōtei-nin** troubleshooter

調停者 **chōteisha** mediator

調停する **chōtei suru** arbitrate, mediate

頂点 **chōten** culmination; high point; summit *fig*

ちょうつがい **chōtsugai** hinge

ちょっと **chotto** a little ◊ excuse me!, hello! (*to get attention*); 五十ちょっと **gojū chotto** 50 odd; ちょっと違いますね **chotto chigai masu ne** not exactly; ちょっといいですか **chotto ii desu ka** do you have a minute?; ちょっと聞いてもいいですか **chotto kiite mo ii desu ka** can I ask you something?; ちょっと待ちなさい **chotto machinasai** just you wait!; ちょっと待って下さい **chotto matte kudasai** just a second, please; ちょっと見てもいいですか **chotto mite mo ii desu ka** can I have a quick look?; ちょっと立ち寄る **chotto tachiyoru** drop in for a while

調和 **chōwa** harmony; unity; reconciliation

調和させる **chōwa saseru** harmonize; reconcile

調和しない **chōwa shinai** incongruous

調和した **chōwa shita** harmonious

調和して **chōwa shite** in keeping with

調和する **chōwa suru** match

跳躍 **chōyaku** leap; spring

調剤室 **chōzaishitsu** dispensary

貯蔵品 **chozōhin** stock, supplies (*food*)

貯蔵室 **chozō-shitsu** stockroom

貯蔵する **chozō suru** stock; store up

注 **chū** note, annotation

中 **-chū** during; within; throughout; 午前中 **gozenchū** in the morning

チューブ **chūbu** tube; inner tube

中部 **Chūbu** central region of *Honshu*

中断する **chūdan suru** interrupt, stop; put aside; pause

中道派 **chūdōha** center POL

中毒 **chūdoku** poisoning; addiction; 中毒になっている **chūdoku ni natte iru** be addicted to

中毒者 **chūdoku-sha** addict

中元 **chūgen** midsummer gift

中国 **Chūgoku** China; western region of Honshu

中国語 **Chūgoku-go** Chinese

中国語(の) **Chūgoku-go (no)** Chinese

中国人 **Chūgoku-jin** Chinese

中国系の **Chūgokukei no** of Chinese descent

中国(の) **Chūgoku (no)** Chinese

中位(の) **chūgurai (no)** medium, average

注意 **chūi** attention, heed; mind; …に注意を払う **… ni chūi o harau** heed *advice*; take notice of

注意深い **chūi-bukai** careful, cautious; observant; watchful

注意深く **chūibukaku** carefully, attentively

チューインガム **chūingamu** (chewing) gum

注意する **chūi suru** beware of; look out for; take note of

忠実(な) **chūjitsu (na)** loyal; staunch

仲介者 **chūkai-sha** go-between; intermediary

仲介する **chūkai suru** mediate

中華人民共和国 **Chūkajinmin-kyōwakoku** People's Republic of China

中間管理職 **chūkan-kanrishoku** middle management

中間(の) **chūkan (no)** halfway; neutral (*color*)

中華料理 **Chūka-ryōri** Chinese cuisine

中継放送 **chūkei-hōsō** outside broadcast

中継する **chūkei suru** relay

中近東 **Chūkintō** Middle East

中古で **chūko de** secondhand

忠告 **chūkoku** advice

忠告する **chūkoku suru** advise

中古(の) **chūko (no)** secondhand, used

中級(の) **chūkyū (no)** intermediate

注目 **chūmoku** publicity; 注目の的になる **chūmoku no mato ni naru** be the focus of attention

注目に値する **chūmoku ni atai suru** notable

注目する **chūmoku suru** pay attention

注文 **chūmon** order

注文する **chūmon suru** order

チューナー **chūnā** tuner

中年(の) **chūnen (no)** middle-aged

中二階 **chūnikai** mezzanine (floor)

注入 **chūnyū** injection; transfusion

注入する **chūnyū suru** inject

中央 **chūō** center

中央分離帯 **chūō-bunritai** median strip

中央処理装置 **chūō-shori-sōchi** CPU, central processing unit

チューリップ **chūrippu** tulip

中立 **chūritsu** neutrality

中立(の) **chūritsu (no)** neutral, nonaligned

中流階級 **chūryū-kaikyū** the middle class(es)

中流階級(の) **chūryū-kaikyū (no)** middle class

仲裁 **chūsai** arbitration

仲裁する **chūsai suru** arbitrate; intercede

忠誠 **chūsei** devotion; 会社への忠誠心 **kaisha e no chūseishin** sense of corporate loyalty

中世 **Chūsei** the Middle Ages

中西部 **Chūseibu** Midwest

注射 **chūsha** injection, shot

駐車 **chūsha** parking

注射針 **chūshabari** hypodermic needle

駐車違反 **chūsha-ihan** parking violation

駐車違反の切符 **chūsha-ihan no kippu** parking ticket

駐車場 **chūshajō** car port; parking lot; parking garage

注射器 **chūshaki** syringe

駐車禁止 **chūsha-kinshi** no parking

注射する **chūsha suru** inject

駐車する **chūsha suru** park

中心 **chūshin** center; core; focus; heart

中止 **chūshi** stoppage

中止になる **chūshi ni naru** be off, be canceled

中心(の) **chūshin (no)** central; …に中心を置く *… ni chūshin o oku* center on

中心的(な) **chūshinteki (na)** central

中止する **chūshi suru** abandon; abort

中傷 **chūshō** slur, smear

抽象派(の) **chūshōha (no)** abstract

中小企業 **chūshō-kigyō** small and medium-sized enterprises

昼食 **chūshoku** lunch

昼食時 **chūshokudoki** lunch hour, lunchtime

中傷する **chūshō suru** libel;

slander; smear; blacken

抽象的(な) **chūshōteki (na)** abstract

チューター **chūtā** tutor

中東 **Chūtō** the Middle East

中等教育 **chūtō-kyōiku** secondary education

中途に **chūto ni** midway

駐屯している **chūton shite iru** be stationed at

中途退学者 **chūto-taigaku-sha** dropout

中途退学する **chūto-taigaku suru** drop out

中和する **chūwa suru** counteract; neutralize

中絶 **chūzetsu** interruption; abortion

中絶する **chūzetsu suru** interrupt; abort

D

だ **da** be → *desu*

打撲症 **dabokushō** bruise

だぶだぶ(の) **dabudabu (no)** baggy

ダブル **daburu** double

ダブルベッド **daburu-beddo** double bed

ダブル(の) **daburu (no)** double; double-breasted

ダブルルーム **daburu-rūmu** double room

ダブルス **daburusu** doubles

だ液 **daeki** saliva

だ円 **daen** ellipse

だ円形(の) **daenkei (no)** oval

だが **daga** but

打楽器 **dagakki** percussion instrument; percussion section

駄菓子屋 **dagashi-ya** confectioner; confectionery

打撃 **dageki** blow; hit; …に打撃を与える *… ni dageki o ataeru* deal a

blow to; 打撃を受ける *dageki o ukeru* receive a blow; suffer damage

台 **dai** pedestal; stand

題 **dai** title

代 -**dai** generation; 六十代の人 *rokujū dai no hito* someone in their sixties

大 **dai** large, big; 大都市 *daitoshi* big city

第… **dai…** (*ordinal prefix*): 第一 *daiichi* first; 第二 *daini* second; 第三 *daisan* third

ダイバー **daibā** diver, frogman

大便 **daiben** feces; shit; 大便をする *daiben o suru* defecate; shit

代弁する **daiben suru** speak for

ダイビング **daibingu** dive (*underwater*)

大部分 **daibubun** bulk

大仏 **daibutsu** great Buddha

台地 **daichi** terrace; plateau

台帳 **daichō** ledger

台所 **daidokoro** kitchen; kitchenette

台所用品 **daidokoro-yōhin** kitchen utensil

ダイエット **daietto** diet

ダイエットする **daietto suru** diet, slim

大学 **daigaku** college; university

大学院(の) **daigakuin (no)** postgraduate

大学院生 **daigakuinsei** postgraduate (*person*)

大学(の) **daigaku (no)** university

大学生 **daigakusei** college student

代議士 **daigishi** Member of the Diet

大虐殺 **daigyakusatsu** carnage; massacre; holocaust

大ヒット **dai hitto** smash hit

代表 **daihyō** delegate; representative; representation

代表団 **daihyō-dan** delegation; deputation

代表する **daihyō suru** represent

大臣 **daijin** minister; secretary POL

大事(な) **daiji (na)** important

大事にする **daiji ni suru** value; prize; treat as important

大臣(の) **daijin (no)** ministerial

大丈夫 **daijōbu**: 大丈夫ですか **daijōbu desu ka** are you ok?

大丈夫(な) **daijōbu (na)** OK; safe

大韓民国 **Daikan-minkoku** the Republic of Korea, South Korea

大規模(な) **daikibo (na)** large-scale

代金 **daikin** charge; price; bill

代金引き換え払い **daikin-hikikaebarai** COD, collect on delivery

大嫌い(な) **daikirai (na)** hateful; ゴキブリは大嫌いです **gokiburi wa daikirai desu** I hate cockroaches

大混乱 **daikonran** chaos; havoc

大工 **daiku** carpenter

代名詞 **daimeishi** pronoun

大名 **daimyō** feudal lord

ダイナマイト **dainamaito** dynamite

台無しにする **dainashi ni suru** mess up, ruin

大人気 **daininki** sensation; phenomenon

ダイレクトメール **dairekuto-mēru** junk mail

代理 **dairi** representative; substitute

代理母 **dairibo** surrogate mother

代理人 **dairi-nin** agent; proxy; deputy

代理(の) **dairi (no)** acting; 代理をする **dairi o suru** represent; stand in for

大理石 **dairiseki** marble

代理店 **dairiten** agency

大流行 **dairyūkō** craze

大災害 **daisaigai** catastrophe

第三世界 **Daisan-sekai** Third World

大聖堂 **daiseidō** cathedral

大成功 **daiseikō** coup *fig*; hit, success

大失敗 **daishippai** fiasco; mistake

大好き(な) **daisuki (na)** favorite; …が大好きだ **...ga daisuki da** have a soft spot for; adore; チョコレートは大好きです **chokorēto wa daisuki desu** I love chocolate

だいたい **daitai** more or less; roughl, approximately

大胆不敵(な) **daitanfuteki (na)** fearless

大胆(な) **daitan (na)** adventurous; bold; flamboyant

大胆さ **daitan-sa** audacity

大多数 **daitasū** majority

大邸宅 **daiteitaku** mansion

大統領 **daitōryō** president

大統領(の) **daitōryō (no)** presidential

大都市 **daitoshi** metropolis

大都市(の) **daitoshi (no)** metropolitan

ダイヤ **daiya** schedule (*for bus, train*); diamond

ダイヤモンド **daiyamondo** diamond

ダイヤル **daiyaru** dial

ダイヤルする **daiyaru suru** dial

代用品 **daiyōhin** replacement; substitute

代用する **daiyō suru** substitute

題材 **daizai** subject matter; topic

大豆 **daizu** soy bean

だじゃれ **dajare** pun

打開する **dakai suru** thrash out, resolve

だから **dakara** because; since; that's why, so; あなたがそれを嫌いだから **anata ga sore o kirai dakara** since you don't like it

…だけ **... dake** only; solely

だけど **dakedo** but

…だけれども **... da keredomo** although; however

抱き合う **dakiau** embrace

抱き締める **dakishimeru** clasp; cuddle; hug

抱き締めたくなる **dakishimetaku naru** cuddly

奪還する **dakkan suru** recapture

脱穀する **dakkoku suru** thresh

脱きゅうさせる **dakkyū saseru** dislocate

抱く **daku** embrace

妥協 **dakyō** compromise

妥協しない **dakyō shinai** uncompromising

妥協する **dakyō suru** compromise

黙らせる **damaraseru** silence, gag

黙る **damaru** shut up, pipe down

だまされる **damasareru** fall for

だまされやすい **damasare-yasui** credulous; gullible

だます **damasu** deceive; trick; rip off, cheat

黙っている **damatte iru** keep quiet about; keep ... in the dark

だまし取る **damashitoru** swindle, cheat

ダメージ **damēji** damage

だめになる **dame ni naru** screwed up ◊ come unstuck

だめになって **dame ni natte** in ruins; spoilt

だめにする **dame ni suru** ruin, screw up

ダム **damu** dam

段 **dan** step; stair; rung

弾圧 **dan'atsu** repression

弾圧的(な) **dan'atsuteki (na)** repressive

暖房 **danbō** heating

段ボール紙 **danbōru-gami** corrugated cardboard

団地 **danchi** *apartment provided by local authorities*

だんだん **dandan** gradually; …にだんだんと向かう **... ni dandan to mukau** lead up to; だんだん激しくなる **dandan hageshiku naru** escalate; get more violent; だんだんと聞こえなくなる **dandan to kikoenaku naru** die away

断言 **dangen** declaration; assertion

断言する **dangen suru** declare

だんご **dango** dumpling

断食 **danjiki** fast (*not eating*)

男女 **danjo** men and women; the two sexes

男女同権主義(の) **danjo-dōkenshugi (no)** feminist

男女共学(の) **danjo-kyōgaku (no)** co-educational

段階 **dankai** stage; phase; point

段階的(な) **dankaiteki (na)** progressive

段階的に **dankaiteki ni** gradually, progressively; 段階的に導入する **dankaiteki ni dōnyū suru** phase in; 段階的に廃止する **dankaiteki ni haishi suru** phase out

団結心 **danketsushin** team spirit

団結する **danketsu suru** unite

断固とした **danko to shita** determined; firm; strong-minded

断熱 **dannetsu** insulation

断熱する **dannetsu suru** insulate

断熱材 **dannetsuzai** insulation (*material*)

断片 **danpen** shred; fragment; piece

断片的(な) **danpenteki (na)** fragmentary

段落 **danraku** paragraph

暖炉 **danro** fireplace

弾力性 **danryokusei** elasticity

弾力性のある **danryokusei no aru** elastic; springy

段差 **dansa** bump; ramp (*in road*)

ダンサー **dansā** dancer

男性 **dansei** male

男性(の) **dansei (no)** male; masculine

男性的(な) **danseiteki (na)** masculine

男性用トイレ **dansei-yō toire** men's room, gents

男子生徒 **danshi-seito** schoolboy

男娼 **danshō** male prostitute

男尊女卑 **danson-johi** male domination

ダンス **dansu** dance; dancing

団体 **dantai** group

団体交渉 **dantai-kōshō** collective bargaining

断定する **dantei suru** conclude

弾薬 **dan'yaku** ammunition

だらだら長引く **daradara nagabiku** drag (of day); drag on (of meeting)

堕落させる **daraku saseru** corrupt

堕落した **daraku shita** tainted

堕落する **daraku suru** degenerate

だらしない **darashinai** untidy; loose morals; undisciplined

誰 **dare** who

誰でも **dare de mo** whoever; 彼女を知っている人誰でもと話した **kanojo o shitte iru hito dare demo to hanashita** I've spoken to everyone who knew her

誰か **dareka** anybody; someone

誰も **dare mo** nobody; anybody; 誰も知らない **dare mo shiranai** nobody knows

誰(の) **dare (no)** whose

だれる **dareru** stagnate; lose enthusiasm

誰それ **daresore** so-and-so

だろう **-darō** will probably ◊ suppose

だるま **daruma** Dharma doll

ダサい **dasai** dowdy; provincial; awkward

駄作 **dasaku** trash; poor work

打算的(な) **dasanteki (na)** calculating, sly

惰性で **dasei de** out of habit

惰性で走る **dasei de hashiru** freewheel

出し物 **dashimono** act; turn (in vaudeville)

出し抜けに **dashinuke ni** abruptly

出し抜く **dashinuku** outwit

出し惜しみする **dashioshimi suru** grudge; be unwilling to give

出しっぱなしにする **dashippanashi ni suru** leave lying around; leave running

脱線 **dassen** digression

脱線する **dassen suru** be derailed

脱脂綿 **dasshimen** absorbent cotton

ダッシュボード **dasshubōdo** dash(board)

脱出する **dasshutsu suru** escape, break out; eject

脱走 **dassō** escape; desertion

脱走する **dassō suru** escape; desert; bolt

脱水機 **dassui-ki** spin-dryer

脱水症状 **dassui-shōjō** dehydration; 脱水症状を起こした **dassui-shōjō o okoshita** dehydrated

脱水する **dassui suru** spin-dry

ダース **dāsu** dozen

出す **dasu** issue warning; publish, bring out; put question; give; serve dish; hold out; take out; submit; send; show; stick out; break out (of fever); gather speed; open

ダストシュート **dasuto-shūto** chute

妥当でない **datō de nai** invalid; inappropriate

妥当(な) **datō (na)** reasonable; valid; appropriate

妥当性 **datōsei** validity

打倒する **datō suru** overturn, bring down government

脱毛剤 **datsumōzai** hair remover

脱落する **datsuraku suru** drop out

脱税 **datsuzei** tax evasion

脱退する **dattai suru** break away, secede

ダウ平均 **Dau-heikin** Dow Jones Average

ダウン **daun** down

ダウンロードする **daunrōdo suru** download

…で **... de** ◊ in; at; on; 家で **ie de** at home; …で休暇を過ごす **...de kyūka o sugosu** go to ... on vacation; 一時間で着く **ichijikan de tsuku** I'll be there in an hour ◊ by; with; 自転車で **jitensha de** by bicycle; 鉛筆で **enpitsu de** with a pencil ◊ owing to; 病気で **byōki de** owing to illness

…である **... de aru** be

出会い **deai** encounter, meeting

出会う **deau** meet *person*; encounter *difficulty etc*

デビットカード **debitto-kādo** debit card

でぶ **debu** fatty, fatso

デビュー **debyū** début

出口 **deguchi** exit, way out

出入口 **deiriguchi** doorway

デジタル **dejitaru** digital

デジタルディバイド **dejitaru-dibaido** digital divide

デジタル式(の) **dejitaru-shiki (no)** digital

出かける **dekakeru** go out

デカンター **dekantā** decanter

出来 **deki** result

出来上がり **dekiagari** completion

出来上がる **dekiagaru** be finished

出来上がっている **dekiagatte iru** tight, smashed

出来合い(の) **dekiai (no)** ready-made

出来栄え **dekibae** workmanship; result

出来事 **dekigoto** event; occurrence

できもの **dekimono** spot; boil

出来のいい **deki no ii** good *result, quality*

出来の悪い **deki no warui** poor *result, quality*

できれば **dekireba** if possible; hopefully; preferably; できれば手伝います **dekireba tetsudai masu** I would help if I could

できる **dekiru** be able to; be ready; be finished; be capable of

できるだけ **dekiru dake** as … as possible; できるだけ早く **dekiru dake hayaku** as soon as possible; …をできるだけ活用する **… o dekiru dake katsuyō suru** make the most of; できるだけよい **dekirudake yoi** the best possible

でき死させる **dekishi saseru** drown

デッキ **dekki** deck

デッキチェア **dekkichea** deckchair

でこぼこ(な) **dekoboko (na)** irregular; uneven; bumpy; lumpy

出くわす **dekuwasu** run across, meet; run into *person, problem*; come across

出前 **demae** home delivery

デモ **demo** demonstration, demo; デモをする **demo o suru** demonstrate POL

でも **demo** ◊ but; though; でも私は行かない **demo watashi wa ikanai** but I am not going ◊: 誰でも **dare demo** anyone; どこでも **doko demo** anywhere ◊ even: 雨でも **ame demo** even if it rains ◊ or something; コーヒーでもいかがですか **kōhī demo ikaga desu ka** would you like to have coffee or something?

デモ行進 **demo-kōshin** march, demo

デモ行進する **demo-kōshin suru** march

でもね、 **demo ne,** mind you,

デモンストレーション **demonsutorēshon** demonstration (*of equipment*)

デモテープ **demo-tēpu** demo (tape)

出迎える **demukaeru** meet

…でない **… de nai** not; un-; 本気でない **honki de nai** not serious; 安全でない **anzen de nai** unsafe; insecure

電圧 **den'atsu** voltage

電池 **denchi** battery

伝道師 **dendōshi** evangelist

伝導する **dendō suru** conduct ELEC

電源 **dengen** switch; power supply

電撃 **dengeki** shock ELEC

伝言 **dengon** message

デニム(の) **denimu (no)** denim

デニッシュ **Denisshu** Danish (pastry)

電化製品 **denka-seihin** appliance

伝記 **denki** biography

電気 **denki** electricity

電気技師 **denki-gishi** electrician

電気配線 **denki-haisen** wiring

電気いす **denki-isu** the (electric) chair

電気かみそり **denki-kamisori** shaver

電気(の) **denki (no)** electric; electrical

電気通信 **denki-tsūshin** telecommunications

電極 **denkyoku** electrode

電球 **denkyū** (light) bulb

デンマーク **Denmāku** Denmark

デンマーク(の) **Denmāku (no)** Danish

電熱器 **dennetsuki** hotplate

電報 **denpō** telegram, wire

でんぷん質 **denpunshitsu** carbohydrate; starch

電力 **denryoku** power

電流 **denryū** current

電線 **densen** power line; wire; run (in pantyhose)

伝染 **densen** transmission; infection

伝染性(の) **densensei (no)** contagious, catching

伝説 **densetsu** legend

電車 **densha** train

電子 **denshi** electron

電子データ処理 **denshi-dēta-shori** EDP, electronic data processing

電子工学 **denshi-kōgaku** electronics

電子工学(の) **denshi-kōgaku (no)** electronic

電子メール **denshi-mēru** e-mail

電信柱 **denshinbashira** telegraph pole

電子レンジ **denshi-renji** microwave (oven)

電卓 **dentaku** calculator; pocket calculator

伝達 **dentatsu** transmission; communication

伝統 **dentō** tradition

伝統的(な) **dentōteki (na)** traditional, conventional

電話 **denwa** (phone)call; (tele)phone; 電話をかける **denwa o kakeru** dial number; 電話を切る **denwa o kiru** cut off; 電話をかけ直す **denwa o kakenaosu** call back

電話番号 **denwa-bangō** (tele)phone number

電話帳 **denwachō** telephone directory, phone book

電話機 **denwaki** (tele)phone

電話交換室 **denwa-kōkanshitsu** telephone exchange

電話に出る **denwa ni deru** answer the telephone

電話線 **denwasen** line TELEC

電話セールス **denwa-sērusu** telesales

電話する **denwa suru** dial number; (tele)phone, call

デオドラント **deodoranto** deodorant

デオキシリボ核酸 **deokishiribo-kakusan** DNA, deoxyribonucleic acid

デパート **depāto** department store

デリカテッセン **derikatessen** delicatessen

デリケート(な) **derikēto (na)** delicate

デリケートさ **derikēto-sa** delicacy

出る **deru** come out (of sun, results, product); get out; be given; infuse; leave; make it (to party, meeting etc); run (of faucet); be issued; stick out; break out; show; attend; graduate

弟子 **deshi** disciple; pupil; apprentice

デシベル **deshiberu** decibel

でしょう **deshō** polite form of darō

です **desu** polite form of da; 学生です **gakusei desu** he's a student; どこです **doko desu** where is it?; 雨です **ame desu** it's raining; チャーリーです **Chārī desu** it's Charlie here

デスクトップパブリッシング **desukutoppu-paburisshingu** DTP, desktop publishing

ですが **desu ga** but

ですから **desu kara** so; therefore; because

データ **dēta** data

データベース **dēta-bēsu** database

データ保護 **dēta-hogo** data protection

データ管理 **dēta-kanri** data storage; data management

デタント **detanto** détente

でたらめ(な) **detarame (na)** haphazard; nonsensical

でたらめを言う **detarame o iu** bullshit

データ処理 **dēta-shori** data

processing

でっちあげる **detchiageru** concoct;
帳簿をでっちあげる **chōbo o
detchi ageru** fiddle the accounts

出て行く **dete iku** go out (*of person*);
leave; clear out; move out; walk
out; 出て行け **dete ike** (get) out!

出ている **dete iru** be out (*of sun*)

出てくる **dete kuru** leave; come out
(*on date*)

では **dewa** well then; right

デート **dēto** date (*romantic*)

デザイン **dezain** design

デザイナー **dezainā** designer

デザインする **dezain suru** design

デザート **dezāto** dessert

DNA **dī-enu-ē** DNA

ディフェンス **difensu** defense

DJ **dī-jē** disc jockey

ディナー **dinā** dinner

ディーラー **dīrā** dealer

ディスコ **disuko** disco

ディスク **disuku** disk

ディスクドライブ **disuku-doraibu**
disk drive

ディスクジョッキー **disuku-jokkī** disc
jockey

ディスプレー **disupurē** display

ディーゼル **dīzeru** diesel

度 **do** degree; …に度が過ぎる *… ni
do ga sugiru* go overboard for

どう **dō** how; what; どうですか *dō
desu ka* how is it?; どうしますか *dō
shimasu ka* what are you going to
do?; 彼なんてどうでもいい *kare
nante dō demo ii* to hell with him;
どうでもよい *dō de mo yoi* it
doesn't make any difference; …は
どうですか *… wa dō desu ka* how
about …?; どうしたの *dō shita no*
what's the matter (with you)?,
what's wrong?

銅 **dō** copper

胴 **dō** trunk (*of body*)

同 … **dō…** same; 同時代 **dōjidai**
(*no*) contemporary

ドア **doa** door

土木技師 **doboku-gishi** civil
engineer

動物 **dōbutsu** animal

動物園 **dōbutsuen** zoo

動物学 **dōbutsugaku** zoology

動物学(の) **dōbutsugaku (no)**
zoological

同着 **dōchaku** dead heat

土着(の) **dochaku (no)** native

どちら **dochira** which

どちらでも **dochira demo** either;
whichever

どちらか(の) **dochira ka no** either

どちらも **dochira mo** both

どちら(の) **dochira (no)** which

同調する **dōchō suru** sympathize

土台 **dodai** foundations

堂々とした **dōdō to shita** dignified;
majestic; regal

同封する **dōfū suru** enclose

動議 **dōgi** motion (*at conference*)

どぎまぎさせる **dogimagi saseru**
disconcert; embarrass

どぎまぎした **dogimagi shita**
disconcerted; embarrassed

どぎまぎする **dogimagi suru** be
disconcerted; feel embarrassed

道具 **dōgu** tool, device, implement

同輩 **dōhai** peer, equal

土俵 **dohyō** sumo ring

同意 **dōi** agreement, consent

同意語 **dōigo** synonym

同意する **dōi suru** concur, agree,
consent

どういたしまして **dō itashimashite**
don't mention it, you're welcome

ドイツ **Doitsu** Germany

ドイツ語 **Doitsu-go** German

ドイツ人 **Doitsu-jin** German

ドイツ(の) **Doitsu (no)** German

同時に **dōji ni** at the same time,
together; simultaneously

同情 **dōjō** compassion; sympathy

同情する **dōjō suru** commiserate,
sympathize

同情的(な) **dōjōteki (na)**
sympathetic

どうか **dō ka** ◊ please; どうか手伝って
ください **dō ka tetsudatte kudasai**
please help ◊ whether (or not);買う
かどうか **kau ka dō ka** whether to
buy or not; どうかと思う **dō ka to
omou** I wonder

同化する **dōka suru** assimilate

同感する **dōkan suru** feel the same, agree

同形異義語 **dōkei-igigo** homograph

どける **dokeru** remove

動機 **dōki** motivation; motive

動悸 **dōki** palpitations

どきどきする **dokidoki suru** flutter; pound (*of heart*)

ドック **dokku** dock

どこ **doko** where

瞳孔 **dōkō** pupil (*of eye*)

どこでも **doko demo** anywhere; everywhere

どこか **dokoka** somewhere

どこかで **dokoka de** anywhere

どこかに **dokoka ni** anywhere; somewhere

同国人 **dōkoku-jin** (fellow) countryman

どこも **doko mo** everywhere; anywhere

どこに **doko ni** where

どこにも **doko ni mo** anywhere; nowhere

どころか **dokoro ka** as well as; on the contrary

どことなく **dokotonaku** somehow

毒 **doku** poison; venom; ...に毒を盛 る ...**ni doku o moru** poison

独房 **dokubō** solitary cell

独自(の) **dokuji (no)** original; unique

毒きのこ **doku kinoko** toadstool

独立 **dokuritsu** independence

独立記念日 **Dokuritsu-kinenbi** Independence Day

独立(の) **dokuritsu (no)** independent

独立した **dokuritsu shita** sovereign

独立して **dokuritsu shite** independently

独力で **dokuryoku de** single-handedly

独力(の) **dokuryoku (no)** single-handed

独裁政治 **dokusai-seiji** dictatorship, tyranny

独裁者 **dokusai-sha** dictator

独裁的(な) **dokusaiteki (na)** dictatorial

独占する **dokusen suru** monopolize

独占的(な) **dokusenteki (na)** exclusive

独占欲の強い **dokusen'yoku no tsuyoi** possessive

読者 **dokusha** reader

独身(の) **dokushin (no)** single

読唇する **dokushin suru** lipread

読書 **dokusho** reading

読書する **dokusho suru** read

独奏 **dokusō** solo

独創性 **dokusōsei** originality; creativity

独特(な) **dokutoku (na)** distinctive

独特(の) **dokutoku (no)** unique

ドキュメンタリー **dokyumentarī** documentary

同級生 **dōkyūsei** classmate; peer

同盟 **dōmei** alliance

どうも **dōmo** ◊ thank you ◊ very much ◊ I suspect that; どうもありがと う **dōmo arigatō** thanks very much

どう猛(な) **dōmō (na)** ferocious; vicious

どもる **domoru** stammer, stutter

ドーム **dōmu** dome

動脈 **dōmyaku** artery

どなる **donaru** bawl, bellow; shout

どうなる **dō naru**: どうなるかわかりま せんね **dō naru ka wakarimasen ne** you never know; 彼女はどうなっ た **kanojo wa dō natta** what's become of her?

ドーナッツ **dōnattsu** donut

丼もの **donburimono** bowl of rice with topping of meat, egg, fish etc

どんちゃん騒ぎ **donchansawagi** drinking session

どんぐり **donguri** acorn

どうにか **dōnika** somehow; どうにか 暮していく **dōnika kurashite iku** manage to survive; どうにか...する **dōnika ... suru** contrive

鈍感 **donkan** insensitivity

鈍感(な) **donkan (na)** insensitive

どんな **donna** what?; what kind of?; 彼女はどんな人ですか **kanojo wa** *donna hito desu ka* what is she like?; どんな…でも *donna ... demo* whatever kind; どんな事情があっても *donna jijō ga atte mo* under no circumstances

どの **dono** which; any; どの辺り *dono atari* where abouts?; あなたがどのスタイルを選ぶにしても *anata ga dono sutairu o erabu ni shite mo* whichever style you choose; どのくらい *dono kurai* how much?; how many?; how far? how soon?

殿 **-dono** polite title suffix used in formal letters after addressee's name

どん欲 **don'yoku** greed

どん欲(な) **don'yoku (na)** acquisitive; greedy; voracious

どんよりした **don'yori shita** glazed; dull; lackluster

導入 **dōnyū** introduction

導入する **dōnyū suru** bring in

どん底に落ちる **donzoko ni ochiru** reach rock bottom

ドラゴン **doragon** dragon

ドライバー **doraibā** driver, motorist; screwdriver

ドライブ **doraibu** ride (in vehicle); run (in car); drive (also COMPUT)

ドライブインシアター **doraibuin-shiatā** drive-in

ドライクリーニングする **dorai-kurīningu suru** dryclean

ドライクリーニング屋 **dorai-kurīningu-ya** dry cleaner's

ドラマ **dorama** drama; play

ドラマー **doramā** drummer

ドラマチック(な) **doramachikku (na)** dramatic

ドラム **doramu** drum

動乱 **dōran** upheaval; disturbance

どれ **dore** which

どれでも **dore demo** whichever; どれでもいいから取りなさい *dore demo ii kara torinasai* take one, it doesn't matter which

どれほど **dore hodo** how much; どれほど大きくても / 金持ちでも *dore hodo ōkikute mo / kanemochi demo* however big / rich he / she is

奴隷 **dorei** slave

どれくらい **dore kurai** how; どれくらいかかりますか *dore kurai kakarimasu ka* how long does it take?; どれくらい前ですか *dore kurai mae desu ka* how long ago?

ドレッシング **doresshingu** (salad) dressing

ドレス **doresu** frock

ドレスアップする **doresuappu suru** dress up

ドリブルする **doriburu suru** dribble SP

ドリル **doriru** drill (tool)

泥 **doro** earth; muck; mud; …に泥を塗る *...ni doro o nuru* bring dishonor on

道路 **dōro** road

泥棒 **dorobō** thief

道路地図 **dōro-chizu** road map

泥だらけ(の) **doro darake (no)** muddy

道路標識 **dōro-hyōshiki** roadsign

道路工事 **dōro-kōji** road repairs

ドル **doru** dollar, buck

同僚 **dōryō** associate, colleague; peer

努力 **doryoku** effort; exertion; endeavor

動力 **dōryoku** power

努力する **doryoku suru** endeavor; exert oneself

同量(の) **dōryō (no)** equivalent

動作 **dōsa** movement

洞察 **dōsatsu** insight

洞察力 **dōsatsuryoku** insight, perception

どうせ **dōse** anyhow; at best

同棲 **dōsei** cohabitation

同性愛(の) **dōseiai (no)** homosexual

同性愛者 **dōseiai-sha** homosexual

同棲する **dōsei suru** cohabit

土砂降り(の) **doshaburi (no)** torrential

同志 **dōshi** comrade

動詞 **dōshi** verb

どうして **dōshite** how come?; what for?; why?; どうしていいか分からなくなる *dōshite ii ka wakaranakunaru* be at one's wits' end; どうしていやなの *dōshite iya na no* *na no* why not?

どうしても **dōshite mo** by any means

同室する **dōshitsu suru** double up

どうしようもない **dō shiyō mo nai** hopeless

同窓会 **dōsōkai** reunion

どっしりした **dosshiri shita** massive

同数(の) **dōsū (no)** equivalent

どっち **dotchi** which one?; どっちでもいいです **dotchi demo ii desu** I don't mind

どっちつかずの場合 **dotchitsukazu no bāi** borderline case

土手 **dote** bank (of river)

童貞 **dōtei** virgin; virginity (male)

同点 **dōten** tie (in sports); 二対二の同点 **ni-tai-ni no dōten** two all

同点にする **dōten ni suru** even the score

同点(の) **dōten (no)** level, tied

動転した **dōten shita** shattered, shocked

同等である **dōtō de aru** match; be equal to; be on a par with

道徳 **dōtoku** ethics; morals; morality

道徳的(な) **dōtokuteki (na)** ethical; moral

同等(の) **dōtō (no)** equivalent

同等の人 **dōtō no hito** equal

ドット **dotto** dot

どうやって **dō yatte** how

動揺 **dōyō** agitation; upheaval; unrest

童謡 **dōyō** nursery rhyme

同様 **dōyō** same; similar; …と同様に … *to dōyō ni* in the same way as; as well as

土曜日 **doyōbi** Saturday

動揺させる **dōyō saseru** disturbing ◊ ruffle

動揺した **dōyō shita** agitated

動揺する **dōyō suru** be shaken; get ruffled

同然である **dōzen de aru** verge on; be equal to

どうぞ **dōzo** please; come in!; go ahead!; どうぞ試してみてください *dōzo tameshite mite kudasai* you're welcome to try some

銅像 **dōzō** bronze

E

柄 **e** handle; shaft

絵 **e** painting; picture; 絵をかく *e o kaku* draw; paint

へ **e** to; for; on; in

ええ **ē** yes; no; ええ、わかっています *ē wakatte imasu* yes, I know; え、どうぞ *ē, dōzo* please do

エーッ **ē'** (expression of surprise, doubt or hesitation) eh?; uh?; well, well!

エアコン **eakon** air conditioner; air conditioning

エアロビクス **earobikusu** aerobics

エアターミナル **eatāminaru** air terminal

えび **ebi** shrimp; prawn

枝 **eda** branch

エディター **editā** editor

江戸時代 **Edo-jidai** Edo period

絵筆 **efude** paintbrush

描く **egaku** depict, portray

笑顔 **egao** smiling face

エゴ **ego** ego

絵はがき **ehagaki** (picture) postcard

絵本 **ehon** picture book

英文学 **Eibungaku** English literature

HIV陽性(の) **eichi-ai-bui-yōsei (no)** HIV-positive

永遠 **eien** eternity

永遠(の) **eien (no)** eternal,

everlasting

映画 **eiga** movie, picture

映画界 **eigakai** cinema

映画館 **eigakan** movie theater

映画監督 **eiga-kantoku** movie director

英語 **Eigo** English; 英語で *Eigo de* in English

営業 **eigyō** selling

営業部 **eigyō-bu** sales (department)

営業中(の) **eigyōchū (no)** open for business

営業時間 **eigyō-jikan** business hours, office hours

営業課長 **eigyō-kachō** sales manager

営業する **eigyō suru** operate

栄光 **eikō** glory

栄光ある **eikō aru** glorious

英国 **Eikoku** GB, (Great) Britain; UK

英国人 **Eikoku-jin** the British; Briton

英国(の) **Eikoku (no)** British

影響 **eikyō** effect; impact; influence; repercussions; 影響を及ぼす *eikyō o oyobosu* affect; influence; 影響を受けやすい *eikyō o ukeyasui* susceptible; …に影響されない *... ni eikyō sarenai* impervious to

影響力 **eikyōryoku** clout, influence, pull; leverage

影響力のある **eikyōryoku no aru** influential

永久に **eikyū ni** forever; permanently

永久的(な) **eikyūteki (na)** permanent; perpetual

衛生 **eisei** hygiene

衛星 **eisei** satellite

衛生局 **eiseikyoku** sanitation department

衛生設備 **eisei-setsubi** sanitary facilities

衛生的(な) **eiseiteki (na)** hygienic, sanitary

衛星テレビ **eisei-terebi** satellite TV

映写機 **eishaki** projector

映写する **eisha suru** screen

英和辞典 **Eiwa jiten** English-Japanese dictionary

栄養 **eiyō** nourishment; nutrition

栄養分 **eiyōbun** goodness

栄養不足(の) **eiyōbusoku (no)** underfed

栄養のある **eiyō no aru** nourishing, nutritious

栄養失調 **eiyō-shitchō** malnutrition

英雄 **eiyū** hero

英雄的(な) **eiyūteki (na)** heroic

永続させる **eizoku saseru** perpetuate

永続する **eizoku suru** enduring

エイズ **eizu** Aids

エジプト **Ejiputo** Egypt

エジプト(の) **Ejiputo (no)** Egyptian

絵かき **ekaki** painter

駅 **eki** (railroad) station; stop; depot

駅弁 **ekiben** lunch box

疫病 **ekibyō** plague

液晶表示 **ekishō-hyōji** LCD, liquid crystal display

エキスパート **ekisupāto** expert

液体 **ekitai** liquid

液体(の) **ekitai (no)** liquid

エキゾチック(な) **ekizochikku (na)** exotic

エックス線 **ekkususen** X-ray

eコマース **e komāsu** e-commerce

エコノミークラス **ekonomī-kurasu** economy class

えくぼ **ekubo** dimple

エメラルド **emerarudo** emerald

エメラルド色 **emerarudo-iro** emerald

獲物 **emono** prey

エムサイズ **em-saizu** medium

円 **en** circle; yen

縁 **en** karma, fate

エナメル **enameru** enamel

円盤 **enban** discus; disk

えん尾服 **enbifuku** tail coat

延長 **enchō** extension

延長コード **enchō-kōdo** extension cable

延長する **enchō suru** extend; roll over; prolong

円柱 **enchū** column

演台 **endai** dais

円高 **endaka** appreciation of the yen

演壇 **endan** platform; rostrum; pulpit

縁談 **endan** marriage proposal

えんどう豆 **endōmame** pea

えんえんと **en'en to** on and on, endlessly

エネルギー **enerugī** energy

沿岸警備隊 **engan-keibitai** coastguard

沿岸(の) **engan (no)** coastal

園芸 **engei** gardening; horticulture

園芸家 **engei-ka** gardener

演劇 **engeki** drama

演劇(の) **engeki (no)** dramatic; theatrical

演技 **engi** acting; performance; portrayal

縁起 **engi** sign; omen; 縁起をかつぐ **engi o katsugu** be superstitious

縁起のいい **engi no ii** lucky

縁起の悪い **engi no warui** unlucky

援護 **engo** backup; protection

援軍 **engun** reinforcements

エンジン **enjin** engine, motor

エンジニア **enjinia** engineer

演じる **enjiru** interpret, play role

援助 **enjo** aid, assistance; input

炎上している **enjō shite iru** be ablaze

援助する **enjo suru** aid, stake

宴会 **enkai** dinner party; banquet

円形(の) **enkei (no)** circular

延期 **enki** postponement; reprieve

延期する **enki suru** postpone, put off

えん曲曲法 **enkyoku-gohō** euphemism

円満(な) **enman (na)** amiable; peaceful; harmonious

絵の具 **enogu** paint

鉛筆 **enpitsu** pencil

鉛筆削り **enpitsu-kezuri** pencil sharpener

遠慮 **enryo** reserve; personal restraint

遠征試合 **ensei-jiai** away match

遠視(の) **enshi (no)** far-sighted, long-sighted

炎症 **enshō** inflammation

円周 **enshū** circumference

演出 **enshutsu** direction

演出家 **enshutsu-ka** director

演出する **enshutsu suru** direct

塩素 **enso** chlorine

演奏 **ensō** performance; rendering

遠足 **ensoku** excursion, outing

演奏者 **ensō-sha** musician; player

演奏する **ensō suru** interpret; perform; play MUS

円すい形 **ensuikei** cone

エンストする **ensuto suru** stall (of vehicle)

エンターテイナー **entāteinā** entertainer

円筒形(の) **entōkei (no)** cylindrical

煙突 **entotsu** chimney

円安 **en'yasu** depreciation of the yen

遠洋航海(の) **en'yō-kōkai (no)** seagoing

演説をする **enzetsu o suru** make a speech

演説者 **enzetsu-sha** speaker, orator

演説する **enzetsu suru** speak; speak to

演ずる **enzuru** perform

エピローグ **epirōgu** epilog

えら **era** gills

選ばれた **erabareta** selected

選び出す **erabidasu** select, pick on

選ぶ **erabu** choose, pick, plump for; single out

偉い **erai** eminent; great

エラーメッセージ **erā-messēji** error message

偉そうに **erasō ni** self-importantly; ...に偉そうに指図する **... ni erasō ni sashizu suru** boss around

エレベーター **erebētā** elevator

エレガント(な) **ereganto (na)** elegant; dressy

エレクトロン **erekutoron** electron

襟 **eri** collar

エリート **erīto** elite

エリート(の) **erīto (no)** elite

エロティック(な) **erotikku (na)** erotic

エロティシズム **erotishizumu** eroticism

得る **eru** earn; gain; obtain, get
えさ **esa** bait; えさをやる **esa o yaru** feed
エッセイ **essei** essay
エース **ēsu** ace

エスカレーター **esukarētā** escalator
エッチ(な) **etchi (na)** naughty; warped; perverted
エッチング **etchingu** etching
えーっと… **ētto …** well …

F

ファイバーグラス **faibā-gurasu** fiberglass
ファインダー **faindā** viewfinder
ファイル **fairu** file; folder
ファイルマネジャー **fairu-manejā** file manager
ファイルする **fairu suru** file
ファックス **fakkusu** fax; …をファックスする **… o fakkusu suru** send by fax
ファン **fan** fan; enthusiast; follower; supporter; 映画ファン **eiga-fan** moviegoer
ファンベルト **fanberuto** fan belt
ファシスト **fashisuto** fascist
ファシズム **fashizumu** fascism
ファッション **fasshon** fashion
ファッションデザイナー **fasshon-dezainā** fashion designer
ファッションモデル **fasshon-moderu** model
ファスナー **fasunā** fastener; zipper; ファスナーを下げる **fasunā o sageru** unzip
ファーストフード **fāsuto fūdo** fast food
ファーストクラス **fāsuto kurasu** firstclass
ファウル **fauru** foul
フェミニスト **feminisuto** feminist
フェミニスト(の) **feminisuto (no)** feminist
フェミニズム **feminizumu** feminism
フェンダー **fendā** fender
フェンス **fensu** fence
フェラチオ **ferachio** fellatio; blow job

フェリー **ferī** ferry
フェルト **feruto** felt
フェルトペン **ferutopen** felt tip
フィギュアスケート **figyua-sukēto** figure skating
フィンランド **Finrando** Finland
フィンランド(の) **Finrando (no)** Finnish
フィリピン(の) **Firipin(no)** Philippine
フィリピン諸島 **Firipin-shotō** the Philippines
フィールド種目 **fīrudo-shumoku** field events
フィルム **firumu** film; …にフィルムを入れる **… ni firumu o ireru** load
フィルター **firutā** filter; filter tip
フィート **fīto** foot
フィットネスクラブ **fittonesu kurabu** fitness center
フォアハンド **foahando** forehand
フォーク **fōku** fork
フォークダンス **fōku-dansu** folk dance
フォークミュージック **fōku-myūjikku** folk music
フォークソング **fōku-songu** folk song
フォーマットする **fōmatto suru** format
フォーメーション **fōmēshon** formation
フォント **fonto** font
フォローする **forō suru** follow up
フォルダ **foruda** folder
フォワード **fowādo** forward
不… **fu …** non…; un…
封 **fū** seal

不安 **fuan** insecurity; misgiving; unrest

不安(な) **fuan (na)** perturbing

不安にさせる **fuan ni saseru** disturb; upset; perturb

不安定 **fuantei** instability

不安定(な) **fuantei (na)** erratic; unstable; wobbly; precarious; uncertain; uneasy

不安定に **fuantei ni** precariously

不払い **fubarai** nonpayment

不便(な) **fuben (na)** inconvenient

不便さ **fuben-sa** inconvenience

不備(な) **fubi (na)** unsatisfactory; defective

吹雪 **fubuki** blizzard, snowstorm

不文律 **fubunritsu** unwritten law

不平等 **fubyōdō** inequality

不平等(な) **fubyōdō (na)** unequal

縁 **fuchi** frame; brink; edge

縁取る **fuchidoru** edge

不調 **fuchō** malfunction; failure

不注意(な) **fuchūi (na)** careless; slack; inattentive

札 **fuda** tag

普段着 **fudangi** casual wear

普段着(の) **fudangi (no)** casual

普段(の) **fudan (no)** informal

不断(の) **fudan (no)** tireless; perpetual

筆 **fude** writing brush

フード **fūdo** hood (*on head*)

不動産 **fudōsan** real estate

不動産屋 **fudōsan-ya** real estate agent

不道徳 **fudōtoku** immorality

不道徳(な) **fudōtoku (na)** immoral

笛 **fue** whistle

増える **fueru** increase; multiply

夫婦 **fūfu** married couple

不服従 **fufukujū** disobedience

夫婦(の) **fūfu no** marital

風変わり(な) **fūgawari (na)** eccentric

不合理(な) **fugōri (na)** illogical; irrational

ふぐ **fugu** blowfish; puffer

不具 **fugu** physically handicapped person

腐敗 **fuhai** decay, rot

腐敗した **fuhai shita** corrupt

腐敗する **fuhai suru** decompose

不平 **fuhei** grievance, beef; fuss; 不平をいう **fuhei o iu** complain, beef

普遍的(な) **fuhenteki (na)** universal

不必要(な) **fuhitsuyō (na)** unnecessary

不法(な) **fuhō (na)** illicit

不法侵入者 **fuhō-shinnyū-sha** trespasser

不法侵入している **fuhō-shinnyū shite iru** trespass on

不法侵入する **fuhō-shinnyū suru** trespass

不評(の) **fuhyō (no)** unpopular

不意に **fui ni** just like that; unexpectedly

ふいにする **fui ni suru** blow; miss an opportunity

不一致 **fuitchi** clash

不意打ち **fuiuchi** surprise attack; …に不意打ちをくらわせる *… ni fuiuchi o kurawaseru* catch unawares

藤 **fuji** wisteria

不時着 **fujichaku** crash landing; forced landing

藤色 **fujiiro** lilac

不死身 **fujimi** immortal

婦人科 **fujinka** gynecologist

婦人警官 **fujin-keikan** policewoman

富士山 **Fuji-san** Mt Fuji

不実 **fujitsu** deception; faithlessness

不自由(な) **fujiyū (na)** physically handicapped; inconvenient

不十分(な) **fujūbun (na)** inadequate; scarce; inconclusive

不純(な) **fujun (na)** impure

負荷 **fuka** load ELEC; …に負荷をかけすぎる *… ni fuka o kakesugiru* overload

深い **fukai** deep; profound

不快(な) **fukai (na)** offensive

不可解(な) **fukakai (na)** baffling; enigmatic

ふ化器 **fukaki** incubator

深く **fukaku** profoundly

不確実 **fukakujitsu** uncertainty

深くなる **fukaku naru** deepen

深くする **fukaku suru** deepen

深まる **fukamaru** deepen

不可能 **fukanō** impossibility

不可能(な) **fukanō (na)** impossible

不感症(の) **fukanshō (no)** frigid

不完全な **fukanzen (na)** imperfect; incomplete; patchy

不活発(な) **fukappatsu (na)** inactive

深さ **fuka-sa** depth

ふかす **fukasu** rev up; puff at *cigarette*

ふけ **fuke** dandruff

父兄 **fukei** parents (*of schoolchildren*)

風景画 **fūkeiga** landscape painting

不景気 **fukeiki** slump

不景気になる **fukeiki ni naru** slacken off

不敬(な) **fukei (na)** irreverent

不経済(な) **fukeizai (na)** uneconomic; wasteful

不健康(な) **fukenkō (na)** unhealthy *person*

不健全(な) **fukenzen (na)** unhealthy *atmosphere, economy*

ふける **fukeru** immerse oneself in; indulge in

不潔(な) **fuketsu (na)** filthy; foul; squalid

不潔さ **fuketsu-sa** squalor

吹きだまり **fukidamari** snowdrift

吹きだまる **fukidamaru** drift

噴き出す **fukidasu** spurt out; burst out laughing

不機嫌である **fukigen de aru** be in a temper

吹替えする **fukikae suru** dub

噴きかける **fukikakeru** squirt *water*

吹き消す **fukikesu** blow out, extinguish

吹き込む **fukikomu** indoctrinate

ふきん **fukin** cloth; tea towel

付近 **fukin** neighborhood

不謹慎(な) **fukinshin (na)** indiscreet

不謹慎な行動 **fukinshin na kōdō** indiscretion

封切り **fūkiri** première, film release

不規則(な) **fukisoku (na)** erratic; irregular

不規則に **fukisoku ni** unevenly

吹き倒す **fukitaosu** blow over

吹き飛ばす **fukitobasu** blow away; blow off

吹き飛ぶ **fukitobu** be blown away

不吉(な) **fukitsu (na)** ominous

吹っかける **fukkakeru** rip off

復活 **fukkatsu** revival

復活祭 **Fukkatsusai** Easter

復活させる **fukkatsu saseru** revive; bring back, reintroduce

復活する **fukkatsu suru** revive

復帰させる **fukki saseru** reinstate

復帰する **fukki suru** return

フック **fukku** hook; peg

ふっくらする **fukkura suru** put on weight

ふっくらする **fukkura suru** fill out, put on weight

不幸 **fukō** unhappiness

不幸(な) **fukō (na)** unfortunate, unlucky; unhappy

不公正 **fukōsei** injustice

ふく **fuku** mop up; wipe

吹く **fuku** blow

服 **fuku** clothes; 服を着る **fuku o kiru** dress; 服を着せる **fuku o kiseru** dress; 服を脱ぐ **fuku o nugu** get undressed, undress

福 **fuku** good fortune

副… **fuku…** vice-; deputy; 副大統領 **fuku-daitōryō** vice-president; 副リーダー **fuku-rīdā** deputy leader

副木 **fukuboku** splint

腹部 **fukubu** abdomen; belly

腹部(の) **fukubu (no)** abdominal

複合(の) **fukugō (no)** multiple

副業 **fukugyō** sideline

服従 **fukujū** obedience

含める **fukumeru** include

含めて **fukumete** including, inclusive, inclusive of

含む **fukumu** embrace, take in; include

ふくらはぎ **fukurahagi** calf (*of leg*)

膨らます **fukuramasu** inflate, blow up

膨らますことができる **fukuramasu koto ga dekiru** inflatable

膨らみ **fukurami** bulge

膨れ上がった **fukureagatta** bloated

膨れる **fukureru** bulge; pout

膨れた **fukureta** swollen

複利 **fukuri** compound interest

袋 **fukuro** bag; pack

ふくろう **fukurō** owl

袋小路 **fukurokōji** impasse; dead end

袋に入れる **fukuro ni ireru** pack

副産物 **fukusanbutsu** by-product; spin-off

副作用 **fukusayō** side effect

複製 **fukusei** copy; replica; reproduction

複製する **fukusei suru** copy, duplicate; reproduce

副社長 **fuku-shachō** vice president

副詞 **fukushi** adverb

福祉 **fukushi** welfare

副支配人 **fukushihai-nin** assistant manager

福祉事業 **fukushi-jigyō** welfare work

福祉国家 **fukushi-kokka** welfare state

副署する **fukusho suru** countersign

復習 **fukushū** review (of lessons)

復しゅう **fukushū** revenge, vengeance; ...に復しゅうする ... ni fukushū suru take one's revenge

復しゅう心に燃えた **fukushūshin ni moeta** vindictive

復習する **fukushū suru** review; revise

服装 **fukusō** dress, clothing

副操縦士 **fuku-sōjūshi** copilot

複数形 **fukusūkei** plural

複数(の) **fukusū (no)** multiple; plural

副店長 **fukutenchō** assistant manager

腹痛 **fukutsū** stomach ache; colic

腹話術師 **fukuwajutsu-shi** ventriloquist

服用法 **fukuyō-hō** directions MED

複雑(な) **fukuzatsu (na)** complex; intricate; mixed feelings

不況 **fukyō** depression (economic)

不協和音 **fukyō-waon** discord

不満 **fuman** discontent; dissatisfaction

不満(な) **fuman (na)** unhappy; dissatisfied; discontented

不満(の) **fuman (no)** disgruntled

不満足(な) **fumanzoku (na)** unsatisfactory

不明 **fumai** unclear

不明りょう(な) **fumeiryō (na)** indistinct; unclear; vague

不名誉 **fumeiyo** dishonor, disgrace

不名誉(な) **fumeiyo (na)** dishonorable, disgraceful

不滅 **fumetsu** immortality

不滅(の) **fumetsu (no)** immortal

風味 **fūmi** flavor

踏み入れる **fumiireru** step into; set foot in

踏切 **fumikiri** grade crossing

不眠 **fumin** insomnia

踏みつける **fumitsukeru** trample (on)

不毛 **fumō** infertility

不毛(な) **fumō (na)** barren

不毛(の) **fumō (no)** infertile

ふもと **fumoto** bottom

踏む **fumu** tread on

不向き(な) **fumuki (na)** unfit

ふん **fun** dung

分 **fun** minute; 十五分 **jūgo fun** 15 minutes

船便 **funabin** shipping; 船便で送る **funabin de okuru** ship

船旅 **funatabi** cruise; voyage

船酔い(の) **funayoi (no)** seasick

船酔いする **funayoi suru** get seasick

分別のある **funbetsu no aru** reasonable

船 **fune** boat; ship; vessel

船(の) **fune (no)** nautical

不燃性(の) **funensei (no)** fireproof, non(in)flammable

憤慨 **fungai** indignation

雰囲気 **fun'iki** atmosphere; mood; tone

不妊 **funin** infertility

不妊(の) **funin (no)** infertile; sterile

噴火 **funka** eruption

噴火口 **funkakō** crater

噴火する **funka suru** erupt

粉砕する **funsai suru** pulverize

紛失 **funshitsu** loss

噴出 **funshutsu** eruption

噴出口 **funshutsu-kō** nozzle

紛争 **funsō** dispute; trouble

紛争地帯 **funsō-chitai** hot spot

噴水 **funsui** fountain

ふぬけ **funuke** sissy; coward

フラッドライト **furaddo-raito** floodlight

ふらふら(の) **furafura (no)** shaky

ふらふらした **furafura shita** unsteady

フライにする **furai ni suru** deep-fry

フライパン **furaipan** frying pan; pan

フライトレコーダー **furaito-rekōdā** flight recorder

フランス **Furansu** France

フランス語 **Furansu-go** French

フランス人 **Furansu-jin** the French

フランス(の) **Furansu (no)** French

フラッシュ **furasshu** flash(light)

フラッシュバック **furasshu-bakku** flashback

フレアー **fureā** flare

フレックスタイム **furekkusutaimu** flexitime

フレーム **furēmu** frame, rim (of eyeglasses)

フレームワーク **furēmuwāku** framework

フレンチフライ **furenchi-furai** (French) fries

触れる **fureru** touch

不利 **furi** disadvantage

フリー **furī** freelancer

フリーダイアル **furī-daiaru** toll-free

振り出しに戻る **furidashi ni modoru** go back to the drawing board; we're back to square one

フーリガン **fūrigan** hooligan

ふりがな **furigana** small kana written beside kanji as a pronunciation aid

振り返る **furikaeru** turn around

ふりかける **furikakeru** sprinkle

フリーキック **furī-kikku** free kick

振り回す **furimawasu** brandish; thrash around

不倫 **furin** adultery

不利(な) **furi (na)** disadvantageous

不利にする **furi ni suru** penalize

フリー(の) **furī (no)** freelance

ふりをする **furi o suru** pretend; act; playact

振り落とす **furiotosu** throw off; shake off

フリル **furiru** frill

振り袖 **furisode** long-sleeved kimono

振り付け **furitsuke** choreography

振り付け師 **furitsukeshi** choreographer

風呂 **furo** bath; 風呂に入る **furo ni hairu** take a bath, bathe

フロア **furoa** floor

フロアランプ **furoarampu** floor lamp

フローチャート **furōchāto** flowchart

浮浪児 **furōji** street urchin

付録 **furoku** appendix

フロンガス **furongasu** CFC, chlorofluorocarbon

フロント **furonto** reception desk; reception; room clerk

フロント係 **furonto-gakari** desk clerk; receptionist

フロントガラス **furonto-garasu** windshield

風呂おけ **furooke** tub

フロッピーディスク **furoppī-disuku** floppy (disk)

浮浪者 **furō-sha** tramp, bum, hobo

降る **furu** fall (of rain, snow)

振る **furu** shake; wag; waggle; wave; swing; jilt

振るう **furū** wield

震える **furueru** shudder; quiver; shake (of voice, hand); tremble; shiver ◊ wobbly

ふるい **furui** sieve; ふるいにかける **furui ni kakeru** sift

古い **furui** old; old-fashioned

奮い立たせる **furuitataseru** summon up

ふるい分ける **furui wakeru** sift through

古くなった **furuku natta** stale

古くさい **furukusai** antiquated; old-fashioned; stale; stuffy person

ふるまい **furumai** behavior; conduct; goings-on

ふるまう **furumau** behave; conduct oneself; treat (to food and drink)

フルート **furūto** flute

フルーツ **furūtsu** fruit

不良 **furyō** juvenile delinquent

房 **fusa** lock (of hair); tassel

封鎖 **fūsa** blockade

ふさふさした髪 **fusafusa shita kami** bushy hair

ふさぎ込む **fusagikomu** mope; feel gloomy

ふさぐ **fusagu** obstruct, block

夫妻 **fusai** husband and wife; 山田夫妻 **Yamada fusai** Mr and Mrs Yamada

負債者 **fusai-sha** debtor

不採用 **fusaiyō** rejection

不採用にする **fusaiyō ni suru** reject

不賛成 **fusansei** disapproval

封鎖する **fūsa suru** blockade; seal off

ふさわしい **fusawashii** fit (*morally*); fitting, appropriate

防ぐ **fusegu** prevent; save

不正 **fusei** wrong; injustice

不誠実 **fuseijitsu** insincerity; unfaithfulness; …に対して不誠実である … **ni taishite fuseijitsu de aru** be unfaithful to

不誠実(な) **fuseijitsu (na)** unfaithful; insincere; dishonest

不正確(な) **fuseikaku (na)** incorrect

不正(な) **fusei (na)** crooked; fraudulent; unjust

不正資金 **fusei-shikin** slush fund

不正操作する **fuseisōsa suru** rig

風船 **fūsen** balloon

風船ガム **fūsengamu** bubble gum

風車 **fūsha** windmill

不死 **fushi** immortality

風刺(な) **fūshi** satire

不幸せ(な) **fushiawase (na)** unhappy

ふしだら(な) **fushidara (na)** dissolute; sloppy

不思議(な) **fushigi (na)** mysterious

不思議なことに **fushigi na koto ni** mysteriously

不思議にも **fushigi ni mo** strangely enough

父子家庭 **fushi katei** single parent family (*father only*)

節くれだった **fushikuredatta** gnarled

風刺漫画 **fūshi-manga** caricature

節目 **fushime** turning point

不信感 **fushinkan** distrust, mistrust

不審(な) **fushin (na)** questionable

不死(の) **fushi (no)** immortal

不親切(な) **fushinsetsu (na)** unfriendly; unkind

風刺的(の) **fūshiteki (na)** satirical

不自然(な) **fushizen (na)** unnatural

不正直 **fushōjiki** dishonesty

不正直(な) **fushōjiki (na)** deceitful; dishonest

腐食 **fushoku** corrosion; decay

腐食させる **fushoku saseru** corrode

腐食する **fushoku suru** corrode; erode

負傷者 **fushō-sha** the injured

負傷する **fushō suru** injure

不足 **fusoku** deficiency; shortage; shortfall; …が不足している … **ga fusoku shite iru** be deficient in …; 不足する **fusoku suru** be in short supply

不相応(な) **fusōō (na)** undeserved; disproportionate; out of keeping

風水 **fūsui** feng shui

ふすま **fusuma** sliding screen

ふた **futa** cap; flap; lid; top

双子 **futago** twin

二けた(の) **futaketa no** double

二股(の) **futamata (no)** forked

負担 **futan** burden; strain; 負担をかける **futan o kakeru** strain

負担する **futan suru** bear (*costs*)

二人 **futari** two people

二人組 **futarigumi** couple; pair

再び現れる **futatabi** again; 再び現れる **futatabi arawareru** reappear

不貞 **futei** infidelity

不定冠詞 **futei-kanshi** indefinite article

不定(の) **futei (no)** indefinite

不定詞 **futeishi** infinitive

不適切(な) **futekisetsu (na)** improper

不適当(な) **futekitō (na)** inadequate; inappropriate; unsuitable

ふと **futo** suddenly; …をふと思いつく … **o futo omoitsuku** hit on

ふ頭 **futō** wharf

封筒 **fūtō** envelope

不凍液 **futōeki** antifreeze

太い **futoi** thick *rope*; deep *voice*; shameless

太字 **futoji** bold *letters*

不登校 **futōkō** refusal to attend school

不透明(な) **futōmei (na)** opaque

ふとん **futon** futon

不当(な) **futō (na)** undeserved; unfair

不当に **futō ni** unduly; unjustly

太りすぎ(の) **futorisugi (no)** overweight

太る **futoru** put on weight

太った **futotta** fat; stout

普通株式 **futsū-kabushiki** equities

二日前 **futsuka-mae** two days ago

二日酔い **futsukayoi** hangover

二日酔い(の) **futsukayoi (no)** hung-over

普通(の) **futsū (no)** normal; ordinary; usual

不つり合い(な) **futsuriai (na)** disproportionate

普通は **futsū wa** mostly; usually

普通預金口座 **futsū-yokin-kōza** savings account

普通郵便 **futsū-yūbin** surface mail

沸騰させる **futtō saseru** boil

沸騰する **futtō suru** boil

不運 **fuun** bad luck

不運(な) **fuun (na)** ill-fated

不和 **fuwa** breach; discord; friction

ふわふわした **fuwafuwa shita** fluffy; spongy

不渡り手形 **fuwatari-tegata** bounced check

増やす **fuyasu** boost; increase

扶養家族 **fuyō-kazoku** dependent

不用(の) **fuyō (no)** waste

扶養料 **fuyōryō** maintenance (*of family*)

扶養する **fuyō suru** maintain, provide for

冬 **fuyu** winter

不愉快(な) **fuyukai (na)** distasteful; unpleasant; repulsive

冬らしい **fuyurashii** wintry

不在 **fuzai** absence

不在(の) **fuzai (no)** absent

ふざける **fuzakeru** fool around

ふざけて **fuzakete** jokingly

風俗 **fūzoku** manners; customs

風俗犯罪取り締まり班 **fūzokuhanzai-torishimarihan** vice squad

付属(の) **fuzoku (no)** affiliated

付属装置 **fuzoku-sōchi** add-on

ふぞろい(の) **fuzoroi (no)** irregular; uneven

付随的(な) **fuzuiteki (na)** incidental

G

が **ga** but ◊ (*subject particle*): 私が やった **watashi ga yatta** I did it

蛾 **ga** moth

画板 *gaban* drawing board

画鋲 *gabyō* thumbtack

がちょう **gachō** goose

ガードマン **gādoman** guard

ガード下 **gādo shita** underpass

雅楽 **gagaku** court music

害 **gai** harm

外部 **gaibu** exterior

外部(の) **gaibu (no)** exterior, external

害虫 **gaichū** pest; vermin

害虫駆除 **gaichū-kujo** pest control

ガイド **gaido** guide

ガイドブック **gaido-bukku** guide(book)

外人 **gaijin** foreigner *pej*

害獣 **gaijū** pest; vermin

外貨 **gaika** foreign currency

外観 **gaikan** façade

外見 **gaiken** appearance; exterior (*of person*)

外交 **gaikō** diplomacy

外交儀礼 **gaikō-girei** protocol

外交官 **gaikōkan** diplomat

外交官(の) **gaikōkan (no)** diplomatic

外交官特権 **gaikōkan-tokken** diplomatic immunity

外国 **gaikoku** foreign country

外国で **gaikoku de** abroad

外国へ **gaikoku e** abroad

外国語 **gaikoku-go** foreign language

外国人 **gaikoku-jin** foreigner; alien

外国為替 **gaikoku-kawase** foreign exchange

外国(の) **gaikoku (no)** foreign; alien

外国通貨 **gaikoku-tsūka** foreign currency

外交(の) **gaikō (no)** diplomatic

外交政策 **gaikō-seisaku** foreign policy

外向的(な) **gaikōteki (na)** outgoing, extrovert

外向的な人 **gaikōteki na hito** extrovert

がい骨 **gaikotsu** skeleton

街区 **gaiku** block

外務 **gaimu** foreign affairs

外務大臣 **Gaimu-daijin** (Japanese) Secretary of State

外務省 **Gaimu-shō** (Japanese) State Department

概念 **gainen** concept

外来語 **gairaigo** loanword

概算で **gaisan de** approximately

概説 **gaisetsu** survey; outline

概して **gaishite** as a rule; typically

外食する **gaishoku suru** eat out

外出中である **gaishutsuchū de aru** be out

街灯 **gaitō** lamppost; streetlight

該当する **gaitō suru** satisfy *requirements*; apply

概要 **gaiyō** gloss (*general explanation*); profile, description

画家 **gaka** artist; painter

がけ **gake** cliff

がき **gaki** kid; brat; urchin

学科 **gakka** department

学会 **gakkai** academic association; academic conference

がっかりした **gakkari shita** disappointed; disheartened; downcast

楽器 **gakki** (musical) instrument

学期 **gakki** semester

学校 **gakkō** school; academy; 学校に行く **gakkō ni iku** go to school

がっくりさせる **gakkuri saseru** depress, get down

学級崩壊 **gakkyū-hōkai** classroom disruption

額 **gaku** amount, sum; frame

学 **gaku** learning; knowledge; study; 言語学 **gengo-gaku** linguistics; 地理学 **chiri-gaku** geography

学部 **gakubu** department; faculty

学部長 **gakubuchō** dean

学長 **gakuchō** college president

楽団 **gakudan** band; orchestra

楽譜 **gakufu** score MUS

学費 **gakuhi** tuition fees

学位 **gakui** degree; 学位を取る **gakui o toru** get one's degree

額面 **gakumen** denomination; face value; …を額面通りに受け取る *… o gakumen dōri ni uketoru* take at face value

学問 **gakumon** scholarship

学問的(な) **gakumonteki (na)** academic

学年 **gakunen** academic year; grade; class (*in school*)

学歴 **gakureki** educational background

学生 **gakusei** student

学生時代 **gakusei-jidai** school days

学生かばん **gakusei-kaban** schoolbag, satchel

学生寮 **gakuseiryō** college dorm; hostel

学者 **gakusha** academic; scholar

楽章 **gakushō** movement MUS

学習 **gakushū** learning

学習曲線 **gakushū-kyokusen** learning curve

学習者 **gakushū-sha** learner

学習する **gakushū suru** study

楽屋 **gakuya** dressing room

楽屋口 **gakuya-guchi** stage door

学友 **gakuyū** school pal

我慢できない **gaman dekinai** unbearable ◊ I won't tolerate it

我慢できる **gaman dekiru** tolerable

我慢する **gaman suru** bear; tolerate; stand for; endure; resist

我慢強い **gamanzuyoi** patient

我慢強く **gamanzuyoku** patiently

画面 **gamen** screen

画面に出る **gamen ni deru** be on (the) screen

がん **gan** cancer

がんばる **ganbaru** persevere

がんばって **ganbatte** good luck!

願望 **ganbō** longing

がにまた(の) **ganimata (no)** bandy-legged

元日 **Ganjitsu** New Year's Day

頑丈(な) **ganjō (na)** strong; solid; robust; heavy-duty

眼科医 **gankai** ophthalmologist

頑健(な) **ganken (na)** rugged, robust

頑固 **ganko** obstinacy

頑固(な) **ganko (na)** stubborn; headstrong; confirmed, inveterate *bachelor*

眼球 **gankyū** eyeball

眼精疲労 **gansei-hirō** eye strain

岩石 **ganseki** rock

元旦 **Gantan** New Year's Day

合併 **gappei** merger

合併症 **gappeishō** complications MED

合併する **gappei suru** combine; merge; amalgamate

がら **gara** character; build; pattern; がらが悪い **gara ga warui** vulgar; ill-mannered; がらの大きい **gara no ōkii** well-built; 派手ながら **hade na gara** a loud pattern

がらがら **garagara** rattle; ...にがらがら音を立てさせる **... ni garagara oto o tatesaseru** rattle

がらがらへび **garagarahebi** rattlesnake

がらくた **garakuta** garbage; junk; odds and ends; trash

がらくた市 **garakuta-ichi** rummage sale

がらんとした **garan to shita** bare, empty

ガラス **garasu** glass

ガレージ **garēji** garage

がれき **gareki** rubble

がり **-gari** sensitive to; 怖がり **kowagari** timid person

がり勉 **gariben** plodder

画廊 **garō** art gallery

ガロン **garon** gallon

がる **-garu** be sensitive to; 寒がる **samugaru** be sensitive to the cold

ガールフレンド **gārufurendo** girlfriend

ガールスカウト **gārusukauto** girl scout

ガソリン **gasorin** gas, gasoline

ガソリンスタンド **gasorin-sutando** gas station, filling station

がっしりした **gasshiri shita** hefty; stocky; sturdy

合唱団 **gasshōdan** chorus

合唱する **gasshō suru** sing in unison

合宿する **gasshuku suru** go to training camp

ガス **gasu** wind, flatulence

ガーター **gātā** garter

がたがた(の) **gatagata (no)** ramshackle; shaky

がたがた動く **gatagata ugoku** jerky

合致する **gatchi suru** check with, tally with

ガッツ **gattsu** guts

ガウン **gaun** gown

側 **gawa** side

ガーゼ **gāze** gauze

下 **ge** low grade

解毒剤 **gedokuzai** antidote

下品(な) **gehin (na)** vulgar; indelicate

芸術 **geijutsu** art

芸術家 **geijutsuka** artist

芸術作品 **geijutsu-sakuhin** work of art

芸術的(な) **geijutsuteki (na)** artistic; cultural

芸能人 **geinō-jin** show business people

芸能界 **geinōkai** show business

芸者 **geisha** geisha

外科 **geka** surgery; 外科手術を受ける **geka-shujutsu o ukeru** undergo surgery

外科医 **gekai** surgeon

外科的(な) **gekateki (na)** surgical

劇 **geki** play, drama

激怒 **gekido** fury, rage

激怒させる **gekido saseru** incense, infuriate

激怒した **gekido shita** furious, livid

激怒する **gekido suru** fly into a rage, go wild

激減する **gekigen suru** decimate

劇場 **gekijō** theater

激化 **gekika** escalation, intensification

激流 **gekiryū** torrent

劇作家 **geki-sakka** dramatist, playwright

撃退する **gekitai suru** repel

劇的(な) **gekiteki (na)** dramatic; spectacular

激痛 **gekitsū** acute pain; twinge

月刊(の) **gekkan (no)** monthly

月刊誌 **gekkanshi** monthly (magazine)

月桂樹 **gekkeiju** laurel

月給 **gekkyū** monthly salary

ゲーム **gēmu** game

ゲームセンター **gēmu-sentā** arcade

弦 **gen** string (on instrument)

現場 **genba** scene

原爆 **genbaku** atom bomb

現地時間 **genchi-jikan** local time

現代(の) **gendai (no)** modern, contemporary, present-day

現代的(な) **gendaiteki (na)** modern way of thinking

限度 **gendo** limit; ...に限度を置く... **ni gendo o oku** draw the line at

現役(の) **gen'eki (no)** active; 現役で合格する **gen'eki de gōkaku suru** pass straight from high school college entrance exam

弦楽器 **gengakki** stringed instrument

言語 **gengo** language

元号 **gengō** era name

言語学者 **gengogaku-sha** linguist

言語(の) **gengo (no)** linguistic

言語療法士 **gengo-ryōhōshi** speech therapist

言語障害 **gengo-shōgai** speech impediment, speech defect

原因 **gen'in** cause

源氏物語 **Genji-monogatari** The Tale of Genji

現実主義 **genjitsu-shugi** realism

現実主義者 **genjitsu-shugi-sha** realist

現実的(な) **genjitsuteki (na)** realistic; practical; hardheaded

原住民 **genjūmin** native

厳重に **genjū ni** strictly

原価 **genka** cost price

限界 **genkai** limit, threshold; limitation; frontier fig

厳格(な) **genkaku (na)** austere; puritanical; straightlaced

厳格さ **genkaku-sa** rigor

玄関 **genkan** entrance; doorway; front door; hall

原型 **genkei** prototype

減刑する **genkei suru** commute sentence

元気 **genki** vigor; vitality; 元気である **genki de aru** be well; be full of life; 元気がない **genki ga nai** be feeling low; 元気-元気です **genki - genki desu** how are you? – fine; 元気を出す **genki o dasu** cheer up

現金 **genkin** cash

元気(な) **genki (na)** frisky

現金自動支払機 **genkin-jidō-shiharaiki** ATM

現金化する **genkinka suru** cash check

現金割引 **genkin-waribiki** cash discount

元気づける **genkizukeru** cheer up, perk up; refresh

原稿 **genkō** copy (written material); manuscript

現行犯で **genkōhan de** in the very act; 現行犯で捕まえる **genkōhan de tsukamaeru** catch red-handed

原告 **genkoku** claimant, plaintiff

現行(の) **genkō (no)** going, current

言及 **genkyū** reference

言及しない **genkyū shinai** stay silent

幻滅 **genmetsu** disillusionment

幻滅させる **genmetsu saseru** disillusion

幻滅する **genmetsu suru** disenchanted with

厳密(な) **genmitsu (na)** strict; rigorous; meticulous

現なま **gennama** dough; cash

原理 **genri** principle

原料 **genryō** raw materials

減産 **gensan** slowdown; decrease in output

原産(の) **gensan (no)** native

原子 **genshi** atom

原子物理学 **genshi-butsurigaku** nuclear physics

原子(の) **genshi (no)** atomic

原始(の) **genshi (no)** primitive

原子炉 **genshiro** nuclear reactor

原子力 **genshiryoku** atomic energy, nuclear energy,

原子力爆弾 **genshiryoku-bakudan** atom bomb

原子力発電所 **genshiryoku-hatsudensho** nuclear power station

原子力(の) **genshiryoku (no)** nuclear

原始的(な) **genshiteki (na)** primitive

減少 **genshō** decrease; reduction; decline

現象 **genshō** phenomenon

減少させる **genshō saseru** decrease

減少する **genshō suru** decrease; diminish; slide

厳粛(な) **genshuku (na)** solemn

元素 **genso** element CHEM

幻想 **gensō** illusion; fantasy

原則 **gensoku** general principle

減速する **gensoku suru** throttle back

原則的には **gensokuteki ni wa** in principle

限定された **gentei sareta** qualified, limited

限定する **gentei suru** qualify, limit, restrict

原油 **gen'yu** crude (oil)

現在 **genzai** right now ◊ the present

現在形 **genzaikei** present GRAM

現在(の) **genzai (no)** present, current; existing

現像 **genzō** development (of film)

現存(の) **genzon (no)** in existence

現像する **genzō suru** develop film

げっぷ **geppu** belch, burp; げっぷをする **geppu o suru** belch, burp

げっぷさせる **geppu saseru** burp baby

下落 **geraku** fall, decline

下落する **geraku suru** fall, decline

ゲレンデ **gerende** ski run

下劣(な) **geretsu (na)** vile

下痢 **geri** diarrhea

ゲリラ兵 **gerira-hei** guerrilla

下船する **gesen suru** disembark

下宿人 **geshuku-nin** boarder, lodger

下宿する **geshuku suru** board with

げっ歯類 **gesshirui** rodent

月食 **gesshoku** eclipse (of the moon)

下水 **gesui** sewage

下水道 **gesuidō** sewer

下水処理場 **gesui-shorijō** sewage plant

下駄 **geta** thonged clogs

ゲート **gēto** gate

月曜日 **getsuyōbi** Monday

下剤 **gezai** laxative

下山 **gezan** descent

下山する **gezan suru** descend

ギア **gia** gear

議案 **gian** bill POL

議長 **gichō** chair; chairperson; chairman; …の議長を務める **… no gichō o tsutomeru** chair; preside at

議題 **gidai** agenda

ギフト **gifuto** gift

ギガバイト **gigabaito** gigabyte

議員 **giin** councilor; member of the Diet

議事録 **gijiroku** minutes (of meeting)

技術 **gijutsu** skill; craft; expertise; technique

議会 **gikai** Congress; assembly, council; parliament

議会(の) **gikai (no)** Congressional; parliamentary

ぎこちない **gikochinai** awkward; stiff

疑問 **gimon** doubt; skepticism; qualm; 疑問がある **gimon ga aru** be in doubt; 疑問のある **gimon no aru** debatable

疑問符 **gimonfu** question mark

疑問詞 **gimonshi** interrogative GRAM

義務 **gimu** duty, responsibility; obligation; liability

義務教育 **gimu-kyōiku** compulsory education

義務（の）**gimu (no)** obligatory

義務づける **gimuzukeru** bind LAW

銀 **gin** silver

銀行 **ginkō** bank FIN

銀行振替為替 **ginkō-furikae-kawase** giro

銀行家 **ginkōka** banker

銀行口座 **ginkō-kōza** bank account

銀めっき（の）**gin mekki (no)** silver-plated

ぎんなん **ginnan** gingko nut

銀（の）**gin (no)** silver

銀髪（の）**ginpatsu (no)** gray-haired; silver-haired

ギプス **gipusu** plaster cast

ぎらぎら光る **giragira hikaru** glare

義理 **giri**: …に義理がある **… ni giri ga aru** be under an obligation to

義理と人情 **giri to ninjō** duty and human feelings

義理（の）**giri (no)** in-law; 義理の姉 **giri no ane** sister-in-law

ギリシア **Girishia** Greece

ギリシア（の）**Girishia (no)** Greek

議論 **giron** argument, reasoning; discussion

議論する **giron suru** argue

議論好きな **gironzuki (na)** argumentative

犠牲 **gisei** cost *fig*; sacrifice; 犠牲にする **gisei ni suru** sacrifice *fig*; victimize; 犠牲をはらう **gisei o harau** make sacrifices

犠牲者 **gisei-sha** martyr *fig*; victim

犠牲者の数 **gisei-sha no kazu** toll (*deaths*)

議席 **giseki** seat POL

技師 **gishi** engineer

儀式 **gishiki** ceremony; ritual

儀式（の）**gishiki (no)** ceremonial

儀式的（な）**gishikiteki (na)** ritual

偽証 **gishō** perjury

偽証する **gishō suru** perjure oneself

ぎっしり詰まって **gisshiri tsumatte** chock-full

ギター **gitā** guitar

ギタリスト **gitarisuto** guitarist

ぎざぎざ（の）**gizagiza (no)** jagged

偽善 **gizen** hypocrisy

偽善者 **gizen-sha** hypocrite

偽善的（な）**gizenteki (na)** hypocritical

偽造 **gizō** forgery

偽造文書 **gizō-bunsho** forgery

偽造（の）**gizō (no)** counterfeit

偽造者 **gizō-sha** forger

偽造する **gizō suru** counterfeit, forge

五 **go** five

語 **go** word

碁 **go** game of Go

後 -**go** after; in; 三日後 **mikkago** after three days; in three days

御 …、ご … **go …** (*honorific prefix*): ご家族 **gokazoku** your family; ご案内致します **goannai itashimasu** I'll show you the way

合弁事業 **gōben-jigyō** joint venture

語尾 **gobi** ending GRAM

五分五分に **gobugobu ni** fifty-fifty

ごちゃごちゃ **gochagocha** muddle

ごちゃごちゃにする **gochagocha ni suru** muddle up

ごちゃ混ぜにする **gochamaze ni suru** mix up

ごちそう **gochisō** feast, spread

ごちそうさまでした **gochisōsama deshita** that was delicious

護衛 **goei** escort; guard

護衛する **goei suru** escort; guard

語学 **gogaku** language

五月 **gogatsu** May

午後 **gogo** afternoon; 午後に **gogo ni** in the afternoon; 午後（の）**gogo (no)** pm

ゴーグル **gōguru** goggles

ご飯 **gohan** rice (*cooked*)

ご飯茶碗 **gohan-jawan** rice bowl

合法化する **gōhōka suru** legalize

合法的(な) **gōhōteki (na)** legal; legitimate

語い **goi** vocabulary

合意 **gōi** consensus, agreement; understanding

強引(な) **gōin (na)** assertive; pushy

合意する **gōi suru** agree

強情(な) **gōjō (na)** pigheaded

五十 **gojū** fifty

誤解 **gokai** misunderstanding; misconception; misinterpretation; …の誤解を招く **… no gokai o maneku** mislead; 誤解をしている **gokai o shite iru** be under a misapprehension; be mistaken

誤解する **gokai suru** misinterpret, misread; misunderstand

合格点 **gōkakuten** pass mark

合格する **gōkaku suru** pass *exam*

語幹 **gokan** root, stem (*of word*)

強かん **gōkan** rape

豪華(な) **gōka (na)** luxurious; de luxe; plush

互換性 **gokansei** compatibility

互換性のある **gokansei no aru** compatible

互換性のない **gokansei no nai** incompatible

強かん者 **gōkan-sha** rapist

強かんする **gōkan suru** rape

合計 **gōkei** sum, total

合計(の) **gōkei (no)** total

合計する **gōkei suru** add; add up

ごきぶり **gokiburi** cockroach

合金 **gōkin** alloy

…ごっこをして遊ぶ **… gokko o shite asobu** play

後光 **gokō** halo

ごく **goku** extremely

極悪(の) **gokuaku (no)** wicked

ごくごく飲む **gokugoku nomu** gulp down

ご苦労さま **gokurōsama** well done!; thanks for your help

極小型(の) **gokushōgata (no)** midget; miniature

ごくわずか(の) **goku wazuka (no)** least

ごまかし **gomakashi** deception;

whitewash

ごまかす **gomakasu** fiddle *accounts, results*; stall (*for time*)

ごう慢 **gōman** arrogance

ごう慢(な) **gōman (na)** arrogant, superior *pej*

ごまをする **goma o suru** suck up to

ごめんなさい **gomen nasai** I beg your pardon?, pardon me?; I'm sorry

ごみ **gomi** garbage; litter

ごみ入れ **gomiire** ash can

ごみの山 **gomi no yama** scrap heap

ごみ捨て場 **gomi-suteba** refuse dump

拷問 **gōmon** torture; 拷問にかける **gōmon ni kakeru** torture

ゴム **gomu** rubber

ゴムボート **gomu-bōto** dinghy

ゴムひも **gomuhimo** piece of elastic

ごう音 **gōon** roar

娯楽 **goraku** recreation, entertainment

娯楽施設 **goraku-shisetsu** amusements

合理化 **gōrika** rationalization

合理化された **gōrika sareta** streamlined

合理化する **gōrika suru** rationalize; streamline

ゴリラ **gorira** gorilla

合理性 **gōrisei** rationality

合理的(な) **gōriteki (na)** rational

…頃 **…goro** around

ごろごろとのどを鳴らす **gorogoro to nodo o narasu** purr

ゴロゴロ鳴る **gorogoro naru** rumble

ごろつき **gorotsuki** ruffian

ゴール **gōru** finish, finishing line; goal

ゴールデンアワー **gōruden-awā** prime time

ゴールデンウィーク **gōruden-wīku** Golden Week (*string of national holidays between April 29 and May 5*)

ゴルファー **gorufā** golfer

ゴルフ **gorufu** golf

ゴルフコース **gorufu-kōsu** golf course

ゴルフクラブ **gorufu-kurabu** golf club

ゴールキーパー **gōru-kīpā** goalkeeper

ゴールポスト **gōru-posuto** goalpost

合流する **gōryū suru** join; link up

誤算 **gosan** miscalculation

合成(の) **gōsei (no)** synthetic

ごしごし洗う **goshigoshi arau** scour; scrub

誤審 **goshin** miscarriage of justice

誤植 **goshoku** misprint

強盗 **gōtō** robber; mugger; robbery; mugging; raid; 強盗に入る **gōtō ni hairu** raid

ごとに **-goto ni** every, each

ごと(の) **-goto (no)** every; each

強盗する **gōtō suru** burglarize; raid

豪雨 **gōu** deluge; monsoon

誤用 **goyō** misuse

誤用する **goyō suru** misuse

ございます **gozaimasu** polite form of **aru**, **desu**

午前 **gozen** a.m.

午前0時 **gozen reiji** midnight

具合 **guai** condition; 体の具合 **karada no guai** health; 具合の悪い **guai no warui** ill

ぐち **guchi** complaint; beef; ぐちを言う **guchi o iu** complain; beef

郡 **gun** county

軍 **gun** army; troops

軍備縮小 **gunbi-shukushō** disarmament; arms reduction

軍備縮小する **gunbi-shukushō suru** disarm; cut down on armaments

軍事演習 **gunji-enshū** exercise MIL

軍事教練 **gunji-kyōren** drill MIL

軍人 **gunjin** serviceman; soldier

軍事(の) **gunji (no)** military

軍事施設 **gunji-shisetsu** military installation

軍艦 **gunkan** warship

軍法会議 **gunpō-kaigi** court martial

群衆 **gunshū** crowd; mob; throng

軍隊 **guntai** armed forces; the military; troops

軍隊(の) **guntai (no)** military

軍用機 **gunyōki** warplane

グラビア雑紙 **gurabia-zasshi** glossy (magazine)

グラフ **gurafu** graph

ぐらぐらした **guragura shita** unsteady

ぐらぐらする **guragura suru** wobble

ぐらい **gurai** around; これぐらい大きい/高い **koregurai ōkii / takai** this big / high

グライダー **guraidā** glider

グラマー(な) **guramā (na)** busty

グラム **guramu** gram

グランドピアノ **gurando-piano** grand piano

グラニュー糖 **guranyū-tō** granulated sugar

グラス **gurasu** tumbler

グレードアップする **gurēdo appu suru** upgrade

グレープフルーツ **gurēpufurūtsu** grapefruit

グリニッジ標準時 **gurinidji-hyōjun ji** GMT, Greenwich Mean Time

グリーン車 **gurīn-sha** first class (on bullet train)

グリップ **gurippu** grip SP

グリル **guriru** grill

グローバルスタンダード **gurōbaru-sutandādo** global standard

グローブ **gurōbu** glove

ぐるぐる巻く **guruguru maku** coil (up)

グルメ **gurume** gourmet, food freak

グループ **gurūpu** bunch; group; in-group

ぐるっと **gurutto** all around

ぐっすり **gussuri** soundly

ぐっすり眠らせる **gussuri nemuraseru** knock out

偶数(の) **gūsū (no)** even

具体化させる **gutaika saseru** crystallize

具体化する **gutaika suru** crystallize

具体的(な) **gutaiteki (na)** concrete

偶然 **gūzen** coincidence; 偶然見つける **gūzen mitsukeru** stumble across

偶然に **gūzen ni** by accident, by chance

偶然(の) **gūzen (no)** accidental

偶像 **gūzō** icon; idol

ぐずぐずする **guzuguzu suru**
dawdle; delay

ギャグ **gyagu** gag, joke

逆 **gyaku** opposite, converse

逆風 **gyakufū** headwind

逆効果(の) **gyakukōka (no)**
counterproductive

逆に **gyaku ni** conversely

逆にする **gyaku ni suru** invert,
reverse

逆(の) **gyaku (no)** opposite;
reverse

虐殺 **gyakusatsu** slaughter;
bloodshed

虐殺する **gyakusatsu suru**
massacre; slaughter

逆説 **gyakusetsu** paradox

逆説的(な) **gyakusetsuteki (na)**
paradoxical

虐待 **gyakutai** abuse, maltreatment

虐待する **gyakutai suru** abuse,
maltreat, illtreat

ギャンブル **gyanburu** gamble;
gambling

ギャング **gyangu** gangster, mobster

行 **gyō** line (of text)

行儀 **gyōgi** manners; behavior; 行儀
良くする **gyōgi yoku suru** behave
(oneself)

行儀のいい **gyōgi no ii** well-
behaved

行儀の悪い **gyōgi no warui**
naughty

行事 **gyōji** festivities; function,
reception; occasion, event

魚介類 **gyokairui** seafood

漁獲 **gyokaku** haul, catch

凝結する **gyōketsu suru** condense

凝固する **gyōko suru** coagulate;
congeal; curdle

行列 **gyōretsu** procession

行政 **gyōsei** administration

行政(の) **gyōsei (no)**
administrative

業績 **gyōseki** achievement

漁船 **gyosen** fishing boat

凝視 **gyōshi** stare

仰天 **gyōten** amazement

仰天させる **gyōten saseru** amaze

仰天する **gyōten suru** be amazed

ぎゅうぎゅう詰めである **gyūgyūzume
de aru** be crowded, be jammed

ぎゅうぎゅう詰め(の) **gyūgyūzume
(no)** jam-packed

牛肉 **gyūniku** beef

牛乳 **gyūnyū** milk

ぎゅっと **gyutto** firmly; tightly; ぎゅっ
と絞る **gyutto shiboru** squeeze

H

刃 **ha** blade

歯 **ha** tooth; cog; 歯をくいしばる **ha o
kuishibaru** clench one's teeth; 歯
(の) **ha (no)** dental

葉 **ha** leaf; foliage

幅 **haba** breadth; range; 幅十メート
ル **haba jū mētoru** 10m across; 幅
を広げる **haba o hirogeru** let out

把握する **haaku suru** comprehend;
grasp

羽ばたく **habataku** flap

幅跳び **habatobi** broadjump, long
jump

派閥 **habatsu** in-group

ハブ **habu** hub

ハーブ **hābu** herb

省く **habuku** leave out

歯ブラシ **ha-burashi** toothbrush

はち **hachi** wasp

鉢 **hachi** bowl

八 **hachi** eight

八月 **hachigatsu** August

はちまき **hachimaki** headband

はちみつ **hachimitsu** honey

はちの巣 **hachi no su** hive;
honeycomb

波長 **hachō** wavelength; 波長が合う *hachō ga au* be on the same wavelength; 波長を変える *hachō o kaeru* scramble

ハ長調 **hachōchō** C major

は虫類 **hachūrui** reptile

肌 **hada** skin

裸で **hadaka de** in the nude

裸にする **hadaka ni suru** strip

裸(の) **hadaka (no)** naked, nude, bare

肌の色 **hada no iro** coloring

裸足(の) **hadashi (no)** barefoot

肌寒い **hadazamui** chilly

派手(な) **hade (na)** loud, flamboyant; ostentatious, showy

ハードディスク **hādo disuku** hard disk

ハードカバー **hādo kabā** hardback

ハードル **hādoru** hurdle; hurdles

ハードウェア **hādowea** hardware

ハエ **hae** fly

生える **haeru** grow

ハーフタイム **hāfu-taimu** half time

葉書 **hagaki** postcard

はがれる **hagareru** come unstuck; peel off

はがす **hagasu** rub off; strip, remove; take up *carpet etc*

はげ **hage** baldness

励まし **hagemashi** encouragement

励ます **hagemasu** encourage, urge on

励ますよう(な) **hagemasu yō (na)** encouraging

励みになる **hagemi ni naru** encouraging

はげ落ちる **hageochiru** flake off; peel

激しい **hageshii** stormy *relationship*; violent *emotion, storm*; acute *pain*; fiery; heavy *rain*; intense; strenuous

激しく **hageshiku** severely; violently

激しくなる **hageshiku naru** intensify

激しさ **hageshi-sa** intensity; violence

はげた **hageta** bald; bare

はげたか **hagetaka** vulture; condor

はげてきている **hagete kite iru**

receding

歯ぐき **haguki** gum (*in mouth*)

はぐらかす **hagurakasu** evade, dodge

はぐれる **hagureru** stray

はぐれた **hagureta** stray

歯車 **haguruma** cogwheel

母 **haha** mother; 母の日 *Haha no hi* Mother's Day

母方(の) **hahakata (no)** maternal

母親 **hahaoya** mother

破片 **hahen** fragment; splinter

はい **hai** yes; no (*see* yes *p670*); uh-huh (*I'm listening*); はい、ここにあります **hai, koko ni arimasu** here it is

灰 **hai** ash; ashes

胚 **hai** embryo

肺 **hai** lung

敗北 **haiboku** defeat, whipping

ハイボール **haibōru** whiskey and soda

ハイブリッド **haiburiddo** hybrid

配置 **haichi** arrangement

配置する **haichi suru** arrange; position; post; station

肺炎 **haien** pneumonia

配布 **haifu** distribution

ハイフン **haifun** hyphen

肺がん **haigan** lung cancer

配偶者 **haigū-sha** partner; spouse

ハイヒール **haihīru** stilettos

灰色(の) **haiiro (no)** gray

ハイジャック **haijakku** hijack

ハイジャックする **haijakku suru** hijack

ハイジャンプ **haijanpu** high jump

ハイカー **haikā** hiker; rambler

配管 **haikan** plumbing

配管工 **haikankō** plumber

廃止にする **haikan ni suru** be discontinued; fold

背景 **haikei** background; context; scenes THEA; ...の背景を考えて *...no haikei o kangaete* looking at ... in context

拝啓 **haikei** Dear Sir

肺結核 **haikekkaku** pulmonary tuberculosis

拝見する **haiken suru** H see

敗血症 **haiketsushō** blood

廃棄 **haiki** disposal

廃棄物 **haikibutsu** waste; waste product

排気ガス **haiki-gasu** exhaust fumes

排気管 **haikikan** exhaust (pipe)

ハイキング **haikingu** hike; ramble; rambling; walking

ハイキングする **haikingu suru** walk; ramble

排気量 **haikiryō** capacity

俳句 **haiku** haiku

配給する **haikyū suru** ration; distribute

排尿する **hainyō suru** urinate

ハイパーテキスト **haipātekisuto** hypertext

ハイライト **hairaito** highlight

排卵誘発剤 **hairan-yūhatsuzai** fertility drug

はいる **hairu** percolate

入る **hairu** enter, come in; fit, slot in; 入ることができる **hairu koto ga dekiru** be able to enter; have access to

配線盤 **haisenban** circuit board

歯医者 **haisha** dentist

敗者 **haisha** loser

廃止する **haishi suru** abolish, ax; discontinue; dismantle

配色 **haishoku** color scheme

排出 **haishutsu** emission

排水 **haisui** drainage

排水管 **haisuikan** drain, drainpipe; drainage

排水口 **haisuikō** overflow (pipe)

排水溝 **haisuikō** storm drain

排水する **haisui suru** drain

歯痛 **haita** toothache

敗退 **haitai** elimination; defeat

敗退する **haitai suru** be eliminated, be out (*from competition*)

配達 **haitatsu** delivery

配達状 **haitatsu-jō** delivery note

配達する **haitatsu suru** deliver

ハイテク **haiteku** hi-tech

ハイテク(の) **haiteku (no)** hi-tech

配当金 **haitōkin** dividend

配役する **haiyaku suru** cast

俳優 **haiyū** actor, player

灰皿 **haizara** ashtray

配属 **haizoku** posting

配属する **haizoku suru** post; assign

恥 **haji** disgrace; shame; embarrassment; humiliation; 恥を かかせる *haji o kakaseru* embarrass; humiliate

はじく **hajiku** flip, flick

初まり **hajimari** beginning, start; onset; dawn

始まる **hajimaru** begin, start

初め **hajime** beginning; outset; 十月 の初め *jūgatsu no hajime* early October

はじめまして **hajimemashite** how do you do?, pleased to meet you

初め(の) **hajime (no)** initial

始める **hajimeru** begin, start; mount *campaign*; take up *new job*

初めて **hajimete** for the first time

初めは **hajime wa** at first, initially

恥さらし **hajisarashi** a disgrace

恥知らず(の) **hajishirazu (no)** shameless

墓 **haka** grave; tomb

破壊 **hakai** destruction; ruin

破壊できない **hakai dekinai** indestructible

破壊行動 **hakai-kōdō** vandalism

破壊工作 **hakai-kōsaku** sabotage

破壊される **hakai sareru** be ruined

墓石 **hakaishi** gravestone; tombstone

破壊する **hakai suru** destroy; knock out *power lines etc*; sabotage; vandalize

破壊的(な) **hakaiteki (na)** destructive; subversive

はかま **hakama** *traditional pants, like culottes*

はかり **hakari** scales

はかりしれない **hakari-shirenai** incalculable, inestimable; inscrutable; untold

測る **hakaru** measure

計る **hakaru** take *temperature*

量る **hakaru** weigh

図る **hakaru** plan; plot

博士号 **hakase-gō** doctorate, PhD

はけ **hake** paintbrush

はけ口 **hakeguchi** outlet

派遣 **haken** temp

派遣で働く **haken de hataraku** temp

派遣する **haken suru** send in; dispatch

吐き出す **hakidasu** exhale; spit out; give vent to

吐き気 **hakike** sickness, vomiting; nausea

吐き気がする **hakike ga suru** feel nauseous

はきもの **hakimono** footwear

破棄する **haki suru** break off *engagement*; tear up *agreement*

掃き寄せる **hakiyoseru** sweep up

ハッカー **hakkā** hacker

発覚 **hakkaku** disclosure

発覚する **hakkaku suru** be out (*of scandal etc*); be discovered

発汗 **hakkan** perspiration

発見 **hakken** detection; discovery; strike (*of oil*)

発見者 **hakken-sha** discoverer

発見する **hakken suru** discover; unearth; strike *oil*

白血病 **hakketsubyō** leukemia

はっきり **hakkiri** clearly; …にはっきり言う *... ni hakkiri iu* give ... a piece of one's mind; はっきり物を言う *hakkiri mono o iu* vocal; はっきりは言えませんが *hakkiri wa iemasen ga* I couldn't say for sure

はっきりさせる **hakkiri saseru** clarify

はっきりしない **hakkiri shinai** dull, inarticulate; uncertain; vague ◊ be a bit hazy

はっきりした **hakkiri shita** clear; decided, definite; distinct; vivid

はっきりする **hakkiri suru** become clear

はっきりと **hakkiri to** clearly, distinctly; explicitly

発揮する **hakki suru** exhibit; display; show

発酵 **hakkō** fermentation

発行 **hakkō** issue

発行部数 **hakkō-busū** circulation

発行物 **hakkōbutsu** issue

発光ダイオード **hakkō-daiōdo** LED, light-emitting diode

発行者 **hakkō-sha** publisher

発効する **hakkō suru** come into

発酵する **hakkō suru** ferment

発行する **hakkō suru** issue

発光する **hakkō suru** emit light

発掘 **hakkutsu** excavation

発掘する **hakkutsu suru** excavate; uncover; unearth

箱 **hako** box; carton; crate; pack

運ぶ **hakobu** carry; convey

はく **haku** wear; put on *footwear, pants*

吐く **haku** blow; vomit, throw up; 息を吐く *iki o haku* breathe; breathe out

掃く **haku** sweep

泊 **-haku** overnight stay; 二泊する *ni-haku suru* stay for two nights

白亜 **hakua** chalk

博物学者 **hakubutsugaku-sha** naturalist

博物館 **hakubutsukan** museum

白鳥 **hakuchō** swan

白昼 **hakuchū** broad daylight

白昼夢 **hakuchūmu** daydream

迫害 **hakugai** persecution

迫害する **hakugai suru** persecute

白人 **hakujin** white (person)

白人(の) **hakujin (no)** white

白状する **hakujō suru** confess, own up

博識(の) **hakushiki (no)** well-read

白紙(の) **hakushi (no)** blank

拍手 **hakushu** applause

拍手する **hakushu suru** applaud, clap

破局 **hakyoku** bust-up, catastrophe

浜辺 **hamabe** beach

はまぐり **hamaguri** clam

葉巻き **hamaki** cigar

ハマる **hamaru** get caught out; be crazy about

はまった **hamatta** be trapped

はめ込む **hamekomu** slot in

はめる **hameru** wear *gloves, rings*

破滅 **hametsu** doom; devastation

歯みがき粉 **ha-migakiko** toothpaste

ハミングする **hamingu suru** hum

ハーモニー **hāmonī** harmony

ハーモニカ **hāmonika** mouthorgan

ハム **hamu** ham

ハムスター **hamusutā** hamster

班 **han** crew

版 **han** edition

判 **han** stamp; seal

半 **-han** half; 十時半 **jūji han** half (past) ten

藩 **han** clan

反… **han…** anti; 反政府団体 **hanseifu-dantai** anti-government group

花 **hana** bloom; blossom; flower

鼻 **hana** nose; snout; trunk; 鼻をかむ **hana o kamu** blow one's nose

鼻柱 **hanabashira** bridge (*of nose*)

花火 **hanabi** fireworks

花びら **hanabira** petal

鼻血 **hanaji** nosebleed; 鼻血が出る **hanaji ga deru** have a nosebleed

鼻くそ **hanakuso** snot; 鼻くそをほじる **hanakuso o hojiru** pick one's nose

花見 **hanami** blossom viewing

鼻水 **hanamizu** mucus; 鼻水が垂れる **hanamizu ga tareru** run (*of nose*)

花模様(の) **hanamoyō (no)** flowery

花婿 **hanamuko** bridegroom

鼻にかかった **hana ni kakatta** nasal

鼻の穴 **hana no ana** nostril

離れられない **hanarerarenai** inseparable

離れる **hanareru** break away; leave

離れた **hanareta** remote

離れて **hanarete** apart (*in distance*); off (*in distance*)

離れている **hanarete iru** stay away

話 **hanashi** story; あなたに話があります **anata ni hanashi ga arimasu** I need to talk to you

話し合い **hanashiai** discussion

話し合う **hanashiau** talk; talk over, discuss

話中(の) **hanashichū (no)** busy TELEC; 話中である **hanashichū de aru** be on the telephone

話しかける **hanashikakeru** speak to; address

話し方 **hanashikata** speech; way of speaking

話し言葉 **hanashi-kotoba** vernacular

話好き(な) **hanashizuki (na)** communicative

話好き(の) **hanashizuki (no)** chatty

離す **hanasu** separate; disengage

放す **hanasu** release; let go; let off

話す **hanasu** speak; talk; relate; tell; …に話す **…ni hanasu** have a word with

花束 **hanataba** bouquet, bunch of flowers

鼻歌を歌う **hanauta o utau** hum

花輪 **hanawa** garland; wreath

花屋 **hana-ya** florist

華やか(な) **hanayaka (na)** gorgeous; flowery; brilliant

花嫁 **hanayome** bride

花盛り(の) **hanazakari (no)** in full bloom

鼻詰まり **hanazumari** congestion

ハンバーガー **hanbāgā** hamburger

販売 **hanbai** sale; 販売されている **hanbai sarete iru** be on sale

販売業者 **hanbai-gyō-sha** dealer

販売会議 **hanbai-kaigi** sales meeting

販売促進 **hanbai-sokushin** promotion

販売する **hanbai suru** sell; distribute

販売店 **hanbaiten** outlet

半分 **hanbun** half

半分にする **hanbun ni suru** halve

半分(の) **hanbun (no)** half

判断 **handan** judgment; 判断の尺度 **handan no shakudo** yardstick; 判断を誤る **handan o ayamaru** misjudge

判断する **handan suru** judge

ハンディ **handi** handicap

反動 **handō** backlash

ハンドバッグ **handobaggu** bag; pocketbook, purse

ハンドブック **handobukku** handbook

ハンドル **handoru** handlebars; (steering) wheel

半導体 **handōtai** semiconductor

反動的(な) **handōteki (na)** reactionary

羽 **hane** wing; feather; propeller

羽根 **hane** feather; shuttlecock

跳ね上る **haneagaru** buck (of horse)

羽ぶとん **hanebuton** eiderdown

繁栄 **han'ei** prosperity

繁栄した **han'ei shita** prosperous

繁栄する **han'ei suru** flourish, prosper

はね返る **hanekaeru** rebound

跳ねかける **hanekakeru** splash; splatter

ハネムーン **hanemūn** honeymoon

半円 **han'en** semicircle

半円(の) **han'en (no)** semicircular

はねる **haneru** bound; knock down, knock over

はねつける **hanetsukeru** scorn; shoot down *suggestion*

ハンガー **hangā** clothes hanger, coathanger

版画 **hanga** engraving; woodblock print

半額(の) **hangaku (no)** half-price

ハンガリー **Hangarī** Hungary

ハンガリー(の) **Hangarī (no)** Hungarian

反撃 **hangeki** counter-attack

反撃する **hangeki suru** counter, counter-attack, retaliate

反逆 **hangyaku** revolt

反逆者 **hangyaku-sha** rebel; traitor

反逆する **hangyaku suru** revolt

反逆罪 **hangyakuzai** treason

範囲 **han'i** area; scope; spectrum; sphere; …の範囲内で **…no han'inai de** within

はにかんだ **hanikanda** coy; shy

判事 **hanji** judge

繁盛している **hanjō shite iru** prospering; flourishing

ハンカチ **hankachi** handkerchief

繁華街 **hankagai** busy shopping district

繁華街(の) **hankagai (no)** downtown

反感 **hankan** antipathy; 反感を買う **hankan o kau** alienate

半径 **hankei** radius

半券 **hanken** stub

判決 **hanketsu** judgment; 判決を下す **hanketsu o kudasu** pass sentence; Xに有罪／無罪判決を下す **X ni yūzai／muzai hanketsu o kudasu** find X innocent／guilty

はんこ **hanko** signature seal

反抗 **hankō** defiance; rebellion

反抗する **hankō suru** rebel

反抗的(な) **hankōteki (na)** defiant; rebellious; disobedient; insubordinate

半狂乱(の) **hankyōran (no)** frantic

反響する **hankyō suru** echo

半球 **hankyū** hemisphere

ハンマー **hanmā** hammer; sledgehammer

ハンモック **hanmokku** hammock

反目 **hanmoku** antagonism

犯人 **hannin** culprit

反応 **hannō** reaction; response

反応する **hannō suru** react

歯(の) **ha (no)** dental

反乱 **hanran** mutiny, rebellion; 反乱を起こす **hanran o okosu** rebel, mutiny

反乱軍 **hanran-gun** rebel troops

はんらんさせる **hanran saseru** flood

はんらんする **hanran suru** overflow

判例 **hanrei** precedent; case LAW

販路 **hanro** market; outlet

反論する **hanron suru** contradict; dispute

ハンサム(な) **hansamu (na)** handsome

反省する **hansei suru** reflect on; be sorry

帆船 **hansen** sailing ship

反射 **hansha** reflection

反社会的(な) **hanshakaiteki (na)** antisocial

反射能力 **hansha-nōryoku** reflex

反射する **hansha suru** reflect

反射的(な) **hanshateki (na)** involuntary

反射運動 **hansha-undō** reflex reaction

反して **hanshite** contrary to

繁殖 **hanshoku** breeding; reproduction

繁殖(の) **hanshoku (no)**

reproductive
繁殖させる **hanshoku saseru** breed
繁殖する **hanshoku suru** breed;
reproduce; multiply
半そで(の) **hansode (no)** short-
sleeved
反則する **hansoku suru** foul SP
半数(の) **hansū (no)** half
反する **hansuru** oppose
反証する **hanshō suru** disprove
反対 **hantai** dissent; opposition
ハンター **hantā** hunter
反対である **hantai de aru** be
opposed to; be disapprove of
反対尋問を行う **hantai-jinmon o
okonau** cross-examine
反対(の) **hantai (no)** contrary;
opposite
反体制になる **hantaisei ni naru**
become anti-establishment; go
underground
反対する **hantai suru** object;
oppose; protest
半島 **hantō** peninsula
犯罪 **hanzai** crime, offense
犯罪(の) **hanzai (no)** criminal
犯罪者 **hanzai-sha** criminal,
offender
半ズボン **han-zubon** shorts
はおり **haori** half-length Japanese
coat
葉っぱ **happa** leaf
発破をかける **happa o kakeru** urge
on; give a pep talk
発砲される **happō sareru** go off (of
gun)
発泡ワイン **happō-wain** sparkling
wine
発表 **happyō** announcement
発表する **happyō suru** announce;
bring out; air
ハープ **hāpu** harp
腹 **hara** belly; gut; insides; 腹を立て
る **hara o tateru** lose one's temper;
resent; …に対して腹を立てている
… ni taishite hara o tatete iru be
angry with
腹ごしらえする **haragoshirae suru**
grab a quick bite
腹黒い **haraguroi** scheming; wicked
払い込む **haraikomu** pay in

払い戻し **haraimodoshi** rebate;
refund
払い戻す **haraimodosu** refund,
reimburse; repay
払いのける **harainokeru** brush;
brush off
波乱に富んだ **haran ni tonda**
eventful
腹ペコ(の) **harapeko (no)** ravenous
払う **harau** pay, fork out; 注意を払う
chūi o harau pay attention
腫れ **hare** swelling
腫れぼったい **harebottai** puffy
晴れ(の) **hare (no)** fine day
晴れる **hareru** brighten up; clear;
lift; swell (of wound, limb)
晴れた **hareta** bright; clear; sunny;
swollen
破裂 **haretsu** burst; rupture
破裂させる **haretsu saseru** burst;
bust, break
破裂した **haretsu shita** burst
破裂する **haretsu suru** burst;
rupture
晴やかさ **hareyaka-sa** brightness
はり **hari** beam; rafter
針 **hari** hand (of clock); needle;
spike; spine (on hedgehog)
張り **hari** strain, tension
ハリ治療 **harichiryō** acupuncture
張り出す **haridasu** jut out
はり紙 **harigami** notice
針金 **harigane** wire
ハリケーン **harikēn** hurricane
張り切る **harikiru** be enthusiastic; be
in high spirits
はりねずみ **harinezumi** hedgehog
はり付ける **haritsukeru** stick (up);
paste
張り付く **haritsuku** stick to, follow
張り詰めた **haritsumeta** tense;
anxious
はる **haru** post; affix; stick up
張る **haru** stretch; spread; tense up;
pitch tent
春 **haru** spring
春一番 **haruichiban** first south
wind of spring
はるかに **haruka ni** far, much
挟まれている **hasamarete iru** lie
between; be caught between

はさみ **hasami** scissors; shears

挟み込む **hasamikomu** tuck; tuck in

挟む **hasamu** sandwich, squeeze

破産 **hasan** bankruptcy

破産させる **hasan saseru** bankrupt, ruin

破産した **hasan shita** bankrupt, insolvent

破産する **hasan suru** go bankrupt, go bust, go under; be ruined (*financially*)

派生(の) **hasei (no)** derivative

はし **hashi** chopsticks

橋 **hashi** bridge

端 **hashi** edge; end

はしご **hashigo** ladder

はしか **hashika** measles

はしけ **hashike** barge NAUT

はし置き **hashioki** chopstick rest

柱 **hashira** pillar; post

走り書き **hashirigaki** scribble

走る **hashiru** run

はした金 **hashitagane** chickenfeed, peanuts

橋渡し **hashiwatashi** mediation; buffer *fig*

破傷風 **hashōfū** tetanus

破損 **hason** break; breakage

発生 **hassei** creation; eruption (*of violence*)

発生する **hassei suru** erupt; flare up

発車 **hassha** departure

発射 **hassha** launch; shot

発射する **hassha suru** launch; blast off; fire, shoot

発しん **hasshin** rash

発信音 **hasshin'on** dial tone

発送 **hassō** shipping, sending

発送する **hassō suru** dispatch, send off

発する **hassuru** give off; utter; issue

ハッスル **hassuru** hustle

はす **hasu** lotus

ハスキー(な) **hasukī (na)** husky

旗 **hata** flag; colors MIL

はたち, 二十歳 **hatachi** twenty (years old)

畑 **hatake** field

はためく **hatameku** flap; flutter

破たん **hatan** breakup, failure

働かせる **hatarakaseru** exercise *caution, restraint*; (make) work

働き者(の) **hatarakimono (no)** hard-working

働きすぎる **hataraki-sugiru** overwork

働く **hataraku** function; work

果たす **hatasu** fulfill

ハッチ **hatchi** hatch

ハッチバック車 **hatchibakku-sha** hatchback

果てしない **hateshinai** never-ending, unending

はと **hato** dove; pigeon

ハート **hāto** hearts

波止場 **hatoba** jetty; wharf

はと派 **hatoha** dove *fig*

初(の) **hatsu (no)** first

発 **-hatsu** departure; 大阪発 *Ōsakahatsu* departure from Osaka

発売 **hatsubai** launch, release (*of product*)

発売する **hatsubai suru** launch, release *new product*

発病 **hatsubyō** onset

発病させる **hatsubyō saseru** develop

発電機 **hatsudenki** dynamo; generator

発電所 **hatsudensho** power station

発電する **hatsuden suru** generate electricity

発煙筒 **hatsuentō** flare

発がん性物質 **hatsugansei-busshitsu** carcinogen

発がん性(の) **hatsugansei (no)** carcinogenic

発芽する **hatsuga suru** sprout

発言 **hatsugen** remark; contribution (*to debate*)

発言する **hatsugen suru** contribute

はつかだいこん **hatsuka-daikon** radish

発明 **hatsumei** invention

発明者 **hatsumei-sha** inventor

発明する **hatsumei suru** invent

初耳 **hatsumimi**: 初耳だ *hatsumimi da* it's the first time I've heard that

初詣 **hatsumōde** first visit to a shrine in New Year

発音 **hatsuon** pronunciation

発音する **hatsuon suru** pronounce

はったり **hattari** bluff; はったりをきかせる **hattari o kikaseru** bluff

発達 **hattatsu** development; growth

発達する **hattatsu suru** develop; grow

発展 **hatten** growth; development; evolution

発展させる **hatten saseru** develop

発展する **hatten suru** grow; grow up; develop; evolve

発展途上国 **hatten-tojōkoku** developing country

はう **hau** crawl; wriggle

ハウスボート **hausubōto** houseboat

早い **hayai** early

速い **hayai** fast, quick, swift, speedy

早死に **hayajini** untimely death

早く **hayaku** early ◊ be quick!

速く **hayaku** fast

早まった **hayamatta** premature

早め(の) **hayame (no)** early

早める **hayameru** precipitate; hasten

早送り **hayaokuri** fast forward

早送りする **hayaokuri suru** fast forward

はやり(の) **hayari (no)** trendy, in

はやる **hayaru** become popular; become fashionable; flourish

速さ **haya-sa** speed, rapidity

早過ぎた **hayasugita** premature

はず **-hazu** should; ought; be supposed to

恥ずべき **hazubeki** disgraceful; shameful

恥ずかしがり(の) **hazukashigari (no)** shy

恥ずかしい **hazukashii** ashamed; embarrassing; ...を恥ずかしく思う *... o hazukashiku omou* be ashamed of

辱める **hazukashimeru** disgrace; shame

恥ずかしそう(な) **hazukashisō (na)** sheepish

弾ませる **hazumaseru** bounce

弾み **hazumi** bound

はずみ **hazumi** impetus

弾む **hazumu** bounce

はずれ **hazure** fringe, edge; miss; outskirts

はずす **hazusu** undo, unfasten; ボタンをはずす *botan o hazusu* unbutton

屁 **he** fart; 屁をこぐ *he o kogu* fart

ヘアブラシ **heaburashi** hairbrush

ヘアダイ **headai** rinse

ヘアドライヤー **headoraiyā** hairdrier, hairdryer

ヘアカット **heakatto** haircut

ヘアピン **heapin** barrette; hairpin

ヘアピンカーブ **heapin-kābu** hairpin curve

ヘアスプレー **heasupurē** lacquer

ヘアスタイル **heasutairu** hairstyle

へび **hebi** snake

ヘビー級(の) **hebī-kyū (no)** heavyweight

ヘビースモーカー **hebī-sumōkā** heavy smoker

隔たり **hedatari** gap, distance

ヘッドハンター **heddo-hantā** headhunter

ヘッドホン **heddo-hon** headphones

ヘッドライト **heddo-raito** headlamp, headlight

ヘディング **hedingu** header (in soccer)

ヘディングする **hedingu suru** head ball

平凡 **heibon** mediocrity; triviality

平凡(な) **heibon (na)** average; mediocre; indifferent; conventional; humdrum

平地 **heichi** plain

兵役 **heieki** military service

平服 **heifuku** clothes for everyday wear

併合する **heigō suru** annex; merge

平方 **heihō** square MATH; 平方マイル *heihō mairu* square mile

平日 **heijitsu** weekday

陸下 **Heika** Your Majesty

閉館時間 **heikan-jikan** closing time

兵器 **heiki** armaments

平均 **heikin** average

平気(な) **heiki (na)** OK; unconcerned

平均寿命 **heikin-jumyō** life
expectancy

平均して **heikin shite** on average

平均的(な) **heikinteki (na)** average

平行(の) **heikō (no)** parallel

平衡を保つ **heikō o tamotsu**
maintain a balance

閉口させる **heikō saseru** stump,
perplex

平行線 **heikōsen** parallel lines

平面図 **heimenzu** ground plan

平熱 **heinetsu** normal temperature

平穏(な) **heion (na)** quiet, peaceful

閉鎖 **heisa** closure

閉鎖される **heisa sareru** be closed
down

閉鎖された **heisa sareta** disused

閉鎖する **heisa suru** close down,
shut down

平成時代 **Heisei-jidai** Heisei era
(1989-)

平静 **heisei** calm; 平静を保つ *heisei
o tamotsu* keep one's temper

閉所恐怖症 **heisho-kyōfushō**
claustrophobia

閉店 **heiten** closure

閉店時間 **heiten-jikan** closing time

閉店する **heiten suru** close

平和 **heiwa** peace

平和部隊 **Heiwa-butai** Peace Corps

平和主義 **heiwa-shugi** pacifism

平和主義者 **heiwa-shugi-sha**
pacifist

平和的(な) **heiwateki (na)** peaceful

平然と **heizen to** calmly; coolly; in
cold blood

平然とした **heizen to shita**
nonchalant; unflappable

壁画 **hekiga** mural

へこませる **hekomaseru** dent

へこみ **hekomi** dent

へま **hema** blunder; へまをする
hema o suru blunder; goof, trip up

偏 **hen** radical of a Chinese
character

変圧器 **hen'atsuki** transformer

変動 **hendō** fluctuation; upheaval

変動する **hendō suru** fluctuate;
float FIN

返事 **henji** answer, reply; 返事をする
henji o suru answer

変人 **henjin** crank; freak; eccentric

変化 **henka** change; shift; variation;
variety

変換 **henkan** conversion

変化に富んだ **henka ni tonda**
checkered; varied

変換する **henkan suru** export
COMPUT; convert COMPUT

変化する **henka suru** vary; change;
transform

変形 **henkei** transformation

変形させる **henkei saseru**
transform

偏見 **henken** bias; prejudice; myth
fig; ...に偏見を抱かせる *... ni
henken o idakaseru* prejudice

偏見に基づいた **henken ni
motozuita** bias(s)ed

偏見のある **henken no aru**
prejudiced

変更 **henkō** alteration, change;
revision

変更できない **henkō dekinai**
irrevocable

変更する **henkō suru** change

返却 **henkyaku** return

返却する **henkyaku suru** return

編曲 **henkyoku** arrangement

編曲する **henkyoku suru** arrange

偏狭(な) **henkyō (na)** intolerant;
narrow-minded

変(な) **hen (na)** odd, strange, weird

変な風に **hen na fū ni** funnily,
oddly

へんぴ(な) **henpi (na)** out-of-the-
way; remote

返済 **hensai** repayment

返済する **hensai suru** wipe out

変色させる **henshoku saseru**
discolor

編集長 **henshūchō** editor-in-chief
(*of magazine*)

編集局長 **henshū-kyokuchō** editor
(*of newspaper*)

編集(の) **henshū (no)** editorial

編集者 **henshū-sha** editor (*of
book*)

編集する **henshū suru** compile; edit

変装 **hensō** disguise; ...に変装する
... ni hensō suru disguise oneself
as

変速機 **hensokuki** transmission MOT

変速レバー **hensoku-rebā** gear lever, gear shift

返送する **hensō suru** send back

変数 **hensū** variable MATH

変態 **hentai** pervert

変態(の) **hentai (no)** kinky

扁桃腺 **hentōsen** tonsils

扁桃腺炎 **hentōsen-en** tonsillitis

変造する **henzō suru** falsify; forge

偏頭痛 **henzutsū** migraine

減らす **herasu** reduce, cut down (on); run down; work off *flab*

へり **heri** border; hem; fringe

ヘリコプター **herikoputā** helicopter

ヘロイン **heroin** heroin

減る **heru** decline, drop off; shrink

ヘルメット **herumetto** helmet, crash helmet

ヘルニア **herunia** hernia

ヘルパー **herupā** helper

ヘルペス **herupesu** herpes

ヘルプ画面 **herupu-gamen** help screen

へそ **heso** navel

へそ曲がり **hesomagari** contrary; sullen

へその緒 **heso no o** umbilical cord

下手(な) **heta (na)** incompetent; poor; lame *excuse*

下手に **heta ni** badly, poorly

へとへとになる **hetoheto ni naru** worn-out

へとへと(の) **hetoheto (no)** grueling; run-down

へつらう **hetsurau** butter up; flatter

部屋 **heya** room; apartment

部屋ばき **heyabaki** slippers

日 **hi** day

火 **hi** fire; 火がつく *hi ga tsuku* catch fire; light up *cigarette*; Xに火をつける *X ni hi o tsukeru* set X on fire

比 **hi** ratio; equal

費 **-hi** expenses

非… **hi...** non-; un-; im-

干上がる **hiagaru** parch; dry up

火花 **hibana** spark

非番である **hiban de aru** be off duty

ひばり **hibari** skylark

ひび **hibi** crack; ひびが入る *hibi ga hairu* crack

響き **hibiki** ring (*of voice*)

響く **hibiku** reverberate

非暴力 **hi-bōryoku** nonviolence

非暴力(の) **hi-bōryoku (no)** nonviolent

ひだ飾り **hidakazari** ruffle (*on dress*)

左 **hidari** left

左側 **hidarigawa** left

左側(の) **hidarigawa (no)** left-hand

左利き(の) **hidarikiki (no)** left-handed

左(の) **hidari (no)** left

左手(の) **hidarite (no)** left-hand

ひどい **hidoi** bad, awful; acute *embarrassment*; gross *exaggeration*; heavy *cold*; murderous *look*; total *disaster* ◊ it's a disgrace

日時計 **hidokei** sundial

ひどく **hidoku** badly; bitterly *cold*; dreadfully *expensive, sorry, pretty*; seriously; violently *object*

冷え **hie** chill

非衛生的(な) **hieiseiteki (na)** unsanitary, unhygienic

冷える **hieru** freeze

皮膚 **hifu** skin

日帰り旅行 **higaeri-ryokō** daytrip

被害 **higai** damage; loss; 被害を受ける *higai o ukeru* be damaged

被害者 **higai-sha** victim

彼岸 **higan** the Equinoctial Week

日傘 **higasa** sunshade

東 **higashi** east

東から(の) **higashi kara (no)** east, easterly

東(の) **higashi (no)** east, eastern

東シナ海 **Higashi-shinakai** East China Sea

ひげ **hige** beard; whiskers; ひげをそる *hige o soru* have a shave

悲劇 **higeki** tragedy

悲劇(の) **higeki (no)** tragic

非現実的(な) **higenjitsuteki (na)** impractical; unrealistic; unreal

ひげそり **higesori** shaver; razor

非合法(の) **higōhō (no)** illegal

日ごとに **higoto ni** day by day

ひぐま **higuma** brown bear

批判 **hihan** criticism

批判する **hihan suru** criticize

批判的(な) **hihanteki (na)** critical; unfavorable

批評 **hihyō** review, write-up

批評する **hihyō suru** review

ひいき **hiiki** favor; partiality

ひいき目 **hiikime** bias

ひいき目に見て **hiikime ni mite** bias(s)ed

ひいきにする **hiiki ni suru** patronize

ひじ **hiji** elbow

ひじ掛け **hijikake** armrest

ひじ掛け椅子 **hijikakeisu** armchair

非常口 **hijōguchi** emergency exit, fire escape

非常階段 **hijō-kaidan** fire escape

非常勤(の) **hijōkin (no)** part-time

非情(な) **hijō (na)** heartless

非常に **hijō ni** very; highly; greatly; much; unusually

非常識(な) **hijōshiki (na)** thoughtless; lacking common sense

控え目(な) **hikaeme (no)** modest; reserved; unobtrusive; unpretentious

日陰 **hikage** out of the sun, in the shade

日陰(の) **hikage (no)** shady

比較 **hikaku** comparison

非核地帯 **hikakuchitai** nuclear-free zone

比較できる **hikaku dekiru** comparable

比較する **hikaku suru** compare

比較的 **hikakuteki** comparative ◊ comparatively, relatively

悲観論 **hikanron** pessimism

悲観論者 **hikanron-sha** pessimist

悲観的(な) **hikanteki (na)** pessimistic

ひかれる **hikareru** have an affinity for; be fascinated by; be attracted to

光 **hikari** light; 光を注ぐ *hikari o sosogu* shed light on

光り輝く **hikari-kagayaku** brilliant

光る **hikaru** gleam; glint; shine

光った **hikatta** shiny

非建設的(な) **hikensetsuteki (na)** destructive

秘訣 **hiketsu** formula; secret; key

ひき **hiki** *countword for animals, fish etc*

引き上げ *hikiage* rise, hike

引き上げる **hikiageru** raise *wages*; withdraw *army*

引き合う **hikiau** pay off; be profitable

引き出し **hikidashi** drawer; withdrawal

引き出す **hikidasu** draw, withdraw, take out

引き戸 **hikido** sliding door

ひきがえる **hikigaeru** toad

引き金 **hikigane** trigger; 引き金になる *hikigane ni naru* trigger; set off

引き離す **hikihanasu** separate, pull apart; pull away

率いる **hikiiru** head, lead

引き換えに **hikikae ni** in exchange

引き返す **hikikaesu** turn back, double back; retrace

引き込まれる **hikikomareru** compelling

引き逃げ事故 **hikinige-jiko** hit-and-run accident

ひき肉 **hikiniku** ground meat

引き伸ばし **hikinobashi** enlargement, blow-up *(of photo)*

引き伸ばす **hikinobasu** enlarge, blow up *photo*; pad *speech*; spin out

引き抜く **hikinuku** extract; pull; pull up

引き起こす **hikiokosu** cause; create; generate; provoke; rouse; stir up

引き落し **hikiotoshi** debit

引き落しされる **hikiotoshi sareru** be debited

引き下がる **hikisagaru** retreat; back off; climb down

引き下げる **hikisageru** lower; reduce

引き裂く **hikisaku** tear *paper, cloth*

引き締まった **hikishimatta** firm; lean; trim

引き潮 **hikishio** ebb tide

引き止める **hikitomeru** detain, keep, stall

引き継ぐ **hikitsugu** take over

引き付ける **hikitsukeru** attract

引き続いて **hikitsuzuite** in the wake of, following

引き受ける **hikiukeru** undertake

引き分け **hikiwake** draw, tie

引き分ける **hikiwakeru** draw

引き渡し **hikiwatashi** extradition; surrender

引き渡し条約 **hikiwatashi-jōyaku** extradition treaty

引き渡す **hikiwatasu** extradite; hand over (*to authorities*); surrender

引き寄せる **hikiyoseru** draw, attract; draw up *chair*

引き算 **hikizan** subtraction

引きずり出す **hikizuridasu** drag out

引きずる **hikizuru** drag; 足を引きずって歩く *ashi o hikizutte aruku* shuffle

引っかける **hikkakeru** hitch; suspend; catch; throw on *clothes*; splash *water*; deceive; pick up *man, woman*

引っかき傷 **hikkakikizu** scratch

引っかく **hikkaku** scratch

ひっきりなしに **hikkirinashi ni** perpetually

引っ込める **hikkomeru** retract; draw back

引っ込み思案(の) **hikkomijian (no)** retiring; conservative

引っ込んでいる **hikkonde iru** make oneself scarce

引っ越す **hikkosu** move out, move house

ひっくり返る **hikkurikaeru** overturn; capsize

ひっくり返す **hikkurikaesu** capsize; knock over; overturn; reverse *decision*

飛行 **hikō** flight; navigation

非行 **hikō** delinquency

飛行時間 **hikō-jikan** flight time

飛行場 **hikōjō** airfield; landing field, landing strip

被後見人 **hikōken-nin** ward (*child*)

飛行機 **hikōki** airplane; 飛行機で *hikōki de* by air

飛行機雲 **hikōki-gumo** vapor trail

被告 **hikoku** defendant

被告弁護人 **hikoku-bengo-nin** defense lawyer

被告側証人 **hikokugawa-shō-nin** defense witness

被告人 **hikoku-nin** the accused; defendant

非行に走った **hikō ni hashitta** delinquent

非公式には **hikōshiki ni wa** unofficially; 非公式に言う *hikōshiki ni iu* say off the record

非公式(の) **hikōshiki (no)** informal

非行少年 **hikō-shōnen** juvenile delinquent

飛行する **hikō suru** navigate

ひく **hiku** run down, knock down; grind *coffee, meat*; saw *wood*

引く **hiku** attract, draw; go down (*of swelling*); subtract

弾く **hiku** play MUS

低い **hikui** deep; low

低くする **hikuku suru** lower; muffle

低さ **hiku-sa** depth

非居住者 **hi-kyojūsha** nonresident

卑きょう(な) **hikyō (na)** unfair; cowardly

非協力的(な) **hikyōryokuteki (na)** uncooperative

暇 **hima** leisure

ひ孫 **himago** great-grandchild

肥満 **himan** obesity

暇(な) **hima (na)** idle

悲鳴 **himei** scream; shriek; yelp; 悲鳴をあげる *himei o ageru* scream; shriek; yelp

秘密 **himitsu** secret, confidence

秘密(の) **himitsu (no)** secret; confidential; clandestine; hidden

ひも **himo** band; cord; string

ひな祭り **Hina-matsuri** Doll Festival

非難 **hinan** accusation; blame; attack; reproach; condemnation

避難 **hinan** shelter; refuge

ひな人形 **hinaningyō** set of ornamental dolls

避難させる **hinan saseru** evacuate

非難すべき **hinansubeki** reprehensible

避難する **hinan suru** shelter, take refuge; evacuate

非難する **hinan suru** attack; accuse; condemn; rebuke

日なた **hinata** sunshine; sunny place

日なたぼっこする **hinatabokko suru** bask in the sun

頻度 **hindo** frequency

ひねくれた **hinekureta** warped, twisted

皮肉 **hiniku** cynicism; sarcasm; irony

皮肉(な) **hiniku (na)** cynical; ironic(al); dry

皮肉屋 **hiniku-ya** cynic

避妊 **hinin** birth control, contraception

避妊具 **hinin-gu** contraceptive device

否認する **hinin suru** disclaim; deny

避妊薬 **hinin-yaku** contraceptive

貧弱(な) **hinjaku (na)** lamentable

貧血である **hinketsu de aru** be anemic

貧困 **hinkon** poverty

品目 **hinmoku** item

日の出 **hinode** sunrise

日の丸 **hinomaru** Japanese national flag, Rising Sun

非能率的(な) **hinōritsuteki (na)** inefficient

頻繁(な) **hinpan (na)** frequent

品詞 **hinshi** part of speech

品質 **hinshitsu** quality

品質管理 **hinshitsu-kanri** quality control

品種 **hinshu** breed; type; category

ヒント **hinto** hint

ひいおばあさん **hīobāsan** great-grandmother

ひいおじいさん **hīojīsan** great-grandfather

引っ張りだこである **hipparidako de aru** in demand, very popular

引っ張る **hipparu** pull, draw; yank; tow

引っぱたく **hippataku** whack; smack

ひらがな **hiragana** *the rounded Japanese syllabary*

避雷針 **hiraishin** lightning conductor

開いた **hiraita** open

開く **hiraku** open; unfold; throw *party*

ひらめ **hirame** plaice; sole

ひらめき **hirameki** brainstorm

ひらめく **hirameku** have a flash of inspiration

平泳ぎ **hiraoyogi** breaststroke

平手打ち **hirateuchi** smack; slap

ひれ **hire** fin

比例した **hirei shita** proportional

ヒレ肉 **hireniku** fillet

ヒレステーキ **hire sutēki** fillet steak

卑劣(な) **hiretsu (na)** contemptible; rotten; shabby

ひりひり痛む **hirihiri itamu** sting; smart

ひりひりする **hirihiri suru** sting; smart

疲労 **hirō** fatigue

ヒーロー **hīrō** hero

広場 **hiroba** square

広々とした **hirobiro to shita** open; roomy, spacious

披露宴 **hirōen** wedding reception

広がり **hirogari** expanse; spread; stretch

広がる **hirogaru** dilate; extend; unfold; stretch ◊ pervasive

広がった **hirogatta** widespread

広げる **hirogeru** broaden; enlarge; expand; unfold; unroll; spread, lay

広い **hiroi** broad, wide; great

ヒロイン **hiroin** heroine

拾い読み **hiroiyomi**: 本を拾い読みする **hon o hiroiyomi suru** browse through a book

広く **hiroku** widely

広くなる **hiroku naru** broaden, widen

広くする **hiroku suru** widen

広まる **hiromaru** become widespread; pervade

広める **hiromeru** spread

広さ **hiro-sa** breadth, width

拾う **hirou** pick up

昼 **hiru** midday; daytime

ヒール **hīru** heel

昼ごはん **hirugohan** lunch

昼間 **hiruma** day

昼休み **hiruyasumi** lunch break

被災地 **hisaichi** disaster area

悲惨(な) **hisan (na)** disastrous

悲惨さ **hisan-sa** misery

ひさし **hisashi** eaves

ひさしぶり **hisashiburi** a long time; ひさしぶりです **hisashiburi desu** long time no see

非生産的(な) **hiseisanteki (na)** unproductive

ひし形 **hishi-gata** diamond (*shape*); lozenge

秘書 **hisho** secretary

秘書(の) **hisho (no)** secretarial

ひそか(な) **hisoka (na)** furtive, stealthy; covert

ひそかに **hisoka ni** secretly; ひそかに...する **hisoka ni ... suru** do ... in secret

筆跡 **hisseki** handwriting

必死で **hisshi de** like mad

必死に **hisshi ni** madly

必死(の) **hisshi (no)** desperate

必修(の) **hisshū (no)** compulsory

必須(の) **hissu (no)** mandatory; imperative

ひすい **hisui** jade

ヒステリー **hisuterī** hysteria

ヒーター **hītā** heater

額 **hitai** forehead, brow

ひたむき(な) **hitamuki (na)** single-minded

悲嘆 **hitan** lament; 悲嘆にくれている **hitan ni kurete iru** be prostrate with grief

浸す **hitasu** steep; dip

ヒッチハイクする **hitchi-haiku suru** hitch, hitchhike

否定 **hitei** denial

否定できない **hitei dekinai** undeniable

否定(の) **hitei (no)** negative

否定する **hitei suru** contradict; deny, repudiate

人 **hito** man; person; character; creature

―... **hito...** (*prefix*) one; a; 一きれ **hitokire** a slice; 一口 **hitokuchi** a bite; a gulp; 一組 **hitokumi** a deck, a pack (*of cards*); a block (*of shares*)

人々 **hitobito** people, folk

ひとで **hitode** starfish

人手 **hitode** hand, worker

人手不足(の) **hitode-busoku (no)** short-staffed, understaffed

ひとでなし **hitodenashi** beast (*person*); brute; monster

人柄 **hitogara** character; personality

人込み **hitogomi** crowd, crush

人殺し **hitogoroshi** killer; murderer

人質 **hitojichi** hostage; 人質にとられる **hitojichi ni torareru** be taken hostage

一言 **hitokoto** a (brief) word

人前で **hitomae de** in public

ひとまとめにする **hitomatome ni suru** bundle up

ひと目 **hitome** a glimpse

ヒト免疫不全ウィルス **hito-men'eki-fuzen-uirusu** human immunodeficiency virus, HIV

人並みはずれた **hitonami-hazureta** uncanny

人なつこい **hitonatsukoi** friendly

人(の) **hito (no)** human

ひとり **hitori** one person; ひとり息子/娘 **hitori-musuko** / **musume** only son / daughter

ひとりで **hitori de** alone; by oneself, on one's own

独り言 **hitorigoto** talking to oneself

ひとりっこ **hitorikko** only child

一人(の) **hitori (no)** one (*person*)

ひとりよがり(の) **hitoriyogari (no)** self-righteous; smug

ひとさじ **hitosaji** a spoonful; a portion; a drop

人さし指 **hitosashiyubi** index finger, forefinger

一騒ぎ **hitosawagi** a fuss

等しい **hitoshii** equal

等しく **hitoshiku** equally

一坪 **hitotsubo** *area measure of 3.6 square yards*

一つ **hitotsu** one

ひとつまみ **hitotsumami** a pinch

一つにする **hitotsu ni suru** unite

一つ(の) **hitotsu (no)** one (*thing*); single, sole

一山 **hitoyama** a pile; a heap

人里離れた **hitozato hanareta** secluded

ひつぎ **hitsugi** casket, coffin

羊 **hitsuji** sheep

羊の肉 **hitsuji no niku** mutton

必需品 **hitsujuhin** commodity; necessity

悲痛(な) **hitsū (na)** heartbreaking; poignant

必要 **hitsuyō** necessity; need

必要経費 **hitsuyō-keihi** expense account

必要(な) **hitsuyō (na)** necessary, required; obligatory

必要とする **hitsuyō to suru** require, necessitate

必然的に **hitsuzenteki ni** inevitably; necessarily

ひったくる **hittakuru** snatch, grab

匹敵する **hitteki suru** be comparable; be similar ◊ equal, rival

匹敵するもの **hitteki suru mono** equal

ヒット **hitto** hit

ヒットチャート **hitto-chāto** charts MUS

ヒット作 **hittosaku** blockbuster

引っつける **hittsukeru** tape; stick

引っつく **hittsuku** stick; stick to

悲運 **hiun** misfortune; doom

冷や **hiya** cold sake

冷やかす **hiyakasu** tease; make fun of

日焼け **hiyake** sunburn; suntan, tan

日焼け止め **hiyake-dome** sunblock

日焼けする **hiyake suru** get a suntan

飛躍的発展 **hiyakuteki-hatten** breakthrough

冷やす **hiyasu** chill *wine*

費用 **hiyō** cost, expense

日よけ **hiyoke** awning; sunshade

ひよこ **hiyoko** chick

肥沃(な) **hiyoku (na)** fertile, rich

比喩的(な) **hiyuteki (na)** figurative, metaphorical

膝 **hiza** knee, lap

日差し **hizashi** sunlight

ひざ掛け **hizakake** (travel) rug

膝小僧 **hizakozō** kneecap

ひざまずく **hizamazuku** kneel down

日付 **hizuke** date; 日付を入れる *hizuke o ireru* date *check etc*

帆 **ho** sail

ほお **hō** cheek

法 **hō** act, law

方 **hō** direction; side; …の方へ *... no hō e* to; toward; やめておいた方がいい *yamete oita hō ga ii* I'd really better not; …のほうを好む *... no hō o konomu* prefer

法案 **hōan** bill POL

ホバークラフト **hobākurafuto** hovercraft

ほお紅 **hōbeni** blusher

ほうび **hōbi** reward

保母 **hobo** nursery school teacher

ほお骨 **hōbone** cheekbone

放置 **hōchi** neglect

補聴器 **hochōki** hearing aid

程 **hodo** around; 一週間程 *isshūkan hodo* around a week; 早ければ早い程いい *hayakereba hayai hodo ii* the sooner the better

歩道 **hodō** sidewalk; walk

報道 **hōdō** journalism; coverage (*by media*); report; publication

ほどほどに **hodohodo ni** in moderation

報道陣 **hōdōjin** the press

報道記事 **hōdō-kiji** news report

ほどく **hodoku** disentangle; undo; unfold; untie

歩道橋 **hodōkyō** footbridge

報道する **hōdō suru** report

ほどよい **hodoyoi** moderate

放映されている **hōei sarete iru** be on (*of TV program*)

ほえる **hoeru** bark; bellow; roar

報復 **hōfuku** reprisal; retaliation

報復する **hōfuku suru** take reprisals; retaliate

豊富(な) **hōfu (na)** abundant; plentiful; rich

豊富にする **hōfu ni suru** enrich

豊富さ **hōfu-sa** abundance; plenty

邦画 **hōga** Japanese movie

法外(な) **hōgai (na)** exorbitant, prohibitive

方角 **hōgaku** direction; compass point

法学 **hōgaku** law (*as subject*)

捕鯨 **hogei** whaling

砲撃 **hōgeki** shellfire

砲撃される **hōgeki sareru** come under shellfire

砲撃する **hōgeki suru** shell

方言 **hōgen** dialect

保護 **hogo** conservation; protection

縫合 **hōgō** stitches; seam; suture

保護観察官 **hogo-kansatsukan** probation officer

保護区域 **hogo-kuiki** sanctuary

保護する **hogo suru** protect; safeguard; shield

縫合する **hōgō suru** stitch up

ほぐす **hogusu** relax; unravel

方法 **hōhō** manner, way; means; method; system

ほほ笑み **hohoemi** smile

ほほ笑む **hohoemu** smile

包囲 **hōi** siege

方位磁針 **hōi-jishin** compass

保育 **hoiku** nursing

保育園 **hoikuen** nursery (school)

ホイル **hoiru** tinfoil, foil

保持者 **hoji-sha** holder

補助教材 **hojo-kyōzai** teaching aid

補助(の) **hojo (no)** auxiliary

補助的(な) **hojoteki (na)** subsidiary; subordinate

補充する **hojū suru** refill; supplement

他、ほか **hoka** etc

放火 **hōka** arson

放課後 **hōkago** after school; 放課後に残す **hōkago ni nokosu** keep in (*at school*)

崩壊 **hōkai** fall, collapse (*of government*)

崩壊した **hōkai shita** broken *home*

崩壊する **hōkai suru** crumble; disintegrate; fall

捕獲 **hokaku** capture

保管 **hokan** storage

他に **hoka ni** apart from, besides; as well as, in addition to; 他にだれが そこにいましたか **hoka ni dare ga soko ni imashita ka** who else was there?; 他にだれも…ない **hoka ni dare mo i nai** there's no one else

here; ほかに何か **hoka ni nani ka** anything else?

他(の) **hoka (no)** other; 他の人 **hoka no hito** the other; 他の人た ち **hoka no hitotachi** (other) people; 他の物 **hoka no mono** another; the other; 他の場所では **hoka no basho de wa** elsewhere; 他の人たちは皆行く **hoka no hitotachi wa mina iku** everyone else is going

保管されている **hokan sarete iru** be in storage

保管する **hokan suru** keep safe; look after

包括的(な) **hōkatsuteki (na)** comprehensive

保険 **hoken** insurance; 保険に入って いる **hoken ni haitte iru** be insured; 保険をかける **hoken o kakeru** insure

保険会社 **hoken-gaisha** insurance company

保険料 **hokenryō** insurance premium; 保険料運賃込み価格 **hokenryō-unchin-komi kakaku** CIF, cost insurance freight

保険証 **hokenshō** health insurance identity card

保険証券 **hoken-shōken** (insurance) policy

保険証書 **hoken-shōsho** (insurance) policy

補欠 **hoketsu** reserve, substitute

ほうき **hōki** broom

保菌者 **hokin-sha** carrier (*of disease*)

放棄する **hōki suru** renounce

北海道 **Hokkaidō** Hokkaido

ホッケー **hokkē** (ice) hockey

ホック **hokku** hook; snap fastener

北極 **Hokkyoku** North Pole

北極(の) **hokkyoku (no)** polar

方向 **hōkō** direction

歩行器 **hokōki** walker

報告 **hōkoku** account; submission

報告書 **hōkoku-sho** report

報告する **hōkoku suru** report

ほこり **hokori** dust ; ほこりを払う **hokori o harau** dust

誇り **hokori** pride; 誇りに思う **hokori**

ni omou be proud of; 誇りにする

hokori ni suru pride oneself on

ほこりっぽい **hokorippoi** dusty

歩行者 **hokō-sha** pedestrian

方向転換 **hōkō-tenkan** turn

方向転換する **hōkō-tenkan suru** turn; turn around

方向づける **hōkōzukeru** shape

北米 **Hokubei** North America

ほくろ **hokuro** mole (*on skin*)

北西 **hokusei** northwest

北東 **hokutō** northeast

補強する **hokyō suru** reinforce

ほめ言葉 **homekotoba** compliment

方面 **hōmen** direction; district; line (of business)

ほめる **homeru** compliment

ホモ **homo** homosexual, gay; fag

訪問 **hōmon** visit

ホモ(の) **homo (no)** homosexual, gay

訪問者 **hōmon-sha** caller

訪問する **hōmon suru** visit

ホーム **hōmu** home; home base; (railroad) platform

ホームムービー **hōmu-mūbī** home movie

ホームラン **hōmu ran** home run

ホームレス **hōmuresu** the homeless, streetpeople

ホームレス(の) **hōmuresu (no)** homeless

ホームシックになる **homushikku ni naru** be homesick

法務省 **Hōmushō** Japanese Ministry of Justice

本 **hon** book

本 **-hon** countword for long thin things

本… **hon…** real, genuine

本部 **honbu** headquarters

本文 **honbun** text

本題 **hondai** the main issue; 本題に入る *hondai ni hairu* get to the point

本棚 **hondana** bookcase

本土 **hondo** mainland

本堂 **hondō** main building of a temple

骨 **hone** bone; 骨の折れる *hone no oreru* painstaking

骨組 **honegumi** frame; framework

本格的(な) **honkakuteki (na)** real; authentic

本気でない **honki de nai** playful; not serious

本気になる **honki ni naru** knuckle down

香港 **Honkon** Hong Kong

本拠地 **honkyochi** base, center; 本拠地にする *honkyochi ni suru* be based in

本物 **honmono** the real thing

本物(の) **honmono (no)** authentic; original; real

本音と建て前 **honne to tatemae** what you really think and the face you put on

本人 **honnin** the person in question

ほんの **hon no** mere; 彼はほんの六歳です *kare wa hon no rokusai desu* he's only 6

本能 **honnō** instinct

本能的に **honnōteki ni** instinctively

ほのお **honō** flame

ほのか(な) **honoka (na)** vague; faint

ほのめかす **honomekasu** imply, insinuate

本来 **honrai** originally; from the beginning; fundamentally

本籍地 **honsekichi** official address (*for registration purposes*)

本社 **honsha** head office

本質 **honshitsu** nature; essence

本質的に **honshitsuteki ni** essentially

本州 **Honshū** Honshu

本当に **hontō ni** absolutely; completely; actually; really, truly; indeed; very much

本当(の) **hontō (no)** real; true

本屋 **hon-ya** bookseller; bookstore

翻訳 **hon'yaku** translation

翻訳者 **hon'yaku-sha** translator

翻訳する **hon'yaku suru** translate; 英語に翻訳する *Eigo ni hon'yaku suru* translate into English

ほ乳びん **honyūbin** bottle

ほ乳動物 **honyū-dōbutsu** mammal

北方領土 **Hoppō-ryōdo** Northern Territories

ホップ **hoppu** hop

ほら **hora** hey; ほら、やってごらんなさ
い *hora, yatte goran nasai* go on,
do it!; ほらを吹く *hora o fuku* brag;
tell a tall story

洞穴 **hora-ana** cave

ほら話 **horabanashi** yarn, tall story

ホラー映画 **horā-eiga** horror movie

ほうれん草 **hōrensō** spinach

掘り出し物 **horidashimono** catch;
lucky find; bargain

ほうり出す **hōridasu** fling out, throw
out

掘り起こす **horiokosu** dig up,
dredge up

法律 **hōritsu** law; statute; legislation

法律違反 **hōritsu-ihan** violation of
the law

法律(の) **hōritsu (no)** legal

ほうろう **hōrō** enamel

滅びる **horobiru** be ruined; die out;
become extinct

ホログラム **horoguramu** hologram

放浪する **hōrō suru** wander around

掘る **horu** dig; excavate; drill

彫る **horu** engrave

ホール **hōru** hall

ホルモン **horumon** hormone

捕虜 **horyo** captive; prisoner of war

保留する **horyū suru** reserve;
withhold

補佐官 **hosakan** assistant, aide

宝石 **hōseki** gem; jewel; (precious)
stone

宝石類 **hōseki-rui** jewelry

宝石商 **hōseki-shō** jeweler

保釈 **hoshaku** bail; 保釈中で
hoshakuchū de on bail

保釈金 **hoshakukin** bail (*money*)

保釈させる **hoshaku saseru** bail
out

放射能 **hōshanō** radiation,
radioactivity

放射性(の) **hōshasei (no)**
radioactive

放射線療法 **hōshasen-ryōhō**
radiotherapy

放射する **hōsha suru** radiate

星 **hoshi** star

欲しい **hoshii** want; would like to;
wish, hope

干しぶどう **hoshibudō** currant;
raisin

星印 **hoshijirushi** asterisk

干し草 **hoshikusa** hay

方針 **hōshin** course of action; policy

星占い **hoshiuranai** astrology;
horoscope

星占い師 **hoshiuranai-shi**
astrologer

保証 **hoshō** guarantee; warranty;
assurance; security (*in job*)

保障 **hoshō** guarantee

補償 **hoshō** compensation

補償額 **hoshō-gaku** (insurance)
cover

保証期間 **hoshō-kikan** guarantee
period

補償金 **hoshō-kin** compensation

捕食動物 **hoshoku-dōbutsu**
predator

保証人 **hoshō-nin** guarantor;
witness; sponsor; 保証人となる
hoshō-nin to naru sponsor; 保証
人としてサインする *hoshō-nin
toshite sain suru* witness

保証する **hoshō suru** guarantee;
answer for, vouch for

補償する **hoshō suru** compensate

報酬 **hōshū** compensation;
remuneration

保守的(な) **hoshuteki (na)**
conservative, conventional

放送 **hōsō** broadcast; broadcasting

包装 **hōsō** packaging

細い **hosoi** fine; thin

補足料金 **hosoku-ryōkin**
supplementary fee

包装紙 **hōsōshi** wrapping paper

舗装する **hosō suru** pave

放送する **hōsō suru** broadcast

包装する **hōsō suru** package

発作 **hossa** bout; fit; seizure

発足する **hossoku suru** inaugurate

ほっそりした **hossori shita** slender,
slim

干す **hosu** dry

ホース **hōsu** hose

ホスピス **hosupisu** hospice

ホステス **hosutesu** hostess

包帯 **hōtai** bandage; dressing; 包帯
をする *hōtai o suru* bandage

ほたる **hotaru** firefly

ホッチキス **hotchikisu®** stapler

法廷 **hōtei** court; courtroom; law court

方程式 **hōteishiki** equation

ほてる **hoteru** glow; feel warm

ホテル **hoteru** hotel

放とう **hōtō** debauchery

仏 **Hotoke** Buddha

仏 **hotoke** the deceased

ほとんど **hotondo** almost; nearly, all but ◊ most; ほとんど…ない *hotondo…nai* scarcely; ほとんど…しない *hotondo... shinai* little; ほとんど…と同じ *hotondo ... to onaji* in comparison with, next to; ほとんど残っていない *hotondo nokotte inai* there are very few of them left

ほととぎす **hototogisu** Japanese cuckoo

ほったらかしにされた **hottarakashi ni sareta** neglected

ほったらかしにする **hottarakashi ni suru** neglect

ほったらかし(の) **hottarakashi (no)** unattended

ホットドッグ **hotto-doggu** hot dog

ホットケーキ **hotto-kēki** pancake

ほっとした **hotto shita** that's a relief

ホワイトハウス **Howaito-hausu** White House

ホワイトカラー **howaito-karā** white-collar worker

抱擁 **hōyō** cuddle; embrace

保存 **hozon** preservation

保存する **hozon suru** preserve; save COMPUT; store COMPUT; cure *meat, fish*

保存剤 **hozonzai** preservative

百科辞典 **hyakka-jiten** encyclopedia

百 **hyaku** hundred; 百番目(の) *hyakubanme (no)* hundredth

百万 **hyakuman** million

百万長者 **hyakuman-chōja** millionaire

百周年 **hyakushūnen** centenary, centennial

百日ぜき **hykunichizeki** whooping cough

ひょう **hyō** hail; leopard

表 **hyō** table (*of figures*)

票 **hyō** vote

評判 **hyōban** reputation; standing

評判の良い **hyōban no yoi** reputable

表題 **hyōdai** heading, title

氷河 **hyōga** glacier

表現 **hyōgen** expression; show, display

表現力 **hyōgenryoku** expressive power

表現する **hyōgen suru** express; phrase; represent

標本 **hyōhon** specimen MED

表示 **hyōji** sign

表情 **hyōjō** expression

表情に富む **hyōjō ni tomu** expressive

表情の豊か(な) **hyōjō no yutaka (na)** expressive

標準 **hyōjun** standard; 標準以下である *hyōjun ika de aru* not be up to standard

標準語 **hyōjungo** standard Japanese / English etc; standard language

標準以下(の) **hyōjun-ika (no)** substandard

評価 **hyōka** valuation; evaluation

評価する **hyōka suru** assess; evaluate; consider

票決 **hyōketsu** vote

標高 **hyōkō** altitude

表明する **hyōmei suru** voice *opinions*

表面 **hyōmen** surface

表面(の) **hyōmen (no)** cosmetic *changes, reasons*

表面上は **hyōmenjō wa** on the surface, superficially

表面的(な) **hyōmenteki (na)** outward; superficial

評論 **hyōron** criticism; review

評論家 **hyōronka** critic, reviewer

漂流する **hyōryū suru** drift

表紙 **hyōshi** (front) cover

標識 **hyōshiki** sign

氷点 **hyōten** freezing point

氷山 **hyōzan** iceberg

ヒューズ **hyūzu** fuse; ヒューズが飛んだ *hyūzu ga tonda* the fuse blew

I

胃 **i** stomach

位 **-i** rank; position; 第4位 *daiyon'i* fourth

医 **-i** doctor; 外科医 *gekai* surgeon

いばる **ibaru** brag; be arrogant

居場所 **ibasho** whereabouts

いびき **ibiki** snoring; いびきをかく *ibiki o kaku* snore

いぼ **ibo** wart

異母兄弟 **ibo-kyōdai** stepbrother

異母姉妹 **ibo-shimai** stepsister

イブニングドレス **ibuningu-doresu** evening dress

いぶす **ibusu** smoke *bacon*

遺物 **ibutsu** relic

一 **ichi** one; 一か八かやってみる *ichi ka bachi ka yatte miru* take a chance

位置 **ichi** position

市場 **ichiba** market; marketplace

一番 **ichiban** the best, the top

一番に **ichiban ni** first

一番(の) **ichiban (no)** foremost

一番好き(な) **ichiban suki (na)** favorite

一番少ない **ichiban sukunai** least

一番遠く(の) **ichiban tōku (no)** furthest

一番年上(の) **ichiban toshiue (no)** eldest

一番上(の) **ichiban ue (no)** topmost

一べつ **ichibetsu** glance

一部 **ichibu** part; fraction; segment; patch

一部分は **ichibubun wa** part, partly

一部始終 **ichibu-shijū** all the details; the whole story

一団 **ichidan** batch; convoy; corps; group

一度 **ichido** once

一度に **ichido ni** all at once

一月 **ichigatsu** January

いちご **ichigo** strawberry

一合 **ichigō** *measure of 0.38 pints*

一群 **ichigun** a cluster

一員 **ichiin** member

いちじく **ichijiku** fig

一陣の風 **ichijin no kaze** blast; gust

一時(の) **ichiji (no)** temporary

著しい **ichijirushii** marked; conspicuous; remarkable

著しく **ichijirushiku** eminently

一時停止標識 **ichijiteishi-hyōshiki** stop sign

一時停止する **ichiji-teishi suru** pause

一時的(な) **ichijiteki (na)** momentary

一畳 **ichijō** *area measure of a tatami mat*

一枚 **ichimai** a copy (*of record, CD*); an exposure; 紙切れ一枚 *kami ichimai* a piece of paper

一面 **ichimen** front page; 一面の ニュース *ichimen no nyūsu* front page news

一面の **ichimen no** a blanket of

一味 **ichimi** gang

一文なし(の) **ichimon-nashi (no)** broke, penniless

一年間(の) **ichinenkan (no)** annual, yearly

一日 **ichinichi** one day

一人前 **ichinin-mae** a portion

一応 **ichiō** for the time being; roughly

一卵性双生児 **ichiransei-sōseiji** identical twins

一連(の) **ichiren (no)** stream of; string of; sequence

一律に **ichiritsu ni** across the board; evenly

一流(の) **ichiryū (no)** first-class, first-rate; classic, definitive

位置している **ichi shite iru** be situated

一話 **ichiwa** one episode, one installment

一族 **ichizoku** clan

いちょう **ichō** gingko

偉大(な) **idai (na)** great

遺伝 **iden** inheritance

遺伝性(の) **idensei (no)** hereditary

遺伝子 **idenshi** gene

遺伝子学 **idenshi-gaku** genetics

遺伝子学者 **idenshi-gakusha** geneticist

遺伝子工学 **idenshi-kōgaku** genetic engineering

遺伝子(の) **idenshi (no)** genetic

イデオロギー **ideologī** ideology

緯度 **ido** latitude

井戸 **ido** well

移動 **idō** migration; transfer

移動させる **idō saseru** move; transfer

移動する **idō suru** move; transfer; relocate; migrate

家 **ie** house

家出する **iede suru** run away from home

家柄 **iegara** pedigree; lineage

家元 **iemoto** principal of a school of one of the Japanese arts

イエローページ **ierōpēji** yellow pages

イエス **Iesu** Jesus

イエスキリスト **Iesu Kirisuto** Jesus Christ

イエスマン **iesuman** yesman

衣服 **ifuku** garment

以外 **igai** except; 八月以外なら **hachigatsu igai nara** except (for) August

意外 **igai** surprising; unexpected

医学 **igaku** medicine

医学博士 **igaku-hakushi** MD, Doctor of Medicine

医学(の) **igaku (no)** medical

鋳型 **igata** cast, mold

異議 **igi** objection

意義 **igi** significance

意義のある **igi no aru** meaningful

異議を唱える **igi o tonaeru** challenge; raise an objection

イギリス **Igirisu** Britain

イギリス人 **Igirisu-jin** British; Briton

イギリスポンド **Igirisu-pondo** pound sterling

以後 **igo** after; since; from now on

囲碁 **igo** the game of Go

居心地 **igokochi**: 居心地のいい **igokochi no ii** friendly; comfortable; 居心地の悪い **igokochi no warui** uncomfortable

偉業 **igyō** exploits; great undertaking

違反 **ihan** breach, violation

違反(の) **ihan (no)** illegal

違反する **ihan suru** violate, contravene

違法(の) **ihō (no)** illegal

違法行為 **ihō-kōi** misconduct

いい **ii** good; いいですね **ii desu ne** good idea!; いいですよ **ii desu yo** you're on; no problem; …といい仲になる **... to ii naka ni naru** have a good time with (*sexually*)

言い表せない **iiarawasenai** indescribable; inexpressible

言い表す **iiarawasu** describe; express

言い分 **iibun**: 言い分がある **iibun ga aru** have one's say

いいえ **iie** no; yes (*see* **no** *p504*)

言い張る **iiharu** insist

言いかえる **iikaeru** paraphrase

言い返す **iikaesu** retort

いい加減(な) **iikagen (na)** perfunctory; slack; いいかげんにしなさい **iikagen ni shinasai** that's enough, calm down!; いいかげんにしてよ **iikagen ni shite yo** do me a favor!

言い方 **iikata** phrase

いい子ぶりっこ **iikoburikko** goody-goody

言い回し **iimawashi** expression; wording

委員 **iin** committee member

委員長 **iinchō** chairperson

委員会 **iinkai** board; committee; commission

言い逃れする **iinogare suru** stonewall

言い伝え **iitsutae** tradition

言い訳 **iiwake** excuse

言いようのない **iiyō no nai**

indescribable

言い寄る **iiyoru** proposition; make advances

維持 **iji** maintenance

意地 **iji** nature; pride; 意地の悪い **iji no warui** mean; nasty

維持管理 **iji-kanri** upkeep

いじくる **ijikuru** meddle; toy with

いじめ **ijime** bullying

いじめっ子 **ijimekko** bully

いじめる **ijimeru** bully; pick on; tease

いじる **ijiru** fumble; interfere with; tinker with; twiddle

維持する **iji suru** hold, maintain; preserve

意地悪(な) **ijiwaru (na)** bitchy; spiteful; wicked

異常 **ijō** freak

以上 **ijō** not less than; plus; それはい やなんです, 以上 **sore wa iya nan desu, ijō** I don't want to, period!; ...以上(で) ... **ijō (de)** above; これ 以上言う必要がありますか **kore ijō iu hitsuyō ga arimasu ka** need I say more?

異常(な) **ijō (na)** abnormal; freak

異常に **ijō ni** extraordinarily; remarkably

移住 **ijū** emigration; immigration

移住者 **ijū-sha** emigrant; immigrant

移住する **ijū suru** emigrate; immigrate; migrate

いか **ika** squid

以下 **ika** below; not more than ◊ the following; 以下次号 **ika-jigō** to be continued

...以下に ... **ika ni** below

以下の事 **ika no koto** the following

いかだ **ikada** raft

いかが **ikaga** how; how about; クッ キーはいかがですか **kukkī wa ikaga desu ka** would you like some cookies?

いかがわしい **ikagawashii** disreputable; indecent; shady; unsavory; juicy *news*

いかに **ika ni** how

いかにも **ika ni mo** really; indeed; very

いかれている **ikarete iru** be mentally unbalanced

いかり **ikari** anchor; いかりを下ろす **ikari o orosu** anchor

怒り **ikari** anger; displeasure

怒り出す **ikaridasu** erupt

怒り狂う **ikarikuruu** rage

いかさま **ikasama** cheat; deception; con; いかさまをする **ikasama o suru** cheat

生かす **ikasu** keep alive; make the best use of

池 **ike** pond

生け花 **ikebana** flower arrangement

生け垣 **ikegaki** hedge

胃けいれん **ikeiren** stomach cramps

いけません **ikemasen** not permitted; forbidden; bad ◊ must; must not

意見 **iken** opinion, (point of) view; observation; judgment; verdict; 意 見が合わない **iken ga awanai** differ; disagree; disagree with

いけにえ **ikenie** sacrifice

生ける **ikeru** arrange *flowers*

息 **iki** breath; 息が切れる **iki ga kireru** be out of breath; 息が詰まる **iki ga tsumaru** choke; 息を切らし た **iki o kirashita** breathless; 息をこ らす **iki o korasu** hold one's breath; 息をのむ **iki o nomu** gasp; 息をする **iki o suru** breathe; 息を吸 う **iki o suu** breathe

行き **iki** : ...行きである ... **iki de aru** be going to; be bound for

遺棄 **iki** abandonment; desertion

行き止まり **ikidomari** cul-de-sac; dead end

憤り **ikidōri** indignation; outrage

息切れする **ikigire suru** pant

息苦しい **ikigurushii** stifling, suffocating

生き生きした **ikiiki shita** lively

生き返る **ikikaeru** be resurrected; be revived

生き物 **ikimono** being; creature

いき(な) **iki (na)** stylish

生き延びる **ikinobiru** survive

生き残る **ikinokoru** survive

勢い **ikioi** momentum; power; energy

勢いのある **ikioi no aru** vigorous

生きる **ikiru** live

生きている **ikite iru** be alive ◊ living

生き写しである **ikiutsushi de aru** be the (spitting) image

生き写し(の) **ikiutsushi (no)** lifelike

行き詰まり **ikizumari** blind alley; deadlock

一ヶ月(の) **ikkagetsu (no)** monthly

一回 **ikkai** once; one episode; first inning; one round

一階 **ikkai** first floor

一回分 **ikkaibun** one dose

一貫性 **ikkansei** consistency

一貫した **ikkan shita** consistent

一括払い **ikkatsubarai** lump sum

一括契約 **ikkatsu-keiyaku** package deal

一見 **ikken** a look

一斤 **ikkin** a loaf

一気に **ikki ni** in one go; at a stretch

いっこうに **ikkō ni**: いっこうに平気だ **ikkō ni heiki da** I couldn't care less

一曲 **ikkyoku** piece of music

一級(の) **ikkyū (no)** choice, top quality

…以降 **… ikō** from … onward

eコマース **ī-komāsu** e-commerce

遺骨 **ikotsu** ashes

行く **iku** come; go; visit; cover distance

意気地のない **ikuji no nai** spineless, cowardly

幾人か **ikuninka** a few people

幾人か(の) **ikuninka (no)** a few; several

いくら **ikura** how much?

いくらか **ikuraka** some

いくらか(の) **ikuraka (no)** some, a number of

いくつ **ikutsu** how many; how old

いくつか **ikutsuka** a few; several

いくつか(の) **ikutsuka (no)** a few; some; several

異教徒 **ikyōto** heathen

今 **ima** now; right now

居間 **ima** living room, lounge

今風(の) **imafū (no)** fashionable

今頃 **imagoro** about this time; by now

いまいましい **imaimashii** damn, cursed

今から **ima kara** from now on

今までで **ima made de** ever

今までに **ima made ni** ever; till now

今にも…しそうである **ima ni mo …shisō de aru** be on the verge of

今のところ **ima no tokoro** at present, at the moment, currently; for the time being

います **imasu** *polite form of iru*

今すぐ **ima sugu** straight away

イメージ **imēji** image

Eメール **īmēru** email

意味 **imi** meaning; point, purpose; implication

意味ありげ(な) **imiarige (na)** meaningful

移民 **imin** immigrant

意味する **imi suru** mean, imply; signify

イミテーション **imitēshon** imitation

芋 **imo** sweet potato

妹 **imōto** (younger) sister

医務室 **imushitsu** dispensary; medical office

韻 **in** rhyme; …と韻を踏む **… to in o fumu** rhyme with

稲光 **inabikari** lightning

いなご **inago** locust

いない **inai** there is/are not

…以内で **…inai de** within

田舎 **inaka** countryside; country; the sticks

田舎者 **inakamono** hick, hillbilly

田舎(の) **inaka (no)** rural

いななく **inanaku** neigh

稲荷神社 **inari-jinja** *shrine for the celebration of the harvest*

陰謀 **inbō** plot; conspiracy; intrigue

インチ **inchi** inch

いんちき(の) **inchiki (no)** bogus

インデックス **indekkusu** index

インディアン **Indian** American Indian, Native American

インド **Indo** India

インドア(の) **indoa (no)** indoor

インドネシア **Indoneshia** Indonesia

インドネシア(の) **Indoneshia (no)** Indonesian

インド(の) **Indo (no)** Indian

インドシナ **Indoshina** Indochina

稲 **ine** rice plant

居眠り **inemuri** snooze

居眠りする **inemuri suru** snooze; have a snooze; nod off

インフレ **infure** inflation; インフレを引き起こす *infure o hikiokosu* inflationary

インフレ(の) **infure (no)** inflationary

インフルエンザ **infuruenza** influenza

隠語 **ingo** slang

イングランド **Ingurando** England

イングランド人 **Ingurando-jin** English person; the English

イングランド(の) **Ingurando (no)** English

委任 **inin** delegation; proxy

委任権 **ininken** power of attorney

イニシャル **inisharu** initial

イニシアチブ **inishiachibu** initiative

印鑑 **inkan** signature seal

陰険(な) **inken (na)** insidious; sneaky

陰気(な) **inki (na)** dingy; dreary; dismal, sad

インコース **inkōsu** inside lane SP

インク **inku** ink

陰毛 **inmō** pubic hair

命 **inochi** life

命にかかわる **inochi ni kakawaru** life-threatening

命取り **inochitori** killer

居残る **inokoru** stay behind; work overtime

祈り **inori** praying, prayer

祈る **inoru** pray

いのしし **inoshishi** wild boar

インポ **inpo** impotence

インポ(の) **inpo (no)** impotent

インプット **inputto** input

引力 **inryoku** gravity

飲料水 **inryōsui** drinking water

飲料用(の) **inryōyō (no)** drinkable

インサイダー取り引き **insaidā-torihiki** insider trading

印刷物 **insatsubutsu** printed matter

印刷業者 **insatsu-gyōsha** printer

印刷機 **insatsuki** printing press

印刷する **insatsu suru** print; run off

いん石 **inseki** meteorite

印象 **inshō** impression

印章 **inshō** seal, stamp

印象的(な) **inshōteki (na)** impressive; memorable

飲酒 **inshu** drinking

インシュリン **inshurin** insulin

飲酒運転 **inshu-unten** drunk driving

インスピレーション **insupirēshon** inspiration

インスタントコーヒー **insutanto-kōhī** instant coffee

インスタント食品 **insutanto-shokuhin** convenience food

インストラクター **insutorakutā** instructor

インストール **insutōru** installation

インストールする **insutōru suru** install

インタビュー **intabyū** interview

インタビューア **intabyūa** interviewer

インタビューする **intabyū suru** interview

インターチェンジ **intāchenji** exit; interchange

インターホン **intāhon** intercom

インターネット **intānetto** Internet

インテリ **interi** intellectual, egghead

インテリア **interia** décor; decoration

インテリアデザイナー **interia-dezainā** interior decorator; interior designer

犬 **inu** dog

犬小屋 **inugoya** kennel

引用 **in'yō** quotation, quote

引用符 **in'yōfu** quotation marks

引用する **inyō suru** quote

印税 **inzei** royalty

硫黄 **iō** sulfur

…一杯 **… ippai** a drink of …; お茶一杯 *ocha ippai* a cup of tea

いっぱいになる **ippai ni naru** fill up

いっぱい(の) **ippai (no)** full, full up

一泊 **ippaku** night

一泊(の) **ippaku (no)** overnight

一般化 **ippanka** generalization

一般化する **ippanka suru** generalize

一般に **ippan ni** in general

一般(の) **ippan (no)** civilian; popular

一般的(な) **ippanteki (na)** general; prevailing

一般的に **ippanteki ni** generally

一片 **ippen** piece; fragment; flake

一匹おおかみ **ippikiōkami** loner

一品 **ippin** course; dish

逸品 **ippin** gem; superb specimen

一歩 **ippo** pace; step

一方では...で、もう一方では...だ **ippō dewa ... de, mō ippō dewa ... da** on the one hand ..., on the other hand

一本 **ippon** length (*of cloth, wood*); strand

一方的(な) **ippōteki (na)** one-sided; unilateral

一方通行 **ippō-tsūkō** one-way street

いらだち **iradachi** annoyance, irritation

いらだたせる **iradataseru** vex

依頼 **irai** commission; request

以来 **irai** since; あなたが去って以来 **anata ga satte irai** since you left

依頼人 **irai-nin** client

いらいらさせる **iraira saseru** annoy, irritate, bug

いらいらして **iraira shite** impatiently

いらいらする **iraira suru** frustrating; nerve-racking ◊ get worked up

依頼する **irai suru** commission; request

イラク **Iraku** Iraq

イラク(の) **Iraku (no)** Iraqi

いらくさ **irakusa** nettle

イラン **Iran** Iran

イラン(の) **Iran (no)** Iranian

いらっしゃいませ **irasshaimase** welcome

いらっしゃる **irassharu** (*polite*) be; come; go

イラスト **irasuto** illustration

イラストレーター **irasutorētā** illustrator

入れ歯 **ireba** dentures, false teeth

入れ物 **iremono** container; holder; tub

入れる **ireru** make, brew; turn on *faucet, heater*; pour; engage *clutch, gear*; include; insert

いれずみ **irezumi** tattoo

入り江 **irie** cove; inlet; estuary

入り口 **iriguchi** entrance, way in; gateway

色 **iro** color; hue

色合い **iroai** shade; tint

色々(な) **iroiro (na)** varied; various

色気 **iroke** sex appeal

いる **iru** be; be present; live; have; ...がいる **... ga iru** there is / are; 彼女は子供が二人いる **kanojo wa kogomo ga futari iru** she has two children

要る **iru** need; require

炒る **iru** roast; toast

鋳る **iru** cast *metal*; mint *coins*

射る **iru** shoot, fire *arrow*

衣類 **irui** clothing

いるか **iruka** dolphin

イルミネーションで飾る **iruminēshon de kazaru** illuminate

医療 **iryō** medical treatment, medical care

衣料品 **iryōhin** clothing

医療過誤 **iryō-kago** malpractice

威力 **iryoku** power

医療(の) **iryō (no)** medical

いさかい **isakai** fight; quarrel

遺産 **isan** heritage; inheritance; legacy

異性 **isei** opposite sex

異性愛者 **isei-aisha** heterosexual

遺跡 **iseki** ruins

医者 **isha** client

石 **ishi** stone; rock

意志 **ishi** will, willpower; 意志が弱い **ishi ga yowai** weak-willed

意思 **ishi** intention; wish; mind

医師 **ishi** doctor

意識 **ishiki** awareness; consciousness; 意識を失う/取り戻す **ishiki o ushinau / torimodosu** lose / regain consciousness

意識不明(の) **ishiki-fumei (no)** unconscious

意識もうろう **ishiki-mōrō** stupor

意識のある **ishiki no aru** conscious

石切り場 **ishikiriba** quarry

意識的(な) **ishikiteki (na)** conscious, deliberate

意志の強い **ishi no tsuyoi** strong-willed

意思疎通 **ishi-sotsū** communication; mutual understanding

遺失物取扱所 **ishitsubutsu-toriatsukaijo** lost-and-found (office)

衣装 **ishō** costume; clothes

移植 **ishoku** graft; transplant

移植する **ishoku suru** transplant

急がせる **isogaseru** rush *person*

忙しい **isogashii** busy; full; eventful

急がす **isogasu** hustle

急ぐ **isogu** hurry (up); rush; speed; 急いで **isoide** hurry up!; don't be long!

急いでいる **isoide iru** be in a rush

一切込み **issaikomi (no)** inclusive

一酸化炭素 **issanka-tanso** carbon monoxide

一冊 **issatsu** a copy

一斉 **issei** volley

一節 **issetsu** passage; stanza

一式 **isshiki** set (*of tools, books etc*)

一生 **isshō** life; lifetime

一升 **isshō** *liquid measure of 3.8 pints*

一生涯 **isshōgai** all his/her/my life

一緒に **issho ni** together; along (with); with; ...と一緒に暮らす **...to issho ni kurasu** live with

一生(の) **isshō (no)** lifelong

一周 **isshū** circuit, lap

一週間 **isshūkan** one week

一掃する **issō suru** clean up; sweep away

いす **isu** chair

イスラエル **Isuraeru** Israel

イスラエル(の) **Isuraeru (no)** Israeli

イスラム教 **Isuramu-kyō** Islam

イスラム教(の) **Isuramu-kyō (no)** Islamic

イースト **īsuto** yeast

板 **ita** board; plank

板ばさみになる **itabasami ni naru** be in a dilemma, be torn between two alternatives

いただけますか **-itadakemasu ka** could you...?

いただきます **itadakimasu** *words spoken before eating*

痛い **itai** painful, sore; tender

遺体 **itai** remains

板前 **itamae** chef

痛ましい **itamashii** miserable; poignant

傷める **itameru** hurt; injure; strain; bruise

炒める **itameru** (stir-)fry

痛めつける **itametsukeru** torment; treat harshly

痛み **itami** pain; prick; ache; tenderness; 痛みがある **itami ga aru** be in pain

痛み止め **itamidome** painkiller

痛む **itamu** hurt; ache

傷む **itamu** bruise

イタリア **Itaria** Italy

イタリア語 **Itaria-go** Italian

イタリア人 **Itaria-jin** Italian

イタリア(の) **Itaria (no)** Italian

いたるところに **itaru tokoro ni** everywhere

いたします **itashimasu** H する

いたわる **itawaru** be kind to

いたずら **itazura** practical joke; prank; mischief; hoax; いたずらをする **itazura o suru** play a prank; molest

いたずらっ子 **itazurakko** rascal, monkey

いたずら(な) **itazura (na)** mischievous

一致 **itchi** correspondence, match; agreement

一致した **itchi shita** concerted ◊ in unison

一致して **itchi shite** in line with ...

一致する **itchi suru** correspond, match; agree

意図 **ito** intention; aim

糸 **ito** thread, yarn; 糸を通す **ito o tōsu** thread

いとこ **itoko** cousin

糸巻き **itomaki** spool

意図的(な) **itoteki (na)** intentional

いつ **itsu** when

逸脱 **itsudatsu** departure; deviation

いつでも **itsu demo** whenever; いつでも協力します *itsu demo kyōryoku shimasu* I am at your disposal

いつか **itsuka** sometime; one day; once; ever; before

いつかは **itsuka wa** sooner or later

慈しみ **itsukushimi** fondness; affection

いつまでも **itsu made mo** for ever; persistently

いつも(の) **itsumo (no)** usual; customary; habitual; いつもの手順で *itsumo no tejun de* as a matter of routine; いつものように *itsumo no yō ni* as usual; as is his/her/my custom

いつのまにか **itsu no ma ni ka** before you know it; unnoticed

一体… **ittai …** … on earth; 一体誰が *ittai dare ga* who on earth?; whoever?; 一体どこに… *ittai doko ni* where on earth?; wherever?

いったん…すれば **ittan … sureba** once

行ったり来たり **ittari kitari** to and fro

一定(の) **ittei (no)** uniform; fixed; definite

いってきます **itte kimasu** see you; I'm off now

いってらっしゃい **itterasshai** good luck!; have a nice day

一等 **ittō** first class

言う **iu** say; describe; …は言うまでもなく *… wa iu made mo naku* to say nothing of

岩 **iwa** rock

岩だらけ(の) **iwadarake (no)** rocky

祝い **iwai** celebration; congratulations

いわし **iwashi** sardine

祝う **iwau** celebrate

岩山 **iwayama** crag

いわゆる **iwayuru** so-called

いやがらせ **iyagarase** harassment; …にいやがらせをする *… ni iyagarase o suru* harass

イヤホン **iyahon** earphones

いやいやながら **iyaiya-nagara** reluctantly

違約条項 **iyaku-jōkō** penalty clause

嫌み **iyami** unpleasantness; sarcasm; bad taste

嫌み(な) **iyami (na)** sarcastic; in bad taste

嫌(な) **iya (na)** unpleasant; disagreeable; dismal; nasty; disgusting; hideous

嫌なやつ **iya na yatsu** a pain in the neck; prick (*person*); swine

嫌になる **iya ni naru** turn off (*sexually*)

いやらしい **iyarashii** unpleasant; disgusting; indecent

イヤリング **iyaringu** earring

癒し **iyashi** healing; soothing; stress-relieving

卑しい **iyashii** humble; vulgar; despicable

卑しめる **iyashimeru** degrade

意欲 **iyoku** will; aspiration; desire

意欲的(な) **iyokuteki (na)** enthusiastic

居酒屋 **izakaya** bar

いざこざ **izakoza** misunderstanding; quarrel

以前 **izen** before; 私は以前彼が好きだった *watashi wa izen kare ga suki datta* I used to like him

以前(の) **izen (no)** former, past

以前は **izen wa** formerly

イーゼル **īzeru** easel

遺族 **izoku** the bereaved

依存 **izon** dependence, dependency; reliance

依存心の強い **izonshin no tsuyoi** clingy

依存する **izon suru** depend on, rely on

泉 **izumi** spring (*of water*)

いずれ **izure** some day; some other time; いずれの場合においても *izure no bāi ni oite mo* in any case; いずれも *izure mo* all; each one; any

J

じゃあ **jā** well; then; in that case; じゃあ、また **jā, mata** see you later!

邪悪(な) **jaaku (na)** evil

じゃがいも **jagaimo** potato

蛇口 **jaguchi** faucet

ジャージー **jājī** jersey

ジャケット **jaketto** jacket

ジャッキ **jakki** jack MOT

ジャック **jakku** jack (in cards)

ジャクージ **jakūji** whirlpool, jacuzzi®

弱者 **jakusha** underdog

弱点 **jakuten** weakness

邪魔 **jama** disruption; interruption; hindrance; intrusion; 邪魔になる **jama ni naru** be in the way; 邪魔を する **jama o suru** interrupt; disrupt; distract; thwart

ジャム **jamu** jam, conserve; jelly

ジャーナリスト **jānarisuto** journalist

ジャーナリズム **jānarizumu** journalism

ジャングル **janguru** jungle

じゃんけん **janken** game of stone, paper, scissors

ジャンパー **janpā** jumper SP

ジャンプ **janpu** jump

砂利 **jari** gravel; grit; shingle

ジャズ **jazu** jazz

ジェイアール **jei-āru** Japan Railways, JR

ジェル **jeru** gel

ジェットエンジン **jetto-enjin** jet engine

ジェット機 **jetto-ki** jet

ジェットコースター **jetto-kōsutā** roller coaster

字 **ji** written character; letter

時 **-ji** o'clock

ぢ **ji** piles MED

耳鼻科 **jibika** ear and nose department; otorhinology

自分 **jibun** oneself

自分で **jibun de** personally, in person; by oneself

自治権 **jichiken** autonomy

時代 **jidai** age, era, epoch

時代劇 **jidaigeki** historical drama

時代後れで **jidaiokure de** out of date

時代後れ(の) **jidaiokure (no)** dated; outdated; out-of-date

自動振替 **jidō-furikae** banker's order

自動販売機 **jidōhanbaiki** slot machine, vending machine

自動化する **jidōka suru** automate

自動(の) **jidō (no)** automatic

自動車 **jidōsha** auto, automobile

自動車教習 **jidōsha-kyōshū** driving lesson

自動車教習所 **jidōsha-kyōshūjo** driving school

自動詞 **jidōshi** intransitive verb

自動的(な) **jidōteki (na)** automatic

自営業(の) **jieigyō (no)** self-employed

自衛隊 **jieitai** Japan Self-Defense Forces

ジーエヌピー **jī-enu-pī** GNP, gross national product

時限爆弾 **jigen bakudan** time bomb

地獄 **jigoku** hell

ジグソー(パズル) **jigusō(pazuru)** jigsaw (puzzle)

ジグザグ **jiguzagu** zigzag; ジグザグ に進む **jiguzagu ni susumu** zigzag

事業 **jigyō** business enterprise; concern

自白 **jihaku** confession

自白する **jihaku suru** admit, confess

自発的(な) **jihatsuteki (na)** voluntary; spontaneous

自発的に **jihatsuteki ni** of one's own accord

自閉症(の) **jiheishō (no)** autistic

慈悲 **jihi** mercy

慈悲深い **jihibukai** benevolent; charitable; merciful

時事問題 **jiji-mondai** current affairs, current events

事実 **jijitsu** reality; fact

事実上(の) **jijitsujō (no)** virtual

事情 **jijō** circumstances; situation; matter

二乗 **jijō** square MATH

自叙伝 **jijoden** autobiography

事情通(の) **jijōtsū (no)** streetwise

自覚 **jikaku** consciousness; awareness

時間 **jikan** time; hour; 時間どおり **jikan dōri** on time; 時間を合わせる **jikan o awaseru** synchronize

時間切れである **jikangire de aru** time is up

時間給で **jikankyū de** at an hourly rate of

時間のずれ **jikan no zure** time-lag

時間を守る **jikan o mamoru** prompt

時間割 **jikan-wari** schedule

自家製(の) **jikasei (no)** homemade

自活している **jikatsu shite iru** independent

自活する **jikatsu suru** support oneself

事件 **jiken** case (*for police*); incident

時期 **jiki** season; time

磁器 **jiki** porcelain

磁器(の) **jiki (no)** porcelain

実感 **jikkan** realization

実感する **jikkan suru** realize

実験 **jikken** experiment

実験台 **jikkendai** guinea pig

実験する **jikken suru** experiment

実験的(な) **jikkenteki (na)** experimental

実行 **jikkō** execution

実行する **jikkō suru** carry out; execute, put into effect; set things in motion

じっくり **jikkuri** properly; じっくり考える **jikkuri kangaeru** ponder; contemplate

実況放送 **jikkyō-hōsō** live broadcast

実況(の) **jikkyō (no)** live

事故 **jiko** accident; mishap

自己 **jiko** self

自己防衛 **jiko-bōei** self-defense

自己中心(の) **jiko-chūshin (no)** self-centered

自己中心的(な) **jiko-chūshinteki (na)** egocentric

自己不信 **jiko-fushin** self-doubt

自己規制 **jiko-kisei** self-discipline

時刻 **jikoku** time; hour

時刻表 **jikoku-hyō** schedule, timetable

自己満足 **jiko-manzoku** complacency

自己満足(の) **jiko-manzoku (no)** self-satisfied

自己満足した **jiko-manzoku shita** complacent

自己紹介 **jikoshōkai** self-introduction

自己主張する **jiko-shuchō suru** assert oneself

軸 **jiku** axle; shaft; axis

持久力 **jikyūryoku** endurance; stamina

字幕 **jimaku** subtitles; 字幕をつける **jimaku o tsukeru** subtitle

自慢 **jiman** boast; pride

自慢する **jiman suru** boast, talk big

自明(の) **jimei (no)** self-evident

じめじめした **jimejime shita** swampy; damp

地面 **jimen** ground

地道な人 **jimichi na hito** steady worker

地味(な) **jimi (na)** conservative, modest

地元で **jimoto de** locally

地元(の) **jimoto (no)** local

ジム **jimu** gym

事務 **jimu** business; office work

事務員 **jimuin** clerk

事務室 **jimushitsu** office

事務所 **jimusho** firm; office

事務的(な) **jimuteki (na)** matter-of-fact; businesslike; mechanical

ジン **jin** gin

人 **-jin** person; アメリカ人 **Amerika-jin** American; 日本人 **Nihon-jin** Japanese

人文科学 **jinbun-kagaku** the arts

陣地 **jinchi** position

人道的(な) **jindōteki (na)** humanitarian

人員 **jin'in** manpower; staff; personnel

辞任 **jinin** resignation

辞任する **jinin suru** resign, step down

自認する **jinin suru** acknowledge

人為的(な) **jin'iteki (na)** human; man-made

神社 **jinja** shrine

人事 **jinji** personnel affairs

人事部 **jinjibu** human resources, personnel (*department*)

人事部長 **jinji-buchō** personnel manager

人格 **jinkaku** personality

人口 **jinkō** population

人工知能 **jinkō-chinō** artificial intelligence

人工衛星 **jinkō-eisei** satellite

人工保育器 **jinkō-hoikuki** incubator

人工呼吸装置 **jinkōkokyū-sōchi** respirator

人口密度 **jinkō-mitsudo** population density

人工(の) **jinkō (no)** artificial, man-made

ジンクス **jinkusu** jinx

人命 **jinmei** human life

人命救助用(の) **jinmei-kyūjoyō (no)** life-saving

尋問 **jinmon** interrogation

尋問者 **jinmon-sha** interrogator

尋問する **jinmon suru** question; interrogate

人類 **jinrui** humanity; mankind; human race

人生 **jinsei** human life

人生観 **jinseikan** outlook on life; philosophy of life

人種 **jinshu** race

人種平等 **jinshu-byōdō** racial equality

人種(の) **jinshu (no)** racial

人種差別 **jinshu-sabetsu** racism

迅速(な) **jinsoku (na)** prompt; rapid

じん帯 **jintai** ligament

人体 **jintai** human body

地主 **jinushi** land owner

人材スカウト係 **jinzai-sukauto-gakari** headhunter

腎臓 **jinzō** kidney

ジーンズ **jīnzu** jeans, denims

ジーパン **jīpan** jeans

ジープ **jīpu** jeep

ジプシー **jipushī** gypsy, gipsy

地雷 **jirai** landmine

地雷原 **jiraigen** minefield

じらした **jirashita** tantalizing

ジレンマ **jirenma** dilemma

じりじりと進む **jirijiri to susumu** edge forward

自立した **jiritsu shita** emancipated; self-reliant

時差ぼけ **jisa-boke** jetlag

自殺 **jisatsu** suicide

自殺する **jisatsu suru** commit suicide, kill oneself

自制 **jisei** self control

時制 **jisei** tense GRAM

自制する **jisei suru** contain oneself, control oneself

磁石 **jishaku** magnet

磁石(の) **jishaku (no)** magnetic

自信 **jishin** confidence; self-confidence; 自信がある **jishin ga aru** be confident

地震 **jishin** earthquake

自信がない **jishin ga nai** insecure

自信のある **jishin no aru** confident; self-confident

辞書 **jisho** dictionary

地所 **jisho** estate; plot (*land*)

自首する **jishu suru** surrender; 警察へ自首する **keisatsu e jishu suru** give oneself up to the police

自主的(な) **jishuteki (na)** independent

時速…マイル **jisoku ... mairu** mph, miles per hour

自尊心 **jisonshin** ego; pride; self-respect

自尊心の強い **jisonshin no tsuyoi** proud

実際には **jissai ni wa** in practice

実際(の) **jissai (no)** actual

実際的(な) **jissaiteki (na)** businesslike; practical

実際は **jissai wa** in fact, as a matter of fact

実績 **jisseki** achievement; accomplishment

実践 **jissen** practice

実践的(な) **jissenteki (na)** hands-on

実施される **jisshi sareru** come into force

実施されて **jisshi sarete** effective

実施する **jisshi suru** enforce; put into effect

実質的(な) **jisshitsuteki (na)** substantive

実質的には **jisshitsuteki ni** practically; essentially; virtually

地滑り **jisuberi** landslide

自炊 **jisui** self-catering

辞退する **jitai suru** refuse

自宅 **jitaku** home

実地(の) **jitchi (no)** practical

時点 **jiten** point in time

辞典 **jiten** dictionary

自転車 **jitensha** bicycle, cycle, bike

実物 **jitsubutsu** the real thing; 実物に会う *jitsubutsu ni au* meet/see a person in the flesh

実物大(の) **jitsubutsudai (no)** lifesized

実現 **jitsugen** fulfillment; realization

実現する **jitsugen suru** realize; come true

実業家 **jitsugyōka** businessman; industrialist

実は **jitsu wa** actually

実力 **jitsuryoku** capability; competence; ability

実用性 **jitsuyōsei** usefulness, utility

実用主義 **jitsuyō-shugi** pragmatism

実用的(な) **jitsuyōteki (na)** practical; pragmatic

じっと **jitto** quietly; intently; without moving

じっと見る **jitto miru** peer at; scrutinize

じっと見つめる **jitto mitsumeru** stare at; gaze at

じっとりした **jittori shita** clammy; damp

じっとしている **jitto shite iru** stand still

自由 **jiyū** freedom; scope; liberty; latitude

自由経済 **jiyū-keizai** free market economy

自由民主党 **Jiyū-minshu-tō** LDP, Liberal Democratic Party

自由(な) **jiyū (na)** free; liberated; open

自由にする **jiyū ni suru** liberate

自由の女神像 **Jiyū no Megamizō** Statue of Liberty

自由主義(の) **jiyū-shugi (no)** liberal

自在ドア **jizai-doa** swing-door

慈善 **jizen** charity

慈善団体 **jizen-dantai** charitable organization

慈善事業 **jizen-jigyō** philanthropy

慈善家 **jizen-ka** philanthropist; do-gooder

事前(の) **jizen (no)** prior

地蔵 **jizō** *guardian deity of children and travelers*

持続 **jizoku** persistence

持続する **jizoku suru** maintain; endure; hold out

上 **jō** best; top

情 **jō** emotion; feelings; affection

状-**jō** letter; card; 招待状 *shōtaijō* invitation 乗馬 **jōba** ride; riding; 乗馬をする *jōba o suru* ride

序文 **jobun** introduction; preface

丈夫(な) **jōbu (na)** hardy; sturdy; indestructible

上部(の) **jōbu (no)** upper

情緒不安定(な) **jōcho-fuantei (na)** emotionally unstable; emotionally disturbed

助長する **jochō suru** encourage, foster

冗談 **jōdan** joke, crack; witticism; 冗談を言う *jōdan o iu* joke; jest; kid; quip; 冗談じゃない *jōdan ja nai* you've got to be joking!

上映される **jōei sareru** show, be screened

上映する **jōei suru** perform *play*; enact; show *movie*

上演する **jōen suru** put on, perform

除外 **jogai** omission

除外する **jogai suru** eliminate; exclude; omit; drop

助言 **jogen** advice; hint, pointer

ジョギング **jogingu** jog; jogging, running

ジョギングシューズ **jogingu-shūzu** jogger

ジョギングする **jogingu suru** go for a run

蒸発させる **jōhatsu saseru** vaporize

蒸発する **jōhatsu suru** evaporate

城壁 **jōheki** rampart; castle wall

上品(な) **jōhin (na)** distinguished; dignified; stylish

譲歩 **jōho** concession; information; intelligence (*news*)

情報 **jōhō** information

情報部 **jōhōbu** intelligence service

情報源 **jōhōgen** source of information

情報科学 **jōhō-kagaku** information science

情報工学 **jōhō-kōgaku** information technology, IT

情報処理 **jōhō-shori** data processing

譲歩する **jōho suru** back down; concede

情報提供者 **jōhō-teikyō-sha** informant

除氷する **johyō suru** de-ice; defrost

女医 **joi** woman doctor

上院 **Jōin** Senate; Upper House

上院議員 **jōin-giin** senator

上位(の) **jōi (no)** senior

ジョイントベンチャー **jointo-benchā** joint venture

情事 **jōji** (love) affair

徐々(の) **jojo (no)** gradual

情状酌量 **jōjō-shakuryō** mitigating circumstances

ジョーカー **jōkā** joker

助監督 **jokantoku** assistant director

浄化する **jōka suru** purify

条件 **jōken** condition, term, requirement; proviso

条件付き(の) **jōkentsuki (no)** conditional; provisional

条件付け **jōkenzuke** conditioning

蒸気 **jōki** vapor; steam

上機嫌(の) **jōkigen (no)** good-humored

常勤で **jōkin de** full-time

常勤(の) **jōkin (no)** full-time

上記(の) **jōki (no)** above-mentioned

ジョッキー **jokkī** jockey

条項 **jōkō** article (*section*); clause (*in agreement*); provision

除光液 **jokōeki** nail polish remover

乗客 **jōkyaku** passenger; occupant (*of vehicle*)

除去 **jokyo** removal, elimination

状況 **jōkyō** conditions, circumstances; matter

情況 **jōkyō** scene

助教授 **jokyōju** associate professor

序曲 **jokyoku** overture

上級(の) **jōkyū (no)** advanced

錠前屋 **jōmae-ya** locksmith

常務 **jōmu** managing director

乗務員 **jōmuin** crew; crew member

静脈 **jōmyaku** vein

静脈内(の) **jōmyakunai (no)** intravenous

静脈瘤 **jōmyakuryū** varicose vein

情熱 **jōnetsu** passion

情熱的(な) **jōnetsuteki (na)** intense; passionate

女王 **joō** queen

女王ばち **joō-bachi** queen bee

常連 **jōren** regular (customer)

上陸する **jōriku suru** go ashore

じょうろ **jōro** watering can

常緑樹 **jōryokuju** evergreen

助力する **joryoku suru** assist

上流階級 **jōryū-kaikyū** upper classes

上流階級(の) **jōryū-kaikyū (no)** upper class

上流に **jōryū ni** upstream

上流(の) **jōryū (no)** upper-class

上流社会 **jōryū-shakai** high society

蒸留酒 **jōryūshu** distilled spirits

如才ない **josainai** tactful; shrewd

如才なさ **josainasa** diplomacy

助産婦 **josanpu** midwife

女性 **josei** woman; female

情勢 **jōsei** situation; state of affairs

女性実業家 **josei-jitsugyōka** businesswoman

女性形 **joseikei** feminine GRAM

助成金 **joseikin** subsidy

女性(の) **josei (no)** female

女性らしい **josei-rashii** feminine

女性用トイレ **joseiyō toire** ladies' room

乗船している **jōsen shite iru** be aboard

乗船する **jōsen suru** embark, go aboard

除雪車 **josetsuki** snowplow

乗車している **jōsha shite iru** be aboard

乗車する **jōsha suru** go aboard

上司 **jōshi** boss; superior

常識 **jōshiki** (common) sense

常識のある **jōshiki no aru** sensible; well-balanced

常識的に **jōshikiteki ni** reasonably

女子 **joshi** girl; woman

女子大 **joshi-dai** women's college

女子生徒 **joshi-seito** schoolgirl

上昇 **jōshō** rise

上昇させる **jōshō saseru** boost

上昇する **jōshō suru** climb; look up, improve

助手 **joshu** assistant

助手席 **joshuseki** passenger seat

常習的(な) **jōshūteki (na)** habitual

助走 **josō** run-up SP

上訴 **jōso** appeal

上訴する **jōso suru** appeal

除草剤 **josōzai** weedkiller

除隊 **jotai** discharge MIL

状態 **jōtai** circumstances; condition, state

上達 **jōtatsu** improvement

上達させる **jōtatsu saseru** improve

上達する **jōtatsu suru** improve; progress

譲渡できる **jōto dekiru** transferable

上等(の) **jōtō (no)** excellent; very good

除夜のかね **joya no kane** temple bells on New Year's Eve

条約 **jōyaku** treaty

常用漢字 **Jōyō kanji** Chinese characters in common use

情欲 **jōyoku** passion; lust

女優 **joyū** actress

錠剤 **jōzai** tablet

醸造業者 **jōzō-gyōsha** brewer

醸造所 **jōzōjo** brewery

醸造する **jōzō suru** brew

上手である **jōzu de aru** be good at

上手(な) **jōzu (na)** good, skillful

銃 **jū** gun

十 **jū** ten

中 **-jū** throughout; 年中 **nenjū** throughout the year, all year round

重圧 **jūatsu** heavy pressure

十分, 充分 **jūbun** enough

十分(な) **jūbun (na)** adequate; enough; ample; plentiful

十分に **jūbun ni** enough; sufficiently; fully

十代 **jūdai** adolescence

重大(な) **jūdai (na)** important; drastic; grave; serious

十代(の) **jūdai (no)** adolescent

充電する **jūden suru** charge; recharge

柔道 **jūdō** judo

樹液 **jueki** sap

十月 **jūgatsu** October

銃撃 **jūgeki** gunfire

授業 **jugyō** class, lesson

従業員 **jūgyōin** employee

獣医 **jūi** veterinary surgeon, vet

十一月 **jūichigatsu** November

十字架 **jūjika** cross REL

充実感 **jūjitsu-kan** fulfillment

充実した **jūjitsu shita** fulfilling

従順(な) **jūjun (na)** docile; submissive

受刑者 **jukei-sha** convict; inmate

受験 **juken** taking an exam

受験者 **juken-sha** candidate; entrant (*for exam*)

熟考 **jukkō** consideration, reflection, thought

熟考する **jukkō suru** deliberate; ponder; pore over

重婚 **jūkon** bigamy

受講手続 **jukō-tetsuzuki** course registration; lecture enrollment

塾 **juku** crammer

ジュークボックス **jūku-bokkusu** jukebox

熟読する **jukudoku suru** pore over

熟練 **jukuren** proficiency

熟練工 **jukuren-kō** skilled worker

熟練(の) **jukuren (no)** skilled

熟練した **jukuren shita** accomplished; expert; experienced; proficient

熟する **juku suru** ripen

熟達 **jukutatsu** mastery

儒教 **Jukyō** Confucianism

住民 **jūmin** inhabitant; people

住民投票 **jūmin-tōhyō** referendum

寿命 **jumyō** life

順 **jun** order, sequence

柔軟(な) **jūnan (na)** flexible; supple; pliable

柔軟仕上げ剤 **jūnan-shiagezai** conditioner

順番に **junban ni** in sequence

準備 **junbi** organization; preparation(s) ; …の準備で … **no junbi de** in preparation for; 準備ができた **junbi ga dekita** ready; …の準備をする … **no junbi o suru** get … ready

準備中は **junbichū de** in the pipeline

準備金 **junbikin** reserves FIN

準備する **junbi suru** arrange; prepare; set up; lay on; get oneself ready; set the table

順調(な) **junchō (na)** smooth, trouble-free

順位 **jun'i** place, position (in race, competition)

十二月 **jūnigatsu** December

十二支 **jūnishi** the twelve Chinese year signs

順序 **junjo** order; sequence

準々決勝 **junjun-kesshō** quarter-final

巡回 **junkai** patrol; round (of mailman, doctor)

巡回中である **junkaichū de aru** be on patrol

巡回する **junkai suru** patrol

循環 **junkan** circulation

循環する **junkan suru** circulate

潤滑油 **junkatsuyu** lubricant

準決勝 **junkesshō** semifinal

純潔 **junketsu** purity

純潔(な) **junketsu (na)** pure

純血(の) **junketsu (no)** pedigree

殉教者 **junkyōsha** martyr

順応する **junnō suru** conform to; adapt to

巡礼 **junrei** pilgrimage

巡礼者 **junrei-sha** pilgrim

純利益 **junrieki** net profit

巡査 **junsa** patrolman

巡査部長 **junsa-buchō** police sergeant

潤色する **junshoku suru** embellish

純粋(な) **junsui (na)** pure

純粋(の) **junsui (no)** solid

純粋さ **junsui-sa** purity

十億 **jū-oku** billion

重量挙げ **jūryōage** weightlifting

重力 **jūryoku** gravity

受領書 **juryō-sho** receipt

受領通知 **juryō-tsūchi** acknowledgment of receipt

銃声 **jūsei** sound of gunfire

受精する **jusei suru** be fertilized

樹脂 **jushi** resin

受信機 **jushinki** receiver TV, RAD

住所 **jūsho** address

重傷 **jūshō** serious injury

受賞者 **jushō-sha** prizewinner

受賞した **jushō shita** prizewinning

ジュース **jūsu** juice; deuce

受胎 **jutai** conception

渋滞 **jūtai** congestion

重体で **jūtai de** critically ill

重体(な) **jūtai (na)** critical

渋滞した **jūtai shita** congested

渋滞している **jūtai shite iru** be jammed

住宅 **jūtaku** housing; residence

住宅地 **jūtakuchi** residential district

住宅ローン **jūtaku-rōn** mortgage

受託者 **jutaku-sha** trustee

じゅうたん **jūtan** carpet; rug

重点 **jūten** emphasis, stress

充てん **jūten** filling; plugging

充当する **jūtō suru** commit; allot; appropriate

受話器 **juwaki** receiver TELEC; 受話器をはずして **juwaki o hazushite** off the hook

重役 **jūyaku** executive

重役会議 **jūyaku-kaigi** board meeting
受容 **juyō** acceptance
需要 **juyō** demand COM
重要である **jūyō de aru** count, matter; be important
重要でない **jūyō de nai**

insignificant; unimportant
重要(な) **jūyō (na)** important; vital; prominent; significant
重要性 **jūyōsei** importance
授与する **juyo suru** confer, award
重罪 **jūzai** felony
じゅず **juzu** prayer beads; rosary

K

か **ka** ◊ (*question particle*): いいです か *ii desu ka* is it OK? ◊: …か…か *… ka … ka* either … or…
日 -**ka** (*countword for days*); 二日 *futsu-ka* two days; the second (*of the month*)
下 -**ka** below; under; 支配下 *shihai-ka* under the control of
化 -**ka** transform into; make into; 自由化 *jiyū-ka* liberalization
科 -**ka** department; 日本語科 *Nihongo-ka* Department of Japanese
家 -**ka** person; profession; 音楽家 *ongaku-ka* musician; 小説家 *shōsetsu-ka* novelist
課 **ka** section; department; lesson; 第一課 *dai-ikka* Lesson 1
蚊 **ka** mosquito
かば **kaba** hippopotamus
カバー **kabā** cover; jacket (*of book*)
かばん **kaban** bag
カバーレター **kabā-retā** covering letter
かばう **kabau** protect; defend; cover up
かばやき **kabayaki** broiled eels
壁 **kabe** wall
壁紙 **kabegami** wallpaper
かび **kabi** mold
かび臭い **kabikusai** musty
花瓶 **kabin** vase
かびのはえた **kabi no haeta** moldy
過敏症 **kabinshō** hypersensitive
かぼちゃ **kabocha** pumpkin

かぶ **kabu** turnip
株 **kabu** share FIN
カーブ **kābu** bend; curve; twist
歌舞伎 **Kabuki** Kabuki
株主 **kabunushi** stockholder, shareholder
株式 **kabushiki** stock
株式会社 **kabushiki-gaisha** incorporated ◊ limited company
株式公開買付 **kabushiki-kōkai-kaitsuke** takeover bid
株式市場 **kabushiki-shijō** stockmarket; securities market
かぶと **kabuto** helmet
かぶと虫 **kabutomushi** beetle
価値 **kachi** merit; value; valuation; 価値がある *kachi ga aru* be good value; be worth; 価値が下がる *kachi ga sagaru* depreciate; 価値がない *kachi ga nai* worthless
勝ち **kachi** win; victory
かちあう **kachiau** clash; coincide
カチカチなる **kachikachi naru** tick
家畜 **kachiku** domestic animal
勝ち目のない人 **kachime no nai hito** outsider (*in race etc*); underdog
かちんと鳴る **kachin to naru** clink; click
課長 **kachō** section chief
課題 **kadai** assignment
過大評価された **kadai-hyōka sareta** overrated
過大に評価する **kadai ni hyōka**

suru overestimate

花壇 **kadan** (flower)bed

カーディガン **kādigan** cardigan

角 **kado** corner

カード **kādo** card

…かどうか **...ka dō ka** whether

門松 **kadomatsu** New Year's pine decoration

過度に **kado ni** overly

可動性 **kadōsei** mobility

替え玉 **kaedama** double; stand-in

かえで **kaede** maple; sycamore

帰り **kaeri** return journey

帰りの便 **kaeri no bin** return flight

かえる **kaeru** frog ◊ hatch out (*of eggs*)

変える **kaeru** change; shift

代える、替える **kaeru** replace; convert

帰る **kaeru** return

返す **kaesu** return, give back; put back; take back; pay back

カフェイン **kafein** caffeine

カフェテラス **kafeterasu** sidewalk café

カフェテリア **kafeteria** cafeteria

花粉 **kafun** pollen

花粉症 **kafunshō** hay fever

カフス **kafusu** cuff

カフスボタン **kafusubotan** cuff link

化学 **kagaku** chemistry

科学 **kagaku** science

科学技術 **kagaku-gijutsu** technology

科学技術恐怖症 **kagaku-gijutsu-kyōfushō** technophobia

科学技術(の) **kagaku-gijutsu (no)** technological

化学兵器戦争 **kagaku-heiki-sensō** chemical warfare

化学肥料 **kagaku-hiryō** fertilizer

化学(の) **kagaku (no)** chemical

化学療法 **kagaku-ryōhō** chemotherapy

化学者 **kagaku-sha** chemist

科学者 **kagaku-sha** scientist

科学的(な) **kagakuteki (na)** scientific

化学薬品 **kagaku-yakuhin** chemicals

かがめる **kagameru** bend; bow

鏡 **kagami** mirror

かがむ **kagamu** bend; stoop; crouch

輝き **kagayaki** glow

輝く **kagayaku** glow; shine; sparkle; twinkle

輝く(よう)(な) **kagayaku yō (na)** radiant

陰 **kage** shadow; 陰で *kage de* behind the scenes; 陰で糸を引く *kage de ito o hiku* mastermind

影 **kage** shadow; silhouette

過激派 **kagekiha** extremist

過激(な) **kageki (na)** extreme; radical

加減 **kagen** adjustment; extent; physical condition

加減する **kagen suru** adjust; moderate

鍵 **kagi** key; lock; 鍵を開ける *kagi o akeru* unlock; 鍵をかける *kagi o kakeru* lock

鍵穴 **kagiana** keyhole

かぎ回る **kagimawaru** nose around

限られた **kagirareta** restricted

限りのない **kagiri no nai** boundless

限り **kagiri**: …である限りは *... de aru kagiri wa* so long as; 今度限り *kondo kagiri* just this once

限る **kagiru** confine

かぎつける **kagitsukeru** detect; get wind of

かご **kago** basket; cage

化合物 **kagōbutsu** compound CHEM

化合する **kagō suru** combine

かぐ **kagu** smell; sniff

家具 **kagu** furniture

家具一式 **kagu-isshiki** suite

加虐的(な) **kagyakuteki (na)** sadistic

下半身麻痺の人 **kahanshin-mahi no hito** paraplegic

過半数を占める **kahansū o shimeru** be in the majority

かい **kai** paddle

会 **kai** association

階 **kai** floor; story

回 **kai** round (*of drinks*); time; occasion

貝 **kai** seashell; shellfish

海抜 **kaibatsu** altitude; elevation ◊ above sea level

解剖学 **kaibō-gaku** anatomy

怪物 **kaibutsu** monster

会長 **kaichō** president; chairman

懐中電灯 **kaichū-dentō** flashlight

買いだめする **kaidame suru** stock up on

階段 **kaidan** stairs; staircase

会談 **kaidan** consultation; discussion

解読する **kaidoku suru** decipher; decode

回復 **kaifuku** recovery; restoration; revival

回復期 **kaifuku-ki** convalescence

回復させる **kaifuku saseru** revive

回復する **kaifuku suru** recover; recuperate; pull through; survive

絵画 **kaiga** painting

海外で **kaigai de** overseas

海外に **kaigai ni** overseas

海外(の) **kaigai (no)** overseas

海岸 **kaigan** coast

海岸通り **kaigandōri** seafront

海岸線 **kaigansen** coastline

貝殻 **kaigara** shell

戒厳令 **kaigenrei** martial law

会議 **kaigi** conference; congress; meeting

会議場 **kaigijō** convention center

会議室 **kaigishitsu** board room; conference room

懐疑的 **kaigiteki** skeptical

介護 **kaigo** care; nursing (of the elderly)

会合 **kaigō** meeting; assembly

海軍 **kaigun** navy

海軍基地 **kaigun-kichi** naval base

海軍大尉 **kaigun-taii** lieutenant

開業医 **kaigyōi** doctor in private practice

開業する **kaigyō suru** set up, establish

開発 **kaihatsu** development

開発業者 **kaihatsu-gyōsha** developer

開発する **kaihatsu suru** develop

回避 **kaihi** evasion

会費 **kaihi** membership fee

回避する **kaihi suru** evade; shirk; deflect

回避的(な) **kaihiteki (na)** evasive

解放 **kaihō** emancipation; release

解放する **kaihō suru** free

開票 **kaihyō** counting (of votes)

会員 **kaiin** member

会員資格 **kaiin-shikaku** membership

会員証 **kaiinshō** pass

会場 **kaijō** venue

開会式 **kaikaishiki** opening ceremony

開会する **kaikai suru** begin a session; open a meeting

改革 **kaikaku** reform

改革する **kaikaku suru** reform

快感 **kaikan** pleasant feeling; kick

階下に **kaika ni** downstairs

階下(の) **kaika (no)** downstairs

快活 **kaikatsu** vivacity

快活(な) **kaikatsu (na)** irrepressible; sunny disposition

会計 **kaikei** accounts

会計係 **kaikei-gakari** accountant; cashier; treasurer

会計上(の) **kaikei-jō (no)** fiscal

会計課 **kaikeika** accounts department

会計監査 **kaikei-kansa** audit

会計監査官 **kaikei-kansakan** auditor

会計年度 **kaikei-nendo** financial year, fiscal year

会計士 **kaikeishi** accountant

会見 **kaiken** meeting; interview; 会見する **kaiken suru** meet with

解決 **kaiketsu** answer; resolution; 解決できない **kaiketsu dekinai** insoluble

解決法 **kaiketsu-hō** fix; way out

解決する **kaiketsu suru** resolve; settle; work out

回帰線 **kaikisen** the tropics

解雇 **kaiko** dismissal

回顧 **kaiko** retrospective

蚕 **kaiko** silkworm

回顧録 **kaikoroku** memoirs

解雇される **kaiko sareru** be laid off

解雇する **kaiko suru** dismiss; lay off; fire

海峡 **kaikyō** strait; channel

階級 **kaikyū** social class; rank

階級社会 **kaikyū-shakai** class society

階級闘争 **kaikyū-tōsō** class warfare

解明する **kaimei suru** unravel

買い物 **kaimono** purchase; shopping; 買い物に行く *kaimono ni iku* go shopping; 買い物をする *kaimono o suru* shop

買い物客 **kaimono-kyaku** shopper

下院 **Kain** House of Representatives; Lower House

飼い慣らされた **kainarasareta** tame

飼い慣らす **kainarasu** domesticate

下院議員 **Kain-giin** Congressman; representative

下位(の) **kai (no)** inferior

飼い主 **kainushi** owner; keeper (*of pet*)

介入 **kainyū** intervention

介入する **kainyū suru** intervene

かいらい政権 **kairai-seiken** puppet government

回覧する **kairan suru** circulate

海里 **kairi** nautical mile

回路 **kairo** circuit

カイロプラクター **kairopurakutā** chiropractor

改良 **kairyō** improvement; reform

海流 **kairyū** current (*in sea*)

開催地 **kaisaichi** venue

開催する **kaisai suru** hold; open

解散する **kaisan suru** dismiss; dissolve; break up

改札係 **kaisatsugakari** ticket collector

改札口 **kaisatsuguchi** ticket barrier

快晴 **kaisei** fine weather

改正 **kaisei** reform; revision

改正する **kaisei suru** reform; revise

懐石料理 **kaiseki-ryōri** Japanese-style haute cuisine

回戦 **kaisen** round (*in tournament*)

回線 **kaisen** telephone line

会戦 **kaisen** battle, encounter

開戦 **kaisen** outbreak of war

解説 **kaisetsu** comment

解説者 **kaisetsu-sha** commentator

会社 **kaisha** business, company, firm

解釈 **kaishaku** interpretation

解釈する **kaishaku suru** interpret

開始 **kaishi** initiation

買い占める **kaishimeru** buy up

開始する **kaishi suru** commence; initiate; open; inaugurate

会衆 **kaishū** congregation REL

回収 **kaishū** recovery; recall

改宗させる **kaishū saseru** convert REL

改修する **kaishū suru** repair; renovate

回収する **kaishū suru** repossess; retrieve

階層 **kaisō** layer

海草 **kaisō** seaweed

快速 **kaisoku** fast train

改装する **kaisō suru** redecorate

回数 **kaisū** frequency

回数券 **kaisūken** multi-journey ticket

開拓する **kaitaku suru** cultivate; develop; open up

買い手 **kaite** buyer, purchaser

快適(な) **kaiteki (na)** pleasant

快適さ **kaiteki-sa** comfort

回転 **kaiten** revolution, turn; rotation; spin

回転盤 **kaitenban** turntable

回転ドア **kaiten-doa** revolving door

回転させる **kaiten saseru** spin; turn

回転する **kaiten suru** revolve; rotate; spin

開店する **kaiten suru** open (for business); establish

解答 **kaitō** answer; response; solution

買い取る **kaitoru** buy out

解答する **kaitō suru** answer; respond; solve

解凍する **kaitō suru** defrost, thaw; 圧縮ファイルを解凍する *asshuku fairu o kaitō suru* unzip

会話 **kaiwa** conversation; talk

会話集 **kaiwa-shū** phrasebook

会話(の) **kaiwa (no)** conversational

かいよう **kaiyō** ulcer

海洋(の) **kaiyō (no)** seafaring

改善 **kaizen** improvement

改善する **kaizen suru** improve

改造 **kaizō** conversion; modification; renovation

解像力 **kaizō-ryoku** resolution

改造する **kaizō suru** adapt, modify; renovate

海図 **kaizu** (nautical) chart

かじ **kaji** rudder

火事 **kaji** blaze, fire

家事 **kaji** housekeeping; housework

かじかんだ **kajikanda** numb

かじき **kajiki** swordfish

カジノ **kajino** casino

かじる **kajiru** chew; gnaw; nibble

箇条書にする **kajōgaki ni suru** itemize

過剰(の) **kajō (no)** excess; excessive

カジュアル(な) **kajuaru (na)** casual

カジュアルウェア **kajuaru-wea** casual wear

果樹園 **kajuen** orchard

抱える **kakaeru** embrace; hold; employ

掲げる **kakageru** put up; hoist; hold up; publish

価格 **kakaku** value

係り **kakari** person in charge; subsection of an office

係り長 **kakarichō** assistant manager

かかる **kakaru** cost; take *time*; catch

掛かる **kakaru** hang

かかと **kakato** heel

かかっていない **kakatte inai** be off (*of brake*)

かかっている **kakatte iru** be on (*of brake*); span

かかわらず **kakawarazu** …にかかわらず *… ni kakawarazu* whatever; regardless of

かかわり合い **kakawariai** involvement; …とかかわり合いになる *… to kakawariai ni naru* get mixed up with

かかわる **kakawaru** engage in; get involved with

賭け **kake** bet

駆け足 **kakeashi** run

掛け布団 **kakebuton** quilt, duvet

かけがえのない **kakegae no nai** indispensable; invaluable; irreplaceable

掛け金 **kakegane** latch

掛け声 **kakegoe** chant; 掛け声を掛ける *kakegoe o kakeru* chant

賭け事 **kakegoto** gamble; gambling; 賭け事をする *kakegoto o suru* bet

家計 **kakei** budget

家系 **kakei** descent; lineage

掛け軸 **kakejiku** hanging scroll

賭け金 **kakekin** stake

駆け落ちする **kakeochi suru** elope

かけら **kakera** bit; piece; fragment

かける **kakeru** put on *glasses, necklace*; build; cover; sprinkle; impose *tax*; switch on; tie up

賭ける **kakeru** bet, stake; back

掛ける **kakeru** hang; multiply; sit down

欠ける **kakeru** lack; wane

欠けている **kakete iru** be lacking; be devoid of

可決する **kaketsu suru** pass, carry *proposal*

掛け算 **kakezan** multiplication

かき **kaki** oyster

柿 **kaki** persimmon

夏期 **kaki** summer; summer semester

かき氷 **kakigōri** *crushed ice with syrup*

かき込む **kakikomu** tuck away; shovel in

かき混ぜる **kakimazeru** stir; toss

書き直す **kakinaosu** rewrite

かき鳴らす **kakinarasu** strum

下記に **kaki ni** below

下記参照 **kaki-sanshō** see below

書き手 **kakite** writer

書留で送る **kakitome de okuru** send a letter registered

書き留める **kakitomeru** write down, note down

書留書簡 **kakitome-shokan** registered letter

書き取り **kakitori** dictation

書き初め **kakizome** New Year calligraphy

活気 **kakki** activity; vitality; dynamism; …に活気を与える *… ni kakki o ataeru* enliven

活気のある **kakki no aru** lively; exuberant

活気のない **kakki no nai** dead *place*; sleepy *town*; slack *period*

画期的(な) **kakkiteki (na)** epoch-making

活気づける **kakkizukeru** stimulate; inspire; give life to

活気づく **kakkizuku** become lively; boom

かっこ岩 **kakkō** bracket

格好 **kakkō** form; appearance

格好いい **kakkō ii** stylish; attractive

確固たる **kakko taru** solid, firm; determined

確固とした **kakko to shita** pronounced, definite; unswerving

格好悪い **kakkō warui** unattractive, ugly

過去 **kako** past

下降 **kakō** downturn

河口 **kakō** mouth (*of river*)

過去分詞 **kako-bunshi** past participle

花こう岩 **kakōgan** granite

囲い **kakoi** enclosure; compound; pen; fold; corral

囲い込む **kakoikomu** fence in

過去形 **kakokei** past tense

囲む **kakomu** enclose; surround; 囲まれている **kakomarete iru** be surrounded by

加工していない **kakō shite inai** raw

加工する **kakō suru** process

かく **kaku** scratch

欠く **kaku** be lacking; neglect; chip; crack

描く **kaku** paint; draw

書く **kaku** write, put down (in writing)

核 **kaku** core; nucleus

各 **kaku** each; every

格上げする **kakuage suru** upgrade; promote

核分裂 **kakubunretsu** nuclear fission

拡張 **kakuchō** enlargement; expansion

拡張する **kakuchō suru** expand; extend

拡大 **kakudai** enlargement; expansion; escalation

拡大鏡 **kakudaikyō** magnifying glass

拡大する **kakudai suru** expand; enlarge; magnify

角度 **kakudo** angle

角刈り **kakugari** crew cut

覚悟 **kakugo** readiness

核廃棄物 **kaku-haikibutsu** nuclear waste

核兵器 **kaku-heiki** nuclear weapon

確保する **kakuho suru** secure, obtain

確実(な) **kakujitsu (na)** definite; sure; safe; hard *facts, evidence*

確実に **kakujitsu ni** reliably

確実にする **kakujitsu ni suru** ensure

確実性 **kakujitsusei** certainty; safety (*of prediction*)

かくまう **kakumau** harbor, shelter

革命 **kakumei** revolution; 革命を起こす *kakumei o okosu* revolutionize

革命家 **kakumei-ka** revolutionary

革命(の) **kakumei (no)** revolutionary

革命的(な) **kakumeiteki (na)** revolutionary

確認 **kakunin** confirmation, verification

確認する **kakunin suru** check; confirm; recognize

核(の) **kaku (no)** nuclear

架空(の) **kakū (no)** fictitious, imaginary

格納庫 **kakunōko** hangar

隠れ家 **kakurega** retreat

かくれんぼ **kakurenbo** hide-and-seek

隠れる **kakureru** hide; go into hiding

隠れている **kakurete iru** be in hiding

隔離 **kakuri** seclusion; quarantine

隔離病棟 **kakuri-byōtō** isolation ward

確率 **kakuritsu** probability

確立する **kakuritsu suru** establish

隠された **kakusareta** hidden

覚せい剤 **kakuseizai** stimulant

かくしゃくとした **kakushaku to shita** sprightly

隠しきれない **kakushikirenai** telltale

確信 **kakushin** assurance; certainty; belief

核心 **kakushin** core, heart (of problem)

革新 **kakushin** innovation

確信のある **kakushin no aru** assured

確信させる **kakushin saseru** convince

革新者 **kakushin-sha** innovator

確信している **kakushin shite iru** be certain

革新的(な) **kakushinteki (na)** innovative

隠す **kakusu** hide; cover; disguise; mask; withhold

確定申告書 **kakutei-shinkokusho** tax return

確定する **kakutei suru** determine, establish

カクテル **kakuteru** cocktail

獲得する **kakutoku suru** capture; land job; poll votes

格闘する **kakutō suru** fight; wrestle

獲得する **kakutoku suru** win; obtain

格付けする **kakuzuke suru** rank; grade

窯 **kama** kiln

かま **kama** sickle

かまう **kamau** mind, object to; かまうものか **kamau mono ka** I don't care!

かまわずに **kamawazu ni** regardless

かめ **kame** tortoise; turtle; tub

カメラ **kamera** camera

カメラマン **kameraman** photographer; cameraman

神 **kami** God, Lord; deity; god

紙 **kami** paper

髪 **kami** hair

かみ合わせる **kamiawaseru** engage, mesh

紙挟み **kamibasami** clipboard

紙袋 **kamibukuro** paper bag

神棚 **kamidana** Shinto altar

髪型 **kamigata** hairdo

神風 **kamikaze** kamikaze

紙コップ **kamikoppu** paper cup

紙くず **kamikuzu** wastepaper

雷 **kaminari** bolt (of lightning); thunder

神(の) **kami (no)** divine

紙(の) **kami (no)** paper

髪の毛 **kami no ke** hair

仮眠する **kamin suru** grab some sleep

神様 **kamisama** god; ace; champion

かみそり **kamisori** razor

紙テープ **kami-tēpu** streamer

かみつきそう(な) **kamitsukisō (na)** snappy

かみつく **kamitsuku** bite; snap

紙やすり **kami-yasuri** sandpaper

かも **kamo** duck; sucker (person)

科目 **kamoku** subject

かもめ **kamome** (sea)gull

…かもしれない … **kamo shirenai** may, might; 彼は決心したかもしれない **kare wa kesshin shita kamo shirenai** he may have decided

貨物 **kamotsu** freight

貨物機 **kamotsu-ki** freighter, cargo plane

貨物列車 **kamotsu-ressha** freight train

貨物船 **kamotsu-sen** freighter

貨物室 **kamotsushitsu** hold

貨物輸送 **kamotsu-yusō** shipment

かむ **kamu** bite; chew

カムバックする **kamubakku suru** make a comeback

カムフラージュ **kamufurāju** camouflage

カムフラージュする **kamufurāju suru** camouflage

缶 **kan** can

勘 **kan** feeling; intuition; 勘が鈍る **kan ga niburu** be losing one's grip

間 **-kan** for; during; between; 一時間 **ichiji-kan** for an hour; 東京-シカゴ間 **Tōkyō-Shikago-kan** between Tokyo and Chicago

巻 **-kan** countword for books, volumes

かな **kana** (question particle): 雨かな **ame kana** is it raining?

仮名 **kana** Japanese syllabary

金網 **kanaami** wire netting

カナダ **Kanada** Canada

カナダ人 **Kanada-jin** Canadian

カナダ（の）**Kanada (no)** Canadian

かなえる **kanaeru** grant

家内 **kanai** wife

金切り声 **kanakirigoe** screech; squeal; 金切り声をあげる **kanakirigoe o ageru** screech; squeal

金物類 **kanamonorui** hardware

必ず **kanarazu** without fail

必ずしも **kanarazushimo** not necessarily

かなり **kanari** considerably; rather; fairly, quite; quite a lot

カナリア **kanaria** canary

かなり（の）**kanari (no)** considerable, substantial; significant; a good deal of ◊ quite a few; a number of

かなりたくさん（の）**kanari takusan (no)** a good many

悲しげ（な）**kanashige (na)** mournful

悲しい **kanashii** sad; disconsolate

悲しませる **kanashimaseru** upset

悲しみ **kanashimi** sadness; sorrow; grief; 悲しみに沈んだ **kanashimi ni shizunda** mournful

悲しむ **kanashimu** grieve; feel sad

悲しそう（な）**kanashisō (na)** sad; plaintive

かなう **kanau** come true; be fulfilled; measure up to; be consistent with; 法にかなう **hō ni kanau** follow the rules

かなづち **kanazuchi** hammer; non-swimmer

干ばつ **kanbatsu** drought

勘弁 **kanben** forgiveness

カンボジア **Kanbojia** Cambodia

カンボジア（の）**Kanbojia (no)** Cambodian

かん木 **kanboku** shrub

陥没 **kanbotsu** cave-in; subsidence

幹部 **kanbu** executive

看病する **kanbyō suru** nurse; look after

干潮 **kanchō** low tide

館長 **kanchō** curator

寛大（な）**kandai (na)** generous; lenient

かん高い **kandakai** high-pitched; strident

感動させる **kandō saseru** move, touch (*emotionally*)

勘当する **kandō suru** disown; disinherit

感動する **kandō suru** be impressed

感動的（な）**kandōteki (na)** emotional; moving; stirring

金 **kane** money

鐘 **kane** bell

金貸し **kanekashi** moneylender; moneylending

金持ち **kanemochi** the rich

金持ち（の）**kanemochi (no)** rich; well-heeled

肝炎 **kan'en** hepatitis

金のかかる **kane no kakaru** expensive

金の無駄 **kane no muda** waste of money

可燃性（の）**kanensei (no)** (in)flammable, combustible

兼ねる **kaneru** combine; serve several functions

カーネーション **kānēshon** carnation

加熱する **kanetsu suru** heat up

金づる **kanezuru** financial supporter; meal ticket

考え **kangae** idea, notion; thought; mind; plan; intention

考え出す **kangaedasu** dream up; think up; come up with

考え方 **kangaekata** mentality, mindset; viewpoint

考え込む **kangaekomu** brood

考え込んだ **kangaekonda** thoughtful

考え直す **kangaenaosu** reconsider

考えられない **kangaerarenai** inconceivable, unthinkable

考えられる **kangaerareru** conceivable

考える **kangaeru** think; assume; figure

かんがい **kangai** irrigation

かんがいする **kangai suru** irrigate

管楽器 **kangakki** wind instrument

歓迎 **kangei** welcome, reception

歓迎する **kangei suru** welcome

感激する **kangeki suru** be touched; be moved

看護 **kango** nursing; care

看護婦 **kangofu** nurse

看護士 **kangoshi** male nurse

かに **kani** crab

カーニバル **kānibaru** carnival

果肉 **kaniku** flesh; pulp (*of fruit*)

患者 **kanja** patient

漢字 **kanji** Chinese character

感じ **kanji** sense

肝心(の) **kanjin (no)** essential

感じのいい **kanji no ii** agreeable; pleasant; pleasing

感じられる **kanjirareru** feel

感じる **kanjiru** feel; sense

勘定 **kanjō** bill; check; counting; 勘定を払う **kanjō o harau** pay

感情 **kanjō** emotion; feeling

冠状動脈血栓 **kanjō-dōmyaku-kessen** coronary

勘定書き **kanjōgaki** check (*in restaurant etc*)

感情的(な) **kanjōteki (na)** emotional

感覚 **kankaku** feeling; sensation; sense

間隔 **kankaku** interval

感覚のない **kankaku no nai** numb

かんかんになっている **kankan ni natte iru** be fuming

関係 **kankei** connection; relationship; dealings; involvement; …と関係がある *... to kankei ga aru* be connected with; be mixed up in

関係のない **kankei no nai** unrelated

関係者以外立ち入り禁止 **kankeisha-igai-tachiiri-kinshi** private

関係している **kankei shite iru** be associated with

関係する **kankei suru** be concerned; be involved

簡潔(な) **kanketsu (na)** concise, succinct

歓喜 **kanki** jubilation

換気 **kanki** ventilation

換気孔 **kankikō** ventilation shaft

監禁 **kankin** confinement

換気性 **kankinsei** liquidity

缶切り **kankiri** can opener

換気装置 **kanki-sōchi** ventilator

換気する **kanki suru** ventilate; air

観光 **kankō** sightseeing

観光案内所 **kankō annaisho** tourist (information) office

観光事業 **kankō jigyō** tourism

韓国 **Kankoku** Korea

韓国語 **Kankoku-go** Korean

韓国人 **Kankoku-jin** Korean

韓国(の) **Kankoku (no)** Korean

観光客 **kankō-kyaku** tourist; visitor; sightseer

観客 **kankyaku** audience; spectator

観客席 **kankyakuseki** auditorium

環境 **kankyō** environment; setting; surroundings; 環境にやさしい *kankyō ni yasashii* environmentally friendly

環境庁 **Kankyōchō** Environment Agency

環境保護 **kankyō-hogo** environmental protection

環境保護(の) **kankyō-hogo (no)** ecological, green

環境保護論者 **kankyō-hogo-ronsha** environmentalist

環境(の) **kankyō (no)** environmental

環境汚染 **kankyō-osen** environmental pollution

緩慢(な) **kanman (na)** sluggish

甘味料 **kanmiryō** sweetener

かんな **kanna** plane (*tool*)

カンニングをする **kanningu o suru** cheat

観音 **kannon** goddess of mercy

官能的(な) **kannōteki (na)** sensual; voluptuous; sultry

かんぬき **kannuki** bolt; bar

神主 **kannushi** Shinto priest

彼女 **kanojo** she ◊ girlfriend

彼女(の) **kanojo (no)** her

可能(な) **kanō (na)** feasible; possible

可能性 **kanōsei** chance; possibility; potential; liability

化膿する **kanō suru** fester

乾杯 **kanpai** toast ◊ cheers!, your health!

完敗する **kanpai suru** be wiped out, be totally beaten

乾杯する **kanpai suru** toast

完ぺき **kanpeki** perfection

完ぺき(な) **kanpeki (na)** perfect; flawless

完ぺき主義者 **kanpeki-shugi-sha** perfectionist

漢方薬 **kanpōyaku** Chinese herbal medicine

慣例 **kanrei** institution

関連 **kanren** link; relevance

関連させる **kanren saseru** link

関連する **kanren suru** relevant

関連づける **kanrenzukeru** connect; implicate

管理 **kanri** administration; control

管理人 **kanri-nin** caretaker; superintendent

管理(の) **kanri (no)** administrative

管理する **kanri suru** look after; control; manage

管理者 **kanri-sha** administrator

管理職 **kanrishoku** administration; management

簡略 **kanryaku** informality; simplicity

官僚 **kanryō** bureaucracy; bureaucrat

完了形 **kanryōkei** perfect GRAM

官僚主義 **kanryō-shugi** bureaucracy, red tape

完了する **kanryō suru** accomplish

官僚的(な) **kanryōteki (na)** bureaucratic

関西 **Kansai** *area around Osaka, Kyoto and Hyogo*

閑散期(の) **kansanki (no)** offpeak

監査する **kansa suru** audit

観察 **kansatsu** observation

観察地点 **kansatsu-chiten** viewpoint (*place*)

観察者 **kansatsu-sha** observer

観察する **kansatsu suru** observe; study

観察点 **kansatsuten** vantage point

歓声 **kansei** cheer; cheering; 歓声を上げる **kansei o ageru** cheer

完成 **kansei** completion

完成する **kansei suru** complete; perfect

艦船 **kansen** fleet

感染 **kansen** infection

幹線道路 **kansen-dōro** highway; main road

感染した **kansen shita** septic

感染する **kansen suru** become infected; go septic ◊ infectious

関節 **kansetsu** joint ANAT

関節炎 **kansetsuen** arthritis

間接経費 **kansetsu-keihi** overhead FIN

間接的(な) **kansetsuteki (na)** indirect

間接的に **kansetsuteki ni** indirectly

感謝 **kansha** gratitude; appreciation; thanks

かんしゃく **kanshaku** tantrum

感謝している **kansha shite iru** thankful

感謝する **kansha suru** grateful ◊ thank; be grateful to

冠詞 **kanshi** article GRAM

感心 **kanshin** admiration

関心 **kanshin** concern; 関心がある **kanshin ga aru** care about; 関心のない **kanshin no nai** unconcerned

関心事 **kanshinji** a matter of concern

感心する **kanshin suru** admire

監視されている **kanshi sarete iru** come under scrutiny

監視する **kanshi suru** monitor; observe

関して **kan shite**: …に関して *...ni kan shite* in connection with, with reference to, as regards

鑑賞 **kanshō** appreciation

干渉 **kanshō** interference; intervention

感傷 **kanshō** sentiment, sentimentality

感触 **kanshoku** touch

干渉する **kanshō suru** interfere, meddle; intervene

感傷的(な) **kanshōteki (na)** sentimental; sloppy

看守 **kanshu** guard

慣習 **kanshū** convention; custom

感想 **kansō** thoughts; impressions; feedback

乾燥機 **kansō-ki** dryer, drier

観測所 **kansokujo** observatory

観測する **kansoku suru** observe; survey

簡素(な) **kanso (na)** plain; austere

乾燥した **kansō shita** arid; dried; seasoned

感嘆符 **kantanfu** exclamation point

簡単(な) **kantan (na)** easy, simple

簡単にする **kantan ni suru** simplify

簡単さ **kantan-sa** simplicity

感嘆させる **kantan saseru** dazzle

観点 **kanten** point of view

関東 **Kantō** *central eastern district of Tokyo, Kanagawa*

監督 **kantoku** direction; director; supervisor

監督する **kantoku suru** direct; oversee; supervise

かんと鳴る **kan to naru** clang

カントリー **kantorī** country and western

貫通する **kantsū suru** penetrate; pierce

カヌー **kanū** canoe

緩和 **kanwa** relief; easing

慣用 **kan'yō** usage

寛容 **kan'yō** tolerance

慣用句 **kan'yōku** idiom

寛容(な) **kan'yō (na)** tolerant

慣用的(な) **kan'yōteki (na)** idiomatic

加入する **kanyū suru** join; take out *insurance*

換算 **kanzan** conversion

換算表 **kanzan-hyō** conversion table

換算する **kanzan suru** convert

関税 **kanzei** tariff

完全(な) **kanzen (na)** complete; full; perfect

肝臓 **kanzō** liver (*in body*)

缶詰にする **kanzume ni suru** can

缶詰(の) **kanzume (no)** canned

顔 **kao** face; 顔に泥を塗る *kao ni doro o nuru* bring shame on; 顔を赤くする *kao o akaku suru* go red in the face; 顔を出す *kao o dasu* put in an appearance; 顔をしかめる *kao o shikameru* frown; scowl; 顔を背ける *kao o somukeru* turn away, look away; 顔をつぶす *kao o tsubusu* make lose face; 顔をつぶされる *kao o tsubusareru* lose face

顔立ち **kaodachi** features

顔色 **kaoiro** color; complexion; 顔色が悪い *kaoiro ga warui* look pale; have a bad complexion

香り **kaori** scent; perfume; aroma; bouquet

カーペット **kāpetto** carpet

かっぱ **kappa** water imp

活発(な) **kappatsu (na)** vigorous; vivacious; brisk

カップ **kappu** cup

カップル **kappuru** couple

カプセル **kapuseru** capsule

から **kara** from; after; off; because; so; 十八世紀から *jūhasseiki kara* from the 18th century; 十人から十五人まで *jū-nin kara jūgo-nin made* from 10 to 15 people; 五時から *goji kara* after five o'clock; 雨が降っているから *ame ga futte iru kara* because it's raining

殻 **kara** husk; shell

カラー **karā** color; collar

カーラー **kārā** roller

体 **karada** body; 体に合わない *karada ni awanai* disagree with (*of food*)

辛い **karai** hot, spicy

からかう **karakau** make fun of; play a joke on

辛口(の) **karakuchi (no)** dry *wine*

絡まる **karamaru** become entangled in

絡ませる **karamaseru** wind

絡み付く **karamitsuku** wind (*of ivy etc*)

空になる **kara ni naru** empty

空にする **kara ni suru** empty

空(の) **kara (no)** blank

カラオケ **karaoke** karaoke

空っぽ **karappo** emptiness

空っぽ(の) **karappo (no)** empty, hollow

カラー写真 **karā-shashin** color photograph

からし **karashi** (Japanese) mustard

からす **karasu** crow

枯らす **karasu** kill *plant*; parch *crops*

空手 **karate** karate

空手チョップ **karate choppu** karate chop

カラーテレビ **karā-terebi** color TV

カラット **karatto** carat

彼 **kare** he; him ◊ boyfriend

かれい **karei** plaice; flounder

華麗に **karei ni** gorgeously; magnificently

カレンダー **karendā** calendar

彼の **kare no** his

彼ら **karera** they; them

彼らの **karera no** their ◊ theirs

枯れる **kareru** wither

枯れ山水 **karesanzui** rock garden with raked gravel

彼氏 **kareshi** boyfriend

狩り **kari** hunt

借り **kari** debt

カリフラワー **karifurawā** cauliflower

刈り込み **karikomi** trim

刈り込む **karikomu** clip; crop

借り越す **karikosu** overdraw

カリキュラム **karikyuramu** curriculum

借りる **kariru** borrow; rent

仮出所 **karishussho** parole

カリスマ **karisuma** charisma

借りている **karite iru** on loan ◊ owe

過労 **karō** overwork

かろうじて **karōjite** barely; narrowly; only just

カロリー **karorī** calorie

過労死 **karōshi** death from overwork

狩る **karu** hunt

刈る **karu** mow

カール **kāru** curl

カルチャーショック **karuchā-shokku** culture shock

軽い **karui** frivolous; minor; light; idle *threat*

軽くなる **karuku naru** ease up

軽くする **karuku suru** lighten

軽さ **karu-sa** lightness

カルシウム **karushiumu** calcium

カールする **kāru suru** curl

カルテル **karuteru** cartel

カルテット **karutetto** quartet

かさ **kasa** lampshade

傘 **kasa** umbrella

かさばった **kasabatta** bulky

かさぶた **kasabuta** scab

火災 **kasai** fire

火災報知機 **kasai-hōchiki** fire alarm

かさかさと鳴る **kasakasa to naru** rustle

重なる **kasanaru** overlap

重ねる **kasaneru** pile up; repeat

稼ぎ手 **kasegite** breadwinner

稼ぐ **kasegu** earn, make

家政婦 **kaseifu** housekeeper

化石 **kaseki** fossil

下線を引く **kasen o hiku** underline

仮説 **kasetsu** hypothesis

仮説上(の) **kasetsujō (no)** hypothetical

カセット **kasetto** cassette

カセットテープ **kasetto-tēpu** tape

貨車 **kasha** freight car

かし **kashi** oak

華氏 **kashi** Fahrenheit

歌詞 **kashi** lyrics

菓子 **kashi** cake; candy

貸し倒れ金 **kashidaorekin** bad debt

貸し家あり **kashiie ari** house for rent

賢い **kashikoi** wise

かしこまりました **kashikomarimashita** (*acknowledging order, request etc*) yes, sir; sure; thank you (*said by sales clerk*)

カシミヤ(の) **kashimiya (no)** cashmere

かしら **kashira** I wonder; I hope

頭文字 **kashira-moji** initial

貸付金 **kashitsukekin** loan

加湿器 **kashitsuki** humidifier

柏餅 **kashiwamochi** *rice cake wrapped in an oak leaf with sweetbean paste*

過小評価する **kashō-hyōka suru** undervalue

歌手 **kashu** singer

火葬 **kasō** cremation; 火葬にする **kasō ni suru** cremate

仮装 **kasō** fancy dress

火葬場 **kasō-ba** crematorium

仮想現実 **kasō-genjitsu** virtual reality

加速 **kasoku** acceleration

加速する **kasoku suru** accelerate

カーソル **kāsoru** cursor

仮装する **kasō suru** dress up

滑車 **kassha** pulley

滑走路 **kassōro** runway

かす **kasu** dregs; scum

課す **kasu** impose

貸す **kasu** loan; rent (out)

かすか(な) **kasuka (na)** dim; faint; vague

かすかな光 **kasuka na hikari** glimmer

かすめる **kasumeru** graze; skim past; steal

かすみ **kasumi** haze

かすむ **kasumu** glaze over; mist over

かすんだ **kasunda** misty

かすり傷 **kasurikizu** graze

かする **kasuru** brush; brush against

カスタードクリーム **kasutādo-kurīmu** custard

カースト **kāsuto** caste

方 **kata** person (*polite*)

方 **-kata** how to...; 書き方 **kakikata** how to write

...方 **... kata** care of, c/o

過多 **kata** excess

型 **kata** version; kind; 型にはまらない *kata ni hamaranai* unconventional; 型にはまる *kata ni hamaru* be in a rut; 型にはまった *kata ni hamatta* conventional; set *views, ideas*

潟 **kata** lagoon

肩 **kata** shoulder; 肩をすくめる *kata o sukumeru* shrug (one's shoulders)

形 **katachi** figure; form; shape

形になる **katachi ni naru** form

形作る **katachizukuru** form

かたどる **katadoru** model on; imitate

肩書き **katagaki** title

型紙 **katagami** pattern

方々 **katagata** people (*polite*)

肩口 **kataguchi** socket

肩ひも **katahimo** strap

片方 **katahō** one side; one of a pair

硬い、固い、堅い **katai** rigid; solid; stiff; tough; tight *drawer, screw*; serious *company*

かたかな **katakana** the angular *Japanese syllabary*

堅くなる **kataku naru** harden; stiffen up

かたくり粉 **katakuriko** cornstarch

堅苦しい **katakurushii** uptight; stiff (*in manner*); stilted

堅く絞める **kataku shimeru** tighten

家宅捜索令状 **katakusōsaku-reijō** search warrant

固まり **katamari** block; chunk; clot

固まる **katamaru** harden; solidify; set

片道切符 **katamichi-kippu** one-way ticket

傾ける **katamukeru** lean

傾き **katamuki** slope

傾く **katamuku** lean; slant; tilt

刀 **katana** samurai sword

片親(の) **kataoya (no)** single parent

カタログ **katarogu** catalog; literature

語る **kataru** relate; talk

固さ, 硬さ, 堅さ **kata-sa** hardness; rigidity

片手 **katate** one hand

片手なべ **katate-nabe** saucepan

かたつむり **katatsumuri** snail

偏らない **katayoranai** impartial; fair; varied

偏った, 片寄った **katayotta** biased; unfair

固ゆで(の) **katayude (no)** hard-boiled

片付ける **katazukeru** clear away; tidy up

仮定 **katei** assumption

家庭 **katei** home

過程 **katei** process

家庭教師 **katei-kyōshi** (private) tutor

家庭(の) **katei (no)** domestic

仮定する **katei suru** assume

家庭的(な) **kateiteki (na)** homeloving, homely

カーテン **kāten** drapes, curtains

カート **kāto** baggage cart

過渡期(の) **kato (no)** transitional

カートリッジ **kātoridji** cartridge

カトリック(の) **katorikku (no)** Roman Catholic

カトリック信者 **katorikku-shinja** Roman Catholic

勝つ **katsu** win; prevail; ...に勝つ *... ni katsu* win a victory over ...

活動 **katsudō** activity

活動家 **katsudōka** activist

活動的(な) **katsudōteki (na)** active; dynamic

担ぐ **katsugu** shoulder; carry; play tricks on

活字 **katsuji** type (*printing*)

活字体 **katsujitai** block letters

かつお **katsuo** bonito

かつら **katsura** wig

活力 **katsuryoku** dynamism; spirit

かつて **katsute** once; long ago

活躍する **katsuyaku suru** be active

活用する **katsuyō suru** use, employ; conjugate

飼っている **katte iru** have, keep *pet*

勝手気ままにさせる **katte kimama ni saseru** run wild

勝手(な) **katte (na)** arbitrary; 勝手にしなさい *katte ni shinasai* please yourself!

カット **katto** cut

かっとなる **katto naru** lose one's cool; blow up

カットする **katto suru** cut

買う **kau** buy

カウボーイ **kaubōi** cowboy

カウチポテト **kauchi-poteto** couch potato

カウンセラー **kaunserā** counselor

カウンセリング **kaunseringu** counseling

カウンター **kauntā** bar, counter

カウント **kaunto** count

皮 **kawa** crust; peel; leather; hide (*of animal*); 皮をはぐ *kawa o hagu* skin; 皮をむく *kawa o muku* peel; 皮をなめす *kawa o namesu* tan *leather*

川, 河 **kawa** river

革 **kawa** leather

川床 **kawadoko** riverbed

川岸 **kawagishi** riverside

かわいがる **kawaigaru** fondle

かわいい **kawaii** cute; sweet

かわいらしい **kawairashii** endearing; pretty

かわいそう(な) **kawaisō (na)** pitiful; poor

乾いた **kawaita** dry

皮ジャン **kawajan** bomber jacket

乾かす **kawakasu** dry

乾く **kawaku** drain; dry

皮(の) **kawa (no)** leather

かわら **kawara** roof tile

代わり **kawari** substitute; exchange; fill in

代わりに **kawari ni** instead (of)

代わり(の) **kawari (no)** alternate; alternative

変わりやすい **kawariyasui** unsettled; changeable

変わる **kawaru** swing (*of opinion*); change; break (*of boy's voice*)

代わる **kawaru** replace

為替相場 **kawase-sōba** exchange rate

かわす **kawasu** evade; ward off; duck

変わった **kawatta** unusual

かわうそ **kawauso** otter

蚊帳 **kaya** mosquito net

火薬 **kayaku** gunpowder

火曜日 **kayōbi** Tuesday

通う **kayou** attend *school*; commute; frequent *place*

かゆい **kayui** itchy

かゆみ **kayumi** itch

火山 **kazan** volcano

火山灰 **kazanbai** ash

飾り **kazari** decoration; ornament; trimming

飾り(の) **kazari (no)** decorative; ornamental

飾る **kazaru** decorate; garnish; trim

風 **kaze** wind; 風の強い *kaze no tsuyoi* windy

風邪 **kaze** cold; 風邪を引く *kaze o hiku* catch (a) cold

課税 **kazei** taxation

課税する **kazei suru** tax

風通しのよい **kazetōshi no yoi** airy

数えきれない **kazoekirenai** countless

数える **kazoeru** count

家族 **kazoku** family; household

家族計画 **kazoku-keikaku** family planning

数 **kazu** count; number; 数に入る **kazu ni hairu** count; qualify; 数に入れる **kazu ni ireru** count

毛 **ke** hair (*single*); bristles

気 **ke** touch; sign; indication

家-**ke** family

毛穴 **keana** pore

けばだった **kebadatta** fuzzy

けばけばしい **kebakebashii** flashy; garish, gaudy

毛深い **kebukai** hairy

ケーブルカー **kēburu-kā** cable car; funicular

ケーブルテレビ **kēburu-terebi** cable television, cable (TV)

ケチャップ **kechappu** ketchup

けち **kechi** miser; けちをつける **kechi o tsukeru** find fault with

けちけちした **kechikechi shita** niggardly

けち(な) **kechi (na)** mean; miserly; tight-fisted

けちる **kechiru** be stingy with

けだもの **kedamono** brute

怪我 **kega** injury; 怪我をさせる **kega o saseru** injure; 怪我をする **kega o suru** injure

怪我をした **kega o shita** injured

汚す **kegasu** ruin; violate; tarnish

毛皮 **kegawa** fur; coat (*of animal*)

刑 **kei** punishment; sentence

敬愛する **keiai suru** revere

競馬 **keiba** the races

競馬場 **keiba-jō** racecourse

刑罰 **keibatsu** punishment

軽べつ **keibetsu** contempt; scorn

軽べつした **keibetsu shita** scornful

軽べつする **keibetsu suru** despise; pour scorn on

軽べつ的(な) **keibetsuteki (na)** derogatory, pejorative

警備 **keibi** security guard

警備部門 **keibi-bumon** security

警備員 **keibiin** security guard

警備する **keibi suru** guard

警備隊 **keibitai** guard

警棒 **keibō** nightstick

経度 **keido** longitude

経営 **keiei** administration; management

経営学 **keieigaku** business studies; management studies

経営学大学院 **keieigaku-daigakuin** business school

経営学修士 **keieigaku-shūshi** MBA, master in business administration

経営陣 **keieijin** management team

経営コンサルタント **keiei-konsarutanto** management consultant

経営(の) **keiei (no)** managerial; administrative

経営者 **keiei-sha** manager; administrator

経営者側 **keieisha-gawa** management

経営する **keiei suru** manage; run; administer

軽減する **keigen suru** alleviate

敬語 **keigo** honorific language

敬具 **keigu** (Kind) regards; Yours truly

経費 **keihi** expenses

景品 **keihin** free gift; giveaway

警報 **keihō** alarm; alert; 暴風警報 **bōfū-keihō** storm warning; 警報を発する **keihō o hassuru** raise the alarm

敬意 **keii** respect; deference; 敬意を払う **keii o harau** show respect to

掲示 **keiji** notice

刑事 **keiji** detective

掲示板 **keijiban** bulletin board

軽自動車 **kei-jidōsha** compact MOT

経過 **keika** passage

警戒警報 **keikai-keihō** security alert

軽快(な) **keikai (na)** nimble; springy

警戒している **keikai shite iru** be on the alert

計画 **keikaku** project; plan, scheme

計画性のない **keikakusei no nai** disorganized

計画する **keikaku suru** plan; propose; stage *demonstration*

計画的(な) **keikakuteki (na)** premeditated

警官 **keikan** policeman

経過する **keika suru** elapse

経験 **keiken** experience

敬けん(な) **keiken (na)** devout; pious

経験のない **keiken no nai** inexperienced

経験する **keiken suru** experience; undergo

経験豊か(な) **keiken yutaka (na)** experienced; seasoned

計器 **keiki** gauge

景気 **keiki** economic conditions; the market; 景気沈滞している *keiki-chintai shite iru* be sluggish (*of business*); be in the doldrums

景気後退 **keiki-kōtai** recession

けいこ **keiko** practice

傾向 **keikō** tendency, inclination; trend

警告 **keikoku** caution; warning

渓谷 **keikoku** ravine

警告する **keikoku suru** warn

蛍光(の) **keikō (no)** fluorescent

蛍光ペン **keikō-pen** marker, highlighter

啓もうする **keimō suru** enlighten

刑務所 **keimu-sho** jail, prison; 刑務所に入れる *keimusho ni ireru* imprison, lock up

敬礼 **keirei** salute

経歴 **keireki** career history; background

けいれん **keiren** cramp; spasm; convulsion; twitch

けいれんする **keiren suru** twitch; have a fit; get cramp

経理部 **keiribu** accounts (department)

敬老の日 **Keirō no hi** Respect-for-the-Aged Day

計略 **keiryaku** trick; plot

計算 **keisan** calculation; count

計算まちがい **keisan machigai** miscalculation

計算する **keisan suru** calculate; count; figure out

警察 **keisatsu** police

警察庁 **Keisatsuchō** National Police Agency

警察官 **keisatsukan** officer

警察国家 **keisatsu-kokka** police state

警察署 **keisatsu-sho** police station

警察署長 **keisatsu-shochō** police chief; marshal

形成外科 **keisei-geka** plastic surgery

形成外科医 **keisei-gekai** plastic surgeon

形成する **keisei suru** mold, shape

形跡 **keiseki** signs; traces; evidence

傾斜 **keisha** slant

警視庁 **Keishichō** Metropolitan Police Department

形式 **keishiki** formality

敬称 **keishō** polite form of address; honorific

軽食 **keishoku** refreshments; snack

軽食堂 **keishokudō** snack bar; truck stop

軽率(な) **keisotsu (na)** hasty, rash; indiscreet; thoughtless

携帯電話 **keitai-denwa** cell phone, mobile phone *Br*

携帯用(の) **keitaiyō (no)** portable

携帯用テレビ **keitaiyō terebi** portable (TV)

毛糸 **keito** wool; yarn

系統 **keitō** system

系統的に **keitōteki ni** systematically

契約 **keiyaku** agreement; contract

契約不履行 **keiyaku-furikō** breach of contract

契約上(の) **keiyakujō (no)** contractual

契約書 **keiyakusho** contract

形容詞 **keiyōshi** adjective

経由で **keiyu de** via, by way of

経済 **keizai** economy

経済学 **keizai-gaku** economics

経済学者 **keizai-gakusha** economist

経済状態 **keizai-jōtai** economic circumstances

経済企画庁 **Keizai-kikakuchō** Economic Planning Agency of Japan

経済緊縮 **keizai-kinshuku** austerity

経済的(な) **keizaiteki (na)** economical

ケーキ **kēki** cake

結果 **kekka** effect; result; ...の結果
... **no kekka** result from; ...の結果
である ... **no kekka de aru** be due
to
結核 **kekkaku** tuberculosis
血管 **kekkan** blood vessel
欠陥 **kekkan** defect
欠陥のある **kekkan no aru**
defective, faulty
欠勤 **kekkin** absence
欠勤(の) **kekkin (no)** absent
結婚 **kekkon** marriage; matrimony
結構(な) **kekkō (na)** decent; good;
sufficient; enough; adequate; 結構
です **kekkō desu** no, thank you
結婚記念日 **kekkon-kinenbi**
wedding anniversary
結婚式 **kekkon-shiki** marriage,
wedding
結婚した **kekkon shita** married
結婚する **kekkon suru** get married;
marry
結婚指輪 **kekkon-yubiwa** wedding
ring
決行する **kekkō suru** carry out
結局 **kekkyoku** after all; ultimately
血球 **kekkyū** corpuscle
獣 **kemono** beast
煙い **kemui** smoky
煙に巻く **kemu ni maku** mystify
煙 **kemuri** fumes; smoke
毛虫 **kemushi** caterpillar
圏 **ken** sphere; circle; bloc
腱 **ken** tendon
県 **ken** prefecture
券 **ken** ticket
軒 **-ken** *countword for houses*
件 **ken** matter, affair
剣 **ken** sword
けなした **kenashita** disparaging
けなす **kenasu** criticize; get at; put
down
顕微鏡 **kenbikyō** microscope
見物 **kenbutsu** sightseeing
見物人 **kenbutsu-nin** sightseer;
visitor; onlooker
建築 **kenchiku** architecture
建築現場 **kenchiku-genba**
construction site
建築業者 **kenchiku-gyōsha**
builder

建築家 **kenchiku-ka** architect
剣道 **kendō** kendo
検閲 **ken'etsu** censorship
検閲する **ken'etsu suru** censor
見学する **kengaku suru** visit; tour
権限 **kengen** authority; mandate;
power
権威 **ken'i** authority
献辞 **kenji** dedication (*in book*)
検事 **kenji** public prosecutor
堅実(な) **kenjitsu (na)** sound;
sensible
けんか **kenka** argument; quarrel;
fight
けんかっぱやい **kenkappayai**
quarrelsome
けんかする **kenka suru** argue; fall
out; quarrel; fight; brawl
献血 **kenketsu** blood donation
献金 **kenkin** contribution; donation
健康 **kenkō** fitness; health
健康保険 **kenkō-hoken** health
insurance
肩甲骨 **kenkōkotsu** shoulder blade
建国記念日 **Kenkoku-kinenbi**
National Foundation Day
健康(な) **kenkō (na)** healthy
健康に悪い **kenkō ni warui**
unhealthy
健康に良い **kenkō ni yoi**
wholesome
健康診断 **kenkō-shindan** medical,
checkup
健康診断書 **kenkō-shindansho**
medical certificate
健康食品 **kenkō-shokuhin** health
food
健康的(な) **kenkōteki (na)** healthy
謙虚 **kenkyo** modesty
検挙 **kenkyo** arrest
謙虚(な) **kenkyo (na)** modest
検挙する **kenkyo suru** arrest; round
up
研究 **kenkyū** research; study
研究所 **kenkyū-jo** laboratory, lab
研究開発 **kenkyū-kaihatsu** R&D,
research and development
研究休暇 **kenkyū-kyūka** sabbatical
研究者 **kenkyū-sha** researcher
研究室 **kenkyū-shitsu** laboratory,
lab (*room*)

賢明(な) **kenmei (na)** judicious; wise

賢明さ **kenmei-sa** wisdom

検問所 **kenmonjo** checkpoint

嫌悪 **ken'o** hatred; disgust; revulsion

憲法 **kenpō** constitution POL

憲法記念日 **kenpō-kinenbi** Constitution Day

憲法(の) **kenpō (no)** constitutional

権利 **kenri** claim; right; 権利を与える **kenri o ataeru** entitle

権力 **kenryoku** power

検査 **kensa** inspection; check; examination

検査係 **kensa-gakari** inspector

検索する **kensaku suru** retrieve

検査する **kensa suru** examine; inspect

検札係 **kensatsu-gakari** inspector (on bus etc)

検察側 **kensatsugawa** prosecution

検察官 **kensatsukan** public prosecutor

建設 **kensetsu** building, construction; 建設中で **kensetsu-chū de** under construction

建設現場 **kensetsu-genba** building site

建設業 **kensetsugyō** building trade

建設業界 **kensetsu-gyōkai** construction industry

建設する **kensetsu suru** construct

建設的(な) **kensetsuteki (na)** constructive

検死 **kenshi** autopsy, postmortem

検死官 **kenshi-kan** coroner

検診 **kenshin** checkup

献身 **kenshin** dedication; devotion

献身的(な) **kenshinteki (na)** devoted

研修 **kenshū** training

研修会 **kenshū-kai** refresher course

研修コース **kenshū kōsu** training course

研修生 **kenshūsei** trainee

研修する **kenshū suru** train

検出器 **kenshutsu-ki** detector

謙そん **kenson** humility; modesty

検討 **kentō** examination; investigation; exploration

見当 **kentō** speculation; aim; direction; 見当もつかない **kentō mo tsukanai** I haven't a clue

見当違いで **kentō-chigai de** beside the point

見当はずれ(な) **kentōhazure (na)** misplaced

検討する **kentō suru** explore possibility; discuss; take stock

倹約 **ken'yaku** thrift

健全(な) **kenzen (na)** healthy; robust; wholesome

建造物 **kenzōbutsu** construction

潔白 **keppaku** innocence

けれど(も) **keredo(mo)** but; however; though

ける **keru** kick; kick around

けさ **kesa** this morning

消しゴム **keshi-gomu** eraser

消印 **keshiin** postmark

景色 **keshiki** landscape; scenery; sights; view

化身 **keshin** embodiment; incarnation

化粧 **keshō** make-up; 化粧をする **keshō o suru** make up, put on make-up

化粧品 **keshōhin** cosmetics

化粧ポーチ **keshō-pōchi** vanity case

化粧室 **keshōshitsu** powder room

決済 **kessai** settlement

傑作 **kessaku** masterpiece

決算 **kessan** settlement; financial results

欠席 **kesseki** absence

欠席(の) **kesseki (no)** absent

欠席する **kesseki suru** miss

血栓症 **kessenshō** thrombosis

決心 **kesshin** resolution

決心する **kesshin suru** decide, make up one's mind

決して...ない **kesshite... nai** never

血色の良い **kesshoku no yoi** ruddy

決勝戦 **kesshōsen** final

決勝点 **kesshōten** winning post

傑出した **kesshutsu shita** outstanding

結束 **kessoku** unity; solidarity

消す **kesu** switch off; put out; erase; delete; extinguish; drown *sound*

ケース **kēsu** holder; case; housing

けた **keta** figure; digit; beam; girder

ケータイ **kētai** cell phone

決着 **ketchaku** conclusion; settlement; 決着をつける *ketchaku o tsukeru* settle

けつ **ketsu** ∨ ass

血圧 **ketsuatsu** blood pressure

欠乏 **ketsubō** lack

血液型 **ketsuekigata** blood group

血液銀行 **ketsueki-ginkō** blood bank

血液検査 **ketsueki-kensa** blood test

血縁関係(の) **ketsuen-kankei (no)** related by birth

決議 **ketsugi** resolution

結合する **ketsugō suru** unite

決意 **ketsui** determination

欠員 **ketsuin** opening

結膜炎 **ketsumakuen** conjunctivitis

結末 **ketsumatsu** conclusion

けつの穴 **ketsu no ana** ∨ asshole

欠落 **ketsuraku** omission; lack

決裂 **ketsuretsu** breakdown; rupture

結露 **ketsuro** condensation

結論 **ketsuron** conclusion; decision; 結論に達しない *ketsuron ni tasshinai* inconclusive; 結論を下す *ketsuron o kudasu* conclude

血流 **ketsuryū** bloodstream

決定 **kettei** decision; ruling

決定戦 **ketteisen** decider

決定者 **kettei-sha** decision-maker

決定する **kettei suru** decide; shape *future*

決定的(な) **ketteiteki (na)** conclusive; decisive; definitive; fatal *error*

欠点 **ketten** drawback; flaw; shortcoming

欠点のない **ketten no nai** faultless; immaculate

血統 **kettō** pedigree; blood line

険しい **kewashii** rugged; steep

毛染め **kezome** dye; tint

削る **kezuru** whittle; shave; sharpen

木 **ki** tree

気 **ki** mood; feeling; will; mind; 気が重い *ki ga omoi* feel down; mind; 気が変わった *ki ga kawatta* have changed one's mind; 気を失う *ki o ushinau* lose consciousness; 気が強い *ki ga tsuyoi* strong-willed; ... 気がする ... *ki ga suru* have a feeling that; 気をつけて *ki o tsukete* take care; 気がいい *ki ga ii* good-natured; 気を静めなさい *ki o shizumenasai* calm down; ...気がない ... *ki ga nai* don't want to ...; → *also ki ga ..., ki ni ..., ki no ..., ki o ...*

キー **kī** key COMPUT, MUS

気圧 **kiatsu** air pressure

気圧計 **kiatsukei** barometer

きば **kiba** fang; tusk

基盤 **kiban** base; foundation

気晴らし **kibarashi** amusement; distraction

きびきびした **kibikibi shita** brisk; energetic

機敏(な) **kibin (na)** agile

厳しい **kibishii** strict; severe; rigorous; grim; bitter *weather*; inhospitable *climate*; rigid *principles*; tight *security*

厳しく **kibishiku** severely; strictly

厳しくする **kibishiku suru** tighten

厳しさ **kibishi-sa** difficulty; severity

規模 **kibo** scale, size

希望 **kibō** hope; wish; 希望を持つ *kibō o motsu* hope

キーボード **kībōdo** keyboard

希望的観測 **kibōteki-kansoku** wishful thinking

気分 **kibun** frame of mind; 行きたい気分です *ikitai kibun desu* I feel like going

気分がいい **kibun ga ii** feel well

気分がさわやかになる **kibun ga sawayaka ni naru** feel refreshed

気分がすぐれない **kibun ga sugurenai** poorly

気分が悪い **kibun ga warui** unwell

気分転換に **kibun-tenkan ni** for a change

基地 **kichi** base MIL

気違い **kichigai** insane; lunatic

気違いじみた **kichigaijimita** insane

きちんと **kichin to** properly; conscientiously; tight *shut*

きちんとした **kichin to shita** neat, tidy; きちんとした服装をする *kichin to shita fukusō o suru* dress up

きちんとする **kichin to suru** tidy oneself up

機長 **kichō** captain (*of aircraft*)

基調演説 **kichō-enzetsu** keynote speech

貴重品 **kichōhin** valuables

きちょうめんな **kichōmen na** methodical; scrupulous

貴重(な) **kichō (na)** precious, valuable

気立てのよい **kidate no yoi** good-natured

軌道 **kidō** orbit; …を軌道に乗せる *… o kidō ni noseru* send into orbit

機動部隊 **kidō-butai** task force

気取らない **kidoranai** unassuming

気取る **kidoru** put on airs

起動させる **kidō saseru** boot up

起動する **kidō suru** boot up; log on

気取った **kidotta** pretentious

消える **kieru** disappear; go away; go out (*of light*); fade

寄付 **kifu** contribution; donation

寄付者 **kifu-sha** contributor

寄付する **kifu suru** contribute; donate

飢餓 **kiga** starvation

気が合う **ki ga au** compatible

着替え **kigae** change of clothes

着替える **kigaeru** change *clothes*

気がかりである **kigakari de aru** be on tenterhooks

気が変わる **ki ga kawaru** change one's mind

気が狂う **ki ga kuruu** go mad; be out of one's mind

気が狂った **ki ga kurutta** crazy

気軽(な) **kigaru (na)** cheerful; lighthearted

気が進まない **ki ga susumanai** disinclined; reluctant

気が立つ **ki ga tatsu** get worked up

気がついている **ki ga tsuite iru** be conscious; be aware of, be conscious of

気がつかない **ki ga tsukanai** be unaware of, be unconscious of

気がつく **ki ga tsuku** regain consciousness, come to; become aware of; notice; observe

喜劇 **kigeki** comedy

喜劇(の) **kigeki (no)** comic

機嫌 **kigen** humor; mood; temper; 機嫌がよい／悪い *kigen ga yoi / warui* be in a good/bad mood

起源 **kigen** origin

期限 **kigen** deadline; time limit; 期限が切れる *kigen ga kireru* be up, have expired

期限切れ **kigengire** expiry

期限切れで **kigengire de** out of date

記号 **kigō** symbol

器具 **kigu** instrument; gadget; appliance; apparatus

企業 **kigyō** enterprise; company

企業秘密 **kigyō-himitsu** trade secret

企業家 **kigyō-ka** entrepreneur

企業家(の) **kigyō-ka (no)** entrepreneurial

企業(の) **kigyō (no)** corporate

規範 **kihan** norm; model

気品 **kihin** elegance; grace; dignity

基本 **kihon** basis; foundation

基本的(な) **kihonteki (na)** basic; fundamental; underlying

キーホルダー **kī-horudā** key-ring

黄色 **kiiro** yellow; 黄色で *kiiro de* at amber MOT

黄色(の) **kiiro (no)** yellow

きじ **kiji** pheasant

記事 **kiji** article; item; story

生地 **kiji** dough; fabric; material

期日 **kijitsu** deadline; 期日が来ている *kijitsu ga kite iru* be due

基準 **kijun** standard; benchmark; criterion

基準利率 **kijun-riritsu** base rate

幾何学 **kikagaku** geometry

幾何学的(な) **kikagakuteki (na)** geometric(al)

機会 **kikai** chance, opportunity

機械 **kikai** machine; mechanism

機械化する **kikaika suru** mechanize

機械工 **kikaikō** mechanic

機械(の) **kikai (no)** mechanical

機械類 **kikairui** machinery

機械的(な) **kikaiteki (na)** mechanical

規格 **kikaku** standard

企画 **kikaku** plan; project

規格化する **kikakuka suru** standardize

期間 **kikan** duration; period; term

機関 **kikan** institution

器官 **kikan** organ ANAT

帰還 **kikan** return

季刊(の) **kikan (no)** quarterly

機関銃 **kikanjū** machine gun

機関士 **kikanshi** engineer NAUT, RAIL

気管支炎 **kikanshi-en** bronchitis

帰化する **kika suru** become naturalized

着飾る **kikazaru** dress up

奇形 **kikei** deformity

棄権 **kiken** abstention

危険 **kiken** risk; danger; hazard; 危険にさらされている **kiken ni sarasarete iru** be at stake; 危険にさらす **kiken ni sarasu** endanger; jeopardize; risk; 危険を冒す **kiken o okasu** take a risk; risk

危険人物 **kiken-jinbutsu** security risk

危険(な) **kiken (na)** dangerous; risky

棄権する **kiken suru** abstain

危機 **kiki** crisis

聞き出す **kikidasu** extract *information*; worm out of

聞き返す **kikikaesu** ask back; ask again

聞き間違える **kikimachigaeru** mishear

効き目 **kikime** effect; 効き目がある **kikime ga aru** effective; potent ◊ tell, have an effect

ききん **kikin** famine

基金 **kikin** foundation; fund

聞き覚えがある **kikioboe ga aru** that sounds familiar

危機的(な) **kikiteki (na)** critical

聞き取る **kikitoru** catch

きっかけ **kikkake** cue; hint; opportunity

きっかりに **kikkari ni** promptly, on the dot

キック **kikku** kick

キックオフ **kikku-ofu** kickoff

気候 **kikō** climate

寄稿 **kikō** contribution

聞こえない **kikoenai** inaudible

聞こえる **kikoeru** hear; sound; seem ◊ audible

帰国 **kikoku** return to one's own country

着込む **kikomu** wrap up warmly

寄稿する **kikō suru** contribute

菊 **kiku** chrysanthemum

聞く **kiku** listen; ask; listen to

効く **kiku** work, take effect

気配り **kikubari** consideration; care

気球 **kikyū** balloon

気前がいい **kimae ga ii** generous

気前のよさ **kimae no yosa** generosity

気まぐれ **kimagure** whim

気まぐれ(な) **kimagure (na)** inconsistent; fickle; quirky; volatile

決まり **kimari** rule

決まり文句 **kimarimonku** cliché

きまりの悪い **kimari no warui** embarrassed

決まった **kimatta** fixed

決まっていない **kimatte inai** undecided

気まずい **kimazui** awkward; embarrassing; 気まずい思いをさせる **kimazui omoi o saseru** embarrass

決める **kimeru** arrange; decide

黄身 **kimi** yolk

君 **kimi** you (*familiar*)

気味 **kimi** feeling; a touch of ; 気味の悪い **kimi no warui** eerie; 風邪気味だ **kazegimi da** I have a slight cold

君が代 **Kimigayo** Kimigayo (*Japanese national anthem*)

君(の) **kimi (no)** your (*familiar*)

君達 **kimitachi** you (*plural familiar*)

君達(の) **kimitachi (no)** your (*plural familiar*)

機密 **kimitsu** secret

機密(の) **kimitsu (no)** classified

気持ち **kimochi** feeling

気持ちのいい **kimochi no ii** delightful; pleasant

気持ちの悪い **kimochi no warui** disgusting; lousy

気持ちよく **kimochi yoku** nicely

キモい **kimoi** lousy, crap

着物 **kimono** kimono

気難しい **kimuzukashii** demanding; morose

奇妙なことに **kimyō na koto ni** strangely enough

金 **kin** gold

機内(の) **kinai (no)** inflight

勤勉(な) **kinben (na)** industrious; painstaking

緊張 **kinchō** tension

緊張緩和 **kinchō-kanwa** détente

緊張した **kinchō shita** tense

緊張して **kinchō shite** keyed-up

緊張する **kinchō suru** tense up

近代化する **kindaika suru** modernize

近代的(な) **kindaiteki (na)** modern

禁断症状 **kindan-shōjō** withdrawal symptoms

禁煙 **kin'en** smoking forbidden, no smoking

記念 **kinen** commemoration; memento

記念日 **kinenbi** anniversary

記念碑 **kinenhi** memorial; monument

記念品 **kinenhin** memento

記念(の) **kinen (no)** memorial

記念する **kinen suru** commemorate; 記念して **kinen shite** in memory of

金額 **kingaku** sum, amount

近眼(の) **kingan (no)** shortsighted

キング **kingu** king (*in cards*)

キングサイズ(の) **kingu-saizu (no)** king-size(d)

金魚 **kingyo** gold fish

気に入る **ki ni iru** take a liking to; appeal to

気にかかる **ki ni kakaru** bother; worry

気にかける **ki ni kakeru** care

気になる **ki ni naru** worry

キニーネ **kinīne** quinine

金色(の) **kin'iro (no)** golden

気にさわる **ki ni sawaru** obnoxious; offensive

気にする **ki ni suru** mind

均一料金 **kin'itsu-ryōkin** flat rate

禁じられた **kinjirareta** forbidden

禁じる **kinjiru** forbid; prohibit

近所 **kinjo** vicinity

金欠(の) **kinketsu (no)** broke

近畿 **Kinki** *western district of Osaka, Kyoto and Hyogo etc*

金庫 **kinko** safe

近郊 **kinkō** environs; suburbs

均衡 **kinkō** equilibrium; balance

禁固刑 **kinkokei** imprisonment

金婚式 **kinkonshiki** golden wedding anniversary

金庫室 **kinkoshitsu** vaults

緊急着陸 **kinkyū-chakuriku** emergency landing

緊急脱出装置 **kinkyū-dasshutsu-sōchi** escape chute

緊急事態 **kinkyū-jitai** emergency; state of emergency

緊急(な) **kinkyū (na)** urgent

金めっき **kinmekki** gilt

勤務日 **kinmubi** workday

勤務中である **kinmuchū de aru** be on duty

勤務時間 **kinmu-jikan** office hours

勤務時間中 **kinmu-jikanchū** during work hours

筋肉 **kinniku** muscle

金(の) **kin (no)** gold

機能 **kinō** faculty; function

昨日 **kinō** yesterday

気の合う **ki no au** congenial

気の小さい **ki no chiisai** nervous

気の毒に思う **ki no doku ni omou** pity; take pity on

気のきいた **ki no kiita** clever

きのこ **kinoko** mushroom

気の狂った **ki no kurutta** mad, loony, nutty, crackbrained

気の狂っている **ki no kurutte iru** mental

気の短い **ki no mijikai** impatient

気の抜けた **ki no nuketa** flat *beer*

気乗りのしない **kinori no shinai** half-hearted; lukewarm

気の強い **ki no tsuyoi** strong-willed; tough

緊迫 **kinpaku** tension

金髪(の) **kinpatsu (no)** fair *hair*

きんぽうげ **kinpōge** buttercup

勤労感謝の日 **Kinrō-kansha no hi** Labor Thanksgiving Day

禁止 **kinshi** ban, prohibition

近視眼的(な) **kinshiganteki (na)** shortsighted, myopic

近視(の) **kinshi (no)** near-sighted, myopic

近親相かん **kinshin-sōkan** incest

禁止する **kinshi suru** ban, prohibit

禁酒 **kinshu** abstinence from alcohol

きんたま **kintama** ∨ balls, nuts

均等に **kintō ni** evenly; equally

絹 **kinu** silk

絹(の) **kinu (no)** silk

金曜日 **kin'yōbi** Friday

金融(の) **kin'yū (no)** monetary

金融市場 **kin'yū-shijō** money market

記入する **kinyū suru** complete; enter; fill out

金細工師 **kinzaikushi** goldsmith

金属 **kinzoku** metal

金属(の) **kinzoku (no)** metal, metallic

金属的(な) **kinzokuteki (na)** metallic

禁ずる **kinzuru** forbid

記憶 **kioku** memory

記憶力 **kiokuryoku** memory

記憶容量 **kioku-yōryō** storage capacity COMPUT

気温 **kion** temperature

気を落ち着ける **ki o ochitsukeru** compose oneself; calm oneself

気を静める **ki o shizumeru** pull oneself together

気をそらす **ki o sorasu** create a diversion

キオスク **kiosuku** kiosk

気を使う **ki o tsukau** worry about; 気を使わないで下さい **ki o tsukawanaide kudasai** you needn't have bothered

気をつける **ki o tsukeru** take care, watch out; make sure

気を失う **ki o ushinau** faint, pass out

きっぱりした **kippari shita** decisive

きっぱりと **kippari to** point-blank

切符 **kippu** ticket

切符売場 **kippu-uriba** ticket office; box office

嫌い **kirai** hate; dislike

きらきら光る **kirakira hikaru** glisten; twinkle

気楽(な) **kiraku (na)** easygoing; lighthearted

きらめき **kirameki** blaze; glint

きらめく **kirameku** glint; twinkle

嫌う **kirau** dislike

嫌われている **kirawarete iru** be in the doghouse

切れ **-kire** countword for slices of bread, meat, cakes etc

切れ端 **kirehashi** shred; scrap

きれい(な) **kirei (na)** nice, pretty, lovely; clean

きれいにする **kirei ni suru** clean; clean out

切れ目 **kireme** nick, cut

切れる **kireru** run out; be cut off; be sharp; expire

キレる **kireru** snap, lose control

切れた **kireta** flat; off (*of switch*); 電話が切れた **denwa ga kireta** I was disconnected

切れている **kirete iru** worn out; be out (*of light*)

亀裂 **kiretsu** rift; crack

きり **kiri** paulownia

霧 **kiri** fog; mist; 霧のかかった **kiri no kakatta** misty

切り上げる **kiriageru** revalue; round up *figure*; cut short

切り出す **kiridasu** broach; begin to talk about; quarry

切り離す **kiri hanasu** isolate

切り開く **kirihiraku** slit, cut open

切り株 **kirikabu** stump

切り替える **kirikaeru** switch; change; transfer

切り傷 **kirikizu** cut; slash

切り口 **kirikuchi** cut, slit

きりん **kirin** giraffe

切り抜ける **kirinukeru** negotiate; wriggle out of

切り抜き **kirinuki** clipping, cutting

切り抜く **kirinuku** cut out

切り落とす **kiriotosu** lop off; shave

切り下げ **kirisage** devaluation; reduction

切り下げる **kirisageru** devalue; reduce

霧雨 **kirisame** drizzle

切りそろえる **kirisoroeru** trim

キリスト **Kirisuto** Christ

キリスト教 **Kirisuto-kyō** Christianity

キリスト教(の) **Kirisuto-kyō (no)** Christian

キリスト教徒 **Kirisuto-kyōto** Christian

切り倒す **kiritaosu** chop down, cut down

切り立った **kiritatta** sheer

切り取る **kiritoru** cut off

規律 **kiritsu** discipline, order

起立 **kiritsu** stand up; all stand!

切り詰める **kiritsumeru** cut back; trim, prune

規律正しい **kiritsutadashii** orderly

切り分ける **kiriwakeru** carve

キロバイト **kirobaito** kilobyte

キログラム **kiroguramu** kilogram

記録 **kiroku** chronicle; record(s); log; reading (*from meter etc*)

記録文書 **kiroku-bunsho** transcript

記録係 **kiroku-gakari** scorer

記録保持者 **kiroku-hojisha** record holder

記録する **kiroku suru** record; document; keep score

記録破り(の) **kirokuyaburi (no)** record-breaking

キロメーター **kiromētā** kilometer

切る **kiru** cut; disconnect; switch off; hang up; shuffle *cards*; write *check*

着る **kiru** wear; put on

気力 **kiryoku** spirit; mental energy

器量の悪い **kiryō no warui** homely, ugly

気さく(な) **kisaku (na)** approachable, friendly

規制 **kisei** controls; regulation

寄生虫 **kiseichū** parasite

既製服(の) **kiseifuku (no)** ready-to-wear

既製(の) **kisei (no)** off the peg, ready-made

規制する **kisei suru** control,

regulate

奇跡 **kiseki** miracle

奇跡的(な) **kisekiteki (na)** miraculous

着せる **kiseru** dress; help … dress

季節 **kisetsu** season

記者 **kisha** journalist, reporter; correspondent

記者会見 **kisha-kaiken** press conference

岸 **kishi** shore

きしむ **kishimu** creak; squeak

気質 **kishitsu** disposition, temperament

気性 **kishō** nature; temperament

気象学 **kishōgaku** meteorology

気象学者 **kishōgaku-sha** meteorologist

気象(の) **kishō (no)** meteorological

騎手 **kishu** rider; jockey

基礎 **kiso** basis, foundation; rudiments

起訴 **kiso** prosecution LAW

基礎知識 **kiso-chishiki** working knowledge

基礎準備 **kiso-junbi** groundwork

規則 **kisoku** regulation, rule

規則的(な) **kisokuteki (na)** even, regular

起訴する **kiso suru** charge, prosecute

基礎的(な) **kisoteki (na)** basic, fundamental, rudimentary

喫茶店 **kissaten** coffee shop

キス **kisu** kiss; キスをする *kisu o suru* kiss

奇数(の) **kisū (no)** odd *number*

北 **kita** north

北アメリカ **Kita-Amerika** North America

北アメリカ人 **Kita-Amerika-jin** North American

北アメリカ(の) **Kita-Amerika (no)** North American

北ベトナム **Kita-Betonamu** North Vietnam

北ベトナム(の) **Kita-Betonamu (no)** North Vietnamese

北朝鮮 **Kita-Chōsen** North Korea

北朝鮮人 **Kita-Chōsen-jin** North Korean

北朝鮮(の) **Kita-Chōsen (no)** North Korean

鍛える **kitaeru** exercise; train

期待 **kitai** expectation(s)

機体 **kitai** fuselage

気体 **kitai** gas

期待はずれ **kitaihazure** disappointment

期待はずれ(な) **kitaihazure (na)** disappointing

期待する **kitai suru** expect

帰宅する **kitaku suru** return home

汚い **kitanai** dirty, grubby; sordid

北(の) **kita (no)** north; northerly; northern

キッチン **kitchin** kitchen; kitchenette

きっちり **kitchiri** tightly; punctually; exactly

既定値(の) **kiteichi (no)** default COMPUT

起点 **kiten** starting point

気転, 機転 **kiten** tact; 気転のきかない **kiten no kikanai** tactless; 機転のきく **kiten no kiku** quickwitted

喫煙 **kitsuen** smoking

喫煙家 **kitsuen-ka** smoker

喫煙車 **kitsuen-sha** smoking car

きつい **kitsui** demanding; punishing; tight

きつね **kitsune** fox

切手 **kitte** stamp

きっと **kitto** no doubt, surely

きっと...する **kitto ... suru** be bound to do

際立って **kiwadatte** striking, conspicuous

きわどい **kiwadoi** narrow; risky; きわどい差で **kiwadoi sa de** by a narrow margin

きわめて **kiwamete** extremely

器用(な) **kiyō (na)** deft; ingenious

器用さ **kiyō-sa** dexterity; ingenuity

刻む **kizamu** cut; carve; chop

兆し **kizashi** hint; symptom

気絶させる **kizetsu saseru** stun

気絶する **kizetsu suru** faint

寄贈 **kizō** donation

寄贈者 **kizō-sha** donor

寄贈する **kizō suru** donate

傷 **kizu** damage; wound; blemish;

flaw; blot; 傷を負わせる **kizu o owaseru** wound; 傷を付ける **kizu o tsukeru** damage

傷跡 **kizuato** scar; 傷跡を残す **kizuato o nokosu** leave a scar

傷口 **kizuguchi** sore; wound

気づいていない **kizuite inai** unsuspecting

気づいている **kizuite iru** be conscious of

気づかって **kizukatte** concerned, caring

気付 **kizuke** c/o, care of

築き上げる **kizukiageru** build up

気づく **kizuku** become aware of

気詰まり **kizumari**: 彼と居ると気詰まりである **kare to iru to kizumari de aru** I feel uncomfortable with him

きずな **kizuna** bond

傷ついた **kizutsuita** injured

傷ついていない **kizutsuite inai** undamaged; uninjured

傷つける **kizutsukeru** wound; hurt; bruise

傷つきやすい **kizutsukiyasui** vulnerable

傷つく **kizutsuku** get hurt; be injured

子 **ko** child; 男の子 **otoko no ko** boy

故 **ko** the late; deceased

個 **ko** countword for small objects

香 **kō** incense

考案者 **kōan-sha** designer; inventor

考案する **kōan suru** devise

高圧ガス **kōatsu-gasu** propellant

高圧的(な) **kōatsuteki (na)** strongarm; high-pressure; authoritative

こう配 **kōbai** gradient, slope

購買意欲 **kōbai-iyoku** consumer confidence

購買契約 **kōbai-keiyaku** subscription

交番 **kōban** police box

こびる **kobiru** flatter; flirt

小人 **kobito** dwarf

こぼれる **koboreru** spill

こぼす **kobosu** spill, slop

こぶ **kobu** bump; hump

後部 **kōbu** back, rear

子分 **kobun** protégé; follower; henchman

後部(の) **kōbu (no)** rear

こぶし **kobushi** fist; こぶしで殴る *kobushi de naguru* punch; こぶし を握り締める *kobushi o nigirishimeru* clench one's fist

子豚 **kobuta** piglet

好物 **kōbutsu** favorite (food)

鉱物 **kōbutsu** mineral

紅茶茶碗 **kōcha-jawan** teacup

こう着状態 **kōchaku-jōtai** stalemate; deadlock

コーチ **kōchi** coach

こちら **kochira** this (*polite*) ◊ this way ◊ this person; this person; こちら へどうぞ *kochira e dōzo* please come this way

拘置する **kōchi suru** detain

校長 **kōchō** principal EDU

好調(な) **kōchō (na)** in good condition; good

誇張する **kōchō suru** exaggerate; magnify

広大(な) **kōdai (na)** vast

古代(の) **kōdai (no)** ancient

誇大宣伝 **kōdai-senden** hype

こだま **kodama** echo

こだわらない **kodawaranai** easy-going

こだわる **kodawaru** be obsessive; dwell on

鼓動 **kodō** beat; heartbeat; throb (*of heart*)

コード **kōdo** cable, cord

高度 **kōdo** altitude; height

行動 **kōdō** behavior; action; 行動を 起こす *kōdō o okosu* take action

小道具 **kodōgu** stage props

孤独 **kodoku** loneliness; solitude

孤独(な) **kodoku (na)** lonely; solitary

子供 **kodomo** child, kid; offspring

子供の日 **Kodomo no hi** Children's Day

子供だまし **kodomo damashi** childish nonsense

子供じみた **kodomojimita** childish

高度(な) **kōdo (na)** sophisticated

コードレス電話 **kōdoresu-denwa** cordless phone

鼓動する **kodō suru** beat; throb; pulsate

行動する **kōdō suru** behave; act

コーデュロイ **kōdyuroi** corduroy

声 **koe** voice; 声を出して *koe o dashite* aloud

小枝 **koeda** twig

光栄(な) **kōei (na)** privileged

公園 **kōen** park

後援 **kōen** patronage, sponsorship

公演 **kōen** performance

声(の) **koe (no)** vocal

後援者 **kōen-sha** backer; patron

公演する **kōen suru** patronize

公演する **kōen suru** perform

越える **koeru** exceed, surpass

越えて **koete** beyond

校閲者 **kōetsu-sha** editor

校閲する **kōetsu suru** edit

坑夫 **kōfu** miner

交付金 **kōfukin** subsidy

幸福 **kōfuku** bliss; well-being

降伏 **kōfuku** submission, surrender

降伏する **kōfuku suru** surrender

古墳 **kofun** burial mound

興奮 **kōfun** excitement, buzz

古風(な) **kofū (na)** quaint

興奮させる **kōfun saseru** excite; stimulate; turn on (*sexually*)

興奮した **kōfun shita** excited; wild *applause*; heated *discussion*; horny (*sexually*)

興奮している **kōfun shite iru** be in a flap

興奮する **kōfun suru** get excited

交付する **kōfu suru** grant

郊外 **kōgai** outskirts; suburbs

口がい **kōgai** palate

公害 **kōgai** environmental pollution

戸外で **kogai de** in the open air

郊外(の) **kōgai (no)** suburban

子会社 **kogaisha** subsidiary

工学 **kōgaku** engineering

高額(の) **kōgaku (no)** expensive

こう丸 **kōgan** testicle

小柄(な) **kogara (no)** undersized

焦がす **kogasu** burn; scorch; singe

小型化する **kogataka suru** downsize

小型(の) **kogata (no)** miniature, pocket; compact

小型トラック **kogata-torakku** pick-up (truck)

攻撃 **kōgeki** aggression; attack, offensive

攻撃する **kōgeki suru** attack, lay into

攻撃的(な) **kōgekiteki (na)** aggressive

高原 **kōgen** plateau

公言する **kōgen suru** profess

焦げる **kogeru** burn

焦げた **kogeta** charred

抗議 **kōgi** outcry; protest

講義 **kōgi** lecture; talk; 講義をする **kōgi o suru** lecture, give a lecture

こぎれい(な) **kogirei (na)** tidy; neat

こぎれいにする **kogirei ni suru** smarten up

抗議者 **kōgi-sha** protester

抗議集会 **kōgi-shūkai** protest

抗議する **kōgi suru** protest

小切手 **kogitte** check FIN

皇后 **kōgō** empress

凍えた **kogoeta** frozen

交互に **kōgo ni** alternately; mutually

口語(の) **kōgo (no)** colloquial

小言を言う **kogoto o iu** nag

こぐ **kogu** paddle; row

工業 **kōgyō** industry

鉱業 **kōgyō** mining

工業団地 **kōgyō-danchi** industrial park

工業化する **kōgyōka suru** industrialize

工業(の) **kōgyō (no)** industrial

後輩 **kōhai** junior

荒廃して **kōhai shite** in ruins

後半 **kōhan** second half

小春日和 **koharu-biyori** Indian summer

公平(な) **kōhei (na)** fair; sporting; impartial, unbias(s)ed

公平さ **kōhei-sa** fairness

コーヒー **kōhī** coffee

コーヒーブレイク **kōhī-bureiku** coffee break

コーヒーメーカー **kōhī-mēkā** coffee maker

コーヒーポット **kōhī-potto** coffee pot

子羊 **kohitsuji** lamb

公報 **kōhō** bulletin; official report

広報活動 **kōhō-katsudō** PR, public relations

候補者 **kōho-sha** candidate; contender

候補する **kōho suru** be a candidate; run for office

公表 **kōhyō** disclosure, publication

好評 **kōhyō** rave review

公表されていない **kōhyō sarete inai** unofficial

公表する **kōhyō suru** publicize; release *information*; post *profits*

こい **koi** koi, carp

恋 **koi** romantic love; 恋に落ちる **koi ni ochiru** fall in love

濃い **koi** thick; strong; dense; dark

行為 **kōi** act, deed; action

好意 **kōi** willingness; goodwill

恋人 **koibito** boyfriend; girlfriend; partner

故意でない **koi de nai** unintentional

コイン **koin** coin; token

故意に **koi ni** knowingly; intentionally

故意(の) **koi (no)** deliberate, intentional

こいのぼり **koinobori** carp banners

コインランドリー **koin-randorī** laundromat

子犬 **koinu** puppy, pup

小石 **koishi** pebble

恋しがる **koishigaru** pine for

恋しい **koishii** dear; cherished; beloved ◊ miss

恋している **koi shite iru** be in love

更衣室 **kōishitsu** changing room

好意的(な) **kōiteki (na)** favorable; sympathetic; high *opinion*

孤児 **koji** orphan

工事 **kōji** construction

こじ開ける **kojiakeru** force open

こじき **kojiki** beggar

故人 **kojin** the deceased

個人 **kojin** individual

個人秘書 **kojin-hisho** personal assistant

個人(の) **kojin (no)** individual; personal

個人主義者 **kojin-shugisha** individualist

個人的(な) **kojinteki (na)** intimate; personal; private

口実 **kōjitsu** pretext; excuse

控除 **kōjo** deduction

工場 **kōjō** factory, plant

甲状腺 **kōjōsen** thyroid (gland)

口述する **kōjutsu suru** dictate

硬貨 **kōka** coin

降下 **kōka** descent

効果 **kōka** effect

高架道路 **kōka-dōro** overpass

航海 **kōkai** crossing; sailing

後悔 **kōkai** regret; penitence; 激しい後悔 **hageshii kōkai** remorse

公会堂 **kōkaidō** auditorium; public hall

航海術 **kōkaijutsu** navigation

コカイン **kokain** cocaine, coke

航海(の) **kōkai (no)** nautical

公開(の) **kōkai (no)** public

航海士 **kōkaishi** mate; navigator

後悔している **kōkai shite iru** penitent

航海する **kōkai suru** cruise

公開する **kōkai suru** exhibit; release

後悔する **kōkai suru** regret; repent

コカコーラ **koka-kōra** Coke®

甲殻類 **kōkakurui** crustaceans

降格する **kōkaku suru** downgrade; demote

高官 **kōkan** dignitary

交換 **kōkan** exchange

高価(な) **kōka (na)** expensive, dear; valuable

交換できる **kōkan dekiru** interchangeable; exchangeable

高架(の) **kōka (no)** overhead, elevated

効果のない **kōka no nai** ineffective

交換留学 **kōkan-ryūgaku** (academic) exchange

交換する **kōkan suru** trade, swap, exchange

効果的(な) **kōkateki (na)** effective; forcible

こけ **koke** moss

口径 **kōkei** caliber

光景 **kōkei** image; sight

後継者 **kōkei-sha** replacement; successor

貢献 **kōken** contribution

後見人 **kōken-nin** guardian

貢献する **kōken suru** contribute

こけし **kokeshi** kokeshi doll

高潔 **kōketsu** integrity

高血圧 **kōketsuatsu** high blood pressure; hypertension

高潔(な) **kōketsu (na)** virtuous, high-minded

後期 **kōki** second semester; second half; 20世紀後期 **nijusseiki-kōki** the late 20th century

高気圧 **kōkiatsu** high pressure

拘禁 **kōkin** detention

高貴(な) **kōki (na)** noble

拘禁する **kōkin suru** confine; detain; intern

こきおろす **kokiorosu** disparage; criticize

高貴さ **kōki-sa** nobility

好奇心 **kōkishin** curiosity; 好奇心の強い **kōkishin no tsuyoi** curious

国家 **kokka** nation, state

国歌 **kokka** national anthem

国会 **Kokkai** the Diet; Congress; national assembly

国会議員 **Kokkai-giin** member of Congress

国家(の) **kokka (no)** national

こっけい(な) **kokkei (na)** comical

国旗 **kokki** national flag

コック **kokku** cook

コックピット **kokkupitto** cockpit

国境 **kokkyō** border, frontier

ここ **koko** here; ここだけの話 **koko dake no hanashi** between you and me

航行 **kōkō** navigation

高校 **kōkō** high school, high

ココア **kokoa** cocoa

心地悪い **kokochiwarui** uncomfortable

心地よい **kokochiyoi** pleasing

考古学 **kōkogaku** archeology

考古学者 **kōkogaku-sha** archeologist

故国 **kokoku** home, native country

広告 **kōkoku** advertisement, advertising; 広告を出す **kōkoku o dasu** advertise

公告 **kōkoku** notice

広告代理店 **kōkoku-dairiten** advertising agency

広告業界 **kōkoku-gyōkai** advertising

広告主 **kōkokunushi** advertiser

ココナッツ **kokonattsu** coconut

ここに **koko ni** in here; here

個々(の) **koko (no)** individual

心 **kokoro** mind; 心に抱く **kokoro ni idaku** harbor; cherish

心当たりがある **kokoroatari ga aru** happen to know of; 心当たりがありますか **kokoroatari ga arimasu ka** any idea …?

心細い **kokorobosoi** downhearted

心がける **kokorogakeru** bear in mind

心から **kokoro kara** dearly; sincerely; warmly

心から(の) **kokoro kara (no)** heartfelt; whole-hearted; warm

試み **kokoromi** try, attempt

試みる **kokoromiru** try, attempt

心無い **kokoronai** thoughtless; heartless

心に浮かぶ **kokoro ni ukabu** strike

心の温かい **kokoro no atatakai** warm-hearted

心の広い **kokoro no hiroi** broadminded, open-minded, liberal

心のこもった **kokoro no komotta** loving

心の中で **kokoro no naka de** inwardly, mentally

心の狭い **kokoro no semai** narrow-minded, petty

心の安らぎ **kokoro no yasuragi** peace of mind

心をかき乱す **kokoro o kakimidasu** stir up

心を奪う **kokoro o ubau** enthrall

快く **kokoroyoku** gladly

志 **kokorozashi** ambition; aspiration; wish

志ざす **kokorozasu** aspire to; aim to

心遣い **kokorozukai** thoughtfulness

心付け **kokorozuke** gratuity

心強い **kokorozuyoi** encouraging; reassuring

高校生 **kōkōsei** high school student

航行する **kōkō suru** navigate

航空 **kōkū** aviation

黒板 **kokuban** blackboard

航空便で **kōkūbin de** by air, by airmail

航空母艦 **kōkū-bokan** aircraft carrier

国防省長官 **Kokubōshō-chōkan** Defense Secretary

国防総省 **Kokubō-sōshō** Department of Defense

国土 **kokudo** country; land

国道 **kokudō** national route

克服できない **kokufuku dekinai** insurmountable

克服する **kokufuku suru** overcome; master

航空会社 **kōkū-gaisha** airline

国外退去命令 **kokugai-taikyo-meirei** deportation order

航空学(の) **kōkūgaku (no)** aeronautical

国語 **kokugo** national language; Japanese

告白 **kokuhaku** admission, confession

告白する **kokuhaku suru** confess

告発 **kokuhatsu** accusation

告発する **kokuhatsu suru** accuse

酷評する **kokuhyō suru** criticize severely; hit out at

刻印 **kokuin** stamp; imprint

黒人 **kokujin** black (*person*)

航空管制 **kōkū-kansei** air-traffic control

航空管制塔 **kōkū-kanseitō** control tower

航空機 **kōkūki** aircraft

国民 **kokumin** subject; fellow citizen; the public

国民の休日 **Kokumin no kyūjitsu** 4th of May holiday

国民総生産 **kokumin-sōseisan**

GNP, gross national product

穀物 **kokumotsu** cereal, grain

国務長官 **Kokumu-chōkan** Secretary of State

国務省 **Kokumushō** State Department

国内(の) **kokunai (no)** domestic, internal

国内線 **kokunai-sen** domestic flight

国内総生産 **kokunai-sōseisan** GDP, gross domestic product

国王 **kokuō** king

国連 **Kokuren** UN

国立公園 **kokuritsu-kōen** national park

コクる **kokuru:** …にコクった **… ni kokutta** he/she said he/she loved

国債 **kokusai** national debt

国際 **kokusai** international

国際電話 **kokusai-denwa** international call

国際競技会 **kokusai-kyōgikai** international competition

国際連合 **Kokusai-rengō** United Nations

国際収支 **kokusai-shūshi** balance of payments

国際的(な) **kokusaiteki (na)** international, cosmopolitan

国際通貨基金 **Kokusai-tsūka-kikin** IMF, International Monetary Fund

国籍 **kokuseki** nationality

航空写真 **kōkū-shashin** aerial photograph

酷使 **kokushi** abuse

航空書簡 **kōkū-shokan** air letter

告訴されている **kokuso sarete iru** be accused of

告訴する **kokuso suru** accuse; sue

航空宇宙産業 **kōkū-uchū-sangyō** aerospace industry

国有化する **kokuyūka suru** nationalize

国税庁 **Kokuzeichō** Internal Revenue (Service); National Tax Administration

航空図 **kōkūzu** chart

顧客 **kokyaku** client, patron

故郷 **kokyō** home; home town

皇居 **Kōkyo** Imperial Palace

公共事業 **kōkyō-jigyō** public utilities

交響曲 **kōkyōkyoku** symphony

公共(の) **kōkyō (no)** public

呼吸 **kokyū** respiration, breathing

高級官僚 **kōkyū-kanryō** mandarin; high-ranking official

高級(な) **kōkyū (na)** exclusive; high-class; high-quality

こま **koma** counter, piece, man

細かい **komakai** detailed; finicky; fine *distinction*

鼓膜 **komaku** eardrum

コマ漫画 **koma-manga** (comic) strip

小間物 **komamono** notions

こま結び **komamusubi** square knot; reef knot

高慢ちき(な) **kōmanchiki (na)** conceited; stuck-up

高慢(な) **kōman (na)** haughty

困らせる **komaraseru** puzzle; put on the spot

困る **komaru** be in trouble; be badly off

コマーシャル **komāsharu** commercial, ad

コマーシャルソング **komāsharu-songu** (advertising) jingle

困った **komatta** troubled; vexed

困っている **komatte iru** be in a fix

米 **kome** rice (*uncooked*)

コメディアン **komedian** comedian

こめかみ **komekami** temple ANAT

コメント **komento** comment

込み合った **komiatta** packed, crowded

小道 **komichi** lane; path; track

小見出し **komidashi** subheading

込み入った **komiitta** involved, complex

項目 **kōmoku** item

顧問 **komon** adviser, consultant

顧問料 **komon-ryō** fee, retainer

こうもり **kōmori** bat

子守歌 **komoriuta** lullaby

込む **komu** be crowded

小麦 **komugi** wheat

小麦粉 **komugiko** flour

公務員 **kōmuin** civil servant, official

こうむる **kōmuru** incur, suffer; receive

鉱脈 **kōmyaku** deposit; vein (*of ore*)

巧妙(な) **kōmyō (na)** ingenious; subtle

コミュニケーション **komyunikēshon** communication

コミュニティー **komyunitī** community

コーン **kōn** cone

粉 **kona** powder

粉々になる **konagona ni naru** smash; ...を粉々にする **... o konagona ni suru** smash to pieces

粉々に割れる **konagona ni wareru** shatter

粉々に割る **konagona ni waru** shatter

構内 **kōnai** campus; yard

コーナーキック **kōnā kikku** corner kick, corner

粉ミルク **konamiruku** formula

コンバイン **konbain** combine harvester

今晩 **konban** this evening, tonight;

こんばんは **konbanwa** good evening

コンビニエンスストア **konbiniensu-sutoa** convenience store

こん棒 **konbō** club; stick

こんぶ **konbu** kelp

昆虫 **konchū** insect

込んだ **konda** crowded

込んでいる **konde iru** busy

コンデンスミルク **kondensu-miruku** condensed milk

今度 **kondo** this time; next time

コンドミニアム **kondominiamu** condo(minium)

コンドーム **kondōmu** condom

今度(の) **kondo (no)** forthcoming

混同する **kondō suru** confuse, muddle

子猫 **koneko** kitten

光年 **kōnen** light year

更年期 **kōnenki** menopause

こねる **koneru** knead

コーンフレーク **kōnfurēku** cereal

婚外(の) **kongai (no)** extramarital

懇願する **kongan suru** plead with

根源 **kongen** root

今月 **kongetsu** this month

混合 **kongō** mixture

公認会計士 **kōnin-kaikeishi** certified public accountant

公認されていない **kōnin sarete inai** unofficial

後任者 **kōnin-sha** successor

紺色 **kon'iro** navy blue

根気 **konki** perseverance

根気強さ **konkizuyo-sa** patience; persistence

コンクリート **konkurīto** concrete

根拠 **konkyo** ground, reason; cause; basis (*of argument*)

根拠のない **konkyo no nai** groundless, unfounded

コンマ **konma** comma

こんな **konna** this kind of; such

困難 **konnan** hardship

こんなに **konna ni** so; to this extent; こんなにたくさん **konna ni takusan** so many

困難(な) **konnan (na)** painful

こんにちは **konnichiwa** good afternoon; hello, hi; how are you?

この **kono** this; the

このあいだ **kono aida** the other day; that time

このごろは **kono goro wa** nowadays

この辺に **kono hen ni** around here

この前(の) **kono mae (no)** the last; the one before this

好ましい **konomashii** agreeable; pleasant

好ましくない **konomashiku nai** undesirable; unsavory

好み **konomi** choice, preference, inclination; taste

木の実 **konomi** nut

好む **konomu** like; be fond of

このよう(な) **kono yō (na)** such

この世の **kono yo no** earthly

コンパクトディスク **konpakuto-disuku** CD, compact disc

コンパス **konpasu** compasses

根本 **konpon** foundation; base

根本的(な) **konponteki (na)** radical; basic

コンプレックス **konpurekkusu** complex

コンピューター **konpyūtā** computer

コンピューターゲーム **konpyūtā-gēmu** computer game

混乱 **konran** confusion, muddle; disruption

混乱させる **konran saseru** confuse, muddle; muddle up

混乱した **konran shita** confused, disoriented

混乱している **konran shite iru** be mixed up

コンサルタント **konsarutanto** consultant

コンサルタント業 **konsarutanto-gyō** consultancy

コンサート **konsāto** concert

コンサートマスター **konsāto-masutā** concertmaster

コンセント **konsento** outlet

今週 **konshū** this week

コンタクトレンズ **kontakuto-renzu** contact lens

コンテナ **kontena** container

コンテスト **kontesuto** competition, contest

コントラバス **kontorabasu** double-bass

コントラスト **kontorasuto** contrast

コントロール **kontorōru** control

コントロールパネル **kontorōru-paneru** control panel

コントロールする **kontorōru suru** control

困惑させる **konwaku saseru** baffle

困惑する **konwaku suru** be baffled

コニャック **konyakku** cognac

婚約 **kon'yaku** engagement

婚約者 **kon'yaku-sha** fiancé; fiancée

婚約している **kon'yaku shite iru** engaged

婚約する **kon'yaku suru** get engaged

婚約指輪 **kon'yaku-yubiwa** engagement ring

購入 **kōnyū** purchase; purchasing

購入品 **kōnyūhin** purchase

購入する **kōnyū suru** purchase

混雑する **konzatsu suru** be crowded

婚前(の) **konzen (no)** premarital

根絶する **konzetsu suru** eradicate, stamp out

コピー **kopī** photocopy; copy

コピー犯罪 **kopī-hanzai** copycat crime

コピー機 **kopī-ki** photocopier, copier

コピーライター **kopī-raitā** copy-writer

コピーする **kopī suru** photocopy; copy

こっぴどく **koppidoku** soundly; severely

コップ **koppu** glass

甲羅 **kōra** shell

こらえる **koraeru** bear; persevere; repress

こらこら **korakora** now, now!

行楽地 **kōrakuchi** resort

行楽客 **kōrakukyaku** vacationer

コラム **koramu** column

コラムニスト **koramunisuto** columnist

凍らせる **kōraseru** freeze

コーラス **kōrasu** chorus

これ **kore** this; this one; これだけです **kore dake desu** that's all, thanks; これでおしまい **kore de oshimai** that's it!

高齢者 **kōrei-sha** senior citizen

これから **kore kara** from now on

コレクション **korekushon** collection; selection, assortment

コレクトコール **korekuto-kōru** collect call

これまでで **kore made de** yet

これら **korera** these

これらの **korera no** these

コレステロール **koresuterōru** cholesterol

氷 **kōri** ice; ice cube

凝り固まった **korikatamatta** entrenched; fanatical

こりる **koriru** learn one's lesson

孤立 **koritsu** isolation

公立学校 **kōritsu-gakkō** public school

公立(の) **kōritsu (no)** public

孤立させる **koritsu saseru** isolate, cut off

孤立した **koritsu shita** isolated

効率的(な) **kōritsuteki (na)** efficient

頃 **koro** time ◊ when; 子供の頃 **kodomo no koro** when I was a child

転ぶ **korobu** fall over

転がる **korogaru** roll

転がす **korogasu** roll over

こおろぎ **kōrogi** cricket

ころころ変わる **korokoro kawaru** changeable ◊ change a lot

ころころ転がる **korokoro korogaru** roll over and over

コロン **koron** colon

殺し屋 **koroshi-ya** hired killer; hitman

殺す **korosu** kill; slay

こる **koru** become stiff; be absorbed in

凍る **kōru** freeze, freeze over

コルク **koruku** cork

コールスロー **kōrusurō** coleslaw

凍るよう(な) **kōru yō (na)** freezing

攻略する **kōryaku suru** capture; conquer

考慮 **kōryo** consideration; 考慮に入れる **kōryo ni ireru** make allowances

綱領 **kōryō** summary; outline; platform

考慮する **kōryo suru** consider; think about

荒涼とした **kōryō to shita** desolate, stark

交流 **kōryū** alternating current

拘留されている **kōryū sarete iru** be in custody

拘留する **kōryū suru** detain; hold

濃さ **ko-sa** depth (of color); shade; thickness

こう彩 **kōsai** iris (of eye)

交際する **kōsai suru** associate with; go out with

耕作 **kōsaku** cultivation

小作人 **kosaku-nin** farmworker

耕作する **kōsaku suru** cultivate

降参する **kōsan suru** give in, surrender

交差する **kōsa suru** cross, intersect

交差点 **kōsaten** intersection; junction

個性 **kosei** individuality; personality

構成 **kōsei** composition; formation; organization; structure

後世 **kōsei** posterity

抗生物質 **kōsei-busshitsu** antibiotic

公正(な) **kōsei (na)** unbias(s)ed, just

高性能(の) **kōseinō (no)** high performance; high-powered

構成されている **kōsei sarete iru** be comprised of, be made up of

厚生省 **Kōseishō** Ministry of Health and Welfare

構成する **kōsei suru** compose, comprise, constitute; structure, plan

校正する **kōsei suru** proofread

校正刷り **kōseizuri** proof (of book)

鉱石 **kōseki** ore

航跡 **kōseki** wake (of ship)

戸籍係 **koseki-gakari** registrar

戸籍登記所 **koseki-tōkisho** registrar's office

交戦 **kōsen** engagement MIL

光線 **kōsen** ray

好戦的(な) **kōsenteki (na)** belligerent

後者 **kōsha** the latter

校舎 **kōsha** school building

腰 **koshi** hip; waist

孔子 **Kōshi** Confucius

公使 **kōshi** envoy; minister

格子 **kōshi** grate, grating, grid

講師 **kōshi** lecturer

腰掛ける **koshikakeru** sit; perch

こし器 **koshiki** strainer

公式 **kōshiki** formula

公式訪問 **kōshiki-hōmon** official visit; state visit

公式(の) **kōshiki (no)** formal; official; ceremonial

行進 **kōshin** march

更新 **kōshin** renewal; update

香辛料 **kōshinryō** spice; 香辛料の利いた **kōshinryō no kiita** spicy

行進する **kōshin suru** march; parade

更新する **kōshin suru** renew, roll over; update

行使する **kōshi suru** use; exercise *right*

こうして **kōshite** thus

個室 **koshitsu** private room

固執する **koshitsu suru** persist, keep on; cling to

こしょう **koshō** pepper

故障 **koshō** breakdown

呼称 **koshō** form of address

交渉 **kōshō** negotiation

故障中で **koshōchū de** out of order

故障のない **koshō no nai** trouble-free

故障する **koshō suru** break down

交渉する **kōshō suru** negotiate

絞首台 **kōshudai** gallows

公衆電話 **kōshū-denwa** pay phone

公衆電話ボックス **kōshū-denwa-bokkusu** (tele)phone booth

絞首刑にする **kōshukei ni suru** hang

こそ **-koso** (*intensifier*): これこそぼくが見たものだ **kore-koso boku ga mita mono da** this is the very one that I saw

高僧 **kōsō** high priest

構想 **kōsō** idea; blueprint; plan

高層ビル **kōsō-biru** high rise

こそ泥 **kosodoro** thief; pilferer

高速道路 **kōsoku-dōro** expressway, freeway

高速ギヤ **kōsoku-giya** high (gear)

拘束力のある **kōsokuryoku no aru** binding

拘束する **kōsoku suru** tie down

酵素洗剤 **kōso-senzai** biological detergent

骨折 **kossetsu** break, fracture

骨折した **kossetsu shita** broken

骨折する **kossetsu suru** break, fracture

こっそり **kossori** stealthily; secretly

こっそりと **kossori to** on the sly

こす **kosu** filter, strain

越す **kosu** exceed

コース **kōsu** track; course

香水 **kōsui** perfume, scent

降水量 **kōsuiryō** rainfall

こする **kosuru** rub; scrape

コスト **kosuto** cost

答え **kotae** answer, response

こたえる **kotaeru** affect; respond; 暑さが彼の身にこたえる **atsusa ga kare no mi ni kotaeru** the heat is telling on him; 期待にこたえる **kitai ni kotaeru** live up to expectations

答える **kotaeru** respond; answer

固体 **kotai** solid

抗体 **kōtai** antibody

後退 **kōtai** retreat; regression; setback

交替 **kōtai** alternation; shift; 交替で…をする **kōtai de ... o suru** take turns in doing; do ... in rotation

交替する, 交代する **kōtai suru** alternate; change places; take over

光沢 **kōtaku** luster

こたつ **kotatsu** heated table with quilt cover

こっち **kotchi** this; this one

こて **kote** curling tongs

皇帝 **kōtei** emperor

行程 **kōtei** journey; stage (*of journey*)

公定歩合 **kōtei-buai** bank rate

固定概念 **koteigainen** stereotype

皇帝(の) **kōtei (no)** imperial

固定された **kotei sareta** secure; fixed

固定した **kotei shita** fixed

固定する **kotei suru** secure, fix

肯定する **kōtei suru** answer in the affirmative

公的(な) **kōteki (na)** official

古典 **koten** classic

好転 **kōten** upturn; improvement

こてんぱんにやっつける **kotenpan ni yattsukeru** massacre

好転させる **kōten saseru** turn around; change for the better

鋼鉄 **kōtetsu** steel

鋼鉄製(の) **kōtetsusei (no)** steel

事, こと **koto** business; matter, affair, thing

琴 **koto** *Japanese string instrument*

コート **kōto** court SP

こう頭 **kōtō** larynx

言葉 **kotoba** language; phrase; word

言葉につまる **kotoba ni tsumaru** be lost for words

言葉の壁 **kotoba no kabe**
language barrier

言葉を選ぶ **kotoba o erabu** choose
one's words

言葉遣い **kotobazukai** wording;
language

…ことができる **… koto ga dekiru**
can, be able to

高等(な) **kōtō (na)** advanced; high-
level

異なる **kotonaru** differ ◊ dissimilar

口頭(の) **kōtō (no)** oral

今年 **kotoshi** this year

断る **kotowaru** refuse, turn down

ことわざ **kotowaza** proverb, saying

こつ **kotsu** knack, trick

交通 **kōtsū** traffic

骨盤 **kotsuban** pelvis

好都合 **kōtsugō** convenience

交通標識 **kōtsū-hyōshiki** traffic
sign

交通違反 **kōtsū-ihan** traffic
violation

交通事故 **kōtsū-jiko** traffic accident

交通渋滞 **kōtsū-jūtai** traffic
congestion; (traffic) jam; gridlock

交通機関 **kōtsū-kikan** means of
transportation

こつこつ **kotsukotsu**: こつこつやる
kotsukotsu yaru plug away,
persevere

凝った **kotta** elaborate; ornate;
fussy

凍った **kōtta** frozen

こってりした **kotteri shita** thick;
heavy; rich

骨とう品 **kottō-hin** antique

コットン **kotton** cotton

骨とう屋 **kottō-ya** antique dealer

幸運, 好運 **kōun** good luck; lucky
break; fortune; 幸運を祈る *kōun o
inoru* keep one's fingers crossed;
wish … well

幸運(な) **kōun (na)** fortunate;
happy

幸運(の) **kōun (no)** lucky

小売業者 **kouri-gyōsha** retailer

小売価格 **kouri-kakaku** retail price

小売値で **kourine de** retail

小売りされる **kouri sareru** retail

子牛 **koushi** calf

子牛肉 **koushiniku** veal

こわばる **kowabaru** stiffen; 顔がこわ
ばる *kao ga kowabaru* wince

こわばった **kowabatta** stiff

怖がらせる **kowagaraseru** frighten,
scare

怖がる **kowagaru** be afraid; be
frightened of; dread

怖い **kowai** scary

壊れない **kowarenai** unbreakable;
indestructible

壊れる **kowareru** break, come apart

壊れた **kowareta** broken

壊れやすい **kowareyasui**
breakable, fragile

壊す **kowasu** break; ruin

小屋 **koya** hut, shed

荒野 **kōya** the wilds; wilderness

肥やし **koyashi** manure

雇用 **koyō** employment

こよみ **koyomi** calendar

雇用者 **koyō-sha** employer

小指 **koyubi** little finger; little toe

口座 **kōza** account

講座 **kōza** course

小細工 **kozaiku** gimmick; cheap
trick

鉱山 **kōzan** mine

小銭 **kozeni** change, small change

公然(の) **kōzen (no)** public

公然と **kōzen to** publicly

構造 **kōzō** mechanism; structure

構造工学 **kōzō-kōgaku** structural
engineering

構造的(な) **kōzōteki (na)** structural

洪水 **kōzui** flood; flooding

小遣い **kozukai** allowance

小突く **kozuku** poke; nudge; jog

小包 **kozutsumi** package, parcel

句 **ku** phrase

区 **ku** ward (*of city*); district; zone

配る **kubaru** deal; distribute, give
out

区別 **kubetsu** distinction; 区別をす
る *kubetsu o suru* differentiate
between, distinguish between;
mark out, single out

首 **kubi** neck; 首を切る *kubi o kiru*
decapitate; fire

首になる **kubi ni naru** be fired

首にする **kubi ni suru** fire

くぼみ **kubomi** dip; recess

くぼんだ **kubonda** hollow

口 **kuchi** mouth; 口が軽い *kuchi ga karui* be talkative; 口がうまい *kuchi ga umai* have a smooth tongue; 口が悪い *kuchi ga warui* have a sharp tongue; 口をはさむ *kuchi o hasamu* interrupt, break in

くちばし **kuchibashi** beak

口紅 **kuchibeni** lipstick

唇 **kuchibiru** lip

口笛 **kuchibue** whistle; 口笛をふく *kuchibue o fuku* whistle

口げんか **kuchigenka** row

口げんかする **kuchigenka suru** have words

口汚い **kuchigitanai** abusive

口答えする **kuchigotae suru** answer back

口ひげ **kuchihige** mustache

口(の) **kuchi (no)** oral

口のきけない **kuchi no kikenai** dumb, mute

口先だけ **kuchisaki dake** lip service

口うるさい **kuchiurusai** nagging

口調 **kuchō** tone of voice

空調 **kūchō** air-conditioning

空中で **kūchū de** in midair

空中(の) **kūchū (no)** aerial

管 **kuda** tube

砕ける **kudakeru** splinter; be smashed

砕けた **kudaketa** chatty; informal; plain; easy

果物 **kudamono** fruit

くだらない **kudaranai** trashy; trifling

下りになる **kudari ni naru** descend

下り坂(の) **kudarizaka (no)** downhill

下さい **kudasai** please; ドアを締めて下さい *doa o shimete kudasai* would you close the door, please?

下さる **kudasaru** give (*polite*); be kind enough to do

下す **kudasu** bring in; hand down; lower

クーデター **kūdetā** coup

くどい **kudoi** persistent; repetitive; tedious

口説く **kudoku** make advances; seduce

空腹 **kūfuku** hunger

九月 **kugatsu** September

くぎ **kugi** nail; spike

空軍 **kūgun** air force

空軍基地 **kūgun-kichi** airbase

空白 **kūhaku** vacuum

くい **kui** stake, post

食いぶち **kuibuchi** keep; *kuibuchi o kasegu* earn one's keep

食い違う **kuichigau** clash

区域 **kuiki** area; sector

食い込む **kuikomu** eat into; encroach on

食い物にする **kuimono ni suru** prey on

食い止める **kuitomeru** keep in check, hold in check

食いつく **kuitsuku** bite

クイズ **kuizu** quiz

クイズ番組 **kuizu-bangumi** quiz program

くじゃく **kujaku** peacock

くじ **kuji** raffle

くじ引き **kujibiki** draw

鯨 **kujira** whale

苦情 **kujō** complaint; 苦情を言う *kujō o iu* complain

駆除する **kujo suru** exterminate

茎 **kuki** stalk; stem

空気 **kūki** air

クッキー **kukkī** cookie

屈強(な) **kukkyō (na)** brawny

空港 **kūkō** airport

苦境 **kukyō** plight, predicament

空虚 **kūkyo** void, emptiness

くま **kuma** bear

くま手 **kumade** rake

組 **kumi** class; team

組合 **kumiai** association

組み合わせ **kumiawase** combination

組み合わせる **kumiawaseru** combine

組曲 **kumikyoku** suite MUS

組み立て **kumitate** assembly

組み立てる **kumitateru** assemble, put together

くも **kumo** spider

雲 **kumo** cloud

苦もん **kumon** agony

クモの巣 **kumo no su** cobweb, spiderweb

くもりガラス **kumori-garasu** opaque glass

曇り **kumori** cloudy weather

曇り(の) **kumori (no)** dull

曇る **kumoru** cloud over; mist up

曇った **kumotta** cloudy; overcast

組む **kumu** unite; pair; assemble; fold *arms*; cross *legs*

君 **-kun** Mr; Ms (*to address younger people*)

宮内庁 **Kunaichō** Imperial Household Agency

くねくねした **kunekune shita** wavy; zigzag

くねくねする **kunekune suru** wriggle

くねらす **kunerasu** wiggle

くねる **kuneru** crooked; wind round; twist

国 **kuni** country, nation; 国の内外で **kuni no naigai de** at home and abroad

くんくんかぐ **kunkun kagu** sniff

くんくん泣く **kunkun naku** whine

苦悩 **kunō** anguish; distress

苦悩した **kunō shita** martyred

訓練する **kunren suru** drill; train; groom

君臨する **kunrin suru** reign

勲章 **kunshō** medal; decoration

クーポン **kūpon** voucher, coupon

くら **kura** saddle

倉 **kura** storehouse

比べものにならない **kurabemono ni naranai** there's no comparison

比べる **kuraberu** compare

クラブ **kurabu** club, society

暗がり **kuragari** dark; gloom

くらげ **kurage** jellyfish

くらい **-kurai** around, approximately ◊ like ◊ at least

位 **kurai** rank; grade; throne

暗い **kurai** dark; somber; dismal

暗い色(の) **kurai iro (no)** dark

クライマックス **kuraimakkusu** climax, high point

クラッカー **kurakkā** cracker

暗くなる **kuraku naru** darken, dim

くらくらする **kurakura suru** feel dizzy; be in a whirl

クラクション **kurakushon** horn MOT

クラリネット **kurarinetto** clarinet

暮し **kurashi** living

クラシック(な) **kurashikku (na)** classical

暮しに困らない **kurashi ni komaranai** be comfortable

クラッシュ **kurasshu** crash COMPUT

クラッシュする **kurasshu suru** crash COMPUT

クラス **kurasu** class

暮らす **kurasu** live

クラスメート **kurasumēto** classmate

クラッチ **kuratchi** clutch MOT

暗やみ **kurayami** darkness

クレジット **kurejitto** credit

クレジットカード **kurejitto-kādo** credit card, charge card

クレーン **kurēn** crane

くれる **kureru** give

暮れる **kureru** get dark; come to an end; be absorbed in

クレヨン **kureyon** crayon

くり **kuri** chestnut

クリアランスセール **kuriaransu-sēru** clearance sale

繰り返し **kurikaeshi** chorus, refrain; repetition

繰り返し(の) **kurikaeshi (no)** repetitive

繰り返している **kurikaeshite iru** duplicate

繰り返して言う **kurikaeshite iu** repeat

繰り返す **kurikaesu** repeat; echo

クリック **kurikku** click COMPUT; ...をクリックする **... o kurikku suru** click on

クリーム **kurīmu** cream

クリームチーズ **kurīmu-chīzu** cream cheese

クリーム色 **kurīmu-iro** cream

クリームソーダ **kurīmu sōda** soda

クリーニングする **kurīningu suru** clean

クリーニング店 **kurīningu-ten** laundry

クリップ **kurippu** clip; paperclip

クリスマス **Kurisumasu** Christmas;

Christmas Day

クリスタルガラス **kurisutaru-garasu** crystal

黒 **kuro** black

苦労 **kurō** effort, struggle, trouble; toil

黒い **kuroi** black

黒字で **kuroji de** in the black, in credit

黒子 **kuroko** puppeteer in Bunraku

クロコダイル **kurokodairu** crocodile

クローク **kurōku** checkroom, cloakroom

黒幕 **kuromaku** mastermind

クロム **kuromu** chrome, chromium

黒帯 **kuro-obi** black belt

黒っぽい **kuroppoi** dark

クロール **kurōru** crawl

クロスカントリー(スキー) **kurosu-kantorī (sukī)** cross-country (skiing)

苦労する **kurō suru** struggle ◊ you'll/he'll etc have a job

クロスワードパズル **kurosuwādo-pazuru** crossword (puzzle)

クローズアップ **kurōzu-appu** close-up

クローズアップする **kurōzu-appu suru** close up, move closer; zoom in

来る **kuru** come; fall (of night)

くるくる回る **kurukuru mawaru** whirl

くるくる回す **kurukuru mawasu** twirl

車 **kuruma** vehicle; car

車いす **kurumaisu** wheelchair

車回し **kuruma-mawashi** driveway

くるみ **kurumi** walnut

くるみ割り **kurumiwari** nutcrackers

くるむ **kurumu** wrap; tuck in (in bed)

苦しい **kurushii** agonizing

苦しめる **kurushimeru** distress

苦しみ **kurushimi** suffering; torment

苦しむ **kurushimu** suffer

狂った **kurutta** unbalanced

クルーズ **kurūzu** cruise

草 **kusa** grass

くさび **kusabi** wedge

くさい **kusai** smelly

鎖 **kusari** chain; lead, leash

腐る **kusaru** decay, rot, go bad

腐った **kusatta** rotten, bad, tainted; rancid; sick *society*

癖 **kuse** habit; peculiarity

くせに **kuse ni** although; in spite of

癖になる **kuse ni naru** be addictive

くしゃくしゃにする **kushakusha ni suru** rumple

くしゃみ **kushami** sneeze; くしゃみをする *kushami o suru* sneeze

くし **kushi** comb

苦心した **kushin shita** labored

くそ **kuso** ∨ fuck!; shit!

空想 **kūsō** fantasy; 空想にふける *kūsō ni fukeru* daydream

くそったれ **kusottare** ∨ asshole

クッション **kusshon** cushion

くすぶる **kusuburu** smolder

くすぐる **kusuguru** tickle

くすぐったがり(の) **kusuguttagari (no)** ticklish

くすぐったい **kusuguttai** ticklish

くすくす笑い **kusukusu warai** chuckle, giggle

くすくす笑う **kusukusu warau** chuckle, giggle, titter

薬 **kusuri** drug, medicine

薬指 **kusuri-yubi** ring finger

くたばっちまえ **kutabatchimae** ∨ fuck off!

くたびれる **kutabireru** get tired; become worn out

くたくた(の) **kutakuta (no)** exhausted; worn out

苦闘 **kutō** struggle

苦闘する **kutō suru** struggle

句読点 **kutōten** punctuation marks

句読点の打ち方 **kutōten no uchikata** use of punctuation

靴 **kutsu** shoe

苦痛 **kutsū** distress; pain; agony

靴べら **kutsu-bera** shoehorn

覆す **kutsugaesu** demolish

靴ひも **kutsu-himo** shoelace

屈辱 **kutsujoku** humiliation

屈辱的(な) **kutsujokuteki (na)** degrading, humiliating

靴直し **kutsunaoshi** heel bar

くつろぐ **kutsurogu** relax, unwind; make oneself at home

くつろいだ **kutsuroida** free and easy

靴下 **kutsushita** sock

靴屋 **kutsu-ya** shoestore

靴墨 **kutsuzumi** shoe polish

くっついている **kuttsuite iru** stick together

くっつける **kuttsukeru** knit together

くっつく **kuttsuku** adhere

桑 **kuwa** mulberry

加える **kuwaeru** add; ...に加えて ... **ni kuwaete** in addition to

くわがたむし **kuwagatamushi** stag beetle

詳しい **kuwashii** detailed; knowledgeable ◊ be well versed in

詳しく **kuwashiku** at length

加わらない **kuwawaranai** keep out

加わる **kuwawaru** join; be a party to

悔やむ **kuyamu** regret

悔しい **kuyashii** regrettable

くよくよ悩む **kuyokuyo nayamu** fret

空輸する **kūyu suru** fly, send by air

くず **kuzu** crumb; scrap; trash, garbage

くず入れ **kuzuire** trashcan

くずかご **kuzukago** waste basket

崩れ落ちる **kuzureochiru** topple

崩れる **kuzureru** collapse, give way; crumble

崩す **kuzusu** change *money*; destroy; crumble

キャベツ **kyabetsu** cabbage

キャビア **kyabia** caviar

キャディー **kyadī** caddie

キャド-キャム **kyado-kyamu** CAD-CAM

客観的(な) **kyakkanteki (na)** objective

却下する **kyakka suru** throw out, reject

客 **kyaku** customer; diner (*person*); guest, visitor

脚注 **kyakuchū** footnote

脚本 **kyakuhon** script

脚本家 **kyakuhon-ka** scriptwriter

客間 **kyakuma** guestroom

客船 **kyakusen** cruise liner

客車 **kyakusha** coach

客室 **kyakushitsu** cabin; compartment

客室係 **kyakushitsu-gakari** cabin crew; maid

脚色 **kyakushoku** dramatization, adaptation

脚色する **kyakushoku suru** dramatize, adapt

キャンバス **kyanbasu** canvas

キャンデー **kyandē** candy; toffee

キャンパス **kyanpasu** campus

キャンピングカー **kyanpingu-kā** camper, motor home

キャンプ **kyanpu** camp; camping

キャンプ場 **kyanpu-jō** camp ground, campsite

キャンプする **kyanpu suru** camp

キャンセル待ち(の) **kyanseru machi (no)** on standby

キャピタルゲイン税 **kyapitarugein-zei** capital gains tax

キャップ **kyappu** cap

キャプテン **kyaputen** captain

キャラバン **kyaraban** trailer

キャリア **kyaria** career

きゃしゃ(な) **kyasha (na)** petite; slight

キャスター **kyasutā** broadcaster; newscaster; caster (*on chair*)

脚立 **kyatatsu** stepladder

キャッチャー **kyatchā** catcher

今日 **kyō** today

競売 **kyōbai** auction; 競売にかける **kyōbai ni kakeru** auction

狂暴になる **kyōbō ni naru** go berserk

共謀する **kyōbō suru** conspire

強調 **kyōchō** accent, emphasis, stress

共著者 **kyōcho-sha** co-author

強調する **kyōchō suru** accentuate, stress

強打 **kyōda** bang, whack, sock

鏡台 **kyōdai** dressing table

巨大(な) **kyodai (na)** enormous, huge

兄弟(の) **kyōdai (no)** fraternal

兄弟姉妹 **kyōdai-shimai** brothers and sisters

強打する **kyōda suru** smash; punch, sock

共同ビル **kyōdō-biru** complex

共同経営事業 **kyōdō-keiei-jigyō** partnership

共同経営者 **kyōdō-keiei-sha** partner; partnership

共同研究する **kyōdō-kenkyū suru** collaborate

協同組合(の) **kyōdō-kumiai (no)** cooperative

共同(の) **kyōdō (no)** collective, joint

虚栄心 **kyoeishin** vanity

恐怖 **kyōfu** fright, terror; horror; 恐怖にかられた **kyōfu ni karareta** be terrified

強風 **kyōfū** gale

恐怖症 **kyōfushō** phobia

狂言 **kyōgen** Noh comedy

協議 **kyōgi** consultation; conference

教義 **kyōgi** dogma; doctrine

競技 **kyōgi** athletics competition; 競技に出る **kyōgi ni deru** race

競技場 **kyōgijō** stadium, arena; field

競技会 **kyōgikai** meet

協議する **kyōgi suru** confer, discuss

競合できる **kyōgō dekiru** competitive

脅迫 **kyōhaku** threat

強迫観念 **kyōhaku-kannen** compulsion, obsession

強迫されて **kyōhaku sarete** under duress

脅迫する **kyōhaku suru** threaten

共犯者 **kyōhan-sha** accomplice, accessory

拒否 **kyohi** refusal; denial

拒否権 **kyohiken** veto; …に拒否権を行使する **... ni kyohiken o kōshi suru** veto

拒否する **kyohi suru** deny, refuse

脅威 **kyōi** menace, threat

教育 **kyōiku** education

教育実習生 **kyōiku-jisshūsei** student teacher

教育(の) **kyōiku (no)** educational

教育のある **kyōiku no aru** educated

教育する **kyōiku suru** educate; train

教育的(な) **kyōikuteki (na)** educational

教員研修 **kyōin-kenshū** teacher training

虚弱 **kyojaku** weakling

巨人 **kyojin** giant

狂人 **kyojin** maniac

狂女 **kyojo** madwoman

教条主義的(な) **kyōjō-shugiteki (na)** dogmatic

教授 **kyōju** professor

居住可能(な) **kyojū-kanō (na)** inhabitable

居住者 **kyojū-sha** resident

居住する **kyojū suru** reside

許可 **kyoka** permission; authority; clearance; 許可を得る **kyoka o eru** get permission; 許可を与える **kyoka o ataeru** clear; authorize

協会 **kyōkai** association, organization, society

境界 **kyōkai** boundary, limit

教会 **kyōkai** church

共感 **kyōkan** sympathy; empathy; …に共感する **... ni kyōkan suru** sympathize with; empathize with

許可証 **kyokashō** permit

教科書 **kyōkasho** textbook

許可する **kyoka suru** allow; permit

強化する **kyōka suru** strengthen; reinforce

恐喝者 **kyōkatsu-sha** blackmailer

狂犬病 **kyōkenbyō** rabies

狂気 **kyōki** insanity, madness

狂気(の) **kyōki (no)** insane

狂喜する **kyōki suru** go wild with joy

強硬派 **kyōkōha** hardliner

強固(な) **kyōko (na)** strong; stubborn

局 **kyoku** bureau

極 **kyoku** pole (of the earth)

曲 **kyoku** musical composition

極地(の) **kyokuchi (no)** polar

極度の疲労 **kyokudo no hirō** exhaustion

教訓 **kyokun** moral (of story)

曲線 **kyokusen** curve

局所麻酔 **kyokusho-masui** local anesthetic

極端 **kyokutan** extreme

極端(な) **kyokutan (na)** drastic, extreme

極東 **Kyokutō** Far East

極右 **kyokuu** extreme right

供給 **kyōkyū** provision, supply

供給する **kyōkyū suru** furnish, supply, provide

興味 **kyōmi** interest; ...に興味がある **... ni kyōmi ga aru** be interested in; 興味を持つ **kyōmi o motsu** take up; have an interest in

去年 **kyonen** last year

狂乱した **kyōran shita** raving mad

強烈(な) **kyōretsu (na)** forceful; overpowering

距離 **kyori** distance

協力 **kyōryoku** collaboration; cooperation; interaction

強力(な) **kyōryoku (na)** strong, powerful

協力者 **kyōryoku-sha** collaborator

協力する **kyōryoku suru** collaborate; cooperate

協力的(な) **kyōryokuteki (na)** cooperative

狭量(な) **kyōryō (na)** narrow-minded

恐竜 **kyōryū** dinosaur

恐妻家 **kyōsai-ka** henpecked husband

共産主義 **Kyōsan-shugi** Communism

共産主義者 **Kyōsan-shugisha** Communist

共産党 **Kyōsan-tō** Japanese Communist Party

虚勢 **kyosei** bravado

強勢 **kyōsei** stress, emphasis

矯正器 **kyōseiki** brace (*on teeth*)

強制送還 **kyōsei-sōkan** deportation

強制送還する **kyōsei-sōkan suru** deport

去勢する **kyosei suru** castrate, neuter

強制する **kyōsei suru** force, compel

強制的(な) **kyōseiteki (na)** compulsory; forced

教師 **kyōshi** teacher; 教師をする **kyōshi o suru** teach

狭心症 **kyōshinshō** angina

教室 **kyōshitsu** classroom

教職 **kyōshoku** teaching

拒食症 **kyoshokushō** anorexia

郷愁 **kyōshū** nostalgia

競争 **kyōsō** competition; race; 競争 の激しい **kyōsō no hageshii** competitive

競走 **kyōsō** race; running

競争相手 **kyōsō-aite** competition, competitor(s)

競走馬 **kyōsō-ba** racehorse

競争社会 **kyōsō-shakai** rat race

競争する **kyōsō suru** compete; race

競走する **kyōsō suru** race

強壮剤 **kyōsōzai** tonic

協定 **kyōtei** pact; 協定を結ぶ **kyōtei o musubu** reach agreement on

拠点 **kyoten** stronghold; base

京都 **Kyōto** Kyoto

共通に **kyōtsū ni** in common

共通(の) **kyōtsū (no)** common, mutual, shared

共和国 **kyōwakoku** republic

共和党員 **Kyōwatōin** Republican

共和党(の) **Kyōwatō (no)** Republican

教養のある **kyōyō no aru** cultivated, cultured

教養のない人 **kyōyō no nai hito** philistine

許容量 **kyoyōryō** limit

共用する **kyōyō suru** share

許容する **kyoyō suru** allow; permit

共有(の) **kyōyū (no)** communal

拒絶 **kyozetsu** rebuff; rejection; refusal

拒絶される **kyozetsu sareru** get the brushoff

拒絶する **kyozetsu suru** reject

共存 **kyōzon** coexistence

共存する **kyōzon suru** coexist

キュー **kyū** cue

九 **kyū** nine

球 **kyū** sphere

旧 **kyū** old; former

宮殿 **kyūden** palace

休業 **kyūgyō** closure, shutdown

吸引 **kyūin** suction

求人 **kyūjin** employment opportunity

求人広告 **kyūjin-kōkoku** want ad

休日 **kyūjitsu** holiday

救助 **kyūjo** rescue

救助員 **kyūjoin** lifeguard

急上昇 **kyūjōshō** jump, sudden rise

急上昇する **kyūjōshō suru** soar, rocket

救助する **kyūjo suru** rescue

救助隊 **kyūjo-tai** rescue party

九十 **kyūjū** ninety

休暇 **kyūka** vacation; leave; day off

休会 **kyūkai** recess, adjournment

休会する **kyūkai suru** adjourn

休火山 **kyūkazan** dormant volcano

休憩 **kyūkei** rest; break

休憩時間 **kyūkei-jikan** intermission, interval

休憩する **kyūkei suru** take a break

急行 **kyūkō** fast train

急行バス **kyūkō-basu** express bus

急降下 **kyūkōka** dive

急降下する **kyūkōka suru** dive; take a dive

球根 **kyūkon** bulb

急行(の) **kyūkō (no)** express

急行列車 **kyūkō-ressha** express train

窮屈(な) **kyūkutsu (na)** narrow; tight; formal; ill at ease

究極(の) **kyūkyoku (no)** ultimate

救急箱 **kyūkyū-bako** first-aid box, first-aid kit

救急車 **kyūkyūsha** ambulance

救急処置 **kyūkyū-shochi** first aid

救命ベルト **kyūmei-beruto** life belt

救命ボート **kyūmei-bōto** dinghy; lifeboat

救命胴衣 **kyūmei-dōi** life vest

救命具 **kyūmeigu** life preserver

休眠中(の) **kyūminchū (no)** dormant

急(な) **kyū (na)** urgent; sudden

急に **kyū ni** suddenly

吸入器 **kyūnyūki** inhaler

急落 **kyūraku** plunge

急落する **kyūraku suru** plummet, plunge

きゅうり **kyūri** cucumber

給料 **kyūryō** pay, salary, wage; payroll (*money*); pay check

給料日 **kyūryōbi** payday

給料体系 **kyūryō-taikei** salary scale

急流 **kyūryū** rapids

旧姓 **kyūsei** maiden name ◊ née

休戦 **kyūsen** truce

急進派 **kyūshin-ha** radical

急進的(な) **kyūshinteki (na)** radical

休職 **kyūshoku** leave of absence

給食 **kyūshoku** school meals

求職 **kyūshoku** job hunting

九州 **Kyūshū** Kyushu

吸収性(の) **kyūshūsei (no)** absorbent

吸収する **kyūshū suru** absorb, soak up

急襲する **kyūshū suru** pounce

救出する **kyūshutsu suru** extricate, free

休息 **kyūsoku** respite

急速に **kyūsoku ni** rapidly

吸水しやすい **kyūsui shiyasui** porous

休廷する **kyūtei suru** adjourn

急用 **kyūyō** urgent business

給油ポンプ **kyūyu-ponpu** gas pump

急増 **kyūzō** surge, sudden increase

M

間 **ma** interval; pause; 間をあける **ma o akeru** pause

まあ **mā** well!; oh!

まあじ **maaji** horse mackerel

真新しい **maatarashii** brand-new

まばたきする **mabataki suru** blink

幻 **maboroshi** vision REL

まぶしい **mabushii** blinding; dazzling

まぶた **mabuta** eyelid

町 **machi** town

待合室 **machiaishitsu** waiting room

待ち合わせ **machiawase** rendez-vous

待ち合わせる **machiawaseru** arrange to meet; rendezvous

待ち針 **machibari** pin

待ちぼうけを食わす **machibōke o kuwasu** break an appointment; stand up

待ち伏せ **machibuse** ambush

待ち伏せする **machibuse suru** ambush; lurk

待ち遠しい **machidōshii** long for; look forward to

間違える **machigaeru** mistake, confuse

間違えて **machigaete** by mistake

間違え様のない **machigae-yō no nai** unmistakable

間違い **machigai** error, mistake, slip

間違った **machigatta** false, wrong

間違っている **machigatte iru** be in the wrong; be wrong

間違う **machigau** make a mistake, go wrong

待ち時間 **machi-jikan** wait; waiting

マチネ **machine** matinée

待ち受ける **machiukeru** wait for; expect

まだ **mada** still, as yet; まだです *mada desu* it's not ready; まだ一時です *mada ichiji desu* it's only one o'clock

…まで **… made** until; …までどれくらいですか *… made dore kurai desu ka* how far is it to …?

…までに **… made ni** by; 月曜日までに *getsuyōbi made ni* by Monday

窓 **mado** window

窓ガラス **mado-garasu** glazing; pane; windowpane

窓口 **madoguchi** teller; wicket

前 **mae** front ◊ before; ago

前払い **maebarai** advance payment, cash in advance

前払いする **maebarai suru** pay in advance

前触れ **maebure** foretaste

前書き **maegaki** foreword

前髪 **maegami** fringe

前借り **maegari** receive in advance

前金 **maekin** (money paid in) advance

前もって **maemotte** in advance; beforehand

前向き(な) **maemuki (na)** positive; facing the front; …に前向きである *… ni maemuki de aru* be receptive to

前に **mae ni** before, previously; forward; in front

前(の) **mae (no)** front; previous, old; preceding

前売り **maeuri** advance booking

マフィア **mafia** the Mafia

マフィン **mafin** muffin

マフラー **mafurā** muffler MOT; scarf

真冬 **mafuyu** midwinter

曲り角 **magarikado** corner; turn

曲がりくねる **magarikuneru** twist

曲がりくねった **magarikunetta** twisting, winding

マーガリン **māgarin** margarine

曲がる **magaru** bend, curve; turn; wind; round

曲がった **magatta** crooked

曲げる **mageru** bend; compromise

紛らわしい **magirawashii** confusing; misleading

孫 **mago** grandchild

孫息子 **mago-musuko** grandson

孫娘 **mago-musume** granddaughter

まごつく **magotsuku** be confused

マグカップ **magukappu** mug

まぐれ(の) **magure (no)** lucky

まぐろ **maguro** tuna

麻ひ **mahi** paralysis

麻ひさせる **mahi saseru** cripple; paralyze

魔法 **mahō** magic; magic spell

魔法瓶 **mahōbin** thermos flask, vacuum flask

魔法(の) **mahō (no)** magical

まい **-mai** (*negative suffix*) not; 言うまい *iumai* I won't say

枚 **-mai** *countword for flat items*

毎… **mai…** every; 毎分 *maifun* every minute; per minute; 毎度 *maido* every time; always

舞い上がる **maiagaru** soar

迷子 **maigo** lost child

マイコン **maikon** microcomputer

マイク **maiku** microphone, mike

マイクロバス **maikurobasu** minibus

マイクロチップ **maikurochippu** (micro)chip

マイクロフィルム **maikurofirumu** microfilm

マイナス **mainasu** minus

マイナス(の) **mainasu (no)** negative

毎日 **mainichi** every day

毎日(の) **mainichi (no)** daily

舞い下りる **maioriru** fly down; swoop

マイル **mairu** mile

参る **mairu** be defeated; surrender; be exhausted; be in love; visit *temple, grave*; H go; H come

毎週 **maishū** weekly

埋葬 **maisō** burial

埋葬する **maisō suru** bury

毎年 **maitoshi** yearly

毎月 **maitsuki** monthly

麻雀 **mājan** mah-jong

間仕切り **majikiri** partition wall

まじめ(な) **majime (na)** earnest, serious; straight; conservative

混じる **majiru** be mixed

魔女 **majo** witch

任せる **makaseru** entrust; delegate

負かす **makasu** beat, defeat

負け **make** defeat

負け惜しみ **make-oshimi** sour grapes

負ける **makeru** lose

負けている **makete iru** be behind SP

マーケティング **māketingu** marketing

まき **maki** firewood

巻き **maki** reel; roll

巻き上げる **makiageru** hoist

巻き毛(の) **makige (no)** curly

巻尺 **makijaku** tape measure

巻き戻す **makimodosu** rewind

巻き物 **makimono** scroll

巻き付ける **makitsukeru** wind

巻き添え **makizoe** involvement

真っ赤(な) **makka (na)** crimson; 真っ赤なうそ *makka na uso* a downright lie

末期(の) **makki (no)** terminal; 末期 の病気 *makki no byōki* terminally ill

真っ暗(な) **makkura (na)** pitch dark

真っ黒(な) **makkuro (na)** jet-black

誠に **makoto ni** really; truly; 誠にあ りがとうございます *makoto ni arigatō gozaimasu* thank you very much indeed

まく **maku** scatter; sow

幕 **maku** act; curtain THEA; screen

膜 **maku** membrane

巻く **maku** coil; curl; wrap

幕あい **makuai** intermission; interlude

枕 **makura** pillow

枕カバー **makura-kabā** pillowcase, pillowslip

マクロ **makuro** macro

まくる **makuru** roll up; tuck up

まま **mama** like that; as is: そのまま にして*sono mama ni shite* leave it as it is

ママ **mama** mom

まあまあ **māmā** so-so

まま父 **mama-chichi** stepfather

まま母 **mama-haha** stepmother

まま息子 **mama-musuko** stepson

まま娘 **mama-musume** stepdaughter

まあまあ(の) **māmā (no)** moderate; ok, passable

マーマレード **māmarēdo** marmalade

まめ **mame** blister; corn

豆 **mame** bean

豆まき **mamemaki** bean scattering (*at the Setsubun festival*)

真水 **mamizu** freshwater

まもなく **mamonaku** before long; presently, soon

守られている **mamorarete iru** sheltered

守る **mamoru** uphold; protect; defend, stand up for; meet, keep to *deadline*

まむし **mamushi** pit viper

万 **man** ten thousand

学ぶ **manabu** learn; study

真夏 **manatsu** midsummer

万引き **manbiki** shoplifter; shoplifting

満潮 **manchō** high tide, high water

まね **mane** imitation, impersonation

マネージャー **manējā** manager

招き猫 **maneki-neko** beckoning cat (*small figure seen in shops and restaurants to invite customers in*)

招く **maneku** invite; beckon; incur

まねる **maneru** copy, imitate

まねし **maneshi** copycat

まねする **mane suru** copy; imitate

漫画 **manga** comic; cartoon

満月 **mangetsu** full moon

マニア **mania** fan; enthusiast; fanatic

間に合う **ma ni au** be suitable; be enough; be in time; catch

間に合わせ(の) **ma ni awase (no)** makeshift

間に合わせる **ma ni awaseru** make do with

万一の事 **man'ichi no koto** contingency

マニキュア **manikyua** manicure; (nail) varnish, (nail) polish

満員 **man'in** full

満場一致(の) **manjō-itchi (no)** unanimous

満期 **manki** maturity; 満期になる **manki ni naru** mature

真ん中 **mannaka** middle; ...の真ん中に... **no mannaka ni** in the middle of

万年筆 **mannenhitsu** (fountain) pen

間の取り方 **ma no torikata** timing

満杯(の) **manpai (no)** full

満腹(の) **manpuku (no)** full (up)

慢性(の) **mansei (no)** chronic

マンション **manshon** apartment; apartment block; condominium

満州 **Manshū** Manchuria

免れる **manugareru** escape from; be relieved of; be excepted from; absolve

まぬけ **manuke** dope, moron

マニュアル **manyuaru** manual

漫才 **manzai** comic duo, comic

double act

満足 **manzoku** contentment, satisfaction

満足で **manzoku de** content

満足感 **manzoku-kan** gratification; feeling of satisfaction

満足(な) **manzoku (na)** satisfactory; adequate

満足させる **manzoku saseru** gratify; indulge; satisfy

満足した **manzoku shita** full; satisfied

満足する **manzoku suru** be satisfied

マラソン **marason** marathon

まれ(な) **mare (na)** rare

マレーシア **Marēshia** Malaysia

マレーシア人 **Marēshia-jin** Malay

マレーシア(の) **Marēshia (no)** Malaysian

マリファナ **marifana** joint; marijuana, pot

マリーナ **marīna** marina

マリネ **marine** marinade

丸 **maru** circle; 丸で囲む *maru de kakomu* encircle; 丸一日 *maru ichinichi* an entire day ◊ (*suffix for names of ships*)

マルチメディア **maruchi-media** multimedia

まるで **marude** completely, entirely; まるで...であるかのように *marude ... de aru ka no yō ni* as if

丸裸で **maruhadaka de** stark naked

丸い **marui** round

丸首セーター **marukubi sētā** crew neck

丸くなる **maruku naru** curl

円くなる **maruku naru** mellow

丸くする **maruku suru** round off

マルクス主義 **Marukusu-shugi** Marxism

マルクス主義者 **Marukusu-shugi-sha** Marxist

丸める **marumeru** roll up; screw up *paper etc*

丸ぽちゃ(の) **marupocha (no)** chubby

丸太 **maruta** log

丸太小屋 **maruta-goya** log cabin

魔力 **maryoku** magic power

まさぐる **masaguru** grope; feel around

まさか **masaka** surely not!; come on! (*in disbelief*)

まさか...ない **masaka ... nai** never

まさに **masa ni** exactly

勝る **masaru** outdo; surpass; predominate

摩擦 **masatsu** friction

マシュマロ **mashumaro** marshmallow

マッサージ **massāji** massage

マッサージ師 **massāji-shi** masseur; masseuse

真っ盛り **massakari** height (*of season*); heyday

真っ逆さまに **massakasama ni** head over heels, headlong

真っ青(の) **massao (no)** pale, pallid

抹殺 **massatsu** elimination, murder

抹殺する **massatsu suru** eliminate, kill

真っ白(な) **masshiro (na)** pure white

マッシュポテト **masshupoteto** mashed potatoes

マッシュルーム **masshurūmu** mushroom

真っすぐ **massugu** straight

真っすぐ(な) **massugu (na)** straight

真っすぐにする **massugu ni suru** straighten

真っ直ぐ(の) **massugu (no)** straight; erect

ます **masu** square (*in board game*); trout; box seat (*for sumo*)

ます **-masu** (*polite verbal suffix*): 私が行きます **watashi ga ikimasu** I'm going

増す **masu** increase; build up; mount; enhance *taste*

麻酔 **masui** anesthetic

麻酔医 **masui** anesthetist

マスカラ **masukara** mascara

マスコミ **masukomi** the media

マスコミ業界 **masukomi-gyōkai** journalism; mass media

マスコット **masukotto** mascot

マスク **masuku** mask

ますます **masumasu** increasingly,

more and more; ますます長い時間 *masumasu nagai jikan* more and more time

ますます良い **masumasu yoi** all the better

マスメディア **masumedia** mass media

マスターベーションをする **masutābēshon o suru** masturbate

マスタード **masutādo** mustard

マスターキー **masutā-kī** master key; skeleton key

マスト **masuto** mast

また **mata** again; also; またね *mata ne* see you!

又貸しする **matagashi suru** sublet

マタニティーウェア **matanitī-wea** maternity dress

または **mata wa** or

抹茶 **matcha** powdered green tea

マッチ **matchi** match

マッチ箱 **matchibako** matchbox

的 **mato** target; butt (*of joke*); 的にする *mato ni suru* target

まとまりのない **matomari no nai** disjointed, rambling

まとまる **matomaru** be settled; be concluded; have coherence

まとめ **matome** round-up

まとめる **matomeru** settle; conclude; form; collect; arrange

まとも(な) **matomo (na)** decent; straight

まともにする **matomo ni suru** straighten out

まとわりつく **matowari tsuku** cling

松 **matsu** pine

待つ **matsu** wait, hold on

松葉杖 **matsubazue** crutch

まつげ **matsuge** (eye)lash

松かさ **matsukasa** pinecone

祭り **matsuri** festival

まったく **mattaku** altogether, completely; decidedly; honestly!; まったく構いません *mattaku kamaimasen* not at all!

まったく(の) **mattaku (no)** absolute, total; downright

まったく同じよう(な) **mattaku onaji yō (na)** identical

待っている **matte iru** expectant ◊ watch for

マット **matto** mat; doormat

まっとう(な) **mattō (na)** decent

マットレス **mattoresu** mattress

マウンド **maundo** mound

マウンテンバイク **mauntenbaiku** mountain bike

マウス **mausu** mouse COMPUT

マウスパッド **mausupaddo** mouse mat

マウスピース **mausupīsu** mouthpiece

マウスウォッシュ **mausu-wosshu** mouthwash

回り **mawari** circumference; rotation; spread ◊ via

回り道 **mawarimichi** detour ◊ indirect

回りに **mawari ni** around

回る **mawaru** turn; spin; rotate; swivel

まわし **mawashi** belt

回す **mawasu** pass around; pass on

回っている **mawatte iru** be spinning

麻薬 **mayaku** drug; narcotic; dope; 麻薬をやっている *mayaku o yatte iru* be on drugs

麻薬常用者 **mayaku-jōyō-sha** drug addict

麻薬密売 **mayaku-mitsubai** drug trafficking

麻薬密売人 **mayaku-mitsubai-nin** (drug) dealer, pusher

麻薬捜査官 **mayaku-sōsakan** narcotics agent

麻薬取り引き **mayaku-torihiki** (drug) dealing

真夜中 **mayonaka** midnight

マヨネーズ **mayonēzu** mayonnaise

迷う **mayou** stray, wander; lose one's way; 道に迷った *michi ni mayotta* I'm lost

まゆ **mayu** eyebrow

混ざる、交ざる **mazaru** mingle

混ぜ合わせる **mazeawaseru** combine

混ぜる **mazeru** mix, blend in

マゾヒスト **mazohisuto** masochist

マゾヒズム **mazohizumu** masochism

まず **mazu** first of all; まず第一に

mazu daiichi ni in the first place; まず最初に *mazu saisho ni* firstly, first of all

まずい **mazui** tasteless; unfortunate *choice of words*

貧しい **mazushii** poor; deprived; needy

貧しくなった **mazushiku natta** impoverished

目 **me** eye; 目が回る *me ga mawaru* heady; dizzy; 目をくらませる *me o kuramaseru* blind, dazzle; 目をくらます *me o kuramasu* blinding; 目をそらす *me o sorasu* look away; 目を奪う *me o ubau* mesmerize

芽 **me** germ; sprout

目新しい **meatarashii** novel; fresh

目新しさ **meatarashi-sa** novelty

めちゃくちゃ(な) **mechakucha (na)** disorganized

めちゃくちゃに **mechakucha ni** absurdly; めちゃくちゃに壊す *mechakucha ni kowasu* smash

めちゃめちゃにする **mechamecha ni suru** mangle

目立ちたがり屋 **medachitagariya** exhibitionist

目玉焼き **medamayaki** fried egg

メダリスト **medarisuto** medalist

メダル **medaru** medal

目立たない **medatanai** discreet; inconspicuous; unobtrusive

目立つ **medatsu** conspicuous; imposing; predominant ◊ stand out, stick out

目立って **medatsu** striking

目立った **medatta** noticeable

メドレー **medorē** medley

メガバイト **megabaito** megabyte

女神 **megami** goddess

目がない **me ga nai** have a weakness for

眼鏡 **megane** (eye)glasses

眼鏡屋 **megane-ya** optician

目が覚める **me ga sameru** wake (up)

目が覚めて **me ga samete** awake

恵まれない **megumarenai** underprivileged

恵まれている **megumarete iru** be blessed with

目薬 **megusuri** (eye)drops

銘 **mei** inscription

名 **mei** excellent; renowned; 名ピアニスト **mei-pianisuto** a renowned pianist ◊ (*countword for people*): 三名 **san-mei** three people

名案 **meian** brainwave

名簿 **meibo** directory; list, roll

命中する **meichū suru** hit; strike

めい福を祈る **meifuku o inoru** pay one's last respects (to)

銘柄 **meigara** brand

銘柄名 **meigara-mei** brand name

明白(な) **meihaku (na)** clear, plain explicit; glaring; pronounced *accent*

明治維新 **Meiji-ishin** Meiji Restoration

明治時代 **Meiji-jidai** Meiji period

名人 **meijin** virtuoso

命じる **meijiru** give orders; order

明確(な) **meikaku (na)** definite; precise

明確さ **meikaku-sa** precision

名門 **meimon** dynasty; distinguished family

名門(の) **meimon (no)** prestigious; renowned

命令 **meirei** command, order

命令形 **meireikei** imperative GRAM

命令する **meirei suru** command

迷路 **meiro** maze

明朗(な) **meirō (na)** bright; cheerful; hearty

明りょうさ **meiryō-sa** clarity

名作 **meisaku** masterpiece

名声 **meisei** fame, renown; prestige

明せきさ **meiseki-sa** clarity

名刺 **meishi** (business) card

名詞 **meishi** noun

迷信 **meishin** superstition

迷信深い **meishin-bukai** superstitious

名所 **meisho** famous place

めい想 **meisō** meditation

めい想する **meisō suru** meditate

迷惑 **meiwaku** inconvenience; 迷惑をかける **meiwaku o kakeru** trouble; bother; impose oneself on; 人に迷惑をかける **hito ni meiwaku**

o kakeru make a nuisance of oneself

迷惑(な) **meiwaku (na)** disruptive

名誉 **meiyo** credit; honor; privilege

名誉棄損 **meiyo-kison** defamation; libel; 名誉棄損にあたる **meiyo-kison ni ataru** defamatory

目隠し **mekakushi** blindfold

メキシコ **Mekishiko** Mexico

メキシコ人 **Mekishiko-jin** Mexican

メキシコ(の) **Mekishiko (no)** Mexican

メークアップをする **mēkuappu o suru** make up

めくる **mekuru** turn over, turn

めまい **memai** giddiness; vertigo

めまいがする **memai ga suru** feel dizzy, feel giddy

メモ **memo** memo; note

メモ帳 **memochō** notepad

目盛り **memori** scale; divisions on a scale

メモリー **memorī** memory COMPUT

メモする **memo suru** jot down

めん **men** noodles

面 **men** mask; face; aspect; 面と向かって **men to mukatte** face to face

綿 **men** cotton

メンバー **menbā** member

めん棒 **menbō**; rolling pin

綿棒 **menbō** absorbent cotton swab

面目 **menboku** reputation; face; …の面目をつぶす **... no menboku o tsubusu** embarrass, make lose face; 面目を失う **menboku o ushinau** lose face

面目を失って **menboku o ushinatte** in disgrace

面倒 **mendō** bother, nuisance, trouble

面倒くさい **mendō-kusai** annoying, tiresome

面倒(な) **mendō (na)** laborious; troublesome; 面倒なことになる **mendō na koto ni naru** get into trouble

めんどり **mendori** hen

免疫 **men'eki** immunity

免疫のある **men'eki no aru** immune

目に見えない **me ni mienai** invisible

目に見える **me ni mieru** visible

目にみえて **me ni miete** visibly

免除 **menjo** exemption; immunity

免除される **menjo sareru** be exempt from

免除された **menjo sareta** exempt; immune

免除する **menjo suru** exempt; excuse; exonerate

面会 **menkai** interview; meeting

面会時間 **menkai-jikan** visiting hours

めんくらわせる **menkurawaseru** fluster

免許 **menkyo** license

免許証 **menkyoshō** license; certificate

綿密(な) **menmitsu (na)** detailed; scrupulous

綿(の) **men (no)** cotton

目の不自由(な) **me no fujiyū (na)** blind; visually impaired

面積 **menseki** area

面接 **mensetsu** interview

面接者 **mensetsu-sha** interviewer

面接する **mensetsu suru** interview

面している **menshite iru** facing, looking on to

メンテナンス **mentenansu** maintenance

メニュー **menyū** menu

免税品 **menzei-hin** duty-free

免税(の) **menzei (no)** duty-free, tax-free

メリーゴーラウンド **merī-gōraundo** carousel, merry-go-round

メロディー **merodī** melody, tune

メロン **meron** melon

メールボックス **mērubokkusu** mailbox COMPUT

メル友 **merutomo** e-mail pen pal

めし **meshi** rice; food; meal (familiar)

召し上がる **meshiagaru** (polite) eat; drink

メッセージ **messēji** message

メス **mesu** scalpel

雌 **mesu** female

メーター **mētā** meter

メートル **mētoru** meter

メートル法(の) **mētoruhō (no)** metric

めったに…ない **metta ni … nai** rarely, seldom

目上ぶった **meuebutta** patronizing

目上の人 **meue no hito** superior

目覚まし時計 **mezamashi-dokei** alarm clock

めざす **mezasu** aim at

目ざわり **mezawari** eyesore

めずらしい **mezurashii** rare, uncommon

めずらしく **mezurashiku** unusually

実 **mi** fruit; nut; ear

身 **mi** body; person; meat; 身の毛のよだつ **mi no ke no yodatsu** hair-raising; 身を引く **mi o hiku** stand down, withdraw; 身をかがめる **mi o kagameru** get down

未… **mi…** not yet; 未解決 (の) **mikaiketsu (no)** unsolved

見上げる **miageru** look up

見合い **miai** arranged marriage meeting

未亡人 **mibōjin** widow

身分 **mibun** status

身分証明書 **mibun-shōmeisho** identity card, (identity) papers

身ぶり **miburi** gesture; 身ぶりで話す **miburi de hanasu** gesticulate; 身ぶりでまねる **miburi de maneru** mime

身震い **miburui** shudder

道 **michi** road; way; means; path, trail

道案内する **michiannai suru** guide; show the way

導く **michibiku** guide; steer

未知(の) **michi (no)** unknown

道のり **michinori** distance; journey; drive

満ちる **michiru** come in ◊ incoming

満ち潮 **michishio** flood tide; incoming tide

みだら **midara** sensuality

乱れる **midareru** be disordered; be chaotic; be corrupt

乱れた **midareta** disheveled; tousled

見出し **midashi** header; headline

身だしなみ **midashinami** personal hygiene; 身だしなみのよい *midashinami no yoi* well-groomed

乱す **midasu** disrupt; ruffle

ミディアム **midiamu** medium

緑の日 **Midori no hi** Green Day

緑色(の) **midori-iro (no)** green

見えなくする **mienaku suru** blot out

見える **mieru** show, show up; look; see

見え透いた **miesuita** transparent

磨く **migaku** clean; polish

身代わり **migawari** scapegoat

右 **migi** right

右側に **migigawa ni** on the right-hand side

右側(の) **migigawa (no)** right-hand

右ハンドル(の) **migi-handoru (no)** right-hand drive

右利き(の) **migikiki (no)** right-handed

右に **migi ni** right; on the right

右(の) **migi (no)** right, right-hand

右腕 **migiude** right-hand man

身ごもっている **migomotte iru** be pregnant

見事(な) **migoto (na)** splendid, wonderful

見事に **migoto ni** beautifully, marvellously

見苦しい **migurushii** unsightly; disgraceful

未払い(の) **miharai (no)** unpaid, outstanding

見晴らし **miharashi** view

見張り **mihari** lookout; sentry; 見張りをする *mihari o suru* keep watch; 見張っている *mihatte iru* keep an eye on

見本 **mihon** pattern; sample, specimen

見本市 **mihon'ichi** trade fair

短い **mijikai** brief, short

短くする **mijikaku suru** abbreviate, shorten; take up *dress etc*

身近(な) **mijika (na)** familiar; closely related

みじめ(な) **mijime (na)** dismal; miserable

みじん切りにする **mijingiri ni suru** shred

未熟児 **mijukuji** premature baby

未熟(な) **mijuku (na)** immature; unskilled

未開地 **mikaichi** wilderness

未解決(の) **mikaiketsu (no)** unsolved

未開の地 **mikai no chi** bush

見かけ **mikake** look, appearance

見かけ倒し(の) **mikake-daoshi (no)** shoddy

見かける **mikakeru** see; catch sight of

味覚 **mikaku** palate; taste *(sense)*

みかん **mikan** mandarin orange; tangerine

未完成(の) **mikansei (no)** incomplete, unfinished

味方 **mikata** ally; 味方をする *mikata o suru* take sides; be behind; side with

見方 **mikata** slant; viewpoint

三日月 **mikazuki** crescent moon

未決定(の) **mikettei (no)** pending; undecided

幹 **miki** stem; trunk

ミキサー **mikisā** blender

密告者 **mikkoku-sha** informer

密告する **mikkoku suru** turn in, inform on

密航者 **mikkō-sha** stowaway

密航する **mikkō suru** stow away

ミックスした **mikkusu shita** mixed

みこ (巫女) **miko** shrine maiden

見込み **mikomi** likelihood, probability; prospect

見込みなし **mikominashi** no-hoper

見込みのある **mikomi no aru** prospective

見込みのない **mikomi no nai** improbable

見込む **mikomu** allow for; expect; anticipate

未婚(の) **mikon (no)** unmarried

みこし **mikoshi** ceremonial palanquin

見くびる **mikubiru** underestimate, underrate

見下す **mikudasu** look down on

見舞い **mimai** visit *(to sick person)*

...未満で **... miman de** under, less than

見回る **mimawaru** patrol

耳 **mimi** ear; 耳が聞こえない *mimi ga kikoenai* deaf; 耳が遠い *mimi ga tōi* hard of hearing; 耳に心地よい *mimi ni kokochi yoi* pleasant-sounding; musical; 耳にする *mimi ni suru* overhear; 耳をそば立てる *mimi o sobadateru* strain the ears; prick up one's ears; 耳を立てる *mimi o tateru* prick up its ears

耳あか **mimiaka** wax

耳寄りの情報 **mimiyori no jōhō** tip, piece of advice

耳障り(な) **mimizawari (na)** grating; unmusical

身もだえする **mimodae suru** writhe, squirm

身元 **mimoto** identity; background

身元保証人 **mimoto-hoshō-nin** referee (*for job*)

身元確認 **mimoto-kakunin** identification

皆 **mina** all

南 **minami** south

南から(の) **minami kara (no)** southerly

源 **minamoto** source

見直す **minaosu** overhaul

見習い **minarai** apprentice

見習い看護婦 **minarai-kangofu** student nurse

見習う **minarau** learn by observation

身なり **minari** appearance; clothes

身なりの良い **minari no yoi** well-dressed

皆さん **mina-san** everyone, folks; ladies and gentlemen

みなす **minasu** consider

港 **minato** harbor, port

港町 **minatomachi** seaport

峰 **mine** mountain, peak

ミネラルウォーター **mineraru-wōtā** mineral water

民芸品 **mingeihin** folkcraft

醜い **minikui** ugly, hideous

身にしみる **mi ni shimiru** piercing

ミニスカート **minisukāto** miniskirt

身につける **mi ni tsukeru** put on; wear; carry; acquire

身につけている **mi ni tsukete iru** have on

民間放送 **minkan-hōsō** independent television

民間人 **minkan-jin** civilian

民間企業 **minkan-kigyō** private sector

民間(の) **minkan (no)** independent; private *industry*; civil (*not military*)

ミンク **minku** mink

皆 **minna** everyone; ねえ、みんな *nē, minna* hey, you guys

見逃す **minogasu** overlook

実りある **minori aru** fruitful

実りのない **minori no nai** unproductive

実る **minoru** bear fruit

身代金 **minoshirokin** ransom

民宿 **minshuku** Japanese B&B

民主主義 **minshu-shugi** democracy

民主主義国家 **minshu-shugi-kokka** democracy

民主主義者 **minshu-shugisha** democrat

民主的(な) **minshuteki (na)** democratic

ミント **minto** mint

民謡 **min'yō** folk music

民族 **minzoku** people

民族(の) **minzoku (no)** ethnic

民族集団 **minzoku-shūdan** ethnic group

民族主義 **minzoku-shugi** nationalism

見覚え **mioboe** recollection; recognition

見送る **miokuru** see off; give a send-off; pass up; miss

見下ろす **miorosu** overlook

見落とし **miotoshi** oversight

見落とす **miotosu** miss, overlook

身を寄せ合う **mi o yoseau** huddle together

密閉(の) **mippei (no)** airtight; sealed

密閉する **mippei suru** seal

未来 **mirai** future

未来形 **miraikei** future tense

ミリグラム **miriguramu** milligram

ミリメーター **mirimētā** millimeter

見る **miru** look; watch; see; view; look at; ...と見る *... to miru* characterize as

みる **-miru** try to; 説得してみる *settoku shite miru* try to persuade

ミルク **miruku** milk

魅力 **miryoku** attraction; appeal

魅力的(な) **miryokuteki (na)** attractive; appealing; fascinating

魅了する **miryō suru** attract; enchant; fascinate

ミサイル **misairu** missile

岬 **misaki** cape

店 **mise** store, shop; place (*bar, restaurant*)

見せびらかす **misebirakasu** parade, show off

見せかけ **misekake** act, pretense; make-believe; 全部見せかけだけである *zenbu misekake dake de aru* it's all done for show

見せかけ(の) **misekake (no)** mock

魅せられた **miserareta** spellbound

見せる **miseru** demonstrate; show; display; exhibit

ミシン **mishin** sewing machine

見知らぬ人 **mishiranu hito** stranger

見知っている **mishitte iru** know by sight

未使用(の) **mishiyō (no)** unused

みそ **miso** soybean paste

みそ汁 **miso shiru** miso soup

密生した **missei shita** dense; thick

密接して **missetsu shite** close together

密集した **misshū shita** crowded; dense

密集する **misshū suru** cluster; crowd; mass

ミス **misu** mistake; unmarried woman

みすぼらしい **misuborashii** scruffy; seedy

未遂 **misui** failed attempt

見捨てない **misutenai** stick by

ミステリー **misuterī** mystery

見捨てる **misuteru** abandon; walk out on; leave; jettison

みたい **-mitai**: 夢みたい *yume-mitai* like a dream; 金持ちみたい *kanemochi-mitai* wealthy-looking; ばかみたい *baka-mitai* idiotic

満たす **mitasu** fill; fulfill; meet; satisfy

見たところ **mita tokoro** apparently; on the face of it

未定 **mitei** undecided

ミートボール **mītobōru** meatball

認められない **mitomerarenai** unacceptable

認められる **mitomerareru** acceptable; discernible

認める **mitomeru** accept; admit; acknowledge; attach *importance*; award *damages*; discern; vindicate

見通し **mitōshi** outlook, prospects; 見通しの利かない *mitōshi no kikanai* blind *corner*

ミツバチ **mitsubachi** bee

密売する **mitsubai suru** push *drugs*

密度 **mitsudo** density

三つ子 **mitsugo** triplets

見つかる **mitsukaru** be found

見つけ出す **mitsukedasu** discover; track down

見つける **mitsukeru** find; observe; gaze; catch sight of; spot; notice; work out *solution*

見つめる **mitsumeru** stare at; gaze at

見積もり **mitsumori** quotation, quote; estimate; projection

見積もる **mitsumoru** calculate; estimate; cost

密林地帯 **mitsurin-chitai** jungle

密漁する **mitsuryō suru** poach (*for fish etc*)

密輸 **mitsuyu** smuggling

密輸業者 **mitsuyu-gyōsha** smuggler

密輸する **mitsuyu suru** smuggle

ミット **mitto** mitt

みっともない **mittomonai** disreputable; shameful

身動きする **miugoki suru** stir

見失う **miushinau** lose sight of

見分けがつく **miwake ga tsuku** recognizable

見分けのつかない **miwake no tsukanai** indistinguishable

見分ける **miwakeru** identify, distinguish; make out, see

魅惑する **miwaku suru** fascinate; charm

魅惑的(な) **miwakuteki (na)** ravishing; seductive; tempting

見渡す **miwatasu** scan; survey

みやげ **miyage** souvenir

溝 **mizo** ditch; drain (*under street*); gutter; gulf; groove

みぞれ **mizore** sleet

水 **mizu** water; 水をやる *mizu o yaru* water; 水を跳ねる *mizu o haneru* splash; 水を通さない *mizu o tōsanai* watertight

水辺(の) **mizube (no)** waterside

水浸し(の) **mizubitashi (no)** soggy

水ぼうそう **mizubōsō** chicken pox

水ぶくれ **mizubukure** blister

水着 **mizugi** swimsuit

水気を切る **mizuke o kiru** strain

湖 **mizūmi** lake

みずみずしい **mizumizushii** juicy

水っぽい **mizuppoi** runny, watery

水差し **mizusashi** carafe; pitcher

水玉 **mizutama** dewdrop; polka dot

水玉(の) **mizutama (no)** spotted

水たまり **mizutamari** puddle

水割り **mizuwari** whiskey and water

...も ... **mo** also, as well; ...も...も ... *mo ...mo* both...and...; ...も...もない *... mo ... mo nai* neither ... nor ...

喪 **mo** mourning

もう **mō** already; still; more ◊ another; もう彼はきましたか -まだです *mō kare wa kimashita ka – mada desu* is he here yet? - not yet; 彼はもうここでは働いていません *kare wa mō koko de wa hataraite imasen* he no longer works here; もう一度 *mō ichido* again, once more; もう少し *mō sukoshi* a little bit more; もう一つ

もう一つ **mō hitotsu** another (one); もう、我慢できない *mō gaman dekinai* that's the last straw!; もう限界だ *mō genkai da* that's the limit!

モバイル **mobairu** cell phone; palmtop; organizer; PDA

もち **mochi** rice cake

持ち上がる **mochiagaru** arise, crop up; be raised

持ち上げる **mochiageru** elevate; lift, raise

持ち歩く **mochiaruku** carry

持ち場 **mochiba** post (*of soldier*)

持ち出す **mochidasu** bring up *subject*; run away with

持ち運ぶ **mochihakobu** carry

持ちこたえる **mochikotaeru** endure; hold out

持ち物 **mochimono** belongings, things

持ち逃げする **mochinige suru** make off with

持ち主 **mochinushi** owner

もちろん **mochiron** of course, certainly; surely

持ちよる **mochiyoru** pool *resources*

盲腸 **mōchō** appendix

盲腸炎 **mōchōen** appendicitis

喪中である **mochū de aru** be in mourning

もだえる **modaeru** squirm, writhe

モデム **modemu** modem

モデル **moderu** model

モード **mōdo** mode

盲導犬 **mōdōken** seeing-eye dog

戻る **modoru** return; go back; come back; resume

戻す **modosu** return, put back

戻ってくる **modotte kuru** come back

燃え上がる **moeagaru** flare up

燃える **moeru** burn

燃え立つ **moetatsu** blaze ◊ fiery

燃えている **moete iru** alight ◊ be on fire

毛布 **mōfu** blanket

喪服 **mofuku** mourning (clothes)

もがく **mogaku** struggle; wriggle

模擬(の) **mogi (no)** mock

もぎ取る **mogitoru** wrench; break off; pull off; snatch

もぐ **mogu** pick, pluck

模範 **mohan** model; example

模範的(な) **mohanteki (na)** exemplary

猛威 **mōi** ferocity; fury

もじゃもじゃ(の) **mojamoja (no)** bushy; shaggy, unkempt

文字 **moji** character (*in writing*); letter; script, writing

文字盤 **moji-ban** dial

文字どおり(の) **mojidōri (no)** literal

もじもじする **mojimoji suru** squirm; fidget

盲人 **mōjin** the blind

もうかる **mōkaru** pay, be profitable

模型 **mokei** miniature; model; mock-up

模型(の) **mokei (no)** model

もうけになる **mōke ni naru** profitable

設ける **mōkeru** institute, set up

木管楽器 **mokkan-gakki** woodwind (instrument)

目撃者 **mokugeki-sha** (eye)witness

目撃する **mokugeki suru** witness

目標 **mokuhyō** goal, target; landmark

目標期日 **mokuhyō- kijitsu** target date

目次 **mokuji** table of contents

木目 **mokume** grain

目録 **mokuroku** inventory, list

木製(の) **mokusei (no)** wooden

目的 **mokuteki** aim, purpose, objective

目的地 **mokutekichi** destination

目的語 **mokutekigo** object GRAM

木曜日 **mokuyōbi** Thursday

木材 **mokuzai** wood

木造(の) **mokuzō (no)** made of wood; wooden

…もまた …**mo mata** too; …もまた…ない … **mo mata …nai** nor

木綿 **momen** cotton

もめる **momeru** have a dispute; be at odds

もみじ **momiji** Japanese maple

もみ消し **momikeshi** coverup

もみ消す **momikesu** cover up, hush up

もみの木 **momi no ki** fir

もも **momo** thigh

桃 **momo** peach

盲目(の) **mōmoku (no)** blind

もむ **momu** massage; rub

門 **mon** gate

文部省 **Monbushō** Ministry of Education, Science, Sports and Culture

もん着 **monchaku** trouble; dispute; もん着を起こす **monchaku o okosu** cause trouble; make a fuss

問題 **mondai** matter, affair; problem; 問題の **mondai no** in question; 問題を生む **mondai o umu** pose a problem

問題解決 **mondai- kaiketsu** troubleshooting

門限 **mongen** curfew

モンゴル **Mongoru** Mongolia

モンゴル (の) **Mongoru (no)** Mongolian

モーニングコール **mōningu-kōru** wake-up call

モニター **monitā** display; visual display unit

文句 **monku** phrase; complaint; 文句を言う **monku o iu** complain; make a fuss

文句無し(の) **monku nashi (no)** entirely satisfactory; undisputed

文盲(の) **monmō (no)** illiterate

物, もの **mono** object, thing; stuff

者 **mono** person

ものだ **-monoda** used to

物語 **monogatari** narrative; story, tale

物乞いする **monogoi suru** beg

ものまね **monomane** impression; …のものまねをする … **no monomane o suru** impersonate; mimic

もの珍しそうに **monomezurashisō ni** curiously, inquisitively

もの覚えがいい **mono-oboe ga ii** have a good memory

もの覚えが悪い **mono-oboe ga warui** have a poor memory

物置 **mono-oki** storeroom; shed

もの思いにふける **mono-omoi ni fukeru** muse

もの思いに沈んだ **mono-omoi ni shizunda** pensive

もの惜しみしない **mono-oshimi shinai** lavish

物音を立てる **mono-oto o tateru** make a noise

モノローグ **monorōgu** monolog(ue)

物差し, ものさし **monosashi** rule, ruler; gauge

ものしり顔(の) **monoshiri gao (no)** knowing

もの静か(な) **mono-shizuka (na)** quiet

ものすごい **monosugoi** terrific, awesome

もの笑いの種になる **monowarai no tane ni naru** become a laughing stock

もの好き(な) **monozuki (na)** curious; inquisitive

もっぱら **moppara** entirely

モップ **moppu** mop

モラルハザード **moraru-hazādo** decline in moral standards

漏らす **morasu** divulge

もらう **morau** receive

もらう **-morau** (*causative*): 洗っても らった *aratte moratta* I had it washed; ちょっと手伝ってもらえます か *chotto tetsudatte moraemasu ka* can you help me?

漏れ **more** escape, leak

漏れる **moreru** escape, leak out

猛烈(な) **mōretsu (na)** fierce; intense; impetuous

猛烈に **mōretsu ni** fiercely; with a vengeance

森 **mori** forest

盛り上がり **moriagari** upsurge; climax; hump

もろい **moroi** brittle; frail; fragile

もうろく **mōroku** senility

もうろくした **mōroku shita** senile

もうろうとした **mōrō to shita** hazy; dim

漏る **moru** leak

モルヒネ **moruhine** morphine

モルモット **morumotto** guinea pig

モルタル **morutaru** mortar

もし **moshi** if; もし必要なら *moshi hitsuyō nara* if need be; もし...の

場合に備えて *moshi ... no bāi ni sonaete* in case ...

申し分ないほど **mōshibun nai hodo** perfectly, impeccably

申し分のない **mōshibun no nai** impeccable; irreproachable

申し出 **mōshide** approach, offer; proposal

申し入れをする **mōshiire o suru** make overtures to

もしかしたら **moshikashitara** maybe

申し込み **mōshikomi** application

申込用紙 **mōshikomi-yōshi** application form

申し込む **mōshikomu** apply for; challenge

もしもし **moshimoshi** hello TELEC

申し立て **mōshitate** allegation; statement; testimony

申す **mōsu** H say; ...と申しますが ... *to mōshimasu ga* this is TELEC

もうすぐ **mōsugu** soon, directly

モスクワ **Mosukuwa** Moscow

モーター **mōtā** motor

モーターボート **mōtābōto** motorboat, speedboat

毛沢東 **Mō Takutō** Mao Zedong

もたらす **motarasu** bring; produce, bring about; yield

もたれる **motareru** recline on; lean on

持たせる **motaseru** give; stretch; make last

もたつく **motatsuku** fumble; dawdle

盲点 **mōten** blind spot

もてなす **motenasu** entertain

もてる **moteru** be popular

モーテル **mōteru** motel

もと, 基, 元 **moto** origin; cause; 元に 戻す *moto ni modosu* reinstate; replace, put back; 基にする *moto ni suru* be based on

元... **moto ...** ex-

求める **motomeru** seek; ask for

もともと **motomoto** naturally; originally

もと(の) **moto (no)** original, first

基づかせる **motozukaseru** base

基づく **motozuku** rest on ...

もつ **motsu** hold out (*of supplies*); keep (*of food, milk*); last

持つ **motsu** have; hold

もつれ **motsure** tangle

もつれる **motsureru** get tangled up

もったいぶった **mottaibutta** pompous

もったいない **mottainai** wasteful

持って行く **motte iku** take away; bring along

持っている **motte iru** possess, have; hang on to; keep

持ってくる **motte kuru** bring; take along

もっと **motto** more; もっと大きな *motto ōki na* bigger

モットー **mottō** motto

最も **mottomo** most; 最も上手(な) *mottomo jōzu (na)* best

もっとも(な) **mottomo (na)** justifiable; reasonable

もっともらしい **mottomorashii** plausible

燃やす **moyasu** burn

模様 **moyō** motif; design; pattern

模様替え **moyōgae** reorganization

模様替えする **moyōgae suru** reorganize *room*; remodel

模様入り(の) **moyō-iri (no)** patterned

催し **moyōshi** meeting; event

モザイク **mozaiku** mosaic

模造品 **mozōhin** imitation

無… **mu…** non-; un-

無防備(な) **mubōbi (na)** defenseless, helpless

無茶(な) **mucha (na)** reckless

無知 **muchi** ignorance

むち **muchi** whip

無知(な) **muchi (na)** ignorant

無秩序 **muchitsujo** anarchy; chaos

無秩序(の) **muchitsujo (no)** chaotic

むち打ち **muchiuchi** hiding; whipping

むち打つ **muchiutsu** flog; whip

夢中である **muchū de aru** be hooked on; be engrossed in

無駄 **muda** useless; unnecessary

無駄足 **mudaashi** wildgoose chase

無駄話をする **mudabanashi o suru** prattle

無駄である **muda de aru** it's no use

無駄(な) **muda (na)** feeble; futile; vain; 彼等の努力は無駄だった *karera no doryoku wa muda datta* their efforts were in vain

無断で **mudan de** without permission

無駄にする **muda ni suru** undo; waste; spoil

無駄使いする **mudazukai suru** waste

無鉛(の) **muen (no)** lead-free, unleaded

無害(な) **mugai (na)** harmless

無学(な) **mugaku (na)** uneducated

無限 **mugen** infinity

無限(の) **mugen (no)** infinite

麦 **mugi** barley; wheat

麦わら **mugiwara** straw

無言で **mugon de** in silence

無言(の) **mugon (no)** mute

むごたらしい **mugotarashii** bloody; cruel; tragic

無法(の) **muhō (no)** lawless

無表情(な) **muhyōjō (na)** impassive

無一文(の) **muichimon (no)** penniless

無意味(な) **muimi (na)** meaningless, empty; pointless, senseless

無意識に **muishiki ni** mechanically; unintentionally

無意識(の) **muishiki (no)** unconscious

むいていない **muite inai** incompetent

無邪気 **mujaki** innocence

無邪気(な) **mujaki (na)** innocent

無慈悲(な) **mujihi (na)** merciless

無人(の) **mujin (no)** uninhabited; unmanned

無地(の) **muji (no)** plain

無尽蔵(の) **mujinzō (no)** inexhaustible

無条件(の) **mujōken (no)** unconditional

矛盾 **mujun** contradiction; discrepancy

矛盾した **mujun shita** contradictory; inconsistent

矛盾する **mujun suru** conflict; …と矛盾する *… to mujun suru* be at odds with

迎えに行く **mukae ni iku** collect, pick up

迎えに来る **mukae ni kuru** come for

向かい風 **mukaikaze** headwind

むかむかさせる **mukamuka saseru** nauseate

無関係(な) **mukankei (na)** irrelevant

無関心 **mukanshin** indifference

無関心(な) **mukanshin (na)** indifferent

昔 **mukashi** ancient times; the old days

昔から(の) **mukashi kara (no)** old

昔々 **mukashimukashi** once upon a time

むかつかせる **mukatsukaseru** disgust; repel; sicken ◊ revolting

ムカつく **mukatsuku** be mad, be pissed

むかつく(よう)な **mukatsuku yō (na)** nauseating

向かう **mukau** head for, make for

向けである **muke de aru** be meant for

むける **mukeru** peel

向ける **mukeru** direct; point; steer; ...に向けたものである **... ni muketa mono de aru** be meant for

無血(の) **muketsu (no)** bloodless

向き **muki** direction; 向きを変える **muki o kaeru** turn around; 向きを変えて立ち去る **muki o kaete tachisaru** turn away

無機物(の) **mukibutsu (no)** inorganic

むき出しにする **mukidashi ni suru** expose

無期限(の) **mukigen (no)** open-ended; indefinite

無記名投票 **mukimei-tōhyō** secret ballot

無気力(な) **mukiryoku (na)** apathetic; lethargic

無傷(の) **mukizu (no)** intact; unscathed

婿 **muko** bridegroom

無効で **mukō de** null and void

向こう側に **mukōgawa ni** across, over

向こう側(の) **mukōgawa (no)** opposite

むこうみず(な) **mukōmizu (na)** foolhardy

無効(な) **mukō (na)** invalid

向こうに **mukō ni** beyond

無効にする **mukō ni suru** annul; invalidate; revoke; overrule

向うずね **mukōzune** shin

むく **muku** peel; scrape; shell

向く **muku** face

無口(な) **mukuchi (na)** reticent

むくどり **mukudori** starling

むくんだ **mukunda** swollen, puffy

無許可(の) **mukyoka (no)** unauthorized

無給(の) **mukyū (no)** unpaid

無名(の) **mumei (no)** obscure

むなしい **munashii** empty ◊ in vain

むなしさ **munashi-sa** emptiness; vanity (of hopes)

胸 **mune** chest; bosom; breast ; 胸に秘める **mune ni himeru** cherish; 胸をうつ **mune o utsu** touching

胸やけ **muneyake** heartburn

無認可(の) **muninka (no)** unauthorized

無能 **munō** incompetence

無能(な) **munō (na)** incapable; incompetent

無農薬(の) **munōyaku (no)** organic

村 **mura** village

群がる **muragaru** mob; cluster; swarm

むら気(な) **muraki (na)** capricious; erratic

むらのある **mura no aru** inconsistent; patchy

紫色(の) **murasakiiro (no)** violet; purple

群れ **mure** clump; crop; flock; herd; swarm

無理 **muri** impossible; unreasonable

無理強い(の) **murijii (no)** forced

無理に **muri ni** by force

無理に抑える **muri ni osaeru** bottle up

無理やり **muriyari** forcibly; 無理やり開き出す **muriyari kikidasu** extract; drag out of; Xを無理やりYに引きずり込む **X o muriyari Y ni hikizurikomu** drag X into Y

ムール貝 **mūru-gai** mussel

無類(の) **murui (no)** incomparable

無料 **muryō** free of charge

無料で **muryō de** for free

無力(な) **muryoku (na)** helpless; powerless

無料(の) **muryō (no)** complimentary, free

無差別(な) **musabetsu (na)** indiscriminate

無差別(の) **musabetsu (no)** indiscriminate; wholesale

むさぼる **musaboru** devour

無作為抽出 **musakui-chūshutsu** random sample

無作為(の) **musakui (no)** random

無生物(の) **museibutsu (no)** inanimate

無制限(の) **museigen (no)** unlimited

無声(の) **musei (no)** silent

無責任(な) **musekinin (na)** irresponsible

無せきつい動物 **musekitsui-dōbutsu** invertebrate

無線 **musen** radio

無線電話 **musen-denwa** radio telephone

無線タクシー **musen-takushī** radio taxi

虫 **mushi** bug; worm

無視 **mushi** disregard

蒸し暑い **mushiatsui** humid, muggy, sultry

虫歯 **mushiba** bad tooth; cavity; 虫歯になる **mushiba ni naru** decay, rot

蒸し器 **mushiki** steamer

虫眼鏡 **mushi-megane** magnifying glass

無神経(な) **mushinkei (na)** insensitive

無神論者 **mushinron-sha** atheist

むしろ **mushiro** rather

虫刺され **mushisasare** bite; sting

無視する **mushi suru** ignore; dismiss; brush off, discount

虫よけ **mushiyoke** (insect) repellent

夢想家 **musō-ka** dreamer

蒸す **musu** steam

結び目 **musubime** knot

結び付ける **musubitsukeru** bind; knit together; XとYを結び付ける **X to Y o musubitsukeru** relate X to Y

結ぶ **musubu** form; tie up, do up; knot

息子 **musuko** son

息子さん **musuko-san** son

娘 **musume** daughter

娘さん **musume-san** daughter

無敵(の) **muteki (no)** invincible; unbeaten

むとんちゃく(な) **mutonchaku (na)** nonchalant; casual

無痛(の) **mutsū (no)** painless

むっとした **mutto shita** annoyed; stuffy, airless

むっとしている **mutto shite iru** be in a huff

むっとする **mutto suru** be annoyed

むっつりした **muttsuri shita** glum; sullen

無欲(の) **muyoku (no)** selfless

夢遊病者 **muyūbyō- sha** sleepwalker

無罪 **muzai** innocence; 無罪にする **muzai ni suru** acquit; exonerate; 無罪を主張する **muzai o shuchō suru** plead not guilty

無罪(の) **muzai (no)** innocent

無造作(な) **muzōsa (na)** offhand ◊ easily

難しい **muzukashii** difficult, hard

難しさ **muzukashi-sa** difficulty

脈拍 **myakuhaku** pulse

脈打つ **myakuutsu** pulsate

ミャンマー **Myanmā** Burma, Myanmar

ミャンマー (の) **Myanmā (no)** Burmese, Myanmar

妙案 **myōan** inspiration

名字 **myōji** family name, surname

妙(な) **myō (na)** peculiar

妙に **myō ni** curiously

ミュージカル **myūjikaru** musical

ミュージシャン **myūjishan** musician

N

な **-na** ◊ (*forms negative imperative*): 忘れるな **wasureru-na** don't forget ◊ (*for emphasis*): きれいだな **kirei da na** it's beautiful, isn't it!

な **na** (*forms adjectives*): 憶病(な) **okubyō (na)** cowardly

名 **na** name; renown

名ばかり(の) **nabakari (no)** so-called

なべ **nabe** pot

ナビゲーター **nabigētā** navigator

名高い **nadakai** prestigious

なだめる **nadameru** soothe; pacify

なだれ **nadare** avalanche

なでる **naderu** caress, stroke

なでつける **nadetsukeru** smooth

など **nado** et cetera, and so on

苗 **nae** seedling

苗床 **naedoko** nursery

名札 **nafuda** nametag

長引いた **nagabiita** protracted

長引かせる **nagabikaseru** drag out

長靴 **nagagutsu** boots

長い **nagai** lengthy, long

長い間 **nagai aida** a long while

長生きする **nagaiki suru** live for a long time

長い目で見れば **nagai me de mireba** in the long term

長いす **nagaisu** couch

長く **nagaku** long

眺め **nagame** view

眺める **nagameru** look at; gaze at

長持ちする **nagamochi suru** last ◊ resilient

長年にわたる **naganen ni wataru** long-standing

ながら **-nagara** (*linking two actions*) while; though; 歩きながら食べる **arukinagara taberu** eat while walking

流れ **nagare** current; flow; timescale

流れ星 **nagare-boshi** shooting star

流れ者 **nagare-mono** drifter

流れる **nagareru** break (*of news*); flow (*of current, traffic*); run (*of river, paint*); flush

流れ作業 **nagare-sagyō** assembly line

長さ **naga-sa** length

流し **nagashi** sink

長袖(の) **nagasode (no)** long-sleeved

流す **nagasu** flush; flush away; shed

長続きする **nagatsuzuki suru** durable ◊ endure, last

長屋 **nagaya** row houses

投げかける **nagekakeru** cast; throw; hurl

嘆かわしい **nagekawashii** deplorable; lamentable; sad

嘆き悲しむ **nagekikanashimu** mourn

嘆く **nageku** deplore; lament

投げる **nageru** throw, pitch; toss; throw up

投げつける **nagetsukeru** hurl; pelt

なごませる **nagomaseru** disarming; calming

名残 **nagori** remains; traces; 名残を惜しむ **nagori o oshimu** be reluctant to leave

なごやか(な) **nagoyaka (na)** peaceful; gentle

なぐり書き **nagurigaki** scrawl, scribble

なぐり書きする **nagurigaki suru** scrawl

殴る **naguru** thump; knock around

慰め **nagusame** consolation, comfort

慰める **nagusameru** console, comfort

慰めようのない **nagusameyō no nai** inconsolable

ない **-nai** (*negative suffix*) not; 私は行かない **watashi wa ikanai** I won't go

無い、ない **nai** there is / are not; do not have

内部 **naibu** inside

内部情報 **naibu-jōhō** inside information

内部(の) **naibu (no)** interior, internal

内縁の妻 **naien no tsuma** common-law wife

ナイフ **naifu** knife

内服薬 **naifukuyaku** medicine for internal use

内報する **naihō suru** tip off

内耳 **naiji** inner ear

内科医 **naikai** physician

内閣 **naikaku** cabinet POL

内閣総理大臣 **naikaku-sōridaijin** Japanese Prime Minister

内向的(な) **naikōteki (na)** introverted

内面(の) **naimen (no)** inner

内密で **naimitsu de** secretly

内密(の) **naimitsu (no)** undercover

内務省 **Naimushō** Department of the Interior

内陸(の) **nairiku (no)** inland; interior (of country)

ナイロン **nairon** nylon

内政不干渉 **naisei-fukanshō** noninterference, nonintervention (in the affairs of other nations)

内戦 **naisen** civil war

内線 **naisen** extension TELEC

内心(の) **naishin (no)** inward, innermost

内緒(の) **naisho (no)** secret

内装 **naisō** décor, decoration

内装業者 **naisō-gyōsha** interior decorator

内装する **naisō suru** decorate

ナイトクラブ **naitokurabu** nightclub

ナイトスポット **naitosupotto** nightspot

内容 **naiyō** content

内臓 **naizō** internal organs

内蔵(の) **naizō (no)** built-in

なじみのない **najimi no nai** alien, unfamiliar

なじむ **najimu** become familiar with

なじる **najiru** taunt; rebuke; blame

中 **naka** inside

仲 **naka** relationship; relations

半ば **nakaba** half; middle

中だるみする **naka-darumi suru** sag

中で **naka de** inside

仲買人 **nakagai-nin** middle man

中ごろに **nakagoro ni** in the middle of

中から **naka kara** from within

仲間 **nakama** circle, group, set; company; crony; comrade

仲間意識 **nakama-ishiki** comradeship

中身、中味 **nakami** contents; filling; …の中身をあける **… no nakami o akeru** empty

なかなか **nakanaka** very; quite; rather; なかなか消えない **nakanaka kienai** linger; なかなか立ち去らない **nakanaka tachisaranai** linger

仲直りをする **nakanaori o suru** make up, be reconciled

仲直りさせる **nakanaori saseru** reconcile, patch up

中に **naka ni** in; inside; 中に入る **naka ni hairu** go in

中庭 **nakaniwa** courtyard, quadrangle; patio

中(の) **naka (no)** inside

仲のよい **naka no yoi** harmonious; on good terms

なければならない **-nakereba naranai** must; 勉強しなければならない **benkyō shinakereba naranai** I have to study

泣き声 **nakigoe** wail; 泣き声をあげる **nakigoe o ageru** give a wail

泣き言を言う **nakigoto o iu** whine

泣きじゃくる **nakijakuru** sob

泣き崩れる **nakikuzureru** break down

泣き叫ぶ **nakisakebu** bawl; wail

仲人 **nakōdo** go-between

泣く **naku** cry, have a cry

なくなる **nakunaru** run out; go (of pain etc)

亡くなる **nakunaru** pass away

なくす **nakusu** abolish, do away with; eliminate; lose

なくてはならない **-nakute wa naranai** must; 行かなくてはならない **ikanakute wa naranai** I must leave

ナマあし **namaashi** *not wearing socks or pantyhose*

生ビール **nama-bīru** draft (beer)

名前 **namae** name; given name

生臭い **namagusai** smelly; smelling of fish

生意気 **namaiki** impertinence

生意気(な) **namaiki (na)** impertinent, fresh; saucy

生意気になる **namaiki ni naru** get smart with

怠け者 **namakemono** layabout

怠け者(の) **namakemono (no)** idle

怠ける **namakeru** idle away; laze around

怠けている **namakete iru** lazy

生(の) **nama (no)** live *broadcast*; raw

なまぬるい **namanurui** tepid

なまり **namari** accent

鉛 **namari** lead

生焼け(の) **namayake (no)** underdone

なまず **namazu** catfish

なめくじ **namekuji** slug

なめらか(な) **nameraka (na)** smooth

なめらかにする **nameraka ni suru** smooth down

なめらかさ **nameraka-sa** fluency

なめる **nameru** lick

波 **nami** wave (*in sea*)

涙 **namida** tear; 涙が出る **namida ga deru** run, water; be wet (*of eyes*); 涙にくれる **namida ni kureru** be in tears

涙でいっぱい(の) **namida de ippai (no)** tearful

並はずれた **namihazureta** uncommon; extraordinary

波に揺れる **nami ni yureru** bob

並(の) **nami (no)** average; satisfactory

七 **nana** seven

斜めになる **naname ni naru** slope

斜め(の) **naname (no)** diagonal; slanting

ナンバー **nanbā** number; license (plate) number

ナンバープレート **nanbāpurēto** license plate

南米 **Nanbei** South America

南米人 **Nanbei-jin** South American

南米(の) **Nanbei (no)** South American

南部 **nanbu** south

南部(の) **nanbu (no)** southern

難題 **nandai** difficult problem; challenge

何だか **nandaka** somehow; kind of, sort of

何でも **nan demo** whatever; 私は何でもかまいません **watashi wa nan demo kamaimasen** it's all the same to me; 私は何でも食べられます **watashi wa nan demo taberaremasu** I could eat anything

難読症 **nandokushō** dyslexia

難読症患者 **nandokushō-kanja** dyslexic

何度も **nando mo** many times

何 **nani** what; 何があったの **nani ga atta no** what has happened?

何気ない **nanigenai** casual; unconcerned

何か **nani ka** anything; something; 何かあった **nani ka atta** what's up?

何も **nani mo** nothing; anything; 何も不自由していない **nani mo fujiyū shite inai** want for nothing; 何も残っていません **nani mo nokotte imasen** there isn't/aren't any left

何よりも **nani yori mo** most of all

何よりもまず **nani yori mo mazu** above all

軟弱(な) **nanjaku (na)** weak; soft; effeminate

何時 **nanji** what time?; what time is it?

何時間でも **nanjikan demo** for hours on end

何十もの… **nanjū mono …** dozens of

何回も **nankai mo** time and again

軟化する **nanka suru** soften

南京錠 **nankinjō** padlock

軟こう **nankō** ointment

南極 **Nankyoku** Antarctic, South Pole

南極(の) **Nankyoku (no)** polar

難民 **nanmin** refugee

難問 **nanmon** difficult problem; puzzle

難なく **nannaku** without difficulty

何年も **nannen mo** for years

何(の) **nan (no)** what; 何のために **nanno tame ni** what for?

…なので **… na node** as; …なので私も来れます **…na node watashi mo koremasu** so I can come too

菜の花 **nanohana** rape blossom

名乗り出る **nanorideru** come forward; give oneself up; claim

難破 **nanpa** shipwreck

難破させる **nanpa saseru** wreck

難破船 **nanpasen** wreck

難破する **nanpa suru** be shipwrecked

南西 **nansei** southwest

南西部(の) **nanseibu (no)** southwestern

ナンセンス **nansensu** nonsense

何て **nante** what; 何て言った **nante itta** what (did you say)?; 何てきれいな娘だろう **nante kirei na ko darō** what a beautiful girl!; 何ておかしいんだろう **nante okashiin darō** how funny!

南東 **nantō** southeast

南東部(の) **nantōbu (no)** southeastern

何と **nan to** what; 彼女が何と言おうとも **kanojo ga nan to iō tomo** no matter what she says

何とか **nantoka** somehow; 何とかパスする **nantoka pasu suru** scrape through; 何とか生活する **nantoka seikatsu suru** scrape a living; どう一日とかやっているよ **dō – nantoka yatte iru yo** how are you? – surviving

何とかして **nantoka shite** somehow

何とかする **nantoka suru** stretch rules

何とかという **nantoka to iu** thingumajig

何となく **nantonaku** vaguely; somehow

南東(の) **nantō (no)** southeast

直る **naoru** be repaired

治る **naoru** heal; be cured; feel better

直す **naosu** correct; put right

治す **naosu** heal

ナプキン **napukin** napkin

なら **nara** Japanese oak

… なら **… nara** if; provided that

並べ直す **narabenaosu** rearrange

並べる **naraberu** lay, set out

並ぶ **narabu** line up; form a line; stand in line

習い始める **narai hajimeru** take up, begin to learn

ならない **-naranai** should not ; 行ってはならない **itte wa naranai** you should not go

並んで **narande** side by side

慣らす **narasu** condition; familiarize

鳴らす **narasu** beep; honk; ring

習う **narau** learn

なれなれしい **narenareshii** familiar

慣れる **nareru** get accustomed to, get used to

ナレーション **narēshon** narration

ナレーター **narētā** narrator

成り上がり **nariagari** upstart

鳴り響く **narihibiku** go off; ring out; reverberate

なりすます **narisumasu** impersonate

成り立っている **naritatte iru** be composed of

なる **naru** go, become sad, green, quiet etc; result in; work out to; constitute; follow

鳴る **naru** sound; crash; ring; toll

なるべく **narubeku** as … as possible

なるほど **naruhodo** I see, indeed

情け深い **nasakebukai** compassionate; philanthropic

情けない **nasakenai** pitiful; disappointing; shameful

なさる **nasaru** polite form of **suru**

なし **nashi** pear

なしで **nashi de** without

なす **nasu** eggplant

夏 **natsu** summer

懐かしい **natsukashii** nostalgic ◊ miss

ナット **natto** nut

納豆 **nattō** fermented soybeans

納得する **nattoku suru** understand

縄 **nawa** rope; cord

縄跳びする **nawatobi suru** skip

納屋 **naya** barn

悩ませる **nayamaseru** perplex; trouble, worry

悩ます **nayamasu** annoy; bother; plague

悩み **nayami** distress; worry

悩む **nayamu** bother; get worried

なぜ **naze** why

なぜか **nazeka** somehow

なぞ **nazo** enigma, mystery

なぞめいた **nazomeita** enigmatic, mysterious

なぞなぞ **nazonazo** riddle (*game*)

名づける **nazukeru** name

ね **-ne** (*for emphasis*): きれいだね *kirei da ne* it's beautiful, isn't it!

根 **ne** root

値 **ne** price

ねえ **nē** hey

値上がりする **neagari suru** go up in price; appreciate FIN

値上げする **neage suru** mark up

ねばねばした **nebaneba shita** sticky

粘り強い **nebarizuyoi** dogged; persistent

粘る **nebaru** persist; be sticky

値引きする **nebiki suru** mark down, discount

寝坊する **nebō suru** sleep late

寝袋 **nebukuro** sleeping bag

値段 **nedan** price

ねだる **nedaru** pester for

値札 **nefuda** price tag

寝返りをうつ **negaeri o utsu** roll over (in bed); toss about (in bed)

願い **negai** desire

願う **negau** request; desire; ask for; hope

ねぎ **negi** leek; spring onion

値切る **negiru** bargain; haggle

音色 **neiro** tone

ネイティブスピーカー **neitibu-**

supīkā native speaker

ねじ **neji** screw; ねじを巻く *neji o maku* wind up

ねじれ **nejire** twist

ねじれる **nejireru** be twisted

ねじる **nejiru** contort; twist

寝かせる **nekaseru** lay, put down

ネックレス **nekkuresu** necklace; beads

ネック **nekku** bottleneck; neckline

熱狂 **nekkyō** mania

熱狂的(な) **nekkyōteki (na)** enthusiastic; ecstatic; fanatical

猫 **neko** cat

寝転ぶ **nekorobu** lie down

根こそぎにする **nekosogi ni suru** root out

ネクタイ **nekutai** necktie

寝巻き **nemaki** nightshirt

眠い **nemui** drowsy, sleepy

眠れる **nemureru** sleep well; have a good night

眠れない **nemurenai** have a restless night ◊ sleepless

眠り込む **nemurikomu** drop off

眠る **nemuru** fall asleep; sleep

年 **nen** (*countword for years, grades*) year; grade; 三年 *san-nen* third years

粘着テープ **nenchaku-tēpu** adhesive tape

年長(の) **nenchō (no)** senior

年代順(の) **nendaijun (no)** chronological

粘土 **nendo** clay

年度 **nendo** (academic) year; fiscal year

ねーねー **nēnē** hey

年賀状 **nengajō** New Year's card

年号 **nengō** era name

根に持って **ne ni motte** bitter

念入り(な) **nen'iri (na)** careful; elaborate

年次総会 **nenji-sōkai** annual general meeting

年中 **nenjū** throughout the year

年中無休 **nenjū-mukyū** open all year

年間 **nenkan:** 十年間 *jū-nenkan* ten years; 年間を通じて *nenkan o tsūjite* throughout the year; 昭和

年間 *Shōwa-nenkan ni* in the Hirohito years

年金 **nenkin** pension

年末 **nenmatsu** year end

年配(の) **nenpai (no)** elderly

年齢 **nenrei** age

年利 **nenri** APR, annual percentage rate

燃料 **nenryō** fuel

年生 **-nensei** -grade student; 二年生 *ni nensei* second grade student, sophomore

燃焼 **nenshō** combustion

ねんざ **nenza** sprain, wrench

ねんざする **nenza suru** sprain, wrench; twist one's ankle

ネオン灯 **neon-tō** neon light

ネパール **Nepāru** Nepal

ネパール(の) **Nepāru (no)** Nepalese

熱波 **neppa** heatwave

ねらい **nerai** aim; message

ねらう **nerau** aim

寝る **neru** go to bed; go to sleep; go to bed with

練る **neru** knead; polish up

寝る時間 **nerujikan** bedtime

値下がりする **nesagari suru** go down in price

値下げ **nesage** reduction (in price)

値下げした **nesage shita** reduced (in price)

寝そべる **nesoberu** lie; sprawl

熱射病 **nesshabyō** heatstroke

熱心(な) **nesshin (na)** enthusiastic; eager

熱心さ **nesshin-sa** eagerness

寝過ごす **nesugosu** oversleep

寝たきり(の) **netakiri (no)** bedridden

ねたみ **netami** envy

ねたむ **netamu** be jealous; envy; grudge

熱中している **netchū shite iru** be mad about, be crazy about ◊ enthusiastic

熱中する **netchū suru** be enthusiastic about; go in for

熱 **netsu** temperature, fever; heat; 熱がある *netsu ga aru* have a temperature; 熱をあげる *netsu o*

ageru have a crush on

熱意 **netsui** enthusiasm, zest

熱意のない **netsui no nai** lukewarm

熱情 **netsujō** zeal; passion

根付け **netsuke** netsuke (*small carved toggle*)

熱っぽい **netsuppoi** feverish

熱烈(な) **netsuretsu (na)** ardent; impassioned; effusive; glowing

熱帯地方 **nettai-chihō** tropics

熱帯(の) **nettai (no)** tropical

熱帯雨林 **nettai-urin** tropical rain forest

ネット **netto** basket; net

ネットサーフィンをする **netto-sāfin o suru** surf the Net

ネットワーク **nettowāku** network

値打ち **neuchi** value; worth; merit

値打ちのある **neuchi no aru** valuable

値打ちのない **neuchi no nai** worthless; poor quality; bad

寝酒 **nezake** nightcap

ねずみ **nezumi** mouse; rat

…に **...** ni at; in; to; by; on; for ◊ and ◊ (*forms adverbs*): 段階的に *dankaiteki ni* gradually

二 **ni** two; 二、三人 *ni, san-nin* two or three people; 二、三の *ni, san no* two or three; a couple of

ニアミス **niamisu** near miss

似合う **niau** flattering ◊ suit

二倍 **nibai** double, twice as much

二倍になる **nibai ni naru** double

鈍い **nibui** blunt; dull; stupid

二分 **nibun** dichotomy

日米安全保障条約 **Nichibei-anzen-hoshō-jōyaku** Japan-US Security Treaty

日没 **nichibotsu** sunset

日時 **nichiji** date (and time)

日常(の) **nichijō (no)** everyday; routine

日露戦争 **Nichiro-sensō** Russo-Japanese War

日曜日 **nichiyōbi** Sunday

日曜大工 **nichiyō-daiku** DIY, do-it-yourself

荷台 **nidai** roofrack; pallet

二段ベッド **nidan-beddo** bunk beds

煮える **nieru** boil; be boiled

苦い **nigai** bitter

逃がす **nigasu** set free; let go; lose

苦手である **nigate de aru** be bad at

二月 **nigatsu** February

逃げ出す **nigedasu** run off

逃げる **nigeru** escape, break away; flee; run away

握り **nigiri** grip

にぎわう **nigiwau** be crowded; be active

にぎやか(な) **nigiyaka (na)** busy; lively

にぎやかにする **nigiyaka ni suru** jazz up

濁る **nigoru** not be clear (of water etc); become muddy

荷車 **niguruma** cart

日本 **Nihon** Japan

日本晴れ **Nihon-bare** very fine day without a cloud in the sky

日本舞踊 **Nihon-buyō** Japanese dance

日本髪 **Nihon-gami** traditional Japanese hairstyle

日本銀行 **Nihon-ginkō** The Bank of Japan

日本語 **Nihon-go** Japanese

日本人 **Nihon-jin** Japanese

日本海 **Nihon-kai** Sea of Japan

日本国憲法 **Nihon-koku-kenpō** Constitution of Japan

日本(の) **Nihon (no)** Japanese

日本列島 **Nihon-rettō** the Japanese Islands

日本製 **Nihon-sei** made in Japan

日本庭園 **Nihon-teien** Japanese garden

虹 **niji** rainbow

にじませる **nijimaseru** spread

にじみ出る **nijimideru** spread; ooze

にじむ **nijimu** run (of color); spread

二次的(な) **nijiteki (na)** secondary

二十 **nijū** twenty

二重あご **nijū-ago** double chin

二重ガラス **nijū-garasu** double glazing

二重人格 **nijū-jinkaku** split personality

二重にする **nijū ni suru** double

二重(の) **nijū (no)** double; dual

二重唱 **nijūshō** duo (singing)

二重奏 **nijūsō** duo (instrumental)

24時間営業 **nijūyojikan-eigyō** open 24 hours

二回 **nikai** twice

二階 **nikai** second story; upper floor

にきび **nikibi** spot; pimple

日刊紙 **nikkan-shi** daily

日記 **nikki** diary, journal

日光 **nikkō** sunshine

にっこり笑う **nikkori warau** grin

日光浴する **nikkōyoku suru** sunbathe

ニックネーム **nikkunēmu** nickname

肉 **niku** flesh; meat; 肉が付く **niku ga tsuku** fill out; put on weight

肉眼では **nikugan de wa** to the naked eye

にくい **-nikui** difficult to...; 食べにくい **tabe-nikui** difficult to eat

憎い **nikui** detestable

憎む **nikumu** hate

憎しみ **nikushimi** hate, hatred

肉親 **nikushin** blood relation, blood relative

肉体 **nikutai** body; flesh

肉体関係 **nikutai-kankei** intimacy; relationship

肉体労働者 **nikutai-rōdō-sha** blue-collar worker; laborer

肉体的(な) **nikutaiteki (na)** physical

肉屋 **niku-ya** butcher

二枚舌を使う **nimaijita o tsukau** doublecross

...にも...にも... **... ni mo ... ni mo** neither ... nor ...

にもかかわらず **ni mo kakawarazu** fml despite

荷物 **nimotsu** luggage; baggage; cargo

荷物受け取り所 **nimotsu-uketorijo** baggage reclaim

人 **-nin** (countword for people): 十人 **jū-nin** ten people

人間 **ningen** human (being); man, humanity

人間味のある **ningenmi no aru** humane

人間味のない **ningenmi no nai** impersonal; inhumane

人間らしい **ningenrashii** human

人間性 **ningensei** humanity

人形 **ningyō** doll

任意(の) **nin'i (no)** optional

にんじん **ninjin** carrot

人情 **ninjō** → *giri*

認可 **ninka** permission; sanction; 認可を受ける *ninka o ukeru* be licensed

認可する **ninka suru** authorize, sanction; license

人気 **ninki** popularity

任期 **ninki** term of office; stint; 大統領の任期 *daitōryō no ninki* presidency

人気がある **ninki ga aru** be popular ◊ popular

人気のない **ninki no nai** unpopular

にんまりする **ninmari suru** gloat

任命 **ninmei** appointment, nomination

任命する **ninmei suru** appoint, nominate; assign; delegate

任務 **ninmu** assignment; mission; mandate

にんにく **ninniku** garlic

妊婦 **ninpu** expectant mother

認識 **ninshiki** awareness; perception; recognition

認識票 **ninshiki-hyō** dog tag

認識する **ninshiki suru** recognize; perceive; acknowledge

妊娠 **ninshin** pregnancy

妊娠中絶 **ninshin-chūzetsu** abortion; 妊娠中絶をする *ninshin-chūzetsu o suru* have an abortion

妊娠している **ninshin shite iru** pregnant ◊ be pregnant

妊娠する **ninshin suru** conceive

人称代名詞 **ninshō-daimeishi** personal pronoun

人相 **ninsō** features; looks

忍耐 **nintai** endurance; patience

認定された **nintei sareta** qualified

人数 **ninzū** number of people

におい **nioi** smell; においがする *nioi ga suru* smell; においをかぐ *nioi o kagu* smell, sniff

におう **niou** smell, odor; reek, stink

日本 **Nippon** Japan

日本語 **Nippon-go** Japanese

日本人 **Nippon-jin** Japanese

日本(の) **Nippon (no)** Japanese

にらむ **niramu** glare at; stare at

煮る **niru** boil; cook

似る **niru** resemble

二流(の) **niryū (no)** second-rate

偽物 **nisemono** fake

偽(の) **nise (no)** fake, phony

西 **nishi** west

西側(の) **Nishigawa (no)** Western

西側諸国 **Nishigawa-shokoku** the West

にしん **nishin** herring

二進法(の) **nishinhō (no)** binary

日射病 **nisshabyō** sunstroke

日誌 **nisshi** log(book)

日清戦争 **Nisshin-sensō** Sino-Japanese War (*1894-95*)

日食 **nisshoku** eclipse

日数 **nissū** number of days

ニス **nisu** varnish

日中 **nitchū** by day

日中戦争 **Nitchū-sensō** Chinese-Japanese War (*1937-45*)

似ている **nite iru** be alike; be close; resemble

二等 **nitō** second class

日程 **nittei** daily schedule

ニットウェア **nitto-wea** knitwear

庭 **niwa** garden

…には **…niwa** concerning; about

にわか雨 **niwaka-ame** scattered showers

にわとり **niwatori** chicken

にやにや笑い **niyaniya-warai** smirk

にやにや笑う **niyaniya warau** smirk

荷造りをする **nizukuri o suru** pack

…の **…no** of; from; with; at; on ◊ (*forms adjectives*): 文法(の) *bunpō (no)* grammatical

能 **Nō** No play

脳 **nō** brain

延ばす **nobasu** defer, delay

伸ばす **nobasu** lengthen; spread; stretch; smooth out

延べ **nobe** total; 延べ時間 *nobe jikan* the total number of hours

述べる **noberu** extend *thanks, congratulations*; state

伸びをする **nobi o suru** stretch

延びる **nobiru** be postponed

伸びる **nobiru** grow; stretch

上る **noboru** mount, go up

登る **noboru** climb; be up (*of sun*)

昇る **noboru** rise, come up

のぼせる **noboseru** feel hot; be crazy about

ノブ **nobu** handle; knob

…ので **…node** because; as; since

のど **nodo** throat; gullet; のどがからからである **nodo ga karakara de aru** be parched; のどを鳴らす **nodo o narasu** gurgle; purr

のど飴 **nodo-ame** throat lozenges

のどか(な) **nodoka (na)** calm; peaceful

のどが渇いて **nodo ga kawaite** thirsty; dehydrated

逃れる **nogareru** elude; escape

逃す **nogasu** miss out on; set free

脳外科医 **nōgekai** brain surgeon

農業 **nōgyō** agriculture

農業(の) **nōgyō (no)** agricultural

野原 **nohara** field

ノウハウ **nōhau** expertise, knowhow

ノイローゼ **noirōze** nervous breakdown

農場 **nōjō** farm

農場主 **nōjōshu** farmer

野宿する **nojuku suru** sleep rough

農家 **nōka** farmhouse

ノック **nokku** knock

ノックアウト **nokku-auto** knockout

ノックアウトする **nokku-auto suru** knock out

ノックする **nokku suru** knock

のこぎり **nokogiri** saw

ノーコメント **nō komento** no comment

残らず **nokorazu** completely; without exception

残り **nokori** remainder, rest; remnant

残り物 **nokorimono** left-overs

残る **nokoru** remain, be left

残す **nokosu** leave, bequeath

能面 **Nōmen** No mask

のめり込む **nomerikomu** be into, get enthusiastic about

のみ **nomi** chisel; flea

のみ **-nomi** *fml* only

飲み干す **nomihosu** drink up; lap up

飲み込む **nomikomu** swallow; engulf

飲物 **nomimono** drink

農民 **nōmin** peasant

飲みに行く **nomi ni iku** go for a drink

のみ屋 **nomi-ya** bookmaker, bookie

飲む **nomu** drink; consume

飲んべえ **nonbē** heavy drinker

のんびりした **nonbiri shita** carefree; laidback; lazy *day*

飲んだくれ **nondakure** drunk; drunkard

ノンフィクション **non-fikushon** nonfiction

のに **-noni** although; if only; in order to; 熱いのに **atsui noni** although it's hot; 勉強しておけばよかったのに **benkyō shite okeba yokatta noni** if only I'd studied

のんき(な) **nonki (na)** happy-go-lucky

ののしり **nonoshiri** abuse

ののしる **nonoshiru** abuse; call names; curse; swear at

納入日 **nōnyūbi** delivery date

納入業者 **nōnyū-gyōsha** supplier

野良犬 **nora-inu** stray

のらくら暮らす **norakura kurasu** laze around; loaf around

野良猫 **nora-neko** stray (*cat*)

のれん **noren** *short cloth curtain at the entrance to a restaurant or store*

のり **nori** paste (*adhesive*); sheet of seaweed

乗り出す **noridasu** set out; embark on

乗り物酔い **norimonoyoi** travelsick

乗り換え **norikae** transfer

乗り換える **norikaeru** change

乗り切る **norikiru** get over; overcome; weather

乗り越える **norikoeru** surmount; get over *fence, disappointment etc*

乗組員 **norikumiin** crew

乗り物 **norimono** vehicle

乗り遅れる **noriokureru** miss *bus, train etc*

乗捨てる **norisuteru** abandon *ship*; drop off *one-way rental car*

乗り手 **norite** rider

能率的に **nōritsuteki ni** efficiently

のろい **noroi** slow; sluggish; dull-witted ◊ curse

のろのろ進む **noronoro susumu** crawl; drag (*of time*)

のろのろと **noronoro to** at a crawl

のろう **norou** curse

乗る **noru** board, get on; get in (*to car*), catch, get; mount; ride

載る **noru** be on top of; be printed

ノルマ **noruma** norm

能力 **nōryoku** ability; capacity; competence

乗せる **noseru** carry; pick up (*in car*)

載せる **noseru** load; put; place; print

乗せて行く **nosete iku** drive; take; give a ride to

脳しんとう **nōshintō** concussion

濃縮された **nōshuku sareta** concentrated

濃淡 **nōtan** light and shade; tone

ノート **nōto** notebook

ノートブック **nōto-bukku** notebook (computer)

乗っ取り **nottori** hijack

乗っ取り犯 **nottorihan** hijacker

乗っ取る **nottoru** hijack; take over *company*

…のうち **… no uchi** between; among; within ; 十人のうち一人 **jū-nin no uchi hitori** one in ten

納税者 **nōzei-sha** tax payer

除いて **nozoite** except for, aside from

のぞき穴 **nozokiana** peephole

のぞき見する **nozokimi suru** peek, peep

除く **nozoku** exclude

望ましい **nozomashii** advisable; desirable

望み **nozomi** hope; prospect; wish

望む **nozomu** wish; hope

ノズル **nozuru** nozzle

ヌード **nūdo** nude (*painting*)

ヌード雑誌 **nūdo-zasshi** girlie magazine

ヌガー **nugā** nougat

脱ぐ **nugu** remove, take off *clothes*; undo *shirt*

ぬぐう **nuguu** mop; wipe

ぬいぐるみ **nuigurumi** stuffed toy, cuddly toy

縫い目 **nuime** seam; stitching

縫い物 **nuimono** sewing; needlework

縫いつける **nuitsukeru** sew on

抜け穴 **nukeana** loophole

抜け出す **nukedasu** slip out; sneak away

抜け目のない **nukeme no nai** shrewd, smart

抜ける **nukeru** fall out; come off; escape; be missing

抜き取り検査 **nukitori-kensa** spot check

抜き打ち検査をする **nukiuchi kensa o suru** carry out spot checks

抜く **nuku** extract, take out *tooth*; pull out; draw *gun, knife*; drain; pluck

沼地 **numachi** marsh; swamp

布 **nuno** cloth, fabric

ぬらす **nurasu** soak

ぬれた **nureta** wet

塗りたくる **nuritakuru** daub

塗る **nuru** spread; paint

ぬるい **nurui** lukewarm

ぬるぬるした物 **nurunuru shita mono** slimy; slippery

盗み **nusumi** theft

盗み聞きする **nusumigiki suru** eavesdrop; listen in

盗み見する **nusumimi suru** sneak a glance at

盗む **nusumu** steal

縫う **nuu** sew; stitch

にゃあ **nyā** miaow

尿 **nyō** urine

入学願書 **nyūgaku-gansho** application form

入学させる **nyūgaku saseru** admit (*to school*)

入学式 **nyūgaku-shiki** admission ceremony

入学する **nyūgaku suru** enroll; matriculate; enter *school, college*

入学手続 **nyūgaku-tetsuzuki** registration; 入学手続きをする **nyūgaku-tetsuzuki o suru** register

乳がん **nyūgan** breast cancer

入院患者 **nyūin-kanja** inmate; in-patient

入院させる **nyūin saseru** admit (*to hospital*); keep in the hospital

入院する **nyūin suru** go into *hospital*

ニュージーランド **Nyū-Jīrando** New Zealand

ニュージーランド人 **Nyū-Jīrando-jin** New Zealander

入場 **nyūjō** admission, entry

入場券 **nyūjōken** pass; platform ticket

入場無料 **nyūjō-muryō** admission free

入場料 **nyūjōryō** entrance fee

入場させる **nyūjō saseru** admit (*to a place*)

入会させる **nyūkai saseru** admit (*to organization*)

入館者 **nyūkan-sha** visitor (*to museum etc*)

入金 **nyūkin** credit (*payment received*)

入国 **nyūkoku** entry (*to country*)

入国ビザ **nyūkoku-biza** entry visa

入国管理局 **Nyūkoku-kanrikyoku** Immigration

入国審査 **nyūkoku-shinsa** passport control

入力 **nyūryoku** input

入力する **nyūryoku suru** enter, input, key (in) COMPUT

入札 **nyūsatsu** bid; tender COM

乳製品 **nyū-seihin** dairy products

入社式 **nyūsha-shiki** induction ceremony

入社する **nyūsha suru** join a company

入賞する **nyūshō suru** win a prize

ニュース **nyūsu** news

ニュースキャスター **nyūsu-kyasutā** anchor man

ニュース速報 **nyūsu-sokuhō** news flash

ニュートラル **nyūtoraru** neutral (*gear*)

ニューヨーク **Nyū-Yōku** New York

入浴する **nyūyoku suru** take a bath

O

お **o** (*honorific*): お友達 *o-tomodachi* your friend; また明日お電話いたします *mata ashita o-denwa itashimasu* I'll call you again tomorrow

を **o** (*direct object particle*): 映画を見に行く *eiga o mi ni iku* go to see a movie

尾 **o** tail

王 **ō** king

オアシス **oashisu** oasis

おば **oba** aunt

オーバー **ōbā** overcoat

おばあちゃん **obāchan** grandma, granny

大ばか **ōbaka** lunatic

お化けの出そう(な) **obake no desō** (na) spooky

オーバーオール **ōbāōru** dungarees

おばさん **obasan** aunt

おばあさん **obāsan** grandmother; granny

欧米 **ōbei** the West; Europe and the US

お弁当 **obentō** lunch box

おび **obi** cloth belt (*kimono sash*)

おびえさせる **obiesaseru** terrorize

おびえる **obieru** be frightened

おびき寄せる **obikiyoseru** lure

脅かす **obiyakasu** threaten, menace

応募 **ōbo** application

覚えがある **oboe ga aru** recognize

覚え書き **oboegaki** reminder

覚える **oboeru** remember; memorize; feel; pick up *language, skill*

覚えやすい **oboeyasui** catchy

お盆 **Obon** O-bon (*Buddhist festival in August*)

横暴(な) **ōbō (na)** domineering; high-handed

おぼれる **oboreru** drown; be drowned

お坊さん **obōsan** Buddhist priest

応募者 **ōbo-sha** applicant

応募する **ōbo suru** apply for

オーブン **ōbun** oven

オーブン皿 **ōbun-zara** oven tray

お茶 **ocha** Japanese tea

落ち **ochi** punch line

落ち込む **ochikomu** sink, fall; have the blues

落ちる **ochiru** come out, go (*of stain*); fail *exam*; fall down; drop; land (*of ball*); slacken off (*of pace*)

落ち着いた **ochitsuita** calm, composed; balanced

落ち着かない **ochitsukanai** feel ill at ease ◊ restless; unsettled; uncomfortable

落ち着かせる **ochitsukaseru** cool down

落ち着き **ochitsuki** balance, composure, poise

落ち着く **ochitsuku** calm; cool (down); wind down; settle (down); feel at ease

王朝 **ōchō** dynasty

お中元 **o-chūgen** mid-year gift

殴打 **ōda** blow; thrashing

お大事に **odaiji ni** bless you (*when s.o. sneezes*); take care (*said to s.o. who is ill*)

オーダーメイド(の) **ōdāmēdo (no)** made-to-measure

黄だん **ōdan** jaundice

横断できない **ōdan dekinai** impassable

横断歩道 **ōdan-hodō** crosswalk

横断幕 **ōdanmaku** banner

横断する **ōdan suru** go across

穏やか(な) **odayaka (na)** calm; mild; peaceable; serene

穏やかさ **odayaka-sa** mildness

おでき **odeki** boil; skin eruption

オーディオ(の) **ōdio (no)** audio

オーディション **ōdishon** audition; screen test; オーディションを受ける **ōdishon o ukeru** audition

オードブル **ōdoburu** hors d'oeuvre

踊り **odori** dance

大通り **ōdōri** main street; avenue

踊り場 **odoriba** landing (*top of staircase*)

驚かす **odorokasu** astonish, surprise; startle

驚き **odoroki** astonishment; surprise; wonder; fright; alarm

驚く **odoroku** be astonished

驚くべき **odoroku beki** amazing, surprising

驚くほど **odoroku hodo** suprisingly

驚くほど(の) **odoroku hodo (no)** astonishing, phenomenal

踊る **odoru** dance

脅し **odoshi** intimidation; menace

脅しつける **odoshitsukeru** browbeat

脅す **odosu** intimidate; menace

応援する **ōen suru** support

終える **oeru** cease; end, finish; round off; conclude

OL **ōeru** *female clerical employee*

オフィス **ofisu** office

オフィスビル **ofisubiru** office block

オフホワイト(の) **ofuhowaito (no)** off-white

往復 **ōfuku** round trip ◊ there and back

往復切符 **ōfuku-kippu** round trip ticket

往復する **ōfuku suru** shuttle

オフライン式(の) **ofurain-shiki (no)** off-line

オフサイド(の) **ofusaido (no)** offside SP

オフシーズン **ofushīzun** low season

大がかり(な) **ōgakari (na)** ambitious; large scale

おがくず **ogakuzu** sawdust

拝む **ogamu** pray; worship

オーガニック **ōganikku** organic

大型(の) **ōgata (no)** large-sized

小川 **ogawa** stream, creek

オーガズム **ōgazumu** orgasm

お元気で **ogenki de** all the best!

(お)元気ですか **(o) genki desu ka** how are you?

大げさ **ōgesa** exaggeration

大げさ(な) **ōgesa (na)** melodramatic; ornate

補い合う **oginaiau** complementary

補う **oginau** compensate for; supplement; complement

大声 **ōgoe** shout; 大声を出す **ōgoe o dasu** cry out; 大声で呼ぶ **ōgoe de yobu** call out

おごる **ogoru** buy a drink / meal for, treat; 一杯おごらせてください **ippai ogorasete kudasai** can I buy you a drink?

大幅に **ōhaba ni** greatly; drastically

お払い箱にする **oharaibako ni suru** dismiss; sack; pension off

おはよう(ございます) **ohayō (gozaimasu)** good morning

横柄(な) **ōhei (na)** insolent; arrogant

尾ひれをつける **ohire o tsukeru** embroider

大広間 **ōhiroma** hall

お昼 **ohiru** lunch

お冷や **ohiya** iced water

オホーツク海 **Ohōtsuku-kai** Sea of Okhotsk

おい **oi** hey! ◊ nephew

覆い **ōi** coating, layer; hood (*over cooker*)

多い **ōi** much; many; frequent

追い出す **oidasu** throw out, kick out

追い払う **oiharau** repel; chase away, see off; send away

追いかける **oikakeru** chase

覆い隠す **ōikakusu** hide; screen

追い風 **oikaze** tail wind

王位継承 **ōi-keishō** succession (*to the throne*)

追い込む **oikomu** drive into *situation, corner*; condemn

追い越し車線 **oikoshi-shasen** fast lane

追い越す **oikosu** pass, overtake

大いに **ōi ni** very much

オイル **oiru** oil

お医者さん **oishasan** doctor

おいしい **oishii** good; nice; delicious

おいしそう(な) **oishisō (na)** appetizing; tempting; gorgeous *smell*

大急ぎ **ōisogi** hurry, rush; ...を大急ぎで病院に連れていった **... o ōisogi de byōin ni tsurete itta** rush ... to the hospital

おいて **oite**: この点において **kono ten ni oite** in this respect

置いてある **oite aru** stand; be placed

置いて行く **oite iku** deliver, drop off; leave behind

追いつく **oitsuku** catch up; overtake

追い詰める **oitsumeru** corner

お祝い **oiwai** celebration; お祝いの言葉 **oiwai no kotoba** congratulations

おじ **oji** uncle

王子 **ōji** prince

おじぎ **ojigi** bow (*greeting*); おじぎをする **ojigi o suru** bow

おじいちゃん **ojiichan** granddad, grandpa

おじいさん **ojiisan** grandfather; grandpa

おじけづく **ojikezuku** lose courage; get frightened

応じる **ōjiru** respond, react; live up to, come up to

おじさん **ojisan** uncle

王女 **ōjo** princess

お嬢さん **ojōsan** daughter; ma'am

お上手(の) **ojōzu (no)** flattering

丘 **oka** hill; mound

おかえりなさい **okaerinasai** welcome home

おかげで **okage de** thanks to

横隔膜 **ōkakumaku** diaphragm

お構いなく **okamainaku** with no regard for

おおかみ **ōkami** wolf

お金 **okane** money

お金持ち(の) **okanemochi (no)** loaded, rich

お勘定 **o-kanjō** check, bill; お勘定

お願い **o-kanjō o-negai** the check, please

オカルト **okaruto** occult

お母さん **okāsan** mother

お菓子 **okashi** confectionery

おかしい **okashii** humorous; odd; suspicious

おかし(な) **okashi (na)** funny, strange

おかしなことに **okashi na koto ni** funnily enough

冒す **okasu** brave *danger*; affect

犯す **okasu** commit

侵す **okasu** invade; infringe

おかわり **okawari**: 紅茶のおかわりは **kōcha no okawari wa** some more tea?

おかず **okazu** side dishes

おけ **oke** bucket

オーケー **ōkē** ok

オーケストラ **ōkesutora** orchestra

置き場 **okiba** storage space; yard

大きい **ōkii** big; loud

置き換え **okikae** substitution

大きくする **ōkiku suru** enlarge

お決まり(の) **okimari (no)** routine

大き(な) **ōki (na)** great, big; large; 大きなお世話だ **ōkina osewa da** that's none of your business

起き直る **okinaoru** sit up (in bed)

沖縄 **Okinawa** Okinawa

お気に入り **oki ni iri** favorite

置きに **oki ni** every other ; 一日置きに **ichi-nichi oki ni** every other day

起きる **okiru** get up (*in morning*); be up (*out of bed*)

大きさ **ōki-sa** size, magnitude

起きている **okite iru** sit up, stay up (*at night*)

置き忘れる **okiwasureru** leave (behind); mislay

おこがましい **okogamashii** impertinent; presumptuous

王国 **ōkoku** kingdom

行い **okonai** conduct; deed

行う **okonau** perform; carry out; transact

行われる **okonawareru** take place

お好み焼き **okonomiyaki** Japanese savory pancake

怒らせる **okoraseru** anger; displease; offend, insult; provoke

怒り出す **okoridasu** flare up

怒りっぽい **okorippoi** bad-tempered, cranky; irritable

起こりうる **okoriuru** potential

怒る **okoru** get angry

起こる **okoru** happen, occur; break out (*of fight*); get up (*of wind*); arise

起こす **okosu** wake, rouse

…お断り **…okotowari** please do not …

怒った **okotta** angry; exasperated; annoyed

怒っている **okotte iru** cross, angry; resentful

奥 **oku** back (*of room, drawer*)

億 **oku** hundred million

置く **oku** deposit, place, put, set

オーク **ōku** oak (tree)

奥歯 **okuba** molar

臆病 **okubyō** cowardice

臆病者 **okubyō-mono** coward

臆病(な) **okubyō (na)** cowardly; timid

屋外(の) **okugai (no)** outdoor, open-air

屋内(の) **okunai (no)** indoor

多く(の) **ōku (no)** much; many

大蔵大臣 **Ōkura-daijin** Minister of Finance

遅らせる **okuraseru** hold up, make late; set back, delay; slow down

大蔵省 **Ōkura-shō** Treasury Department; Japanese Ministry of Finance

遅れ **okure** delay, hold up

遅れる **okureru** be delayed; lag behind; lose (*of clock*)

遅れた **okureta** backward; late; overdue

遅れている **okurete iru** be slow (*of clock*); be behind

送り出す **okuridasu** see out, see to the door

送りがな **okurigana** *syllabary letters added to Chinese characters to show inflection*

贈り物 **okurimono** gift

贈る **okuru** present, give

送る **okuru** send, ship; transmit; see off (*at airport etc*); take back *person*

奥さん **okusan** wife; ma'am

オークション **ōkushon** auction

憶測 **okusoku** speculation, guess

憶測する **okusoku suru** speculate, guess

お悔やみ **okuyami** condolences

奥行き **okuyuki** depth

奥行きの深い **okuyuki no fukai** deep

オーク材 **ōku-zai** oak

お経 **okyō** Buddhist sutra

応急(の) **ōkyū (no)** emergency

応急処置 **ōkyū-shochi** first aid; emergency treatment

お前 **omae** you (*familiar*)

お孫さん **omago-san** grandchild; grandson; granddaughter

お参りする **omairi suru** visit a shrine

おまけ **omake** bonus, extra; free gift

おまけに **omake ni** on top of that

お守り **omamori** lucky charm

おまる **omaru** potty; bedpan

大また **ōmata** stride; 大またで歩く **ōmata de aruku** stride

お待たせしました **omatase shimashita** sorry to keep you waiting

お祭り **omatsuri** festival

お巡りさん **omawari-san** cop

おめでとう **omedetō** best wishes; congratulations on …; well done; …におめでとうと言う **... ni omedetō to iu** congratulate

汚名 **omei** stigma, shame

お目にかかる **ome ni kakaru** (*polite*) see *person*

大目に見る **ōme ni miru** make allowances

お見合い **omiai** meeting to discuss an arranged marriage

おみくじ **omikuji** written oracle received at shrine

大みそか **Ōmisoka** New Year's Eve

おもちゃ **omocha** toy

重い **omoi** heavy; serious; tough

思い上った **omoiagatta** conceited

思い違い **omoichigai** misunderstanding

思い出させる **omoidasaseru** bring back; be reminiscent of

思い出す **omoidasu** remember, recollect; remind

思い出 **omoide** memory, recollection

思い出話をする **omoidebanashi o suru** reminisce

思い通りにする **omoidōri ni suru** have one's (own) way

思いがけない **omoigakenai** unexpected, unforeseen

思い切り **omoikiri** with all one's might; as hard / fast as you can; 思い切り遊ぶ **omoikiri asobu** have a great time

思い切って…する **omoikitte ... suru** dare; venture; 思い切ってやってみる **omoikitte yatte miru** take the plunge

思い込む **omoikomu** have the impression that; be convinced that

思い過ごしです **omoisugoshi desu** it's all in your imagination

思いとどまらせる **omoi-todomaraseru** dissuade, put off

思いつき **omoitsuki** plan; idea

思いつく **omoitsuku** hit on a plan

思いやり **omoiyari** consideration; empathy

思いやりのある **omoiyari no aru** caring; considerate; understanding; unselfish

思いやりのない **omoiyari no nai** inconsiderate

思いやる **omoiyaru** consider

大文字 **ōmoji** capital letter

大もうけする **ōmōke suru** make a killing, clean up

主(な) **omo (na)** chief, main

重荷 **omoni** burden, millstone

主に **omo ni** mainly, mostly

大物 **ōmono** tycoon

重さ **omo-sa** weight; 重さが…である **omo-sa ga ... de aru** weigh; 重さを量る **omo-sa o hakaru** weigh

おもしろがる **omoshirogaru** be amused at

おもしろ半分で **omoshiro hanbun de** (just) for kicks; for fun

おもしろい **omoshiroi** entertaining; amusing; hilarious; interesting

おもしろく **omoshiroku** funnily

重たい **omotai** heavy

表 **omote** front

表向き **omotemuki** front, cover

表向きは **omotemuki wa** officially

おもてなし **omotenashi** hospitality

思う **omou** think; expect; feel; reckon; ...と思う ... **to omou** regard as; ...と思われる ... **to omowareru** it appears that; ...と思われている ... **to omowarete iru** it is considered to be

思う存分 **omouzonbun** to one's heart's content

思わず **omowazu** involuntarily, in spite of oneself; 思わず笑ってしまう **omowazu waratte shimau** I couldn't help laughing

おうむ **ōmu** parrot

大麦 **ōmugi** barley

オムレツ **omuretsu** omelet

おむすび **omusubi** rice ball

おむつ **omutsu** diaper

恩 **on** debt of gratitude; indebtedness

オーナー **ōnā** owner

同じ **onaji** the same; ...と同じだけ ... **to onaji dake** as much as

同じくらいに **onaji kurai ni**; ...と同じくらい高い/かわいい ... **to onaji kurai takai / kawaii** as high / pretty as

おなか **onaka** tummy; belly; おなかが一杯になる **onaka ga ippai ni naru** be full up; おなかがペコペコである **onaka ga pekopeko de aru** I'm starving; おなかがすいた **onaka ga suita** I'm hungry; おなか一杯食べる **onaka-ippai taberu** eat one's fill; おなかをこわしている **onaka o kowashite iru** have an upset stomach

おなか痛 **onakaita** stomach-ache

おんぶ **onbu** piggyback

御中 **onchū** *fml* to; Messrs

温度 **ondo** temperature

温度計 **ondokei** thermometer

おんどり **ondori** cock, cockerel

尾根 **one** ridge

お願い **onegai** favor; request

お願いします **onegai shimasu** please

お願いする **onegai suru** request

恩返しする **ongaeshi suru** repay

お姉さん **onēsan** elder sister

音楽 **ongaku** music

音楽家 **ongakuka** musician

音楽(の) **ongaku (no)** musical

音楽的でない **ongakuteki de nai** unmusical

音楽的(な) **ongakuteki (na)** melodious

音楽好き(な) **ongakuzuki (na)** musical

鬼 **oni** devil

鬼ばば **onibaba** dragon; nag

おにぎり **onigiri** rice ball

大人数 **ōninzū** large number of people

お兄さん **onīsan** elder brother

恩人 **onjin** benefactor

音階 **onkai** scale MUS

音感のよい **onkan no yoi** musical

穏健派 **onkenha** moderate

穏健(な) **onken (na)** moderate

恩着せがましい **onkisegamashii** condescending

音響効果 **onkyō-kōka** acoustics

女 **onna** woman; female; chick

女形 **onnagata** *female impersonator in Kabuki*

女の子 **onna no ko** girl

女らしい **onna-rashii** feminine

女主人 **onna-shujin** landlady; mistress (*of servant*)

女たらし **onnatarashi** womanizer, wolf

女友達 **onna-tomodachi** girlfriend (*of girl*)

おの **ono** ax; chopper (*tool*)

音符 **onpu** note MUS

オンライン(の) **onrain (no)** on-line

オンラインサービス **onrain-sābisu** on-line service

温泉 **onsen** hot spring

音節 **onsetsu** syllable

恩赦 **onsha** amnesty; pardon

恩知らず **onshirazu** ingratitude

恩知らず(の) **onshirazu (no)** ungrateful

温室 **onshitsu** conservatory; greenhouse

温室効果 **onshitsu-kōka** greenhouse effect

温床 **onshō** breeding ground

オンス **onsu** ounce

温水 **onsui** heated water

温帯 **ontai** temperate zone

音訳する **on'yaku suru** transliterate

オンザロック **on-za-rokku** on the rocks ◊ whiskey and water

おおやまねこ **ōyamaneko** lynx

オペラ **opera** opera

オペラグラス **operagurasu** opera glasses

オペレーター **operētā** operator TELEC

オペレーティングシステム **operētingu-shisutemu** operating system

オープンチケット **ōpun-chiketto** open ticket

オープンカー **ōpun-kā** convertible

オープンプランオフィス **ōpun-puran-ofisu** open plan office

オプション **opushon** optional extras

往来 **ōrai** traffic

オランダ **Oranda** Holland

オランダ語 **Oranda-go** Dutch

オーラルセックス **ōraru-sekkusu** oral sex

おれ **ore** (*familiar, used by men*) I

お礼 **orei** bow; thanks; remuneration

オレンジ **orenji** orange

オレンジ色 **orenji-iro** orange

折れる **oreru** break

おり **ori** cage; occasion

オリーブオイル **orību-oiru** olive oil

折り紙 **origami** origami

オリジナル **orijinaru** original *painting etc*

折り返し **orikaeshi** cuff (*of pants*)

折り返し(で) **orikaeshi (de)** by return (*of mail*); …に折り返し電話する **… ni orikaeshi denwa suru** call back

折返し運転 **orikaeshi-unten** shuttle service

折り返す **orikaesu** turn back *edges, sheets*; turn up *collar*

折り込み広告 **orikomi kōkoku** insert

折り目 **orime** crease (*in pants*); fold

織物 **orimono** textile; tissue

折りの悪い **ori no warui** untimely

オリンピック **Orinpikku** Olympics

降りる, 下りる **oriru** descend; come down; go down; come down; disembark; get off

折りたたみ式ベッド **oritatami-shiki-beddo** folding bed

折りたたみ式(の) **oritatami-shiki (no)** folding

折りたたむ **oritatamu** fold (up)

往路 **ōro** outward journey

愚か(な) **oroka (na)** stupid; mindless

愚かさ **oroka-sa** stupidity; folly

卸で **oroshi de** wholesale

おろし金 **oroshigane** grater

卸(の) **oroshi (no)** wholesale

下ろす **orosu** let down *hair, blinds*

降ろす **orosu** drop (off) (*from car*); lower

折る **oru** break; break off

織る **oru** weave

オール **ōru** oar

オルガン **orugan** organ MUS

横領 **ōryō** misappropriation

横領する **ōryō suru** misappropriate

抑えきれない **osaekirenai** irrepressible

抑える **osaeru** check, restrain; keep back; keep down *costs etc*; repress; bring under control

押さえつける **osaetsukeru** pin, hold down

おさげ髪 **osagegami** braid; plait; pigtail

大さじ **ōsaji** tablespoon

大阪 **Ōsaka** Osaka

収まる **osamaru** subside, blow over, quieten down

納まる **osamaru** fit, go in

治める **osameru** govern

納める **osameru** settle *debts*

お産 **osan** confinement MED

幼い **osanai** very young; infantile

大騒ぎ **ōsawagi** scene (*argument*); uproar; 大騒ぎをする *ōsawagi o suru* make a scene

大騒ぎ(の) **ōsawagi (no)** wild

オセアニア **Oseania** Oceania

おせち料理 **osechi-ryōri** *traditional New Year food*

お歳暮 **o-seibo** year-end gift

おう盛(な) **ōsei (na)** hearty; active

お世辞 **oseji** flattery; お世辞のうまい *oseji no umai* smooth; お世辞を言う *oseji o iu* flatter

おせっかいな人 **osekkai na hito** busybody

お説教をする **osekkyō o suru** preach

汚染 **osen** pollution; contamination

汚染物質 **osen-busshitsu** pollutant

汚染する **osen suru** pollute; infect

応接室 **ōsetsushitsu** drawing room; room for visitors

おしゃべり **oshaberi** gossip; chat; banter; chatterbox

おしゃべり(な) **oshaberi (na)** talkative

おしゃべりする **oshaberi suru** chat

おしゃぶり **oshaburi** pacifier

おしゃれ(な) **oshare (na)** stylish

押し上げる **oshiageru** push off *lid*; push up *prices*

押しボタン **oshi-botan** button, push-button

おしどり **oshidori** mandarin duck

教える **oshieru** educate; teach, instruct

惜しい **oshii** regrettable; unfortunate ◊ be precious

押し入れ **oshiire** storage space

押し入る **oshiiru** jam, squeeze

押しかける **oshikakeru** gatecrash

おしっこをする **oshikko o suru** pee

押し込み強盗 **oshikomi-gōtō** burglary, break-in; housebreaking

押し込む **oshikomu** jam, ram; squeeze in

おしまい **oshimai** conclusion, end

おしめ **oshime** diaper

惜しむ **oshimu** regret; be

ungenerous; begrudge

押しのける **oshinokeru** elbow out of the way

おしろい **oshiroi** face powder; …におしろいを塗る *... ni oshiroi o nuru* powder

押し進む **oshisusumu** push along

押し倒す **oshitaosu** overpower

押しつぶす **oshitsubusu** crush

押しつける **oshitsukeru** coerce; force

押し売り **oshiuri** high-pressure selling

押し売り(の) **oshiuri (no)** high-pressure *salesman*

押し寄せる **oshiyoseru** close in

汚職 **oshoku** corruption; bribery

押収 **ōshū** seizure

押収する **ōshū suru** seize

遅い **osoi** late (*in day*); tardy; slow

襲いかかる **osoikakaru** attack; pounce on; go for

大掃除 **ōsōji** spring-cleaning

遅くなった **osoku natta** belated; 遅くなってきた *osoku natte kita* it's getting late; 遅くなります *osoku narimasu* I won't be back until late

お粗末(な) **osomatsu (na)** flimsy; poor; crude

お供え **osonae** offering

おそらく **osoraku** possibly, perhaps; おそらく…しない *osoraku ... shinai* hardly; not likely

恐れ **osore** fear

恐れいります **osore irimasu** (*polite*) thank you

恐れる **osoreru** fear

おそろい(の) **osoroi (no)** matching

恐ろしい **osoroshii** terrifying; frightening

襲う **osou** attack; break (*of storm*)

おっしゃる **ossharu** (*polite*) say; tell

雄 **osu** male (*animal*)

押す **osu** press; push, shove

雄猫 **osuneko** tomcat

オーストラレーシア **Ōsutorarēshia** Australasia

オーストラリア **Ōsutoraria** Australia

オーストラリア人 **Ōsutoraria-jin** Australian

オーストラリア(の) **Ōsutoraria (no)** Australian

オーストリア **Ōsutoria** Austria

オーストリア (の) **Ōsutoria (no)** Austrian

おたふくかぜ **otafukukaze** mumps

お互いに **otagai ni** one another, each other

応対に出る **ōtai ni deru** answer the door

応対する **ōtai suru** deal with customers

おたま **otama** ladle

おたまじゃくし **otamajakushi** tadpole

お誕生日おめでとう **otanjōbi omedetō** happy birthday!

王手 **ōte** checkmate

お手洗 **otearai** rest room, washroom

お手柄 **otegara** great feat

おてんば **otenba** tomboy

お手伝い **otetsudai** maid

音 **oto** noise, sound

おう吐 **ōto** vomiting

オートバイ **ōtobai** motorbike, motorcycle

おとぎ話 **otogi-banashi** fairy tale

男 **otoko** man

男の子 **otoko no ko** boy

男っぽい **otokoppoi** macho

男っぽさ **otokoppo-sa** machismo

男らしい **otokorashii** manly; virile

男らしさ **otokorashi-sa** masculinity; virility

男やもめ **otokoyamome** widower

お得意さん **otokuisan** good customer

お徳用 **otokuyō** economy size

オートマチック **ōtomachikku** automatic

オートメーション **ōtomēshon** automation

大人 **otona** adult, grown-up

おとなしい **otonashii** meek, mild

おとなしく **otonashiku** meekly

おとり **otori** decoy, diversion

衰える **otoroeru** weaken; ebb away

劣る **otoru** be inferior

お父さん **otōsan** father; dad

落し穴 **otoshiana** catch, pitfall

落し物 **otoshimono** lost and found

お年寄り **otoshiyori** old person

落とす **otosu** drop; droop (*of shoulders*); slacken; shed *leaves*

弟 **otōto** younger brother

おととい **ototoi** the day before yesterday

弟さん **otōtosan** younger brother

おととし **ototoshi** year before last

劣った **ototta** inferior

訪れる **otozureru** visit; arrive

おつまみ **otsumami** nibbles; snacks

お釣り **otsuri** change

追っ手 **otte** those in pursuit; 追って 通知する **otte tsūchi suru** until further notice

夫 **otto** husband

追う **ou** chase; pursue; follow

負う **ou** bear *responsibility, debt*; carry on one's back

覆う **ōu** coat, cover; cover up; envelop

大売り出し **ōuridashi** clearance sale

雄牛 **oushi** bull; ox

おわび **owabi** apology

おわん **owan** bowl

大笑い **ōwarai** hysterics

大笑いする **ōwarai suru** howl, roar with laughter

終わらせる **owaraseru** terminate; finish off; put an end to

終わり **owari** end; ending

終わりである **owari de aru** be over, be finished

終わりのない **owari no nai** endless

終わる **owaru** finish; end; be through (*of couple*); result in

親 **oya** parent; dealer (*in card games*)

おや、まあ **oya, mā** oh dear!, good heavens!

親会社 **oyagaisha** holding company; parent company

公(の) **ōyake (no)** public

親子 **oyako** parent and child; family

親(の) **oya (no)** parental

親知らず **oyashirazu** wisdom tooth

おやすみ(なさい) **oyasumi (nasai)** good night

親指 **oyayubi** thumb
及び **oyobi** and; as well as
及ぼす **oyobosu** influence; affect; exert
及ぶ **oyobu** reach; extend to
泳ぎ **oyogi** swimming; 泳ぎに行く **oyogi ni iku** go swimming, go for a swim
泳ぐ **oyogu** swim
大喜び **ōyorokobi** delight
大喜び(の) **ōyorokobi (no)** elated; overjoyed; jubilant
大喜びする **ōyorokobi suru** exult
およそ **oyoso** around, approximately

おおよそ(の) **ōyoso (no)** approximate
王座 **ōza** throne
大酒 **ōzake** heavy drinking; bender
大ざっぱ(な) **ōzappa (na)** broad, general; sketchy; 大ざっぱに言って **ōzappa ni itte** broadly speaking
大皿 **ōzara** platter
大勢 **ōzei** crowd
大関 **ōzeki** sumo champion
王族 **ōzoku** royalty
オゾン **ozon** ozone
オゾン層 **ozon-sō** ozone layer
応ずる **ōzuru** comply

P

パー **pā** par (*in golf*)
パブ **pabu** pub
パチンコ **pachinko** Japanese pinball
ぱちぱちと音を立てる **pachipachi to oto o tateru** crackle
パッド **paddo** pad
パイ **pai** flan; pie
パイ生地 **pai-kiji** pastry
パイナップル **painappuru** pineapple
パイプ **paipu** pipe
パイロット **pairotto** pilot
パジャマ **pajama** pajamas
パーキングメーター **pākingu-mētā** parking meter
パキスタン **Pakisutan** Pakistan
パック **pakku** carton; pack; packet
パック旅行 **pakku-ryokō** package tour
パーコレーター **pākorētā** percolator
パーマ **pāma** perm; パーマをかける **pāma o kakeru** perm
パン **pan** bread
パンチ **panchi** punch
パンダ **panda** panda
パネル **paneru** panel

パンフレット **panfuretto** brochure; booklet; pamphlet
パニック **panikku** panic, scare; パニック状態になる **panikku-jōtai ni naru** panic
パンジー **panjī** pansy (*flower*)
パン粉 **panko** breadcrumbs
パンク **panku** blow-out (*of tire*)
パンクした **panku shita** flat
パンクする **panku suru** blow (*of tire*)
パンくず **pankuzu** breadcrumbs
パノラマ **panorama** panorama
パンティー **pantī** panties
パンティーストッキング **pantī-sutokkingu** pantyhose
パンツ **pantsu** underpants
パン屋 **pan-ya** baker; bakery
パパ **papa** dad
パラボラアンテナ **parabora-antena** satellite dish
パラサイトシングル **parasaito-shinguru** person who lives with his/her parents for a long time
パラシュート **parashūto** parachute; パラシュートで降りる **parashūto de oriru** parachute

パラソル **parasoru** parasol

パレード **parēdo** parade

パレードする **parēdo suru** parade

ぱりっとした **paritto shita** crisp *shirt, bank bills*

パルプ **parupu** pulp (*for papermaking*)

パーセント **pāsento** percent

パセリ **paseri** parsley

パソコン **pasokon** PC, personal computer

パス **pasu** pass SP

パスポート **pasupōto** passport

パスする **pasu suru** pass SP

パステル **pasuteru** pastel (*color*)

パステル調(の) **pasuteru-chō** (**no**) pastel

パスワード **pasuwādo** password

パターン **patān** pattern

パッチワーク **patchiwāku** patchwork

パーティー **pātī** party

パート **pāto** part MUS; part-time job

パトカー **patokā** patrol car

パートナー **patonā** partner (*in particular activity*)

パトロール **patorōru** patrol

パートタイム(の) **pātotaimu** (**no**) part-time

パワーシャベル **pawā-shaberu** excavator

パワーステアリング **pawā-sutearingu** power(-assisted) steering

パワーユニット **pawā-yunitto** power unit

パズル **pazuru** puzzle

ペア **pea** pair

ぺちゃくちゃしゃべる **pechakucha shaberu** yap; chatter

ペチコート **pechikōto** underskirt

ペダル **pedaru** pedal; ペダルを踏む *pedaru o fumu* pedal

ページ **pēji** page

北京語 **Pekingo** Mandarin Chinese

ぺこぺこする **pekopeko suru** fawn (on); kowtow (to)

ペン **pen** pen

ペナント **penanto** pennant

ペナルティー **penarutī** penalty SP;

ペナルティーを科す *penarutī o kasu* penalize

ペナルティーエリア **penarutī-eria** penalty area

ペンチ **penchi** pliers

ペンダント **pendanto** pendant

ペンフレンド **pen-furendo** pen friend

ペニシリン **penishirin** penicillin

ペンキ **penki** paint; ペンキを塗る *penki o nuru* paint

ペンキ塗り **penki-nuri** painting (*decorating*)

ペンキ塗りたて **penki-nuritate** wet paint

ペンキ屋 **penki-ya** painter (*decorator*)

ペンネーム **pen-nēmu** pseudonym, pen name

ペーパーバック **pēpābakku** paperback

ペパーミント **pepāminto** peppermint

ぺらぺら(の) **perapera** (**no**) fluent; talkative

ペッサリー **pessarī** diaphragm (*contraceptive*)

ペース **pēsu** pace, speed

ペースメーカー **pēsumēkā** pacemaker

ペストリー **pesutorī** pastry

ぺてん師 **peten-shi** swindler; impostor

ペッティングする **pettingu suru** pet (*of couple*)

ペット **petto** pet, domestic animal

ペットホテル **petto-hoteru** pet hotel

ピアニスト **pianisuto** pianist

ピアノ **piano** piano

ピーアール **pīāru** public relations

ピアスをする **piasu o suru** pierce

ピエロ **piero** clown

ぴかぴか(の) **pikapika** (**no**) sparkling; flashing

ぴかぴか光る **pikapika hikaru** glitter; flash

ピーク **pīku** peak, high point

ピーク時 **pīku-ji** peak hours

ピクニック **pikunikku** picnic

ぴくぴく動く **pikupiku ugoku**

twitch; move jerkily

ピクルス **pikurusu** pickles

ピーマン **pīman** pepper

ピン **pin** pin; ピンで留める **pin de tomeru** pin; attach

ピーナッツ **pīnattsu** ground nut, peanut

ピーナッツバター **pīnattsu-batā** peanut butter

ピンチ **pinchi** pinch; fix; difficulty

ピンク色 **pinku-iro** pink

ピンポン **pinpon** ping-pong ◊ *used to indicate a correct answer*

ピンセット **pinsetto** forceps; tweezers

ピンストライプ **pinsutoraipu** pinstripe

ピント **pinto** focus; ピントが合っている/ずれている **pinto ga atte iru / zurete iru** be in / out of focus; …にピントを合わせる **… ni pinto o awaseru** focus on

ぴんと張った **pin to hatta** taut; tense

ぴりぴりした **piripiri shita** uptight, nervous, jittery

ぴりぴりする **piripiri suru** sting; smart

ぴりっとした **piritto shita** savory; sharp *taste*

ピル **piru** the pill; ピルを飲んでいる **piru o nonde iru** be on the pill

ぴしゃりとたたく **pishari to tataku** slap

ピシャッと打つ **pishatto utsu** slap; smack

ピストン **pisuton** piston

ピストル **pisutoru** pistol

ピッチャー **pitchā** pitcher

ぴったり **pittari**: ぴったり合った **pittari atta** snug, tight-fitting; ぴったりだ **pittari da** it's a good fit; 体にぴったり(の) **karada ni pittari (no)** skin-tight

ピザ **piza** pizza

ポーチ **pōchi** pouch; porch

ぽい**-poi**: 子供っぽい **kodomoppoi** childish

ポーカー **pōkā** poker

ポケット **poketto** pocket

ポケットベル **poketto-beru** pager

ぽきんと折れる **pokin to oreru** snap, break

ぽきんと折る **pokin to oru** snap, break

ポン引き **ponbiki** pimp

ポニー **ponī** pony

ポニーテール **ponītēru** ponytail

ポンプ **ponpu** pump

ぽんという音 **pon to iu oto** pop

ぽんと抜く **pon to nuku** pop

ポピー **popī** poppy

ポップコーン **poppukōn** popcorn

ポップス **poppusu** pop; pop song

ポップス(の) **poppusu (no)** pop

ポーランド **Pōrando** Poland

ポリエチレン **poriechiren** polyethylene

ポリ塩化ビニール **pori-enka-binīru** PVC

ポリエステル **poriesuteru** polyester

ポリスチレン **porisuchiren** polystyrene

ポロシャツ **poroshatsu** polo shirt

ポルノ **poruno** pornography, porn

ポルトガル **Porutogaru** Portugal

ポルトガル語 **Porutogaru-go** Portuguese (*language*)

ポスター **posutā** poster

ポスト **posuto** mailbox

ぽっちゃりした **potchari shita** plump

ポテトチップス **poteto-chippusu** potato chip

ポテトフライ **poteto-furai** fried potatoes

ポット **potto** pot

ポーズをとる **pōzu o toru** pose

プードル **pūdoru** poodle

プンプンにおう **punpun niou** have a strong smell

プンプン怒る **punpun okoru** be furious

プラチナ **purachina** platinum

プラチナ製(の) **purachina-sei (no)** platinum

プラグ **puragu** plug ELEC

プライバシー **puraibashī** privacy

プライド **puraido** pride

プラカード **purakādo** placard

プラム **puramu** plum

プランテーション **purantēshon** plantation

プラス **purasu** plus (sign)

プラス(の) **purasu (no)** positive ELEC

プラスチック **purasuchikku** plastic

プラスチック製(の) **purasuchikku-sei (no)** plastic, made of plastic

プラトニック(な) **puratonikku (na)** platonic

プラットホーム **purattohōmu** platform

プレー **purē** play SP

プレハブ(の) **purehabu (no)** prefabricated

プレイボーイ **purei-bōi** flirt (*male*)

プレイガール **purei-gāru** flirt (*female*)

プレッシャー **puresshā** pressure; プレッシャーを感じる *puresshā o kanjiru* be under pressure

プレーする **purē suru** play

プレゼン **purezen** presentation

プレゼント **purezento** present

プリンター **purintā** printer

プリント **purinto** print, photograph; handout (*for class*); hard copy

プリントアウト **purinto-auto** printout

プリントアウトする **purinto-auto suru** print out

ぷりぷりする **puripuri suru** be in a huff

プリーツ **purītsu** pleat

プロ **puro** professional, pro; プロに転向する *puro ni tenkō suru* turn professional

プロバイダー **purobaidā** service provider

プロデューサー **purodyūsā** filmmaker; producer

プログラマー **puroguramā** programmer

プログラム **puroguramu** program

プロモーション **puromōshon** promotion

プロ並み(の) **puro-nami (no)** professional

プロンプト **puronputo** prompt COMPUT

プロパガンダ **puropaganda** propaganda

プロポーズ **puropōzu** proposal

プロポーズする **puropōzu suru** propose

プロテスタント **Purotesutanto** Protestant

プール **pūru** (swimming) pool; pool (*game*)

プルーン **purūn** prune

プルタブ **puru-tabu** ring-pull

ぴょんと飛ぶ **pyon to tobu** hop

R

らば **raba** mule

ラベンダー **rabendā** lavender

ラベル **raberu** label; ラベルをはる *raberu o haru* label

ラブ **rabu** love

ラブレター **raburetā** love letter

ラード **rādo** lard

ラフ **rafu** rough

ラガービール **ragābīru** lager

ライバル **raibaru** competition; rival

ライダー **raidā** motorcyclist

ライフル **raifuru** rifle

来月 **raigetsu** next month

来客 **raikyaku** guest; visitor

ライム **raimu** lime

ライン **rain** line

来年 **rainen** next year

来日する **ranichi suru** visit Japan

ラインズマン **rainzuman** linesman

ライオン **raion** lion

ライラック **rairakku** lilac (*flower*)

来週 **raishū** next week

ライス **raisu** rice (*cooked*)

ライター **raitā** lighter

ライトアップする **raitoappu suru** light, light up, illuminate

ライト級 **raito-kyū** lightweight

ライトウイング **raito-uingu** right wing SP

雷雨 **raiu** thunderstorm

ラジエーター **rajiētā** radiator

ラジオ **rajio** radio

ラジオ放送局 **rajio-hōsōkyoku** radio station

ラケット **raketto** bat; racket

楽観論 **rakkanron** optimism

楽観論者 **rakkanron-sha** optimist

楽観的(な) **rakkanteki (na)** optimistic

楽観要因 **rakkan-yōin** feelgood factor

落下傘兵 **rakkasanhei** paratrooper

ラック **rakku** rack

楽 **raku**: 楽である **raku de aru** be comfortable; 楽をする **raku o suru** live comfortably; take the easy course

落第する **rakudai suru** fail an exam (*and not be able to move up a grade*)

落書き **rakugaki** graffiti

落書きする **rakugaki suru** scribble

落語 **rakugo** comic story-telling

落語者 **rakugo-sha** dropout; loser

楽に走る **raku ni hashiru** cruise

楽々とした **rakuraku to shita** effortless

落成する **rakusei suru** be completed; inaugurate

落選する **rakusen suru** be defeated

楽勝 **rakushō** walkover

落胆した **rakutan shita** dejected, downhearted

ラーメン **rāmen** Chinese noodles

ラム **ramu** lamb; RAM

ラム酒 **ramu-shu** rum

らん **ran** orchid

欄 **ran** box (*on form*); column (*of text*)

乱暴 **ranbō** violence; hooliganism

乱暴(な) **ranbō (na)** rough, violent; rowdy; destructive

ランチ **ranchi** lunch; launch (*boat*)

ランチョンマット **ranchonmatto** place mat

ランドリー **randorī** laundry

ランジェリー **ranjerī** lingerie

乱気流 **rankiryū** turbulence

ランプ **ranpu** lamp; ramp

卵子 **ranshi** ovum, egg

卵巣 **ransō** ovary

乱闘 **rantō** scuffle

乱用 **ran'yō** abuse

乱用する **ran'yō suru** abuse

乱雑 **ranzatsu** disorder

乱雑(な) **ranzatsu (na)** disorderly

ラオス **Raosu** Laos

ラオス(の) **Raosu (no)** Laotian

ラップ **rappu** clingfilm; shrink-wrapping; lap (*in athletics*); rap MUS

ラップで包む **rappu de tsutsumu** shrink-wrap

ラップトップ **rapputoppu** laptop

られる **-rareru** ◊ (*polite*): 学長は来られますか **gakuchō wa koraremasu ka** will the college president come? ◊ (*ability*): 信じられない **shinjirarenai** I can't believe it ◊ (*passive*): 部屋は白く塗られていた **heya wa shiroku nurarete ita** the room had been painted white ◊ (*intuition*): 何か起こったと感じられた **nani ka okotta to kanjirareta** I felt that something must have happened

ラリー **rarī** rally

ら旋階段 **rasen kaidan** spiral staircase

ら旋形 **rasenkei** spiral

らしい **-rashii** apparently ◊ it appears that ◊ typical of; あなたらしい **anatarashii** that's typical of you!

ラッシュアワー **rasshu-awā** rush hour

ラストスパートをかける **rasuto-supāto o kakeru** put on a final spurt

ラテンアメリカ **Raten-Amerika** Latin America

ラテンアメリカ人 **Raten-Amerika-jin** Latin American, Hispanic

ラテンアメリカ(の) **Raten-Amerika-(no)** Latin American, Hispanic

ラウンド **raundo** round (*in boxing*)

ラズベリー **razuberī** raspberry

レア **rea** rare

レバー **rebā** lever; liver (*food*)

レベル **reberu** level, amount

レビュー **rebyū** revue

レーダー **rēdā** radar

レフトウイング **refuto-uingu** left wing SP

例 **rei** case, example

礼 **rei** etiquette; thanks; reward; fee; bow

零 **rei** zero

霊 **rei** spirit (*of dead person*)

霊安室 **reianshitsu** mortuary

レイアウトする **reiauto suru** lay out

霊媒師 **reibaishi** medium

冷房 **reibō** air conditioning

例外 **reigai** exception

例外的(な) **reigaiteki (na)** exceptional, special

礼儀 **reigi** courtesy; decency; social niceties

礼儀知らず(の) **reigishirazu (no)** ignorant; impolite

礼儀正しい **reigi-tadashii** polite, civil; respectful; well-mannered

礼儀正しさ **reigitadashi-sa** politeness

礼拝 **reihai** worship

礼拝堂 **reihaidō** chapel

令状 **reijō** warrant

零下 **reika** below zero

霊感 **reikan** inspiration; …から霊感を得る *… kara reikan o eru* be inspired by

冷血(の) **reiketsu (no)** cold-blooded

礼金 **reikin** key money (*deposit on apartment*)

冷酷 **reikoku** ruthlessness

冷酷(な) **reikoku (na)** ruthless; cold-blooded; unfeeling; remorseless

冷酷に **reikoku ni** in cold blood

冷却期間 **reikyaku-kikan** cooling-off period; break

冷却する **reikyaku suru** cool; refrigerate

霊きゅう車 **reikyū-sha** hearse

例年(の) **reinen (no)** annual

レインコート **reinkōto** raincoat

冷静(な) **reisei (na)** cool; level-headed; objective; philosophical

冷静さ **reisei-sa** detachment, objectivity

冷笑 **reishō** sneer

冷淡(な) **reitan (na)** cool, icy *welcome*; callous

冷淡に **reitan ni** coolly; indifferently

霊的(な) **reiteki (na)** spiritual

冷凍庫 **reitōko** freezer, deep freeze; freezing compartment

冷凍(の) **reitō (no)** frozen

冷凍室 **reitō-shitsu** icebox

冷凍食品 **reitō-shokuhin** (deep-) frozen food

冷凍する **reitō suru** freeze

冷蔵庫 **reizōko** refrigerator, fridge

冷蔵する **reizō suru** refrigerate

レジ **reji** checkout, cash desk

レジデント(の) **rejidento (no)** resident

レジ係 **reji-gakari** cashier

レジスター **rejisutā** cash register

歴史 **rekishi** history

歴史上(の) **rekishijō (no)** historical

歴史家 **rekishi-ka** historian

レッカー車 **rekkā-sha** wrecker, tow truck

列挙する **rekkyo suru** recite, enumerate

レコード **rekōdo** record MUS

レコードプレイヤー **rekōdo-pureiyā** record player

レモン **remon** lemon

レモネード **remonēdo** lemonade

レモンティー **remon-tī** lemon tea

恋愛 **ren'ai** love; romance

恋愛映画 **ren'ai-eiga** romance (*movie*)

恋愛関係 **ren'ai-kankei** love affair

恋愛小説 **ren'ai-shōsetsu** romance (*novel*)

恋愛する **ren'ai suru** fall in love

れんが **renga** brick

連合 **rengō** confederation; union

連合王国 **Rengō-ōkoku** United Kingdom

レンジ **renji** stove; burner

連日 **renjitsu** day after day

連盟 **renmei** league

練乳 **rennyū** condensed milk

連発 **renpatsu** torrent

連邦 **renpō** federation

連邦(の) **renpō (no)** federal

連絡 **renraku** contact; liaison; から連絡がある *kara renraku ga aru* hear from; 連絡が途絶える *renraku ga todaeru* lose touch with

連絡道路 **renraku-dōro** access road

連絡先 **renraku-saki** contact number; contact address

連絡している **renraku shite iru** keep in touch with

連絡する **renraku suru** contact; communicate

連絡役を務める **renrakuyaku o tsutomeru** liaise with

連立内閣 **renritsu-naikaku** coalition cabinet

連鎖反応 **rensa-hannō** chain reaction

連載される **rensai sareru** be serialized

練習 **renshū** practice; training; 練習不足である *renshū-busoku de aru* be out of practice; be out of training

練習帳 **renshūchō** exercise book

練習計画 **renshū-keikaku** training scheme

練習問題 **renshū-mondai** exercise EDU

練習する **renshū suru** practice

レンタカー **renta-kā** rental car

レントゲン **rentogen** X -ray; レントゲン写真を取る *rentogen-shashin o toru* X-ray

連続 **renzoku** sequence, series, succession

連続ホームコメディー **renzoku hōmu-komedī** sitcom

連続公演 **renzoku-kōen** run (*of play*)

連続公演する **renzoku-kōen suru** run (*of play*)

連続メロドラマ **renzoku merodorama** soap (opera)

連続(の) **renzoku (no)** consecutive

連続殺人犯 **renzoku-satsujinhan** serial killer

連続性 **renzokusei** continuity

連続して **renzoku shite** in succession

連続する **renzoku suru** continue

レンズ **renzu** aperture; lens

レオタード **reotādo** leotard

レポート **repōto** report; paper

レプリカ **repurika** replica

れる **-reru** → *rareru*

レール **rēru** rail

レーサー **rēsā** racing driver

列車 **ressha** train

レシーバー **reshībā** receiver

レーシングカー **rēshingu-kā** racing car

レシピ **reshipi** recipe

レシート **reshīto** receipt

レッスン **ressun** lesson

レス **rēsu** lace; race

レスラー **resurā** wrestler

レスリング **resuringu** wrestling

レストラン **resutoran** restaurant

レタス **retasu** lettuce

レート **rēto** rate

列 **retsu** column; row; tier; line; 列に並ぶ *retsu ni narabu* stand in line

劣等感 **rettōkan** inferiority complex

レーザー **rēzā** laser

レーザー光線 **rēzā-kōsen** laser beam

レーザープリンター **rēzā-purintā** laser printer

レズビアン **rezubian** lesbian

リアルタイム **riarutaimu** real time

リバイバル **ribaibaru** revival

リベート **ribēto** kickback

リビア **Ribia** Libya

リビングルーム **ribingu-rūmu** living room, sitting room

リボン **ribon** ribbon

リボルバー **riborubā** revolver

リーダー **rīdā** chief; leader

リーダーシップ **rīdā-shippu** leadership

リード **rīdo** lead (*in race*); リードして

rīdo shite in the lead, in front

リードする **rīdo suru** lead *race*

利益 **rieki** benefit; profit; yield; 利益を上げる *rieki o ageru* realize a profit; yield a profit FIN;利益を得る *rieki o eru* benefit; profit

利益のない **rieki no nai** unprofitable

リフレーション **rifureishon** reflation

リーグ **rīgu** league

利幅 **rihaba** mark-up; profit margin

リハーサル **rihāsaru** rehearsal; リハーサルをする *rihāsaru o suru* rehearse

理科 **rika** science; science department

理解 **rikai** understanding, comprehension

理解できない **rikai dekinai** incomprehensible ◊ be puzzled

理解できる **rikai dekiru** intelligible

理解し合う **rikai shiau** communicate

理解する **rikai suru** understand; assimilate; take on board

立候補 **rikkōho** candidacy

リコーダー **rikōdā** recorder MUS

離婚 **rikon** divorce

利口(な) **rikō (na)** intelligent, clever, bright

離婚した **rikon shita** divorced

離婚する **rikon suru** divorce, get divorced

離婚手当 **rikon-teate** alimony

利口さ **rikō-sa** intelligence

利己主義 **riko-shugi** self-interest

陸 **riku** land

リクエスト **rikuesuto** request

陸軍 **rikugun** army

陸上で **rikujō de** on land

陸上競技場 **rikujō-kyōgijō** athletics stadium

陸路で **rikuro de** by land, overland

理屈 **rikutsu** reason; argument; pretext

リキュール **rikyūru** liqueur

リモートアクセス **rimōto-akusesu** remote access

リモートコントロール **rimōto-**

kontorōru remote control

リム **rimu** rim

リムジン **rimujin** limo, limousine

リネン **rinen** linen

りんご **ringo** apple

リング **ringu** ring

林業 **ringyō** forestry

臨時(の) **rinji (no)** temporary; extraordinary

臨時職員 **rinji-shokuin** temp

輪郭 **rinkaku** contour; outline

臨機応変(の) **rinki-ōhen (no)** resourceful

リンク **rinku** rink

輪ね **rinne** reincarnation

リンパ腺 **rinpasen** lymph gland

倫理学 **rinri-gaku** ethics

リンリンと鳴る音 **rinrin to naru oto** tinkle; jingle

倫理的(な) **rinriteki (na)** ethical

隣接(の) **rinsetsu (no)** adjacent

隣接した **rinsetsu shita** neighboring

隣接する **rinsetsu suru** border on

臨床(の) **rinshō (no)** clinical

リンス **rinsu** conditioner

輪タク **rintaku** pedicab

立派(な) **rippa (na)** honorable; noble; admirable; respectable

立法府 **rippōfu** legislature

立法権のある **rippōken no aru** legislative

立法(の) **rippō (no)** legislative

立方体 **rippōtai** cube

リレー **rirē** relay (race)

履歴書 **rirekisho** résumé

離陸 **ririku** takeoff

離陸する **ririku suru** rise; take off (of airplane)

リリースする **rirīsu suru** bring out video, CD

利率 **riritsu** interest rate

理論 **riron** theory

理論的(な) **rironteki (na)** theoretical

理論的には **rironteki ni wa** in theory

リール **rīru** reel, spool

リサイクル **risaikuru** recycling

リサイタル **risaitaru** recital

理性 **risei** mind, sanity; reason

理性的(な) **riseiteki (na)** rational

利子 **rishi** interest; rate of interest

理想 **risō** role model

理想の高い **risō no takai** idealistic

理想的(な) **risōteki (na)** ideal,
model

立証 **risshō** demonstration, proof

立食 **risshoku** buffet

立証する **risshō suru** demonstrate,
prove

りす **risu** squirrel

リスト **risuto** list

リターン **ritān** return

利他的(な) **ritateki (na)** altruistic

立地条件 **ritchi-jōken** location;
neighborhood

利点 **riten** advantage, plus

率 **ritsu** rate

立案者 **ritsuan-sha** draftsman;
planner

立案する **ritsuan suru** form a plan

立体映像 **rittaieizō** hologram

立体交差 **rittai-kōsa** (overhead)
interchange

立体的 **rittaiteki** three-dimensional

リットル **rittoru** liter

利用できる **riyō dekiru** have access
to ◊ available

利用する **riyō suru** utilize; use *pej:
person*; exploit *resources*; take
advantage of *opportunity*

理由 **riyū** reason; 理由もなく *riyū
mo naku* for nothing, for no reason

利ざや **rizaya** (profit) margin

リゾート **rizōto** resort

リズム **rizumu** rhythm; throb; リズムを
打つ *rizumu o utsu* throb

ろうあ(の) **rōa (no)** deaf-and-dumb

ろば **roba** donkey

ろうばい **rōbai** consternation

ろうばい売り **rōbai uri** panic selling

ロビー **robī** lobby; lounge (*in hotel,
airport*)

ロボット **robotto** robot

ロブスター **robusutā** lobster

労働 **rōdō** labor

労働ビザ **rōdō-biza** work permit

労働組合 **rōdō-kumiai** labor union

朗読する **rōdoku suru** read out;
recite

労働力 **rōdōryoku** workforce

労働者 **rōdō-sha** worker; laborer

労働者階級 **rōdōsha-kaikyū**
working class

労働争議 **rōdō-sōgi** industrial
dispute

漏えい **rōei** leak; disclosure

ローファー **rōfā** loafer (*shoe*)

ロゴ **rogo** logo

浪費 **rōhi** waste

浪費家 **rōhi-ka** spendthrift

浪費する **rōhi suru** waste;
squander

路地 **roji** alley, lane

老人 **rōjin** elderly person

老人ホーム **rōjin-hōmu** nursing
home

廊下 **rōka** corridor

路肩 **rokata** verge

ロケ中で **roke-chū de** on location

ロケット **roketto** locket; rocket

ロッカー **rokkā** locker

ろっ骨 **rokkotsu** rib

ロック **rokku** rock MUS

ロックンロール **rokkun-rōru**
rock'n'roll

ロックスター **rokku-stā** rock star

六 **roku** six

録画 **rokuga** video recording

録画する **rokuga suru** video

六月 **rokugatsu** June

録音 **rokuon** recording

録音する **rokuon suru** tape

録音スタジオ **rokuon-sutajio**
recording studio

ロム **ROM** ROM, read only
memory

ローマ法王 **Rōma-hōō** Pope

ローマ字 **rōmaji** Roman script,
romaji

ロマンチック(な) **romanchikku (na)**
romantic

路面電車 **romen-densha** streetcar

論 **ron** theory

ローン **rōn** bank loan

論文 **ronbun** paper (*academic*);
thesis

老年 **rōnen** old age

老年医学 **rōnen-igaku** geriatric

ロングドレス **rongu-doresu** gown

ロング(の) **rongu (no)** full-length

浪人 **rōnin** *student who will resit*

college entrance examinations

論じる **ronjiru** discuss; maintain, assert; argue

論破 **ronpa** refutation; demolition

論理 **ronri** logic

論理的(な) **ronriteki (na)** logical

論争 **ronsō** conflict, dispute; controversy

ロープ **rōpu** rope

ローラーブレード **rōrā-burēdo** roller blade

ローラースケート **rōrā-sukēto** roller skate

老齢身障者医療保険制度 **rōrei-shinshōsha-iryō-hoken-seido** Medicare

老練(な) **rōren (na)** experienced; veteran

ロールパン **rōru-pan** bread roll

労力 **rōryoku** labor; workforce

ロシア **Roshia** Russia

ロシア語 **Roshia-go** Russian (*language*)

ロシア人 **Roshia-jin** Russian (*person*)

ローション **rōshon** lotion

露出不足(の) **roshutsu-busoku (no)** underexposed

露出狂 **roshutsukyō** exhibitionist

露出する **roshutsu suru** expose

ろうそく **rōsoku** candle

ろうそく立て **rōsokutate** candlestick

ロースト **rōsuto** roast

ローストビーフ **rōsuto-bīfu** roast beef

ロータリー **rōtarī** traffic circle

露天風呂 **rotenburo** open-air hot spa

ルビー **rubī** ruby

類似 **ruiji** analogy; similarity

類人猿 **ruijin'en** ape

類似した **ruiji shita** similar

類似点 **ruijiten** resemblance, likeness; parallel

ルームサービス **rūmu-sābisu** room service

ルール **rūru** rule

留守番電話 **rusuban-denwa** answerphone; voicemail

留守番する **rusuban suru** look after

the house / apartment

留守である **rusu de aru** be out; be away

ルート **rūto** route

ルーツ **rūtsu** roots

るつぼ **rutsubo** melting pot

略 **ryaku** abbreviation; …の略である *… no ryaku de aru* stand for

略奪者 **ryakudatsu-sha** looter

略奪する **ryakudatsu suru** loot

略す **ryaku suru** abbreviate

量 **ryō** amount, quantity; volume

寮 **ryō** dormitory

漁 **ryō** fishing

猟 **ryō** hunting

両開き(の) **ryōbiraki (no)** double *doors*

領土 **ryōdo** territory

領土(の) **ryōdo (no)** territorial

両替する **ryōgae suru** exchange

両側 **ryōgawa** both sides

両端 **ryōtan** both ends

両方(の) **ryōhō (no)** both; 両方とも *ryōhō tomo* both of them

領域 **ryōiki** preserve; domain

領事 **ryōji** consul

領事館 **ryōji-kan** consulate

領海 **ryōkai** territorial waters

了解する **ryōkai suru** agree; understand

旅館 **ryokan** Japanese-style inn

旅券 **ryoken** passport

料金 **ryōkin** fee; charge; rate

料金表 **ryōkinhyō** price list; tariff

料金ブース **ryōkin-jo** toll booth

旅行 **ryokō** journey; trip; travels

旅行代理店 **ryokō-dairiten** tour operator

旅行会社 **ryokō-gaisha** tour operator

旅行保険 **ryokō-hoken** travel insurance

旅行かばん **ryokō-kaban** suitcase

旅行者 **ryokō-sha** traveler

旅行者用小切手 **ryokōshayō-kogitte** traveler's check

旅行する **ryokō suru** travel; tour

領空 **ryōkū** airspace

緑茶 **ryokucha** green tea

両極化する **ryōkyokuka suru** polarize

料理 **ryōri** cooking (*food*); dish (*part of meal*)

料理(の) **ryōri (no)** cookery; culinary

料理する **ryōri suru** cook

両立する **ryōritsu suru** be compatible

量産する **ryōsan suru** mass produce

寮生 **ryōsei** *student who lives on campus*

良性(の) **ryōsei (no)** benign

漁師 **ryōshi** fisherman

猟師 **ryōshi** hunter

良心 **ryōshin** conscience; 良心のとがめ **ryōshin no togame** scruples

両親 **ryōshin** parents

良心的(な) **ryōshinteki (na)** conscientious

領収書 **ryōshū-sho** receipt

両手 **ryōte** both hands

料亭 **ryōtei** quality restaurant

療養所 **ryōyō-jo** sanitarium

竜 **ryū** dragon

留置場 **ryūchijō** police cell; lockup

流ちょうに **ryūchō ni** fluently

流動体 **ryūdōtai** fluid

留学する **ryūgaku suru** study abroad

留学生 **ryūgakusei** overseas student

流儀 **ryūgi** fashion; style

流感 **ryūkan** flu

流血 **ryūketsu** bloodshed

リュックサック **ryukku-sakku** rucksack

流行 **ryūkō** epidemic; fashion, style

流行(の) **ryūkō (no)** fashionable

流行遅れである **ryūkō-okure de aru** be out (of fashion)

流行遅れになる **ryūkō-okure ni naru** go out of style

流行する **ryūkō suru** be in fashion; break out (*of disease*)

竜骨 **ryūkotsu** keel

琉球 **Ryūkyū** *historical name for Okinawa*

リューマチ **ryūmachi** rheumatism

留年する **ryūnen suru** repeat a year

流星 **ryūsei** meteor

流星のよう(な) **ryūsei no yō (na)** meteoric

流線形(の) **ryūsenkei (no)** streamlined

粒子 **ryūshi** particle

流出する **ryūshutsu suru** drain away, drain off

流通 **ryūtsū** distribution

流通業者 **ryūtsū-gyōsha** distributor

流産 **ryūzan** miscarriage

S

さ **-sa** (*familiar emphatic particle used mostly by men*): もう、いいさ **mō iisa** that's enough

差 **sa** difference; gap; remainder; 2、3分の差で **ni, sanpun no sa de** by a couple of minutes

さあ **sā** well; right; come on!

さば **saba** mackerel

サーバー **sābā** scoop; server (*in tennis*), COMPUT; サーバーにデータを送る **sābā ni dēta o okuru** upload

さばけた **sabaketa** down-to-earth; wordly-wise

砂漠 **sabaku** desert

差別 **sabetsu** discrimination; segregation

差別する **sabetsu suru** discriminate

さび **sabi** rust

さびない **sabinai** rust-proof

さびれた **sabireta** bleak; deserted

さびれている **sabirete iru** run-down

さびる **sabiru** rust

寂しい **sabishii** lonely; ...がいなくなって寂しい *... ga inaku natte sabishii* miss

サービス **sābisu** service

サービスエリア **sābisu-eria** service area

サービス(の) **sābisu (no)** complimentary

サービス料 **sābisu-ryō** service charge

サービス産業 **sābisu-sangyō** service industry, service sector

さびた **sabita** rusty

さび取り剤 **sabitorizai** rust remover

さぼる **saboru** skip *class*; 学校をさぼる *gakkō o saboru* play hooky

サボタージュ **sabotāju** go-slow

さぼてん **saboten** cactus

サーブ **sābu** serve (*in tennis*)

サーブする **sābu suru** serve (*in tennis*)

サーチ **sāchi** search COMPUT

サーチライト **sāchiraito** searchlight

定まらない **sadamaranai** variable

定める **sadameru** set, arrange

サディスト **sadisuto** sadist

サディズム **sadizumu** sadism

茶道 **sadō** tea ceremony

作動していない **sadō shite inai** be down (*not working*)

作動する **sadō suru** go, work; run; start to operate

...さえ **... sae** even

さえぎる **saegiru** obstruct; block

さえない **saenai** drab; plain

さえずる **saezuru** twitter; warble (*of birds*)

サーファー **sāfā** (wind)surfer

サファイア **safaia** sapphire

サーフィン **sāfin** surfing

サーフボード **sāfu-bōdo** sailboard; surfboard

差額 **sagaku** balance, remainder

砂岩 **sagan** sandstone

下がる **sagaru** drop, come down (*in price etc*)

捜し出す **sagashidasu** trace; dig out, root out

探し回る、捜しまわる **sagashimawaru** poke around; scour, search

探す、捜す **sagasu** search for, hunt for, seek

下がっている **sagatte iru** be down (*of price, rate*); stand back, keep back

下げる **sageru** reduce, lower; keep down *voice, noise*; bow *head*

下げ相場 **sagesōba** bear market

さぎ **sagi** heron

詐欺 **sagi** fraud; racket (*criminal*), scam; rip-off

詐欺師 **sagishi** fraud, trickster

探り出す **saguridasu** dig up *information*

さぐる **saguru** spy on; grope for, feel for

作業 **sagyō** work; operation

作業場 **sagyōba** workshop

作業台 **sagyōdai** (work)bench

左派 **saha** left POL

さい **sai** rhinoceros

際 **sai** occasion

才 **sai** ability; gift; years old

歳 **-sai** years old

最愛(の) **saiai (no)** beloved

最悪(の) **saiaku (no)** worst; 最悪の場合には *saiaku no bāi ni wa* if the worst comes to worst; 最悪の事態 *saiaku no jitai* the worst

栽培する **saibai suru** cultivate; grow *flowers, vegetables*

裁判 **saiban** trial, court case; judgment

裁判官 **saibankan** judge; 裁判にかけられて *saiban ni kakerarete* on trial

裁判所 **saiban-sho** courthouse

裁判所命令 **saibansho-meirei** court order

裁判する **saiban suru** try LAW

サイバースペース **saibāsupēsu** cyberspace

細胞 **saibō** cell BIO

再分割する **saibunkatsu suru** subdivide

再調整する **saichōsei suru** rearrange, reschedule

最中 **saichū** middle

再注文 **saichūmon** repeat order

最大限 **saidaigen** maximum; 最大限に利用する **saidaigen ni riyō suru** make the best of

最大にする **saidai ni suru** maximize

最大(の) **saidai (no)** maximum; utmost

祭壇 **saidan** altar

サイドブレーキ **saidoburēki** parking brake

サイドライン **saidorain** sideline

サイドライト **saidoraito** sidelight

財布 **saifu** pocketbook, wallet

災害 **saigai** disaster

再現する **saigen suru** reconstruct *crime*; reproduce *atmosphere*

さい疑心 **saigishin** paranoia

最期 **saigo** last moments; death

最後に **saigo ni** in conclusion, finally, lastly

最後(の) **saigo (no)** final, last; latest; 最後は…になる **saigo wa … ni naru** end up (*doing something*)

最後通ちょう **saigotsūchō** ultimatum

再軍備する **saigunbi suru** rearm

再発 **saihatsu** relapse

再発する **saihatsu suru** have a relapse; recur

再編成 **saihensei** reorganization; shake-up

再編成する **saihensei suru** reorganize

裁縫 **saihō** sewing

再放送 **saihōsō** repeat

細字部分 **saiji-bubun** small print

再上演する **saijōen suru** revive *play etc*

最上階 **saijōkai** top *floor*

最上(の) **saijō (no)** best

最重要(の) **saijūyō (no)** of prime importance

再開 **saikai** renewal

再開発する **saikaihatsu suru** redevelop

再会させる **saikai saseru** reunite

再開する **saikai suru** renew *discussions*; reopen *business*

債券 **saiken** bond FIN

債権者 **saiken-sha** creditor

再建する **saiken suru** reconstruct *city*

再検討 **saikentō** review

再検討する **saikentō suru** review

細菌 **saikin** bacteria

最近 **saikin** recently, lately, of late

細菌戦争 **saikin-sensō** germ warfare

最高 **saikō** top *speed, note*

最後尾(の) **saikōbi (no)** rearmost

最高幹部 **saikō-kanbu** top *management, official*

最高機密(の) **saikō-kimitsu (no)** top secret

最高記録 **saikō-kiroku** high (*in statistics*); record SP

最高(の) **saikō (no)** best; maximum; supreme; utmost; top

再婚する **saikon suru** remarry

さいころ **saikoro** dice

最高裁判所 **Saikō-saibansho** Supreme Court

最高責任者 **Saikō-sekininsha** CEO, Chief Executive Officer

最高司令官 **saikō-shireikan** commander-in-chief, supreme commander

サイクリング **saikuringu** cycling

サイクル **saikuru** cycle

採掘 **saikutsu** extraction (*of coal, oil*)

採掘する **saikutsu suru** mine; extract

催眠状態 **saimin-jōtai** hypnosis

催眠術をかける **saiminjutsu o kakeru** hypnotize

催眠療法 **saimin-ryōhō** hypnotherapy

サイン **sain** autograph

最年長者 **sainenchō-sha** eldest

才能 **sainō** aptitude; talent, flair; 才能がある **sainō ga aru** talented; gifted ◊ be gifted

さいの目に切る **sai no me ni kiru** dice, cut

歳入 **sainyū** revenue

サイレン **sairen** siren

再利用できる **sairiyō dekiru** reusable

再利用する **sairiyō suru** recycle, reuse

催涙ガス **sairui-gasu** tear gas

再三(の) **saisan (no)** repeated

再生 **saisei** playback, replay; reproduction

再生する **saisei suru** play; rerun *tape*

さい銭 **saisen** money offering REL

最先端 **saisentan** frontier

最先端(の) **saisentan (no)** leading-edge

妻子 **saishi** family; wife and children

再試合 **saishiai** replay

最新版 **saishinban** update; latest edition

最新技術(の) **saishin-gijutsu (no)** state-of-the-art

最新(の) **saishin (no)** latest; up-to-date

細心(の) **saishin (no)** meticulous

最新流行(の) **saishin-ryūkō (no)** up-to-date

最新式(の) **saishinshiki (no)** up-to-date

最初は **saisho wa** at first; originally

最小限(の) **saishōgen (no)** minimal

菜食主義(の) **saishoku-shugi (no)** vegetarian

菜食主義者 **saishoku-shugisha** vegetarian

最初に **saisho ni** beforehand

最小にする **saishō ni suru** minimize

最初のうちは **saisho no uchi wa** to begin with, at first

最終 **saishū** end

最終決定する **saishū-kettei suru** finalize

最終(の) **saishū (no)** final, last

最終的(な) **saishūteki (na)** eventual

最終的には **saishūteki ni wa** at the last count

催促状 **saisokujō** reminder (*for payment*)

催促する **saisoku suru** remind; urge

咲いた **saita** open *flower*

再逮捕する **saitaiho suru** recapture

最低 **saitei** a minimum of

最低賃金 **saitei-chingin** minimum wage

最低記録 **saitei-kiroku** low (*in statistics*)

最低にする **saitei ni suru** minimize

最低(の) **saitei (no)** lousy; minimum

咲いている **saite iru** be out, be open (*of flower*)

最適条件 **saiteki-jōken** optimum

最適(な) **saiteki (na)** optimum

再点検する **saitenken suru** doublecheck

採点する **saiten suru** correct, mark

再統合する **saitōgō suru** reunite

再統一 **saitōitsu** reunification

幸いにも **saiwai ni mo** luckily, happily

採用 **saiyō** adoption (*of plan*)

採用する **saiyō suru** adopt *plan*

最善を尽くす **saizen o tsukusu** do one's best, do one's utmost

最前列 **saizenretsu** front row

サイズ **saizu** format; size

さじ **saji** spoon

坂 **saka** slope; hill

酒場 **sakaba** bar

栄える **sakaeru** thrive

境 **sakai** border; boundary

魚 **sakana** fish

魚屋 **sakana-ya** fishmonger

盛ん(な) **sakan (na)** flourishing

さかのぼる **sakanoboru** date back, go back ◊ retroactive

逆らう **sakarau** contradict; disobey

盛りにある **sakari ni aru** be in one's prime

盛りを過ぎる **sakari o sugiru** go to seed; go down in the world

逆さまに **sakasama ni** upside down

逆さま(の) **sakasama (no)** topsy-turvy

サーカス **sākasu** circus

酒屋 **sakaya** liquor store

酒 **sake** alcohol; liquor; rice wine; 酒を飲む **sake o nomu** drink *alcohol*; 酒を絶つ **sake o tatsu** stop drinking

さけ **sake** salmon

叫び声 **sakebigoe** cry, call; yell; shouting

叫ぶ **sakebu** cry, call; yell; exclaim

裂け目 **sakeme** rip, tear; split (*in fabric, wood*); 裂け目をいれる **sakeme o ireru** crack, decipher *code*

酒飲み **sakenomi** drinker

避けられない **sakerarenai** inevitable, unavoidable

避ける **sakeru** avoid; avert; evade; shun

裂ける **sakeru** split, tear

先 **saki** point, tip; 先へ進む **saki e susumu** continue, push on; 先を考える **saki o kangaeru** think ahead

先駆け **sakigake** pioneer

先物取引 **sakimono-torihiki** futures FIN

先(の) **saki (no)** former; recent; future

サーキット **sākitto** circuit

作家 **sakka** writer

サッカー **sakkā** soccer, football

錯覚 **sakkaku** delusion, illusion

サッカリン **sakkarin** saccharin

さっき **sakki** a little while ago; some time ago

殺菌した **sakkin shita** sterile

殺菌する **sakkin suru** sterilize

作曲 **sakkyoku** composition MUS

作曲家 **sakkyoku-ka** composer

作曲する **sakkyoku suru** compose MUS

鎖国 **sakoku** national seclusion

鎖骨 **sakotsu** collarbone

さく **saku** barrier; fence; railings

策 **saku** plan; scheme; policy

咲く **saku** open (of flower); 花が咲く **hana ga saku** bloom, flower

裂く **saku** rip; split

作文 **sakubun** composition, essay

削減 **sakugen** cut, cutback

削減する **sakugen suru** ax; reduce, cut back

作品 **sakuhin** work (of art, literature)

索引 **sakuin** index (of book)

昨日 **sakujitsu** yesterday

削除 **sakujo** deletion

削除する **sakujo suru** delete

昨年 **sakunen** last year

桜 **sakura** cherry blossom

さくらんぼ **sakuranbo** cherry (fruit)

策略 **sakuryaku** maneuver; trap, set-up; 策略に富む **sakuryaku ni tomu** tactical

作成する **sakusei suru** prepare, draw up document

作戦 **sakusen** maneuver; tactics

作者 **sakusha** author

作詞家 **sakushi-ka** lyricist, songwriter

搾取 **sakushu** exploitation

搾取する **sakushu suru** exploit

サクソフォーン **sakusofōn** saxophone

昨夜 **sakuya** last night

砂丘 **sakyū** sand dune

…様 **... sama** Mr / Mrs / Ms (in addresses)

冷ます **samasu** cool down

覚ます **samasu** wake up

妨げる **samatageru** hinder, hamper; prevent; obstruct

さまよう **samayou** roam; drift (of person)

様々(な) **samazama (na)** diverse, varied; various, several

さめ **same** shark

冷める **sameru** cool, cool down; die down (of excitement)

覚める **sameru** wake up; sober up

サミット **samitto** summit

さもないと **samonai to** otherwise, or else

サーモスタット **sāmostatto** thermostat

寒い **samui** cold; fresh weather

寒気 **samuke** chill (illness); 寒気がする **samuke ga suru** chilly ◊ I'm chilly

侍 **samurai** samurai

寒さ **samu-sa** cold; freshness

酸 **san** acid

…さん **... san** Mr; Mrs; Ms; 賢さん **Ken-san** Ken

…山 **... san** Mount

三 **san** three

三倍になる **sanbai ni naru** treble

賛美歌 **sanbika** hymn

散文 **sanbun** prose

産地 **sanchi** home

散弾銃 **sandanjū** shotgun

サンダル **sandaru** sandal

サンドイッチ **sandoitchi** sandwich

産婦人科 **sanfujinka** obstetrics and gynecology

三月 **sangatsu** March

参議院 **sangiin** House of Councilors

さんご **sango** coral

サングラス **sangurasu** sunglasses, dark glasses

産業 **sangyō** industry

産業廃棄物 **sangyō-haikibutsu** industrial waste

三乗(の) **sanjō (no)** cubic

三重奏 **sanjūsō** trio MUS

参加 **sanka** participation

酸化物 **sankabutsu** oxide

産科病棟 **sanka-byōtō** maternity ward

産科医 **sankai** obstetrician

三角形 **sankakkei** triangle

三角巾 **sankakukin** sling (*for arm*)

三角(の) **sankaku (no)** triangular

参加させる **sanka saseru** involve, bring in

参加者 **sanka-sha** participant; competitor

参加する **sanka suru** participate; compete, take part

参考 **sankō** reference

参考図書 **sankōtosho** reference book

三脚 **sankyaku** tripod

産休 **sankyū** maternity leave

さんま **sanma** saury

山脈 **sanmyaku** range (*of mountains*)

参入 **sannyū** penetration (*of market*)

参入する **sannyū suru** penetrate

散髪する **sanpatsu suru** have a haircut

賛否両論 **sanpi-ryōron** the pros and cons

散歩 **sanpo** stroll

山腹 **sanpuku** hillside, slope

サンプル **sanpuru** sample

三輪車 **sanrinsha** tricycle

三流(の) **sanryū (no)** third-rate

山菜 **sansai** edible wild plant

賛成 **sansei** approval, blessing

賛成している **sansei shite iru** agreeable, in agreement

賛成する **sansei suru** agree, assent; approve; go along; hold with

酸性雨 **sanseiu** acid rain

参照する **sanshō suru** refer to, consult *dictionary etc*

酸素 **sanso** oxygen

算数 **sansū** arithmetic

サンタクロース **santakurōsu** Santa Claus

さっぱりした **sappari shita** refreshing

さっぱりする **sappari suru** freshen up

皿 **sara** dish; plate

サラブレッド **sarabureddo** thoroughbred

サラダ **sarada** salad

再来年 **sarainen** the year after next

再来週 **saraishū** the week after next

さらに **sara ni** in addition, moreover; even more, still more；さらに大きく/よく **sara ni ōkiku / yoku** even bigger / better

サラリーマン **sararīman** salaried office worker, salaryman

さらさらと鳴る **sarasara to naru** rustle

さらされる **sarasareru** bear the brunt of; be exposed; 風雨にさらされた **fūu ni sarasareta** weather-beaten

さらす **sarasu** subject; expose

さらう **sarau** dredge; drag *canal, river*; kidnap

される **sareru** ◊ (*polite form of* **suru**): 教授が講演される **kyōju ga kōen sareru** the professor will also give us a lecture ◊ (*passive of* **suru**): 連載される **rensai sareru** be serialized

さりげない **sarigenai** throw-away, casual *remark*

去る **saru** go (*of people*); leave

猿 **saru** monkey

猿ぐつわ **sarugutsuwa** gag; 猿ぐつわをかませる **sarugutsuwa o kamaseru** gag

支える **sasaeru** bear *weight*; support; prop up; keep in place

捧げる **sasageru** dedicate, devote; donate

ささい(な) **sasai (na)** trivial; little

ささいなこと **sasai na koto** detail, trifle, irrelevancy

ささやか（な）**sasayaka (na)** modest *house*

ささやき **sasayaki** whisper

ささやく **sasayaku** whisper

…させられる … **saserareru** be made to

…させる … **saseru** let, allow; make; 彼の思うようにさせる **kare no omou yō ni saseru** leave himself to his own resources; 意識を回復させる **ishiki o kaifuku saseru** bring around

差し上げる **sashiageru** (*polite*) give; present; offer

差し当たり **sashiatari** for the moment

差出人 **sashidashi-nin** sender

差し出す **sashidasu** hold out, put out *hand*

挿絵 **sashie** illustration, picture

差し引く **sashihiku**: YからXを差し引く **Y kara X o sashihiku** deduct X from Y

差し込む **sashikomu** insert

さしみ **sashimi** sashimi

差し迫った **sashisematta** impending, imminent; dire

差し迫っている **sashisematte iru** pending, be about to happen

指し示す **sashishimesu** point out, indicate

指図 **sashizu** directions; instructions

査証 **sashō** visa

誘う **sasou** entice; invite

サッシ **sasshi** sash (*in window*)

早速 **sassoku** immediately; at once

察する **sassuru** guess; infer; imagine

刺す **sasu** bite; sting; prick, jab; stab; ナイフで刺す **naifu de sasu** knife, stab

指す **sasu** point; point to

さすがに **sasuga ni** as expected

サスペンダー **sasupendā** suspenders

サスペンション **sasupenshon** suspension (*of vehicle*)

サスペンス **sasupensu** suspense

刺すよう（な）**sasu yō (na)** piercing

殺虫剤 **satchūzai** insecticide; pesticide

さて **sate** right; now; well

査定 **satei** evaluation, assessment

査定する **satei suru** assess, evaluate

サテン **saten** satin

砂糖 **satō** sugar

里帰り **satogaeri** homecoming

里子 **satogo** foster child

砂糖きび **satō kibi** sugar cane

里親 **satooya** foster parents

悟り **satori** enlightenment

悟る **satoru** be enlightened; realize

冊 **satsu** countword for books

札 **satsu** paper money; bill

撮影現場 **satsuei-genba** (film) set

撮影所 **satsuei-sho** (film) studio

撮影する **satsuei suru** film; shoot *movie*

殺害する **satsugai suru** murder

札入れ **satsuire** billfold

殺人 **satsujin** homicide, murder, killing

殺人犯 **satsujin-han** killer, murderer

殺人鬼 **satsujinki** butcher, murderer

殺人捜査課 **satsujin-sōsa-ka** homicide (*department*)

さつま芋 **satsuma-imo** sweet potato

さっと **satto** suddenly; quickly

殺到 **sattō** stampede; rush; deluge

殺到する **sattō suru** flood

サウジアラビア **Sauji-Arabia** Saudi Arabia

サウジアラビア（の）**Sauji-Arabia (no)** Saudi Arabian

サウナ **sauna** sauna

サウンドトラック **saundotrakku** soundtrack

騒がしい **sawagashii** noisy; boisterous

騒ぎ **sawagi** commotion, hullabaloo; noise; trouble; 騒ぎを起こす **sawagi o okosu** make a fuss; cause a stir

騒ぎ立てる **sawagitateru** carry on, make a fuss

さわら **sawara** Spanish mackerel

触る **sawaru** touch; feel

障る **sawaru** grate; jar on

さわやか（な）**sawayaka (na)** fresh, cool; invigorating *climate*; crisp *weather*

さわやかさ **sawayaka-sa** freshness *(of weather)*

さや **saya** husk; pod; sheath *(for knife)*

左翼 **sayoku** left-wing

さようなら **sayōnara** goodbye

左右する **sayū suru** affect; influence; decide

さざえ **sazae** top shell

さざ波 **sazanami** ripple

さぞ **sazo** how; surely

授かる **sazukaru** be given; be blessed with; be taught

授ける **sazukeru** give; award; teach

背 **se** back; spine *(of book)*; height; 背が高い *se ga takai* tall; 背の低い *se no hikui* short; …に背を向ける *... ni se o mukeru* turn one's back on

背広 **sebiro** suit *(for men)*

背骨 **sebone** spine; spinal column;

セーブ **sēbu** save SP

セーブする **sēbu suru** save SP

世代 **sedai** generation; 世代の断絶 *sedai no danzetsu* generation gap

セダン **sedan** sedan

セーフティーコーン **sēfutī-kōn** (traffic) cone

せがむ **segamu** press for *reform*, *payment*

せい **sei** fault; あなた/私のせいです *anata/watashi no sei desu* it's your/my fault; せいにする *sei ni suru* blame

性 **sei** gender

姓 **sei** family name

性別 **seibetsu** sex, gender

整備された **seibi sareta** roadworthy; tuned up; serviced

整備する **seibi suru** provide; equip

西部 **seibu** west *(of a country)*

西部劇 **seibugeki** western *(movie)*

生物 **seibutsu** organism

生物学 **seibutsugaku** biology

性病 **seibyō** venereal disease

成長 **seichō** growth

成長できる **seichō dekiru** viable *(able to survive)*

成長する **seichō suru** grow up

静電気 **seidenki** static (electricity)

制度 **seido** system

青銅 **seidō** bronze *(metal)*

精鋭（の）**seiei (no)** elite

精液 **seieki** semen; sperm

声援する **seien suru** cheer, cheer on

政府 **seifu** government

征服 **seifuku** conquest

制服 **seifuku** uniform

征服者 **seifuku-sha** conqueror

征服する **seifuku suru** conquer

製粉工場 **seifun-kōjō** mill *(for grain)*

請願書 **seigansho** petition

制限 **seigen** limit, restriction

制限速度 **seigen-sokudo** speed limit

制限する **seigen suru** limit, restrict

正義 **seigi** justice

正義感の強い **seigikan no tsuyoi** moral

制御盤 **seigyoban** control panel

正反対（の）**seihantai (no)** inverse; opposite; diametrically opposed

製品 **seihin** product

正方形 **seihōkei** square *(shape)*

製本 **seihon** binding *(of book)*

声域 **seiiki** range *(of voice)*

聖域 **seiiki** sanctuary

誠意のない **seii no nai** insincere

静寂 **seijaku** silence; tranquility

政治 **seiji** politics

政治部記者 **seijibu-kisha** political correspondent

政治犯 **seijihan** political detainee

政治家 **seijika** politician

成人の日 **Seijin no hi** Adult's Day

成人映画 **seijin-eiga** adult film

成人教育 **seijin-kyōiku** adult education

政治（の）**seiji (no)** political

政治体制 **seiji-taisei** political system; regime

政治的（な）**seijiteki (na)** political

誠実 **seijitsu** fidelity; sincerity

誠実（な）**seijitsu (na)** truthful; sincere; faithful

正常 **seijō** normality

正常化する **seijōka suru** normalize

relationship
星条旗 **Seijōki** Stars and Stripes
正常に **seijō ni** normally
成熟 **seijuku** maturity; ripeness
成熟期 **seijukuki** maturity, adulthood
成熟する **seijuku suru** mature (*of person*)
正解 **seikai** correct answer
性格 **seikaku** character, nature; 性格の不一致 *seikaku no fuitchi* incompatibility (*of people*); 性格の悪い *seikaku no warui* ill-natured; 性格のいい *seikaku no ii* good-natured
正確である **seikaku de aru** be right (*of clock*)
正確(な) **seikaku (na)** accurate; exact, precise
正確さ **seikaku-sa** accuracy; precision
聖歌隊 **seikatai** choir
生活 **seikatsu** life; livelihood
生活費 **seikatsu-hi** cost of living; housekeeping (money); keep
生活保護を受けている **seikatsu-hogo o ukete iru** be on welfare
生活協同組合 **seikatsu-kyōdō-kumiai** cooperative (*store*)
生活習慣病 **seikatsu-shūkanbyō** lifestyle disease
生活水準 **seikatsu-suijun** standard of living
生活様式 **seikatsu-yōshiki** way of life
生計 **seikei** livelihood; 生計を立てる *seikei o tateru* earn one's living
整形外科(の) **seikei-geka (no)** orthopedic
整形手術 **seikei-shujutsu** plastic surgery
政権 **seiken** political power; government, administration; 政権を握った *seiken o nigitta* in power
清潔(な) **seiketsu (na)** clean; spotless
生気 **seiki** animation, liveliness; 生気のない *seiki no nai* lifeless
世紀 **seiki** century
性器 **seiki** genitals
正規(の) **seiki (no)** regular; formal;

full-time *student*
成功 **seikō** success
性交 **seikō** (sexual) intercourse
性交感染病 **seikō-kansen-byō** sexually transmitted disease
成功した **seikō shita** prosperous, successful
成功する **seikō suru** succeed
請求 **seikyū** claim (*for damages, insurance*)
請求書 **seikyūsho** bill; invoice; 請求書を送る *seikyūsho o okuru* bill; invoice
請求する **seikyū suru** charge *sum of money*; claim
声明 **seimei** statement, announcement
生命 **seimei** life; existence
姓名 **seimei** full name
青年 **seinen** youth; young person
生年月日 **seinengappi** date of birth
成年期 **seinenki** manhood, maturity
性能 **seinō** performance (*of machine*)
性能が悪い **seinō ga warui** perform badly
性能がよい **seinō ga yoi** perform well
生来(の) **seirai (no)** innate
聖霊 **Seirei** Holy Spirit
西暦 **Seireki** Western calendar; AD
整列する **seiretsu suru** line up
生理 **seiri** menstruation; period; 生理がある *seiri ga aru* menstruate
セーリングする **sēringu suru** sail
整理する **seiri suru** order, sort out; arrange
成立する **seiritsu suru** come into existence; be established
生理用ナプキン **seiriyō napukin** (sanitary) napkin
清涼飲料水 **seiryō-inryōsui** soft drink
精力 **seiryoku** energy (*of person*); strength (*of organization*); 精力を傾けた *seiryoku o katamuketa* energetic *measures*; 精力を使い果たす *seiryoku o tsukaihatasu* burn oneself out
勢力 **seiryoku** power; influence

精力的(な) **seiryokuteki (na)** energetic; spirited

制裁 **seisai** punishment; penalty

政策 **seisaku** policy

製作 **seisaku** production (of movie etc)

製作費 **seisakuhi** production costs

製作する **seisaku suru** produce movie etc

清算 **seisan** settlement of debts; liquidation

生産 **seisan** production

生産物 **seisanbutsu** product

生産高 **seisandaka** output

生産力 **seisanryoku** capacity (of factory); 生産力の高い **seisanryoku no takai** productive

生産性 **seisansei** productivity

生産者 **seisan-sha** producer

清算する **seisan suru** go into liquidation; settle, pay bill

生産する **seisan suru** produce

生産的(な) **seisanteki (na)** productive

精製所 **seisei-jo** refinery

生成する **seisei suru** generate

精製する **seisei suru** refine

成績 **seiseki** grade; result; performance

正社員 **seishain** permanent employee

正社員(の) **seishain (no)** full-time

生死 **seishi** life and death

精子 **seishi** sperm

精子銀行 **seishi-ginkō** sperm bank

正式(の) **seishiki (no)** formal

精神 **seishin** soul, spirit; 精神が錯乱した **seishin ga sakuran shita** delirious

精神安定剤 **seishin-anteizai** tranquilizer

精神分裂症 **seishin-bunretsushō** schizophrenia

精神分析 **seishin-bunseki** psychoanalysis

精神分析医 **seishin-bunsekii** psychoanalyst

精神分析をする **seishin-bunseki o suru** psychoanalyse

精神病 **seishin-byō** mental illness

精神病院 **seishin-byōin** (mental) asylum, mental hospital

精神医学 **seishin-igaku** psychiatry

精神異常者 **seishin-ijōsha** psychopath

精神科医 **seishinkai** psychiatrist

精神科(の) **seishinka (no)** psychiatric

精神力 **seishinryoku** willpower

精神的虐待 **seishinteki-gyakutai** mental cruelty

精神的(な) **seishinteki (na)** mental

制止する **seishi suru** stop; restrain

静止する **seishi suru** stand still; freeze video

性質 **seishitsu** nature (of person)

聖書 **seisho** Bible, the (Holy) Scriptures

清書 **seisho** clean copy

生殖力 **seishokuryoku** fertility

聖職者 **seishoku-sha** clergy

青少年 **seishōnen** youth, young people

青春 **seishun** adolescence

正装 **seisō** formal clothes

生息地 **seisokuchi** habitat; home

整体 **seitai** manipulation (of bones)

声帯 **seitai** vocal cords

整体治療する **seitai-chiryō suru** manipulate bones

生態学 **seitaigaku** ecology

生態系 **seitaikei** ecosystem

整体師 **seitaishi** chiropractor

生誕地 **seitanchi** birthplace

制定する **seitei suru** enact; 法律を制定する **hōritsu o seitei suru** legislate

性的いやがらせ **seiteki iyagarase** sexual harassment

性的(な) **seiteki (na)** sexual

性的能力 **seiteki-nōryoku** virility (sexual)

性的倒錯 **seiteki-tōsaku** (sexual) perversion

性的欲求不満 **seiteki-yokkyūfuman** sexual frustration

晴天 **seiten** good weather

青天のへきれき **seiten no hekireki** like a bolt from the blue

生徒 **seito** pupil; student; schoolchild

政党 **seitō** political party

正当化する **seitōka suru** justify; rationalize

正当(な) **seitō (na)** just, right; lawful; rightful

正当に **seitō ni** duly, properly

整とんされた **seiton sareta** neat, tidy

整とんする **seiton suru** arrange, put in order

精通している **seitsū shite iru** knowledgeable ◊ be conversant

制約 **seiyaku** constraint, restriction

製薬(の) **seiyaku (no)** pharmaceutical

西洋 **Seiyō** the West

西洋人 **Seiyō-jin** Westerner

西洋化 **seiyōka** westernized

西洋なし **seiyōnashi** pear

星座 **seiza** signs of the zodiac

正座 **seiza** *formal Japanese sitting position, kneeling, with legs tucked under*

せいぜい **seizei** at (the) most

整然とした **seizen to shita** in order, shipshape

製造 **seizō** manufacture

製造番号 **seizō bangō** serial number

製造中止にする **seizō-chūshi ni suru** discontinue *product*

製造業 **seizōgyō** manufacturing (*industry*)

製造業者 **seizō-gyōsha** manufacturer

生存 **seizon** survival; existence

生存者 **seizon-sha** survivor

生存する **seizon suru** exist; live on, continue living

製造する **seizō suru** manufacture

製図法 **seizuhō** graphics

製図工 **seizukō** draftsman

セージ **sēji** sage (*herb*)

世界 **sekai** world

世界経済 **sekai-keizai** global economy

世界市場 **sekai-shijō** global market

世界大戦 **sekaitaisen** world war

世界的(な) **sekaiteki (na)** worldwide

セカンド **sekando** second (gear)

せかす **sekasu** hurry; press, urge

世間話 **sekenbanashi** small talk

世間知らず(な) **sekenshirazu (na)** naive

せき **seki** family register; cough; barrier; dam; せきをする **seki o suru** cough

席 **seki** seat, place; 席に着く **seki ni tsuku** sit down; take one's seat

隻 **seki** *countword for boats*

籍 **seki** family register

せき払い **seki-barai** cough

赤道 **sekidō** equator

せき止め薬 **sekidome-yaku** cough medicine, cough syrup

赤外線(の) **sekigaisen (no)** infra-red

赤十字 **Sekijūji** Red Cross

赤面 **sekimen** blush

赤面する **sekimen suru** blush

責任 **sekinin** fault; accountability; liability; guilt; blame; 責任がある **sekinin ga aru** be responsible, be to blame; 責任を取る **sekinin o toru** accept responsibility

責任感 **sekininkan** sense of responsibility; commitment (*in professional relationship*)

責任(の) **sekinin (no)** responsible; guilty

責任のある **sekinin no aru** be liable

責任の重い **sekinin no omoi** responsible *job*

責任者である **sekinin-sha de aru** be in charge

責任転嫁をする **sekinin-tenka o suru** pass the buck

セキセイインコ **sekiseiinko** budgerigar

石炭 **sekitan** coal

せきたてる **sekitateru** hurry up; push, pressure

関取 **sekitori** ranking sumo wrestler

せきつい **sekitsui** spine; vertebra

せきつい動物 **sekitsui-dōbutsu** vertebrate

石油 **sekiyu** oil; petroleum

石油会社 **sekiyu-gaisha** oil company

石油化学(の) **sekiyu-kagaku (no)** petrochemical

石油タンカー **sekiyu-tankā** oil tanker

切開 **sekkai** incision

石灰 **sekkai** lime (*substance*)

設計 **sekkei** design

設計ミス **sekkei-misu** design fault

設計者 **sekkei-sha** designer

設計する **sekkei suru** design, plan

石けん **sekken** soap

接近 **sekkin** approach; access

セックス **sekkusu** sex; セックスをする *sekkusu o suru* make love (to), have sex (with); sleep with

セックスライフ **sekkusu-raifu** lovelife

セックスする **sekkusu suru** make love (to), have sex (with)

説教 **sekkyō** sermon; lecture, criticism; 説教をする *sekkyō o suru* preach

積極的(な) **sekkyokuteki (na)** positive, optimistic

施行 **sekō** execution (*of work, law*)

施行する **sekō suru** execute *work, law*

セクハラ **sekuhara** sexual harrassment

セクシー(な) **sekushī (na)** sexy

セキュリティーチェック **sekyuritī-chekku** security check

狭い **semai** narrow; small; cramped

狭苦しい **semakurushii** poky, cramped

迫る **semaru** approach; draw near; compel

迫っている **sematte iru** brew (*of trouble*)

セメント **semento** cement

責める **semeru** blame; persecute

せめて **semete** at least

せみ **semi** cicada

セミナー **seminā** seminar

千 **sen** thousand

線 **sen** line; 線を引く *sen o hiku* draw a line; mark out, set apart

栓 **sen** plug, stopper; 栓をする *sen o suru* plug

背中 **senaka** back (*of person*)

専売 **senbai** monopoly

旋盤 **senban** lathe

選抜 **senbatsu** selection (*that/those chosen*)

選抜方法 **senbatsu-hōhō** selection process

せんべい **senbei** rice cracker

戦没者追悼記念日 **Senbotsusha-tsuitōkinenbi** Memorial Day

センチメートル **senchimētoru** centimeter

船長 **senchō** captain, skipper

宣伝 **senden** publicity; endorsement

宣伝文句 **senden-monku** blurb (*on book*)

宣伝する **senden suru** publicize; promote

扇動者 **sendō-sha** agitator

扇動する **sendō suru** incite (*to riot*)

洗顔料 **senganryō** facial cleanser

宣言 **sengen** declaration (*of independence etc*)

宣言する **sengen suru** declare; proclaim; pronounce

先月 **sengetsu** last month

戦後(の) **sengo (no)** postwar

繊維 **sen'i** fiber, roughage

繊維光学 **sen'i-kōgaku** fiber optics

船員 **sen'in** seaman

戦時 **senji** wartime

先日 **senjitsu** the other day, recently

戦場 **senjō** battlefield, battleground

旋回する **senkai suru** circle (*of plane, bird*)

先見の明 **senken no mei** foresight

せん光 **senkō** flash

線香 **senkō** incense

専攻 **senkō** major (*academic*); specialty

宣告 **senkoku** sentence LAW

専攻する **senkō suru** specialize in *subject*; major in

先駆者 **senku-sha** forerunner; pioneer

先駆的(な) **senkuteki (na)** pioneering

占拠 **senkyo** occupation; capture

選挙 **senkyo** election

選挙人 **senkyo-nin** elector

選挙制度 **senkyo-seido** electoral system

選挙する **senkyo suru** elect

選挙運動 **senkyo-undō** election campaign; 選挙運動をする **senkyo-undō o suru** campaign, canvass

洗面台 **senmendai** (wash)basin

洗面所 **senmenjo** bathroom

洗面器 **senmenki** washbowl; basin

洗面用具 **senmen yōgu** toiletries

専門 **senmon** specialty

専門医 **senmon-i** specialist MED

専門家 **senmonka** specialist

専門家(の) **senmonka (no)** professional

専門にする **senmon ni suru** specialize in

専門職の人 **senmonshoku no hito** professional

専門的(な) **senmonteki (na)** technical

専門用語 **senmon-yōgo** terminology, jargon

専務取締役 **senmu-torishimariyaku** managing director

専念する **sennen suru** concentrate; focus

せん熱 **sennetsu** glandular fever

洗脳 **sennō** brainwashing

洗脳する **sennō suru** brainwash

栓抜き **sennuki** bottle-opener; corkscrew

先入観 **sennyūkan** preconceived idea

先輩 **senpai** one's senior at school or work

船舶 **senpaku** shipping, sea traffic

戦犯 **senpan** war criminal

扇風機 **senpūki** fan (electric)

洗礼 **senrei** baptism

先例 **senrei** precedent

洗礼する **senrei suru** christen

洗練された **senren sareta** sophisticated; refined

洗練する **senren suru** civilize; refine

戦利品 **senrihin** spoils of war; booty; loot

線路 **senro** track; rail

戦略 **senryaku** strategy

戦略的(な) **senryakuteki (na)** strategic

染料 **senryō** dye

占領 **senryō** occupation (of country)

戦力 **senryoku** military capability

占領する **senryō suru** occupy country

繊細(な) **sensai (na)** delicate

繊細さ **sensai-sa** delicacy

せん索する **sensaku suru** pry; poke one's nose into

せん索好き(な) **sensakuzuki (na)** nosy

先生 **sensei** (school)teacher; doctor (form of address)

宣誓 **sensei** oath LAW

占星術 **senseijutsu** astrology

宣誓供述書 **senseikyōjutsusho** deposition

宣誓就任する **sensei-shūnin suru** swear in witnesses

宣誓する **sensei suru** swear (on oath)

センセーション **sensēshon** sensation (event)

センセーショナル(な) **sensēshonaru (na)** sensational

洗車 **sensha** car wash

戦車 **sensha** tank MIL

戦士 **senshi** warrior

戦死 **senshi** death in action

先史時代(の) **senshi-jidai (no)** prehistoric

線審 **senshin** linesman, touch judge

先進(の) **senshin (no)** advanced

船首 **senshu** bow (of ship)

船主 **senshu** shipowner

選手 **senshu** player; contender; 飛び込みの選手 **tobikomi no senshu** diver

先週 **senshū** last week

選手権 **senshuken** championship (title)

選手権大会 **senshuken-taikai** championship (event)

選出する **senshutsu suru** select; elect

戦争 **sensō** war; warfare

戦争の放棄 **sensō no hōki** renunciation of war

戦争中である **sensōchū de aru** be at war

センス **sensu** good sense; taste

扇子 **sensu** fan (handheld)

潜水艦 **sensuikan** submarine

潜水する **sensui suru** submerge

センター **sentā** center (building)

船体 **sentai** hull (of ship)

選択 **sentaku** choice, option; selection; 選択の余地がなかった **sentaku no yochi ga nakatta** I had no choice

洗濯できる **sentaku dekiru** washable

洗濯機 **sentakuki** washing machine

洗濯物 **sentaku-mono** laundry, washing

選択(の) **sentaku (no)** elective; optional

選択肢 **sentakushi** alternative

洗濯室 **sentakushitsu** laundry (place)

洗濯する **sentaku suru** do the laundry; do the washing

先端 **sentan** tip (of cigarette); top (of mountain, tree)

せん定ばさみ **senteibasami** pruning shears

せん定する **sentei suru** prune

先天性(の) **sentensei (no)** congenital

セント **sento** cent

せん塔 **sentō** spire, steeple

先頭 **sentō** head; leader; 先頭に立つ **sentō ni tatsu** take the lead

戦闘 **sentō** combat

銭湯 **sentō** public bath

戦闘機 **sentōki** fighter (airplane)

先頭(の) **sentō (no)** leading

セントラルヒーティング **sentoraru-hītingu** central heating

洗剤 **senzai** detergent; dishwashing liquid

潜在意識 **senzai-ishiki** the subconscious (mind)

潜在的(な) **senzaiteki (na)** insidious effect; potential customer

戦前(の) **senzen (no)** prewar

先祖 **senzo** forefathers

背負う **seou** carry on one's back; be burdened with

背泳ぎ **seoyogi** backstroke

セラピー **serapī** therapy

セラピスト **serapisuto** therapist

せりふ **serifu** speech (in play); …に

せりふをつける … **ni serifu o tsukeru** prompt

セーリング **sēringu** sailing

セロハン **serohan** cellophane

世論 **seron** public opinion

世論調査 **seron-chōsa** poll, survey

世論調査員 **seron-chōsain** pollster

セロリ **serori** celery

せる **seru** compete

セール **sēru** sale (at reduced price)

セルフサービス(の) **serufu-sābisu (no)** self-service

セールスマン **sērusuman** salesman, (sales) rep

セールスポイント **sērusu-pointo** selling point

節制のない **sessei no nai** immoderate

せっせと働く **sesse to hataraku** work hard; beaver away

摂氏 **sesshi** centigrade

摂氏零度 **sesshi-reido** freezing

接触 **sesshoku** contact

接触する **sesshoku suru** touch

セッション **sesshon** session

節操のない **sessō no nai** unprincipled

接する **sessuru** touch; contact; serve; receive; border on

セーター **sētā** sweater

接着する **setchaku suru** glue; bond (of glue)

接着テープ **setchaku-tēpu** sticky tape

接着剤 **setchakuzai** adhesive, glue

設置する **setchi suru** set up

瀬戸際 **setogiwa** brink

瀬戸物 **setomono** ceramics

節 **setsu** clause; verse

設備 **setsubi** facilities, amenities; equipment

設備完備(の) **setsubi-kanbi (no)** self-contained

切望 **setsubō** longing

切望する **setsubō suru** long, yearn; be anxious for

節分 **setsubun** last day of winter

切断する **setsudan suru** amputate; sever; mutilate

節度 **setsudo** moderation, restraint

接合する **setsugō suru** cement; fuse; link

切除 **setsujo** removal MED

切除する **setsujo suru** remove MED

雪辱を果たす **setsujoku o hatasu** get even; get revenge

説明 **setsumei** explanation; account; illustration

説明文 **setsumeibun** caption

説明できない **setsumei dekinai** unaccountable; inexplicable

説明する **setsumei suru** explain, set out; illustrate (with examples)

設立 **setsuritsu** foundation, setting up

設立する **setsuritsu suru** establish, set up

節約 **setsuyaku** saving, economy

節約して **setsuyaku shite** economically, thriftily

節約する **setsuyaku suru** save; conserve; economize

接続 **setsuzoku** connection

接続便 **setsuzoku-bin** connecting flight

接続詞 **setsuzoku-shi** conjunction GRAM

接続する **setsuzoku suru** connect

設定 **settei** setting

設定する **settei suru** set movie, novel etc; establish; create

セット **setto** scenery; set (in tennis)

窃盗 **settō** theft; larceny

接頭辞 **settōji** prefix

説得 **settoku** persuasion

説得力のある **settokuryoku no aru** be convincing ◊ persuasive; compelling; forceful

説得する **settoku suru** persuade; reason with

セットメニュー **setto-menyū** set menu

セットする **setto suru** do hair; 髪をセットしてもらう **kami o setto shite morau** have one's hair done

窃盗罪 **settōzai** larceny

世話 **sewa** care (of baby, pet etc); 世話をする **sewa o suru** attend to; take care of; look after; 世話をやく **sewa o yaku** meddle; interfere

せわしなく動き回る **sewashinaku ugokimawaru** bustle around

世話やき(の) **sewayaki (no)** interfering; over-protective

世俗(の) **sezoku (no)** common; secular

世俗的(な) **sezokuteki (na)** worldly

しゃべる **shaberu** talk; chat

シャベル **shaberu** shovel

シャボン玉 **shabondama** (soap) bubble

しゃぶしゃぶ **shabushabu** fondue-style dish with beef

社長 **shachō** head, president (of company)

遮断する **shadan suru** block out light; cut off; insulate

車道 **shadō** roadway

しゃがむ **shagamu** squat

しゃがれ声 **shagaregoe** husky voice; croak; しゃがれ声を出す **shagaregoe o dasu** croak

しゃがれ声(の) **shagaregoe (no)** hoarse; husky

社員 **shain** staff; employee

写実的(な) **shajitsuteki (na)** graphic, vivid

社会 **shakai** community; society

社会復帰させる **shakai-fukki saseru** rehabilitate

社会福祉事業 **shakaifukushi-jigyō** social work

社会学 **shakai-gaku** sociology

社会(の) **shakai (no)** social; 社会のくず **shakai no kuzu** the dregs of society

社会主義 **shakai-shugi** socialism

社会主義(の) **shakai-shugi (no)** socialist

社会主義者 **shakai-shugi-sha** socialist

社会党 **Shakaitō** Social Democratic Party

しゃきしゃきした **shakishaki shita** crisp lettuce, apple

借金 **shakkin** debt; 借金をしている **shakkin o shite iru** be in debt, be in the red; …に借金をしている **... ni shakkin o shite iru** owe

しゃっくり **shakkuri** hiccup

しゃっくりする **shakkuri suru** have

the hiccups

車庫 **shako** garage

社交(の) **shakō (no)** social

社交的(な) **shakōteki (na)** sociable

借地人 **shakuchi-nin** tenant

赤銅色 **shakudōshoku** tan (*color*)

尺八 **shakuhachi** bamboo flute

釈放 **shakuhō** release

釈放する **shakuhō suru** release

釈明 **shakumei** defense, justification

釈明する **shakumei suru** defend, justify

しゃくし定規(な) **shakushi-jōgi (na)** pedantic

借用証書 **shakuyō-shōsho** IOU

斜面 **shamen** slope

赦免する **shamen suru** pardon; absolve

三味線 **shamisen** Japanese banjo

シャム双生児 **Shamu-sōseiji** Siamese twins

車内 **shanai** *inside of a train car*

社内(の) **shanai (no)** in-house

シャンデリア **shanderia** chandelier

シャンパン **shanpan** champagne

シャンプー **shanpū** shampoo

シャンプーする **shanpū suru** shampoo

しゃれ **share** joke; pun

しゃれた **shareta** classy; stylish, elegant

車両 **sharyō** car (*of train*)

車両立ち入り禁止区域 **sharyō-tachiiri-kinshi-kuiki** pedestrian precinct

射殺する **shasatsu suru** gun down

写生する **shasei suru** sketch

車線 **shasen** lane MOT

斜線 **shasen** oblique

社説 **shasetsu** editorial

写真 **shashin** photo(graph); 写真を とる *shashin o toru* photograph

写真撮影 **shashin-satsuei** photography

写真うつりのよい **shashin'utsuri no yoi** photogenic

車掌 **shashō** ticket inspector; conductor

射手 **shashu** marksman; archer

車体 **shatai** bodywork

射程距離 **shatei-kyori** range (*of gun*)

シャトル **shatoru** shuttlecock

シャトルバス **shatoru-basu** shuttlebus

シャツ **shatsu** shirt

シャッター **shattā** shutter

シャワー **shawā** shower; シャワーを 浴びる *shawā o abiru* take a shower, shower

シャワーカーテン **shawā-kāten** shower curtain

シャワーキャップ **shawā-kyappu** shower cap

社用車 **shayō-sha** company car

謝罪 **shazai** apology

シェフ **shefu** chef

シェイク **sheiku** milk shake

し-**shi** and; and besides that; りんごも 好きだし、みかんも好きだ *ringo mo suki da shi, mikan mo suki da* I like both apples and tangerines

死 **shi** death; loss

四 **shi** four

詩 **shi** poem; poetry, verse

市 **shi** city

氏 **shi** *polite form of san*; Mr; Ms

仕上がり **shiagari** finish (*of product*)

仕上げをする **shiage o suru** polish up *work*

試合 **shiai** competition; match; game (*in tennis*); 試合をする *shiai o suru* play

シーアイエー(中央情報局) **Shī-ai-ē (Chūō-jōhō-kyoku)** CIA, Central Intelligence Agency

試合開始 **shiai-kaishi** kickoff

指圧 **shiatsu** shiatsu (*massage*)

幸せ **shiawase** happiness; welfare

幸せ(な) **shiawase (na)** happy; …を 幸せにする *… o shiawase ni suru* make happy

芝生 **shibafu** lawn; grass

芝居 **shibai** play; drama

芝刈り機 **shibakariki** lawn mower

しばらく **shibaraku** for a while, for a time

縛り付ける **shibaritsukeru** tie down (*with rope*)

縛る **shibaru** bind, tie up

しばしば **shibashiba** frequently

しびれる **shibireru** go numb; have pins and needles

しびれた **shibireta** numb

志望 **shibō** wish; hope

脂肪 **shibō** fat

死亡 **shibō** death

死亡事故 **shibō-jiko** fatality

死亡記事 **shibō-kiji** obituary

死亡率 **shibō-ritsu** mortality, death rate

絞る **shiboru** press *grapes, olives*; wring out

死亡者数 **shibō-sha-sū** death toll

志望する **shibō suru** wish; hope

死亡する **shibō suru** die

渋い **shibui** sour; astringent; sullen; austere; tasteful

しぶき **shibuki** spray; splash

四分音符 **shibu-onpu** quarternote

渋る **shiburu** hesitate; falter

試着する **shichaku suru** try on *clothes*

七福神 **Shichi-fukujin** the Seven Deities of Good Luck

七月 **shichigatsu** July

七五三 **Shichigosan** Shichi-Go-San *(festival for children aged 3, 5 and 7)*

七面鳥 **shichimenchō** turkey

質に入れる **shichi ni ireru** pawn

質屋 **shichi-ya** pawnbroker; pawnshop

市長 **shichō** mayor

視聴覚(の) **shichōkaku (no)** audiovisual

視聴者 **shichō-sha** audience; viewer

シチュー **shichū** stew

支柱 **shichū** support

シダ **shida** fern

次第 **shidai**: あなた次第です **anata shidai desu** it's up to you

次第に **shidai ni** by degrees, gradually

仕出し業者 **shidashi-gyōsha** caterer

仕出しをする **shidashi o suru** cater for

CD **shī-dī** CD, compact disc

指導 **shidō** guidance; tuition

私道 **shidō** private road

シード **shīdo** seed *(in tennis)*

指導権争い **shidōken-arasoi** leadership contest

指導者 **shidō-sha** mentor; advisor; coach

指導する **shidō suru** coach, teach

始動する **shidō suru** start

指導的地位 **shidōteki-chii** leadership

支援 **shien** support, backing

支援者 **shien-sha** sympathizer

支援する **shien suru** support, back up

シーフード **shīfūdo** seafood

私服 **shifuku de** plain clothes

至福感 **shifukukan** euphoria

私腹をこやす **shifuku o koyasu** line one's own pockets

シフトキー **shifuto kī** shift key

…しがちである **… shigachi de aru** be liable to, be prone to

市外 **shigai** suburbs; area beyond city limits

市外局番 **shigai-kyokuban** area code

紫外線(の) **shigaisen (no)** ultraviolet

しがみつく **shigamitsuku** cling to *(of child)*

志願者 **shigan-sha** volunteer

四月 **shigatsu** April

刺激 **shigeki** incentive; stimulation; irritation MED

刺激する **shigeki suru** arouse *(sexually)*; goad; stimulate; irritate MED

刺激的(な) **shigekiteki (na)** pungent; stimulating; electric *fig*

茂み **shigemi** bush

資源 **shigen** resource; stock, reserves

茂る **shigeru** grow thickly; be luxuriant

死後(の) **shigo (no)** posthumous

仕事 **shigoto** work; job, task; business affair

仕事中である **shigotochū de aru** be at work

仕事中毒 **shigoto-chūdoku** workaholic

支配 **shihai** control; domination;

reign; sway, influence

支配人 **shihai-nin** manager (*of restaurant, hotel etc*)

支配者 **shihai-sha** ruler (*of state*)

支配する **shihai suru** rule; reign; control; dominate

支配的(な) **shihaiteki (na)** dominant

四半期(の) **shihanki (no)** quarterly

支払い **shiharai** payment (*of bill*); 支払いをする **shiharai o suru** pay

支払う **shiharau** meet *payment*; pay

支払うべき **shiharaubeki** payable

支払われるべき **shiharawarerubeki** due, owed

始発 **shihatsu** the first train

紙幣 **shihei** bank bill

司法権 **shihōken** jurisdiction

資本 **shihon** capital (*money*)

資本家 **shihon-ka** capitalist

司法(の) **shihō (no)** judicial

資本主義 **shihon-shugi** capitalism

資本主義(の) **shihon-shugi (no)** capitalist

資本主義者 **shihon-shugi-sha** capitalist, believer in capitalism

指標 **shihyō** index; indicator; guidelines

子音 **shiin** consonant

仕入れる **shiireru** purchase; buy in

虐げる **shiitageru** tyrannize; oppress

指示 **shiji** directions, instructions

詩人 **shijin** poet

支持者 **shiji-sha** follower, supporter

支持する **shiji suru** bear out, confirm; support; stand by

指示する **shiji suru** instruct

市場 **shijō** market; market place

市場調査 **shijō-chōsa** market research

市場経済 **shijō-keizai** market economy

市場シェア **shijō-shea** market share

しか **shika** deer

しか -**shika** only, just

仕返しをする **shikaeshi o suru** take revenge; get even with, pay back

視界 **shikai** visual field; visibility

市会議員 **shikai-giin** councilman

司会をする **shikai o suru** front *TV program*

司会者 **shikai-sha** host (*of TV program*); master of ceremonies

仕掛け **shikake** device; mechanism

仕掛ける **shikakeru** begin; set *trap*

四角形 **shikakkei** quadrangle

資格 **shikaku** certificate; qualification; 資格を与える **shikaku o ataeru** qualify; 資格を得る **shikaku o eru** qualify (*in competition*); 資格を取る **shikaku o toru** qualify (*get degree etc*)

死角 **shikaku** blind spot

資格のある **shikaku no aru** eligible

資格のない **shikaku no nai** ineligible; unqualified

視覚障害 **shikaku-shōgai** visual deficiency

視覚的(な) **shikakuteki (na)** visual

しかめる **shikameru** contort; screw up *eyes*

しかめっ面 **shikamettsura** frown; scowl; grimace

しかも **shikamo** besides; in addition; and also

士官 **shikan** officer

歯冠 **shikan** crown (*on tooth*)

しか肉 **shikaniku** venison

歯科(の) **shika (no)** dental

しかりとばす **shikaritobasu** bawl out, chew out

しかる **shikaru** scold

しかし **shikashi** at the same time, however, but

仕方 **shikata** method; way

しかたがない **shikata ga nai**: 待っていてもしかたがない **matte itemo shikata ga nai** it's no use waiting; 寂しくてしかたがない **sabishikute shikata ga nai** I cannot help feeling sad; …をしかたがないと受け入れる **... o shikata ga nai to ukeireru** reconcile oneself to

死刑 **shikei** capital punishment; death penalty; 電気いすで死刑になる **denki-isu de shikei ni naru** go to the chair

死刑執行人 **shikei-shikkō-nin** executioner

死刑執行猶予 **shikeishikkō-yūyo** reprieve from the death penalty

試験 **shiken** examination; paper; 試験に合格する **shiken ni gōkaku suru** pass an exam; 試験に受かる／落ちる **shiken ni ukaru／ochiru** pass／fail an exam; 試験を受ける **shiken o ukeru** take an exam

試験官 **shiken-kan** examiner

試験管 **shikenkan** test tube

試験管ベビー **shikenkan-bebī** test tube baby

試験採用期間 **shiken-saiyō-kikan** probation period

試験する **shiken suru** examine

式 **shiki** ceremony; style

士気 **shiki** morale, spirits

指揮 **shiki** conducting; command

四季 **shiki** the four seasons

敷布団 **shikibuton** bottom futon

敷地 **shikichi** location; premises

指揮台 **shikidai** podium

式服 **shikifuku** ceremonial robe

敷居 **shikii** threshold

色覚異常(の) **shikikaku-ijō (no)** color-blind

敷物 **shikimono** carpet; rug

資金 **shikin** fund; 資金を出す **shikin o dasu** fund, finance

至近距離で **shikin-kyori de** at point-blank range

仕切り **shikiri** partition; compartment

しきりに **shikiri ni** eagerly

仕切り屋 **shikiri-ya** control freak

仕切る **shikiru** partition off

色彩 **shikisai** color; 色彩に富んだ **shikisai ni tonda** colorful

指揮者 **shiki-sha** conductor MUS

指揮する **shiki suru** conduct MUS

式典 **shikiten** ceremony

失格する **shikkaku suru** be disqualified; be eliminated

しっかり **shikkari** tight; しっかり焼けた **shikkari yaketa** well-done meat

しっかりした **shikkari shita** solid; stalwart; steady

湿気 **shikke** humidity

漆器 **shikki** lacquerware

失効となる **shikkō to naru** expire

執行猶予 **shikkō-yūyo** probation

しっくい **shikkui** plaster

失脚 **shikkyaku** downfall

失脚する **shikkyaku suru** fall from power

歯こう **shikō** plaque (on teeth)

四国 **Shikoku** Shikoku

しこり **shikori** lump, swelling

敷く **shiku** lay cable, carpet

しくじる **shikujiru** botch, bungle ◊ put one's foot in it

仕組み **shikumi** structure; device; mechanism

しくしく泣く **shikushiku naku** weep

死去 **shikyo** demise

至急 **shikyū** urgently; immediately

子宮 **shikyū** uterus, womb

子宮摘出手術 **shikyū-tekishutsu-shujutsu** hysterectomy

支給する **shikyū suru** supply; issue supplies

しま **shima** stripe

島 **shima** island

姉妹 **shimai** sisters

しまい込む **shimaikomu** put away

姉妹都市 **shimai-toshi** twin town

しま模様(の) **shimamoyō (no)** striped

閉まる **shimaru** close, shut

します **shimasu** (polite present tense of suru): 私がします **watashi ga shimasu** I'll do it

始末する **shimatsu suru** dispose of; put away animal

閉まった **shimatta** closed

しまった **shimatta** damn!

閉まっている **shimatte iru** be on (of lid, top)

しまっておく **shimatte oku** keep (in specific place)

しまう **shimau** store, stow; put away (in closet etc)

しまうま **shimauma** zebra

締め出す **shimedasu** bar; exclude; lock out (of house)

締め金 **shimegane** clamp

氏名 **shimei** full name

指名する **shimei suru** designate, nominate

指名手配中(の) **shimei-tehai chū (no)** wanted (by police)

締め切り **shimekiri** deadline; time limit

締め切る **shimekiru** close; keep shut; refuse to accept because a deadline has passed

絞め殺す **shimekorosu** strangle

締めくくる **shimekukuru** finish, wind up

湿っぽい **shimeppoi** damp

湿らせる **shimeraseru** dampen, moisten

湿り気 **shimerike** moisture

湿る **shimeru** get damp

占める **shimeru** account for, constitute; occupy, take up

閉める **shimeru** close; shut; wind up *car window*

締める **shimeru** fasten *seat belt*; tighten *screw*; tie *necktie*

示す **shimesu** show; indicate, point to; mark; reveal

湿った **shimetta** damp, moist

染み **shimi** stain, mark; blot; smear; 染みがつく **shimi ga tsuku** mark (*of fabric*)

染み込む **shimikomu** sink in

市民 **shimin** citizen; fellow citizen; the people

市民権 **shiminken** citizenship; civil rights

市民(の) **shimin (no)** civic; civil

染み抜き **shiminuki** stain remover

しみる **shimiru** penetrate; pierce; sting

霜 **shimo** frost; 霜の降りた **shimo no orita** frosty

指紋 **shimon** fingerprint

霜取りをする **shimotori o suru** defrost

しもやけ **shimoyake** frostbite; chilblain

シミュレートする **shimyurēto suru** simulate

しん **shin** core (*of fruit*); しんをくり抜く **shin o kurinuku** core

新... **shin...** new

竹刀 **shinai** bamboo sword

市内 **shinai** area within city limits

市内通話 **shinai-tsūwa** local call

シナモン **shinamon** cinnamon

品物 **shinamono** article; thing; goods

シナリオ **shinario** scenario

しなやか(な) **shinayaka (na)** supple; flexible

シンボルマーク **shinboru-māku** emblem

辛抱する **shinbō suru** be patient; endure

新聞 **shinbun** (news)paper

新聞雑誌 **shinbun-zasshi** the press

新聞雑誌販売店 **shinbun-zasshi-hanbaiten** newsagent

新陳代謝 **shinchin-taisha** metabolism

身長 **shinchō** height

慎重(な) **shinchō (na)** cautious, prudent

慎重に **shinchō ni** carefully; gingerly

慎重さ **shinchō-sa** discretion; prudence

真ちゅう **shinchū** brass

死んだ **shinda** dead; lifeless

寝台 **shindai** berth, bunk; couchette

寝台車 **shindai-sha** sleeping car

診断 **shindan** diagnosis

診断する **shindan suru** diagnose

神殿 **shinden** *main building of a shrine*

震度 **shindo** magnitude (*of quake*)

進度 **shindo** progress

震動 **shindō** tremor

振動 **shindō** vibration; oscillation; swing

震動する **shindō suru** quake; tremble

振動する **shindō suru** vibrate

深えん **shin'en** abyss; depths

深遠(な) **shin'en (na)** profound, deep

心不全 **shinfuzen** heart failure

侵害 **shingai** infringement; violation

侵害する **shingai suru** violate; encroach on; trespass on

神学 **shingaku** theology

シンガポール **Shingapōru** Singapore

シンガポール (の) **Shingapōru (no)** Singaporean

震源地 **shingenchi** epicenter

新月 **shingetsu** new moon

審議会 **shingikai** council

信号 **shingō** traffic light; signal

信号無視 **shingō-mushi** jaywalking

寝具 **shingu** bedclothes; bedding

シングル盤 **shinguru-ban** single MUS

シングルマザー **shinguru-mazā** single mother

シングル(の) **shinguru (no)** single-breasted

シングルス **shingurusu** singles (in tennis)

新方針 **shin-hōshin** new direction; new departure

死に物狂い **shinimonogurui** desperation

シニヨン **shiniyon** chignon; bun (hairstyle)

信者 **shinja** believer

信じがたい **shinjigatai** farfetched

信心深い **shinjinbukai** pious, religious

新人類 **shinjinrui** pej younger generation

信じられない **shinjirarenai** incredible; unbelievable

信じる **shinjiru** believe

真実 **shinjitsu** truth

信条 **shinjō** creed (beliefs)

真珠 **shinju** pearl

心中 **shinjū** double suicide

真珠湾 **Shinjuwan** Pearl Harbor

進化 **shinka** evolution

新幹線 **shinkansen** bullet train

進化論 **shinka-ron** evolution

進化する **shinka suru** evolve

神経 **shinkei** nerve; 神経が参っている **shinkei ga maitte iru** be a nervous wreck; 神経にさわる **shinkei ni sawaru** jar, grate

神経過敏 **shinkei-kabin** hypersensitivity

神経過敏(の) **shinkei-kabin (no)** neurotic; hypersensitive

神経科医 **shinkeikai** neurologist

神経(の) **shinkei (no)** nervous

神経質(な) **shinkeishitsu (na)** nervous; high-strung; sensitive

神経症 **shinkeishō** neurosis

真剣(な) **shinken (na)** serious; intense; solemn

しん気楼 **shinkirō** mirage

信仰 **shinkō** faith, belief

進行中である **shinkōchū de aru** be under way

深刻(な) **shinkoku (na)** deep trouble; somber; serious

深刻さ **shinkoku-sa** severity

申告する **shinkoku suru** declare (at customs)

深呼吸をする **shinkokyū o suru** take a deep breath

新婚カップル **shinkon-kappuru** newlyweds

信仰する **shinkō suru** believe in

進行する **shinkō suru** proceed, progress

真空 **shinkū** vacuum

真紅色(の) **shinkuiro (no)** scarlet

真空パック(の) **shinkū-pakku (no)** vacuum-packed

新境地 **shin-kyōchi** new departure

進級する **shinkyū suru** move up (in school)

新芽 **shinme** shoot

新年 **Shinnen** New Year

新任(の) **shinnin (no)** incoming

侵入 **shinnyū** penetration

進入禁止 **shinnyū-kinshi** no entry

新入生 **shinnyūsei** freshman

侵入者 **shinnyū-sha** intruder

新入社員 **shinnyū-shain** newcomer, recruit (to company)

侵入する **shinnyū suru** break in (of burglar); encroach on

市(の) **shi (no)** civic; municipal

忍び寄る **shinobiyoru** creep; sneak

しのぐ **shinogu** eclipse, outdo; overtake

死の灰 **shi no hai** fallout

しのんで **shinonde** in memory of

心配 **shinpai** anxiety, concern, worry

心配(な) **shinpai (na)** disturbed, concerned; worrying

心配させる **shinpai saseru** alarm; worry, concern

心配して **shinpai shite** anxious

心配している **shinpai shite iru** be worried ◊ apprehensive; concerned

心配そう(な) **shinpaisō (na)** worried

心配する **shinpai suru** worry

審判 **shinpan** referee; umpire; judge

審判する **shinpan suru** judge

新兵 **shinpei** recruit

神秘的(な) **shinpiteki (na)** mystical; occult; enigmatic

進歩 **shinpo** advance, progress

進歩させる **shinpo saseru** advance

信奉者 **shinpō-sha** believer

進歩する **shinpo suru** make progress, advance, come on

進歩的(な) **shinpoteki (na)** progressive

新婦 **shinpu** bride

信ぴょう性 **shinpyōsei** reliability; credibility

信頼 **shinrai** belief; faith; confidence, trust

信頼できない **shinrai dekinai** unreliable

信頼できる **shinrai dekiru** authoritative; credible; reliable; responsible

信頼性 **shinraisei** reliability

信頼する **shinrai suru** trust; rely on

辛らつ(な) **shinratsu (na)** cutting; hurtful; pointed *remark, question*

真理 **shinri** truth

心理 **shinri** state of mind

心理学 **shinrigaku** psychology

心理学者 **shinri-gakusha** psychologist

心理学的(な) **shinrigakuteki (na)** psychological

森林 **shinrin** woods; forest

森林警備隊員 **shinrin-keibi-taiin** forest ranger

心理的(な) **shinriteki (na)** psychological

針路 **shinro** course (*of ship, plane*)

新郎 **shinrō** groom

侵略 **shinryaku** invasion

侵略する **shinryaku suru** invade; overrun

診療 **shinryō** medical treatment

診療所 **shinryōjo** clinic

審査する **shinsa suru** screen, vet; process *application*

診察 **shinsatsu** examination (*of patient*)

診察料 **shinsatsu-ryō** medical fee

診察する **shinsatsu suru** examine *patient*

申請 **shinsei** application

神聖(な) **shinsei (na)** holy, sacred

神聖さ **shinsei-sa** sanctity

申請書 **shinseisho** application form

申請する **shinsei suru** apply for; put in for

親せき **shinseki** relation, relative

新鮮(な) **shinsen (na)** fresh

新鮮さ **shinsen-sa** freshness

親切 **shinsetsu** kindness

親切(な) **shinsetsu (na)** genial; obliging; kind

紳士 **shinshi** gentleman

紳士的(な) **shinshiteki (na)** gallant

寝室 **shinshitsu** bedroom

侵食 **shinshoku** encroachment; erosion

侵食する **shinshoku suru** encroach on; erode

伸縮性のある **shinshukusei no aru** elastic; flexible

進出する **shinshutsu suru** advance

進水 **shinsui** launch

浸水した **shinsui shita** waterlogged

進水する **shinsui suru** launch

身体障害 **shintai-shōgai** physical disability, physical handicap; 身体障害のある **shintai-shōgai no aru** be disabled

身体障害者 **shintai-shōgai-sha** the disabled

身体的(な) **shintaiteki (na)** physical; bodily

信託 **shintaku** trust FIN

進展 **shinten** breakthrough; development

親展 **shinten** private, confidential

新展開 **shin-tenkai** new departure, new development

進展させる **shinten saseru** develop, improve on

神道 **Shintō** Shinto

死ぬ **shinu** die

神話 **shinwa** myth; mythology

神話学 **shinwagaku** mythology

深夜料金 **shin'ya-ryōkin** late-night fare

信用できない **shin'yō dekinai** untrustworthy

信用できる **shinyō dekiru** trustworthy; credible; reliable

針葉樹 **shinyōju** conifer

信用された **shin'yō sareta** trusted

信用性 **shinyōsei** credibility

信用しない **shinyō shinai** distrust, mistrust

信用照会状 **shinyō-shōkaijō** letter of credit

信用する **shinyō suru** trust; rely on

親友 **shin'yū** close friend

親善 **shinzen** friendship

新参者 **shinzanmono** newcomer

心臓 **shinzō** heart; heart attack

心臓発作 **shinzō-hossa** heart attack

心臓移植 **shinzo-ishoku** heart transplant

心臓(の) **shinzō (no)** cardiac, coronary

塩 **shio** salt

潮 **shio** tide; 潮が満ちる/引く **shio ga michiru / hiku** the tide is in / out

塩味(の) **shioaji (no)** savory; salty

塩辛い **shiokarai** salty

しおれる **shioreru** wilt, droop; be depressed

失敗 **shippai** failure, flop; 失敗に終わる **shippai ni owaru** break down (of talks)

失敗した **shippai shita** unsuccessful

失敗する **shippai suru** fail; flunk; misfire (of scheme)

しっぺ返し **shippegaeshi** retort; tit for tat

尻尾 **shippo** tail

湿布 **shippu** compress

調べ **shirabe** investigation; enquiry

調べる **shiraberu** check; find out; study, examine; look at; look up

しらふ(の) **shirafu (no)** sober

白髪(の) **shiraga (no)** gray-haired

しらかば **shirakaba** silver birch

しらみ **shirami** louse

知らない **shiranai** strange, unknown; unfamiliar

知られていない **shirarete inai** unheard of, unknown

知らせ **shirase** word, news

知らせる **shiraseru** break news; keep posted

試練 **shiren** trial; ordeal

しり **shiri** bottom, buttocks, butt; しりに敷かれた **shiri ni shikareta** henpecked

知り合い **shiriai** acquaintance

知り合いである **shiriai de aru** be acquainted with; know

知り合いになる **shiriai ni naru** get to know

知り合う **shiriau** know; get to know

しりごみさせる **shirigomi saseru** daunt

しりごみする **shirigomi suru** flinch

シリコン **shirikon** silicon

シリコンチップ **shirikon chippu** silicon chip

シリンダー **shirindā** cylinder

知りたがり(の) **shiritagari (no)** inquisitive

私立(の) **shiritsu (no)** private

市立(の) **shiritsu (no)** municipal

私立探偵 **shiritsu-tantei** private detective

退ける **shirizokeru** dismiss; reject; repel

白 **shiro** white

城 **shiro** castle

白い **shiroi** white; fair complexion

しろかび **shirokabi** mildew

白くま **shirokuma** polar bear

白黒(の) **shirokuro (no)** black and white

しろめ **shirome** pewter

白身 **shiromi** (egg) white

素人 **shirōto** amateur; layman

素人(の) **shirōto (no)** unprofessional; amateurish

汁 **shiru** soup; juice; sap

知る **shiru** know

白ワイン **shiro wain** white wine

印 **shirushi** mark, sign; brand; checkmark; 印を付ける **shirushi o tsukeru** check, check off

資料 **shiryō** data, material

飼料 **shiryō** fodder

視力 **shiryoku** eyesight, vision

資料請求券 **shiryō-seikyū-ken** coupon

支流 **shiryū** tributary

示唆 **shisa** suggestion, implication

資産 **shisan** asset; equity

示唆する **shisa suru** suggest, imply

視察 **shisatsu** inspection

視察する **shisatsu suru** inspect

姿勢 **shisei** position, stance; posture

私生児 **shiseiji** bastard, illegitimate child

視線 **shisen** gaze

施設 **shisetsu** establishment; institute

使節団 **shisetsudan** mission

支社 **shisha** branch office

死者 **shisha** dead person; the deceased

四捨五入 **shisha-gonyū** *rounding off to the nearest whole number*

試写会 **shishakai** preview

指針 **shishin** pointer, indication

司書 **shisho** librarian

私書箱 **shishobako** PO Box

死傷者 **shishō-sha** casualty

ししゅう **shishū** embroidery; needlework

思春期 **shishunki** puberty

支出 **shishutsu** expenditure

しそ **shiso** perilla (*plant*)

思想 **shisō** idea; thought

子孫 **shison** descendant; ...の子孫である ... *no shison de aru* be descended from...

湿疹 **shisshin** eczema

失神させる **shisshin saseru** knock unconscious

失そう **shissō** disappearance

質素(な) **shisso (na)** humble; thrifty; plain; simple

質素さ **shisso-sa** modesty, simplicity

失そうする **shissō suru** disappear

システム **shisutemu** system COMPUT

システムアナリスト **shisutemu-anarisuto** systems analyst

システムキッチン **shisutemu-kitchin** fitted kitchen

下 **shita** bottom (*of pile*); lower part; 下で **shita de** under; 下に **shita ni** below; down; 下(の) **shita (no)** junior, subordinate

舌 **shita** tongue

下取り **shitadori** part exchange

下取りする **shitadori suru** trade in; take in part exchange

下書き **shitagaki** (rough) draft

したがって **shitagatte** accordingly; therefore; thus; ...にしたがって ... *ni shitagatte* in accordance with

従う **shitagau** abide by; comply with; follow; obey

下着 **shitagi** underwear

死体 **shitai** corpse, cadaver

支度 **shitaku** preparations; arrangements

下町 **shitamachi** downtown

下向き(の) **shitamuki (no)** downward

舌なめずりする **shitanamezuri suru** lick one's lips

親しい **shitashii** close; intimate; ...と親しい ... *to shitashii* be friendly with

親しくなる **shitashiku naru** make friends with; get involved with

親しくしている **shitashiku shite iru** be close to

親しさ **shitashi-sa** intimacy; familiarity

舌足らず **shitatarazu** lisp

したたる **shitataru** drip

下手投げ(の) **shitate nage (no)** underarm

仕立て(の) **shitate (no)** tailor-made

仕立てる **shitateru** tailor; sew; train; prepare

慕っている **shitatte iru** be attached to

慕う **shitau** adore

下請け会社 **shitauke-gaisha** subcontractor

下請けさせる **shitauke saseru** subcontract

舌触り **shitazawari** texture (*of food*)

指定する **shitei suru** designate; specify

指定図書 **shitei-tosho** set book; set reading

私的(な) **shiteki (na)** personal, private

詩的(な) **shiteki (na)** poetic

指摘する **shiteki suru** point out; bring to the attention of

支店 **shiten** branch (*of bank, company*)

私鉄 **shitetsu** private railroad

シートベルト **shīto-beruto** seat belt

しとしと **shitoshito**: 雨がしとしと降っ
ている **ame ga shitoshito futte iru**
it's spitting with rain

質 **shitsu** quality (of goods etc)

シーツ **shītsu** sheet

失望 **shitsubō** disappointment;
dismay; frustration

湿度 **shitsudo** humidity

失業 **shitsugyō** unemployment

失業中(の) **shitsugyōchū (no)** idle

失業者 **shitsugyō-sha** the
unemployed

失業した **shitsugyō shita**
unemployed

失業している **shitsugyō shite iru** be
out of work

しつけ **shitsuke** upbringing; training

しつける **shitsukeru** discipline; train

しつこい **shitsukoi** insistent; nagging
pain; strident demands; heavy food

失明させる **shitsumei saseru** blind

質問 **shitsumon** question, query

質問する **shitsumon suru** ask a
question; query; question

室内(の) **shitsunai (no)** interior (of
house)

室内装飾 **shitsunai-sōshoku**
interior design

室温 **shitsuon** room temperature

失礼 **shitsurei** disrespect; 失礼です
が **shitsurei desu ga** excuse me
(interrupting s.o.); 失礼します
shitsurei shimasu excuse me

失礼(な) **shitsurei (na)**
disrespectful; offensive

知ったかぶり屋 **shittakaburi-ya**
wise guy

知っている **shitte iru** know

しっと **shitto** jealousy

しっと深い **shittobukai** jealous

しわ **shiwa** crease, wrinkle; しわがよ
る **shiwa ga yoru** shrivel; wrinkle,
crease; しわにする **shiwa ni suru**
crumple, crease; しわを寄せる
shiwa o yoseru wrinkle

視野 **shiya** field of vision; 視野の狭
い **shiya no semai** narrow-minded

市役所 **shiyakusho** city hall, town
hall

しよう **shiyō** let's; 仕事をしよう
shigoto o shiyō let's do business;

...しようと努力する **...shiyō to
doryoku suru** try to; resolve to

仕様 **shiyō** means; method;
specifications

使用 **shiyō** use

使用できる **shiyō dekiru** usable

使用法 **shiyō-hō** directions (for
use)

使用可能(な) **shiyō-kanō (na)** live
ammunition

試用期間 **shiyō-kikan** trial period
(for employee); 試用期間中で
shiyōkikan chū de on probation
(in job)

使用説明 **shiyō-setsumei**
instruction; operating instructions

使用者 **shiyō-sha** user

私有(の) **shiyū (no)** private

死産した **shizan shita** be stillborn

自然 **shizen** nature

自然保護区域 **shizen-hogo-kuiki**
nature reserve

自然保護論者 **shizen-hogo-
ronsha** conservationist

自然科学 **shizen-kagaku** natural
science

自然科学者 **shizen-kagakusha**
natural scientist

自然に **shizen ni** naturally

自然(の) **shizen (no)** natural

静か(な) **shizuka (na)** peaceful;
quiet; subdued; still water, trees;
smooth ride

静かに **shizuka ni** quiet!, silence!
◊ softly

静かにさせる **shizuka ni saseru**
quieten down

静けさ **shizuke-sa** calm; peace

滴 **shizuku** drip; drop

静まる **shizumaru** die down (of
storm); drop (of wind); settle down;
calm down

沈める **shizumeru** sink ship

沈む **shizumu** sink, go under

シーズン **shīzun** season (for tourism
etc)

シーズンオフ **shīzun'ofu** off-season

ショー **shō** cabaret; show

賞 **shō** award, prize

章 **shō** chapter; section

省 **shō** department, ministry,

商売 **shōbai** business; 商売をする *shōbai o suru* do business; deal

処罰する **shobatsu suru** penalize, punish

小便 **shōben** urine; 小便をする *shōben o suru* urinate

消防車 **shōbō-sha** fire truck

消防士 **shōbō-shi** firefighter

消防署 **shōbō-sho** fire department

勝負 **shōbu** match; game; victory or defeat, result; ここが勝負だ *koko ga shōbu da* this is the crucial moment

処分 **shobun** disposal; punishment

処分する **shobun suru** dispose of; punish

承知する **shōchi suru** consent; understand; be aware of

所長 **shochō** director; warden

象徴 **shōchō** symbol

象徴する **shōchō suru** symbolize

象徴的(な) **shōchōteki (na)** symbolic

承諾 **shōdaku** acceptance; compliance

承諾する **shōdaku suru** accept

商談をまとめる **shōdan o matomeru** clinch a deal

書道 **shodō** calligraphy

衝動 **shōdō** impulse, urge

衝動買い **shōdōgai** impulse buy; 衝動買いをする *shōdōgai o suru* go on a shopping spree

消毒綿 **shōdokumen** swab

消毒(の) **shōdoku (no)** antiseptic

消毒する **shōdoku suru** disinfect

消毒剤 **shōdokuzai** antiseptic; disinfectant

衝動的(な) **shōdōteki (na)** impulsive

衝動的に **shōdōteki ni** on the spur of the moment

省エネ(の) **shō-ene (no)** energy-saving

しょうが **shōga** ginger

障害 **shōgai** barrier; obstacle; hindrance; disorder MED

渉外 **shōgai** public relations; customer relations

生涯 **shōgai** lifetime

障害物 **shōgaibutsu** obstacle, obstruction; blockage

障害物走 **shōgaibutsu-sō** steeplechase

小学校 **shōgakkō** elementary school

小学校教師 **shōgakkō-kyōshi** elementary teacher

奨学金 **shōgakukin** grant; scholarship

小学生 **shōgakusei** elementary school student

しょうがない **shō ga nai** it can't be helped

正月 **shōgatsu** New Year season

衝撃 **shōgeki** impact (*of new manager etc*); knock, blow

衝撃的(な) **shōgekiteki (na)** devastating; traumatic; shocking

証言する **shōgen suru** testify, give evidence

将棋 **shōgi** Japanese chess

正午 **shōgo** midday, noon

将軍 **shōgun** general MIL

商業 **shōgyō** commerce

商業化する **shōgyōka suru** commercialize

商業(の) **shōgyō (no)** commercial

商業的(な) **shōgyōteki (na)** commercial

消費 **shōhi** consumption

商品 **shōhin** goods, merchandise; stock

賞品 **shōhin** prize

商品化 **shōhinka** merchandising

商品券 **shōhinken** gift token, gift voucher

消費量 **shōhi-ryō** consumption

消費者 **shōhi-sha** consumer

消費社会 **shōhi-shakai** consumer society

消費する **shōhi suru** consume, use

消費財 **shōhi-zai** consumer goods

初歩(の) **shoho (no)** elementary, rudimentary

処方せん **shohōsen** prescription

処方する **shohō suru** prescribe

初歩的(な) **shohoteki (na)** rudimentary

所持 **shoji** possession (*of gun, drugs*)

障子 **shoji** sliding paper door

正直 **shōjiki** honesty

正直(な) **shōjiki (na)** honest, straight; upright

正直に **shōjiki ni** honestly; 正直に言うと **shōjiki ni iu to** to be brutally frank; to be honest with you

所持規制薬物 **shojikisei-yakubutsu** controlled substance

精進料理 **shōjin-ryōri** vegetarian Japanese cuisine

所持する **shoji suru** possess *gun, drugs*

処女 **shojo** virgin (*female*); virginity (*female*)

少女 **shōjo** girl

症状 **shōjō** symptom; 症状がある **shōjō ga aru** be symptomatic of

賞状 **shōjō** certificate of merit

処女航海 **shojo-kōkai** maiden voyage

消化 **shōka** digestion

消化不良 **shōka-furyō** indigestion

紹介 **shōkai** introduction (*to person*); presentation (*of product*)

照会番号 **shōkai-bangō** reference number

紹介する **shōkai suru** introduce

消火器 **shōka-ki** fire extinguisher

昇格する **shōkaku suru** move up (*in league*)

召喚状 **shōkan-jō** subpoena

召喚する **shōkan suru** subpoena

償還する **shōkan suru** repay; redeem *debt*

消火栓 **shōkasen** hydrant

消化する **shōka suru** digest

処刑 **shokei** execution (*of criminal*)

処刑する **shokei suru** execute *criminal*

証券 **shōken** bonds; securities; stocks

証券ブローカー **shōken-burōkā** broker

証券市場 **shōken-shijō** stock market; 証券市場の暴落 **shōken-shijō no bōraku** stockmarket crash

証券取引所 **shōken-torihiki-sho** stock exchange

初期 **shoki** infancy (*of state, institution*)

正気 **shōki** sanity

初期化する **shokika suru** format

賞金 **shōkin** reward; winnings; 賞金を与える **shōkin o ataeru** reward

初期(の) **shoki (no)** early; initial

正気(の) **shōki (no)** sane, lucid

触角 **shokkaku** antenna, feeler

食券 **shokken** voucher (*for food*)

食器 **shokki** tableware

食器棚 **shokkidana** dresser; sideboard

ショッキング(な) **shokkingu (na)** shocking

ショック **shokku** shock; ショックを与える **shokku o ataeru** stun, shock; electrify *fig*

ショック状態にある **shokku jōtai ni aru** be in shock

証拠 **shōko** evidence, proof; testament (*to s.o.*)

証拠物件 **shōko-bukken** evidence

商工会議所 **Shōkō-kaigisho** Chamber of Commerce

しょう紅熱 **shōkōnetsu** scarlet fever

職 **shoku** job, post; office, position; 職探しをしている **shokusagashi o shite iru** be job hunting

触媒 **shokubai** catalyst

植物 **shokubutsu** plant

植物学 **shokubutsugaku** botany

植物(の) **shokubutsu (no)** botanical

食中毒 **shoku-chūdoku** food poisoning

食堂 **shokudō** canteen; diner; dining room

食堂車 **shokudōsha** dining car, restaurant car

職業 **shokugyō** employment; business; profession

職業(の) **shokugyō (no)** vocational

職業倫理に反する **shokugyōrinri ni hansuru** unprofessional

職業紹介所 **shokugyō-shōkaijo** employment agency

触発する **shokuhatsu suru** touch off; trigger; provoke

食費 **shokuhi** spending on food

食品 **shokuhin** food products

職員 **shokuin** personnel, staff

職員室 **shokuin-shitsu** staffroom

食事 **shokuji** meal; 食事を出す

食事を出す **shokuji o dasu** serve food, give out food; 食事をする **shokuji o suru** dine

食事時間 **shokuji-jikan** mealtime; sitting (*for meal*)

食事療法 **shokuji-ryōhō** diet (*for health reasons*)

植民地 **shokuminchi** colony

植民地化する **shokuminchika suru** colonize

職務 **shokumu** duty, responsibility

職務内容 **shokumu-naiyō** job description

職人 **shokunin** tradesman, workman; craftsman

食料 **shokuryō** food

食料雑貨屋 **shokuryō-zakka-ya** grocer

食生活 **shokuseikatsu** diet (*regular food*)

触手 **shokushu** feeler; antenna; tentacle

食卓 **shokutaku** dining table

食欲 **shokuyoku** appetite

食前酒 **shokuzenshu** appetizer, apéritif

焼却炉 **shōkyakuro** incinerator

消極的(な) **shōkyokuteki (na)** passive; negative

初級 **shokyū** beginner's course; elementary level

昇給 **shōkyū** raise, rise (*in salary*)

署名 **shomei** signature

照明 **shōmei** lighting

証明 **shōmei** verification; identification; proof

証明書 **shōmeisho** certificate

署名する **shomei suru** sign

証明する **shōmei suru** certify; prove

正面 **shōmen** front (*of building, book*)

書面で **shomen de** in writing

正面入り口 **shōmen-iriguchi** front entrance

正面観覧席 **shōmen-kanranseki** grandstand

正面の **shōmen (no)** head-on

消滅 **shōmetsu** disappearance

賞味期限の日付け **shōmikigen no hizuke** best before date

庶民 **shomin** the people, the masses

正味(の) **shōmi (no)** net *weight, amount*

消耗する **shōmō suru** consume; exhaust

少年 **shōnen** boy

少年非行 **shōnen-hikō** delinquency

少年(の) **shōnen (no)** juvenile

少年のような(な) **shōnen no yō(na)** boyish

初日 **shonichi** première

小児科 **shōnika** pediatrics

小児科医 **shōnikai** pediatrician

小児まひ **shōni-mahi** polio

承認 **shōnin** acknowledg(e)ment; recognition (*of state, s.o.'s achievements*); approval

証人 **shōnin** witness

商人 **shōnin** merchant; shopkeeper

証人席 **shōnin-seki** witness stand

承認する **shōnin suru** approve; grant *request*; recognize

しょう乳洞 **shōnyūdō** limestone cave

消音装置 **shōon-sōchi** silencer

ショッピングセンター **shoppingu-sentā** shopping mall, plaza

将来 **shōrai** future

症例 **shōrei** case MED

奨励 **shōrei** encouragement

奨励する **shōrei suru** encourage

勝利 **shōri** win, victory; triumph; 勝利を得た **shōri o eta** victorious

勝利者 **shōri-sha** victor

処理する **shori suru** handle, take care of; process *data*; treat *materials*

小論文 **shōronbun** essay

ショール **shōru** shawl

書類 **shorui** documentation, papers

ショールーム **shōrūmu** showroom

省略 **shōryaku** omission

省略形 **shōryakukei** abbreviation

省略する **shōryaku suru** omit; abbreviate

少量 **shōryō** dash, drop

書斎 **shosai** den; study

詳細 **shōsai** detail

詳細に **shōsai ni** in minute detail, minutely

称賛 **shōsan** applause, praise; 称賛に値する **shōsan ni atai suru** creditable; praiseworthy

称賛する **shōsan suru** applaud, praise

小冊子 **shōsasshi** booklet

小説 **shōsetsu** fiction; novel

小説家 **shōsetsu-ka** novelist

勝者 **shō-sha** winner

商社 **shōsha** trading company

昇進 **shōshin** promotion

昇進させる **shōshin saseru** promote *employee*

初心者 **shoshin-sha** beginner, novice

正真正銘(の) **shōshin-shōmei (no)** genuine

昇進する **shōshin suru** be promoted

証書 **shōsho** (title) deed; certificate

少々 **shōshō** a bit; a little; mildly

招集する **shōshū suru** call, summon, convene

召集する **shōshū suru** summon, call out

消息通 **shōsokutsū** insider

小数 **shōsū** decimal; minority ◊ few, not many

少数派である **shōsūha de aru** be in the minority

少数民族 **shōsū-minzoku** ethnic minority

少数(の) **shōsū (no)** few, not many

小数点 **shōsūten** decimal point

招待 **shōtai** invitation

正体 **shōtai** true character; 正体を現わす **shōtai o arawasu** give oneself away

招待状 **shōtaijō** invitation (*card*)

招待する **shōtai suru** invite, ask

焦点 **shōten** focus; …の焦点を絞る **… no shōten o shiboru** focus on

商店 **shōten** store

商店主 **shōten-shu** storekeeper; merchant

ショート **shōto** short circuit

所得 **shotoku** earnings; 所得から控除される **shotoku kara kōjo sareru** tax deductible

所得税 **shotokuzei** income tax

衝突 **shōtotsu** crash, collision

衝突させる **shōtotsu saseru** crash, collide

衝突する **shōtotsu suru** collide; run into

ショーツ **shōtsu** briefs

ショット **shotto** photograph, shot

小宇宙 **shōchū** microcosm

昭和時代 **Shōwa-jidai** Showa period (*1926-1989*)

昭和天皇 **Shōwa-tennō** Emperor Hirohito

ショーウィンドウ **shō-windō** store window

賞与 **shōyo** bonus; reward

所有 **shoyū** possession, ownership

しょうゆ **shōyu** soy sauce

所有物 **shoyūbutsu** possession; possessions, property

所有地 **shoyūchi** land (*property*)

所有格(の) **shoyūkaku (no)** possessive GRAM

所有権 **shoyū-ken** ownership

所有者 **shoyū-sha** holder, owner

所有する **shoyū suru** own, possess

肖像画 **shōzōga** portrait

所属する **shozoku suru** belong to

種 **shu** species

州 **shū** province, state

週 **shū** week

守備 **shubi** defense; fielding SP

首謀者 **shubō-sha** ringleader

秋分 **shūbun** autumnal equinox

秋分の日 **Shūbun no hi** Day of the Autumnal Equinox

執着 **shūchaku** attachment; persistence; obsession

執着する **shūchaku suru** be attached; stick

主張 **shuchō** case, argument; cause; claim; assertion

しゅう長 **shūchō** chief; headman

主張する **shuchō suru** claim, maintain; argue that; protest

集中治療室 **shūchū-chiryōshitsu** intensive care (unit)

集中コース **shūchū-kōsu** crash course

集中講座 **shūchū-kōza** intensive course

集中力 **shūchūryoku** concentration

集中する **shūchū suru** concentrate

集中的(な) **shūchūteki (na)** intensive

主題 **shudai** subject, topic

手段 **shudan** avenue *fig*; vehicle *fig*; expedient

集団 **shūdan** group

集団療法 **shūdan-ryōhō** group therapy

終電 **shūden** last train of the day

修道院 **shūdōin** abbey; monastery

修道女 **shūdōjo** nun

主導権 **shudōken** initiative

修道士 **shūdōshi** monk

収益 **shūeki** proceeds; profits

収益性 **shūekisei** profitability

主演させる **shuen saseru** star

主演する **shuen suru** star

主夫 **shufu** house-husband

主婦 **shufu** housewife

修復 **shūfuku** restoration (*of building*)

修復できない **shūfuku dekinai** irreparable

修復する **shūfuku suru** restore

手芸 **shugei** handicraft

襲撃 **shūgeki** assault, attack; raid

襲撃する **shūgeki suru** assault, attack; raid

主義 **shugi** doctrine; principle; 主義として *shugi to shite* on principle

衆議院 **Shūgiin** House of Representatives

集合 **shūgō** gathering; assembly; set MATH

主語 **shugo** subject GRAM

就業時間 **shūgyō-jikan** work day

宗派 **shūha** cult, sect; denomination

周波数 **shūhasū** frequency, wavelength

周辺 **shūhen** periphery

周辺機器 **shūhen-kiki** peripheral

首位 **shui** first place; leader

周囲 **shūi** perimeter

周囲(の) **shūi (no)** surrounding

習字 **shūji** calligraphy

主人 **shujin** landlord; master

囚人 **shūjin** prisoner

手術 **shujutsu** operation MED; 手術をする *shujutsu o suru* operate on; 手術を受ける *shujutsu o ukeru* have an operation

手術室 **shujutsushitsu** operating room

手術する **shujutsu suru** operate MED

集会 **shūkai** rally POL

臭覚 **shūkaku** sense of smell

収穫 **shūkaku** crop; harvest; yield; catch (*of fish*)

収穫する **shūkaku suru** reap

習慣 **shūkan** habit; routine; practice, custom

週間 **shūkan** week

週刊 **shūkan** weekly *magazine*

主観的(な) **shukanteki (na)** subjective

主権 **shuken** sovereignty, independence

集結地点 **shūketsu-chiten** rendezvous MIL

周期 **shūki** cycle (*series of events*)

周期的(な) **shūkiteki (na)** periodic

集金 **shūkin** collecting money; bill collection

出血 **shukketsu** hemorrhage

出血している **shukketsu shite iru** bleeding

出血する **shukketsu suru** bleed

出勤する **shukkin suru** go off to work

出国審査 **shukkoku-shinsa** passport control (*for departure*)

出港する **shukkō suru** sail, depart

宿題 **shukudai** homework

祝福 **shukufuku** blessing

祝福する **shukufuku suru** bless

宿泊客 **shukuhaku-kyaku** guest; visitor; resident

宿泊させる **shukuhaku saseru** accommodate

宿泊設備 **shukuhaku-setsubi** accommodations

宿泊する **shukuhaku suru** stay

祝日 **shukujitsu** holiday (*one day*)

縮小 **shukushō** decrease

縮小する **shukushō suru** decrease; wind down (*of business*)

宿敵 **shukuteki** old enemy; mortal enemy

縮図 **shukuzu** scale (*of map*); scale drawing

宗教 **shūkyō** religion

宗教(の) **shūkyō (no)** religious

週末 **shūmatsu** weekend

趣味 **shumi** hobby; pastime, pursuit

趣味のよい **shumi no yoi** tasteful; esthetic

種目 **shumoku** event SP

春分 **shunbun** vernal equinox

春分の日 **Shunbun no hi** Day of the Vernal Equinox

周年 **-shūnen** anniversary

執念深い **shūnen-bukai** relentless; persistent

就任式(の) **shūninshiki (no)** inaugural

就任する **shūnin suru** be inaugurated; be appointed

瞬間 **shunkan** instant, moment

春期 **shunki** springtime

州(の) **shū (no)** state

収納箱 **shūnōbako** chest

首脳会議 **shunō-kaigi** summit

シュノーケル **shunōkeru** snorkel

収入 **shūnyū** income, revenue

出版 **shuppan** publication (of book, report); publishing

出版物 **shuppanbutsu** publication (book, newspaper)

出版されている **shuppan sarete iru** be published, be out

出版社 **shuppan-sha** publisher, publishing company

出版する **shuppan suru** publish, bring out

出発 **shuppatsu** departure

出発便 **shuppatsubin** outgoing flight

出発地点 **shuppatsu-chiten** starting point

出発時刻 **shuppatsu-jikoku** departure time

出発ラウンジ **shuppatsu-raunji** departure lounge

出発する **shuppatsu suru** leave

出品物 **shuppinbutsu** exhibit; entry, item submitted

シュレッダー **shureddā** shredder; シュレッダーにかける **shureddā ni kakeru** shred

修理工 **shūrikō** mechanic

修理工場 **shūri-kōjō** body shop; garage (for repairs)

修理する **shūri suru** repair, mend; fix; recondition

種類 **shurui** brand, make; sort, variety; form (of government, address)

狩猟 **shuryō** hunting

終了 **shūryō** termination

終了する **shūryō suru** log off; shut down COMPUT; complete

修了する **shūryō suru** complete

手りゅう弾 **shuryūdan** grenade

主催者 **shusai-sha** organizer; promoter

主催する **shusai suru** sponsor; host

修正 **shūsei** amendment; revision

修正液 **shūseieki** white-out, correcting fluid

修正する **shūsei suru** amend; revise text, figures; touch up photo

臭跡 **shūseki** scent (of animal)

集積回路 **shūseki-kairo** integrated circuit

収支 **shūshi** income and expenditure; 収支を合わせる **shūshi o awaseru** balance the books

終止符 **shūshifu** full stop

修士号 **shūshigō** master's (degree)

首相 **shushō** prime minister, premier

主食 **shushoku** staple diet

就職する **shūshoku suru** find work; get a job

収集家 **shūshūka** collector

収縮する **shūshuku suru** contract, shrink

収集した **shūshū shita** collected works

収集する **shūshū suru** collect (as hobby)

しゅうしゅうという音を立てる **shūshū to iu oto o tateru** hiss; sizzle

出産 **shussan** birth, labor; childbirth; delivery (of baby)

出産前(の) **shussanmae (no)** antenatal, prenatal

出生証明書 **shussei-shōmeisho** birth certificate

出席 **shusseki** attendance

出席者 **shusseki-sha** those attending; turnout (of people)

出席している **shusseki shite iru** be present

出席する **shusseki suru** attend

出世する **shusse suru** be promoted

出身である **shusshin de aru** originate from, come from

出資者 **shusshi-sha** investor; financier

出生率 **shusshōritsu** birthrate

出所する **shussho suru** get out (*from prison*); be released

首都 **shuto** capital

シュート **shūto** chute

取得する **shutoku suru** acquire

習得する **shūtoku suru** master *skill, language*

しゅうとめ **shūtome** mother-in-law

主として **shu to shite** chiefly, largely

出馬する **shutsuba suru** run (*in election*); 大統領選に出馬する **daitōryō-sen ni shutsuba suru** run for President

出演 **shutsuen** appearance (*in movie etc*)

出演者 **shutsuen-sha** cast

出演する **shutsuen suru** appear (*in movie etc*)

出願 **shutsugan** application

出願する **shutsugan suru** apply for

出現 **shutsugen** birth, appearance

出現させる **shutsugen saseru** materialize

出場させる **shutsujō saseru** enter (*in race*)

出場者 **shutsujō-sha** contestant

出場する **shutsujō suru** enter (*in competition*); play, take part SP

出力 **shutsuryoku** output

出張 **shutchō** business trip

出張旅費 **shutchō-ryohi** travel expenses

出廷 **shuttei** appearance (*in court*)

出廷する **shuttei suru** appear (*in court*)

出頭命令 **shuttō-meirei** summons (*to court*)

出頭する **shuttō suru** report (*to police*); present oneself

手話 **shuwa** sign language

手腕 **shuwan** prowess

しゅよう **shuyō** growth MED; tumor

主要（な）**shuyō (na)** main; major, primary

収容力 **shūyōryoku** capacity

収容する **shūyō suru** accommodate; take in; intern

取材する **shuzai suru** collect *news*; gather *material*; cover (*of journalist*)

種族 **shuzoku** tribe

そう **sō** so; yes; in that way ◊ seeming; うれしそうな顔 **ureshi-sō na kao** a happy-looking face; そうですね **sō desu ne** that's right, isn't it?; そうではないだろう **sō dewa nai darō** I guess not; そう希望します/そう思います **sō kibō shimasu / omoimasu** I hope / think so

層 **sō** layer; tier

粗悪さ **soaku-sa** inferiority

そば **soba** buckwheat noodles

相場 **sōba** market; market price

そばかす **sobakasu** freckles

そばに **soba ni** beside; by

送別会 **sōbetsukai** farewell party

装備 **sōbi** gear, equipment

そびえる **sobieru** tower over; soar over; dominate

そびえ立つ **sobietatsu** lofty

ソビエト連邦 **Sobieto-renpō** Soviet Union

装備されている **sōbi sarete iru** be supplied with

祖母 **sobo** grandmother

素朴（な）**soboku (na)** simple, unsophisticated

装置 **sōchi** device

そうだ **sō da** that's right; I hear that …; looks like; そうだとは思いません **sō da to wa omoimasen** I don't think so; そうだとよいと思う **sō da to yoi to omou** I hope so; みんなうまくいきそうだ **minna umaku ikisō da** it looks like everything is going to be fine

ソーダ **sōda** soda (*water*)

壮大（な）**sōdai (na)** grand, magnificent

壮大さ **sōdai-sa** magnificence

相談 **sōdan** session

相談料 **sōdan-ryō** fee

相談する **sōdan suru** consult

相談役 **sōdan'yaku** adviser

そうだろう **sō darō** I guess so

育てる **sodateru** raise, bring up *child*

育つ **sodatsu** develop, grow; thrive

そで **sode** sleeve

そでなし(の) **sodenashi (no)** sleeveless

騒動 **sōdō** tumult; 騒動を起こす **sōdō o okosu** make a scene

疎遠になる **soen ni naru** drift apart

ソファ **sofa** sofa

ソファベッド **sofa-beddo** sofa-bed

祖父 **sofu** grandfather

祖父母 **sofubo** grandparents

ソフト **sofuto** software

双眼鏡 **sōgankyō** binoculars

狙撃班 **sogekihan** hit squad

狙撃兵 **sogekihei** sniper

草原 **sōgen** prairie

争議 **sōgi** dispute (*industrial*)

葬儀場 **sōgijō** funeral home

葬儀屋 **sōgiya** mortician

相互依存した **sōgo-izon shita** interdependent

相互(の) **sōgo (no)** mutual, reciprocal

相互作用 **sōgo-sayō** interaction; reciprocal action

総合的(な) **sōgōteki (na)** comprehensive

操業短縮する **sōgyō-tanshuku suru** be on short time; reduce operations

双方で **sōhō de** bilateral

相違 **sōi** disparity; 意見の相違 **iken no sōi** difference; disagreement; dissension

そういう **sō iu** such a ◊ so; そういうつもりはなかった **sō iu tsumori wa nakatta** that's not what I intended

掃除 **sōji** cleaning

掃除夫 **sōjifu** cleaner (*male*)

掃除婦 **sōjifu** cleaner (*female*); cleaning woman

掃除機 **sōjiki** vacuum cleaner; 掃除機をかける **sōjiki o kakeru** vacuum

掃除する **sōji suru** clean, clean up

早熟(な) **sōjuku (na)** precocious

操縦室 **sōjū-shitsu** flight deck

操縦装置 **sōjū-sōchi** controls

操縦する **sōjū suru** fly *airplane*

総会 **sōkai** general meeting; plenary session

送還する **sōkan suru** repatriate

総計...になる **sōkei ... ni naru** amount to...

ソケット **soketto** socket, outlet

送金 **sōkin** transfer (*of money*)

速記 **sokki** shorthand

即金で払う **sokkin de harau** cash down

そっくりである **sokkuri de aru** be the spitting image of

即興で演じる **sokkyō de enjiru** improvise

そこ **soko** over there; down there

底 **soko** base, bottom; bed (*of sea, river*); 底をつく **soko o tsuku** bottom out (*of recession etc*)

倉庫 **sōko** storehouse; warehouse; storeroom

そこで **soko de** there; then; accordingly

走行距離 **sōkō-kyori** mileage

損なう **sokonau** deface; harm; spoil

底値(の) **sokone (no)** rock-bottom

そこに **soko ni** down there; there

装甲車 **sōkōsha** armored vehicle

足 **-soku** *countword for footwear*

束縛 **sokubaku** restriction; tie

速度 **sokudo** rate; velocity; 速度を増す **sokudo o masu** gain speed

速度計 **sokudo-kei** speedometer

即時(の) **sokuji (no)** instant, instantaneous

即時再生ビデオ **sokuji-saisei-bideo** action replay

側面 **sokumen** side; flank MIL

測量 **sokuryō** survey (*of building*)

測量技師 **sokuryō-gishi** surveyor

測量する **sokuryō suru** survey *building*

側線 **sokusen** sidetrack

促進 **sokushin** promotion

促進する **sokushin suru** encourage; promote; facilitate; further

速達 **sokutatsu** express delivery

測定 **sokutei** measurement

測定する **sokutei suru** gauge

即座に **sokuza ni** instantly; promptly

染まる **somaru** dye; be dyed; be tainted

粗末(な) **somatsu (na)** cheap; poor; shabby; low *quality*

染める **someru** dye

そもそも **somosomo** in the first place

背く **somuku** go against; defy; offend

損 **son** loss; 損をする **son o suru** lose out; be out of pocket

備える **sonaeru** provide; be equipped with

供える **sonaeru** offer (*at an altar*)

備え付けられている **sonaetsukerarete iru** be fixed

備え付ける **sonaetsukeru** equip; install; provide

遭難信号 **sōnan-shingō** distress signal

遭難する **sōnan suru** meet with disaster

尊重する **sonchō suru** respect; value

尊大(な) **sondai (na)** dictatorial; haughty; arrogant

損益分岐点 **son'eki-bunkiten** break-even point

損害 **songai** damage; 損害を与える **songai o ataeru** damage

損害賠償 **songai-baishō** damages

損害賠償保険 **songaibaishō-hoken** third-party insurance

尊敬 **sonkei** deference; respect

尊敬する **sonkei suru** respect

そんな **sonna** such a, so; そんなばかなことはない **sonna baka na koto wa nai** that's not acceptable; そんなこと知ったことじゃない **sonna koto shitta koto ja nai** I don't give a damn!; そんなにかかるのですか **sonna ni kakaru no desu ka** as much as that?; そんなにたくさん **sonna takusan** so much

その **sono** that; those; the

その間に **sono aida ni** meanwhile

その後 **sono ato** subsequently

その後(の) **sono ato (no)** subsequent; succeeding

その場で **sono ba de** on the spot, immediately

その場しのぎ(の) **sono ba shinogi (no)** temporary; stopgap

その辺 **sono hen** somewhere near

その代わりに **sono kawari ni** instead; alternatively

その結果 **sono kekka** consequently; so, for that reason

そのくらい **sono kurai** thereabouts

そのまま **sono mama**: そのまま真っすぐ行く **sono mama massugu iku** carry straight on; そのままお待ちください **sono mama omachi kudasai** please hold the line; そのまま立っていて **sono mama tatte ite** stand still!

その当時 **sono tōji** then, at that time

その当時は **sono tōji wa** in those days

そのとおり **sono tōri** exactly!; that's it!; that's right

そのうち **sono uchi** sometime

そのうちに **sono uchi ni** in due course; eventually

そのうえ **sono ue** besides

そのよう(な) **sono yō (na)** such

損失 **sonshitsu** loss; 損失を出す **sonshitsu o dasu** make a loss

挿入 **sōnyū** insertion, inserting

存在 **sonzai** existence; presence

存在しない **sonzai shinai** nonexistent

存在する **sonzai suru** exist

騒音 **sōon** din, racket

ソプラノ **sopurano** soprano

空 **sora** sky

そらす **sorasu** avert; distract; divert

それ **sore** that; that one

それで **sore de** so, and then; in order that ◊ so what?; それでいい―ちょっと違う **sore de ii - chotto chigau** is that right? - not quite; それで十分だ **sore de jūbun da** that will do!

それでも **soredemo** still, ◊ yet; nevertheless

それでもなお **sore demo nao** nonetheless

それどころか **sore dokoro ka** on the contrary

それ程 **sore hodo** so; that

それ以上(の) **sore ijō (no)** further; additional

それ以来 **sore irai** ever since; since

それじゃ **sore ja** well; so

それから **sore kara** then, after that; since then

それまで **sore made** until then

それなら **sore nara** in that case, then

それに加えて **sore ni kuwaete** plus; in addition to that

それにもかかわらず **sore ni mo kakawarazu** nevertheless

それに応じて **sore ni ōjite** accordingly

それら **sorera** they; those

それらの **sorera no** their; those ◊ theirs

それる **soreru** stray, wander; swerve

それとも **sore tomo** or

それぞれ **sorezore** each; respectively

それぞれ(の) **sorezore (no)** each ◊ respective

そり **sori** sled(ge), sleigh, toboggan

総理大臣 **sōri-daijin** prime minister, premier

そりおとす **soriotosu** shave off

創立者 **sōritsu-sha** founder

創立する **sōritsu suru** found; start, establish

そろばん **soroban** abacus

そろえる **soroeru** put in order; arrange; make uniform

そろそろ **sorosoro** soon; slowly

そろう **sorou** be complete; be equal; gather

そる **soru** shave

総領事 **sōryōji** consul general

ソリューション **soryūshon** solution, fix

操作 **sōsa** operation; handling

捜査 **sōsa** investigation

捜査方針 **sōsa-hōshin** line of inquiry

創作 **sōsaku** creation

捜索 **sōsaku** hunt

創作者 **sōsaku-sha** creator

創作する **sōsaku suru** create

捜索する **sōsaku suru** search; hunt

捜索隊 **sōsaku-tai** search party

操作する **sōsa suru** manipulate; operate

ソーセージ **sōsēji** sausage

祖先 **sosen** ancestor

総選挙 **sōsenkyo** general election

総選挙日 **sōsenkyobi** election day

創設者 **sōsetsu-sha** creator

走者 **sōsha** runner

ソーシャルワーカー **sōsharu-wākā** social worker, welfare worker

組織 **soshiki** outfit, organization; system; set-up, structure; tissue ANAT

葬式 **sōshiki** funeral

組織する **soshiki suru** organize; put together

組織的(な) **soshikiteki (na)** methodical, systematic

装身具 **sōshingu** accessories; trinkets

送信機 **sōshinki** transmitter

送信する **sōshin suru** transmit; beam

阻止する **soshi suru** check, stop; deter

そして **soshite** and (then)

素質 **soshitsu** nature; character; predisposition

訴訟 **soshō** lawsuit

装飾する **sōshoku suru** decorate; embellish

そう祖父 **sōsofu** great-grandfather

そう祖母 **sōsobo** great-grandmother

注ぎ口 **sosogiguchi** spout

注ぐ **sosogu** pour; devote oneself to

そそのかす **sosonokasu** instigate; egg on

そそる **sosoru** excite; incite; arouse

ソース **sōsu** sauce

そうすると **sō suru to** in that case; if so; then

相対的(な) **sōtaiteki (na)** relative

そっち **sotchi** over there ◊ you (*informal*)

率直(な) **sotchoku (na)** candid; open; direct; outspoken

率直さ **sotchoku-sa** candor

外 **soto** outside; 外を見る **soto o miru** look out

外側 **sotogawa** outside

外側(の) **sotogawa (no)** outer; outside

相当(な) **sōtō (na)** substantial; suitable

外に **soto ni** outdoors, outside; 外に出す **soto ni dasu** let out (*of room, building*); 外に出ている **soto ni dete iru** be out, be outside

ソートする **sōto suru** sort COMPUT

相当する **sōtō suru** correspond to; be equivalent to

卒業 **sotsugyō** graduation

卒業生 **sotsugyō-sei** graduate

卒業式 **sotsugyō-shiki** graduation ceremony

卒業証書 **sotsugyō-shōsho** diploma

卒業する **sotsugyō suru** graduate; leave *school*

そつのない **sotsu no nai** diplomatic, tactful

そった **sotta** shaven

そっと **sotto** quietly; softly; stealthily

沿う **sou** run along; follow; go along

添う **sou** meet; answer; accompany

そわそわする **sowasowa suru** fidget

そよ風 **soyokaze** breeze

総菜屋 **sōzai-ya** delicatessen

粗雑(な) **sozatsu (na)** crude

想像 **sōzō** imagination; 想像がつく **sōzō ga tsuku** I can just imagine it

創造 **sōzō** creation

想像できない **sōzō dekinai** unimaginable

想像できる **sōzō dekiru** imaginable

相続人 **sōzoku-nin** heir; heiress

相続する **sōzoku suru** inherit

想像力 **sōzōryoku** imagination; 想像力の豊か(な) **sōzōryoku no yutaka (na)** imaginative

騒々しい **sōzōshii** boisterous; rowdy; tumultuous

想像する **sōzō suru** imagine; visualize

創造する **sōzō suru** create

巣 **su** nest; 巣をつくる **su o tsukuru** spin (*of spider*)

酢 **su** vinegar

巣箱 **subako** nesting box; hive

素晴らしい **subarashii** amazing, wonderful, brilliant, great

素晴らしく **subarashiku** beautifully

素早い **subayai** nimble

素早く **subayaku** quickly, speedily

滑らない **suberanai** nonslip

滑らせる **suberaseru** slide

滑り台 **suberidai** slide

滑る **suberu** glide; slip

すべて(の) **subete (no)** all; every

スチュワーデス **suchuwādesu** flight attendant; stewardess

スチュワード **suchuwādo** steward

すだれ **sudare** bamboo blind

すでに **sude ni** already

末 **sue** end; trifle; tip; future

スエード **suēdo** suede

末っ子 **suekko** youngest child

据え付ける **suetsukeru** install; set up

スエットスーツ **suetto-sūtsu** jogging suit

数学 **sūgaku** math

数学者 **sūgaku-sha** mathematician

数学的(な) **sūgakuteki (na)** mathematical

すがすがしい **sugasugashii** refreshing

姿 **sugata** image; 姿を表す **sugata o arawasu** surface

すっごく **suggoku** really; extremely; way

杉 **sugi** Japanese cedar

過ぎる **sugiru** pass by; slip away (*of time*); expire; go too far

…すぎる **...sugiru** too; ごはんが多すぎる **gohan ga ō-sugiru** there is too much rice

過ぎ去る **sugisaru** speed by

すごい **sugoi** super, terrific; unbelievable

すごく **sugoku** very; extremely

過ごす **sugosu** spend, pass the time

すぐ **sugu** right away; directly; すぐ近くに **sugu chikaku ni** nearby; すぐそば **sugu soba** right next door; close; すぐそこです **sugu soko desu** it's around the corner; it's just down the road

すぐに **sugu ni** immediately; soon; right now

優れる **sugureru** shine; excel

優れた **sugureta** excellent

すぐさま **sugusama** immediately

崇拝 **sūhai** worship

崇拝者 **sūhai-sha** worshiper; admirer

崇拝する **sūhai suru** idolize; worship

水分 **suibun** moisture; water

垂直(の) **suichoku (no)** perpendicular; vertical

水中翼船 **suichū-yokusen** hydrofoil

水田 **suiden** ricefield

水道 **suidō** water supply

水道管 **suidōkan** water pipe

水道水 **suidōsui** running water

水泳 **suiei** swimming; swim

吸い殻 **suigara** butt, stub

水源地 **suigenchi** source

水銀 **suigin** mercury, quicksilver

水兵 **suihei** sailor

水平(の) **suihei (no)** horizontal

水平線 **suiheisen** horizon

水位 **suii** water level

衰弱した **suijaku shita** emaciated; worn out

衰弱する **suijaku suru** become weak; be worn out

炊事 **suiji** cooking

水蒸気 **suijōki** steam

水上スキー **suijō-sukī** waterskiing

水準 **suijun** level; standard

スイカ **suika** water melon

吸い込む **suikomu** inhale, breathe in

水面 **suimen** surface

睡眠 **suimin** sleep

睡眠薬 **suimin'yaku** sleeping pill

推理 **suiri** inference; speculation

推理小説 **suiri-shōsetsu** detective novel

水路 **suiro** waterway

推論 **suiron** deduction

推論する **suiron suru** deduce

水力 **suiryoku** water power

水力発電(の) **suiryoku-hatsuden (no)** hydroelectric

水彩絵の具 **suisai-enogu** watercolor (*paint*)

水彩画 **suisaiga** watercolor (*painting*)

すい星 **suisei** comet

水性白色塗料 **suisei-hakushoku-toryō** whitewash

推薦 **suisen** endorsement; recommendation; nomination

水仙 **suisen** daffodil

推薦状 **suisenjō** reference, testimonial

推薦する **suisen suru** endorse; recommend

推進力 **suishin-ryoku** driving force

推進する **suishin suru** propel

水晶 **suishō** crystal; quartz

水素 **suiso** hydrogen

水素爆弾 **suiso-bakudan** hydrogen bomb

吹奏楽団 **suisō-gakudan** brass band

推測 **suisoku** conjecture; guess

推測する **suisoku suru** gather; guess

スイス **Suisu** Switzerland

スイス(の) **Suisu (no)** Swiss

スイッチ **suitchi** switch

推定 **suitei** estimate; inference; presumption

推定する **suitei suru** presume; assume

吸い取り紙 **suitorishi** blotter; blotting paper

吸い取る **suitoru** absorb

スイートルーム **suīto-rūmu** suite (*of rooms*)

水曜日 **suiyōbi** Wednesday

水族館 **suizokukan** aquarium

筋 **suji** action; plot; gristle; tendon; 筋の通った **suji no tōtta** coherent

数字 **sūji** digit, figure, number; numeral

筋張った **sujibatta** wiry

筋違い **sujichigai** crick in the neck

筋書き **sujigaki** scenario

数字に強い **sūji ni tsuyoi** numerate

スカーフ **sukāfu** headscarf

スカイライン **sukairain** skyline

数か国語を話せる **sūkakokugo o hanaseru** multilingual *person*

好かれる **sukareru** likeable

スカッシュ **sukasshu** squash

スカート **sukāto** skirt

すけすけ(の) **sukesuke (no)** see-through

スケーター **sukētā** skater

スケッチ **suketchi** drawing; sketch

スケッチブック **suketchi bukku** sketchbook

スケート **sukēto** skate; skating

スケートボード **sukēto-bōdo** skateboard

すき **suki** plow; spade

スキー **sukī** ski; skiing

好きである **suki de aru** like ◊ be enthusiastic about; be into

すき間 **sukima** chink; gap; slit

すきま風 **sukimakaze** draft; すきま風の入る **sukimakaze no hairu** drafty

すき間のない **sukima no nai** solid

スキムミルク **sukimu miruku** skimmed milk

好きになる **suki ni naru** like, take to

スキップ **sukippu** skip

スキップする **sukippu suru** skip

スキーリフト **sukī-rifuto** chair lift, ski lift

透き通る **sukitōru** be transparent

スキーヤー **sukīyā** skier

すきやき **sukiyaki** sukiyaki

すっからかんになる **sukkarakan ni naru** go broke, go bankrupt

すっかり **sukkari** right, completely; head over heels *fall in love*; in full; すっかり目が覚めている **sukkari me ga samete iru** be wide awake; すっかりなくなる **sukkari nakunaru** be all gone; すっかり大人になった **sukkari otona ni natta** full-grown

すっきりする **sukkiri suru** feel refreshed; be satisfied

スコア **sukoa** score MUS, SP

崇高(な) **sūkō (na)** lofty; sublime

スコップ **sukoppu** scoop; spade

少し **sukoshi** a little, a bit; scrap; touch ◊ rather, somewhat; slightly ◊ some; 少しだけ **sukoshi dake** just a bit; not a lot

少しも…ない **sukoshi mo …nai** not at all; not in the least; 少しも残って

いない **sukoshi mo nokotte inai** there is none left

少し(の) **sukoshi (no)** a little; a bit (of)

少しの間 **sukoshi no aida** briefly

少しずつ **sukoshi zutsu** bit by bit, little by little

スコッチウイスキー **sukotchi-uisukī** Scotch (whiskey)

スコットランド **Sukottorando** Scotland

すく **suku** become less full; be hungry; be transparent; plow

救い **sukui** rescue; relief; help

すくい上げる **sukuiageru** scoop up

救い出す **sukuidasu** salvage

救いがたい **sukuigatai** incorrigible

少ない **sukunai** few

少なくとも **sukunaku tomo** at least

スクープ **sukūpu** scoop (*story*)

スクランブルエッグ **sukuranburu eggu** scrambled eggs

スクラップブック **sukurappu-bukku** scrapbook

スクリーン **sukurīn** monitor; screen

スクリーンセーバー **sukurīn-seibā** screen saver

スクロールする **sukurōru suru** scroll up/down

スクリュー **sukuryū** propeller

スクーター **sukūtā** motorscooter; scooter

すくう **sukuu** scoop

救う **sukuu** redeem; save, rescue

スキャン **sukyan** scan; scanner; スキャンをかける **sukyan o kakeru** scan

スキャナー **sukyanā** scanner; スキャナーで読み込む **sukyanā de yomikomu** scan in

スキャンダル **sukyandaru** scandal

スキューバダイビング **sukyūba-daibingu** scuba diving

住まい **sumai** house; residence

すまない **sumanai** inexcusable; sorry; すまないと思う **sumanai to omou** regret

住ませる **sumaseru** settle

すまし汁 **sumashijiru** clear soup

スマッシュ **sumasshu** smash

済ます **sumasu** finish

スマートカード **sumāto-kādo** smart

card

スマート(な) **sumāto (na)** stylish; slim

住める **sumeru** habitable

炭 **sumi** charcoal

隅 **sumi** corner; nook

墨 **sumi** Chinese ink

炭火焼き(の) **sumibiyaki (no)** charbroiled

墨絵 **sumie** ink painting

すみません **sumimasen** excuse me; (I'm) sorry!; thank you; ちょっとすみません **chotto sumimasen** excuse me; すみませんが、塩をとっていただけますか **sumimasen ga, shio o totte itadakemasu ka** will you pass the salt please

住みにくい **suminikui** inhospitable

すみれ **sumire** violet (*plant*)

相撲 **sumō** sumo

相撲取り **sumō-tori** sumo wrestler

スモッグ **sumoggu** smog

住む **sumu** live, reside; live in

澄む **sumu** be clear

済む **sumu** be finished; manage without

砂 **suna** grit; sand

砂場 **sunaba** sandpit

砂袋 **suna-bukuro** sandbag

素直(な) **sunao (na)** docile; obedient

スナップ写真 **sunappu shashin** snap(shot)

すなわち **sunawachi** namely

澄んだ **sunda** clear; pure

すね **sune** shin

すねる **suneru** sulk

すねた **suneta** sulky; sullen

スニーカー **sunīkā** sneakers

寸法 **sunpō** dimension, measurement

寸法直し **sunpō-naoshi** alteration

寸前 **sunzen** immediately before; 寸前である **sunzen de aru** be on the verge of

スロットル **surottoru** throttle

スパゲティ **supageti** spaghetti

スパイ **supai** secret agent, spy; スパイをする **supai o suru** spy

スパイ防止活動 **supai-bōshi-katsudō** counterespionage

スパイ行為 **supai-kōi** espionage

スパイク **supaiku** spike (*on shoe*)

スーパーマーケット **sūpāmāketto** supermarket

スパナ **supana** wrench (*tool*)

スパート **supāto** spurt

スペアミント **supeaminto** spearmint

スペアリブ **supearibu** spare ribs

スペアタイヤ **supea-taiya** spare tire; spare wheel

スペード **supēdo** spades (*in card game*)

スペイン **Supein** Spain

スペイン語 **Supein-go** Spanish

スペイン人 **Supein-jin** Spaniard

スペイン(の) **Supein (no)** Spanish

スペクタクル **supekutakuru** spectacle

スペリング **superingu** spelling

スペルチェッカー **superu-chekkā** spellchecker

スペルチェック **superu-chekku** spellcheck

スペースバー **supēsu-bā** space bar

スペースシャトル **supēsu-shatoru** space shuttle

スピーチ **supīchi** speech

スピード **supīdo** speed; ...のスピードを上げる **... no supīdo o ageru** accelerate; スピードを出す **supīdo o dasu** speed up, put one's foot down; スピードを落とす **supīdo o otosu** slow down

スピード違反 **supīdo-ihan** speeding

スピーカー **supīkā** speaker; loudspeaker

スポーク **supōku** spoke

スポークスマン **supōkusuman** spokesperson

スポンジ **suponji** sponge

スポンサー **suponsā** sponsor; スポンサーになる **suponsā ni naru** sponsor

スポーティー(な) **supōtī (na)** sporty

スポーツ **supōtsu** sport

スポーツカー **supōtsu-kā** sportscar

スポーツクラブ **supōtsu-kurabu** health club

スポーツマン **supōtsu-man** sportsman

スポーツ(の) **supōtsu (no)** athletic; sporting

スポーツニュース **supōtsu-nyūsu** sports news

スポーツ欄 **supōtsu-ran** sports page

スポーツウーマン **supōtsu-ūman** sportswoman

スポットライト **supottoraito** spotlight

酸っぱい **suppai** sour (not sweet)

酸っぱくなった **suppaku natta** sour (not fresh)

素っぴん(の) **suppin (no)** unmade-up

スープ **sūpu** soup, broth

スプーン **supūn** spoon

スプレー **supurē** atomizer; spray

スプレッドシート **supureddoshīto** spreadsheet

スプレー缶 **supurē-kan** aerosol

スプリンクラー **supurinkurā** sprinkler

スープ皿 **sūpu-zara** soup bowl

すら **-sura** even

スライド **suraido** slide PHOT

スラックス **surakkusu** slacks

スラム街 **suramugai** slum

スラング **surangu** slang

スラッシュ **surasshu** slash

すらすら言う **surasura iu** rattle off

すれば **sureba**: …とすれば **…to sureba** supposing that

すれ違う **surechigau** brush past; pass each other

すり **suri** pickpocket

すりガラス **suri-garasu** frosted glass

擦り減らす **suriherasu** wear away; wear out

擦り減る **suriheru** wear away; wear out

擦り切れる **surikireru** wear (of carpet, fabric)

擦り切れた **surikireta** threadbare

擦り傷 **surikizu** abrasion

擦りむく **surimuku** chafe; graze

すりおろす **suriorosu** grate

スリッパ **surippa** slipper

スリップ **surippu** skid; slip

スリップする **surippu suru** skid

スリラー **surirā** thriller

スリル **suriru** thrill

スリーサイズ **surī-saizu** vital statistics

スリット **suritto** slit

スローガン **surōgan** slogan

スローイン **surō-in** throw-in

スローモーションで **surō-mōshon de** in slow motion

スロープ **surōpu** ramp

スロットマシン **surotto-mashin** slot machine

スロットル **surottoru** throttle

する **suru** ◊ do; have meal, walk, wash; play game; lift; render service; wear make-up; choose; decide on; cost; …すること **… suru koto** to (with verbs); …することができない **… suru koto ga deki nai** be incapable of doing … ◊ (forms verbs): 大量生産する **tairyō-seisan suru** mass produce

擦る **suru** rub; grind; chafe

刷る **suru** print

…する間 **… suru aida** while

鋭い **surudoi** acute, sharp; incisive mind; penetrating analysis; perceptive

鋭くする **surudoku suru** sharpen

鋭さ **surudo-sa** edge (in voice)

すると **suruto** and then; just then

すし **sushi** sushi

すそ **suso** hem; bottom edge; foot (of mountain)

すす **susu** soot

すすぐ **susugu** rinse

すすき **susuki** Japanese pampas grass

勧められない **susumerarenai** inadvisable

進める **susumeru** advance; go ahead with

勧める **susumeru** advise; offer

薦める **susumeru** recommend

進む **susumu** progress, come along; flow (of work); proceed

進んで **susunde** readily, willingly

進んでいる **susunde iru** be fast (of clock)

すすり泣き **susurinaki** sob

すする **susuru** sip; slurp; はなをすする **hana o susuru** sniff

スター **sutā** star
スタイリスト **sutairisuto** stylist
スタイル **sutairu** figure (*of person*); style; スタイルのいい **sutairu no ii** shapely
スタジアム **sutajiamu** stadium
スタジオ **sutajio** television studio
スタミナ **sutamina** energy; stamina
スタンド **sutando** stand; stall; the bleachers; lamp
スタンプ **sutanpu** stamp; スタンプを押す **sutanpu o osu** postmark
スタント **sutanto** stunt
スタントマン **sutantoman** stuntman
すたれる **sutareru** decline; be abolished; die out
すたれた **sutareta** obsolete
スターター **sutātā** starter
ステアリング **sutearingu** steering
ステイタスシンボル **suteitasu-shinboru** status symbol
素敵(な) **suteki (na)** cute; gorgeous; swell
ステーキ **sutēki** steak
ステッカー **sutekkā** sticker
ステッキ **sutekki** walking stick
ステンドグラス **sutendo-gurasu** stained-glass
ステンレス **sutenresu** stainless steel
ステレオ **sutereo** stereo
ステレオタイプ **sutereotaipu** stereotype
ステロイド **suteroido** steroids
捨てる **suteru** abandon; discard; throw out
スト **suto** strike, industrial action
ストーブ **sutōbu** stove
ストーカー **sutōkā** stalker
ストッキング **sutokkingu** stocking
ストップする **sutoppu suru** stop
ストップウォッチ **sutoppu-wotchi** stopwatch
ストライキ **sutoraiki** strike, industrial action; ストライキに入る **sutoraiki ni hairu** go on strike; ストライキをする

sutoraiki o suru strike
ストライク **sutoraiku** strike (*in baseball*)
ストライキ中である **sutoraikichū de aru** be on strike
ストラップ **sutorappu** strap
ストレス **sutoresu** stress; ストレスがたまっている **sutoresu ga tamatte iru** stressed out; ストレスのある **sutoresu no aru** be under stress ◊ stressful
ストレート(の) **sutorēto (no)** black *tea*; neat, straight-up *whiskey etc*
ストリッパー **sutorippā** stripper
ストリップ小屋 **sutorippu-goya** strip club
ストリップショー **sutorippu-shō** strip show; striptease
ストロー **sutorō** straw
スーツ **sūtsu** suit
スーツケース **sūtsukēsu** suitcase
スツール **sutsūru** stool
吸う **suu** inhale; suck; smoke
座り心地のよい **suwarigokochi no yoi** comfortable
座る **suwaru** sit, sit down
スウェーデン **Suwēden** Sweden
スウェーデン(の) **Suwēden (no)** Swedish
スウェットスーツ **suwetto-sūtsu** tracksuit
すやすや眠る **suyasuya nemuru** sleep peacefully; be fast asleep
すず **suzu** tin
鈴 **suzu** bell
酢漬けにする **suzuke ni suru** pickle
すずき **suzuki** sea bass
すずめ **suzume** sparrow; すずめの涙 **suzume no namida** pittance
すずめばち **suzumebachi** hornet
鈴虫 **suzumushi** cricket (*insect*)
すずらん **suzuran** lily of the valley
涼しい **suzushii** cool
涼しくなる **suzushiku naru** cool down

T

田 **ta** paddy field; rice field

他 **ta** other

束 **taba** bundle; wad; tuft

タバコ **tabako** cigarette; tobacco; タバコを吸う *tabako o suu* smoke; have a smoke

束ねる **tabaneru** bundle; tie up

食べ物 **tabemono** food

食べられない **taberarenai** uneatable; inedible

食べられる **taberareru** eatable; edible

食べる **taberu** eat

旅 **tabi** journey

足袋 **tabi** *traditional split-toed Japanese socks*

タービン **tābin** turbine

度々 **tabitabi** often; repeatedly; 度々起こる *tabitabi okoru* recurrent

タブ **tabu** tab (*in text*)

たぶん **tabun** maybe, perhaps; probably; presumably

タブー(の) **tabū (no)** taboo

タブロイド **taburoido** tabloid

立ち上がる **tachiagaru** get up, rise, stand up; set up

立場 **tachiba** position

たちどころに **tachidokoro ni** at once; there and then; like magic

立ち止まる **tachidomaru** stop

立入禁止 **tachiiri-kinshi** no admittance; no trespassing; keep out

たちまち **tachimachi** instantly; at once

立ち見席 **tachimiseki** standing room

立ち向かう **tachimukau** stand up to; confront

立ち直る **tachinaoru** recover; make a comeback

立ち退かせる **tachinokaseru** evict

立ち去る **tachisaru** leave, go away; get away

立ち寄る **tachiyoru** call, come by; stop over

ただ **tada** just, only

ただで **tada de** for nothing, for free

ただいま **tadaima** I'm home

ただし **tadashi** however; but

正しい **tadashii** correct, right ◊ be right; be in the right

正しく **tadashiku** right, correctly

正す **tadasu** rectify; correct

漂う **tadayou** drift

たどり着く **tadoritsuku** arrive at; struggle along to

耐えがたい **taegatai** excruciating, unbearable

絶え間ない **taema nai** continual, perpetual

絶え間なく **taema naku** incessantly; nonstop

耐えられない **taerarenai** intolerable, unbearable

耐えられる **taerareru** bearable

耐える **taeru** withstand

耐え忍ぶ **taeshinobu** endure

絶えず **taezu** continuously

タフガイ **tafu gai** tough guy

互いに **tagai ni** mutually; (with) each other

多額(の) **tagaku (no)** a lot of; a large sum of

たがる **-tagaru** want; 知りたがる *shiri-tagaru* want to know

耕す **tagayasu** plow, till

タグボート **tagubōto** tug

タイ **Tai** Thailand

たい **-tai** want; 行きたい *ikitai* want to go

対 **tai** versus; 三対一 *san tai ichi* three to one

体罰 **taibatsu** corporal punishment

大病 **taibyō** severe illness

体調 **taichō** condition (*of health*)

怠惰 **taida** indolence

怠惰(な) **taida (na)** indolent

対談する **taidan suru** talk; converse

態度 **taido** attitude, manner

台風 **taifū** typhoon

たいがい **taigai** mostly; generally

退学処分 **taigaku-shobun** expulsion

体現する **taigen suru** embody

タイ語 **Tai-go** Thai (*language*)

待遇 **taigū** service; treatment

退廃的(な) **taihaiteki (na)** decadent

太平洋 **Taiheiyō** Pacific (Ocean)

太平洋横断(の) **Taiheiyō-ōdan (no)** transpacific

太平洋戦争 **Taiheiyō-sensō** Pacific War

大変 **taihen** most, very

大変(な) **taihen (na)** difficult; terrible; tough; enormous

待避所 **taihijo** pull-in (*at roadside*)

対比する **taihi suru** contrast

逮捕 **taiho** arrest; capture

大砲 **taihō** artillery

逮捕されている **taiho sarete iru** be under arrest

逮捕する **taiho suru** arrest; pick up

体育 **taiiku** gymnastics

体育の日 **Taiiku no hi** Sports Day

体育館 **taiikukan** gymnasium, gym

退院 **taiin** discharge

退院させる **taiin saseru** discharge

退位する **taii suru** abdicate

胎児 **taiji** embryo; fetus; unborn baby

タイ人 **Tai-jin** Thai

退治する **taiji suru** exterminate; subdue; conquer

退場 **taijō** exit

退場させる **taijō saseru** expel from the game

体重 **taijū** weight

体重計 **taijūkei** scales

大会 **taikai** convention

体格 **taikaku** build, physique

耐火性(の) **taikasei (no)** fireproof

体系 **taikei** system

体系的 **taikeiteki** systematic

体験 **taiken** experience

対決 **taiketsu** confrontation, showdown

大気 **taiki** atmosphere

大気圏 **taikiken** atmosphere

大金 **taikin** a large sum of money

大気汚染 **taiki-osen** air pollution, atmospheric pollution

待機する **taiki suru** stand by, be ready

太鼓 **taiko** drum

太鼓腹 **taikobara** paunch

太鼓橋 **taikobashi** arched bridge

対抗する **taikō suru** counter; oppose

退屈(な) **taikutsu (na)** boring; dull

退屈させる **taikutsu saseru** bore

退屈する **taikutsu suru** be bored

退却 **taikyaku** retreat

退却する **taikyaku suru** retreat

耐久性 **taikyūsei** endurance; 耐久性のある **taikyūsei no aru** durable

大麻 **taima** hemp; cannabis

タイマー **taimā** timer, time switch

怠慢 **taiman** neglect; negligence

たいまつ **taimatsu** torch

タイミング **taimingu** timing; タイミングがいい **taimingu ga ii** timely; well-timed

タイムアウト **taimu-auto** time out SP

タイムレコーダー **taimu-rekōdā** time clock

耐熱(の) **tainetsu (no)** resistant to heat

タイ(の) **Tai (no)** Thai

滞納金 **tainōkin** arrears

滞納している **tainō shite iru** be in arrears

体温 **taion** (body) temperature

体温計 **taionkei** clinical thermometer

対応する **taiō suru** correspond (to); cope (with)

タイピスト **taipisuto** typist

タイプ **taipu** type; sort; タイプを打つ **taipu o utsu** type

タイプライター **taipu-raitā** typewriter

タイプする **taipu suru** type

平らげる **tairageru** eat up; put away; subjugate

平ら(な) **taira (na)** even, level; flat

平らにする **taira ni suru** flatten

大陸 **tairiku** continent

大陸(の) **tairiku (no)** continental

対立 **tairitsu** conflict, clash; rift

対立する **tairitsu suru** confront

タイル **tairu** tile

大量 **tairyō** mass; 大量に *tairyō ni* in bulk

体力 **tairyoku** strength; stamina

大量生産 **tairyō-seisan** mass production

大量生産する **tairyō-seisan suru** mass produce

大作 **taisaku** epic

対策 **taisaku** measures; steps

体制 **taisei** system; structure; Establishment

体勢 **taisei** footing, balance

大勢 **taisei** general situation; current trend

大西洋(の) **Taiseiyō (no)** Atlantic

大西洋横断(の) **Taiseiyō-ōdan (no)** transatlantic

体積 **taiseki** volume

対戦する **taisen suru** meet SP

大切(な) **taisetsu (na)** important; valuable

大切にする **taisetsu ni suru** cherish, prize, treasure

貸借対照表 **taishaku-taishōhyō** balance sheet

退社する **taisha suru** leave work; resign; retire

大使 **taishi** ambassador

大使館 **taishikan** embassy

たいした **taishita** great; important ; たいしたことではない *taishita koto de wa nai* it doesn't matter; nothing much

対して **taishite** against; concerning

体質 **taishitsu** constitution (*of person*)

対称 **taishō** symmetry

対象 **taishō** target; object

対照 **taishō** contrast; comparison

大正時代 **Taishō-jidai** Taisho period

退職 **taishoku** retirement; departure

大食 **taishoku** gluttony

大食家 **taishokuka** glutton

退職金 **taishokukin** golden handshake

退職した **taishoku shita** retired

退職する **taishoku suru** retire

対処する **taisho suru** cope with; deal with; tackle

対称的(な) **taishōteki (na)** symmetrical; regular

対照的(な) **taishōteki (na)** contrasting

対照的に **taishōteki ni** as opposed to; in contrast to

体臭 **taishū** BO, body odor

大衆 **taishū** the masses; 大衆向けに *taishūmuke ni* downmarket

体操 **taisō** gymnastics

体操選手 **taisō-senshu** gymnast

たいてい **taitei** most of the time

たいてい(の) **taitei (no)** most

対等(の) **taitō (no)** equal

タイトル **taitoru** title

対話 **taiwa** dialog

台湾 **Taiwan** Taiwan

台湾語 **Taiwan-go** Taiwanese (*dialect*)

台湾人 **Taiwan-jin** Taiwanese

タイヤ **taiya** tire

太陽 **taiyō** sun

太陽電池板 **taiyō-denchiban** solar panel

太陽エネルギー **taiyō-enerugī** solar energy

耐用年数 **taiyō nensū** life (*of a building*)

滞在 **taizai** stay

滞在する **taizai suru** stay

たか **taka** hawk

たか派 **takaha** hawk *fig*

高い **takai** high; tall; expensive; prominent

多角経営 **takaku-keiei** diversification

多角経営する **takaku-keiei suru** diversify

高まり **takamari** upsurge; build-up; rise

高める **takameru** boost, enhance

宝 **takara** treasure

宝くじ **takara-kuji** lottery

たかり **takari** scrounger, sponger; blackmailer

たかる **takaru** bum, cadge; sponge off; extort; swarm; be infested with

高さ **takasa** height

竹 **take** bamboo

丈 **take** height; size; stature

竹の子 **takenoko** bamboo shoot

竹馬 **takeuma** stilts

滝 **taki** waterfall

たき火 **takibi** bonfire

タキシード **takishīdo** tuxedo

タックル **takkuru** tackle SP

タックルする **takkuru suru** tackle

卓球 **takkyū** table tennis

宅急便 **takkyūbin®** express home delivery service

たこ **tako** kite; octopus; callus

多国籍企業 **takokuseki-kigyō** multinational (company)

多国籍(の) **takokuseki (no)** multinational

たく **taku** burn; heat

宅 **taku** home; house

炊く **taku** boil; cook

たくましい **takumashii** strong; robust

巧み(な) **takumi (na)** professional, workmanlike

巧みに **takumi ni** professionally; 巧みに操る **takumi ni ayatsuru** maneuver

たくらみ **takurami** scheme, plot

たくらむ **takuramu** engineer; plot, scheme

たくさん **takusan** a lot, lots; much

たくさん(の) **takusan (no)** many, much; big

タクシー **takushī** cab, taxi

タクシードライバー **takushī-doraibā** cab driver

タクシー乗り場 **takushī-noriba** cab rank, cab stand

タクシー運転手 **takushī-untenshu** cab driver, taxi driver

蓄え **takuwae** hoard; store

蓄える **takuwaeru** hoard

玉 **tama** ball; bead; jewel

球 **tama** ball

弾 **tama** bullet

卵 **tamago** egg

卵焼き **tamagoyaki** Japanese omelet

たまねぎ **tamanegi** onion

たまに **tama ni** occasionally

たまには **tama ni wa** for a change

たま(の) **tama (no)** infrequent, occasional

たまらない **tamaranai** unendurable

たまらない **-tamaranai** be desperate; 飲みたくてたまらない **nomitakute tamaranai** be desperate for a drink

たまり **tamari** puddle; pool

たまり場 **tamariba** meeting place; haunt; joint

たまる **tamaru** accumulate, mount up; pile up

貯まる **tamaru** be saved up

魂 **tamashii** soul REL

たまたま **tamatama** accidentally; by chance

玉突き場 **tamatsukijō** pool hall

玉突き衝突 **tamatsuki-shōtotsu** pile-up

ため息 **tameiki** sigh; ため息をつく **tameiki o tsuku** sigh

ため(に) **tame (ni)** due to; owing to; because of; in favor of; for the sake of

ためになる **tame ni naru** rewarding; worthwhile

ためらい **tamerai** hesitation

ためらいがち(な) **tameraigachi (na)** tentative

ためらう **tamerau** hesitate; hold back

ためる **tameru** accumulate, collect; straighten; remedy

貯める **tameru** save; put by

試してみる **tameshite miru** try out; experiment with

試す **tamesu** test; try

ターミナル **tāminaru** terminal; terminus

保つ **tamotsu** keep, retain

棚 **tana** ledge; shelf; shelves; rack; cabinet

七夕 **Tanabata** Star Festival

棚ぼた **tanabota** windfall; godsend

棚卸し **tanaoroshi** stocktaking

田んぼ **tanbo** paddy field

探知 **tanchi** detection

探知器 **tanchi-ki** detector

探知する **tanchi suru** detect

短調 **tanchō** minor; ニ短調 **ni tanchō** D minor

単調 **tanchō** monotony

単調(な) **tanchō (na)** flat; monotonous; uneventful

単独(の) **tandoku (no)** isolated; solo

種 **tane** pip, seed; cause; trick; topic; quality

種馬 **taneuma** stallion; stud

嘆願 **tangan** plea; appeal

嘆願する **tangan suru** plead for; implore

単語 **tango** word

タンゴ **tango** tango

谷 **tani** valley

単位 **tan'i** unit

他人 **tanin** outsider, stranger

単一(の) **tan'itsu (no)** single

誕生 **tanjō** birth

誕生日 **tanjōbi** birthday

単純(な) **tanjun (na)** menial; simple; straightforward

単価 **tanka** unit cost

担架 **tanka** stretcher

短歌 **tanka** tanka (*31-syllable Japanese poem*)

タンカー **tankā** tanker

短剣 **tanken** dagger

探検 **tanken** expedition; exploration

探検家 **tankenka** explorer

探検する **tanken suru** explore

探検隊 **tankentai** expedition

短気 **tanki** impatience

短期間(の) **tankikan (no)** short-term

短気(な) **tanki (na)** short-tempered, testy

炭鉱 **tankō** coal mine

炭坑 **tankō** pit, coal mine

タンク **tanku** cistern; tank

タンクローリー **tanku-rōrī** tanker (*truck*)

短距離競走 **tankyori-kyōsō** sprint

短距離選手 **tankyori-senshu** sprinter

端末 **tanmatsu** terminal

単に **tan ni** purely, simply, merely

胆のう **tannō** gall bladder

頼み **tanomi** request; X の頼みを聞く *X no tanomi o kiku* do X a favor

頼む **tanomu** ask; request; beg

楽しい **tanoshii** pleasant; enjoyable; delightful

楽しませる **tanoshimaseru** amuse, entertain

楽しみ **tanoshimi** amusement; entertainment; fun; enjoyment, pleasure; 楽しみにする *tanoshimi ni suru* anticipate; look forward to

楽しむ **tanoshimu** enjoy, relish; have a good time

楽しそうに **tanoshisō ni** happily

短波 **tanpa** high-frequency; short wave

たんぱく質 **tanpakushitsu** protein

短編小説 **tanpen-shōsetsu** short story

担保 **tanpo** security; mortgage

タンポン **tanpon** tampon

たんぽぽ **tanpopo** dandelion

炭酸入り(の) **tansan'iri (no)** carbonated

胆石 **tanseki** gallstone

端子 **tanshi** terminal ELEC

単身赴任 **tanshinfunin** *living away from one's family after a job transfer*

短所 **tansho** shortcoming; fault

短縮する **tanshuku suru** condense, make shorter; curtail

たんす **tansu** bureau, chest of drawers

単数 **tansū** singular GRAM

淡水 **tansui** freshwater

炭水化物 **tansuika-butsu** carbohydrate

単刀直入(な) **tantō-chokunyū (na)** point-blank

担当する **tantō suru** be in charge of

たぬき **tanuki** raccoon dog

倒れる **taoreru** collapse; tumble; fall down; fall over

タオル **taoru** towel

倒す **taosu** bring down; knock down; overthrow; topple

タペストリー **tapesutorī** tapestry

タップダンス **tappu-dansu** tap dance

たっぷり(の) **tappuri (no)** abundant; hearty; lavish

たっぷりした **tappuri shita** substantial

たら **tara** cod

たら **-tara** if; when; how about; まじめに勉強したら *majime ni benkyō* *shitara* if you study hard; 駅に着いたら電話してください *eki ni tsuitara denwa shite kudasai* call me when you get to the station; 映画を見に行ったらどう *eiga o mi ni ittara dō* how about going to see a movie?

たらふく食う **tarafuku kuu** gorge oneself

タラップ **tarappu** airbridge; landing steps; gangway

垂らす **tarasu** drop; let fall; suspend

垂れる **tareru** dribble; droop

垂れている **tarete iru** floppy

たり **-tari** (*for example actions*): 彼は本を読んだりなど決してしない *kare wa hon o yondari nado kesshite shinai* he never does things like reading books ◊ (*for successive actions*): 食べたり飲んだりする *tabetari nondari suru* eating and drinking; 雨が降ったりやんだりしている *ame ga futtari yandari shite iru* it's raining on and off

足りない **tarinai** be short of, be low on

足りる **tariru** be enough; suffice

たる **taru** barrel

タール **tāru** tar

たるみ **tarumi** flab

たるむ **tarumu** sag

たるんだ **tarunda** flabby; loose, slack

タルト **taruto** tart

多量(の) **taryō (no)** a large quantity of

多才 **tasai** versatility

多才(の) **tasai (no)** versatile

多作(な) **tasaku (na)** prolific

確かめる **tashikameru** make certain

確か(な) **tashika (na)** certain; sure; 確かな筋から聞いたところによると *tashika na suji kara kiita tokoro ni yoru to* I am reliably informed that

確かに **tashika ni** certainly, definitely; sure; by far

足し算 **tashizan** addition MATH

足し算する **tashizan suru** add

たそがれ **tasogare** dusk, twilight

達成 **tassei** achievement

達成する **tassei suru** accomplish, achieve

達する **tassuru** arrive at, reach;

meet

足す **tasu** add; 2足す2は4だ *ni tasu ni wa yon da* 2 plus 2 is 4

多数 **tasū** many

助かる **tasukaru** be saved; be helpful; survive

助け **tasuke** favor; help

助ける **tasukeru** help

多数(の) **tasū (no)** numerous; many

多胎(の) **tatai (no)** of a multiple birth

戦い **tatakai** battle; fight

闘い **tatakai** battle, fight

戦う **tatakau** fight

闘う **tatakau** battle, fight, combat; contend with

たたき上げの人 **tatakiage no hito** self-made man

たたき出す **tatakidasu** throw out; evict; flush out

たたく **tataku** beat, hit; hammer; swat

畳 **tatami** tatami mat

たたむ **tatamu** fold up; close *umbrella*; wind up *company*

タッチ **tatchi** touch SP

タッチダウン **tatchi-daun** touchdown

タッチダウンする **tatchi-daun suru** touch down

縦 **tate** length; height

盾 **tate** shield

たてがみ **tategami** mane

縦書き **tategaki** writing in vertical lines

建具屋 **tategu-ya** joiner

建て替える **tatekaeru** rebuild; remodel

立てかける **tatekakeru** lean against

建て前 **tatemae** → *honne*

建物 **tatemono** building

縦向き **tatemuki** vertical; portrait *print*

建て直す **tatenaosu** rebuild

立て直す **tatenaosu** rebuild, reconstruct

建てる **tateru** build, erect, put up

立てる **tateru** raise; stand

たとえ **tatoe** example; simile; metaphor

例えば **tatoeba** for example

たとえ...でも **tatoe ... de mo** even if;

even as; たとえそうでも **tatoe sō de mo** even so

タートル **tātoru** turtleneck (sweater)

たつ **tatsu** pass, go by; get on (*of time*)

立つ **tatsu** stand

発つ **tatsu** leave

絶つ **tatsu** sever; discontinue

建つ **tatsu** be up, be built

達人 **tatsujin** master

竜巻 **tatsumaki** tornado

たった **tatta** only

立っている **tatte iru** stand, be

建っている **tatte iru** stand, be situated (*of building*)

田植え **taue** rice-planting

たわごと **tawagoto** nonsense, garbage

たわみ **tawami** sag; bend

たやすい **tayasui** easy

便り **tayori** news

頼りになる **tayori ni naru** dependable

頼りにする **tayori ni suru** rely on

頼る **tayoru** rely on

多様性 **tayōsei** diversity

頼っている **tayotte iru** dependent

たゆまぬ **tayumanu** steady; untiring

手綱 **tazuna** rein

尋ねる **tazuneru** ask, check with

訪ねる **tazuneru** visit (with), come around

て **-te** and; 安くて汚い **yasukute kitanai** cheap and dirty ◊ -ing; 雨が降っている **ame ga futte imasu** it's raining ◊ since; 雨が降って行けなかった **ame ga futte ikenakatta** since it was raining, I couldn't go ◊ (*as imperative*): 早く起きて **hayaku okite** quick, wake up! ◊ (*as a participle in combination with other verbs*): 送ってもらう **okutte morau** have ... sent; 試してみる **tameshite miru** try out

手 **te** hand; move (*in board game*); 手が空いている **te ga aite iru** available; 手に入りやすい **te ni hairiyasui** accessible; 手に入れられる **te ni irerareru** available, obtainable; 手に入れる **te ni ireru** get; pick up, buy; 手に負えない **te**

ni oenai disorderly, unruly; uncontrollable; 手の届かないところ **te no todokanai tokoro** out of reach; 手の届くところ **te no todoku tokoro** within reach; 手をあげろ **te o agero** hands up!; 手を出す **te o dasu** dabble in; mess with; 手を振る **te o furu** wave; 手を引く **te o hiku** back out, pull out; 手を伸ばす **te o nobasu** reach out; 手をつなぐ **te o tsunagu** hold

手足 **teashi** limbs

手当たり次第に **teatari shidai ni** at random

手当たり次第(の) **teatari shidai (no)** random

手当 **teate** allowance; medical treatment; 手当をする **teate o suru** dress; treat

手放す **tebanasu** part with

早く **tebayaku** lightly; quickly

手引き **tebiki** guidebook

手袋 **tebukuro** glove

手振り **teburi** gesture

テーブル **tēburu** table

テーブルクロス **tēburu-kurosu** tablecloth

テーブルスプーン **tēburu-supūn** tablespoon

手違い **techigai** mix-up; mistake

手帳 **techō** small notebook; diary

手取り給料 **tedori-kyūryō** take-home pay

テフロン加工(の) **tefuron-kakō (no)** nonstick

手がかり **tegakari** clue; purchase, grip

手書き(の) **tegaki (no)** handwritten

手紙 **tegami** letter; correspondence

手柄 **tegara** credit

手軽(な) **tegaru (na)** handy; light; easy

手際 **tegiwa** skill; 手際がいい **tegiwa ga ii** skillful; 手際が悪い **tegiwa ga warui** awkward; clumsy

手ごろ(な) **tegoro (na)** handy; convenient; reasonably priced

手配 **tehai** arrangements

手配する **tehai suru** fix, fix up; arrange for

手本 **tehon** model; example

提案 **teian** proposal, suggestion, proposition

提案する **teian suru** propose, suggest

堤防 **teibō** dike (*wall*); embankment

停電 **teiden** power outage, blackout

程度 **teido** degree, extent, measure

定義 **teigi** definition

定義する **teigi suru** define

停泊場所 **teihaku-basho** berth

定員 **teiin** capacity (*of elevator, vehicle*)

提示 **teiji** presentation

定住所 **teijūsho** permanent address

定住する **teijū suru** settle down

低下 **teika** decline, drop, fall

定価 **teika** list price

定冠詞 **teikanshi** definite article

低カロリー(の) **tei-karorī (no)** low-calorie

低下させる **teika saseru** decrease

低下する **teika suru** decline, decrease, fall

提携する **teikei suru** link up TV

定期 **teiki** commuter pass

低気圧 **teikiatsu** depression, low (*in weather*)

低気圧域 **teikiatsu-iki** low-pressure area

定期便 **teikibin** scheduled flight

定期券 **teikiken** season ticket, pass (*for transport*)

定期購読者 **teiki-kōdokusha** subscriber

定期購読する **teiki-kōdoku suru** subscribe to

定期船 **teikisen** liner

提起する **teiki suru** raise *question*

定期的(な) **teikiteki (na)** regular

定期的に **teikiteki ni** periodically

抵抗 **teikō** resistance

帝国 **teikoku** empire

定刻 **teikoku** scheduled time

定刻どおり **teikoku dōri** on schedule

抵抗力 **teikō-ryoku** resistance

抵抗する **teikō suru** resist

テイクアウト **teikuauto** take-away

提供 **teikyō** offer; donation MED

提供者 **teikyō-sha** donor MED

提供する **teikyō suru** contribute; put up *money*; offer *services*;

present TV, RAD donate MED

定休日 **teikyūbi** closing day

ていねい語 **teinei-go** polite word

ていねい(な) **teinei (na)** polite

ていねいに **teinei ni** politely

定年 **teinen** retirement age

帝王切開 **teiō-sekkai** Cesarean

手入れをする **teire o suru** take care of

手入れされた **teire sareta** trim

手入れされて **teire sarete** in good shape trim

手入れする **teire suru** swoop on; make a raid

停留所 **teiryū-jo** depot; bus stop

体裁 **teisai** appearance; format

偵察 **teisatsu** reconnaissance

訂正 **teisei** correction

訂正する **teisei suru** correct

停戦 **teisen** cease-fire

停車禁止 **teisha-kinshi** no stopping

停車する **teisha suru** stop; call at

停止 **teishi** cessation; halt

低脂肪(の) **teishibō (no)** low-fat

低姿勢(な) **teishisei (na)** low profile

停止信号 **teishi-shingō** stoplight

停止している **teishi shite iru** be at a standstill

停止する **teishi suru** come to a halt

定職 **teishoku** permanent job

停職 **teishoku** suspension (*from duty*)

定食 **teishoku** set menu

停職処分にする **teishoku-shobun ni suru** suspend (*from office, duties*)

提出する **teishutsu suru** advance *theory*; submit; put in

停滞した **teitai shita** stagnant

停滞している **teitai shite iru** be backed up

抵当 **teitō** pledge, security

手近に **tejika ni** close at hand

手品 **tejina** conjuring tricks, magic; magic trick

手品師 **tejina-shi** conjurer, magician

手錠 **tejō** handcuffs

手順 **tejun** process; procedure

敵 **teki** adversary, enemy

的中する **tekichū suru** hit the bull's-eye

適度(な) **tekido (na)** modest

適度に **tekido ni** within limits; moderately

適度(の) **tekido (no)** moderate

適合性 **tekigōsei** compatibility

適合している **tekigō shite iru** be compatible

適合する **tekigō suru** conform; fit; suit

敵意 **tekii** animosity, hostility, ill will; 敵意のある **tekii no aru** hostile

的確(な) **tekikaku (na)** precise; accurate

適応させる **tekiō saseru** adjust; accommodate

適応性 **tekiōsei** compatibility; 適応性のある **tekiōsei no aru** adaptable

適応する **tekiō suru** adapt

適性 **tekisei** aptitude

適切(な) **tekisetsu (na)** appropriate, apt; neat *solution*; right, fair

適している **tekishite iru** be suited for, be cut out for

適所 **tekisho** niche; the right place

適する **teki suru** be suitable

テキスト **tekisuto** text; textbook

敵対行為 **tekitai-kōi** hostilities

適当(な) **tekitō (na)** proper, right, suitable

適用できない **tekiyō dekinai** inapplicable

適用できる **tekiyō dekiru** applicable

適用させる **tekiyō sareru** apply; apply to

適用する **tekiyō suru** apply

撤回する **tekkai suru** retract, withdraw

鉄筋コンクリート **tekkin-konkurīto** reinforced concrete

てこ **teko** lever; てこの作用 **teko no sayō** leverage

手首 **tekubi** wrist

手間 **tema** time; trouble

テーマ **tēma** theme

手前 **temae** this side; front

手招きする **temaneki suru** beckon

テーマ音楽 **tēma-ongaku** signature tune

テーマソング **tēma-songu** theme song

ても **-te mo** even if; whether; however; 雪が降っても **yuki ga futte mo** even if it snows; 高くても **takakute mo** however expensive it is

…てもいい **…temo ii** can; タクシーで行ってもいい **takushii de itte mo ii** can we go by taxi?

点 **ten** dot; point

天 **ten** heaven; sky

手直し **tenaoshi** correction; touching up

店長 **tenchō** manager

天国 **tengoku** heaven, paradise

手荷物 **tenimotsu** (hand) luggage, baggage

手荷物預かり所 **tenimotsu-azukarijo** (baggage) checkroom

店員 **ten'in** sales clerk

テニス **tenisu** tennis

テニスコート **tenisu-kōto** tennis court

テニスプレイヤー **tenisu-pureiyā** tennis player

点字 **tenji** braille

展示 **tenji** display

展示中 **tenjichū** on show, on display

展示品 **tenjihin** exhibit

展示している **tenji shite aru** be on display

展示する **tenji suru** exhibit, display, show

天井 **tenjō** ceiling

添乗員 **tenjōin** courier, tour conductor

天井桟敷 **tenjō-sajiki** gallery THEA

添加物 **tenkabutsu** additive

展開する **tenkai suru** unfold, develop

てんかん **tenkan** epilepsy

転換 **tenkan** shift, switch; convert

てんかん患者 **tenkan-kanja** epileptic

点火装置 **tenka-sōchi** ignition

点火する **tenka suru** ignite

典型 **tenkei** model; pattern; type; cross-section

典型である **tenkei de aru** representative

典型的(な) **tenkeiteki (na)** typical, representative; vintage, classic

点検修理 **tenken-shūri** service (for car)

点検修理する **tenken-shūri suru** service car

点検する **tenken suru** check, look over

天気 **tenki** weather

転勤する **tenkin suru** be transferred

天気予報 **tenki-yohō** weather forecast

点呼 **tenko** roll call

転向させる **tenkō saseru** convert

転向者 **tenkō-sha** convert

転校する **tenkō suru** change schools

天窓 **tenmado** skylight

点滅 **tenmetsu** blip

点滅する **tenmetsu suru** blink; flash on and off

天文学 **tenmongaku** astronomy

天文学者 **tenmongaku-sha** astronomer

天文学的(な) **tenmongakuteki (na)** astronomical

天然 **tennen** nature

天然ガス **tennen-gasu** natural gas

天然痘 **tennentō** smallpox

天皇 **tennō** emperor

天皇誕生日 **Tennō-tanjōbi** Emperor's Birthday

手のひら **tenohira** palm (of hand)

テノール **tenōru** tenor

テンポ **tenpo** tempo

転覆させる **tenpuku saseru** turn over, put upside down

転覆する **tenpuku suru** overturn; capsize

てんぷら **tenpura** tempura (deep-fried food)

転落 **tenraku** fall

転落する **tenraku suru** fall

展覧会 **tenrankai** exhibition

天才 **tensai** genius, prodigy

天災 **tensai** natural disaster

点線 **tensen** dotted line

天使 **tenshi** angel

転職 **tenshoku** career change

天職 **tenshoku** vocation, calling

店主 **tenshu** shopkeeper

転送する **tensō suru** forward

点数 **tensū** mark, point; 点数かせぎをする **tensūkasegi o suru** earn Brownie points

点滴 **tenteki** drip MED

テント **tento** marquee; tent

店頭 **tentō** storefront

転倒 **tentō** fall

てんとうむし **tentōmushi** ladybug

転倒する **tentō suru** fall

手ぬるい **tenurui** lax; permissive

点在している **tenzai shite iru** be scattered

点在する **tenzai suru** be dotted about

手遅れ(の) **teokure (no)** too late

手おの **teono** hatchet

手押し車 **teoshi-guruma** wheelbarrow; pushcart

鉄板 **teppan** iron plate; hot plate

鉄砲 **teppō** gun

テープデッキ **tēpu-dekki** tape deck

テープレコーダー **tēpu-rekōdā** tape recorder

寺 **tera** temple

テラコッタ **terakotta** terracotta

照らす **terasu** shine

テラス **terasu** terrace, patio

テラスハウス **terasu-hausu** row house

テレビ **terebi** television set, TV

テレビ番組 **terebi-bangumi** TV program

テレビ電話 **terebi-denwa** videophone

テレビゲーム **terebi-gēmu** video game

テレビ放送 **terebi-hōsō** television

テレビ会議 **terebi-kaigi** video conference

テレホンカード **terehon-kādo** phonecard

テレパシー **terepashī** telepathy

テロ **tero** terrorism

テロリスト **terorisuto** terrorist

テロ組織 **tero-soshiki** terrorist organization

照る **teru** shine

手探りする **tesaguri suru** fumble around, grope

手作業(の) **tesagyō (no)** manual

手先 **tesaki** fingers; agent; pawn fig

手製(の) **tesei (no)** handmade

手仕事 **teshigoto** handiwork

手数 **tesū** trouble; inconvenience

手すり **tesuri** handrail; banister

手数料 **tesūryō** commission; handling fee

テスト **tesuto** test, trial

テスト期間 **tesuto-kikan** trial period

鉄 **tetsu** iron

鉄棒 **tetsubō** bar (*gymnastics*)

手伝い **tetsudai** helper

手伝う **tetsudau** help

鉄道 **tetsudō** railroad

鉄道線路 **tetsudō-senro** track

哲学 **tetsugaku** philosophy

哲学者 **tetsugaku-sha** philosopher

哲学的(な) **tetsugakuteki (na)** philosophical

手付け金 **tetsukekin** deposit

鉄製品 **tetsuseihin** ironworks

徹夜する **tetsuya suru** stay up all night

手続き **tetsuzuki** procedure

撤退 **tettai** withdrawal

撤退させる **tettai saseru** pull out, withdraw

撤退する **tettai suru** pull out, withdraw

徹底している **tettei shite iru** be thorough

徹底する **tettei suru** be thorough

徹底的(な) **tetteiteki (na)** thorough; exhaustive

徹底的に **tetteiteki ni** thoroughly; downright; systematically

鉄塔 **tettō** steel tower; mast

…てはいけない **...te wa ikenai** must not

手分けする **tewake suru** divide

手渡す **tewatasu** hand on; hand over, pass

手触り **tezawari** texture; touch

手詰まり **tezumari** stalemate; deadlock

ティー **tī** tee

ティーバッグ **tībaggu** teabag

ティーンエイジャー **tīn'eijā** teenager

ティーポット **tīpotto** teapot

ティールーム **tīrūmu** tearoom

ティーセット **tīsetto** tea service, tea set

ティーシャツ **tī-shatsu** T-shirt

ティースプーン **tīspūn** teaspoon

ティッシュペーパー **tisshu-pēpā** tissue paper

…と… **to** and; パンとバター **pan to batā** bread and butter ◊ with; 友達と映画を見に行った **tomodachi to eiga o mi ni itta** I went with a friend to see a movie ◊ if; 入試に合格しないと **nyūshi ni gōkaku shinai to** if you don't pass your entrance exams ◊ whenever; 雨が降ると **ame ga furu to** whenever it rains ◊: 彼と同じ大学を卒業した **kare to onaji daigaku o sotsugyō shita** I graduated from the same university as him; 何といいましたか **nan to iimashita ka** what did you say?

戸 **to** door

都 **to** metropolis; capital; city

塔 **tō** pagoda; tower

党 **tō** political party

頭 **-tō** countword for large animals

答案 **tōan** answer sheet

当番 **tōban** duty; person on duty

当番表 **tōbanhyō** duty rota

飛ばす **tobasu** skip; blow *fuse*

飛び上がる **tobiagaru** spring

飛び散る **tobichiru** splash; scatter

飛び出す **tobidasu** rush out; jump out; jut out

飛び道具 **tobidōgu** missile; projectile

飛び跳ねる **tobihaneru** bounce

飛び石 **tobiishi** stepping stone

飛び板 **tobiita** springboard

飛びかかる **tobikakaru** jump, attack; tackle

とびきり(の) **tobikiri (no)** exceptional; out of this world

跳び越える **tobikoeru** jump, leap

飛び込み **tobikomi** dive; plunge; high diving

飛び込み台 **tobikomi-dai** diving board

飛び込む、跳び込む **tobikomu** dive; plunge; leap

飛び回る **tobimawaru** jump around; fly around

飛びのく **tobinoku** jump back; jump

aside

飛び乗る **tobinoru** jump into *car*

飛び下りる **tobioriru** jump down; jump out; jump off

扉 **tobira** (double) door

飛びつく **tobitsuku** jump at

逃亡 **tōbō** flight, escape

逃亡者 **tōbō-sha** fugitive

乏しい **toboshii** scarce; meager

とぼとぼ歩く **tobotobo aruku** plod, trudge

飛ぶ **tobu** blow (*of fuse*); fly; fly in

跳ぶ **tobu** jump, leap

東部 **tōbu** east

等分する **tōbun suru** divide into equal parts

到着 **tōchaku** arrival, appearance

到着ロビー **tōchaku-robī** arrivals

到着する **tōchaku suru** arrive

到着予定時刻 **tōchaku-yotei-jikoku** ETA, estimated time of arrival

父ちゃん **tōchan** pop, dad

土地 **tochi** land, property; 土地の人 **tochi no hito** local

統治 **tōchi** rule

土地開発業者 **tochi-kaihatsu-gyōsha** property developer

統治する **tōchi suru** rule; administer

盗聴器 **tōchōki** bug (*device*); 盗聴器を仕掛ける **tōchōki o shikakeru** bug

盗聴する **tōchō suru** listen in; tap

途中 **tochū** midway; on the way

途中下車 **tochū-gesha** stopover

灯台 **tōdai** lighthouse

戸棚 **todana** closet; cupboard

都道府県 **todōfuken** prefectures

届出 **todokede** report; notification; registration

届け出る **todokederu** notify; register

届ける **todokeru** deliver, pass on

滞りなく **todokōri naku** duly; without a hitch

届く **todoku** reach, come to (*of hair, dress, water*); be through (*of news etc*)

とどまる **todomaru** remain, stay put

頭取 **tōdori** bank president

とどろき **todoroki** boom; roll (*of thunder*)

とどろく **todoroku** boom

とうふ **tōfu** tofu, bean curd

塗布する **tofu suru** apply *ointment*

とがめる **togameru** find fault; blame

とうがらし **tōgarashi** chili (pepper)

とがる **togaru** taper; be pointed

とげ **toge** prickle; spine; thorn; splinter

峠 **tōge** pass (*in mountains*)

とげだらけ(の) **togedarake (no)** prickly

陶芸 **tōgei** ceramics; pottery

遂げる **togeru** achieve; accomplish

討議 **tōgi** debate

途切れなく **togirenaku** uninterrupted

途切れ途切れ(の) **togiretogire no** fitful

投獄 **tōgoku** imprisonment

統語論 **tōgoron** syntax

研ぐ **togu** sharpen; wash *rice*

戸口 **toguchi** doorstep

徒歩 **toho** walk

東北 **Tōhoku** *northern region of Honshu*

途方もない **tohō mo nai** absurd; preposterous; fantastic

途方に暮れる **tohō ni kureru** be at a loss

徒歩旅行 **toho-ryokō** walking tour, hike

投票 **tōhyō** polls; vote; voting

投票箱 **tōhyō-bako** ballot box

投票所 **tōhyō-jo** polling booth, voting booth

投票者 **tōhyō-sha** voter

投票数 **tōhyō-sū** vote, votes cast

投票用紙記入所 **tōhyō-yōshi-kinyūjo** voting booth

投票する **tōhyō suru** go to the polls, vote

とい **toi** gutter (*on roof*)

遠い **tōi** distant, remote

問い合わせ **toiawase** inquiry

問い合わせる **toiawaseru** inquire; apply to

トイレ **toire** bathroom, toilet; トイレに行く **toire ni iku** go to the toilet

トイレットペーパー **toiretto-pēpā**

toilet paper

問いただす **toitadasu** question; grill

統一 **tōitsu** unification

統一する **tōitsu suru** unify

…といって **… to itte** just because

当時 **tōji** at that time; then

冬至 **tōji** winter solstice

陶磁器 **tōjiki** ceramics; china; crockery

閉じ込める **tojikomeru** confine; lock in; block in

戸締り **tojimari** locking up

閉じる **tojiru** close

閉じた **tojita** closed

当日 **tōjitsu** (on) that day; the scheduled day

登場 **tōjō** entrance

登場人物 **tōjō-jinbutsu** character

搭乗券 **tōjōken** boarding card, boarding pass

搭乗している **tōjō shite iru** be aboard

搭乗する **tōjō suru** go aboard

登場する **tōjō suru** appear; enter THEA

…とか **… toka** and so on; something like; 山田とかいう人 *Yamada toka iu hito* somebody called Yamada or something like that

とかげ **tokage** lizard

都会 **tokai** city

投かんする **tōkan suru** mail

とかす **tokasu** comb

溶かす **tokasu** dissolve; melt; melt down

時計 **tokei** clock

統計 **tōkei** statistics (*figures*)

統計学 **tōkei-gaku** statistics (*science*)

時計仕掛け **tokeijikake** clockwork

統計上 **tōkeijō** statistically

時計回り **tokeimawari** clockwise

時計屋 **tokei-ya** watchmaker

溶け込ませる **tokekomaseru** integrate

溶け込む **tokekomu** merge; blend in; fit in

溶けない **tokenai** insoluble

溶ける **tokeru** dissolve; melt; thaw ◊ soluble

凍結路面 **tōketsu-romen** black ice

凍結する **tōketsu suru** freeze

時 **toki** when; 子供/学生の時 *kodomo / gakusei no toki* as a child / student; 道をわたっている時に *michi o watatte iru toki ni* when crossing the road

陶器 **tōki** earthenware, china; pottery

投機 **tōki** venture; speculation

冬季 **tōki** winter; the winter season

登記 **tōki** registration

時々 **tokidoki** now and again, sometimes

解き放す **tokihanasu** release; set free

投機家 **tōki-ka** speculator

時には **toki ni wa** sometimes

投棄する **tōki suru** dump, throw away

投機する **tōki suru** speculate

特権 **tokken** privilege; 特権のある *tokken no aru* privileged

取っ組み合う **tokkumiau** grapple with

とっくに **tokku ni** long ago; long since; already

とっくり **tokkuri** sake flask

特許 **tokkyo** patent

特急 **tokkyū** express train

床 **toko** floor; bed; 床についている *toko ni tsuite iru* be confined to one's bed

陶工 **tōkō** potter

床の間 **tokonoma** alcove

所, ところ **tokoro** place; area; point; space; house ◊ about to; on the point of; have only just; ちょうど寝たところ *chōdo neta tokoro* when I had just gone to bed

ところで **tokoro de** incidentally, by the way

所々 **tokoro dokoro** here and there

ところが **tokoro ga** but; while; however

床屋 **tokoya** barber

得 **toku** advantage; profit; benefit; 得をする *toku o suru* profit; gain an advantage

解く **toku** answer; solve

特売 **tokubai** sale (*reduced prices*)

特別(な) **tokubetsu (na)** special

特別に **tokubetsu ni** specially;

particularly

特別(の) **tokubetsu (no)** particular, special

特別対策本部 **tokubetsu-taisaku-honbu** task force

特徴 **tokuchō** character, personality; special feature

特徴づける **tokuchōzukeru** characterize

特大(の) **tokudai (no)** king-size(d); outsize

特派員 **tokuhain** correspondent, reporter

得意(な) **tokui (na)** skillful; …が得意である **… ga tokui de aru** be good at…

得意先 **tokuisaki** customer; client

特異点 **tokuiten** idiosyncrasy

匿名(の) **tokumei (no)** anonymous

特に **toku ni** especially, particularly; exceptionally

遠くに **tōku ni** in the distance ◊ far

トークショー **tōku-shō** talk show

特色 **tokushoku** characteristic, trait; specialty

特集記事 **tokushū-kiji** feature article

特殊(な) **tokushu (na)** special; particular; unique

特定(の) **tokutei (no)** particular, specific

得点 **tokuten** goal; score

特典 **tokuten** privilege; advantage

得点者 **tokuten-sha** scorer

得点する **tokuten suru** score

特有(の) **tokuyū (no)** characteristic

東京 **Tōkyō** Tokyo

当局 **tōkyoku** the authorities

等級 **tōkyū** grade, quality; 等級をつける **tōkyū o tsukeru** grade

投球する **tōkyū suru** pitch

とまどい **tomadoi** perplexity, puzzlement

とまどった **tomadotta** perplexed

止り木 **tomarigi** perch

止まる **tomaru** stop; bring to a standstill; perch

泊まる **tomaru** stay the night; ホテルに泊まる **hoteru ni tomaru** stay in a hotel

留まる **tomaru** fasten

トマト **tomato** tomato

トマトケチャップ **tomato-kechappu** tomato ketchup

止まっている **tomatte iru** be off (*of machine*) ◊ stationary

遠回りする **tōmawari suru** make a detour; go the long way around

遠回し(な) **tōmawashi (na)** coy; indirect

遠回しに言う **tōmawashi ni iu** beat around the bush

留め金 **tomegane** catch

留め具 **tomegu** clasp, fastener

透明度 **tōmeido** transparency

透明(の) **tōmei (no)** transparent

当面(の) **tōmen (no)** in hand

止める **tomeru** disconnect; turn off; stop; stall; halt; break up

泊める **tomeru** put up, take in *person*

留める **tomeru** do up; staple

富 **tomi** wealth

冬眠する **tōmin suru** hibernate

糖蜜 **tōmitsu** molasses; syrup

とも **-tomo** both; all ◊ wherever; 両方とも **ryōhō tomo** both of them　どこへ行こうとも **doko e ikō tomo** wherever you go; 少なくとも **sukunaku tomo** at least; 遅くとも **osoku tomo** at the latest

友 **tomo** friend

共働き **tomo-bataraki** dual-income family

友達 **tomodachi** friend, buddy, pal; 友達ができる **tomodachi ga dekiru** make a friend; 友達になる **tomodachi ni naru** make friends

伴う **tomonau** take along; be accompanied; involve; entail

とうもろこし **tōmorokoshi** corn; sweetcorn

富む **tomu** be wealthy; abound in

トン **ton** ton

トナー **tonā** toner

唱える **tonaeru** recite; chant; advocate

トーナメント **tōnamento** tournament

東南アジア **Tōnan Ajia** Southeast Asia

盗難報知機 **tōnan-hōchiki** burglar alarm

隣 **tonari** house next door; neighbor

隣り合わせ(の) **tonariawase (no)** adjoining

隣に **tonari ni** next-door; ...の隣に ... **no tonari ni** next to

隣(の) **tonari (no)** next; next-door; 隣の人 **tonari no hito** neighbor

とんぼ **tonbo** dragonfly

とんぼ返り **tonbogaeri** somersault

とんぼ返りする **tonbogaeri suru** somersault

とんだ **tonda** unexpected; terrible; serious

飛んで行く **tonde iku** fly, rush; fly off (of hat etc)

飛んで帰る **tonde kaeru** fly back

とんでもない **tondemonai** absolutely not!; of course not; my pleasure! ◊ unreasonable; scandalous, shocking; 彼はとんでもない **kare wa tondemonai** he's unbelievable

とんでもなく **tondemonaku** dreadfully

とにかく **tonikaku** anyhow; in any case, at all events

とんかち **tonkachi** hammer

とんま **tonma** clown, fool

トンネル **tonneru** tunnel

とんとんたたく **tonton tataku** rap

問屋 **ton'ya** wholesaler

糖尿病 **tōnyōbyō** diabetes

糖尿病患者 **tōnyōbyō-kanja** diabetic

糖尿病(の) **tōnyōbyō (no)** diabetic

投入 **tōnyū** injection (of capital), investment

投入口 **tōnyūguchi** slot

投入する **tōnyū** inject, invest

突破する **toppa suru** break through; smash through

突飛(な) **toppi (na)** wild; erratic

トッピング **toppingu** topping

トップ **toppu** leader; top

突風 **toppū** gusty wind

トップギア **toppu-gia** top (gear)

トップレベル(の) **toppureberu (no)** high-level

トップレス(の) **toppuresu (no)** topless

とら **tora** tiger

トラベラーズチェック **toraberāzu-chekku** traveler's check

トラブル **toraburu** problem

トラブルメーカー **toraburu-mēkā** troublemaker

捕らえる **toraeru** capture, portray; seize

トラック **torakku** racetrack; rig, truck

トラクター **torakutā** tractor

トランク **toranku** trunk

トランクス **torankusu** swimsuit

トランペット **toranpetto** trumpet

トランポリン **toranporin** trampoline

トランプ **toranpu** playing card

トランシーバー **toranshībā** walkie-talkie

トランジスター **toranjistā** transistor

とらわれの身 **toraware no mi** prisoner; captive

トレイ **torei** tray

トレーナー **torēnā** sweatshirt; trainer

トレーニング **torēningu** workout

トレーニングする **torēningu suru** work out

トレーラー **torērā** semi; trailer

取れる **toreru** come away; come off; be obtained; be interpreted

採れる **toreru** be extracted; be picked

鳥 **tori** bird

通り **tōri** street

通り **-tōri** as; 先生のいう通りにしなさい **sensei no iu tōri ni shinasai** do as your teacher tells you

とりあえず **toriaezu** for the time being

取り上げる **toriageru** pick up; take away; bring up

取り扱い **toriatsukai** treatment

取り扱い注意 **toriatsukai-chūi** (handle) with care

取扱説明 **toriatsukai-setsumei** instructions for use

取扱説明書 **toriatsukai-setsumeisho** instruction manual

取り扱う **toriatsukau** handle, deal with

取り違える **torichigaeru** mix up

取り散らかした **torichirakashita** messy

取り散らかす **torichirakasu** mess up

取り出す **toridasu** eject; extract,

take out; produce, bring out

とりで **toride** fort

取柄 **torie** merit; redeeming feature

鳥肌 **torihada** gooseflesh

取り計らう **torihakarau** arrange; see about, look into

取り払う **toriharau** remove, clear away

取りはずせる **torihazuseru** detachable

取りはずす **torihazusu** detach; disconnect

取り引き **torihiki** bargain, deal; transaction

取り引きする **torihiki suru** trade; deal with

鳥居 **torii** *gateway to Shinto shrine*

取り入れる **toriireru** incorporate; introduce

取り入る **toriiru** ingratiate oneself with

取替部品 **torikae-buhin** replacement part

取り替える **torikaeru** change; exchange; switch

取り返しのつかない **torikaeshi no tsukanai** irretrievable

取り返す **torikaesu** get back; retrieve

取りかかる **torikakaru** go ahead; launch; start

取り囲む **torikakomu** encircle

取り交わす **torikawasu** exchange

取り消し **torikeshi** cancelation; withdrawal

取り消す **torikesu** cancel; withdraw

取り決める **torikimeru** arrange; settle; negotiate

とりこになる **toriko ni naru** be captivated

取り壊し **torikowashi** demolition

取り壊す **torikowasu** demolish, pull down

取り組み方 **torikumi kata** approach

取り組む **torikumu** tackle *problem*; grapple with, wrestle with

通り道 **tōrimichi** route

取り巻く **torimaku** surround

取り乱した **torimidashita** distraught; confused

取り戻す **torimodosu** recover, get

back; regain; recapture; 遅れを取り戻す **okure o torimodosu** catch up on

取りにいく **tori ni iku** collect, pick up

鳥肉 **toriniku** chicken (*food*); poultry (*meat*)

取りにくる **tori ni kuru** come for, collect

取り除く **torinozoku** clear; remove; weed out; take away

通り抜けられない **tōrinukerarenai** impassable

通り抜ける **tōrinukeru** get by, pass; pass through

取り下げる **torisageru** drop

取り去る **torisaru** take away; remove

取り締まり **torishimari** management; discipline; crackdown

取締役 **torishimariyaku** director

取り締まる **torishimaru** clamp down on

取り調べ **torishirabe** investigation

取り調べる **torishiraberu** investigate

通り過ぎる **tōrisugiru** go by, pass (by)

とりとめのない **toritome no nai** rambling; incoherent *speech*

取り次ぐ **toritsugu** act as an agent; pass on; convey

取りつかれたよう(な) **toritsukareta yō (na)** obsessive

取りつかれている **toritsukarete iru** be obsessed by / with

取り付け **toritsuke** installation; fittings

取り付ける **toritsukeru** attach; fix; install

取り止める **toriyameru** call off, cancel

とろ火 **torobi** low flame

トローチ **torōchi** lozenge

トロフィー **torofī** cup, trophy

登録 **tōroku** enrolment, registration

登録簿 **tōrokubo** register

登録商標 **tōroku-shōhyō** registered trademark

登録する **tōroku suru** enroll, register

討論 **tōron** debate, discussion

トロンボーン **toronbōn** trombone

討論する **tōron suru** debate

トロール船 **torōru-sen** trawler

とろとろ歩く **torotoro aruku** trudge

とる **toru** have *meal*

取る **toru** remove; seize; take *math, French etc*; take off (*discount*); take on *job*; occupy *time*; steal; subscribe to; record

捕る **toru** catch *fish*

撮る **toru** take *photograph, photocopy*

通る **tōru** penetrate

トルコ **Toruko** Turkey

トルコ(の) **Toruko (no)** Turkish

取るに足らない **toru ni taranai** unimportant; insignificant; negligible; petty

塗料 **toryō** paint

倒産 **tōsan** bankruptcy; crash

倒産させる **tōsan saseru** bankrupt

倒産した **tōsan shita** bankrupt

倒産する **tōsan suru** go bankrupt

と殺 **tosatsu** slaughter

と殺する **tosatsu suru** slaughter

当選者 **tōsen-sha** winner

当選する **tōsen suru** win

年 **toshi** year; age; 年をとる *toshi o toru* age, get on; 年をとった *toshi o totta* old

都市 **toshi** city

投資 **tōshi** investment, stake

闘士 **tōshi** fighter; activist; militant

都市化 **toshika** urbanization

都心部 **toshinbu** inner city

都市(の) **toshi (no)** urban

投資家 **tōshi-sha** investor

年下(の) **toshishita (no)** junior

投資する **tōshi suru** invest

…として **… to shite** as; by way of, in the form; …として機能する *… to shite kinō suru* function as; …として務める *… to shite tsutomeru* act as

通して **tōshite** through the medium of; 通して読む *tōshite yomu* go through, read through

年上 **toshiue** elder

年寄り **toshiyori** elderly person

図書 **tosho** books

投書 **tōsho** letter to the editor; contribution

凍傷 **tōshō** frostbite

図書館 **toshokan** library

党首 **tōshu** leadership

とそ **toso** New Year spiced sake

塗装 **tosō** paintwork

逃走 **tōsō** escape; flight; getaway

逃走車 **tōsō-sha** getaway car

闘争的(な) **tōsōteki (na)** militant

とっさに **tossa ni** at once; instantly

突進する **tosshin suru** dart, dash; surge forward

通す **tōsu** run through *details*; send in; thread

トースト **tōsuto** toast

…とたん **… totan** just when, the moment that; as soon as

到達する **tōtatsu suru** arrive at, reach

とうてい **tōtei** absolutely, utterly

とても **totemo** very; much; really

とうとう **tōtō** at last; after all

整える **totonoeru** organize, prepare; make *bed*; typeset

整う **totonou** be prepared; be completed

突撃する **totsugeki suru** charge, attack

突然 **totsuzen** all at once, suddenly

突然(の) **totsuzen (no)** abrupt, sudden

とって **totte**: …にとって *… ni totte* to; for; 私にとって非常に不便だった *watashi ni totte hijō ni fuben datta* it was very inconvenient for me

取っ手 **totte** handle, knob

取って食う **totte kuu** prey on

取ってくる **totte kuru** get, fetch

とっても **tottemo** very; much; really

取っておく **totte oku** keep; set aside *money*; save; reserve

当惑 **tōwaku** discomfort, embarrassment

当惑させる **tōwaku saseru** perplex; embarrass; bewilder; dismay

投薬量 **tōyaku-ryō** dosage

東洋 **Tōyō** East, Orient

東洋人 **Tōyō-jin** Oriental

東洋(の) **Tōyō (no)** Eastern, Oriental

投与する **tōyo suru** administer, give *medication*

灯油 **tōyu** kerosene

東西 **Tōzai** East and West

当座借越 **tōza-karikoshi** overdraft

遠ざかる **tōzakaru** go away; get faint; drift apart

遠ざける **tōzakeru** shun; keep at a distance; abstain from

登山 **tozan** climb; mountaineering

登山家 **tozanka** mountaineer

登山者 **tozan-sha** climber

登山する **tozan suru** climb

当座預金口座 **tōza-yokin-kōza** checking account

当然 **tōzen** justly, rightly; naturally, of course; 当然だ **tōzen da** no wonder

当然(の) **tōzen (no)** due, proper; natural, obvious; 当然のこととして **tōzen no koto to shite** as a matter of course

盗賊 **tōzoku** bandit

つ **tsu** countword for small objects

通 **tsū** connoisseur

つば **tsuba** saliva; brim (of hat); guard (on sword); つばを吐く **tsuba o haku** spit

つばき **tsubaki** camellia

つばめ **tsubame** swallow (bird)

翼 **tsubasa** wing

つぼ **tsubo** urn

坪 **tsubo** unit of area, 3. 6 square yards

つぼみ **tsubomi** bud

粒 **tsubu** grain; speck ◊ countword for small round objects and grain

つぶれる **tsubureru** be crushed; go bankrupt; fold

つぶれそう(な) **tsuburesō(na)** tumbledown

つぶれた **tsubureta** broken

つぶす **tsubusu** kill time; smash; crush; thwart

つぶやき **tsubuyaki** murmur; muttering

つぶやく **tsubuyaku** murmur, mutter

土 **tsuchi** earth, soil

通知票 **tsūchi-hyō** report card

通知する **tsūchi suru** inform, notify

通帳 **tsūchō** bank book

つえ **tsue** cane; walking stick

つがい **tsugai** pair

つがいになる **tsugai ni naru** mate

告げ口する **tsugeguchi suru** snitch; inform on

告げ口屋 **tsugeguchi-ya** snitch, telltale

つぎ **tsugi** patch

接ぎ木 **tsugiki** graft BOT

つぎ込む **tsugikomu** invest, sink funds; put in

継ぎ目 **tsugime** join; joint

次に **tsugi ni** next

次(の) **tsugi (no)** next, following; 次の方どうぞ **tsugi no kata dōzo** next, please; 次のとおり **tsugi no tōri** as follows; 次の次 **tsugi no tsugi** the next but one

都合 **tsugō** circumstances; convenience; 都合のいい **tsugō no ii** suitable, convenient; 都合の悪い **tsugō no warui** inconvenient; あなた/私の都合の良い時に **anata/ watashi no tsugō no yoi toki ni** at your/my convenience

つぐ **tsugu** join; piece together; pour, pour out

継ぐ **tsugu** inherit; succeed to

償う **tsugunau** compensate; make amends

通報する **tsūhō suru** report

つい **tsui** just; only; by accident; in spite of oneself; つい笑ってしまった **tsui waratte shimatta** I couldn't help laughing; ついさっき **tsui sakki** just now, a few moments ago

対 **tsui** pair

ついでに **tsuide ni** while I'm/you're etc about it

追放 **tsuihō** expulsion

追放された **tsuihō sareta** outcast

追放する **tsuihō suru** eject, expel, oust; exile

追加 **tsuika** addition

つい間板ヘルニア **tsuikanban herunia** slipped disc

追加(の) **tsuika (no)** additional

追加料金 **tsuika-ryōkin** surcharge

追加する **tsuika suru** add

追求 **tsuikyū** pursuit, search

追求する **tsuikyū suru** pursue

ツインベッド **tsuin-beddo** twin beds

ついに **tsui ni** in the end, eventually; at last; ついに…となる **tsui ni … to naru** culminate in

墜落 **tsuiraku** crash

墜落する **tsuiraku suru** crash

ついさっき **tsui sakki** a few moments ago

追跡 **tsuiseki** chase, pursuit; 犯人追跡 **hannin-tsuiseki** manhunt

追跡者 **tsuiseki-sha** pursuer

追伸 **tsuishin** PS, postscript

追体験する **tsuitaiken suru** relive

ついたて **tsuitate** partition, screen

ついて **tsuite** per; about; concerning; …について聞く **… ni tsuite kiku** hear about; …についてよく知っている **… ni tsuite yoku shitte iru** have a good knowledge of; …については **… ni tsuite wa** as for

ついて行けない **tsuite ikenai** be out of one's depth

ついて行く **tsuite iku** follow; accompany; keep up with

ついている **tsuite iru** be lucky; be on (of light, TV etc); hold

ついてくる **tsuite kuru** keep up

ついて回る **tsuite mawaru** dog

追悼(の) **tsuitō (no)** memorial

費やす **tsuiyasu** spend

通じない **tsūjinai** dead phone

通じる **tsūjiru** lead to; reach by phone; communicate; …に通じる **… ni tsūjiru** give onto

つじつまが合う **tsujitsuma ga au** add up, make sense; be consistent

つじつまの合わない **tsujitsuma no awanai** incoherent; inconsistent

通常(の) **tsūjō (no)** regular, normal

通貨 **tsūka** currency; money

使えない **tsukaenai** useless

使える **tsukaeru** run (of software); be usable

仕える **tsukaeru** serve

使い **tsukai** errand

使い古し(の) **tsukaifurushi (no)** battered

使い古した **tsukaifurushita** well-worn; worn-out; dog-eared

使い古す **tsukaifurusu** wear

使い果たす **tsukaihatasu** exhaust, use up

使い込み **tsukaikomi** embezzlement

使い込む **tsukaikomu** embezzle

使いこなす **tsukaikonasu** master

使い道の多い **tsukaimichi no ōi** versatile

使い慣れる **tsukainareru** get used to

使いにくい **tsukainikui** unfriendly, not easy to use

使いすぎる **tsukaisugiru** overwork

使い捨て(の) **tsukaisute (no)** disposable

使い尽くす **tsukaitsukusu** eat up, use up

使いやすい **tsukaiyasui** user-friendly, easy to use

捕まえにくい **tsukamaenikui** elusive

捕まえる **tsukamaeru** capture, catch

捕まらないで **tsukamaranaide** at large

つかむ **tsukamu** grab; seize; catch hold of

通貨(の) **tsūka (no)** monetary

つかの間(の) **tsuka no ma (no)** fleeting; short-lived

通関手続 **tsūkan-tetsuzuki** customs formalities

疲れ果てた **tsukarehateta** weary

疲れ切った **tsukarekitta** exhausted

疲れる **tsukareru** wearing, tiring ◊ tire

疲れさせる **tsukare saseru** wear out, tire

疲れた **tsukareta** tired

通過する **tsūka suru** pass through

使う **tsukau** use; spend; take credit cards; run car

つけ **tsuke** charge account; credit

付け合わせ **tsukeawase** relish, sauce; side dish

つけ込む **tsukekomu** cash in on; take advantage of

付け加える **tsukekuwaeru** add, say; add on

漬物 **tsukemono** pickled vegetables

付け値 **tsukene** bid

つけっぱなしにする **tsukeppanashi ni suru** leave on computer etc

つける **tsukeru** immerse; dunk

cookie; soak; mop up *liquid* ; strike *match*; switch on, turn on *light etc*

着ける **tsukeru** put on; wear

付ける **tsukeru** fit, attach; build up

月 **tsuki** month; moon

月(の) **tsuki (no)** lunar; 月の光 *tsuki no hikari* moonlight

つき **tsuki**: ...につき ... *ni tsuki* per

付き合い **tsukiai** companionship, company ◊ *afterwork socializing with people from work*; ...と付き合い を続ける ... *to tsukiai o tsuzukeru* keep up with

突き当たり **tsukiatari** bottom (*of street*)

付き合う **tsukiau** date, go out with; mix, socialize; keep ... company

突き出す **tsukidasu** poke

突き出る **tsukideru** project, stick out

突き出た **tsukideta** prominent *chin*

月日 **tsukihi** time; days; years

通気孔 **tsūkikō** vent

つきまとう **tsukimatou** stalk *person*; lurk (*of doubt*); haunt

通勤ラッシュ **tsūkin-rasshu** commuter traffic

通勤列車 **tsūkin-ressha** commuter train

通勤者 **tsūkin-sha** commuter

通勤する **tsūkin suru** commute

尽きる **tsukiru** be used up

突き刺す **tsukisasu** plunge

突き刺すよう(な) **tsukisasu yō (na)** penetrating

付き添い **tsukisoi** nurse; orderly

付き添う **tsukisou** accompany; attend

突き飛ばす **tsukitobasu** push away

つきとめる **tsukitomeru** isolate, pinpoint; ascertain

月夜 **tsukiyo** moonlit night

つっかえさせる **tsukkaesaseru** jam

突っ込む **tsukkomu** plunge; poke, stick; shove in

通行権 **tsūkō-ken** right of way

通告 **tsūkoku** notice; ...に通告する ... *ni tsūkoku suru* give ... his/her notice

通行人 **tsūkō-nin** passer-by

通行料 **tsūkō-ryō** toll

通行証 **tsūkōshō** pass, permit

つく **tsuku** increase; tell *lie*; leave for; pound; strike *bell*

付く **tsuku** be joined to; stick; be smeared; accompany; cost; be in luck

突く **tsuku** jab, prod; thrust

着く **tsuku** arrive; come; reach, come to; get

机 **tsukue** desk

作り上げる **tsukuriageru** make out *list*

作り話 **tsukuribanashi** lie, story

作り出す **tsukuridasu** make; produce; devise

作り付け(の) **tsukuritsuke (no)** built-in

繕い **tsukuroi** darning, mending

繕う **tsukurou** darn, mend

作る **tsukuru** create; make; fix *lunch*; form *past tense etc*

造る **tsukuru** build; manufacture; construct

尽くす **tsukusu** use up; exhaust

妻 **tsuma** wife

つまみ **tsumami** pinch (*of salt*); knob; snacks; 塩ひとつまみ *shio hito-tsumami* a pinch of salt

つまらない **tsumaranai** uninteresting; unsuccessful; tame *joke*

つまらなさ **tsumaranasa** boredom

詰まらせる **tsumaraseru** clog up; 彼 はのどに骨を詰まらせた *kare wa nodo ni hone o tsumaraseta* he choked on a bone

つまり **tsumari** that is to say

詰まり **tsumari** blockage

つまる **tsumaru** be at a loss for words

詰まる **tsumaru** clog up, stop up; be packed; shrink; run short

つま先 **tsumasaki** toe (*of shoe*); つま 先立ちで *tsumasakidachi de* on tippy-toe

つましい **tsumashii** economical, thrifty

つまようじ **tsumayōji** toothpick

つまずく **tsumazuku** stumble, trip

つめ **tsume** claw; fingernail

詰め合わせ **tsumeawase** assortment

つめ切り **tsume-kiri** nail clippers; nail scissors

詰め込まれる **tsumekomareru** be squeezed in

詰め込む **tsumekomu** cram

詰めもの **tsumemono** padding; stuffing

詰める **tsumeru** move up, squeeze up; pack; take in *clothes*

冷たい **tsumetai** cold; cool *drink*; frosty *welcome*

つめやすり **tsume-yasuri** nail file

罪 **tsumi** sin, crime; 罪を犯す *tsumi o okasu* sin

積み上げる **tsumiageru** heap up, pile up

罪深い **tsumibukai** sinful

積み重ね **tsumikasane** heap

積み重ねる **tsumikasaneru** stack

積み込み渡し **tsumikomi-watashi** FOB, free on board

積み荷 **tsumini** cargo, load

つもり **tsumori** intention; ...のつもりはまったくない *... no tsumori wa mattaku nai* I have no intention of; つもりである *tsumori de aru* mean, intend

摘む **tsumu** pick

積む **tsumu** load

つむぐ **tsumugu** spin *wool, cotton*

つむじ風 **tsumujikaze** whirlwind

つむじ曲り(の) **tsumujimagari (no)** perverse

綱 **tsuna** cable

ツナ **tsuna** tuna

つながり **tsunagari** link

つながる **tsunagaru** link up

つなげる **tsunageru** connect; link

つなぎ合わせる **tsunagiawaseru** piece together

つなぐ **tsunagu** connect, join; moor, tie up *boat*; tether *horse*; tie *hands*

津波 **tsunami** tidal wave, tsunami

常に **tsune ni** always

つねる **tsuneru** pinch

角 **tsuno** horn; 角で突く *tsuno de tsuku* butt

ツーピース **tsūpīsu** two-piece

面 **tsura** mug (*face*)

つらい **tsurai** upsetting, painful; trying, annoying

貫く **tsuranuku** pierce, penetrate

つらら **tsurara** icicle

連れ **tsure** companion

通例 **tsūrei** usually; as a rule ◊ standard

連れて行く **tsurete iku** take, accompany

連れてかえる **tsurete kaeru** fetch *person*

連れてくる **tsurete kuru** bring *person*

痛烈(な) **tsūretsu (na)** scathing

釣り **tsuri** fishing; change; 釣りをする *tsuri o suru* fish

つり上がった **tsuriagatta** slanting *eyes*

釣り合い **tsuriai** balance; proportions, dimensions; 釣り合いのとれた *tsuriai no toreta* balanced, fair; 釣り合いを取る *tsuriai o toru* balance

釣り合っていない **tsuriatte inai** unevenly matched

釣り合わせる **tsuriawaseru** counterbalance

釣り針 **tsuribari** hook

つり橋 **tsuribashi** suspension bridge

釣り道具 **tsuri-dōgu** fishing tackle

釣り糸 **tsuri-ito** fishing line

釣ざお **tsuri-zao** fishing rod

通路 **tsūro** aisle; passage, passageway; 通路側の席 *tsūrogawa no seki* aisle seat

つる **tsuru** crane (*bird*)

釣る **tsuru** catch *fish with rod*

つるす **tsurusu** suspend, hang

通信衛星 **tsūshin-eisei** communications satellite

通信販売カタログ **tsūshin-hanbai-katarogu** mail-order catalog

通信社 **tsūshinsha** news agency

通信手段 **tsūshin-shudan** communications

通信する **tsūshin suru** correspond; communicate

通商産業省 **Tsūshō-Sangyōshō** Ministry of International Trade and Industry

つた **tsuta** creeper; ivy

伝える **tsutaeru** communicate, convey, pass on, relay; hand down

伝わる **tsutawaru** carry (*of sound*);

come across; be communicated

つて **tsute** connection, contact; つて
がある **tsute ga aru** be well
connected

勤まる **tsutomaru** be fit for; be
equal to

勤める **tsutomeru** serve; be
employed

務める **tsutomeru** make efforts;
work (*for a company*); 議長を務め
る *gichō o tsutomeru* act as
chairperson

勤め先 **tsutomesaki** place of
employment

筒 **tsutsu** cylinder

つつく **tsutsuku** peck, bite; poke;
incite; criticize

つつましい **tsutsumashii** humble,
modest; frugal

包み **tsutsumi** bundle; wrapper

包む **tsutsumu** envelop, wrap

慎み **tsutsushimi** modesty; self-
control

慎む **tsutsushimu** refrain from; be
discreet

つや **tsuya** gloss, shine

つや出し **tsuyadashi** polishing

つや消し(の) **tsuyakeshi (no)** matt;

frosted

通訳 **tsūyaku** interpretation;
interpreter

通訳する **tsūyaku suru** interpret

強火でいためる **tsuyobi de itameru**
stir-fry

強い **tsuyoi** strong; forceful
argument; vigorous *denial*;
profound *shock, effect*

強く **tsuyoku** strongly

強くなる **tsuyoku naru** intensify;
strengthen

強くする **tsuyoku suru** strengthen;
turn up

強める **tsuyomeru** heighten,
intensify

強み **tsuyomi** advantage; strength

強さ **tsuyo-sa** strength

つゆ **tsuyu** soup; sauce

梅雨 **tsuyu** rainy season

露 **tsuyu** dew

続ける **tsuzukeru** carry on,
continue

続き **tsuzuki** continuation, sequel

続く **tsuzuku** continue; persist, last;
to be continued

つづり **tsuzuri** spelling

つづる **tsuzuru** spell

U

乳母車 **ubaguruma** baby carriage,
buggy

奪う **ubau** rob; deprive; fascinate

家 **uchi** house; home; family ◊ I
(*familiar*); 家に帰る *uchi ni kaeru*
come home

内 **uchi** inside; indoors; in-group; ◊
between; 両者の内で *ryōsha no
uchi de* between the two of them

打ち上げ **uchiage** blast-off, lift-off

打ち上げられる **uchiagerareru** lift
off (*of rocket*)

打ち明ける **uchiakeru** confide

打ち合わせ **uchiawase** prior

arrangement; briefing

打ち合わせる **uchiawaseru** make a
prior arrangement

内側 **uchigawa** inside

内側(の) **uchigawa (no)** inner;
inside

内側車線 **uchigawa-shasen** inside
lane

打ち掛け **uchikake** *traditional
Japanese wedding dress*

打ち勝つ **uchikatsu** conquer;
overcome

内気 **uchiki** shyness

内気(な) **uchiki (na)** shy

打ち消す **uchikesu** deny; contradict

打ち込む **uchikomu** drive in, hammer in

打ち切る **uchikiru** break off; discontinue

撃ち殺す **uchikorosu** shoot (*and kill*)

打ち壊す **uchikowasu** break down *door*

打ち砕く **uchikudaku** dash *hopes*

打ち負かす **uchimakasu** defeat, whip, thrash

内に **uchi ni** in ◊ while

家の内の (*familiar*) my **uchi no**

打ちのめされる **uchinomesareru** go to pieces

打ちのめす **uchinomesu** devastate; beat up

撃ち落とす **uchiotosu** shoot down, bring down

内ポケット **uchi-poketto** inside pocket

打ち解ける **uchitokeru** open up (*of person*)

うちわ **uchiwa** fan (*round, made of paper*)

内輪 **uchiwa** family circle; inner circle

内訳 **uchiwake** breakdown; details

打ち寄せる波 **uchiyoseru nami** surf; breakers

有頂天 **uchōten** ecstasy, rapture; 有頂天になった **uchōten ni natta** entranced

有頂天(の) **uchōten (no)** ecstatic

宇宙 **uchū** universe

宇宙服 **uchū-fuku** spacesuit

宇宙飛行士 **uchū-hikōshi** astronaut

宇宙人 **uchū-jin** alien

宇宙旅行 **uchū-ryokō** voyage (in space); space travel

宇宙船 **uchū-sen** space module, spacecraft

宇宙ステーション **uchū-sutēshon** space station

うだるよう(な) **udaru yō (na)** sweltering

腕 **ude** arm

腕時計 **udedokei** wrist watch

腕組みをする **udegumi o suru** fold

one's arms

腕前 **udemae** ability; skill

腕立て伏せ **udetatefuse** push-up

うどん **udon** noodles

上 **ue** top; upper part; brow (*of hill*); 兄は僕より三歳上です **ani wa boku yori sansai ue desu** my elder brother is three years older than me; 上に **ue ni** on; on top of; upstairs; 山の上を飛ぶ **yama no ue o tobu** fly over the mountains; ピアニストである上に **pianisuto de aru ue ni** as well as being a pianist

飢え **ue** hunger

ウエーブのかかった **uēbu no kakatta** wavy

ウエハース **uehāsu** wafer

ウエディングドレス **uedingu-doresu** wedding dress

ウエディングケーキ **uedingu-kēki** wedding cake

上側 **uegawa** top part

ウエイター **ueitā** waiter; ウエイターをする **ueitā o suru** wait table

ウエイトレス **ueitoresu** waitress

飢え死にする **uejini suru** starve to death

植木 **ueki** garden plant; potted plant

植木鉢 **uekibachi** flowerpot; pot

植え込み **uekomi** shrubbery

上向きに **uemuki ni** upward

上に **ue ni** above ◊ up

植える **ueru** plant

飢える **ueru** starve

ウエスト **uesuto** waist; waistline

ウエストポーチ **uesuto pōchi** fanny pack

うがいをする **ugai o suru** gargle

動いていない **ugoite inai** idle *machinery*

動かない **ugokanai** be out of action ◊ motionless

動かなくなる **ugokanaku naru** jam, stick; seize up

動かす **ugokasu** move, shift; work *machine*; drive TECH

動き **ugoki** activity; movement; move; motion

動き回る **ugokimawaru** get around, be mobile; move around

動く **ugoku** move, budge, shift;

operate, work (*of machine*) ◊ moving (*which can move*)

うぐいす **uguisu** bush warbler

右派 **uha** right wing

ウイークデー **uīkudē** weekday

ウイークエンド **uīkuendo** weekend

ウィンドサーフィン **uindosāfin** windsurfing, sailboarding

ウインドーショッピングをする **uindō-shoppingu o suru** go window-shopping

ウイング **uingu** wing SP

ウインカー **uinkā** indicator MOT; ウインカーを出す **uinkā o dasu** indicate

ウインク **uinku** wink

ウインクする **uinku suru** wink

ウイルス **uirusu** virus

ウイルス(の) **uirusu (no)** viral

ウイスキー **uisukī** whiskey

うじゃうじゃしている **ujauja shite iru** crawl with, swarm with

うじ **uji** maggot

うじ虫 **ujimushi** grub (*of insect*)

浮かべる **ukaberu** set afloat; sail; picture, imagine

浮かぶ **ukabu** float

うかがう **ukagau** H call on; visit; ask; hear

う回路 **ukairo** detour, diversion

う回させる **ukai saseru** divert, reroute

う回する **ukai suru** bypass

浮かんで **ukande** afloat

受かる **ukaru** pass *exam*

受け入れ **ukeire** acceptance

受け入れる **ukeireru** accept; take on board

受身 **ukemi** passive GRAM

受け持ち(の) **ukemochi (no)** in charge; having responsibility

受け持つ **ukemotsu** take charge

受ける **ukeru** take *exam, degree*; undergo *surgery*; take up, accept

受取人 **uketori-nin** addressee; recipient; payee

受け取る **uketoru** accept, take; get, receive; perceive, view

受け継ぐ **uketsugu** inherit; succeed to; take over

受付 **uketsuke** reception, reception desk

受付係 **uketsuke-gakari** receptionist

受け付けない **uketsukenai** reject

受け付ける **uketsukeru** accept

受け皿 **ukezara** saucer

雨季, 雨期 **uki** monsoon season

浮き彫り **ukibori** relief (*in art*)

浮き沈み **ukishizumi** ups and downs

浮き浮きした **ukiuki shita** cheerful; excited; buoyant; exhilarating

浮世絵 **ukiyoe** wood block print

うっかり **ukkari** carelessly; うっかり言う **ukkari iu** blurt out; let slip

浮く **uku** float

馬 **uma** horse

うまい **umai** delicious; skillful; clever; good; lucrative

うまく **umaku** cleverly; nicely; successfully; うまくいかない **umaku ikanai** go wrong, fail; うまくいく **umaku iku** do well; turn out well; うまくなる **umaku naru** get better; うまくやる **umaku yaru** do well (*of person*); うまくやっていく **umaku yatte iku** get on; be friendly with

ウーマンリブ **ūman ribu** women's lib

生まれ故郷(の) **umarekokyō (no)** native

生まれる **umareru** be born; originate

生まれたて(の) **umaretate (no)** newborn

生まれつき(の) **umaretsuki (no)** inborn

梅 **ume** (Japanese) plum

埋め合せ **umeawase** compensation

埋め合わせる **umeawaseru** compensate for

梅干し **umeboshi** pickled plum

うめき **umeki** groan; moan

うめき声 **umekigoe** groan

うめく **umeku** groan, moan

埋める **umeru** bridge *gap*; bury; fill in *hole*

埋め立て **umetate** (land) reclamation

埋め立てる **umetateru** reclaim *land*

うみ **umi** pus

海 **umi** sea; ocean

海辺 **umibe** seaside

生み出す **umidasu** generate, create

海(の) **umi (no)** marine; maritime

海の日 **Umi no hi** Sea Day

羽毛 **umō** down; feather

有無 **umu** presence; existence

うむ **umu** fester

生む **umu** yield; bring in *interest, income*

産む **umu** bear *children*; lay *eggs*; give birth to

うん **un** yes; OK; that's right

運 **un** chance, luck; 運のいい **un no ii** lucky; 運の悪い事に **un no warui koto ni** unluckily

うなぎ **unagi** eel

うなじ **unaji** nape of the neck

うなり声 **unarigoe** bellow; growl

うなる **unaru** growl; wail; whirr

うなずき **unazuki** nod

うなずく **unazuku** nod; agree

運賃 **unchin** fare

運賃込み価格 **unchin-komi kakaku** cost and freight

運動 **undō** campaign, drive; crusade; movement; exercise; 運動を起こす **undō o okosu** campaign

運動不足(の) **undōbusoku (no)** unfit

運動場 **undōjō** playing field

運動家 **undō-ka** campaigner

運動(の) **undō (no)** athletic

運動させる **undō saseru** exercise

運動する **undō suru** exercise, take exercise

運営 **un'ei** management; operation

運営する **un'ei suru** manage; operate; run

うねり **uneri** swell (*of sea*)

運河 **unga** canal

うに **uni** sea urchin

うんこ **unko** shit

運行 **unkō** running (*of trains etc*); movement (*of planets*)

運行する **unkō suru** run, operate (*of trains etc*); move (*of planet*)

運命 **unmei** destiny, fate

うのみにする **unomi ni suru** lap up; swallow

運搬する **unpan suru** transport; convey

運送 **unsō** haulage

運送会社 **unsō-gaisha** haulage company, haulier

運送業 **unsō-gyō** haulage

運送業者 **unsō-gyōsha** forwarding agent; movers

運送料 **unsō-ryō** freight

運転 **unten** driving; navigation

運転台 **untendai** driver's cab

運転免許試験 **unten-menkyo-shiken** driving test

運転免許証 **unten-menkyoshō** driver's license

運転者 **unten-sha** operator

運転士 **unten-shi** engineer RAIL

運転手 **unten-shu** driver; chauffeur

運転する **unten suru** drive; steer

うんと **unto** a great deal; severely

うぬぼれ **unubore** conceit; pride, arrogance

うぬぼれた **unuboreta** conceited; big-headed

うぬぼれている **unuborete iru** vain

うぬぼれや **unubore-ya** show-off

運よく **un'yoku** luckily

運輸業者 **un'yu-gyōsha** carrier

運輸省 **Un'yushō** Department of Transportation

うんざりした **unzari shita** bored; fed up

うんざりする **unzari suru** be fed up with

魚 **uo** fish

うっぷんを晴らす **uppun o harasu** work off *bad mood*; vent *anger*

裏 **ura** back; bottom; reverse; 裏をかく **ura o kaku** foil, outwit

裏返しに **uragaeshi ni** inside out

裏切り **uragiri** disloyalty; betrayal; treachery

裏切り者(の) **uragirimono (no)** disloyal

裏切る **uragiru** betray; 期待を裏切る **kitai o uragiru** let down

裏口 **uraguchi** backdoor

裏地 **uraji** lining; backing

裏階段 **urakaidan** backstairs

裏目に出る **urame ni deru** backfire

恨み **urami** feud; rancor; grudge; resentment; 恨みを晴らす **urami o harasu** have a score to settle with; 恨みを持っている **urami o motte iru** bear a grudge

恨む **uramu** bear a grudge

裏道 **uramichi** back road

占い師 **uranaishi** fortune teller

ウラニウム **uraniumu** uranium

裏庭 **uraniwa** backyard, yard

裏表 **uraomote** both sides; 裏表のある **uraomote no aru** two-faced

うらやましげ(な) **urayamashige (na)** envious

うらやましい **urayamashii** enviable ◊ envy; be jealous of

裏付け **urazuke** confirmation; backing, support

裏付ける **urazukeru** back up; corroborate; confirm; reinforce

売れる **ureru** sell; be in demand

熟れる **ureru** ripen; be ripe

うれしい **ureshii** glad

熟れた **ureta** ripe

売れていない **urete inai** unsuccessful

売り上げ **uriage** takings; turnover

売上高 **uriagedaka** sales figures

売り場 **uriba** department (*of store*)

売り出す **uridasu** offer for sale

売り切れ **urikire** sold out

売り込み **urikomi** sales patter

売り崩し **urikuzushi** raid FIN

売り物(の) **urimono (no)** for sale

売りに出す **uri ni dasu** put up for sale

うり類 **urirui** squash (*vegetable*)

売り手 **urite** seller, vendor

売り渡し証 **uriwatashishō** bill of sale

うろこ **uroko** scale (*on fish*)

うろたえる **urotaeru** be in a flap; get flustered

うろつく **urotsuku** loiter; prowl

うろうろする **urouro suru** mill around; hang around

売る **uru** sell

ウール **ūru** wool

うるう年 **urūdoshi** leap year

ウール(の) **ūru (no)** woolen

うるさい **urusai** noisy; loud; persistent; annoying; fussy

漆 **urushi** lacquer

うさぎ **usagi** rabbit

牛 **ushi** cow; bull; cattle

失う **ushinau** lose; forfeit

失われた **ushinawareta** lost

後ろ **ushiro** back (*of car, bus*)

後ろへ **ushiro e** backward

後ろ前 **ushiromae** back to front

うしろめたい **ushirometai** have a guilty conscience

うしろめたさ **ushirometa-sa** guilt feelings

後ろに **ushiro ni** backward; behind;

後ろに下がる **ushiro ni sagaru** draw back, back off

後ろ(の) **ushiro (no)** back, rear

うそ **uso** lie; うそをつく **uso o tsuku** lie

うそ(の) **uso (no)** false, untrue; phony

うそつき **usotsuki** liar

うっ積した **usseki shita** pent-up

薄茶色 **usuchairo** buff; light brown

薄汚ない **usugitanai** dingy

薄暗い **usugurai** dim; obscure

薄い **usui** thin; light; weak; flimsy; 薄いピンク色 **usui pinku-iro** pale pink

薄く **usuku** thinly

薄める **usumeru** dilute

うすのろ(の) **usunoro (no)** dumb, stupid

薄っぺらい **usupperai** superficial; thin; flimsy

薄れる **usureru** abate; wane

歌 **uta** song

疑い **utagai** doubt; suspicion; reservation; 疑いのある **utagai no aru** suspected; 疑いをもっている **utagai o motte iru** be doubtful (*of person*)

疑い深い **utagaibukai** skeptical; suspicious

疑いもなく **utagai mo naku** unquestionably

疑いない **utagai nai** doubtless

疑いなく **utagai naku** distinctly, decidedly

疑う **utagau** question, doubt; suspect

疑う余地なく **utagau yochi naku** undoubtedly

疑わない **utagawanai** unquestioning

疑わしげ(な) **utagawashige (na)** questioning

疑わしげに **utagawashige ni** doubtfully

疑わしい **utagawashii** doubtful, dubious; questionable

うたた寝 **utatane** doze; nap; うたた寝をする **utatane o suru** doze; have a nap

歌う **utau** sing

うとうとする **utouto suru** doze off

打つ **utsu** hit; thrash; bat; bounce; strike (*of clock*)

撃つ **utsu** shoot

うつ病 **utsubyō** depression MED

美しい **utsukushii** beautiful

美しさ **utsukushi-sa** beauty

うつむく **utsumuku** hang one's head; look down

移り変わり **utsurikawari** change; transition

うつりやすい **utsuri-yasui** contagious

うつろ(な) **utsuro (na)** hollow; empty; vacant

うつる **utsuru** be infectious

移る **utsuru** move; transfer; change

映る **utsuru** be reflected; be shown (*on a screen*); suit

うつす **utsusu** transfer; transmit; pass on; 病気をうつす **byōki o utsusu** infect

映す **utsusu** project; reflect; mirror

写す **utsusu** take a photo; copy; trace; draw

訴え **uttae** lawsuit; complaint

訴える **uttaeru** complain of; bring an action against

うってつけ(の) **uttetsuke (no)** perfect, ideal

うっとりさせる **uttori saseru** charm

うっとりする **uttori suru** go into a trance

うっとりするよう(な) **uttori suru yō (na)** enchanting

うっとうしい **uttōshii** gloomy; oppressive

うわべだけ(の) **uwabe dake (no)** glib; hollow

上着 **uwagi** coat, jacket; top

うわ言を言う **uwagoto o iu** be delirious MED; rave

浮気(な) **uwaki (na)** unfaithful

浮気をする **uwaki o suru** fool around; have an affair

うわの空(の) **uwa no sora (no)** preoccupied; distracted

うわさ **uwasa** rumor

うわさ話 **uwasabanashi** gossip; うわさ話をする **uwasabanashi o suru** gossip

うわさで **uwasa de** by hearsay

上役 **uwayaku** superior; senior official

敬う **uyamau** respect; honor

うやうやしい **uyauyashii** reverent

右翼 **uyoku** right wing; right-winger

渦 **uzu** whirlpool; eddy; curl (*of smoke*)

うずく **uzuku** hurt; ache; smart; throb

渦巻 **uzumaki** whirlpool

渦巻く **uzumaku** whirl

うずら **uzura** quail

W

わ **wa** bundle; sheaf ◊ (*familiar softening or emphasizing particle used mostly by women*): 私が一緒に行くわ **watashi ga issho ni ikuwa** I'll come with you

は **wa** (*subject particle*): 私はアメリカ

人です **watashi wa Amerika-jin desu** I'm American

和 **wa** peace; harmony; sum

和... **wa...** Japanese(-style)

羽 **-wa** countword for birds and rabbits

輪 **wa** hoop, loop; link (*in chain*); ring, circle

わーっ **wā'** wow!

わび **wabi** apology

わびる **wabiru** apologize

わび寂び **wabisabi** *restrained quiet beauty of stark simplicity*

わびしい **wabishii** lonely; miserable

わだち **wadachi** rut (*in road*)

話題 **wadai** topic; subject

話題(の) **wadai (no)** in question ◊ topical

ワッフル **waffuru** waffle

和服 **wafuku** Japanese clothes (*traditional*)

和風(の) **wafū (no)** Japanese-style

我が **waga** my; our

わがまま(な) **wagamama (na)** selfish; willful

和菓子 **wagashi** Japanese candy and cakes

輪ゴム **wagomu** rubber band

ワゴン車 **wagon-sha** station wagon

ワイン **wain** wine

ワインリスト **wainrisuto** wine list

ワイパー **waipā** windshield wiper

わいろ **wairo** bribe; kickback

わいせつ(な) **waisetsu (na)** obscene, lewd; dirty, smutty

ワイシャツ **waishatsu** shirt

和歌 **waka** waka (*31-syllable poem*)

分かち合う **wakachiau** share

若鶏 **wakadori** chicken; broiler

若い **wakai** young

和解 **wakai** reconciliation

和解できない **wakai dekinai** irreconcilable

わかめ **wakame** seaweed

若者 **wakamono** youngster

わからない **wakaranai** not understand; not know

わからせる **wakaraseru** get through

別れ **wakare** farewell, parting

別れる **wakareru** break up, split up; leave; finish with

わかりにくい **wakarinikui** obscure, hard to understand

わかりやすい **wakariyasui** clear, lucid; illuminating

わかる **wakaru** understand; tell *the difference*; わかりません

わかりません **wakarimasen** I don't know; わかりました **wakarimashita** I see

沸かす **wakasu** boil; heat; excite

若々しい **wakawakashii** youthful

訳, わけ **wake** reason; cause; meaning; sense; どういうわけで**dō iu wake de** why?; そういうわけで **sō iu wake de** that's the reason why; そういうわけなら **sō iu wake nara** if that's the case; 心配しないわけにはいかない **shinpai shinai wake ni wa ikanai** I can't help worrying; わけのわからない **wake no wakaranai** puzzling

分け前 **wakemae** share, slice

分け目 **wakeme** part (*in hair*)

分ける **wakeru** divide, share; part, separate

わき **waki** side; わきへ入る **waki e hairu** turn off (*of car, driver*)

わき腹 **wakibara** flank; わき腹が痛む **wakibara ga itamu** have a stitch

わき道 **wakimichi** side street; わき道へそれる **wakimichi e soreru** digress

わき見する **wakimi suru** look away

わきに **waki ni** aside

わきの下 **waki no shita** armpit

ワックス **wakkusu** wax

沸く **waku** boil; be heated; be enthusiastic

枠 **waku** frame

ワクチン **wakuchin** vaccine

惑星 **wakusei** planet

ワークショップ **wāku-shoppu** workshop

ワークステーション **wāku-sutēshon** work station

わくわくさせる **wakuwaku saseru** thrilling

わくわくする **wakuwaku suru** exciting ◊ be thrilled

わめき声 **wamekigoe** shout; yell; roar

わめく **wameku** shout; howl; roar; rave

湾 **wan** bay; gulf

わな **wana** setup, trap; わなにかける **wana ni kakeru** frame, set up; trap

わに **wani** crocodile

ワンマン(な) **wanman (na)** dictatorial; one-man

ワンピース **wanpīsu** dress

ワンルームマンション **wanrūmu-manshon** studio apartment

わんわん **wanwan** doggie, bow-wow

和音 **waon** chord

ワープ **wāpu** timewarp

ワープロ **wāpuro** word processor

わら **wara** straw

笑い **warai** laugh; laughter

笑い声 **waraigoe** laughter

笑い事じゃない **waraigoto ja nai** it's no joke

笑いもの **waraimono** mockery, travesty; 笑いものになる **waraimono ni naru** make a fool of oneself

笑う **warau** laugh

笑わせる **warawaseru** amuse

割れ目 **wareme** crevice; split

我を忘れる **ware o wasureru** be beside oneself

割れる **wareru** break; break up; split

割れた **wareta** broken

我々 **wareware** we

割 **wari** rate; ratio; 10%; 二割 **niwari** 20%; 割に合わない **wari ni awanai** thankless; 割の合う **wari no au** remunerative

割合 **wariai** percentage; proportion; part

割り当て **wariate** quota

割り当てる **wariateru** allocate, allot, assign

割りばし **waribashi** disposable chopsticks

割引 **waribiki** discount

割引券 **waribiki-ken** coupon

割り引く **waribiku** discount

割り勘にする **warikan ni suru** go Dutch

割り切れる **warikireru** divisible

割り込む **warikomu** interrupt; cut in

割増料金 **warimashi-ryōkin** surcharge

わりに **wari ni** rather; somewhat

割り算 **warizan** division MATH

割る **waru** divide MATH; break; crack; split; chop

悪ふざけ **warufuzake** practical joke

悪賢い **warugashikoi** devious, cunning

悪賢さ **warugashiko-sa** cunning

悪気 **warugi** ill will; malice

悪口 **waruguchi** slander

悪い **warui** bad; evil

悪く **waruku** badly

悪くない **waruku nai** it's not bad ◊ fair, not bad

悪くなる **waruku naru** deteriorate, go downhill

ワルツ **warutsu** waltz

わさび **wasabi** Japanese horse radish

わし **washi** eagle

和紙 **washi** Japanese paper

ワシントン **Washinton** Washington

和室 **washitsu** Japanese room

和食 **washoku** Japanese cuisine

忘れ物 **wasuremono** something left behind; lost and found

わすれなぐさ **wasurenagusa** forget-me-not

忘れっぽい **wasureppoi** forgetful

忘れられない **wasurerarenai** memorable, unforgettable

忘れられる **wasurerareru** be forgotten, fall into oblivion

忘れられた **wasurerareta** neglected

忘れる **wasureru** forget; get over *lover etc*

綿 **wata** cotton

綿あめ **wata-ame** cotton candy

私 **watakushi** I (*polite*)

渡る **wataru** cross, go across

私 **watashi** I; me

私の **watashi no** ◊ mine

私達 **watashitachi** we; us

私達の **watashitachi no** our ◊ ours

渡す **watasu** give in, hand in

ワット **watto** watt

わっと泣き出す **watto nakidasu** burst into tears

わざと **wazato** deliberately, intentionally, on purpose

わざとらしい **wazatorashii** artificial; theatrical

わざわざ **wazawaza** expressly

わずか(な) **wazuka (na)** slender, slight; meager; miserly

わずかに **wazuka ni** remotely;

slightly

わずらわしい **wazurawashii** annoying

わずらわしさ **wazurawashi-sa** annoyance

ウェブページ **webu-pēji** web page

ウェブサイト **webu-saito** web site

ウェールズ **Wēruzu** Wales

ウォッカ **wokka** vodka

ウォークマン **wōkuman** personal stereo, Walkman®

ウォームアップする **wōmu-appu suru** warm up

ウォール街 **Wōru-gai** Wall Street

Y

や **ya** (*particle linking nouns used as examples*) and; or; 肉や魚を食べない **niku ya sakana o tabenai** I don't eat things like meat or fish

矢 **ya** arrow

やばい **yabai** dangerous; terrible

野蛮人 **yaban-jin** savage

野蛮(な) **yaban (na)** savage

やぶ医者 **yabuisha** quack

破れる **yabureru** be ripped; be broken; break down

敗れる **yabureru** lose; be defeated

破る **yaburu** break; tear up ◊ outrage

破ることのできない **yaburu koto no dekinai** unbreakable

家賃 **yachin** rent, rental

宿 **yado** inn; hotel

ヤード **yādo** yard (*measurement*)

宿屋 **yadoya** inn

野外(の) **yagai (no)** outdoor

やがて **yagate** before long; soon

やぎ **yagi** goat

やはり **yahari** after all; as expected; also

やじ **yaji** jeering

やじる **yajiru** boo; heckle

矢印 **yajirushi** arrow

やじ馬 **yajiuma** curious bystander; rubber-neck

やかましい **yakamashii** noisy; particular; strict

やかん **yakan** kettle

夜間 **yakan** night time

夜間フライト **yakan-furaito** night flight

夜間外出禁止令 **yakan-gaishutsu-kinshirei** curfew

夜間学校 **yakan-gakkō** night school

夜間勤務 **yakan-kinmu** night shift

やけど **yakedo** burn

やけどさせる **yakedo saseru** scald

やけどする **yakedo suru** get burned

焼け焦げ **yakekoge** burn

焼ける **yakeru** burn; roast (*of food*)

焼き網 **yakiami** grill; broiler (*on stove*)

焼き増し **yakimashi** additional print of a photo

やきもち **yakimochi** toasted rice cake; jealousy; やきもちをやく **yakimochi o yaku** be jealous

焼き肉 **yakiniku** grilled meat

夜勤する **yakin suru** work nights

焼きすぎる **yaki-sugiru** overdo *meat etc*

焼きすぎた **yaki-sugita** overdone *meat etc*

やきとり **yakitori** grilled chicken and vegetables on a skewer

焼き尽くす **yakitsukusu** burn down

やっかい者 **yakkai mono** menace, pest

やっかい(な) **yakkai (na)** troublesome; awkward; messy

薬局 **yakkyoku** drugstore; pharmacy

焼く **yaku** burn; get a tan; bake; fry; grill; roast; toast; broil

約 **yaku** in the region of, roughly

訳 **yaku** translation

役 **yaku** part (*in play, movie*); 役を割り当てる *yaku o wariateru* cast

薬品 **yakuhin** medicine; chemical

役員会 **yakuinkai** board (of directors)

役目 **yakume** role; duty

役人 **yakunin** public servant; bureaucrat

役に立たない **yaku ni tatanai** useless

役に立つ **yaku ni tatsu** be worthwhile; be helpful; pay; benefit ◊ helpful

役者 **yakusha** actor

役者になる **yakusha ni naru** go on the stage

役所 **yakusho** government office

役職 **yakushoku** managerial position

約束 **yakusoku** appointment, date; meeting; promise, pledge; 約束を守る *yakusoku o mamoru* keep a promise

約束する **yakusoku suru** promise; commit oneself

訳す **yakusu** translate

役立たず **yakutatazu** good-for-nothing

役立たず(の) **yakutatazu (no)** useless, worthless

役得 **yakutoku** perk (*of job*)

役割 **yakuwari** function, role

薬用(の) **yakuyō (no)** medicated; medicinal

やくざ **yakuza** yakuza, gangster

薬剤師 **yakuzaishi** druggist, pharmacist

野球 **yakyū** baseball; ball game; 野球のバット *yakyū no batto* baseball bat; 野球のボール *yakyū no bōru* baseball (*ball*)

野球帽 **yakyū-bō** baseball cap

野球場 **yakyū-jō** ballpark

野球選手 **yakyū-senshu** baseball player

山 **yama** hill; mountain; pile, mound, stack; guess; 山が当たった *yama ga atatta* my guess was right!; 山の多い *yama no ōi* mountainous

やまあらし **yama-arashi** porcupine

山歩き **yamaaruki** hike

山ほどの **yamahodo no** a pile of

山のような(な) **yama no yō (na)** mammoth, enormous

やましい **yamashii** remorseful; やましいところのない *yamashii tokoro no nai* clear *conscience*

やますそ **yamasuso** foothills

山分けする **yamawake suru** divide equally

やめる **yameru** drop, give up, abandon; stop

辞める **yameru** resign; quit

やめさせる **yamesaseru** stop, put a stop to

やみ **yami** darkness

やみ経済 **yamikeizai** black economy

やみ市場 **yamishijō** black market

病みつき(の) **yamitsuki (no)** compulsive

やむ **yamu** stop, let up; subside

やむを得ない **yamuoenai** unavoidable

やむを得ず **yamuoezu** unwillingly, reluctantly

柳 **yanagi** willow tree

屋根 **yane** roof

屋根裏 **yaneura** loft

屋根裏部屋 **yaneura-beya** attic, garret

ヤンキー **Yankī** Yank

八百長する **yaochō suru** fix *boxing match etc*

八百屋 **yaoya** greengrocer

やっぱり **yappari** after all; as expected; also

やれやれ **yareyare** thank God!

やり合う **yariau** compete; argue; haggle

やりがいのある **yarigai no aru** worthwhile

やり返す **yarikaesu** hit back

やり方 **yarikata** method; way

やりくりする **yarikuri suru** manage (*financially*); stretch *income*

やり直す **yarinaosu** brush up; go over

やりすぎ **yari-sugi** overdose; excess;

やりすぎだ **yari-sugi da** you went too far

やりすぎる **yari-sugiru** overdo, exaggerate; be over the top

やりたがる **yaritagaru** be enthusiastic to do

やり遂げる **yaritogeru** accomplish; pull off *deal etc*

やりとり **yaritori** give and take; exchange (*of letters*)

やる **yaru** play; do; give; ∨ fuck

やる気 **yaruki** drive, energy; やる気がわいて **yaruki ga waite** in a burst of energy; やる気にさせる **yaruki ni saseru** motivate; やる気をなくす **yaruki o nakusu** become demoralized

野菜 **yasai** vegetable

やさしい **yasashii** easy

優しい **yasashii** loving, affectionate, tender; gentle; soft, kind, lenient; gracious

やさしさ **yasashi-sa** ease

優しさ **yasashi-sa** tenderness

野生動物 **yasei-dōbutsu** wildlife

野生(の) **yasei (no)** wild

やせこけた **yasekoketa** gaunt; haggard; sunken

やせ衰える **yaseotoroeru** waste away

やせっぽち(の) **yaseppochi (no)** puny

やせる **yaseru** get thin; lose weight

やせた **yaseta** lanky; skinny

やし **yashi** palm (tree)

野心 **yashin** ambition *pej*

養う **yashinau** support, provide for, keep

野心的(な) **yashinteki (na)** ambitious

安い **yasui** cheap, inexpensive; downmarket; low *salary, price*; weak *currency*

やすい **-yasui** easy to; 使いやすい **tsukai-yasui** easy to use, user-friendly

休まず **yasumazu** without a letup

休み **yasumi** break, rest; vacation; 休みである **yasumi de aru** be off

休み時間 **yasumi-jikan** recess (*at school*)

休みなく **yasumi naku** without respite

休みなしで **yasumi nashi de** without a break

休む **yasumu** rest

安物 **yasumono** cheap item

安っぽい **yasuppoi** cheap, tacky; sleazy

やすり **yasuri** file; やすりをかける **yasuri o kakeru** sand; file

安売り(の) **yasuuri (no)** cut-price

安売りされている **yasuuri sarete iru** be on sale (*at reduced prices*)

やすやすと **yasuyasu to** with ease

屋台 **yatai** street stall

やたら(に) **yatara (ni)** at random; indiscriminately; recklessly; extremely; やたら忙しい **yatara isogashii** hectic; やたらかわいがる **yatara kawaigaru** dote on

野党 **yatō** opposition POL

雇う **yatou** employ, hire, take on

雇われている **yatowarete iru** be on the payroll

やつ **yatsu** fellow, guy

やつれた **yatsureta** careworn, haggard

やっていく **yatte iku** get along, progress

やって来る **yatte kuru** come along, turn up

やってみる **yatte miru** have a try at; やってみよう **yatte miyō** let's risk it

やっと **yatto** finally; barely

やっとこ **yattoko** pincers

やっつける **yattsukeru** defeat; finish; criticize

和らげる **yawarageru** deaden; cushion, soften; defuse; ease, relieve; soothe

和らぐ **yawaragu** soften; ease off, moderate

柔らかい **yawarakai** muted, subdued; soft; tender

柔らかくなる **yawarakaku naru** soften

柔らか(な) **yawaraka na** soft; tender; mellow

柔らかさ **yawaraka-sa** tenderness

やや **yaya** rather; somewhat

ややこしい **yayakoshii** tricky

よ **yo** (*exclamatory particle*): 行こうよ *ikō yo* come on, let's go!; 何をしてるんだよ *nani o shiterun da yo* what the hell are you doing?

夜 **yo** night

世 **yo** world; 世が世なら *yo ga yo nara* if times hadn't changed

よう **-yō** let's; 食べよう *tabeyō* let's eat

用 **yō** business; use; service

洋... **yō...** Western(-style)

夜明け **yoake** dawn, daybreak

夜遊び **yoasobi** nightlife

曜日 **yōbi** day of the week

呼び出し **yobidashi** call; summon

呼び出す **yobidasu** page (*with pager*); ask for

呼び入れる **yobiireru** call in, summon

呼びかける **yobikakeru** call out; call out to

予備校 **yobikō** prep school

呼び戻す **yobimodosu** call back, recall

呼び物 **yobimono** special attraction, draw

予備(の) **yobi (no)** auxiliary; spare

呼び起こす **yobiokosu** arouse; evoke, conjure up; inspire

予備選挙 **yobi-senkyo** primary POL

呼び捨て **yobisute** *using a person's name without courtesy titles*

予備的(な) **yobiteki (na)** preliminary

予防 **yobō** prevention

容ぼう **yōbō** looks; features

要望 **yōbō** request; requirement

予防注射する **yobō-chūsha suru** vaccinate

予防(の) **yobō (no)** preventive

予防接種 **yobō-sesshu** inoculation, vaccination

予防接種する **yobō-sesshu suru** inoculate

予防する **yobō suru** prevent

呼ぶ **yobu** call, shout; summon

養分 **yōbun** nutrient

余分(な) **yobun (na)** extra; spare; redundant; 余分に五個あります *yobun ni goko arimasu* there are 5 to spare

余分(の) **yobun (no)** extra

余地 **yochi** room, scope

予知 **yochi** prediction; prognosis

幼稚園 **yōchien** kindergarten

よちよち歩く **yochiyochi aruku** waddle; toddle

幼虫 **yōchū** larva

ようだ **yō da → yō na**

容態 **yōdai** condition MED

余談 **yodan** padding (*in speech etc*)

よだれ **yodare** dribble; よだれが出ている *yodare ga dete iru* my mouth is watering; よだれを垂らす *yodare o tarasu* dribble; slobber

よだれ掛け **yodarekake** bib

よだれの出そう(な) **yodare no desō (na)** mouthwatering

よどんだ **yodonda** stagnant; stale

夜更かしする **yofukashi suru** stay up late

溶液 **yōeki** solution, mixture

洋服ダンス **yōfuku-dansu** wardrobe

洋服一式 **yōfuku-isshiki** wardrobe (*clothes*)

洋服掛け **yōfuku-kake** hanger; hook

洋服屋 **yōfuku-ya** tailor

洋風(の) **yōfū (no)** Western

洋画 **yōga** Western movie

溶岩流 **yōganryū** lava flow

洋菓子 **yōgashi** cake; pastries

予言 **yogen** prediction, prophecy

予言する **yogen suru** foretell, predict; prophesy

容疑 **yōgi** suspicion; charge LAW; 容疑を晴らす *yōgi o harasu* clear, acquit

容疑者 **yōgi-sha** suspect

用語 **yōgo** language; term

擁護 **yōgo** defense; protection

汚れ **yogore** dirt, filth

汚れる **yogoreru** stain

擁護者 **yōgo-sha** champion (*of cause*)

養護施設 **yōgo-shisetsu** orphanage

用語集 **yōgoshū** glossary; vocabulary

汚す **yogosu** dirty, soil, stain; smudge

擁護する **yōgo suru** defend, champion *cause*

夜ごとに **yogoto ni** nightly

用具 **yōgu** equipment; materials; utensil

ヨーグルト **yōguruto** yoghurt

余白 **yohaku** blank, space; margin

よう兵 **yōhei** mercenary *(soldier)*

予報 **yohō** weather forecast

余程 **yohodo** very much; almost

予報する **yohō suru** forecast

よい, 良い, 善い **yoi** good; nice

酔い **yoi** drunkenness; 酔いが覚める **yoi ga sameru** sober up; 酔いがすぐ回る **yoi ga sugu mawaru** heady *drink*

用意 **yōi** preparations

養育権 **yōikuken** custody

要因 **yōin** main cause; primary factor

容易(な) **yōi (na)** simple; easy

容易に **yōi ni** easily, with ease

容易さ **yōi-sa** ease

用意する **yōi suru** prepare; arrange

幼児 **yōji** infant

用事 **yōji** engagement; business

用心 **yōjin** caution; precaution

要人 **yōjin** very important person, VIP

用心棒 **yōjinbō** bodyguard; bouncer

用心深い **yōjin-bukai** cautious; alert; wary

用心のため(の) **yōjin no tame (no)** precautionary

用心する **yōjin suru** be careful; be wary of; guard against

よじれ **yojire** kink; twist

よじれる **yojireru** be twisted

余剰 **yojō** surplus

余剰(の) **yojō (no)** surplus

余暇 **yoka** leisure time; spare time

溶解した **yōkai shita** molten

予感 **yokan** foreboding, premonition; hunch

よかれと思ってする **yokare to omotte suru** mean well

余計(な) **yokei (na)** unnecessary; superfluous

用件 **yōken** business

よければ **yokereba** if you like

よける **yokeru** avoid; shun; dodge

予期 **yoki** expectation; anticipation

容器 **yōki** container

預金 **yokin** deposit

陽気(な) **yōki (na)** cheerful; lively

預金する **yokin suru** deposit; ...銀行に預金する *... ginkō ni yokin suru* bank with

預金残高 **yokin-zandaka** bank balance

予期する **yoki suru** expect; anticipate

欲求不満 **yokkyū-fuman** frustration

欲求不満にさせる **yokkyū-fuman ni saseru** frustrate

欲求不満(の) **yokkyū-fuman (no)** frustrated

横 **yoko** side; width

横笛 **yokobue** flute

横書き **yokogaki** write horizontally

横顔 **yokogao** profile *(of face)*

横切る **yokogiru** cross; go across

横切って **yokogitte** through, across

横浜 **Yokohama** Yokohama

予告 **yokoku** warning

予告編 **yokokuhen** preview *(of movie)*

横道にそれる **yokomichi ni soreru** get sidetracked; wander *(of attention)*

横向きに **yokomuki ni** sideways

横になる **yoko ni naru** lie; lie down

溶鉱炉 **yōkōro** blast furnace

横綱 **yokozuna** grand champion

よく **yoku** often; well

欲 **yoku** appetite; greed

翌朝 **yokuasa** the following morning

抑圧する **yokuatsu suru** repress; stifle; oppress

欲張り **yokubari** greedy person

欲張る **yokubaru** be greedy

欲望 **yokubō** desire, lust

翌日 **yokujitsu** the following day

良くない **yoku nai** poor; unfavorable; wrong

良くなる **yoku naru** improve, pick up; look up

翌年 **yokunen** the following year

抑制 **yokusei** control; restraint; suppression

抑制されない **yokusei sarenai** unrestrained

抑制されている **yokusei sarete iru** inhibited

抑制した **yokusei shita** muted

抑制する **yokusei suru** curb; inhibit

抑止力 **yokushiryoku** deterrent

浴室 **yokushitsu** bathroom

翌週 **yokushū** the following week

浴槽 **yokusō** bathtub

欲得ずくの **yokutokuzuku no** selfish; mercenary *attitude*

抑揚 **yokuyō** intonation; inflection

要求 **yōkyū** demand; call; requirement; 要求を満たす **yōkyū o mitasu** cater for

要求者 **yōkyū-sha** claimant

要求する **yōkyū suru** demand; insist on

嫁 **yome** daughter-in-law

読める **yomeru** readable

読み **yomi** reading (*of a character*)

読み違える **yomichigaeru** misread

よみがえる **yomigaeru** come back to life; revive

読み書きができる **yomikaki ga dekiru** be literate

読み方 **yomikata** reading; pronunciation

読み物 **yomimono** reading matter

読みにくい **yominikui** difficult to read; illegible

読み取る **yomitoru** read *diskette*

読みやすい **yomiyasui** easy to read; legible

よもぎ **yomogi** mugwort

読む **yomu** read

四 **yon** four

よう(な) **yō (na)**: ...のよう(な) **... no yō (na)** like; such as; ...のようである **... no yō de aru** be like, look like; seem like; 彼は来ないようだ **kare wa konai yō da** it looks like he's not coming

夜中 **yonaka** middle of the night; small hours

幼年時代 **yōnen-jidai** infancy

...ように **... yō ni** as, like; ...のように **... no yō ni** as though; ...のように見える **... no yō ni mieru** appear; seem

容認できる **yōnin dekiru** acceptable

容認する **yōnin suru** accept; allow; condone

四十 **yonjū** forty

世の中 **yo no naka** the world; society

酔っ払い **yopparai** drunk

酔っ払い(の) **yopparai (no)** drunken

酔っ払った **yopparatta** drunk

酔っ払う **yopparau** get drunk

よれば **yoreba** according to

より **yori** from; than; 五月一日より **gogatsu tsuitachi yori** effective as from May 1; ...より金がある **... yori kane ga aru** be better off than; ...より前に **... yori mae ni** prior to; Y よりXのほうが好きである **Y yori X no hō ga suki de aru** prefer X to Y

より好みする **yorigonomi suru** pick and choose

寄りかかる **yorikakaru** lean against; rely on

寄り目(の) **yorime (no)** cross-eyed

寄り道する **yorimichi suru** stop over; drop in

寄り添う **yorisou** snuggle up to

より優れた **yori sugureta** superior, better

より分ける **yoriwakeru** classify; sort out

よろいかぶと **yoroikabuto** armor

養老院 **yōrōin** rest home

喜ばす **yorokobasu** please

喜び **yorokobi** pleasure; joy

喜んだ **yorokonda** pleased

喜んで **yorokonde** gladly, willingly

喜んでいる **yorokonde iru** be delighted

よろめく **yoromeku** lurch, stagger; wobble; totter

ヨーロッパ **Yōroppa** Europe

ヨーロッパ人 **Yōroppa-jin** European

ヨーロッパ(の) **Yōroppa (no)** European

よろしい **yoroshii** good; OK

よろしく **yoroshiku** please do; はじめましてどうぞよろしくお願いします

hajimemashite, dōzo yoroshiku onegai shimasu hello, how do you do?; 彼女によろしく kanojo ni yoroshiku give her my love; give her my best wishes

よろよろする yoroyoro suru stagger; totter

よる yoru according to ◊ be based on; be relative to

夜 yoru night

夜中 yorujū the whole night ◊ in the night

要領 yōryō main point; knack; 要領がいい yōryō ga ii shrewd; clever; 要領が悪い yōryō ga warui awkward; clumsy

容量 yōryō volume, quantity

要さい yōsai fortress

予算 yosan budget; 予算がある yosan ga aru be on a budget; 予算にいれる yosan ni ireru budget for; 予算を立てる yosan o tateru budget

寄せ集め yoseatsume mixture; jumble; medley

寄せ集める yoseatsumeru gather up; put together

よう精 (妖精) yōsei fairy

要請 yōsei request

陽性(の) yōsei (no) positive medical test

養成する yōsei suru train; educate

容積 yōseki cubic capacity, volume

溶接工 yōsetsu-kō welder

溶接する yōsetsu suru weld

容赦ない yōsha nai remorseless, unrelenting; cut-throat

養子 yōshi adopted child; 養子にする yōshi ni suru adopt

用紙 yōshi form (document)

善し悪し yoshiashi good and bad

様式 yōshiki mode, form; style, method

洋室 yōshitsu Western-style room

洋書 yōsho book written in a Western language

洋食 yōshoku Western cuisine

養殖 yōshoku cultivation; breeding

予習する yoshū suru prepare one's lessons

よそ yoso another place; another

person; out-group

予想 yosō anticipation, expectation; forecast; 予想のつく yosō no tsuku predictable

ヨウ素 yōso iodine

要素 yōso element; factor; ingredient

予想できない yosō dekinai unpredictable

予測できる yosoku dekiru foreseeable

予想する yosō suru anticipate, expect; envisage

よそよそしい yosoyososhii cold; distant

様子 yōsu appearance; aspect; state of affairs; 様子を聞く yōsu o kiku ask after

用水路 yōsuiro irrigation canal

要する yō suru need; cost; entail

要するに yō suru ni in short; in a nutshell

世捨て人 yosutebito hermit

よたよた歩く yotayota aruku hobble; totter; waddle

予定 yotei arrangement, plan; 予定で一杯になる yotei de ippai ni naru be booked up; 予定がある yotei ga aru have on, have planned

予定である yotei de aru intend to; plan on

予定どおりである yotei dōri de aru be on schedule

予定されている yotei sarete iru on, be scheduled

予定説 yoteisetsu predestination

予定する yotei suru intend; plan

要点 yōten main point; gist

与党 yotō ruling party

用途 yōto use; application

腰痛 yōtsū lumbago

四つ足(の) yotsuashi (no) quadruped

四つ子 yotsugo quadruplets

四つ角 yotsukado intersection

酔った yotta intoxicated

よって yotte: ...によって ...ni yotte with; by; by means of; according to; depending on

ヨット yotto yacht, sailboat

ヨットマン **yottoman** yachtsman, sailor

酔う **you** get drunk; get sick; 飛行機に酔う *hikōki ni you* get airsick

弱い **yowai** delicate *health*; floppy, weak; light

弱い者いじめ **yowaimono-ijime** bullying

弱気(な) **yowaki (na)** timid; weak-minded

弱気になる **yowaki ni naru** weaken

弱くなる **yowaku naru** weaken

弱くする **yowaku suru** weaken; turn down *heating*

弱まる **yowamaru** die down

弱める **yowameru** undermine

弱虫 **yowamushi** chicken, wimp; weakling

弱らせる **yowaraseru** sap

弱る **yowaru** weaken; flag, tire

弱さ **yowa-sa** weakness; frailty

酔わせる **yowaseru** make drunk

弱った **yowatta** impaired; infirm

弱っている **yowatte iru** be weak

弱々しい **yowayowashii** feeble

予約 **yoyaku** reservation; advance booking; appointment; 予約で一杯になる *yoyaku de ippai ni naru* be booked up

ようやく **yōyaku** finally; just, barely

要約 **yōyaku** summary, précis, résumé

予約帳 **yoyakuchō** appointments diary

予約係 **yoyaku-gakari** booking clerk

予約(の) **yoyaku (no)** reserved

予約する **yoyaku suru** book, reserve

要約する **yōyaku suru** summarize, sum up; compress *information*; abridge

余裕 **yoyū** leeway; margin; 余裕を持つ *yoyū o motsu* allow for; calculate for; 余裕がない *yoyū ga nai* have none to spare; not be able to afford to

湯 **yu** hot water

優 **yū** grade A; excellent

油圧式(の) **yuatsushiki (no)** hydraulic

ゆうべ **yūbe** last night

雄弁 **yūben** eloquence

雄弁家 **yūben-ka** speaker, orator

雄弁(な) **yūben (na)** eloquent

指 **yubi** finger

郵便 **yūbin** mail

優美(な) **yūbi (na)** dainty; exquisite; graceful

郵便番号 **yūbin-bangō** zip code

郵便振替為替 **yūbin-furikae-kawase** giro

指人形 **yubiningyō** finger puppet

郵便為替 **yūbin-kawase** money order

郵便局 **yūbinkyoku** post office

郵便(の) **yūbin (no)** postal

郵便受け **yūbin'uke** mailbox

指貫 **yubinuki** thimble

郵便屋さん **yūbin'ya-san** mailman

優美さ **yūbi-sa** grace

指先 **yubisaki** fingertip

指さす **yubisasu** point at

指輪 **yubiwa** ring

有望(な) **yūbō (na)** hopeful; promising

夕立 **yūdachi** evening shower

雄大(な) **yūdai (na)** grand; epic

雄大さ **yūdai-sa** grandeur

油断する **yudan suru** be careless; be off guard

ユダヤ人 **Yudaya-jin** Jew

ユダヤ(の) **Yudaya (no)** Jewish

ゆでる **yuderu** boil; poach

ゆで卵 **yude-tamago** boiled egg

湯豆腐 **yudōfu** hot bean curd

有毒(な) **yūdoku (na)** poisonous, toxic

有益(な) **yūeki (na)** informative; instructive; beneficial; salutary

遊園地 **yūenchi** amusement park, funfair

裕福(な) **yūfuku (na)** wealthy, well-off

有害(な) **yūgai (na)** detrimental, harmful

ゆがめる **yugameru** distort, warp

ゆがむ **yugamu** buckle; warp

優雅(な) **yūga (na)** elegant; gracious

優雅さ **yūga-sa** elegance, style

夕方 **yūgata** evening

湯気 **yuge** steam

融合 **yūgō** fusion

夕暮れ **yūgure** twilight

夕飯 **yūhan** dinner; evening meal

夕日 **yūhi** setting sun

遊歩道 **yūhodō** promenade; boardwalk

遺言 **yuigon** will LAW; 遺言で譲る *yuigon de yuzuru* bequeath

唯一(の) **yuiitsu (no)** exclusive, sole; only

友人 **yūjin** friend

友情 **yūjō** friendship

優柔不断 **yūjū-fudan** indecisiveness

優柔不断(の) **yūjū-fudan (no)** indecisive; wishy-washy

床 **yuka** floor (*of room*)

誘拐 **yūkai** kidnapping

誘拐犯 **yūkai-han** kidnapper

愉快(な) **yukai (na)** pleasant

誘拐する **yūkai suru** abduct; kidnap, snatch

床板 **yukaita** floorboard

夕刊 **yūkan** evening paper

勇敢(な) **yūkan (na)** brave, valiant; intrepid

勇敢さ **yūkan-sa** bravery

有価証券 **yūka-shōken** securities

浴衣 **yukata** summer kimono

有権者 **yūken-sha** elector, voter; electorate

輸血 **yuketsu** blood transfusion

雪 **yuki** snow; 雪が降る *yuki ga furu* snow

行き **yuki** going to; bound for; …行きの列車 *…yuki no ressha* a train for

勇気 **yūki** courage; nerve; 勇気のある *yūki no aru* courageous

雪玉 **yukidama** snowball

雪だるま **yukidaruma** snowman

有機肥料 **yūki-hiryō** organic fertilizer

勇気を出す **yūki o dasu** pluck up courage

ゆっくり **yukkuri** slowly; at leisure; ゆっくり歩く *yukkuri aruku* stroll; ゆっくり考える *yukkuri kangaeru* reflect, think; sleep on

ゆっくりした **yukkuri shita** easy

有効期限 **yūkō-kigen** expiry date; 有効期限が切れる *yūkō-kigen ga kireru* expire

有効(な) **yūkō (na)** valid

有効にする **yūkō ni suru** validate

有効性 **yūkōsei** validity

友好的(な) **yūkōteki (na)** friendly

行方不明である **yukue-fumei de aru** be missing

行方不明(の) **yukue-fumei (no)** missing

油膜 **yumaku** oil slick

夢 **yume** dream, ambition; 夢が実現する *yume ga jitsugen suru* a dream come true; 夢を見る *yume o miru* have a dream

有名人 **yūmei-jin** celebrity, personality

有名(な) **yūmei (na)** famous, well-known

有名になる **yūmei ni naru** make a name for oneself

夢見る **yumemiru** daydream

夢見るよう(な) **yumemiru yō (na)** dreamy

夢にも思わない **yume ni mo omowanai** undreamt-of

夢のよう(な) **yume no yō (na)** dream *house etc*

夢うつつ **yumeutsutsu** trance; *state between sleep and wakefulness*

弓 **yumi** bow MUS

ユーモア **yūmoa** humor, wit; ユーモアのある *yūmoa no aru* be witty; ユーモアのセンス *yūmoa no sensu* sense of humor

ユーモラス(な) **yūmorasu (na)** humorous

ユニフォーム **yunifōmu** uniform

ユニーク(な) **yunīku (na)** unique

ユニット **yunitto** module, unit

ユニット式(の) **yunitto-shiki (no)** modular

ゆのみ **yunomi** Japanese tea cup

有能(な) **yūnō (na)** able, skillful; capable

輸入 **yunyū** import

輸入業者 **yunyū-gyōsha** importer

輸入する **yunyū suru** import

揺らぐ **yuragu** waver; flicker; swing; shake

由来する **yurai suru** be derived from

揺れ **yure** shake; motion; swing; tremor

幽霊 **yūrei** ghost

揺れる **yureru** sway; rock; shake, shudder, quake; quiver; swing; wag (*of tail*)

揺れ動く **yure ugoku** rock

ゆり **yuri** lily

揺りいす **yuriisu** rocking chair

揺りかご **yurikago** cradle

有利(な) **yūri (na)** advantageous

揺り動かす **yuri ugokasu** rock

ユーロ **yūro** euro FIN

揺るがす **yurugasu** shake; shock; undermine

緩い **yurui** loose, slack; runny

緩く **yuruku** loosely

緩める **yurumeru** ease off; loosen; relax; slacken

許されない **yurusarenai** inexcusable

許される **yurusareru** permissible; 許されていない **yurusarete inai** it's not allowed

許せない **yurusenai** unforgivable

許し **yurushi** forgiveness

許しがたい **yurushigatai** outrageous

許す **yurusu** allow, permit; excuse, forgive, pardon

有料 **yūryō** charge; fee; toll

有料道路 **yūryō-dōro** toll road

優良株 **yūryō-kabu** blue chip; gilts

有料高速道路 **yūryō-kōsoku-dōro** turnpike

有力(な) **yūryoku (na)** important; leading; powerful; strong

優良(な) **yūryō (na)** high-grade

揺さぶる **yusaburu** shake; jolt; sway

油井 **yusei** oil well

優勢 **yūsei** dominance; supremacy

優勢(な) **yūsei (na)** superior; dominant

優性(の) **yūsei (no)** dominant

優先事項 **yūsen-jikō** priority

優先権 **yūsen-ken** right of way

優先(の) **yūsen (no)** preferential

優先される **yūsen sareru** give priority to; take precedence

優先する **yūsen suru** have priority

融資する **yūshi suru** finance

有刺鉄線 **yūshi-tessen** barbed wire

夕食 **yūshoku** dinner, supper

有色人種(の) **yūshoku-jinshu (no)** non-white; colored

優勝する **yūshō suru** win; be victorious

優秀(な) **yūshū (na)** brilliant, distinguished

輸出 **yushutsu** export

輸出業者 **yushutsu-gyōsha** exporter

輸出品 **yushutsuhin** export (*product*)

輸出禁止 **yushutsu-kinshi** export ban; embargo

輸出する **yushutsu suru** export

輸送 **yusō** transport

輸送貨物 **yusō-kamotsu** consignment

輸送機関 **yusō-kikan** (means of) transportation

郵送料 **yūsōryō** postage

郵送先名簿 **yūsōsaki-meibo** mailing list

郵送する **yūsō suru** mail; transport

ゆすぐ **yusugu** rinse

ユースホステル **yūsu-hosuteru** youth hostel

ゆすり **yusuri** blackmail, extortion

ゆする **yusuru** blackmail; extort; shake

豊か(な) **yutaka (na)** affluent; lavish; rich

豊かにする **yutaka ni suru** enrich

Uターン **yū-tān** U-turn

ゆとり **yutori** room; space; clearance

優等生 **yūtōsei** honor student

ゆったりした **yuttari shita** leisurely; loose, roomy *clothes*

憂うつ **yūutsu** gloom, melancholy

憂うつである **yūutsu de aru** be down, be depressed

憂うつ(な) **yūutsu (na)** depressed; dismal, gloomy; depressing

誘惑 **yūwaku** lure; seduction; temptation; 誘惑に負ける **yūwaku ni makeru** succumb to temptation

誘惑する **yūwaku suru** seduce; tempt

ゆうゆうと **yūyū to** calmly; in a relaxed way; easily

有罪 **yūzai** guilt LAW

有罪判決 **yūzai-hanketsu** conviction LAW; 有罪判決を下す *yūzai-hanketsu o kudasu* convict

有罪にする **yūzai ni suru** incriminate

有罪(の) **yūzai (no)** guilty LAW

ゆず **yuzu** yuzu (*small citrus fruit*)

融通の利かない **yūzū no kikanai** inflexible, rigid

融通の利く **yūzū no kiku** adaptable, flexible

譲る **yuzuru** yield, give way; transfer; sell

Z

ザブンという音 **zabun to iu oto** splash (*noise*)

ざぶとん **zabuton** (floor) cushion

座談会 **zadankai** meeting; round-table discussion

罪悪感 **zaiakukan** feelings of guilt

財閥 **zaibatsu** financial conglomerate

財団 **zaidan** foundation (*organization*)

在学する **zaigaku suru** be in school; attend school

財宝 **zaihō** treasure

在住 **zaijū** residence, stay

在庫 **zaiko** stock; 在庫がある/ない *zaiko ga aru / nai* be in / out of stock

在庫品 **zaikohin** supplies

材木 **zaimoku** lumber, timber

罪人 **zainin** sinner

材料 **zairyō** ingredient

在留許可 **zairyū-kyoka** residence permit

財産 **zaisan** assets; estate; wealth; means (*financial*)

財政 **zaisei** finance

財政上(の) **zaiseijō (no)** financial

在籍する **zaiseki suru** be enrolled; be registered

在席する **zaiseki suru** be in one's own seat; be at one's desk

在宅勤務する **zaitaku-kinmu suru** work from home

在宅する **zaitaku suru** be at home

雑貨 **zakka** sundries

座骨神経痛 **zakotsu-shinkeitsū** sciatica

ざくざく音を立てる **zakuzaku oto o tateru** crunch

残高 **zandaka** balance (*of bank account*)

残がい **zangai** debris, wreckage; wreck

ざんげする **zange suru** confess

ざんごう **zangō** trench

残虐行為 **zangyaku-kōi** atrocity

残業 **zangyō** overtime

残酷 **zankoku** cruelty

残酷(な) **zankoku (na)** cruel; savage, vicious

残酷に **zankoku ni** brutally

残念 **zannen** hard luck!; what a pity!; what a shame!

残念(な) **zannen (na)** regrettable; sorry

残念ながら **zannen-nagara** regrettably, unfortunately; 残念ながらそう思います *zannen-nagara sō omoimasu* I'm afraid so

残念なことに **zannen na koto ni** sadly, regrettably

残念に思う **zannen ni omou** feel bad about

残忍(な) **zannin (na)** brutal, savage

残忍さ **zannin-sa** brutality

残留物 **zanryūbutsu** residue

雑費 **zappi** incidental expenses

ざらざらした **zarazara shita** rough; gritty; sandy

ざりがに **zarigani** crayfish

ざるをえない **-zaru o enai** cannot help but; have to

座席 **zaseki** seat

ざ折させる **zasetsu saseru** defeat; frustrate *plans*

ざ折する **zasetsu suru** fall through

座礁する **zashō suru** strand

雑誌 **zasshi** magazine; journal, periodical

雑誌売り場 **zasshi uriba** bookstall

雑種 **zasshu** hybrid; mongrel

雑草 **zassō** weed

雑談 **zatsudan** chat

雑(な) **zatsu (na)** careless; scrappy

雑音 **zatsuon** noise, interference

雑用 **zatsuyō** chores

雑然とした **zatsuzen to shita** jumbled; confused

雑多(な) **zatta (na)** miscellaneous; unsorted

ざっと **zatto** briefly; ざっと目を通す **zatto me o tōsu** skim through, scan

雑踏 **zattō** hustle and bustle

座薬 **zayaku** suppository

座右の銘 **zayū no mei** motto

座禅 **zazen** Zen meditation

ぜ **ze** (*familiar exclamatory particle used mostly by men*): やろうぜ **yarō ze** let's do it!

ぜひ **zehi** by all means; ぜひどうぞ **zehi dōzo** by all means, of course

税 **zei** duty (*on goods*)

税関 **zeikan** customs

税関審査 **zeikan-shinsa** customs inspection

税金 **zeikin** tax; taxation; 税金を払う **zeikin o harau** pay a tax

税金を加えて **zeikin o kuwaete** plus tax

税引き後 **zeibikigo** after tax

税込み **zeikomi** including tax

税務査察官 **zeimu-sasatsukan** tax inspector

税務署 **zeimusho** tax office

税抜き(の) **zeinuki (no)** net *price*

ぜいたく **zeitaku** extravagance; luxury

ぜいたく(な) **zeitaku (na)** luxurious

ゼイゼイ言う **zeizei iu** wheeze

絶好(の) **zekkō (no)** ideal; perfect

絶交する **zekkō suru** drop; sever relations

絶叫する **zekkyō suru** scream; shout; exclaim

禅 **Zen** Zen

善 **zen** virtue; good

全…**zen…** (*prefix*) all, the whole; 全国 *zenkoku* the whole country

前…**zen…** (*prefix*) former; previous; ex-

善悪 **zen'aku** good and evil

全部 **zenbu** all; everything ◊ fully; 全部払う *zenbu harau* pay in full; 全部飲む *zenbu nomu* drink up

前部 **zenbu** front

全部で **zenbu de** altogether, in all

全部(の) **zenbu (no)** complete; overall

前置詞 **zenchishi** preposition

前代未聞(の) **zendaimimon (no)** unheard-of

前衛的(な) **zen'eiteki (na)** avant-garde; futuristic

前夫 **zenfu** ex (*former husband*)

前言を撤回する **zengen o tekkai suru** backpedal *fig*

前後 **zengo** around; about; before and after; back and forth

前半 **zenhan** first half

善意 **zen'i** goodwill

全員 **zen'in** everybody; all the members

善意(の) **zen'i (no)** well-meaning

前日 **zenjitsu** the previous day

前科 **zenka** criminal record

全会一致である **zenkai itchi de aru** be unanimous on

全快する **zenkai suru** recover completely

前景 **zenkei** foreground

前期 **zenki** first semester

全国 **zenkoku** entire country

全国的(な) **zenkokuteki (na)** nationwide

全面的(な) **zenmenteki (na)** sweeping

全面的に **zenmenteki ni** overall; entirely

全滅させる **zenmetsu saseru** wipe out, destroy, kill

全滅する **zenmetsu suru** be

completely destroyed

前任者 **zennin-sha** predecessor (*in job*)

全般的(な) **zenpanteki (na)** overall; general

前方へ **zenpō e** onward

前例のない **zenrei no nai** unprecedented

全輪駆動 **zenrin-kudō** all-wheel drive

前輪駆動 **zenrin-kudō** front-wheel drive

前略 **zenryaku** hi there (*at start of informal letters*)

全力 **zenryoku** with all one's might; 全力で走る **zenryoku de hashiru** they pelted along the road

全力疾走 **zenryoku-shissō** sprint, race

前菜 **zensai** appetizer; starter

前妻 **zensai** ex (*former wife*)

全世界 **zensekai** entire world

全世界的(な) **zensekaiteki (na)** global, worldwide

前線 **zensen** weather front

前者 **zensha** the former

全身 **zenshin** the whole body; all over

全身(の) **zenshin (no)** full-length

前進する **zenshin suru** advance

全焼する **zenshō suru** burn down

禅宗 **Zenshū** Zen Buddhism

ぜんそく **zensoku** asthma

全速力で **zensokuryoku de** at full speed; flat out *work, run, drive*

全体 **zentai** whole; 町全体 **machi-zentai** the whole town

全体(の) **zentai (no)** entire, whole

全体主義(の) **zentai-shugi (no)** totalitarian

全体的(な) **zentaiteki (na)** general, widespread; global

全体として **zentai to shite** on the whole

前提 **zentei** premise; presupposition; prerequisite

前提条件 **zentei-jōken** precondition

前途有望(な) **zento-yūbō (na)** promising

前夜 **zen'ya** eve

全然 **zenzen**: 全然…ではない **zenzen… de wa nai** not at all; anything but; 全然かまいません **zenzen kamaimasen** it's no bother; 全然思い当たりませんか **zenzen omoiatarimasen ka** have you any idea at all?

絶版で **zeppan de** out of print

ゼリー **zerī** jelly

ゼロ **zero** zero; ゼロから始める **zero kara hajimeru** start from scratch

ゼロエミッション **zero-emisshon** zero emission

ゼロ成長 **zero-seichō** zero growth

絶頂 **zetchō** pinnacle

絶望 **zetsubō** despair

絶望して **zetsubō shite** in despair

絶望する **zetsubō suru** despair; despair of

絶望的(な) **zetsubōteki (na)** desperate, hopeless

絶縁 **zetsuen** breaking off relations; insulation ELEC

絶縁する **zetsuen suru** break off relations; insulate ELEC

絶縁体 **zetsuentai** insulation

絶縁テープ **zetsuen-tēpu** friction tape

絶滅 **zetsumetsu** extinction

絶滅した **zetsumetsu shita** extinct

絶滅する **zetsumetsu suru** die out; exterminate

絶対 **zettai**: 彼は絶対休暇をとるべきだ **kare wa zettai kyūka o toru beki da** he badly needs a rest; 絶対に確実(な) **zettai ni kakujitsu (na)** infallible; 絶対に…ない **zettai ni …nai** on no account

絶対的(な) **zettaiteki (na)** absolute *power*; implicit *trust*

ぞ **zo** (*exclamatory particle used by men*): 無理だぞ **muri da zo** it's impossible!

象 **zō** elephant

像 **zō** statue

増築 **zōchiku** extension (*to house*)

増大 **zōdai** increase

象眼細工 **zōgan-zaiku** inlay

象牙 **zōge** ivory

増減する **zōgen suru** fluctuate; go up and down

増加 **zōka** increase; growth

増加する **zōka suru** increase; grow

造形(の) **zōkei (no)** figurative; formative

ぞうきん **zōkin** duster; cloth, rag

俗物 **zokubutsu** person with vulgar taste; snob

俗物(の) **zokubutsu (no)** snobbish

俗語 **zokugo** slang; colloquial word

属性 **zokusei** attribute

属する **zoku suru** belong

続々 **zokuzoku** successively; one after another; 続々出てくる *zokuzoku dete kuru* stream, pour

ぞくぞくさせる **zokuzoku saseru** thrill

ぞくぞくする **zokuzoku suru** be excited; have the shivers

増強する **zōkyō suru** reinforce; build up

雑煮 **zōni** rice cake soup

存じる **zon jiru** Ｈ know; think

ぞんざい(な) **zonzai (na)** rude; coarse; cursory; slipshod

ぞうり **zōri** Japanese sandals

増量 **zōryō** increase

増収 **zōshū** rise in income

増刷 **zōsatsu** reprint

増刷する **zōsatsu suru** reprint

造船 **zōsen** shipbuilding

造船所 **zōsen-jo** dockyard, shipyard

増進 **zōshin** boost

蔵書 **zōsho** (personal) library

贈呈票 **zōteihyō** compliments slip

ぞっとさせる **zotto saseru** appall; give the creeps

図 **zu** diagram; drawing; graphic

ズボン **zubon** pants; ズボンのチャック **zubon no chakku** fly (*on pants*)

ずぶぬれになる **zubunure ni naru** get drenched

ずぶぬれにする **zubunure ni suru** drench

ずぶぬれ(の) **zubunure (no)** dripping (wet)

図太さ **zubuto-sa** audacity, impudence

頭がい骨 **zugaikotsu** skull

図表 **zuhyō** chart

ずいぶん **zuibun** really; very; a lot

随筆 **zuihitsu** essay

髄膜炎 **zuimakuen** meningitis

頭上(の) **zujō (no)** overhead

図面 **zumen** plan (*drawing*)

ズームレンズ **zūmu-renzu** zoom lens

ずんぐりした **zunguri shita** stocky; thickset

頭脳 **zunō** brains, intelligence

づらい **-zurai** difficult to; 聞きづらい *kiki-zurai* difficult to hear

ずらす **zurasu** shift; stagger *breaks etc*

ずれ **zure** difference; gap (*in the market*)

ずれる **zureru** be shifted; be postponed

ずる賢い **zurugashikoi** wily

ずるい **zurui** crafty, sly; shifty

ずるずる滑る **zuruzuru suberu** slither; be slippery

ずさん(な) **zusan (na)** sloppy, slipshod

ずたずたになって **zutazuta ni natte** in tatters, in shreds

ずつ **-zutsu** each; of each; at a time; ひとつずつ *hitotsu-zutsu* one of each; 少しずつ *sukoshi-zutsu* little by little

頭痛 **zutsū** headache

ずっと **zutto** all the time, all along; a whole lot; ずっと前に *zutto mae ni* long ago; ずっと遠くに *zutto tōku ni* far off

ずうずうしい **zūzūshii** shameless; nervy

ずうずうしさ **zūzūshi-sa** nerve, impudence

a, an ◊ (*no translation*): *a cat* neko 猫; *an apple* ringo りんご ◊ (*with countword*): *a pencil and an eraser* enpitsu ippon to keshigomu ikko 鉛筆一本と消しゴム一個; *five men and a woman* go-nin no otoko to hitori no onna 五人の男と一人の女 ◊ (*per*): *$50 a ride* ikkai gojū doru 一回五十ドル; *once a week* isshūkan ni ikkai 一週間に一回

abacus soroban そろばん

abalone awabi あわび

abandon *object* suteru 捨てる; *person* misuteru 見捨てる; *car* norisuteru 乗捨てる; *plan* chūshi suru 中止する

abbreviate mijikaku suru 短くする

abbreviation shōryakukei 省略形

abdomen fukubu 腹部

abdominal fukubu (no) 腹部(の)

abduct yūkai suru 誘拐する

♦ **abide by** ... ni shitagau ...に従う

ability nōryoku 能力

ablaze: *be ~* enjō shite iru 炎上している

able (*skillful*) yūnō (na) 有能(な); *be ~ to* ... koto ga dekiru ...ことができる; *I wasn't ~ to see / hear* watashi wa miru koto ga dekinakatta / kiku koto ga dekinakatta 私は見ることができなかった/聞くことができなかった

abnormal ijō (na) 異常(な)

aboard 1 *prep* ... ni notte ...に乗って **2** *adv*: *be ~* (*on ship*) jōsen shite iru 乗船している; (*on plane*) tōjō shite iru 搭乗している; (*on train*) jōsha shite iru 乗車している; *go ~* (*onto ship*) jōsen suru 乗船する; (*onto plane*) tōjō suru 搭乗する; (*onto train*) jōsha suru 乗車する

abolish haishi suru 廃止する

abort *v/t launch, program* chūshi suru 中止する

abortion ninshin-chūzetsu 妊娠中絶; *have an ~* ninshin-chūzetsu o suru 妊娠中絶をする

about 1 *prep* (*concerning*) ... ni tsuite (no) ...について(の); *a book ~ France* Furansu ni tsuite no hon フランスについての本; *what's it ~?* (*book, movie*) nani ni tsuite desu ka 何についてですか **2** *adv* (*roughly: number*) ... gurai ...ぐらい; (*time*) ...goro ...頃; *be ~ to* ... tokoro desu ...ところです; *I was just ~ to leave* watashi wa chōdo deru tokoro deshita 私はちょうど出るところでした

above 1 *prep* (*higher than*) ... no ue (ni) ...の上(に); (*more than*) ... ijō (de) ...以上(で); *~ all* nani yori mo mazu 何よりもまず **2** *adv* ue ni 上に; *on the floor ~* ikkai ue ni 一階上に

above-mentioned jōki (no) 上記(の)

abrasion surikizu 擦り傷

abrasive *person* hageshii 激しい

abridge yōyaku suru 要約する

abroad *live* gaikoku de 外国で; *go* gaikoku e 外国へ

abrupt *departure* totsuzen (no) 突然(の); *manner* bukkirabō (na) ぶっきらぼう(な)

abscess nōyō 膿瘍

absence (*of person*) fuzai 不在; (*from school*) kesseki 欠席; (*from work*) kekkin 欠勤; (*lack*) ketsuraku 欠落

absent *adj* fuzai (no) 不在(の); (*from school*) kesseki (no) 欠席(の); (*from work*) kekkin (no) 欠勤(の)

absent-minded bon'yari shita ぼんやりした

absolute *power* zettaiteki (na) 絶対的(な); *idiot* mattaku (no) まったく(の)

absolutely (*completely*) hontō ni 本当に; **~ not!** tondemonai とんでもない; **do you agree?** - ~ sansei desu ka - mochiron 賛成ですか - もちろん

absolve manugareru 免れる

absorb kyūshū suru 吸収する; **~ed in ...** ... ni muchū ni natte ...に夢中になって

absorbent kyūshūsei (no) 吸収性 (の)

absorbent cotton dasshimen 脱脂綿

abstain (*from voting*) kiken suru 棄権する

abstention (*in voting*) kiken 棄権

abstract *adj* chūshōteki (na) 抽象的(な); *art* chūshōha (no) 抽象派 (の)

absurd bakageta ばかげた

absurdity bakabakashi-sa 馬鹿馬鹿しさ

abundance hōfu-sa 豊富さ

abundant hōfu (na) 豊富(な)

abuse¹ *n* (*insults*) nonoshiri ののしり; (*of child*) gyakutai 虐待; (*of thing*) kokushi 酷使; (*of drug*) ran'yō 乱用

abuse² *v/t* (*physically*) gyakutai suru 虐待する; (*verbally*) nonoshiru ののしる; (*take advantage of*) ran'yō suru 乱用する

abusive *language* kuchigitanai 口汚い; **become ~** akutai o tsukidasu 悪態をつきだす

abysmal (*very bad*) hidoi ひどい

abyss shin'en 深え ん

academic 1 *n* gakusha 学者 **2** *adj* gakumonteki (na) 学問的(な); *person* atama no yoi 頭の良い; **~ year** gakunen 学年

academy gakkō 学校

accelerate 1 *v/i* kasoku suru 加速する **2** *v/t production* ... no supīdo o ageru ...のスピードを上げる

acceleration (*of car*) kasoku 加速

accelerator akuseru アクセル

accent (*when speaking*) namari なまり; (*emphasis*) kyōchō 強調

accentuate kyōchō suru 強調する

accept 1 *v/t offer*, *suggestion* ukeireru 受け入れる; *present* uketoru 受け取る; *behavior*, *conditions* mitomeru 認める **2** *v/i* shōdaku suru 承諾する; **thank you, I'd be pleased to ~** arigatō, yorokonde o-uke shimasu 有り難う、喜んでお受けします

acceptable konomashii 好ましい

acceptance (*of offer*) shōdaku 承諾; (*recognition*) juyō 受容

access 1 *n*: **have ~ to** *building* ... ni hairu koto ga dekiru ...に入ることができる; *computer* ... o riyō dekiru ...を利用できる; *child* ... to no menkaiken ga aru ...との面会権がある; *information* ... ni chikazukeru ...に近付ける **2** *v/t information* ... ni chikazuku ...に近付く; *files* ... ni akusesu suru ...にアクセスする

access code COMPUT akusesu kōdo アクセスコード

accessible ikiyasui 行きやすい; *information* te ni hairiyasui 手に入りやすい

accessory (*for wearing*) akusesarī アクセサリー; LAW kyōhan-sha 共犯者

access road renraku-dōro 連絡道路

access time COMPUT akusesu-taimu アクセスタイム

accident jiko 事故; **by ~** gūzen ni 偶然に

accidental gūzen (no) 偶然(の)

acclimate, acclimatize *v/t* ... ni narasu ...に慣らす

accommodate shukuhaku saseru 宿泊させる; *special requirements* tekiō saseru 適応させる

accommodations shukuhaku-setsubi 宿泊設備

accompaniment MUS bansō 伴奏

accompany ... ni tsuite iku ...について行く; MUS bansō o suru 伴奏をする

accomplice kyōhan-sha 共犯者

accomplish *task* kanryō suru 完了する

accomplished jukuren shita 熟練した

accord: *of one's own* ~ jihatsuteki ni 自発的に

accordance: *in* ~ *with* ... ni shitagatte ...に従って

according: ~ *to* ... ni yoru to ...によると

accordingly (*consequently*) shitagatte したがって; (*appropriately*) sore ni ōjite それに応じて

account *n* (*financial*) kōza 口座; (*report, description*) hōkoku 報告; *give an* ~ *of* ... no setsumei o suru ...の説明をする; *on no* ~ zettai ni...nai 絶対に...ない; *on* ~ *of* ... no tame (ni) ...のため(に); *take* ... *into* ~, *take* ~ *of* ... ... o kōryo ni ireru ...を考慮に入れる

♦ **account for** (*explain*) ... no setsumei o suru ...の説明をする; (*make up, constitute*) shimeru 占める

accountability sekinin 責任

accountable: *be held* ~ sekinin ga aru 責任がある

accountant kaikeishi 会計士

accounts kaikei 会計; (*department*) keiribu 経理部

accumulate 1 *v/t* tameru ためる **2** *v/i* tamaru たまる

accuracy seikaku-sa 正確さ

accurate seikaku (na) 正確(な)

accusation hinan 非難; (*public*) kokuhatsu 告発

accuse hinan suru 非難する; (*publicly*) kokuhatsu suru 告発する; *he* ~*d me of lying* kare wa watashi ga uso o tsuita to hinan shita 彼は私が嘘をついたと非難した; *be* ~*d of* ... LAW ... de kokuso sarete iru ...で告訴されている; *the* ~*d* hikoku-nin 被告人

accustom: *get* ~*ed to* ... ni nareru ...に慣れる; *be* ~*ed to* ... ni narete iru ...に慣れている

ace (*in cards, tennis*) ēsu エース

ache 1 *n* itami 痛み **2** *v/i* itamu 痛む

achieve tassei suru 達成する

achievement (*of ambition*) tassei 達成; (*thing achieved*) gyōseki 業績

acid *n* san 酸

acid rain sanseiu 酸性雨

acid test *fig* genkaku na kijun 厳格な基準

acknowledge mitomeru 認める

acknowledg(e)ment shōnin 承認; (*letter*) juryō-tsūchi 受領通知

acorn donguri どんぐり

acoustics onkyō-kōka 音響効果

acquaint: *be* ~*ed with* ... to shiriai de aru ...と知り合いである

acquaintance (*person*) shiriai 知り合い

acquire *skill, knowledge* mi ni tsukeru 身に付ける; *property* shutoku suru 取得する

acquisitive don'yoku (na) どん欲(な)

acquit LAW muzai ni suru 無罪にする

acre ēkā エーカー

acrobat akurobatto アクロバット

acrobatics akurobatto アクロバット

across 1 *prep* (*on other side of*) ... no mukōgawa ni ...の向こう側に; (*to other side of*) ... o ōdan shite ...を横断して; ~ *the table from me* tēburu o hasande shōmen ni テーブルをはさんで正面に; *sail* ~ *the Atlantic* Taiseiyō o ōdan suru 大西洋を横断する **2** *adv* (*to other side*) mukōgawa e 向こう側へ; *10m* ~ haba jūmētoru 幅十メートル; *walk* / *run* ~ aruite / hashtte wataru 歩いて/走って渡る

act 1 *v/i* THEA enjiru 演じる; (*pretend*) furi o suru ふりをする; ~ *as* ... to shite tsutomeru ...として務める **2** *n* (*deed*) kōi 行為; (*of play*) maku 幕; (*in vaudeville*) dashimono 出し物; (*pretense*) misekake 見せかけ; (*law*) hō 法

acting 1 *n* engi 演技 **2** *adj* (*temporary*) dairi no 代理(の)

action kōi 行為; (*in movie*) jiken 事件; *be out of* ~ ugokanai 動かない; *take* ~ kōdō o okosu 行動を起こす; *bring an* ~ *against* LAW ... o uttaeru ...を訴える; *full of* ~ *novel, movie* akushon no ōi アクションの多い

action replay TV sokuji-saisei-bideo 即時再生ビデオ

active katsudōteki (na) 活動的(な); *party member* gen'eki (no) 現役 (の); GRAM nōdō (no) 能動(の)

activist POL katsudōka 活動家

activity (*doing things*) katsudō 活動; (*economic, mental etc*) ugoki 動き; (*on the streets etc*) kakki 活気; (*pastime, thing to do*) goraku 娯楽

actor haiyū 俳優

actress joyū 女優

actual jissai (no) 実際(の)

actually (*in fact, to tell the truth*) jitsu wa 実は; (*surprise*) hontō ni 本当に; *~ I do know him* (*stressing converse*) jitsu wa kare o shitte imasu 実は彼を知っています

acupuncture harichiryō ハリ治療

acute *pain* hageshii 激しい; *embarrassment* hidoi ひどい; *sense* surudoi 鋭い

ad kōkoku 広告

adapt 1 v/t (*for the stage, TV etc*) kyakushoku suru 脚色する; *machine* kaizō suru 改造する **2** v/i (*of person*) tekiō suru 適応する

adaptable *person, plant* tekiōsei no aru 適応性のある; *vehicle etc* yūzū no kiku 融通の利く

adaptation (*of play etc*) kyakushoku 脚色

adapter ELEC adaputā アダプター

add 1 v/t MATH gōkei suru 合計する; (*say*) tsukekuwaeru 付け加える; *comment, sugar etc* kuwaeru 加える **2** v/i MATH tashizan suru 足し算する

♦ **add on** *15% etc* ... o tsukekuwaeru ...を付け加える

♦ **add up 1** v/t ... o gōkei suru ...を合計する **2** v/i fig tsujitsuma ga au つじつまが合う

addict n chūdoku-sha 中毒者

addicted: *be ~ to* ... no chūdoku ni natte iru ...の中毒になっている

addiction (*to drugs, TV etc*) chūdoku 中毒

addictive: *be ~* (*of drugs*) shūkansei no aru 習慣性のある; (*of TV, chocolate etc*) kuse ni naru 癖になる

る

addition MATH tashizan 足し算; (*to list, company etc*) tsuika 追加; *in ~* sara ni さらに; *in ~ to* ... ni kuwaete ...に加えて

additional tsuika (no) 追加(の)

additive tenkabutsu 添加物

add-on fuzoku-sōchi 付属装置

address 1 n jūsho 住所; *form of ~* keishō 敬称 **2** v/t *letter* ... ni atena o kaku ...に宛名を書く; *audience* ... ni enzetsu suru ...に演説する; *person* ... ni hanashikakeru ...に話しかける

address book adoresuchō アドレス帳

addressee uketori-nin 受取人

adequate jūbun (na) 十分(な); (*satisfactory*) manzoku (na) 満足 (な)

adhere kuttsuku くっつく

♦ **adhere to** *surface* ... ni shikkari to kuttsuku ...にしっかりとくっつく; *rules* mamoru 守る

adhesive setchakuzai 接着剤

adhesive plaster bansōkō ばんそうこう

adhesive tape nenchaku-tēpu 粘着テープ

adjacent rinsetsu (no) 隣接(の)

adjective keiyōshi 形容詞

adjoining tonariawase (no) 隣り合わせ(の)

adjourn v/i (*of court*) kyūtei suru 休廷する; (*of meeting*) kyūkai suru 休会する

adjust v/t chōsetsu suru 調節する; *behavior* tekiō saseru 適応させる

adjustable chōsetsu dekiru 調節できる

administer *medicine* tōyo suru 投与する; *company* keiei suru 経営する; *country* tōchi suru 統治する

administration kanri 管理; (*of company*) keiei 経営; (*of country*) gyōsei 行政; (*government*) seiken 政権

administrative keiei (no) 経営(の); *tasks* kanri (no) 管理(の); (*in government*) gyōsei (no) 行政(の)

administrator (*in company*) kanri-

sha 管理者; (*civil servant*)
gyōseikan 行政官

admirable rippa (na) りっぱ(な)

admiral teitoku 提督

admiration kanshin 感心

admire kanshin suru 感心する

admirer sūhai-sha 崇拝者

admissible yōnin dekiru 容認できる

admission (*confession*) kokuhaku
告白; ~ **ceremony** nyūgaku-shiki
入学式; ~ **free** nyūjō-muryō 入場無
料

admit (*to a place*) nyūjō saseru 入場
させる; (*to school*) nyūgaku saseru
入学させる; (*to hospital*) nyūin
saseru 入院させる; (*to
organization*) nyūkai saseru 入会
させる; (*confess*) jihaku suru 自白
する; (*accept*) mitomeru 認める

admittance: *no* ~ tachiiri-kinshi 立
入禁止

adolescence jūdai 十代

adolescent 1 *n* jūdai 十代 **2** *adj* jūdai
(no) 十代(の)

adopt *child* yōshi ni suru 養子にする;
plan saiyō suru 採用する

adoption (*of child*) yōshi-engumi 養
子縁組み; (*of plan*) saiyō 採用

adorable aikurushii 愛くるしい

adore *person* shitau 慕う; *chocolate,
movie, book etc* ... ga daisuki de aru
...が大好きである

adult 1 *n* otona 大人 **2** *adj* otona (no)
大人(の); ~ **movie** seijin-eiga 成人
映画

Adult's Day Seijin no hi 成人の日

adultery furin 不倫

advance 1 *n* (*on payment*) maekin 前
金; (*on salary*) maegari 前借り; (*in
science etc*) shinpo 進歩; MIL
shingun 進軍; *in* ~ maemotte 前もっ
て; (*get money*) maekin de 前金で;
make ~**s** (*progress*) shinpo suru 進
歩する; (*sexually*) kudoku 口説く
2 *v/i* MIL zenshin suru 前進する;
(*make progress*) shinpo suru 進歩す
る **3** *v/t* *theory* teishutsu suru 提
出する; *money* maebarai suru 前払
いする; *cause* susumeru 進める;
knowledge shinpo saseru 進歩させ
る

advance booking yoyaku 予約

advanced *country* senshin (no) 先進
(の); *level, learner* jōkyū (no) 上級
(の)

advance payment maebarai 前払い

advantage riten 利点; (*of person*)
tsuyomi 強み; *it's to your* ~ sore ga
anata no tame ni naru それがあなた
のためになる; *take* ~ *of
opportunity* ... o riyō suru ...を利用
する

advantageous yūri (na) 有利(な)

adventure bōken 冒険

adventurous daitan (na) 大胆(な)

adverb fukushi 副詞

adversary teki 敵

advertise 1 *v/t* kōkoku suru 広告する
2 *v/i* kōkoku o dasu 広告を出す

advertisement kōkoku 広告

advertiser kōkokunushi 広告主

advertising kōkoku 広告; (*industry*)
kōkoku-gyōkai 広告業界

advertising agency kōkoku-
dairiten 広告代理店

advice chūkoku 忠告, adobaisu アド
バイス; *take X's* ~ X no chūkoku o
kiku Xの忠告を聞く

advisable nozomashii 望ましい

advise *person* ... ni chūkoku suru ...
に忠告する; *caution* susumeru 勧め
る; ~ *X to* ... X ni ...suru yō
susumeru Xに...するよう勧める

adviser sōdan'yaku 相談役; (*to
company*) komon 顧問

aerial kūchū (no) 空中(の)

aerial photograph kōkū-shashin 航
空写真

aerobics earobikusu エアロビクス

aerodynamic kūki-rikigaku o ōyō
shita 空気力学を応用した

aeronautical kōkūgaku (no) 航空学
(の)

aerosol supurē-kan スプレー缶

aerospace industry kōkū-uchū-
sangyō 航空宇宙産業

affair (*matter*) koto こと; (*business*)
shigoto 仕事; (*love*) jōji 情事;
foreign ~**s** gaimu 外務; *have an* ~
with ... to uwaki suru ...と浮気する

affect MED okasu 冒す; (*influence,
concern*) ... ni eikyō o oyobosu ...に

影響を及ぼす

affection aijō 愛情

affectionate yasashii 優しい

affinity ruijisei 類似性; *have an ~ with / for* … ni hikareru …にひかれる

affirmative: *answer in the ~* kōtei suru 肯定する

affluent yutaka (na) 豊か(な); *~ society* yutaka na shakai 豊かな社会

afford (*financially*) suru yoyū ga aru する余裕がある

Afghan 1 *adj* Afuganisutan (no) アフガニスタン(の) **2** *n* (*person*) Afuganisutan-jin アフガニスタン人

Afghanistan Afuganisutan アフガニスタン

afloat *boat* ukande 浮かんで

afraid: *be ~* kowagaru 怖がる; *be ~ of cats etc* … o kowagaru …を怖がる; *of upsetting him etc* … o shinpai suru …を心配する; *I'm ~* (*regretting*) zannen-nagara 残念ながら; *I'm ~ so* zannen-nagara sō omoimasu 残念ながらそう思います; *I'm ~ not* zannen-nagara sō de wa naiyō desu 残念ながらそうではないようです

Africa Afurika アフリカ

African 1 *adj* Afurika (no) アフリカ(の) **2** *n* Afurika-jin アフリカ人

after 1 *prep* (*in order*) … no tsugi ni …の次に; (*in position*) … no ushiro ni …の後ろに; (*in time*) … no ato de …の後で; (*with names of months, telling the time etc*) … ikō …以降; *~ 2 o'clock / March* niji sn-gatsu ikō 二時/三月以降; *~ all* kekkyoku 結局; *~ that* sorekara それから; *it's ten-two* niji juppun sugi desu 二時十分過ぎです **2** *adv* ato ni 後に; *the day ~* sono yokujitsu ni その翌日に; *~ you* dōzo osaki ni どうぞお先に

afternoon gogo 午後; *in the ~* gogo ni 午後に; *this ~* kyō no gogo 今日の午後; *good ~* konnichi wa こんにちは

after sales service afutā sābisu アフターサービス

aftershave afutā shēbu アフター

シェーブ

aftertaste atoaji 後味

afterward ato de 後で

again mōichido もう一度

against (*lean etc: ~ person*) … ni yorikakatte …に寄り掛かって; (*~ thing*) … ni tatekakete …に立て掛けて; *America ~ Brazil* SP Amerika tai Burajiru アメリカ対ブラジル; *I'm ~ the idea* watashi wa sono kangae ni hantai desu 私はその考えに反対です; *what do you have ~ her?* anata wa kanojo no nani ga kirai nan desu ka あなたは彼女の何がきらいなんですか; *~ the law* hōritsu-ihan 法律違反

age 1 *n* nenrei 年齢; (*era*) jidai 時代; *at the ~ of* …sai de …歳で; *under ~* miseinen de 未成年で; *she's five years of ~* kanojo wa gosai desu 彼女は五歳です **2** *v/i* toshi o toru 年をとる

agency dairiten 代理店

agenda gidai 議題; *on the ~* gidai to natte 議題となって

agent dairi-nin 代理人

aggravate akka saseru 悪化させる

aggression kōgeki 攻撃

aggressive sekkyokuteki (na) 積極的(な); (*dynamic*) kōgekiteki (na) 攻撃的(な)

agile kibin (na) 機敏(な)

agitated dōyō shita 動揺した

agitation dōyō 動揺

agitator sendō-sha 扇動者

ago: *2 days ~* futsuka-mae 二日前; *long ~* zutto mae ni ずっと前に; *how long ~?* dore kurai mae desu ka どれくらい前ですか

agonizing kurushii 苦しい

agony kumon 苦もん

agree 1 *v/i* sansei suru 賛成する; (*of figures, accounts*) itchi suru 一致する; (*reach agreement*) gōi suru 合意する; *I ~* watashi wa sansei desu 私は賛成です; *I don't ~* watashi wa sansei dekimasen 私は賛成できません; *~ with* … ni dōi suru …に同意する; *it doesn't ~ with me* (*of food*) watashi no karada ni aimasen 私の体に合いま

せん **2** *v/t price, date* ... ni gōi suru ...に合意する; *~ that something should be done* nanika shinakereba naranai to iu koto ni gōi shita 何かしなければならないということに合意した

agreeable (*pleasant*) kanji no ii 感じのいい; (*in agreement*) sansei shite iru 賛成している

agreement (*consent*) dōi 同意; (*contract*) keiyaku 契約; *reach ~ on* ... no kyōtei o musubu ...の協定を結ぶ

agricultural nōgyō (no) 農業(の)

agriculture nōgyō 農業

ahead: *be ~ of* ... ni katte iru ...に勝っている; *plan ~* saki no keikaku o tateru 先の計画をたてる; *think ~* saki o kangaeru 先を考える

aid 1 *n* enjo 援助 **2** *v/t* enjo suru 援助する

Aids eizu エイズ

aikido aikidō 合気道

ailing byōki (no) 病気(の); *economy* fushin (no) 不振(の)

aim 1 *n* (*in shooting*) nerai ねらい; (*objective*) mokuteki 目的 **2** *v/i* (*in shooting*) nerau ねらう; *~ to do* ... ... suru tsumori de aru ...するつもりである **3** *v/t*: *be ~ed at* (*of remark etc*) ... ni muketa mono de aru ...に向けたものである; (*of guns*) ... o neratte iru ...をねらっている

air 1 *n* kūki 空気; *by ~ travel* hikōki de 飛行機で; *send mail* kōkūbin de 航空便で; *in the open* ~ kogai de 戸外で; *on the ~* RAD, TV hōsō sarete 放送されて **2** *v/t room* kanki suru 換気する; *fig: views* happyō suru 発表する

airbase kūgun-kichi 空軍基地; **air-conditioned** eakon-tsuki (no) エアコン付き(の); **air-conditioning** kūchō 空調; **aircraft** kōkūki 航空機; **aircraft carrier** kōkū-bokan 航空母艦; **air cylinder** akuarangu アクアラング; **airfield** hikōjō 飛行場; **air force** kūgun 空軍; **air hostess** suchuwādesu スチュワーデス; **air letter** kōkū-shokan 航空書簡;

airline kōkū-gaisha 航空会社; **airmail**: *by ~* kōkūbin de 航空便で; **airplane** hikōki 飛行機; **air pollution** taiki-osen 大気汚染; **airport** kūkō 空港; **airsick**: *get ~* hikōki ni you 飛行機に酔う; **airspace** ryōkū 領空; **air terminal** eatāminaru エアターミナル; **airtight** *container* mippei (no) 密閉(の); **air traffic** kōkū-kōtsūryō 航空交通量; **air-traffic control** kōkū-kansei 航空管制; **air-traffic controller** kōkū-kanseikan 航空管制官

airy *room* kazetōshi no yoi 風通しのよい; *attitude* kaikatsu (na) 快活(な)

aisle tsūro 通路

aisle seat tsūrogawa no seki 通路側の席

alarm 1 *n* keihō 警報; *raise the ~* keihō o hassuru 警報を発する **2** *v/t* shinpai saseru 心配させる

alarm clock mezamashi-dokei 目覚まし時計

album arubamu アルバム

alcohol arukōru アルコール; (*alcoholic drink*) sake 酒

alcoholic 1 *n* arukōru-chūdoku-kanja アルコール中毒患者 **2** *adj* arukōru-iri (no) アルコール入り(の)

alert 1 *n* (*signal*) keihō 警報; *be on the ~* keikai shite iru 警戒している **2** *v/t* ... ni keihō o dasu ...に警報を出す **3** *adj* yōjin-bukai 用心深い

alibi aribai アリバイ

alien 1 *n* gaikokujin 外国人; (*from space*) uchūjin 宇宙人 **2** *adj* gaikoku (no) 外国(の); (*strange*) najimi no nai なじみのない; *be ~ to* ... no shō ni awanai ...の性にあわない

alienate ... no hankan o kau ...の反感を買う

alight *adj* moete iru 燃えている

alike 1 *adj*: *be ~* nite iru 似ている **2** *adv*: *old and young ~* rōjin mo wakamono mo onajiyō ni 老人も若者も同じように

alimony rikon-teate 離婚手当

alive: *be ~* ikite iru 生きている

all 1 *adj* subete (no) すべて(の)
2 *pron* zenbu 全部, mina 皆; *he ate ~ of it* kare wa zenbu tabemashita 彼は全部食べました; *~ of us / ~ of them* watashitachi wa mina / karera wa mina 私達は皆/彼等は皆; *that's ~, thanks* kore dake desu これだけです; *for ~ I care* watashi no shitta koto ja nai 私の知ったことじゃない; *for ~ I know* tabun たぶん; *~ at once* totsuzen 突然; *~ but...* (*except*) ... o nozoite ... を除いて; *~ the time* zutto ずっと **3** *adv*: *~ the better* masumasu yoi ますます良い; *~ but* (*nearly*) hotondo ほとんど; *they're not at ~ alike* karera wa mattaku nite inai 彼らはまったく似ていない; *not at ~!* (*you're welcome*) zenzen kamaimasen 全然構いません; *two ~* (*in score*) ni-tai-ni no dōten 二対二の同点

allegation shuchō 主張; LAW mōshitate 申し立て

alleged ... to sarete iru ...とされている; *an ~ murderer* satsujinhan to sarete iru hito 殺人犯とされている人

allergic: *be ~ to ...* ... ni arerugī ga aru ...にアレルギーがある

allergy arerugī アレルギー

alleviate keigen suru 軽減する

alley roji 路地

alliance dōmei 同盟

alligator arigētā アリゲーター

allocate wariateru 割り当てる

allot wariateru 割り当てる

allow yurusu 許す; (*of person in authority*) kyoka suru 許可する; (*calculate for*) yoyū o motsu 余裕を持つ; *it's not ~ed* yurusarete inai 許されていない; *~ X to ...* X ni ...sasete oku Xに...させておく

♦ **allow for** ... o mikomu ...を見込む

allowance (*money*) teate 手当; (*to child*) kozukai 小遣い; *make ~s* (*for thing, weather etc*) kōryo ni ireru 考慮に入れる; (*for person*) ōme ni miru 大目に見る

alloy gōkin 合金

all-purpose bannō (no) 万能(の); **all-round** *athlete* bannō (no) 万能(の); *improvement* tahōmen ni wataru 多方面にわたる; **all-time**: *be at an ~ low* saitei-kiroku de aru 最低記録である

♦ **allude to** ... o honomekasu ...をほのめかす

alluring miryokuteki (na) 魅力的(な)

all-wheel drive zenrin-kudō 全輪駆動

ally *n* mikata 味方

almond āmondo アーモンド

almost hotondo ほとんど◊ (*negative consequences*) ayauku あやうく; *he was ~ killed* kare wa ayauku korosareru tokoro datta 彼はあやうく殺されるところだった

alone hitori de ひとりで

along 1 *prep* (*moving forward*) tōtte 通って; (*situated beside*) ... ni sotte ...に沿って; *walk ~ this path* kono michi o zutto aruku この道をずっと歩く **2** *adv*: *~ with ...* to issho ni ...と一緒に; *all ~* (*all the time*) zutto ずっと

aloud koe o dashite 声を出して

alphabet arufabetto アルファベット

alphabetical arufabetto-jun (no) アルファベット順(の)

already sude ni すでに

alright: *that's ~* (*doesn't matter*) sore de kamaimasen それで構いません; (*when s.o. says thank you*) dōitashimashite どう致しまして; (*is quite good*) nakanaka ii desu なかなかいいです; *I'm ~* (*not hurt*) daijōbu 大丈夫; (*have got enough*) kekkō desu 結構です; *~, that's enough!* hai, kekkō desu はい、結構です; *don't do it again – ~* mata shinaide ne – wakarimashita またしないでね−わかりました

also ... mo ...も

altar saidan 祭壇

alter *v/t* kaeru 変える

alteration henkō 変更; (*to clothes*) sunpō-naoshi 寸法直し

alternate 1 *v/i* kōtai suru 交替する; (*of mood*) kokoro-o kawaru ころこ

ろ変わる **2** *adj* hitotsu-oki (no) 一つ置き(の); *plan* kawari (no) 代わり(の)

alternating current kōryū 交流

alternative 1 *n* kawari no hōhō 代わりの方法; *(choice)* sentakushi 選択肢 **2** *adj* kawari (no) 代わり(の)

alternatively sono kawari ni その代わりに

although … keredomo …けれども; ~ *he hadn't paid for it* kare wa sore o haratte inai keredomo 彼はそれを払っていないけれども

altitude *(of plane)* kōdo 高度; *(of mountain)* hyōkō 標高; *(of city)* kaibatsu 海抜

altogether *(completely)* mattaku まったく; *(in all)* zenbu de 全部で

altruistic ritateki (na) 利他的(な)

aluminum aruminiumu アルミニウム

always itsumo いつも

a.m. gozen 午前; **10 ~** gozen jūji 午前十時

amalgamate *v/i (of companies)* gappei suru 合併する

amateur *n* shirōto 素人; SP amachua アマチュア

amaze gyōten saseru 仰天させる

amazement gyōten 仰天

amazing odoruku beki 驚くべき; *(very good)* subarashii 素晴らしい

ambassador taishi 大使

amber: *at* ~ kiiro de 黄色で

ambiguous aimai (na) あいまい(な)

ambition yume 夢; *pej* yashin 野心

ambitious yashinteki (na) 野心的(な); *plan* ōgakari (na) 大がかり(な)

ambulance kyūkyūsha 救急車

ambush 1 *n* machibuse 待ち伏せ **2** *v/t* machibuse suru 待ち伏せする

amend shūsei suru 修正する

amendment shūsei 修正

amends: *make* ~ tsugunau 償う

amenities setsubi 設備

America Amerika アメリカ

American 1 *adj* Amerika (no) アメリカ(の) **2** *n* Amerika-jin アメリカ人

amiable aisō no yoi 愛想のよい

amicable enman (na) 円満(な)

ammunition dan'yaku 弾薬; *fig* kōgeki-zairyō 攻撃材料

amnesty onsha 恩赦

among(st) … ni kakomarete …に囲まれて; *(in the set of)* … no naka ni …のなかに; *this is just one ~ many* kore wa tan ni takusan no naka no hitotsu desu これは単にたくさんの中のひとつです

amount ryō 量; *(of money)* gaku 額

♦ **amount to** sōkei … ni naru 総計…になる; *(of work)* … ni hitoshii …に等しい

ample jūbun (na) 十分(な)

amplifier anpu アンプ

amplify *sound* kakudai suru 拡大する

amputate setsudan suru 切断する

amuse *(make laugh etc)* warawaseru 笑わせる; *(entertain)* tanoshimaseru 楽しませる

amusement *(merriment)* tanoshimi 楽しみ; *(entertainment)* kibarashi 気晴らし; **~s** *(games)* goraku-shisetsu 娯楽施設; *to our great ~* totemo omoshiroi koto ni とても面白いことに

amusement park yūenchi 遊園地

amusing omoshiroi おもしろい

anabolic steroid anaborikku-suteroido アナボリック・ステロイド

analog COMPUT anarogu-shiki (no) アナログ式(の)

analogy ruiji 類似

analysis bunseki 分析; PSYCH seishin-bunseki 精神分析

analyze bunseki suru 分析する; PSYCH … no seishin-bunseki o suru …の精神分析をする

anarchy muchitssujo 無秩序

anatomy kaibō-gaku 解剖学; *(body)* karada 体

ancestor sosen 祖先

anchor 1 *n* NAUT ikari いかり **2** *v/i* NAUT ikari o orosu いかりを下ろす

anchor man TV nyūsu-kyasutā ニュースキャスター

ancient *adj* kodai (no) 古代(の)

and ◊ *(joining nouns, adjectives for*

distinct properties) … to …と; *cats
~ dogs* inu to neko 犬と猫; *yellow ~
green* kiiro to midori 黄色と緑◊
(*with verbs*) …shi…し; *he can play
the violin ~ sing* kare wa baiorin
mo hikerushi uta mo utaeru 彼はバ
イオリンもひけるし歌も歌える◊
(*in order to, joining adjectives
jointly describing*) …te…て; *I ate
too much ~ I have a stomach-
ache* tabesugite onaka ga itaku
natta 食べ過ぎておなかが痛くなっ
た; *it is small ~ inexpensive*
chiisakute yasui 小さくて安い◊
(*and then*) soshite そして、…te…
て; *I want to go there ~ take some
photos* soko e itte shashin o toritai
そこへ行って写真を撮りたい◊
(*doing two things at the same time*)
…tari…tari; *we drank ~ talked*
nondari hanashitari shita 飲んだり
話したりした◊; *he talked ~ talked*
kare wa hanashi tsuzuketa 彼は話
し続けた; *he ran faster ~ faster*
kare wa masumasu hayaku
hashitta 彼はますます速く走った; *~
so on* nadonado 等々

anemia hinketsushō 貧血症
anemic: be ~ MED hinketsu de aru 貧
血である
anesthetic *n* masui 麻酔
anesthetist masui 麻酔医
anger 1 *n* ikari 怒り **2** *v/t* okoraseru
怒らせる
angina kyōshinshō 狭心症
angle *n* kakudo 角度
angry okotta 怒った; *be ~ with* …ni
taishite hara o tatete iru …に対し
て腹を立てている; *get ~* okoru 怒る
anguish kunō 苦悩
animal dōbutsu 動物
animated ikiiki shita 生き生きした
animated cartoon anime-eiga アニ
メ映画
animation seiki 生気; (*movie*)
animēshon-seisaku アニメーショ
ン製作
animosity tekii 敵意
ankle ashikubi 足首
annex 1 *n* (*building*) bekkan 別館
2 *v/t state* heigō suru 併合する

anniversary kinenbi 記念日;
wedding ~ kekkon-kinenbi 結婚記
念日
announce happyōsuru 発表する
announcement happyō 発表; (*at
airport*) anaunsu アナウンス
announcer RAD, TV, anaunsā アナウ
ンサー
annoy iraira saseru いらいらさせる;
be ~ed mutto suru むっとする
annoyance (*anger*) iradachi いら立
ち; (*nuisance*) wazurawashi-sa わ
ずらわしさ
annoying wazurawashii わずらわし
い; *person* urusai うるさい
annual *adj* (*once a year*) reinen (no)
例年(の); (*of a year*) ichinenkan
(no) 一年間(の)
annul *marriage* mukō ni suru 無効に
する
anonymous tokumei (no) 匿名(の)
anorak anorakku アノラック
anorexia kyoshokushō 拒食症
anorexic: be ~ kyoshokushō de aru
拒食症である
another 1 *adj* (*different*) betsu (no)
別(の); (*additional: thing, way*) mō
hitotsu (no) もう一つ(の);
(*person*) mō hitori (no) もう一人
(の) **2** *pron* (*different one*) hoka no
mono 他のもの; (*additional one*)
mō hitotsu もう一つ; (*person*) mō
hitori もう一人; *one ~* otagai ni お
互いに; *they helped one ~* karera
wa otagai ni tasukeatta 彼等はお互
いに助け合った
answer 1 *n* henji 返事; (*to problem*)
kaiketsu 解決; (*to question*) kotae
答え **2** *v/t* …ni henji o suru …に返事
をする; *question* toku 解く; *~ the
door* ōtai ni deru 応対に出る; *~ the
telephone* denwa ni deru 電話に出
る
♦**answer back 1** *v/t person* …ni
kuchigotae suru …に口答えする
2 *v/i* kuchigotae suru 口答えする
♦**answer for** … no sekinin o toru …
の責任をとる
answerphone rusuban-denwa 留守
番電話
ant ari あり

antagonism hanmoku 反目

Antarctic n Nankyoku 南極

antenatal shussan mae (no) 出産前 (の)

antenna shokkaku 触角; (*for TV*) antena アンテナ

antibiotic n kōsei-busshitsu 抗生物質

antibody kōtai 抗体

anticipate yosō suru 予想する; (*look forward to*) tanoshimi ni suru 楽しみにする

anticipation yosō 予想

antidote gedokuzai 解毒剤

antifreeze futōeki 不凍液

antipathy hankan 反感

antiquated furukusai 古くさい

antique n kottō-hin 骨とう品

antique dealer kottō-ya 骨とう屋

antiseptic 1 adj shōdoku (no) 消毒 (の) 2 n shōdokuzai 消毒剤

antisocial hanshakaiteki (na) 反社会的(な)

antivirus program uirusu-chekkā ウイルスチェッカー

anxiety shinpai 心配

anxious shinpai shite 心配して; (*eager*) setsubō shite 切望して; **be ~ for ...** (*for news etc*) ... o setsubō suru ...を切望する

any 1 adj ◊ (*usually not translated*): **are there ~ diskettes / glasses?** furoppī / gurasu wa arimasu ka フロッピー/グラスはありますか; **is there ~ bread?** pan wa arimasu ka パンはありますか; ◊ (*with abstracts*) nanika 何か; **is there ~ improvement?** nanika kaizen saremashita ka 何か改善されましたか; **there isn't ~ improvement** nani mo kaizen sarete imasen 何も改善されていません ◊ (*emphatic*) **have you ~ idea (at all)?** zenzen omoi-atarimasen ka 全然思い当たりませんか; **take ~ one you like** dore demo suki na mono o totte kudasai どれでも好きなものを取ってください 2 pron: **do you have ~?** motte imasu ka 持っていますか; **there isn't / aren't ~ left** nani mo nokotte imasen 何も残っていませ

ん; **~ of them could be guilty** karera no uchi dare ka ga yūzai kamo shiremasen 彼らのうち誰かが有罪かもしれません 3 adv: **is that ~ better?** sukoshi wa yoku narimashita ka 少しは良くなりましたか; **is that ~ easier?** sukoshi wa kantan ni nari mashita ka 少しは簡単になりましたか; **I don't like it ~ more** watashi wa sore ga mō suki de nakunarimashita わたしはそれがもう好きでなくなりました

anybody ◊ (*with questions, conditionals*) dareka 誰か; **is ~ at home?** dareka iru 誰かいる; **if ~ thinks ...** moshi dareka ga ... to kangaetara もし誰かが...と考えたら... ◊ (*with negatives*) dare mo 誰も; **there wasn't ~ there** soko ni wa dare mo inakatta そこには誰もいなかった ◊ (*in statements, emphatic*) dare demo 誰でも; **~ who has ...** ... o motte iru hito wa dare demo ...を持っている人は誰でも; **it could have been ~** dare de atte mo okashiku nai 誰であってもおかしくない

anyhow (*regardless*) tonikaku とにかく; **he did it ~** (*carelessly*) kare wa ozanari ni yarimashita 彼はおざなりにやりました

anyone → anybody

anything ◊ (*with questions, conditionals*) nanika 何か; **~ else?** hoka ni nanika ほかに何か ◊ (*with negatives*) nani mo 何も; **I didn't hear ~** watashi ni wa nani mo kikoenakatta 私には何も聞こえなかった; ◊ (*in statements, emphatic*) nan demo 何でも; **I could eat ~** watashi wa nan demo taberaremasu 私は何でも食べられますが; **~ but** zenzen ... de wa nai 全然...ではないが; **~ but sad** zenzen kanashiku nai 全然悲しくない

anyway → anyhow

anywhere ◊ (*with questions, conditionals*) dokoka de どこかで; **do you see him ~?** dokoka de kare o mikake mashita ka どこかで彼を

見かけましたか; **if you see one ~**
moshi dokoka de sore o
mikaketara もしどこかでそれを見
かけたら◊ (*with negatives*) doko ni
mo どこにも; **I can't find it ~** doko
ni mo mitsukaranai どこにも見つか
らない◊ (*in statements, emphatic*)
doko demo どこでも; **you can go ~
you like** doko demo suki na tokoro
ni ikeru どこでも好きなところにい
ける

apart (*in distance*) hanarete 離れて;
keep the two sides ~ ryōgawa o
hanashite oku 両側を離しておく;
live ~ bekkyo shite iru 別居してい
る; **~ from** (*excepting*) ... wa betsu
to shite ...は別として; (*in addition
to*) ... no hoka ni ...のほかに

apartment apāto アパート, manshon
マンション

apartment block apāto アパート,
manshon マンション

apathetic mukiryoku (na) 無気力
(な)

ape n ruijin'en 類人猿

aperture PHOT renzu レンズ

apologize ayamaru 謝る

apology shazai 謝罪

apostrophe aposutorofī アポストロ
フィー

appall zotto saseru ぞっとさせる

appalling osoroshii 恐ろしい;
language hidoi ひどい

apparatus kigu 器具

apparent (*clear*) akiraka (na) 明ら
か(な); (*seeming*) mitatokoro 見た
所; **become ~ that ...** ... to iu koto
ga akiraka ni naru ...ということが
明らかになる

apparently ... rashii ...らしい; **~ they
have all been sold** sorera wa zenbu
ureta rashii それらは全部売れたら
しい

appeal 1 n (*charm*) miryoku 魅力;
(*for funds etc*) apīru アピール; LAW
jōso 上訴 **2** v/i LAW jōso suru 上訴す
る

◆**appeal for** ... o motomete uttaeru
...を求めて訴える

◆**appeal to** (*be attractive to*) ... no ki
ni iru ...の気に入る

appear arawareru 現れる; (*in movie
etc*) shutsuen suru 出演する; (*of new
product*) tōjō suru 登場する; (*in
court*) shuttei suru 出廷する; (*look,
seem*) ... no yōni mieru ...のように
見える; **it ~s that ...** ... to
omowareru ...と思われる

appearance (*arrival*) tōchaku 到着;
(*look*) gaiken 外見; (*in movie etc*)
shutsuen 出演; (*in court*) shuttei 出
廷; **put in an ~** kao o dasu 顔を出す

appendicitis mōchōen 盲腸炎

appendix MED mōchō 盲腸; (*of book
etc*) furoku 付録

appetite shokuyoku 食欲; *fig* yoku 欲

appetizer (*food*) zensai 前菜;
(*drink*) shokuzenshu 食前酒

appetizing oishisō (na) おいしそう
(な)

applaud 1 v/i hakushu suru 拍手する
2 v/t ... ni hakushu o okuru ...に拍
手を送る; *fig* shōsan suru 称賛する

applause hakushu 拍手; (*praise*)
shōsan 称賛

apple ringo りんご

apple pie appurupai アップルパイ

apple sauce ringo-sōsu りんごソー
ス

appliance kigu 器具; (*household*)
denka-seihin 電化製品

applicable tekiyōdekiru 適用できる

applicant ōbo-sha 応募者

application (*for job etc*) ōbo 応募;
(*for passport, visa*) shinsei 申請;
(*for university*) shutsugan 出願

application form mōshikomi-yōshi
申込用紙; (*for visa*) shinseisho 申
請書; (*for university*) nyūgaku-
gansho 入学願書

apply 1 v/t tekiyō suru 適用する;
ointment tofu suru 塗布する **2** v/i
(*of rule, law*) tekiyō sareru 適用さ
れる

◆**apply for** *job* ... ni ōbo suru ...に応
募する; *passport* ... o shinsei suru
...を申請する; *university* ... ni
shutsugan suru ...に出願する

◆**apply to** (*contact*) ... ni
toiawaseru ...に問い合わせる;
(*affect*) ... ni tekiyō sareru ...に適
用される

appoint (*to position*) ninmei suru 任命する

appointment (*meeting*) yakusoku 約束; (*at hairdresser, dentist*) yoyaku 予約; (*to position*) ninmei 任命

appointments diary yoyakuchō 予約帳

appreciate 1 *v/t* (*value*) hyōka suru 評価する; (*be grateful for*) arigataku omou ありがたく思う; (*acknowledge*) rikai suru 理解する; *thanks, I ~ it* arigatō, kansha shite imasu ありがとう、感謝しています 2 *v/i* FIN neagari suru 値上がりする

appreciation (*of kindness etc*) kansha 感謝; (*of music etc*) kanshō 鑑賞; (*understanding*) rikai 理解

apprehensive shinpai shite iru 心配している

apprentice minarai 見習い

approach 1 *n* sekkin 接近; (*offer etc*) mōshide 申し出, apurōchi アプローチ; (*to problem*) torikumi kata 取り組み方 2 *v/t* (*get near to*) ... ni chikazuku ...に近づく; (*contact*) ... ni hanashi o mochikakeru ...に話を持ちかける; *problem ... to torikumu* ...と取り組む

approachable *person* kisaku (na) 気さく(な)

appropriate *adj* tekisetsu (na) 適切(な)

approval sansei 賛成; (*of something official*) shōnin 承認

approve 1 *v/i* sansei suru 賛成する 2 *v/t* ... ni sansei suru ...に賛成する; *sth official* shōnin suru 承認する

♦ **approve of** ... o yoi to omou ...を良いと思う

approximate *adj* ōyoso (no) おおよそ(の)

approximately ōyoso おおよそ

APR (= *annual percentage rate*) nenri 年利

apricot anzu あんず

April shigatsu 四月

apt *pupil* rikō (na) 利口(な); *remark* tekisetsu (na) 適切(な); *be ~ to ...* ... suru keikō ga aru ...する傾向がある

aptitude sainō 才能

aquarium suizokukan 水族館

aquatic suisei (no) 水生(の)

Arab 1 *adj* Arabu (no) アラブ(の) 2 *n* Arabu-jin アラブ人

Arabic 1 *adj* Arabia (no) アラビア(の); *~ numerals* Arabia-sūji アラビア数字 2 *n* Arabia-go アラビア語

arable kōsaku ni tekishita 耕作に適した

arbitrary shiiteki (na) 恣意的(な); *remark* katte (na) 勝手(な); *attack* musabetsu (na) 無差別(な)

arbitrate *v/i* (*in public affair*) chōtei suru 調停する; (*in private*) chūsai suru 仲裁する

arbitration (*in public affair*) chōtei 調停; (*in private*) chūsai 仲裁

arcade (*with slot machines*) gēmu-sentā ゲームセンター

arch *n* āchi アーチ

archeologist kōko-gakusha 考古学者

archeology kōko-gaku 考古学

archer shashu 射手

architect kenchiku-ka 建築家

architecture kenchiku 建築

archives kōbunsho-hozonjo 公文書保存所

archway āchi no kakatta iriguchi アーチの架かった入り口

Arctic *n* Hokkyoku-chihō 北極地方

ardent netsuretsu (na) 熱烈(な)

area (*region*) chiiki 地域; (*part*) han'i 範囲; (*of activity*) bun'ya 分野; (*square metres etc*) menseki 面積

area code TELEC shigai-kyokuban 市外局番

arena SP kyōgijō 競技場

Argentina Aruzenchin アルゼンチン

Argentinian 1 *adj* Aruzenchin (no) アルゼンチン (の) 2 *n* Aruzenchin-jin アルゼンチン人

arguably osoraku おそらくは

argue 1 *v/i* (*quarrel*) kenka suru けんかする; (*reason*) giron suru 議論する 2 *v/t*: *~ that* ... to ronjiru ...と論じる

argument (*quarrel*) kenka けんか;

(*reasoning*) giron 議論

argumentative gironzuki (na) 議論好き(な)

arid *land* kansō shita 乾燥した

arise (*of situation*) okoru おこる

arithmetic sansū 算数

arm¹ *n* ude 腕; (*of chair*) hijikake ひじ掛け

arm² *v/t* busō saseru 武装させる

armaments heiki 兵器

armchair hijikakeisu ひじ掛け椅子

armed busō shita 武装した

armed forces guntai 軍隊

armed robbery busō-gōtō 武装強盗

armor bōdan-chokki 防弾チョッキ; (*for Samurai*) yoroikabuto よろいかぶと

armored vehicle sōkōsha 装甲車

armpit waki no shita わきの下

arms (*weapons*) buki 武器

army rikugun 陸軍

aroma kaori 香り

around 1 *prep* (*in circle*) ... no mawari ni ...の回りに; (*roughly*) oyoso ...およそ...; (*with expressions of time*) ... goro ...ごろ; *it's ~ the corner* kado o magatta tokoro desu 角を曲がったところです; *Christmas is just ~ the corner* kurisumasu wa mō sugu desu クリスマスはもうすぐです **2** *adv* (*in the area*) chikaku ni 近くに; (*encircling*) mawari ni 回りに; *there are a lot of people ~* atari ni wa takusan no hito ga iru 辺りにはたくさんの人がいる; *he lives ~ here* kare wa konohen ni sunde iru 彼はこの辺に住んでいる; *walk ~* burabura aruku ぶらぶら歩く; *she has been ~* (*has traveled, is experienced*) kanojo wa keiken ga hōfu de aru 彼女は経験が豊富である

arouse yobiokosu 呼び起こす; (*sexually*) shigeki suru 刺激する

arrange (*put in order*) seiton suru 整とんする; *furniture* haichi suru 配置する; *flowers* ikeru 生ける; *music* henkyoku suru 編曲する; *meeting, party* junbi suru 準備する; *time, place* kimeru 決める; *I've ~d to*

meet her watashi wa kanojo ni au yakusoku o shimashita 私は彼女と会う約束をしました

♦ **arrange for** ... o tehai suru ...を手配する

arranged marriage omiai-kekkon お見合い結婚

arrangement (*plan*) yotei 予定; (*agreement*) yakusoku 約束; (*layout: of furniture etc*) haichi 配置; (*of flowers*) ikebana 生け花; (*of music*) henkyoku 編曲

arrears tainōkin 滞納金; *be in ~* tainō shite iru 滞納している

arrest 1 *n* taiho 逮捕; *be under ~* taiho sarete iru 逮捕されている **2** *v/t* taiho suru 逮捕する

arrival tōchaku 到着; *~s* (*at airport*) tōchaku-robī 到着ロビー

arrive tsuku 着く

♦ **arrive at** *place* ... ni tōchaku suru ...に到着する; *decision etc* ... ni tassuru ...に達する

arrogance gōman 傲慢

arrogant gōman (na) 傲慢(な)

arrow ya 矢; (*on sign*) yajirushi 矢印

arson hōka 放火

art geijutsu 芸術; *the ~s* jinbun-kagaku 人文科学; *~s degree* bunkei no gakui 文系の学位

artery MED dōmyaku 動脈

art gallery bijutsukan 美術館; (*private*) garō 画廊

arthritis kansetsuen 関節炎

article buppin 物品; (*in newspaper*) kiji 記事; (*section*) jōkō 条項; GRAM kanshi 冠詞

articulate *adj* hyōgen no meikaku (na) 表現の明確(な)

artificial jinkō (no) 人工(の); (*not sincere*) wazatorashii わざとらしい

artificial intelligence jinkō-chinō 人工知能

artillery taihō 大砲

artisan shokunin 職人

artist gaka 画家; (*artistic person*) geijutsuka 芸術家

artistic geijutsuteki (na) 芸術的(な)

as 1 *conj* (*at the same time as*) ... (suru) toki ni ...(する)ときに; *he*

came in – I was going out kare wa watashi ga dekakeru toki ni kita 彼は私が出かけるときに来た◊ (while) …(shi)nagara …(し)ながら; **she whistled – she worked** kanojo wa shigoto o shinagara kuchibue o fuita 彼女は仕事をしながら口笛を吹いた◊ (because) … no de …ので; **– it is still raining** mada ame ga futte iru no de まだ雨が降っているので◊ (like) … yō ni …ように; **– I do** watashi ga suru yō ni 私がするように◊; **– if** marude … de aru ka no yō ni まるで…であるかのように; **– usual** itsumo no yō ni いつものように; **– necessary** hitsuyō na dake 必要なだけ 2 adv onaji kurai 同じくらい; **– high/pretty** …to onaji kurai takai/kawaii …と同じくらい高い/かわいい; **will it cost – much – that?** sonna ni kakaru no desu ka そんなにかかるのですか 3 prep (in capacity of) … to shite …として; (when) … no toki ni …のときに; **– a child/student** kodomo no/gakusei no toki 子供の/学生の時; **work – a teacher/ – a translator** sensei to shite /hon'yaku-sha to shite hataraite iru 先生として/翻訳者として働いている; **– for** … ni tsuite wa …について は; **– Hamlet** Hamuretto yaku de ハムレット役で

asap (= as soon as possible) dekiru dake hayaku できるだけ早く

ash hai 灰; (volcanic) kazanbai 火山灰; **–es** (after cremation) ikotsu 遺骨

ashamed hazukashii 恥ずかしい; **be – of** … o hazukashiku omou …を恥ずかしく思う; **you should be – of yourself** haji o shirinasai 恥を知りなさい

ash can gomiire ごみ入れ

ashore riku de 陸で; **go –** jōriku suru 上陸する

ashtray haizara 灰皿

Asia Ajia アジア

Asian 1 adj Ajia (no) アジア(の) **2** n Ajia-jin アジア人

aside waki ni わきに; **– from** … o nozoite …を除いて

ask 1 v/t (put question to) kiku 聞く; (inquire) tazuneru 尋ねる; (invite) shōtai suru 招待する; (favor) tanomu 頼む; **can I – you something?** chotto kiite mo ii desu ka ちょっと聞いてもいいですか; **– a question** shitsumon suru 質問する; **– X for …** X ni … o tanomu Xに…を頼む; **– X to do** X ni Y suru yō tanomu Xに Yするよう頼む; **– X about Y** X ni Y ni tsuite kiku XにYについて聞く **2** v/i tazuneru 尋ねる

♦ **ask after** person … no yōsu o kiku …の様子を聞く

♦ **ask for** … o motomeru …を求める; person … o yobidasu …を呼び出す

♦ **ask out** … o sasou …を誘う

asking price iine 言い値

asleep: be (fast) – (gussuri) nemutte iru (ぐっすり) 眠っている; **fall –** nemuru 眠る

asparagus asuparagasu アスパラガス

aspect (angle) men 面; (appearance) yōsu 様子

aspirin asupirin アスピリン

ass¹ (idiot) baka 馬鹿

ass² V ketsu けつ; (sex) sekkusu セックス

assassin ansatsu-sha 暗殺者

assassinate ansatsu suru 暗殺する

assassination ansatsu 暗殺

assault 1 n bōkō 暴行 **2** v/t … ni bōkō suru …に暴行する

assemble 1 v/t parts kumitateru 組み立てる **2** v/i (of people) atsumaru 集まる

assembly (of parts) kumitate 組み立て; POL gikai 議会

assembly line nagaresagyō 流れ作業

assembly plant kumitate-kōjō 組み立て工場

assent v/i sansei suru 賛成する

assert: – oneself jiko-shuchō suru 自己主張する

assertive person gōin (na) 強引(な)

assess situation satei suru 査定する; value hyōka suru 評価する

asset FIN shisan 資産; *fig* zaisan 財産

asshole V ketsu no ana けつの穴; (*idiot*) kusottare くそったれ

assign *person* ninmei suru 任命する; *thing* wariateru 割り当てる

assignment (*task, study*) kadai 課題; (*job*) ninmu 任務; *his ~ to this position* kare no kono pozishon e no ninmei 彼のこのポジションへの任命

assimilate *v/t information* rikai suru 理解する; *person into group* … ni dōka suru …に同化する

assist joryoku suru 助力する

assistance enjo 援助

assistant joshu 助手, ashisutanto アシスタント; (*of minister etc*) hosakan 補佐官

assistant director (*in movies*) jokantoku 助監督

assistant manager ashisutanto-manējā アシスタントマネージャー; (*of hotel, restaurant*) fuku-shihainin 副支配人; (*of store*) fuku-tenchō 副店長

associate 1 *v/t: ~ X with Y* X o Y to musubitsukete kangaeru XをYと結び付けて考える; *be ~ed with* (*organization*) … to kankei shite iru …と関係している **2** *v/i: ~ with* … to kōsai suru …と交際する **3** *n* dōryō 同僚

associate professor jokyōju 助教授

association kyōkai 協会, kumiai 組合; *in ~ with* … to kyōdō shite …と共同して

assortment (*of food*) tsumeawase 詰め合わせ; (*of people*) iroiro na hito いろいろな人

assume (*suppose*) … to kangaeru …と考える; (*take for granted*) … to katei suru …と仮定する

assumption katei 仮定

assurance hoshō 保証; (*confidence*) kakushin 確信

assure (*reassure*) … ni hoshō suru …に保証する

assured (*confident*) kakushin no aru 確信のある

asterisk hoshi-jirushi 星印

asthma zensoku ぜんそく

astonish odorokasu 驚かす; *be ~ed* odoroku 驚く

astonishing odorokuhodo (no) 驚くほど(の)

astonishment odoroki 驚き

astrologer hoshiuranai-shi 星占い師

astrology senseijutsu 占星術

astronaut uchū-hikōshi 宇宙飛行士

astronomer tenmon-gakusha 天文学者

astronomical tenmongaku (no) 天文学(の); *price etc* tenmongakuteki (na) 天文学的(な)

astronomy tenmongaku 天文学

asylum (*mental*) seishin-byōin 精神病院; POL hinansho 避難所

at ◊ (*place*) … ni …に; (*with verbs of activity*) … de …で; *it's still ~ the cleaner's* sore wa mada drai-kurīningu-ya no tokoro ni aru それはまだドライクリーニング屋のところにある; *we all met ~ Joe's* Jō no tokoro de aou Jō のところで会おう ◊ *~ 10 dollars* jū doru de 十ドルで; ◊ *~ the age of 18* jūhassai de 十八歳で ◊ *~ 5 o'clock* goji ni 五時に; *~ 150 mph* jisoku hyakugojū mairu de 時速百五十マイルで ◊ *be good / bad ~* … ga tokui / … ga nigate de aru …が得意/…が苦手である

atheist mushinron-ja 無神論者

athlete supōtsu-senshu スポーツ選手

athletic undō (no) 運動(の), supōtsu (no) スポーツ(の)

athletics undō-kyōgi 運動競技

Atlantic *n* Taiseiyō 大西洋

atlas chizuchō 地図帳

ATM (= *automated teller machine*) genkin-jidō-shiharaiki 現金自動支払機, ATM (*always in romaji*)

atmosphere (*of earth*) taiki 大気; (*ambience*) fun'iki 雰囲気

atmospheric pollution taiki-osen 大気汚染

atom genshi 原子

atom bomb genshiryoku-bakudan 原子力爆弾

atomic genshi (no) 原子(の)

atomic energy genshiryoku 原子力

atomic waste kaku-haikibutsu 核廃棄物

atomizer supurē スプレー

atrocious hidoi ひどい

atrocity zangyaku-kōi 残虐行為

attach toritsukeru 取り付ける; *be ~ed to* (*fond of: thing*) ... ni aichaku o motte iru ...に愛着を持っている; (*person*) ... o shitatte iru ...を慕っている; *don't ~ too much importance to what he says* kare no iu koto o jyūyōshi shinai de 彼の言うことを重要視しないで

attack 1 n shūgeki 襲撃; MIL kōgeki 攻撃; (*verbal*) hinan 非難 **2** v/t osou 襲う; MIL kōgeki suru 攻撃する; (*verbally*) hinan suru 非難する

attempt 1 n kokoromi 試み **2** v/t kokoromiru 試みる

attend ... ni shusseki suru ...に出席する

♦ **attend to** ... o shori suru ...を処理する; *customer* ... no sewa o suru ...の世話をする

attendance shusseki 出席

attendant (*in museum etc*) annaigakari 案内係

attention chūi 注意; *bring to the ~ of* ... ... o shiteki suru ...を指摘する; *your ~ please* chotto okiki kudasai ちょっとお聞きください; *pay ~* chūi o harau 注意を払う

attentive *listener* nesshin (na) 熱心 (な)

attic yaneura-beya 屋根裏部屋

attitude taido 態度

attn (= *for the attention of*) ... sama ate ...様宛て

attorney bengoshi 弁護士; *power of ~* ininken 委任権

attract hikitsukeru 引き付ける; *attention* hiku 引く; *be ~ed to* ... ni hikarete iru ...にひかれている

attraction (*charm*) miryoku 魅力; (*asset: of city*) yobimono 呼び物, atorakushon アトラクション

attractive miryokuteki (na) 魅力的 (な)

attribute¹ v/t: *~ X to* ... X o ... no sei ni suru X を...のせいにする; *painting, poem* X o ... no saku to

kangaeru X を...の作と考える

attribute² n zokusei 属性

auction 1 n kyōbai 競売, ōkushon オークション **2** v/t kyōbai ni kakeru 競売にかける

♦ **auction off** ... o kyōbai ni kakete shobun suru ...を競売にかけて処分する

audacious daitan (na) 大胆 (な)

audacity daitan-sa 大胆さ

audible kikoeru 聞こえる

audience (*of speaker*) chōshū 聴衆; (*in theater, at show*) kankyaku 観客; (*of TV program*) shichō-sha 視聴者

audio *adj* ōdio (no) オーディオ(の)

audiovisual shichōkaku (no) 視聴覚 (の)

audit 1 n kaikei-kansa 会計監査 **2** v/t ... no kaikei o kansa suru ...の会計を監査する; *course* chōkō suru 聴講する

audition 1 n ōdishon オーディション **2** v/i ōdishon o ukeru オーディションを受ける

auditor kaikei-kansakan 会計監査官

auditorium (*of theater etc*) kankyakuseki 観客席; (*building*) kōkaidō 公会堂

August hachigatsu 八月

aunt (*own*) oba おば; (*s.o. else's*) obasan おばさん

austere *interior* kanso (na) 簡素 (な); *person* genkaku (na) 厳格 (な)

austerity (*economic*) keizai-kinshuku 経済緊縮

Australasia Ōsutorarēshia オーストラレーシア

Australia Ōsutoraria オーストラリア

Australian 1 *adj* Ōsutoraria (no) オーストラリア(の) **2** n Ōsutoraria-jin オーストラリア人

Austria Ōsutoria オーストリア

Austrian 1 *adj* Ōsutoria (no) オーストリア (の) **2** n Ōsutoria-jin オーストリア人

authentic honmono (no) 本物 (の)

authenticity honmono de aru koto 本物であること

author sakusha 作者; *(of text)* chosha 著者

authoritative ken'i no aru 権威のある; *source* shinrai dekiru 信頼できる

authority *(of officials, ministers)* kengen 権限; *(of parent, teacher)* ken'i 権威; *(permission)* kyoka 許可; *be an ~ on ...* ... no ken'i de aru ...の権威である; *the authorities* tōkyoku 当局

authorize ninka suru 認可する; *be ~d to ...* ... suru kengen o ataerarete iru ...する権限を与えられている

autistic jiheishō (no) 自閉症(の)

auto *n* jidōsha 自動車

autobiography jijoden 自叙伝

autograph sain サイン

automate jidōka suru 自動化する

automatic 1 *adj* jidō (no) 自動(の); *gesture, response* jidōteki (na) 自動的(な) **2** *n (car, gun etc)* ōtomatikku オートマティック

automatically jidōteki ni 自動的に

automation ōtomēshon オートメーション

automobile jidōsha 自動車

automobile industry jidōsha-gyōkai 自動車業界

autonomy jichiken 自治権

autopilot jidō-sōjū-sōchi 自動操縦装置

autopsy kenshi 検死

Autumn Equinox Day Shūbun no hi 秋分の日

auxiliary *adj services etc* hojo (no) 補助(の); *generator etc* yobi (no) 予備(の)

available *service* riyō dekiru 利用できる; *book, information* te ni irerareru 手に入れられる; *person* te ga aite iru 手が空いている

avalanche nadare なだれ

avenue ōdōri 大通り; *fig* shudan 手段

average 1 *adj* heikinteki (na) 平均的(な); *(ordinary)* nami (no) 並(の); *(mediocre)* heibon (na) 平凡(な) **2** *n* heikin 平均; *above / below ~* heikin ijō / ika de 平均以上/以下で; *on ~* heikin shite 平均して **3** *v/t* heikin ... to naru 平均...となる

♦ **average out** *v/t* heikin o ... to mitsumoru 平均を...と見積もる

♦ **average out at** heikin suru to ... ni naru 平均すると...になる

aversion: have an ~ to ... ga daikirai de aru ...が大嫌いである

avert *one's eyes* sorasu そらす; *crisis* sakeru 避ける

aviary tori yō no ori 鳥用のおり

aviation kōkū 航空

avid nesshin (na) 熱心(な)

avoid sakeru 避ける

awake *adj* me ga samete 目が覚めて; *it's keeping me ~* watashi o nemurasezu ni iru 私を眠らせずにいる

award 1 *n (prize)* shō 賞 **2** *v/t* ataeru 与える; *damages* mitomeru 認める

aware: be ~ of ... ni ki ga tsuite iru ...に気が付いている; *become ~ of* ... ni ki ga tsuku ...に気が付く

awareness ninshiki 認識; *(knowledge)* ishiki 意識

away: be ~ *(traveling, sick etc)* rusu ni suru 留守にする; *walk ~* arukisaru 歩き去る; *run ~* hashirisaru 走り去る; *look ~* me o sorasu 目をそらす; *it's 2 miles ~* ni-mairu hanarete iru 二マイル離れている; *Christmas is still six weeks ~* Kurisumasu wa mada roku-shūkan mo saki da クリスマスはまだ六週間も先だ; *take X from Y* Y kara X o torisaru YからXを取り去る

away game SP ensei-jiai 遠征試合

awesome F *(terrific)* monosugoi ものすごい

awful hidoi ひどい

awkward *(clumsy)* gikochinai ぎこちない; *(difficult)* yakkai (na) やっかい(な); *(embarrassing)* kimazui 気まずい; *feel ~* kimazui 気まずい

awning hiyoke 日よけ

ax 1 *n* ono おの **2** *v/t project etc* haishi suru 廃止する; *budget, job* sakugen suru 削減する

axle jiku 軸

B

BA (= *Bachelor of Arts*) gakushi-gō 学士号
baby *n* akanbō 赤ん坊
baby carriage ubaguruma 乳母車;
baby-sit bebīshittā o suru ベビーシッターをする; **baby-sitter** bebīshittā ベビーシッター
bachelor dokushin no otoko 独身の男
back 1 *n* (*of person*) senaka 背中; (*of car, bus*) ushiro 後ろ, kōbu 後部; (*of paper, clothes, house, book*) ura 裏; (*of drawer*) oku 奥; (*of chair*) se 背; SP bakku バック; **in ~** ura ni 裏に; **in the ~ of the car** kuruma no kōbu-zaseki ni 車の後部座席に; **at the ~ of the bus** basu no kōbu-zaseki ni バスの後部座席に; **~ to front** ushiromae 後ろ前; **at the ~ of beyond** henpi na tokoro へんぴなところ **2** *adj* ushiro (no) 後ろ(の); **~ road** uramichi 裏道 **3** *adv*: **please move ~/stand ~** ushiro ni sagatte kudasai/sagattete kudasai 後ろに下がって下さい/下がってて下さい; **two meters ~ from the edge** hashi kara ni mētoru bakku shita 端からニメートルバックした; **~ in 1935** sen-kyūhyaku-sanjūgo nen ni modotte 千九百三十五年に戻って; **give X ~ to Y** Y ni X o kaesu YにXを返す; **she'll be ~ tomorrow** kanojo wa ashita modotte kuru deshō 彼女は明日戻ってくるでしょう; **when are you coming ~?** itsu modotte kimasu ka いつ戻ってきますか; **I'm ~** tadaima ただいま; **take X ~ to the store** (*because unsatisfactory*) X o mise ni henpin suru Xを店に返品する; **they wrote ~/phoned ~** karera wa henji o kureta/orikaeshi denwa o kureta 彼らは返事をくれた/折り返し電話をくれた; **he hit me ~** kare wa watashi o nagurikaeshita 彼は私を殴り返した **4** *v/t* (*support*) shien suru 支援する; *car* bakku saseru バックさせる; *horse* ... ni kakeru ...に賭ける **5** *v/i* (*of person*) ... ni modoru ...に戻る

♦ **back away** atozusari suru 後ずさりする
♦ **back down** jōho suru 譲歩する
♦ **back off** ushiro ni sagaru 後ろにさがる; (*from danger*) hikisagaru 引き下がる
♦ **back onto** ushirogawa de ... ni menshite iru 後ろ側で...に面している
♦ **back out** (*of commitment*) te o hiku 手を引く
♦ **back up 1** *v/t* (*support*) ... o shien suru ...を支援する; *claim, argument* urazukeru 裏付ける; *file* bakku-appu バックアップ; **be backed up** (*of traffic*) teitai shiteiru 停滞している; (*in car*) bakku suru バックする **2** *v/i* (*in car*) bakku suru バックする

back burner: **put ... on the ~** ... o atomawashi ni suru ...を後回しにする; **backdate** sakanobotte yūkō ni suru さかのぼって有効にする; **backdoor** uraguchi 裏口
backer kōen-sha 後援者
backfire *v/i fig* urame ni deru 裏目に出る; **background** haikei 背景; (*of person*) keireki 経歴; **backhand** *n* (*in tennis*) bakku バック
backing (*support*) shien 支援; MUS bansō 伴奏
backing group MUS bansō-gurūpu 伴奏グループ
backlash handō 反動; **backlog** tamatta shigoto たまった仕事; **backpack 1** *n* bakku-pakku バックパック **2** *v/i* bakku-pakku o seotte ryokō suru バックパックを背負っ

て旅行する; **backpacker** bakku-
pakkā バックパッカー; **backpedal**
fig zengen o tekkai suru 前言を撤
回する; **backspace (key)** bakkusupēsu (kī) バックスペース(キー);
backstairs urakaidan 裏階段;
backstroke SP seoyogi 背泳ぎ

backup (*support*) bakku-appu バック
アップ, engo 援護; COMPUT
bakku-appu バックアップ; *take a ~*
COMPUT bakku-appu shiteoku
バックアップしておく

backup disk bakku-appu no furoppī
バックアップのフロッピー

backward 1 *adj child* chieokure
(no) 知恵遅れ(の); *society* okureta
遅れた; *glance* ushiro e (no) 後ろ
へ(の) **2** *adv* ushiro ni 後ろに

backyard *also fig* uraniwa 裏庭; *the
not in my ~ syndrome*
watashitachi ni wa kankei nai
shōkōgun 私達には関係ない症候群

bacon bēkon ベーコン

bacteria saikin 細菌

bad warui 悪い; *weather, conditions,
cold, etc* hidoi ひどい; *mistake,
accident* ōki (na) 大き(な);
(*rotten*) kusatta 腐った; *it's not ~
waruku nai* 悪くない; *that's really
too ~* hontō ni zannen desu 本当に
残念です; *feel ~ about* ... o zannen
ni omou ...を残念に思う; *be ~ at*
nigate de aru 苦手である; *Friday's
~, how about Thursday?* kin'yōbi
wa tsugō ga warui desu, mokuyōbi
wa dō desu ka 金曜日は都合が悪い
です、木曜日はどうですか

bad debt kashidaorekin 貸し倒れ金

bad language akutai 悪態

badge badji バッジ

badger *v/t* nayamasu 悩ます

badly waruku 悪く; *work* heta ni 下
手に; *injured, damaged* hidoku ひ
どく; (*very much*) totemo とても;
he ~ needs a haircut / rest kare wa
zettai kami no ke o kiru beki da /
kyūka o torubeki da 彼は絶対髪
の毛をきるべきだ／休暇をとるべき
だ; *he is ~ off* kare wa seikatsu ga
kurushii 彼は生活が苦しい

badminton badominton バドミント

ン

baffle konwaku saseru 困惑させる;
be ~d konwaku suru 困惑する

baffling fukakai (na) 不可解(な)

bag (*plastic, paper*) fukuro 袋; (*for
school, traveling*) kaban かばん

baggage tenimotsu 手荷物

baggage car RAIL tenimotsu-sha 手
荷物車; **baggage cart** kāto カート;
baggage check tenimotsu-ichiji-
azukarijo 手荷物一時預り所;
baggage reclaim nimotsu-
uketorijo 荷物受け取り所

baggy dabudabu (no) だぶだぶ(の)

bail *n* LAW hoshaku 保釈; (*money*)
hoshakukin 保釈金; *on ~*
hoshakuchū de 保釈中で

♦**bail out 1** *v/t* LAW ... o hoshaku
saseru ...を保釈させる; *fig* ... o
kyūsai suru ...を救済する **2** *v/i*
(*from airplane*) parashūto de
dasshutsu suru パラシュートで脱
出する

bait *n* esa えさ

bake *v/t* yaku 焼く

baked potato beikuto-poteto ベイク
ト・ポテト

baker pan-ya パン屋

bakery pan-ya パン屋

balance 1 *n* tsurai 釣り合い,
baransu バランス; (*mental*)
ochitsuki 落ち着き; (*remainder*)
sagaku 差額; (*of bank account*)
zandaka 残高 **2** *v/t* ... no tsurai o
toru ...の釣り合いを取る; *~ the
books* shūshi o awaseru 収支を合
わせる **3** *v/i* heikō o tamotsu 平衡
を保つ; (*of accounts*) chōjiri ga au
帳尻が合う

balanced (*fair*) tsurai no toreta 釣
り合いのとれた; *diet* baransu no
toreta バランスのとれた;
personality ochitsuita 落ち着いた

balance of payments kokusai-
shūshi 国際収支; **balance of trade**
bōeki-shūshi 貿易収支; **balance
sheet** taishaku-taishōhyō 貸借対
照表

balcony (*of house*) beranda ベラン
ダ; (*in theater*) nikai-sajiki 二階桟
敷

bald hageta はげた; **he's going ~** kare wa hagete kita 彼ははげてきた

ball bōru ボール; **on the ~** fig yūnō na na ban da できる; **play ~ with ...** fig ... to kyōryoku suru ...と協力する; **the ~'s in his court** fig kondo wa kare no ban da 今度は彼の番だ

ball bearing bōru-bearingu no tama ボール・ベアリングの球

ballerina barerīna バレリーナ

ballet baree バレエ

ballet dancer baree dansā バレエダンサー

ball game (baseball) yakyū 野球; **that's a different ~** sore wa zenzen betsu no hanashi desu それは全然別の話です

ballistic missile dandōdan 弾道弾

balloon (child's) fūsen 風船; (for flight) kikyū 気球

ballot 1 n mukimei-tōhyō 無記名投票 **2** v/t tōhyō de kimeru 投票で決める

ballot box tōhyōbako 投票箱

ballpark yakyūjō 野球場; **in the right ~** fig gaisan de 概算で

ballpark figure ōyoso no sūji おおよその数字

ballpoint (pen) bōrupen ボールペン

balls V kintama きんたま; (courage) yūki 勇気

bamboo take 竹

bamboo flute shakuhachi 尺八

bamboo shoots takenoko 竹の子

ban 1 n kinshi 禁止 **2** v/t kinshi suru 禁止する

banana banana バナナ

band gakudan 楽団; (pop) bando バンド; (material) himo ひも

bandage 1 n hōtai 包帯 **2** v/t hōtai o suru 包帯をする

Band-Aid® bando-eido バンドエイド

bandit tōzoku 盗賊

bandwagon: jump on the ~ binjō suru 便乗する

bandy legs ganimata (no) がにまた (の)

bang 1 n (noise) batan to iu oto ばたんという音; (blow) kyōda 強打 **2** v/t door batan to shimeru ばたん

と閉める; (hit) butsukeru ぶつける **3** v/i batan to shimaru ばたんと閉まる

banjo banjō バンジョー; **Japanese ~** shamisen 三味線

bank¹ (of river) dote 土手

bank² **1** n FIN ginkō 銀行; **The Bank of Japan** Nihon-ginkō 日本銀行 **2** v/i: **~ with** (of individual) ginkō ni yokin suru 銀行に預金する; **~** (of company) ginkō to torihiki suru 銀行と取り引きする **3** v/t money ginkō ni yokin suru 銀行に預金する

♦ **bank on ...** o ate ni suru ...を当てにする; **don't ~ it** sore o ate ni shinaide それを当てにしないで

bank account ginkō-kōza 銀行口座;
bank balance yokin-zandaka 預金残高; **bank bill** shihei 紙幣

banker ginkō-ka 銀行家

banker's card chekku kādo, kogitte o tsukau toki ni hitsuyō na kādo チェックカード、小切手を使うときに必要なカード

banker's order jidō-furikae 自動振替

bank loan rōn ローン; **bank manager** ginkō-shitenchō 銀行支店長; **bank rate** kōtei-buai 公定歩合; **bankroll** v/t ... ni shikin o teikyō suru ...に資金を提供する

bankrupt 1 adj person hasan shita 破産した; company tōsan shita 倒産した; **go ~** hasan suru 破産する; (of company) tōsan suru 倒産する **2** v/t hasan saseru 破産させる; company tōsan saseru 倒産させる

bankruptcy hasan 破産; (of company) tōsan 倒産

bank statement kōzashūshi-hōkokusho 口座収支報告書

banner ōdanmaku 横断幕

banns kekkon-yokoku 結婚予告

banquet enkai 宴会

banter n oshaberi おしゃべり

baptism senrei 洗礼

baptize ... ni senrei o hodokosu ...に洗礼を施す

bar¹ (iron) bō 棒; (for drinks) sakaba 酒場; (counter) kauntā カ

ウンター; **a ~ of soap** sekken ikko
石けん一個; **a ~ of chocolate**
itachoko ichimai 板チョコ一枚; **be
behind ~s** keimusho ni hairu 刑務
所に入る

bar² v/t shimedasu 締め出す

bar³ prep (except) ... o nozoite ...を
除いて

barbecue 1 n bābekyū バーベ
キュー; (equipment) bābekyū-dai
バーベキュー台 **2** v/t bābekyū ni
suru バーベキューにする

barbed wire yūshi-tessen 有刺鉄線

barber tokoya 床屋

bar code bākōdo バーコード

bare adj arms earth hadaka (no) 裸
(の); room, shelf garan to shita が
らんとした; mountainside hageta
はげた; floor jūtan no shiite inai
じゅうたんの敷いていない

barefoot: be ~ hadashi de aru 裸足
である

bare-headed bōshi nashi de 帽子な
しで

barely karōjite かろうじて

bargain 1 n (deal) torihiki 取り引き;
(good buy) yasui kaimono 安い買
物; **it's a ~!** (deal) sore de kimari
それで決まり **2** v/i nebiki no kōshō
o suru 値引きの交渉をする

♦ **bargain for** (expect) ... o yoki
suru ...を予期する

barge n NAUT hashike はしけ

bark¹ 1 n (of dog) hoeru koe ほえる
声 **2** v/i hoeru ほえる

bark² (of tree) ki no kawa 木の皮

barley ōmugi 大麦

barn naya 納屋

barometer kiatsukei 気圧計; fig
baromētā バロメーター

barracks MIL heisha 兵舎

barrel taru たる

barren land fumō (na) 不毛(な)

barrette baretta バレッタ

barricade n barikēdo バリケード

barrier saku さく; (cultural) shōgai
障害; **language ~** kotoba no kabe
言葉の壁

bartender bāten バーテン

barter 1 n butsubutsu-kōkan 物々交
換 **2** v/t: **~ X for Y** X o Y to

butsubutsu-kōkan suru X を Y と
物々交換する

base 1 n (bottom) soko 底; (center)
honkyochi 本拠地; MIL kichi 基地
2 v/t motozukaseru 基づかせる; ~
X on Y X wa Y o moto ni shite iru
X は Y を基にしている; **be ~d in** (in
city, country) ... o honkyochi ni
suru ...を本拠地にする

baseball (ball) yakyū no bōru 野球
のボール; (game) yakyū 野球

baseball bat yakyū no batto 野球の
バット; **baseball cap** yakyūbō 野球
帽; **baseball player** yakyū-senshu
野球選手

basement (of house) chika 地下; (of
store) chikai 地階

base rate FIN kijun-ritsu 基準利率

basic (rudimentary) kisoteki (na)
基礎的(な); (fundamental)
kihonteki (na) 基本的(な)

basically kihonteki ni 基本的に

basics: the ~ kisoteki na koto 基礎
的なこと; **get down to ~** kihonteki
na koto ni torikakaru 基本的なこ
とに取り掛かる

basis kiso 基礎; (of argument)
konkyo 根拠

bask hinatabokko suru ひなたぼっ
こする

basket kago かご, basuketto バス
ケット; (in basketball) netto ネッ
ト

basketball basukettobōru バスケッ
トボール

bass 1 n (part) basu バス; (singer)
basu-kashu バス歌手; (instrument)
bēsu ベース **2** adj basu (no) バス
(の)

bastard shiseiji 私生児; F kusoyarō
くそ野郎; **poor / stupid ~** kawaisō
na / baka na yatsu かわいそうな/
ばかなやつ

bat¹ 1 n (for baseball) batto バット;
(for table tennis) raketto ラケット
2 v/i (in baseball) utsu 打つ

bat²: he didn't ~ an eyelid sukoshi
mo odorokanakatta 少しも驚かな
かった

bat³ (animal) kōmori こうもり

batch n (of bread) hitokama 一かま;

(*of goods*) hitoyama 一山; (*of students*) ichidan 一団

bath furo 風呂; *have a ~, take a ~* furo ni hairu 風呂に入る

bathe *v/i* (*have a bath*) furo ni hairu 風呂に入る

bath mat basu-matto バスマット; **bathrobe** basu-rōbu バスローブ; **bathroom** (*for bath*) yokushitsu 浴室; (*for washing hands*) senmenjo 洗面所; (*toilet*) toire トイレ; **bath towel** basu-taoru バスタオル; **bathtub** yokusō 浴槽

batter *n* tane たね; (*in baseball*) battā バッター

battery denchi 電池; MOT batterī バッテリー

battle 1 *n* tatakai 戦い; *fig* tatakai 闘い **2** *v/i* *fig* tatakau 闘う

battlefield, battleground senjō 戦場

bawdy waisetsu (na) わいせつ(な)

bawl (*shout*) donaru どなる; (*weep*) nakisakebu 泣き叫ぶ

♦ **bawl out** *v/t* F … o shikaritobasu …をしかりとばす

bay (*inlet*) wan 湾

bay window demado 出窓

be ◊ (*written form*) … de aru …である; (*plain form*) … da …だ; (*polite form*) … desu …です; *it's me* watashi desu 私です; *I'm 15* watashi wa jūgo sai da 私は十五歳だ; *how much is / are …?* … wa ikura desu ka …はいくらですか ◊ (*written and plain form: of humans, animals*) iru いる; (*polite form*) imasu います; (*written and plain form of objects*) aru ある; (*polite form*) arimasu あります; *was he there?* kanojo wa soko ni imashita ka 彼女はそこにいましたか; *there is / are* (*of humans, animals*) … ga iru …がいる; (*polite form*) … ga imasu …がいます; (*of objects*) … ga aru …がある; (*polite form*) … ga arimasu …があります ◊ (*imperatives*) …te … て; *~ careful* ki o tsukete 気をつけて; *don't ~ sad* kanashi-garanaide 悲しがらないで ◊ *has the mailman been?* yūbin'ya-san wa mō kimashita ka 郵便屋さんはもう来ましたか; *I've never been to Japan* watashi wa Nihon ni itta koto ga arimasen 私は日本に行ったことがありません; *I've been here for hours* watashi wa koko ni nanjikan mo imasu 私はここに何時間もいます ◊ (*tags*): … ne …ね; *that's right, isn't it?* sō desu ne そうですね; *she's Chinese, isn't she?* kanojo wa Chūgoku-jin desu ne 彼女は中国人ですね ◊ (*auxiliary*): *I am thinking* watashi wa kangaete imasu 私は考えています; *he was running* kare wa hashitte imashita 彼は走っていました; *you're ~ing silly* anata wa baka na mane o shite imasu あなたはばかなまねをしています ◊ (*obligation*): *you are to do what I tell you* watashi no iu tōri ni shinasai 私の言う通りにしなさい; *I was to tell you this* watashi wa kore o iu koto ni natte imashita 私はこれを言うことになっていました; *you were not to tell anyone* anata wa dare ni mo iubeki de wa nakatta あなたは誰にもいうべきではなかった ◊ (*passive*): *he was killed* kare wa korosareta 彼は殺された; *they have been sold* sorera wa urete shimatta それらは売れてしまった

♦ **be in for** … ni kitto au …にきっとあう

beach hamabe 浜辺

beachwear bīchiwea ビーチウェア

beads nekkuresu ネックレス; (*rosary*) juzu じゅず

beak kuchibashi くちばし

beaker bīkā ビーカー

be-all: *the ~ and end-all* mottomo jūyō na koto 最も重要なこと

beam 1 *n* (*in ceiling etc*) hari はり **2** *v/i* (*smile*) egao 笑顔 **3** *v/t* (*transmit*) sōshin suru 送信する

bean mame 豆; *be full of ~s* genki ippai de aru 元気いっぱいである

bear¹ (*animal*) kuma くま

bear² **1** *v/t* *weight* sasaeru 支える; *costs* futan suru 負担する;

(*tolerate*) gaman suru 我慢する;
child umu 産む **2** v/i: **bring
pressure to ~ on** ... ni atsuryoku o
kakeru ...に圧力をかける
♦ **bear out** (*confirm*) ... o shiji suru
...を支持する

bearable taerareru 耐えられる

beard hige ひげ

bearing (*in machine*) bearingu ベア
リング; *that has no ~ on the case*
sore wa jiken to mattaku kankei
ga nai それは事件とまったく関係
がない

bear market FIN sagesōba 下げ相場

beast kemono 獣

beat 1 n (*of heart*) kodō 鼓動; (*of
music*) bīto ビート **2** v/i (*of heart*)
kodō suru 鼓動する; (*of rain*) utsu
打つ; **~ about the bush** tōmawashi
ni iu 遠回しに言う **3** v/t (*in
competition*) makasu 負かす; (*hit*)
butsu ぶつ; (*pound*) tataku たたく;
~ it! F deteke 出てけ; **it ~s me** F
sore ni wa maitta それにはまいっ
た
♦ **beat up** ... o uchinomesu ...を打ち
のめす

beaten: *off the ~track* henpi na
tokoro へんぴなところ

beating (*physical*) bōkō 暴行

beat-up F tsukaifurushi (no) 使い古
し(の)

beautician biyōshi 美容師

beautiful utsukushii 美しい; *meal,
vacation, story, movie* subarashii
素晴らしい; *thanks, that looks ~!*
arigatō, mattaku subarashii あり
がとう、まったくすばらしい

beautifully *cooked, done* migoto ni
見事に; *simple* subarashiku 素晴ら
しく

beauty (*of woman, sunset*)
utsukushi-sa 美しさ

beauty parlor biyōin 美容院

♦ **beaver away** F sesse to hataraku
せっせと働く

because ... kara ...から; *we can't
go there - it is too expensive* sore
wa takasugiru kara ikenai それは
高すぎるから行けない; *~ of* ... no
tame ni ...のために; (*referring to

sth negative) ... no seide ...のせい
で

beckon v/i ... ni temaneki suru ...に
手招きする

become ... ni naru ...になる; *what's
~ of her?* kanojo wa dō natta 彼女
はどうなった

bed beddo ベッド; (*of flowers*)
kadan 花壇; (*of sea, river*) soko 底;
go to ~ neru 寝る; *he's still in ~*
kare wa mada nete iru 彼はまだ寝
ている; *go to ~ with* ... to neru ...と
寝る

bedclothes shingu 寝具

bedding shingu 寝具

bedridden netakiri (no) 寝たきり
(の); **bedroom** shinshitsu 寝室;
bedspread beddokabā ベッドカ
バー; **bedtime** nerujikan 寝る時間

bee mitsubachi ミツバチ

beech buna ぶな

beef 1 n gyūniku 牛肉; F
(*complaint*) fuhei 不平 **2** v/i F
(*complain*) fuhei o iu 不平をいう
♦ **beef up** ... o kyōka suru ...を強化
する

beefburger hanbāgā ハンバーガー

beehive mitsubachi no subako ミツ
バチの巣箱

beeline: *make a ~ for* ... e massugu
ni iku ...へまっすぐに行く

beep 1 n bītto naru oto ビーッと鳴
る音 **2** v/i bītto naru ビーッと鳴る
3 v/t (*on pager*) narasu 鳴らす

beeper pokettoberu ポケットベル

beer bīru ビール

beetle kabutomushi かぶと虫

before 1 prep (*time, space, order*) ...
no mae ni ...の前に **2** adv mae ni
前に; *I've seen this movie ~* kono
eiga maeni mita koto ga aru この
映画前に見たことがある; *I didn't
know that ~* ima made
shiranakatta 今まで知らなかった;
you should have told me ~ motto
hayaku itte kurereba yokatta no
ni もっと早く言ってくれればよ
かったのに; *the week / day ~*
isshūkan / ichinichi mae 一週間／
一日前 **3** conj ... (suru) mae ni ...
(する)前に

beforehand maemotte 前もって

beg 1 *v/i* monogoi suru 物ごいする
2 *v/t*: **~ X to ...** X ni ... o tanomu X
に...を頼む

beggar kojiki こじき

begin 1 *v/i* hajimaru 始まる; **to ~
with** (*at first*) saisho no uchi wa 最
初のうちは; (*in the first place*)
mazu saisho ni まず最初に **2** *v/t*
hajimeru 始める

beginner shoshin-sha 初心者

beginner driver unten-renshū-sha
運転練習者

beginning hajime 初め; (*origin*)
hajimari 初まり

behalf: **on** or **in ~ of** ... ni kawatte ...
に代わって; **on my / his ~** watashi
no/kare no kawari ni 私の/彼の代
わりに

behave *v/i* furumau ふるまう; **~
(oneself)** gyōgi yoku suru 行儀良
くする; **~ (yourself)!** gyōgi yoku
shinasai 行儀良くしなさい

behavior kōdō 行動

behind 1 *prep* (*in position*) ... no
ushiro ni ...の後ろに; (*in race,
competition etc*) ... yori okurete
...より遅れて; **be ~ ...** (*responsible
for*) ... no ura ni iru ...の裏にいる;
(*support*) ... ni mikata suru ...に
味方する **2** *adv* (*at the back*)
ushiro ni 後ろに; (*leave, stay*) ato ni
あとに; **be ~ with** ...ga okurete iru
...が遅れている

being (*existence*) sonzai 存在;
(*creature*) ikimono 生き物

belated osokunatta 遅くなった

belch 1 *n* geppu げっぷ **2** *v/i* geppu
o suru げっぷをする

Belgian 1 *adj* Berugī (no) ベルギー
(の) **2** *n* Berugī-jin ベルギー人

Belgium Berugī ベルギー

belief shinrai 信頼; (*religious*)
shinkō 信仰

believe shinjiru 信じる

♦ **believe in** REL ... o shinkō suru ...
を信仰する; *ghosts* ... no sonzai o
shinjiru ...の存在を信じる; (*trust*)
... o shinrai suru ...を信頼する;
(*have confidence in abilities of*) ...
o yoi to omou ...を良いと思う

believer shinja 信者; *fig* shinpō-sha
信奉者

bell beru ベル

bellhop bōi ボーイ

belligerent *adj* kōsenteki (na) 好戦
的(な)

bellow 1 *n* unarigoe うなり声; (*of
bull*) hoegoe ほえ声 **2** *v/i* donaru
どなる; (*of bull*) hoeru ほえる

belly (*of person*) hara 腹; (*fat
stomach*) onaka おなか; (*of
animal*) fukubu 腹部

bellyache *v/i* F guchi o iu ぐちを言
う

belong *v/i*: **where does this ~?** kore
wa doko no mono desu ka これは
どこのものですか; **I don't ~ here**
watashi wa koko ni wa awanai 私
はここには合わない

♦ **belong to** ... no mono de aru ...の
ものである; *club, organization* ...
ni shozoku suru ...に所属する

belongings mochimono 持ち物

beloved *adj* saiai (no) 最愛(の)

below 1 *prep* ... no shita ni ...の下
に; (*in amount, rate, level*) ... ika
ni ...以下に **2** *adv* shita ni 下に; (*in
text*) kaki ni 下記に; **see ~** kaki-
sanshō 下記参照; **10 degrees ~**
reika jūdo 零下十度

belt beruto ベルト; **tighten one's ~**
fig taibō-seikatsu o suru 耐乏生活
をする

bench benchi ベンチ; (*work~*)
sagyōdai 作業台

benchmark kijun 基準

bend 1 *n* kābu カーブ **2** *v/t* mageru
曲げる **3** *v/i* magaru 曲がる; (*of
person*) kagamu かがむ

♦ **bend down** karada o kagameru 体
をかがめる

bender F ōzake 大酒

beneath 1 *prep* ... no shita ni ...の下
に; (*in status, value*) ... yori ototte
...より劣って **2** *adv* shita ni 下に

benefactor onjin 恩人

beneficial yūeki (na) 有益(な)

benefit 1 *n* rieki 利益 **2** *v/t* ... no
yaku ni tatsu ...の役に立つ **3** *v/i*
rieki o eru 利益を得る

benevolent jihibukai 慈悲深い

benign yasashii 優しい; MED ryōsei (no) 良性(の)

bequeath yuigon de yuzuru 遺言で譲る; fig nokosu 残す

bereaved 1 adj ato ni nokosareta あとに残された 2 n: **the** ~ ato ni nokosareta hitobito あとに残された人々; (family) izoku 遺族

berry ichigo-rui いちご類

berserk: **go** ~ kyōbō ni naru 狂暴になる

berth (for sleeping) shindai 寝台; (for ship) teihaku-basho 停泊場所; **give ... a wide** ~ ... o keien suru ...を敬遠する

beside ... no soba ni ...のそばに; **be** ~ **oneself** ware o wasureru 我を忘れる; **that's** ~ **the point** sore wa mato hazure de aru それは的はずれである

besides 1 adv sono ue そのうえ 2 prep (apart from) ... no hoka ni ...のほかに

best 1 adj mottomo yoi 最もよい 2 adv mottomo yoku 最もよく; **it would be** ~ **if** ... ...suru no ga ichiban da to omou ...するのが一番だと思う; **I like her** ~ kanojo ga ichiban suki da 彼女がいちばん好きだ 3 n: **do one's** ~ saizen o tsukusu 最善を尽くす; **the** ~ (thing) saikō no mono 最高のもの; (person) ichiban 一番; **I did the** ~ **I could** watashi wa jibun de dekiru saikō no koto o shimashita 私は自分でできる最高のことをしました; **make the** ~ **of** ... o saidaigen ni riyō suru ...を最大限に利用する; **all the** ~! ogenki de お元気で

best before date shōmikigen no hizuke 賞味期限の日付け; **best man** (at wedding) shinrō-tsukisoi-nin 新郎付添人; **best-seller** besuto-serā ベストセラー

bet 1 n kake 賭け 2 v/i (gamble) kakegoto o suru 賭け事をする; (on horse etc) kakeru 賭ける; **you** ~! mochiron もちろん 3 v/t (reckon) ... o dangen suru ...と断言する

betray uragiru 裏切る

betrayal uragiri 裏切り

better 1 adj motto yoi もっとよい; actor, swimmer, driver etc motto jōzu (na) もっと上手な; **get** ~ umaku naru うまくなる; (in health) kaifuku suru 回復する; **he's** ~ (in health) kare wa daibu yoi 彼はだいぶよい 2 adv motto yoku もっとよく; act, swim, drive etc motto jōzu ni もっと上手に; **you'd** ~ **ask permission** kyoka o morau beki da 許可をもらうべきだ; **I'd really** ~ **not** yamete oita hō ga ii やめておいた方がいい; **all the** ~ **for us** watashitachi no tame ni wa sono hōga ii その方がいい; **I like her** ~ kanojo no hō ga suki da 彼女のほうが好きだ

better-off ...yori kane ga aru ...より金がある

between prep ... no aida ni ...の間に; ~ **you and me** koko dake no hanashi da ga ここだけの話だが

beverage fml nomimono 飲み物

beware: ~ **of** chūi suru 注意する

bewilder tōwaku saseru 当惑させる

beyond 1 prep ... o koete ...を越えて; **it's** ~ **me** (don't understand) watashi ni wa wakaranai 私にはわからない; (can't do it) watashi ni wa dekinai 私にはできない 2 adv mukō ni 向こうに

Bhutan Būtan ブータン

Bhutanese 1 adj Būtan (no) ブータン(の) 2 n (person) Būtan-jin ブータン人

bias n henken 偏見; (favorable) hiikime ひいき目

bias(s)ed henken ni motozuita 偏見に基づいた; (favorably) hiikime ni mite ひいき目に見て

bib (for baby) yodarekake よだれ掛け

Bible seisho 聖書

bibliography bunken-mokuroku 文献目録

biceps chikarakobu 力こぶ

bicker kenka suru けんかする

bicycle n jitensha 自転車, F charinko ちゃりんこ

bid 1 n (at auction) tsukene 付け値; (attempt) kokoromi 試み 2 v/i (at

auction) kyōbai ni sanka suru 競
売に参加する
biennial adj ni-nen goto (no) 二年ご
と(の)
big 1 adj ōkii 大きい; **~ brother** ani
兄; **~ sister** ane 姉; **~ name** ichiryū
一流 **2** adv: **talk ~** jiman suru 自慢
する
bigamy jūkon 重婚
big-headed unuboreta うぬぼれた
bike 1 n jitensha 自転車 **2** v/i
jitensha ni noru 自転車に乗る
bikini bikini ビキニ
bilingual bairingaru (no) バイリン
ガル(の)
bill 1 n (money) shihei 紙幣; (for
electricity etc) seikyūsho 請求書;
Br (in restaurant) o-kanjō お勘定;
POL gian 議案; (poster) bira ビラ
2 v/t (invoice) … ni seikyūsho o
okuru …に請求書を送る
billboard kōkokuban 広告板
billfold satsuire 札入れ
billiards biriyādo ビリヤード
billion jū-oku 十億
bill of exchange kawase tegata 為替
手形
bill of sale uriwatashishō 売り渡し証
bin (for storage) chozōbako 貯蔵箱
binary nishinhō (no) 二進法(の)
bind v/t (connect) musubi-tsukeru 結
び付ける; (tie) shibaru 縛る; (LAW:
oblige) gimuzukeru 義務づける
binder (for papers) baindā バイン
ダー
binding 1 adj agreement, promise
kōsokuryoku no aru 拘束力のある
2 n (of book) seihon 製本
binoculars sōgankyō 双眼鏡
biodegradable mugai-busshitsu ni
kangen dekiru 無害物質に還元で
きる
biography denki 伝記
biological seibutsugaku-jō (no) 生
物学上(の)
biological detergent kōso-senzai 酵
素洗剤
biological parents jitsu no ryōshin
実の両親
biology seibutsugaku 生物学
biotechnology baiotekunorojī バイ

オテクノロジー
birch: **silver ~** shirakaba しらかば
bird tori 鳥
bird of prey mōkin 猛きん
bird sanctuary chōrui-hogoku 鳥類
保護区
birth (of child) tanjō 誕生; (labor)
shussan 出産; fig (of country)
shutsugen 出現; **give ~ to child** … o
umu …を産む; **date of ~**
seinengappi 生年月日
birth certificate shussei-shōmeisho
出生証明書; **birth control** hinin 避
妊; **birthday** tanjōbi 誕生日; **happy
~!** otanjōbi omedetō お誕生日おめ
でとう; **birthplace** seitanchi 生誕
地; **birthrate** shusshōritsu 出生率
biscuit bisuketto ビスケット
bisexual 1 adj baisekusharu (no) バ
イセクシャル(の) **2** n
baisekusharu バイセクシャル
bishop (catholic) shikyō 司教;
(protestant) shukyō 主教
bit n (of a whole) kakera かけら;
(part, section) bubun 部分; (in
book, movie) tokoro ところ;
COMPUT bitto ビット; **a ~ (a little)**
sukoshi 少し; **a ~ of (a little)**
sukoshi (no) 少し(の); **a ~ of
news / advice** chotto shita nyūsu /
adobaisu ちょっとしたニュース/
アドバイス; **~ by ~** sukoshi zutsu
少しずつ; **I'll be there in a ~**
watashi wa soko ni sukoshi
shitara ikimasu 私はそこに少しし
たら行きます
bitch 1 n (dog) mesuinu 雌犬; F
(woman) ama あま **2** v/i F
(complain) monku o iu 文句を言う
bitchy F ijiwaru (na) 意地悪(な)
bite 1 n kamikizu かみ傷; (of
mosquito, flea) mushisasare 虫刺
され; (of food) hitokuchi 一口; **get
a ~** (of angler) kuitsuki 食い付き;
a ~ (to eat) tabemono 食べ物 **2** v/t
kamu かむ; (of mosquito, flea)
sasu 刺す **3** v/i kamitsuku かみつ
く; (of mosquito, flea) sasu 刺す;
(of fish) kuitsuku 食いつく
bitter taste nigai 苦い; person ne ni
motte 根に持って; weather kibishii

厳しい; *argument* hageshii 激しい
bitterly *cold* hidoku ひどく
black 1 *adj* kuroi 黒い; *person* kokujin (no) 黒人(の); *coffee* burakku (no) ブラック(の); *tea* sutorēto (no) ストレート(の); *fig* ankoku (no) 暗黒(の) **2** *n* (*color*) kuro 黒; (*person*) kokujin 黒人; *in the ~* FIN kuroji de 黒字で
♦**black out** *v/i* ishiki o ushinau 意識を失う
black belt kuro-obi 黒帯; **blackberry** burakkuberī ブラックベリー; **blackbird** kurōtadori クロウタドリ; **blackboard** kokuban 黒板; **black box** burakku-bokkusu ブラックボックス; **black economy** yamikeizai やみ経済
blacken *name* chūshō suru 中傷する
black eye aoaza 青あざ; **black ice** tōketsu-romen 凍結路面; **blacklist 1** *n* burakkurisuto ブラックリスト **2** *v/t* burakkurisuto ni noseru ブラックリストに載せる; **blackmail 1** *n* yusuri ゆすり; *emotional* ~ hito no yowami ni tsukekomu koto 人の弱味に付け込むこと **2** *v/t* yusuru ゆする; **blackmailer** kyōkatsu-sha 恐喝者; **black market** yamishijō やみ市場
blackness ankoku 暗黒
blackout ELEC teiden 停電; MED ishikisōshitsu 意識喪失
bladder bōkō 膀胱
blade (*of knife, sword*) ha 刃; (*of helicopter*) hane 羽根; *a ~ of grass* kusa ippon 草一本
blame 1 *n* hinan 非難; (*responsibility*) sekinin 責任 **2** *v/t* … no sei ni suru …のせいにする; ~ *X for Y* Y o X no sei ni suru YをXのせいにする
bland ajikenai 味気ない
blank 1 *adj* (*not written on*) hakushi (no) 白紙(の); *tape* kara (no) から(の); *look* bon'yari shita ぼんやりした **2** *n* (*empty space*) yohaku 余白; *my mind's a* ~ atama ga karappo de aru 頭が空っぽである
blank check kingaku no kaite inai kogitte 金額の書いていない小切手

blanket *n* mōfu 毛布; *a ~ of fig* ichimen (no)… 一面(の)…
blare *v/i* yakamashiku naru やかましく鳴る
♦**blare out 1** *v/i* yakamashiku naru やかましく鳴る **2** *v/t* … o yakamashiku narasu …をやかましく鳴らす
blaspheme bōtoku suru 冒とくする
blast 1 *n* (*explosion*) bakuhatsu 爆発; (*gust*) ichijin no kaze 一陣の風 **2** *v/t* bakuha suru 爆破する **3** *interj* che' ちぇっ
♦**blast off** (*of rocket*) hassha suru 発射する
blast furnace yōkōro 溶鉱炉
blast-off uchiage 打ち上げ
blatant zūzūshii ずうずうしい
blaze 1 *n* (*fire*) kaji 火事; *a ~ of color* kagayaku yō na iro 輝くような色 **2** *v/i* (*of fire*) moetatsu 燃え立つ
♦**blaze away** (*with gun*) tsuzukete happō suru 続けて発砲する
blazer burezā ブレザー
bleach 1 *n* burīchi ブリーチ **2** *v/t* *hair* burīchi suru ブリーチする
bleak *countryside* sabireta さびれた; *weather* samuzamu shita 寒々した; *future* kurai 暗い
bleary-eyed me ga shoboshobo shita 目がしょぼしょぼした
bleat *v/i* (*of sheep*) mē to naku めーと泣く
bleed 1 *v/i* shukketsu suru 出血する **2** *v/t fig* kane o shibori toru 金を搾り取る
bleeding *n* shukketsu 出血
bleep 1 *n* pī to iu oto ぴーという音 **2** *v/i* pī to naru ぴーと鳴る
bleeper pokettoberu ポケットベル
blemish 1 *n* kizu 傷 **2** *v/t reputation* … o sokonau …を損なう
blend 1 *n* burendo ブレンド **2** *v/t* burendo suru ブレンドする
♦**blend in 1** *v/i* tokekomu 溶け込む **2** *v/t* (*in cooking*) … o mazeru …を混ぜる
blender mikisā ミキサー
bless shukufuku suru 祝福する; (*God*) ~ *you!* kamisama no

omegumi ga arimasuyō ni 神様の
お恵みがありますように; **~ you** (*in
response to sneeze*) odaiji ni お大
事に; **be ~ed with** ... ni
megumarete iru ...に恵まれている
blessing REL shukufuku 祝福; *fig*
(*approval*) sansei 賛成
blind 1 *adj* mōmoku (no) 盲目(の);
corner mitōshi no kikanai 見通し
の利かない; **~ to** ... ni ki ga
tsukanai ...に気がつかない 2 *n*: **the
~** mōjin 盲人 3 *v/t* shitsumei
saseru 失明させる; *fig* me o
kuramaseru 目をくらませる
blind alley *also fig* ikizumari 行き詰
まり; **blind date** buraindo-dēto ブ
ラインド・デート; **blindfold 1** *n*
mekakushi 目隠し 2 *v/t* ... ni
mekakushi o suru ...に目隠しをす
る 3 *adv* mekakushi o shite 目隠し
をして
blinding me o kuramasu 目をくらま
す
blind spot (*in road*) shikaku 死角;
fig mōten 盲点
blink *v/i* (*of person*) mabataki suru
まばたきする; (*of light*) chiratsuku
ちらつく
blip (*on radar screen*) tenmetsu 点
滅; *fig* tankiteki na mono 短期的な
もの
bliss kōfuku 幸福
blister 1 *n* mizubukure 水ぶくれ
2 *v/i* mizubukure ni naru 水ぶくれ
になる; (*of paint*) butsubutsu ga
dekiru ぶつぶつができる
blizzard fubuki 吹雪
bloated fukureagatta ふくれ上がっ
た
blob (*of liquid*) hitotarashi ひとた
らし
bloc POL ken 圏
block 1 *n* katamari かたまり; (*in
town*) burokku ブロック, gaiku 街
区; (*blockage*) shōgaibutsu 障害物
2 *v/t* fusagu ふさぐ
♦**block in** (*with vehicle*) ... o
tojikomeru ...を閉じ込める
♦**block out** *light* ... o shadan suru
...を遮断する
♦**block up** *v/t sink etc* ... o sukkari

fusagu ...をすっかりふさぐ
blockade 1 *n* fūsa 封鎖 2 *v/t* fūsa
suru 封鎖する
blockage tsumari 詰まり
blockbuster hittosaku ヒット作
block letters katsujitai 活字体
blond *adj* kinpatsu (no) 金髪(の)
blonde *n* (*woman*) kinpatsu no josei
金髪の女性
blood chi 血; *in cold ~* reikoku ni 冷
酷に
blood bank ketsueki-ginkō 血液銀
行; **blood donor** kenketsu-sha 献血
者; **blood group** ketsuekigata 血液
型
bloodless *coup* muketsu (no) 無血
(の)
blood poisoning haiketsushō 敗血症;
blood pressure ketsuatsu 血圧;
blood relation, blood relative
nikushin 肉親; **blood sample**
ketsueki-sanpuru 血液サンプル;
bloodshed ryūketsu 流血;
bloodshot chibashitta 血走った;
bloodstain kekkon 血こん;
bloodstream ketsuryū 血流; **blood
test** ketsueki-kensa 血液検査;
blood transfusion yuketsu 輸血;
blood vessel kekkan 血管
bloody *hands etc* chidarake (no) 血
だらけ(の); *battle* mugotarashii む
ごたらしい
bloody mary buradī-marī ブラ
ディーマリー
bloom 1 *n* hana 花; *in full ~*
hanazakari (no) 花盛り(の) 2 *v/i*
hana ga saku 花が咲く; *fig*
massakari de aru 真っ盛りである
blossom 1 *n* hana 花; **~ viewing**
hanami 花見 2 *v/i* hana o tsukeru
花をつける; *fig* kaikatsu ni naru 快
活になる
blot 1 *n* shimi 染み; *fig* kizu 傷 2 *v/t*
(*dry*) suitotte kawakasu 吸い取っ
て乾かす
♦**blot out** ... o kesu ...を消す; *view* ...
o mienaku suru ...を見えなくする
blotch hasshin 発疹
blotchy shimi darake (no) 染みだら
け(の)
blouse burausu ブラウス

blow¹ *n* ōda 殴打; *fig* dageki 打撃

blow² 1 *v/t* (*of wind*) fukitobasu 吹き飛ばす; *smoke* haku 吐く; *whistle* fuku 吹く; F (*spend*) rōhi suru 浪費する; F *opportunity* fui ni suru ふいにする; **~ one's nose** hana o kamu 鼻をかむ 2 *v/i* (*of wind*) fuku 吹く; (*of whistle*) naru 鳴る; (*of person*) haku 吐く; (*of fuse*) tobu 飛ぶ; (*of tire*) panku suru パンクする

♦ **blow off** 1 *v/t* ... o fukitobasu ...を吹き飛ばす 2 *v/i* fukitobu 吹き飛ぶ

♦ **blow out** 1 *v/t* *candle* ... o fukikesu ...を吹き消す 2 *v/i* (*of candle*) kaze de kieru 風で消える

♦ **blow over** 1 *v/t* ... o fukitaosu ...を吹き倒す 2 *v/i* fukitobasareru 吹き飛ばされる; (*of storm*) shizumaru 静まる; (*of argument*) osamaru 収まる

♦ **blow up** 1 *v/t* (*with explosives*) ... o bakuha suru ...を爆破する; *balloon* fukuramasu 膨らます; *photograph* hikinobasu 引き伸ばす 2 *v/i* bakuhatsu suru 爆発する; F (*get angry*) katto naru かっとなる

blow-dry *n* burō-dorai ブロードライ; **blow job** V ferachio フェラチオ; **blow-out** (*of tire*) panku パンク; F (*big meal*) gochisō ごちそう; **blow-up** (*of photo*) hikinobashi 引き伸ばし

blue 1 *adj* aoi 青い; *movie* poruno (no) ポルノ(の) 2 *n* ao 青

blueberry burūberī ブルーベリー; **blue chip** yūryō kabu 優良株; **blue-collar worker** nikutai-rōdōsha 肉体労働者; **blueprint** aojashin 青写真; (*plan*) keikaku 計画

blues MUS burūsu ブルース; **have the ~** ochikomu 落ち込む

blues singer burūsu-kashu ブルース歌手

bluff 1 *n* (*deception*) hattari はったり 2 *v/t* hattari o kikaseru はったりをきかせる

blunder 1 *n* hema へま 2 *v/i* hema o suru へまをする

blunt *adj* nibui 鈍い; *person* bukkirabō (na) ぶっきらぼう(な)

bluntly *speak* bukkirabō ni ぶっきら

ぼうに

blur 1 *n* bon'yari shita mono ぼんやりしたもの 2 *v/t* bokasu ぼかす

blurb (*on book*) senden-monku 宣伝文句

♦ **blurt out** ... o dashinuke ni iidasu ...を出し抜けに言い出す

blush 1 *n* sekimen 赤面 2 *v/i* sekimen suru 赤面する

blusher (*cosmetic*) hōbeni ほお紅, chīku チーク

BO (= *body odor*) taishū 体臭

board 1 *n* ita 板; (*for game*) bōdo ボード; (*for notices*) keijiban 掲示板; (*committee*) iinkai 委員会; **~ (of directors)** yakuinkai 役員会; **on ~** (*plane*) hikōki ni notte 飛行機に乗って; (*train*) ressha ni notte 列車に乗って; (*boat*) fune ni notte 船に乗って; **take on ~** *comments etc* rikai suru 理解する; (*fully realize truth of*) ukeireru 受け入れる; **across the ~** ichiritsu ni 一律に 2 *v/t* *airplane etc* ... ni noru ...に乗る 3 *v/i* (*of passengers*) noru 乗る

♦ **board up** ... ni ita o haru ...に板を張る

♦ **board with** ... ni geshuku suru ...に下宿する

board and lodging makanai-tsuki geshuku 賄い付き下宿

boarder geshukunin 下宿人; EDU ryōsei 寮生

board game bōdo-gēmu ボードゲーム

boarding card tōjōken 搭乗券; **boarding house** geshukuya 下宿屋; **boarding pass** tōjōken 搭乗券; **boarding school** kishuku-gakkō 寄宿学校

board meeting jūyaku-kaigi 重役会議; **board room** kaigishitsu 会議室; **boardwalk** yūhodō 遊歩道

boast 1 *n* jiman 自慢 2 *v/i* jiman suru 自慢する

boat fune 船; (*small, for leisure*) bōto ボート; **go by ~** fune de iku 船で行く

bob¹ (*haircut*) bobu ボブ

bob² *v/i* (*of boat etc*) nami ni yureru 波に揺れる

◆ **bob up** arawareru 現れる
bobsleigh, bobsled bobusurē ボブス
レー
bodice bodīsūtsu ボディースーツ
bodily 1 *adj* shintaiteki (na) 身体的
(な) **2** *adv eject* karada goto 体ごと
body karada 体; (*dead*) shitai 死体;
~ *of water* koshō 湖沼; ~ (*suit*)
(*undergarment*) bodīsūtsu ボ
ディースーツ
bodyguard bodīgādo ボディーガー
ド; **body language** bodīrangēji ボ
ディーランゲージ; **body odor**
taishū 体臭; **body shop** MOT shūri-
kōjō 修理工場; **bodywork** MOT
shatai 車体
boggle: *it ~s the mind!* shinjirarenai
信じられない
bogus inchiki (no) いんちき(の)
boil¹ *n* (*swelling*) odeki おでき
boil² **1** *v/t liquid* futtō saseru 沸騰さ
せる; *egg, vegetables* yuderu ゆで
る **2** *v/i* futtō suru 沸騰する
◆ **boil down to** ... to naru ...となる
◆ **boil over** (*of milk etc*) ... ga
fukikoboreru ...が吹きこぼれる
boiler boirā ボイラー
boisterous sōzōshii 騒々しい
bold 1 *adj* daitan (na) 大胆(な) **2** *n*
(*print*) futoji 太字; *in* ~ futojitai de
太字体で
bolster *v/t confidence* shiji suru 支
持する
bolt 1 *n* boruto ボルト; (*on door*)
kannuki かんぬき; (*of lightning*)
kaminari 雷; *like a ~ from the blue*
seiten no hekireki no yō ni 青天の
へきれきのように **2** *adv*: ~ *upright*
massugu ni まっすぐに **3** *v/t* (*fix
with bolts*) boruto de shimeru ボ
ルトで締める; *door* ... ni kannuki o
kakeru ...にかんぬきを掛ける **4** *v/i*
(*run off*) hashiridasu 走り出す;
(*of prisoner*) dassō suru 脱走する
bomb 1 *n* bakudan 爆弾 **2** *v/t*
bakuha suru 爆破する; MIL
bakugeki suru 爆撃する
bombard: ~ *with questions*
shitsumonzeme ni suru 質問ぜめに
する
bomb attack bakugeki 爆撃

bomber (*airplane*) bakugekiki 爆撃
機; (*terrorist*) bakugeki-hannin 爆
撃犯人
bomber jacket kawajan 皮ジャン
bomb scare bakudan-sawagi 爆弾
騒ぎ
bond 1 *n* (*tie*) kizuna きずな; FIN
saiken 債券 **2** *v/i* (*of glue*)
setchaku suru 接着する
bone 1 *n* hone 骨 **2** *v/t meat, fish* ...
no hone o nuku ...の骨を抜く
bonfire takibi たき火
bonsai bonsai 盆栽
bonus (*money*) bōnasu ボーナス;
(*something extra*) omake おまけ
boo 1 *n* būingu ブーイング **2** *v/t &
v/i* yajiru やじる
book 1 *n* hon 本; ~ *of matches*
hagitori matchi はぎ取りマッチ
2 *v/t* (*reserve*) yoyaku suru 予約す
る; (*of policeman*) chōsho o toru
調書をとる **3** *v/i* (*reserve*) yoyaku
suru 予約する
bookcase hondana 本棚
booked up: *be* ~ (*of hotel, flight*)
yoyaku de ippai ni naru 予約で一杯
になる; (*of person*) yotei de
ippai ni naru 予定で一杯になる
bookie F nomi-ya のみ屋
booking (*reservation*) yoyaku 予約
booking clerk yoyaku-gakari 予約
係
bookkeeper boki-gakari 簿記係
bookkeeping boki 簿記
booklet shōsasshi 小冊子
bookmaker baken-ya 馬券屋
books (*accounts*) chōbo 帳簿; *do the
~* chōbo o tsukeru 帳簿をつける
bookseller hon-ya 本屋; **bookstall**
zasshi uriba 雑誌売り場;
bookstore hon-ya 本屋
boom¹ **1** *n* būmu ブーム **2** *v/i* (*of
business*) kakkizuku 活気づく
boom² **1** *n* (*noise*) todoroki とどろ
き **2** *v/i* todoroku ととどろく
boonies: *out in the* ~ F henpi na
tokoro へんぴなところ
boost 1 *n* (*to sales, confidence*) zōka
増加; (*to economy*) zōshin 増進
2 *v/t production, sales* fuyasu 増や
す; *prices* jōshō saseru 上昇させる;

morale takameru 高める

boot *n* būtsu ブーツ

♦ **boot out** F ... o oidasu ...を追い出す

♦ **boot up 1** *v/i* COMPUT kidō suru 起動する **2** *v/t* COMPUT ... o kidō saseru ...を起動させる

booth (*at market, fair*) baiten 売店; (*in restaurant*) shikiriseki 仕切り席

booze *n* F sake 酒

booze-up *Br* F donchansawagi どんちゃん騒ぎ

border 1 *n* (*between countries*) kokkyō 国境; (*edge*) heri へり **2** *v/t country, river* ... to rinsetsu suru ...と隣接する

♦ **border on** *country* ... to rinsetsu suru ...と隣接する; (*be almost*) ... ni chikai ...に近い

borderline: *a ~ case* dotchitsukazu no bāi どっちつかずの場合

bore[1] *v/t hole* akeru あける

bore[2] **1** *n* (*person*) taikutsu na hito 退屈な人 **2** *v/t* taikutsu saseru 退屈させる; *be ~d* taikutsu suru 退屈する

bored unzari shita うんざりした

boredom tsumaranasa つまらなさ

boring taikutsu (na) 退屈(な)

born: *be ~* umareru 生まれる; *where were you ~?* anata wa doko de umaremashita ka あなたはどこで生まれましたか; *be a ~ ...* umarenagara no ... de aru 生まれながらの...である

borrow kariru 借りる

bosom (*of woman*) mune 胸

boss jōshi 上司

♦ **boss around** ... ni erasō ni sashizu suru ...に偉そうに指図する

bossy ibarichirasu いばり散らす

botanical shokubutsu-sa 植物の

botany shokubutsugaku 植物学

botch *v/t* shikujiru しくじる

both 1 *adj & pron* ryōhō (no) 両方(の); (*as subject of sentence*) ... wa ryōhō tomo ...は両方とも; *I know ~* (*of the*) *brothers* ryōhō no kyōdai o shitte iru 両方の兄弟を知っている; *~* (*of the*) *brothers were there* kyōdai wa ryōhō tomo soko ni ita 兄

弟は両方ともそこにいた; *~ of them* (*things*) ryōhō tomo 両方とも; (*people*) futari tomo 二人とも **2** *adv*: *~ my mother and I* haha mo watashi mo 母も私も; *he's ~ handsome and intelligent* kare wa hansamu de shikamo kashikoi 彼はハンサムでしかも賢い; *is it business or pleasure? - ~* sore wa shigoto desu ka, asobi desu ka - ryōhō それは仕事ですか、遊びですか - 両方

bother 1 *n* mendō 面倒; *it's no ~* zenzen kamaimasen 全然かまいません **2** *v/t* (*disturb*) ... ni meiwaku o kakeru ...に迷惑をかける; *person working* ... no jama o suru ...の邪魔をする; (*worry*) shinpai saseru 心配させる **3** *v/i* nayamu 悩む; *don't ~!* yamete やめて; *you needn't have ~ed* ki o tsukawanai de kudasai 気を使わないで下さい

bottle 1 *n* bin びん; (*for baby*) honyūbin ほ乳びん **2** *v/t* bin ni ireru びんに入れる

♦ **bottle up** *feelings* ... o muri ni osaeru ...を無理に抑える

bottle bank akibin-kaishūbako 空きびん回収箱

bottled water botoru-iri mineraru-wōtā ボトル入りミネラルウォーター

bottleneck *n* (*in road*) kyū ni semaku natte iru michi 急に狭くなっている道; (*in production*) nekku ネック

bottle-opener sennuki 栓抜き

bottom 1 *adj* mottomo shita (no) 最も下(の) **2** *n* (*underside*) ura 裏; (*on the inside*) soko 底; (*of hill*) fumoto ふもと; (*of pile*) shita 下; (*of street*) tsukiatari 突き当たり; (*of garden*) ichiban oku いちばん奥; (*buttocks*) shiri 尻; *at the ~ of the screen* sukurīn no shita no bubun ni スクリーンの下の部分に

♦ **bottom out** soko o tsuku 底をつく

bottom line (*outcome*) kekka 結果; (*the real issue*) hondai 本題

boulder ōkina maruishi 大きな丸石

bounce 1 *v/t ball* hazumaseru 弾ま

せる; SP baundo saseru バウンドさ
せる **2** v/i (of ball) hazumu 弾む; SP
baundo suru バウンドする; (on
sofa etc) tobihaneru 飛び跳ねる;
(of rain etc) utsu 打つ; (of check)
fuwatari de modoru 不渡りで戻る

bouncer yōjinbō 用心棒

bound[1] **1** n (as greeting) ojigi おじぎ
2 v/i ojigi o suru おじぎをする
3 v/t head sageru 下げる

bound[1]: **be ~ to do ...** (sure to) kitto
... suru きっと...する; (obliged to)
... suru gimu ga aru ...する義務が
ある

bound[2]: **be ~ for** (of ship) ... iki de
aru ...行きである

bound[3] **1** n (jump) hazumi 弾み **2** v/i
haneru はねる

boundary kyōkai 境界

boundless kagiri no nai 限りのない

bouquet hanataba 花束; (of wine)
kaori 香り

bourbon bābon バーボン

bout MED hossa 発作; (in boxing)
ichishiai 一試合

boutique butikku ブティック

bow[1] **1** n (as greeting) ojigi おじぎ
2 v/i ojigi o suru おじぎをする
3 v/t head sageru 下げる

bow[2] (knot) chōmusubi 蝶結び; MUS
yumi 弓

bow[3] (of ship) senshu 船首

bowels chō 腸

bowl[1] (container) hachi 鉢; (for
rice) chawan 茶わん; (for Japanese
soup) owan おわん; (for cooking,
salad) bōru ボール

bowl[2] v/i (in bowling) bōringu o
suru ボーリングをする

♦ **bowl over** fig ... o bikkuri saseru
...をびっくりさせる

bowling bōringu ボーリング

bowling alley bōringu-jō ボーリング
場

bow tie chōnekutai 蝶ネクタイ

box[1] n (container) hako 箱; (on
form) ran 欄

box[2] v/i bokushingu o suru ボクシ
ングをする

boxer bokusā ボクサー

boxing bokushingu ボクシング

boxing match bokushingu no shiai
ボクシングの試合

box office kippu-uriba 切符売り場

boy otoko no ko 男の子; (son)
musuko 息子

boycott 1 n boikotto ボイコット
2 v/t boikotto suru ボイコットする

boyfriend bōifurendo ボーイフレン
ド, kareshi 彼氏

boyish shōnen no yō (na) 少年のよ
う(な)

boyscout bōisukauto ボーイスカウ
ト

bra burajā ブラジャー

brace (on teeth) kyōsei 矯正器

bracelet buresuretto ブレスレット

bracket (for shelf) udeki 腕木; (in
text) kakko かっこ

brag v/i hora o fuku ほらを吹く

braid n (in hair) osagegami おさげ
髪; (trimming) mōru モール

braille tenji 点字

brain n nō 脳

brainless F nōmiso no taranai 脳み
その足らない

brains (intelligence) zunō 頭脳

brainstorm (bright idea) hirameki
ひらめき; **brainstorming**
burēnsutōmingu ブレーンストーミ
ング; **brain surgeon** nōgekai 脳外
科医; **brainwash** sennō suru 洗脳す
る; **brainwashing** sennō 洗脳;
brainwave (brilliant idea) meian
名案

brainy F atama no ii 頭のいい

brake 1 n burēki ブレーキ **2** v/i
burēki o kakeru ブレーキをかける

brake light burēki-ranpu ブレーキ
ランプ

brake pedal burēki-pedaru ブレー
キペダル

branch n (of tree) eda 枝; (of bank,
company) shiten 支店

♦ **branch off** (of road) bunki suru 分
岐する

♦ **branch out** jigyō o kakuchō suru
事業を拡張する

brand 1 n meigara 銘柄, burando ブ
ランド **2** v/t: **be ~ed a liar** usotsuki
no rakuin o osareru うそつきのら
く印を押される

brand image burando-imēji ブラン
ドイメージ

brandish furimawasu 振り回す

brand leader ichiban urete iru burando いちばん売れているブランド; **brand loyalty** burando-shikō ブランド志向; **brandname** meigara-mei 銘柄名, burando-mei ブランド名

brand-new maatarashii 真新しい

brandy burandē ブランデー

brass (*alloy*) shinchū 真ちゅう

brass band burasu-bando ブラスバンド

brassiere burajā ブラジャー

brat *pej* gaki がき

bravado kyosei 虚勢

brave *adj* yūkan (na) 勇敢(な)

bravery yūkan-sa 勇敢さ

brawl 1 *n* kenka けんか **2** *v/i* kenka suru けんかする

brawny kukkyō (na) 屈強(な)

Brazil Burajiru ブラジル

Brazilian 1 *adj* Burajiru (no) ブラジル(の) **2** *n* Burajiru-jin ブラジル人

breach (*violation*) ihan 違反; (*in party*) fuwa 不和

breach of contract LAW keiyaku-furikō 契約不履行

bread *n* pan パン

breadcrumbs (*for cooking*) panko パン粉; (*for bird*) pankuzu パンくず

breadth (*of road*) haba 幅; (*of knowledge*) hiro-sa 広さ

breadwinner kasegite 稼ぎ手

break 1 *n* hason 破損; (*in bone*) kossetsu 骨折; (*rest*) yasumi 休み; (*in relationship*) reikyaku-kikan 冷却期間; **give ... a ~** (*opportunity*) ... ni chansu o ataeru ...にチャンスを与える; **take a ~** kyūkei suru 休憩する; **without a ~** *work, travel* yasumi nashi de 休みなしで **2** *v/t device, toy* kowasu 壊す; *stick* oru 折る; *arm, leg* kossetsu suru 骨折する; *china, glass, egg* waru 割る; *law, promise, record* yaburu 破る; *news* shiraseru 知らせる **3** *v/i* (*of device, toy*) kowareru 壊れる; (*of china, glass, egg*) wareru 割れる; (*of news*) oreru 折れる; (*of news*) nagareru 流れる; (*of storm*) osou 襲う; (*of boy's voice*) kawaru 変わる

♦ **break away** *v/i* (*escape*) nigeru 逃げる; (*from family, tradition*) hanareru 離れる; (*from organization*) dattai suru 脱退する

♦ **break down 1** *v/i* (*of vehicle, machine*) koshō suru 故障する; (*of talks*) shippai ni owaru 失敗に終わる; (*in tears*) nakikuzureru 泣き崩れる; (*mentally*) seishinteki ni mairu 精神的に参る **2** *v/t door* uchikowasu 打ち壊す; *figures* bunrui suru 分類する

♦ **break even** COM sontoku nashi ni owaru 損得なしに終わる

♦ **break in** (*interrupt*) kuchi o hasamu 口をはさむ; (*of burglar*) shinnyū suru 侵入する

♦ **break off 1** *v/t* ... o mogitoru ...をもぎ取る; *damage* ... o oru ...を折る; *engagement* ... o haki suru ...を破棄する; **they've broken it off** karera wa kon'yaku haki ni natta 彼等は婚約破棄になった **2** *v/i* (*stop talking*) kyū ni hanashi o yameru 急に話をやめる

♦ **break out** (*start up*) okoru 起こる; (*of disease*) ryūkō suru 流行する; (*of prisoners*) dasshutsu suru 脱出する; **he broke out in a rash** kare wa totsuzen hasshin ga deta 彼は突然発しんが出た

♦ **break up 1** *v/t* (*into component parts*) ... o bunkai suru ...を分解する; *fight* ... o tomeru ...をとめる **2** *v/i* (*of ice*) wareru 割れる; (*of couple*) wakareru 別れる; (*of band, meeting*) kaisan suru 解散する

breakable kowareyasui 壊れやすい

breakage hason 破損

breakdown (*of vehicle, machine*) koshō 故障; (*of talks*) ketsuretsu 決裂; (*nervous ~*) noirōze ノイローゼ; (*of figures*) uchiwake 内訳

break-even point son'eki-bunkiten 損益分岐点

breakfast *n* chōshoku 朝食, asagohan 朝ごはん; **have ~** chōshoku o toru 朝食をとる

break-in oshikomi-gōtō 押し込み強盗

breakthrough (*in talks*) shinten 進

展; (*in science, technology*)
hiyakuteki-hatten 飛躍的発展;
(*personal achievement*) toppa 突破

breakup (*of marriage, partnership*)
hatan 破たん

breast (*of woman*) mune 胸

breastfeed *v/t* bonyū de sodateru
母乳で育てる

breaststroke hiraoyogi 平泳ぎ

breath hitoiki ひと息; *be out of ~* iki
ga kireru 息が切れる; *take a deep
~* shinkokyū o suru 深呼吸をする

Breathalyzer®, breath analyzer
inshu-kenchiki 飲酒検知器

breathe *v/i* iki o suru 息をする
2 *v/t* (*inhale*) suu 吸う; (*exhale*)
haku 吐く

♦ **breathe in 1** *v/i* iki o suikomu 息を
吸い込む **2** *v/t* ... o suikomu ...を吸
い込む

♦ **breathe out** *v/i* iki o haku 息を吐く

breathing kokyū 呼吸

breathless iki o kirashita 息を切ら
した

breathlessness ikigurushi-sa 息苦
しさ

breathtaking iki o nomu yō (na) 息
を飲むような(な)

breed 1 *n* hinshu 品種 **2** *v/t*
hanshoku saseru 繁殖させる; *fig*
hikiokosu 引き起こす **3** *v/i* (*of
animals*) hanshoku suru 繁殖する

breeding (*of animals*) hanshoku 繁
殖

breeding ground *fig* onshō 温床

breeze soyokaze そよ風

brew 1 *v/t beer* jōzō suru 醸造する;
tea ireru 入れる **2** *v/i* (*of storm*)
okorō to shite iru 起ころうとして
いる; (*of trouble*) sematte iru 迫っ
ている

brewer jōzō-gyōsha 醸造業者

brewery jōzōjo 醸造所

bribe 1 *n* wairo わいろ **2** *v/t* baishū
suru 買収する

bribery oshoku 汚職

brick renga れんが

bricklayer renga-shokunin れんが
職人

bride hanayome 花嫁

bridegroom hanamuko 花婿

bridesmaid hanayome-tsukisoi-nin
花嫁付添人

bridge¹ 1 *n* hashi 橋; (*of nose*)
hanabashira 鼻柱; (*of ship*) buridji
ブリッジ **2** *v/t gap* umeru うめる

bridge² (*card game*) buridji ブリッ
ジ

brief¹ *adj* mijikai 短い

brief² 1 *n* (*mission*) ninmu 任務
2 *v/t*: ~ *X on Y* X ni Y ni tsuite no
jōhō o ataeru XにYについての情
報を与える

briefcase burīfukēsu ブリーフケー
ス

briefing uchiawase 打合せ

briefly sukoshi no aida 少しの間; (*in
a few words*) kantan ni 簡単に; (*to
sum up*) kantan ni ieba 簡単に言え
ば

briefs (*for women*) shōtsu ショーツ;
(*for men*) burīfu ブリーフ

bright *color, smile, future* akarui 明
るい; (*sunny*) hareta 晴れた;
(*intelligent*) rikō (na) 利口(な)

brighten (*of face, person*) akaruku
naru 明るくなる

♦ **brighten up 1** *v/t* ... o akaruku
suru ...を明るくする **2** *v/i* (*of
weather*) hareru 晴れる

brightly akaruku 明るく

brightness (*of weather*) hareyaka-
sa 晴やかさ; (*of smile*) akaru-sa 明
るさ; (*intelligence*) rikō-sa 利口さ

brilliance (*of person*) meiseki-sa 明
せきさ; (*of color*) azayaka-sa 鮮や
かさ

brilliant *sunshine* hikarikagayaku
光り輝く; *idea, performance*
subarashii 素晴らしい; (*very
intelligent*) yūshū (na) 優秀(な)

brim (*of container, hat*) fuchi ふち

brimful afurenbakari (no) あふれん
ばかり(の)

bring *object* motte kuru 持ってくる;
person tsurete kuru 連れてくる;
peace, happiness etc motarasu も
たらす; ~ *it here, will you* koko e
motte kite kudasai ne ここへ持っ
てきて下さいね; *can I ~ a friend?*
tomodachi o tsuretekite iidesu ka
友達を連れてきていいですか

♦ **bring about** ... o motarasu ...をもたらす

♦ **bring around** (*from a faint*) ... no ishiki o kaifuku saseru ...の意識を回復させる; (*persuade*) ... o settoku suru ...を説得する

♦ **bring back** (*return*) ... o kaesu ...を返す; (*re-introduce*) ... o fukkatsu saseru ...を復活させる; *memories* ... o omoidasaseru ...を思い出させる; *the song brought back memories of my childhood* sono uta o kiku to kodomo no koro o omoidasu その歌を聞くと子どものころを思い出す

♦ **bring down** *fence, tree* o taosu ...を倒す; *government* ... o datō suru ...を打倒する; *bird, airplane* ... o uchiotosu ...を撃ち落とす; *inflation, price* ... o sageru ...を下げる

♦ **bring in** *interest, income* ... o umu ...を生む; (*earn*) ... no kane ga hairu ...の金が入る; *legislation* ... o dōnyū suru ...を導入する; *verdict* ... o kudasu ...を下す; (*involve*) ... o sanka saseru ...を参加させる

♦ **bring out** (*produce: book*) ... o shuppan suru ...を出版する; *video, CD* ... o rirīsu suru ...をリリースする; *new product* ... o happyō suru ...を発表する

♦ **bring to** (*from a faint*) ... no ishiki o kaifuku saseru ...の意識を回復させる

bring up *child* ... o sodateru ...を育てる; *subject* ... o mochidasu ...を持ち出す; (*vomit*) ... o haku ...を吐く

brink fuchi ふち; *fig* setogiwa 瀬戸際

brisk *person, voice, walk* kibikibi shita きびきびした; *trade* kappatsu (na) 活発(な)

bristles (*on chin*) bushōhige 不精ひげ; (*of brush*) ke 毛

bristling: *be ~ with* ... de ippai de aru ...でいっぱいである

Britain Eikoku 英国, Igirisu イギリス

British 1 *adj* Eikoku (no) 英国(の),

Igirisu (no) イギリス(の) **2** *n the ~* Eikoku-jin 英国人, Igirisu-jin イギリス人

Briton Eikoku-jin 英国人, Igirisu-jin イギリス人

brittle *adj* moroi もろい

broach *subject* kiridasu 切り出す

broad 1 *adj* hiroi 広い; (*general*) ōzappa (na) 大ざっぱ(な); *in ~ daylight* hakuchū ni 白昼に **2** *n* F (*woman*) onna 女

broadcast 1 *n* hōsō 放送 **2** *v/t* hōsō suru 放送する

broadcaster kyasutā キャスター

broadcasting hōsō 放送

broaden 1 *v/i* hiroku naru 広くなる **2** *v/t* hirogeru 広げる

broadjump habatobi 幅跳び

broadly: *~ speaking* ōzappa ni itte 大ざっぱに言って

broadminded kokoro no hiroi 心の広い

broccoli burokkori ブロッコリ

brochure panfuretto パンフレット

broil *v/t* yakiami de yaku 焼き網で焼く

broiler *n* (*on stove*) yakiami 焼き網; (*chicken*) wakadori 若鶏

broke F (*temporarily*) kinketsu (no) 金欠(の); (*long term*) ichimon-nashi (no) 一文なし(の); *go ~* (*bankrupt*) sukkarakan ni naru すっからかんになる

broken *adj* kowareta 壊れた; *glass, window* wareta 割れた; *neck, arm* kossetsu shita 骨折した; *home* hōkai shita 崩壊した; *marriage* hatan shita 破綻した; *English* burōkun (na) ブロークン(な)

broken-hearted kanashimi ni kureta 悲しみにくれた

broker (*stock~*) shōken-burōkā 証券ブローカー; (*insurance ~*) hoken-dairinin 保険代理人

bronchitis kikanshi-en 気管支炎

bronze *n* seidō 青銅; (*medal*) buronzu ブロンズ

brooch burōchi ブローチ

brood *v/i* (*of person*) kangaekomu 考え込む

broom hōki ほうき

broth (*soup*) sūpu スープ; (*stock*) niku no dashijiru 肉のだし汁

brothel baishun'yado 売春宿

brother (*own, elder*) ani 兄; (*somebody else's, elder*) onīsan お兄さん; (*own, younger*) otōto 弟; (*somebody else's, younger*) otōtosan 弟さん; **they're ~s** karera wa kyōdai desu 彼らは兄弟です; **~s and sisters** kyōdai-shimai 兄弟姉妹

brother-in-law (*own, elder*) giri no ani 義理の兄; (*somebody else's, elder*) giri no onīsan 義理のお兄さん; (*own, younger*) giri no otōto 義理の弟; (*somebody else's, younger*) giri no otōtosan 義理の弟さん; **they're brothers-in-law** karera wa giri no kyōdai desu 彼らは義理の兄弟です

brotherly kyōdai no yō (na) 兄弟のよう(な)

browbeat odoshitsukeru 脅しつける

brow (*forehead*) hitai 額; (*of hill*) ue 上

brown 1 *n* chairo 茶色 **2** *adj* chairo (no) 茶色(の); (*tanned*) hi ni yaketa 日に焼けた **3** *v/t* (*in cooking*) chairoku itameru 茶色く炒める **4** *v/i* (*in cooking*) chairo ni irozuku 茶色に色づく

brownbag: **~ it** F bentō o jisan suru 弁当を持参する

Brownie Buraunī ブラウニー

Brownie points: **earn ~** tensūkasegi o suru 点数かせぎをする

brownie (*cake*) buraunī ブラウニー

brown-nose *v/t* F ... ni pekopeko suru ...にぺこぺこする

browse (*in store*) busshoku suru 物色する; **~ through a book** hon o hiroiyomi suru 本を拾い読みする

browser COMPUT burauzā ブラウザー

bruise 1 *n* dabokushō 打撲症 **2** *v/t* aza o tsukeru あざをつける; *fruit* itameru 傷める **3** *v/i* (*of person*) aza ni naru あざになる; (*of fruit*) itamu 傷む

bruising *adj fig* tsurai つらい

brunch buranchi ブランチ

brunette burunetto ブルネット

brunt: **bear the ~ of ...** ... ni sarasareru ...にさらされる

brush 1 *n* burashi ブラシ; (*for hair*) hea-burashi ヘアブラシ; (*for paint*) fude 筆; (*for teeth*) ha-burashi 歯ブラシ; (*conflict*) isakai いさかい **2** *v/t* burashi o kakeru ブラシをかける; (*touch lightly*) kasuru かする; (*move away*) harainokeru 払いのける

◆ **brush against** ... o kasuru ...をかする

◆ **brush aside** ... o mushi suru ...を無視する

◆ **brush off** ... o harainokeru ...を払いのける; *criticism* ... o mushi suru ...を無視する

◆ **brush up** ... o yarinaosu ...をやり直す

brushoff F kyozetsu 拒絶; **get the ~** kyozetsu sareru 拒絶される

brusque bukkirabō (na) ぶっきらぼう(な)

Brussels sprouts mekyabetsu 芽キャベツ

brutal zannin (na) 残忍(な)

brutality zannin-sa 残忍さ

brutally zankoku ni 残酷に; **be ~ frank** shōjiki ni iu to 正直に言うと

brute kedamono けだもの

brute force chikara 力; (*dispelling crowd*) bōryoku 暴力

bubble *n* awa 泡; (*soap ~*) shabondama しゃぼん玉

bubble gum fūsengamu 風船ガム

buck¹ *n* F (*dollar*) doru ドル

buck² *v/i* (*of horse*) haneagaru 跳ね上る

buck³: **pass the ~** sekinin-tenka o suru 責任転嫁をする

bucket *n* baketsu バケツ

buckle¹ 1 *n* bakkuru バックル **2** *v/t belt* ... o bakkuru de shimeru ...をバックルで締める

buckle² *v/i* (*of metal*) yugamu ゆがむ

bud *n* BOT tsubomi つぼみ

Buddha Budda 仏陀; **Great ~** daibutsu 大仏

Buddhism Bukkyō 仏教

Buddhist 1 *n* Bukkyōto 仏教徒 **2** *adj* Bukkyō (no) 仏教(の); **~ altar** butsudan 仏壇; **~ monk** bōzu 坊主; **~ sutra** okyō お経

buddy F aibō 相棒; **hey ~, move your car, will you?** anta, kuruma dokete kurenai あんた車どけてくれない

budge 1 *v/t* ugokasu 動かす; (*make reconsider*) … no iken o kaeru … の意見を変える **2** *v/i* ugoku 動く; (*change one's mind*) iken o kaeru 意見を変える

budgerigar sekiseiinko セキセイインコ

budget 1 *n* yosan 予算; (*of a family*) kakei 家計; **be on a ~** yosan ga aru 予算がある **2** *v/i* yosan o tateru 予算を立てる

♦ **budget for** … o yosan ni ireru … を予算にいれる

buff[1] *adj* (*color*) usuchairo 薄茶色

buff[2] *n*: **a movie/jazz ~** eiga/jazu-kyō 映画/ジャズ狂

buffalo baffarō バッファロー

buffer RAIL kanshōki 緩衝器; COMPUT kanshōkioku-sōchi 緩衝記憶装置; *fig* hashiwatashi 橋渡し

buffet[1] *n* (*meal*) risshoku 立食

buffet[2] *v/t* (*of wind*) … ni uchitsukeru …に打ちつける

bug 1 *n* (*insect*) mushi 虫; (*virus*) baikin ばい菌; (*spying device*) tōchōki 盗聴器; COMPUT bagu バグ **2** *v/t room, telephone* … ni tōchōki o shikakeru …に盗聴器を仕掛ける; F (*annoy*) iraira saseru いらいらさせる

buggy (*for baby*) ubaguruma 乳母車

build 1 *n* (*of person*) taikaku 体格 **2** *v/t* tateru 建てる

♦ **build up 1** *v/t strength* … o tsukeru …をつける; *relationship* … o kizukiageru …を築き上げる; *collection* … o fuyashite iku …を増やしていく **2** *v/i* masu 増す

builder kenchiku-gyōsha 建築業者

building kensetsu 建設; (*house, office block etc*) tatemono 建物, birudingu ビルディング

building site kensetsu-genba 建設現場

building trade kensetsugyō 建設業

build-up (*accumulation*) chikuseki 蓄積; (*publicity*) senden 宣伝

built-in tsukuritsuke (no) 作り付け(の); *flash* naizō (no) 内蔵(の)

built-up area jūtakugai 住宅街

bulb BOT kyūkon 球根; (*light ~*) denkyū 電球

bulge 1 *n* fukurami 膨らみ; (*bigger and noticeable*) deppari 出っ張り **2** *v/i* (*of pocket*) fukureru 膨れる; (*of wall, eyes*) depparu 出っ張る

bulk daibubun 大部分; **in ~** tairyō ni 大量に

bulky kasabatta かさばった

bull (*animal*) oushi 雄牛

bulldoze (*demolish*) burudōzā de sarachi ni suru ブルドーザーでさら地にする; **~ X into Y** *fig* X ni Y o gorioshi suru XをYにごり押しする

bulldozer burudōzā ブルドーザー

bullet tama 弾

bulletin kōhō 公報

bulletin board *also* COMPUT keijiban 掲示板

bullet-proof bōdan (no) 防弾(の)

bullet train (*in Japan*) shinkansen 新幹線

bull market FIN agesōba 上げ相場

bull's-eye mato no chūshin 的の中心; **hit the ~** tekichū suru 的中する

bullshit V **1** *n* tawagoto たわごと **2** *v/i* detarame o iu でたらめを言う

bully 1 *n* yowaimono-ijime suru hito 弱い者いじめする人; (*child*) ijimekko いじめっ子 **2** *v/t* ijimeru いじめる

bum 1 *n* F (*tramp*) furō-sha 浮浪者; (*worthless person*) yōnashi 用無し **2** *adj* (*useless*) yaku ni tatanai 役に立たない **3** *v/t cigarette etc* takaru たかる

♦ **bum around** F (*travel*) burabura tabi o suru ぶらぶら旅をする; (*be lazy*) bōtto shite sugosu ぼーっとして過ごす

bumblebee maruhanabachi まるはなばち

bump 1 n (*swelling*) kobu こぶ; (*in road*) dansa 段差; **get a ~ on the head** atama o butsukeru 頭をぶつける **2** v/t butsukeru ぶつける

♦ **bump into** *table* ... ni butsukaru ...にぶつかる; (*meet*) ... ni hyokkori au ...にひょっこり会う

♦ **bump off** F ... o korosu ...を殺す

♦ **bump up** F *prices* ... o ageru ...を上げる

bumper n MOT banpā バンパー

bumpy dekoboko (na) でこぼこ(な)

bun (*hairstyle*) shiniyon シニョン; (*for eating*) marupan 丸パン

bunch (*of people*) gurūpu グループ; **a ~ of flowers** hanataba 花束; **a ~ of grapes** hitofusa no budō 一房のぶどう; **thanks a ~** (*ironic*) sore wa dōmo それはどうも

bundle (*of clothes*) tsutsumi 包み; (*of wood*) taba 束

♦ **bundle up** v/t ... o hitomatome ni suru ...をひとまとめにする; (*dress warmly*) ... o atsugi saseru ...を厚着させる

bungle v/t shikujiru しくじる

bunk shindai 寝台

bunk beds nidan-beddo 二段ベッド

buoy n bui ブイ

buoyant ukiuki shita 浮き浮きした; *economy* kakki no aru 活気のある

burden 1 n omoni 重荷; *fig* futan 負担 **2** v/t: **~ X with Y** Y de X o nayamasu YでXを悩ます

bureau (*chest of drawers*) tansu たんす; (*government department*) kyoku 局; (*office*) ka 課

bureaucracy (*red tape*) kanryō-shugi 官僚主義; (*system*) kanryō 官僚

bureaucrat kanryō 官僚

bureaucratic kanryōteki (na) 官僚的(な)

burger hanbāgā ハンバーガー

burglar gōtō 強盗

burglar alarm tōnan-hōchiki 盗難報知機

burglarize gōtō suru 強盗する

burglary gōtō 強盗

burial maisō 埋葬

burly takumashii たくましい

Burma Biruma ビルマ, Myanmā ミャンマー

Burmese 1 adj Biruma (no) ビルマ(の), Myanmā (no) ミャンマー(の) **2** n (*person*) Biruma-jin ビルマ人, Myanmā-jin ミャンマー人

burn 1 n yakekoge 焼け焦げ; (*on finger etc*) yakedo やけど **2** v/t moyasu 燃やす; *toast, meat* kogasu 焦がす; *finger, tongue etc* yakedo suru やけどする; (*consume*) moyasu 燃やす **3** v/i moeru 燃える; (*of house*) yakeru 焼ける; (*of toast*) kogeru 焦げる; (*get sunburnt*) hi ni yakeru 日に焼ける

♦ **burn down 1** v/t yakitsukusu 焼き尽くす **2** v/i zenshō suru 全焼する

♦ **burn out** v/t: **burn oneself out** seiryoku o tsukaihatasu 精力を使い果たす; **a burned-out car** yaketa kuruma 焼けた車

burner (*on cooker*) konro コンロ

burp 1 n geppu げっぷ **2** v/i geppu suru げっぷする **3** v/t *baby* geppu saseru げっぷさせる

burst 1 n (*in water pipe*) haretsu 破裂; (*of gunfire*) rensha 連射; **in a ~ of energy** yaruki ga waite やる気がわいて **2** adj *tire* haretsu shita 破裂した **3** v/t *balloon* haretsu saseru 破裂させる **4** v/i (*of balloon*) haretsu suru 破裂する; **~ into a room** heya ni tobikomu 部屋に飛び込む; **~ into tears** watto nakidasu わっと泣き出す; **~ out laughing** kyū ni waraidasu 急に笑い出す

bury *person* maisō suru 埋葬する; *animal* umeru 埋める; (*conceal*) umete kakusu 埋めて隠す; **be buried under** (*covered by*) ... no shita ni umatte iru ...の下に埋まっている; **~ oneself in one's work** shigoto ni bottō suru 仕事に没頭する

bus 1 n basu バス **2** v/t basu de idō saseru バスで移動させる

busboy shokudō-kyūji no joshu 食堂給仕の助手

bush (*plant*) shigemi 茂み; (*land*) mikai no chi 未開の地

bushed F (*tired*) kutakuta (no) くた
くた(の)

bushy *beard* mojamoja (no) もじゃ
もじゃ(の)

business (*trade*) shōbai 商売;
(*company*) kaisha 会社; (*work*)
shigoto 仕事; (*sector*) shokugyō 職
業; (*affair, matter*) koto 事; (*as
subject of study*) keieigaku 経営
学; **on ~** shigoto de 仕事で; *that's
none of your ~!*, *mind your own ~!*
ōkina osewa da 大きなお世話だ

business card meishi 名刺;
business class bijinesu-kurasu ビ
ジネスクラス; **business hours**
eigyō-jikan 営業時間;
businesslike jissaiteki (na) 実際
的(な); **business lunch** bijinesu-
ranchi ビジネスランチ;
businessman jitsugyōka 実業家;
business meeting kaigō 会合;
business school keieigaku-
daigakuin 経営学大学院; **business
studies** keieigaku 経営学;
business suit sūtsu スーツ, sebiro
背広; **business trip** shutchō 出張;
businesswoman josei-jitsugyōka
女性実業家

bus station basu-tāminaru バスター
ミナル

bus stop basutei バス停

bust¹ *n* (*of woman*) basuto バスト

bust² F **1** *adj* (*broken*) tsubureta つ
ぶれた; **go ~** hasan suru 破産する
2 *v/t* haretsu saseru 破裂させる

♦ **bustle around** sewashinaku
ugokimawaru せわしなく動き回る

bust-up F hakyoku 破局

busty guramā (na) グラマー(な)

busy 1 *adj* isogashii 忙しい; *street*
nigiyaka (na) にぎやか(な); *shop,
restaurant: making money* hanjō
shite iru 繁盛している; (*full of
people*) konde iru 混んでいる;
TELEC hanashichū (no) 話中(の);
be ~ doing ... ... shite iru isogashii
... していて忙しい **2** *v/t: ~ oneself
with ...** ... de isogashii ...で忙しい

busybody osekkai na hito おせっか
いな人

busy signal hanashichū no oto 話中

の音

but 1 *conj* keredomo けれども; *I
tried, ~ I couldn't* tameshite mita
keredomo dekinakatta 試してみた
けれどもできなかった; *that's not
fair!* demo sore wa fukōhei da で
もそれは不公平だ; *it's not me ~
my father you want* hitsuyō na no
wa watashi de wa naku chichi desu
必要なのは私ではなく父です; *~
then* (*again*) shikashi しかし
2 *prep: all ~ him* kare no nozoite
をのぞいて; *the last ~ one* saigo
kara nibanme 最後から二番目; *the
next ~ one* tsugi no tsugi 次の次; *~
for you* kimi ga inakattara 君がい
なかったら; *nothing ~ the best*
saikō no mono dake 最高のものだ
け; *nothing ~ problems* mondai
bakari 問題ばかり

butcher *n* niku-ya 肉屋; (*murderer*)
satsujinki 殺人鬼

butt 1 *n* (*of cigarette*) suigara 吸い
殻; (*of joke*) mato 的; F (*buttocks*)
shiri 尻 **2** *v/t* atama de tsuku 頭で
突く; (*of goat, bull*) tsuno de tsuku
角で突く

♦ **butt in** ... ni kuchi o hasamu ...に
口をはさむ

butter 1 *n* batā バター **2** *v/t* ... ni
batā o nuru ...にバターを塗る

♦ **butter up** F ... ni hetsurau ...にへ
つらう

buttercup kinpōge きんぽうげ

butterfly (*insect*) chō ちょう

buttocks shiri 尻

button 1 *n* botan ボタン; (*on
machine*) oshi-botan 押しボタン;
(*badge*) badji バッジ **2** *v/t* botan o
tomeru ボタンを留める

buttonhole 1 *n* (*in suit*) botanhōru
ボタンホール **2** *v/t* hikitomete
hanasu 引きとめて話す

buxom nikuzuki no yoi 肉づきのよい

buy 1 *n* kaimono 買い物 **2** *v/t* kau 買
う; *can I ~ you a drink?* ippai
ogorasete kudasai 一杯おごらせて
ください; *$50 doesn't ~ much*
gojū doru de wa amari kaenai 50
ドルではあまり買えない

♦ **buy off** (*bribe*) ... o baishū suru ...

を収収する

♦ **buy out** COM ... o kaitoru ...を買い取る

♦ **buy up** ... o kaishimeru ...を買い占める

buyer kaite 買い手; (*for store*) shiiregakari 仕入れ係; (*for luxury goods*) baiyā バイヤー

buzz 1 *n* bunbun iu oto ぶんぶんいう音; F (*thrill*) kōfun 興奮 **2** *v/i* (*of insect*) bunbun iu ぶんぶんいう; (*with buzzer*) buzā o narasu ブザーを鳴らす **3** *v/t* (*with buzzer*) buzā de yobu ブザーで呼ぶ

♦ **buzz off**: ～*!* F dete ike 出て行け

buzzer buzā ブザー

by 1 *prep* ◊ (*agency*) ... ni ...に; *she was knocked down ~ a bus* kanojo wa basu ni hikareta 彼女はバスにひかれた; *a painting ~ Picasso* Pikaso no e ピカソの絵; *a play ~ ...* ... no kaita shibai ...の書いた芝居 ◊ (*near, next to*) ... no soba ni ...のそばに; *~ the window* mado no soba ni 窓のそばに ◊ (*past*) soba o tōri sugite そばを通り過ぎて; *we drove ~ the church* ◊ (*mode of transport*) ... de ...で; *~*

bus / *train* basu / densha de バス / 電車で ◊ (*no later than*) ... made ni ...までに; *~ Friday* kin'yōbi made ni 金曜日までに; *~ 9 o'clock* kuji made ni 九時までに; *~ this time tomorrow* ashita no kono jikan ni wa 明日のこの時間には ◊ (*during*): *~ day* / *~ night* nitchū / yorujū 日中 / 夜中 ◊ (*according to*): *~ my watch* watashi no tokei de wa 私の時計では ◊ (*measuring*): *~ the hour* / *ton* jikan / ton tan'i de 時間 / トン単位で; *~ a couple of minutes* ni, sanpun no sa de 2、3分の差で; *2 ~ 4* ni kakeru yon 2掛ける4 ◊: *~ oneself* hitori de ひとりで **2** *adv*: *~ and ~* yagate やがて

bye(-bye) baibai バイバイ

bygone: *let ~s be ~s* sugita koto wa mizu ni nagase 過ぎたことは水に流せ

bypass 1 *n* (*road*) baipasu バイパス; MED baipasu バイパス **2** *v/t* ukai suru う回する

by-product fukusanbutsu 副産物

bystander yaji umatachi やじ馬たち

byte baito バイト

C

cab (*taxi*) takushī タクシー; (*of truck*) untendai 運転台

cabaret furoā-shō フロアーショー

cabbage kyabetsu キャベツ

cab driver takushī-doraibā タクシードライバー

cabin (*of plane, ship*) kyakushitsu 客室

cabin crew kyakushitsu-gakari 客室係

cabinet todana 戸棚; POL naikaku 内閣

cable (*of electrical appliance, telephone*) kōdo コード; (*for*

securing) tsuna 綱; *~ (TV)* kēburu-terebi ケーブルテレビ

cable car kēburu-kā ケーブルカー; **cable television** kēburu-terebi ケーブルテレビ; **cab stand** takushī noriba タクシー乗り場

cactus saboten さぼてん

cadaver shitai 死体

CAD-CAM kyado-kyamu キャド-キャム

caddie 1 *n* (*in golf*) kyadī キャディー **2** *v/i*: *~ for* ... no kyadī o suru ...のキャディーをする

cadet shikan-gakkō-seito 士官学校

生徒

cadge: ~ *X* from *Y* Y に X を たかる
YにXをたかる

café kafe カフェ

cafeteria kafeteria カフェテリア

caffeine kafein カフェイン

cage (*for bird*) kago かご; (*for lion*) ori おり

cagey keikai shite iru 警戒している

cahoots: *be in ~ with* ... to guru ni natte iru ...とぐるになっている

cake 1 *n* kēki ケーキ; *be a piece of ~ fig* asameshimae desu 朝飯前です 2 *v/i* katamaru 固まる

calcium karushiumu カルシウム

calculate (*work out*) mitsumoru 見積もる; (*in arithmetic*) keisan suru 計算する

calculating dasanteki (na) 打算的 (な)

calculation keisan 計算

calculator dentaku 電卓

calendar karendā カレンダー

calf[1] (*young cow*) koushi 子牛

calf[2] (*of leg*) fukurahagi ふくらはぎ

caliber (*of gun*) kōkei 口径; *a man of his ~* sugoude no hito すご腕の人

call 1 *n* TELEC denwa 電話; (*shout*) koe 声; (*demand*) yōkyū 要求; *there's a ~ for you* anata ni denwa desu あなたに電話です 2 *v/t* (*on phone*) ... ni denwa o suru ...に電話をする; (*summon*) shōshū suru 招集する; (*shout*) yobu 呼ぶ; *he ~ed me a liar* kare wa watashi o usotsuki da to itta 彼は私をうそつきだと言った; *what have they ~ed the baby?* karera wa akanbō o nan to nazukemashita ka 彼らは赤ん坊を何と名付けましたか; *but we ~ him Tom* dakedo watashitachi wa kare o Tomu to yonde imasu だけど私たちは彼をトムと呼んでいます; *... names* ... o nonoshiru ...をののしる 3 *v/i* (*on phone*) denwa o kakeru 電話をかける; (*shout*) yobu 呼ぶ; (*visit*) tachiyoru 立ち寄る

♦ **call at** (*stop at*) ... ni chotto tachiyoru ...にちょっと立ち寄る; (*of train*) ... ni teisha suru ...に停車する

♦ **call back** 1 *v/t* (*on phone*) ... ni orikaeshi denwa suru ...に折り返し電話する; (*summon*) ... o yobimodosu ...を呼び戻す 2 *v/i* (*on phone*) denwa o kakenaosu 電話をかけ直す; (*make another visit*) ato de mata tachiyoru あとでまた立ち寄る

♦ **call for** (*collect*) ... o tori ni tachiyoru ...を取りに立ち寄る; (*demand*) ... o yōkyū suru ...を要求する; (*require*) ... o hitsuyō to suru ...を必要とする

♦ **call in** 1 *v/t* (*summon*) ... o yobiireru ...を呼び入れる 2 *v/i* (*phone*) denwa o ireru 電話を入れる

♦ **call off** (*cancel*) ... o toriyameru ...を取り止める

♦ **call on** (*urge*) ... ni yōkyū suru ...に要求する; (*visit*) ... o hōmon suru ...を訪問する

♦ **call out** (*shout*) ōgoe de yobu 大声で呼ぶ; (*summon*) ... o shōshū suru ...を招集する

♦ **call up** *v/t* (*on phone*) ... ni denwa o kakeru ...に電話をかける; COMPUT ... o konpyūtā de yobidasu ...をコンピューターで呼び出す

caller (*on phone*) denwa o kaketa hito 電話をかけた人; (*visitor*) hōmon-sha 訪問者

call girl baishunfu 売春婦

calligraphy shodō 書道

callous reitan (na) 冷淡 (な)

calm 1 *adj sea* odayaka (na) 穏やか (な); *person* ochitsuita 落ち着いた 2 *n* (*of countryside*) shizuke-sa 静けさ; (*of person*) heisei 平静 3 *v/t* shizumeru 静める

♦ **calm down** 1 *v/t* ... o shizumeru ...を静める 2 *v/i* (*of sea, wind*) shizuka ni naru 静かになる; (*of person*) ochitsuku 落ち着く

calorie karorī カロリー

Cambodia Kanbojia カンボジア

Cambodian 1 *adj* Kanbojia (no) カンボジア(の) 2 *n* (*person*) Kanbojia-jin カンボジア人

camcorder bideo-kamera ビデオカメラ

camellia tsubaki つばき

camera kamera カメラ

cameraman kameraman カメラマン

camouflage 1 n kamufurāju カムフラージュ 2 v/t kamufurāju suru カムフラージュする

camp 1 n kyanpu キャンプ 2 v/i kyanpu suru キャンプする

campaign 1 n undō 運動 2 v/i undō o okosu 運動を起こす

campaigner undō-ka 運動家

camper (*person*) kyanpu o suru hito キャンプをする人; (*vehicle*) kyanpingu-kā キャンピングカー

camp ground kyanpu-jō キャンプ場

camping kyanpu キャンプ

campsite kyanpu-jō キャンプ場

campus kōnai 構内, kyanpasu キャンパス

can[1] (*ability*) ... koto ga dekiru ...ことができる; *I ~ use a computer* konpyūtā o tsukau koto ga dekiru コンピューターを使うことができる; *~ you hear me?* kikoemasu ka 聞こえますか; *I ~'t see* mienai 見えない; *~ you speak French?* Furansu-go ga hanasemasu ka フランス語が話せますか; *I ~'t speak French* Furansu-go ga hanasemasen フランス語が話せません; *as fast as you ~* dekiru dake hayaku できるだけ速く ◊ (*request*) ... te mo ii desu ka ...てもいいですか; *~ he call me back?* kare ni denwa o kakenaoshite morattemo ii desu ka 彼に電話をかけなおしてもらってもいいですか; *~ you help me?* tetsudatte morattemo ii desu ka 手伝ってもらってもいいですか; *~ I have a beer / coffee?* bīru / kōhī o itadakimasu te mo ii desu ka ビール / コーヒーをいただいてもいいですか ◊ (*permission*) ... te mo ii desu ka ...てもいいですか; *~ I borrow the car?* kuruma o karite mo ii desu ka 車を借りてもいいですか ◊ (*prohibition*): *~not* ... te wa ikenai ...てはいけない; *you ~not stay*

without a visa vizanashi de taizai shite wa ikenai ビザなしで滞在してはいけない ◊ (*offer*): *~ I help you?* nanika otetsudai shimashō ka 何かお手伝いしましょうか ◊ (*disbelief*): *that ~'t be right* sore wa machigatte iru ni chigainai それは間違っているに違いない

can[2] 1 n (*for drinks etc*) kan 缶 2 v/t kanzume ni suru 缶詰にする

Canada Kanada カナダ

Canadian 1 adj Kanada (no) カナダ(の) 2 n Kanada-jin カナダ人

canal (*waterway*) unga 運河

canary kanaria カナリア

cancel torikesu 取り消す

cancellation torikeshi 取り消し

cancer gan がん

c & f (= *cost and freight*) unchin-komi kakaku 運賃込み価格

c & i (= *cost and insurance*) hokenryō-komi kakaku 保険料込み価格

candid sotchoku (na) 率直(な)

candidacy rikkōho 立候補

candidate (*for position*) kōho-sha 候補者; (*in exam*) juken-sha 受験者

candle rōsoku ろうそく

candlestick rōsokutate ろうそく立て

candor sotchoku-sa 率直さ

candy kyandī キャンディー

cannabis taima 大麻

canned *fruit, tomatoes* kanzume (no) 缶詰(の); (*recorded*) rokuon sareta 録音された

cannibalize bunkai suru 分解する

cannot → **can**[1]

canoe kanū カヌー

can opener kankiri 缶切り

cant tatemae 建て前

can't → **can**[1]

canteen (*in factory*) shokudō 食堂

canvas (*for painting*) kyanbasu キャンバス; (*material*) kyanbasu-ji キャンバス地

canvass 1 v/t (*seek opinion of*) ... no iken o kiku ...の意見を聴く 2 v/i POL senkyo-undō o suru 選挙運動をする

canyon kyōkoku 峡谷

cap (*hat*) bōshi 帽子; (*of bottle, jar*) futa ふた; (*of pen, lens ~*) kyappu キャップ

capability (*of person*) nōryoku 能力; (*of military*) senryoku 戦力

capable (*efficient*) yūnō (na) 有能 (な); *be ~ of* ... ga dekiru ...ができる

capacity (*of container*) yōseki 容積; (*of building*) shūyōryoku 収容力; (*of elevator*) teiin 定員; (*of car engine*) haikiryō 排気量; (*of factory*) seisanryoku 生産力; (*ability*) nōryoku 能力; *in my ~ as ...* ... no shikaku de ...の資格で

cape (*land*) misaki 岬

capital *n* (*of country*) shuto 首都; (*letter*) ōmoji 大文字; (*money*) shihon 資本

capital expenditure shihon-shishutsu 資本支出; **capital gains tax** kyapitarugein-zei キャピタルゲイン税; **capital growth** shihon-seichō 資本成長

capitalism shihon-shugi 資本主義

capitalist 1 *adj* shihon-shugi (no) 資本主義(の) **2** *n* shihon-shugisha 資本主義者; (*businessman*) shihon-ka 資本家

capital letter ōmoji 大文字

capital punishment shikei 死刑

capitulate kōfuku suru 降伏する

capsize 1 *v/i* hikkurikaesu ひっくり返る **2** *v/t* hikkurikaesu ひっくり返す

capsule (*of medicine*) kapuseru カプセル; (*space ~*) roketto no kapuseru ロケットのカプセル

captain *n* (*of ship*) senchō 船長; (*of aircraft*) kichō 機長; (*of team*) kyaputen キャプテン

caption *n* setsumeibun 説明文

captivate miryō suru 魅了する

captive horyo 捕虜

captivity toraware no mi とらわれの身

capture 1 *n* (*of city*) senkyo 占拠; (*of criminal*) taiho 逮捕; (*of animal*) hokaku 捕獲 **2** *v/t person, animal* tsukamaeru 捕まえる; *city, building* kōryaku suru 攻略する;

market share kakutoku suru 獲得する; (*portray*) toraeru 捉える

car kuruma 車; (*of train*) sharyō 車両; *by ~* kuruma de 車で

carafe (*for wine*) karafu カラフ

carat karatto カラット

carbohydrate denpunshitsu でんぷん質, tansuika-butsu 炭水化物

carbonated tansan'iri (no) 炭酸入り(の)

carbon monoxide issanka-tanso 一酸化炭素

carburetor kyaburetā キャブレター

carcinogen hatsugansei-busshitsu 発がん性物質

carcinogenic hatsugansei (no) 発がん性(の)

card (*to mark special occasion*) kādo カード; (*post~*) hagaki 葉書; (*business ~*) meishi 名刺; (*playing ~*) toranpu トランプ

cardboard bōrugami ボール紙

cardiac shinzō (no) 心臓(の)

cardiac arrest shinzō-teishi 心臓停止

cardigan kādigan カーディガン

card index kādoshiki-sakuin カード式索引

card key kādoshiki no kagi カード式のかぎ

care 1 *n* (*of baby, pet*) sewa 世話; (*of the elderly*) kaigo 介護; (*of sick person*) kango 看護; (*medical ~*) iryō 医療; (*worry*) nayami 悩み; *~ of ...* ... kata ...方, ... kizuke ...気付; *take ~* (*be cautious*) ki o tsukeru 気をつける; *take ~ (of yourself)!* (*goodbye*) ki o tsukete 気をつけて; *take ~ of baby, dog ...* no sewa o suru ...の世話をする; *tools, house, garden ...* no teire o suru ...の手入れをする; (*deal with*) ... o shori suru ...を処理する; (*handle*) *with ~!* (*on label*) toriatsukai-chūi 取り扱い注意 **2** *v/i* ki ni kakeru 気にかける; *I don't ~!* kamau mono ka かまうものか; *I couldn't ~ less* zenzen ki ni shinai 全然気にしない

♦**care about** ... ni kanshin ga aru

…に関心がある

◆ **care for** (*look after*) … no sewa o suru …の世話をする; (*like, be fond of*) … ga suki de aru …が好きである; *would you ~ …?* … ga hoshii desu ka …が欲しいですか

career (*profession*) shokugyō 職業; (*path through life*) kyaria キャリア

carefree nonbiri shita のんびりした

careful (*cautious*) chūibukai 注意深い; (*thorough*) nen'iri (na) 念入り(な); (*be*) ~! ki o tsukete 気をつけて

carefully (*with caution*) shinchō ni 慎重に; (*worded etc*) nen'iri ni 念入りに

careless fuchūi (na) 不注意(な); *you are so ~!* anata mo zuibun ukkari shite imasu ne あなたもずいぶんうっかりしていますね

caress 1 *n* naderu koto なでること **2** *v/t* naderu なでる

caretaker kanri-nin 管理人

careworn yatsureta やつれた

cargo tsumini 積み荷

caricature *n* fūshi-manga 風刺漫画

caring *adj* omoiyari no aru 思いやりのある

carnage daigyakusatsu 大虐殺

carnation kānēshon カーネーション

carnival idō-yūenchi 移動遊園地; (*festival*) kānibaru カーニバル

carol *n* kurisumasu-kyaroru クリスマスキャロル

carousel (*at airport*) enkei-beruto-konbeyā 円形ベルトコンベヤー; (*for slide projector*) enkei-suraido-torē 円形スライドトレー; (*merry-go-round*) merī-gōraundo メリーゴーラウンド

carpenter daiku 大工

carpet kāpetto カーペット

carpool 1 *n* ainori-hōshiki 相乗り方式 **2** *v/i* ainori suru 相乗りする

car port chūshajō 駐車場

carrier (*company*) un'yu-gyōsha 運輸業者; (*of disease*) hokin-sha 保菌者

carrot ninjin にんじん; *~ and stick* ame to muchi あめとムチ

carry 1 *v/t* (*of person: in hand*)

mochihakobu 持ち運ぶ; (*from one place to another*) hakobu 運ぶ; (*have on one's person*) mochiaruku 持ち歩く; (*of pregnant woman*) migomotte iru 身ごもっている; *disease* kin o motte iru 菌を持っている; (*of ship, plane, bus etc*) noseru 乗せる; *proposal* kaketsu suru 可決する; *get carried away* muchū ni naru 夢中になる **2** *v/i* (*of sound*) tsutawaru 伝わる

◆ **carry on 1** *v/i* (*continue*) tsuzukeru 続ける; (*make a fuss*) sawagitateru 騒ぎ立てる; (*have an affair*) uwaki suru 浮気する **2** *v/t* (*conduct*) … o tsuzukeru …を続ける

◆ **carry out** *survey etc* … o okonau …を行う; *orders etc* … o jikkō suru …を実行する

car seat (*for child*) chairudo-shīto チャイルドシート

cart niguruma 荷車

cartel karuteru カルテル

carton (*for storage, transport*) hako 箱; (*for milk, eggs, cigarettes etc*) pakku パック

cartoon (*in newspaper, magazine*) manga 漫画; (*on TV, movie*) anime アニメ

cartridge (*for gun*) kātoridji カートリッジ

carve *meat* kiriwakeru 切り分ける; *wood* chōkoku suru 彫刻する

carving (*figure*) horimono 彫り物

car wash sensha 洗車

case¹ (*container*) kēsu ケース; (*of Scotch, wine*) hitohako ひと箱; *Br* (*suitcase*) sūtsu-kēsu スーツケース

case² *n* (*instance*) rei 例; (*situation*) ba-ai 場合; (*argument*) shuchō 主張; (*for police etc*) jiken 事件; MED shōrei 症例; LAW hanrei 判例; *in ~ …* moshi … no ba-ai ni sonaete もし…の場合に備えて; *in any ~* tonikaku とにかく; *in that ~* sore nara それなら

case history MED byōreki 病歴

cash 1 *n* genkin 現金; *~ down* sokkin de harau 即金で払う; *pay* (*in*) ~ genkin de shiharau 現金で支払う; ~ *in advance* maebarai de 前払いで **2** *v/t check* genkinka suru 現金化する

♦**cash in on** ... ni tsukekomu ...につけ込む

cash cow kane no naru ki 金のなる木; **cash desk** reji レジ; **cash discount** genkin-waribiki 現金割引; **cash flow** kyasshu-furō キャッシュフロー

cashier *n* (*in store etc*) reji-gakari レジ係

cash machine genkin-jidō-shiharaiki 現金自動支払機, ATM (*always in romaji*)

cashmere *adj* kashimiya (no) カシミヤ(の)

cash register rejisutā レジスター

casino (*kajino*) カジノ

casket (*coffin*) hitsugi ひつぎ

cassette kasetto カセット

cassette player kasetto-pureiyā カセットプレイヤー

cassette recorder kasetto-rekōdā カセットレコーダー

cast 1 *n* (*of play*) shutsuen-sha 出演者; (*mold*) igata 鋳型 **2** *v/t doubt, suspicion* nagekakeru 投げかける; *metal* chūzō suru 鋳造する; *play* haiyaku suru 配役する; *actor* yaku o wariateru 役を割り当てる

♦**cast off** *v/i* (*of ship*) nawa o toku 綱を解く

caste kāsuto カースト

caster (*on chair etc*) kyasutā キャスター

cast iron *n* chūtetsu 鋳鉄

cast-iron chūtetsu (no) 鋳鉄(の)

castle shiro 城

castor → **caster**

castor oil himashiyu ひまし油

castrate kyosei suru 去勢する

casual (*chance*) nanigenai 何気ない; (*offhand*) mutonchaku (na) むとんちゃく(な); (*not formal*) kajuaru (na) カジュアル(な), fudangi (no) 普段着(の); (*not permanent*) rinji (no) 臨時(の)

casualty shishō-sha 死傷者

casual wear kajuaru-wea カジュア

ruwea, fudangi 普段着

cat neko 猫

catalog *n* katarogu カタログ

catalyst *fig* shokubai 触媒

catalytic converter shokubai-konbātā 触媒コンバーター

catastrophe daisaigai 大災害

catch 1 *n* hokyū 捕球; (*of fish*) shūkaku 収穫; (*locking device*) tomegane 留め金; (*problem*) otoshiana 落し穴 **2** *v/t ball, escaped prisoner* tsukamaeru 捕まえる; (*get on: bus, train*) ... ni noru ...に乗る; (*not miss: bus, train*) ... ni ma ni au ...に間に合う; *fish with rod* tsuru 釣る; *fish with net* toru 捕る; (*in order to speak to*) tsukamaeru 捕まえる; (*hear*) kikitoru 聞き取る; *illness* ... ni kakaru ...にかかる; ~ *(a) cold* kaze o hiku 風邪を引く; ~ *X's eye* (*of person, object*) X no chūi o hiku Xの注意を引く; ~ *sight of* ... o miru ... を見る; ~ *X doing Y* X ga Y shite iru tokoro o mitsukeru XがYしているところを見つける

♦**catch on** (*become popular*) ninki o haku suru 人気を博する; (*understand*) wakaru わかる

♦**catch up** *v/i* oitsuku 追いつく

♦**catch up on** ... no okure o torimodosu ...の遅れを取り戻す

catch-22: *it's a ~ situation* dōshiyōmonai jōkyō de aru どうしようもない状況である

catcher (*in baseball*) kyatchā キャッチャー

catching *disease* densensei (no) 伝染性(の); *fear, panic* utsuru 移る

catchy *tune* oboeyasui 覚えやすい

category burui 部類

♦**cater for** (*meet the needs of*) ... no yōkyū o mitasu ...の要求を満たす; (*provide food for*) ... no shidashi o suru ...の仕出しをする

caterer shidashi-gyōsha 仕出し業者

caterpillar kemushi 毛虫

cathedral daiseidō 大聖堂

Catholic 1 *adj* Katorikku (no) カトリック(の) **2** *n* Katorikku-kyōto カトリック教徒

catsup kechappu ケチャップ

cattle ushi 牛

catty ijiwaru 意地悪(na)

cauliflower karifurawā カリフラワー

cause 1 n gen'in 原因; (grounds) konkyo 根拠; (aim of movement) shuchō 主張 **2** v/t hikiokosu 引き起こす

caution 1 n (carefulness) yōjin 用心; ~ is advised gochūi negaimasu 御注意願います **2** v/t (warn) keikoku suru 警告する

cautious shinchō (na) 慎重(な)

♦**cave in** (of roof) kanbotsu 陥没

caviar kyabia キャビア

cavity mushiba 虫歯

cc 1 n kopī-haifusaki コピー配布先 **2** v/t ... no kopī o okuru ...のコピーを送る

CD (= compact disc) shī-dī ＣＤ

CD-ROM shīdī-romu ＣＤロム

CD-ROM drive shīdī-romu-doraibu ＣＤロムドライブ

cease 1 v/i owaru 終わる **2** v/t oeru 終える

cease-fire teisen 停戦

cedar: Japanese ~ sugi 杉

ceiling tenjō 天井; (limit) saikō-gendo 最高限度

celebrate v/t & v/i iwau 祝う

celebrated yūmei (na) 有名(な); be ~ for ... de yūmei de aru ...で有名である

celebration oiwai お祝い

celebrity yūmei-jin 有名人

celery serori セロリ

cell (for prisoner) dokubō 独房; BIO saibō 細胞

cello chero チェロ

cellophane serohan セロハン

cell(ular) phone keitai-denwa 携帯電話

cement 1 n semento セメント **2** v/t setsugō suru 接合する; friendship katameru 固める

cemetery bochi 墓地

censor v/t ken'etsu suru 検閲する

censorship ken'etsu 検閲

cent sento セント

centennial n hyakushūnen 百周年

center 1 n (middle) chūshin 中心; (building) sentā センター; (region) chūshin 中心; POL chūdōha 中道派; in the ~ of ... no chūshin de ...の中心で **2** v/t chūshin ni oku 中心に置く

♦**center on** ... ni chūshin o oku ...に中心を置く

centigrade sesshi 摂氏; **10 degrees ~** sesshi jū-do 摂氏十度

centimeter senchimētoru センチメートル

central chūshin (no) 中心(の); location, apartment chūshinbu de benri (na) 中心部で便利(な); (main) chūshinteki (na) 中心的(な); be ~ to kore ga ... no chūshin to naru これが...の中心となる

central heating sentoraru-hītingu セントラル・ヒーティング

centralize chūō ni atsumeru 中央に集める

central locking MOT sentoraru-rokku セントラルロック

central processing unit → **CPU**

century seiki 世紀

CEO (= Chief Executive Officer) saikō-sekininsha 最高責任者

ceramic tōjiki (no) 陶磁器(の)

ceramics (objects) tōjiki 陶磁器; (art) tōgei 陶芸; (Japanese ~) setomono 瀬戸物

cereal (grain) kokumotsu 穀物; (breakfast ~) shiriaru シリアル

ceremonial 1 adj gishiki (no) 儀式(の) **2** n gishiki 儀式

ceremony (event) shikiten 式典; (ritual) gishiki 儀式

certain (sure) kakushin shite iru 確信している; (particular) aru ある; it's ~ that ... ... wa hobo kakujitsu da ...はほぼ確実だ; a ~ Mr S. esu-shi toka iu hito S氏とかいう人; make ~ tashikameru 確かめる; know / say for ~ hakkiri shitte iru / iu はっきり知っている/言う

certainly (definitely) tashika ni 確かに; (of course) mochiron もちろん; ~ not! tondemonai とんでもない

certainty (*confidence*) kakushin 確信; (*inevitability*) kakujitsusei 確実性; **it's / he's a ~** sore/kare wa kakujitsu da それ/彼は確実だ

certificate (*qualification*) shikaku 資格; (*official paper*) shōmeisho 証明書

certified public accountant kōnin-kaikeishi 公認会計士

certify shōmei suru 証明する

Cesarean *n* teiō-sekkai 帝王切開

cessation teishi 停止

CFC (= *chlorofluorocarbon*) furongasu フロンガス

chafe *v/t* surimuku すりむく

chain 1 *n* kusari 鎖; (*for bicycle, of stores, hotels*) chēn チェーン **2** *v/t*: **~ X to Y** X o Y ni kusari de tsunagu XをYに鎖でつなぐ

chain reaction rensa-hannō 連鎖反応; **chain smoke** tsuzukezama ni tabako o suu 続けざまにたばこを吸う; **chain smoker** chēn-sumōkā チェーンスモーカー; **chain store** chēn-sutoa チェーンストア

chair 1 *n* isu いす; (*arm~*) hijikake-isu ひじ掛けいす; (*at university*) shunin-kyōju 主任教授; **the ~** (*electric ~*) denki-isu 電気いす; (*at meeting*) gichō 議長; **take the ~** gichō o tsutomeru 議長を務める **2** *v/t* meeting gichō o tsutomeru 議長を務める

chair lift sukī-rifuto スキーリフト; **chairman** gichō 議長; **chairperson** gichō 議長; **chairwoman** gichō 議長

chalk (*for writing*) chōku チョーク; (*in soil*) hakua 白亜

challenge 1 *n* (*difficulty*) nandai 難題; (*in race, competition*) chōsen 挑戦 **2** *v/t* (*defy*) yōkyū suru 要求する; (*to race, debate*) mōshikomu 申し込む; (*call into question*) igi o tonaeru 異議を唱える

challenger chōsen-sha 挑戦者

challenging yarigai no aru やりがいのある

chambermaid mēdo メード

Chamber of Commerce shōkō-kaigisho 商工会議所

chamois (*leather*) sēmu-gawa セーム皮

champagne shanpan シャンパン

champion 1 *n* SP chanpion チャンピオン; (*of cause*) yōgo-sha 擁護者 **2** *v/t* cause yōgo suru 擁護する

championship (*event*) senshuken-taikai 選手権大会; (*title*) senshuken 選手権

chance (*possibility*) kanōsei 可能性; (*opportunity*) kikai 機会; (*risk*) kiken 危険; (*luck*) un 運; **by ~** gūzen ni 偶然に; **take a ~** ichi ka bachi ka yatte miru 一か八かやってみる; **I'm not taking any ~s** kiken o okashitari shinai 危険を冒したりしない

Chancellor (*in Germany*) shushō 首相; **~ (of the Exchequer)** (*in Britain*) ōkura-daijin 大蔵大臣

chandelier shanderia シャンデリア

change 1 *n* (*to plan, idea, script*) henkō 変更; (*in society, climate, condition*) henka 変化; (*small coins*) kozeni 小銭; (*from purchase*) otsuri お釣り; (*different situation etc*) kibun-tenkan 気分転換; **for a ~** tama ni たまには; **a ~ of clothes** kigae 着替え **2** *v/t* (*alter*) kaeru 変える; bank bill kuzusu くずす; (*replace*) torikaeru 取り替える; trains, planes norikaeru 乗り換える; one's clothes kigaeru 着替える **3** *v/i* kawaru 変わる; (*put on different clothes*) kigaeru 着替える; (*take different train / bus*) norikaeru 乗り換える

channel RAD, TV channeru チャンネル; (*waterway*) suiro 水路

chant 1 *n* kakegoe 掛け声 **2** *v/i* kakegoe o kakeru 掛け声を掛ける

chaos daikonran 大混乱

chaotic muchitsujo (no) 無秩序(の)

chapel reihaidō 礼拝堂

chapped hibi no kireta ひびの切れた

chapter (*of book*) shō 章; (*of organization*) chihō-shibu 地方支部

character (*nature*) seikaku 性格; (*person*) hito 人; (*in book, play*)

tōjō-jinbutsu 登場人物;
(*personality*) tokuchō 特徴; (*in writing*) moji 文字; *he's a real ~* kare wa taishita jinbutsu da 彼は たいした人物だ; *Chinese ~* kanji 漢字

characteristic 1 *n* tokushoku 特色 **2** *adj* tokuyū (no) 特有(の)

characterize (*be typical of*) tokuchōzukeru 特徴づける; (*describe*) … to miru …と見る

charbroiled sumibiyaki (no) 炭火焼き(の)

charcoal (*for barbecue*) sumi 炭; (*for drawing*) mokutan 木炭

charge 1 *n* (*fee*) ryōkin 料金; LAW yōgi 容疑; *free of ~* muryō 無料; *will that be cash or ~?* genkin to kādo no dochira desu ka 現金と カードのどちらですか; *be in ~* sekinin-sha de aru 責任者である; *take ~* ukemotsu 受け持つ **2** *v/t sum of money* seikyū suru 請求する; (*put on account*) kādo de harau カードで払う; LAW kiso suru 起訴する; *battery* jūden suru 充電する **3** *v/i* (*attack*) totsugeki suru 突撃する

charge account tsuke つけ

charge card ka-do カード

charisma karisuma カリスマ

charitable *institution, donation* jizen-katsudō (no) 慈善活動(の); *person* jihibukai 慈悲深い

charity (*assistance*) charitī チャリティー, jizen 慈善; (*organization*) jizen-dantai 慈善団体

charm 1 *n* (*appealing quality*) miryoku 魅力; (*on bracelet etc*) omamori お守り **2** *v/t* (*delight*) uttori saseru うっとりさせる

charming miryokuteki (na) 魅力的(な)

charred kogeta 焦げた

chart (*diagram*) zuhyō 図表; NAUT kaizu 海図; (*for airplane*) kōkūzu 航空図; *the ~s* MUS hitto-chāto ヒットチャート

charter *v/t* chātā suru チャーターする

charter flight chātā-bin チャーター

chase 1 *n* tsuiseki 追跡 **2** *v/t* oikakeru 追いかける

♦ **chase away** … o oiharau …を追い払う

chaser (*drink*) chēsā チェーサー

chassis (*of car*) shāshi シャーシー

chat 1 *n* oshaberi おしゃべり **2** *v/i* oshaberi suru おしゃべりする

chatter 1 *n* oshaberi おしゃべり **2** *v/i* pechakucha to shaberu ぺちゃくちゃとしゃべる; (*of teeth*) katakata naru かたかた鳴る

chatterbox oshaberi おしゃべり

chatty *person* hanashizuki (no) 話好き(の); *letter* kudaketa くだけた

chauffeur *n* untenshu 運転手

chauvinist (*male ~*) danson-johi no hito 男尊女卑の人

cheap *adj* (*inexpensive*) yasui 安い; (*nasty*) yasuppoi 安っぽい; (*mean*) kechi (na) けち(な)

cheat 1 *n* (*person*) ikasamashi いかさま師 **2** *v/t* ~ *X out of Y* X kara Y o damashitoru XからYをだまし取る **3** *v/i* (*in exam*) kanningu o suru カンニングをする; (*in cards etc*) ikasama o suru いかさまをする; ~ *on one's wife* okusan ni kakurete uwaki o suru 奥さんにかくれて浮気をする

check[1] 1 *adj shirt* chekku (no) チェック(の) **2** *n* chekku チェック

check[2] *n* FIN kogitte 小切手; (*in restaurant etc*) kanjōgaki 勘定書き; ~ *please* o-kanjō o-negai お勘定お願い

check[3] 1 *n* (*to verify sth*) kensa 検査; *keep in ~, hold in ~* … o kuitomeru …を食い止める; *keep a ~ on* … o kanri suru …を管理する **2** *v/t* (*verify*) kakunin suru 確認する; *machinery* tenken suru 点検する; (*restrain*) osaeru 抑える; (*stop*) soshi suru 阻止する; (*with a mark*) shirushi o tsukeru 印を付ける; *coat, package etc* azukeru 預ける **3** *v/i shiraberu 調べる; ~ *for* … o shiraberu …を調べる

♦ **check in** (*at airport, hotel*) chekku-in suru チェックインする

- ◆ **check off** shirushi o tsukeru 印を付ける
- ◆ **check on** ... o shiraberu ...を調べる
- ◆ **check out 1** *v/i* (*of hotel*) chekku-auto suru チェックアウトする **2** *v/t* (*look into*) ... o chōsa suru ...を調査する; *club, restaurant etc* ... ni itte miru ...に行ってみる
- ◆ **check up on** ... o shiraberu ... を調べる
- ◆ **check with** (*of person*) ... ni tazuneru ...に尋ねる; (*tally: of information*) gatchi suru 合致する
- **checkbook** kogittechō 小切手帳
- **checked** *material* chekku (no) チェック(の)
- **checkerboard** chekkā-ban チェッカー盤
- **checkered** *pattern* chekku (no) チェック(の); *career* haran ni tonda 波乱に富んだ
- **checkers** chekkā チェッカー
- **check-in** (**counter**) chekku-in (kauntā) チェックイン (カウンター)
- **checking account** tōza-yokin-kōza 当座預金口座
- **check-in time** chekku-in no jikan チェックインの時間; **checklist** chekku-risuto チェックリスト; **checkmark** chekku no shirushi チェックの印; **checkmate** *n* chekku-meito チェックメイト、ōte 王手; **checkout** reji レジ; **checkout time** (*from hotel*) chekku-auto no jikan チェックアウトの時間; **checkpoint** (*military, police*) kenmonjo 検問所; (*in race etc*) chekku-pointo チェックポイント; **checkroom** (*for coats*) kurōku クローク; (*for baggage*) tenimotsu-azukarisho 手荷物預かり所; **checkup** (*medical*) kenkō-shindan 健康診断; (*dental*) kenshin 検診
- **cheek** hō ほほ
- **cheekbone** hōbone ほお骨
- **cheer 1** *n* kansei 歓声; *~s!* (*toast*) kanpai 乾杯 **2** *v/t* seien suru 声援する **3** *v/i* kansei o ageru 歓声を上げる

- ◆ **cheer on** ... o seien suru ...を声援する
- ◆ **cheer up 1** *v/i* genki o dasu 元気を出す; *~!* genki dashite 元気出して **2** *v/t* genki zukeru 元気づける
- **cheerful** kigen no ii 機嫌のいい
- **cheering** kansei 歓声
- **cheerleader** chiarīdā チアリーダー
- **cheese** chīzu チーズ
- **cheeseburger** chīzubāgā チーズバーガー
- **cheesecake** chīzukēki チーズケーキ
- **chef** shefu シェフ; (*for Japanese cuisine*) itamae 板前
- **chemical 1** *adj* kagaku (no) 化学(の) **2** *n* kagaku-yakuhin 化学薬品
- **chemical warfare** kagakuheiki-sensō 化学兵器戦争
- **chemist** kagaku-sha 化学者
- **chemistry** kagaku 化学; *fig* aishō 相性
- **chemotherapy** kagaku-ryōhō 化学療法
- **cherish** taisetsu ni suru 大切にする; *memory, hope* mune ni himeru 胸に秘める
- **cherry** (*fruit*) sakuranbo さくらんぼ; (*tree*) sakura no ki 桜の木; *~ blossom* sakura 桜
- **chess** chesu チェス
- **chessboard** chesu-ban チェス盤
- **chest** (*of person*) mune 胸; (*box*) shūnōbako 収納箱; *get ... off one's ~* ... o uchiakeru ...を打ち明ける; *~ of drawers* tansu たんす
- **chestnut** kuri くり; (*tree*) kuri no ki くりの木
- **chew** *v/t* kamu かむ; (*of dog, rats*) kajiru かじる
- ◆ **chew out** F ... o shikaritobasu ...をしかりとばす
- **chewing gum** chūingamu チューインガム
- **chick** hiyoko ひよこ; F (*girl*) onna 女
- **chicken 1** *n* niwatori にわとり; (*food*) toriniku とり肉; F (*coward*) yowamushi 弱虫 **2** *adj* F (*cowardly*) okubyō (na) おくびょう(な)
- ◆ **chicken out** ojikezuite yameru お

じけづいてやめる

chickenfeed F hashitagane はした金

chicken pox mizubōsō 水ぼうそう

chief 1 n (head) rīdā リーダー; (of tribe) shūchō しゅう長 **2** adj omo (na) 主(な)

chiefly shu to shite 主として

chilblain shimoyake しもやけ

child kodomo 子供; pej kodomojimita hito 子供じみた人

childbirth shussan 出産

childhood kodomo no koro 子供の頃

childish pej kodomojimita 子供じみた

childishness kodomoppo-sa 子供っぽさ

childless kodomo no inai 子供のいない

childlike kodomo no yō (na) 子供のよう(な)

Children's Day Kodomo no hi 子供の日

chill 1 n (in air) hie 冷え; (illness) samuke 寒気 **2** v/t wine hiyasu 冷やす

chilli (pepper) tōgarashi とうがらし

chilly weather hadazamui 肌寒い; welcome hiyayaka (na) 冷やか(な); I'm ~ samuke ga suru 寒気がする

chime v/i chaimu チャイム

chimney entotsu 煙突

chimpanzee chinpanjī チンパンジー

chin ago あご

china tōjiki 陶磁器; (material) setomono 瀬戸物

China Chūgoku 中国

Chinese 1 adj Chūgoku (no) 中国(の); (in Chinese) Chūgoku-go (no) 中国語(の); ~ character kanji 漢字 **2** n (language) Chūgoku-go 中国語; (person) Chūgoku-jin 中国人

chink (gap) sukima すきま; (sound) kachin to iu oto かちんという音

chip 1 n (fragment) kakera かけら; (damage) kaketa tokoro 欠けたところ; (in gambling) chippu チップ; COMPUT maikuro-chippu マイクロチップ; ~s potetochippu ポテトチップ **2** v/t (damage) kaku 欠く

♦ **chip in** (interrupt) kuchi o hasamu

口をはさむ; (with money) sukoshi zutsu dashiau 少しずつ出し合う

chiropractor seitaishi 整体師, kairopurakutā カイロプラクター

chirp v/i chunchun naku ちゅんちゅん鳴く

chisel n nomi のみ

chivalrous kishidō-seishin no aru 騎士道精神のある

chives chaibu チャイブ

chlorine enso 塩素

chockfull gisshiri tsumatte ぎっしり詰まって

chocolate chokorēto チョコレート; hot ~ hotto-chokorēto ホットチョコレート

chocolate cake chokorēto-kēki チョコレートケーキ

choice 1 n sentaku 選択; (selection) sentaku no haba 選択の幅; (preference) konomi 好み; I had no ~ sentaku no yochi ga nakatta 選択の余地がなかった **2** adj (top quality) ikkyū (no) 一級(の)

choir gasshōdan 合唱団; REL seikatai 聖歌隊

choke 1 n MOT chōku チョーク **2** v/i iki ga tsumaru 息が詰まる; he ~d on a bone kare wa nodo ni hone o tsumaraseta 彼はのどに骨をつまらせた **3** v/t chissoku saseru 窒息させる

cholesterol koresuterōru コレステロール

choose v/t & v/i erabu 選ぶ

choosey F urusai うるさい

chop 1 n (meat) choppu チョップ **2** v/t wood waru 割る; meat, vegetables kiru 切る

♦ **chop down** tree ... o kiritaosu ... を切り倒す

chopper (tool) ono おの; F (helicopter) herikoputā ヘリコプター

chopsticks hashi はし; disposable ~ waribashi わりばし; ~ rest hashioki はし置き

chord MUS waon 和音

chore zatsuyō 雑用

choreographer furitsukeshi 振り付け師

choreography furitsuke 振り付け

chorus (*singers*) gasshōdan 合唱団, kōrasu コーラス; (*of song*) kurikaeshi 繰り返し

Christ Iesu Kirisuto イエスキリスト; **~/** chikushō 畜生

christen senrei suru 洗礼する

Christian 1 *n* Kirisuto-kyōto キリスト教徒 **2** *adj* Kirisuto-kyō (no) キリスト教(の)

Christianity kirisuto-kyō キリスト教

Christian name namae 名前

Christmas Kurisumasu クリスマス; *at ~* Kurisumasu no koro ni クリスマスの頃に; **Merry ~/** Merī Kurisumasu メリークリスマス

Christmas card Kurisumasu-kādo クリスマスカード; **Christmas Day** Kurisumasu クリスマス; **Christmas Eve** Kurisumasu-ibu クリスマスイブ; **Christmas present** Kurisumasu-purezento クリスマスプレゼント; **Christmas tree** Kurisumasu-tsurī クリスマスツリー

chrome, chromium kuromu クロム

chronic mansei (no) 慢性(の)

chronological nendaijun (no) 年代順(の); *in ~ order* nendaijun ni 年代順に

chrysanthemum kiku 菊

chubby marupocha (no) 丸ぽちゃ (の)

chuck *v/t* F hōru ほうる

♦**chuck out** *object* ... o suteru ...を捨てる; *person* ... o oidasu ...を追い出す

chuckle 1 *n* kusukusu warai くすくす笑い **2** *v/i* kusukusu warau くすくす笑う

chunk katamari かたまり

church kyōkai 教会

chute shūto シュート; (*for garbage*) dasuto-shūto ダストシュート

CIA (= *Central Intelligence Agency*) shī-ai-ē シーアイエー(中央情報局)

cicada semi せみ

cider ringo-shu リンゴ酒

CIF (= *cost insurance freight*) hokenryō unchin-komi kakaku 保

険料運賃込み価格

cigar hamaki 葉巻き

cigarette tabako たばこ

cinema (*Br: building*) eigakan 映画館; (*as institution*) eigakai 映画界

cinnamon shinamon シナモン

circle 1 *n* en 円; (*group*) nakama 仲間 **2** *v/t* (*draw circle around*) maru de kakomu 丸で囲む **3** *v/i* (*of plane, bird*) senkai suru 旋回する

circuit kairo 回路; (*lap*) isshū 一周

circuit board haisenban 配線盤

circuit breaker burēkā ブレーカー

circular 1 *n* (*giving information*) chirashi ちらし **2** *adj* enkei (no) 円形(の)

circulate 1 *v/i* junkan suru 循環する **2** *v/t memo* kairan suru 回覧する

circulation BIO junkan 循環; (*of newspaper, magazine*) hakkō-busū 発行部数

circumference enshū 円周

circumstances jijō 事情; (*financial*) keizai-jōtai 経済状態; *under no ~* donna jijō ga atte mo どんな事情があっても; *under the ~* sō iu jijō na node そういう事情なので

circus sākasu サーカス

cistern tanku タンク

citizen shimin 市民

citizenship shiminken 市民権

city toshi 都市; *~ center* hankagai 繁華街; *~ hall* shiyakusho 市役所

civic *adj* shi (no) 市(の); *pride, responsibilities* shimin (no) 市民 (の)

civil (*not military*) minkan (no) 民間(の); *disobedience, duties etc* shimin (no) 市民(の); (*polite*) reigi-tadashii 礼儀正しい

civil engineer doboku-gishi 土木技師

civilian 1 *n* minkan-jin 民間人 **2** *adj clothes* ippan (no) 一般(の)

civilization bunmei 文明

civilize *person* senren suru 洗練する

civil rights shiminken 市民権; **civil servant** kōmuin 公務員; **civil service** seifu-kanchō(gun igai) 政府官庁(軍以外); **civil war** naisen 内戦

claim 1 n (*request*) seikyū 請求; (*right*) kenri 権利; (*assertion*) shuchō 主張 **2** v/t (*ask for as a right*) seikyū suru 請求する; (*assert*) shuchō suru 主張する; *lost property* nanorideru 名乗り出る; ***they have ~ed responsibility for the attack*** karera wa shūgeki no hankō-seimei o dashita 彼らは襲撃の犯行声明を出した

claimant yōkyū-sha 要求者; LAW genkoku 原告

clam hamaguri はまぐり

♦ **clam up** F totsuzen kuchi o tsugumu 突然口をつぐむ

clammy jittori shita じっとりした

clamor (*noise*) sakebi 叫び; (*outcry*) koe 声

♦ **clamor for** ... o yakamashiku yōkyū suru ...をやかましく要求する

clamp 1 n (*fastener*) shimegane 締め金, kuranpu クランプ **2** v/t (*fasten*) shimegane de shimeru 締め金で締める

♦ **clamp down** genjū ni torishimaru 厳重に取り締まる

♦ **clamp down on** ... o genjū ni torishimaru ...を厳重に取り締まる

clan ichizoku 一族

clandestine himitsu (no) 秘密(の)

clang 1 n kān to iu oto カーンという音 **2** v/i kān to naru カーンと鳴る

clap 1 v/i hakushu suru 拍手する **2** v/t ... ni hakushu suru ...に拍手する

clarify hakkiri saseru はっきりさせる

clarinet kurarinetto クラリネット

clarity meiryō-sa 明りょうさ

clash 1 n shōtotsu 衝突; (*of personalities*) fuitchi 不一致 **2** v/i shōtotsu suru 衝突する; (*of opinions*) kuichigau 食い違う; (*of colors*) awanai 合わない; (*of events*) kachiau かちあう

clasp 1 n tomegu 留め具 **2** v/t (*in hand*) nigirishimeru 握りしめる; (*to self*) dakishimeru 抱き締める

class 1 n (*lesson*) jugyō 授業; (*group of people*) kurasu クラス;

(*category*) burui 部類; (*social ~*) kaikyū 階級 **2** v/t minasu みなす

classic 1 adj (*typical*) tenkeiteki (na) 典型的(な); (*definitive*) ichiryū (no) 一流(の) **2** n meisaku 名作

classical *music, style* kurashikku (no) クラシック(の); *literature* koten (no) 古典(の)

classification bunrui 分類

classified *information* kimitsu (no) 機密(の)

classified ad(vertisement) kōmokubetsu-kōkoku 項目別広告

classify (*categorize*) bunrui suru 分類する

classmate dōkyūsei 同級生, kurasumēto クラスメート

classroom kyōshitsu 教室

class warfare kaikyū-tōsō 階級闘争

classy F shareta しゃれた

clatter 1 n katakata to iu oto かたかたという音 **2** v/i katakata oto o tateru かたかた音を立てる

clause (*in agreement*) jōkō 条項; GRAM setsu 節

claustrophobia heisho-kyōfushō 閉所恐怖症

claw 1 n tsume つめ **2** v/t (*scratch*) tsume de hikkaku つめでひっかく

clay nendo 粘土

clean 1 adj kirei (na) きれい(な) **2** adv F (*completely*) kanzen ni 完全に **3** v/t kirei ni suru きれいにする; *teeth, shoes* migaku 磨く; *house, room* sōji suru 掃除する; *car, hands, face* arau 洗う; *clothes* kurīningu suru クリーニングする; ***get one's jacket ~ed*** uwagi o kurīningu suru 上着をクリーニングする

♦ **clean out** *room, cupboard* kirei ni suru きれいにする; fig ichimon nashi ni suru 一文なしにする

clean up 1 v/t katazukeru 片付ける; fig issō suru 一掃する **2** v/i sōji suru 掃除する; (*wash*) arau 洗う; (*on stock market etc*) ōmōke suru 大もうけする

cleaner (*male*) sōjifu 掃除夫; (*female*) sōjifu 掃除婦; ***dry ~*** dorai-kurīningu-ya ドライクリー

ニング屋

cleaning woman sōfu 掃除婦

cleanse *skin* kurenjingu suru クレンジングする

cleanser senganryō 洗顔料

clear 1 *adj voice, photograph, vision* hakkiri shita はっきりした; (*easy to understand*) wakariyasui わかりやすい; (*obvious*) akiraka (na) 明らか(な); *weather, sky* hareta 晴れた; *water, eyes* sunda 澄んだ; *skin* kenkō-sō (na) 健康そう(な); *conscience* yamashii tokoro no nai やましいところのない; *I'm not ~ about it* watashi ni wa yoku wakaranai 私にはよくわからない; *I didn't make myself ~* watashi wa hakkiri sasenakatta 私ははっきりさせなかった **2** *adv*: *stand ~ of* ... kara hanarete tatsu ...から離れて立つ; *steer ~ of* ... o sakeru ...を避ける **3** *v/t roads etc* torinozoku 取り除く; (*acquit*) yōgi o harasu 容疑を晴らす; (*authorize*) kyoka o ataeru 許可を与える; (*earn*) kasegu 稼ぐ; *~ one's throat* sekibarai o suru せき払いをする **3** *v/i* (*of sky, mist*) hareru 晴れる; (*of face*) akaruku naru 明るくなる

♦ **clear away** *v/t* ... o katazukeru ...を片付ける

♦ **clear off** *v/i* isoide tachisaru 急いで立ち去る

♦ **clear out 1** *v/t* (*cupboard*) ... o kara ni suru ...を空にする **2** *v/i* dete iku 出ていく

♦ **clear up 1** *v/i* katazuke o suru 片付けをする; (*of weather*) hareagaru 晴れ上がる; (*of illness, rash*) naoru 治る **2** *v/t* (*tidy*) katazukeru 片付ける; *mystery, problem* kaiketsu suru 解決する

clearance (*space*) yutori ゆとり; (*authorization*) kyoka 許可

clearance sale kurabarai-ōuridashi 蔵払い大売り出し, kuriaransu-sēru クリアランスセール

clearly (*with clarity*) hakkiri to はっきりと; (*evidently*) akiraka ni 明らかに

clemency kandai na shochi 寛大な処置

clench *teeth* ha o kuishibaru 歯をくいしばる; *fist* kobushi o nigirishimeru こぶしを握り締める

clergy seishoku-sha 聖職者

clergyman bokushi 牧師

clerk jimuin 事務員; (*in store*) ten'in 店員

clever *person, animal* rikō (na) 利口(な); *idea* umai うまい; *gadget, device* ki no kiita 気のきいた

♦ **click on** COMPUT ... o kurikku suru ...をクリックする

client (*of lawyer etc*) irainin 依頼人; (*customer*) kokyaku 顧客

cliff gake がけ

climate kikō 気候

climax *n* kuraimakkusu クライマックス

climb 1 *n* (*up mountain*) tozan 登山 **2** *v/t* ... ni noboru ...に登る **3** *v/i* noboru 登る; (*up mountain*) tozan suru 登山する; *fig* (*increase*) jōshō suru 上昇する

♦ **climb down** oriru 降りる; *fig* hikisagaru 引き下がる

climber (*person*) tozan-sha 登山者

clinch: *~ a deal* shōdan o matomeru 商談をまとめる

cling (*of clothes*) matowari tsuku まとわりつく

♦ **cling to** (*of child*) ... ni shigamitsuku ...にしがみつく; *ideas, tradition* ... ni koshitsu suru ...に固執する

clingfilm rappu ラップ

clingy *child, boyfriend* izonshin no tsuyoi 依存心の強い

clinic shinryōjo 診療所

clinical rinshō (no) 臨床(の)

clink 1 *n* (*noise*) kachin to iu oto かちんという音 **2** *v/i* kachin to naru かちんと鳴る

clip¹ 1 *n* (*fastener*) kurippu クリップ **2** *v/t*: *~ X to Y* X o Y ni kurippu de tomeru XをYにクリップで止める

clip² 1 *n* (*extract*) kurippu クリップ

click 1 *n* COMPUT kurikku クリック **2** *v/i* kachiri to oto ga suru かちりと音がする

2 v/t hair, hedge karikomu 刈り込む

clipboard kamibasami 紙挟み

clippers (for hair) barikan バリカン; (for nails) tsume-kiri つめ切り; (for gardening) senteibasami せん定ばさみ

clipping (from newspaper) kirinuki 切り抜き

cloakroom kurōku クローク

clock tokei 時計

clock radio tokei-tsuki rajio 時計付きラジオ; **clockwise** tokeimawari 時計回り; **clockwork** tokeijikake 時計仕掛け; **it went like ~** todokōri naku itta 滞りなく行った

clog: thonged ~s geta 下駄

◆**clog up** v/i tsumaru 詰まる **2** v/t ...o tsumaraseru ...を詰まらせる

close¹ 1 adj family, friend shitashii 親しい; resemblance nite iru 似ている **2** adv sugu soba すぐそば; ~ **at hand** tejika ni 手近に; ~ **by** chikaku ni 近くに; **be ~ to** (emotionally) ... to shitashiku shite iru ...と親しくしている

close² 1 v/t shimeru 閉める; (permanently: business) yameru やめる; factory heisa suru 閉鎖する **2** v/i (of door, store) shimaru 閉まる; (of eyes) tojiru 閉じる; (of store: permanently) heiten suru 閉店する

◆**close down 1** v/t heisa suru 閉鎖する **2** v/i (permanently) heisa sareru 閉鎖される

◆**close in** v/i oshiyoseru 押し寄せる

◆**close up** v/t building ...o shimeru ...を閉める **2** v/i (move closer) kurōzu-appu suru クローズアップする

closed store shimatta 閉まった; eyes tojita 閉じた

closed-circuit television kurōzudo-sākitto-terebi クローズドサーキットテレビ

closely listen, watch chūibukaku 注意深く; cooperate missetsu shite 密接して

closet todana 戸棚

close-up kurōzu-appu クローズアップ

closing time (of store) heiten-jikan 閉店時間; (of museum, library) heikan-jikan 閉館時間

closure (permanent) heisa 閉鎖; (of shop) heiten 閉店

clot 1 n (of blood) katamari 固まり **2** v/i (of blood) katamaru 固まる

cloth (fabric) nuno 布; (for kitchen) fukin ふきん; (for cleaning etc) zōkin ぞうきん

clothes fuku 服; (traditional) Japanese~ wafuku 和服

clothes brush ifukuyō-burashi 衣服用ブラシ

clothes hanger hangā ハンガー

clothing irui 衣類

cloud n kumo 雲; **a ~ of smoke/dust** mōmō to shita kemuri/hokori もうもうとした煙/ほこり

◆**cloud over** (of sky) kumoru 曇る

cloudburst doshaburi どしゃ降り

cloudy kumotta 曇った

clout fig (influence) eikyōryoku 影響力

clown n (in circus) piero ピエロ; (joker) itazuramono いたずら者; pej tonma とんま

club n (weapon) konbō こん棒; (golf iron) gorufu-kurabu ゴルフクラブ; (organization) kurabu クラブ; ~**s** (in cards) kurōbā クローバー

clue tegakari 手がかり; **I haven't a ~** kentō mo tsukanai 見当もつかない

clued-up seitsū shite iru 精通している

clump n (of earth) katamari かたまり; (group) mure 群れ

clumsiness bukiyō 不器用

clumsy person bukiyō (na) 不器用 (な)

cluster 1 n (of people) ichidan 一団; (of houses) ichigun 一群 **2** v/i (of people) muragaru 群がる; (of houses) misshū suru 密集する

clutch n MOT kuratchi クラッチ **2** v/t shikkari nigiru しっかり握る

◆**clutch at** ...o tsukamō to suru ...をつかもうとする

Co. (= Company) kaisha 会社

c/o (= care of) kizuke 気付, kata 方

coach 1 n (trainer) kōchi コーチ

2 v/t shidō suru 指導する

coagulate (of blood) gyōko suru 凝固する

coal sekitan 石炭

coalition renritsu 連立

coal-mine tankō 炭鉱

coarse kime no arai きめの粗い; *hair* katai 硬い; (vulgar) gehin (na) 下品(な)

coast n kaigan 海岸; *at the ~* kaigan de 海岸で

coastal engan (no) 沿岸(の)

coastguard engan-keibitai 沿岸警備隊; (person) engan-keibitaiin 沿岸警備隊員

coastline kaigansen 海岸線

coat 1 n uwagi 上着; (over~) ōbā オーバー; (of animal) kegawa 毛皮; (of paint etc) nuri 塗り **2** v/t (cover) ōu 覆う

coathanger hangā ハンガー

coating ōi 覆い

coax settoku suru 説得する

cobweb kumo no su クモの巣

cocaine kokain コカイン

cock n (chicken) ondori おんどり; (any male bird) osu 雄

cockeyed idea etc bakageta ばかげた

cockpit kokkupitto コックピット

cockroach gokiburi ごきぶり

cocktail kakuteru カクテル

cocoa kokoa ココア

coconut kokonattsu ココナッツ

coconut palm kokoyashi no ki ココヤシの木

COD (= collect on delivery) chakubarai 着払い

cod tara たら

coddle sick person daiji ni suru 大事にする; child amayakasu 甘やかす

code n angō 暗号

co-educational danjo-kyōgaku (no) 男女共学(の)

coerce kyōsei suru 強制する

coexist kyōzon suru 共存する

coexistence kyōzon 共存

coffee kōhī コーヒー

coffee break kōhī-bureiku コーヒーブレイク; **coffee maker** kōhī-mēkā コーヒーメーカー; **coffee**

pot kōhī-potto コーヒーポット; **coffee shop** kissaten 喫茶店; **coffee table** kōhī-tēburu コーヒーテーブル

coffin hitsugi ひつぎ

cog ha 歯

cognac konyakku コニャック

cogwheel haguruma 歯車

cohabit dōsei suru 同棲する

coherent suji no tōtta 筋の通った

coil 1 n (of rope) hitomaki ひと巻き **2** v/t maku 巻く

coin n kōka 硬貨

coincide dōji ni okoru 同時に起こる

coincidence gūzen 偶然

coke F (cocaine) kokain コカイン

Coke® koka-kōra コカコーラ

cold 1 adj tsumetai 冷たい; weather, day, room samui 寒い; I'm (feeling) ~ samui desu 寒いです; it's ~ samui desu 寒いです; in ~ blood heizen to 平然と; get ~ feet fig ojikezuku おじけづく **2** n samu-sa 寒さ; I have a ~ kaze o hiite iru 風邪をひいている

cold-blooded reiketsu (no) 冷血(の); fig reikoku (na) 冷酷(な); **cold cuts** hamu-rui ハム類; **cold sore** kōshin-herupesu 口唇ヘルペス

coleslaw kōrusurō コールスロー

colic fukutsū 腹痛

collaborate kyōryoku suru 協力する; (in research) kyōdō-kenkyū suru 共同研究する; (on book) kyōdō de kaku 共同で書く

collaboration kyōryoku 協力

collaborator kyōryoku-sha 協力者; (in writing book) kyōcho-sha 共著者

collapse kuzureru 崩れる; (of person) taoreru 倒れる

collapsible oritatameru 折りたためる

collar eri 襟

collarbone sakotsu 鎖骨

colleague dōryō 同僚

collect 1 v/t person mukae ni iku 迎えにいく; tickets, cleaning etc tori ni iku 取りにいく; (as hobby) shūshū suru 収集する; (gather) atsumeru 集める **2** v/i (gather together) atsumaru 集まる **3** *adv*: **call ~** ... ni korekuto-kōru o kakeru ...にコレクトコールをかける

collect call korekuto-kōru コレクトコール

collected *works, poems etc* shūshū shita 収集した; *person* ochitsuita 落ち着いた

collection korekushon コレクション; *(in church)* bokin 募金

collective kyōdō (no) 共同(の)

collective bargaining dantai-kōshō 団体交渉

collector shūshūka 収集家

college daigaku 大学

collide shōtotsu suru 衝突する

collision shōtotsu 衝突

colloquial kōgo (no) 口語(の)

colon *(punctuation)* koron コロン; ANAT ketchō 結腸

colonel taisa 大佐

colonial *adj* shokuminchi (no) 植民地(の)

colonize *country* shokuminchika suru 植民地化する

colony shokuminchi 植民地

color 1 *n* iro 色; *(in cheeks)* kaoiro 顔色; **in ~** *(movie etc)* karā de カラーで; **~s** MIL hata 旗 **2** *v/t one's hair* iro o tsukeru 色をつける **3** *v/i (blush)* kao o akaku suru 顔を赤くする

color-blind shikikaku-ijō (no) 色覚異常(の)

colored *adj person* yūshoku-jinshu (no) 有色人種(の)

color fast iro-ochi shinai 色落ちしない

colorful shikisai ni tonda 色彩に富んだ

coloring hada no iro 肌の色

color photograph karā-shashin カラー写真; **color scheme** haishoku 配色; **color TV** karā-terebi カラーテレビ

colt osu no kouma 雄の子馬

column retsu 列; *(architectural)* enchū 円柱; *(of text)* ran 欄; *(newspaper feature)* koramu コラム

columnist koramunisuto コラムニスト

comb 1 *n* kushi くし **2** *v/t* tokasu とかす; *area* tetteiteki ni sagasu 徹底的に捜す

combat 1 *n* sentō 戦闘 **2** *v/t* ... to tatakau ...と闘う

combination kumiawase 組み合わせ; *(of safe)* kumiawase-bangō 組み合わせ番号

combine 1 *n* COM gappei suru 合併する **2** *v/t* kumiawaseru 組み合わせる; *ingredients* mazeawaseru 混ぜ合わせる **3** *v/i (of chemical elements)* kagō suru 化合する

combine harvester konbain コンバイン

combustible kanensei (no) 可燃性(の)

combustion nenshō 燃焼

come *(toward speaker)* kuru 来る; *(toward listener)* iku 行く; *(of train, bus)* tsuku 着く; **you'll ~ to like it** sore o suki ni naru to omoimasu それを好きになると思います; **how ~?** F dōshite どうして

♦**come about** *(happen)* okoru 起こ

♦**come across 1** *v/t (find)* ... ni dekuwasu ...に出くわす **2** *v/i (of idea, humor)* tsutawaru 伝わる; **she comes across as ...** kanojo wa ... to iu inshō o ataeru 彼女は...という印象を与える

♦**come along** *(come too)* issho ni kuru いっしょに来る; *(turn up)* yatte kuru やって来る; *(progress)* susumu 進む

♦**come apart** barabara ni naru ばらばらになる; *(break)* kowareru 壊れる

♦**come around** *(to place)* tazuneru 訪ねる; *(regain consciousness)* ki ga tsuku 気がつく

♦**come away** *(leave)* dete kuru 出て来る; *(of button etc)* toreru とれる

♦**come back** modotte kuru 戻ってくる; **it came back to me** omoidashita 思い出した

♦**come by 1** *v/i* tachiyoru 立ち寄る **2** *v/t (acquire)* ... o te ni ireru ...を手に入れる

♦**come down** *v/i* oriru 降りる; *(in*

price, amount etc) sagaru 下がる; (*of rain, snow*) furu 降る; *he came down the stairs* kare wa kaidan o orita 彼は階段を降りた

♦ **come for** (*collect: thing*) ... o tori ni kuru ...を取りにくる; *person* ... o mukae ni kuru ...を迎えにくる; (*attack*) ... ni osoi kakaru ...に襲いかかる

♦ **come forward** nanorideru 名乗り出る

♦ **come from** ... shusshin de aru ... 出身である

♦ **come in** hairu 入る; (*of train*) haittekuru 入ってくる; (*of tide*) michiru 満ちる; *~ I* dōzo どうぞ

♦ **come in for**: *~ criticism* hihan o ukeru 批判を受ける

♦ **come in on**: *~ a deal* keiyaku ni sanka suru 契約に参加する

♦ **come off** (*of handle etc*) toreru とれる

♦ **come on** (*progress*) shinpo suru 進歩する; *~ I* sā, hayaku さあ早く; (*in disbelief*) masaka まさか

♦ **come out** (*of person*) dete kuru 出てくる; (*of sun, results, product*) deru 出る; (*of stain*) ochiru 落ちる

♦ **come to** 1 *v/t place* tsuku 着く; (*of hair, dress, water*) todoku 届く; *that comes to $70* nana-jū doru ni naru 70ドルになる 2 *v/i* (*regain consciousness*) ki ga tsuku 気がつく

♦ **come up** agatte kuru 上がってくる; (*of sun*) noboru 昇る; *something has ~* nanika ga okotta 何かが起こった

♦ **come up with** *new idea etc* ... o kangaedasu ...を考え出す

comeback: *make a ~* kamubakku suru カムバックする

comedian komedian コメディアン; *pej* tonma とんま

comedown kitaihazure 期待外れ

comedy kigeki 喜劇

comet suisei すい星

comeuppance: *he'll get his ~* sono uchi kare wa tōzen no mukui o ukeru darō そのうち彼は当然の報いを受けるだろう

comfort 1 *n* kaiteki-sa 快適さ;

(*consolation*) nagusame 慰め 2 *v/t* nagusameru 慰める

comfortable *chair* suwarigokochi no yoi 座り心地のよい; *house, room* igokochi no yoi 居心地のよい; *be ~* (*of person*) raku de aru 楽である; (*financially*) kurashi ni komaranai 暮しに困らない

comic 1 *n* (*to read*) manga 漫画 2 *adj* kigeki (no) 喜劇(の)

comical kokkei (na) こっけい(な)

comic book mangabon 漫画本

comics rensai-manga 連載漫画

comma konma コンマ

command 1 *n* meirei 命令 2 *v/t* meirei suru 命令する

commander shireikan 司令官

commander-in-chief saikō-shireikan 最高司令官

commemorate kinen suru 記念する

commemoration: *in ~ of* ... o kinen shite ...を記念して

commence 1 *v/i* hajimaru 始まる 2 *v/t* kaishi suru 開始する

comment 1 *n* kaisetsu 解説, komento コメント; *no ~ I* nōkomento ノーコメント 2 *v/i* iken o noberu 意見を述べる

commentary jikkyō-hōsō 実況放送

commentator kaisetsu-sha 解説者

commerce shōgyō 商業

commercial 1 *adj firm, bank, English, college* shōgyō (no) 商業(の); *success* shōgyōteki (na) 商業的(な) 2 *n* (*advert*) komāsharu コマーシャル

commercial break komāsharu コマーシャル

commercialize *v/t* shōgyōka suru 商業化する

commercial traveler sērusuman セールスマン

commiserate dōjō suru 同情する

commission 1 *n* (*payment*) buai 歩合; (*job*) irai 依頼; (*committee*) iinkai 委員会 2 *v/t* (*for a job*) irai suru 依頼する

commit *crime* okasu 犯す; *money* jūtō suru 充当する; *~ oneself* yakusoku suru 約束する

commitment (*in professional*

compete

relationship) sekininkan 責任感;
(*in personal relationship*) kenshin
献身; (*responsibility*) sekinin 責任
committee iinkai 委員会
commodity shōhin 商品
common (*not rare*) arifureta あり
ふれた; (*shared*) kyōtsū (no) 共通
(の); *in* ~ kyōtsū ni 共通に; *have
something in* ~ *with* … to nanika
kyōtsūten ga aru …と何か共通点
がある
common law wife naien no tsuma
内縁の妻; **commonplace** *adj*
arifureta ありふれた; **common
sense** jōshiki 常識
commotion sawagi 騒ぎ
communal kyōyū (no) 共有(の)
communicate 1 *v/i* (*have contact*)
renraku o toru 連絡をとる; (*make
self understood*) rikai shiau 理解
し合う 2 *v/t* tsutaeru 伝える
communication komyunikēshon コ
ミュニケーション, ishi-sotsū 意思
疎通
communications tsūshin-shudan 通
信手段
communications satellite tsūshin-
eisei 通信衛星
communicative *person* hanashizuki
(na) 話好き(な)
Communism kyōsan-shugi 共産主
義
Communist 1 *adj* kyōsan-shugi
(no) 共産主義(の) 2 *n* Kyōsan-
shugi-sha 共産主義者
community shakai 社会, komyunitī
コミュニティー
commute 1 *v/i* tsūkin suru 通勤する
2 *v/t* LAW genkei suru 減刑する
commuter tsūkin-sha 通勤者
commuter pass teikiken 定期券;
commuter traffic tsūkin rasshu 通
勤ラッシュ; **commuter train**
tsūkin-ressha 通勤列車
compact 1 *adj* kogata (no) 小型(の)
2 *n* MOT kei-jidōsha 軽自動車
compact disc konpakuto-disuku コ
ンパクトディスク
companion aite 相手
companionship tsukai-付き合い
company COM kaisha 会社;

(*companionship*) tsukai 付き合い;
(*guests*) raikyaku 来客; *he's good
~* kare wa omoshiroi nakama da
彼はおもしろい仲間だ; *keep X* ~ X
ni tsukiau Xにつきあう
company car shayō-sha 社用車
company law kaisha-hō 会社法
comparable (*which can be
compared*) hikaku dekiru 比較でき
る; (*similar*) hitteki suru 匹敵する
comparative 1 *adj* (*relative*)
hikakuteki 比較的; *study* hikaku
(no) 比較(の); GRAM hikakukyū
(no) 比較級(の) 2 *n* GRAM
hikakukyū 比較級
comparatively hikakuteki 比較的
compare 1 *v/t* hikaku suru 比較する;
~ *X with Y* X o Y to kuraberu Xを
Yと比べる; ~*d with* … to
kuraberu to …と比べると 2 *v/i*
hitteki suru 匹敵する
comparison hikaku 比較; *there's no
~* kurabemono ni naranai 比べも
のにならない
compartment shikiri 仕切り
compass hōi-jishin 方位磁針; NAUT
rashinban 羅針盤; (*for geometry*)
konpasu コンパス
compassion dōjō 同情
compassionate nasakebukai 情け
深い
compatibility (*of people*) tekiōsei 適
応性; (*of software*) gokansei 互換性;
(*of blood types*) tekigōsei 適合性
compatible *people* ki ga au 気が合
う; *blood types, life styles* tekigō
shite iru 適合している; COMPUT
gokansei no aru 互換性のある;
we're not ~ watashitachi wa uma
ga awanai 私達はうまが合わない
compel kyōsei suru 強制する
compelling *argument* settokuryoku
no aru 説得力のある; *movie, book*
hikikomareru 引き込まれる
compensate 1 *v/t* (*with money*)
hoshō suru 補償する 2 *v/i*: ~ *for* …
o umeawaseru …を埋め合わせる
compensation (*money*) hoshō-kin
補償金; (*reward*) hōshū 報酬;
(*comfort*) umeawase 埋め合わせ
compete kyōsō suru 競争する; (*take*

part) sanka suru 参加する; **~ for** … o mezashite kyōsō suru …をめざして競争する

competence nōryoku 能力

competent *person* yūnō (na) 有能 (な); *work* deki no ii できのいい; **I'm not ~ to judge** watashi wa handan suru shikaku ga nai 私は判断する資格がない

competition kyōsō 競争; SP shiai 試合; *(competitors)* kyōsō-aite 競争相手, raibaru ライバル; **the government wants to encourage ~** seifu wa kyōsō o shōrei shite iru 政府は競争を奨励している

competitive *person* kyōsōshin ga tsuyoi 競争心が強い; *price, offer* kyōgō dekiru 競合できる; *profession* kyōsō no hageshii 競争の激しい

competitor *(in contest)* sanka-sha 参加者; COM kyōsō-aite 競争相手

compile henshū suru 編集する

complacency jiko-manzoku 自己満足

complacent jiko-manzoku shita 自己満足した

complain *v/i* fuhei o iu 不平を言う; *(to shop, manager)* kujō o iu 苦情を言う; **~ of** MED … o uttaeru …を訴える

complaint *(grumble)* monku 文句; *(of striker)* uttae 訴え; MED byōki 病気

complement *v/t* oginau 補う; **they ~ each other** karera wa tarinai tokoro o oginaiatte iru 彼等は足りない所をを補い合っている

complementary oginaiau 補い合う

complete 1 *adj (total)* kanzen (na) 完全(な); *(full)* zenbu (no) 全部 (の); *(finished)* kansei shite 完成して **2** *v/t task, building etc* kansei suru 完成する; *course* shūryō suru 修了する; *form* kinyū suru 記入する

completely kanzen ni 完全に

completion kansei 完成

complex 1 *adj (total)* fukuzatsu (na) 複雑 (な) **2** *n* PSYCH konpurekkusu コンプレックス; *(of buildings)* kyōdō-biru 共同ビル

complexion *(facial)* kao no irotsuya 顔の色つや

compliance shōdaku 承諾

complicate fukuzatsu ni suru 複雑にする

complicated fukuzatsu (na) 複雑 (な)

complication mondai 問題; **~s** MED gappeishō 合併症

compliment 1 *n* homekotoba ほめ言葉 **2** *v/t* homeru ほめる

complimentary shōsan o hyōshita 賞賛を表した; *(free)* muryō (no) 無料(の); *(in restaurant, hotel)* sābisu (no) サービス(の)

compliments slip zōteihyō 贈呈票

comply ōzuru 応ずる; **~ with** … ni shitagau …に従う

component bubun 部分

compose *v/t* kōsei suru 構成する; MUS sakkyoku suru 作曲する; **be ~d of** … kara naritatte iru …から成り立っている; **~ oneself** ki o ochitsukeru 気を落ち着ける

composed ochitsuita 落ち着いた

composer MUS sakkyoku-ka 作曲家

composition *(make-up)* kōsei 構成; MUS sakkyoku 作曲; *(essay)* sakubun 作文

composure ochitsuki 落ち着き

compound *n* CHEM kagōbutsu 化合物

compound interest fukuri 複利

comprehend *(understand)* rikai suru 理解する

comprehension rikai 理解

comprehensive hōkatsuteki (na) 包括的(な); *account* sōgōteki (na) 総合的(な)

compress 1 *n* MED shippu 湿布 **2** *v/t air, gas* asshuku suru 圧縮する; *information* yōyaku suru 要約する

comprise kōsei suru 構成する; **be ~d of** … de kōsei sarete iru …で構成されている

compromise 1 *n* dakyō 妥協 **2** *v/i* dakyō suru 妥協する **3** *v/t principles* mageru 曲げる; *(jeopardize)* ayauku suru 危うくする; **~ oneself** taimen o kizutsukeru 体面を傷付ける

compulsion PSYCH kyōhaku-kannen

強迫観念

compulsive *behavior* byōteki (na) 病的(な); *reading* yamitsuki (no) 病みつき(の)

compulsory kyōseiteki (na) 強制的 (な); *subject* hisshū (no) 必修(の); *~ education* gimu-kyōiku 義務教育

computer konpyūtā コンピューター; *have ... on ~* konpyūtā ni ... ga nyūryoku shite aru コンピューターに...が入力してある

computer-controlled konpyūtā-seigyo (no) コンピューター制御 (の)

computer game konpyūtā-gēmu コンピューターゲーム

computerize konpyūtā de shori suru コンピューターで処理する; *workplace ... ni konpyūtā o sonaeru ...に コンピューターを備える

computer literate konpyūtā o tsukaeru hito コンピューターを使 える人; **computer science** konpyūtā-kagaku コンピューター 科学; **computer scientist** konpyūtā-kagaku-sha コンピューター科学者

computing (*use of computers*) konpyūtā-sōsa コンピューター操 作; (*computers*) konpyūtā-riyō コンピューター利用

comrade nakama 仲間; POL dōshi 同 志

comradeship nakama-ishiki 仲間意 識

con 1 *n* F ikasama いかさま **2** *v/t* F damasu だます

conceal kakusu 隠す

concede (*admit*) mitomeru 認める

conceit unubore うぬぼれ

conceited omoiagatta 思い上った

conceivable kangaerareru 考えら れる

conceive *v/i* (*of woman*) ninshin suru 妊娠する; *~ of* (*imagine*) ... o sōzō suru ...を想像する

concentrate 1 *v/i* shūchū suru 集中 する; (*on task*) sennen suru 専念す る **2** *v/t* one's attention, energies shūchū suru 集中する

concentrated *juice etc* nōshuku

sareta 濃縮された

concentration shūchūryoku 集中力

concept gainen 概念

conception (*of child*) jutai 受胎

concern 1 *n* (*anxiety*) shinpai 心配; (*care*) kanshin 関心; (*business*) kanshinji 関心事; (*company*) jigyō 事業 **2** *v/t* (*involve*) ... ni kankei ga aru ...に関係がある; (*worry*) shinpai saseru 心配させる; *~ oneself with* ... ni kanshin o motsu ...に関心を持つ

concerned (*anxious*) shinpai shite iru 心配している; (*caring*) kizukatte 気づかって; (*involved*) kankei suru 関係する; *as far as I'm ~* watashi no mikata to shite wa 私の見方としては

concerning *prep* ... ni kanshite ...に 関して

concert konsāto コンサート

concerted itchi shita 一致した

concertmaster konsāto-masutā コ ンサートマスター

concerto kyōsōkyoku 協奏曲

concession (*giving in*) jōho 譲歩

conciliatory kaijūteki (na) 壊柔的 (な)

concise kanketsu (na) 簡潔(な)

conclude 1 *v/t* (*deduce*) ketsuron o kudasu 結論を下す; (*end*) oeru 終 える **2** *v/i* owaru 終わる

conclusion (*deduction*) ketsuron 結 論; (*end*) ketsumatsu 結末; *in ~* saigo ni 最後に

conclusive ketteiteki (na) 決定的 (な)

concoct *meal, drink* mazeawasete tsukuru 混ぜ合わせて作る; *excuse, story* detchiageru でっちあげる

concoction (*food, drink*) chōgōbutsu 調合物

concrete[1] *adj* (*not abstract*) gutaiteki (na) 具体的(な)

concrete[2] *n* konkurīto コンクリート

concur *v/i* dōi suru 同意する

concussion nōshintō 脳しんとう

condemn *action* hinan suru 非難す る; *building* futeki to nintei suru 不適と認定する; (*doom*) oikomu 追 い込む

condemnation (*of action*) hinan 非難

condensation ketsuro 結露

condense 1 *v/t* (*make shorter*) tanshuku suru 短縮する **2** *v/i* (*of steam*) gyōketsu suru 凝結する

condensed milk kondensu-miruku コンデンスミルク, rennyū 練乳

condescend: *he ~ed to speak to me* kare wa onkisegamashiku hanashikakete kita 彼は恩着せがましく話しかけてきた

condescending (*patronizing*) onkisegamashii 恩着せがましい

condition 1 *n* (*state*) jōtai 状態; (*of health*) taichō 体調; MED yōdai 容態; (*requirement, term*) jōken 条件; *~s* (*circumstances*) jōkyō 状況; *on ~ that ...* ... to iu jōken de ...という条件で **2** *v/t* PSYCH narasu 慣らす

conditional 1 *adj acceptance* jōkentsuki (no) 条件付き(の) **2** *n* GRAM jōkenhō 条件法

conditioner (*for hair*) rinsu リンス; (*for fabric*) jūnan-shiagezai 柔軟仕上げ剤

conditioning PSYCH jōkenzuke 条件付け

condo kondominiamu コンドミニアム, bunjō-manshon 分譲マンション

condolences okuyami お悔やみ

condom kondōmu コンドーム

condominium → *condo*

condone yōnin suru 容認する

conducive: *~ to* ... no tame ni naru ...のためになる

conduct 1 *n* (*behavior*) okonai 行い **2** *v/t* (*carry out*) okonau 行う; ELEC dendō suru 伝導する; MUS shiki suru 指揮する; *~ oneself* furumau ふるまう

conducted tour gaido-tsuki kengaku ガイド付き見学

conductor MUS shiki-sha 指揮者; (*on train*) shashō 車掌

cone ensuikei 円すい形; (*for ice cream*) kōn コーン; (*of pine tree*) matsukasa 松かさ; (*on highway*) sēfutī-kōn セーフティーコーン

confectioner dagashi-ya 駄菓子屋

confectioners' sugar aishingu-yō shugā アイシング用シュガー

confectionery (*candy*) okashi お菓子

confederation rengō 連合

confer 1 *v/t* (*bestow*) juyo suru 授与する **2** *v/i* (*discuss*) kyōgi suru 協議する

conference kaigi 会議

conference room kaigishitsu 会議室

confess 1 *v/t* hakujō suru 白状する; REL zange suru ざんげする; (*admit*) mitomeru 認める; (*to the police*) jihaku suru 自白する; *I ~ I don't know* zannen desu ga shirimasen 残念ですが知りません **2** *v/i* mitomeru 認める; (*to police*) jihaku suru 自白する; REL zange suru ざんげする; *~ to a weakness for ...* ... ni taisuru yowasa o mitomeru ...に対する弱さを認める

confession kokuhaku 告白; (*to police*) jihaku 自白; REL zange ざんげ

confessional REL zange-shitsu ざんげ室

confessor REL chōzai-shisai 聴罪司祭

confide 1 *v/t* uchiakeru 打ち明ける **2** *v/i: ~ in* ... ni himitsu o uchiakeru ...に秘密を打ち明ける

confidence (*assurance*) jishin 自信; (*trust*) shinrai 信頼; (*secret*) himitsu 秘密; *in ~* himitsu de 秘密で

confident (*self-assured*) jishin no aru 自信のある; (*convinced*) kakushin shite 確信して

confidential himitsu (no) 秘密(の)

confine (*imprison*) tojikomeru 閉じ込める; (*restrict*) kagiru 限る; *be ~d to one's bed* toko ni tsuite iru 床についている

confined *space* semai 狭い

confinement (*imprisonment*) kankin 監禁; MED osan お産

confirm *v/t* kakunin suru 確認する; *theory, fears* urazukeru 裏付ける

confirmation kakunin 確認; (*of theory, fears*) urazuke 裏付け

confirmed (*inveterate*) ganko (na) 頑固(な)

confiscate bosshū suru 没収する
conflict 1 n (disagreement) ronsō 論争; (clash) tairitsu 対立; (war) arasoi 争い **2** v/i (clash) kachiau かちあう; (of theories) mujun suru 矛盾する
conform junnō suru 順応する; (of product) tekigō suru 適合する; ~ **to government standards** seifu no kijun ni shitagau 政府の基準に従う
conformist n taisei ni tsuku hito 大勢につく人
confront ... ni tachimukau ...に立ち向かう
confrontation taiketsu 対決
Confucianism Jukyō 儒教
Confucius Kōshi 孔子
confuse (muddle) konran saseru 混乱させる; ~ **X with Y** X to Y o kondō suru XとYを混同する
confused konran shita 混乱した
confusing magirawashii 紛らわしい
confusion konran 混乱
congeal gyōko suru 凝固する
congenial tanoshii 楽しい
congenital MED sentensei (no) 先天性(の)
congested roads jūtai shita 渋滞した
congestion (on roads) jūtai 渋滞; (in lungs) kikan-heisoku 気管閉塞; (in nose) hanazumari 鼻詰まり; traffic ~ kōtsū-jūtai 交通渋滞
congratulate ... ni omedetō to iu ...におめでとうと言う
congratulations oiwai no kotoba お祝いの言葉; ~ **on** ... omedetō ... おめでとう
congregate atsumaru 集まる
congregation REL kaishū 会衆
congress (conference) kaigi 会議; **Congress** (of US) Gikai 議会
Congressional Gikai (no) 議会(の)
Congressman Kain-giin 下院議員
Congresswoman Kain-giin 下院議員
conifer shinyōju 針葉樹
conjecture n (speculation) suisoku 推測
conjugate v/t GRAM katsuyō suru 活用する

conjunction GRAM setsuzoku-shi 接続詞; in ~ **with** ... to tomo ni ...とともに
conjunctivitis ketsumakuen 結膜炎
♦ **conjure up** (produce) ... o tachidokoro ni tsukuridasu ...をたちどころに作り出す; (evoke) ... o yobiokosu ...を呼び起こす
conjurer, conjuror tejina-shi 手品師
conjuring tricks tejina 手品
con man F ikasama-shi いかさま師
connect (join), TELEC tsunagu つなぐ; (link) kanrenzukeru 関連づける; (to power supply) setsuzoku suru 接続する
connected: be well ~ tsute ga aru つてがある; **be** ~ **with** ... ... to kankei ga aru ...と関係がある
connecting flight setsuzoku-bin 接続便
connection (in wiring) setsuzoku 接続; (link) kankei 関係; (when traveling) setsuzoku 接続; (personal contact) tsute つて; in ~ **with** ... ... ni kanshite ...に関して
connoisseur tsū 通
conquer seifuku suru 征服する; fear etc uchikatsu 打ち勝つ
conqueror seifuku-sha 征服者
conquest (of territory) seifuku 征服
conscience ryōshin 良心; **a guilty** ~ yamashii kokoro やましい心; **it has been on my** ~ ki ni kakatte ita 気にかかっていた
conscientious ryōshinteki (na) 良心的(な)
conscientious objector ryōshinteki-heieki-kyohi-sha 良心的兵役拒否者
conscious adj (aware) ki ga tsuite iru 気がついている; (deliberate) ishikiteki (na) 意識的(な); MED ishiki no aru 意識のある; **be ~of** ... ... ni kizuite iru ...に気付いている
consciousness (awareness) jikaku 自覚; MED ishiki 意識; **lose / regain** ~ ishiki o ushinau / torimodosu 意識を失う/取り戻す
consecutive renzoku (no) 連続(の)
consensus gōi 合意
consent 1 n dōi 同意 **2** v/i dōi suru

同意する

consequence (*result*) kekka 結果

consequently sono kekka その結果

conservation hogo 保護

conservationist n shizen-hogoron-sha 自然保護論者, kankyō-hozenron-sha 環境保全論者

conservative adj (*conventional*) hoshuteki (na) 保守的(な); *clothes* jimi (na) 地味(な); *estimate* hikaeme (no) 控え目の(の)

conservatory (*for plants*) onshitsu 温室; MUS ongaku-gakkō 音楽学校

conserve 1 n (*jam*) jamu ジャム **2** v/t *energy, strength* setsuyaku suru 節約する

consider (*regard*) ... to minasu ... とみなす; (*show regard for*) omoiyaru 思いやる; (*think about*) yoku kangaeru よく考える; *it is ~ed to be ...* ... to omowarete iru ...と思われている

considerable kanari (no) かなり(の)

considerably kanari かなり

considerate omoiyari no aru 思いやりのある

consideration (*thought*) jukkō 熟考; (*thoughtfulness, concern*) omoiyari 思いやり; (*factor*) kōryo subeki ten 考慮すべき点; *take ... into ~* ... o kōryo ni ireru ...を考慮に入れる

consignment COM yusō-kamotsu 輸送貨物

♦**consist of** ... kara naru ...から成る

consistency (*texture*) kata-sa 固さ; (*unchangingness*) ikkansei 一貫性

consistent (*unchanging*) ikkan shita 一貫した

consolation nagusame 慰め

console v/t nagusameru 慰める

consonant n GRAM shiin 子音

consortium kyōkai 協会

conspicuous medatsu 目立つ

conspiracy inbō 陰謀

conspire kyōbō suru 共謀する

constant (*continuous*) taezu tsuzuku 絶えず続く

consternation rōbai ろうばい

constipated benpi shite iru 便秘している

constipation benpi 便秘

constituent n (*component*) kōsei-yōso 構成要素

constitute (*account for*) kōsei suru 構成する; (*represent*) ... to naru ...となる

constitution POL kenpō 憲法; (*of person*) taishitsu 体質

constitutional adj POL kenpō (no) 憲法(の)

Constitution Day Kenpō-kinenbi 憲法記念日

constraint seiyaku 制約

construct v/t *building etc* kensetsu suru 建設する

construction (*of building etc*) kensetsu 建設; (*building*) kenzōbutsu 建造物; (*trade*) kensetsu-gyō 建設業; *under ~* kensetsu-chū de 建設中で

construction industry kensetsu-gyōkai 建設業界; **construction site** kenchiku-genba 建築現場; **construction worker** kensetsu-rōdō-sha 建設労働者

constructive kensetsuteki (na) 建設的(な)

consul ryōji 領事

consulate ryōji-kan 領事館

consult ... ni sōdan suru ...に相談する

consultancy (*company*) konsarutanto-gyō コンサルタント業; (*advice*) adobaisu アドバイス

consultant komon 顧問, konsarutanto コンサルタント

consultation kyōgi 協議

consume (*eat*) taberu 食べる; (*drink*) nomu 飲む; (*use*) shōhi suru 消費する

consumer (*purchaser*) shōhi-sha 消費者

consumer confidence kōbai-iyoku 購買意欲; **consumer goods** shōhi-zai 消費財; **consumer society** shōhi-shakai 消費社会

consumption shōhi 消費; (*of energy*) shōhi-ryō 消費量; *~ tax* shōhi-zei 消費税

contact 1 n (*person*) tsute つて; (*communication*) renraku 連絡;

(*physical*) sesshoku 接触; *keep in ~ with ...* to renraku o toru ...と連絡をとる **2** *v/t* ... *ni renraku suru* ...に連絡する

contact lens kontakuto-renzu コンタクトレンズ

contact number renraku-saki 連絡先

contagious densensei (no) 伝染性(の); *fig* utsuri-yasui うつりやすい

contain *tears, laughter* osaeru 抑える; *it ~ed my camera* sono naka ni watashi no kamera ga haitte ita その中に私のカメラが入っていた;~ *oneself* jisei suru 自制する

container iremono 入れ物; COM kontena コンテナ

container ship kontena-sen コンテナ船

contaminate osen 汚染する

contamination osen 汚染

contemplate *v/t* (*look at*) jitto mitsumeru じっと見つめる; (*think about*) jikkuri kangaeru じっくり考える

contemporary 1 *adj* gendai (no) 現代(の) **2** *n* dōjidai no hito 同時代の人

contempt keibetsu 軽べつ; *be beneath ~* keibetsu ni mo atai shinai 軽べつにも値しない

contemptible hiretsu (na) 卑劣(な)

contemptuous hito o baka ni shita 人をばかにした

contend: ~ for ... ... o arasou ...を争う; *~ with ...* ... to tatakau ...と闘う

contender SP senshu 選手; (*in competition*) sanka-sha 参加者; (*against champion*) chōsen-sha 挑戦者; POL kōho-sha 候補者

content¹ *n* naiyō 内容

content² 1 *adj* manzoku de 満足で **2** *v/t: ~ oneself with ...* ... de manzoku suru ...で満足する

contented manzokusō (na) 満足そう(な)

contention (*assertion*) shuchō 主張; *be in ~ for ...* ... o arasotte iru ...を争っている

contentment manzoku 満足

contents nakami 中身

contest¹ (*competition*) kontesuto コンテスト; (*struggle, for power*) arasoi 争い

contest² *leadership etc* ... o arasou ...を争う; (*oppose*) ... ni igi o tonaeru ...に異議を唱える

contestant kyōsō-sha 競争者; (*in competition*) shutsujō-sha 出場者

context bunmyaku 文脈; *look at X in ~* X no haikei o kangaete Xの背景を考えて

continent *n* tairiku 大陸

continental tairiku (no) 大陸(の)

contingency man'ichi no koto 万一の事

continual taema nai 絶え間ない

continuation tsuzuki 続き

continue 1 *v/t* tsuzukeru 続ける; *to be ~d* tsuzuku 続く **2** *v/i* tsuzuku 続く

continuity renzokusei 連続性

continuous taema nai 絶え間ない

contort *face* shikameru しかめる; *body* nejiru ねじる

contour rinkaku 輪郭

contraception hinin 避妊

contraceptive *n* (*device*) hinin-gu 避妊具; (*pill*) hinin-yaku 避妊薬

contract¹ *n* keiyaku 契約

contract² 1 *v/i* (*shrink*) shūshuku suru 収縮する **2** *v/t illness* ... ni kakaru ...にかかる

contractor ukeoinin 請負人

contractual keiyakujō (no) 契約上(の)

contradict *statement* hitei suru 否定する; *colleague* hanron suru 反論する; *parent, teacher* sakarau 逆らう

contradiction mujun 矛盾

contradictory mujun shita 矛盾した

contraption F kikai 機械

contrary¹ 1 *adj* hantai (no) 反対(の); *~ to ...* ... ni hanshite ...に反して **2** *n: on the ~* soredokoroka それどころか

contrary² (*perverse*) hesomagari へそ曲り

contrast 1 *n* chigai 違い, kontorasuto コントラスト **2** *v/t* taihi suru 対比する **3** *v/i* ... *to ijirushiku chigau* ...と著しく違う

contrasting taishōteki (na) 対照的
(な)

contravene ... ni ihan suru ...に違
反する

contribute 1 v/i (with money,
material) kifu suru 寄付する; (with
time) kōken suru 貢献する; (to
magazine, paper) kikō suru 寄稿す
る; (to discussion) hatsugen suru
発言する; (help to cause) ichiin to
naru 一因となる **2** v/t money kifu
suru 寄付する; time, suggestion
teikyō suru 提供する

contribution (money) kifu 寄付; (to
political party, church) kenkin 献
金; (of time, effort) kōken 貢献; (to
debate) hatsugen 発言; (to
magazine) kikō 寄稿

contributor (of money) kifu-sha 寄
付者; (to magazine) kikō-sha 寄稿
者

contrive dōnika ... suru どうにか...
する

control 1 n (of country,
organization) shihai 支配;
(domination) kanri 管理; (of
emotion) yokusei 抑制; (in ball
game) kontorōru コントロール; **be
in ~ of** ... o shihai shite iru ...を
支配している; **bring ... under ~** ...o
osaeru ...を抑える; **get out of ~** ... o
seishikirenaku naru ...を制しきれ
なくなる; **lose ~ of** ... ...o
seishikirenaku naru ...を制しきれ
なくなる; **lose ~ of oneself** jibun no
kanjō o osaekirenaku naru 自分の
感情を抑えきれなくなる; **the
situation is under ~** banji umaku
itte iru 万事うまくいっている;
circumstances beyond our ~
jōkyō ga te ni oenai 状況が手に負え
ない; **~s** (of aircraft, vehicle) sōjū-
sōchi 操縦装置; (restrictions) kisei
規制 **2** v/t (govern) shihai suru 支配
する; class kontorōru suru コント
ロールする; (restrict) kisei suru 規
制する; (regulate) kanri suru 管理
する; **~ oneself** jisei suru 自制する

control center kontorōru-sentā コ
ントロールセンター

control freak F shikiri-ya 仕切り屋

controlled substance shojikisei-
yakubutsu 所持規制薬物

controlling interest FIN shihai-
mochibun 支配持ち分

control panel kontorōru-paneru コ
ントロールパネル, seigyoban 制御
盤

control tower kōkū-kanseitō 航空管
制塔

controversial ronsō no mato ni
natte iru 論争の的になっている

controversy ronsō 論争

convalesce kaifuku suru 回復する

convalescence kaifuku-ki 回復期

convene v/t shōshū suru 招集する

convenience benri 便利; (of
arrangement, time) kōtsugō 好都
合; **at your/my ~** anata / watashi no
tsugō no yoi toki ni あなた/私の都
合の良い時に; **all (modern) ~s**
(gendaiteki) setsubi-kanbi (現代
的)設備完備

convenience food insutanto-
shokuhin インスタント食品

convenience store konbini コンビ
ニ

convenient location, device benri
(na) 便利(な); time, arrangement
tsugō no yoi 都合のよい

convent joshi-shūdōin 女子修道院

convention (tradition) kanshū 慣習;
(conference) taikai 大会

conventional person, ideas kata ni
hamatta 型にはまった; family
heibon (na) 平凡(な); method
dentōteki (na) 伝統的(な)

convention center kaigijō 会議場

conventioneer taikai-sanka-sha 大
会参加者

conversant: be ~ with ... ... ni
seitsū shite iru ...に精通している

conversation kaiwa 会話

conversational kaiwa (no) 会話(の)

converse n (opposite) gyaku 逆

conversely gyaku ni 逆に

conversion henkan 変換; (of part of
house etc) kaizō 改造; (of yards to
meters etc) kanzan 換算; REL
kaishū 改宗

conversion table kanzan-hyō 換算表

convert 1 n tenkō-sha 転向者 **2** v/t

kaeru 変える; *unit of measurement* kanzan suru 換算する; *person* tenkō saseru 転向させる; REL kaishū saseru 改宗させる

convertible *n* (*car*) ōpun-kā オープンカー

convey (*transmit*) tsutaeru 伝える; (*carry*) hakobu 運ぶ

conveyor belt beruto-konbeyā ベルトコンベヤー

convict 1 *n* jukei-sha 受刑者 **2** *v/t* LAW yūzai-hanketsu o kudasu 有罪判決を下す; ~ *X of Y* Y ni tsuite X ni yūzai-hanketsu o kudasu Y についてXに有罪判決を下す

conviction LAW yūzai-hanketsu 有罪判決; (*belief*) kakushin 確信

convince kakushin saseru 確信させる

convincing settokuryoku no aru 説得力のある

convivial yōki (na) 陽気(な)

convoy (*of ships*) sendan 船団; (*of vehicles*) ichidan 一団

convulsion MED keiren けいれん

cook 1 *n* kokku コック, ryōri-nin 料理人 **2** *v/t* ryōri suru 料理する; *a ~ed meal* atatakai shokuji 暖かい食事 **3** *v/i* ryōri suru 料理する

cookbook ryōri no hon 料理の本

cookery ryōri (no) 料理(の)

cookie kukkī クッキー

cooking (*food*) ryōri 料理

cool 1 *n* F: *keep one's ~* katto naranai かっとならない; *lose one's ~* katto naru かっとなる **2** *adj weather, breeze* suzushii 涼しい; *drink* tsumetai 冷たい; (*calm*) reisei (na) 冷静(な); (*unfriendly*) reitan (na) 冷淡(な); F (*great*) kakko ii かっこいい **3** *v/i* (*of food*) sameru さめる; (*of tempers*) ochitsuku 落ち着く; (*of interest*) sameru さめる **4** *v/t*: ~ *it!* F ochitsuite 落ち着いて

♦ **cool down 1** *v/i* sameru さめる; (*of weather*) suzushiku naru 涼しくなる; (*of tempers*) ochitsuku 落ち着く **2** *v/t food* samasu さます; *fig* ochitsukaseru 落ち着かせる

cooperate kyōryoku suru 協力する

cooperation kyōryoku 協力

cooperative 1 *n* COM seikatsu-kyōdō-kumiai 生活協同組合 **2** *adj* COM seikatsu-kyōdō-kumiai (no) 生活協同組合(の); (*helpful*) kyōryokuteki (na) 協力的(な)

coordinate *activities* chōsei suru 調整する

coordination (*of activities*) chōsei 調整; (*of body*) baransu バランス

cop F omawari-san お巡りさん

cope taiō suru 対応する; ~ *with ...* ... ni taiō suru ...に対応する; *how does she ~ when she has six kids?* kodomo ga rokunin mo ite kanjo wa dō yatte iru no kashira 子供が六人もいて彼女はどうやっているのかしら

copier (*machine*) kopī-ki コピー機

copilot fuku-sōjūshi 副操縦士

copious takusan (no) たくさん(の)

copper *n* (*metal*) dō 銅

copy 1 *n* (*duplicate, imitation*) fukusei 複製; (*photo~*) kopī コピー; (*of book*) issatsu 一冊; (*of record, CD*) ichimai 一枚; (*written material*) genkō 原稿; *make a ~ of a file* COMPUT fairu o kopī suru ファイルをコピーする **2** *v/t* (*imitate*) maneru まねる; *painting* fukusei suru 複製する; (*on photocopier, computer*) kopī suru コピーする; (*from blackboard, another person's work*) utsusu 写す

copy cat F maneshi まねし; **copycat crime** kopī-hanzai コピー犯罪; **copyright** *n* chosaku-ken 著作権; **copy-writer** (*in advertising*) kopī-raitā コピーライター

coral (*on seabed*) sango さんご

cord (*string*) himo ひも; (*cable*) kōdo コード

cordial *adj* atatakai 温かい

cordless phone kōdoresu-denwa コードレス電話

cordon hijōsen 非常線

♦ **cordon off** hijōsen o haru 非常線を張る

cords (*pants*) kōdyuroi no zubon コーデュロイのズボン

corduroy kōdyuroi コーデュロイ

core 1 *n* (*of fruit*) shin しん; (*of problem*) kakushin 核心; (*of organization, party*) chūshin 中心 2 *adj* issue, meaning jūyō (na) 重要(な)

cork (*in bottle*) koruku-sen コルク栓; (*material*) koruku コルク

corkscrew sennuki 栓抜き

corn tōmorokoshi とうもろこし

corner 1 *n* (*of page, room*) sumi 隅; (*of table, street*) kado 角; (*bend: on road*) magarikado 曲り角; (*in soccer*) kōnā kikku コーナーキック; **in the ~** sumi ni 隅に; **on the ~** (*of street*) kado de/ni 角で/に 2 *v/t* person oitsumeru 追い詰める; **~ the market** shijō o shihai suru 市場を支配する 3 *v/i* (*of driver, car*) kado o magaru 角を曲がる

corner kick kōnā kikku コーナーキック

cornstarch katakuriko かたくり粉

corny F tsumaranai つまらない

coronary 1 *adj* shinzō (no) 心臓(の) 2 *n* kanjō-dōmyaku-kessen 冠状動脈血栓

coroner kenshi-kan 検死官

corporal *n* gochō 伍長

corporal punishment taibatsu 体罰

corporate COM kigyō (no) 企業(の); **~ image** kigyō no imēji 企業のイメージ; **sense of ~ loyalty** kaisha e no chūseishin 会社への忠誠心

corporation (*business*) kigyō 企業

corps ichidan 一団

corpse shitai 死体

corpulent himan(no) 肥満(の)

corpuscle kekkyū 血球

corral *n* kakoi 囲い

correct 1 *adj* tadashii 正しい 2 *v/t* naosu 直す; *homework* saiten suru 採点する; *proofs* teisei suru 訂正する

correction teisei 訂正

correspond (*match*) itchi suru 一致する; (*write letters*) buntsū suru 文通する; **~ to ...** ... ni sōtō suru ...に相当する; **~ with ...** ... to itchi suru ...と一致する

correspondence (*matching*) itchi 一致; (*letters*) tegami 手紙; (*exchange of letters*) buntsū 文通

correspondent *letter writer* buntsū-aite 文通相手; (*reporter: abroad*) tokuhain 特派員; (*reporter: domestic*) kisha 記者

corresponding (*equivalent*) taiō suru 対応する

corridor (*in building*) rōka 廊下

corroborate urazukeru 裏付ける

corrode 1 *v/t* fushoku saseru 腐食させる 2 *v/i* fushoku suru 腐食する

corrosion fushoku 腐食

corrugated cardboard danbōru-gami 段ボール紙

corrugated iron hajō-totan'ita 波状トタン板

corrupt 1 *adj* fuhai shita 腐敗した; COMPUT mojibake suru 文字化けする 2 *v/t* daraku saseru 堕落させる; (*bribe*) baishū suru 買収する

corruption oshoku 汚職

cosmetic *adj* biyō (no) 美容(の); *fig* hyōmen dake (no) 表面だけ(の)

cosmetics keshōhin 化粧品

cosmetic surgeon biyō-seikei-gekai 美容整形外科医

cosmetic surgery biyō-seikei 美容整形

cosmonaut uchū-hikōshi 宇宙飛行士

cosmopolitan *city* kokusaiteki (na) 国際的(な)

cost 1 *n* hiyō 費用; *fig* gisei 犠牲; **~s** COM kosuto コスト 2 *v/t* kakaru かかる; *time* yō suru 要する; FIN *proposal, project* mitsumoru 見積もる; **how much does it ~?** kore wa ikura desu ka これはいくらですか; **it ~ me my health** watashi no kenkō ga gisei ni natta 私の健康が犠牲になった

cost and freight COM unchinkomi no nedan de 運賃込みの値段で; **cost-conscious** kosuto ishiki o motte コスト意識を持って; **cost-effective** hiyō-kōka no takai 費用効果の高い; **cost, insurance and freight** COM hokenryō unchinkomi no nedan de 保険料運賃込みの値段で

costly *mistake etc* takaku tsuku 高

くつく

cost of living seikatsu-hi 生活費

cost price genka 原価

costume (*for actor*) ishō 衣装

costume jewelry mozō-hōsekirui 模造宝石類

cot (*folding*) oritatami-shiki beddo 折りたたみ式ベッド

cottage shōkaoku 小家屋

cottage cheese kotēji-chīzu コテージチーズ

cotton 1 *n* wata 綿, kotton コットン **2** *adj* men (no) 綿(の)

♦ **cotton on** F wakaru わかる

♦ **cotton on to** F ... ga wakaru ...がわかる

♦ **cotton to** F ... ga suki ni naru ...が好きになる

cotton candy wataame 綿あめ

couch *n* nagaisu 長いす

couch potato kauchi-poteto カウチポテト

couchette shindai 寝台

cough 1 *n* seki せき; (*to get attention*) seki-barai せき払い **2** *v/i* seki o suru せきをする; (*to get attention*) seki-barai o suru せき払いをする

♦ **cough up 1** *v/t blood etc* ... o haku ...を吐く; F *money* ... o shibushibu dasu ...をしぶしぶ出す **2** *v/i* F (*pay*) okane o shibushibu harau お金をしぶしぶ払う

cough medicine, cough syrup sekidome-yaku せき止め薬

could: ~ *I have my key?* kagi o totte itadakemasu ka かぎを取って頂けますか; ~ *you help me?* tetsudatte itadakemasu ka 手伝って頂けますか; *this* ~ *be our bus* kore ga watashitachi no basu kamo shiremasen これが私達のバスかもしれません; *you* ~ *be right* anata ga tadashii kamo shiremasen あなたが正しいかもしれません; *I* ~ *n't say for sure* hakkiri wa iemasen ga はっきりは言えませんが; *he* ~ *have got lost* kare wa mayotte ita kamo shiremasen 彼は迷っていたかもしれません; *you* ~ *have warned me!* anata wa watashi ni keikoku dekita no ni あなたは私に警告できたのに

council (*assembly*) gikai 議会; (*advisory body*) shingikai 審議会

councilman shikai-giin 市会議員

councilor giin 議員

counsel 1 *n* (*advice*) jogen 助言; (*lawyer*) bengo-shi 弁護士 **2** *v/t course of action* susumeru 勧める; *person* ... ni jogen o ataeru ...に助言を与える

counseling kaunseringu カウンセリング

counselor (*adviser*) kaunserā カウンセラー; LAW bengo-nin 弁護人

count 1 *n* (*number arrived at*) kazu 数; (*action of ~ing*) kanjō 勘定; (*in baseball, boxing*) kaunto カウント; *keep* ~ *of* ... ... no kazu o oboete oku ...の数を覚えておく; *lose* ~ *of* ... ... no kazu o wasureru ...の数を忘れる; *at the last* ~ saishūteki ni wa 最終的には **2** *v/i* (*to ten etc*) kazu o kazoeru 数を数える; (*calculate*) keisan suru 計算する; *be important* jūyō de aru 重要である; *qualify* kazu ni hairu 数に入る **3** *v/t* (~ *up*) kazoeru 数える; (*calculate*) keisan suru 計算する; (*include*) kazu ni ireru 数に入れる

♦ **count on** ... o ate ni suru ...を当てにする

countdown byōyomi 秒読み

countenance *v/t* yōnin suru 容認する

counter[1] (*in shop, café*) kauntā カウンター; (*in game*) koma こま

counter[2] 1 *v/t* ... ni taikō suru ...に対抗する **2** *v/i* (*retaliate*) hangeki suru 反撃する

counter[3]: *run* ~ *to* ... ... ni han suru ...に反する

counteract chūwa suru 中和する; **counter-attack 1** *n* hangeki 反撃 **2** *v/i* hangeki suru 反撃する; **counterbalance** tsuriawaseru 釣り合わせる; **counterclockwise** han-tokeimawari (no) 反時計回り(の); **counterespionage** supai-bōshi-katsudō スパイ防止活動; **counterfeit** *v/t* gizō suru 偽造す

る **2** *adj* gizō (no) 偽造(の);
counterpart (*person*) sōtō suru
hito 相当する人;
counterproductive gyakukōka
(no) 逆効果(の);**countersign** *v/t*
… ni fukusho suru …に副署する
countless kazoekirenai 数えきれな
い
country kuni 国; (*as opposed to
town*) inaka 田舎; **in the ~** inaka ni
田舎に
country and western MUS kantorī
カントリー
countryman (*fellow ~*) dōkoku-jin
同国人
countryside inaka 田舎
county gun 郡
coup POL kūdetā クーデター; *fig*
daiseikō 大成功
couple (*married*) fūfu 夫婦;
(*romantically involved*) kappuru
カップル; (*two people*) futarigumi
二人組; *just a ~* sukoshi dake 少し
だけ; *a ~ of* ni, san no 二、三の;
(*people*) ni, san-nin no 二、三人の
coupon (*form*) shiryō-seikyū-ken
資料請求券; (*voucher*) waribiki-
ken 割引券
courage yūki 勇気
courageous yūki no aru 勇気のある
courier (*messenger*) kūrie クーリエ;
(*with tourist party*) tenjōin 添乗員;
motorcycle ~ baiku-bin バイク便
course *n* (*series of lessons*) kōza 講
座, kōsu コース; (*part of meal*)
ippin 一品; (*of ship, plane*) shinro
針路; (*for sports event*) kōsu コー
ス; *of ~* mochiron もちろん; *of ~
not* tondemonai とんでもない; *~ of
action* hōshin 方針; *~ of treatment*
chiryō-katei 治療過程; *in the ~ of
…* … no aida ni …の間に; *can I
open the window? - of ~!* mado o
akete mo ii desu ka - ē dōzo 窓を
開けてもいいですか - ええどうぞ
court *n* LAW hōtei 法廷; (*~house*)
saiban-sho 裁判所; SP kōto コート;
take … to ~ … o kiso suru …を起
訴する
court case saiban 裁判
court dance (*Japanese-style*)

bugaku 舞楽
courteous reigi-tadashii 礼儀正しい
courtesy reigi 礼儀
courthouse saiban-sho 裁判所;
court martial 1 *n* gunpō-kaigi 軍法
会議 **2** *v/t* gunpō-kaigi ni kakeru
軍法会議にかける; **court music**
(*Japanese-style*) gagaku 雅楽;
court order saibansho-meirei 裁
判所命令; **courtroom** hōtei 法廷;
courtyard nakaniwa 中庭
cousin itoko いとこ
cove (*small bay*) irie 入り江
cover 1 *n* (*protective*) kabā カバー;
(*of book, magazine*) hyōshi 表紙;
(*for bed*) beddo-kabā ベッドカ
バー; (*shelter*) kakure-basho 隠れ
場所; (*shelter from rain*)
amayadori no basho 雨宿りの場所;
(*insurance*) hoshō-gaku 補償額
2 *v/t* ōu 覆う; (*hide*) kakusu 隠す;
(*of insurance policy*) … ni hoken
o kakeru …に保険をかける;
distance iku 行く; (*of journalist*)
shuzai suru 取材する
♦ cover up 1 *v/t* … o ōu …を覆う;
fig momikesu もみ消す **2** *v/i fig*
kabau かばう; *~ for* (*for person*)
… o kabau …をかばう
coverage (*by media*) hōdō 報道
covering letter dōfu no tegami 同封
の手紙, kabā-retā カバーレター
covert hisoka (na) ひそか(な)
coverup (*of crime etc*) momikeshi
もみ消し
cow *n* ushi 牛
coward okubyō-mono おくびょう者
cowardice okubyō おくびょう
cowardly okubyō (na) おくびょう
(な)
cowboy kaubōi カウボーイ
cower chijikomaru ちぢこまる
coy (*evasive*) tōmawashi (na) 遠回
し(な); (*flirtatiously*) hanikanda
はにかんだ
cozy igokochi no yoi 居心地のよい
CPU (= *central processing unit*)
chūō-shori-sōchi 中央処理装置
crab *n* kani かに
crack 1 *n* hibi ひび; (*joke*) jōdan 冗
談 **2** *v/t cup, glass* hibi o ireru ひび

を入れる; *nut* waru 割る; (*solve*) kaiketsu suru 解決する; *code* sakeme o ireru 裂け目をいれる; *~ a joke* jōdan o tobasu 冗談を飛ばす 3 *v/i* hibi ga hairu ひびが入る; *get ~ing* sassoku shigoto ni torikakaru 早速仕事に取りかかる

♦ **crack down on** ... o kibishiku torishimaru ...を厳しく取り締まる

♦ **crack up** *F* (*have breakdown*) noirōze ni naru ノイローゼになる; *F* (*laugh*) warau 笑う

crackdown torishimari 取り締まり

cracked *cup, glass* hibiwareta ひび割れた

cracker (*to eat*) kurakkā クラッカー

crackle *v/i* (*of fire*) pachipachi to oto o tateru ぱちぱちと音を立てる

cradle *n* (*of baby*) yurikago 揺りかご

craft[1] NAUT fune 船

craft[2] (*skill*) gijutsu 技術; (*trade*) shokugyō 職業

craftsman shokunin 職人

crafty zurui ずるい

crag (*rocky*) iwaba 岩場

cram *v/t* tsumekomu 詰め込む

cramped *apartment* semai 狭い

cramps ikeiren 胃けいれん

cranberry kuranberī クランベリー, kiichigo 木いちご

crane 1 *n* (*machine*) kurēn クレーン; (*bird*) tsuru つる 2 *v/t:* **~ one's neck** kubi o nobasu 首を伸ばす

crank *n* (*person*) henjin 変人

crankshaft kuranku-jiku クランク軸

cranky (*bad-tempered*) okorippoi 怒りっぽい

crap *n* kuso くそ; *fig* V (*nonsense*) tawagoto たわごと; (*poor quality item*) dekisokonai 出来そこない

crash 1 *n* (*noise*) gachan to iu oto がちゃんという音; (*accident*) shōtotsu 衝突; (*plane ~*) tsuiraku 墜落; COM tōsan 倒産; COMPUT kurasshu クラッシュ 2 *v/i* (*make noise*) monosugoi oto o tateru ものすごい音を立てる; (*of thunder*) naru 鳴る; (*of car*) shōtotsu suru 衝突する; (*of airplane*) tsuiraku suru 墜落する; (*of market*) bōraku

suru 暴落する; COMPUT kurasshu suru クラッシュする; F (*sleep*) neru 寝る; *the vase ~ed to the ground* kabin ga jimen ni ochite oto o tatete wareta 花瓶が地面に落ちて音をたてて割れた 3 *v/t car* shōtotsu saseru 衝突させる

♦ **crash out** F (*fall asleep*) neru 寝る

crash course shūchū-kōsu 集中コース; **crash diet** shūchū-daietto 集中ダイエット; **crash helmet** herumetto ヘルメット; **crash landing** fujichaku 不時着

crate (*packing case*) hako 箱

crater (*of volcano*) funkakō 噴火口

crave hidoku hoshigaru ひどく欲しがる

craving tsuyoi yokkyū 強い欲求

crawl 1 *n* (*in swimming*) kurōru クロール; *at a ~* (*very slowly*) noronoro to のろのろと; (*on floor*) hau はう; (*move slowly*) noronoro susumu のろのろ進む

♦ **crawl with** ... de ujauja shite iru ...でうじゃうじゃしている

crayon kureyon クレヨン

craze dairyūkō 大流行; *the latest ~* saishin-ryūkō 最新流行

crazy *adj* ki ga kurutta 気が狂った, *be ~ about* ... ni netchū shite iru ...に熱中している

creak 1 *n* kiikii iu oto きいきいいう音 2 *v/i* kishimu きしむ

cream 1 *n* (*for skin, coffee, cake*) kurīmu クリーム; (*color*) kurīmu-iro クリーム色 2 *adj* kurīmu-iro (no) クリーム色(の)

cream cheese kurīmu-chīzu クリームチーズ

creamer (*pitcher*) mirukuire ミルク入れ; (*for coffee*) kōhī-yō kurīmu コーヒー用クリーム

creamy (*with lots of cream*) kurīmu tappuri (no) クリームたっぷり(の)

crease 1 *n* (*accidental*) shiwa しわ; (*deliberate*) orime 折り目 2 *v/t* (*accidentally*) shiwa o tsukeru しわをつける

create 1 *v/t* hikiokosu 引き起こす; *garden, jobs, opportunity* tsukuru 作る 2 *v/i* (*be creative*) sōzō suru

創造する

creation hassei 発生; (*of employment, opportunity*) sōshutsu 創出; (*something created*) sōsaku 創作; *Creation* REL tenchi-sōzō 天地創造

creative sōzōsei ga aru 創造性がある

creator sōsaku-sha 創作者; (*author*) saku-sha 作者; (*founder*) sōsetsu-sha 創設者; *the Creator* REL sōzō-shu 創造主

creature (*animal*) ikimono 生き物; (*person*) hito 人

credibility (*of person*) shinrai dekiru koto 信頼できること; (*of story*) shin'yōsei 信用性

credible (*believable*) shin'yō dekiru 信用できる; *candidate etc* shinrai dekiru 信頼できる

credit 1 *n* FIN tsuke つけ; (*use of ~ cards*) kurejitto クレジット; (*honor*) meiyo 名誉; (*payment received*) nyūkin 入金; *be in ~* kuroji de aru 黒字である; *get the ~ for ...* ... ni kansuru shin'yō o eru ...に関する信用を得る 2 *v/t* (*believe*) shinjiru 信じる; *~ an amount to an account* aru kingaku o kōza ni nyūkin suru ある金額を口座に入金する

creditable shōsan ni atai suru 称賛に値する

credit card kurejitto-kādo クレジットカード

credit limit (*of credit card*) kādo-shiyō-gendogaku カード使用限度額

creditor saiken-sha 債権者

creditworthy shinyōgashi dekiru 信用貸しできる

credulous damasare-yasui だまされやすい

creed shinjō 信条

creek (*stream*) ogawa 小川

creep 1 *n pej* kobiru yatsu こびるやつ 2 *v/i* shinobiyoru 忍び寄る

creeper BOT tsuru-shokubutsu つる植物

creeps: *the house gives me the ~* zotto suru yō na ie da ぞっとするような家だ

creepy zotto suru ぞっとする

cremate kasō ni suru 火葬にする

cremation kasō 火葬

crematorium kasō-ba 火葬場

crescent *n* (*shape*) mikazuki 三日月

crest (*of hill*) chōjō 頂上; (*of bird*) tosaka とさか

crestfallen gakkari shita がっかりした

crevice wareme 割れ目

crew *n* (*of ship, plane*) norikumiin 乗組員; (*of repairmen etc*) han 班; (*crowd, group*) nakama 仲間

crew cut kakugari 角刈り

crew neck marukubi sētā 丸首セーター

crib *n* (*for baby*) bebī-beddo ベビーベッド

crick: *~ in the neck* sujichigai 筋違い

cricket (*insect*) kōrogi こおろぎ

crime (*offense*) hanzai 犯罪; (*shameful act*) tsumi 罪

criminal 1 *n* hanzai-sha 犯罪者 2 *adj* (*relating to crime*) hanzai (no) 犯罪(の); (LAW: *not civil*) keiji (no) 刑事(の); (*shameful*) keshikaran けしからん

crimson *adj* makka (na) 真っ赤(な)

cringe chijimiagaru 縮み上がる

cripple 1 *n* (*disabled person*) fugu 不具 2 *v/t* person fugu ni suru 不具にする; *fig* mahi saseru 麻ひさせる

crisis kiki 危機

crisp *adj* weather, air sawayaka (na) さわやか(な); *lettuce, apple* shakishaki shita しゃきしゃきした; *bacon, toast* karitto shita かりっとした; *shirt* paritto shita ぱりっとした; *bank bill* te no kireru yō (na) 手の切れるよう(な)

criterion (*standard*) kijun 基準

critic hyōron-ka 評論家

critical (*making criticisms*) hihanteki (na) 批判的(な); (*serious*) kikiteki (na) 危機的(な); *moment etc* jūdai (na) 重大(な); MED jūtai (no) 重体(の)

critically *speak etc* hihanteki ni 批判的に; *~ ill* jūtai de 重体で

criticism hihan 批判

criticize *v/t* hihan suru 批判する

croak 1 *n* (*of frog*) gerogero to naku koe げろげろと鳴く声; (*of person*) shagaregoe しゃがれ声 **2** *v/i* (*of frog*) gerogero naku げろげろ鳴く; (*of person*) shagaregoe o dasu しゃがれ声を出す

crockery tōjiki 陶磁器

crocodile wani わに, kurokodairu クロコダイル

crony F nakama 仲間

crook *n* (*dishonest*) akutō 悪党

crooked (*not straight*) magatta 曲がった; (*dishonest: person*) fuseijitsu (na) 不誠実(な); *business* fusei (na) 不正(な)

crop 1 *n* shūkaku 収穫; *fig* mure 群れ **2** *v/t hair* karikomu 刈り込む; *photo* hashi o kiriotosu 端を切り落とす

♦ **crop up** mochiagaru 持ち上がる

cross 1 *adj* (*angry*) okotte iru 怒っている **2** *n* (X) batsujirushi ばつ(印); (*Christian symbol*) jūjika 十字架 **3** *v/t* (*go across*) wataru 渡る; ~ *oneself* REL jūji o kiru 十字を切る; ~ *one's legs* ashi o kumu 足を組む; *keep one's fingers ~ed* kōun o inoru 幸運を祈る; *it never ~ed my mind* sore wa omoitsukanakatta それは思いつかなかった **4** *v/i* (*go across*) wataru 渡る; (*of lines*) kōsa suru 交差する

♦ **cross off, cross out** … o kesu … を消す

crossbar (*of goal*) yokogi 横木; (*of bicycle*) ue-paipu 上パイプ; (*in high jump*) bā バー

cross-country (**skiing**) kurosu-kantorī (sukī) クロスカントリー(スキー)

crossed check senbiki-kogitte 線引き小切手

cross-examine LAW hantai-jinmon o okonau 反対尋問を行う

cross-eyed yorime (no) 寄り目の

crossing NAUT kōkai 航海

crossroads kōsaten 交差点; **cross-section** (*of people*) tenkei 典型

crosswalk ōdan-hodō 横断歩道;

crossword (**puzzle**) kurosuwādo-pazuru クロスワードパズル

crouch *v/i* kagamu かがむ

crow *n* (*bird*) karasu からす; *as the ~ flies* massugu ni ikeba 真っ直ぐに行けば

crowd *n* gunshū 群衆; (*at sports event*) kankyaku 観客; (*in department store, bar etc*) hitogomi 人込み; *I don't like ~s* hitogomi ga kirai desu 人込みがきらいです

crowded konda 込んだ

crown 1 *n* (*on tooth*) shikan 歯冠, kuraun クラウン **2** *v/t tooth … ni* kuraun o kabuseru …にクラウンをかぶせる

crucial jūdai (na) 重大(な)

crude 1 *adj* (*vulgar*) gehin (na) 下品(な); (*unsophisticated*) sozatsu (na) 粗雑(な) **2** *n*: ~ (*oil*) gen'yu 原油

cruel zankoku (na) 残酷(な)

cruelty gyakutai-kōi 虐待行為

cruise 1 *n* funatabi 船旅, kurūzu クルーズ **2** *v/i* (*in ship*) kōkai suru 航海する; (*of car*) raku ni hashiru 楽に走る; (*of plane*) junkō-sokudo de hikō suru 巡航速度で飛行する

cruise liner kyakusen 客船

cruising speed junkō-sokudo 巡航速度

crumb kuzu くず

crumble 1 *v/t* kuzusu 崩す **2** *v/i* (*of bread, stonework*) kuzureru 崩れる; *fig* (*of opposition etc*) hōkai suru 崩壊する

crumple 1 *v/t* (*crease*) shiwa ni suru しわにする **2** *v/i* (*collapse*) kuzureru 崩れる

crunch *n* F: *when it comes to the ~* iza to iu toki ni wa いざというときには **2** *v/i* (*of snow, gravel*) zakuzaku oto o tateru ざくざく音を立てる

crusade *n fig* undō 運動

crush 1 *n* (*crowd*) hitogomi 人込み; *have a ~ on* … ni netsu o ageru …に熱をあげる **2** *v/t* oshitsubusu 押しつぶす; (*crease*) shiwakucha ni suru しわくちゃにする; *they were*

~ed to death karera wa gekitotsushi shita 彼等は激突死した

crust (on bread) kawa 皮

crutch (for injured person) matsubazue 松葉杖

cry 1 n (call) sakebigoe 叫び声; **have a** ~ naku 泣く 2 v/t (call) sakebu 叫ぶ 3 v/i (weep) naku 泣く

♦ **cry out** 1 v/t ... o ōgoe de iu ...を大声で言う 2 v/i ōgoe o dasu 大声を出す

♦ **cry out for** (need) ... o ōi ni hitsuyō to suru ...を多いに必要とする

crystal (mineral) suishō 水晶; (glass) kurisutaru-garasu クリスタルガラス

crystallize 1 v/t gutaika saseru 具体化させる 2 v/i (of thoughts etc) gutaika suru 具体化する

cub ko 子

cube (shape) rippōtai 立方体

cubic sanjō (no) 三乗 (の)

cubic capacity TECH yōseki 容積

cubicle (changing room) kōishitsu 更衣室

cucumber kyūri きゅうり

cuddle 1 n hōyō 抱擁 2 v/t dakishimeru 抱き締める

cuddly kitten etc dakishimetaku naru 抱き締めたくなる; (liking cuddles) dakko saretagaru だっこされたがる

cue n (for actor, pool) kyū キュー; **that's my ~ to leave** sore ga kaeru kikkake to natta それが帰るきっかけとなった

cuff n (of shirt) kafusu カフス; (of pants) orikaeshi 折り返し; (blow) hirateuchi 平手打ち; **off the ~** tossa no kiten de とっさの機転で

cuff link kafusubotan カフスボタン

cuisine: **Japanese ~** washoku 和食; **western ~** yōshoku 洋食; **Chinese ~** chūka-ryōri 中華料理

cul-de-sac ikidomari 行き止まり

culinary ryōri (no) 料理 (の)

culminate: **~ in ...** tsui ni ... to naru ついに...となる

culmination chōten 頂点

culprit hannin 犯人

cult (sect) shūha 宗派

cultivate land kōsaku suru 耕作する; person kankei o kizuku 関係を築く

cultivated person kyōyō no aru 教養のある

cultivation (of land) kōsaku 耕作

cultural (of the arts) geijutsuteki (na) 芸術的 (な); (of a country's identity) bunkateki (na) 文化的 (な)

culture n (artistic) geijutsu 芸術; (of a country) bunka 文化

Culture Day Bunka no hi 文化の日

cultured (cultivated) kyōyō no aru 教養のある

culture shock karuchā-shokku カルチャーショック

cumbersome yakkai (na) やっかい (な)

cunning 1 n warugashiko-sa 悪賢さ 2 adj warugashikoi 悪賢い

cup n kappu カップ; (trophy) torofī トロフィー; **a ~ of tea** ippai no ocha 一杯のお茶

cupboard todana 戸棚

curable chiryō-kanō (na) 治療可能 (な)

curator (of museum) kanchō 館長

curb 1 n (of street) fuchiishi 縁石; (on powers etc) yokusei 抑制 2 v/t yokusei suru 抑制する

curdle v/i (of milk) gyōko suru 凝固する

cure 1 n MED chiryōhō 治療法 2 v/t MED chiryō suru 治療する; meat, fish hozon suru 保存する

curfew MIL yakan-gaishutsu-kinshirei 夜間外出禁止令; fig mongen 門限

curiosity (inquisitiveness) kōkishin 好奇心

curious (inquisitive) kōkishin no tsuyoi 好奇心の強い; (strange) kimyō (na) 奇妙 (な)

curiously (inquisitively) monomezurashisō ni もの珍しそうに; (strangely) myō ni 妙に; **~ enough** kimyō ni mo 奇妙にも

curl 1 n (in hair) kāru カール; (of smoke) uzu 渦 2 v/t hair kāru saseru カールさせる; (*wind*) maku 巻く **3** *v/i* (*of hair*) kāru suru カールする; (*of leaf, paper etc*) maruku naru 丸くなる

♦ **curl up** maruku natte neru 丸くなって寝る

curly *hair* makige (no) 巻き毛(の); *tail* kāru shita カールした

currant hoshibudō 干しぶどう

currency (*money*) tsūka 通貨; *foreign* ~ gaika 外貨

current 1 *n* (*in river*) nagare 流れ; (*in sea*) kairyū 海流; ELEC denryū 電流 **2** *adj* (*present*) genzai (no) 現在(の)

current affairs, **current events** jiji-mondai 時事問題

current affairs program jiji-mondai-bangumi 時事問題番組

currently ima no tokoro 今のところ

curriculum karikyuramu カリキュラム

curse 1 *n* (*spell*) noroi のろい; (*swearword*) akutai 悪態 **2** *v/t* norou のろう; (*swear at*) nonoshiru ののしる **3** *v/i* nonoshiru ののしる

cursor COMPUT kāsoru カーソル

cursory zonzai (na) ぞんざい(な)

curt bukkirabō (na) ぶっきらぼう(な)

curtail tanshuku suru 短縮する

curtain kāten カーテン; THEA maku 幕

curve 1 *n* kyokusen 曲線, kābu カーブ **2** *v/i* magaru 曲がる

cushion 1 *n* (*for couch etc*) kusshon クッション **2** *v/t* *blow, fall* yawarageru 和らげる

custard kasutādo-kurīmu カスタードクリーム

custody (*of children*) yōikuken 養育権; *in* ~ LAW kōryū sarete 拘留されて

custom (*tradition*) kanshū 慣習; (*habit*) shūkan 習慣; COM hiiki ひいき; *as was his* ~ itsumo no yō ni いつものように

customary itsumo (no) いつも(の); (*required by tradition*) kanshū (no) 慣習(の); *it is* ~ *to ...* ... suru no ga kanshū to natte iru ...する

が慣習となっている

customer kyaku 客

customer relations shōgai 渉外

custom-made ōdāmeido (no) オーダーメイド(の)

customs zeikan 税関

customs clearance tsūkan-tetsuzuki 通関手続; **customs inspection** zeikan-shinsa 税関審査; **customs officer** zeikanri 税官吏

cut 1 *n* (*with knife, scissors*) kirikuchi 切り口; (*injury*) kirikizu 切り傷; (*of garment, hair*) katto カット; (*reduction*) katto カット, sakugen 削減; *my hair needs a* ~ kami o katto shitai 髪をカットしたい **2** *v/t* kiru 切る; (*reduce*) katto suru カットする, sakugen suru 削減する; *get one's hair* ~ kami o kitte morau 髪を切ってもらう

♦ **cut back 1** *v/i* (*in costs*) kiritsumeru 切り詰める **2** *v/t* *employees ...* o sakugen suru ...を削減する

♦ **cut down 1** *v/t* *tree ...* o kiritaosu ...を切り倒す **2** *v/i* (*in smoking etc*) herasu 減らす

♦ **cut down on** *smoking etc ...* o herasu ...を減らす

♦ **cut off** (*with knife, scissors etc*) kiritoru 切り取る; (*isolate*) koritsu saseru 孤立させる; TELEC denwa o kiru 電話を切る; *we were* ~ kirete shimai mashita 切れてしまいました

♦ **cut out** (*with scissors*) ... o kirinuku ...を切り抜く; (*eliminate*) ... o yameru ...をやめる; *cut that out!* F yamenasai やめなさい; *be* ~ *for* ... ni tekishite iru ...に適している

♦ **cut up** *v/t* *meat etc ...* o kiru ...を切る

cutback sakugen 削減

cute (*pretty*) kawaii かわいい; (*sexually attractive*) suteki (na) 素敵(な); (*smart, clever*) nukeme no nai 抜け目のない

cuticle amakawa あま皮

cut-price yasuuri (no) 安売り(の)

cut-throat *competition* yōsha no nai

容赦のない

cutting 1 *n* (*from newspaper etc*) kirinuki 切り抜き **2** *adj remark* shinratsu (na) 辛らつ(な)

cyberspace saibāsupēsu サイバースペース

cycle 1 *n* (*bicycle*) jitensha 自転車; (*series of events*) shūki 周期 **2** *v/i*: **~ to work** jitensha de shigoto ni iku 自転車で仕事に行く

cycling saikuringu サイクリング

cyclist saikuringu suru hito サイクリングする人; (*in race*) jitensha no senshu 自転車の選手

cylinder (*container*) tsutsu 筒; (*in engine*) shirindā シリンダー

cylindrical entōkei (no) 円筒形(の)

cynic hiniku-ya 皮肉屋

cynical hiniku (na) 皮肉(な)

cynicism hiniku 皮肉

cyst nōshu のうしゅ

Czech 1 *adj* Cheko (no) チェコ(の); **the ~ Republic** Cheko-kyōwakoku チェコ共和国 **2** *n* (*person*) Cheko-jin チェコ人; (*language*) Cheko-go チェコ語

D

DA (= *district attorney*) chihō-kenji 地方検事

dab 1 *n* (*small amount*) hitonuri ひと塗り **2** *v/t* (*remove*) tebayaku fuku 手早くふく; (*apply*) tebayaku nuru 手早く塗る

♦ **dabble in** ... ni te o dasu ...に手を出す

dad otōsan お父さん, papa パパ; (*when talking to outsiders about own father*) chichi 父

daffodil suisen 水仙

dagger tanken 短剣

daily 1 *n* (*paper*) nikkan-shi 日刊紙 **2** *adj* mainichi (no) 毎日(の)

dainty yūbi (na) 優美(な)

dairy products nyū-seihin 乳製品

dais endai 演台

dam 1 *n* (*for water*) damu ダム **2** *v/t river* ... ni damu o tsukuru ...にダムを造る

damage 1 *n* songai 損害; *fig* (*to reputation etc*) kizu 傷, damēji ダメージ **2** *v/t* songai o ataeru 損害を与える; *fig: reputation etc* kizu o tsukeru 傷を付ける

damages LAW songai-baishō 損害賠償

damaging songai o ataeru 損害を与える

dame F (*woman*) onna 女

damn 1 *interj* shimatta しまった **2** *n*: **I don't give a ~!** sonna koto shitta koto ja nai そんなこと知ったことじゃない **3** *adj* imaimashii いまいましい **4** *adv* hidoku ひどく **5** *v/t* (*condemn*) hinan suru 非難する; **~ it!** chikushō 畜生; **I'm ~ed if ...** ... da nante jōdan ja nai ...だなんて冗談じゃない

damned → **damn** *adj*, *adv*

damp *building, room* shimeppoi 湿っぽい; *cloth* shimetta 湿った

dampen shimeraseru 湿らせる

dance 1 *n* dansu ダンス; (*social event*) dansu-pātī ダンスパーティー; *Japanese ~* Nihon-buyō 日本舞踊 **2** *v/i* odoru 踊る; *would you like to ~?* odorimasen ka 踊りませんか

dancer odoru hito 踊る人; (*performer*) dansā ダンサー

dancing dansu ダンス

dandelion tanpopo たんぽぽ

dandruff fuke ふけ

Dane Denmāku-jin デンマーク人

danger kiken 危険; **out of ~** (*of patient*) kiki o dasshite 危機を脱える

して

dangerous kiken (na) 危険(な)

dangle 1 v/t burasageru ぶら下げる **2** v/i burasagaru ぶら下がる

Danish 1 adj Denmāku (no) デンマーク(の) **2** n (language) Denmāku-go デンマーク語

Danish (pastry) Denisshu デニッシュ

dare 1 v/t omoikitte ... suru 思い切って...する; **how ~ you!** yoku mo mā よくもまあ **2** v/i: **~ X to do Y** X ni Y dekiru nara yatte miro to keshikakeru XにY できるならやってみろとけしかける

daring adj daitan (na) 大胆(な)

dark 1 n kuragari 暗がり; **after ~** kurai natte kara 暗くなってから; **keep ... in the ~** fig ... ni damatte oku ...に黙っておく **2** adj room, night kurai 暗い; hair, eyes kuroppoi 黒っぽい; color koi 濃い; clothes kurai iro (no) 暗い色(の); **~ blue** kon 紺; **~ green** fukamidori 深緑; **a ~er blue** koi ao 濃い青

darken (of sky) kuraku naru 暗くなる

dark glasses sangurasu サングラス

darkness kurayami 暗やみ

darling 1 n (woman to man) anata あなた; (man to woman) nē ねえ; **he's a ~** kare wa kawaii hito da 彼はかわいい人だ **2** adj aisubeki 愛すべき

darn[1] **1** n (mend) tsukuroi 繕い **2** v/t (mend) tsukurou 繕う

darn[2], **darned** → **damn** adj, adv

dart 1 n (for throwing) dātsu ダーツ **2** v/i tosshin suru 突進する

dash 1 n (punctuation) dasshu ダッシュ; (small amount) shōryō 少量; (MOT: dashboard) dasshubōdo ダッシュボード; **a ~ of brandy** shōryō no burandē 少量のブランデー; **make a ~ for** ... ni tosshin suru ...に突進する **2** v/i tosshin suru 突進する **3** v/t hopes uchikudaku 打ち砕く

◆ **dash off 1** v/i isoide iku 急いで行く **2** v/t (write quickly) ... o isoide kaku ...を急いで書く

dashboard dasshubōdo ダッシュボード

data shiryō 資料, dēta データ

database dēta-bēsu データベース; **data capture** dēta-shūshū データ収集; **data processing** jōhō-shori 情報処理, dēta-shori データ処理; **data protection** dēta-hogo データ保護; **data storage** dēta-kanri データ管理

date[1] (fruit) natsumeyashi no mi なつめやしの実

date[2] **1** n hizuke 日付; (romantic) dēto デート; (person) dēto no aite デートの相手; **what's the ~ today?** kyō wa nannichi desu ka 今日は何日ですか; **out of ~** clothes jidaiokure de 時代後れで; passport kigengire de 期限切れで; **up to ~** saishinshiki de 最新式で **2** v/t letter hizuke o ireru 日付を入れる; (go out with) tsukiau つき合う; **that ~s you** toshi ga bareru 年がばれる

dated jidaiokure (no) 時代後れ(の)

daub v/t nuritakuru 塗りたくる

daughter (own) musume 娘; (s.o. else's) ojō-san お嬢さん, musume-san 娘さん

daughter-in-law giri no musume 義理の娘; (s.o. else's) giri no musume-san 義理の娘さん

daunt v/t shirigomi saseru しりごみさせる

dawdle v/i guzuguzu suru ぐずぐずする

dawn 1 n yoake 夜明け; fig (of new age) hajimari 始まり **2** v/i: **it ~ed on me that ...** ... da to wakatte kita ...だとわかってきた

day hi 日; (daytime) hiruma 昼間; **what ~ is it today?** nan'yōbi desu ka 今日は何曜日ですか; **~ off** kyūka 休暇; **by ~** nitchū ni 日中に; **~ by ~** higoto ni 日ごとに; **the ~ after** sono tsugi no hi その次の日; **the ~ after tomorrow** asatte あさって; **the ~ before** sono mae no hi その前の日; **the ~ before yesterday** ototoi おととい; **~ in ~ out** kuru hi mo kuru hi mo 来る日も来る日も; **in those ~s** sono tōji wa そのとうじは

その当時は; **one ~** (*in past*) aru hi ある日; (*in future*) itsuka いつか; **the other ~** (*recently*) senjitsu 先日; **let's call it a ~!** kyō wa kore de o-shimai ni shiyō 今日はこれでおしまいにしよう ◊ (*with count word*) nichi 日; **a ~** ichi nichi 一日; **two ~s** futsuka 二日; **three ~s** mikka 三日; **four ~s** yokka 四日; **five ~s** itsuka 五日; **six ~s** muika 六日; **seven ~s** nanoka 七日; **eight ~s** yōka 八日; **nine ~s** kokonoka 九日; **ten ~s** tōka 十日; **twenty ~s** hatsuka 二十日

daybreak yoake 夜明け; **daydream 1** *n* hakuchūmu 白昼夢 **2** *v/i* kūsō ni fukeru 空想にふける; **daylight** hi no hikari 日の光; **daytime: in the ~** hiruma 昼間に; **daytrip** higaeri-ryokō 日帰り旅行

daze: in a ~ bōzen to shite ぼう然として

dazed (*by news*) bōzen to shita ぼう然とした; (*by a blow*) bon'yari shite ぼんやりして

dazzle *v/t* ... no me o kuramaseru ...の目をくらませる; *fig* kantan saseru 感嘆させる

dead 1 *adj* person shinda 死んだ; *plant* kareta 枯れた; *battery* kirete iru 切れている; *phone* tsūjinai 通じない; *flashlight, light bulb* tsukenai つかない; F *place* kakki no nai 活気のない **2** *adv* F (*very*) sugoku すごく; **~ beat, ~ tired** hetoheto ni tsukareta へとへとに疲れた; **that's ~ right** hontō ni tadashii 本当に正しい **3** *n*: **the ~** shinda hito 死んだ人; **in the ~ of night** mayonaka ni 真夜中に

deaden *pain, sound* yawarageru 和らげる

dead end (*street*) ikidomari 行きどまり; **dead-end job** shōraisei no nai shigoto 将来性のない仕事; **dead heat** dōchaku 同着; **deadline** saishū-kigen 最終期限; (*for submissions*) shimekiri 締め切り; **deadlock** *n* (*in talks*) ikizumari 行き詰まり

deadly *adj* (*fatal*) chimeiteki (na) 致命的(な); F (*boring*) hidoku

tsumaranai ひどくつまらない

deaf mimi ga kikoenai 耳が聞こえない

deaf-and-dumb rōa (no) ろうあ(の)

deafen mimi o kikoenaku suru 耳を聞こえなくする

deafening mimi o tsunzaku yō (na) 耳をつんざくような

deafness mimi no kikoenai koto 耳の聞こえない事

deal 1 *n* torihiki 取り引き; **it's a ~** COM kore de kimari desu ne これで決まりですね; (*I agree*) notta のった; (*it's a promise*) yakusoku desu yo 約束ですよ; **a good ~** (*bargain*) toku na kaimono 得な買い物; (*a lot*) kanari (no) かなり(の); **a great ~ of** (*lots*) takusan (no) たくさん(の) **2** *v/t cards* kubaru 配る; **~ a blow to** ... ni dageki o ataeru ...に打撃を与える

♦ **deal in** (*trade in*) ... no baibai o suru ...の売買をする

♦ **deal out** *cards* ... o kubaru ...を配る

♦ **deal with** (*handle*) ... o atsukau ...を扱う; (*do business with*) ... to torihiki suru ...と取り引きする

dealer (*merchant*) hanbai-gyō-sha 販売業者, dīrā ディーラー; (*drug ~*) mayaku-mitsubainin 麻薬密売人; (*at cards*) dīrā ディーラー, oya 親

dealing (*drug ~*) mayaku-torihiki 麻薬取り引き

dealings (*business*) kankei 関係

dean (*of college*) gakubuchō 学部長

dear *adj* shin'ai (na) 親愛(な); (*expensive*) kōka (na) 高価(な); **Dear Sir** haikei 拝啓; **Dear Richard / Margaret** richādo-san / māgaretto-san リチャードさん/マーガレットさん, *fml* richādo-sama / māgaretto-sama リチャード様/マーガレット様; **(oh) ~!, ~ me!** oya, mā おや、まあ

dearly *love* kokoro kara 心から

death shi 死

death penalty shikei 死刑

death toll shibōsha-sū 死亡者数

debatable gimon no aru 疑問のある

debate 1 *n* tōgi 討議; POL tōron 討論

2 *v/t* & *v/i* tōron suru 討論する

debauchery hōtō 放とう

debit 1 *n* hikiotoshi 引き落し **2** *v/t*
account hikiotoshi sareru 引き落
しされる; *amount* karikata ni
kinyū suru 借り方に記入する

debris zangai 残がい

debt shakkin 借金; **be in ~** shakkin
shite iru 借金している

debtor fusai-sha 負債者

debug *room* tōchōki o torinozoku 盗
聴器を取り除く; COMPUT konpyūta
no puroguramu o tenaoshi suru コ
ンピューターのプログラムを手直
しする

début *n* debyū デビュー

decade jūnenkan 十年間

decadent taihaiteki (na) 退廃的(な)

decaffeinated kafein o nuita カフェ
インを抜いた

decanter dekantā デカンター

decapitate kubi o kiru 首を切る

decay 1 *n* (*process*) fuhai 腐敗;
(*decayed matter*) fushoku 腐食; (*in
teeth*) mushiba 虫歯 **2** *v/i* kusaru
腐る; (*of teeth*) mushiba ni naru 虫
歯になる

deceased: **the ~** kojin 故人

deceit damashi だまし

deceitful fushōjiki (na) 不正直(な)

deceive damasu だます

December jūnigatsu 十二月

decency reigi 礼儀; **he had the ~ to
...** kare wa ... suru reigi o
wakimaeteita 彼は...する礼儀をわ
きまえていた

decent *person* mattō (na) まっとう
(な); *salary, price* kekkō (na) 結構
(な); *meal, sleep* matomo (na) まと
も(な); (*adequately dressed*)
chanto fuku o kite iru ちゃんと服
を着ている

decentralize *administration* chihō-
bunken ni suru 地方分権にする

deception gomakashi ごまかし;
(*sexual*) fujitsu 不実

deceptive mikake to nakami no
chigatta 見かけと中身の違った

deceptively: *it looks ~ simple*
mikake wa shinpuru da ga 見かけ
はシンプルだが

decibel deshiberu デシベル

decide 1 *v/t* kimeru 決める, kettei
suru 決定する; (*settle*) sayū suru 左
右する; *I haven't ~d what I'm
going to do* watashi wa nani o suru
ka kimete inai 私は何をするか決め
ていない **2** *v/i* kimeru 決める; *you ~*
kimete kudasai 決めて下さい

decided (*definite*) hakkiri shita
はっきりした

decider (*game*) ketteisen 決定戦

decimal *n* shōsū 小数

decimal point shōsūten 小数点

decimate gekigen suru 激減する

decipher kaidoku suru 解読する

decision kettei 決定; *it's your ~*
anata ga kimeru koto desu あなた
が決めることです; *it was your ~ to
come here* koko e kuru no wa
anata ga kimeta koto desu ここへ
来るのはあなたが決めたことです;
come to a ~ on ... ni kimeru ...に
決める; *we need a ~*
kimenakereba narimasen 決めな
ければなりません

decision-maker kettei-sha 決定者

decisive kippari shita きっぱりした;
(*crucial*) ketteiteki (na) 決定的
(な)

deck (*of ship*) dekki デッキ; (*of
cards*) hitokumi 一組

deckchair dekkichea デッキチェア

declaration (*statement*) dangen 断
言; (*of independence*) sengen 宣言;
(*of war*) fukoku 布告

declare (*state*) dangen suru 断言す
る; *independence* sengen suru 宣言
する; *war* fukoku suru 布告する; (*at
customs*) shinkoku suru 申告する

decline 1 *n* (*fall*) genshō 減少; (*in
standards, health*) teika 低下 **2** *v/t*
invitation kotowaru 断わる; **~ to
comment** komento o sashihikaeru
コメントをさしひかえる **3** *v/i*
(*refuse*) kotowaru 断わる;
(*decrease*) genshō suru 減少する;
(*of health*) teika suru 低下する

declutch kuratchi o kiru クラッチを
切る

decode kaidoku suru 解読する

decompose fuhai suru 腐敗する

décor naisō 内装, interia インテリア

decorate (*with paint, paper*) naisō suru 内装する; (*adorn*) kazaru 飾る; *soldier* ... ni kunshō o sazukeru ...に勲章を授ける

decoration (*paint, paper*) naisō 内装, interia インテリア; (*ornament*) kazari 飾り

decorative kazari (no) 飾り(の)

decorator (*interior ~*) naisō-gyōsha 内装業者

decoy n otori おとり; (*model duck*) dekoi デコイ

decrease 1 n (*in number*) genshō 減少; (*in size*) shukushō 縮小; (*in value, production, speed*) teika 低下 **2** v/t *number* genshō saseru 減少させる; *size* shukushō suru 縮小する; *value, speed, production* teika saseru 低下させる **3** v/i (*of number*) genshō suru 減少する; (*of size*) shukushō suru 縮小する; (*of value, speed, production*) teika suru 低下する

dedicate *book etc* sasageru 捧げる; **~ oneself to ...** ... ni sennen suru ...に専念する

dedication (*in book*) kenji 献辞; (*to cause, work*) kenshin 献身

deduce suiron suru 推論する

deduct: **~ X from Y** Y kara X o sashihiku YからXを差し引く

deduction (*from salary*) kōjo 控除; (*conclusion*) suiron 推論

deed n (*act*) okonai 行い; LAW shōsho 証書

deep *hole, water* fukai 深い; *shelf* okuyuki no fukai 奥行きの深い; *trouble* shinkoku (na) 深刻(な); *voice* hikui 低い; *color* koi 濃い; *thinker* kangae no fukai 考えの深い

deepen 1 v/t fukaku suru 深くする **2** v/i fukaku naru 深くなる; (*of mystery*) fukamaru 深まる; (*of crisis*) masu 増す

deep freeze n reitōko 冷凍庫; **deep-frozen food** reitō-shokuhin 冷凍食品; **deep-fry** ageru 揚げる, furai ni suru フライにする

deer shika しか

deface sokonau 損なう

defamation meiyo-kison 名誉棄損

defamatory meiyo-kison ni ataru 名誉棄損にあたる

default adj COMPUT kiteichi (no) 既定値(の)

defeat 1 n haiboku 敗北 **2** v/t *makasu* 負かす; (*of task, problem*) zasetsu saseru ざ折させる

defeatist adj attitude haiboku-shugi (no) 敗北主義(の)

defect n kekkan 欠陥

defective kekkan no aru 欠陥のある

defend mamoru 守る; *cause* bōgo suru 擁護する; (*stand by*) kabau かばう; (*justify*) shakumei suru 釈明する; LAW bengo suru 弁護する

defendant hikoku 被告; (*in criminal case*) hikoku-nin 被告人

defense n bōei 防衛; SP difensu ディフェンス; LAW bengo 弁護; (*justification*) shakumei 釈明; (*of cause*) yōgo 擁護; **come to X's ~** X o tasukeru Xを助ける; (*verbally*) ... o bengo suru ...を弁護する

defense budget bōei-yosan 防衛予算

defense lawyer hikoku-bengonin 被告弁護人

defenseless mubōbi (na) 無防備(な)

defense player SP difensu no senshu ディフェンスの選手; **Defense Secretary** Kokubōshō-chōkan 国防省長官; **defense witness** hikokugawa-shōnin 被告側証人

defensive 1 n: **on the ~** mamori ni mawatte 守りに回って; **go on the ~** shusei ni tatsu 守勢に立つ **2** adj *weaponry* bōeiyō (no) 防衛用(の); *person* benkai-gamashii 弁解がましい

defer v/t nobasu 延ばす

deference sonkei 尊敬; keii 敬意

deferential keii o arawasu 敬意を表す

defiance hankō 反抗; **in ~ of ...** ... o mushi shite ...を無視して

defiant hankōteki (na) 反抗的(な)

deficiency (*lack*) fusoku 不足

deficient: *be ~ in ...* ... ga fusoku shite iru ...が不足している

deficit akaji 赤字

define *word* teigi suru 定義する; *goal* akiraka ni suru 明らかにする

definite *date, time* hakkiri to kimatta はっきりと決まった; *answer, improvement* meikaku (na) 明確(な); *(certain)* kakujitsu (na) 確実(な); *are you ~ about that?* sore wa tashika desu ka それは確かですか; *nothing ~ has been arranged* nani mo hakkiri to kimatte inai 何もはっきりと決まっていない

definite article teikanshi 定冠詞

definitely tashika ni 確かに

definition *(of word)* teigi 定義; *(of objective)* setsumei 説明

definitive ketteiteki (na) 決定的(な)

deflect *ball, blow* kawasu かわす; *criticism* kaihi suru 回避する; *(from course of action)* magesaseru 曲げさせる; *be ~ed from ...* o kaeru ...を変える

deform bukakkō ni suru 不格好にする

deformity kikei 奇形

defraud ... kara damashitoru ...からだまし取る

defrost *v/t food* kaitō suru 解凍する; *fridge* ... no shimotori o suru ...の霜取りをする

deft kiyō 器用(な)

defuse *bomb* shinkan o torinozoku 信管を取り除く; *situation* yawarageru 和らげる

defy mushi suru 無視する

degenerate *v/i (of behavior)* daraku suru 堕落する; MED akka suru 悪化する; *the discussion ~d into a fight* giron kara kenka ni hatten shita 議論からけんかに発展した

degrade iyashimeru 卑しめる

degrading *position, work* kutsujokuteki (na) 屈辱的(な)

degree do 度; *(from university)* gakui 学位; *(amount)* teido 程度; *by ~s* shidai ni 次第に; *get one's ~* gakui o toru 学位を取る

dehydrated dassui-shōjō o okoshite

脱水症状を起こして

de-ice johyō suru 除氷する

de-icer johyō-supurē 除氷スプレー

deign: *~ to ...* ...shite kudasatta ...して下さった

deity kami 神

dejected rakutan shita 落胆した

delay 1 *n* okure 遅れ **2** *v/t nobasu* 延ばす; *be ~ed* okureru 遅れる **3** *v/i* guzuguzu suru ぐずぐずする

delegate 1 *n* daihyō 代表 **2** *v/t task* makaseru 任せる; *person* ninmei suru 任命する

delegation *(of task)* inin 委任; *(people)* daihyō-dan 代表団

delete sakujo suru 削除する; *(cross out)* kesu 消す

deletion *(act)* sakujo 削除; *(that deleted)* sakujo-bubun 削除部分

deli → **delicatessen**

deliberate 1 *adj* koi (no) 故意(の) **2** *v/i* jukkō suru 熟考する

deliberately waza to わざと

delicacy *(of fabric)* sensai-sa 繊細さ; *(of problem)* bimyō-sa 微妙さ, derikēto-sa デリケートさ; *(of health)* yowa-sa 弱さ; *(tact)* kikubari 気配り; *(food)* chinmi 珍味

delicate *fabric* sensai (na) 繊細(な), derikēto (na) デリケート(な); *problem* bimyō (na) 微妙(な), derikēto (na) デリケート(な); *health* yowai 弱い

delicatessen derikatessen デリカテッセン, sōzai-ya 総菜屋

delicious oishii おいしい; *that was ~* oishikatta おいしかった; *(to hostess, waiter etc)* gochisōsama deshita ごちそうさまでした

delight *n* ōyorokobi 大喜び

delighted yorokonde iru 喜んでいる; *be ~ to ...* yorokonde... suru 喜んで...する

delightful tanoshii 楽しい

delimit han'i o sadameru 範囲を定める

delinquent *n* hikō ni hashitta 非行に走った

delirious MED uwagoto o iu うわ言をいう; *(ecstatic)* uchōten (no) 有

頂天(の)

deliver haitatsu suru 配達する;
message todokeru 届ける; *baby*
shussan o tasukeru 出産を助ける;
~ a speech enzetsu o suru 演説を
する

delivery (*of goods, mail*) haitatsu
配達; (*of baby*) shussan 出産

delivery date nōnyūbi 納入日;
delivery note haitatsu-jō 配達状;
delivery van haitatsuyō-torakku
配達用トラック

delude damasu だます; *you're
deluding yourself* anata wa jibun o
damashite iru あなたは自分をだま
している

deluge 1 *n* gōu 豪雨; *fig* sattō 殺到
2 *v/t fig* sattō saseru 殺到させる

delusion sakkaku 錯覚

de luxe gōka (na) 豪華(な)

demand 1 *n* yōkyū 要求; COM juyō
需要; *in ~* hipparidako de aru 引っ
張りだこである **2** *v/t* yōkyū suru
要求する; (*require*) hitsuyō to suru
必要とする

demanding *job* kitsui きつい; *person*
kimuzukashii 気難しい

demented hakkyō shita 発狂した

demise shikyo 死去; *fig* shōmetsu 消
滅

demitasse demitasu デミタス

demo (*protest*) demo デモ; (*tape*)
demo-tēpu デモテープ

democracy (*system*) minshu-shugi
民主主義; (*country*) minshu-shugi-
kokka 民主主義国家

democrat minshu-shugi-sha 民主主
義者; *Democrat* POL minshutō-in
民主党員

democratic minshuteki (na) 民主的
(な)

demo disk demo-disuku デモディス
ク

demolish *building* torikowasu 取り
壊す; *argument* kutsugaesu 覆す

demolition (*of building*)
torikowashi 取り壊し; (*of
argument*) ronpa 論破

demon akuma 悪魔

demonstrate 1 *v/t* (*prove*) risshō
suru 立証する; *machine* miseru 見

せる **2** *v/i* (*politically*) demo o
suru デモをする

demonstration (*show*) risshō 立証;
(*protest*) demo デモ; (*of machine*)
demonsutorēshon デモンストレー
ション

demonstrative: *be ~* kanjō o soto ni
dasu 感情を外に出す

demonstrator (*protester*) demo-
sankasha デモ参加者

demoralized yaru ki o nakusaseru
やる気をなくさせる

demoralizing yaru ki o nakusu やる
気をなくす

den (*study*) shosai 書斎

denial (*of rumor, accusation*) hitei
否定; (*of request*) kyohi 拒否

denim denimu (no) デニム(の)

denims (*jeans*) jīnzu ジーンズ

Denmark Denmāku デンマーク

denomination (*of money*) gakumen
額面; (*religious*) shūha 宗派

dense (*thick*) koi 濃い; *foliage*
missei shita 密生した; *crowd*
misshū shita 密集した; (*stupid*)
atama no warui 頭の悪い

densely: *~ populated* jinkō no
misshū shita 人口の密集した

density (*of population*) mitsudo 密度

dent 1 *n* hekomi へこみ **2** *v/t*
hekomaseru へこませる

dental *treatment* ha (no) 歯(の);
hospital shika (no) 歯科(の)

dentist haisha 歯医者

dentures ireba 入れ歯

deny *charge, rumor* hitei suru 否定
する; *right, request* kyohi suru 拒
否する

deodorant deodoranto デオドラン
ト, bōshūzai 防臭剤

depart shuppatsu suru 出発する; *~
from* (*deviate from*) ... kara
soreru ...からそれる

department (*of company*) bu 部; ka
課; (*of university*) gakubu 学部,
gakka 学科; (*of government*) shō
省; (*of store*) uriba 売り場

Department of Defense Kokubō-
sōshō 国防総省; **Department of
the Interior** Naimushō 内務省;
Department of State Kokumushō

国務省; **department store** depāto デパート

departure (*leaving*) shuppatsu 出発; (*of train, bus*) hassha 発車; (*of person from job*) taishoku 退職; (*deviation*) itsudatsu 逸脱; **a new ~** (*for goverment, organization*) shin-hōshin 新方針; (*for company*) shin-tenkai 新展開; (*for actor, writer*) shin-kyōchi 新境地

departure lounge shuppatsu-raunji 出発ラウンジ

departure time shuppatsu-jikoku 出発時刻

depend: *that ~s* bāi ni yoru 場合による; *it ~s on the weather* tenki ni yoru 天気による; *I ~ on you* anata o tayori ni shite imasu あなたを頼りにしています

dependable tayori ni naru 頼りになる

dependence, dependency izon 依存

dependent 1 *n* fuyō-kazoku 扶養家族 **2** *adj* tayotte iru 頼っている

depict (*in painting, writing*) egaku 描く

deplorable nagekawashii 嘆かわしい

deplore nageku 嘆く

deport kyōsei-sōkan suru 強制送還する

deportation kyōsei-sōkan 強制送還

deportation order kokugaitaikyo-meirei 国外退去命令

deposit 1 *n* (*in bank*) yokin 預金; (*of mineral*) kōmyaku 鉱脈; (*on purchase*) tetsukekin 手付け金 **2** *v/t money* yokin suru 預金する; (*put down*) oku 置く; *silt, mud* taiseki suru 堆積する

deposition LAW sensei-kyōjutsusho 宣誓供述書

depot (*train station*) eki 駅; (*bus station*) teiryū-jo 停留所; (*for storage*) chōzō-jo 貯蔵所

depreciate *v/i* FIN kachi ga sagaru 価値が下がる

depreciation FIN kachi no teika 価値の低下

depress *person* yūutsu ni saseru 憂うつにさせる

depressed *person* yūutsu (na) 憂うつ(な)

depressing yūutsu (na) 憂うつ(な)

depression MED utsubyō うつ病; (*economic*) fukyō 不況; (*meteorological*) teikiatsu 低気圧

deprive: *~ X of Y* X kara Y o ubau X からYを奪う

deprived mazushii 貧しい

depth fuka-sa 深さ; (*of shelf*) okuyuki 奥行き; (*of voice*) hiku-sa 低さ; (*of color*) ko-sa 濃さ; (*of thought*) fuka-sa 深さ; *in ~* (*thoroughly*) tettei shite 徹底して; *in the ~s of winter* fuyu no massaichū 冬の真最中; *be out of one's ~* (*in water*) se no tatanai 背の立たない; (*in discussion etc*) tsuite ikenai ついていけない

deputation daihyō-dan 代表団

♦**deputize for** ... no kawari o suru ...の代わりをする

deputy dairi-nin 代理人

deputy leader fuku-rīdā 副リーダー

derail: *be ~ed* (*of train*) dassen suru 脱線する

deranged hakkyō shita 発狂した

derelict *adj* hōki sareta 放棄された

deride baka ni suru ばかにする

derision azakeri あざけり

derisive *remarks, laughter* azakeruyō (na) あざけるよう(な)

derisory *sum* kushō shite shimauyō (na) 苦笑してしまうよう(な)

derivative (*not original*) hasei (no) 派生(の)

derive *v/t* eru 得る; *be ~d from* (*of word*) ... ni yurai suru ...に由来する

derogatory keibetsuteki (na) 軽べつ(の)

descend 1 *v/t* oriru 下りる; *be ~ed from* ... no shison de aru ...の子孫である **2** *v/i* (*of airplane*) oriru 降りる; (*of climber*) gezan suru 下山する; (*of road*) kudari ni naru 下りになる; (*of darkness*) oriru 下りる

descendant shison 子孫

descent (*from mountain*) gezan 下山; (*of airplane*) kōka 降下; (*ancestry*) kakei 家系; *of Chinese*

~ chūgokukei no 中国系の

describe iiarawasu 言い表す; **~ X as Y** X o Y da to iu X を Y だと言う

description byōsha 描写; (*of criminal*) ninsō 人相

desegregate jinshu, seibetsu ni yoru sabetsu o nakusu 人種、性別による差別をなくす

desert¹ *n* sabaku 砂漠; *fig* fumō no chi 不毛の地

desert² **1** *v/t* (*abandon*) misuteru 見捨てる **2** *v/i* (*of soldier*) dassō suru 脱走する

deserted sabireta さびれた

deserter MIL dassōhei 脱走兵

desertion iki 遺棄; MIL dassō 脱走

deserve ... ni atai suru ...に値する

design **1** *n* dezain デザイン; (*for building*) sekkei 設計; (*pattern*) moyō, 模様, dezain デザイン **2** *v/t* sekkei suru 設計する; *clothes* dezain suru デザインする; *not -ed for heavy use* tashiyō ni taeru yō ni dezain sarete inai 多使用に耐える様にデザインされていない

designate *v/t person* shimei suru 指名する; *area* shitei suru 指定する

designer dezainā デザイナー; (*of building, car, ship*) sekkei-sha 設計者

designer clothes burando-mono ブランド物

design fault sekkei-misu 設計ミス

design school dezain-sukūru デザインスクール

desirable nozomashii 望ましい

desire *n* (*wish*) negai 願い; (*sexual*) yokubō 欲望

desk tsukue 机; (*in hotel*) furonto フロント

desk clerk furonto-gakari フロント係

desktop publishing desukutoppu-paburisshingu デスクトップパブリッシング

desolate *adj place* kōryō to shita 荒涼とした

despair **1** *n* zetsubō 絶望; *in ~* zetsubō shite 絶望して **2** *v/i* zetsubō suru 絶望する; *~ of* ... ni zetsubō suru ...に絶望する, *doing*

sth ... o akirameru ...をあきらめる

desperate *person, action* hisshi (no) 必死(の); *situation* zetsubōteki (na) 絶望的(な); *be ~ for a drink/cigarette* nomitakute/tabako o suitakute tamaranai 飲みたくて/タバコを吸いたくてたまらない

desperation shinimonogurui 死に物狂い; *an act of ~* hisshi no kōdō 必死の行動

despise keibetsu suru 軽べつする

despite ... nimo kakawarazu ...にもかかわらず

despondent rakutan shita 落胆した

despot bōkun 暴君

dessert dezāto デザート

destination mokutekichi 目的地

destiny unmei 運命

destitute konkyū no 困窮(の)

destroy hakai suru 破壊する

destroyer NAUT kuchikukan 駆逐艦

destruction hakai 破壊

destructive *power* hakaiteki (na) 破壊的(な); *criticism* hikensetsuteki (na) 非建設的(な); *child* ranbō (na) 乱暴(な)

detach torihazusu 取りはずす

detachable torihazuseru 取りはずせる

detached (*objective*) reisei (na) 冷静(な)

detachment (*objectivity*) reisei-sa 冷静さ

detail *n* (*small point*) komakai ten 細かい点; (*piece of information*) shōsai 詳細; (*irrelevancy*) sasai na koto さいさいなこと; *in ~* saibu ni watatte 細部にわたって

detailed komakai 細かい

detain (*hold back*) hikitomeru 引き止める; (*as prisoner*) kōryū suru 拘留する

detainee POL seijihan 政治犯

detect ... ni kizuku ...に気づく; (*of device*) tanchi suru 探知する

detection (*of crime*) hakken 発見; (*of smoke etc*) tanchi 探知

detective keiji 刑事; (*private*) shiritsu-tantei 私立探偵

detective novel suiri-shōsetsu 推理
小説
detector (*for metal*) tanchi-ki 探知
器; (*for drugs*) kenshutsu-ki 検出
器
détente POL kinchō-kanwa 緊張緩
和, detanto デタント
detention (*imprisonment*) kōkin 拘
禁
deter soshi suru 阻止する; ~ **X from
doing Y** X ni Y suru no o omoi
todomaseru XにYするのを思いと
どませる
detergent senzai 洗剤
deteriorate waruku naru 悪くなる
determination (*resolution*) ketsui
決意
determine (*establish*) kakutei suru
確定する
determined kataku kesshin shite 堅
く決心して; *effort* danko to shita
断固とした
deterrent *n* yokushiryoku 抑止力
detest hidoku kirau ひどく嫌う
detonate 1 *v/t* bakuhatsu saseru 爆
発させる **2** *v/i* bakuhatsu suru 爆
発する
detour *n* mawarimichi 回り道;
(*diversion*) ukairo う回路
detract: ~ **from** ... o sokonau ... を損
なう
detriment: **to the** ~ **of** ... ni songai o
ataete ... に損害を与えて
detrimental yūgai (na) 有害(な)
deuce (*in tennis*) jūsu ジュース
devaluation (*of currency*) heika-
kirisage 平価切り下げ
devalue *currency* ... no heika o
kirisageru ... の平価を切り下げる
devastate *crops, countryside, city*
... ni ōki na higai o motarasu ... に
大きな被害をもたらす; *fig*: *person*
uchinomesu うちのめす
devastating shōgekiteki (na) 衝撃
的(な)
develop 1 *v/t film* genzō suru 現像す
る; *land, site* kaihatsu suru 開発す
る; *activity, business* hatten saseru
発展させる; (*design*) kaihatsu
suru 開発する; (*improve on*)
shinten saseru 進展させる; *illness,*

cold hatsubyō saseru 発病させる
2 *v/i* (*grow*) sodatsu 育つ; (*of
country, business*) hatten suru 発
展する
developer (*of property*) kaihatsu-
gyōsha 開発業者
developing country hatten-
tojōkoku 発展途上国
development (*of film*) genzō 現像;
(*of land, new drug*) kaihatsu 開発;
(*of business, country*) hatten 発展;
(*event*) shinten 進展; (*improving*)
shinten 進展
device (*tool*) dōgu 道具; (*gadget*)
sōchi 装置
devil akuma 悪魔
devious (*sly*) warugashikoi 悪賢い
devise kōan suru 考案する
devoid: ~ **of** ... ni kakete iru ... に欠
けている
devote *time, effort, money* ateru 充
てる; *life* sasageru 捧げる
devoted *son etc* kenshinteki (na) 献
身的(な); **be** ~ **to a person** hito ni
kenshinteki de aru 人に献身的で
ある
devotion (*to person*) kenshin 献身;
(*to job*) chūsei 忠誠
devour *food* musaborikuu むさぼり
食う; *book* musaboruyō ni yomu む
さぼるように読む
devout keiken (na) 敬けん(な)
dew tsuyu 露
dexterity kiyō-sa 器用さ
diabetes tōnyōbyō 糖尿病
diabetic 1 *n* tōnyōbyō-kanja 糖尿病
患者 **2** *adj* tōnyōbyō (no) 糖尿病
(の)
diagonal *adj* naname (no) 斜め(の)
diagram zu 図
dial 1 *n* (*of clock*) moji-ban 文字盤;
(*of meter*) keiki-ban 計器盤 **2** *v/i*
TELEC denwa o kakeru 電話をかけ
る **3** *v/t number* daiyaru suru ダイ
ヤルする
dialect hōgen 方言
dialog taiwa 対話
dial tone hasshin'on 発信音
diameter chokkei 直径
diametrically: ~ **opposed** seihantai
(no) 正反対(の)

diamond (*jewel, in cards*)
daiyamondo ダイヤモンド;
(*shape*) daiyamondo-gata ダイヤ
モンド形, hishi-gata ひし形

diaper oshime おしめ

diaphragm ANAT ōkakumaku 横隔
膜; (*contraceptive*) pessarī ペッサ
リー

diarrhea geri 下痢

diary (*for thoughts*) nikki 日記; (*for
appointments*) techō 手帳

dice 1 *n* saikoro さいころ **2** *v/t* (*cut*)
sai no me ni kiru さいの目に切る

dichotomy nibun 二分

dictate *v/t letter* kōjutsu suru 口述す
る

dictation kakitori 書き取り

dictator dokusai-sha 独裁者

dictatorial *tone of voice* sondai (na)
尊大(な); *person* wanman (na) ワ
ンマン(な); *powers* dokusaiteki
(na) 独裁的(な)

dictatorship dokusai-seiji 独裁政治

dictionary jisho 辞書

die shinu 死ぬ; ~ *of cancer/AIDS*
gan / eizu de shinu がん/エイズで
死ぬ; *I'm dying to know/leave*
shiritakute / tachisaritakute
tamaranai 知りたくて/立ち去りた
くてたまらない

♦ **die away** (*of noise*) dandan to
kikoenaku naru だんだんと聞こえ
なくなる

♦ **die down** (*of noise*) chiisaku naru
小さくなる; (*of storm*) shizumaru
静まる; (*of fire*) kiete iku 消えてい
く; (*of excitement*) sameru 冷める

♦ **die out** (*of custom*) sutareru すた
れる; (*of species*) zetsumetsu suru
絶滅する

diesel (*fuel*) dīzeru ディーゼル

diet 1 *n* (*regular food*)
shokuseikatsu 食生活; (*for losing
weight*) daietto ダイエット; (*for
health reasons*) shokuji-ryōhō 食
事療法 **2** *v/i* daietto suru ダイエッ
トする

differ (*be different*) kotonaru 異な
る; (*disagree*) iken ga awanai 意見
が合わない

difference chigai 違い; (*argument*)

iken no sōi 意見の相違; *it doesn't
make any ~* (*doesn't change
anything*) nani mo kawaranai 何
も変わらない; (*doesn't matter*)
dōdemo yoi どうでもよい

different (*dissimilar*) chigau 違う;
(*distinct*) betsu (no) 別(の)

differentiate: ~ *between things* …
no kubetsu o suru …の区別をする;
people sabetsu suru 差別する

differently chigau fū ni 違う風に; *he
expressed it ~* kare wa chigau
hyōgen o shita 彼は違う表現をし
た; *they do things ~* karera wa
betsubetsu no yarikata o suru 彼
等は別々のやり方をする

difficult muzukashii 難しい

difficulty muzukashi-sa 難しさ; *have
~ doing* … … suru no wa
muzukashii …するのは難しい;
with ~ kurō shite 苦労して

dig 1 *v/t* horu 掘る **2** *v/i*: *it was ~ging
into me* … ni kuikomu …に食い込
む

♦ **dig out** (*find*) … o sagashidasu …
を捜し出す

♦ **dig up** … o horiokosu …を掘り起
こす; *information* … o saguridasu
…を探り出す

digest *v/t* shōka suru 消化する;
information yoku rikai suru よく
理解する

digestible *food* shōka-shiyasui 消化
しやすい

digestion shōka 消化

digit (*number*) sūji 数字; *a* **4** ~
number yonketa no sūji 4けたの数
字

digital dejitaru-shiki (no) デジタル
式(の)

dignified dōdō to shita 堂々とした

dignitary kōkan 高官

dignity kihin 気品

digress wakimichi e soreru わき道
へそれる

digression dassen 脱線

dike (*wall*) teibō 堤防

dilapidated arehateta 荒れ果てた

dilate (*of pupils*) hirogaru 広がる

dilemma jirenma ジレンマ; *be in a* ~
itabasami ni naru 板ばさみになる

diligent nesshin (na) 熱心(な)

dilute v/t usumeru 薄める

dim 1 adj room, light usugurai 薄暗い; outline bon'yari shita ぼんやりした; (stupid) atama no nibui 頭の鈍い; prospects kasuka (na) かすか(な) **2** v/t: **~ the headlights** heddoraito o shita ni mukeru ヘッドライトを下に向ける **3** v/i (of lights) kuraku naru 暗くなる

dime jussento-kōka 十セント硬貨

dimension (measurement) sunpō 寸法

diminish 1 v/t herasu 減らす **2** v/i genshō suru 減少する

diminutive 1 n aishō 愛称 **2** adj chiisai 小さい

dimple ekubo えくぼ

din n sōon 騒音

dine shokuji o suru 食事をする

diner (person) kyaku 客; (restaurant) shokudō 食堂

dinghy (sailboat) kogata yotto 小型ヨット; (row boat) gomu-bōto ゴムボート; (inflatable) kyūmei-bōto 救命ボート

dingy (gloomy) inki (na) 陰気(な); (dirty) usugitanai 薄汚い

dining car shokudō-sha 食堂車; **dining room** shokudō 食堂; **dining table** shokutaku 食卓

dinner (in the evening) yūshoku 夕食; (midday) chūshoku 昼食; (gathering) dinā ディナー, enkai 宴会

dinner guest dinā no kyaku ディナーの客; **dinner jacket** takishīdo タキシード; **dinner party** dinā-pātī ディナーパーティー, enkai 宴会

dinosaur kyōryū 恐竜

dip 1 n (swim) hito-oyogi ひと泳ぎ; (for food) dippu ディップ; (in road) kubomi くぼみ **2** v/t ... ni hitasu ...に浸す; **~ the headlights** heddoraito o shita ni mukeru ヘッドライトを下に向ける **3** v/i (of road) kudarizaka ni naru 下り坂になる

diploma sotsugyō-shōsho 卒業証書

diplomacy gaikō 外交; (tact) josainasa 如才なさ

diplomat gaikōkan 外交官

diplomatic corps gaikōkan (no) 外交官(の); solution gaikō (no) 外交(の); (tactful) sotsu no nai そつのない

dire sashisematta 差し迫った

direct 1 adj chokusetsu (no) 直接(の); flight chokkō (no) 直行(の); train chokutsū (no) 直通(の); person sotchoku (na) 率直(な) **2** v/t (to a place) ... ni michi o oshieru ...に道を教える; play enshutsu suru 演出する; movie kantoku suru 監督する; attention mukeru 向ける

direct current ELEC chokuryū 直流

direction hōkō 方向; (of play) enshutsu 演出; (of movie) kantoku 監督; **~s** (instructions) shiji 指示; (to a place) michi 道; (for use) shiyō-hō 使用法; (for medicine) fukuyō-hō 服用法

direction indicator MOT winkā ウィンカー

directly 1 adv (straight) massugu ni 真っ直ぐに; (soon) mō sugu もうすぐ; (immediately) sugu ni すぐに **2** conj ... suru to sugu ni ...すると すぐに

director (of company) torishimariyaku 取締役; (of movie) kantoku 監督; (of play) enshutsu-ka 演出家

directory meibo 名簿; TELEC denwachō 電話帳

dirt yogore 汚れ

dirt cheap baka-yasui ばか安い

dirty 1 adj kitanai 汚い; (pornographic) waisetsu (na) わいせつ(な) **2** v/t yogosu 汚す

dirty trick hikyō na te 卑怯な手

disability shintai-shōgai 身体障害

disabled 1 n: **the ~** shintai-shōgai-sha 身体障害者 **2** adj shintai-shōgai no aru 身体障害のある

disadvantage (drawback) furi na koto 不利なこと; **be at a ~** furi na tachiba ni iru 不利な立場にいる

disadvantaged konkyū shite iru 困窮している

disadvantageous furi (na) 不利(な)

disagree iken ga awanai 意見が合わない

♦**disagree with**: *of person* ... to iken ga awanai ...と意見が合わない; *of food* ... no karada ni awanai ...の体に合わない

disagreeable iya (na) いや(な)

disagreement iken no sōi 意見の相違; *argument* kenka けんか

disappear kieru 消える; *run away* shissō suru 失そうする

disappearance shissō 失そう

disappoint gakkari saseru がっかりさせる

disappointed gakkari shita がっかりした

disappointing kitaihazure (na) 期待はずれ(な)

disappointment shitsubō 失望

disapproval fusansei 不賛成

disapprove sansei shinai 賛成しない; **~ of** X X ni hantai de aru Xに反対である

disarm 1 *v/t robber* ... no buki o toriageru ...の武器を取り上げる; *militia* busō-kaijo suru 武装解除する 2 *v/i* gunbi-shukushō suru 軍備縮小する

disarmament *of militia* busō-kaijo 武装解除; *of country* gunbi-shukushō 軍備縮小

disarming kokoro o nagomaseru 心をなごませる

disaster saigai 災害

disaster area hisaichi 被災地; *fig* *person* shippai-sha 失敗者

disastrous hisan (na) 悲惨(な)

disbelief: *in ~* shinjirarenai to iu fū ni 信じられないという風に

discard suteru 捨てる

discern mitomeru 認める

discernible mitomerareru 認められる

discerning chigai no wakaru 違いのわかる

discharge 1 *n* *from hospital* taiin 退院; *from army* jotai 除隊 2 *v/t* *from hospital* taiin saseru 退院させる; *from army* jotai saseru 除隊させる; *from job* kaiko suru 解雇する

disciple *religious* deshi 弟子

disciplinary chōkai (no) 懲戒(の)

discipline 1 *n* kiritsu 規律 2 *v/t* *child, dog* shitsukeru しつける; *employee* bassuru 罰する

disc jockey disuku-jokkī ディスクジョッキー, dī-jē D J

disclaim hinin suru 否認する

disclose akiraka ni suru 明らかにする

disclosure *of information, name* kōhyō 公表; *about scandal etc* hakkaku 発覚

disco disuko ディスコ

discolor henshoku saseru 変色させる

discomfort *pain* karui itami 軽い痛み; *embarrassment* tōwaku 当惑

disconcert dogimagi saseru どぎまぎさせる

disconcerted dogimagi shita どぎまぎした; **be ~** dogimagi suru どぎまぎする

disconnect *hose, appliance* torihazusu 取りはずす; *supply, service* tomeru 止める

disconsolate kanashii 悲しい

discontent fuman 不満

discontented fuman no aru 不満のある

discontinue *product* seizō-chūshi ni suru 製造中止にする; *train service* haishi suru 廃止する; *magazine* haikan ni suru 廃刊にする

discord MUS fukyō-waon 不協和音; *in relations* fuwa 不和

discotheque →**disco**

discount 1 *n* waribiki 割引 2 *v/t* *goods* waribiite baibai suru 割り引いて売買する; *theory* mushi suru 無視する

discourage *dissuade* ... ni omoitodomaru yō ni iu ...に思いとどまるようにいう; *dishearten* jishin o ushinawaseru 自信を失わせる

discover hakken suru 発見する; *talent* mitsukedasu 見つけ出す

discoverer hakken-sha 発見者

discovery hakken 発見

discredit *v/t person* … no shin'yō o kizutsukeru …の信用を傷つける; *theory* … ni gimon o nagekakeru …に疑問を投げかける

discreet *person* shinchō (na) 慎重 (な); *restaurant* medatanai 目立たない

discrepancy mujun 矛盾

discretion shinchō-sa 慎重さ; *at your ~* anata no handan de あなたの判断で

discriminate: *~ against* … o sabetsu suru …を差別する; *~ between* … o kubetsu suru …を区別する

discriminating chigai no wakaru 違いのわかる

discrimination *(sexual, racial etc)* sabetsu 差別

discus SP enban 円盤

discuss hanashiau 話し合う; *(of article)* ronjiru 論じる

discussion *(talk)* hanashiai 話し合い; *(debate)* tōron 討論; *(in the press)* giron 議論

disease byōki 病気

disembark *v/i (from plane)* oriru 降りる; *(from ship)* gesen suru 下船する

disenchanted: *~ with* … ni genmetsu suru …に幻滅する

disengage hanasu 離す

disentangle hodoku ほどく

disfigure minikuku suru 醜くする

disgrace 1 *n* haji 恥; *a ~ (person)* hajisarashi 恥さらし; *it's a ~* hidoi ひどい; *in ~* menboku o ushinatte 面目を失って **2** *v/t* hazukashimeru 辱める

disgraceful hazukbeki 恥ずべき

disgruntled fuman (no) 不満(の)

disguise 1 *n* hensō 変装; *(costume, make-up)* hensō-dōgu 変装道具 **2** *v/t* kaeru 変える; *fear, anxiety* kakusu 隠す; *~ oneself as* … ni hensō suru …に変装する; *he was ~d as* kare wa … ni hensō shite ita 彼は…に変装していた

disgust 1 *n* ken'o 嫌悪 **2** *v/t* mukatsukaseru むかつかせる

disgusting *habit* iya (na) いや(な); *smell, food* kimochi no warui 気持

ちの悪い; *it is ~ that* … … da to wa hidosugiru …だとはひどすぎる

dish *(part of meal)* ryōri 料理; *(container)* sara 皿

dishcloth shokkiaraiyō kurosu 食器洗い用クロス

disheartened gakkari shita がっかりした

disheartening gakkari saseru がっかりさせる

disheveled *hair, clothes* midareta 乱れた; *person* darashi no nai だらしのない

dishonest fushōjiki (na) 不正直(な)

dishonesty fushōjiki 不正直

dishonor *n* fumeiyo 不名誉; *bring ~ on* … ni doro o nuru …に泥を塗る

dishonorable fumeiyo (na) 不名誉(な)

dishwasher saraarai-ki 皿洗い機

dishwashing liquid senzai 洗剤

dishwater saraarai o shita mizu 皿洗いをした水

disillusion genmetsu saseru 幻滅させる

disillusionment genmetsu 幻滅

disinclined ki ga susumanai 気が進まない

disinfect shōdoku suru 消毒する

disinfectant shōdokuzai 消毒剤

disinherit … kara sōzokuken o ubau …から相続権を奪う

disintegrate barabara ni naru ばらばらになる; *(of marriage, building)* hōkai suru 崩壊する

disinterested *(unbiased)* kōhei (na) 公平(な)

disjointed matomari no nai まとまりのない

disk *(shape)* enban 円盤; COMPUT disuku ディスク; *on ~* furoppī ni hozon shite フロッピーに保存して

disk drive COMPUT disuku-doraibu ディスクドライブ

diskette furoppī-disuku フロッピーディスク

dislike 1 *n* hankan 反感 **2** *v/t* kirau 嫌う

dislocate *shoulder* dakkyū saseru 脱きゅうさせる

dislodge torihazusu 取り外す

disloyal uragirimono (no) 裏切り者 (の)

disloyalty uragiri 裏切り

dismal *weather* iya (na) いや(な); *news, prospect* kurai 暗い; *person (sad)* inki (na) 陰気(な); *person (negative)* yūutsu (na) 憂うつ(な); *failure* mijime (na) みじめ(な)

dismantle *machine* bunkai suru 分解する; *organization* haishi suru 廃止する

dismay 1 *n (alarm)* tōwaku 当惑; *(disappointment)* shitsubō 失望 **2** *v/t* tōwaku saseru 当惑させる

dismiss *employee* kaiko suru 解雇する; *suggestion* shirizokeru 退ける; *idea, thought* suteru 捨てる; *possibility* mushi suru 無視する

dismissal *(of employee)* kaiko 解雇

disobedience fufukujū 不服従

disobedient hankōteki (na) 反抗的 (な)

disobey ... ni sakarau ...に逆らう

disorder *(untidiness)* ranzatsu 乱雑; *(unrest)* bōdō 暴動; MED shōgai 障害

disorderly *room, desk* ranzatsu (na) 乱雑(な); *crowd* te ni oenai 手に負えない

disorganized mechakucha (na) め ちゃくちゃ(な); *person* keikakusei no nai 計画性のない

disoriented konran shita 混乱した

disown kandō suru 勘当する

disparaging kenashita けなした

disparity sōi 相違

dispassionate *(objective)* reisei (na) 冷静(な)

dispatch *v/t (send)* hassō suru 発送する

dispensary *(in pharmacy)* chōzaishitsu 調剤室

dispense: ~ **with** ... nashi de sumaseru ...なしで済ませる

disperse 1 *v/t* chirasu 散らす **2** *v/i (of crowd)* chitte iku 散っていく; *(of mist)* kieru 消える

displace *(supplant)* ... ni totte kawaru ...にとって代わる

display 1 *n* tenji 展示; *(in store window)* disupurē ディスプレー;

COMPUT monitā モニター; *be on ~ (at exhibition)* tenji shite aru 展示してある; *(be for sale)* chinretsu shite iru 陳列している **2** *v/t emotion* miseru 見せる; *(at exhibition)* tenji suru 展示する; *(for sale)* chinretsu suru 陳列する; COMPUT sukurīn ni hyōji suru スクリーンに表示する

display cabinet *(in museum, shop)* chinretsudana 陳列棚

displease okoraseru 怒らせる

displeasure ikari 怒り

disposable tsukaisute (no) 使い捨て(の); ~ **income** tedori 手取り

disposal shobun 処分; *(of pollutants, nuclear waste)* haiki 廃棄; **I am at your** ~ itsudemo kyōryoku shimasu いつでも協力します; **put X at Y's** ~ X o Y no jiyū ni tsukaeru yōni suru XをYの自由に使えるようにする

dispose: ~ **of** ... o shimatsu suru ...を始末する

disposed: **be** ~ **to** ... *(willing)* ... ga aru ...気がある; **be well** ~ **toward** ... ni kōiteki de aru ...に好意的である

disposition *(nature)* kishitsu 気質

disproportionate futsuriai (na) 不つり合い(な)

disprove hanshō suru 反証する

dispute 1 *n* ronsō 論争; *(between countries)* funsō 紛争; *(industrial)* sōgi 争議 **2** *v/t* hanron suru 反論する; *(fight over)* arasou 争う

disqualify shikkaku ni suru 失格とする

disregard 1 *n* mushi 無視 **2** *v/t* mushi suru 無視する

disrepair: **in a state of** ~ hidoku itanda jōtai de ひどく傷んだ状態で

disreputable mittomonai みっともない; *area* ikagawashii いかがわしい

disrespect shitsurei 失礼

disrespectful shitsurei (na) 失礼 (な)

disrupt *train service* midasu 乱す; *meeting, class* jama suru 邪魔する; *(intentionally)* bōgai suru 妨害する

disruption *(of train service)* konran

混乱; (*minor*) jama 邪魔; (*major*) bōgai 妨害

disruptive meiwaku (na) 迷惑(な)

dissatisfaction fuman 不満

dissatisfied fuman (na) 不満(な)

dissension iken no sōi 意見の相違

dissent 1 *n* hantai 反対 **2** *v/i: ~ from* ... ni hantai suru ...に反対する

dissident *n* iken no chigau hito 意見の違う人

dissimilar kotonaru 異なる

dissociate: ~ oneself from ... to no kankei o hitei suru ...との関係を否定する

dissolute fushidara (na) ふしだら(な)

dissolve 1 *v/t substance* tokasu 溶かす **2** *v/i* (*of substance*) tokeru 溶ける

dissuade omoi-todomaraseru 思いとどまらせる; **~ X from Y** X ni Y o omoi-todomaraseru XにYを思いとどまらせる

distance 1 *n* kyori 距離; *in the ~* tōku ni 遠くに **2** *v/t: ~ oneself from* ... kara kyori o oku ...から距離をおく

distant tōi 遠い; (*aloof*) yosoyososhii よそよそしい

distaste ken'o 嫌悪

distasteful fuyukai (na) 不愉快(な)

distinct (*clear*) hakkiri shita はっきりした; (*different*) betsu (no) 別(の); *as ~ from* ... to wa chigatte ...とは違って

distinction (*differentiation*) kubetsu 区別; *hotel of ~* kōkyū-hoteru 高級ホテル; *product of ~* kōkyū-hin 高級品

distinctive dokutoku (na) 独特(な)

distinctly hakkiri to はっきりと; (*decidedly*) utagai naku 疑いなく

distinguish (*see*) hakkiri to mieru はっきりと見える; (*hear*) hakkiri to kikoeru はっきりと聞こえる; *~ between X and Y* X to Y no kubetsu o suru XとYの区別をする

distinguished (*famous*) yūmei (na) 有名(な); (*dignified*) jōhin (na) 上品(な)

distort yugameru ゆがめる

distract *person* jama suru 邪魔する; *attention* sorasu そらす

distracted (*worried*) uwa no sora (no) 上の空(の)

distraction (*of attention*) ki o chirasu mono 気を散らすもの; (*amusement*) kibarashi 気晴らし; *drive ... to ~* ... o gyakujō saseru ...を逆上させる

distraught torimidashita 取り乱した

distress 1 *n* (*mental suffering*) kunō 苦悩; (*physical pain*) kutsū 苦痛; *in ~, ship, aircraft* sōnan shite 遭難して **2** *v/t* (*upset*) kurushimeru 苦しめる

distress signal sōnan-shingō 遭難信号

distribute bunpai o kubaru 分配を配る; *wealth* bunpai suru 分配する; COM hanbai suru 販売する

distribution haifu 配布; (*of wealth*) bunpai 分配; COM ryūtsū 流通

distribution arrangement COM ryūtsū no tehai 流通の手配

distributor COM ryūtsū-gyōsha 流通業者

district chiku 地区

district attorney chihō-kenji 地方検事

distrust 1 *n* fushinkan 不信感 **2** *v/t* shinyō shinai 信用しない

disturb (*interrupt*) ... no jama o suru ...の邪魔をする; (*upset*) fuan ni saseru 不安にさせる; *do not ~* nyūshitsu goenryo kudasai 入室ご遠慮下さい

disturbance (*interruption*) jama 邪魔; *~s* bōdō 暴動

disturbed (*concerned, worried*) shinpai (na) 心配(な); (*mentally*) jōcho-fuantei (no) 情緒不安定(の)

disturbing dōyō saseru 動揺させる

disused heisa sareta 閉鎖された

ditch 1 *n* mizo 溝 **2** *v/t* F (*get rid of*) suteru 捨てる

dive 1 *n* tobikomi 飛び込み; (*underwater*) daibingu ダイビング; (*of plane*) kyūkōka 急降下; F (*bar etc*) ikagawashii bā いかがわしいバー; *take a ~* (*of dollar etc*) kyūkōka suru 急降下する **2** *v/i* tobikomu 飛

び込む; (*underwater*) daibingu o suru ダイビングをする; (*of plane*) kyūkōka suru 急降下する

diver (*off board*) tobikomi no senshu 飛び込みの選手; (*underwater*) daibā ダイバー

diverge bunki suru 分岐する

diverse samazama (na) 様々(な)

diversification COM takaku-keiei 多角経営

diversify *v/i* COM takaku-keiei suru 多角経営する

diversion (*for traffic*) ukairo う回路; *create a ~* ki o sorasu 気をそらす

diversity tayōsei 多様性

divert *traffic* ukai saseru う回させる; *attention* sorasu そらす

divest: *~ X of Y* X kara Y o ubau X からYを奪う

divide wakeru 分ける; MATH waru 割る; *family* bunretsu saseru 分裂させる; *country* bunkatsu suru 分割する

dividend FIN haitōkin 配当金; *pay ~s* *fig* yaku ni tatsu 役に立つ

divine REL kami (no) 神(の); F subarashii すばらしい

diving (*from board*) tobikomi 飛び込み; (*scuba ~*) sukyūba-daibingu スキューバダイビング

diving board tobikomi-dai 飛び込み台

divisible warikireru 割り切れる

division MATH warizan 割り算; (*in party etc*) bunretsu 分裂; (*splitting into parts*) bunkatsu 分割; (*of company*) bu 部

divorce 1 *n* rikon 離婚; *get a ~* suru 離婚する 2 *v/t* ... to rikon suru ...と離婚する 3 *v/i* rikon suru 離婚する

divorced rikon shita 離婚した; *get ~d* rikon suru 離婚する

divorcee (*man*) rikon shita dansei 離婚した男性; (*woman*) rikon shita josei 離婚した女性

divulge morasu 漏らす

DIY (= *do-it-yourself*) nichiyō-daiku 日曜大工

DIY store doito ドイト

dizzy: *feel ~* memai ga suru めまいがする

DNA (= *deoxyribonucleic acid*) deokishiribo-kakusan デオキシリボ核酸, dī-enu-ē DNA

do 1 *v/t* suru する; *one's hair* setto suru セットする; *Spanish, chemistry* benkyō suru 勉強する; *100mph etc* ... no sokudo de susumu ...の速度で進む; *what are you ~ing tonight?* kyō no yoru wa nani o suru no desu ka 今日の夜は何をするのですか; *I don't know what to ~* dō shitara ii ka wakarimasen どうしたらいいか分かりません; *no, I'll ~ it* iie, watashi ga shimasu いいえ、私がします; *~ it right now!* ima sugu shinasai 今すぐしなさい; *have you done this before?* kore o mae ni shita koto ga arimasu ka これを前にした事がありますか; *have one's hair done* kami o setto shite morau 髪をセットしてもらう 2 *v/i* (*be suitable, enough*) ma ni au 間に合う; *that will ~!* sore de jūbun da それで十分だ; *~ well* (*of person*) umaku yaru うまくやる; (*of business*) umaku iku うまくいく; *well done!* (*congratulations!*) omedetō おめでとう; *how ~ you* hajimemashite はじめまして 3 (*auxiliary*): *~ you know him?* kare o shitte imasu ka 彼を知っていますか; *I don't know* wakarimasen わかりません; *~ be quick* isoide yo 急いでよ; *you like San Francisco? – yes I* ~ San Furanshisuko wa suki desu ka – hai, suki desu サンフランシスコは好きですか – はい、好きです; *he works hard, doesn't he?* kare wa nesshin ni hatarakimasu ne 彼は熱心に働きますね; *don't you believe me?* shinjiraremasen ka 信じられませんか; *you believe me, don't you?* shinjite kuremasu ne 信じてくれますね; *you don't know the answer, ~ you? – no I don't* kotae o shirimasen ne – hai, shirimasen 答えを知りませんね – はい、知りません

◆**do away with** (*abolish*) ... o

nakusu ...をなくす

♦ **do in** F: *I'm done in* hetoheto desu へとへとです

♦ **do out of**: *do X out of Y* X o damashite Y o toriageru XをだましてYを取り上げる

♦ **do over** (*do again*) ... o yarinaosu ...をやり直す

♦ **do up** (*renovate*) ... o kaishū suru ...を改修する; (*fasten*) ... o shimeru ...を閉める; *buttons* ... o tomeru ...を留める; *laces* ... o musubu ...を結ぶ

♦ **do with**: *I could ~ ...* ... ga hoshii ...が欲しい; *he won't have anything to ~ it* kare wa sore to mattaku kakawaritakunai 彼はそれとまったくかかわりたくない

♦ **do without 1** v/i nashi de sumaseru なしで済ませる **2** v/t ... nashi de sumaseru ...なしで済ませる

docile *person* sunao (na) 素直(な); *animal* jūjun (na) 従順(な)

dock¹ **1** n NAUT dokku ドック **2** v/i (*of ship*) dokku ni hairu ドックに入る; (*of spaceship*) dokkingu suru ドッキングする

dock² LAW hikoku-seki 被告席

dockyard zōsen-jo 造船所

doctor n MED isha 医者; (*form of address*) sensei 先生

doctorate hakase-gō 博士号

doctrine shugi 主義

docudrama dokyumentarī-dorama ドキュメンタリードラマ

document n bunsho 文書

documentary n dokyumentarī ドキュメンタリー

documentation shorui 書類

dodge v/t *blow* yokeru よける; *person, issue* sakeru 避ける; *question* hagurakasu はぐらかす

doe (*deer*) mejika 雌鹿

dog 1 n inu 犬 **2** v/t (*of bad luck*) ... ni tsuite mawaru ...について回る

dog catcher yaken-hokaku-nin 野犬捕獲人

dog-eared *book* tsukaifurushita 使い古した

dogged nebarizuyoi 粘り強い

doggie wanwan わんわん

doggy bag dogī-baggu ドギーバッグ

doghouse: *be in the ~* kirawarete iru 嫌われている

dogma kyōgi 教義

dogmatic kyōjō-shugiteki (na) 教条主義的(な)

do-gooder osekkai na jizen-ka おせっかいな慈善家

dog tag MIL ninshiki-hyō 認識票

dog-tired hetoheto ni tsukareta へとへとに疲れた

do-it-yourself nichiyō-daiku 日曜大工

doldrums: *be in the ~* (*of person*) yūutsu de aru 憂うつである; (*of economy*) keiki-chintai shite iru 景気沈滞している

♦ **dole out** ... o wakeru ...を分ける

doll (*toy*) ningyō 人形; F (*attractive woman*) bijin 美人; F (*nice woman*) kawaii hito かわいい人

♦ **doll up**: *get dolled up* kikazaru 着飾る

dollar doru ドル

dollop n hitosaji ひとさじ

dolphin iruka いるか

dome dōmu ドーム

domestic adj *chores* katei (no) 家庭(の); *news, policy* kokunai (no) 国内(の)

domestic animal petto ペット; (*for agriculture*) kachiku 家畜

domesticate *animal* kainarasu 飼い慣らす; *be ~d* (*of person*) kaji ni narete iru 家事に慣れている

domestic flight kokunai-sen 国内線

dominant omo (na) 主(な); *member* yūsei (na) 優勢(な); *opinion* shihaiteki (na) 支配的(な); BIO yūsei (no) 優性(の)

dominate shihai suru 支配する; *landscape* ... ni sobieru ...にそびえる

domination shihai 支配

domineering ōbō (na) 横暴(な)

donate *money* kifu suru 寄付する; *time* sasageru 捧げる; *toys, books* kizō suru 寄贈する; MED teikyō suru 提供する

donation (*of money*) kifu 寄付; (*of time*) kiyo 寄与; (*of toys, books*) kizō 寄贈; MED teikyō 提供

donkey roba ろば

donor (of money) kizō-sha 寄贈者; MED teikyō-sha 提供者

donut dōnattsu ドーナッツ

doom n (fate) hiun 悲運; (ruin) hametsu 破滅

doomed project kanarazu shippai suru unmei (no) 必ず失敗する運命 (の); **we are ~** (bound to fail) watashitachi wa shippai suru unmei ni aru 私達は失敗する運命 にある; **the ~ ship** shizumu unmei no fune 沈む運命の船; **the ~ plane** tsuiraku suru unmei no hikōki 墜 落する運命の飛行機

door to 戸, doa ドア; (double ~s) tobira 扉; (entrance) deiriguchi 出 入口; **there's someone at the ~** dare ka kita mitai desu 誰か来た みたいです

doorbell buzā ブザー; **doorknob** doanobu ドアノブ, doa no totte ド アの取っ手; **doorman** doaman ド アマン; **doormat** matto マット; **doorstep** toguchi 戸口; **doorway** deiriguchi 出入口; (in home) genkan 玄関

dope 1 n (drugs) mayaku 麻薬; (idiot) manuke まぬけ; (information) jōhō 情報 2 v/t kōfunzai o ataeru 興奮剤を与える

dormant plant kyūminchū (no) 休眠 中(の); **~ volcano** kyūkazan 休火山

dormitory ryō 寮

dosage tōyaku-ryō 投薬量

dose n ikkaibun 一回分

dot n ten 点; (in e-mail address) dotto ドット; **on the ~** (exactly) kikkari ni きっかりに

♦ **dote on** ... o yatara ni kawaigaru ...をやたらにかわいがる

dotted line tensen 点線

double 1 n (amount) nibai (二)倍; (referring to money) baigaku 倍額; (person) sokkuri na hito そっくり な人; (of movie star) kaedama 替 え玉; (room) daburu ダブル **2 adj** (twice as much) (ni)bai (no) (二) 倍(の); whiskey daburu (no) ダブ ル(の); sink, oven futatsu aru 二つ

ある; layer nijū (no) 二重(の); digit futaketa no 二けた(の); **in ~ figures** futaketa no sūji de 二けた の数字で **3 adv** bai (no) 倍(の); **4** v/t (ni)bai ni suru (二)倍にする; (fold) nijū ni suru 二重にする **5** v/i (ni)bai ni naru (二)倍になる

♦ **double back** v/i (go back) hikikaesu 引き返す

♦ **double up** (in pain) karada o futatsu ni oru 体を二つに折る; (share) dōshitsu suru 同室する

double-bass kontorabasu コントラ バス; **double bed** daburubeddo ダ ブルベッド; **double-breasted** daburu (no) ダブル(の); **doublecheck** v/t & v/i saitenken suru 再点検する; **double chin** nijū-ago 二重あご; **doublecross** v/t ... ni nimaijita o tsukau ...に二枚舌を 使う; **double door** tobira 扉; **double glazing** nijū-garasu 二重ガラス; **doublepark** v/i nijū-chūsha suru 二重駐車する; **double-quick: in ~ time** ōisogi de 大急ぎで; **double room** daburu-rūmu ダブルルーム

doubles (in tennis) daburusu ダブル ス

doubt 1 n utagai 疑い; (uncertainty) gimon 疑問; **be in ~** gimon ga aru 疑問がある; **no ~** (probably) kitto きっと **2** v/t utagau 疑う

doubtful remark, look utagawashii 疑わしい; **be ~** (of person) utagai o motte iru 疑いをもっている; **it is ~ whether** ... to iu no wa utagawashii ...というのは疑わしい

doubtfully utagawashige ni 疑わし げに

doubtless utagai nai 疑いない

dough kiji 生地; F (money) gennama 現なま

dove hato はと; fig hatoha はと派

dowdy dasai ださい

Dow Jones Average dau-heikin ダ ウ平均

down[1] n (feathers) umō 羽毛, daun ダウン

down[2] 1 adv (downward) shita no hō e 下の方へ; (onto the ground) shita ni 下に; **~ there** (near listener) soko ni そこに; (*far from speaker/ listener*) asoko ni あそこに; **fall ~** ochiru 落ちる; **$200 ~** (*as deposit*) nihyaku doru sokkin de 200ドル即金で; **~ south** (*direction*) minami e 南へ; (*location*) nanbu dewa 南部では; **be ~** (*of price, rate*) sagatte iru 下がっている; (*of numbers amount*) hette iru 減っている; (*not working*) sadō shite inai 作動していない; F (*depressed*) yūutsu de aru 憂うつである **2** *prep*: **run ~ the stairs** kaidan o kakeoriru 階段を駆け降りる; **the lava rolled slowly ~ the hill** yōgan ga yukkuri oka o nagareochite itta 溶岩がゆっくり丘を流れ落ちて行った; **the fish has distinctive markings ~ its back** sakana no se ni wa me o hiku moyō ga aru 魚の背には目を引く模様がある; **I looked ~ the list of names** watashi wa namae no risuto o mita 私は名前のリストを見た; **walk ~ the street** (*along*) michi o aruku 道を歩く; **third door on the left ~ this corridor** kono rōka o zutto itta hidarite sanbanme no doa この廊下をずっと行った左手三番目のドア **3** *v/t* **drink** nomu 飲む; **food** nomikomu のみ込む; (*destroy*) uchiotosu 撃ち落とす

down-and-out *n* ochibureta hito 落ちぶれた人; **downcast** (*dejected*) gakkari shita がっかりした; **downfall** botsuraku 没落; (*of politician*) shikkyaku 失脚; **downgrade** *v/t* ... no tōkyū o sageru ...の等級を下げる; **employee** kōkaku suru 降格する; **downhearted** rakutan shita 落胆した; **downhill** *adv* kudarizaka (no) 下り坂(の); **go ~ fig** waruku naru 悪くなる; **downhill skiing** daunhiru-sukī ダウンヒルスキー; **download** COMPUT daunrōdo suru ダウンロードする; **downmarket 1** *adj* yasui 安い **2** *adv* taishūmuke ni 大衆向けに; **down payment** atamakin 頭金; **downplay** karuku atsukau 軽く扱う; **downpour** doshaburi どしゃ降り; **downright 1** *adj* **idiot** mattaku

(no) まったく(の); **a ~ lie** makka na uso 真っ赤なうそ **2** *adv* **dangerous, stupid etc** tetteiteki ni 徹底的に; **downside** (*disadvantage*) warui men 悪い面; **downsize 1** *v/t* **car** kogataka suru 小型化する; **company** ... no kibo o chiisaku suru ...の規模を小さくする **2** *v/i* (*of company*) kibo o chiisaku suru 規模を小さくする; **downstairs 1** *adj* kaika (no) 階下(の) **2** *adv* kaika ni 階下に; **down-to-earth** *approach, person* genjitsuteki (na) 現実的(な); **down-town 1** *adj* hankagai (no) 繁華街(の) **2** *adv* hankagai ni 繁華街に; **downturn** (*in economy*) kakō 下降; **downward 1** *adj* shitamuki (no) 下向き(の) **2** *adv* shita no hō e 下の方へ

doze 1 *n* utatane うたたね **2** *v/i* utatane suru うたたねする

♦ **doze off** utouto nemurikomu うとうと眠り込む

dozen dāsu ダース; **~s of ...** nanjū mono ... 何十もの...

drab saenai さえない

draft 1 *n* (*of air*) sukimakaze すきま風; (*of document*) shitagaki 下書き; MIL chōhei 徴兵; **beer on ~** nama-bīru 生ビール **2** *v/t* **document** ... no shitagaki o suru ...の下書きをする; MIL chōhei suru 徴兵する

draft dodger chōhei-kihisha 徴兵忌避者

draftee chōshūhei 徴集兵

draftsman seizukō 製図工; (*of plan*) ritsuan-sha 立案者

drafty sukimakaze no hairu すきま風の入る

drag 1 *n*: **it's a ~ having to ...** ... shinakute wa naranai no ga yakkai da ...しなくてはならないのがやっかいだ; **he's a ~** kare wa taikutsu na hito da 彼は退屈な人だ; **the main ~** ōdōri 大通り; **in ~** josō shite 女装して **2** *v/t* (*pull*) hikizuru 引きずる; **person** hikizuridasu 引きずり出す; (*search*) sarau さらう; **I was feeling awful but I managed to ~**

myself into work kibun ga hidoku warukatta ga nantoka shigoto ni dekaketa 気分がひどく悪かったが何とか仕事に出かけた; **~ X into Y** (*involve*) X o muriyari Y ni hikizurikomu X をむりやり Y に引きずり込む; **~ X out of Y** (*get information from*) Y kara X o kikidasu Y から X を聞きだす **3** *v/i* (*of time*) noronoro susumu のろのろ進む; (*of show, movie*) daradara nagabiku だらだら長引く

♦ **drag away**: ***drag ... away from the TV*** ... o terebi kara hikihanasu ...をテレビから引き離す

♦ **drag in** (*into conversation*) ... no koto o mochidasu ...のことを持ちだす

♦ **drag on** daradara to nagabiku だらだらと長引く

♦ **drag out** ... o nagabikaseru ...を長引かせる

♦ **drag up** (*mention*) ... o mochidasu ...を持ちだす

dragon ryū 竜, doragon ドラゴン; *fig* onibaba 鬼ばば

dragonfly tonbo とんぼ

drain 1 *n* (*pipe*) haisuikan 排水管; (*under street*) mizo 溝; ***a ~ on resources*** kane no muda 金の無駄 **2** *v/t water* haisui suru 排水する; *oil* nuku 抜く; *vegetables* ... no mizu o kiru ...の水を切る; *land* ... ni haisui-setsubi o hodokosu ...に排水設備を施す; *glass, tank* kara ni suru 空にする; (*exhaust: person*) shōmō saseru 消耗させる **3** *v/i* (*of dishes*) kawaku 乾く

♦ **drain away** (*of liquid*) ryūshutsu suru 流出する

♦ **drain off** *water* ryūshutsu suru 流出する

drainage (*drains*) haisui-kan 排水管; (*of water from soil*) haisui 排水

drainpipe haisui-kan 排水管

drama dorama ドラマ; (*in theater, as study*) engeki 演劇

dramatic engeki (no) 演劇(の); (*exciting*) doramachikku (na) ドラマチック(な), gekiteki (na) 劇的(な); *gesture* ōgesa (na) 大げさ

(な)

dramatist geki-sakka 劇作家

dramatization (*play*) kyakushoku 脚色

dramatize *story* kyakushoku suru 脚色する; *fig* ōgesa ni hyōgen suru 大げさに表現する

drape *v/t cloth, coat* kakeru 掛ける; **~d in** (*covered with*) ... de ōwareta ...でおおわれた

drapery hida no aru nunoji ひだのある布地

drapes kāten カーテン

drastic (*extreme*) kyokutan (na) 極端(な); *measures* bapponteki (na) 抜本的(な); *change* jūdai (na) 重大(な)

draw 1 *n* (*in match, competition*) hikiwake 引き分け; (*in lottery*) kujibiki くじ引き; (*attraction*) yobimono 呼び物 **2** *v/t picture, map* kaku かく; *cart, curtain* hiku 引く; *gun, knife* nuku 抜く; (*attract*) hikiyoseru 引き寄せる; (*lead*) hipparu 引っ張る; (*from bank account*) hikidasu 引き出す; ***he drew her closer*** kare wa kanojo o hikiyoseta 彼は彼女を引き寄せた **3** *v/i e* o kaku 絵をかく; (*in match, competition*) hikiwakeru 引き分ける; **~ near** chikazuku 近づく

♦ **draw back 1** *v/i* (*recoil*) ushiro ni sagaru 後ろに下がる **2** *v/t* (*pull back*) ... o hikkomeru ...を引っ込める

♦ **draw on 1** *v/i* (*approach*) chikazuku 近づく **2** *v/t* (*make use of*) ... o riyō suru ...を利用する

♦ **draw out** *v/t billfold etc* ... o hikidasu ...を引き出す

♦ **draw up 1** *v/t document* ... o sakusei suru ...を作成する; *chair* ... o hikiyoseru ...を引き寄せる **2** *v/i* (*of vehicle*) tomaru 止まる

drawback ketten 欠点

drawer[1] (*of desk etc*) hikidashi 引き出し

drawer[2]: ***be a good ~*** e o kaku no ga umai 絵を描くのがうまい

drawing suketchi スケッチ

drawing board gaban 画板; *go back to the ~* furidashi ni modoru 振り出しに戻る

drawl *n* yukkuri shita hanashi buri ゆっくりした話しぶり

dread *v/t* kowagaru 怖がる

dreadful hidoi ひどい

dreadfully (*very*) hidoku ひどく; *behave* tondemonaku とんでもなく

dream 1 *n* yume 夢 **2** *adj house etc* yume no yō (na) 夢のよう(な) **3** *v/t* ... to iu yume o miru ...という夢を見る; (*day~*) yumemiru 夢見る **4** *v/i* yume o miru 夢を見る; (*day~*) yumemiru 夢見る

♦ **dream up** ... o kangaedasu ...を考え出す

dreamer (*day~*) musō-ka 夢想家

dreamy *voice, look* yumemiru yō (na) 夢見るよう(な)

dreary inki (na) 陰気(な)

dredge *canal* ... no soko o sarau ...の底をさらう

♦ **dredge up** *fig* horiokosu 掘り起こす

dregs (*of coffee*) kasu かす; *the ~ of society* shakai no kuzu 社会のくず

drench *v/t* zubunure ni suru ずぶぬれにする; *get ~ed* zubunure ni naru ずぶぬれになる

dress 1 *n* (*for woman*) wanpīsu ワンピース; (*clothing*) fukusō 服装 **2** *v/t person* ... ni fuku o kiseru ...に服を着せる; *wound* ... no teate o suru ...の手当をする; *get ~ed* ... ni fuku o kiseru ...に服を着せる **3** *v/i* (*get ~ed*) fuku o kiru 服を着る; (*well, in black etc*) fukusō o shite iru 服装をしている

♦ **dress up** *v/i* kichin to shita fukusō o suru きちんとした服装をする; (*in evening wear*) doresuappu suru ドレスアップする; (*wear a disguise*) kasō suru 仮装する; *~ as X* X ni kasō suru Xに仮装する

dress circle nikai-shōmenseki 二階正面席

dresser (*dressing table*) kyōdai 鏡台; (*in kitchen*) shokkidana 食器棚

dressing (*for salad*) doresshingu ドレッシング; (*for wound*) hōtai 包帯

dressing room THEA gakuya 楽屋

dressing table kyōdai 鏡台

dressmaker doresumēkā ドレスメーカー

dress rehearsal butai-geiko 舞台げいこ

dressy ereganto (na) エレガント(な)

dribble *v/i* (*of person*) yodare o tarasu よだれを垂らす; (*of water*) tareru 垂れる; SP doriburu suru ドリブルする

dried *fruit etc* kansō shita 乾燥した

drier = *dryer*

drift 1 *n* (*of snow*) fukidamari 吹きだまり **2** *v/i* (*of snow*) fukidamaru 吹きだまる; (*of ship*) hyōryū suru 漂流する; (*go off course*) kōro ni hazureru 航路をはずれる; (*of person*) samayou さまよう

♦ **drift apart** (*of couple*) soen ni naru 疎遠になる

drifter nagaremono 流れ者

drill 1 *n* (*tool*) doriru ドリル; (*exercise*) bōsai-kunren 防災訓練; MIL gunji-kyōren 軍事教練 **2** *v/t hole* ... ni ana o akeru ...に穴をあける **3** *v/i* (*for oil*) horu 掘る; MIL kunren suru 訓練する

drilling rig (*platform*) kaijō-saiyu-kichi 海上採油基地

drily *remark* reitan ni 冷淡に

drink 1 *n* nomimono 飲物; (*alcoholic*) sake 酒; *a ~ of* ... ippai ...一杯; *go for a ~* nomi ni iku 飲みに行く **2** *v/t* nomu 飲む **3** *v/i* nomu 飲む; (*consume alcohol*) sake o nomu 酒を飲む; *I don't ~* watashi wa osake o nomimasen 私はお酒を飲みません

♦ **drink up 1** *v/i* (*finish drink*) nomihosu 飲み干す **2** *v/t* (*drink completely*) ... o zenbu nomu ...を全部飲む

drinkable inryōyō (no) 飲料用(の)

drinker sakenomi 酒飲み

drinking (*of alcohol*) inshu 飲酒

drinking water inryōsui 飲料水

drip 1 *n* (*liquid*) shizuku 滴; MED tenteki 点滴 **2** *v/i* shitataru し

たたる

dripping: ~ (*wet*) zubunure (no) ず
ぶぬれ(の)

drive 1 *n* (*journey*) michinori 道のり;
(*outing*) doraibu ドライブ;
(*energy*) yaruki やる気; COMPUT
doraibu ドライブ; (*campaign*)
undō 運動; *it's a short ~ from the
station* eki kara kuruma de sugu
desu 駅から車ですぐです; *left-/
right-hand ~* MOT hidari/migi-
handoru no kuruma 左/右ハンドル
の車 **2** *v/t vehicle* unten suru 運転す
る; (*own*) ... ni notte iru ...に乗って
いる; (*take in car*) nosete iku 乗せて
行く; TECH ugokasu 動かす; *that
noise/he is driving me mad* ano
oto/kare no sei de ki ga kuruisō-da
あの音/彼のせいで気が狂いそうだ
3 *v/i* unten suru 運転する

♦ **drive at**: *what are you driving at?*
nani o iitai no 何を言いたいの

♦ **drive away 1** *v/t* ... o kuruma de
tsurete iku ...を車で連れて行く;
(*chase off*) ... o oiharau ...を追い
払う **2** *v/i* hashirisaru 走り去る

♦ **drive in** *v/t nail* ... o uchikomu ...
を打ち込む

♦ **drive off** → **drive away**

drive-in *n* (*movie theater*)
doraibuin-shiatā ドライブインシ
アター

driver untenshu 運転手, doraibā ド
ライバー

driver's license unten-menkyoshō
運転免許証

driveway kuruma-mawashi 車回し

driving 1 *n* unten 運転 **2** *adj rain*
hageshii 激しい

driving force suishin-ryoku 推進力;
driving instructor unten-kyōkan
運転教官; **driving lesson** jidōsha-
kyōshū 自動車教習; **driving school**
jidōsha-kyōshūjo 自動車教習所;
driving test untenmenkyo-shiken
運転免許試験

drizzle 1 *n* kirisame 霧雨 **2** *v/i*
kirisame ga furu 霧雨が降る

drone *n* (*noise*) būn to iu oto ぶーん
という音

droop *v/i* tareru 垂れる; (*of plant*)

shioreru しおれる; *her shoulders
~ed* kanojo wa kata o otoshita 彼
女は肩を落とした

drop 1 *n* (*of rain*) shizuku 滴; (*small
amount*) shōryō 少量; (*in price,
temperature*) teika 低下; (*in
number*) genshō 減少 **2** *v/t object*
otosu 落とす; *person from car*
orosu 降ろす; *person from team*
jogai suru 除外する; (*stop seeing*)
... to zekkō suru ...と絶交する;
(*give up*) yameru やめる; *charges,
demand etc* torisageru 取り下げる;
~ a line to ... ni kantan na tegami o
kaku ...に簡単な手紙を書く **3** *v/i*
ochiru 落ちる; (*decline*) sagaru 下
がる; (*of wind*) shizumaru 静まる

♦ **drop in** *v/i* (*visit*) chotto tachiyoru
ちょっと立ち寄る

♦ **drop off 1** *v/t person* ... o orosu ...
を降ろす; (*deliver*) ... o oite iku ...
を置いて行く **2** *v/i* (*fall asleep*)
nemurikomu 眠り込む; (*decline*)
heru 減る

♦ **drop out** (*withdraw*) datsuraku
suru 脱落する; (*of school*) chūto-
taigaku suru 中途退学する

dropout (*from school*) chūto-
taigaku-sha 中途退学者; (*from
society*) rakugo-sha 落後者

drops (*for eyes*) megusuri 目薬

drought kanbatsu 干ばつ

drown 1 *v/i* oboreshinu おぼれ死ぬ
2 *v/t person* dekishi saseru でき死
させる; *sound* kesu 消す; *be ~ed*
oboreshinu おぼれ死ぬ

drowsy nemui 眠い

drudgery tanchō na shigoto 単調な
仕事

drug 1 *n* MED kusuri 薬; (*illegal*)
mayaku 麻薬; *be on ~s* mayaku o
yatte iru 麻薬をやっている **2** *v/t*
kusuri o nomaseru 薬を飲ませる

drug addict mayaku-jōyō-sha 麻薬
常用者; **drug dealer** mayaku-
mitsubai-nin 麻薬密売人; **drug
trafficking** mayaku-mitsubai 麻薬
密売

druggist yakuzaishi 薬剤師

drugstore yakkyoku 薬局,
doraggusutoa ドラッグストア

drum 1 *n* MUS doramu ドラム; (*Japanese-style*) taiko 太鼓; (*container*) doramu-kan ドラム缶
♦ **drum into**: *drum X into Y* X o Y ni yakamashiku oshiekomu XをYにやかましく教え込む
♦ **drum up**: *~ support* kakki zukeru 活気づける
drummer doramā ドラマー; (*Japanese-style*) taiko-sōsha 太鼓奏者
drumstick MUS bachi ばち; (*of poultry*) tori no momoniku 鶏の腿肉
drunk 1 *n* nondakure 飲んだくれ **2** *adj* yopparatta 酔っ払った; *get ~* yopparau 酔っ払う
drunk driving inshu-unten 飲酒運転
drunken *voices, laughter* yopparatta 酔っ払った; *party* yopparai (no) 酔っ払い(の)
dry 1 *adj skin, clothes, mouth* kawaita 乾いた; *weather* ame no furanai 雨の降らない; *wine* karakuchi (no) 辛口(の); (*ironic*) hiniku (na) 皮肉(な); (*where alcohol is banned*) kinshu (no) 禁酒(の) **2** *v/t* kawakasu 乾かす; *dishes* fuite kawakasu 拭いて乾かす; *~ one's eyes* namida o fuku 涙を拭く **3** *v/i* kawaku 乾く
♦ **dry out** (*of alcoholic*) sake o tatsu 酒を絶つ
♦ **dry up** (*of river*) hiagaru 干上がる; (*of speaker*) kotoba ni tsumaru 言葉につまる; *~!* (*be quiet*) damarinasai 黙りなさい
dry-clean *v/t* doraikurīningu suru ドライクリーニングする; **dry-cleaner** doraikurīningu-ya ドライクリーニング屋; **dry-cleaning** (*clothes*) sentaku-mono 洗濯もの
dryer (*machine*) kansō-ki 乾燥機
DTP (= *desktop publishing*) desukutoppu-paburisshingu デスクトップパブリッシング
dual nijū (no) 二重(の)
dub *movie* ... no fukikae o suru ...の吹替えをする
dubious ikagawashii いかがわしい; (*doubting*) utagawashii 疑わしい

duck 1 *n* (*wild*) kamo かも; (*domestic*) ahiru あひる **2** *v/i* hyoi to karada o kagameru ひょいと体をかがめる **3** *v/t* one's head hyoi to sageru ひょいと下げる; *question* kawasu かわす
due (*owed*) shiharawarerubeki 支払われるべき; (*proper*) tōzen (no) 当然(の); *be ~* (*of train, baby etc*) yotei de aru 予定である; (*of report, announcement*) kijitsu de aru 期日である; *~ to* (*because of*) ... no tame ...のため; *be ~ to* (*be caused by*) ... no kekka de aru ...の結果である; *in ~ course* sono uchi ni そのうちに; *by the ~ date* kijitsu made ni 期日までに
dull *weather* kumori (no) くもり(の); *sound* hakkiri shinai はっきりしない; *pain* nibui 鈍い; (*boring*) taikutsu (na) 退屈(な)
duly (*as expected*) todokōri naku 滞りなく; (*properly*) seitō ni 正当に
dumb (*mute*) kuchi no kikenai 口のきけない; (*stupid*) usunoro (no) うすのろ(の)
dummy (*for clothes*) manekin-ningyō マネキン人形
dump 1 *n* (*for rubbish*) gomi-suteba ごみ捨て場; (*unpleasant place*) usugitanai basho 薄汚い場所 **2** *v/t* (*deposit*) oku buru 置く; (*dispose of*) suteru 捨てる; *nuclear waste* tōki suru 投棄する
dumpling dango だんご
dune sakyū 砂丘
dung fun ふん
dungarees ōbāōru オーバーオール
dunk *biscuit* tsukeru つける
duo (*singing*) nijūshō 二重唱; (*instrumental*) nijūsō 二重奏
duplex (**apartment**) mezonetto メゾネット
duplicate 1 *n* fukusei 複製; *in ~* seifuku nitsū ni shite 正副二通にして **2** *v/t* (*copy*) fukusei suru 複製する; (*repeat*) kurikaeshite iru 繰り返している
duplicate key aikagi 合い鍵
durable *material* taikyūsei no aru 耐久性のある; *relationship*

nagatsuzuki suru 長続きする

duration kikan 期間

duress: *under ~* kyōhaku sarete 強迫されて

during ... no aida ni ...の間に; (*throughout*) ... no aida zutto ...の間ずっと

dusk tasogare たそがれ

dust 1 *n* hokori ほこり **2** *v/t* ... no hokori o harau ...のほこりを払う; *~ X with Y* (*sprinkle*) Y o X ni furikakeru YをXにふりかける

dust cover (*for furniture*) hokoriyoke-kabā ほこりよけカバー; (*for book*) kabā カバー

duster (*cloth*) zōkin ぞうきん

dust jacket (*of book*) kabā カバー

dustpan chiritori ちりとり

dusty hokorippoi ほこりっぽい

Dutch 1 *adj* Oranda (no) オランダ (の); *go ~* warikan ni suru 割り勘にする **2** *n* (*language*) Oranda-go オランダ語; *the ~* Oranda-jin オランダ人

duty gimu 義務; (*task*) shokumu 職務; (*on goods*) zei 税; *be on ~*

kinmuchū de aru 勤務中である; *be off ~* hiban de aru 非番である

duty-free 1 *adj* menzei (no) 免税 (の) **2** *n* menzei-hin 免税品

duty-free shop mezei-ten 免税店

dwarf 1 *n* kobito 小人 **2** *v/t* chiisaku miseru 小さくみせる

♦ **dwell on** ... ni kodawaru ...にこだわる

dwindle genshō suru 減少する

dye 1 *n* senryō 染料; (*for hair*) kezome 毛染め **2** *v/t* someru 染める

dying *person* shinikakatte iru 死にかかっている; *industry, tradition* kiekakatte iru 消えかかっている

dynamic *person* katsudōteki (na) 活動的(な)

dynamism katsuryoku 活力

dynamite *n* dainamaito ダイナマイト

dynamo TECH hatsudenki 発電機

dynasty ōchō 王朝; *fig* meimon 名門

dyslexia nandokushō 難読症

dyslexic 1 *adj* nandokushō (no) 難読症(の) **2** *n* nandokushō-kanja 難読症患者

E

each 1 *adj* sorezore (no) それぞれ (の) **2** *adv* sorezore それぞれ; *they're $1.50 ~* sorezore ichi doru gojū desu それぞれ1ドル50です; *he gave us one ~* kare wa watashitachi ni hitotsuzutsu kureta 彼は私達にひとつずつくれた **3** *pron* sorezore それぞれ; *~ other* otagai ni お互いに

eager nesshin (na) 熱心(な); *he is ~ to buy a house* kare wa shikiri ni ie o kaitagatte iru 彼はしきりに家を買いたがっている

eager beaver shigoto no mushi 仕事の虫

eagerly nesshin ni 熱心に

eagerness nesshin-sa 熱心さ

eagle washi わし

ear[1] (*of person, animal*) mimi 耳

ear[2] (*of corn*) mi 実

earache mimi no itami 耳の痛み

eardrum komaku 鼓膜

early 1 *adj* (*in morning*) hayai 早い; (*ahead of time, in the near future*) hayame (no) 早め(の); (*farther back in time*) shoki (no) 初期(の); *~ October* jūgatsu no hajime 十月の初め **2** *adv* (*not late, ahead of time*) hayaku 早く

early bird (*in morning*) hayaokidori 早起き鳥; (*who arrives before others*) hayaku kuru hito 早く来る人

earmark: **~ X for Y** X o Y no tame ni totte oku X をYのために取っておく

earn kasegu 稼ぐ; *respect, holiday, drink etc* eru 得る

earnest majime (na) まじめ(な); *in ~* majime (na)(ni) まじめ(な)(に); *I'm speaking in ~* watashi wa majime ni hanashite imasu 私はまじめに話しています; *I'm in ~ when I say that ...* watashi ga ... to ittatoki majime datta 私が...と言ったときまじめだった

earnings shotoku 所得

earphones iyahon イヤホン

ear-piercing adj mimi o tsunzaku yō (na) 耳をつんざくよう(な)

earring iyaringu イヤリング

earshot: *within ~* tsuchi no todoku han'i 声の届く範囲; *out of ~* yonde mo kikoenai tokoro ni 呼んでも聞こえないところに

earth (soil) tsuchi 土; (world, planet) chikyū 地球; *where on ~ ...?* ittai doko (ni) (de)... 一体どこ(に)(で)...; *where on ~ did you find it?* ittai doko de mitsuketa no 一体どこで見つけたの; *where on ~ have you been?* ittai doko ni itte ita no 一体どこに行っていたの

earthenware n tōki 陶器

earthly konoyo (no) この世(の); *it's no ~ use ...* ...shite mo muda da ...しても無駄だ

earthquake jishin 地震

earth-shattering sekai o yurugasu 世界を揺るがす

ease 1 n yōi-sa 容易さ; *be or feel at ~* ochitsuku 落ち着く; *be or feel ill at ~* ochitsukanai 落ち着かない; *with ~* yasuyasu to やすやすと 2 v/t (relieve) yawarageru 和らげる 3 v/i (of pain) karuku naru 軽くなる

♦ **ease off** 1 v/t (remove) ... o yurumeru ...をゆるめる 2 v/i (of pain, rain) yawaragu 和らぐ

easel īzeru イーゼル

easily (with ease) yōi ni 容易に; (by far) tashika ni 確かに

east 1 n higashi 東; (of a country) tōbu 東部; *East* (Orient) Tōyō 東洋 2 adj coast higashi (no) 東(の); *wind* higashi kara (no) 東から(の) 3 adv travel higashi e 東へ

East China Sea Higashi-shinakai 東シナ海

Easter Fukkatsusai 復活祭

Easter egg Īsutā-eggu イースターエッグ

easterly direction higashi e (no) 東へ(の); *wind* higashi kara (no) 東から(の)

eastern tōbu (no) 東部(の); (oriental) tōyō (no) 東洋(の)

easterner tōbu-shusshin-sha 東部出身者

eastward higashi e 東へ

easy (not difficult) kantan (na) 簡単(な); (relaxed) yukkuri shita ゆっくりした; life kiraku (na) 気楽(な); *take things ~* (slow down) nonbiri yaru のんびりやる; *take it ~!* (calm down) ochitsuite 落ち着いて

easy chair anrakuisu 安楽いす

easy-going kodawaranai こだわらない

eat v/t & v/i taberu 食べる

♦ **eat out** gaishoku suru 外食する

♦ **eat up** food ... o tabete shimau ...を食べてしまう; fig ... o tsukaitsukusu ...を使い尽くす

eatable taberareru 食べられる

eaves hisashi ひさし

eavesdrop nusumigiki suru 盗み聞きする

ebb v/i (of tide) shio ga hiku 潮が引く

♦ **ebb away** (of courage, strength) otoroeru 衰える

ebb tide hikishio 引き潮

eccentric 1 adj fūgawari (na) 風変わり(な) 2 n henjin 変人

echo 1 n kodama こだま 2 v/i hankyō suru 反響する 3 v/t words kurikaesu 繰り返す; views ... ni dōchō suru ...に同調する

eclipse 1 n (of sun) nisshoku 日食; (of moon) gesshoku 月食 2 v/t fig shinogu しのぐ

ecological kankyō-hogo (no) 環境保護(の); **~ balance** seitaikei no baransu 生態系のバランス

ecologically friendly kankyō ni yasashii 環境にやさしい

ecologist kankyō-hozen-ron-sha 環境保全論者

ecology seitaigaku 生態学

e-commerce ī-komāsu e-コマース

economic keizaigaku (no) 経済学(の)

economical (cheap) keizaiteki (na) 経済的(な); (thrifty) tsumashii つましい

economically (in terms of economics) keizaiteki ni wa 経済的には; (thriftily) setsuyaku shite 節約して

economics (science) keizaigaku 経済学; (financial aspects) keizaiteki-sokumen 経済的側面

economist keizai-gakusha 経済学者

economize setsuyaku suru 節約する

♦economize on ... o setsuyaku suru ...を節約する

economy (of a country) keizai 経済; (saving) setsuyaku 節約

economy class ekonomī-kurasu エコノミークラス; **economy drive** ken'yaku-seishin 倹約精神; **economy size** otokuyō お得用

ecosystem seitaikei 生態系

ecstasy uchōten 有頂天

ecstatic uchōten (no) 有頂天(の); fan, welcome nekkyōteki (na) 熱狂的(な)

eczema shisshin 湿疹

edge 1 n hashi 端; (of knife) hasaki 刃先; (of cliff) fuchi ふち; (in voice) surudo-sa 鋭さ; **on ~** iraira shite いらいらして **2** v/t fuchidoru 縁取る **3** v/i (move slowly) jirijiri to susumu じりじりと進む

edgewise: I couldn't get a word in ~ kuchi o dasu yochi ga nai 口を出す余地がない

edgy iraira shite いらいらして

edible taberareru 食べられる

edit text kōetsu suru 校閲する; book, newspaper, TV program, movie henshū suru 編集する

edition han 版

editor (of text) kōetsu-sha 校閲者; (of book) henshū-sha 編集者; (of magazine) henshūchō 編集長; (of newspaper) henshū-kyokuchō 編集局長; (of TV program, movie) editā エディター; **sports / political ~** supōtsubu / seijibu-kisha スポーツ部/政治部記者

editorial 1 adj henshū (no) 編集(の) **2** n shasetsu 社説

EDP (= electronic data processing) denshi-dēta-shori 電子データ処理

educate child kyōiku suru 教育する; consumers ... ni oshieru ...に教える

educated person kyōiku no aru 教育のある

education kyōiku 教育

educational kyōiku (no) 教育(の); informative kyōikuteki (na) 教育的(な)

eel (fresh water) unagi うなぎ; (marine) anago あなご

eerie kimi no warui 気味の悪い

effect n eikyō 影響; (of overwork, detonation) kekka 結果; **take ~** (of medicine, drug) kiku 効く; **come into ~** (of law) hakkō suru 発効する; **have a positive ~** kōka ga aru 効果がある

effective (efficient) kōkateki (na) 効果的(な); (striking) inshōteki (na) 印象的(な); (valid) yūkō (na) 有効(な); **~ May 1** gogatsu tsuitachi yori yūkō na 五月一日より有効な

effeminate nanjaku (na) 軟弱(な)

effervescent awadatsu 泡立つ; personality ikiiki shita 生き生きした

efficiency (of person, machine) nōryoku 能力

efficient person yūnō (na) 有能(な); machine, method kōritsuteki (na) 効率的(な)

efficiently kōkateki ni 効果的に, nōritsuteki ni 能率的に

effort (struggle) kurō 苦労; (attempt) doryoku 努力; **make an ~ to do ...** ... suru doryoku o suru

...する努力をする

effortless: *he makes it look so ~* kare wa zousa-naku yatte miseru 彼は造作なくやってみせる

effrontery atsukamashi-sa 厚かましさ

effusive netsuretsu (na) 熱烈(な)

e.g. tatoeba 例えば

egalitarian *adj* byōdō-shugi (no) 平等主義(の)

egg tamago 卵; (*of woman*) ranshi 卵子

♦ **egg on** ... o sosonokasu ...をそそのかす

eggcup yudetamago-tate ゆで卵立て; **egghead** interi インテリ; **eggplant** nasu なす; **eggshell** tamago no kara 卵のから

ego PSYCH ego エゴ; (*self-esteem*) jisonshin 自尊心

egocentric jiko-chūshinteki (na) 自己中心的(な)

Egypt Ejiputo エジプト

Egyptian 1 *adj* Ejiputo (no) エジプト(の) 2 *n* Ejiputo-jin エジプト人

eiderdown (*quilt*) hanebuton 羽ぶとん

eight hachi 八; (*with countword 'tsu'*) yattsu 八つ

eighteen jūhachi 十八

eighteenth dai-jūhachi (no) 第十八(の)

eighth 1 *adj* dai-hachi (no) 第八(の) 2 *n* (*of month*) yōka 八日

eightieth *adj* dai-hachijū (no) 第八十(の)

eighty hachijū 八十

either 1 *adj* dochira ka (no) どちらか(の); (*both*) ryōhō (no) 両方(の); ~ *solution is OK* ryōhō no kaiketsuhō tomo daijōbu desu 両方の解決法とも大丈夫です 2 *pron* dochira de mo どちらでも 3 *adv*: *I won't go* ~ watashi mo ikanai 私も行かない 4 *conj*: ~ ... *or* ... ka ... ka ...か...か; (*in negative sentence*) ... mo ... mo ...も...も; *you can have* ~ *rice or potatoes* gohan ka jagaimo ka eraberu ごはんかじゃがいもか選べる; *I haven't seen ~ Mike or Joanne* Maiku ni mo Joannu ni mo

atte imasen マイクにもジョアンヌにも会っていません

eject 1 *v/t cassette etc* toridasu 取り出す; *people* tsuihō suru 追放する 2 *v/i* (*from plane*) dasshutsu suru 脱出する

♦ **eke out** motaseru もたせる

el → *elevated railroad*

elaborate 1 *adj design* kotta 凝った; *scheme* shinchō ni keikaku shita 慎重に計画した 2 *v/i* kuwashiku noberu 詳しく述べる

elapse keika suru 経過する

elastic 1 *adj* danryokusei no aru 弾力性のある 2 *n* gomuhimo ゴムひも

elastic band wagomu 輪ゴム

elasticity danryokusei 弾力性

elasticized *waistband* gomu o tōshita ゴムを通した

elated ōyorokobi (no) 大喜び(の)

elation ōyorokobi 大喜び

elbow 1 *n* hiji ひじ 2 *v/t*: ~ *out of the way* oshinokeru 押しのける

elder 1 *adj* toshiue (no) 年上(の); ~ *brother* ani 兄; ~ *sister* ane 姉 2 *n* toshiue 年上

elderly nenpai (no) 年配(の)

eldest 1 *adj* ichiban toshiue (no) いちばん年上(の) 2 *n* sainenchō-sha 最年長者; *you're the ~* kimi ga ichiban toshiue da 君がいちばん年上だ

elect *v/t* senkyo suru 選挙する; ~ *to* ... suru koto o erabu ...することを選ぶ

elected senkyo ni yotte erabareru 選挙によって選ばれる

election senkyo 選挙

election campaign senkyo-undō 選挙運動

election day sōsenkyobi 総選挙日

elective *subject* sentaku (no) 選択(の); *surgery* shinakutemo yoi しなくてもよい

elector yūken-sha 有権者; (*at Presidential election*) senkyo-nin 選挙人

electoral system senkyo-seido 選挙制度

electorate yūken-sha 有権者

electric denki (no) 電気(の); *fig*

shigekiteki (na) 刺激的(な)

electrical denki (no) 電気(の)

electric blanket denki-mōfu 電気毛布; **electric chair** denki-isu 電気いす; **electric fan** senpūki 扇風機

electrician denki-gishi 電気技師

electricity denki 電気

electrify *railway line, fence* denki o tōsu 電気を通す; *fig* shokku o ataeru ショックを与える

electrocute kandenshi saseru 感電死させる

electrode denkyoku 電極

electron erekutoron エレクトロン

electronic denshi-kōgaku (no) 電子工学(の)

electronic data processing denshi-dēta-shori 電子データ処理

electronic mail ī-mēru eメール

electronics denshi-kōgaku 電子工学

elegance yūga-sa 優雅さ

elegant yūga (na) 優雅(な)

element CHEM genso 元素

elementary (*rudimentary*) shoho (no) 初歩(の)

elementary school shōgakkō 小学校

elementary teacher shōgakkō-kyōshi 小学校教師

elephant zō 象

elevate mochiageru 持ち上げる

elevated railroad kōka-tetsudō 高架鉄道

elevation (*altitude*) kaibatsu 海抜

elevator erebētā エレベーター

eleven jūichi 十一

eleventh dai-jūichi (no) 第十一(の); **at the ~ hour** kiwadoi toki ni きわどいときに

eligible shikaku no aru 資格のある

eligible bachelor otto ni nozomashii dansei 夫に望ましい男性

eliminate *poverty etc* nakusu なくす; *village etc* keshisaru 消し去る; (*from inquiries*) jogai suru 除外する; (*kill*) massatsu suru 抹殺する; **be ~ed** (*from competition*) haitai suru 敗退する

elimination (*from competition*) haitai 敗退; (*of poverty etc*)

bokumetsu 撲滅; (*murder*) massatsu 抹殺

elite 1 *n* erīto エリート **2** *adj* erīto (no) エリート(の); *troops* seiei (no) 精鋭(の)

elk herajika へらじか

ellipse daen だ円

elm nire no ki にれの木

elope kakeochi suru 駆け落ちする

eloquence yūben 雄弁

eloquent yūben (na) 雄弁(な)

eloquently yūben ni 雄弁に

else: *anything ~?* hoka ni nani ka 他に何か; *if you've got nothing ~ to do* moshi hoka ni nani mo nai nara もし他に何もないなら; *no one ~* hoka ni dare mo ... nai 他にだれも...ない; *everyone ~ is going* hoka no hitotachi wa mina iku 他の人たちは皆行く; *who ~ was there?* hoka ni dare ga imashita ka 他にだれがいましたか; *someone ~* dare ka hoka no hito だれか他の人; *something ~* nani ka hoka no mono 何か他のもの; (*abstracts*: *suggestions, ideas*) nani ka hoka no koto 何か他のこと; *let's go somewhere ~* doko ka hoka no tokoro ni ikimashō どこか他のところに行きましょう; *or ~* samonai to さもないと

elsewhere hoka no basho de wa 他の場所では

elude *escape from* ... kara nigeru ...から逃げる; *avoid* nogareru 逃れる; *her name ~s me* kanojo no namae ga omoidasenai 彼女の名前が思い出せない

elusive *person* tsukamaenikui つかまえにくい

emaciated suijaku shita 衰弱した

e-mail 1 *n* ī-mēru eメール **2** *v/t person* ... ni ī-mēru o okuru ...にeメールを送る; *text* ... o ī-mēru de okuru ...をeメールで送る

e-mail address ī-mēru no adoresu eメールのアドレス

emancipated *woman* jiritsu shita 自立した

emancipation kaihō 解放

embalm ... ni bōfu-shori o

hodokosu ...に防腐処理を施す

embankment teibō 堤防

embargo *n* yushutsu-kinshi 輸出禁止

embark (*on ship*) jōsen suru 乗船する; (*on plane*) tōjō suru 搭乗する

♦**embark on** (*begin*) ... ni noridasu ...に乗り出す

embarrass ... ni kimazui omoi o saseru ...に気まずい思いをさせる; (*put in awkward position*) komaraseru 困らせる; (*shame*) ... ni haji o kakaseru ...に恥をかかせる; (*cause to lose face*) ... no menboku o tsubusu ...の面目をつぶす; **am I ~ing you?** kimari ga warukatta desu ka きまりが悪かったですか

embarrassed *smile* kimari no warui きまりの悪い; **I was ~** hazukashikatta 恥ずかしかった

embarrassing hazukashii 恥ずかしい; (*awkward*) kimazui 気まずい; **put ... in an ~ position** ... ni kimari no warui omoi o saseru ...にきまりの悪い思いをさせる

embarrassment kimazu-sa 気まずさ; (*shame*) haji 恥; **I don't want to cause any ~** kimazui omoi o sasetaku nai 気まずい思いをさせたくない

embassy taishikan 大使館

embellish sōshoku suru 装飾する; *story* junshoku suru 潤色する

embers moesashi 燃えさし

embezzle tsukaikomu 使い込む

embezzlement tsukaikomi 使い込み

embitter ... ni nigai omoi o saseru ...に苦い思いをさせる

emblem shinboru-māku シンボルマーク

embodiment keshin 化身

embody arawasu 表す; (*of person*) taigen suru 体現する

embolism sokusenshō そく栓症

emboss *metal* ... ni enbosu-kakō o suru ...にエンボス加工をする; *paper* ... ni kataoshi-insatsu o suru ...に型押し印刷をする; *fabric* ... ni ukiori o hodokosu ...に浮き

織りを施す

embrace 1 *n* hōyō 抱擁 2 *v/t* (*hug*) dakishimeru 抱き締める; (*take in*) fukumu 含む 3 *v/i* (*of two people*) dakiau 抱き合う

embroider ... ni shishū o suru ...に刺しゅうをする; *fig* ... ni ohire o tsukeru ...に尾ひれをつける

embroidery shishū 刺しゅう

embryo BIO hai 胚; (*fetus*) taiji 胎児

emerald (*precious stone*) emerarudo エメラルド; (*color*) emerarudo-iro エメラルド色

emerge (*appear*) arawareru 現れる; (*of truth*) akiraka ni naru 明らかになる; **it has ~d that...** ... koto ga akiraka ni natta ...ことが明らかになった

emergency kinkyū-jitai 緊急事態; **in an ~** kinkyū no bāi ni wa 緊急の場合には

emergency exit hijōguchi 非常口

emergency landing kinkyū-chakuriku 緊急着陸

emigrant *n* ijū-sha 移住者

emigrate ijū suru 移住する

emigration ijū 移住

eminent chomei (na) 著名(な)

eminently ichijirushiku 著しく

emission (*of gases*) haishutsu 排出

emotion kanjō 感情

emotional *problems, development* kanjōteki (na) 感情的(な); (*full of emotion*) kandōteki (na) 感動的(な)

empathize: ~ with ... ni kyōkan suru ...に共感する

emperor kōtei 皇帝; (*of Japan*) Tennō 天皇; **Emperor's Birthday** Tennō-Tanjōbi 天皇誕生日

Emperor Hirohito Shōwa-Tennō 昭和天皇

emphasis (*stress*) kyōchō 強調; (*importance*) jūten 重点

emphasize kyōchō suru 強調する

emphatic hakkiri to shita はっきりとした

empire teikoku 帝国

employ yatou 雇う; *skills* katsuyō suru 活用する; *tool, method* riyō

suru 利用する; **he's ~ed as a ...**
kare wa ... to shite yatowarete iru
彼は...として雇われている

employee jūgyōin 従業員

employer koyō-sha 雇用者

employment koyō 雇用; (*work*)
shokugyō 職業; **be seeking ~** shoku
o sagashite iru 職を探している

employment agency shokugyō-
shōkaijo 職業紹介所

empress jotei 女帝; (*of Japan*) kōgō
皇后

emptiness (*of box, room*) karappo
からっぽ; (*in heart*) munashii-sa む
なしさ; (*of words, life*) kūkyo-sa
空虚さ

empty 1 *adj* karappo (no) からっぽ
(の); *room, street, bus* dare mo
inai だれもいない; *word* munashii
むなしい; **~ promises** kara-
yakusoku から約束 **2** *v/t drawer,*
pockets ... no nakami o akeru ...の
中身をあける; *glass, bottle* kara ni
suru からにする **3** *v/i* (*of room,*
street) kara ni naru からになる

emulate minarau 見習う

enable ... dekiru yō ni suru ...でき
るようにする; **the money ~d him to**
go to university sono okane de
kare wa daigaku ni iku koto ga
dekita そのお金で彼は大学に行く
ことができた

enact *law* seitei suru 制定する;
THEA jōen suru 上演する

enamel *n* hōrō ほうろう; (*on tooth*)
enameru-shitsu エナメル質;
(*paint*) enameru エナメル

encircle torikomu 取り囲む

encl (= **enclosure(s)**) dōfūbutsu 同
封物

enclose (*in letter*) dōfū suru 同封す
る; *area* kakomu 囲む; **please find**
~ ... ... o dōfū itashimasu ...を同
封いたします

enclosure (*with letter*) dōfūbutsu 同
封物

encore *n* ankōru アンコール

encounter 1 *n* deai 出会い **2** *v/t*
person ... ni deau ...に出会う;
problem, resistance ... ni
chokumen suru ...に直面する

encourage *person* hagemasu 励ま
す; *participation* shōrei suru 奨励
する; *violence* jochō suru 助長する;
growth sokushin suru 促進する

encouragement hagemashi 励まし;
(*from government etc*) shōrei 奨励

encouraging *news, report* hagemi ni
naru 励みになる; *smile* hagemasu
yō (na) 励ますような(な)

♦ **encroach on** *land* ... ni shinnyū
suru ...に侵入する; *rights* shingai
suru 侵害する; *time* tsubusu つぶす

encyclopedia hyakka-jiten 百科辞
典

end 1 *n* (*extremity*) hashi 端;
(*conclusion*) owari 終わり;
(*purpose*) mokuteki 目的; **in the ~**
tsui ni ついに; **for hours on ~**
nanjikan demo 何時間でも; **stand**
... on ~ ... o massugu ni tateru ...
をまっすぐに立てる; **at the ~ of**
July shichigatsu no owari ni 七月
の終わりに; **put an ~ to** ... o
owaraseru ...を終わらせる **2** *v/t*
oeru 終える **3** *v/i* owaru 終わる

♦ **end up: we ended up in Nagoya**
watashitachi wa Nagoya ni kite
shimatta 私達は名古屋に来てし
まった; **we ended up buying ...**
watashitachi wa ... o kau koto ni
natte shimatta 私達は...を買うこ
とになってしまった

endanger kiken ni sarasu 危険にさ
らす

endangered species zetsumetsu-
sunzen no shu 絶滅寸前の種

endearing kawairashii かわいらし
い

endeavor 1 *n* doryoku 努力 **2** *v/t*
doryoku suru 努力する

ending owari 終わり; GRAM gobi 語尾

endless *questioning etc* owari no
nai 終わりのない; *desert* hateshi
no nai 果てしのない

endorse *check* ... ni uragaki o suru
...に裏書きをする; *candidacy*
suisen suru 推薦する; *product*
senden suru 宣伝する

endorsement (*of check*) uragaki 裏
書き; (*of candidacy*) suisen 推薦;
(*of product*) senden 宣伝

end product saishū-seisanbutsu 最終生産物

end result saishū-kekka 最終結果

endurance (*physical*) jikyūryoku 持久力; (*mental*) nintai 忍耐

endure 1 v/t (*go through*) taeshinobu 耐え忍ぶ; (*tolerate*) gaman suru 我慢する **2** v/i (*last*) mochikotaeru 持ちこたえる

enduring eizoku suru 永続する

end-user mattan-shōhisha 末端消費者

enemy teki 敵; (*in war*) tekigun 敵軍

energetic *person* seiryokuteki (na) 精力的(な); *activity* seiryoku o tsukau 精力を使う; *fig: measures* seiryoku o katamuketa 精力を傾けた

energy seiryoku 精力; (*gas, electricity etc*) enerugī エネルギー

energy-saving *device* shō-ene (no) 省エネ(の)

enforce jisshi suru 実施する

engage 1 v/t (*hire*) yatou 雇う **2** v/i (*of clutch, gear*) ireru 入れる

♦ **engage in** ... ni kakawaru ...にかかわる

engaged (*to be married*) kon'yaku shite iru 婚約している; **get ~** kon'yaku suru 婚約する

engagement (*appointment*) yakusoku 約束; (*to be married*) kon'yaku 婚約; MIL kōsen 交戦

engagement ring kon'yaku-yubiwa 婚約指輪

engaging *smile, person* hito o hikitsukeru 人を引き付ける

engine enjin エンジン

engineer 1 n gishi 技師; NAUT kikanshi 機関士; RAIL untenshi 運転士 **2** v/t *meeting etc* takuramu たくらむ

engineering kōgaku 工学

England Ingurando イングランド

English 1 adj Ingurando (no) イングランド(の) **2** n (*language*) Eigo 英語; **the ~** Ingurando-jin イングランド人

Englishman Ingurando-jin-dansei イングランド人男性

Englishwoman Ingurando-jin-josei イングランド人女性

engrave horu 彫る

engraving (*drawing*) hanga 版画; (*design*) chōban 彫版

engrossed: **~ in** ... ni muchū de ...に夢中で

engulf nomikomu 飲み込む

enhance *reputation, performance, effect* takameru 高める; *beauty, flavor* masu 増す

enigma nazo なぞ

enigmatic nazomeita なぞめいた

enjoy tanoshimu 楽しむ; **I ~ skiing** sukī ga suki de desu スキーが好きです; **~ oneself** tanoshii omoi o suru 楽しい思いをする; **~!** (*said to s.o. eating*) dōzo どうぞ

enjoyable tanoshii 楽しい

enjoyment tanoshimi 楽しみ

enlarge kakudai suru 拡大する; PHOT hikinobasu 引き伸ばす

enlargement kakudai 拡大; PHOT hikinobashi 引き伸ばし

enlighten (*educate*) keimō suru 啓もうする; (*inform*) ... ni oshieru ...に教える

enlightenment (*in Japanese philosophy*) satori 悟り

enlist 1 v/i MIL nyūtai suru 入隊する **2** v/t: **~ X's help** X no kyōryoku o eru Xの協力を得る

enliven ... ni kakki o ataeru ...に活気を与える

enormity (*of crime*) kyōaku-sa 凶悪さ; (*of task*) bōdai-sa 膨大さ

enormous kyodai (na) 巨大(な); *amount* bakudai (na) 莫大(な); *satisfaction, patience* taihen (na) 大変(な)

enormously hijō ni 非常に

enough 1 adj jūbun (na) 十分(な); **will $50 be ~?** gojū doru de tarimasu ka 五十ドルで足りますか; **I've had ~!** mō takusan もうたくさん; **that's ~, calm down!** iikagen ni shinasai いいかげんにしなさい **3** adv jūbun ni 十分に; **strangely ~** fushigi ni mo 不思議にも

enquire, enquiry → inquire, inquiry

enraged gekido shita 激怒した

enrich *vocabulary* hōfu ni suru 豊富にする; *s.o.'s life* yutaka ni suru 豊かにする

enroll *v/i* (*for a course*) tōroku suru 登録する

enrolment tōroku 登録

ensure ... ni kenri o ataeru ...を確実にする

entail tomonau 伴う; *cost, time* yō suru 要する

entangle: *get ~d in* (*in rope*) ... ni karamaru ...にからまる; (*in love affair*) ... to kankei o motsu ...と関係を持つ

enter *v/t room, house* ... ni hairu ...に入る; *competition* ... ni shutsujō suru ...に出場する; *person, horse in race* shutsujō saseru 出場させる; *write down* kinyū suru 記入する; COMPUT nyūryoku suru 入力する **2** *v/i* hairu 入る; THEA tōjō suru 登場する; (*in competition*) shutsujō suru 出場する

enterprise (*initiative*) shinshu no kishō 進取の気性; (*venture*) jigyō 事業

enterprising shinshu no kishō ni tonda 進取の気性に富んだ

entertain 1 *v/t* (*amuse*) tanoshimaseru 楽しませる; (*as host*) motenasu もてなす; *idea* kōryo suru 考慮する **2** *v/i* (*have guests*) raikyaku o motenasu 来客をもてなす

entertainer (*as profession*) entā teinā エンターテイナー

entertaining *adj* omoshiroi おもしろい

entertainment tanoshimi 楽しみ

enthrall ... no kokoro o ubau ...の心を奪う

enthusiasm netsui 熱意

enthusiast fan ファン

enthusiastic netchū shite iru 熱中している

entice sasou 誘う

entire zentai (no) 全体(の); *the ~ country* zenkoku 全国; *the ~ day* maru ichinichi まる一日; *the ~ family* kazoku-zen'in 家族全員; *the ~ world* zensekai 全世界

entirely (*completely*) mattaku 全く; *I'm not ~ satisfied* watashi wa kanzen ni manzoku shite iru wake de wa nai 私は完全に満足しているわけではない

entitle ... ni kenri o ataeru ...に権利を与える; *you're ~d to be angry* okotte atarimae desu 怒って当たり前です

entitled *book* ... ni taitoru o tsukeru ...にタイトルをつける

entrance *n* (*doorway*) iriguchi 入り口; (*of house*) genkan 玄関; (*act of entering*) tōjō 登場; (*admission*) nyūjō 入場

entranced uchōten ni natta 有頂天になった

entrance fee nyūjōryō 入場料

entrant (*for exam*) juken-sha 受験者; (*in competition*) sanka-sha 参加者

entrenched *attitudes* korikatamatta 凝り固まった

entrepreneur kigyō-ka 企業家

entrepreneurial kigyō-ka (no) 企業家(の)

entrust: *~ X with Y, ~ Y to X* X o Y ni makaseru XをYに任せる

entry (*way in*) iriguchi 入り口; (*admission*) nyūjō 入場; (*of country*) nyūkoku 入国; (*for competition*) sanka-sha 参加者; (*item submitted*) shuppinbutsu 出品物; (*in diary, accounts*) kinyū 記入; *no ~* (*for cars*) shinnyū-kinshi 進入禁止; (*for people*) tachiiri-kinshi 立入禁止

entry form shutsujō-mōshikomi-yōshi 出場申し込み用紙

entry visa nyūkoku-biza 入国ビザ

envelop tsutsumu 包む; (*of mist etc*) ōu 覆う

envelope fūtō 封筒

enviable urayamashii うらやましい

envious urayamashige (na) うらやましげ(な); *be ~ of* ... o netande iru ...をねたんでいる

environment kankyō 環境

environmental *problem* kankyō (no) 環境(の); *consideration* kankyō ni tai suru 環境に対する

environmentalist kankyō-hogo-ronsha 環境保護論者
environmentally friendly kankyō ni yasashii 環境に優しい
environmental pollution kankyō-osen 環境汚染
environmental protection kankyō-hogo 環境保護
environs kinkō 近郊
envisage yosō suru 予想する
envoy kōshi 公使
envy 1 *n* netami ねたみ; *be the ~ of* senbō no mato de aru せん望の的である **2** *v/t* …ga urayamashii …がうらやましい; *I ~ you your success* anata no seikō ga urayamashii あなたの成功がうらやましい
epic 1 *n* taisaku 大作 **2** *adj journey* yūdai (na) 雄大(な)
epicenter shingenchi 震源地
epidemic ryūkō 流行
epilepsy tenkan てんかん
epileptic *n* tenkan-kanja てんかん患者
epileptic fit tenkan no hossa てんかんの発作
epilog epirōgu エピローグ
episode (*of story*) episōdo エピソード; (*of TV series*) ikkai 一回; (*event*) dekigoto 出来事
epitaph bohimei 墓碑銘
epoch jidai 時代
epoch-making kakkiteki (na) 画期的(な)
equal 1 *adj amount, number, value* hitoshii 等しい; *right, opportunity* byōdō (no) 平等(の); *be ~ to task* … ni taerareru …に耐えられる **2** *n* (*person*) dōtō no hito 同等の人; (*object*) hitteki suru mono 匹敵するもの **3** *v/t* (*in quantity*) … ni hitoshii …に等しい; (*be as good as*) … ni hitteki suru …に匹敵する; *2 plus 2 ~s 4* ni tasu ni wa 4 二たす2は4
equality byōdō 平等
equalize 1 *v/t* hitoshiku suru 等しくする **2** *v/i* SP dōten ni naru 同点になる
equalizer SP dōten-gōru 同点ゴール

equally *divide, apportion etc* byōdō ni 平等に; *intelligent, guilty etc* hitoshiku 等しく; *~, …* sore to dōji ni,… それと同時に,…
equate: *~ X with Y* X o Y to hitoshii to minasu XをYと等しいとみなす
equation MATH hōteishiki 方程式
equator sekidō 赤道
equilibrium kinkō 均衡
equinox (*spring*) shunbun 春分; (*autumnal*) shūbun 秋分
equip: *be ~ped with* … o sonaete iru …を備えている; *he's not ~ped to handle it* fig kare wa sore o atsukau kokoro no junbi ga dekite inai 彼はそれを扱う心の準備ができていない
equipment (*machinery*) setsubi 設備; (*tools*) yōgu 用具
equity FIN shisan 資産; *equities* (*shareholdings*) futsū-kabushiki 普通株式
equivalent 1 *adj* sōtō (no) 相当(の); *be ~ to* … ni sōtō suru …に相当する **2** *n* sōtō suru mono 相当するもの
era jidai 時代
eradicate konzetsu suru 根絶する
erase kesu 消す
eraser keshi-gomu 消しゴム; (*for blackboard*) kokuban-keshi 黒板消し
erect 1 *adj posture* chokuritsu shita 直立した **2** *v/t* tateru 建てる
erection (*of building etc*) kensetsu 建設; (*of penis*) bokki ぼっ起
erode (*of acid*) fushoku suru 腐食する; (*of rain, wind*) shinshoku suru 侵食する; *rights, power* okasu 侵す
erosion shinshoku 侵食; fig shingai 侵害
erotic erochikku (na) エロチック(な)
eroticism erochishizumu エロチシズム
errand tsukai 使い; *run ~s* … no tsukaibashiri o suru …の使い走りをする
erratic *behavior* toppi (na) とっぴ(な); *person* muraki (na) むら気(な); *performance, course* fuantei (na) 不安定(な); *heartbeat*

fukisoku (na) 不規則(な)

error machigai 間違い

error message COMPUT erāmessēji エラーメッセージ

erupt (of volcano) funka suru 噴火する; (of violence) hassei suru 発生する; (be very angry) okoridasu 怒り出す

eruption (of volcano) funka 噴火; (of violence) hassei 発生

escalate dandan kakudai suru だんだん拡大する

escalation gekika 激化

escalator esukarētā エスカレーター

escape 1 n (of prisoner) dassō 脱走; (of gas) more 漏れ; **have a narrow ~** karōjite manugareru かろうじて免れる **2** v/i (of prisoner) dassō suru 脱走する; (of animal) nigeru 逃げる; (of gas) moreru 漏れる **3** v/t: nogareru 逃れる; **the name ~s me** namae ga omoidasenai 名前が思い出せない

escape chute kinkyū-dasshutsu-sōchi 緊急脱出装置

escort 1 n dēto no aite デートの相手; (guard) goei 護衛 **2** v/t (socially) okutte iku 送っていく; (as guard) goei suru 護衛する

especial → **special**

especially toku ni 特に

espionage supai-kōi スパイ行為

essay n essei エッセイ; (academic) shōronbun 小論文

essential adj food, equipment kaku koto no dekinai 欠くことのできない; (crucial) kanjin (no) 肝心(の)

essentially honshitsuteki ni 本質的に

establish company setsuritsu suru 設立する; (create) kakuritsu suru 確立する; (determine) kakutei suru 確定する; **~ oneself as** ... to shite no chii o katameru ...としての地位を固める

establishment (firm, shop etc) shisetsu 施設; **the Establishment** taisei 体制

estate (area of land) jisho 地所; (of dead person) zaisan 財産

esthetic value, appeal biteki (na) 美的(な); building etc shumi no yoi 趣味のよい

estimate 1 n mitsumori 見積り **2** v/t mitsumoru 見積もる

estimation: he has gone up / down in my ~ kare ni taisuru watashi no hyōka wa agatta/sagatta 彼に対する私の評価は上がった/下がった; **in my ~** (opinion) watashi no miru tokoro de wa 私の見るところでは

estranged wife, husband bekkyochū (no) 別居中(の)

estuary irie 入り江

ETA (= estimated time of arrival) tōchaku-yotei-jikoku 到着予定時刻

etching etchingu エッチング

eternal eien (no) 永遠(の)

eternity eien 永遠

ethical rinriteki (na) 倫理的(な); (morally correct) dōtokuteki (na) 道徳的(な)

ethics dōtoku 道徳; (academic subject) rinri-gaku 倫理学

ethnic minzoku (no) 民族(の)

ethnic group minzoku-shūdan 民族集団

ethnic minority shōsū-minzoku 少数民族

euphemism enkyoku-gohō えん曲語法

euphoria shifukukan 至福感

Europe Yōroppa ヨーロッパ

European 1 adj Yōroppa (no) ヨーロッパ(の) **2** n Yōroppa-jin ヨーロッパ人

euthanasia anrakushi 安楽死

evacuate (clear people from) ... kara hinan saseru ...から避難させる; (leave) ... kara hinan suru ...から避難する

evade question hagurakasu はぐらかす; person sakeru 避ける; responsibility kaihi suru 回避する

evaluate performance hyōka suru 評価する; damage satei suru 査定する

evaluation (of performance) hyōka 評価; (of situation) satei 査定

evangelist dendōshi 伝道師

evaporate (*of water*) jōhatsu suru 蒸発する; (*of confidence*) kiete nakunaru 消えてなくなる

evasion kaihi 回避; **tax ~** datsuzei 脱税

evasive kaihiteki (na) 回避的(な)

eve zen'ya 前夜

even 1 *adj* (*regular*) kisokuteki (na) 規則的(な); (*equal*) byōdō (na) 平等(な); (*level*) taira (na) 平ら(な); *number* gūsū (no) 偶数(の); **get ~ with** ... ni shikaeshi o suru ...に仕返しをする **2** *adv* ... de sae mo ...でさえも; *it was good* kare de sae mo sore wa yokatta to itta 彼でさえもそれはよかったと言った; *the car ~ has a CD* sono kuruma ni wa shīdī made aru その車にはCDまである; **~ bigger / better** sara ni ōkiku / yoku さらに大きく/よく; *not ~ ... sae ...* nai ...さえ...ない; *he doesn't ~ try* kare wa tamesu koto sae shinai 彼は試すことさえしない; **~ so** tatoe sō demo たとえそうでも; **~ if** tatoe ... demo たとえ...でも **3** *v/t*: **~ the score** dōten ni suru 同点にする

evening ban 晩; **in the ~** yūgata ni 夕方に; *this ~* konban 今晩; *good ~* konban wa こんばんは

evening classes yakan-kōza 夜間講座; **evening dress** (*for woman*) ibuningu-doresu イブニングドレス; (*for man*) seisō 正装; **evening paper** yūkan 夕刊

evenly *distribute* kintō ni 均等に; *breathe* kisokuteki ni 規則的に; **~ matched** gokaku (no) 互角(の)

event dekigoto できごと; SP shumoku 種目; **at all ~s** tonikaku とにかく

eventful haran ni tonda 波乱に富んだ

eventual saishūteki (na) 最終的(な)

eventually (*finally*) tsui ni ついに; (*in time*) sono uchi ni そのうちに

ever *adv* ◊ (*in if clause*) itsuka いつか; *if I ~ see you again* moshi itsu ka mata aetara もしいつか また会えたら; ◊ (*up to now / then*) ima made de 今までで; *the worst movie ~ made* ima made tsukurareta saiaku no eiga 今まで作られた最悪の映画; *the best book I ~ read* imamade yonda saikō no hon 今まで読んだ最高の本; *have you ~ been to Japan?* Nihon ni itta koto ga arimasu ka 日本に行ったことがありますか; *do you ~ see her now?* kanojo ni ima mo atte iru no 彼女に今も会っているの; *for ~* itsu made mo いつまでも; **~ since** sore irai それ以来; **~ since the accident** sono jiko irai その事故以来

evergreen *n* jōryokuju 常緑樹

everlasting *love* eien (no) 永遠(の)

every subete (no) すべて(の); **~ student has a computer** subete no gakusei wa konpyūta o motte iru すべての学生はコンピューターを持っている; **~ week / month** maishū / maitsuki 毎週/毎月; **~ Sunday** mainichiyōbi 毎日曜日; **~ other day** ichinichi oki ni 一日置きに; **~ now and then** tokidoki ときどき

everybody → **everyone**

everyday *incident* arifureta ありふれた; *language* nichijō (no) 日常(の)

everyone minna 皆; *I've spoken to ~ who knew her* kanojo o shitte iru hito dare demo to hanashita 彼女を知っている人誰でもと話した

everything zenbu 全部

everywhere doko demo どこでも; (*wherever*) itaru tokoro ni いたるところに

evict tachinokaseru 立ち退かせる

evidence shōko 証拠; LAW shōko-bukken 証拠物件; *give ~* shōgen suru 証言する

evident akiraka (na) 明らか(な); *it was ~ that* ... wa akiraka datta ... は明らかだった

evidently (*clearly*) akiraka ni 明らかに; (*apparently*) dōyara どうやら

evil 1 *adj* ja-aku (na) 邪悪(な) **2** *n* ja-aku 邪悪

evoke *image* yobiokosu 呼び起こす

evolution (*of animal*) shinka 進化;

(development) hatten 発展

evolve v/i *(of animals)* shinka suru 進化する; *(develop)* hatten suru 発展する

ewe mehitsuji 雌羊

ex- moto ... 元...

ex n F *(wife)* zensai 前妻; *(husband)* zenpu 前夫

exact adj time, word, amount seikaku (na) 正確(な)

exactly *(precisely)* chōdo ちょうど; *you look ~ like your mother* anata wa okāsan ni sokkuri da あなたはお母さんにそっくりだ; *that's ~ what I mean* sore ga masa ni watashi no iō to shita koto da それがまさに私の言おうとしたことだ; *~!* sono tōri そのとおり; *not ~* chotto chigaimasu ne ちょっと違いますね

exaggerate 1 v/t kochō suru 誇張する **2** v/i ōgesa na iikata o suru 大げさな言い方をする

exaggeration ōgesa 大げさ

exam shiken 試験; *sit an ~* shiken o ukeru 試験を受ける; *pass / fail an ~* shiken ni ukaru / ochiru 試験に受かる/落ちる

examination *(of facts)* chōsa 調査; *(chemical analysis etc)* kensa 検査; *(of patient)* shinsatsu 診察; EDU shiken 試験; *take an entrance ~* juken suru 受験する

examine *(study)* chōsa suru 調査する; *(analyse)* kensa suru 検査する; *patient* shinsatsu suru 診察する; EDU shiken suru 試験する

examiner EDU shiken-kan 試験官

example rei 例; *for ~* tatoeba 例えば; *set a good / bad ~* yoi otehon / warui mihon to naru よいお手本/悪い見本となる

exasperated okotta 怒った

excavate v/t *(dig)* horu 掘る; *(of archeologist)* hakkutsu suru 発掘する

excavation hakkutsu 発掘

excavator pawāshaberu パワーシャベル

exceed *(be more than)* koeru 越える; *(go beyond)* kosu 越す

exceedingly kiwamete きわめて

excel 1 v/i sugurete iru 優れている; *~ at* ... ni hiidete iru ...に秀でている **2** v/t: *~ oneself* itsumo yori umaku yaru いつもよりうまくやる

excellence sugurete iru koto 優れていること

excellent sugureta 優れた

except ... igai wa ...以外は; *~ for* ... o nozoite wa ...を除いては; *~ that* ... to iu koto o nozokeba ...ということを除けば

exception reigai 例外; *with the ~ of* ... o nozoite wa ...を除いては; *take ~ to* ... ga ki ni iranai ...が気に入らない

exceptional *(very good)* tokubetsu ni sugureta 特別に優れた; *(special)* reigaiteki (na) 例外的(な)

exceptionally *(extremely)* toku ni 特に

excerpt bassui 抜粋

excess 1 n: *eat / drink to ~* tabe / nomi-sugiru 食べ/飲み過ぎる; *in ~ of* ... yori ōku ...より多く **2** adj kajō (no) 過剰(の)

excess baggage chōka-tenimotsu 超過手荷物

excess fare chōka-ryōkin 超過料金

excessive kajō (no) 過剰(の)

exchange 1 n *(of views, information)* kōkan 交換; *(between schools)* kōkan-ryūgaku 交換留学; *in ~* hikikae ni 引き換えに; *in ~ for* ... to hikikae ni ...と引き換えに **2** v/t *(in store)* torikaeru 取り替える; *addresses* torikawasu 取り交わす; *currency* ryōgae suru 両替する; *~ X for Y* X o Y to kōkan suru X を Y と交換する

exchange rate kawase-sōba 為替相場

excitable kōfun shiyasui 興奮しやすい

excite *(make enthusiastic)* kōfun saseru 興奮させる

excited kōfun shita 興奮した; *get ~* kōfun suru 興奮する; *get ~ about* ... no koto de kōfun suru ...のことで興奮する

excitement kōfun 興奮

exciting wakuwaku suru わくわくする

exclaim sakebu 叫ぶ

exclamation sakebi 叫び

exclamation point kantanfu 感嘆符

exclude nozoku 除く, jogai suru 除外する; (*ban: from club etc*) shimedasu 締め出す

excluding ... o nozoite ...を除いて

exclusive *hotel, restaurant* kōkyū (na) 高級(な); *rights* yuiitsu (no) 唯一(の); *interview* dokusenteki (na) 独占的(な)

excruciating *pain* taegatai 耐えがたい

excursion ensoku 遠足

excuse 1 *n* iiwake 言い訳 **2** *v/t* (*forgive*) yurusu 許す; (*allow to leave*) ... ga chūza suru no o yurusu ...が中座するのを許す; **~ X from Y** X o Y kara menjo suru X をYから免除する; **~ me** (*to get attention*) sumimasen すみません; (*to get past*) chotto sumimasen ちょっとすみません; (*interrupting*) shitsurei desu ga 失礼ですが

execute *criminal* shokei suru 処刑する; *plan* jikkō suru 実行する

execution (*of criminal*) shokei 処刑; (*of plan*) jikkō 実行

executioner shikei-shikkō-nin 死刑執行人

executive *n* jūyaku 重役

executive briefcase kōkyū-burīfukēsu 高級ブリーフケース

executive washroom jūyakuyō-keshōshitsu 重役用化粧室

exemplary *conduct* mohanteki (na) 模範的(な)

exempt: be ~ from ... o menjo sareru ...を免除される

exercise 1 *n* (*physical*) undō 運動, EDU renshū-mondai 練習問題; MIL gunji-enshū 軍事演習; **take ~** undō suru 運動する **2** *v/t muscle* kitaeru 鍛える; *dog* undō saseru 運動させる; *caution, restraint* hatarakaseru 働かせる **3** *v/i* (*do exercise*) undō suru 運動する

exercise book EDU renshūchō 練習帳

exert *authority* kōshi suru 行使する; *influence* oyobosu 及ぼす; **~ oneself** doryoku suru 努力する

exertion doryoku 努力

exhale hakidasu 吐き出す

exhaust 1 *n* (*fumes*) haiki-gasu 排気ガス; (*pipe*) haikikan 排気管 **2** *v/t* (*tire*) tsukarehatesaseru 疲れ果てさせる; (*use up*) tsukaihatasu 使い果たす

exhaust fumes haiki-gasu 排気ガス

exhausted (*tired*) tsukarekitta 疲れ切った

exhausting hidoku tsukareru ひどく疲れる

exhaustion kyokudo no hirō 極度の疲労

exhaustive (*complete*) kanzen (na) 完全(な); (*thorough*) tetteiteki (na) 徹底的(な)

exhaust pipe haikikan 排気管

exhibit 1 *n* (*in exhibition*) tenjihin 展示品 **2** *v/t* (*of gallery*) tenji suru 展示する; (*of artist*) kōkai suru 公開する; (*give evidence of*) miseru 見せる

exhibition tenrankai 展覧会; (*of skill*) hakki 発揮; **make an ~ of oneself** hajisarashi na mane o suru 恥さらしなまねをする

exhibitionist medachitagariya 目立ちたがり屋

exhilarating ukiuki suru yō (na) うきうきするよう(な)

exile 1 *n* bōmei 亡命; (*person*) bōmei-sha 亡命者 **2** *v/t* tsuihō suru 追放する

exist sonzai suru 存在する; (*of animal*) seizon suru 生存する; **~ on** ... de ikite iru ...で生きている

existence sonzai 存在; (*life*) seikatsu 生活; **in ~** genzon (no) 現存(の); **come into ~** seiritsu suru 成立する

existing genzai (no) 現在(の)

exit *n* (*way out*) deguchi 出口; (*from highway*) intāchenji インターチェンジ; THEA taijō 退場

exonerate menjo suru 免除する; (*of*

serious offense) muzai ni suru 無
罪にする

exorbitant hōgai (na) 法外(な)

exotic ekizochikku (na) エキゾチック(な)

expand 1 *v/t market, business*
hirogeru 広げる **2** *v/i (of business)*
kakuchō suru 拡張する; (*of city*)
kakudai suru 拡大する; (*of*
population) zōka suru 増加する;
(*of metal*) bōchō suru 膨張する

♦ **expand on** ... ni tsuite kuwashiku
noberu ...について詳しく述べる

expanse hirogari 広がり

expansion (*of business*) kakuchō 拡
張; (*of city*) kakudai 拡大; (*of*
population) zōka 増加; (*of metal*)
bōchō 膨張

expect 1 *v/t person, phonecall etc*
machiukeru 待ち受ける; *rain etc*
yosō suru 予想する; (*suppose*) ...
to omou ...と思う; (*demand*) kitai
suru 期待する **2** *v/i: be ~ing* (*be*
pregnant) ninshin shite iru 妊娠し
ている; *I ~ so* sō omoimasu そう思
います

expectant matte iru 待っている

expectant mother ninpu 妊婦

expectation (*anticipation*) yosō 予
想; (*hope*) kitai 期待; **~s**
(*demands*) kitai 期待

expedient *n* shudan 手段

expedition tanken 探検; (*group*)
tankentai 探検隊

expel *person* tsuihō suru 追放する

expend *energy* tsuiyasu 費やす

expendable *person* gisei ni shite
yoi 犠牲にしてよい

expenditure shishutsu 支出

expense (*cost*) hiyō 費用; *at the*
company's ~ keihi de 経費で; *a*
joke at my ~ watashi o dashi ni
shita jōdan 私をだしにした冗談; *at*
the ~ *of his health* kenkō o gisei ni
shite 健康を犠牲にして

expense account hitsuyō-keihi 必
要経費

expenses keihi 経費

expensive *car, book, watch* kōka
(na) 高価(な); *meal, hotel* nedan
no takai 値段の高い; *lifestyle* kane

no kakaru 金のかかる

experience 1 *n* keiken 経験 **2** *v/t*
keiken suru 経験する

experienced jukuren shita 熟練した

experiment 1 *n* jikken 実験 **2** *v/i*
jikken suru 実験する; *~ on animals*
... de jikken suru ...で実験する; *~*
with (*try out*) ... o tameshite miru
...を試してみる

experimental jikkenteki (na) 実験
的(な)

expert 1 *adj* jukuren shita 熟練した;
~ advice senmonka no iken 専門家
の意見 **2** *n* senmonka 専門家,
ekisupāto エキスパート

expertise gijutsu 技術, nōhau ノウ
ハウ

expire yūkō-kigen ga kireru 有効期
限が切れる; (*of contract*) shikkō to
naru 失効となる

expiry kigengire 期限切れ

expiry date yūkō-kigen 有効期限

explain *v/t & v/i* setsumei suru 説明
する

explanation setsumei 説明

explicit *instructions* meihaku 明白
(な)

explicitly hakkiri to はっきりと

explode 1 *v/i (of bomb)* bakuhatsu
suru 爆発する **2** *v/t bomb*
bakuhatsu saseru 爆発させる

exploit¹ *n* igyō 偉業

exploit² *v/t person* sakushu suru 搾
取する; *resources* riyō suru 利用す
る

exploitation (*of person*) sakushu 搾
取

exploration tanken 探検; (*of idea*)
kentō 検討

exploratory *surgery* shindan-
mokuteki (no) 診断目的(の)

explore *town* tanken suru 探検する;
possibility kentō suru 検討する

explorer tankenka 探検家

explosion bakuhatsu 爆発; (*in*
population) bakuhatsuteki na
zōka 爆発的な増加

explosive *n* bakuyaku 爆薬

export 1 *n* (*action*) yushutsu 輸出;
(*item*) yushutsuhin 輸出品 **2** *v/t*
goods yushutsu suru 輸出する;

COMPUT waritsuke suru 割り付けする

export campaign yushutsu kyanpēn 輸出キャンペーン

exporter yushutsu-gyōsha 輸出業者

expose (*uncover*) mukidashi ni suru むき出しにする; *scandal* bakuro suru 暴露する; *person ... no shōtai o abaku* ...の正体をあばく; ~ *X to Y* X o Y ni sarasu X を Y にさらす

exposure sarasareru koto さらされること; MED teitaion-shō 低体温症; (*of dishonest behavior*) bakuro 暴露; *36-~ film* sanjūroku mai dori no firumu 36枚取りのフィルム

express 1 *adj* (*fast*) kyūkō (no) 急行(の); (*explicit*) meihaku (na) 明白(な) **2** *n* (*train*) kyūkō-ressha 急行列車; (*bus*) kyūkō-basu 急行バス **3** *v/t* (*speak of, voice*) iiarawasu 言い表す; *feelings* hyōgen suru 表現する; ~ *oneself well / clearly* iitai koto o umaku / hakkiri noberu 言いたいことをうまく/はっきり述べる; ~ *oneself* (*emotionally*) jiko o hyōgen suru 自己を表現する

express elevator kyūkō-erebētā 急行エレベーター

expression (*voiced*) hyōgen 表現; (*on face*) hyōjō 表情; (*phrase*) iimawashi 言い回し; (*expressiveness*) hyōgenryoku 表現力

expressive *face* hyōjō no yutaka (na) 表情の豊か(な); *gesture* hyōjō ni tomu 表情に富む

expressly (*explicitly*) meihaku ni 明白に; (*deliberately*) waza to わざと

expressway kōsoku-dōro 高速道路

expulsion (*from school*) taigaku-shobun 退学処分; (*of diplomat*) tsuihō 追放

exquisite (*beautiful*) yūbi (na) 優美(な)

extend 1 *v/t* (*make longer*) enchō suru 延長する; (*make larger*) kakuchō suru 拡張する; *thanks, congratulations* noberu 述べる **2** *v/i* (*of garden etc*) hirogaru 広がる

extension (*to house*) zōchiku 増築; (*of contract, visa*) enchō 延長; TELEC naisen 内線

extension cable enchō-kōdo 延長コード

extensive kōhan'i ni watatta 広範囲にわたった

extent (*degree*) teido 程度; *to such an ~ that ...* ... suru hodo ...するほど; *to a certain ~* aru teido wa ある程度は

exterior 1 *adj* gaibu (no) 外部(の) **2** *n* (*of building*) gaibu 外部; (*of person*) gaiken 外見

exterminate *vermin* kujo suru 駆除する; *race* zetsumetsu suru 絶滅する

external gaibu (no) 外部(の)

extinct *species* zetsumetsu shita 絶滅した

extinction (*of species*) zetsumetsu 絶滅

extinguish *fire, cigarette* kesu 消す

extinguisher shōka-ki 消火器

extort: ~ *money from ...* kara kane o yusuritoru ...から金をゆすり取る

extortion yusuri ゆすり

extortionate hōgai (na) 法外(な)

extra 1 *n* omake おまけ **2** *adj* yobun (no) 余分(の); *be ~* (*cost more*) warimashi-ryōkin ga iru 割増料金がいる **3** *adv* tokubetsu ni 特別に

extra charge warimashi-ryōkin 割増料金

extract¹ *n* bassui 抜粋

extract² *v/t* nail etc hikinuku 引き抜く; (*from pocket etc*) toridasu 取り出す; *coal, oil* saikutsu suru 採掘する; *tooth* nuku 抜く; *information* muriyari kikidasu 無理やり聞き出す

extraction (*of oil, coal*) saikutsu 採掘; (*of tooth*) basshi 抜歯

extradite hikiwatasu 引き渡す

extradition hikiwatashi 引き渡し

extradition treaty hikiwatashi-jōyaku 引き渡し条約

extramarital kongai (no) 婚外(の)

extraordinarily ijō ni 異常に

extraordinary namihazureta 並はずれた

extravagance zeitaku ぜいたく

extravagant (*with money*) zeitaku (na) ぜいたく(な)

extreme 1 *n* kyokutan 極端 **2** *adj* kyokutan (na) 極端(な); *views* kageki (na) 過激(な)

extremely kiwamete きわめて

extremist *n* kagekiha 過激派

extricate kyūshutsu suru 救出する

extrovert *n* gaikōteki na hito 外向的な人

exuberant *person* kakki no aru 活気のある

exult ōyorokobi suru 大喜びする

eye 1 *n* me 目; (*of needle*) hari no ana 針の穴; *keep an ~ on* ...o mihatte iru ...を見張っている **2** *v/t* jitto miru じっと見る

eyeball gankyū 眼球; **eyebrow** mayu まゆ; **eyeglasses** megane めがね; **eyelash** matsuge まつげ; **eyelid** mabuta まぶた; **eyeliner** airainā アイライナー; **eye shadow** aishadō アイシャドー; **eyesight** shiryoku 視力; **eyesore** mezawari 目ざわり; **eye strain** gansei-hirō 眼精疲労; **eyewitness** mokugeki-sha 目撃者

F

F (= *Fahrenheit*) kashi 華氏

fabric kiji 生地

fabulous subarashii すばらしい

façade (*of building*) gaikan 外観; (*of person*) misekake 見せかけ

face 1 *n* kao 顔; **~ to ~** men to mukatte 面と向かって; *lose ~* menboku o ushinau 面目を失う **2** *v/t person* muku 向く; *the sea menshite iru* 面している

facelift kao no shiwatori seikei-shujutsu 顔のしわ取り整形手術

face value FIN gakumen 額面; *take ... at ~* ...o gakumen dōri ni uketoru ...を額面通りに受け取る

facilitate sokushin suru 促進する

facilities setsubi 設備

fact jijitsu 事実; *in ~, as a matter of ~* jissai wa 実際は

factor yōin 要因

factory kōjō 工場

faculty (*hearing etc*) kinō 機能; (*at university*) gakubu 学部

fade *v/i* (*of color*) iro ga aseru 色があせる; (*of sound, light*) kiete iku 消えていく

faded *color, jeans* aseta あせた

fag F (*homosexual*) homo ホモ

Fahrenheit kashi 華氏

fail 1 *v/i* shippai suru 失敗する **2** *v/t exam* ochiru 落ちる

failure shippai 失敗

faint 1 *adj* kasuka (na) かすか(な) **2** *v/i* ki o ushinau 気を失う

fair[1] *n* (*fun~*) yūenchi 遊園地; COM mihon'ichi 見本市

fair[2] *adj hair* kinpatsu (no) 金髪(の); *complexion* shiroi 白い; (*just*) kōhei (na) 公平(な); (*not bad*) warukunai 悪くない; *it's not ~ sore wa fukōhei desu* それは不公平です

fairly *treat* kōhei ni 公平に; (*quite*) kanari かなり

fairness (*of treatment*) kōhei-sa 公平さ

fairy yōsei 妖精

fairy tale *n* otogi-banashi おとぎ話

faith shinrai 信頼; REL shinkō 信仰

faithful seijitsu (na) 誠実(な); *be ~ to one's partner* pātonā ni seijitsu de aru パートナーに誠実である

fake 1 *n* nisemono 偽物 **2** *adj* nise (no) 偽(の)

fall[1] **1** *v/i* (*of person*) tentō suru 転倒する; (*from height*) tenraku suru 転落する; (*of government*) hōkai suru 崩壊する; (*of prices,* *temperature*) teika suru 低下する; (*of exchange rate*) geraku suru 下落する; (*of night*) kuru 来る; **it ~s on a Tuesday** kayōbi ni ataru 火曜日にあたる; **~ ill** byōki ni naru 病気になる **2** *n* (*of person*) tentō 転倒; (*from height*) tenraku 転落; (*of government*) hōkai 崩壊; (*in price, temperature*) teika 低下; (*of exchange rate*) geraku 下落

♦ **fall back on** ... ni tayoru ...に頼る

♦ **fall down** taoreru 倒れる

♦ **fall for** *person* ... ni muchū ni naru ...に夢中になる; (*be deceived by*) ... ni damasareru ...にだまされる

♦ **fall out** (*of hair*) nukeru 抜ける; (*argue*) kenka suru けんかする

♦ **fall over** (*of person*) korobu 転ぶ; (*of tree*) taoreru 倒れる

♦ **fall through** (*of plans*) zasetsu suru ざ折する

fall² *n* (*autumn*) aki 秋

fallout hōshasei-rakkabutsu 放射性落下物, shi no hai 死の灰

false uso (no) うそ(の); (*mistaken*) machigatta 間違った

false alarm ayamari no keihō 誤りの警報

false teeth ireba 入れ歯

falsify henzō suru 変造する

fame meisei 名声

familiar *adj* (*intimate*) narenareshii なれなれしい; *name, form of address* shitashimi o kometa 親しみをこめた; **be ~ with** ... o yoku shitte iru ...をよく知っている; **that sounds ~** kiita koto ga aru 聞いたことがある

familiarity (*intimacy*) shitashi-sa 親しさ; (*with area etc*) chishiki 知識

familiarize narasu 慣らす; **~ oneself with** ... ni najimu ...になじむ

family kazoku 家族

family doctor kakaritsuke no isha かかりつけの医者; **family name** sei 姓; **family planning** kazoku-keikaku 家族計画

famine kikin ききん

famous yūmei (na) 有名(な); **be ~ for ...** ... de yūmei de aru ...で有名である

fan¹ *n* (*supporter*) fan ファン

fan² **1** *n* (*for cooling: electric*) senpūki 扇風機; (*handheld*) sensu 扇子 **2** *v/t:* **~ oneself** aogu あおぐ

fanatic *n* mania マニア

fanatical nekkyōteki (na) 熱狂的(な)

fan belt MOT fanberuto ファンベルト

fancy dress kasō 仮装

fancy-dress party kasō-pātī 仮装パーティー

fang kiba きば

fanny pack uesuto pōchi ウエストポーチ

fantastic (*very good*) totemo subarashii とてもすばらしい; (*very big*) tohō mo nai 途方もない

fantasy kūsō 空想

far *adv* tōku ni 遠くに; (*much*) haruka ni はるかに; **~ away** haruka tōku ni はるか遠くに; **~ off** zutto tōku ni ずっと遠くに; **how ~ is it to ...** ...made dorekurai desu ka ...までどれくらいですか; **as ~ as the corner / hotel** kado / hoteru made 角/ホテルまで; **as ~ as I can see** watashi no mita kagiri de wa 私の見た限りでは; **as ~ as I know** watashi no shiru kagiri de wa 私の知る限りでは; **you've gone too ~** (*in behavior*) anata wa chotto yarisugita あなたはちょっとやりすぎた; **so ~ so good** ima no tokoro umaku itte iru 今の所うまくいっている

farce chabangeki 茶番劇

fare (*for travel*) unchin 運賃

Far East Kyokutō 極東

farewell wakare 別れ

farewell party sōbetsukai 送別会

farfetched shinjigatai 信じがたい

farm *n* nōjō 農場

farmer nōjōshu 農場主

farmhouse nōka 農家

farmworker kosaku-nin 小作人

farsighted enshi (no) 遠視(の); *fig* senken no mei ga aru 先見の明がある

fart F **1** *n* he 屁 **2** *v/i* he o kogu 屁をこぐ

farther adv sara ni tōku ni さらに遠くに

farthest ichiban tōku ni 一番遠くに

fascinate v/t miryō suru 魅了する; **be ~d by...** ... ni hikareru ...にひかれる

fascinating miryokuteki (na) 魅力的(な)

fascination toriko ni naru koto とりこになること

fascism fashizumu ファシズム

fascist 1 n fashisuto ファシスト **2** adj kyokuu (no) 極右(の)

fashion n fasshon ファッション; (manner) ryūgi de 流儀で; **in ~** ryūkō shite 流行して; **out of ~** ryūkō okure de 流行おくれで

fashionable clothes ryūkō (no) 流行(の); person, idea imafū (no) 今風(の)

fashion-conscious ryūkō o ishiki shita 流行を意識した

fashion designer fasshon-dezainā ファッションデザイナー

fast¹ 1 adj hayai 速い; **be ~** (of clock) susunde iru 進んでいる **2** adv hayaku 速く; **stuck ~** kataku shimatte iru 固くしまっている; **~ asleep** gussuri nemutte ぐっすり眠って

fast² n (not eating) danjiki 断食

fasten 1 v/t shikkari shimeru しっかりしめる; **~ X onto Y** X o Y ni tomeru XをYに留める **2** v/i (of dress etc) tomaru 留まる

fastener (for dress) fasunā ファスナー; (for lid) tomegu 留め具

fast food fāsutofūdo ファーストフード; **fast-food restaurant** fā sutofūdo-restoran ファーストフードレストラン; (video etc) hayaokuri 早送り **2** v/i hayaokuri suru 早送りする; **fast lane** (on road) oikoshi-shasen 追い越し車線; **fast train** kaisoku 快速, kyūkō 急行

fat 1 adj futotta 太った **2** n (on meat) aburami 脂身

fatal chimeiteki (na) 致命的(な); error ketteiteki (na) 決定的(な)

fatality shibō-jiko 死亡事故

fatally: **~ injured** chimeishō o uketa 致命傷を受けた

fate unmei 運命

father n otōsan お父さん; (talking to outsiders about one's own father) chichi 父; **become a ~** chichioya ni naru 父親になる

fatherhood chichioya de aru koto 父親であること

father-in-law (s.o. else's) giri no otōsan 義理のお父さん; (one's own) giri no chichi 義理の父

fatherly chichioya no yō (na) 父親のよう(な)

fathom n NAUT hiro ひろ

fatigue n hirō 疲労

fatso n F debu でぶ

fatty 1 adj aburakkoi 脂っこい **2** n F (person) debu でぶ

faucet jaguchi 蛇口

fault n sekinin 責任; (in machine etc) kekkan 欠陥; (in person) ketten 欠点; **it's your/my ~** anata/watashi no sei desu あなた/私のせいです; **find ~ with** ... no ara o sagasu ...のあらを探す

faultless ketten no nai 欠点のない

faulty goods kekkan no aru 欠陥のある

favor (service) tasuke 助け; (approval) sansei 賛成; **in ~ of** ... vote, decide no tame ni ...のために; **be in ~ of** ... ni sansei shite ...に賛成して; **do ... a ~** ... no tanomi o kiku ...の頼みを聞く; **do me a ~!** (don't be stupid) iikagen ni shite yo いいかげんにしてよ

favorable reply etc kōteki (na) 好意的(な)

favorite 1 n okiniiri お気に入り; (food) kōbutsu 好物 **2** adj ichiban suki (na) 一番好き(な)

fax 1 n fakkusu ファックス; **send ... by ~** ... o fakkusu suru ...をファックスで送る **2** v/t fakkusu de okuru ファックスで送る; **~ X to Y** Y ni X o fakkusu de okuru YにXをファックスで送る

FBI (= Federal Bureau of Investigation) Ef-bī-ai エフ・ビー・アイ

fear 1 n osore 恐れ **2** v/t osoreru 恐

れる

fearless daitanfuteki (na) 大胆不敵
(な)

feasibility study jikkōsei-chōsa 実
行性調査

feasible kanō (na) 可能(な)

feast n gochisō ごちそう

feat otegara お手柄

feather umō 羽毛

feature 1 n (on face) kaodachi 顔立
ち; (of city, building, plan, style)
tokuchō 特徴; (article in paper)
tokushū-kiji 特集記事; (movie)
chōhen-eiga 長編映画; *make a ~ of*
... o ōkiku atsukau ...を大きく扱
う **2** v/t (of movie) shuen to suru
主演とする

February nigatsu 二月

federal renpō (no) 連邦(の)

federation renpō 連邦

fed up adj F unzari shite うんざりし
て; *be ~ with* ... ni unzari shite iru
...にうんざりしている

fee ryōkin 料金; (of lawyer) bengo-
ryō 弁護料; (of doctor) shinsatsu-
ryō 診察料; (paid to professional)
sōdan-ryō 相談料; (for entrance)
nyūjō-ryō 入場料; (for
membership) kaihi 会費

feeble person yowayowashii 弱々し
い; attempt muda (na) 無駄(な);
laugh kasuka (na) かすか(な)

feed v/t ... ni tabemono o ageru ...
に食べ物をあげる; animal ... ni
esa o yaru ...にえさをやる

feedback kansō 感想

feel 1 v/t (touch) ... ni sawaru ...に触
る; (be aware of) kanjiru 感じる;
pleasure, relief etc oboeru 覚える;
pain kanjiru 感じる; (think) ... to
omou ... と思う **2** v/i kanjirareru 感
じられる; *it ~s like silk / cotton*
kinu / men no yō ni kanjirareru 絹/
綿のように感じられる; *your hand
~s hot / cold* anata no te wa atsui /
tsumetai あなたの手は熱い/冷た
い; *I ~ hungry / tired* onaka ga
suita / tsukareta mitai おなかがす
いた/疲れたみたい; *how are you
~ing today?* kyō no kibun wa dō
desu ka 今日の気分はどうですか;

how does it ~ to be rich?
okanemochi no kibun wa dō desu ka
お金持ちの気分はどうですか; *do
you ~ like a drink / meal?* nani ka
nomitai / nani ka tabetai desu ka
何か飲みたい/何か食べたいですか;
I ~ like going / staying ikitai /
koko ni itai kibun desu 行きたい/こ
こにいたい気分です; *I don't ~ like
it* watashi wa shitakunai 私はした
くない

♦ **feel up** (sexually) ... ni chikan
suru ... にちかんする

♦ **feel up to...** ga dekisō na ki ga
suru ...ができそうな気がする

feeler (of insect) shokkaku 触角

feelgood factor rakkan-yōin 楽観要
因

feeling (opinion) kimochi 気持ち;
(emotion) kanjō 感情; (sensation)
kankaku 感覚; *I have mixed ~s
about him* kare ni taishite
fukuzatsu na kanjō o motte iru 彼
に対して複雑な感情を持っている;
what are your ~s about it? sore ni
tsuite anata no kangaekata wa dō
desu ka それについてあなたの考え
方はどうですか

fellow n (man) yatsu やつ

fellow citizen (of country) kokumin
国民; (of city) shimin 市民; **fellow
countryman** dōkokujin 同国人;
fellow man ningen 人間

felony jūzai 重罪

felt n feruto フェルト

felt tip, felt-tip(ped) pen ferutopen
フェルトペン

female 1 adj animal, plant mesu (no)
雌(の); (relating to people) josei
(no) 女性の **2** n (of animals,
plants) mesu 雌; (person) josei 女
性; pej (woman) onna 女

feminine 1 adj qualities josei-rashii
女性らしい; GRAM josei (no) 女性
(の); *she's very ~* kanojo wa
totemo onnarashii 彼女はとても女
らしい **2** n GRAM joseikei 女性形

feminism feminizumu フェミニズム

feminist 1 n feminisuto フェミニス
ト **2** adj group feminisuto (no)
フェミニスト(の); ideas danjo-

dōkenshugi (no) 男女同権主義(の)

fence saku さく, fensu フェンス

♦ **fence in** land … o kakoikomu …を
囲い込む

fencing SP fenshingu フェンシング

fend: ~ **for oneself** jikatsu suru 自活
する

fender MOT fendā フェンダー

feng shui fūsui 風水

ferment[1] v/i (of liquid) hakkō suru
発酵する

ferment[2] n (unrest) konran 混乱

fermentation hakkō 発酵

fern shida シダ

ferocious animal dōmō (na) どう猛
(な); attack hageshii 激しい

ferry n ferī フェリー

fertile soil hiyoku (na) 肥よく(な);
woman, animal ninshinkanō (na)
妊娠可能(な)

fertility (of soil) hiyoku-sa 肥よく
さ; (of woman, animal)
seishokuryoku 生殖力

fertility drug hairan-yūhatsuzai 排
卵誘発剤

fertilize v/t ovum jusei saseru 受精
させる

fertilizer (for soil) hiryō 肥料

fervent admirer netsuretsu (na) 熱
烈(な)

fester (of sore) kanō suru 化膿する

festival omatsuri お祭り

festive omatsurikibun (no) お祭り
気分(の); the ~ season kurisumas
no koro クリスマス(の)頃

festivities gyōji 行事

fetch person tsurete kaeru 連れてか
える; thing totte kuru 取ってくる;
price … de ureru …で売れる

fetus taiji 胎児

feud n hanmoku 反目

fever netsu 熱

feverish netsuppoi 熱っぽい; excitement nekkyōteki (na) 熱狂的(な)

few 1 adj (not many) shōsū (no) 少
数(の); we have ~ friends
watashitachi wa tomodachi ga
hotondo inai 私達は友達がほとん
どいない; there are ~ of them left
hotondo nokotte inai ほとんど
残っていない; a ~ ikutsuka (no) い

くつか(の); (people) ikuninka
(no) 幾人か(の); quite a ~, a good
~ (a lot) kanari (no) かなり(の)
2 pron (not many) shōsū 少数; a ~
ikutsuka 幾つか; a ~ (people)
ikuninka 幾人か; quite a ~, a good
~ (a lot) kanari no hito かなりの人

fewer adj yori sukunai より少ない; ~
than … yori sukunai …より少ない

fiancé kon'yaku-sha 婚約者

fiancée kon'yaku-sha 婚約者

fiasco daishippai 大失敗

fib n uso うそ

fiber sen'i 繊維

fiberglass n faibā-gurasu ファイ
バーグラス; fiber optic cable
hikari faibā kēburu 光ファイバー
ケーブル; fiber optics (subject)
sen'i-kōgaku 繊維光学

fickle kimagure (na) 気まぐれ(な)

fiction (novels etc) shōsetsu 小説;
(lie, exaggeration) tsukuribanashi
作り話

fictitious kakū (no) 架空(の)

fiddle 1 n F (violin) baiorin バイオリ
ン 2 v/i: ~ with … o ijiru …をいじる;
~ (around) with (tamper with) … o
ijiru …をいじる 3 v/t accounts,
results gomakasu ごまかす

fidelity seijitsu 誠実

fidget v/i sowasowa suru そわそわす
る

field n nohara 野原; (with crops)
hatake 畑; SP kyōgi-jō 競技場;
(competitors in race) kyōgi-sha 競
技者; (of research, knowledge etc)
bun'ya 分野; that's not my ~ sore
wa watashi no bun'ya de wa nai そ
れは私の分野ではない

field events fīrudo-shumoku フィー
ルド種目

fierce adj animal dōmō (na) どう猛
(な); wind, storm mōretsu (na) 猛
烈(な)

fiery sunset moetatsu 燃え立つ;
personality hageshii 激しい

fifteen jūgo 十五

fifteenth dai-jūgo (no) 第十五(の)

fifth 1 adj dai-go (no) 第五(の) 2 n
(of month) itsuka 五日

fiftieth dai-gojū (no) 第五十(の)
fifty gojū 五十
fifty-fifty adv gobugobu ni 五分五分に
fig ichijiku いちじく
fight 1 n tatakai 戦い; (argument) kenka けんか; fig (for survival, championship etc) tatakai 闘い; (in boxing) bokushingu no shiai ボクシングの試合 **2** v/t ... to tatakau ...と戦う; disease, injustice ... to tatakau ...と闘う **3** v/i tatakau 戦う; (argue) kenka suru けんかする; (for a cause, against injustice) tatakau 闘う
♦**fight for** rights, cause ... no tame ni tatakau ...のために闘う
fighter tatakau hito 戦う人; (airplane) sentōki 戦闘機; (boxer) bokusā ボクサー; **she's a ~** kanojo wa tōshi da 彼女は闘士だ
figurative usage hiyuteki (na) 比ゆ的(な); art zōkei (no) 造形(の)
figure 1 n (digit) sūji 数字; (of person) sutairu スタイル; (form, shape) katachi 形 **2** v/t F (think) ... to kangaeru ...と考える
♦**figure on** F (plan) ... o keikaku suru ...を計画する
♦**figure out** (understand) ... o rikai suru ...を理解する; calculation keisan suru 計算する
figure skating figyua-sukēto フィギュアスケート
file[1] 1 n also COMPUT fairu ファイル **2** v/t documents fairu suru ファイルする
♦**file away** documents ... o fairu ni irete seiri suru ...をファイルにいれて整理する
file[2] n (for wood, fingernails) yasuri やすり
file cabinet seiriyō kyabinetto 整理用キャビネット
file manager COMPUT fairu-manejā ファイルマネジャー
Filipino 1 adj Firipin (no) フィリピン(の) **2** n (person) Firipin-jin フィリピン人
fill 1 v/t mitasu 満たす; tooth jūten suru 充てんする **2** n: **eat one's ~**

onaka-ippai taberu おなかいっぱい食べる
♦**fill in** form ... o kinyū suru ...を記入する; hole ... o umeru ...を埋める
♦**fill in for** ... no kawari o suru ...の代わりをする
♦**fill out 1** v/t form ... o kinyū suru ...を記入する **2** v/i (get fatter) fukkura suru ふっくらする
♦**fill up 1** v/t ... o ippai ni mitasu ...をいっぱいに満たす **2** v/i (of stadium, theater) ippai ni naru いっぱいになる
fillet n hireniku ヒレ肉
fillet steak hire sutēki ヒレステーキ
filling 1 n (in cake, sandwich etc) nakami 中味; (in tooth) jūten 充てん **2** adj food onaka ga ippai ni naru おなかが一杯になる
filling station gasorin-sutando ガソリンスタンド
film 1 n (for camera) firumu フィルム; (movie) eiga 映画 **2** v/t person, event satsuei suru 撮影する
film-maker eiga-kantoku 映画監督
film star eiga-sutā 映画スター
filter 1 n firutā フィルター **2** v/t coffee, liquid kosu こす
♦**filter through** (of news, reports) jojo ni ikiwataru 徐々にいきわたる
filter tip firutā フィルター; (cigarette) firutā-tsuki no tabako フィルター付きのたばこ
filth yogore 汚れ
filthy fuketsu (na) 不潔(な); language etc gehin (na) 下品(な)
fin (of fish) hire ひれ
final 1 adj saigo (no) 最後(の); decision saishū (no) 最終(の) **2** n SP kesshōsen 決勝戦
finalist kesshōsen-shutsujōsenshu 決勝戦出場選手
finalize plans, design saishū-kettei suru 最終決定する
finally saigo ni 最後に; (at last) tsui ni ついに
finance 1 n zaisei 財政 **2** v/t yūshi suru 融資する
financial zaiseijō (no) 財政上(の)
financial year kaikei-nendo 会計年度

financier shusshi-sha 出資者

find v/t mitsukeru 見つける; **if you ~ it too hot in here** koko ga atsusugiru to omou nara ここが暑すぎると思うなら; **~ X innocent / guilty** LAW X ni yūzai / muzai hanketsu o kudasu Xに有罪/無罪判決を下す

♦**find out 1** v/t (inquire) ... o shiraberu ...を調べる; (discover) ... ga wakaru ...がわかる **2** v/i (inquire) shiraberu 調べる; (discover) wakaru わかる

fine¹ adj day, weather hare (no) 晴れ(の); wine, performance, city subarashii 素晴らしい; distinction komakai 細かい; line hosoi 細い; **how's that? - that's ~** dō datta - yokatta desu どうだった - よかったです; **that's ~ by me** watashi wa ōkē desu 私はOKです; **how are you? - ~** genki - genki desu 元気 - 元気です

fine² n (penalty) bakkin 罰金

finger n yubi 指

fingernail tsume つめ; **fingerprint** n shimon 指紋; **fingertip** yubisaki 指先; **have ... at one's ~s** ... ni seitsū shite iru ...に精通している

finicky person urusai うるさい; design, pattern komakai 細かい

finish 1 v/t oeru 終える; **~ doing ...** ... suru no o oeru ...するのを終える **2** v/i owaru 終わる **3** n (of product) shiagari 仕上がり; (of race) gōru ゴール

♦**finish off** v/t wine ... o nonde shimau ...を飲んでしまう; job ... o oete shimau ...を終えてしまう

♦**finish up** v/t food ... o tabete shimau ...を食べてしまう; **he finished up living there** kare wa kekkyoku soko ni sumu koto ni natta 彼は結局そこに住む事になった

♦**finish with** v/t boyfriend etc ... to wakareru ...と別れる

finishing line gōru ゴール

Finland Finrando フィンランド

Finn Finrando-jin フィンランド人

Finnish 1 adj Finrando (no) フィン

ランド (の) **2** n Finrando-go フィンランド語

fir momi no ki もみの木

fire 1 n hi 火; (electric, gas) hītā ヒーター; (blaze) kaji 火事; (bonfire, campfire etc) takibi たき火; **be on ~** moete iru 燃えている; **catch ~** hi ga tsuku 火がつく; **set ~ to** ... ni hi o tsukeru ...に火をつける **2** v/i (shoot) hassha suru 発射する **3** v/t F (dismiss) kubi ni suru 解雇する

fire alarm kasai-hōchiki 火災報知機; **firearm** jūki 銃器; **fire department** shōbō-sho 消防署; **fire engine** shōbō-sha 消防車; **fire escape** hijō-kaidan 非常階段; route hijō-guchi 非常口; **fire extinguisher** shōka-ki 消火器; **firefighter** shōbō-shi 消防士; **firefly** hotaru ほたる; **fireman** shōbō-shi 消防士; **fireplace** danro 暖炉; **fireproof** adj taikasei (no) 耐火性(の); **fire truck** shōbō-sha 消防車; **firewood** maki まき; **fireworks** hanabi 花火; (display) hanabi no uchiage 花火の打ち上げ

firm¹ adj grip, handshake antei shita 安定した; flesh, muscles hikishimatta 引き締まった; voice, decision danko to shita 断固とした; **a ~ deal** kakujitsu na torihiki 確実な取り引き

firm² n COM kaisha 会社; (of lawyers, accountants) jimusho 事務所

first 1 adj dai-ichi (no) 第一(の) **2** n ichiban 一番; (of month) tsuitachi 一日 **3** adv arrive, finish ichiban ni 一番に; (beforehand) saisho ni 最初に; **~ of all** (for one reason) mazu saisho ni まず最初に; **at ~** hajime wa 初めは

first aid kyūkyū-shochi 救急処置; **first-aid box**, **first-aid kit** kyūkyū-bako 救急箱; **first-born** adj saisho ni umareta 最初に生まれた; **first-class 1** adj (on boat, train) ittō (no) 一等(の); (on bullet train) gurīn-sha (no) グリーン車(の); (on airplane) fāsuto kurasu (no) ファーストクラス(の); (very *good*) ichiryū (no) 一流(の) **2** *adv* (*on boat, train*) ittō de 一等で; (*on bullet train*) gurīn de グリーンで; (*on airplane*) fāsuto kurasu de ファーストクラスで; **first floor** ikkai 一階; **firsthand** *adj* chokusetsu (no) 直接(の)

firstly mazu saisho ni まず最初に

first name namae 名前

first-rate ichiryū (no) 一流(の)

fiscal kaikei-jō (no) 会計上(の)

fish 1 *n* sakana 魚 **2** *v/i* tsuri o suru 釣りをする

fishbone sakana no hone 魚の骨

fisherman ryōshi 漁師

fishing tsuri 釣り

fishing boat gyosen 漁船; **fishing line** tsuri-ito 釣り糸; **fishing rod** tsuri-zao 釣りざお

fishmonger sakana-ya 魚屋

fish stick sakana no furai 魚のフライ

fishy F (*suspicious*) ayashii 怪しい

fist kobushi こぶし

fit¹ *n* MED hossa 発作; **a ~ of rage / jealousy** totsuzen no ikari / shitto 突然の怒り/しっと

fit² *adj* (*physically*) chōshi ga yoi 調子がよい; (*morally*) fusawashii ふさわしい; **keep ~** karada no chōshi o iji suru 体の調子を維持する

fit³ 1 *v/t* (*of clothes*) ... ni au ...に合う; (*attach*) tsukeru 付ける **2** *v/i* (*of clothes*) au 合う; (*of piece of furniture etc*) hairu 入る **3** *n*: **it is a good ~** pittari da ぴったりだ; **it's a tight ~** kitchiri da きっちりだ

♦ **fit in** (*of person in group*) tokekomu 溶け込む; **it fits in with our plans** watashitachi no keikaku ni umaku au 私達の計画にうまく合う

fitful *sleep* togiretogire (no) 途切れ途切れ(の)

fitness (*physical*) kenkō 健康

fitness center fittonesu kurabu フィットネスクラブ

fitted kitchen shisutemu kitchin システムキッチン

fitter *n* kumitatekō 組み立て工

fitting *adj* fusawashii ふさわしい

fittings setsubi 設備

five go 五; (*with count word 'tsu'*) itsutsu 五つ

fix 1 *n* F (*solution*) kaiketsu-hō 解決法; **be in a ~** F komatte iru 困っている **2** *v/t* (*attach*) toritsukeru 取り付ける; (*repair*) shūri suru 修理する; *meeting etc* tehai suru 手配する; *lunch* tsukuru 作る; *boxing match etc* yaochō o shikumu 八百長を仕組む; **~ X onto Y** X o Y ni toritsukeru XをYに取り付ける; **I'll ~ you a drink** watashi ga nomimono o tsukurimasu 私が飲み物を作ります

♦ **fix up** *meeting* ... o tehai suru ...を手配する; **it's all fixed up** zenbu tehai sarete imasu 全部手配されています

fixed (*in one position*) kotei shita 固定した; *timescale, exchange rate* kimatta 決まった

fixture (*in room*) setsubi 設備; SP shiai 試合

flab (*on body*) tarumi たるみ

flabbergast: **be ~ed** F gyōten suru 仰天する

flabby *muscles, stomach* tarunda たるんだ

flag¹ *n* hata 旗

flag² *v/i* (*tire*) yowaru 弱る

flair (*talent*) sainō 才能; **have a natural ~ for** ... no tenpu no sainō ga aru ...の天賦の才能がある

flake *n* usui kakera 薄いかけら; (*of snow*) ippen 一片

♦ **flake off** *v/i* hageochiru はげ落ちる

flaky *adj* *skin, paint* hageochi-yasui はげ落ちやすい

flaky pastry sō ni natta pesutorī 層になったペストリー

flamboyant *person* daitan (na) 大胆(な); *design* hade (na) 派手(な)

flame *n* honō ほのお

flammable kanensei (no) 可燃性(の)

flan pai パイ

flank **1** *n* (*of horse etc*) wakibara わき腹; MIL sokumen 側面 **2** *v/t*: **be ~ed by** ... ni hasamarete iru ...に挟まれている

flap 1 n (of envelope, pocket) futa ふた; (of table) tareita 垂れ板; **be in a ~** F kōfun shite iru 興奮している **2** v/t wings habataku 羽ばたく **3** v/i (of flag etc) hatameku はためく; F (panic) urotaeru うろたえる

flare n (distress signal) hatsuentō 発煙筒; (in dress) furea フレアー

♦ **flare up** (of violence) boppatsu suru ぼっ発する; (of illness, rash) hassei suru 発生する; (of fire) moeagaru 燃え上がる; (get very angry) okoridasu 怒り出す

flash 1 n (of light) senkō せん光; PHOT furasshu フラッシュ; **in a ~** F atto iu ma ni あっという間に; **a ~ of inspiration** hirameku ひらめく; **~ of lightning** inabikari いなびかり **2** v/i (of light) patto hikaru ぱっとひかる **3** v/t headlights tenmetsu saseru 点滅させる

flashback n (in movie) furasshu-bakku フラッシュバック

flashbulb furasshu no denkyū フラッシュの電球

flasher MOT jidō-tenmetsu-sōchi 自動点滅装置

flashlight kaichū-dentō 懐中電灯

flashy pej kebakebashii けばけばしい

flask mahōbin 魔法びん

flat 1 adj surface, land taira (na) 平ら(な); beer ki no nuketa 気の抜けた; battery kireta パンクした; tire panku shita パンクした; shoes hīru no nai ヒールのない; sound, tone tanchō (na) 単調(な); **and that's ~!** F zettai dakara ne 絶対だからね **2** adv MUS han'on sagete 半音さげて; **~ out** work, run, drive zensokuryoku de 全速力で

flat-chested mune no chiisai 胸の小さい

flat rate kin'itsu-ryōkin 均一料金

flatten v/t land, road taira ni suru 平らにする; (by bombing, demolition) hakai suru 破壊する

♦ **flatten out** v/i (of land) taira ni naru 平らになる

flatter v/t ... ni oseji o iu ...にお世辞を言う

flattering comments oseji (no) お世辞(の); color, clothes niau 似合う

flattery oseji お世辞

flavor 1 n fūmi 風味 **2** v/t food ajitsuke suru 味付けする

flavoring n chōmiryō 調味料

flaw n (in glass, design) kizu 傷; (in system, plan etc) ketten 欠点

flawless kanpeki (na) 完璧(な)

flea nomi のみ

flee v/i nigeru 逃げる

fleet n NAUT kansen 艦船; **a ~ of ...** (of taxis, trucks) ... no ichidan ...の一団

fleeting visit etc tsuka no ma (no) つかのま(の); **catch a ~ glimpse of** chirari ni miru ちらりと見る

flesh niku 肉; (of fruit) kaniku 果肉; **meet / see a person in the ~** jitsubutsu ni au 実物に会う

flex v/t muscles magenobashi suru 曲げ伸ばしする

flexible jūnan (na) 柔軟(な); **I'm quite ~** watashi wa yūzū ga kikimasu 私は融通が利きます

flick v/t tail hitofuri 一振り; **he ~ed a fly off his hand** kare wa hae no yubi de hajiita 彼ははえを指ではじいた; **she ~ed her hair out of her eyes** kanojo wa kami no ke ga me ni kakaranai yō ni haratta 彼女は髪の毛が目にかからない様にはらった

♦ **flick through** book, magazine parapara to pēji o mekuru ぱらぱらとページをめくる

flicker v/i (of light, candle, screen) chirachira suru ちらちらする

flies (on pants) zubon no chakku ズボンのチャック

flight (in airplane) bin 便; (flying) hikō 飛行; (escape) tōbō 逃亡; **~ of stairs** hitonobori no kaidan ひと上りの階段

flight crew jōmuin 乗務員; **flight deck** sōjū-shitsu 操縦室; **flight number** binmei 便名; **flight path** hikō-keiro 飛行経路; **flight recorder** furaito-rekōdā フライトレコーダー; **flight time** (departure) shuppatsu-jikoku 出発時刻; (duration) hikō-jikan 飛行時間

flighty karui 軽い

flimsy *structure, furniture* chachi (na) ちゃち(な); *dress, material* usui 薄い; *excuse* osomatsu (na) お粗末(な)

flinch shirigomi suru しりごみする

fling *v/t* hōridasu ほうり出す; *she flung herself into his arms* kanojo wa kare no ude no naka ni tobikonda 彼女は彼の腕のなかに飛び込んだ; *~ oneself into a chair* isu ni dosun to suwaru いすにどすんと座る

♦ **flip through** *book, magazine* parapara to pēji o mekuru ぱらぱらとページをめくる

flipper (*for swimming*) ashihire 足ひれ

flirt 1 *v/i* kobiru こびる **2** *n* (*male*) purei-bōi プレイボーイ; (*female*) purei-gāru プレイガール

flirtatious ki o hiku yō (na) 気を引くよう(な)

float *v/i* uku 浮く; FIN (*of currency*) hendō suru 変動する

flock *n* (*of sheep*) mure 群れ

flog *v/t* (*whip*) muchiutsu むち打つ

flood 1 *n* kōzui 洪水 **2** *v/t* (*of river*) hanran saseru はんらんさせる; *~ its banks* (*of river*) kishi o hanran saseru 岸をはんらんさせる

flooding kōzui 洪水

floodlight *n* tōkō-shōmei 投光照明, furaddo-raito フラッドライト

floor *n* (*of room*) yuka 床, furoa フロア; (*story*) kai 階

floorboard yukaita 床板; **floor cloth** yukayō zōkin 床用雑巾; **floor lamp** furoarampu フロアランプ

flop 1 *v/i* dasatto taorekomu どさっと倒れ込む; F (*fail*) shippai suru 失敗する **2** *n* F (*failure*) shippai 失敗

floppy *adj* (*not stiff*) tarete iru 垂れている; (*weak*) darui だるい

floppy (*disk*) furoppī-disuku フロッピーディスク

florist hana-ya 花屋

flour komugiko 小麦粉

flourish *v/i* han'ei suru 繁栄する

flourishing *business, trade* sakan (na) 盛ん(な)

flow 1 *v/i* (*of river, current, traffic*) nagareru 流れる; (*of work*) susumu 進む **2** *n* (*of river, ideas*) nagare 流れ

flowchart furōchāto フローチャート

flower 1 *n* hana 花 **2** *v/i* hana ga saku 花が咲く

flower arrangement ikebana 生け花; **flowerbed** kadan 花壇; **flowerpot** uekibachi 植木鉢

flowery *pattern* hanamoyō (no) 花模様(の); *style of writing* ōgesa (na) 大げさ(な)

flu infuruenza インフルエンザ

fluctuate *v/i* hendō suru 変動する

fluctuation hendō 変動

fluency (*in a language*) ryūchō-sa 流ちょうさ

fluent *adj* ryūchō (na) 流ちょう(な); *he speaks ~ Japanese* kare wa Nihon-go o ryūchō ni hanasu 彼は日本語を流ちょうに話す

fluently ryūchō ni 流ちょうに

fluff: *a bit of ~* (*material*) chotto shita keba ちょっとした毛羽

fluffy *adj material, hair* fuwatto shita ふわっとした; *clouds* fuwafuwa shita ふわふわした; *~ toy* nuigurumi ぬいぐるみ

fluid *n* ryūdōtai 流動体

flunk *v/t* F *subject* shippai suru 失敗する

fluorescent keikō (no) 蛍光(の)

flush 1 *v/t toilet* nagasu 流す; *~ ... down the toilet* ...o toire ni nagasu ...をトイレに流す **2** *v/i* (*of toilet*) nagareru 流れる; (*go red*) akaku naru 赤くなる **3** *adj* (*level*) ... to onaji takasa (no) ...と同じ高さ(の); *be ~ with...* ... to onaji takasa de aru ...と同じ高さである

♦ **flush away** *v/i* (*down toilet*) nagasu 流す

♦ **flush out** *rebels etc* ... o tatakidasu ...をたたき出す

fluster *v/t* menkurawaseru めんくらわせる; *get ~ed* urotaeru うろたえる

flute furūto フルート, yokobue 横笛

flutter *v/i* (*of bird, wings*) habataki suru 羽ばたきする; (*of flag*) hatameku はためく; (of heart) dokidoki suru どきどきする

fly[1] n (insect) hae ハエ

fly[2] n (on pants) zubon no chakku ズボンのチャック

fly[3] 1 v/i (of bird, airplane) tobu 飛ぶ; (in airplane) hikōki de iku 飛行機で行く; (of flag) agaru 揚がる; (rush) tonde iku 飛んでいく; ~ into a rage gekido suru 激怒する 2 v/t airplane sōjū suru 操縦する; airline ... de ryokō suru ...で旅行する; (transport by air) kūyu suru 空輸する

♦ **fly away** (of bird, airplane) tonde iku 飛んで行く

♦ **fly back** v/i (travel back) tonde kaeru 飛んで帰る

♦ **fly in 1** v/i (of airplane, passengers) tonde kuru 飛んで来る 2 v/t supplies etc ... o hikōki de hakobu ...を飛行機で運ぶ

♦ **fly off** (of hat etc) tonde iku 飛んでいく

♦ **fly out 1** v/i hikōki de iku 飛行機で行く 2 v/t ... o hikōki de hakobu ...を飛行機で運ぶ

♦ **fly past** (in formation) parēdo-hikō o suru パレード飛行をする; (of time) tobu yō ni sugiru 飛ぶようすぎる

flying n hikōki de ryokō suru koto 飛行機で旅行する事

foam n (on liquid) awa 泡

foam rubber kihō-gomu 気泡ゴム

FOB (= free on board) tsumikomi-watashi 積み込み渡し

focus n (of attention) chūshin 中心; PHOT pinto ピント; be the ~ of attention chūmoku no mato ni naru 注目の的になる; be in ~ / out of ~ pinto ga atte iru / zurete iru ピントが合っている/ずれている

♦ **focus on** problem, issue ... no shōten o shiboru ...の焦点を絞る; PHOT ...ni pinto o awaseru ...にピントを合わせる

fodder n shiryō 飼料

fog kiri 霧

foggy adj kiri no tachikometa 霧の立ち込めた

foil[1] n (silver - etc) hoiru ホイル

foil[2] v/t (thwart) ura o kaku 裏をかく

fold 1 v/t paper etc oritatamu 折りたたむ; ~ one's arms udegumi o suru 腕組みをする 2 v/i (of business) tsubureru つぶれる 3 n (in cloth etc) orime 折り目

♦ **fold up 1** v/t ... o oritatamu ...を折りたたむ 2 v/i (of chair, table) oritatameru 折りたためる

folder (for documents) fairu ファイル; COMPUT foruda フォルダ

folding oritatami-shiki (no) 折りたたみ式(の); ~ chair oritatami-isu 折りたたみ椅子

foliage ha 葉

folk (people) hitobito 人々; my ~ (family) watashi no shinseki 私の親せき; come in, ~s F minna みんな

folk dance fōku-dansu フォークダンス; **folk music** fōku-myūjikku フォークミュージック, minzoku-ongaku 民俗音楽; **folk singer** fōku-shingā フォークシンガー; (Japanese-style) min'yō-kashu 民謡歌手; **folk song** fōku-songu フォークソング; (Japanese-style) min'yō 民謡

follow 1 v/t person ato ni tsuite iku 後について行く; road ... ni sotte iku ...に沿って行く; guidelines, instructions ... ni shitagau ...に従う; TV series, news tsuzukete miru 続けて見る; (understand) rikai suru 理解する; ~ me watashi ni tsuite kinasai 私についてきなさい 2 v/i tsuite iku ついていく; (logically) ... to naru ...となる; it ~s from this that ... kono kekka kara ...to iu koto ni naru この結果から...ということになる; as ~s tsugi no tōri 次のとおり

♦ **follow up** v/t letter, inquiry ... o forō suru ...をフォローする

follower shinpō-sha 信奉者; (of politician) shiji-sha 支持者; (of team, TV program) fan ファン

following 1 adj tsugi (no) 次(の) 2 n (people) shiji-sha 支持者; the ~ ika no koto 以下の事

follow-up meeting hikitsuzuki no

mītingu 引き続きのミーティング

follow-up visit (*to doctor etc*) saido no hōmon 再度の訪問

folly (*madness*) oroka-sa 愚かさ

fond (*loving*) yasashii 優しい; *memory* natsukashii 懐かしい; *be ~ of...* ... ga suki de aru ...が好きである

fondle kawaigaru かわいがる

fondness itsukushimi 慈しみ

font (*for printing*) fonto フォント

food tabemono 食べ物

food freak F gurume グルメ; **food mixer** dendō-awadateki 電動泡立て器; **food poisoning** shoku-chūdoku 食中毒

fool *n* baka 馬鹿; *make a ~ of oneself* waraimono ni naru 笑いものになる

♦**fool around** fuzakeru ふざける; (*sexually*) uwaki o suru 浮気をする

♦**fool around with** *knife, drill etc* ... de fuzakeru ...でふざける; (*sexually*) ... to uwaki o suru ...と浮気をする

foolish baka (na) 馬鹿(な)

foolproof machigaeyō no nai 間違えようのない

foot *n* ashi 足; (*measurement*) fīto フィート; *on ~* aruite 歩いて; *at the ~ of the page* pēji no shita no bubun ni ページの下の部分に; *at the ~ of the hill* oka no fumoto ni 丘のふもとに; *put one's ~ in it* F shikujiru しくじる

football amerikan-futtobōru アメリカンフットボール; (*soccer*) sakkā サッカー; (*ball*) bōru ボール; **football player** amefuto-senshu アメフト選手; (*soccer*) sakkā-senshu サッカー選手; **footbridge** hodōkyō 歩道橋; **foothills** yamasuso やますそ

footing (*basis*) taisei 体勢; *lose one's ~* ashi o fumihazusu 足を踏み外す; *be on the same/a different ~* onaji/chigau tachiba ni aru 同じ/違う立場にある; *be on a friendly ~ with ...* ... to shitashii ...と親しい

footlights futtoraito フットライト; **footnote** kyakuchū 脚注; **footpath** komichi 小道; (*in countryside*)

shizen-hodō 自然歩道; **footprint** ashiato 足跡; **footstep** ashioto 足音; *follow in X's ~s* X no kokorozashi o tsugu Xの志を継ぐ; **footwear** hakimono はきもの

for ◊ (*purpose, destination etc*) *a train ~ ...* ...yuki no ressha ...行きの列車; *clothes ~ children* kodomo yō no fuku 子供用の服; *it's too big ~ you* anata ni wa ōkisugiru あなたには大きすぎる; *here's a letter ~ you* anata ni tegami desu あなたに手紙です; *this is ~ you* kore wa anata ni desu これはあなたにです; *what is there ~ lunch?* ohiru wa nan desu ka お昼は何ですか; *the steak is ~ me* sutēki wa watashi desu ステーキは私です; *what is this ~?* kore wa nani ni tsukau no desu ka これは何に使うのですか; *what ~?* nan no tame ni 何のために ◊ (*time*): *~ three days/~ two hours* mikkakan/nijikan 三日間/二時間; *please get it done ~ Monday* getsuyōbi made ni shiagete kudasai 月曜日までに仕上げて下さい ◊ (*distance*): *I walked ~ a mile* ichi-mairu arukimashita 1マイル歩きました; *it stretches for a 100 miles* hyaku-mairu ni watatte iru 100マイルに渡っている ◊ (*in favor of*): *I am ~ the idea* watashi wa sono kangae ni sansei desu 私はその考えに賛成です ◊ (*instead of, in behalf of*): *let me do that ~ you* watashi ni yarasete kudasai 私にやらせて下さい; *we are agents ~ ...* watashitachi wa ... no dairinin desu 私達は...の代理人です ◊ (*in exchange for*): *I bought it ~ $25* nijūgo-doru de kaimashita 二十五ドルで買いました; *how much did you sell it ~* ikura de urimashita ka いくらで売りましたか

forbid kinjiru 禁じる; *~ X to do Y* X ni Y suru koto o kinjiru XにYすることを禁じる

forbidden *adj* kinjirareta 禁じられた; *smoking ~* kin'en 禁煙; *parking ~* chūsha-kinshi 駐車禁止

forbidding *rockface, prospect* kiken (na) 危険(な); *person* kowai 恐い

force 1 n (*violence*) bōryoku 暴力; (*of explosion, wind, punch*) chikara 力; **come into ~** jisshi sareru 実施される; **the ~s** MIL guntai 軍隊 **2** v/t *door, lock* kojiakeru こじ開ける; **~ X to do Y** X ni Y suru yō ni kyōsei suru Xに Yするように強制する;**~open** kojiakeru こじ開ける

forced (*strained*) murijii (no) 無理強い(の); *confession* kyōseiteki (na) 強制的(な); **~ smile** tsukuriwarai 作り笑い

forced landing fujichaku 不時着

forceful *argument* tsuyoi 強い; *speaker* settokuryoku no aru 説得力のある; *character* kyōretsu (na) 強烈(な)

forceps pinsetto ピンセット

forcible *entry* chikarazuku (no) 力ずく(の); *argument* kōkateki (na) 効果的(な)

ford n asase 浅瀬

fore: come to the ~ medatte kuru 目立ってくる

foreboding yokan 予感; **forecast 1** n yosō 予想; (*of weather*) yohō 予報 **2** v/t yosō suru 予想する; *weather* yohō suru 予報する; **forecourt** maeniwa 前庭; **forefathers** senzo 先祖; **forefinger** hitosashi-yubi 人差し指; **foregone: it's a ~ conclusion** sore wa sara ni mieta kekka desu それは目に見えた結果です; **foreground** zenkei 前景; **forehand** (*in tennis*) foahando フォアハンド; **forehead** hitai 額

foreign gaikoku (no) 外国(の)

foreign affairs gaimu 外務

foreign currency gaikoku-tsūka 外国通貨

foreigner gaikoku-jin 外国人; *pej* gaijin 外人

foreign exchange gaikoku-kawase 外国為替; **foreign language** gaikoku-go 外国語; **Foreign Office** *Br* Gaimu-shō 外務省; **foreign policy** gaikō-seisaku 外交政策; **Foreign Secretary** *Br* Gaimu-

daijin 外務大臣

foreman (*of jury*) baishinchō 陪審長; **foremost** ichiban (no) 一番(の); **forerunner** senku-sha 先駆者; **foresee** yosō suru 予想する; **foreseeable** yosoku dekiru 予測できる; **in the ~ future** chikai shōrai ni 近い将来に; **foresight** senken no mei 先見の明

forest mori 森

forestry ringyō 林業

foretaste maebure 前触れ

foretell yogen suru 予言する

forever eikyū ni 永久に

foreword maegaki 前書き

forfeit v/t *right etc* ushinau 失う

forge v/t (*counterfeit*) ... o gizō suru ...を偽造する

forger gizō-sha 偽造者

forgery (*bank bill*) gizō 偽造; (*document*) gizō-bunsho 偽造文書

forget wasureru 忘れる

forgetful wasureppoi 忘れっぽい

forget-me-not (*flower*) wasurenagusa わすれなぐさ

forgive v/t & v/i yurusu 許す

forgiveness yurushi 許し

fork n fōku フォーク; (*in road*) bunkiten 分岐点

♦ **fork out** v/i F (*pay*) harau 払う

forklift (**truck**) fōkurifuto フォークリフト

form 1 n (*shape*) katachi 形; (*type*) shurui 種類; (*document*) yōshi 用紙; **~ of address** hanashikata 話し方 **2** v/t (*in clay etc*) katachizukuru 形作る; *friendship* musubu 結ぶ; *opinion* matomeru まとめる; *past tense etc* tsukuru 作る **3** v/i (*take shape, develop*) katachi ni naru 形になる

formal seishiki (no) 正式(の); *recognition etc* kōshiki (no) 公式(の); **~ clothes** seisō 正装

formality keishiki 形式; **it's just a ~** keishiki dake no koto desu 形式だけの事です

formally *adv speak* seishiki ni 正式に; *recognized* kōshiki ni 公式に; *behave* katakurushiku 堅苦しく

format 1 v/t *diskette* fōmatto suru

フォーマットする, shokika suru 初期化する; *document* keishiki o totonoeru 形式を整える **2** n (*size: of magazine, paper etc*) saizu サイズ; (*make-up: of program*) teisai 体裁

formation (*act of forming*) kōsei 構成; (*of airplanes*) fōmēshon フォーメーション

formative zōkei (no) 造形(の); *in his ~ years* kare no jinkaku keiseiki ni 彼の人格形成期に

former izen (no) 以前(の); *the ~* mae no mono 前のもの

formerly izen wa 以前は

formidable osoroshii 恐ろしい

formula MATH, CHEM kōshiki 公式; (*for success etc*) hiketsu 秘訣; (*for baby*) konamiruku 粉ミルク

formulate amidasu 編み出す

fort MIL toride とりで

forth: *back and ~* ittari kitari shite 行ったり来たりして; *and so ~* nado など

forthcoming (*future*) kondo (no) 今度(の); *personality* sotchoku (na) 率直(な)

fortieth dai-yonjū (no) 第四十(の)

fortnight Br nishūkan 二週間

fortress MIL yōsai 要塞

fortunate kōun (na) 幸運(な)

fortunately kōun ni mo 好運にも

fortune kōun 好運; (*lot of money*) zaisan 財産; *it costs a ~ to live here* koko ni sumu ni wa totemo okane ga kakarimasu ここに住むにはとてもお金がかかります

fortune-teller uranaishi 占い師

forty yonjū 四十

forward 1 adv mae ni 前に **2** adj pej: *person* zūzūshii ずうずうしい **3** n SP fowādo フォワード **4** v/t *letter* tensō suru 転送する

forwarding agent COM unsō-gyōsha 運送業者

forward planning keikaku 計画

fossil kaseki 化石

foster child satogo 里子

foster parents satooya 里親

foul 1 n SP fauru ファウル **2** adj *smell, taste* fuketsu (na) 不潔(な);

weather warui 悪い **3** v/t SP hansoku suru 反則する

found v/t *school etc* sōritsu suru 創立する

foundation (*of theory etc*) kiso 基礎; (*organization*) zaidan 財団, kikin 基金; (*setting up*) setsuritsu 設立

foundations (*of house*) dodai 土台

founder n sōritsu-sha 創立者

foundry chūzō-kōjō 鋳造工場

fountain funsui 噴水

four yon 四, shi 四; (*with count word 'tsu'*) yottsu 四つ

four-star adj *hotel etc* yotsuboshi (no) 四つ星(の)

fourteen jūyon 十四

fourteenth dai-jūyon (no) 第十四(の)

fourth 1 adj dai-yon (no) 第四(の) **2** n (*of month*) yokka 四日

Fourth of May holiday Kokumin no kyūjitsu 国民の休日

fowl kakin 家禽

fox n kitsune きつね

fraction ichibu 一部; (*decimal*) bunsū 分数

fracture 1 n kossetsu 骨折 **2** v/t kossetsu suru 骨折する

fragile koware-yasui 壊れやすい

fragment hahen 破片

fragmentary danpenteki (na) 断片的(な)

fragrance ii kaori いい香り

fragrant kaori no ii 香りのいい

frail moroi もろい

frame 1 n (*of eyeglasses*) furēmu フレーム, fuchi 縁; (*of building, body*) honegumi 骨組み; (*of window*) waku 枠; (*of picture*) gaku 額; *~ of mind* kibun 気分 **2** v/t *picture* gakubuchi ni ireru 額縁に入れる; F *s.o.* wana ni kakeru わなにかける

framework honegumi 骨組, furēmu-wāku フレームワーク

France Furansu フランス

frank sotchoku (na) 率直(な)

frankly sotchoku ni 率直に; *~, it's not worth it* sotchoku ni itte sore wa suru kachi ga nai desu 率直に言ってそれはする価値がないです

frantic hankyōran (no) 半狂乱(の)
fraternal kyōdai (no) 兄弟(の)
fraud sagi 詐欺; (*person*) sagishi 詐欺師
fraudulent fusei (na) 不正(な)
frayed *cuffs* surikireru 擦り切れる
freak 1 *n* (*unusual event*) ijō 異常; (*two-headed person, animal etc*) kikei 奇形; F (*strange person*) henjin 変人; *movie* / *jazz* ~ F (*fanatic*) eiga / jazu mania 映画/ジャズマニア **2** *adj wind, storm etc* ijō (na) 異常(な)
freckle sobakasu そばかす
free 1 *adj* (*at liberty*) jiyū (na) 自由(な); (*no cost*) muryō (no) 無料(の); *room, table* aite iru 空いている; *are you ~ this afternoon?* kyō no gogo aite imasu ka 今日の午後空いていますか; *~ and easy* kutsuroida くつろいだ; *for ~* muryō de 無料で **2** *v/t prisoners* kaihō suru 解放する
freebie F keihin 景品
freedom jiyū 自由
freedom of the press hōdō no jiyū 報道の自由
free kick (*in soccer*) furī-kikku フリーキック; **freelance 1** *adj* furī (no) フリー(の) **2** *adv work* furī de フリーで; **freelancer** furī フリー; **free market economy** jiyū-keizai 自由経済; **free sample** muryō-sanpuru 無料サンプル; **free speech** genron no jiyū 言論の自由; **freeway** kōsoku-dōro 高速道路; **freewheel** *v/i* (*on bicycle*) dasei de hashiru 惰性で走る
freeze 1 *v/t food, river* kōraseru 凍らせる; *wages, bank account* tōketsu suru 凍結する; *video seishi* suru 静止する **2** *v/i* (*of water*) kōru 凍る; (*of weather*) hieru 冷える
♦**freeze over** kōru 凍る
freezer reitōko 冷凍庫
freezing 1 *adj* kōru yō (na) 凍るよう(な); *it's ~ out here* soto wa sugoku hiete imasu 外はすごく冷えています; *it's ~* (*cold*) (*of weather, water*) sugoku samui

desu すごく寒いです; *I'm ~* (*cold*) karada ga sukkari hiete imasu 体がすっかり冷えています **2** *n* sesshi-reido 摂氏零度; *10 degrees below ~* hyōtenka-jūdo 氷点下十度
freezing compartment reitōko 冷凍庫
freezing point hyōten 氷点
freight *n* kamotsu 貨物; (*costs*) unsō-ryō 運送料
freight car (*on train*) kasha 貨車
freighter (*ship*) kamotsu-sen 貨物船; (*airplane*) kamotsu-ki 貨物機
freight train kamotsu-ressha 貨物列車

French 1 *adj* Furansu (no) フランス(の) **2** *n* (*language*) Furansu-go フランス語; *the ~* Furansu-jin フランス人
French doors furansu-mado フランス窓; **French fries** furenchi-furai フレンチフライ; **Frenchman** Furansu-jin dansei フランス人男性; **Frenchwoman** Fransu-jin josei フランス人女性
frequency hindo 頻度; RAD shūhasū 周波数
frequent[1] *adj* hinpan (na) 頻繁(な)
frequent[2] *v/t yoku iku* よく行く; *bar* kayō 通う
frequently shibashiba しばしば
fresh *fruit, meat etc* shinsen (na) 新鮮(な); (*cool*) sawayaka (na) さわやか(な); (*cold*) samui 寒い; (*new*) atarashii 新しい; (*impertinent*) namaiki (na) 生意気(な)
♦**freshen up 1** *v/i* sappari suru さっぱりする **2** *v/t room , paintwork …* o moyōgae suru …を模様替えする
freshman shinnyūsei 新入生
freshness (*of fruit, meat*) shinsen-sa 新鮮さ; (*of style, approach*) atarashi-sa 新しさ; (*of weather: coolness*) sawayaka-sa さわやかさ; (*coldness*) samu-sa 寒さ
freshwater *adj* mamizu 真水, tansui 淡水
fret *v/i* kuyokuyo nayamu くよくよ悩む
friction PHYS masatsu 摩擦; (*between people*) fuwa 不和

friction tape zetsuen-tēpu 絶縁テープ

Friday kin'yōbi 金曜日

fridge reizōko 冷蔵庫

friend tomodachi 友達; **make ~s** (of one person) tomodachi ga dekiru 友達ができる; (of two people) tomodachi ni naru 友達になる; **make ~s with** ... to shitashiku naru ...と親しくなる

friendly adj atmosphere, meeting yūkōteki (na) 友好的(な); restaurant igokochi no ii 居心地のいい; person hitonatsukoi 人なつこい; (easy to use) tsukai-yasui 使いやすい; **be ~ with** ... to shitashii ...と親しい

friendship yūjō 友情

fries furenchi-furai フレンチフライ

fright: **give ... a ~** ... o odorokasu ... を驚かす

frighten v/t kowagaraseru 怖がらせる; **be ~ed** obieta おびえた; **don't be ~ed** kowagaranaide 怖がらないで; **be ~ed of** ... o kowagaru ...を怖がる

frightening osoroshii 恐ろしい

frigid (sexually) fukanshō (na) 不感症(の)

frill (on dress etc) furiru フリル; (extra) yokei na mono 余計な物

fringe (on tablecloth, curtains etc) heri ヘリ; (in hair) maegami 前髪; (edge) hazure はずれ

frisk v/t ... no bodīchekku o suru ... のボディーチェックをする

frisky puppy genki (na) 元気 (な)

♦ **fritter away** time, fortune ... o rōhi suru ...を浪費する

frivolous person karui 軽い; pleasures kudaranai 下らない

frizzy hair chijireta 縮れた

frog kaeru かえる

frogman daibā ダイバー

from ◊ (in time): **~ 9 to 5 (o'clock)** kuji kara goji made 九時から五時まで; **~ the 18th century** jūhasseiki kara 十八世紀から; **~ today (on)** kyō kara 今日から; **~ next Tuesday** tsugi no kayōbi kara 次の火曜日から ◊ (in space):

~ here to there koko kara soko made ここからそこまで; **we drove here ~ Tokyo** watashitachi wa Tōkyō kara koko made kuruma de kita 私達は東京からここまで車で来た ◊ (origin): **a letter ~ Jo** jō kara no tegami ジョーからの手紙; **a gift ~ the management** keieijin kara no okurimono 経営陣からの贈り物; **it doesn't say who it's ~** dare kara kita no ka kaite inai それから来たのか書いていない; **I am ~ New Jersey** watashi wa Nyūjājī no shusshin desu 私はニュージャージーの出身です; **made ~ bananas** banana de tsukurarete iru バナナで作られている ◊ (because of): **tired ~ the journey** tabi de tsukarete iru 旅で疲れている; **it's ~ overeating** tabesugi kara kite iru 食べ過ぎから来ている

front 1 n (of building, book) shōmen 正面; (of piece of paper) omote 表; (of car) zenbu 前部; (cover organization) omotemuki 表向き; MIL senchi 戦地; (of weather) zensen 前線; **in ~** mae ni 前に; (in a race) rīdo shite リードして; **in ~ of** ... no mae no ...の前の; **at the ~** mae no hō ni 前の方に; **at the ~ of** ... no zenbu ni ...の前部に **2** adj wheel, seat mae (no) 前(の) **3** v/t TV program shikai o suru 司会をする

front cover hyōshi 表紙; **front door** genkan 玄関; **front entrance** shōmen-iriguchi 正面入り口

frontier kokkyō 国境; fig (of science) saisentan 最先端; (of knowledge) genkai 限界

front page (of newspaper) ichimen 一面; **front page news** ichimen no nyūsu 一面のニュース; **front row** saizenretsu 最前列; **front seat passenger** (in car) zenbu zaseki no jōkyaku 前部座席の乗客; **front-wheel drive** zenrin-kudō 前輪駆動

frost shimo 霜

frostbite tōshō 凍傷

frostbitten tōshō ni kakatta 凍傷にかかった

frosted glass suri-garasu すりガラス

frosting (on cake) aishingu アイシング

frosty weather shimo no orita 霜の降りた; welcome tsumetai 冷たい

froth awa 泡

frothy cream etc awa no yō (no) 泡のよう(な)

frown 1 n shikamettsura しかめっ面 **2** v/i kao o shikameru 顔をしかめる

frozen feet etc kogoeta 凍えた; wastes of Siberia kōtta 凍った; food reitō (no) 冷凍(の); I'm ~ F sugoku hiete iru すごく冷えている

frozen food reitō-shokuhin 冷凍食品

fruit kudamono 果物, furūtsu フルーツ

fruitful talks minori aru 実りある

fruit juice furūtsu-jūsu フルーツジュース

fruit salad furūtsu-sarada フルーツサラダ

frustrate v/t person yokkyū-fuman ni saseru 欲求不満にさせる; plans zasetsu saseru ざ折させる

frustrated look, sigh yokkyū-fuman (no) 欲求不満(の)

frustrating iraira suru いらいらする

frustratingly slow, hard iraira saseru hodo いらいらさせるほど

frustration yokkyū-fuman 欲求不満; sexual ~ seiteki-yokkyūfuman 性的欲求不満; the ~s of modern life kindaiteki na kurashi o naka no yokkyū-fuman 近代的な暮らしの中の欲求不満; a look of ~ shitsubō no kao 失望の顔

fry v/t (shallow-~) yaku 焼く; (stir-~) itameru 炒める; (deep-~) ageru 揚げる

fried egg medamayaki 目玉焼き

fried potatoes poteto-furai ポテトフライ

frying pan furaipan フライパン

fuck v/t V yaru やる; ~! kuso くそ; ~ him / ~ that! kare nante dō demo ii / sore wa dō demo ii 彼なんてどうでもいい / それはどうでもいい

♦**fuck off** V useru うせる; ~! jama shinaide じゃましないで

fucking V **1** adj kusoimaimashii くそいまいましい **2** adv kusoimaimashiku くそいまいましく; that's ~ stupid suggoku bakabakashii すっごくばかばかしい; that's ~ brilliant suggoku ii すっごくいい

fuel n nenryō 燃料

fugitive n tōbō-sha 逃亡者

fulfill v/t (carry out) hatasu 果たす; (satisfy) mitasu 満たす; feel ~ed (in job, life) mitasarete iru ki ga suru 満たされている気がする

fulfilling job jūjitsu shita 充実した

fulfillment (of contract etc) jitsugen 実現; (moral, spiritual) jūjitsu-kan 充実感

full bottle, hotel, bus, diskette ippai (no) いっぱい(の); account kanzen (na) 完全(な); life manzoku shita 満足した; schedule, day isogashii 忙しい; ~ of ... de ippai no ...で いっぱいの; ~ up hotel etc ippai no いっぱいの; (with food) onaka ga ippai no おなかがいっぱいの; pay in ~ zenbu harau 全部払う

full coverage (insurance) zengaku-hoshō 全額補償; **full-grown** sukkari otona ni natta すっかり大人になった; **full-length** dress rongu (no) ロング(の); mirror zenshin (no) 全身(の); movie katto shite inai カットしていない

full moon mangetsu 満月; **full stop** piriodo ピリオド, shūshifu 終止符; **full-time 1** adj job seishain (no) 正社員(の); teaching jōkin (no) 常勤(の); student seiki (no) 正規(の) **2** adv seishain de 正社員で; teach jōkin de 常勤で; study seiki ni 正規に

fully booked manpai ni 満杯に; recovered kanzen ni 完全に; understand jūbun ni 十分に

fumble v/t catch, job motatsuku もたつく

♦**fumble about** tesaguri suru 手探りする

fume: be fuming F (angry) kankan

ni natte iru かんかんになっている

fumes (*from car*) haiki-gasu 排気ガ
ス; (*from chemicals, machine*)
gasu ガス

fun tanoshimi 楽しみ; *it was great ~*
sore wa sugoku tanoshikatta それ
はすごく楽しかった; *bye, have ~!*
jā tanoshinde ne じゃあ楽しんで
ね; *for ~* omoshirohanbun ni omo
shiro hanbun に; *make ~ of* karakau か
らかう

function 1 n (*of machine part*) kinō
機能; (*of employee*) yakuwari 役割;
(*reception etc*) gyōji 行事 **2** v/i
hataraku 働く; *~ as ...* ... to shite
kinō suru ...として機能する

fund 1 n shikin 資金;
(*governmental*) kikin 基金 **2** v/t
project shikin o dasu 資金を出す

fundamental (*basic*) kisoteki (na)
基礎的(な); (*substantial*)
kihonteki (na) 基本的(な);
(*crucial*) jūyō (na) 重要(な)

fundamentally kihonteki ni 基本的に

funeral sōshiki 葬式

funeral home sōgijō 葬儀場

funfair yūenchi 遊園地

funicular (*railway*) kēburukā ケー
ブルカー

funnel n (*of ship*) jōgo じょうご

funnily (*oddly*) hen na fū ni へんな
風に; (*comically*) omoshiroku おも
しろく; *~ enough* okashi na koto ni
おかしなことに

funny (*comical*) okashi (na) おかし
(な); (*odd*) hen (na) へん(な)

fur kegawa 毛皮

furious (*angry*) gekido shite 激怒し
て; *at a ~ pace* mōretsu na hayasa
de 猛烈な速さで

furnace (*in building*) boirā ボイ
ラー; (*industrial*) ro 炉

furnish *room* sonaetsukeru 備え付け
る; (*supply*) kyōkyū suru 供給する

furniture kagu 家具; *a piece of ~*
kagu itten 家具一点

furry *animal* ke de ōwareta 毛で覆
われた

further 1 adj (*additional*) sore ijō
(no) それ以上(の); (*more distant*)
sara ni susunda さらに進んだ; *until*

~ notice otte tsūchi suru 追って通
知する; *have you anything ~ to
say?* mada nani ka iu koto ga
arimasu ka まだ何か言うことがあ
りますか **2** adv walk, drive motto
saki ni もっと先に; *~, I want to
say ...* kuwaete watashi wa ... to
iitai 加えて私は...と言いたい;
2 miles ~ (*on*) sara ni ni-mairu さ
らに二マイル **3** v/t cause etc
sokushin suru 促進する; *interests*
tsukisusumeru 突き進める

furthest 1 adj ichiban tōku (no) 一
番遠く(の) **2** adv ichiban tōku ni
一番遠くに

furtive *look* hisoka (na) ひそか(な)

fury (*anger*) gekido 激怒

fuse 1 n ELEC hyūzu ヒューズ **2** v/i
ELEC hyūzu ga tobu ヒューズが飛
ぶ **3** v/t ELEC ... no hyūzu o tobasu
...のヒューズを飛ばす

fusebox hyūzu-bokkusu ヒューズ
ボックス

fuselage kitai 機体

fuse wire hyūzu-sen ヒューズ線

fusion yūgō 融合

fuss n hitosawagi 一騒ぎ; fuhei 不
平; *make a ~* (*complain*) monku o
iu 文句を言う; (*behave in
exaggerated way*) ōsawagi o suru
大騒ぎをする; *make a ~ of* (*be very
attentive to*) ... o chiyahoya suru
...をちやほやする

fussy *person* urusai うるさい;
design etc korisugita 凝りすぎた;
be a ~ eater tabemono ni urusai
食べ物にうるさい

futile muda (na) 無駄(な)

futon futon ふとん

future n (*of person, company*)
shōrai 将来; (*of humanity, earth*)
mirai 未来; GRAM miraikei 未来形;
in ~ korekarasaki これから先

futures FIN sakimono-torihiki 先物
取引

futures market FIN sakimono-
torihiki-shijō 先物取引市場

futuristic *design* zen'eiteki (na) 前
衛的(な)

fuzzy *hair* kebadatta けばだった;
(*out of focus*) boyaketa ぼやけた

G

gadget kigu 器具

gag 1 *n* sarugutsuwa 猿ぐつわ; (*joke*) gyagu ギャグ **2** *v/t person* sarugutsuwa o kamaseru 猿ぐつわをかませる; *the press* damaraseru 黙らせる

gain *v/t* (*acquire*) eru 得る; ~ *speed* sokudo o masu 速度を増す; ~ *10 pounds* juppondo fueru 十ポンド増える

gale kyōfū 強風

gall bladder tannō 胆のう

gallery (*for art*) bijutsukan 美術館; (*art dealer's shop*) garō 画廊; (*in theater*) tenjō-sajiki 天井桟敷

galley (*on ship*) chōrishitsu 調理室

gallon garon ガロン; ~*s of tea* tairyō no kōcha 大量の紅茶

gallop *v/i* gyaroppu ギャロップ

gallows kōshudai 絞首台

gallstone tanseki 胆石

gamble gyanburu ギャンブル, kakegoto 賭けごと

gambler bakuchiuchi ばくち打ち

gambling gyanburu ギャンブル, kakegoto 賭けごと

game *n* SP shiai 試合; (*child's*) asobi 遊び; (*in tennis*) gēmu ゲーム

gang ichimi 一味

gangster yakuza やくざ

♦ **gang up on** guru ni natte ... ijimeru ぐるになって...をいじめる

gangway tarappu タラップ

gap (*in teeth, clouds*) sukima すきま; (*between rich and poor etc, in time*) hedatari 隔たり; (*on the market*) zure ずれ

gape *v/i* (*of person*) pokan to kuchi o akete mitoreru ぽかんと口を開けて見とれる; (*of hole*) ōkiku hiraku 大きく開く

♦ **gape at** pokan to kuchi o akete ... ni mitoreru ぽかんと口を開けて...に見とれる

gaping *hole* ōkiku hiraita 大きく開いた

garage (*for parking*) shako 車庫; garēji ガレージ; (*for repairs*) shūri-kōjō 修理工場; *Br* (*for gas*) gasorin-sutando ガソリンスタンド

garbage gomi ごみ; *fig* (*nonsense*) tawagoto たわごと; (*poor quality item*) dekisokonai 出来そこない

garbage can gomi-baketsu ごみバケツ

garden niwa 庭; *Japanese ~* Nihonteien 日本庭園

gardener engei-ka 園芸家; (*professional*) niwashi 庭師

gardening engei 園芸, gādeningu ガーデニング

gargle *v/i* ugai o suru うがいをする

garish kebakebashii けばけばしい

garland *n* hanawa 花輪

garlic ninniku にんにく

garment ifuku 衣服

garnish *v/t* kazaru 飾る

garrison *n* (*place*) chūtonchi 駐屯地; (*troops*) shubitai 守備隊

garter gātā ガーター

gas *n* kitai 気体; (*gasoline*) gasorin ガソリン

gash *n* fukai kizu 深い傷

gasket gasuketto ガスケット

gasoline gasorin ガソリン

gas pump kyūyu-ponpu 給油ポンプ

gasp *v/i* iki o nomu 息をのむ; ~ *for breath* ikigire ga suru 息切れがする

gas pedal akuseru アクセル; **gas station** gasorin-sutando ガソリンスタンド; **gas works** gasu-kōjō ガス工場

gate mon 門; (*at airport*) gēto ゲート

gatecrash ... ni oshikakeru ...に押しかける

gateway iriguchi 入り口; *fig* michi 道

gather *v/t facts, information*

atsumeru 集める; (*understand*) suisoku suru 推測する; *I ~ that ...* ... da to omou ...だと思う; *~ speed* supīdo o masu スピードを増す

♦ **gather up** *possessions* yoseatsumeru 寄せ集める

gathering (*group of people*) atsumari 集まり

gaudy kebakebashii けばけばしい

gauge 1 *n* keiki 計器 **2** *v/t* sokutei suru 測定する

gaunt yasekoketa やせこけた

gauze gāze ガーゼ

gay 1 *n* homo ホモ **2** *adj* homo (no) ホモ(の)

gaze 1 *n* shisen 視線 **2** *v/i* mitsumeru 見つめる

♦ **gaze at** ... o jitto mitsumeru ...を じっと見つめる

GB (= *Great Britain*) Eikoku 英国

GDP (= *gross domestic product*) kokunai-sōseisan 国内総生産

gear *n* (*equipment*) sōbi 装備; (*in vehicles*) gia ギア

gear lever, gear shift hensoku-rebā 変速レバー

geisha geisha 芸者

gel (*for hair*) jeru ジェル; (*for shower*) bodīsōpu ボディーソープ

gem hōseki 宝石; *fig* (*book etc*) ippin 逸品; (*person*) kichō na hito 貴重な人

gender sei 性

gene idenshi 遺伝子; *it's in his ~s* kare no chi da 彼の血だ

general 1 *n* (*in army*) shōgun 将軍; *in ~* ippan ni 一般に **2** *adj* (*overall, miscellaneous*) ippanteki (na) 一般的(の); (*widespread*) zentaiteki (na) 全体的(な)

general election sōsenkyo 総選挙

generalization ippanka 一般化; *that's a ~* sore wa ippanron desu それは一般論です

generalize ippanka suru 一般化する

generally ippanteki ni 一般的に

generate (*create*) umidasu 生み出す; (*in linguistics*) seisei suru 生成する; *feeling* hikiokosu 引き起こす; *~ electricity* hatsuden suru 発電する

generation sedai 世代

generation gap sedai no danzetsu 世代の断絶

generator hatsudenki 発電機

generosity kimae no yosa 気前のよさ

generous (*with money*) kimae no yoi 気前のよい; (*not too critical*) kandai (na) 寛大(な); *portion etc* takusan (no) たくさん(の)

genetic idenshi (no) 遺伝子(の)

genetically idenshiteki ni 遺伝子的に

genetic engineering idenshi-kōgaku 遺伝子工学

genetic fingerprint idenshi-shimon 遺伝子指紋

geneticist idenshi-gakusha 遺伝子学者

genetics idenshi-gaku 遺伝子学

genial *person, company* shinsetsu (na) 親切(な)

genitals seiki 性器

genius tensai 天才

gentle yasashii 優しい

gentleman shinshi 紳士

gents (*toilet*) dansei-yō toire 男性用トイレ

genuine shōshin-shōmei (no) 正真正銘(の); seijitsu (na) 誠実(な)

geographical chiriteki (na) 地理的(な)

geography (*of area*) chiri 地理; (*subject*) chiri-gaku 地理学

geological chishitsugaku (no) 地質学(の)

geologist chishitsu-gakusha 地質学者

geology (*of area*) chishitsu 地質; (*subject*) chishitsu-gaku 地質学

geometric(al) kikagakuteki (na) 幾何学的(な)

geometry kikagaku 幾何学

geriatric 1 *adj* rōnen-igaku (no) 老年医学(の) **2** *n* rōnen-igaku 老年医学

germ baikin ばい菌; (*of idea etc*) me 芽

German 1 *adj* Doitsu (no) ドイツ(の) **2** *n* (*person*) Doitsu-jin ドイツ人; (*language*) Doitsu-go ドイツ語

Germany Doitsu ドイツ

germ warfare saikin-sensō 細菌戦争

gesticulate miburi de hanasu 身ぶりで話す

gesture n miburi 身ぶり; (of friendship) shirushi 印

get 1 v/t (obtain) te ni ireru 手に入れる; (fetch) totte kuru 取ってくる; (receive: letter) uketoru 受け取る; (receive: knowledge, respect etc) eru 得る; (catch: bus, train etc) ... ni noru ...に乗る; (understand) wakaru わかる ◊ (become) ... ni naru ...になる; ~ worried/nervous shinpai/shinkeishitsu ni naru 心配/神経質になる ◊ (causative): ~ X repaired X o shūri shite morau Xを修理してもらう; ~ X to do Y X ni Y saseru XにYさせる; ~ one's hair cut ... no kami o kitte morau ...の髪を切ってもらう; ~ X ready X no junbi o suru Xの準備をする ◊ (have opportunity): I never got to meet her kanojo ni au kikai ga zenzen nakatta 彼女に会う機会が全然なかった; I didn't ~ to go there soko ni iku kikai ga nakatta そこに行く機会がなかった ◊ (possess): have got motte iru 持っている; she's got three of them kanojo wa mittsu motte iru 彼女は三つ持っている ◊ have got to (must): I have got to study/see him benkyōshinakereba/kare ni awanakereba naranai 勉強しなければ/彼に会わなければならない; I don't want to, but I've got to yaritaku nai kedo yaranakya やりたくないけどやらなきゃ ◊ v/i (arrive) ... ni tsuku ...に着く

♦ **get about** (travel) achikochi ryokō suru あちこち旅行する; (be mobile) ugokimawaru 動き回る

♦ **get along** (progress) yatte iku やっていく; (come to party etc) iku 行く; (with s.o.) nakayoku yatte iku 仲よくやっていく

♦ **get at** (criticize) ... o kenasu ...をけなす; (imply, mean) iō to suru 言おうとする

♦ **get away 1** v/i (leave) tachisaru 立ち去る **2** v/t: **get X away from Y** Y kara X o toriageru YからXを取り上げる

♦ **get away with** ... no batsu o ukenaide sumu ...の罰を受けないですむ

♦ **get back 1** v/i (return) modoru 戻る; **I'll ~ to you on that** ato de henji o suru 後で返事をする **2** v/t (obtain again) ... o torimodosu ...を取り戻す

♦ **get by** (pass) tōrinukeru 通り抜ける; (financially) nantoka yatte iku なんとかやっていく

♦ **get down 1** v/i (from ladder etc) oriru 降りる; (duck) mi o kagameru 身をかがめる **2** v/t (depress) ... o gakkuri saseru ...をがっくりさせる

♦ **get down to** (work) ... ni torikakaru ...に取りかかる; (real facts) ... ni tassuru ...に達する

♦ **get in 1** v/i (of train, plane) tōchaku suru 到着する; (come home) uchi ni kaeru 家に帰る; (to car) noru 乗る; **how did they ~?** (of thieves, snakes etc) dō yatte hairikonda no darō どうやって入り込んだのだろう **2** v/t (to suitcase etc) ... o naka ni ireru ...を中に入れる

♦ **get off 1** v/i (from bus etc) oriru 降りる; (finish work) owaru 終わる; (not be punished) manugareru 免れる **2** v/t (remove) ... o toru ...を取る; clothes, footgear ... o nugu ...を脱ぐ; ~ **the grass!** shibafu kara denasai 芝生から出なさい

♦ **get off with** Br (sexually) ... to ii naka ni naru ...といい仲になる; ~ **a small fine** shōgaku no bakkin de sumu 小額の罰金で済む

♦ **get on 1** v/i (to bike, bus, train) noru 乗る; (be friendly) umaku yatte iku うまくやっていく; (of time) tatsu たつ; (become old) toshi o toru 年をとる; (make progress) susumu 進む; **it's getting on** daibu jikan ga tatta だいぶ時間がたった; **he's getting on** kare wa mō toshi da 彼はもう年だ; **he's getting on for 50** kare wa mō sugu go-jū ni naru 彼はもうすぐ五十になる **2** *v/t* … ni noru …に乗る; **the bus / one's bike** basu / jitensha ni noru バス/自転車に乗る; **get one's hat on** bōshi o kaburu 帽子をかぶる; **I can't get these pants on** kono zubon wa hakenai このズボンははけない

♦ **get out 1** *v/i* (*from car etc*) deru 出る; (*from prison*) shussho suru 出所する; **~!** dete ike 出て行け; **let's ~ of here** koko o deyō ここを出よう; **I don't ~ much these days** watashi wa saikin amari gaishutsu shimasen 私は最近あまり外出しません **2** *v/t* nail, sth jammed … o torinozoku …を取り除く; stain … o toru …を取る; gun, pen … o nuku …を抜く

♦ **get over** fence, disappointment etc … o norikoeru …を乗り越える; lover etc … o wasureru …を忘れる

♦ **get over with: let's get it over with** sore o katazukete shimaō それを片付けてしまおう

♦ **get through** TELEC denwa ga tsūjiru 電話が通じる; (*make self understood*) wakaraseru わからせる

♦ **get to** (*reach*) … ni tsuku …に着く

♦ **get up 1** *v/i* (*in morning*) okiru 起きる; (*from chair etc*) tachiagaru 立ち上がる; (*of wind*) okoru 起こる **2** *v/t* hill … o noboru …を登る

getaway (*from robbery*) tōsō 逃走

getaway car tōsō-sha 逃走車

get-together shinbokukai 親睦会

ghastly (*horrible*) hidoi ひどい

gherkin kyūri no pikurusu きゅうりのピクルス

ghetto hinmingai 貧民街

ghost yūrei 幽霊

ghostly bukimi (na) 無気味(な)

giant 1 *n* kyojin 巨人 **2** *adj* kyodai (na) 巨大(な)

gibberish tawagoto たわごと

giblets tori no zōmotsu 鳥の臓物

giddiness memai めまい

giddy memai ga suru めまいがする

gift okurimono 贈り物, gifuto ギフト

gifted sainō no aru 才能のある

giftwrap okurimono yō no hōsō o suru 贈り物用の包装をする

gigabyte COMPUT gigabaito ギガバイト

gigantic kyodai (na) 巨大(な)

giggle 1 *v/i* kusukusu warau くすくす笑う **2** *n* kusukusuwarai くすくす笑い

gill (*of fish*) era えら

gilt *n* kinmekki 金めっき; **~s** FIN yūryō kabu 優良株

gimmick kozaiku 小細工

gin jin ジン; **~ and tonic** jintonikku ジントニック

ginger (*spice*) shōga しょうが; akage 赤毛

gingerbread shōga-iri bisuketto しょうが入りビスケット

gingerly shinchō ni 慎重に

gipsy jipushī ジプシー

giraffe kirin きりん

girder *n* tessei no hari 鉄製の梁

girl onna no ko 女の子

girlfriend (*of boy*) kanojo 彼女; (*of girl*) onnatomodachi 女友達

girl guide gārugaido ガールガイド

girlie magazine nūdo-zasshi ヌード雑誌

girl scout gārusukauto ガールスカウト

gist yōten 要点

give ataeru 与える; (*from viewpoint of the giver*) ageru あげる; (*from viewpoint of the receiver*) kureru くれる; present okuru 贈る; (*supply: electricity etc*) kyōkyū suru 供給する; **I can ~ you $5** go doru ageru koto ga dekiru 五ドルあげることができる; **can you ~ me $5?** go doru kureru 五ドルくれる; **~ her my love** kanojo ni yoroshiku 彼女によろしく◊; **~ a groan** umeku うめく; **~ a talk** hanashi o suru 話をする; **~ a lecture** kōgi o okonau 講義を行なう; **~ a cry** nakigoe o ageru 泣き声をあげる

♦ **give away** (*as present*) … o hito ni ageru …を人にあげる; (*betray*) … o barasu …をばらす; **give oneself** *away* shōtai o arawasu 正体を現わす

♦**give back** ... o kaesu ...を返す

♦**give in 1** *v/i* (*surrender*) kōsan suru 降参する **2** *v/t* (*hand in*) ... o watasu ...を渡す

♦**give off** *smell, fumes* ... o hassuru ...を発する

♦**give onto** (*open onto*) ... ni tsūjiru ...に通じる

♦**give out 1** *v/t leaflets etc* ... o kubaru ...を配る **2** *v/i* (*of supplies, strength*) nakunaru なくなる

♦**give up 1** *v/t smoking etc* ... o yameru ...をやめる; *give oneself up to the police* keisatsu e jishu suru 警察へ自首する **2** *v/i* (*cease habit*) yameru やめる; (*stop trying*) akirameru あきらめる

♦**give way** (*of bridge etc*) kuzureru 崩れる

given name namae 名前
glacier hyōga 氷河
glad ureshii うれしい
gladly yorokonde 喜んで
glamor miryoku 魅力
glamorous miryokuteki (na) 魅力的(な)
glance *v/i* chiratto miru ちらっと見る; *~ at* ... o chiratto miru ...をちらっと見る
gland sen 腺
glandular fever sennetsu 腺熱
glare 1 *n* (*of sun, headlights*) giragira suru hikari ぎらぎらする光 **2** *v/i* (*of sun, headlights*) giragira hikaru ぎらぎら光る
♦**glare at** ... o niramu ...をにらむ
glaring *adj mistake* meihaku (na) 明白(な)
glass (*material*) garasu ガラス; (*for drink*) koppu コップ
glasses megane 眼鏡
glaze *n* uwagusuri 上薬
♦**glaze over** (*of eyes*) kasumu かすむ
glazed *expression* don'yori shita どんよりした
glazier garasu-ya ガラス屋
glazing mado-garasu 窓ガラス
gleam 1 *n* honoka na hikari ほのか

な光 **2** *v/i* hikaru 光る
glee ōyorokobi 大喜び
gleeful ōyorokobi (no) 大喜び(の)
glib uwabe dake (no) うわべだけ(の)
glide *v/i* suberu 滑る
glider guraidā グライダー
gliding *n* (*sport*) guraidā-hikō グライダー飛行
glimmer 1 *n* (*of light*) kasuka na hikari かすかな光; *~ of hope* kasuka na kibō no hikari かすかな希望の光 **2** *v/i* kasuka ni hikaru かすかに光る
glimpse 1 *n* hitome ひと目 **2** *v/t* chirari to hitome miru ちらりとひと目見る
glint 1 *n* kirameki きらめき **2** *v/i* (*of light*) kirameku きらめく; (*of eyes*) hikaru 光る
glisten kirakira hikaru きらきら光る
glitter pikapika hikaru ぴかぴか光る
glitterati yūmei-jin 有名人
gloat ninmari suru にんまりする; *~ over* ... o ninmari to nagameru ...をにんまりと眺める
global (*worldwide*) zensekaiteki (na) 全世界的(な); (*without exceptions*) zentaiteki (na) 全体的(な)
global economy sekai-keizai 世界経済; **global market** sekai-shijō 世界市場; **global warming** chikyū no ondanka 地球の温暖化
globe (*the earth*) chikyū 地球; (*model of earth*) chikyūgi 地球儀
gloom kuragari 暗がり; (*mood*) yūutsu 憂うつ
gloomy *room* kurai 暗い; *mood, person* yūutsu (na) 憂うつ(な)
glorious *weather* subarashii すばらしい; *victory* eikō aru 栄光ある
glory *n* eikō 栄光
gloss *n* (*shine*) tsuya つや; (*general explanation*) gaiyō 概要
glossary yōgoshū 用語集
gloss paint tsuyadashi-penki つや出しペンキ
glossy 1 *adj paper* tsuyadashi-jōshitsushi つや出し上質紙 **2** *n* (*magazine*) gurabia-zasshi グラビ

ア雑紙

glove tebukuro 手袋; (*in baseball*) gurōbu グローブ

glow 1 *n* (*of light, fire*) kagayaki 輝き; (*in cheeks*) akami 赤味 **2** *v/i* (*of light*) kagayaku 輝く; (*of fire*) makka ni moeru 真っ赤に燃える; (*of cheeks*) hoteru ほてる

glowing *description* netsuretsu (na) 熱烈 (な)

glue 1 *n* setchakuzai 接着剤 **2** *v/t* setchakuzai de tsukeru 接着剤でつける; **~ X to Y** X o Y ni setchaku suru XをYに接着する

glum muttsuri shita むっつりした

glutton taishokuka 大食家

gluttony taishoku 大食

GMT (= *Greenwich Mean Time*) gurinidji-hyōjun ji グリニッジ標準時

gnarled *branch* kobudarake (no) こぶだらけ(の); *hands* fushikuredatta 節くれだった

gnat buyo ぶよ

gnaw *v/t bone* kajiru かじる

GNP (= *gross national product*) jī-enu-pī ジー・エヌ・ピー, kokumin-sōseisan 国民総生産

go¹ (*game*) go 碁

go² 1 *n*: **on the ~** (*active*) hatarakizume 働き詰め **2** *v/i* iku 行く; (*leave: of train, plane*) shuppatsu suru 出発する; (*of people*) saru 去る; (*work, function*) sadō suru 作動する; (*become*) naru なる; (*of stain etc*) ochiru 落ちる; (*cease: of pain etc*) nakunaru なくなる; (*match: of colors etc*) au 合う; **~ shopping / jogging** kaimono / jogingu ni iku 買い物/ジョギングに行く; **I must be ~ing** ikanakereba narimasen 行かなければなりません; **let's ~!** sā, ikō さあ、行こう; **~ for a walk** sanpo ni iku 散歩に行く; **~ to bed** neru 寝る; **~ to school** gakkō ni iku 学校に行く; **how's the work ~ing?** shigoto no chōshi wa dō desu ka 仕事の調子はどうですか; **they're ~ing for $50** gojū doru de urarete iru 50ドルで売られている; **hamburger to ~**

teikuauto no hanbāgā テイクアウトのハンバーガー; **be all gone** sukkari nakunaru すっかりなくなる; **be ~ing to** (*future*) tsumori de aru つもりである

♦ **go ahead** (*and do sth*) torikakaru 取りかかる; **~!** (*on you go*) dōzo どうぞ

♦ **go ahead with** *plans etc* ... o susumeru ...を進める

♦ **go along with** *suggestion* ... ni sansei suru ...に賛成する

♦ **go at** (*attack*) ... o kōgeki suru ...を攻撃する

♦ **go away** (*of person*) tachisaru 立ち去る; (*of rain*) yamu 止む; (*of pain, clouds*) kieru 消える

♦ **go back** (*return*) modoru 戻る; (*date back*) sakanoboru さかのぼる; **~ to sleep** mō ichido nemurikomu もう一度眠り込む; **we ~ a long way** watashitachi wa nagai tsukiai da 私たちは長いつきあいだ

♦ **go by** (*of car, people*) tōrisugiru 通り過ぎる; (*of time*) tatsu たつ

♦ **go down** (*descend*) oriru 降りる; (*of sun, ship*) shizumu 沈む; (*of swelling*) hiku 引く; **~ well / ~ badly** (*of suggestion etc*) ukeireru / ukeirerarenai 受け入れる/受け入れられない

♦ **go for** (*attack*) ... ni osoikakaru ...に襲いかかる; (*like*) ... ga suki de aru ...が好きである

♦ **go in** (*to room, house*) naka ni hairu 中に入る; (*of sun*) kumo ni kakureru 雲に隠れる; (*fit: of part etc*) osamaru 納まる

♦ **go in for** *competition, race* ... ni sanka suru ...に参加する; (*like, take part in*) ... ni netchū suru ...に熱中する

♦ **go off 1** *v/i* (*leave*) tachisaru 立ち去る; (*of bomb*) bakuhatsu suru 爆発する; (*of gun*) happō sareru 発砲される; (*of alarm*) narihibiku 鳴り響く **2** *v/t* (*stop liking*) ... ga kirai ni naru ...が嫌いになる

♦ **go on** (*continue*) tsuzukeru 続ける; (*happen*) okoru 起こる; **what's**

going on? dōshitan desu ka どうしたんですか; **~, do it!** hora, yatte gorannasai ほら、やってごらんなさい

♦ **go on at** (*nag*) … ni kogoto o ītsuzukeru …に小言を言い続ける

♦ **go out** (*of person*) dete iku 出て行く; (*of light, fire*) kieru 消える

♦ **go over** v/t (*check*) … o shiraberu …を調べる

♦ **go through** v/t *illness, hard times* … o keiken suru …を経験する; (*check*) … o shōsai ni shiraberu …を詳細に調べる; (*read through*) … o tōshite yomu …を通して読む

♦ **go under** v/i (*sink*) shizumu 沈む; (*of company*) hasan suru 破産する

♦ **go up 1** v/i (*climb*) noboru 上る; (*of prices*) agaru 上がる **2** v/t *mountain* … o noboru …を登る

♦ **go without 1** v/t *food etc* … nashi de sumaseru …なしで済ませる **2** v/i nashi de sumaseru なしで済ませる

goad v/t shigeki suru 刺激する

go-ahead 1 n kyoka 許可; **get the ~** kyoka o eru 許可を得る **2** adj (*enterprising, dynamic*) sekkyokuteki (na) 積極的(な)

goal SP (*target*) gōru ゴール; (*point*) tokuten 得点; (*objective*) mokuhyō 目標

goalkeeper gōru-kīpā ゴールキーパー

goalpost gōru-posuto ゴールポスト

goat yagi やぎ

♦ **gobble up** … o gatsugatsu kuu …をがつがつ食う

go-between chūkai-sha 仲介者; (*for arranged marriage*) nakōdo 仲人

god kami 神; **thank God!** yareyare やれやれ; **oh God!** āa あーあ

godchild nazukego 名づけ子

goddess megami 女神

godfather nazukeoya 名づけ親; (*in mafia*) goddofāzā ゴッドファーザー; **godforsaken** *place, town* arehateta 荒れ果てた; **godmother** nazukeoya 名づけ親; **godparent** nazukeoya 名づけ親; **godson** nazukego 名づけ子

goggles gōguru ゴーグル

going adj *price etc* genkō (no) 現行(の); **~ concern** umaku itte iru うまくいっている

goings-on furumai ふるまい

gold 1 n kin 金 **2** adj kin (no) 金(の)

golden *sky, hair* kin'iro (no) 金色(の)

golden handshake taishokukin 退職金

golden wedding anniversary kinkonshiki 金婚式

goldfish kingyo 金魚; **gold medal** kinmedaru 金メダル; **goldsmith** kinzaikushi 金細工師

golf gorufu ゴルフ

golf club (*organization, stick*) gorufu-kurabu ゴルフクラブ

golf course gorufu-kōsu ゴルフコース

golfer gorufā ゴルファー

gong dora どら; (*in wrestling*) gungu グング

good yoi よい; *food* oishii おいしい; **a ~ many** kanari takusan (no) かなりたくさん(の); **be ~ at** …ga jōzu de aru …が上手である; **it's ~ for you** anata no karada ni yoi あなたの体によい

goodbye sayōnara さようなら; **say ~ to** … ni sayōnara to iu …にさようならと言う

good-for-nothing n yakutatazu 役立たず; **Good Friday** Seikin'yōbi 聖金曜日; **good-humored** jōkigen (no) 上機嫌(の); **good-looking** *woman* bijin (no) 美人(の); *man* hansamu (na) ハンサム(な); **good-natured** kidate no yoi 気立てのよい

goodness (*moral*) hitogara no yosa 人柄のよさ; (*of fruit etc*) eiyōbun 栄養分; **thank ~!** yareyare やれやれ

goods COM shōhin 商品

goodwill zen'i 善意

goody-goody n iikoburikko いい子ぶりっこ

gooey betobeto suru べとべとする

goof v/i F hema o suru へまをする

goose gachō がちょう

gooseberry gūsuberī グースベリー

gooseflesh torihada 鳥肌

gorge 1 n kyōkoku 峡谷 **2** v/t: ~ **oneself on** ... o tarafuku kuu ...をたらふく食う

gorgeous weather subarashii すばらしい; dress suteki (na) すてき (な); woman, hair kirei (na) きれい (な); smell oishisō おいしそう (な)

gorilla gorira ゴリラ

go-slow sabotāju サボタージュ

Gospel (in Bible) Fukuinsho 福音書

gossip 1 n uwasabanashi うわさ話; (person) oshaberi おしゃべり **2** v/i uwasabanashi o suru うわさ話をする

govern country osameru 治める

government seifu 政府

governor chiji 知事

gown (long dress) rongu-doresu ロングドレス; (wedding dress) wedingu-doresu ウェディングドレス; (academic, of judge) gaun ガウン; (of surgeon) shujutsugi 手術着

grab v/t tsukamu つかむ; ~ **a quick bite** haragoshirae suru 腹ごしらえする; ~ **some sleep** kamin suru 仮眠する

grace (of dancer) yūbi-sa 優美さ

graceful yūbi (na) 優美 (な)

gracious person yasashii 優しい; style, living yūga (na) 優雅(な); good ~! oya, mā おや、まあ

grade 1 n (quality) tōkyū 等級; EDU (class) gakunen 学年; (in exam) seiseki 成績 **2** v/t tōkyū o tsukeru 等級をつける

grade crossing fumikiri 踏切

gradient kōbai こう配

gradual jojo (no) 徐々(の)

gradually dandan to だんだんと

graduate n sotsugyō-sei 卒業生

graduation sotsugyō-shiki 卒業式

graffiti rakugaki 落書き

graft n BOT tsugiki 接ぎ木; MED ishoku 移植; (corruption) oshoku 汚職

grain tsubu 粒; (in wood) mokume 木目; **go against the** ~ shō ni awanai 性に合わない

gram guramu グラム

grammar bunpō 文法

grammatical bunpō (no) 文法(の)

grand 1 adj sōdai (na) 壮大(な); F (very good) subarashii すばらしい **2** n F ($1000) sen-doru 千ドル

grandchild mago 孫; (somebody else's) omago-san お孫さん; **granddad** ojiichan おじいちゃん; **granddaughter** mago-musume 孫娘; (somebody else's) omago-san お孫さん

grandeur yūdai-sa 雄大さ

grandfather sofu 祖父; (somebody else's) ojiisan おじいさん; **grandma** obāchan おばあちゃん; **grandmother** sobo 祖母; (somebody else's) obāsan おばあさん; **grandpa** ojiichan おじいちゃん; **grandparents** sofubo 祖父母; (somebody else's) ojiisan-obāsan おじいさんおばあさん; **grand piano** gurando-piano グランドピアノ; **grandson** mago-musuko 孫息子; (somebody else's) omago-san お孫さん; **grandstand** shōmen-kanranseki 正面観覧席

granite kakōgan 花こう岩

granny obāchan おばあちゃん

grant 1 n (money) kōfukin 交付金; (for university, school) shōgakukin 奨学金 **2** v/t wish, peace kanaeru かなえる; visa kōfu suru 交付する; request shōnin suru 承認する; **take ... for ~ed** sth ... o tōzen to omou ...を当然と思う; s.o. ... o karuku miru ...を軽く見る

granule tsubu 粒

grape budō ぶどう

grapefruit gurēpufurūtsu グレープフルーツ; **grapefruit juice** gurēpufurūtsu-jūsu グレープフルーツジュース; **grapevine**: hear ... **through the** ~ ... o uwasa de mimi ni suru ...をうわさで耳にする

graph gurafu グラフ

graphic 1 adj (vivid) shajitsuteki (na) 写実的(な) **2** n COMPUT zu 図

graphics COMPUT seizuhō 製図法

♦ **grapple with** attacker ... to

tokkumiau …と取り組み合う; *problem etc* … ni torikumu …に取り組む

grasp 1 *n* (*mental*) ha-aku 把握; *within one's ~* (*within reach*) … no te no todoku tokoro ni …の手の届くところに **2** *v/t* (*physically*) tsukamaeru つかまえる; (*mentally*) ha-aku suru 把握する

grass kusa 草

grasshopper batta ばった; **grass widow** otto ga rusuchū no tsuma 夫が留守中の妻; **grass widower** tsuma ga rusuchū no otto 妻が留守中の夫

grassy kusa no haeta 草の生えた

grate¹ *n* (*metal grid*) kōshi 格子

grate² **1** *v/t carrots etc* suriorosu すりおろす **2** *v/i* (*of sounds*) … ni sawaru …に障る

grateful kansha shite iru 感謝している; *be ~ to* … ni kansha suru …に感謝する

grater oroshigane おろし金

gratification manzoku-kan 満足感

gratify manzoku saseru 満足させる

grating 1 *n* (*grid*) kōshi 格子 **2** *adj sound* mimizawari (na) 耳障り(な)

gratitude kansha 感謝

gratuity kokorozuke 心付け

grave¹ *n* haka 墓

grave² *adj error* jūdai (na) 重大(な); *voice* shinkoku (na) 深刻(な)

gravel jari 砂利

gravestone hakaishi 墓石

graveyard bochi 墓地

gravity PHYS jūryoku 重力

gravy gurēbī sōsu グレービーソース

gray *adj* haiiro (no) 灰色(の); *be going ~* (*of hair*) dandan shiraga ni naru だんだん白髪になる

gray-haired shiraga (no) 白髪(の)

grayhound gurē-haundo グレーハウンド

graze 1 *v/t arm etc* kasumeru かすめる **2** *n* kasurikizu かすり傷

grease *n* abura 脂

greasy aburappoi 脂っぽい; *food* aburakkoi 脂っこい

great *mistake, disappointment* ōki

(na) 大き(な); *area* hiroi 広い; *amount* bakudai (na) ばく大(な); *composer, writer* idai (na) 偉大(な); F (*very good*) subarashii すばらしい; *~ to see you!* oaidekite totemo ureshii desu お会いできてとてもうれしいです

Great Britain Eikoku 英国

greatly hijō ni 非常に

greatness idai-sa 偉大さ

Greece Girishia ギリシア

greed (*for money*) don'yoku どん欲; *that's just ~* (*for food*) tan ni ijikitanai dake da 単に意地きたないだけだ

greedy (*for money*) don'yoku (na) どん欲(な); (*for food*) ijikitanai 意地きたない

Greek 1 *adj* Girishia (no) ギリシア(の) **2** *n* Girishia-jin ギリシア人; (*language*) Girishia-go ギリシア語

green midoriiro (no) 緑色(の); (*environmentally*) kankyō-hogo (no) 環境保護(の)

Green Day Midori no hi 緑の日;

greengrocer yaoya 八百屋;

greenhorn aonisai 青二才;

greenhouse onshitsu 温室;

greenhouse effect onshitsu-kōka 温室効果; **greenhouse gas** onshitsu-kōka-gasu 温室効果ガス

green tea ryokucha 緑茶

greet aisatsu suru あいさつする

greeting aisatsu あいさつ

grenade shuryūdan 手りゅう弾

grid kōshi 格子

gridiron SP amerikan-futtobōru-kyōgijō アメリカンフットボール競技場

gridlock (*in traffic*) kōtsū-jūtai 交通渋滞; (*in city*) kinō-mahi 機能まひ

grief kanashimi 悲しみ

grievance fuhei 不平

grieve kanashimu 悲しむ; *~ for* … no koto o fukaku kanashimu …のことを深く悲しむ

grill 1 *n Br* (*for cooking*) guriru グリル **2** *v/t Br food* yaku 焼く; (*interrogate*) toitadasu 問いただす

grille (*bars*) kōshimado 格子窓

grim kibishii 厳しい

grimace *n* shikamettsura しかめっ面

grime aka あか

grimy akajimita あかじみた

grin *v/i* nikkori warau にっこり笑う

grind *v/t coffee, meat* hiku ひく

grip 1 *n* (*handle*) nigiribubun 握り部分; (SP: *way of holding*) gurippu グリップ; **lose one's ~** tsukande ita te o hanasu つかんでいた手を放す; **be losing one's ~** (*losing one's skills*) kan ga niburu かんが鈍る **2** *v/t* gyutto nigiru ぎゅっと握る

gristle nankotsu 軟骨

grit suna 砂; (*for roads*) jari 砂利

groan 1 *n* umekigoe うめき声 **2** *v/i* umeku うめく

grocer shokuryō-zakka-ya 食料雑貨屋

groceries shokuryō-zakkarui 食料雑貨類

grocery store shokuryō-zakkaten 食料雑貨店

groin ashi no tsukene 足のつけ根

groom 1 *n* (*for bride*) hanamuko 花婿; (*for horse*) batei 馬丁 **2** *v/t horse* gūmingu suru グルーミングする; (*train, prepare*) kunren suru 訓練する; **well ~ed** midashinami no yoi 身だしなみのよい

groove *n* mizo 溝

grope 1 *v/i* (*in the dark*) tesaguri suru 手探りする **2** *v/t* (*sexually*) masaguru まさぐる

♦ **grope for** *door* ... o tesaguri de sagasu ...を手探りで探す; *word* ... o mosaku suru ...を模索する

gross *adj* (*coarse, vulgar*) gehin (na) 下品(な); *exaggeration* hidoi ひどい; FIN zentai (no) 全体(の)

gross domestic product kokunai-sōseisan 国内総生産

gross national product kokumin-sōseisan 国民総生産

ground 1 *n* jimen 地面; (*reason*) konkyo 根拠; ELEC āsu アース **2** *v/t* ELEC āsu suru アースする

ground control chijō-kanseishitsu 地上管制室

ground crew chijō-seibiin 地上整備員

groundless konkyo no nai 根拠のない

ground meat hikiniku ひき肉; **ground nut** pīnattsu ピーナッツ; **ground plan** heimenzu 平面図; **ground staff** SP kyōgijō-senzoku-kakariin 競技場専属係員; (*at airport*) chijō-seibiin 地上整備員; **groundwork** kiso-junbi 基礎準備

group 1 *n* gurūpu グループ **2** *v/t* ichidan to naru 一団となる

group therapy shūdan-ryōhō 集団療法

grow 1 *v/i* (*of child, animal*) sodatsu 育つ; (*of plants*) haeru 生える; (*of hair, beard*) nobiru 伸びる; (*of amount*) zōka suru 増加する; (*of business*) hatten suru 発展する; **~ old** toshi o toru 年を取る; **~ tired** tsukareru 疲れる **2** *v/t flowers* saibai suru 栽培する

♦ **grow up** (*of person*) seichō suru 成長する; (*of city*) hatten suru 発展する; **~!** motto otona ni narinasai もっと大人になりなさい

growl 1 *n* unarigoe うなり声 **2** *v/i* unaru うなる

grown-up 1 *n* otona 大人 **2** *adj* otona (no) 大人(の)

growth (*of person*) seichō 成長; (*of company*) hatten 発展; (*increase*) zōka 増加; MED shuyō しゅよう

grub (*of insect*) ujimushi うじ虫

grubby kitanai 汚い

grudge 1 *n* urami 恨み; **bear a ~** urami o motte iru 恨みを持っている **2** *v/t* dashioshimi suru 出し惜しみする; **~ X Y** X no Y o netamu Xの Yをねたむ

grudging iyaiya nagara (no) いやいやながら(の)

grueling hetoheto (no) へとへと(の)

gruff bukkirabō (na) ぶっきらぼう(な)

grumble *v/i* butsubutsu fuhei o iu ぶつぶつ不平を言う

grumbler fuhei o iu hito 不平を言う人

grunt 1 *n* būbū iu koe ぶうぶう言う声 **2** *v/i* būbū iu ぶうぶう言う

guarantee 1 n hoshō 保証 **2** v/t hoshō suru 保証する

guarantor hoshōnin 保証人

guarantee period hoshō-kikan 保証期間

guard 1 n (security ~) keibiin 警備員, gādoman ガードマン; MIL keibitai 警備隊; (in prison) kanshu 看守; be on one's ~ against ... ni yōjin suru ...に用心する **2** v/t keibi suru 警備する

♦ **guard against** ... ni yōjin suru ...に用心する

guarded reply shinchō (na) 慎重(な)

guardian LAW kōken-nin 後見人

guerrilla gerira-hei ゲリラ兵

guess 1 n suisoku 推測 **2** v/t answer suisoku suru 推測する; I ~ so darō そうだろう; I ~ not sō darō そうだろう **3** v/i suisoku suru 推測する

guesswork atezuppō あてずっぽう

guest kyaku 客

guesthouse minshuku 民宿

guestroom kyakuma 客間

guffaw 1 n bakawarai ばか笑い **2** v/i bakawarai suru ばか笑いする

guidance shidō 指導

guide 1 n (person) annai-nin 案内人, gaido ガイド; (book) gaido-bukku ガイドブック **2** v/t annai suru 案内する

guidebook gaido-bukku ガイドブック

guided missile yūdō-misairu 誘導ミサイル

guided tour gaido-tsuki ryokō ガイド付き旅行; (in museum, art gallery) gaido-tsuki kengaku ガイド付き見学

guidelines shihyō 指標

guilt LAW yūzai 有罪; (moral responsibility) sekinin 責任; (guilty feeling) zaiakukan 罪悪感

guilty LAW yūzai (no) 有罪(の); (responsible) sekinin (no) 責任(の); smile ushirometasō (na) うしろめたそう(な); have a ~ conscience ushirometaku omou うしろめたく思う

guinea pig morumotto モルモット;

fig jikkendai 実験台

guitar gitā ギター

guitarist gitarisuto ギタリスト

gulf wan 湾; fig mizo 溝

gull kamome かもめ

gullet nodo のど

gullible damasareyasui だまされやすい

gulp 1 n (of water etc) hitokuchi 一口 **2** v/i (in surprise) hatto iki o nomu はっと息をのむ

♦ **gulp down** drink ... o gokugoku nomu ...をごくごく飲む; breakfast, food ... o gatsugatsu taberu ...をがつがつ食べる

gum[1] (in mouth) haguki 歯ぐき

gum[2] n (glue) gomu-nori ゴムのり; (chewing ~) chūingu-gamu チューインガム

gun jū 銃

♦ **gun down** ... o shasatsu suru ...を射殺する

gunfire jūgeki 銃撃; **gunman** (robber) kenjū-gōtō けん銃強盗; **gunpowder** kayaku 火薬; **gunshot** jūsei 銃声; **gunshot wound** jūsō 銃創

gurgle v/i (of baby) nodo o narasu のどを鳴らす; (of drain) gobogobo oto o tateru ごぼごぼ音を立てる

gush v/i (of liquid) hotobashiru ほとばしる

gushy F (enthusiastic) hotobashiru yō (na) ほとばしるよう(な)

gust n ichijin no kaze 一陣の風

gusty weather toppū no fuku 突風が吹く; ~ wind toppū 突風

gut 1 n (of stomach) hara 腹; **~s** F (courage) gattsu ガッツ **2** v/t (of fire) sukkari yaku すっかり焼く

gutter (on sidewalk) mizo 溝; (on roof) toi とい

guy F yatsu やつ; hey, you **~s** nē, minna ねえ、みんな

gym (sports club) jimu ジム; EDU taiikukan 体育館

gymnasium taiikukan 体育館

gymnast taisō-senshu 体操選手

gymnastics taisō 体操

gynecologist fujinka 婦人科

gypsy jipushī ジプシー

H

habit kuse 癖; (*routine*) shūkan 習慣
habitable sumeru 住める
habitat seisokuchi 生息地
habitual itsumo (no) いつも(の);
smoker, drinker jōshūteki (na) 常
習的(な)
hack n (*poor writer*) sanmon-
bunshi 三文文士
hacker COMPUT hakkā ハッカー
hackneyed arifureta ありふれた
haddock tara たら
haggard yatsureta やつれた
haggle (*bargain*) negiru 値切る;
(*argue*) yariau やり合う
haiku haiku 俳句
hail n (*big stones*) hyō ひょう;
(*small stones*) arare あられ
hailstorm hyō/arare no arashi
ひょう/あられの嵐
hair kami no ke 髪の毛; (*single*) ke
毛
hairbrush heaburashi ヘアブラシ;
haircut heakatto ヘアカット;
hairdo kamigata 髪型, heasutairu
ヘアスタイル; hairdresser biyōshi
美容師; *at the ~* biyōin de 美容院
で; hairdrier, hairdryer
headoraiyā ヘアドライヤー;
hairless ke no nai 毛のない; hairpin heapin ヘアピン; hairpin curve
heapin-kābu ヘアピンカーブ; hair-
raising mi no ke no yodatsu yō
(na) 身の毛のよだつよう(な); hair
remover datsumōzai 脱毛剤; hair-
splitting n shōji ni kodawaru koto
詳事にこだわること; hairstyle
heasutairu ヘアスタイル
hairy arm, animal kebukai 毛深い; F
(*frightening*) mi no ke no yodatsu
身の毛のよだつ
half 1 n hanbun 半分; ~ *past ten* jūji
han 十時半; ~ *after ten* jūji han 十
時半; ~ *an hour* sanjuppun 三十分;
~ *a pound* hanpondo 半ポンド; ~

the ... hanbun no ... 半分の... 2 adj
size hanbun (no) 半分(の); *price*
hangaku (no) 半額(の) 3 adv eaten
hanbun dake 半分だけ; *asleep,
hope* nakaba 半ば
half-hearted kinori no shinai 気乗
りのしない; half time n SP hāfu-
taimu ハーフタイム; halfway 1 adj
stage, point chūkan (no) 中間(の)
2 adv: ~ *between the two cities*
futatsu no toshi no chūkan de 二つ
の都市の中間で; *it's ~ finished*
hanbun owatta 半分終わった
hall (*large room*) ōhiroma 大広間,
hōru ホール; (*hallway*) genkan 玄
関
halo gokō 後光
halt 1 v/i tomaru 止まる 2 v/t
tomeru 止める 3 n teishi 停止;
come to a ~ teishi suru 停止する
halve v/t hanbun ni suru 半分にする
ham hamu ハム
hamburger hanbāgā ハンバーガー
hammer 1 n kanazuchi 金づち 2 v/i
tataku たたく; (*with hammer*)
tonkachi de tataku とんかちでたた
く; ~ *at the door* doa o gangan
tataku ドアをがんがんたたく
hammock hanmokku ハンモック
hamper[1] n (*picnic ~*) pikunikku-yō
basuketto ピクニック用バスケット
hamper[2] v/t (*obstruct*) samatageru
妨げる
hamster hamusutā ハムスター
hand 1 n te 手; (*of clock*) hari 針;
(*worker*) hitode 人手; *at ~, to ~*
sugu chikaku ni すぐ近くに; *at
first* ~ chokusetsu ni 直接に; *by ~*
write te de 手で; *deliver* tewatashi
de 手渡しで; *on the one ~ ..., on
the other ~...* ippō dewa ... de, mō
ippō dewa ... da 一方では ... で、も
う一方では ... だ; *be in ~* (*being
done*) ima yatte iru tokoro de 今

やっているところで; *the job in ~*
tōmen no shigoto 当面の仕事; *on
your right ~* migigawa ni 右側に;
~s off! (*do not touch*)
sawaranaide 触らないで; *~s up!* te
o agero 手をあげろ; *change ~s*
mochinushi ga kawaru 持ち主が変
わる; (*of company*) keiei-sha ga
kawaru 経営者が変わる

♦ **hand down** *fig* tsutaeru 伝える
♦ **hand in** teishutsu suru 提出する
♦ **hand on** tewatasu 手渡す; *fig* ... o
tsutaeru ...を伝える
♦ **hand out** ... o watasu ...を渡す
♦ **hand over** *knife, baton* ... o
tewatasu ...を手渡す; *hostage etc*
... o hikiwatasu ...を引き渡す

handbag *Br* handobaggu ハンド
バッグ; **handbook** handobukku ハ
ンドブック; **handbrake** *Br*
saidoburēki サイドブレーキ;
handcuffs tejō 手錠
handicap *n* (*disability*) shintai-
shōgai 身体障害; *fig* furi na jōken
不利な条件, handi ハンディ
handicapped (*physically*) shōgai
no aru 障害のある; *fig* furi de aru
不利である
handicraft shugei 手芸
handiwork teshigoto 手仕事
handkerchief hankachi ハンカチ
handle *n* totte 取っ手; (*of brush,
umbrella*) e 柄; (*on ship*) nobu ノ
ブ **2** *v/t goods* atsukau 扱う; *case,
deal* shori suru 処理する; *difficult
person* atsukau 扱う; *let me ~ this*
watashi ni makasete kudasai 私に
任せてください
handlebars handoru ハンドル
hand luggage tenimotsu 手荷物;
handmade tesei (no) 手製(の);
handrail tesuri 手すり; **handshake**
akushu 握手
hands-off kanshō shinai 干渉しない
handsome hansamu (na) ハンサム
(な)
hands-on jissenteki (na) 実践的(な)
handwriting hisseki 筆跡
handwritten tegaki (no) 手書き(の)
handy *tool, device* benri (na) 便利
(な); *it might come in ~* sore wa

yaku ni tatsu kamo shirenai それ
は役に立つかもしれない

hang 1 *v/t picture* kakeru 掛ける;
person kōshukei ni suru 絞首刑に
する **2** *v/i* kakaru
掛かる **3** *n*: *get the ~ of* ... no kotsu
o nomikomu ...のこつをのみ込む
♦ **hang around** ... o urotsuku ...をう
ろつく
♦ **hang on** *v/i* (*wait*) chotto matsu
ちょっと待つ
♦ **hang on to** (*keep*) ... o motte iru
...を持っている
♦ **hang up** *v/i* TELEC kiru 切る
hangar kakunōko 格納庫
hanger (*for clothes*) hangā ハン
ガー, yōfuku-kake 洋服掛け
hang glider (*device*) hanguraidā ハ
ンググライダー
hang gliding hanguraidingu ハング
ライディング
hangover futsukayoi 二日酔い
♦ **hanker after** ... ni akogareru ...に
あこがれる
hankie, hanky F hankachi ハンカチ
haphazard detarame (na) でたらめ
(な)
happen okoru 起こる; *if you ~ to see
him* moshi kare ni tamatama
attara もし彼にたまたま会ったら;
what has ~ed to you? nani ga atta
no 何があったの
♦ **happen across** ... o gūzen
mitsukeru ...を偶然見つける
happening dekigoto 出来事
happily tanoshisō ni 楽しそうに;
(*willingly*) yorokonde 喜んで;
(*luckily*) saiwai ni mo 幸いにも
happiness shiawase 幸せ
happy shiawase (na) 幸せ(な);
coincidence kōun (na) 幸運(な)
happy-go-lucky nonki (na) のんき
(な)
happy hour sābisutaimu サービスタ
イム
harass ... ni iyagarase o suru ...に
いやがらせをする
harassed tsukareta つかれた
harassment iyagarase いやがらせ;
sexual ~ seiteki iyagarase 性的い
やがらせ, sekuhara セクハラ

harbor 1 *n* minato 港 **2** *v/t criminal* kakumau かくまう; *grudge* kokoro ni idaku 心に抱く

hard *material* katai 硬い; *punch* hageshii 激しい; *training* kibishii 厳しい; *(difficult)* muzukashii 難しい; *facts, evidence* kakujitsu (na) 確実(な); **~ of hearing** mimi ga tōi 耳が遠い

hardback hādo kabā ハードカバー; **hard-boiled** *egg* katayude (no) 固ゆで(の); **hard copy** purinto プリント; **hard core** *n* chūshin-seiryoku 中心勢力; **hard currency** kōkankanō-tsūka 交換可能通貨; **hard disk** hādo disuku ハードディスク

harden 1 *v/t* kataku suru 固くする **2** *v/i (of glue)* katamaru 固まる; *(of attitude)* kataku naru 固くなる

hardheaded genjitsuteki (na) 現実的(な)

hardliner kyōkōha 強硬派

hardly hotondo ... nai ほとんど…ない; **I ~ know him** watashi wa kare o hotondo shiranai 私は彼をほとんど知らない

hardness kata-sa 硬さ; *(difficulty)* kibishii-sa 厳しさ

hardsell oshiuri 押し売り

hardship konnan 困難

hard shoulder rokata 路肩

hard up ichimon-nashi 一文なし

hardware kanamonorui 金物類; COMPUT hādowea ハードウェア

hardware store kanamonoten 金物店

hard-working hatarakimono (no) 働き者(の); *(eager to learn)* benkyōka (no) 勉強家(の)

hardy jōbu (na) 丈夫(な)

hare nousagi 野うさぎ

harm 1 *n* gai 害; **it wouldn't do any ~ to ...** ... shite warui koto wa nai ...して悪いことはない **2** *v/t* sokonau 損なう; *person* ... ni kigai o kuwaeru ...に危害を加える

harmful yūgai (na) 有害(な)

harmless mugai (na) 無害(な)

harmonious *sound* chōwa shita 調和した; *relationship* naka no yoi 仲のよい

harmonize MUS waon o tsukeru 和音をつける; *ideas* chōwa saseru 調和させる

harmony MUS hāmonī ハーモニー; *(in relationship etc)* chōwa 調和

harp hāpu ハープ

♦ **harp on about** F ... o kudokudo hanashitsuzukeru ...をくどくど話し続ける

harpoon mori もり

harsh kibishii 厳しい

harvest *n* shūkaku 収穫

hash: make a ~ of F ... o dainashi ni suru ...を台なしにする

hash browns hasshu-buraun ハッシュブラウン

hashish hasshishi ハッシシ

haste: do ... in ~ ... o awatete suru ...をあわててする

hasty keisotsu (na) 軽率(な)

hat bōshi 帽子

hatch *n (for serving food)* haizenmado 配ぜん窓, hatchi ハッチ; *(on ship)* hatchi ハッチ

♦ **hatch out** *v/i (of eggs)* kaeru かえる

hatchet teono 手おの

hate 1 *n* ken'o 嫌悪; *(deep: of the enemy, a country)* nikushimi 憎しみ **2** *v/t* hidoku kirau ひどく嫌う; *(deeply)* nikumu 憎む

hatred ken'o 嫌悪; *(deep: of enemy, a country)* nikushimi 憎しみ

haughty kōman (na) 高慢(な)

haul 1 *n (from robbery)* shūkaku 収穫; **~ of fish** gyokaku 漁獲 **2** *v/t (pull)* hipparu 引っ張る

haulage unsō 運送

haulage company unsō-gaisha 運送会社

haulier unsō-gaisha 運送会社

haunch shiri 尻

haunt 1 *v/t (of memory)* ... no kokoro ni tsukimatou ...の心につきまとう; **this place is ~ed** kono basho wa yūrei ga deru この場所は幽霊が出る **2** *n* yoku iku basho よく行く場所

have ◊ *(possess)* motte iru 持っている; *brother, sister etc* ... ga iru ...

がいる; *pet* katte iru 飼っている; *do you ~ your passport with you?* pasupōto motte iru パスポート持っている; *I ~ two brothers* watashi ni wa ani ga futari imasu 私には兄が二人います; *he has red hair* kare wa akai kami o shite imasu 彼は赤い髪をしています; *I ~ small hands* watashi no te wa chīsai 私の手は小さい ◊ *breakfast, lunch* toru とる; *we had steak/fish* watashitachi wa sutēki/sakana o tabeta 私達はステーキ/さかなを食べた; *I'll ~ the apple pie* watashi wa appuru pai ni shimasu 私はアップルパイにします ◊ (*requests*): *can I ~ a cup of coffee?* kōhī o itadakemasu ka コーヒーをいただけますか; *can I ~ more time?* mō sukoshi jikan ii desu ka もうすこし時間いいですか; *do you ~ milk?* (*to shopkeeper*) gyūnyū arimasu ka 牛乳ありますか; *do you ~ a pen?* pen mottemasu ka ペン持ってますか ◊ ~ (*got*) *to* (*must*) ... shinakereba naranai ... しなければならない; *you ~ to sign it first* hajime ni shomei shinakereba naranai 初めに署名しなければならない; *you don't ~ to leave* ikanakute mo ii desu 行かなくてもいいです; *if he doesn't want to stay with us, he doesn't ~ to* moshi kare ga watashi-tachi to issho ni itaku nainara sōshinakute mo ii desu もし彼が私達と一緒にいたくないならそうしなくてもいいです ◊ (*causative*): ~ *X done* X shite morau Xしてもらう; *I'll ~ it repaired* shūri shite morau yō ni suru 修理してもらうようにする; *I had my hair cut* kami o kitte moratta 髪を切ってもった ◊ (*past tense*): *I ~ come* kita 来た; ~ *you seen her?* kanojo o mikakemashita ka 彼女を見かけましたか ◊ (*tags*) ne ね; *you ~n't finished already, ~ you?* mō owattain nai yo ne もう終わってんじゃないよね

♦ **have back** ... o kaeshite morau ...

を返してもらう; *when can I have it back?* itsu kaeshite moraemasu ka いつ返してもらえますか

♦ **have on** (*wear*) ... o mi ni tsukete iru ...を身につけている; (*have planned*) yotei ga aru 予定がある; *do you have anything on for tonight?* konban wa nani ka yotei ga arimasu ka 今晩は何か予定がありますか

haven *fig* hinan-basho 避難場所
havoc daikonran 大混乱; *play ~ with* mechamecha ni midasu めちゃめちゃに乱す
hawk taka たか; *fig* takaha たか派
hay hoshikusa 干し草
hay fever kafunshō 花粉症
hazard *n* kiken 危険
hazard lights MOT kiken-keikoku-sōchi 危険警告装置
hazardous kiken (na) 危険(な)
haze *n* kasumi かすみ
hazel (*tree*) hashibami はしばみ
hazelnut hēzerunattsu ヘーゼルナッツ
hazy *view, image* bon'yari shita ぼんやりした; *memories* mōrō to shita もうろうとした; *I'm a bit ~ about it* hakkiri shinai はっきりしない

he kare 彼; ~ *is American* kare wa Amerika-jin desu 彼はアメリカ人です ◊ (*omission of pronoun*): *where is ~? ~ has left* kare wa doko desu ka - mō ikimashita 彼はどこですか-もう行きました
head 1 *n* (*of person, nail*) atama 頭; (*boss, leader*) chō 長; (*of department*) buchō 部長; (*of company*) shachō 社長; (*of delegation*) daihyō-danchō 代表団長; (*on beer*) awa 泡; (*of line*) sentō 先頭; *$15 a ~* hitoribun jūgo doru 一人分十五ドル; ~*s or tails?* ura ka omote ka 裏か表か; *at the ~ of the list* risuto no saisho ni リストの最初に; ~ *over heels fall* massakasama ni 真っ逆さまに; *fall in love* sukkari すっかり; *lose one's ~* (*go crazy*) ki ga kurutta yō ni naru 気が狂ったようになる

2 v/t (*lead*) hikiiru 率いる; *ball* hedingu suru ヘディングする

headache zutsū 頭痛

headband hachimaki はちまき

header (*in soccer*) hedingu ヘディング; (*in document*) midashi 見出し

headhunter COM jinzai-sukauto-gakari 人材スカウト係, heddohantā ヘッドハンター

heading (*in list*) hyōdai 表題

headlamp heddoraito ヘッドライト; **headlight** heddoraito ヘッドライト; **headline** (*in newspaper*) midashi 見出し; *make the ~s* ōkiku midashi ni toriagerareru 大きく見出しに取り上げられる

headlong adv fall massakasama ni 真っ逆さまに; **headmaster** kōchō 校長; **headmistress** kōchō 校長

head office honsha 本社; **head-on 1** adv crash shōmen kara 正面から **2** adj crash shōmen (no) 正面(の);

headphones heddohon ヘッドホン; **headquarters** honbu 本部; **headrest** heddoresuto ヘッドレスト; **headroom** (*under bridge*) akidaka 空き高; (*in car*) tenjō made no yutori 天井までのゆとり;

headscarf sukāfu スカーフ;

headstrong ganko (na) 頑固(な); **head teacher** kōchō 校長; **head waiter** bōi-chō ボーイ長; **headwind** mukaikaze 向かい風

heady me ga mawaru 目が回る; *drink, wine etc* yoi ga sugu mawaru 酔いがすぐ回る

heal 1 v/t naosu 治す **2** v/i naoru 治る

health kenkō 健康; (*condition*) karada no guai 体の具合; *your ~!* kanpai 乾杯

health club supōtsu-kurabu スポーツクラブ; **health food** kenkō-shokuhin 健康食品; **health food store** kenkō-shokuhinten 健康食品店; **health insurance** kenkō-hoken 健康保険; **health resort** kenkō-rizōto 健康リゾート

healthy kenkō (na) 健康(な); *food, lifestyle* kenkōteki (na) 健康的(な); *economy* kenzen (na) 健全(な)

heap n tsumikasane 積み重ね

♦**heap up** v/t ... o tsumiageru ...を積み上げる

hear kikoeru 聞こえる

♦**hear about** ... ni tsuite kiku ...について聞く

♦**hear from** (*have news from*) ... kara renraku ga aru ...から連絡がある

hearing chōkaku 聴覚; LAW chōmonkai 聴聞会; *within ~* kikoeru tokoro de 聞こえるところで; *out of ~* kikoenai tokoro de 聞こえないところで

hearing aid hochōki 補聴器

hearsay: *by ~* uwasa de うわさで

hearse reikyūsha 霊きゅう車

heart shinzō 心臓; (*of problem*) kakushin 核心; (*of city, organization*) chūshin 中心; *know ... by ~* ... o anki shite iru ...を暗記している

heart attack shinzō-hossa 心臓発作; **heartbeat** kodō 鼓動; **heartbreaking** hitsū (na) 悲痛(な); **heartburn** muneyake 胸やけ; **heart failure** shinfuzen 心不全; **heartfelt** sympathy kokoro kara (no) 心から(の)

hearth roshō 炉床

heartless hijō (na) 非情(な)

heartrending hitsū (na) 悲痛(な)

hearts (*in cards*) hāto ハート

heart throb F akogare no mato あこがれの的

heart transplant shinzo-ishoku 心臓移植

hearty appetite ōsei (na) おう盛(な); *meal* tappuri (no) たっぷり(の); *person* meirō (na) 明朗(な)

heat n netsu 熱

♦**heat up** food ... o atatameru ...を温める; *room* ... o atatameru ...を暖める

heated pool onsui (no) 温水(の); *discussion* kōfun shita 興奮した

heater hītā ヒーター

heathen n ikyōto 異教徒

heating danbō 暖房

heatstroke nesshabyō 熱射病

heatwave neppa 熱波

heave v/t (*lift*) mochiageru 持ち上げる

heaven tengoku 天国; *good ~s!* oya, mā おや、まあ

heavy omoi 重い; *overcoat* atsui 厚い; *cold* hidoi ひどい; *rain* hageshii 激しい; *traffic* noroi のろい; *accent* tsuyoi 強い; *food* shitsukoi しつこい; *financial loss* tagaku (no) 多額(の); *loss of life* tasū (no) 多数(の); *bleeding* taryō (no) 多量(の); *~ smoker* hebī-sumōkā ヘビースモーカー; *~ drinker* nonbē 飲んべえ

heavy-duty ganjō (na) 頑丈(な)

heavyweight SP hebī-kyū (no) ヘビー級(の)

heckle v/t yajiru やじる

hectic yatara isogashii やたら忙しい

hedge n ikegaki 生け垣

hedgehog harinezumi はりねずみ

heed chūi 注意; *pay ~ to …* … ni chūi o harau …に注意を払う

heel (*of foot*) kakato かかと; (*of shoe*) hīru ヒール

heel bar kutsunaoshi 靴直し

hefty *person* gasshiri shita がっしりした; *suitcase* omokute ōkii 重くて大きい; *fine, cut* kōgaku (no) 高額(の)

height takasa 高さ; (*of person*) shinchō 身長; (*of plane*) kōdo 高度; (*of season*) massakari 真っ盛り

heighten *effect, tension* tsuyomeru 強める

heir sōzoku-nin 相続人

heiress sōzoku-nin 相続人

helicopter herikoputā ヘリコプター

hell jigoku 地獄; *what the ~ are you doing?* F ittai nani shitenda いったい何してんだ; *what the ~ do you want?* F ittai nani ga hoshiittenda いったい何が欲しいってんだ; *go to ~!* F kutabatchimae くたばっちまえ; *a ~ of a lot* F sugoku すごく; *one ~ of a nice guy* F sugoi ii yatsu すごいいいやつ

hello konnichiwa こんにちは; TELEC moshimoshi もしもし

helm NAUT darin だ輪

helmet herumetto ヘルメット

help 1 n tasuke 助け; *thanks for your ~* tasukete kurete arigatō 助けてくれてありがとう **2** v/t tasukeru 助ける; *~ oneself* (*to food*) jiyū ni toru 自由に取る; *I can't ~ it* shō ga nai しょうがない; *I couldn't ~ laughing* omowazu waratte shimau 思わず笑ってしまう

helper tetsudai 手伝い, herupā ヘルパー

helpful yaku ni tatsu 役に立つ

helping (*of food*) hitomori ひと盛り

helpless (*unable to cope*) muryoku (na) 無力(な); (*powerless*) mubōbi (na) 無防備(な)

help screen COMPUT herupu-gamen ヘルプ画面

hem n (*of dress etc*) heri へり

hemisphere hankyū 半球

hemorrhage 1 n shukketsu 出血 **2** v/i taryō ni shukketsu suru 多量に出血する

hemp asa 麻

hen mendori めんどり

henchman pej kobun 子分

henpecked shiri ni shikareta 尻に敷かれた; *~ husband* kyōsai-ka 恐妻家

hepatitis kan'en 肝炎

her 1 adj ◊ kanojo no 彼女の; *~ ticket* kanojo no kippu 彼女の切符 ◊ (*omission of possessive*): *she broke ~ arm* kanojo wa ude no hone o otta 彼女は腕の骨を折った; *she forgot ~ key* kanojo wa kagi o wasureta 彼女はかぎを忘れた **2** pron kanojo 彼女; *who? ~ ~* dare – kanojo desu 誰 – 彼女です; *this is for ~* kore wa kanojo ni desu これは彼女にです ◊ (*direct object*) kanojo o 彼女を; *I know ~* kanojo o shitte iru 彼女を知っている ◊ (*indirect object*) kanojo ni 彼女に; *can you mail it to ~?* kanojo ni okutte kureru 彼女に送ってくれる

herb kōsō 香草, hābu ハーブ

herb(al) tea hābutī ハーブティー

herd n mure 群れ

here *live, stay, sit down* koko ni こ
こに; *sleep, eat* koko de ここで;

come koko e ここへ; **~'s to you!** kimi ni kanpai 君に乾杯; **~ you are** (*giving sth*) hai, dōzo はい、どうぞ; **~ we are!** (*finding sth*) hora, koko ni atta ほらここにあった

hereditary *disease* idensei (no) 遺伝性(の)

heritage isan 遺産

hermit yosutebito 世捨て人

hernia MED herunia ヘルニア

hero eiyū 英雄, hīrō ヒーロー

heroic eiyūteki (na) 英雄的(な)

heroin heroin ヘロイン

heroine hiroin ヒロイン

heron aosagi アオサギ

herpes MED herupesu ヘルペス

herring nishin にしん

hers kanojo no mono 彼女のもの; **it's ~** kanojo no mono desu 彼女のものです

herself: *she hurt* **~** kanojo wa kega o shita 彼女はけがをした; *she saw* **~** *in the mirror* kanojo wa kagami de jibun o mita 彼女は鏡で自分を見た; *what does she think* **~?** kanojo wa dō kangaete iru no 彼女はどう考えているの; *by* **~** (*without help*) jibun de 自分で; (*alone*) hitori de ひとりで

hesitate tamerau ためらう

hesitation tamerai ためらい

heterosexual *adj* isei-aisha 異性愛者

heyday massakari 真っ盛り

hi konnichiwa こんにちは

hibernate tōmin suru 冬眠する

hiccup *n* shakkuri しゃっくり; (*minor problem*) chotto shita mondai ちょっとした問題; *have the* **~s** shakkuri suru しゃっくりする

hick *pej* F inakamono いなか者

hick town *pej* F inakamachi いなか町

hidden *meaning* kakusareta 隠された; *treasure* himitsu (no) 秘密(の)

hide[1] *v/t* kakusu 隠す **2** *v/i* kakureru 隠れる

hide[2] *n* (*of animal*) kawa 皮

hide-and-seek kakurenbo かくれんぼ

hideaway kakurebasho 隠れ場所

hideous iya (na) いや(な); *crime* osoroshii 恐ろしい; *face* minikui 醜い

hiding[1] (*beating*) muchiuchi むち打ち

hiding[2]: *be in* **~** kakurete iru 隠れている; *go into* **~** kakureru 隠れる

hiding place kakurebasho 隠れ場所

hierarchy kaikyū-soshiki 階級組織

hi-fi haifai-sutereo ハイファイステレオ

high 1 *adj* building, temperature, price, note, salary, speed takai 高い; *wind* tsuyoi 強い; *quality* kōkyū (na) 高級(な); (*on drugs*) hai (na) ハイ(な); *have a* **~** *opinion of* ... o takaku hyōka suru ... を高く評価する; *it is* **~** *time* ... mō ... suru koro da もう...する頃だ **2** *n* MOT kōsoku-giya 高速ギヤ; (*in statistics*) saikō-kiroku 最高記録; EDU kōkō 高校 **3** *adv* takaku 高く; **~** *in the sky* soratakaku 空高く; *that's as* **~** *as we can go* sore ga seiippai da それが精一杯だ

highbrow *adj* interimuke (no) インテリ向けの); **highchair** bebī-isu ベビーいす; **highclass** kōkyū (na) 高級(な); **high diving** taka-tobikomi 高飛び込み; **high-frequency** tanpa 短波; **high-grade** yūryō (na) 優良(な); **high-handed** ōbō (na) 横暴(な); **high-heeled** haihīru o haita ハイヒールをはいた; **high jump** haijanpu ハイジャンプ; **high-level** toppureberu (no) トップレベルの); **high life** zeitaku na seikatsu ぜいたくな生活; **highlight 1** *n* hairaito ハイライト **2** *v/t* (*with pen*, COMPUT) keikō-pen de kyōchō suru 蛍光ペンで強調する; **highlighter** (*pen*) keikō-pen 蛍光ペン

highly *desirable*, *likely* hijō ni 非常に; *be* **~** *paid* kōkyū o moratte iru 高給をもらっている; *think* **~** *of* ... o takaku hyōka shite iru ... を高く評価している

high-performance *drill* kōseinō (no) 高性能(の); *battery* jizoku-jikan no nagai 持続時間の長い; **high-pitched** kandakai かん高い;

high point (*of life, career*) chōten 頂点, pīku ピーク; (*of program*) kuraimakkusu クライマックス;

high-powered *engine* kōseinō (no) 高性能(の); *intellectual* senren sareta 洗練された; *salesman* yūnō (na) 有能(な); **high pressure 1** *n* (*weather*) kōkiatsu 高気圧 **2** *adj* TECH atsuryoku (no) 圧力(の); *salesman* oshiuri (no) 押し売り(の); *job, lifestyle* jūatsu no ōkii 重圧の大きい; **high priest** kōsō 高僧;

high school kōkō 高校; **high society** jōryū-shakai 上流社会; **high-speed train** kōsoku-ressha 高速列車; **high-strung** shinkeishitsu (na) 神経質(な); **high tech 1** *n* haiteku ハイテク **2** *adj* haiteku (no) ハイテク(の); **high technology** haiteku ハイテク; **high-tension** *cable* kōden'atsu (no) 高電圧(の); **high tide** manchō 満潮; **high water** manchō 満潮; **highway** kansen-dōro 幹線道路; **high wire** tsunawatari no tsuna 綱渡りの綱

hijack 1 *v/t plane* haijakku suru ハイジャックする; *bus* nottoru 乗っ取る **2** *n* (*of plane*) haijakku ハイジャック; (*of bus*) nottori 乗っ取り

hijacker (*of plane, bus*) nottorihannin 乗っ取り犯人

hike¹ 1 *n* haikingu ハイキング; (*longer distance*) toho-ryokō 徒歩旅行 **2** *v/i* haikingu ni iku ハイキングに行く; (*longer distance*) toho-ryokō o suru 徒歩旅行をする

hike² *n* (*in prices*) hikiage 引き上げ

hiker haikā ハイカー

hilarious omoshiroi おもしろい

hill oka 丘; (*slope*) saka 坂

hillbilly *pej* F inaka-mono いなか者

hillside oka no chūfuku 丘の中腹

hilltop oka no ue 丘の上

hilly oka no ōi 丘の多い

hilt ken no tsuka 剣の柄

him kare 彼; *who? ~* dare – kare desu 誰 – 彼です; *this is for ~* kore wa kare ni desu これは彼にです◊ (*direct object*) kare o 彼を; *do you know ~?* kare o shitte imasu ka 彼を知っていますか◊ (*indirect object*) kare ni 彼に; *can you mail it to ~?* kare ni okutte kureru 彼に送ってくれる

himself: *he hurt ~* kare wa kega o shimashita 彼はけがをしました; *he saw ~ in the mirror* kare wa kagami de jibun o mita 彼は鏡で自分を見た *what does he think ~?* kare wa dō kangaete iru no 彼はどう考えているの; *by ~* (*without help*) jibun de 自分で; (*alone*) hitori de ひとりで

hinder samatageru 妨げる

hindrance (*bags, person*) jama 邪魔; (*lack of knowledge etc*) shōgai 障害

hindsight atojie あと知恵; *with ~* ato ni shite omoeba あとにして思えば

hinge *n* chōtsugai ちょうつがい

hint (*clue*) hinto ヒント; (*piece of advice*) jogen 助言; (*implied suggestion*) honomekashi ほのめかし; (*of red, sadness etc*) wazuka na ryō わずかな量; (*of spring, recovery*) kizashi 兆し

hip koshi 腰

hip pocket shiri-poketto 尻ポケット

hippopotamus kaba かば

hiragana hiragana ひらがな

hire *workers* yatou 雇う

his 1 *adj* ◊ kare no 彼の; *~ ticket* kare no kippu 彼の切符 ◊ (*omission of possessive*): *he broke ~ arm* kare wa ude no hone o otta 彼は腕の骨を折った; *he forgot ~ key* kare wa kagi o wasureta 彼はかぎを忘れた **2** *pron* kare no mono 彼のもの; *it's ~* kare no desu 彼のです

Hispanic 1 *adj* Raten-Amerika (no) ラテンアメリカ(の) **2** *n* Raten-Amerika-jin ラテンアメリカ人

hiss *v/i* (*of snake*) shūshū to iu oto o tateru しゅうしゅうという音を立てる; (*of audience*) shītto yajiru しーっとやじる

historian rekishi-ka 歴史家

historic rekishiteki ni yūmei (na) 歴史的に有名(な)

historical rekishijō (no) 歴史上(の)

history rekishi 歴史

hit 1 v/t tataku たたく; *ball* utsu 打つ; (*collide with*) … ni butsukaru …にぶつかる; *he was ~ by a bullet* kare wa dangan ni atatta 彼は弾丸に当たった; *it suddenly ~ me* (*I realized*) totsuzen sore o omoitsuita 突然それを思いついた; *~ town* (*arrive*) machi ni ikiataru 町に行き当たる **2** n (*blow*) dageki 打撃; MUS hitto ヒット; (*success*) daiseikō 大成功

♦ **hit back** yarikaesu やり返す

♦ **hit on** *idea* … o futo omoitsuku …をふと思いつく

♦ **hit out at** (*criticize*) … o kokuhyō suru …を酷評する

hit-and-run adj: *~ accident* hikinige-jiko 引き逃げ事故; *~ driver* hikinige-untenshu 引き逃げ運転手

hitch 1 n (*problem*) mondai 問題; *without a ~* todokōrinaku 滞りなく **2** v/t hikkakeru 引っかける; *~ X to Y* X to Y o tsunagu XとYをつなぐ; *~ a ride* kuruma o hitchi-haiku suru 車をヒッチハイクする **3** v/i (*hitchhike*) hitchi-haiku suru ヒッチハイクする

♦ **hitch up** *wagon, trailer* … o tsunagu …をつなぐ

hitchhike hitchi-haiku suru ヒッチハイクする; **hitchhiker** hitchi-haikā ヒッチハイカー; **hitchhiking** hitchi-haikingu ヒッチハイキング

hi-tech 1 n haiteku ハイテク **2** adj haiteku(no) ハイテク(の)

hitlist (*terrorist's*) satsugai-yoteisha-risuto 殺害予定者リスト; (*management's*) kubikiri-taishōsha-risuto 首切り対象者リスト; **hitman** koroshi-ya 殺し屋; **hit-or-miss** ikitaribattari 行き当たりばったり; **hit squad** sogekihan 狙撃班

HIV hito-men'eki-fuzen-uirusu ヒト免疫不全ウィルス

hive (*for bees*) subako 巣箱

hive off v/t COM bunri-dokuritsu saseru 分離独立させる

HIV-positive eichi-ai-bui-yōsei (no) ＨＩＶ陽性(の)

hoard 1 n takuwae 蓄え **2** v/t takuwaeru 蓄える

hoarse shagaregoe (no) しゃがれ声(の)

hoax n itazura いたずら

hobble v/i ashi o hikizutte aruku 足を引きずって歩く

hobby shumi 趣味

hobo furō-sha 浮浪者

hockey (*ice ~*) hokkē ホッケー

hog n (*pig*) buta 豚

hoist 1 n makiageki 巻き上げ機 **2** v/t (*lift*) mochiageru 持ち上げる; *flag* ageru 揚げる

Hokkaido Hokkaidō 北海道

hokum (*nonsense*) kodomodamashi 子供だまし; (*sentimental stuff*) tawagoto たわごと

hold 1 v/t (*in hands*) te ni motsu 手に持つ; (*in arms*) kakaeru 抱える; *s.o.'s hand* te o tsunagu 手をつなぐ; (*support, keep in place*) sasaeru 支える; *passport, license* motte iru 持っている; *prisoner, suspect* kōryū suru 拘留する; (*contain*) ireru koto ga dekiru 入れることができる; *job, post* … ni tsuite iru …についている; *course* iji suru 維持する; *the crate ~s 6 bottles* kono kēsu ni wa roppon ireru koto ga dekiru このケースには六本入れることができる; *~ one's breath* iki o korasu 息を凝らす; *he can ~ his drink* kare wa chotto ya sotto ja yowanai 彼はちょっとやそっとじゃ酔わない; *~ … responsible* … ni sekinin ga aru toomou …に責任があると思う; *~ that …* (*believe, maintain*) … da to shinjite iru …だと信じている; *~ the line* TELEC kirazu ni sono mama matsu 切らずにそのまま待つ **2** n (*in ship, plane*) kamotsu-shitsu 貨物室; *catch ~ of* … o tsukamu …をつかむ; *lose one's ~ on* (*on rope*) … no te o hanasu …の手を離す; *lose one's ~ on reality* genjitsu o miushinau 現実を見失う

♦ **hold against**: *hold X against Y* X o ne ni motte Y o uramu X を根に持ってYを恨む

♦ **hold back 1** v/t *crowds* … o

oshitodomeru ...を押しとどめる;
facts, information ... o kakusu ...
を隠す **2** v/i (not tell all) tamerau
ためらう

♦ **hold on** v/i (wait) matsu 待つ;
TELEC kiranaide matsu 切らない
で待つ; *now ~ a minute!* chotto
matte ちょっと待って

♦ **hold on to** (keep) ... o motte iru ...
を持っている; (belief) ... o
mamoritsuzukeru ...を守り続ける

♦ **hold out 1** v/t hand ... o sashidasu
...を差し出す; prospect ... o
motaseru ...を持たせる **2** v/i (of
supplies) motsu もつ; (of trapped
miners etc) mochikotaeru 持ちこ
たえる

♦ **hold up** v/t hand ... o ageru ...をあ
げる; bank etc ... o osotte kinpin o
toru ...を襲って金品を取る; (make
late) ... o okuraseru ...を遅らせる;
hold ... up as an example ... o rei
to shite shimesu ...を例として示す

♦ **hold with** (approve of) ... ni
sansei suru ...に賛成する

holder (container) iremono 入れ物,
kēsu ケース; (of passport, ticket
etc) shoyū-sha 所有者; (of record)
hoji-sha 保持者

holding company oyagaisha 親会社

holdup (robbery) gōtō 強盗; (delay)
okure 遅れ

hole ana 穴

holiday (single day) shukujitsu 祝
日; (period) kyūka 休暇; *take a ~*
yasumi o toru 休みを取る

holidaymaker kōrakukyaku 行楽客

Holland Oranda オランダ

hollow object karappo (no) 空っぽ
(の); cheeks kubonda くぼんだ;
promise uwabe dake (no) うわべ
だけ(の)

holly seiyō-hiiragi 西洋ひいらぎ

holocaust daigyakusatsu 大虐殺

hologram rittaieizō 立体影像,
horoguramu ホログラム

holster horusutā ホルスター

holy shinsei (na) 神聖(な)

Holy Spirit Seirei 聖霊

Holy Week Seishūkan 聖週間

home 1 n katei 家庭; (native

country) kokoku 故国; (area, part
of country) kokyō 故郷; (for
animals) seisokuchi 生息地; (for
old people) rōjin-hōmu 老人ホー
ム; *at ~* (in my house) ie de で;
(in my country) jibun no kuni de
自分の国で; SP honkyochi de 本拠
地で; *make oneself at ~* kutsurogu
くつろぐ; *at ~ and abroad* kuni no
naigai de 国の内外で; *work from ~*
zaitaku-kinmu suru 在宅勤務する
2 adv jitaku e 自宅へ; (country)
kokoku e 故国へ; (area, part of
country) kokyō e 故郷へ; *go ~*
jitaku e kaeru 自宅へ帰る; (to own
country) kokoku e kaeru 故国へ帰
る; (to area, part of country)
kokyō e kaeru 故郷へ帰る

home address jitaku no jūsho 自宅
の住所; **homecoming** satogaeri 里
帰り; **home computer** pasokon パ
ソコン

homeless adj hōmuresu (no) ホー
ムレス(の); (temporarily) ie no
nai 家のない

homeloving kateiteki (na) 家庭的
(な)

homely kateiteki (na) 家庭的(な);
(not good-looking) kiryō no yoku
nai 器量の良くない

homemade jikasei (no) 自家製(の);
home game honkyochi no shiai
本拠地での試合; **home movie**
hōmu-mūbī ホームムービー

homeopathy homeopashī ホメオパ
シー, dōdoku-ryōhō 同毒療法

homesick: *be ~* homushikku ni naru
ホームシックになる; **home town**
kokyō 故郷; **homeward** adv ie ni
mukatte 家に向かって; (to one's
country) kokoku ni mukau 故国に
向かう; **homework** EDU shukudai
宿題; **homeworking** COM zaitaku-
kinmu (no) 在宅勤務(の)

homicide (crime) satsujin 殺人;
(police department) satsujin-sōsa-
ka 殺人捜査課

homograph dōkei-igigo 同系異義語

homophobia dōsei-girai ホモ嫌い

homosexual 1 adj dōseiai (no) 同性
愛(の), homo (no) ホモ(の) **2** n

dōseiai-sha 同性愛者, homo ホモ
honest shōjiki (na) 正直(な)
honestly (*truthfully*) shōjiki ni 正直に; (*frankly*) sotchoku ni 率直に; **~!** mattaku まったく
honesty shōjiki 正直
honey hachimitsu はちみつ; F (*darling*) kawaii hito かわいい人; (*to husband*) anata あなた; (*to wife*) omae おまえ
honeycomb hachi no su はちの巣
honeymoon n hanemūn ハネムーン
Hong Kong Honkon 香港
honk v/t horn narasu 鳴らす
honor 1 n meiyo 名誉 **2** v/t uyamau 敬う
honorable rippa (na) 立派(な)
honorific language keigo 敬語
Honshu Honshū 本州
hood (*over head*) fūdo フード; (*over cooker*) ōi 覆い; MOT bonnetto ボンネット; F (*gangster*) chinpira チンピラ
hoodlum F chinpira チンピラ
hoof hizume ひづめ
hook (*on wall, door*) yōfuku-kake 洋服掛け; (*on dress*) hokku ホック; (*for fishing*) tsuribari 釣り針; (*in golf, boxing*) fukku フック; **off the ~** TELEC juwaki o hazushite 受話器をはずして
hooked: *be ~ on* ... ni muchū de ...に夢中で; (*on drugs*) ... chūdoku de ...中毒で
hooker F baishunfu 売春婦
hooky: *play ~* gakkō o saboru 学校をさぼる
hooligan fūrigan フーリガン
hooliganism ranbō 乱暴
hoop wa 輪
hoot 1 v/t horn būbū narasu ぶーぶー鳴らす **2** v/i (*of car*) kurakushon ga naru クラクションが鳴る; (*of owl*) hōhō to naku ほーほーと鳴く
hop[1] (*plant*) hoppu ホップ
hop[2] v/i (*of frog*) pyon to tobu ぴょんと飛ぶ; (*of person*) kataashi de tobu 片足で跳ぶ
hope 1 n nozomi 望み; *there's no ~ of that* sono mikomi wa amari nai

その見込みはあまりない **2** v/i kibō o motsu 希望を持つ; **~ for** ... o nozomu ...を望む **3** v/t: *I - you like it* tsumaranai mono desu ga つまらないものですが; *I - so* sō da to yoi to omou そうだとよいと思う; *I - not* sō de nai to yoi to omou そうでないと思う
hopeful kibō o motta 希望を持った; (*promising*) yūbō (na) 有望(な)
hopefully kitai shite 期待して; (*I/we hope*) dekireba できれば
hopeless *position, project* zetsubōteki (na) 絶望的(な); (*useless: person*) dō shiyō mo nai どうしようもない
horizon chiheisen 地平線; (*at sea*) suiheisen 水平線
horizontal suihei (no) 水平(の)
hormone horumon ホルモン
horn (*of animal*) tsuno つの; MOT kurakushon クラクション
hornet suzumebachi すずめばち
horn-rimmed bekkōbuchi (no) べっ甲縁(の)
horny F (*sexually*) kōfun shita 興奮した
horoscope hoshiuranai 星占い
horrible osoroshii 恐ろしい
horrify: *I was horrified* zotto shimashita ぞっとしました
horrifying *experience* osoroshii 恐ろしい; *idea, prices* akireta あきれた
horror kyōfu 恐怖; *the ~s of war* sensō no sanka 戦争の惨禍
horror movie horā-eiga ホラー映画
hors d'oeuvre ōdoburu オードブル
horse uma 馬
horseback: *on ~* uma ni notte 馬に乗って; **horse chestnut** seiyō-tochinoki no mi 西洋とちのきの実; **horsepower** bariki 馬力; **horse race** keiba 競馬; **horse radish** seiyō-wasabi 西洋わさび; *Japanese ~* wasabi わさび; **horseshoe** teitetsu てい鉄
horticulture engei 園芸
hose n hōsu ホース
hospice hosupisu ホスピス
hospitable motenashi no yoi もてなしのよい

hospital byōin 病院; **go into the ~** nyūin suru 入院する

hospitality (o) motenashi (お)もてなし

host n (at party, reception) shujin'yaku 主人役; (of TV program) shikai-sha 司会者

hostage hitojichi 人質; **be taken ~** hitojichi ni torareru 人質にとられる

hostel (for students) gakuseiryō 学生寮; (youth ~) yūsu-hosuteru ユースホステル

hostess (at party, reception) shujin'yaku 主人役; (on airplane) suchuwādesu スチュワーデス; (in bar) hosutesu ホステス

hostile tekii teki na 敵意のある

hostility (of attitude) tekii 敵意; **hostilities** tekitai-kōi 敵対行為

hot weather, day atsui 暑い; object, food, water atsui 熱い; (spicy) karai 辛い; F (good) jōzu (na) 上手(な)

hot dog hottodoggu ホットドッグ

hotel (Western-style) hoteru ホテル; (Japanese-style) ryokan 旅館

hotplate dennetsuki 電熱器; **hotspot** (military, political) funsō-chitai 紛争地帯; **hot spring** onsen 温泉

hour jikan 時間

hourly adj ichijikan goto (no) 1時間ごと(の)

house n ie 家; **at your ~** anata no ie de あなたの家で

houseboat hausubōto ハウスボート; **housebreaking** oshikomi-gōtō 押し込み強盗; **household** kazoku 家族; **household name** dare demo shitte iru namae だれでも知っている名前; **house husband** shufu 主夫; **housekeeper** kaseifu 家政婦; **housekeeping** (activity) kaji 家事; (money) seikatsuhi 生活費; **House of Councilors** Sangiin 参議院, **House of Representatives** (Japanese) Shūgiin 衆議院; (in USA) Kain 下院; **housewarming** (party) hikkoshi-iwai no pātī 引越し祝いのパーティー; **housewife** shufu 主婦; **housework** kaji 家事

housing jūtaku 住宅; TECH kēsu ケース

housing conditions jūkankyō 住環境

hovel abaraya あばら屋

hover kūchū de teishi suru 空中で停止する

hovercraft hobākurafuto ホバークラフト

how dō yatte どうやって; **~ do you open it?** dō yatte akeru no どうやって開けるの; **~ are you?** konnichi wa こんにちは; (long time since you met) (o) genki desu ka (お)元気ですか ...? ... wa dō desu ka ...はどうですか; **~ much?** dono kurai どのくらい; **~ much is it?** (cost) sore wa ikura desu ka それはいくらですか; **~ many?** ikutsu いくつ; **~ funny/sad!** nante okashiin darō/kanashiin darō なんておかしいんだろう/悲しいんだろう

however keredomo けれども; **~ big/small they are** dore hodo ōkikute mo/chiisakute mo どれほど大きくて/小さくても

howl v/i (of dog) tōboe suru 遠ぼえする; (of person in pain) wameku わめく; (with laughter) ōwarai suru 大笑いする

hub (of wheel) habu ハブ

hubcap hoīru-kyappu ホイールキャップ

♦ huddle together mi o yoseau 身を寄せ合う

huff: **be in a ~** mutto shite iru むっとしている

hug v/t dakishimeru 抱き締める

huge building, tree kyodai (na) 巨大(な); debt, difference bakudai (na) ばく大(な)

hull n sentai 船体

hullabaloo sawagi 騒ぎ

hum 1 v/t song, tune hamingu suru ハミングする 2 v/i (of person) hanauta o utau 鼻歌を歌う; (of machine) būn to iu oto o tateru ぶーんという音を立てる

human 1 n ningen 人間 2 adj ningen (no) 人間(の), hito (no) 人(の); attitude, weakness ningen-rashii

人間らしい; *error* jin'iteki (na) 人
為的(な)

human being ningen 人間

humane *society* ningenmi no aru 人
間味のある; *treatment* ningenteki
(na) 人間的(な)

humanitarian jindōteki (na) 人道的
(な)

humanity (*human beings*) jinrui 人
類; (*of attitude*) ningensei 人間性

human race jinrui 人類

human resources (*department*)
jinjibu 人事部; (*personnel*) jinzai
人材

humble *person* tsutsumashii つつま
しい; *origins* iyashii 卑しい; *meal,
house* shisso (na) 質素(な)

humdrum heibon (na) 平凡(な)

humid mushiatsui 蒸し暑い

humidifier kashitsuki 加湿器

humidity shikke 湿気; **70% ~**
shitsudo nanajuppāsento 湿度
70%

humiliate ... ni haji o kakaseru ...に
恥をかかせる

humiliating kutsujokuteki (na) 屈辱
的(な)

humiliation (*embarrassment*) haji
恥; (*indignity*) kutsujoku 屈辱; (*of
enemy*) bujoku 侮辱

humility kenson 謙そん

humor (*comical*) yūmoa ユーモア;
(*mood*) kigen 機嫌; *sense of ~*
yūmoa no sensu ユーモアのセンス;
he has a sense of ~ kare wa
yūmoa ga aru 彼はユーモアがある

humorous *movie, story* okashii お
かしい; *person* yūmorasu (na)
ユーモラス(な)

hump 1 *n* (*of camel, person*) kobu こ
ぶ; (*on road*) moriagari 盛り上が
り **2** *v/t* F (*carry*) katsuide hakobu
担いで運ぶ

hunch F (*idea*) yokan 予感

hundred hyaku 百

hundredth *adj* dai-hyaku (no) 第百
(の)

hundredweight handoreddo-wēto
ハンドレッドウェート

Hungarian 1 *adj* Hangarī (no) ハン
ガリー (の) **2** *n* (*person*) Hangarī-

jin ハンガリー人; (*language*)
Hangarī-go ハンガリー語

Hungary Hangarī ハンガリー

hunger kūfuku 空腹; (*starvation*) ue
飢え

hung-over futsukayoi (no) ふつか
酔い(の)

hungry onaka o sukaseta お腹をす
かせた; *I'm ~* onaka ga suita お腹
がすいた

hunk: (*gorgeous*) ~ F
takumashikute kakko ii otoko た
くましくてかっこいい男

hunky-dory F daijōbu (na) 大丈夫
(な)

hunt 1 *n* (*for animals*) kari 狩り;
(*for criminal, missing child*)
sōsaku 捜索; (*for new leader etc*)
sukauto スカウト **2** *v/t* *animal*
karu 狩る

♦**hunt for** ... o sagasu ...を探す

hunter (*for sport*) kari o suru hito
狩をする人, hantā ハンター; (*for
living*) ryōshi 猟師

hunting shuryō 狩猟

hurdle SP hādoru ハードル; *fig
(obstacle)* shōgai 障害

hurdler SP hādoru-senshu ハードル
選手

hurdles SP hādoru ハードル

hurl nagetsukeru 投げつける

hurray banzai 万歳

hurricane bōfū 暴風雨; harikēn ハ
リケーン

hurried awatadashii あわただしい

hurry 1 *n* ōisogi 大急ぎ; *be in a ~*
awatete iru あわてている **2** *v/i*
isogu 急ぐ

♦**hurry up** *v/i* isogu 急ぐ; *~!* isoide
急いで **2** *v/t* ... o sekitateru ...をせ
きたてる

hurt 1 *v/i* itamu 痛む; *does it ~?* itai
desu ka 痛いですか **2** *v/t* itameru
痛める; (*emotionally*) kizutsukeru
傷つける; *was anybody ~?*
keganin wa imashita ka 怪我人は
いましたか

husband otto 夫

hush *n* chinmoku 沈黙; *~!* shizuka ni
静かに

♦**hush up** *scandal etc* ... o

momikesu ...をもみ消す
husk (*of grain*) kara 殻
husky *adj* shagaregoe (no) しゃがれ声(の); *woman's voice* hasukī (na) ハスキー(な)
hustle 1 *n* hassuru ハッスル; *~ and bustle* zattō 雑踏 2 *v/t person* isogasu 急がす; *~ X into doing Y* X ni muri ni Y saseru Xに無理にYさせる
hut koya 小屋
hyacinth hiyashinsu ヒヤシンス
hybrid *n* (*plant, animal*) zasshu 雑種, haiburiddo ハイブリッド
hydrangea ajisai あじさい
hydrant shōkasen 消火栓
hydraulic suiryoku (no) 水力(の); *brake* yuatsushiki (no) 油圧式(の)
hydroelectric suiryoku-hatsuden (no) 水力発電(の)
hydrofoil (*boat*) suichū-yokusen 水中翼船
hydrogen suiso 水素
hydrogen bomb suiso-bakudan 水素爆弾
hygiene eisei 衛生
hygienic eiseiteki (na) 衛生的(な)
hymn sanbika 賛美歌
hype *n* hade na puromōshon はでなプロモーション; *pej* kodai-senden 誇大宣伝
hyperactive hidoku ochitsuki no nai ひどく落ち着きのない;
hypermarket ōgata-sūpāmāketto

大型スーパーマーケット;
hypersensitive kabin (na) 過敏(な); **hypertension** kōketsuatsu 高血圧; **hypertext** COMPUT haipā tekisuto ハイパーテキスト
hyphen haifun ハイフン
hypnosis saimin-jōtai 催眠状態
hypnotherapy saimin-ryōhō 催眠療法
hypnotize (*by hypnotist*) ... ni saiminjutsu o kakeru ...に催眠術をかける; *fig* miwaku suru 魅惑する
hypochondriac *n* shinkishō-kanja 心気症患者
hypocrisy gizen 偽善
hypocrite gizen-sha 偽善者
hypocritical gizenteki (na) 偽善的(な)
hypothesis kasetsu 仮説
hypothermia teitaion-shō 低体温症
hypothetical kasetsujō (no) 仮説上(の)
hysterectomy shikyū-tekishutsu-shujutsu 子宮摘出手術
hysteria hisuterī ヒステリー
hysterical *person, laugh* hisuterikku (na) ヒステリック(な); (*very funny*) hidoku omoshiroi ひどくおもしろい; *become ~* hisuterī-jōtai ni naru ヒステリー状態になる
hysterics hisuterī no hossa ヒステリーの発作; (*laughter*) ōwarai 大笑い

I

I watashi 私; (*informal use by men*) boku ぼく; (*informal use by women*) atashi あたし; *~ am American / a student* watashi wa Amerika-jin / gakusei desu 私はアメリカ人/学生です ◊ (*omission of pronoun*): *~ don't know* shirimasen 知りません

ice kōri 氷; *break the ~* *fig* kinchō o hogusu 緊張をほぐす
♦ **ice up** (*of engine, wings*) kōri ni ōwareru 氷に覆われる
iceberg hyōzan 氷山; **icebox** reitō shitsu 冷凍室; **icebreaker** (*ship*) saihyōsen 砕氷船; **ice cream** aisukurīmu アイスクリーム;

ice-cream parlor dezāto kafe デザートカフェ; **ice cube** kōri 氷
iced *drink* kōri-iri (no) 氷入り(の)
iced tea aisutī アイスティー; **iced coffee** aisukōhī アイスコーヒー; **iced water** ohiya お冷や
ice hockey aisuhokkē アイスホッケー
ice rink (aisu)sukēto-rinku (アイス)スケートリンク
icicle tsurara つらら
icon (*cultural*) gūzō 偶像; COMPUT aikon アイコン
icy *road, surface* kōri de ōwareta 氷で覆われた; *welcome* reitan (na) 冷淡(な)
idea kangae 考え; *good ~!* ii kangae da いい考えだ; *I have no ~* wakarimasen わかりません; *it's not a good ~ to ...* ... suru no wa ii kangae de wa nai ...するのはいい考えではない
ideal (*perfect*) risōteki (na) 理想的(な)
idealistic risō no takai 理想の高い
identical mattaku onaji 全く同じ; *~ twins* ichiransei-sōseiji 一卵性双生児
identification mimoto-kakunin 身元確認; (*papers etc*) mibun-shōmei ni naru mono 身分証明になるもの
identify *person* miwakeru 見分ける; *cause, problem* akiraka ni suru 明らかにする; (*with a label, by analysis*) shikibetsu suru 識別する
identity mimoto 身元
identity card mibun-shōmeisho 身分証明書
ideology ideorogī イデオロギー
ideological ideorogī (no) イデオロギー(の)
idiom (*saying*) kan'yōku 慣用句
idiomatic kan'yōteki (na) 慣用的(な)
idiosyncrasy (*of style*) tokuisei 特異性; (*of person, behavior*) fūgawari na ten 風変わりな点
idiot baka ばか
idiotic baka (na) ばか(な)
idle 1 *adj* (*lazy*) namakemono (no) 怠け者(の); (*not busy*) hima (na)

暇(な); (*unemployed*) shitsugyōchū (no) 失業中(の); *threat* karui 軽い; *machinery* ugoite inai 動いていない; *in a moment* hima na toki ni 暇なときに 2 *v/i* (*of engine*) aidoringu suru アイドリングする
♦ **idle away** *time etc* namakeru 怠ける
idol aidoru アイドル
idolize sūhai suru 崇拝する
idyllic bokkateki (na) 牧歌的(な)
if moshimo ... naraba もしも...ならば; (*whether or not*) ... kadōka ...かどうか; *you need any more information ...* moshimo hoka ni jōhō ga hitsuyō naraba もしも他に情報が必要ならば; *I don't know ~ he will agree* ... kare ga sansei suru kadōka wakaranai 彼が賛成するかどうかわからない
igloo igurū イグルー
ignite *v/t* tenka suru 点火する
ignition (*in car*) tenka-sōchi 点火装置; *~ key* igunisshon-kī イグニッションキー
ignorance muchi 無知
ignorant muchi (na) 無知(な); (*rude*) reigishirazu (no) 礼儀知らず(の)
ignore mushi suru 無視する
ill guai no warui 具合の悪い; (*with specific illness*) byōki (no) 病気(の); *fall ~, be taken ~* byōki ni naru 病気になる
illegal *strike, trade* higōhō (no) 非合法(の); *immigrant* fuhō (no) 不法(の); *parking* ihan (no) 違反(の); *it's ~ to ...* ... suru no wa hōritsu ihan da ...するのは法律違反だ
illegible yomenai 読めない
illegitimate: *be ~* chakushutsu de nai 嫡出でない; *~ child* shiseiji 私生児
illicit fuhō (no) 不法(の)
illiterate monmō (no) 文盲(の)
ill-mannered busahō (na) 不作法(な)
ill-natured seikaku no warui 性格の悪い
illness byōki 病気

illogical fugōri (na) 不合理(な)

ill-tempered okorippoi 怒りっぽい

illtreat gyakutai suru 虐待する

illuminate building etc iruminēshon de kazaru イルミネーションで飾る

illuminating remarks etc wakariyasui わかりやすい

illusion gensō 幻想; (false belief) sakkaku 錯覚

illustrate book ... ni sashie o ireru ...に挿絵を入れる; (with examples) setsumei suru 説明する

illustration (picture) sashie 挿絵, irasuto イラスト; (with examples) setsumei 説明

illustrator irasutorētā イラストレーター

ill will tekii 敵意

image kōkei 光景; (exact likeness) ikiutsushi 生き写し; (of politician, company) imēji イメージ; (of pop star etc) sugata 姿

image-conscious imēji o ishiki shita イメージを意識した

imaginable sōzō dekiru 想像できる; the biggest / smallest size ~ kangaerareru kagiri ichiban ōki/chiisai saizu 考えられる限り一番大きい/小さいサイズ

imaginary sōzōjō (no) 想像上(の)

imagination (ability to imagine) sōzōryoku 想像力; it's all in your ~ omoisugoshi desu 思い過ごしです

imaginative child sōzōryoku no yutaka (na) 想像力の豊か(な); piece of work sōzōsei ni tomu 想像性に富む

imagine sōzō suru 想像する; I can just ~ it sōzō ga tsuku 想像がつく; you're imagining things kangaesugi desu 考えすぎです

imbecile baka ばか

IMF (= International Monetary Fund) Kokusai-tsūka-kikin 国際通貨基金

imitate maneru まねる

imitation (copying) mane まね; (sth copied) mozōhin 模造品; (jewelry) imitēshon イミテーション

immaculate yogore no nai 汚れのない; (flawless) ketten no nai 欠点のない

immaterial toru ni taranai 取るに足らない

immature mijuku (na) 未熟(な)

immediate (in time) sugu (no) すぐ(の); the ~ family kinshin-sha 近親者; in the ~ neighborhood sugu kinjo ni すぐ近所に

immediately sugusama すぐさま; ~ after the bank / church ginkō/kyōkai no sugu saki 銀行/教会のすぐ先

immense kyodai (na) 巨大(な); relief, longing taihen (na) 大変(な)

immerse tsukeru つける; ~ oneself in ... ni fukeru ...にふける

immersion heater yuwakashiki 湯沸かし器

immigrant n imin 移民

immigrate ijū suru 移住する

immigration (act) ijū 移住; Immigration (government office) nyūkoku-kanrikyoku 入国管理局

imminent sashisematta 差し迫った

immobilize person ugokenaku suru 動けなくする; factory sutoppu saseru ストップさせる; car sadō shinai yō ni suru 作動しないようにする

immoderate sessei no nai 節制のない

immoral fudōtoku (na) 不道徳(な)

immorality fudōtoku 不道徳

immortal fushi (no) 不死(の)

immortality fushi 不死

immune (to illness, infection) men'eki no aru 免疫のある; (from ruling, requirement) menjo sareta 免除された

immune system MED men'eki-shisutemu 免疫システム

immunity (to infection) men'eki 免疫; (from ruling) menjo 免除; diplomatic ~ gaikōkan-tokken 外交官特権

impact n (of meteorite, vehicle) shōtotsu 衝突; (effect) eikyō 影響; (of new manager etc) shōgeki 衝撃

impair sokonau 損なう

impaired hearing, sight yowatta

弱った

impartial kōhei (na) 公平(な)

impassable road tōrenai 通れない

impasse (in negotiations etc) fukurokōji 袋小路

impassioned netsuretsu (na) 熱烈 (な)

impassive face muhyōjō 無表情(な)

impatience tanki 短気

impatient ki no mijikai 気の短い

impatiently iraira shite いらいらして

impeccable turnout mōshibun no nai 申し分のない; English, Japanese kanpeki (na) 完ぺき(な)

impeccably dressed mōshibun nai hodo 申し分ないほど; pronounce, speak kanpeki ni 完ぺきに

impede samatageru 妨げる

impediment: speech ~ gengo-shōgai 言語障害

impending sashisemaiatta 差し迫った

impenetrable mind fukakai (na) 不可解(な)

imperative 1 adj dō shite mo hitsuyō (na) どうしても必要(な) **2** n GRAM meireikei 命令形

imperceptible chikakufunō (na) 知覚不能(な)

imperfect 1 adj fukanzen (na) 不完全(な) **2** n GRAM mikanryō-kei 未完了形

imperial teikoku (no) 帝国(の); palaces kōtei (no) 皇帝(の); Imperial Palace Kōkyo 皇居

impersonal ningenmi no nai 人間味のない

impersonate (as a joke) ... no monomane o suru ...の物まねをする; (illegally) ... ni narisumasu ...になりすます

impertinence namaiki 生意気

impertinent namaiki (na) 生意気(な)

imperturbable ochitsuita 落ち着いた

impervious: ~ to ... ni eikyō sarenai ...に影響されない

impetuous mōretsu (na) 猛烈(な)

impetus (of campaign etc) hazumi

はずみ

implement 1 n dōgu 道具 **2** v/t measures etc jikkō suru 実行する

implicate: ~ X in Y X o Y ni kanrenzukeru XをYに関連付ける

implication (inference) imi 意味

implicit anmoku (no) 暗黙(の); trust zettaiteki (na) 絶対的(な)

implore ... ni tangan suru ...に嘆願する

imply (mean) imi suru 意味する; (hint) honomekasu ほのめかす

impolite reigishirazu (no) 礼儀知らず(の)

import 1 n yunyū 輸入 **2** v/t yunyū suru 輸入する

importance jūyōsei 重要性

important jūyō (na) 重要(な); person yūryoku (na) 有力(な)

importer yunyū-gyōsha 輸入業者

impose tax kasu 課す; ~ oneself on ... ni meiwaku o kakeru ...に迷惑をかける

imposing medatsu 目立つ

impossibility fukanō 不可能

impossible fukanō (na) 不可能(な)

impostor peten-shi ぺてん師

impotence inpo インポ

impotent inpo (no) インポ(の)

impoverished mazushiku natta 貧しくなった

impractical person jōshiki ni kakete iru 常識に欠けている; suggestion higenjitsuteki (na) 非現実的(な)

impress (give an impression to) ... ni yoi inshō o ataeru ...によい印象を与える; (of scenery) ... ni kandō o ataeru ...に感動を与える; be ~ed by (by s.o.) ... ni yoi inshō o ukeru ...によい印象を受ける; (by sth) ... ni kandō suru ...に感動する; I'm not ~ed sore wa kanshin dekimasen ne それは感心できませんね

impression inshō 印象; (impersonation) monomane 物まね; make a good / bad ~ on ... ni yoi / warui inshō o ataeru ...によい/悪い印象を与える; I get the ~ that ... to iu kanji ga suru ...という感じがする

impressionable kanjiyasui 感じや
すい

impressive inshōteki (na) 印象的
(な)

imprint *n* (*of credit card*) kokuin 刻
印

imprison keimusho ni ireru 刑務所
に入れる

imprisonment (*act*) tōgoku 投獄; *10
years'~* jūnen no kinkokei 十年の
禁固刑

improbable mikomi no nai 見込みの
ない

improper *behavior* futekisetsu (na)
不適切(な)

improve 1 *v/t* kaizen suru 改善する;
skills jōtatsu saseru 上達させる
2 *v/i* yoku naru よくなる; (*of
skills*) jōtatsu suru 上達する

improvement kaizen 改善; (*in
skills*) jōtatsu 上達

improvise *v/i* THEA sokkyō de
enjiru 即興で演じる; MUS sokkyō
de ensō suru 即興で演奏する; *we
just had to ~* sono ba o
maniawasete de yarisugosu その場
を間に合わせでやりすごす

impudent atsukamashii 厚かましい

impulse shōdō 衝動; *do ... on ~*
shōdōteki ni ... o suru 衝動的に...
をする; *~ buy* shōdōgai 衝動買い

impulsive shōdōteki (na) 衝動的
(な)

impunity: *with ~* basserarezu ni 罰
せられずに

impure fujun (na) 不純(な)

in 1 *prep* (*with verbs of being*) ... ni
...に; (*with verbs of activity*) ...
de ...で; *~ Washington / Japan*
(*live, stay*) Washinton / Nihon ni
ワシントン/日本に; (*meet, work*)
Washinton / Nihon de ワシントン/
日本で; *~ the box* (*inside*) hako no
naka ni 箱の中に; *he put it ~ his
pocket* kare wa poketto no naka
ni shimatta 彼はポケットの中にし
まった; *wounded ~ the leg / arm*
ashi / ude ni kega o shita 足/腕に
怪我をした; (*time*) ... ni ...に; *~
1999* sen kyūhyaku kyūjū kyū nen
ni 1999年に; *~ two hours* (*from

now*) nijikan go ni 二時間後に;
(*over period of*) nijikan de 二時間
で; *~ the morning* asa ni 朝に; *~ the
summer* natsu ni 夏に; *~ August*
hachigatsu ni 八月に; ◊ (*manner*)
... de ...で; *~ English / Japanese*
Eigo / Nihon-go de 英語/中国語で;
~ a loud voice ōkina koe de 大きな
声で; *~ his style* kare no yarikata
de 彼のやり方で; *dressed ~ yellow*
kiiroi fuku o kite iru 黄色い服を着
ている ◊ (*while*); *~ crossing the
road* michi o watatte iru toki ni 道
をわたっているときに; *~ agreeing
to this* (*by virtue of*) sansei shita
tame ni 賛成したために ◊ *the
characters ~ his novel* kare no
shōsetsu no naka no tōjōjinbutsu
彼の小説の中の登場人物; *~
Faulkner* Fōkunā de wa フォーク
ナーでは ◊ *three ~ all* zenbu de
san 全部で三; *one ~ ten* (*of
objects*) jū no uchi hitotsu 十のう
ち一つ; (*of people*) jūnin no uchi
hitori 十人のうち一人 *2 adj* (*at
home*) ie ni 家に; (*in the building
etc*) uchi ni 内に; (*arrived: train*)
tōchaku shite 到着して; (*in its
position*) naka ni 中に; *~ here*
koko ni ここに *3 adj*
(*fashionable, popular*) hayari
(no) はやり(の)

inability munō 無能

inaccessible ikizurai 行きづらい

inaccurate fuseikaku (na) 不正確
(な)

inactive fukappatsu (na) 不活発(な)

inadequate *supply, space* fujūbun
(na) 不十分(な); *person* muryoku
(na) 無力(な)

inadvisable susumerarenai 勧めら
れない

inanimate museibutsu (no) 無生物
(の)

inapplicable tekiyō dekinai 適用で
きない

inappropriate futekitō (na) 不適当
(な)

inarticulate *person* hakkiri shinai
はっきりしない

inattentive fuchūi (na) 不注意(な)

inaudible kikoenai 聞こえない

inaugural *speech* shūninshiki (no) 就任式(の)

inaugurate *new building* rakusei suru 落成する; *service* kaigyō suru 開業する; *system* kaishi suru 開始する

inauguration (*of president*) shūninshiki 就任式

inborn umaretsuki (no) 生まれつき(の)

inbreeding kinshin-kōhai 近親交配

inc. (= *incorporated*) kabushiki-gaisha 株式会社

incalculable *damage* hakari-shirenai はかりしれない

incapable muryoku (na) 無力(な); **he's ~ of understanding** kare wa rikai suru koto ga dekinai 彼は理解することができない

incendiary device shōdan 焼い弾

incense[1] *n* kō 香; REL senkō 線香

incense[2] *v/t* gekido saseru 激怒させる

incentive shigeki 刺激

incessant taema no nai 絶え間のない

incessantly taema naku 絶え間なく

incest kinshin-sōkan 近親相かん

inch *n* inchi インチ

incident dekigoto できごと; (*more serious*) jiken 事件

incidental fuzuiteki (na) 付随的(な); **~ expenses** zappi 雑費

incidentally tokoro de ところで

incinerator shōkyakuro 焼却炉

incision MED sekkai 切開

incisive *analysis* surudoi 鋭い

incite (*to riot*) sendō suru 扇動する; *violence* aoritateru あおりたてる; **~ X to do Y** X o sosonokashite Y saseru XをそそのかしてYさせる

inclement *weather* kibishii 厳しい

inclination (*tendency*) keikō 傾向; (*liking: for music*) konomi 好み; (*for travel*) ganbō 願望

incline: be ~d to do … (*tend to*) … suru keikō ni aru …する傾向にある; (*be willing to*) … shitai ki ga suru …したい気がする

inclose, inclosure → **enclose,**

enclosure

include ireru 入れる; (*of price*) fukumu 含む

including *prep* … o fukumete …を含めて

inclusive 1 *adj price* issaikomi (no) 一切込み(の) **2** *prep* … o fukumete …を含めて; **~ of** … o fukumete … を含めて **3** *adv*: **from Monday to Thursday ~** getsuyōbi kara mokuyōbi made 月曜日から木曜日まで

incoherent tsujitsuma no awanai つじつまの合わない

income shūnyū 収入

income tax shotokuzei 所得税

incoming *flight* tōchaku suru 到着する; *phonecall* soto kara kakatte kuru 外からかかってくる; *mail* haitatsu sarete kuru 配達されてくる; *president* kōnin (no) 後任の(の); **~ tide** ageshio 上げ潮

incomparable murui (no) 無類(の)

incompatibility (*of personalities*) seikaku no fuitchi 性格の不一致; (*of disk formats, systems*) gokansei no nasa 互換性のなさ

incompatible *personalities* aiirenai 相入れない; *formats, systems* gokansei no nai 互換性のない

incompetence munō 無能

incompetent *person, organization* munō (na) 無能(な); *piece of work* heta (na) 下手(な); **be ~ to teach** oshieru no ni muite inai 教えるのに向いていない

incomplete mikansei (no) 未完成(の); *account, statement* fukanzen (na) 不完全(な)

incomprehensible rikai dekinai 理解できない

inconceivable kangaerarenai 考えられない

inconclusive *argument* ketsuron ni tasshinai 結論に達しない; *evidence* fujūbun (na) 不十分(な)

incongruous chōwa shinai 調和しない

inconsiderate omoiyari no nai 思いやりのない

inconsistent *argument* mujun shita

矛盾した; *person* kimagure (na) 気まぐれ(な); *behavior, work* mura no aru むらのある

inconsolable nagusameyō no nai 慰めようのない

inconspicuous medatanai 目立たない

inconvenience *n* (*caused by s.o./sth*) meiwaku 迷惑; (*of not having a car etc*) fuben-sa 不便さ

inconvenient *time, arrangement* tsugō no warui 都合の悪い; *place, not having a car etc* fuben (na) 不便(な)

incorporate (*include*) toriireru 取り入れる

incorporated COM kabushiki-gaisha 株式会社

incorrect fuseikaku (na) 不正確(な)

incorrectly fuseikaku ni 不正確に

incorrigible sukuigatai 救いがたい

increase 1 *v/t* ageru 上げる; *number, amount* fuyasu 増やす **2** *v/i* agaru 上がる; (*of number, amount*) fueru 増える; (*of confidence*) tsuku つく **3** *n* (*in number*) zōka 増加; (*in amount*) zōryō 増量; (*in value*) zōdai 増大

increasing zōka suru 増加する

increasingly masumasu ますます

incredible (*amazing*) shinjirarenai 信じられない; (*very good*) subarashii すばらしい

incriminate yūzai ni suru 有罪にする; ~ *oneself* tsumi o mitomeru 罪を認める

incubator (*for chicks*) fukaki ふ化器; (*for babies*) jinkō-hoikuki 人工保育器

incur maneku 招く; *anger* kōmuru こうむる

incurable chiryō-fukanō (na) 治療不可能(な)

indebted: *be ~ to* ... ni taihen kansha shite iru ...に大変感謝している

indecent waisetsu (na) わいせつ(な)

indecisive yūjū-fudan (no) 優柔不断(の)

indecisiveness yūjū-fudan 優柔不断

indeed (*in fact*) hontō ni 本当に, tashika ni 確かに; (*yes, agreeing*) sono tōri その通り; *very much ~* hontō ni 本当に

indefinable bakuzen to shita 漠然とした

indefinite *period, time* futei (no) 不定(の); ~ *article* GRAM futei-kanshi 不定冠詞

indefinitely mukigen ni 無期限に

indelicate gehin (na) 下品(な)

indent 1 *n* (*in text*) atamasage 頭下げ **2** *v/t line* gyōtō o sageru 行頭を下げる

independence dokuritsu 独立

Independence Day Dokuritsu-kinenbi 独立記念日

independent *business, country* dokuritsu (no) 独立(の); (*financially*) jikatsu shite iru 自活している; *type of person* jiritsu shita 自立した; (*not state-owned*) minkan (no) 民間(の)

independently *treat* betsubetsu ni 別々に; ~ *of* betsubetsu ni 別々に

indescribable ii yō no nai 言いようのない

indescribably *bad, beautiful* iiarawasenai hodo 言い表せないほど

indestructible hakai dekinai 破壊できない; *faith* kowarenai こわれない

indeterminate *length of time* bakuzen to shita ばく然とした

index (*for book*) sakuin 索引, indekkusu インデックス

index card sakuin-kādo 索引カード

index finger hitosashiyubi 人さし指

India Indo インド

Indian 1 *adj* Indo (no) インド(の) **2** *n* Indo-jin インド人; (*American*) Indian インディアン

Indian summer koharu-biyori 小春日和

indicate 1 *v/t* (*show*) shimesu 示す **2** *v/i* MOT winkā o dasu ウィンカーを出す

indication chōkō 徴候

indicator MOT winkā ウィンカー

indict kiso suru 起訴する
indifference mukanshin 無関心
indifferent mukanshin (na) 無関心 (な); (*mediocre*) heibon (na) 平凡 (な)
indigestible shōka dekinai 消化できない
indigestion shōka-furyō 消化不良
indignant fungaishita 憤慨した
indignation ikidōri 憤り
indirect *link* kansetsuteki (na) 間接的(な); *criticism* tōmawashi (na) 遠回し(な); ~ *route* mawarimichi 回り道
indirectly kansetsuteki ni 間接的に
indiscreet keisotsu (na) 軽率(な)
indiscretion (*act*) keisotsu (na) kōdō 軽率な行動
indiscriminate musabetsu (na) 無差別(な)
indispensable kakegae no nai 掛け替えのない
indisposed (*not well*) kibun ga warui 気分が悪い
indisputable meihaku (na) 明白(な)
indisputably meihaku ni 明白に
indistinct fumeiryō (na) 不明りょう(な)
indistinguishable miwake no tsukanai 見分けのつかない
individual 1 *n* kojin 個人 **2** *adj* (*separate*) koko (no) 個々(の); (*personal*) kojin (no) 個人(の)
individualist kojin-shugisha 個人主義者
individually koko ni 個々に
indivisible bunkatsu dekinai 分割できない
indoctrinate ... ni fukikomu ...に吹き込む
indolence taida 怠惰
indolent taida (na) 怠惰(な)
Indochina Indoshina インドシナ
Indochinese *adj* Indoshina-jin インドシナ人
Indonesia Indoneshia インドネシア
Indonesian 1 *adj* Indoneshia (no) インドネシア(の) **2** *n* (*person*) Indoneshia-jin インドネシア人
indoor okunai (no) 屋内(の), indoa (no) インドア(の)

indoors *go* okunai e 屋内へ; *stay* okunai ni 屋内に; *play* okunai de 屋内で
indulge 1 *v/t* oneself manzoku saseru 満足させる **2** *v/i*: ~ *in* ... ni fukeru ...にふける
indulgence (*of tastes, appetite etc*) tanoshimi 楽しみ; (*laxity*) amayakashi 甘やかし
indulgent (*not strict enough*) amai 甘い
industrial kōgyō (no) 工業(の)
industrial action sutoraiki ストライキ
industrial dispute rōdō-sōgi 労働争議
industrialist jitsugyōka 実業家
industrialize *v/t* & *v/i* kōgyōka suru 工業化する
industrial waste sangyō-haikibutsu 産業廃棄物
industrious kinben (na) 勤勉(な)
industry sangyō 産業, kōgyō 工業
ineffective kōka no nai 効果のない
ineffectual person munō 無能 (な)
inefficient *system* hinōritsuteki (na) 非能率的(な); *person* munō (na) 無能(な)
ineligible shikaku no nai 資格のない
inept *person* munō 無能(な)
inequality fubyōdō 不平等
inescapable sakerarenai 避けられない
inestimable hakari-shirenai はかりしれない
inevitable sakerarenai 避けられない
inevitably hitsuzenteki ni 必然的に
inexcusable yurusarenai 許されない
inexhaustible *person* tsukare o shiranai 疲れを知らない; *supply* mujinzō (no) 無尽蔵(の)
inexpensive yasui 安い
inexperienced keiken no nai 経験のない
inexplicable setsumei no tsukanai 説明のつかない
inexpressible *joy* iiarawasenai 言い表せない

infallible zettai ni machigai no nai 絶対に間違いのない

infamous akumei no takai 悪名の高い

infancy (*of person*) yōnen-jidai 幼年時代; (*of state, institution*) shoki 初期

infant yōji 幼児

infantile *pej* kodomoppoi 子供っぽい

infantry hoheitai 歩兵隊

infantry soldier hohei 歩兵

infatuated: *be ~ with* ... ni muchū ni naru ...に夢中になる

infect ... ni kansen suru ...に感染する; (*of person*) byōki o utsusu 病気を移す; *food, water* osen suru 汚染する; *become ~ed* (*of person*) kansen suru 感染する; (*of wound*) baikin ga hairu ばい菌が入る

infection kansen 感染

infectious *disease* kansen suru 感染する; *laughter* hito ni utsuru 人に移る

infer: *~ X from Y* Y kara X o suiron suru YからXを推論する

inferior *quality, workmanship* ototta 劣った; *be ~ to* MIL ... yori kai de aru ...より下位である

inferiority (*in quality*) soaku-sa 粗悪さ

inferiority complex rettōkan 劣等感

infertile *soil* fumō (no) 不毛(の); *woman* funin (no) 不妊(の)

infertility (*of soil*) fumō 不毛; (*of woman*) funin 不妊

infidelity futei 不貞

infiltrate *v/t* shinnyū saseru 侵入させる

infinite mugen (no) 無限(の); *fig* bakudai (na) 莫大(な)

infinitive futeishi 不定詞

infinity mugen 無限

infirm yowatta 弱った

infirmary byōin 病院

infirmity byōki 病気

inflame *passions* aoritateru あおりたてる

inflammable kansei (no) 可燃性(の)

inflammation MED enshō 炎症

inflatable *dinghy* fukuramasu koto ga dekiru ふくらますことができる

inflate *v/t tire, dinghy* fukuramasu ふくらます; *economy* infure ni suru インフレにする

inflation infure インフレ

inflationary (*of inflation*) infure (no) インフレ(の); (*causing inflation*) infure o hikiokosu インフレを引き起こす

inflection (*of voice*) yokuyō 抑揚

inflexible *attitude, person* yūzū no kikanai 融通のきかない

inflict: *X on Y* Y ni X o ataeru YにXを与える

in-flight kinai (no) 機内(の); *~ entertainment* kinai-entāteinmento 機内エンターテインメント

influence 1 *n* eikyō 影響; (*power to ~*) eikyōryoku 影響力; *be a good / bad ~ on* yoi/warui eikyō o ... ni ataeru よい/悪い影響を...に与える **2** *v/t s.o.'s thinking* ... ni eikyō o oyobosu ...に影響を及ぼす; *decision* sayū suru 左右する

influential eikyōryoku no aru 影響力のある

influenza infuruenza インフルエンザ

inform tsūchi suru 通知する; *~ X of Y* X ni Y no koto o tsūchi suru XにYのことを通知する; *keep me ~ed* shirasenasai 知らせなさい

♦**inform on** ... o mikkoku suru ...を密告する

informal *conversation* kudaketa くだけた; *dress* fudan (no) 普段(の); *meeting* hikōshiki (no) 非公式(の)

informality kudaketa fun'iki くだけた雰囲気; *the ~ of their dress* karera no fudangi 彼らの普段着; *given the ~ of the agreement ...* gōi ga hikōshiki nano de ... 合意が非公式なので...

informant jōhō-teikyō-sha 情報提供者

information jōhō 情報, infomēshon インフォメーション

information science jōhō-kagaku 情報科学; **information scientist** jōhō-kagaku-sha 情報科学者;

information technology jōhō-kōgaku 情報工学

informative yūeki (na) 有益(な)

informer mikkoku-sha 密告者

infra-red *adj* sekigaisen (no) 赤外線(の)

infrastructure (*of economy, society, industry*) kiban 基盤; (*of organization*) kabu-soshiki 下部組織

infrequent tama (no) たま(の)

infuriate gekido saseru 激怒させる

infuriating hidoku haradatashii ひどく腹立たしい

infuse *v/i* (*of tea*) deru 出る

infusion (*of herb tea*) hābutī ハーブティー

ingenious kōmyō (na) 巧妙(な); *person* kiyō (na) 器用(な)

ingenuity kōmyō-sa 巧妙さ; (*of person*) kiyō-sa 器用さ

ingot jigane 地金

ingratiate: **~ oneself with** ... ni toriiru ...に取り入る

ingratitude onshirazu 恩知らず

ingredient (*in cooking*) zairyō 材料; *fig* (*for success*) yōso 要素

inhabit ... ni sumu ...に住む

inhabitable kyojū-kanō (na) 居住可能(な)

inhabitant jūmin 住民

inhale *v/t & v/i* suikomu 吸い込む

inhaler kyūnyūki 吸入器

inherit sōzoku suru 相続する

inheritance isan 遺産; (*characteristics*) iden 遺伝

inhibit *growth, conversation etc* yokusei suru 抑制する

inhibited yokusei sarete iru 抑制されている

inhibition yokusei 抑制

inhospitable *person* buaisō (na) 無愛想(な); *city* suminikui 住みにくい; *climate* kibishii 厳しい

in-house 1 *adj* shanai (no) 社内(の) **2** *adv* *work* shukkin shite 出勤して

inhuman zankoku (na) 残酷(な)

initial 1 *adj* hajime (no) 始め(の); *stage* shoki (no) 初期(の) **2** *n* kashira-moji 頭文字, inisharu イニシャル **3** *v/t* *document* ... ni

kashira-moji de shomei suru ...に頭文字で署名する

initially hajime wa 始めは

initiate *v/t* (*start*) kaishi suru 開始する

initiation (*of new project*) kaishi 開始

initiative shudōken 主導権, inishiachibu イニシアチブ; **do ... on one's own ~** mizukara susunde ... suru 自ら進んで...する

inject *medicine, drug* chūsha suru 注射する; *fuel* chūnyū suru 注入する; *capital* tōnyū suru 投入する

injection MED chūsha 注射; (*of fuel*) chūnyū 注入; (*of cash*) tōnyū 投入

injure *person* kega o saseru 怪我をさせる; *oneself* kega suru 怪我する; *arm, leg* itameru 傷める

injured 1 *adj* kega o shita 怪我をした; *feelings* kizutsuita 傷ついた **2** *n*: **the ~** fushō-sha 負傷者

injury kega 怪我

injustice fukōsei 不公正

ink inku インク; (*Chinese* ~) sumi 墨; **~ painting** sumie 墨絵

inkjet (*printer*) inkujetto purintā インクジェットプリンター

inland nairiku 内陸(の)

in-laws inseki 姻せき

inlay *n* zōgan-zaiku 象眼細工

inlet (*of sea*) irie 入り江; (*in machine*) chūnyūkō 注入口

inmate (*in prison*) jukei-sha 受刑者; (*in mental hospital*) nyūin-kanja 入院患者

inn ryokan 旅館

innate seirai (no) 生来(の)

inner *courtyard* uchigawa (no) 内側(の); *thoughts* naimen (no) 内面(の); **~ ear** naiji 内耳

inner city toshinbu 都心部

innermost mottomo oku (no) 最も奥(の); *feelings* kokoro no oku (no) 心の奥(の)

inner tube chūbu チューブ

innocence mujaki 無邪気; LAW muzai 無罪

innocent mujaki (na) 無邪気(な); LAW muzai (no) 無罪(の)

innovation kakushin 革新

innovative kakushinteki (na) 革新

的(な)

innovator kakushin-sha 革新者

innumerable kazoekirenai 数え切れない

inoculate yobō-sesshu suru 予防接種する

inoculation yobō-sesshu 予防接種

inoffensive gai ni naranai 害にならない

inorganic muki (no) 無機(の)

in-patient nyūin-kanja 入院患者

input 1 n (into project etc) enjo 援助, COMPUT nyūryoku 入力, inputto インプット **2** v/t (into project) enjo suru 援助する; COMPUT nyūryoku suru 入力する

input port COMPUT inputto-pōto インプットポート

inquest chōsa 調査

inquire toiawaseru 問い合わせる; ~ into ... o chōsa suru ...を調査する

inquiry toiawase 問い合わせ

inquisitive shiritagari (no) 知りたがり(の)

insane kichigaijimita 気違いじみた; MED kyōki (no) 狂気(の)

insanitary hieiseiteki (na) 非衛生的(な)

insanity kyōki 狂気

insatiable aku koto no nai 飽くことのない

inscription mei 銘

inscrutable fukakai (na) 不可解(な)

insect konchū 昆虫

insecticide satchūzai 殺虫剤

insect repellent mushiyoke 虫よけ

insecure (anxious) fuan ni omotte iru 不安に思っている; (not confident) jishin ga nai 自信がない

insecurity (anxiety) fuan 不安 (lack of confidence) jishin no nasa 自信のなさ

insensitive person donkan (na) 鈍感(な); remark mushinkei (na) 無神経(な)

insensitivity donkan 鈍感; (of remark) mushinkei-sa 無神経さ

inseparable issues bunri dekinai 分離できない; people hanarerarenai 離れられない

insert 1 n (in magazine etc) orikomi

kōkoku 折り込み広告 **2** v/t sashikomu 差し込む, ireru 入れる; ~ X into Y X o Y ni sashikomu XをYに差し込む

insertion (act) sōnyū 挿入

inside 1 n (of house, box) naka 中, naibu 内部, uchigawa 内側; (of road) uchigawa-shasen 内側車線; somebody on the ~ dare ka naijō ni tsūjite iru hito だれか内情に通じている人; ~ out uragaeshi ni 裏返しに; turn X ~ out X o uragaeshi ni suru Xを裏返しにする; know X ~ out X o yoku shitte iru Xをよく知っている **2** prep ... no naka ni/e ...の中に/へ; ~ the house ie no naka ni 家の中に; ~ of 2 hours nijikan miman de 二時間未満で **3** adv stay naka ni 中に; go, carry naka e 中へ; play, eat naka de 中で; we looked ~ watashitachi wa naka o mita 私達は中を見た **4** adj naka (no) 中(の), uchigawa (no) 内側(の); ~ information naibu-jōhō 内部情報; ~ lane SP inkōsu インコース; (on road) uchigawa-shasen 内側車線; ~ pocket uchi-poketto 内ポケット

insider shōsokutsū 消息通

insider trading FIN insaidā-torihiki インサイダー取り引き

insides onaka おなか, hara 腹

insidious disease shiranai aida ni shinkō suru 知らない間に進行する; means, trick inken (na) 陰険(な); effect senzaiteki (na) 潜在的(な)

insight (understanding) dōsatsu 洞察, (perception) dōsatsuryoku 洞察力

insignificant toru ni taranai 取るに足らない; person jūyō de nai 重要でない

insincere seii no nai 誠意のない

insincerity fuseijitsu 不誠実

insinuate (imply) honomekasu ほのめかす

insist iiharu 言い張る; please keep it, I ~ dōka, totte oite kudasai どうか, 取っておいてください

♦ **insist on** ... o yōkyū suru ...を要求する

insistent shitsukoi しつこい

insolent ōhei (na) 横柄(な)

insoluble *problem* kaiketsu dekinai 解決できない; *substance* tokenai 溶けない

insolvent hasan shita 破産した

insomnia fumin 不眠

inspect *work, tickets, baggage* kensa suru 検査する; *factory, school* shisatsu suru 視察する

inspection (*of work, tickets, baggage*) kensa 検査; (*of factory, school*) shisatsu 視察

inspector (*in factory*) kensa-gakari 検査係; (*on buses*) kensatsu-gakari 検札係

inspiration reikan 霊感, insupirēshon インスピレーション; (*very good idea*) myōan 妙案

inspire *respect etc* yobiokosu 呼び起こす; *be ~d by ...* kara reikan o eru ...から霊感を得る; (*be encouraged by*) ... ni shokuhatsu sareru ...に触発される

instability fuantei 不安定

instal(l) *computer, phone* toritsukeru 取り付ける; *software* insutōru suru インストールする

installation (*of new equipment*) toritsuke 取り付け; (*of software*) insutōru インストール; *military ~* gunji-shisetsu 軍事施設

installment (*of story, TV drama etc*) ichiwa 一話; (*payment*) ikkaibun no shiharai 一回分の支払い

installment plan bunkatsubarai 分割払い

instance (*example*) rei 例; *for ~* tatoeba 例えば

instant 1 *adj* sokuji (no) 即時(の) **2** *n* shunkan 瞬間; *in an ~* sugu ni すぐに

instantaneous sokuji (no) 即時(の)

instant coffee insutanto-kōhī インスタントコーヒー

instantly sokuza ni 即座に

instead sono kawari ni その代わりに; *~ of ...* no kawari ni ...の代わりに

instep ashi no kō 足の甲

instinct honnō 本能

instinctive honnōteki (na) 本能的

(な)

institute 1 *n* (*association*) kyōkai 協会; (*academic*) gakkai 学会; (*educational*) kyōiku kikan 教育機関; (*research*) kenkyū-kikan 研究機関; (*special home*) shisetsu 施設 **2** *v/t new law, inquiry* mōkeru 設ける

institution (*governmental*) kikan 機関; (*something traditional*) kanrei 慣例; (*setting up*) setsuritsu 設立

instruct (*teach*) oshieru 教える; *~ X to do Y* X ni Y suru yō ni shiji suru XにYするように指示する

instruction shiyō-setsumei 使用説明; *~s for use* toriatsukai-setsumei 取扱説明

instruction manual toriatsukai-setsumeisho 取扱説明書

instructive yūeki (na) 有益(な)

instructor insutorakutā インストラクター

instrument MUS gakki 楽器; (*gadget, tool*) kigu 器具

insubordinate hankōteki (na) 反抗的(な)

insufficient fujūbun (na) 不十分(な)

insulate ELEC zetsuen suru 絶縁する; (*against cold*) dannetsu suru 断熱する

insulation ELEC zetsuen 絶縁; (*material*) zetsuentai 絶縁体; (*against cold*) dannetsu 断熱; (*material*) dannetsuzai 断熱材

insulin inshurin インシュリン

insult 1 *n* bujoku 侮辱 **2** *v/t* bujoku suru 侮辱する

insurance hoken 保険

insurance company hoken-gaisha 保険会社

insurance policy hoken-shōsho 保険証書

insure ... ni hoken o kakeru ...に保険をかける; *be ~d* hoken ni haitte iru 保険に入っている

insurmountable kokufuku dekinai 克服できない

intact (*not damaged*) mukizu (no) 無傷(の)

intake (*of college etc*) boshū-jin'in 募集人員

integrate *v/t* tokekomaseru 溶け込ませる

integrated circuit shūseki-kairo 集積回路

integrity (*honesty*) kōketsu 高潔

intellect chisei 知性

intellectual 1 *adj* chiteki (na) 知的(な) **2** *n* chishikijin 知識人, interi インテリ

intelligence chinō 知能; MIL jōhō 情報

intelligence service jōhōbu 情報部

intelligent rikō (na) 利口(な)

intelligible rikai dekiru 理解できる

intend: ~ to ... ... tsumori de aru ... するつもりである; *that's not what I ~ed* sō iu tsumori wa nakatta そういうつもりはなかった

intense mōretsu (na) 猛烈(な); *personality* jōnetsuteki (na) 情熱的(な)

intensify 1 *v/t effect, pressure* tsuyomeru 強める **2** *v/i* (*of pain*) tsuyoku naru 強くなる; (*of battle*) hageshiku naru 激しくなる

intensity hageshi-sa 激しさ

intensive *study, treatment* shūchūteki (na) 集中的(な)

intensive care (**unit**) shūchū-chiryōshitsu 集中治療室, ai-shī-yū ICU

intensive course (*of language study*) shūchū-kōza 集中講座

intent: be ~ on doing ... (*determined to do*) ... shiyō to yonen ga nai ... しようと余念がない; (*concentrating on*) ... suru no ni muchū ni natte iru ...するのに夢中になっている

intention ito 意図; *I have no ~ of ...* (*refuse*) ... no tsumori wa mattaku nai ...のつもりはまったくない

intentional itoteki (na) 意図的(な); (*referring to negative things*) koi (no) 故意(の)

intentionally waza to わざと

interaction (*between departments etc*) kyōryoku 協力; (*between people*) fureai ふれあい; (*between chemicals*) sōgo-sayō 相互作用

interactive *software* taiwashiki (no) 対話式(の); *teaching* fureai no aru ふれあいのある

intercede chūsai suru 仲裁する

intercept *ball* intāseputo suru インターセプトする; *message* bōju suru 傍受する; *missile* tochū de geigeki suru 途中で迎撃する

interchange *n* MOT intāchenji インターチェンジ, rittai-kōsa 立体交差

interchangeable kōkan dekiru 交換できる

intercom intāhon インターホン

intercourse (*sexual*) seikō 性交

interdependent sōgo-izon shita 相互依存した

interest 1 *n* kyōmi 興味; (*financial*) rishi 利子; *take an ~ in ...* ...に興味がある **2** *v/t* kyōmi o motaseru 興味を持たせる; *does that offer ~ you?* sono teian ni wa kyōmi ga arimasu ka その提案には興味がありますか

interested kyōmi o motta 興味を持った; *be ~ in ...* ...に興味がある; *thanks but I'm not ~* sumimasen ga, kyōmi ga arimasen すみませんが、興味がありません

interesting omoshiroi おもしろい

interest rate riritsu 利率

interface 1 *n* intāfeisu インターフェイス **2** *v/i* intāfeisu de rendō suru インターフェイスで連動する

interfere kanshō suru 干渉する

♦ **interfere with** *controls* ... o ijiru ...をいじる; *plans* ... o jama suru ...を邪魔する

interference kanshō 干渉; (*on radio*) jushin-shōgai 受信障害

interior 1 *adj* naibu (no) 内部(の) **2** *n* (*of house*) interia インテリア; (*of country*) nairiku 内陸

interior decorator interia-dezainā インテリアデザイナー; **interior design** shitsunai-sōshoku 室内装飾, interia-dezain インテリアデザイン; **interior designer** interia-dezainā インテリアデザイナー

interlude (*at theater, concert*) makuai 幕あい; (*period*) aima 合間

intermediary *n* chūkai-sha 仲介者
intermediate *adj* chūkyū (no) 中級 (の)
intermission THEA kyūkei-jikan 休憩時間
intern *v/t* kōkin suru 拘禁する
internal *(in body)* naibu (no) 内部(の); *trade* kokunai (no) 国内(の)
internal combustion engine nainen-kikan 内燃機関
internally *(in body)* tainai ni 体内に; *(in organizaton)* naibu ni 内部に
Internal Revenue (Service) Kokuzeichō 国税庁
international *adj* kokusaiteki (na) 国際的(な)
international call kokusai-denwa 国際電話
International Court of Justice Kokusai-shihō-saibansho 国際司法裁判所
internationally kokusaiteki ni 国際的に
International Monetary Fund Kokusai-tsūka-kikin 国際通貨基金
Internet intānetto インターネット; *on the ~* intānetto ni インターネットに
internist naikai 内科医
interpret 1 *v/t* *(linguistically)* tsūyaku suru 通訳する; *comment* kaishaku suru 解釈する; *piece of music* ensō suru 演奏する; *role of Hamlet* enjiru 演じる **2** *v/i* tsūyaku suru 通訳する
interpretation *(linguistic)* tsūyaku 通訳; *(of piece of music, meaning)* kaishaku 解釈
interpreter tsūyaku 通訳
interrelated *facts* sōgo ni kankei shita 相互に関係した
interrogate jinmon suru 尋問する
interrogation jinmon 尋問
interrogative *n* GRAM gimonshi 疑問詞
interrogator jinmon-sha 尋問者
interrupt 1 *v/t* *speaker* … no hanashi ni warikomu …の話に割り込む **2** *v/i* jama o suru 邪魔をする
interruption jama 邪魔

intersect 1 *v/t* … to kōsa suru …と交差する **2** *v/i* kōsa suru 交差する
intersection MOT kōsaten 交差点
interstate *adj* kakushūkan (no) 各州間(の)
interval kankaku 間隔; *(at theater, concert)* kyūkei-jikan 休憩時間
intervene kanshō suru 干渉する; *(of police, military)* kainyū suru 介入する
intervention kanshō 干渉; *(of police, military)* kainyū 介入
interview 1 *n* *(on TV, in paper)* intabyū インタビュー; *(for job)* mensetsu 面接 **2** *v/t* *(on TV, in paper)* … ni intabyū suru …にインタビューする; *(for job)* mensetsu suru 面接する
interviewee *(on TV)* intabyū o ukeru hito インタビューを受ける人; *(for job)* mensetsu-juken-sha 面接受験者
interviewer *(on TV, for paper)* intabyūa インタビューア; *(for job)* mensetsu-sha 面接者
intestine chō 腸
intimacy *(of friendship)* shitashi-sa 親しさ; *(sexual)* nikutai-kankei 肉体関係
intimate *friend* shitashii 親しい; *(sexually)* fukai kankei no aru 深い関係のある; *thoughts* kojinteki (na) 個人的(な)
intimidate odosu 脅す
intimidation odoshi 脅し
into … no naka ni …の中に; *he put it ~ his suitcase* kare wa sūtsukēsu no naka ni shimatta 彼はスーツケースの中にしまった; *translate ~ English* Eigo ni hon'yaku suru 英語に翻訳する; *be ~ F (like)* … ga suki de aru …が好きである; *(be involved with)* … ni nomerikomu …にのめり込む; *when you're ~ the job* shigoto ga wakatte kitara 仕事がわかってきたら
intolerable taerarenai 耐えられない
intolerant henkyō (na) 偏狭(な)
intoxicated yotta 酔った
intransitive verb jidōshi 自動詞

intravenous jōmyakunai (no) 静脈内(の)

intrepid yūkan (na) 勇敢(な)

intricate fukuzatsu (na) 複雑(な)

intrigue 1 *n* inbō 陰謀 2 *v/t*: *I would be ~d to know ...* ... ga wakattara omoshiroi darō ...がわかったらおもしろいだろう

intriguing omoshiroi おもしろい

introduce *person* shōkai suru 紹介する; (*to chess etc*) oshieru 教える; *new technique etc* toriireru 取り入れる; *~ X to Y* X o Y ni shōkai suru XをYに紹介する; *may I ~ ...?* ... o goshōkai shimasu ...をご紹介します

introduction (*to person*) shōkai 紹介; (*to a new food, sport etc*) hajimete no keiken 初めての経験; (*in book*) jobun 序文; (*of new techniques etc*) dōnyū 導入

introvert *n* naikōteki na hito 内向的な人

intrude jama o suru 邪魔をする

intruder shinnyū-sha 侵入者

intrusion jama 邪魔

intuition chokkan 直感

invade shinryaku suru 侵略する

invalid¹ *adj* argument datō de nai 妥当でない; (*legally*) mukō (na) 無効(な)

invalid² *n* MED byōnin 病人

invalidate *claim, theory* mukō ni suru 無効にする

invaluable *help, contributor* kakegae no nai かけがえのない

invariably (*always*) itsumo いつも

invasion shinryaku 侵略

invent hatsumei suru 発明する

invention hatsumei 発明; (*product*) hatsumeihin 発明品

inventive hatsumei no sai no aru 発明の才のある

inventor hatsumei-sha 発明者

inventory mokuroku 目録

inverse *adj* order seihantai (no) 正反対(の)

invert gyaku ni suru 逆にする

inverted commas in'yōfu 引用符

invertebrate *n* musekitsui-dōbutsu 無せきつい動物

invest 1 *v/t* tōshi suru 投資する; *time, energy* tsugikomu つぎ込む 2 *v/i* tōshi suru 投資する

investigate chōsa suru 調査する; *crime* sōsa suru 捜査する

investigation chōsa 調査; (*of crime*) sōsa 捜査

investigative journalism chōsa-hōdō 調査報道

investment (*act*) tōshi 投資; (*amount*) tōshigaku 投資額

investor tōshi-sha 投資者

invigorating *climate* sawayaka (na) さわやか(な)

invincible *army, team* muteki (no) 無敵(の)

invisible me ni mienai 目に見えない

invitation shōtai 招待; (*card*) shōtaijō 招待状

invite shōtai suru 招待する; *can I ~ you for a meal?* issho ni shokuji shimasen ka 一緒に食事しませんか

invoice 1 *n* seikyūsho 請求書 2 *v/t* customer ... no seikyūsho o okuru ...の請求書を送る

involuntary hanshateki (na) 反射的(な)

involve *hard work, expense* hitsuyō to suru 必要とする; (*concern*) ... ni kankei suru ...に関係する; *what does it ~?* sore ni wa nani ga hitsuyō desu ka それには何が必要ですか; *get ~d with* (*with sth*) ... ni kakawaru ...にかかわる; (*with s.o., emotionally*) ... to shitashiku naru ...と親しくなる

involved (*complex*) komiitta 込み入った

involvement (*in a project etc*) kakawariai かかわり合い; (*in crime, accident*) kankei 関係 (*as victim*) makizoe 巻き添え

invulnerable fujimi (no) 不死身(の)

inward 1 *adj* thoughts naishin 内心(の); *direction* naka ni mukau 中に向かう 2 *adv* naka ni mukatte 中に向かって; (*into oneself*) naishin e 内心へ

inwardly (*in one's heart*) kokoro no naka de 心の中で

iodine yōso ヨウ素; (*as disinfectant*)

yōdochinki ヨードチンキ

IOU (= *I owe you*) shakuyō-shōsho 借用証書

IQ (= *intelligence quotient*) chinō-shisū 知能指数, ai-kyū ＩＱ

Iran Iran イラン

Iranian 1 *adj* Iran (no) イラン(の) **2** *n* (*person*) Iran-jin イラン人; (*language*) Iran-goha イラン語派

Iraq Iraku イラク

Iraqi 1 *adj* Iraku (no) イラク (の) **2** *n* (*person*) Iraku-jin イラク人

Ireland Airurando アイルランド

iris (*of eye*) kōsai こう彩; (*flower*) ayame あやめ

Irish 1 *adj* Airurando (no) アイルランド(の) **2** *n*: **the ~** Airurando-jin アイルランド人

Irishman Airurando-jin dansei アイルランド人男性

Irishwoman Airurando-jin josei アイルランド人女性

iron 1 *n* tetsu 鉄; (*for clothes*) airon アイロン **2** *v/t shirts etc* airon o kakeru アイロンをかける

ironic(al) hiniku (na) 皮肉(な)

ironing airon-gake アイロンがけ; **do the ~** airon-gake o suru アイロンがけをする

ironing board airon-dai アイロン台

ironworks seitetsujo 製鉄所

irony hiniku 皮肉

irrational fugōri (na) 不合理(な)

irreconcilable *positions* ryōritsu shinai 両立しない; *people* wakai dekinai 和解できない

irrecoverable torikaeshi no tsukanai 取り返しのつかない

irregular *intervals* fukisoku (na) 不規則(な); *sizes* fuzoroi (no) ふぞろい(の); *surface* dekoboko (no) 凸凹(の); (*against the rules*) kisoku ihan no 規則違反の

irrelevant mukankei (na) 無関係(な)

irreparable shūfuku dekinai 修復できない

irreplaceable *object, person* kakegae no nai かけがえのない

irrepressible *sense of humor* osaekirenai 抑えきれない; *person*

kaikatsu (na) 快活(な)

irreproachable mōshibun no nai 申し分のない

irresistible *offer, smell* kotowarenai 断れない; *pleasures* osaekirenai 抑えきれない

irrespective: ~ of ... ni kakawarazu …にかかわらず

irresponsible musekinin (na) 無責任(な)

irretrievable torikaeshi no tsukanai 取り返しのつかない

irreverent fukei (na) 不敬(な)

irrevocable henkō dekinai 変更できない

irrigate kangai suru かんがいする

irrigation kangai かんがい

irrigation canal yōsuiro 用水路

irritable okorippoi 怒りっぽい

irritate (*annoy*) iraira saseru いらいらさせる; MED shigeki suru 刺激する

irritating *person, itch* iraira suru yō (na) いらいらするよう(な)

irritation iradachi いらだち; MED shigeki 刺激

Islam Isuramu-kyō イスラム教

Islamic Isuramu-kyō (no) イスラム教(の)

island shima 島; (*traffic*) **~** anzen-chitai 安全地帯

islander shima no hito 島の人

isolate (*separate*) kiri hanasu 切り離す; (*cut off*) koritsu saseru 孤立させる; (*identify*) tsukitomeru つきとめる; *gene, bacteria* bunri suru 分離する

isolated *house* koritsu shita 孤立した; *occurrence* tandoku (no) 単独(の)

isolation (*of a region*) koritsu 孤立; **in ~** hoka to kirihanashite 他と切り離して

isolation ward kakuri-byōtō 隔離病棟

Israel Isuraeru イスラエル

Israeli 1 *adj* Isuraeru (no) イスラエル(の) **2** *n* (*person*) Isuraeru-jin イスラエル人

issue 1 *n* (*matter*) mondai 問題; (*result*) kekka 結果; **March ~** (*of*

magazine) sangatsu-gō 三月号;
the point at ~ mondai to natte iru
ten 問題となっている点; **take ~
with** ... ni igi o tonaeru ...に異議を
唱える **2** v/t *coins, passports, visa*
hakkō suru 発行する; *supplies*
shikyū suru 支給する; *warning*
dasu 出す
IT (= *information technology*) jōhō-
kōgaku 情報工学
it ◊ (*as subject*) sore wa/ga それは/
が; (*as object*) sore o それを ◊ (*not
translated*): **~'s raining** ame ga
futte imasu 雨が降っています; **~'s
me/him** watashi/kare desu 私/彼
です; **~'s Charlie here** TELEC Chā
rī desu チャーリーです; **I don't like
~** watashi wa kirai desu 私は嫌い
です; **that's ~!** (*that's right*) sono
tōri そのとおり; (*finished*) kore
de oshimai これでおしまい
Italian 1 *adj* Itaria (no) イタリア(の)
2 n (*person*) Itaria-jin イタリア人;

(*language*) Itaria-go イタリア語
italic shatai 斜体
italics: shatai de 斜体で
Italy Itaria イタリア
itch 1 n kayumi かゆみ **2** v/i kayui
かゆい
item (*on agenda*) kōmoku 項目; (*of
news*) kiji 記事; (*on shopping list*)
hinmoku 品目; (*thing, article*)
shinamono 品物
itemize *invoice* kajōgaki ni suru 箇
条書にする
itinerary ryokō-keikaku 旅行計画
its sore (no) それ(の); **the dog has
hurt ~ leg** sono inu wa ashi o kega
shite iru その犬は足を怪我してい
る
itself: **the dog hurt ~** inu ga kega o
shita 犬がけがをした; **by ~** (*alone*)
jishin de 自身で; (*automatically*)
sorejishin de それ自身で
ivory (*substance*) zōge 象牙
ivy tsuta つた

J

jab v/t tsuku 突く
jack MOT jakki ジャッキ; (*in cards*)
jakku ジャック
♦jack up MOT ... o jakki de
mochiageru ...をジャッキで持ち上
げる
jacket (*coat*) jaketto ジャケット,
uwagi 上着; (*of book*) kabā カバー
jacket potato *kawa goto yaita
jagaimo* 皮ごと焼いたじゃがいも
jack-knife v/i oremagatte tachiōjō
suru 折れ曲がって立ち往生する
jackpot ittōshōkin 一等賞金; **hit the
~** taikin o ateru 大金を当てる
jade n hisui ひすい
jagged gizagiza (no) ぎざぎざ(の)
jail keimu-sho 刑務所
jam[1] jamu ジャム
jam[2] **1** n MOT kōtsū-jūtai 交通渋滞;

F (*difficulty*) pinchi ピンチ; **be in
a ~** pinchi de aru ピンチである
2 v/t (*ram*) oshikomu 押し込む;
(*cause to stick*) tsukkaesaseru
つっかえさせる; *broadcast* bōgai
suru 妨害する; **be ~med** (*very
busy*) gyūgyūzume de aru ぎゅう
ぎゅう詰めである; (*of road*) jūtai
shite iru 渋滞している; (*of door,
window*) ugokanaku natte iru 動か
なくなっている **3** v/i (*stick*)
ugokanaku naru 動かなくなる;
(*squeeze*) oshiiru 押し入る
jam-packed gyūgyūzume (no) ぎゅ
うぎゅう詰め(の)
janitor kanrinin 管理人
January ichigatsu 一月
Japan Nihon 日本, Nippon 日本
Japanese 1 *adj* Nihon (no) 日本

(の), Nippon (no) 日本(の) **2** *n*
Nihon-jin 日本人, Nippon-jin 日本
人; (*language*) Nihon-go 日本語,
Nippon-go 日本語

Japanese-Chinese War (1937-45)
Nitchū-sensō 日中戦争

Japanese tea ocha お茶

Japan Railways Jei-āru ジェイアー
ル

Japan Self-Defense Forces Jieitai
自衛隊

jar¹ *n* (*container*) bin びん

jar² *v/i* (*of noise*) shinkei ni sawaru
神経にさわる; ~ **on** ... ni sawaru ...
にさわる

jargon senmon-yōgo 専門用語

jaundice ōdan 黄だん

jaw *n* ago あご

jaywalker shingō-mushi o suru hito
信号無視をする人

jaywalking shingō-mushi 信号無視

jazz jazu ジャズ

♦**jazz up** *tune* ... o nigiyaka ni suru
...をにぎやかにする; *room etc* ... o
hade ni suru ...を派手にする

jealous shittobukai しっと深い; **be
~ of ...** ... o urayamashiku omou
...をうらやましく思う

jealousy shitto しっと

jeans jīnzu ジーンズ, jīpan ジーパン

jeep jīpu ジープ

jeer 1 *n* yaji やじ **2** *v/i* yajiru やじ
る; ~ **at** ... o yajiru ...をやじる

Jello zerī ゼリー

jelly jamu ジャム

jelly bean zerī-bīn ゼリービーン

jellyfish kurage くらげ

jeopardize kiken ni sarasu 危険に
さらす

jeopardy: **be in ~** kiki ni sarasarete
iru 危機にさらされている

jerk¹ 1 *n* guitto ugoku koto ぐいっ
と動く事 **2** *v/t* guitto hiku ぐいっと
引く

jerk² F baka ばか

jerky *movement* pikupiku ugoku ぴ
くぴく動く; *train* gatagata ugoku
がたがた動く

jest 1 *n* jōdan 冗談; **in ~** jōdan de 冗
談で **2** *v/i* jōdan o iu 冗談を言う

Jesus Iesu イエス

jet 1 *n* (*of water*) funshutsu 噴出;
(*nozzle*) funshutsu-kō 噴出口;
(*airplane*) jetto-ki ジェット機
2 *v/i* (*travel*) jetto-ki de iku
ジェット機で行く

jet-black makkuro (na) 真っ黒(な);
jet engine jetto-enjin ジェットエ
ンジン; **jetlag** jisa-boke 時差ぼけ

jettison suteru 捨てる; *fig* misuteru
見捨てる

jetty tottei 突堤

Jew Yudaya-jin ユダヤ人

jewel hōseki 宝石; *fig* (*person*)
kichō na hito 貴重な人

jeweler hōseki-shō 宝石商

jewelry hōseki-rui 宝石類

Jewish Yudaya (no) ユダヤ(の);
father, girlfriend etc Yudaya-jin
(no) ユダヤ人(の)

jiffy: **in a ~** F sugu ni すぐに

jigsaw (puzzle) jigusō(pazuru) ジ
グソー (パズル)

jilt furu ふる

jingle 1 *n* (*song*) komāsharu-songu
コマーシャルソング **2** *v/i* (*of
coins*) charin to naru oto ちゃりん
と鳴る音

jinx (*person*) engi no warui hito 縁
起の悪い人; (*bad luck*) jinkusu ジ
ンクス; **there's a ~ on this
project** kono purojekuto ni wa
jinkusu ga aru このプロジェクト
にはジンクスがある

jitters: **get the ~** F agaru あがる

jittery F piripiri shita ぴりぴりした

job (*employment*) shoku 職; (*task*)
shigoto 仕事; **out of a ~** shitsugyō
shite 失業して; **it's a good ~
that...** ... shite yokatta ...して良
かった; **you'll have a ~** (*it'll be
difficult*) kurō suru 苦労する

job description shokumu-naiyō 職
務内容; **job hunt:** **be job hunting**
shūshoku-katsudō shite iru 就職活
動している

jobless shitsugyō (no) 失業(の)

job satisfaction shigoto no
jūjitsukan 仕事の充実感

jockey *n* kishu 騎手, jokkī ジョッ
キー

jog 1 *n* jogingu ジョギング; **go for a**

~ jogging shi ni iku ジョギングしに行く **2** v/i (*as exercise*) jogingu suru ジョギングする **3** v/t *elbow etc* kozuku 小突く; **~ one's memory** ... no kioku o yobisamasu ...の記憶を呼びさます

jogger (*person*) jogingu suru hito ジョギングする人

jogging jogingu ジョギング; **go ~** jogingu shi ni iku ジョギングしに行く

jogging suit suetto-sūtsu スエットスーツ

john F (*toilet*) toire トイレ

join 1 n tsugime 継ぎ目 **2** v/i (*of roads, rivers*) gōryū suru 合流する; (*become a member*) kanyū suru 加入する **3** v/t (*connect*) tsunagu つなぐ; *person* ... to issho ni naru ...と一緒になる; *club* ... ni sanka suru ...に参加する; (*go to work for*) ... ni nyūsha suru ...に入社する; (*of road*) gōryū suru 合流する

♦join in ... ni sanka suru ...に参加する

joiner tategu-ya 建具屋

joint 1 n ANAT kansetsu 関節; (*in woodwork*) tsugime 継ぎ目; (*of meat*) katamariniku かたまり肉; F (*place*) tamariba たまり場; (*of cannabis*) marifana マリファナ **2** adj (*shared*) kyōdō (no) 共同(の)

joint account kyōdō-yokin-kōza 共同預金口座; **joint-stock company** gōshi-gaisha 合資会社; **joint venture** gōben-jigyō 合弁事業, jointo-benchā ジョイントベンチャー

joke 1 n (*story*) jōdan 冗談; (*practical ~*) itazura いたずら; **play a ~ on** ... o karakau ...をからかう; **it's no ~** waraigoto ja nai 笑い事じゃない **2** v/i (*pretend*) karakau からかう; (*having a ~*) jōdan o iu 冗談を言う

joker (*person*) jōdan-zuki 冗談好き; *pej* yatsu やつ; (*in cards*) jōkā ジョーカー

joking: ~ apart jōdan wa sateoki 冗談はさておき

jokingly fuzakete ふざけて

jolly adj yōki (na) 陽気(な)

jolt 1 n (*jerk*) yure 揺れ **2** v/t (*push*) ... ni butsukaru ...にぶつかる

jostle v/t osu 押す

♦jot down ... o memo suru ...をメモする

journal (*magazine*) zasshi 雑誌; (*diary*) nikki 日記

journalism hōdō 報道, jānarizumu ジャーナリズム

journalist kisha 記者, jānarisuto ジャーナリスト

journey n ryokō 旅行; **it's a five-hour ~** gojikan no kōtei de aru 五時間の行程である

joy yorokobi 喜び

jubilant ōyorokobi (no) 大喜び(の)

jubilation kanki 歓喜

judge 1 n LAW saibankan 裁判官; (*in competition*) shinpan 審判, jajji ジャッジ **2** v/t handan suru 判断する; *person* hyōka suru 評価する; *competition* shinpan suru 審判する

judgment LAW hanketsu 判決; (*opinion*) iken 意見; (*good sense*) handan 判断

judicial shihō no 司法(の)

judicious kenmei (na) 賢明(な)

judo jūdō 柔道

juggle kyokugei o suru 曲芸をする; *fig* ... no yarikuri o tsukeru ...のやりくりをつける

juggler kyokugei-shi 曲芸師

juice jūsu ジュース

juicy mizumizushii みずみずしい; *news, gossip* omoshiroi おもしろい

July shichigatsu 七月

jumble n yoseatsume 寄せ集め

♦jumble up yoseatsumeru 寄せ集める

jump 1 n jampu ジャンプ; (*increase*) kyūjōshō 急上昇; **give a ~** (*of surprise*) bikkuri saseru びっくりさせる **2** v/i tobu 跳ぶ; (*in surprise*) dokitto suru どきっとする; (*increase*) kyūjōshō suru 急上昇する; **~ to one's feet** satto tachiagaru さっと立ち上がる; **~ to conclusions** karugarushiku ketsuron o dasu 軽々しく結論を出

す 3 v/t fence etc tobikoeru 跳び越える; F (attack) tobikakaru 飛びかかる

♦jump at opportunity … ni tobitsuku …に飛びつく

jumper SP jampā ジャンパー; (horse) shōgai-rēsu-yō kyōsōba 障害レース用競争馬

jumpy bikubiku shite iru びくびくしている

junction (of roads) kōsaten 交差点

June rokugatsu 六月

jungle janguru ジャングル, mitsurin-chitai 密林地帯

junior 1 adj (subordinate) shita (no) 下(の); (younger) toshishita (no) 年下(の) **2** n (in rank) kōhai 後輩; **she is ten years my ~** kanojo wa watashi yori jussai toshishita da 彼女は私より十歳年下だ

junk (trash) garakuta がらくた

junk food janku-fūdo ジャンクフード

junkie mayaku-jōshūsha 麻薬常習者

junk mail dairekuto-mēru ダイレクトメール

junkyard haihin-okiba 廃品置場

jurisdiction LAW shihōken 司法権

juror baishin-in 陪審員

jury baishin 陪審

just 1 adj law kōsei (na) 公正(な); war, cause seitō (na) 正当(な) **2** adv (exactly) chōdo ちょうど; (only) tada ただ; **I've ~ got here** watashi wa koko ni tsuita bakari desu 私はここに着いたばかりです; **I've ~ seen her** chōdo kanojo ni atta tokoro da ちょうど彼女に会っ

たところだ; ~ about (almost) mō sukoshi de もうすこしで; **I was ~ about to leave when …** … shita toki watashi wa chōdo deru tokoro datta …したとき私はちょうど出るところだった; ~ like that (abruptly) fui ni 不意に; (exactly like that) chōdo konna fū ni ちょうどこんな風に; ~ now (a few moments ago) tsui sakki ついさっき; (at the moment) chōdo ima ちょうど今; ~ you wait! chotto machinasai ちょっと待ちなさい; ~ be quiet! chotto shizuka ni shinasai ちょっと静かにしなさい

justice shihō 司法; (of cause) seigi 正義

justifiable mottomo (na) もっとも(な)

justifiably tōzen ni 当然に; **she ~ refused to agree** kanojo ga sansei shinakatta no wa tōzen da 彼女が賛成しなかったのは当然だ

justification seitō na iiwake 正当な言い訳

justify seitōka suru 正当化する; text chōsei suru 調整する

justly (fairly) kōsei ni 公正に; (rightly) tōzen 当然

♦jut out v/i haridasu 張り出す

juvenile 1 adj shōnen (no) 少年(の); pej kodomoppoi 子供っぽい **2** n fml miseinen-sha 未成年者

juvenile delinquency shōnen-hikō 少年非行

juvenile delinquent (male) hikō-shōnen 非行少年; (female) hikō-shōjo 非行少女

K

k (= kilobyte) kirobaito キロバイト; (= thousand) sen 千

Kabuki Kabuki 歌舞伎

kamikaze kamikaze 神風

karaoke karaoke カラオケ

karate karate 空手

karate chop karate choppu 空手チョップ

katakana katakana かたかな

keel n NAUT ryūkotsu 竜骨

keen (*intense*) hageshii 激しい

keep 1 n (*maintenance*) kuibuchi 食いぶち, seikatsu-hi 生活費; **for ~s** F eikyū ni 永久に **2** v/t totte oku 取っておく; (*not give back*) motte iru 持っている; (*not lose*) tamotsu 保つ; (*detain*) hikitomeru 引き止める; (*in specific place*) shimatte oku しまっておく; *family* yashinau 養う; *animals* kau 飼う; ~ *a promise* yakusoku o mamoru 約束を守る; ~ *... company* ... ni tsukiau ...に付き合う; ~ *... waiting* ... o mataseta mama ni suru ...を待たせたままにする; *sorry to have kept you waiting* o-matase shimashita お待たせしました; ~ *... to oneself* (*not tell*) ... o damatte iru ...を黙っている; ~ *X from Y* (*not tell*) X o Y ni shirasenaide oku X を Y に知らせないでおく; ~ *trying* tsuzukete miru 続けてみる; ~ *interrupting* jama shitsuzukeru 邪魔し続ける **3** v/i (*remain*) ... no mama de iru ...のままでいる; (*of food, milk*) motsu もつ

♦ **keep away 1** v/i chikazukanai 近付かない; ~ *from* ... ... ni chikayoranai ...に近寄らない **2** v/t chikazukenai 近付けない

♦ **keep back** v/t (*hold in check*) ... o osaeru ...を抑える; *information* ... o kakushite oku ...を隠しておく

♦ **keep down** v/t *voice, costs etc* ... o osaeru ...を抑える; *he can't keep anything down* kare wa zenbu haite shimau 彼は全部吐いてしまう

♦ **keep in** (*in hospital*) ... o nyūin saseru ...を入院させる; (*in school*) ... o hōkago ni nokosu ...を放課後に残す

♦ **keep off 1** v/t (*avoid*) ... o sakeru ...を避ける; ~ *the grass!* shibafu ni hairanaide 芝生にはいらないで **2** v/i (*of rain*) furanaide iru 降らないでいる

♦ **keep out** v/i naka ni hairanai 中に入らない; (*of argument*) kuwawaranai 加わらない; ~*!* (*as sign*) tachiiri-kinshi 立入禁止

♦ **keep to** *path* ... kara hanarenai ...から離れない; *rules* mamoru 守る

♦ **keep up 1** v/i (*when walking, running etc*) tsuite kuru ついてくる **2** v/t *pace, payments* tsuzukeru 続ける; *bridge* sasaeru 支える; *pants* osaeru 押さえる

♦ **keep up with** ... ni okurenaide tsuite iku ...に遅れないでついていく; (*stay in touch with*) ... to tsukiai o tsuzukeru ...とつき合いを続ける

keeping: *in ~ with* ... to chōwa shite ...と調和して; (*with promises*) ... to itchi shite ...と一致して

keg chiisai taru 小さい樽

kelp konbu こんぶ

kendo kendō 剣道

kennel inugoya 犬小屋

kennels petto-hoteru ペットホテル

kernel tane 種

kerosene tōyu 灯油

ketchup kechappu ケチャップ

kettle yakan やかん

key 1 n (*to door, drawer*) kagi 鍵; COMPUT, MUS kī キー **2** adj (*vital*) jūyō (na) 重要(な) **3** v/t COMPUT nyūryoku suru 入力する

♦ **key in** *data* ... o nyūryoku suru ...を入力する

keyboard COMPUT, MUS kī-bōdo キーボード; **keyboarder** COMPUT nyūryoku-operētā 入力オペレーター; **keycard** kādo-shiki no kagi カード式の鍵

keyed-up kinchō shite 緊張して

keyhole kagiana 鍵穴; **keynote speech** kichō-enzetsu 基調演説; **keyring** kī-horudā キーホルダー

kick 1 n kikku キック; F (*thrill*) kaikan 快感; (*just*) *for ~s* F omoshirohanbun de おもしろ半分で **2** v/t keru ける; F *habit* yameru やめる **3** v/i keru ける

♦ **kick around** v/t *ball* keru ける; (*treat harshly*) kozukimawasu 小突きまわす; F (*discuss*) kentō suru 検討する

♦ **kick in 1** v/t F *money* ... o dashiau ...を出し合う **2** v/i (*of boiler etc*)

sadō suru 作動する

♦ **kick off** v/i kikku-ofu o suru キックオフをする, shiai-kaishi o suru 試合開始をする; F (*start*) hajimeru 始める

♦ **kick out** v/t ... o oidasu ...を追い出す; **be kicked out of the company** / **army** kaisha / rikugun o oidasareru 会社/陸軍を追い出される

kickback F (*bribe*) ribēto リベート, wairo わいろ

kickoff kikku-ofu キックオフ, shiai-kaishi 試合開始

kid 1 n F (*child*) kodomo 子供; *pej* gaki がき; **~ brother** otōto 弟; **~ sister** imōto 妹 **2** v/t F karakau からかう **3** v/i F jōdan o iu 冗談を言う; *only ~ding* chotto karakatta dake desu ちょっとからかっただけです

kidder F itazurazuki いたずら好き

kidnap yūkai suru 誘拐する

kidnap(p)er yūkai-han 誘拐犯

kidnap(p)ing yūkai 誘拐

kidney ANAT jinzō じん臓; (*food*) kidonī キドニー

kill v/t korosu 殺す; *plant* karasu 枯らす; *time* tsubusu つぶす; *be ~ed in an accident* jiko de shinu 事故で死ぬ; *~ oneself* jisatsu suru 自殺する

killer (*murderer*) satsujin-han 殺人犯; (*cause of death*) inochitori 命取り

killing satsujin 殺人; *make a ~* (*lots of money*) ōmōke suru 大もうけする

kiln kama 窯

kilo → *kilogram*

kilobyte kirobaito キロバイト

kilogram kiroguramu キログラム

kilometer kiromētā キロメーター

kimono kimono 着物; *summer ~* yukata 浴衣

kind[1] *adj* shinsetsu (na) 親切(な)

kind[2] *n* shurui 種類; (*make, brand*) kata 型; *what ~ of ...?* donna shurui no ... desu ka どんな種類の ...ですか; *all ~s of people* arayuru hitobito あらゆる人々; *nothing of the ~* zenzen betsumono 全然別物;

~ of sad / *strange* F nandaka sabishii / hen na 何だか寂しい/変な; *it's ~ of green* midoriiro no isshu da 緑色の一種だ

kindergarten yōchien 幼稚園

kind-hearted shinsetsu (na) 親切(な)

kindly 1 *adj* yasashii 優しい **2** *adv* shinsetsu ni mo 親切にも; (*please*) dōzo どうぞ

kindness shinsetsu 親切

king kokuō 国王; (*in cards*) kingu キング

kingdom ōkoku 王国

king-size(d) F kingu-saizu (no) キングサイズ(の), tokudai (no) 特大(の)

kink (*in hose etc*) yojire よじれ

kinky F kimyō (na) 奇妙(な); *sex* hentai (no) 変態(の)

kiosk kiosuku キオスク

kiss 1 n kisu キス **2** v/t ... ni kisu suru ...にキスする **3** v/i kisu o suru キスをする

kit (*equipment*) dōgubako 道具箱; (*for assembly*) kumitateyō buhin-setto 組み立て用部品セット

kitchen daidokoro 台所, kitchin キッチン

kitchenette daidokoro 台所, kitchin キッチン

kitchen sink: *everything but the ~* F ari to arayuru mono ありとあらゆるもの

kite tako たこ

kitten koneko 子猫

kitty (*money*) kyōdō-tsumitatekin 共同積立金

klutz F (*clumsy person*) bukitcho ぶきっちょ

knack kotsu こつ

knead *dough* koneru こねる

knee n hiza ひざ

kneecap n hizakozō ひざ小僧, hiza no sara ひざの皿

kneel hizamazuku ひざまずく

knick-knacks komagoma shita mono こまごました物

knife 1 n naifu ナイフ **2** v/t naifu de sasu ナイフで刺す

knit 1 v/t amu 編む **2** v/i amimono o

suru 編み物をする

♦ **knit together** (of broken bone) kuttsukeru くっつける

knitting amimono 編み物

knitwear nitto-wea ニットウェア

knob totte 取っ手

knock 1 n (at door) nokku ノック; (blow) shōgeki 衝撃 **2** v/t (hit) butsukeru ぶつける; (to the floor) taosu 倒す; F (criticize) kenasu けなす **3** v/i (on the door) nokku suru ノックする

♦ **knock around 1** v/t (beat) ... o naguru ...を殴る **2** v/i F (travel) hōrō suru 放浪する

♦ **knock down** (of car) haneru はねる; wall, building torikowasu 取り壊す; F (in price) nesage shita 値下げした

♦ **knock out** nokku-auto suru ノックアウトする; (of medicine) gussuri nemuraseru ぐっすり眠らせる; power lines etc hakai suru 破壊する

♦ **knock over** hikkurikaesu ひっくり返す; (of car) haneru はねる

knockdown: a ~ price hakaku no nedan 破格の値段

knockout n (in boxing) nokku-auto ノックアウト

knot 1 n musubime 結び目 **2** v/t musubu 結ぶ

knotty problem komiitta 込み入った

know fact, city, subject, (have heard of: person) shitte iru 知っている; (be acquainted with: person) shiriai de aru 知り合いである; (understand) wakatte iru わかっている; language dekiru できる; (recognize) ki ga tsuku 気がつく; get to ~ person ... to shiriai ni naru ...と知り合いになる; city ... ni nareru ...に慣れる; I ~ what you mean anata no itteru koto ga wakaru あなたの言ってることがわかる; I ~ you! (what you're like) anatano koto wakatteiru あなたのことわかっている; don't I ~ you? watashi anata no koto shitte masu ka 私あなたのこと知ってますか **2** v/i shitte iru 知っている; I don't ~ shirimasen 知りません; (in

despair, frustration) wakarimasen わかりません; yes, I ~ ē, shitte imasu ええ、知っています; (I understand) ē, wakatte imasu え え、わかっています; be in the ~ jijō ni tsūjite iru 事情に通じている

knowhow nōhau ノウハウ

knowing monoshiri-gao (no) ものしり顔(の)

knowingly (wittingly) koi ni 故意に; smile etc tokuigao de 得意顔で

know-it-all F shittakaburi suru hito 知ったかぶりする人

knowledge chishiki 知識; to the best of my ~ watashi no shiru kagiri de wa 私の知る限りでは; have a good ~ of ... ... ni tsuite yoku shitte iru ...についてよく知っている

knowledgeable chishiki no aru 知識のある; be ~ about music ongaku ni tsuite yoku shitte iru 音楽について良く知っている

knuckle yubi no tsukene no kansetsu 指の付け根の関節

♦ **knuckle down** honki ni naru 本気になる

♦ **knuckle under** kōsan suru 降参する

KO → knockout

koi (carp) koi こい

Korea (South) Kankoku 韓国, fml Daikan-minkoku 大韓民国; (North) Kita-chōsen 北朝鮮, fml Chōsen-minshu-shugi-jinmin-kyōwakoku 朝鮮民主主義人民共和国; (South & North) Chōsen 朝鮮

Korean 1 adj (South) Kankoku (no) 韓国(の); (North) Kita-chōsen (no) 北朝鮮(の); (South and North) Chōsen (no) 朝鮮(の) **2** n (South) Kankoku-jin 韓国人; (North) Kita-chōsen-jin 北朝鮮人; (South and North) Chōsen-jin 朝鮮人; (language) Kankoku-go 韓国語, Chōsen-go 朝鮮語

kosher REL Yudaya no oshie ni kanatta ユダヤの教えにかなった; F tekitō (na) 適当(な)

kudos shōsan 称賛

Kyoto Kyōto 京都

Kyushu Kyūshū 九州

L

lab *(room)* jikken-shitsu 実験室; *(building)* kenkyū-jo 研究所
label 1 *n* raberu ラベル **2** *v/t bags* raberu o haru ラベルをはる
labor *n (work)* rōdō 労働; *(in pregnancy)* bunben 分べん; **be in ~** bunbenchū de aru 分べん中である
laboratory → **lab**
laboratory technician kenkyū-gishi 研究技師
labored *style, speech* kushin shita 苦心した
laborer nikutai-rōdō-sha 肉体労働者
laborious mendō (na) 面倒(な)
Labor Thanksgiving Day Kinrō-kansha no hi 勤労感謝の日; **labor union** rōdō-kumiai 労働組合; **labor ward** bunben-shitsu 分べん室
lace *n (material)* rēsu レース; *(for shoe)* kutsuhimo 靴ひも
♦ **lace up** *shoes* ... no himo o shimeru ...のひもを締める
lack 1 *n* ketsubō 欠乏 **2** *v/t* ... ni kakeru ...に欠ける **3** *v/i*: **be ~ing** kakete iru 欠けている
lacquer *n (for hair)* heasupurē ヘアスプレー; *(paint)* urushi 漆
lacquerware shikki 漆器
lad wakamono 若者
ladder hashigo はしご
laden: **~ with hay / parcels** hoshikusa/nimotsu o tsunde 干し草/荷物を積んで
ladies' room joseiyō toire 女性用トイレ
ladle *n* shakushi しゃくし
lady shukujo 淑女
ladybug tentōmushi てんとうむし
lag *v/t pipes* dannetsuzai de ōu 断熱材で覆う
♦ **lag behind** okureru 遅れる
lager ragābīru ラガービール
lagoon kata 潟

laid-back nonbiri shita のんびりした
lake mizūmi 湖
lamb kohitsuji 子羊; *(meat)* kohitsuji no niku 子羊の肉, ramu ラム
lame *person* bikko (no) びっこ(の); *excuse* heta (na) 下手(な)
lament 1 *n* hitan 悲嘆 **2** *v/t* nageku 嘆く
lamentable *ignorance* nagekawashii 嘆かわしい; *supplies* hinjaku (na) 貧弱(な)
laminated raminēto sareta ラミネートされた
lamp ranpu ランプ
lamppost gaitō 街灯
lampshade sutando no kasa スタンドのかさ
land 1 *n* tochi 土地; *(property)* shoyūchi 所有地; *(shore)* riku 陸; *(country)* kuni 国; **by ~** rikuro de 陸路で; **on ~** rikujō de 陸上で; **work on the ~** *(as farmer)* nōfu to shite hataraku 農夫として働く **2** *v/t airplane* chakuriku saseru 着陸させる; *job* kakutoku suru 獲得する **3** *v/i (of airplane)* chakuriku suru 着陸する; *(of ball, sth thrown)* ochiru 落ちる
landing *(of airplane)* chakuriku 着陸; *(top of staircase)* ichiban ue no odoriba 一番上の踊り場
landing field kei-hikōjō 軽飛行場; **landing gear** chakuriku-sōchi 着陸装置; **landing strip** chakurikujō 着陸場
landlady *(of hostel)* onna-shujin 女主人; **landlord** *(of hostel)* shujin 主人; **landmark** mokuhyō 目標; *fig* kakkiteki-jiken 画期的な事件; **land owner** jinushi 地主; **landscape 1** *n* keshiki 景色; *(painting)* fūkeiga 風景画 **2** *adv print* yokomuki de

横向きで; **landslide** jisuberi 地滑り; **landslide victory** attōteki na shōri 圧倒的な勝利

lane (*in country*) komichi 小道; (*alley*) roji 路地; MOT shasen 車線

language kotoba 言葉; (*of one's own country*) kokugo 国語; (*technical terms*) yōgo 用語; (*style, type of ~*) kotobazukai 言葉遣い; (*college subject*) gogaku 語学; **foreign ~** gaikokugo 外国語

lank *hair* nobite aburappoi 伸びて脂っぽい

lanky *person* yaseta やせた

lantern tesage-ranpu 手さげランプ

Lao (*language*)Rao-go ラオ語

Laos Raosu ラオス

Laotian 1 *adj* Raosu (no) ラオス(の) **2** *n* (*person*) Raosu-jin ラオス人

lap¹ *n* (*of track*) isshū 一周; (*in athletics*) rappu ラップ

lap² *n* (*of water*) nami no oto 波の音

lap³ *n* (*of person*) hiza ひざ

♦ lap up *drink, milk* ... o nametsukusu ...をなめ尽くす; *flattery* ... o unomi ni suru ...をうのみにする

lapel orieri 折り襟

laptop COMPUT rapputoppu ラップトップ

larceny (*charge*) settōzai 窃盗罪; (*act*) settō 窃盗

larder shokuryō-chozōshitsu 食料貯蔵室

large ōki (na) 大き(な); *sum of money* tagaku (no) 多額(の); *family, number of people* ōninzū (no) 大人数(の); *amount* taryō (no) 多量(の); *the criminal is still at ~* hannin wa mada tōsōchū de aru 犯人はまだ逃走中である

largely shu to shite 主として

lark (*bird*) hibari ひばり

larva yōchū 幼虫

laryngitis kōtōen こう頭炎

larynx kōtō こう頭

laser rēzā レーザー

laser beam rēzā-kōsen レーザー光線

laser printer rēzā-purintā レーザープリンター

lash¹ *v/t* (*with whip*) muchi de utsu むちで打つ

lash² *n* (*eyelash*) matsuge まつげ

♦ lash down (*with rope*) shikkari shibaritsukeru しっかり縛りつける

last¹ *adj* (*in series*) saigo (no) 最後(の); *bus, train* saishū (no) 最終(の); (*preceding*) kono mae (no) この前(の); **~ but one** saigo kara nibanme 最後から二番目; **~ night** yūbe ゆうべ; **~ but not least** (*in speech*) saigo ni daiji na koto o nobemasu ga saigo ni daiji na koto o nobemasu ga つ いに; *at ~* tsui ni ついに; *the week before ~* ni shūkan mae 二週間前

last² *v/i* (*of weather, relationship*) tsuzuku 続く; (*of food, money*) nagamochi suru 長持ちする

lastly saigo ni 最後に

latch kakegane 掛け金

late (*behind time*) okureta 遅れた; (*for school, meeting*) chikoku shita 遅刻した; (*in day*) osoi 遅い; *it's getting ~* osoku natte kita 遅くなってきた; *of ~* saikin 最近; *the ~ 19th/20th century* jūkyūseiki/nijusseiki-kōki 19世紀/20世紀後期; *sorry I'm ~* okurete sumimasen 遅れてすみません; *sleep ~* asane o suru 朝寝をする

lately saikin 最近

late night fare shin'ya-ryōkin 深夜料金

later *adv* ato de あとで; *see you ~!* jā, mata じゃあ、また; **~ on** ato de あとで

latest *news, girlfriend* saishin (no) 最新(の)

lathe *n* senban 旋盤

lather (*from soap*) awa 泡

lather (*sweat*) ase 汗

Latin America Raten-Amerika ラテンアメリカ

Latin American 1 *adj* Raten-Amerika (no) ラテンアメリカ(の) **2** *n* (*person*) Raten-Amerika-jin ラテンアメリカ人

latitude ido 緯度; (*freedom to act*) jiyū 自由

latter: *the ~* kōsha 後者

laugh 1 *n* warai 笑い; *it was a ~* omoshirokatta おもしろかった **2** *v/i* warau 笑う
♦ **laugh at** *person* ... o azawarau ... をあざ笑う; *joke* omoshirogaru おもしろがる

laughing stock: *make oneself a ~* monowarai no tane ni naru もの笑いの種になる

laughter waraigoe 笑い声

launch 1 *n* (*boat*) ranchi ランチ; (*of rocket, missile*) hassha 発射; (*of ship*) shinsui 進水; (*of product*) hatsubai 発売 **2** *v/t rocket, missile* hassha suru 発射する; *ship* shinsui suru 進水する; *new product* hatsubai suru 発売する

launch(ing) ceremony hatsubai-kinenkai 発売記念会

launch(ing) pad hasshadai 発射台

launder sentaku suru 洗濯する; *money* senjō suru 洗浄する

laundromat koinrandorī コインランドリー

laundry (*in apartment building*) sentaku-shitsu 洗濯室; (*shop*) kurīningu-ten クリーニング店, randorī ランドリー; (*clothes*) sentakumono 洗濯もの; *do one's ~* sentaku o suru 洗濯をする

laurel (*tree*) gekkeiju 月桂樹

lavatory (*place*) toire トイレ; (*equipment*) benki 便器

lavender rabendā ラベンダー

lavish *adj meal* tappuri (no) たっぷり(の); *lifestyle* yutaka (na) 豊か(な); *reception* mono-oshimi shinai 物惜しみしない

law hōritsu 法律; (*subject*) hōgaku 法学; *against the ~* ihō de 違法で; *forbidden by ~* hō de kinjirareta 法で禁じられた

law court hōtei 法廷

lawful seitō (na) 正当(な)

lawless muhō (no) 無法(の)

lawn shibafu 芝生

lawn mower shibakariki 芝刈り機

lawsuit soshō 訴訟

lawyer bengoshi 弁護士

lax tenurui 手ぬるい

laxative *n* gezai 下剤

lay *v/t* (*put*) oku 置く; *cable, carpet* shiku 敷く; (*put down flat*) nekaseru 寝かせる; *eggs* umu 産む; ∨ (*sexually*) yaru やる; *get laid* ∨ yaru やる
♦ **lay into** (*attack*) ... o kōgeki suru ...を攻撃する
♦ **lay off** *workers* ... o kaiko suru ...を解雇する
♦ **lay on** *food, entertainment* ... o junbi suru ...を準備する
♦ **lay out** *objects* ... o chinretsu suru ...を陳列する; *page* ... o reiauto suru ...をレイアウトする

layer *n* sō 層; (*of society*) kaisō 階層

layman shirōto 素人

layout reiauto レイアウト
♦ **laze around** namakeru 怠ける

lazy *person* namakete iru 怠けている; *day* nonbiri shita のんびりした

lb (= *pound(s)*) pondo ポンド

LCD (= *liquid crystal display*) ekishō-hyōji 液晶表示

lead¹ *v/t procession* ... no sentō ni tatsu ...の先頭に立つ; *race* rīdo suru リードする; *company, team* hikiiru 率いる; (*guide, take*) annai suru 案内する **2** *v/i* (*in race, competition*) rīdo suru リードする; (*provide leadership*) rīdā ni naru リーダーになる; *a street ~ing off the square* hiroba kara dete iru michi 広場から出ている道; *where is this ~ing?* (*of argument, policy*) kore wa donna kekka o motarasu no ka これはどんな結果をもたらすのか **3** *n* (*in race*) rīdo リード; *be in the ~* rīdo shite iru リードしている; *take the ~* sentō ni tatsu 先頭に立つ; *lose the ~* rīdo o ushinau リードを失う
♦ **lead on** (*go in front*) ... o rīdo suru ...をリードする
♦ **lead up to** (*precede*) ... ni naru to mukau ...にだんだんと向かう; *what are you leading up to?* anata wa ittai nani ga iitai no desu ka あなたはいったい何が言いたいのですか

lead² n (*for dog*) kusari 鎖

lead³ n (*substance*) namari 鉛

leader (*of group, team*) rīdā リーダー; (*in tournament etc*) toppu トップ; (*of league*) shui 首位; (*in race*) sentō 先頭

leadership (*ability to lead*) rīdā shippu リーダーシップ; (*leaders of country, organization*) shidōken 指導権; (*leaders of party*) tōshu 党首; *under his ~* kare no shidō de 彼の指導で; *~ skills* rīdāshippu o toru nōryoku リーダーシップをとる能力

leadership contest shidōken-arasoi 指導権争い; POL tōshu-senkyō 党首選挙

lead-free gas muen (no) 無鉛(の)

leading *runner* sentō (no) 先頭(の); *company, product* yūryoku (na) 有力(な)

leading-edge adj *technology* saisentan (no) 最先端(の)

leaf happa 葉っぱ; (*of book*) pēji ページ

♦ **leaf through** ... no pēji o parapara to mekuru ...のページをぱらぱらとめくる

leaflet chirashi ちらし

league renmei 連盟; SP rīgu リーグ

leak 1 n (*of water, air, gas*) more 漏れ; (*hole*) ana 穴; (*of information*) rōei 漏えい **2** v/i moru 漏る

♦ **leak out** (*of air, gas, news*) moreru 漏れる

leaky *pipe, boat* ana no aru 穴のある

lean¹ 1 v/i (*be at an angle*) katamuku 傾く; *~ against* (*of person*) ... ni yorikakaru ...に寄りかかる; (*of object*) ... ni tatekakaru ...に立てかかる **2** v/t: *~ X against Y* X o Y ni tatekakeru XをYに立てかける

lean² adj *meat* akami (no) 赤身(の); *style, prose* hikishimatta 引き締まった

leap 1 n (*jump*) chōyaku 跳躍; *a great ~ forward* ōkina shinpo 大きな進歩 **2** v/i tobu 跳ぶ; *~ over* ... o tobikoeru ...を跳び越える

leap year urūdoshi うるう年

learn narau 習う; *~ how to* ... no shikata o narau ...の仕方を習う

learner gakushū-sha 学習者

learning (*knowledge*) gakushiki 学識; (*act*) gakushū 学習

learning curve gakushū-kyokusen 学習曲線; *be on the ~* manabi-tsuzukete iru 学び続けている

lease 1 n (*to lend*) chintai-keiyaku 賃貸契約; (*to borrow*) chinshaku-keiyaku 賃借契約 **2** v/t (*of owner*) chintai suru 賃貸する; (*of taker*) chinshaku suru 賃借する

♦ **lease out** ... o chintai suru ...を賃貸する

lease purchase kaitori-opushon tsuki chintai 買い取りオプションつき賃貸

leash n (*for dog*) kusari 鎖

least 1 adj (*slightest*) goku wazuka (no) ごくわずか(の) **2** adv *ichiban ... de nai* いちばん...でない; *he had changed ~ ~* kare ga ichiban kawaranakatta 彼がいちばん変わらなかった; *the ~ expensive car* ichiban yasui kuruma 一番安い車 **3** n: *he drank the ~* kare ga ichiban nomanakatta 彼がいちばん飲まなかった; *not in the ~ surprised / disappointed* sukoshi mo manzoku / gakkari shite inai 少しも満足/がっかりしていない; *at ~* sukunaku tomo 少なくとも

leather 1 n kawa 皮 **2** adj kawa (no) 皮(の)

leave 1 n (*vacation*) kyūka 休暇; *on ~* kyūka de 休暇で **2** v/t *town, city* hanareru 離れる; *park, museum* deru 出る; (*for another town, city, country*) tatsu 発つ; *company* saru 去る; (*graduate from*) sotsugyō suru 卒業する; (*desert*) misuteru 見捨てる; *husband, wife* ... to wakareru ...と別れる; (*not finish: food, drink*) nokosu 残す; *scar, memory* nokosu 残す; (*forget, leave behind*) okiwasureru 置き忘れる; *let's ~ things as they are* kono mama ni shite okō このままにしておこう; *how did you ~ things with him?* kare wa dō suru to itte imashita ka 彼はどうすると言っていましたか; **~ X alone** (*not interfere with*) X o hotte oku Xをほっておく; **~ it to me** watashi ni makasete kudasai 私に任せてください; **be left** nokoru 残る; **there is nothing left** nani mo nokotte inai 何も残っていない 3 *v/i* (*of person*) tachisaru 立ち去る; (*of plane, train, bus*) … ga shuppatsu suru …が出発する; **we left for New York** Nyū Yōku ni shuppatsu shita ニューヨークに出発した

♦ **leave behind** *v/t* (*intentionally*) … o oite iku …を置いていく; (*forget*) okiwasureru 置き忘れる

♦ **leave on** *v/t hat* … o kabutta mama ni suru …をかぶったままにする; *coat* … o kita mama ni suru …を着たままにする; *TV, computer* … o tsukeppanashi ni suru …をつけっぱなしにする

♦ **leave out** *v/t word, figure* … o habuku …を省く; (*not put away*) dashippanashi ni suru 出しっぱなしにする; **leave me out of this** watashi o makikomanaide kudasai 私を巻き込まないでください

leaving party sōbetsukai 送別会
lecture 1 *n* kōgi 講義; (*criticism*) sekkyō 説教 2 *v/i* kōgi o suru 講義をする
lecturer kōshi 講師
LED (= *light-emitting diode*) hakkō-daiōdo 発光ダイオード
ledge tana たな
ledger COM daichō 台帳
leek rīki リーキ
leer *n* (*sexual*) iyarashii metsuki いやらしい目つき; (*evil*) ijiwarui metsuki 意地悪い目つき
left 1 *adj* hidari (no) 左(の); POL saha (no) 左派(の) 2 *n* hidari 左, hidarigawa 左側; POL saha 左派; **on the ~** hidarigawa ni 左側に; **on the ~ of** … no hidarigawa ni …の左側に; **to the ~ turn** hidari e 左へ; 3 *adv turn* hidari ni 左に; **look** hidari o 左を
left-hand hidarite (no) 左手(の);

bend hidarigawa (no) 左側(の); **left-hand drive** hidari-handoru no kuruma 左ハンドルの車; **left-handed** hidarikiki (no) 左利き(の); **left-overs** (*food*) nokorimono 残り物; **left-wing** POL sayoku (no) 左翼(の); **left wing** SP refuto-uingu レフトウイング
leg ashi 足; **he's pulling your ~** kare wa kimi o karakatteiru 彼は君をからかっている
legacy isan 遺産
legal (*allowed*) gōhōteki (na) 合法的(な); (*relating to the law*) hōritsu (no) 法律(の)
legal adviser hōritsu-komon 法律顧問
legality gōhōsei 合法性
legalize gōhōka suru 合法化する
legend densetsu 伝説
legendary yūmei (na) 有名(な)
legible yomeru 読める
legislate hōritsu o seitei suru 法律を制定する
legislation (*laws*) hōritsu 法律; (*passing of laws*) hōritsu-seitei 法律制定
legislative *powers* rippōken no aru 立法権のある; *assembly* rippō (no) 立法(の)
legislature POL rippōfu 立法府
legitimate gōhōteki (na) 合法的(な)
leg room ashimoto no supēsu 足もとのスペース
leisure hima 暇; **at your ~** hima na toki ni 暇なときに
leisurely *pace* yuttari shita ゆったりした
leisure time yoka 余暇
lemon remon レモン
lemonade remonēdo レモネード
lemon juice remon-jūsu レモンジュース
lemon tea remon-tī レモンティー
lend: **~ Y to X** X ni Y o kasu XにYを貸す
length naga-sa 長さ; (*piece: of cloth, wood*) ippon 一本; **at ~** *describe, explain* kuwashiku 詳しく; (*eventually*) tsui ni ついに
lengthen nobasu 伸ばす

lengthy *speech, stay* nagai 長い

lenient kandai (na) 寛大(な)

lens renzu レンズ

lens cover renzu-kabā レンズカバー

Lent Shijunsetsu 四旬節

lentil hiramame ひら豆

leopard hyō ひょう

leotard reotādo レオタード

lesbian 1 *n* rezu レズ **2** *adj* rezu (no) レズ(の)

less: ~ *interesting / serious than ...* ... hodo omoshiroku nai/shinkoku de nai ...ほどおもしろくない/深刻でない; *it cost* ~ *than ...* hiyō ga ... hodo kakaranakatta 費用が...ほどかからなかった; ~ *than* $200 nihyaku doru 200ドル以下; *eat / talk* ~ (*than one used to*) mae yori tabenai/shaberanai 前より食べない/しゃべらない

lesson (*in school*) jugyō 授業; (*for piano, swimming*) ressun レッスン

let *v/t* (*allow*): ~ *X do Y* X ni Y saseru XにYさせる; ~ *me go!* hanashite 放して; ~ *him come in* kare o irete agete 彼をいれてあげて; ~*'s go* ikō 行こう; ~*'s eat* tabeyō 食べよう; ~*'s not argue* iiarasō no wa yameyō 言い争うのはやめよう; *she can hardly walk* ~ *alone run* kanojo wa hashiru no wa iu made mo naku aruku koto mo dekinai 彼女は走るのは言うまでもなく歩くこともできない; ~ *go of* (*of rope, handle*) ... o hanasu ...を放す

♦**let down** (*shades, hair*) ... o orosu ...をおろす; (*disappoint*) ... no kitai o uragiru ...の期待を裏切る; (*make longer*) ... no take o nobasu ...の丈を伸ばす

♦**let in** (*to house*) ... o naka ni ireru ...を中に入れる

♦**let off** (*not punish*) ... o hanasu ...を放す; (*from car*) ... o orosu ...を降ろす

♦**let out** (*of room, building*) soto ni dasu 外に出す; *jacket etc* haba o hirogeru 幅を広げる; *groan, yell* ageru あげる

♦**let up** *v/i* (*stop*) yamu やむ

lethal chishi (no) 致死(の)

lethargic mukiryoku (na) 無気力(な)

letter (*of alphabet*) moji 文字; (*in mail*) tegami 手紙

letterhead (*heading*) retāheddo レターヘッド; (*headed paper*) retā heddo-iri no binsen レターヘッド入りの便せん

letter of credit COM shin'yō-shōkaijō 信用照会状

lettuce retasu レタス

letup: *without a* ~ yasumazu 休まず

leukemia hakketsubyō 白血病

level 1 *adj field, surface* taira (na) 平ら(な); (*in competition, scores*) dōten (no) 同点(の); *draw* ~ *with* ... to hikiwakeru ...と引き分ける **2** *n* (*standard*) suijun 水準; (*in hierarchy*) chii 地位; (*amount, quantity*) reberu レベル; *on the* ~ taira na men de 平らな面で; (*honest*) shōjiki (na) 正直(な)

level-headed reisei (na) 冷静(な)

lever 1 *n* (*on machine*) rebā レバー; (*bar*) teko てこ **2** *v/t* teko de ugokasu てこで動かす; ~ *open* ... o kojiakeru ...をこじあける

leverage teko no sayō てこの作用; (*influence*) eikyōryoku 影響力

levy *v/t taxes* chōshū suru 徴収する

lewd waisetsu (na) わいせつ(な)

liability (*responsibility*) sekinin 責任; (*of taxpayer*) futan 負担

liability insurance songaibaishō-hoken 損害賠償保険

liable (*answerable*) sekinin no aru 責任のある; *be* ~ *to* (*likely*) ... shigachi de aru ...しがちである

♦**liaise with** ... to no renrakuyaku o tsutomeru ...との連絡役を務める

liaison (*contacts*) renraku 連絡

liar usotsuki うそつき

libel 1 *n* hibō-bunsho ひぼう文書; LAW meiyo-kison 名誉棄損 **2** *v/t* chūshō suru 中傷する

liberal *adj* (*broad-minded*) kokoro no hiroi 心の広い; *portion etc* kimae no yoi 気前のよい; POL jiyū-shugi (no) 自由主義(の)

liberate jiyū ni suru 自由にする
liberated *woman* jiyū (na) 自由(な)
liberty jiyū 自由; *at ~ (prisoner etc)* jiyū de 自由で; *be at ~ to ...* jiyū ni ... dekiru 自由に...できる
librarian shisho 司書
library toshokan 図書館
Libya Ribia リビア
Libyan 1 *adj* Ribia (no) リビア(の)
2 *n* Ribia-jin リビア人
license 1 *n* menkyo 免許; *(for car)* unten-menkyoshō 運転免許証 **2** *v/t* ninka suru 認可する; *be ~d* ninka o ukeru 認可を受ける
license number menkyo-bangō 免許番号; MOT nanbā ナンバー
license plate nanbāpurēto ナンバープレート
lick 1 *n* hitoname ひとなめ **2** *v/t* nameru なめる; *~ one's lips* shitanamezuri o suru 舌なめずりをする
licking: *get a ~* F *(defeat)* boromake suru ぼろ負けする
lid futa ふた
lie¹ 1 *n* (*untruth*) uso うそ **2** *v/i* uso o tsuku うそをつく
lie² *v/i (of person)* yoko ni naru 横になる; *(of animal)* nesoberu ねそべる; *(of place, building, object)* aru ある
♦ lie down yoko ni naru 横になる
lieutenant *(in navy)* taii 大尉; *(in army)* chūi 中尉; *(in police)* keibuho 警部補
life *(being alive)* inochi 命; *(way of living)* seikatsu 生活; *(period of being alive)* isshō 一生; *(of machine)* jumyō 寿命; *he had a happy / sad ~* kare wa shiawase na / kanashii isshō o okutta 彼は幸せな/悲しい一生を送った; *all her ~* isshōgai 一生涯; *that's ~!* jinsei to wa sonna mono da 人生とはそんなものだ
life belt kyūmei-beruto 救命ベルト;
lifeboat kyūmei-bōto 救命ボート;
life expectancy heikin-jumyō 平均寿命; **lifeguard** kyūjoin 救助員; **life history** seikatsushi 生活史; **life insurance** seimei-hoken 生命保険;

life jacket kyūmei-dōi 救命胴衣
lifeless *body* shinda 死んだ; *personality* seiki no nai 生気のない
lifelike ikiutsushi (no) 生き写し(の); **lifelong** isshō (no) 一生(の); **life preserver** *(for swimmer)* kyūmeigu 救命具; **life-saving** *adj equipment, drug* jinmei-kyūjoyō (no) 人命救助用(の); **lifesized** jitsubutsudai (no) 実物大(の); **life-threatening** inochi ni kakawaru 命にかかわる; **lifetime** *(of person)* shōgai 生涯; *in my ~* watashi no ikite iru aida ni 私の生きている間に
lift 1 *v/t* mochiageru 持ち上げる **2** *v/i (of fog)* hareru 晴れる **3** *n Br (elevator)* erebētā エレベーター; *give ... a ~ (in car)* ... o kuruma de okuru ...を車で送る
♦ lift off *v/i (of rocket)* uchiagerareru 打ち上げられる
lift-off *(of rocket)* uchiage 打ち上げ
ligament jintai じん帯
light¹ 1 *n* hikari 光; *(lamp)* akari 明り; *in the ~ of fig* ... ni terashite ...に照らして; *do you have a ~?* hi o motte imasu ka 火を持っていますか **2** *v/t fire, cigarette* ... ni hi o tsukeru ...に火をつける; *(illuminate)* raitoappu suru ライトアップする **3** *adj (not dark)* akarui 明るい; *color* usui 薄い
light² 1 *adj (not heavy)* karui 軽い; *traffic* sukunai 少ない; *rain, wind* yowai 弱い **2** *adv: travel ~* migaru ni ryokō suru 身軽に旅行する
♦ light up 1 *v/t (illuminate)* ... o raitoappu suru ...をライトアップする **2** *v/i (start to smoke)* hi o tsukeru 火をつける
light bulb denkyū 電球
lighten¹ *v/t color* akaruku suru 明るくする
lighten² *v/t load* karuku suru 軽くする
♦ lighten up *(cheer up)* genki o dashite 元気を出して
lighter *(for cigarettes)* raitā ライター
light-headed *(dizzy)* atama ga

furafura suru 頭がふらふらする;
light-hearted kiraku (na) 気楽
(な); **lighthouse** tōdai 灯台
lighting shōmei 照明
lightly *touch* karuku かるく; *get off ~*
assari nogareru あっさり逃れる
lightness[1] (*of room, color*) keikai-
sa 軽快さ
lightness[2] (*in weight*) karu-sa 軽さ
lightning inabikari 稲光
lightning conductor hiraishin 避雷
針
light pen raitopen ライトペン;
lightweight (*in boxing*) raito-kyū
ライト級; **light year** kōnen 光年
like[1] **1** *prep* ... no yō (na) ...のよう
(な); *be ~* (*resemble*) ... no yō de
aru ...のようである; *what is she
~?* (*in looks, character*) kanojo wa
donna hito desu ka 彼女はどんな
人ですか; *it's not ~ him* (*not his
character*) karerashiku nai kara-
shiku nai 彼らしくない **2** *conj* F (*as*) ...yō ni ...よう
に; *~ I said* watashi ga itta yō ni
私が言ったように
like[2] *v/t* ... ga suki da ...が好きだ; *I
~ this one* sore ga suki da それが
好きだ; *I ~ her* kanojo ga suki da
彼女が好きだ; *I would ~ ...* ... ga
hoshii ...が欲しい; *I would ~ to ~
... shitai ...したい; *would you ~ ...
... ga hoshii desu ka ...が欲しいで
すか; *would you ~ to ...?* ... shitai
desu ka ...したいですか; *~ to ...* no
ga suki de aru ...のが好きである; *if
you ~* yokereba よければ
likeable sukareru 好かれる
likelihood mikomi 見込み; *in all ~*
tabun 多分
likely (*probable*) arisō (na) ありそ
う(な); *not ~!* tondemonai とんで
もない
likeness (*resemblance*) ruijiten 類
似点
liking: *is it to your ~?* anata no
konomi ni attemasu ka あなたの好
みに合ってますか; *take a ~ to ...*
ga ki ni iru ...が気に入る
lilac (*flower*) rairakku ライラック;
(*color*) fujiiro ふじ色
lily yuri ゆり

lily of the valley suzuran すずらん
limb teashi 手足
lime[1] (*fruit, tree*) raimu ライム
lime[2] (*substance*) sekkai 石灰
limegreen usumidoriiro うすみどり
色
limelight: *be in the ~* chūmoku no
mato ni naru 注目の的になる
limit 1 *n* (*of endurance, patience*)
genkai 限界; (*of age, weight,
speed*) seigen 制限; (*of land, area*)
kyōkai 境界; *within ~s* tekido ni
light guchi ni 適度に; *off ~s* tachiiri-kinshi-chiku
de 立ち入り禁止地区で; *that's the
~!* mō genkai da もう限界だ; *5
glasses is my ~* gurasu gohai ga
watashi no genkai desu グラス五
杯が私の限界です **2** *v/t* seigen
suru 制限する
limitation genkai 限界
limited company *Br* kabushiki-
gaisha 株式会社
limo, limousine rimujin リムジン
limp[1] *adj arm etc* darari to shita だ
らりとした; (*lacking energy*)
genki no nai 元気のない
limp[2] *n*: *he has a ~* kare wa ashi o
hikizutte aruite iru 彼は足を引き
ずって歩いている
line[1] *n* (*on paper, road*) sen 線; (*on
tennis court*) rain ライン; TELEC
denwasen 電話線; (*of people,
trees*) retsu 列; (*of text*) gyō 行; (*of
business*) hōmen 方面; *the ~ is
busy* hanashichū desu 話中です;
hold the ~ please sono mama
omachi kudasai そのままお待ちく
ださい; *draw the ~ at ...* ni gendo
o oku ...に限度を置く; *~ of inquiry*
(*in police investigation*) sōsa-
hōshin 捜査方針; *~ of reasoning*
suiri no hōkō 推理の方向; *stand in
~* retsu ni narabu 列に並ぶ; *in ~
with ...* (*conforming with*) ... to
itchi shite ...と一致して; *he's out
of ~ there* kare wa kisoku yaburi
da 彼は規則破りだ
line[2] *v/t clothes* ... ni ura o tsukeru
...に裏をつける
♦**line up** *v/i* seiretsu suru 整列する
linen (*material*) asa 麻, rinen リネ

ン; (*for bed*) beddo-rinen ベッドリ
ネン

liner (*ship*) teikisen 定期船

linesman SP senshin 線審,
rainzuman ラインズマン

linger (*of person*) nakanaka
tachisaranai なかなか立ち去らな
い; (*of pain*) nakanaka kienai な
かなか消えない

lingerie ranjerī ランジェリー

linguist (*professional*) gengo-
gakusha 言語学者; *she's a good ~*
kanojo wa gaikokugo ga jōzu da
彼女は外国語が上手だ

linguistic gengo (no) 言語(の)

lining (*of clothes*) uraji 裏地

link 1 *n* (*between incidents, facts*)
kanren 関連; (*between people,
countries*) tsunagari つながり; (*in
chain*) wa 輪 **2** *v/t* kanren saseru
関連させる

◆**link up** *v/i* tsunagaru つながる;
(*with person*) gōryū suru 合流する

lion raion ライオン

lip kuchibiru 唇

lipread *v/i* dokushin suru 読唇する

lipstick kuchibeni 口紅

liqueur rikyūru リキュール

liquid 1 *n* ekitai 液体 **2** *adj* ekitai
(no) 液体(の)

liquidation seisan 清算; *go into ~*
seisan suru 清算する

liquidity kankinsei 換金性

liquor sake 酒

liquor store sakaya 酒屋

lisp 1 *n* shitatarazu no hatsuon 舌足
らずの発音 **2** *v/i* shitatarazu ni
hatsuon suru 舌足らずに発音する

list 1 *n* risuto リスト; (*of people*)
meibo 名簿; (*of things*) mokuroku
目録 **2** *v/t* hyō ni suru 表にする

listen kiku 聞く

◆**listen in** nusumigiki suru 盗み聞き
する; (*with listening device*) tōchō
suru 盗聴する

◆**listen to** *radio* ... o kiku ...を聞く;
person ... no iu koto o kiku ...の言
うことを聞く

listener (*to radio*) chōshu-sha 聴取
者; *he's a good ~* kare wa hito no
hanashi o yoku kiku 彼は人の話を

よく聞く

listings magazine terebi-zasshi テ
レビ雑誌

listless genki no nai 元気のない

liter rittoru リットル

literal mojidōri (no) 文字どおり(の)

literary bungaku (no) 文学(の)

literate: *be ~* yomikaki ga dekiru
読み書きができる

literature bungaku 文学;
(*advertising*) insatsubutsu 印刷物;
(*about a product*) katarogu カタロ
グ

litter gomi ごみ; (*of animals*)
hitohara no ko ひと腹の子

little 1 *adj* sukoshi (no) 少し(の);
town, house, hands chīsai 小さい;
problem, mistake sasai (na) ささ
い(な); *child* osanai 幼い; *~ sister*
imōto 妹; *~ brother* otōto 弟; *the
ones* kodomotachi 子供たち; *when
I was ~* watashi ga kodomo no
koro 私が子供の頃; *it's of ~ use*
yaku ni tatanai 役に立たない **2** *n*:
the ~ I know nakenashi no
chishiki なけなしの知識; *a ~*
sukoshi 少し; *a ~ bread / wine*
sukoshi no pan / wain 少しのパン /
ワイン; *a ~ is better than nothing*
sukoshi de mo nai yori mashi da
少しでもないよりましだ **3** *adv*: *~
by* sukoshi zutsu 少しずつ; *a ~
better / bigger* sukoshi yoi / ōkii
少しよい / 大きい; *a ~ before 6*
rokuji sukoshi mae 六時少し前

live¹ *v/i* (*reside*) sumu 住む; (*be
alive*) ikiru 生きる

◆**live on 1** *v/t rice, bread* ... o
tabete ikiru ...を食べて生きる **2** *v/i* (*continue living*) seizon suru
生存する

◆**live up**: *live it up* tanoshiku
sugosu 楽しく過ごす

◆**live up to** ... ni kotaeru ...にこた
える

◆**live with** *person* ... to issho ni
kurasu ...と一緒に暮らす

live² *adj broadcast* nama (no) 生
(の); jikkyō (no) 実況(の);
ammunition shiyō-kanō (na) 使用
可能(な)

livelihood seikei 生計

lively *party* nigiyaka (na) にぎやか (な); *city, place* kakki no aru 活気 のある; *music* yōki (na) 陽気(な); *person* ikiiki shita 生き生きした

liver MED kanzō 肝臓; (*food*) rebā レバー

livestock kachikurui 家畜類

livid (*angry*) gekido shita 激怒した

living *adj* ikite iru 生きている; *language* genzai tsukawarete iru 現在使われている 2 *n* kurashi 暮し; **earn one's ~** seikei o tateru 生計 を立てる; **standard of ~** seikatsu-suijun 生活水準

living room ima 居間, ribingu-rūmu リビングルーム

lizard tokage とかげ

load *n* tsumini 積荷; **~s of** takusan no ... たくさんの ... 2 *v/t car* ... ni noseru ...にのせ る; *camera* ... ni firumu o ireru ... にフィルムを入れる; *gun* ... ni tama o komeru ...に弾を込める; *software* rōdo suru ロードする; **~ X onto Y** X o Y ni tsumu XをYに 積む

loaded F (*very rich*) okanemochi (no) お金持ち(の); (*drunk*) yopparatta 酔っぱらった

loaf ikkin 一斤; **a ~ of bread** ikkin no pan 一斤のパン

♦ **loaf around** norakura suru のらく らする

loafer (*shoe*) rōfā ローファー

loan *n* kashitsukekin 貸付金; **on ~** karite iru 借りている 2 *v/t* kasu 貸 す; **~ Y to X** X ni Y o kasu XにYを 貸す

loathe hidoku kirau ひどく嫌う

lobby robī ロビー; POL atsuryoku-dantai 圧力団体

lobster robusutā ロブスター

local 1 *adj* jimoto (no) 地元(の) 2 *n* (*person*) tochi no hito 土地の人; TELEC naisen 内線

local anesthetic kyokusho-masui 局所麻酔; **local call** TELEC shinai-tsūwa 市内通話; **local government** chihō-jichitai 地方自治体

locality basho 場所

locally *live, work* jimoto de 地元で

local produce jimoto no seisanbutsu 地元の生産物

local time genchi-jikan 現地時間

locate *new factory etc* oku 置く; (*identify position of*) basho o shimesu 場所を示す; **be ~d** aru あ る

location (*siting*) basho 場所; (*identifying position of*) shozai no kakunin 所在の確認; **on ~** *movie* roke-chū de ロケ中で

lock[1] (*of hair*) fusa 房

lock[2] 1 *n* (*on door*) kagi 鍵 2 *v/t door* ... ni kagi o kakeru ...に鍵をかける; **~ X in position** X o teiichi ni kotei suru Xを定位置に固定する

♦ **lock away** ... o genjū ni shimaikomu ...を厳重にしまい込む

♦ **lock in** *person* ... o tojikomeru ... を閉じ込める

♦ **lock out** (*of house*) ... o shimedasu ...を締め出す; **I locked myself out** kagi o naka ni oita mama doa o shimete shimatta 鍵 を中に置いたままドアを閉めてし まった

♦ **lock up** (*in prison*) keimusho ni ireru 刑務所に入れる

locker rokkā ロッカー

locket roketto ロケット

locksmith jōmae-ya 錠前屋

locust inago いなご

lodge 1 *v/t complaint* teishutsu suru 提出する 2 *v/i* (*of bullet etc*) atatte tomaru 当たって止まる

lodger geshukunin 下宿人

loft yaneura 屋根裏; (*as apartment*) rofuto ロフト

lofty *heights* sobietatsu そびえ立つ; *ideals* sūkō (na) 崇高(な)

log (*wood*) maruta 丸太; (*record*) kiroku 記録; (*captain's, driver's*) nisshi 日誌

♦ **log off** shūryō suru 終了する

♦ **log on** kidō suru 起動する

♦ **log on to** ... o kidō suru ...を起動 する

logbook nisshi 日誌

log cabin maruta-goya 丸太小屋

logic ronri 論理

logical ronriteki (na) 論理的(な)

logistics keikaku no jisshi 計画の実施

logo rogo ロゴ

loiter urotsuku うろつく

lollipop bōtsuki kyandī 棒付きキャンディー

London Rondon ロンドン

loneliness (*of person*) kodoku 孤独; (*of place*) sabishi-sa 寂しさ

lonely *person* kodoku (na) 孤独(な); *place* sabishii 寂しい

loner ippiki-ōkami 一匹おおかみ

long¹ **1** *adj* nagai 長い; *it's a ~ way* tōi 遠い **2** *adv* nagaku 長く; *don't be ~* (*be back soon*) hayaku modotte kite 早く戻って来て; (*be quick*) isoide 急いで; *5 weeks is too ~* goshūkan wa nagasugiru 五週間は長過ぎる; *will it take ~?* nagaku kakarimasu ka 長くかかりますか; *that was ~ ago* sore wa daibu mae no koto da それはだいぶ前のことだ; *~ before then* sore yori daibu mae ni それよりだいぶ前に; *we can't wait any ~er* watashitachi wa kore ijō matemasen 私たちはこれ以上待てません; *he no ~er works here* kare wa mō koko de wa hataraite imasen 彼はもうここでは働いていません; *so ~ as* (*provided*) ... de aru kagiri wa ...である限りは; *so ~!* sayōnara さようなら

long² *v/i*: *~ for ...* o machinozomu ...を待ち望む; *I'm ~ing to see her again* watashi wa kanojo ni aitakute tamaranai 私は彼女に会いたくてたまらない

long-distance *adj* chōkyori (no) 長距離(の)

longing *n* setsubō 切望

longingly setsubō shite 切望して

longitude keido 経度

long jump habatobi 幅跳び; **long-range** *missile* chōkyori (no) 長距離(の); *forecast* chōki (no) 長期(の); **long-sighted** enshi (no) 遠視(の); **long-sleeved** nagasode (no) 長袖(の); **long-standing** naganen

ni wataru 長年にわたる; **long-term** *adj* chōki (no) 長期(の); **long wave** chōha 長波

look 1 *n* (*appearance*) mikake 見かけ; (*glance*) ikken 一見; *give ... a ~* ... o chiratto miru ...をちらっと見る; *have a ~ at* (*examine*) ... o chotto miru ...をちょっと見る; *can I have a ~?* chotto mite mo ii desu ka ちょっと見てもいいですか; *can I have a ~ around?* (*in store etc*) gurutto mite mawatte mo ii desu ka ぐるっと見て回ってもいいですか; *~s* (*beauty*) yōbō 容ぼう **2** *v/i* miru 見る; (*seem*) ... ni mieru ...に見える; *you ~ tired / different* tsukarete / itsumo to chigatte mieru 疲れて / いつもと違って見える

♦ **look after** *children* ... no sewa o suru ...の世話をする; *property* ... no kanri o suru ...の管理をする; *own interests* ... o mamoru ...を守る

♦ **look around** *museum, city* ... o gurutto mite mawaru ...をぐるっと見て回る

♦ **look at** ... o miru ...を見る; (*examine*) ... o shiraberu ...を調べる; (*consider*) ... o kangaeru ...を考える

♦ **look back** ... o furikaette miru ...を振り返って見る

♦ **look down on** ... o mikudasu ...を見下す

♦ **look for** ... o sagasu ...を探す

♦ **look forward to** ... o tanoshimi ni shite matsu ...を楽しみにして待つ

♦ **look in on** (*visit*) ... no tokoro ni tachiyoru ...のところに立ち寄る

♦ **look into** (*investigate*) ... no naiyō o shiraberu ...の内容を調べる

♦ **look on 1** *v/i* (*watch*) bōkan suru 傍観する **2** *v/t*: *~ X as Y* (*consider*) X o Y da to minasu Xを Yだとみなす

♦ **look onto** *garden, street* ... ni menshite iru ...に面している

♦ **look out** *v/i* (*of window etc*) soto o miru 外を見る; (*pay attention*) ki o tsukeru 気をつける; *~!* abunai 危ない

look out for 478

♦**look out for** *mailman etc* ... o sagashite miru ...を捜してみる; (*be on guard against*) ... ni chūi suru ...に注意する

♦**look out of** *window* ... kara soto o miru ...から外を見る

♦**look over** *house* ... o tenken suru ...を点検する; *translation* ... o shiraberu ...を調べる

♦**look through** *magazine, notes* ... o yoku shiraberu ...をよく調べる

♦**look to** (*rely on*) ... ni tayoru ...に頼る

♦**look up 1** *v/i* (*from paper etc*) miageru 見上げる; (*improve*) jōshō suru 上昇する; (*of weather*) yoku naru よくなる; *things are looking up* yoku natte kite iru よくなって来ている **2** *v/t word, phone number* ... o shiraberu ...を調べる; (*visit*) ... o hōmon suru ...を訪問する

♦**look up to** (*respect*) ... o sonkei suru ...を尊敬する

lookout (*person*) mihari 見張り; *be on the ~ for* ... no mihari o shite iru ...の見張りをしている

♦**loom up** bon'yari arawareru ぼんやり現れる

loony F **1** *n* kichigai 気違い **2** *adj* ki no kurutta 気の狂った

loop *n* wa 輪

loophole (*in law etc*) nukeana 抜け穴

loose *connection* yurui ゆるい; *rope* tarunda たるんだ; *button* torekakatta 取れかかった; *clothes* yuttari shita ゆったりした; *morals* fushidara (na) ふしだら(な); *wording* aimai (na) あいまい(な); *~ change* bara no kozeni ばらの小銭; *~ ends* mikaiketsu-bubun 未解決部分

loosely *tied* yuruku ゆるく

loosely *worded* aimai ni あいまいに

loosen yurumeru ゆるめる

loot 1 *n* senrihin 戦利品 **2** *v/i* ryakudatsu suru 略奪する

looter ryakudatsu-sha 略奪者

♦**lop off** ... o kiriotosu ...を切り落とす

lop-sided katayotta 片寄った

Lord (*God*) Kamisama 神様; *Lord's Prayer* SP Shu no inori 主の祈り

lorry *Br* torakku トラック

lose 1 *v/t object* nakusu なくす; *match* ... ni makeru ...に負ける **2** *v/i* SP makeru 負ける; (*of clock*) okureru 遅れる; *I'm lost* michi ni mayotta 道に迷った; *get lost!* F (*go away*) usero うせろ; (*don't be stupid*) yamete やめて

♦**lose out** son o suru 損をする

loser SP haisha 敗者; (*in life*) rakugo-sha 落後者

loss (*of object*) funshitsu 紛失; (*through death*) sōshitsu 喪失; (*in business*) sonshitsu 損失; *make a ~* sonshitsu o dasu 損失を出す; *be at a ~* tohō ni kureru 途方に暮れる

lost ushinawareta 失われた

lost-and-found(office) ishitsubutsu-toriatsukaijo 遺失物取扱所

lot: *a ~, ~s* takusan たくさん; (*very, much*) totemo とても; *a ~ of, ~s of* takusan no たくさんの; *a ~ better/easier* totemo yoi/kantan とても良い/簡単

lotion rōshon ローション

lotus hasu はす

loud *voice, noise* ōkii 大きい; *music* urusai うるさい; *color* hade (na) はで(な)

loudspeaker supīkā スピーカー

lounge ima 居間; (*in hotel, airport*) robī ロビー

♦**lounge around** burabura suru ぶらぶらする

louse shirami しらみ

lousy saitei (no) 最低(の); (*ill*) kimochi no warui 気持ちの悪い

lout busahō na otoko 不作法な男

lovable aisubeki 愛すべき

love 1 *n* ai 愛; (*for child, pet*) aijō 愛情; (*romantic*) ren'ai 恋愛; (*for object*) aichaku 愛着; (*in tennis*) rabu ラブ; *be in ~* ... ni koi shite iru ...に恋している; *fall in ~* horeru ほれる; *make ~* sekkusu o suru セックスをする; *what is it, my ~?* (*man to woman*) nāni, anata なに、あなた; (*woman to* *man, mother to child*) nāni なあに **2** *v/t* aisuru 愛する; *~ to ... ... no ga daisuki de aru* ...のが大好きである

love affair ren'ai-kankei 恋愛関係; **love life** sekkusu-raifu セックスライフ; **love letter** raburetā ラブレター

lovely *face, hair* utsukushii 美しい; *color, tune* kirei (na) きれい(な); *person, character, holiday, weather, meal* subarashii すばらしい; *we had a ~ time* totemo tanoshikatta とっても楽しかった

lover aijin 愛人

loving *adj person* aijō no fukai 愛情の深い; *care* kokoro no komotta 心のこもった

low 1 *adj* hikui 低い; *salary, price etc* yasui 安い; *quality* somatsu (na) 粗末(な); *be feeling ~* genki ga nai 元気がない; *be ~ on gas / tea* gasorin/kōcha ga tarinai ガソリン/紅茶が足りない **2** *n* (*in weather*) teikiatsu 低気圧; (*in sales, statistics*) saitei-kiroku 最低記録

lowbrow *adj* kyōyō no hikui 教養の低い; **low-calorie** tei-karorī (no) 低カロリー(の); **low-cut** *dress* eriguri no fukai 襟ぐりの深い

lower *boat, sth to the ground* orosu 降ろす; *flag, hemline, pressure, price* sageru 下げる; *voice* hikuku suru 低くする

low-fat teishibō (no) 低脂肪(の); **lowkey** hishigata (no) 控え目(の); **lowlands** teichi-chihō 低地方; **low-pressure area** teikiatsu-iki 低気圧域; **low season** ofushīzun オフシーズン; **low tide** kanchō 干潮

loyal chūjitsu (na) 忠実(な)

lozenge (*shape*) hishigata ひし形; (*tablet*) torōchi トローチ

Ltd (= *limited*) kabushiki-gaisha 株式会社

lubricant junkatsuyu 潤滑油

lubricate ... ni abura o sasu ...に油をさす

lubrication chūyu 注油

lucid (*clear*) wakariyasui わかりや

すい; (*sane*) shōki (no) 正気(の)

luck un 運; *bad ~* fuun 不運; *hard ~!* zannen 残念; *good ~* kōun 幸運; *good ~!* ganbatte がんばって

♦ **luck out** F tsuite iru ついている

luckily un' yoku 運よく

lucky *person, coincidence, day* un no ii 運のいい; *number, charm* kōun (no) 幸運(の); *guess* magure (no) まぐれ(の); *you were ~* kimi wa un ga yokatta 君は運がよかった; *he's ~ to be alive* ikite iru nante kare wa un ga yokatta 生きているなんて彼は運がよかった; *that's ~!* sore wa tsuite iru それはついている

ludicrous bakageta ばかげた

luggage tenimotsu 手荷物

lukewarm nurui ぬるい; *reception* kinori no shinai 気乗りのしない

lull 1 *n* (*in storm, fighting*) koyami 小やみ; (*in conversation*) ma 間 **2** *v/t*: *~ ... into a false sense of security* ... o damashite anshin da to omowaseru ...をだまして安心だと思わせる

lullaby komoriuta 子守歌

lumbago yōtsū 腰痛

lumber *n* (*timber*) zaimoku 材木

luminous hakkō suru 発光する

lump (*of sugar*) kakuzatō ikko 角砂糖一個; (*swelling*) shikori しこり, kobu こぶ

♦ **lump together** isshokuta ni suru 一緒くたにする

lump sum ikkatsubarai 一括払い

lumpy *sauce* dama ni natta だまになった; *mattress* dekoboko (no) 凸凹(の)

lunacy kyōki 狂気

lunar tsuki (no) 月(の)

lunatic *n* Fōbaka 大ばか

lunch chūshoku 昼食, hirugohan 昼ごはん; *have ~* chūshoku o toru 昼食をとる

lunch box (*packed lunch*) obentō お弁当; (*at station*) ekiben 駅弁; **lunch break** hiruyasumi 昼休み; **lunch hour** chūshokudoki 昼食時; **lunchtime** chūshokudoki 昼食時

lung hai 肺

lung cancer haigan 肺がん
♦ **lunge at** ... o tsuku ...を突く
lurch v/i (of person) yoromeku よろめく; (of ship, car) yureru 揺れる
lure 1 n yūwaku 誘惑 **2** v/t (into a trap) obikiyoseru おびき寄せる
lurid color kebakebashii けばけばしい; details osoroshii 恐ろしい
lurk (of person) machibuse suru 待ち伏せする; (of doubt) tsukimatou つきまとう
luscious fruit, dessert amai 甘い;

woman, man miryokuteki (na) 魅力的(な)
lust n yokubō 欲望
luxurious gōka (na) 豪華(な)
luxury 1 n zeitaku ぜいたく **2** adj gōka (na) 豪華(な)
lymph gland rinpasen リンパ腺
lynch ... ni shikei o kuwaeru ...に私刑を加える
lynx ōyamaneko おおやまねこ
lyricist sakushika 作詞家
lyrics kashi 歌詞

M

MA (= Master of Arts) bungaku-shūshigō 文学修士号
ma'am okusan 奥さん; (to younger woman) ojōsan お嬢さん; (to teacher) sensei 先生
machine 1 n kikai 機械 **2** v/t (on sewing machine) mishin o kakeru ミシンをかける; TECH kikai de tsukuru 機械で作る
machine gun n kikanjū 機関銃
machine-readable konpyūta de yomitori-kanō (no) コンピューターで読み取り可能(の)
machinery (machines) kikairui 機械類
machismo otokoppo-sa 男っぽさ
macho otokoppoi 男っぽい
mackerel saba さば
mackintosh reinkōto レインコート
macro COMPUT makuro マクロ
mad ki no kurutta 気の狂った; idea bakageta ばかげた; (angry) kankan ni hara o tateta かんかんに腹を立てた; be ~ about (enthusiastic) ... ni netchū shite iru ...に熱中している; this is driving me ~ kono sei de ki ga kurui-sō da このせいで気が狂いそうだ; go ~ ki ga kuruu 気が狂う; (with enthusiasm) ki ga kurutta yō

ni kōfun suru 気が狂ったように興奮する; like ~ run, work hisshi de 必死で
madden hidoku iradataseru ひどくいらだたせる
maddening hidoku haradatashii ひどく腹立たしい
made-to-measure ōdāmeido (no) オーダーメイド(の)
madhouse fig sōzōshii basho 騒々しい場所
madly hisshi ni 必死に; ~ in love muchū ni natte iru 夢中になっている
madman kichigai 気違い
madness kyōki 狂気
Mafia: the ~ Mafia マフィア
magazine (printed) zasshi 雑誌
maggot uji うじ
magic 1 n (supernatural force) mahō 魔法; (charm) maryoku 魔力; (tricks) tejina 手品; like ~ tachidokoro ni たちどころに **2** adj mahō no yō (na) 魔法のよう(な)
magical powers mahō (no) 魔法の; moment subarashii すばらしい
magician tejina-shi 手品師, majishan マジシャン
magic spell mahō 魔法
magic trick tejina 手品

magnanimous kandai (na) 寛大(な)

magnet jishaku 磁石

magnetic jishaku (no) 磁石(の); *personality* hito o hikitsukeru 人を引きつける

magnetism (*of person*) hito o hikitsukeru miryoku 人を引きつける魅力

magnificence sōdai-sa 壮大さ

magnificent *view, building* sōdai (na) 壮大(な); *decoration, work* migoto (na) みごと(な)

magnify kakudai suru 拡大する; *difficulties* kochō suru 誇張する

magnifying glass mushi-megane 虫眼鏡

magnitude ōki-sa 大きさ

mah-jong mājan 麻雀

maid otetsudai お手伝い; (*in hotel*) kyakushitsu-gakari 客室係

maiden name kyūsei 旧姓

maiden voyage shojo-kōkai 処女航海

mail 1 *n* (*brand*) shurui 種類; **put X in the ~** X o tōkan suru Xを投かんする **2** *v/t letter* yūsō suru 郵送する

mailbox (*in street*) posuto ポスト; (*of house*) yūbin'uke 郵便受け; COMPUT mērubokkusu メールボックス

mailing list yūsōsaki-meibo 郵送先名簿

mailman yūbin'ya-san 郵便屋さん;
mail-order catalog tsūshin-hanbai-katarogu 通信販売カタログ; **mail-order firm** tsūshin-hanbai no kaisha 通信販売の会社

maim jūshō o owaseru 重傷を負わせる (*fugu ni naru* 不具になる)

main *adj* omo (na) 主(な)

mainframe ōgata-konpyūta 大型コンピューター; **mainland** hondo 本土; **on the ~** hondo ni 本土に; **mainland China** Chūgoku hondo 中国本土

mainly omo ni 主に

main road kansen-dōro 幹線道路

main street ōdōri 大通り

maintain *v/t* iji suru 維持する; *pace, speed* jizoku suru 持続する; *family* fuyō suru 扶養する; *innocence,*

guilt shuchō suru 主張する; **~ that** ... o ronjiru ...を論じる

maintenance (*of machine, house*) mentenansu メンテナンス; (*money*) fuyōryō 扶養料; (*of law and order*) iji 維持

majestic dōdō to shita 堂々とした

major 1 *adj* shuyō (na) 主要(な); **C ~** MUS hachōchō ハ長調 **2** *n* MIL shōsa 少佐

♦**major in** ... o senkō suru ...を専攻する

majority daitasū 大多数; POL tokuhyō sa 得票差; **be in the ~** kahansū o shimeru 過半数を占める

make 1 *n* (*brand*) shurui 種類; **a Japanese ~ of car** Nihonsei no kuruma 日本製の車 **2** *v/t meal, dress, cake* tsukuru 作る; *coffee, tea* ireru 入れる; *movie, TV program* seisaku suru 製作する; *speech, statement etc* suru する; *bed* totonoeru 整える; *hole* akeru 開ける; (*manufacture*) seizō suru 製造する; (*earn*) kasegu 稼ぐ; MATH ... ni naru ...になる; **~ X do Y** (*compel, cause*) X ni Y saseru XにYさせる; **you can't ~ me do it!** muri ni yaraseyō tatte dame desu 無理にやらせようったってだめです; **~ X happy** X o shiawase ni suru Xを幸せにする; **~ X angry** X o okoraseru Xを怒らせる; **~ a noise** mono-oto o tateru 物音を立てる; **made in Japan** Nihonsei 日本製; **~ it** (*come to party, meeting*) deru 出る; (*arrive on time*) ma ni au 間に合う; (*succeed*) seikō suru 成功する; (*survive*) mochikotaeru 持ちこたえる; **what time do you ~ it?** ima nanji desu ka 今何時ですか; **~ believe** (*pretend*) ... de aru furi o suru ...のあるふりをする; **~ do with** ma ni awaseru 間に合わせる; **what do you ~ of it?** sore no dō omoimasu ka それをどう思いますか

♦**make for** (*go toward*) ... ni mukau ...に向かう

♦**make off** isoide tachisaru 急いで立ち去る

♦**make off with** (*steal*) ... o

mochinige suru …を持ち逃げする

♦**make out** v/t *list* … o tsukuriageru …を作り上げる; (*see*) … o miwakeru …を見分ける; (*imply*) … to honomekasu …とほのめかす

♦**make over**: *make X over to Y* X o Y ni yuzuru XをYに譲る

♦**make up 1** v/i (*of woman*) keshō o suru 化粧をする; (*of actor*) mēkuappu o suru メークアップをする; (*after quarrel*) nakanaori suru 仲直りする **2** v/t *story, excuse* … o tsukuridasu …を作り出す; *face* … ni keshō o suru …に化粧をする; *constitute* kōsei suru 構成する; *be made up of* … de tsukurarete iru …で作られている; (*of class, group*) … de kōsei sarete iru …で構成されている; ~ *one's mind* kesshin suru 決心する; *make it up* (*after quarrel*) nakanaori suru 仲直りする

♦**make up for** … no umeawase o suru …の埋め合せをする

make-believe n misekake 見せかけ

maker (*of product*) seizō-gaisha 製造会社

makeshift ma ni awase (no) 間に合わせ(の)

make-up (*cosmetics*) keshōhin 化粧品

maladjusted kankyō-futekiō (no) 環境不適応(の)

Malay (*language*) Marē-go マレー語; (*person*) Marēshia-jin マレーシア人

Malaysia Marēshia マレーシア

Malaysian Marēshia (no) マレーシア(の)

male 1 adj dansei (no) 男性(の); *animal, bird, fish* osu (no) 雄(の) **2** n dansei 男性; (*animal, bird, fish*) osu 雄

male chauvinist (*pig*) danson-johi no (butayarō) 男尊女卑の(ブタ野郎)

male nurse kangoshi 看護士

malevolent akui o motta 悪意をもった

malfunction 1 n fuchō 不調 **2** v/i

seijō ni ugokanai 正常に動かない

malice akui 悪意

malicious akui no aru 悪意のある

malignant *tumor* akusei (no) 悪性(の)

mall (*shopping ~*) shoppingu-sentā ショッピングセンター

malnutrition eiyō-shitchō 栄養失調

malpractice (*of doctor*) iryō-kago 医療過誤

maltreat gyakutai suru 虐待する

maltreatment gyakutai 虐待

mammal honyū-dōbutsu ほ乳動物

mammoth adj yama no yō (na) 山のよう(な)

man n otoko 男; (*human*) hito 人; (*humanity*) ningen 人間; (*in checkers*) koma こま

manage 1 v/t *business* keiei suru 経営する; *money* kanri suru 管理する; ~ *to* nan to ka … suru 何とか…する **2** v/i (*cope*) dō ni ka kurashite iku どうにか暮していく; (*financially*) yarikuri suru やりくりする; *can you* ~? daijōbu desu ka 大丈夫ですか

manageable *hair* atsukai-yasui 扱いやすい; *work* dō ni ka shori suru どうにか処理できる

management keiei 経営; (*managers*) keieisha-gawa 経営者側, kanrishoku 管理職

management buyout keieijin no jishakabu kaishime 経営陣の自社株買い占め; **management consultant** keiei-konsarutanto 経営コンサルタント; **management studies** keiei-gaku 経営学; **management team** keiei-jin 経営陣

manager (*of restaurant, hotel*) shihai-nin 支配人, kanrishoku 管理職; (*of shop*) tenchō 店長

managerial keiei (no) 経営(の)

managing director senmu-torishimariyaku 専務取締役

Manchuria Manshū 満州

Mandarin Pekin-go 北京語

mandarin orange mikan みかん

mandate (*authority*) kengen 権限; (*task*) ninmu 任務

mandatory hissu (no) 必須(の)

mane (*of horse*) tategami たてがみ

maneuver 1 *n* sakusen 作戦; *fig* sakuryaku 策略 **2** *v/t* takumi ni ugokasu 巧みに動かす; *fig* takumi ni ayatsuru 巧みに操る

mangle *v/t* (*crush*) mechamecha ni suru 目茶目茶にする

manhandle *person* teara ni atsukau 手荒に扱う; *object* jinriki de ugokasu 人力で動かす

manhood (*maturity*) seinenki 成年期; (*virility*) otoko to shite no seiteki-nōryoku 男としての性的能力

man-hour jinji 人時

manhunt hannin-tsuiseki 犯人追跡

mania (*craze*) nekkyō 熱狂

maniac kyōjin 狂人

manicure *n* manikyua マニキュア

manifest 1 *adj* meihaku (na) 明白(な) **2** *v/t* akiraka ni suru 明らかにする; **~ itself** arawareru 表れる

manipulate *person* ayatsuru 操る; *bones* seitai-chiryō suru 整体治療する

manipulation (*of bones*) seitai 整体

manipulative hito o kōmyō ni ayatsuru yō (na) 人を巧妙に操るよう(な)

mankind jinrui 人類

manly otoko-rashii 男らしい

man-made jinkō (no) 人工(の)

manner (*of doing something*) hōhō 方法; (*attitude*) taido 態度

manners: good / bad ~ yoi / warui gyōgi よい/悪い行儀; **have no ~** gyōgi ga warui 行儀が悪い

manpower jin'in 人員

mansion daiteitaku 大邸宅

mantelpiece, mantelshelf mantorupīsu マントルピース

manual 1 *adj* tesagyō (no) 手作業(の); *labor* nikutai (no) 肉体(の); *dexterity* tesaki (no) 手先(の) **2** *n* manyuaru マニュアル

manufacture 1 *n* seizō 製造 **2** *v/t* seizō suru 製造する

manufacturer seizō-gyōsha 製造業者

manufacturing (*industry*) seizōgyō 製造業

manure koyashi 肥やし

manuscript genkō 原稿

many 1 *adj* takusan (no) たくさん(の); **~ times** nando mo 何度も **2** *pron* tasū 多数; **how ~ do you need?** ikutsu hitsuyō desu ka いくつ必要ですか; **a great ~** takusan no とてもたくさんの; **a good ~** kanari takusan no かなりたくさんの

map *n* chizu 地図

♦ **map out** ... no keikaku o shikkari tateru ...の計画をしっかり立てる

maple kaede かえで; *Japanese ~* momiji もみじ

mar sokonau 損なう; *event* dainashi ni suru 台無しにする

marathon (*race*) marason マラソン

marble (*material*) dairiseki 大理石

March sangatsu 三月

march 1 *n* kōshin 行進; (*protest*) demo-kōshin デモ行進 **2** *v/i* kōshin suru 行進する; (*in protest*) demo-kōshin suru デモ行進する

Mardi Gras Shanikusai no kayōbi 謝肉祭の火曜日

mare (*horse*) mesu-uma 雌馬

margarine māgarin マーガリン

margin (*of page*) yohaku 余白; (*profit ~*) rizaya 利ざや; **by a narrow ~** kiwadoi sa de きわどい差で

marginal (*slight*) wazuka (na) わずか(な)

marginally wazuka ni わずかに

marijuana, marihuana marifana マリファナ

marina marīna マリーナ

marinade *n* marine マリネ

marinate marine ni suru マリネにする

marine 1 *adj* umi (no) 海(の) **2** *n* (*soldier*) kaihei-taiin 海兵隊員

marital *problems* fūfu (no) 夫婦(の); **~ status** kon'in-kankei no umu 婚姻関係の有無

maritime umi (no) 海(の)

mark 1 *n* (*stain*) shimi 染み; (*sign, token*) shirushi 印; (*trace*) ato 跡; EDU tensū 点数; **leave one's ~** ...

ni eikyō o ataeru ...に影響を与える **2** *v/t* (*stain*) ato o tsukeru 跡をつける; EDU saiten suru 採点する; (*indicate*) shimesu 示す; (*commemorate*) kinen suru 記念する; **~ time** *fig* ashibumi-jōtai de aru 足踏み状態である **3** *v/i* (*of fabric*) shimi ga tsuku 染みがつく

♦ **mark down** *goods* ... o nebiki suru ...を値引きする

♦ **mark out** ... ni sen o hiku ...に線を引く; *fig* ... o kubetsu suru ...を区別する

♦ **mark up** *price* ... o neage suru ...を値上げする

marked ichijirushii 著しい

marker (*highlighter*) keikō-pen 蛍光ペン

market 1 *n* ichiba 市場; (*for particular commodity*) shijō 市場; (*outlet*) hanro 販路; (*stock ~*) kabushiki-shijō 株式市場; **on the ~** shijō de 市場で **2** *v/t* shijō ni uri ni dasu 市場に売りに出す

market economy shijō-keizai 市場経済

market forces shijō-jissei 市場実勢

marketing māketingu マーケティング

market leader māketto līdā マーケットリーダー; **marketplace** (*in town*) ichiba 市場; (*for commodities*) shijō 市場; **market research** shijō-chōsa 市場調査; **market share** shijō-shea 市場シェア

mark-up rihaba 利幅

marmalade māmarēdo マーマレード

marquee tento テント

marriage (*institution*) kekkon 結婚; (*state of being married*) kekkon-seikatsu 結婚生活; (*wedding*) kekkonshiki 結婚式

marriage certificate kekkon-shōmeisho 結婚証明書

marriage counselor maridji-kaunserā マリッジカウンセラー

married kekkon shita 結婚した; **be ~ to ...** ... to kekkon shite iru ...と結婚している

marry ... to kekkon suru ...と結婚する; (*of priest*) ... no kekkonshiki o toriokonau ...の結婚式をとり行う; **get married** kekkon suru 結婚する

marsh numachi 沼地

marshal *n* (*police officer*) keisatsu-shochō 警察署長

marshmallow mashumaro マシュマロ

marshy numachi (no) 沼地(の)

martial arts bujutsu 武術

martial law kaigenrei 戒厳令

martyr *n* REL junkyō-sha 殉教者; *fig* gisei-sha 犠牲者

martyred kunō shita 苦悩した

marvel 1 *n* (*person*) odorokubeki hito 驚くべき人 **2** *v/i*: **~ at ...** ... ni odoroku ...に驚く

marvelous subarashii すばらしい

Marxism Marukusu-shugi マルクス主義

Marxist 1 *adj* Marukusu-shugi (no) マルクス主義(の) **2** *n* Marukusu-shugi-sha マルクス主義者

mascara masukara マスカラ

mascot masukotto マスコット

masculine *pride* dansei (no) 男性(の); *appearance* danseiteki (na) 男性的(な)

masculinity otoko-rashisa 男らしさ; (*virility*) otoko to shite no seiteki-nōryoku 男としての性的能力

mash *v/t* tsubusu つぶす

mashed potatoes masshupoteto マッシュポテト

mask 1 *n* masuku マスク **2** *v/t* *feelings* kakusu 隠す

masochism mazohizumu マゾヒズム

masochist mazohisuto マゾヒスト

masquerade 1 *n* *fig* misekake みせかけ **2** *v/i*: **~ as ...** ... no furi o suru ...のふりをする

mass¹ 1 *n* (*great amount*) tairyō 大量; (*body*) katamari かたまり; **a ~ of** tairyō no ... 大量の...; **be a ~ of** (*be covered in*) ... de ippai de aru ...でいっぱいである; **~es of** tasū no ... 多数の... **2** *v/i* hitokatamari ni naru ひとかたまりになる

mass² REL misa ミサ

massacre 1 n daigyakusatsu 大虐殺; F boromake ボロ負け **2** v/t gyakusatsu suru 虐殺する; F (in sport) kotenpan ni yattsukeru こてんぱんにやっつける

massage 1 n massāji マッサージ **2** v/t massāji suru マッサージする; statistics sōsa suru 操作する

masseur massāji-shi マッサージ師

masseuse massāji-shi マッサージ師

massive effort, increase taihen (na) 大変(な); building dosshiri shita どっしりした

mass media masumedia マスメディア; **mass-produce** tairyō-seisan suru 大量生産する; **mass production** tairyō-seisan 大量生産

mast masuto マスト; RAD tettō 鉄塔

master 1 n (of dog) shujin 主人; (of ship) senchō 船長; **be a ~ of** ... no tatsujin de aru ...の達人である **2** v/t skill, language shūtoku suru 習得する; situation kokufuku suru 克服する

master bedroom mein-beddorūmu メインベッドルーム

master key masutā-kī マスターキー

masterly migoto (na) みごと(な)

mastermind 1 n kuromaku 黒幕 **2** v/t menmitsu ni keikaku o tateru 綿密に計画をたてる; crime kage de ito o hiku 陰で糸を引く; **Master of Arts** bungaku-shūshigō 文学修士号; **master of ceremonies** shikai-sha 司会者; **masterpiece** kessaku 傑作; **master's (degree)** shūshigō 修士号

mastery jukutatsu 熟達

masturbate masutābēshon o suru マスターベーションをする

mat n matto マット

match¹ (for cigarette) matchi マッチ

match² **1** (in competition) shiai 試合; (marriage) kekkon 結婚; **be no ~ for** totemo ... ni wa oyobanai ともに...にはおよばない; **meet one's ~** kyōteki ni deau 強敵に出会う **2** v/t (be the same as) ... to chōwa

suru ...と調和する; (equal) ... to dōtō de aru ...と同等である **3** v/i (of colors, patterns) chōwa suru 調和する

matchbox matchibako マッチ箱

matching osoroi (no) おそろい(の)

mate 1 n (of animal) tsugai no aite つがいの相手; NAUT kōkaishi 航海士 **2** v/i tsugai ni naru つがいになる

material 1 n (fabric) kiji 生地; (substance) busshitsu 物質 **2** adj busshitsuteki (na) 物質的(な)

materialism busshitsu-shugi 物質主義

materialist busshitsu-shugisha 物質主義者

materialistic busshitsu-shugiteki (na) 物質主義的(な)

materialize shutsugen suru 出現する

materials (for specific activity) yōgu 用具

maternal boseiteki (na) 母性的 (な); grandmother hahakata (no) 母方(の)

maternity bosei 母性

maternity dress matanitī-wea マタニティーウェア; **maternity leave** sankyū 産休; **maternity ward** sanka-byōtō 産科病棟

math sūgaku 数学

mathematical calculations sūgaku (no) 数学(の); mind sūgakuteki (na) 数学的(な)

mathematician sūgaku-sha 数学者

mathematics sūgaku 数学

matinée machine マチネ

matriarch onnakachō 女家長

matrimony kekkon 結婚

matt tsuyakeshi (no) つや消し(の)

matter (affair) mondai 問題; PHYS busshitsu 物質; **as a ~ of course** tōzen no koto to shite 当然のこととして; **as a ~ of fact** jitsu o iu to 実を言うと; **it's just a ~ of time** tan ni jikan no mondai da 単に時間の問題だ; **what's the ~ (with you)?** dō shita no どうしたの; **you're making ~s worse** anata wa jijō o akka sasete iru あなた事情を悪化させている; **no ~ what**

she says kanojo ga nan to iō tomo 彼女が何と言おうとも **2** v/i jūyō de aru 重要である; **it doesn't ~ taishita koto de wa nai** たいしたことではない

matter-of-fact jimuteki (na) 事務的(な)

mattress mattoresu マットレス

mature 1 adj (grown-up) seijuku shita 成熟した **2** v/i (of person) seijuku suru 成熟する; FIN manki ni naru 満期になる

maturity (adulthood) seijuku-ki 成熟期; (in behavior) seijuku 成熟; FIN manki 満期

maximize saidai ni suru 最大にする

maximum 1 adj size, effort saidai (no) 最大(の); speed, salary saikō (no) 最高(の) **2** n saidaigen 最大限; **a ~ of ...** saidai ... no 最大...の

May gogatsu 五月

may ◊ (possibility) ... ka mo shirenai ...かもしれない; **he ~ have decided** kare wa kesshin shita ka mo shirenai 彼は決心したかもしれない ◊ (permission) ... shite mo ii ...してもいい; **~ I ...?** ...shite mo ii desu ka ...してもいいですか; **you ~ as well** ...shite mo ii ...してもいい

maybe tabun たぶん; **you could ~ try...** ... o moshikashitara tameseru kamo ...をもしかしたら試せるかも

May Day Mēdē メーデー

mayo, mayonnaise mayonēzu マヨネーズ

mayor shichō 市長

maze meiro 迷路

MB (= **megabyte**) megabaito メガバイト

MBA (= **Master in Business Administration**) keieigaku-shūshigō 経営学修士号

MBO (= **management buyout**) keieijin no jishakabu kaishime 経営陣の自社株買い占め

MD (= **Doctor of Medicine**) igaku-hakushigō 医学博士号

me watashi 私; **with ~** watashi to ... と; **who?, ~?** dare – watashi desu

誰 – 私です ◊ (direct object) watashi o 私を; **he doesn't know ~** kare wa watashi o shiranai 彼は私を知らない ◊ (indirect object) watashi ni 私に; **can you mail it to ~?** watashi ni okutte moraemasu ka 私に送ってもらえますか

meadow bokusōchi 牧草地

meager wazuka (na) わずか(な)

meal shokuji 食事

meal ticket F kanezuru 金づる

mealtime shokuji-jikan 食事時間

mean¹ (with money) kechi (na) けち(な); (nasty) iji no warui 意地の悪い

mean² 1 v/t (intend) tsumori de aru つもりである; (signify) imi suru 意味する; **~ to do X** X suru tsumori de aru X するつもりである; **I really ~ it** hontō ni sono tsumori de itte iru 本当にそのつもりで言っている; **be ~t for** (be intended for) ... muke de aru ...向けである; (of remark) ... ni muketa mono de aru ...に向けたものである; **he ~s nothing to me** kare nante watashi ni wa dōdemo yoi 彼なんて私にはどうでもよい **2** v/i: **~ well** yokare to omotte suru よかれと思ってする

meaning (of word) imi 意味

meaningful (comprehensible) imi o nasu 意味を成す; (constructive) igi no aru 意義のある; glance imiarige (na) 意味ありげ(な)

meaningless muimi 無意味(な)

means (financial) zaisan 財産; (way) hōhō 方法; **~ of transportation** kōtsū-kikan 交通機関; **by all ~** (certainly) zehi dōzo ぜひどうぞ; **by no ~** kesshite ... de nai 決して...でない; **by ~ of ...** ni yotte ...によって

meanwhile sono aida ni その間に

measles hashika はしか

measure 1 n (step) taisaku 対策; (amount) teido 程度 **2** v/t hakaru 測る **3** v/i aru ある

♦ **measure out** ... o hakaritoru ...を測りとる

♦ **measure up to** ... ni kanau ...にかなう

measurement sunpō 寸法; (*action*) sokutei 測定

meat niku 肉

meatball mītobōru ミートボール

meatloaf mītorōfu ミートローフ

mechanic (*for cars*) jidōsha-shūrikō 自動車修理工

mechanical *device* kikai (no) 機械(の); *gesture* kikaiteki (na) 機械的(な)

mechanically *fig* kikaiteki ni 機械的に

mechanism (*device*) kikai 機械; (*workings*) kōzō 構造

mechanize kikaika suru 機械化する

medal medaru メダル

medallion (*medal*) ōgata-medaru 大型メダル

medalist medarisuto メダリスト

meddle (*interfere*) kanshō suru 干渉する; (*tinker*) ijikuru いじくる

media: *the* ~ masukomi マスコミ

median strip chūō-bunritai 中央分離帯

mediate chōtei suru 調停する

mediation chōtei 調停

mediator chōtei-sha 調停者

medical 1 *adj college, student* igaku (no) 医学(の); *insurance* iryō (no) 医療(の); ~ *history* byōreki 病歴; ~ *treatment* iryō 医療 2 *n* kenkō-shindan 健康診断

medical certificate kenkō-shindansho 健康診断書

Medicare rōreisha-shinshōsha tō no iryō-hoken-seido 老齢者身障者等の医療保険制度

medicated yakuyō (no) 薬用(の)

medication kusuri 薬

medicinal yakuyō (no) 薬用(の)

medicine kusuri 薬; (*science*) igaku 医学

medieval chūsei (no) 中世(の)

mediocre heibon (na) 平凡(な)

mediocrity (*of work etc*) heibon 平凡; (*person*) bonjin 凡人

meditate jukkō suru 熟考する; (*in yoga*) meisō suru めい想する

meditation (*thought*) jukkō 熟考; (*relaxation*) meisō めい想; *seated* ~ zazen 座禅

medium 1 *adj* chūgurai (no) 中位(の); *steak* midiamu (no) ミディアム(の) 2 *n* (*in size*) emu-saizu エムサイズ; (*means*) baitai 媒体; (*spiritualist*) reibai 霊媒; *through the* ~ *of* ... o tōshite ...を通して

medium-sized chūgurai no ōki-sa (no) 中位の大きさ(の)

medium wave chūha 中波

medley yoseatsume 寄せ集め; (*race, of songs*) medorē メドレー

meek otonashii おとなしい

meekly otonashiku おとなしく

meet 1 *v/t* ... ni au ...に会う; (*encounter*) ... ni deau ...に出会う; (*at airport etc*) demukaeru 出迎える; (*in competition*) ... to taisen suru ...と対戦する; (*of eyes*) ... to au ...と合う; (*satisfy: need*) mitasu 満たす; *deadline* mamoru 守る; *payment* shiharau 支払う; *standard* ... ni tassuru ...に達する 2 *v/i* au 会う; (*get to know each other*) shiriau 知り合う; (*in competition*) taisen suru 対戦する; (*of eyes*) au 合う; (*of committee*) kaigō suru 会合する 3 *n* kyōgikai 競技会

♦**meet with** *person* ... ni kaiken suru ...と会見する; *opposition, approval etc* ... ni au ...にあう

meeting (*unplanned*) deai 出会い; (*in business*) kaigi 会議; (*of committee*) kaigō 会合

megabyte megabaito メガバイト

Meiji Restoration Meijiishin 明治維新

melancholy yūutsu 憂うつ

mellow 1 *adj* yawaraka (na) 柔らか(な) 2 *v/i* (*of person*) maruku naru 円くなる

melodious ongakuteki (na) 音楽的(な)

melodramatic ōgesa (na) おおげさ(な)

melody merodī メロディー

melon meron メロン

melt 1 *v/i* tokeru 溶ける 2 *v/t* tokasu 溶かす

♦**melt away** *fig* kiete nakunaru 消えてなくなる

♦ **melt down** ... o tokasu ...を溶かす

melting pot rutsubo るつぼ

member ichiin 一員; (of organization) menbā メンバー; **Member of Congress** Kokkai-giin 国会議員

membership kaiin-shikaku 会員資格; (of UN etc) kaiin no chii 会員の地位; (members) kaiinsū 会員数

membrane maku 膜

memento kinenhin 記念品

memo memo メモ

memoirs kaikoroku 回顧録

memorable wasurerarenai 忘れられない

memorial 1 adj concert kinen (no) 記念(の); service tsuitō (no) 追悼(の) **2** n kinenhi 記念碑

Memorial Day Senbotsusha-tsuitō-kinenbi 戦没者追悼記念日

memorize anki suru 暗記する

memory kioku 記憶; (of vacation, childhood) omoide 思い出; (power of recollection) kiokuryoku 記憶力; COMPUT memorī メモリー; **have a good/bad ~** kiokuryoku ga yoi/warui 記憶力がよい/悪い; **in ~ of** ... o kinen shite ...を記念して; (on gravestone) ... o shinonde ...をしのんで

menace 1 n (threat) kyōi 脅威; (pest) yakkai mono やっかい者 **2** v/t (of person) odosu 脅す; (of flood etc) obiyakasu 脅かす

menacing odosu yō (na) 脅すよう(な)

mend 1 v/t shūri suru 修理する **2** n: **be on the ~** kaifuku ni mukatte iru 回復に向かっている

menial adj tanjun (na) 単純(な)

meningitis nōmakuen 脳膜炎

menopause kōnenki 更年期

men's room danseiyō toire 男性用トイレ

menstruate seiri ga aru 生理がある

menstruation seiri 生理

mental health, suffering seishin (no) 精神(の); ability chinō (no) 知能(の); F (crazy) ki no kurutte iru 気の狂っている

mental arithmetic anzan 暗算;

mental cruelty seishinteki-gyakutai 精神的虐待; **mental hospital** seishin-byōin 精神病院; **mental illness** seishinbyō 精神病

mentality (intellect) chisei 知性; (mindset) kangaekata 考え方

mentally kokoro no naka de 心の中で; calculate etc atama no naka de 頭の中で

mentally handicapped chiteki-shōgai no aru 知的障害のある

mentally ill seishinbyō (no) 精神病(の)

mention 1 n: **he made no ~ of it** kare wa sono koto wa nani mo iwanakatta 彼はそのことは何も言わなかった **2** v/t ... no koto o hanasu ...のことを話す; **don't ~ it** dō itashimashite どういたしまして

mentor n shidō-sha 指導者

menu also COMPUT menyū メニュー

mercenary 1 adj yokutokuzuku (no) 欲得ずく(の) **2** n MIL yōhei よう兵

merchandise shōhin 商品

merchandising shōhinka 商品化

merchant shōten-shu 商店主

merciful jihibukai 慈悲深い

mercifully kōun na koto ni 幸運なことに

merciless mujihi (na) 無慈悲(な)

mercury suigin 水銀

mercy jihi 慈悲; **be at X's ~** X no nasu ga mama de aru Xのなすがままである

mere hon no ほんの

merely tan ni ... dake たんに...だけ

merge v/i (of companies) gappei suru 合併する

merger gappei 合併

merit 1 n (worth) kachi 価値; (advantage) chōsho 長所 **2** v/t ... ni atai suru ...に値する

merriment yōki na sawagi 陽気な騒ぎ

merry yōki (na) 陽気(な); **Merry Christmas!** Merī-Kurisumasu メリークリスマス

merry-go-round merīgōraundo メリーゴーラウンド

mesh n amime 網目

mesmerize ... no me o ubau ...の目を奪う

mess: *who made this ~?* konna ni chirakashita no wa dare desu ka こんなに散らかしたのはだれですか; *I'm in a bit of a ~* (*trouble*) komatta koto ni natta 困ったことになった; *be a ~* (*of room, desk*) chirakatte iru 散らかっている; (*of situation*) hidoku yakkai na koto ni natte iru ひどくやっかいなことになっている

♦ **mess around** burabura suru ぶらぶらする

♦ **mess around with** ... o ijikurimawasu ...をいじくり回す

♦ **mess up** *room, papers* ... o torichirakasu ...を取り散らかす; *plans* ... o dainashi ni suru ...を台なしにする

♦ **mess with** (*use*) ... ni te o dasu ...に手を出す; (*get involved with*) ... ni kakawaru ...にかかわる; (*upset, offend*) ... ni chokkai o dasu ...にちょっかいを出す

message messēji メッセージ, dengon 伝言; (*of movie, book*) nerai ねらい

messenger (*courier*) kyūsōbin 急送便; (*biker*) baiku-bin バイク便

messy *room* torichirakashita 取り散らかした; *person* darashi no nai だらしのない; *eater* tabechirakasu 食べ散らかす; *job* te no yogoreru 手の汚れる; *divorce etc* yakkai (na) やっかい(な)

metabolism shinchin-taisha 新陳代謝

metal 1 *n* kinzoku 金属 **2** *adj* kinzoku (no) 金属(の)

metallic *paint* kinzoku (no) 金属(の); *sound, taste* kinzokuteki (na) 金属的(な)

meteor ryūsei 流星

meteoric *fig* ryūsei no yō (na) 流星のよう(な)

meteorite inseki いん石

meteorological kishō (no) 気象(の)

meteorologist kishō-gakusha 気象学者

meteorology kishō-gaku 気象学

meter¹ (*for measuring*) mētā メーター; (*parking ~*) pākingu-mētā パーキングメーター

meter² (*length*) mētoru メートル

method hōhō 方法

methodical *search* soshikiteki (na) 組織的(な); *person* kichōmen (na) きちょうめん(な)

methodically soshikiteki ni 組織的に

meticulous *person* kichōmen (na) きちょうめん(な); *work, planning* genmitsu (na) 厳密(な)

meticulously kichōmen ni きちょうめんに

metric mētoruhō (no) メートル法(の)

metropolis daitoshi 大都市

metropolitan *adj* daitoshi (no) 大都市(の)

mew → miaow

Mexican 1 *adj* Mekishiko (no) メキシコ(の) **2** *n* Mekishiko-jin メキシコ人

Mexico Mekishiko メキシコ

mezzanine (*floor*) chūnikai 中二階

miaow 1 *n* nyā にゃあ **2** *v/i* nyā to naku にゃあと鳴く

mickey mouse *adj pej* F *course, qualification* kudaranai くだらない

microchip maikurochippu マイクロチップ; **microcomputer** maikon マイコン; **microcosm** shōuchū 小宇宙; **microfilm** maikurofirumu マイクロフィルム; **microphone** maiku マイク; **microprocessor** maikuropurosessā マイクロプロセッサー; **microscope** kenbikyō 顕微鏡; **microscopic** bishō (no) 微小(の); **microwave** denshi-renji 電子レンジ

midair: *in ~* kūchū de 空中で

midday shōgo 正午

middle 1 *adj* mannaka (no) 真ん中(の) **2** *n* (*of room, garden*) mannaka 真ん中; (*of week, month*) nakaba 半ば; (*of meeting*) saichū 最中; *in the ~ of* (*room*) ... no mannaka ni ...の真ん中に; (*period of time*) ... no nakagoro ni

...の中ごろに; *be in the ~ of doing X* X o shite iru saichū de aru Xをしている最中である

middle-aged chūnen (no) 中年(の); **the Middle Ages** Chūsei 中世; **middle-class** chūryū-kaikyū (no) 中流階級(の); **middle class(es)** chūryū-kaikyū 中流階級; **Middle East** Chūtō 中東; **middle man** nakagainin 仲買人; **middle name** midori-nēmu ミドルネーム; **middle weight** n (boxer) midoru-kyū-senshu ミドル級選手

middling chūgurai (no) 中位(の)

midget adj gokushōgata (no) 極小型(の)

midnight gozen reiji 午前零時, mayonaka 真夜中; *at ~* mayonaka ni 真夜中に; **midsummer** manatsu 真夏; **midway** chūto ni 中途に; **midweek** adv shū no nakaba ni 週の半ばに; **Midwest** Chūseibu 中西部; **midwife** josanpu 助産婦; **midwinter** mafuyu 真冬

might[1] ... ka mo shirenai ...かもしれない; *I ~ be late* okureru ka mo shirenai 遅れるかもしれない; *you ~ have told me!* itte kuretara yokatta no ni 言ってくれたらよかったのに; *you ~ as well spend the night* hitoban tomaru hō ga ii darō 一晩泊まるほうがいいだろう

might[2] n chikara 力

mighty 1 adj kyōryoku (na) 強力 (な) **2** adv F (very) sugoku すごく

migraine henzutsū 偏頭痛

migrant worker kisetsu-rōdōsha 季節労働者

migrate (of people) ijū suru 移住する; (of bird) idō suru 移動する

migration idō 移動

mike maiku マイク

mild weather odayaka (na) 穏やか(な); person, voice otonashii おとなしい; (not spicy) amakuchi (no) 甘口(の)

mildly (slightly) shōshō 少々; *say odayaka ni* 穏やかに

mildew shirokabi しろかび

mildness (of weather, person, voice) odayaka-sa 穏やかさ

mile mairu マイル

mileage sōkō-kyori 走行距離

milestone fig kakkiteki-jiken 画期的事件

militant 1 adj tōsōteki (na) 闘争的(な) **2** n tōshi 闘士

military 1 adj guntai (no) 軍隊(の); spending, intervention gunji (no) 軍事(の) **2** n: *the ~* guntai 軍隊

military academy rikugun-shikan-gakkō 陸軍士官学校

militia giyūgun 義勇軍

milk 1 n (of cow) gyūnyū 牛乳; (of woman) bonyū 母乳; (of other animal) chichi 乳 **2** v/t ... no chichi o shiboru ...の乳をしぼる

milk chocolate miruku-chokorēto ミルクチョコレート

milk shake sheiku シェイク

mill n (for grain) seifun-kōjō 製粉工場; (for textiles) bōseki-kōjō 紡績工場

♦**mill around** urouro suru うろうろする

millennium sennenkan 千年間

milligram miriguramu ミリグラム

millimeter mirimētā ミリメーター

million hyakuman 百万; *hundred ~* oku 億

millionaire hyakuman-chōja 百万長者

millstone fig omoni 重荷

mime v/t miburi de maneru 身ぶりでまねる

mimic 1 n monomane no umai hito 物まねのうまい人 **2** v/t ... no monomane o suru ...の物まねをする

mince v/t komakaku kizamu 細かく刻む

mincemeat minsumīto ミンスミート

mince pie minsupai ミンスパイ

mind 1 n (intellect) chisei 知性; (sanity) risei 理性; *be out of one's ~* ki ga kuruu 気が狂う; *keep in ~* o oboete oku ...を覚えておく; *I've a good ~ to ...* ... suru ki ga aru ...する気my気がある; *change one's ~* kangae o kaeru 考えを変える; *do you have something in ~?* nani ka kangae ga aru no 何か考えがある

の; *it didn't enter my ~* sore wa omoitsukanakatta それは思いつかなかった; *body and ~* karada to kokoro to 心と体; *give ... a piece of one's ~* ... ni hakkiri iu ...にはっきり言う; *make up one's ~* kesshin suru 決心する; *have something on one's ~* nani ka o ki ni shite iru 何かを気にしている; *keep one's ~ on* ... ni sennen suru ...に専念する 2 *v/t (care)* ki ni suru 気にする; *(object to)* kamau かまう; *(look after)* ... no sewa o suru ...の世話をする; *(heed)* ... no iu koto o kiku ...の言うことを聞く; *do you ~ if I smoke?* tabako o sutte mo kamaimasen ka たばこを吸ってもかまいませんか; *would you ~ opening the window?* mado o akete itadakemasen ka 窓を開けていただけませんか; *~ the step!* ashimoto ni ki o tsukete 足元に気をつけて; *~ your own business!* ōki na osewa da 大きなお世話だ; *you, ...* demo ne, ... でもね、... 3 *v/i: ~!* ki o tsukete 気をつけて; *never ~!* ki ni shinai 気にしない; *I don't ~* dotchi demo ii desu どっちでもいいです

mindful: *be ~ of* ... o ki ni suru ...を気にする

mindless *violence* oroka (na) 愚か (な)

mine[1] *pron* watashi no mono 私のもの; *a friend of ~* watashi no tomodachi 私の友達

mine[2] 1 *n (coal – etc)* kōzan 鉱山 2 *v/i: ~ for* ... o saikutsu suru ...を採掘する

mine[3] 1 *n (explosive)* jirai 地雷 2 *v/t* ... ni jirai o shikakeru ...に地雷をしかける

minefield *also fig* jiraigen 地雷原

miner kōfu 坑夫

mineral kōbutsu 鉱物

mineral water mineraru-wōtā ミネラルウォーター

mingle *v/i (of sounds)* mazaru 混ざる; *(at party)* mazaru 交ざる

mini → **miniskirt**

minibus maikurobasu マイクロバス

miniature *adj* kogata (no) 小型 (の)

minimal saishōgen (no) 最小限 (の); *cost* saiteigen (no) 最低限 (の)

minimize saishō ni suru 最小にする; *cost* saitei ni suru 最低にする; *(downplay)* chiisaku miseru 小さく見せる

minimum 1 *adj* saitei (no) 最低 (の) 2 *n: a ~ of 10 people* saitei jū nin 最低十人

minimum wage saitei-chingin 最低賃金

mining kōgyō 鉱業

miniskirt minisukāto ミニスカート

minister POL daijin 大臣; REL bokushi 牧師

ministerial POL daijin (no) 大臣 (の)

ministry POL shō 省

mink *(fur)* minku ミンク; *(coat)* minku no kōto ミンクのコート

minor 1 *adj* chiisa (na) 小さ (な); *pain, operation* karui 軽い; *D ~* ni tanchō ニ短調 2 *n* miseinen-sha 未成年者

minority shōsū 少数; *be in the ~* shōsūha de aru 少数派である

mint *n (herb)* minto ミント; *(chocolate)* minto-chokorēto ミントチョコレート; *(hard candy)* minto-kyandī ミントキャンディー

minus 1 *n* mainasu マイナス 2 *prep (without)* ... nashi ni ...なしに; *42 ~ 18 is 24* yonjūni hiku jūhachi wa nijūyon 42引く18は24; *~ 10 (temperature)* reika jūdo 零下10度

minuscule hijō ni chiisai 非常に小さい

minute[1] *n (of time)* fun 分; *in a ~* sugu すぐ; *just a ~* chotto matte ちょっと待って; *do you have a ~?* chotto ii desu ka ちょっといいですか

minute[2] *adj (tiny)* kiwamete chiisai きわめて小さい; *(detailed)* shōsai (na) 詳細 (な); *in ~ detail* shōsai ni 詳細に

minutes *(of meeting)* gijiroku 議事録

miracle kiseki 奇跡

miraculous kisekiteki (na) 奇跡的 (な)

miraculously kisekiteki ni 奇跡的に

mirage shinkirō しん気楼

mirror 1 *n* kagami 鏡; MOT bakkumirā バックミラー **2** *v/t* utsusu 映す

misanthropist tsukiai no warui hito つき合いの悪い人

misapprehension: *be under a ~* gokai o shite iru 誤解をしている

misappropriate ōryō suru 横領する

misappropriation ōryō 横領

misbehave busahō ni furumau 不作法にふるまう

misbehavior busahō 不作法

miscalculate 1 *v/t* ... no handan o ayamaru ...の判断を誤る **2** *v/i* keisanchigai o suru 計算違いをする

miscalculation (*misjudgment*) gosan 誤算; (*in sums*) keisanmachigai 計算まちがい

miscarriage MED ryūzan 流産; *~ of justice* goshin 誤審

miscarry (*of plan*) zasetsu suru ざ折する

miscellaneous zatta (na) 雑多(な)

mischief (*naughtiness*) itazura いたずら

mischievous itazura (na) いたずら(な); (*malicious*) akui no aru 悪意のある

misconceived fubi (na) 不備(な)

misconception gokai 誤解

misconduct shokken-ran'yō 職権乱用

misconstrue gokai suru 誤解する

misdemeanor bizai 微罪

miser kechi けち

miserable (*unhappy*) mijime (na) みじめ(な); *life* aware (na) 哀れ(な); *weather* iya (na) いや(な); *news* itamashii 痛ましい

miserly wazuka (na) わずか(な); *person* kechi (na) けち(な)

misery (*wretchedness*) hisan-sa 悲惨さ; (*unhappiness*) mijime-sa みじめさ

misfire (*of scheme*) shippai suru 失敗する

misfit (*in society*) tekiō shinai hito 適応しない人

misfortune fuun 不運

misgiving fuan 不安

mishandle ... no toriatsukai o ayamaru ...の取り扱いを誤る

mishap jiko 事故

misinterpret gokai suru 誤解する

misinterpretation gokai 誤解

misjudge ... no handan o ayamaru ...の判断を誤る

mislay okiwasureru 置き忘れる

mislead ... no gokai o maneku ...の誤解を招く

misleading magirawashii 紛らわしい

mismanage *situation* ... no shochi o shisokonau ...の処置をしそこなう; *economy* ... no kanri o shisokonau ...の管理をしそこなう; *company* ... no keiei ni shippai suru ...の経営に失敗する

mismanagement (*of situation*) ayamatta shochi 誤った処置; (*of economy*) ayamatta kanri 誤った管理; (*of company*) ayamatta keiei 誤った経営

miso soup misoshiru 味噌汁

misplaced kentōhazure (na) 見当はずれ(な)

misprint *n* goshoku 誤植

mispronounce hatsuon o machigaeru 発音を間違える

misread *word, figures* yomichigaeru 読み違える; *situation* gokai suru 誤解する

misrepresent ayamatte tsutaeru 誤って伝える

miss¹: *Miss Smith* Sumisu-san スミスさん

miss² 1 *n: give X a ~* X o yamete oku Xをやめておく **2** *v/t* (*not hit*) hazusu はずす; (*not meet*) ... to ikichigau ...と行き違う; (*emotionally: person*) ... ga inaku natte sabishiku omou ...がいなくなって寂しく思う; (*emotionally: place*) ... ga natsukashii ...がなつかしい; *bus, train, plane* ... ni norisokonau ...に乗りそこなう; (*not notice*) miotosu 見落とす; (*not be present at*) kesseki suru 欠席する **3** *v/i* hazusu はずす

♦ **miss out on** *opportunity* ... o nogasu ...を逃す

misshapen bukakkō (na) 不格好 (な)

missile misairu ミサイル; (*sth thrown*) tobidōgu 飛び道具

missing yukue-fumei (no) 行方不明 (の); **be ~** yukue-fumei de aru 行方不明である

mission (*task*) ninmu 任務; (*people*) shisetsudan 使節団

misspell ... no tsuzuri o machigaeru ...のつづりを間違える

mist kiri 霧

♦ **mist over** (*of eyes*) kasumu かすむ

♦ **mist up** (*of mirror*) kumoru 曇る

mistake 1 *n* machigai 間違い; **make a ~** machigau 間違う; **by ~** machigaete 間違えて 2 *v/t*: **~ X for Y** X o Y to machigaeru XをYと間違える

mistaken: **be ~** gokai shite iru 誤解している

mistress (*lover*) aijin 愛人; (*of servant*) onnashujin 女主人; (*of dog*) kainushi 飼い主

mistrust 1 *n* fushinkan 不信感 2 *v/t* shin'yō shinai 信用しない

misty *weather* kiri no kakatta 霧のかかった; *eyes* kasunda かすんだ; *color* bon'yari shita ぼんやりした

misunderstand gokai suru 誤解する

misunderstanding (*mistake*) gokai 誤解; (*argument*) izakoza いざこざ

misuse 1 *n* goyō 誤用; (*dishonest*) akuyō 悪用 2 *v/t* goyō suru 誤用する; (*dishonestly*) akuyō suru 悪用する

mitigating circumstances jōjō-shakuryō 情状酌量

mitt (*in baseball*) mitto ミット

mitten miton ミトン

mix 1 *n* kongō 混合; (*in cooking*) mazeawaseta mono 混ぜ合わせたもの; **a ~ of people** iroiro na hitotachi no mazatta gurūpu いろいろな人たちの混ざったグループ; *pancake ~* (*ready to use*) pankēki-mikkusu パンケーキミックス 2 *v/t* mazeru 混ぜる 3 *v/i*

(*socially*) tsukiau 付き合う

♦ **mix up** ... o gochamaze ni suru ...をごちゃ混ぜにする; **mix X up with Y** X o Y to torichigaeru XをYと取り違える; **be mixed up** (*of person*) konran shite iru 混乱している; **be mixed up in** ... to kankei ga aru ...と関係がある; **get mixed up with** ... to kakawariai ni naru ...とかかわり合いになる

♦ **mix with** (*associate with*) ... to tsukiau ...と付き合う

mixed *feelings* fukuzatsu (na) 複雑 (な); *reviews* sanpi-ryōron 賛否両論(の); *nuts* mikkusu shita ミックスした; (*racially*) kotonaru jinshu no mazatta 異なる人種の混ざった; (*religiously*) shūkyō no mazatta 異なる宗教の混ざった

mixer (*for food*) mikisā ミキサー; (*drink*) sōda nado kakuteru o tsukuru no ni hitsuyō na mono ソーダなどカクテルをつくるのに必要なもの; **she's a good ~** kanojo wa hitozukiai ga yoi 彼女は人付き合いがよい

mixture (*in cooking*) mazeawaseta mono 混ぜ合わせたもの; (*medicine*) kongōyaku 混合薬; **a ~ of relief and anger** ando to ikari no mazatta kimochi 安どと怒りの混ざった気持ち

mix-up techigai 手違い

moan 1 *n* (*of pain*) umeki うめき; (*complaint*) monku 文句 2 *v/i* (*in pain*) umeku うめく; (*complain*) butsukusa iu ぶつくさ言う

mob 1 *n* gunshū 群衆; (*violent*) bōto 暴徒 2 *v/t* muragaru 群がる

mobile *adj person* ugoku koto no dekiru 動くことのできる 2 *n* (*for decoration*) mobīru モビール

mobile home torērāhausu トレーラーハウス

mobile phone *Br* keitai-denwa 携帯電話

mobility kadōsei 可動性

mobster gyangu ギャング; (*Japanese*) bōryokudan'in 暴力団員

mock 1 *adj surprise* misekake (no)
みせかけ(の); *exams, election* mogi
(no) 模擬(の) **2** *v/t* baka ni suru ば
かにする; *(by mimicking)* ... no
mane o suru ...のまねをする
mockery azakeri あざけり;
(travesty) warai mono 笑いもの
mock-up mokei 模型
mode *(form)* yōshiki 様式; COMPUT
mōdo モード
model 1 *adj employee, husband*
risōteki (na) 理想的(な); *boat,
plane* mokei (no) 模型(の) **2** *n*
(miniature) mokei 模型; *(fashion
~)* fasshon-moderu ファッション
モデル; *male ~* dansei-moderu 男
性モデル **3** *v/t* ... no moderu ni
naru ...のモデルになる **4** *v/i (for
artist, photographer)* moderu ni
naru モデルになる
modem modemu モデム
moderate 1 *adj heat, cold* hodoyoi
ほどよい; *wealth, success, salary*
māmā (no) まあまあ(の); *exercise*
tekido (no) 適度(の); *price* tegoro
(na) 手ごろ(な); POL onken (na)
穏健(な) **2** *n* POL onkenha 穏健派
3 *v/t* yawarageru やわらげる **4** *v/i*
yawaragu やわらぐ
moderately tekido ni 適度に
moderation *(restraint)* setsudo 節
度; *in ~* hodohodo ni ほどほどに
modern *history, medicine* gendai
(no) 現代(の); *way of thinking*
gendaiteki (na) 現代的(な),
kindaiteki (na) 近代的(な)
modernization kindaika 近代化
modernize kindaika suru 近代化す
る
modest *house* sasayaka (na) ささ
やか(な); *amount, rate,
improvement* tekido (na) 適度(な);
request hikaeme (na) 控えめ(な);
clothes, role jimi (na) 地味(な);
(not conceited) kenkyo (na) 謙虚
(な)
modesty *(of house)* shisso-sa 質素
さ; *(of wage, improvement)*
osomatsu-sa お粗末さ; *(lack of
conceit)* kenkyo 謙虚
modification *(to machine)* kaizō 改

造; *(to proposal)* shūsei 修正; *(to
system)* kaisei 改正
modify *machine* kaizō suru 改造す
る; *proposal* shūsei suru 修正する;
system kaisei suru 改正する
modular *furniture* yunitto-shiki
(no) ユニット式(の)
module yunitto ユニット; *space ~*
uchū-sen 宇宙船
moist shimetta 湿った
moisten shimeraseru 湿らせる
moisture shimerike 湿り気; *(in air)*
shikke 湿気
moisturizer moisucharaizā モイス
チャライザー
molar okuba 奥歯
molasses tōmitsu 糖蜜
mold¹ *n (on food)* kabi かび
mold² **1** *n* igata 鋳型 **2** *v/t clay etc*
katadoru かたどる; *character*
keisei suru 形成する
moldy *food* kabi no haeta かびのは
えた
mole *(on skin)* hokuro ほくろ
molecular bunshi (no) 分子(の)
molecule bunshi 分子
molest *child, woman* ... ni itazura o
suru ...にいたずらをする
mollycoddle amayakasu 甘やかす
molten yōkai shita 溶解した
mom F *n* mama ママ; *(talking to
outsiders about one's own ~)* haha
母
moment shunkan 瞬間; *at the ~* ima
no tokoro 今のところ; *for the ~*
sashiatari 差し当たり; *it'll only
take a ~* sore niwa isshun shika
kakara nai それには一瞬しかかか
らない
momentarily *(for a moment)*
ichijiteki ni 一時的に; *(in a
moment)* sugu ni すぐに
momentary ichijiteki (na) 一時的
(な)
momentous jūdai (na) 重大(な)
momentum ikioi 勢い
monarch kunshu 君主
monastery shūdōin 修道院;
(Buddhist) sōbō 僧坊
monastic shūdōshi (no) 修道士(の);
(Buddhist) sō (no) 僧(の); *~ life*

shūdo-seikatsu 修道生活

Monday getsuyōbi 月曜日

monetary *policy* kin'yū (no) 金融
(の); *system* tsūka (no) 通貨(の)

money okane お金; (*currency*)
tsūka 通貨

money-lender kanekashi 金貸し;
money market kin'yū-shijō 金融
市場; **money order** yūbin-kawase
郵便為替

Mongolia Mongoru モンゴル

Mongolian 1 *adj* Mongoru (no) モ
ンゴル (の) **2** *n* (*person*)
Mongoru-jin モンゴル人

mongrel zasshu 雑種

monitor 1 *n* COMPUT sukurīn スク
リーン **2** *v/t* kanshi suru 監視する

monk shūdōshi 修道士; (*Buddhist*)
sō 僧

monkey saru さる; F (*child*)
itazurakko いたずらっ子

♦**monkey around with** F
ijikurimawasu いじくり回す

monkey wrench monkīrenchi モン
キーレンチ

monkfish ankō あんこう

monogram *n* monoguramu モノグラ
ム

monogrammed monoguramu iri
(no) モノグラム入り(の)

monolog monorōgu モノローグ

monopolize dokusen suru 独占する

monopoly senbai 専売

monotonous *voice, song* tanchō
(na) 単調(な); *job, movie* taikutsu
(na) 退屈(な)

monotony tanchō-sa 単調さ

monsoon (*rain*) gōu 豪雨; (*wind*)
kisetsufū 季節風; (*season*) uki 雨
期

monsoon season uki 雨期

monster *n* kaibutsu 怪物; *fig*
(*person*) hitodenashi ひとでなし

monstrosity bakadekkai bakari no
shiromono ばかでっかいばかりの
代物

monstrous (*shocking*) tondemonai
とんでもない

month tsuki 月

monthly 1 *adj payment* maitsuki
(no) 毎月(の); *magazine* gekkan

(no) 月刊(の); *figures* ikkagetsu
(no) 一ヶ月(の) **2** *adv* maitsuki 毎
月 **3** *n* (*magazine*) gekkanshi 月刊
誌

monument kinenhi 記念碑

mood (*frame of mind*) kigen 機嫌;
(*bad ~*) fukigen 不機嫌; (*of
meeting, country*) fun'iki 雰囲気;
be in a good/bad ~ kigen ga yoi/
warui 機嫌がよい/悪い; **be in the
~ for doing X** X ga shitai kimochi
de aru Xがしたい気持ちである

moody (*changing moods*) kibunya
(no) 気分屋(の); (*bad-tempered*)
fukigen (na) 不機嫌(な)

moon *n* tsuki 月

moonlight 1 *n* tsuki no hikari 月の
光 **2** *v/i* F arubaito o suru アルバイ
トをする

moonlit night tsukiyo 月夜

moor *v/t boat* tsunagu つなぐ

moorings keiryūjo 係留所

moose herajika へらじか

mop 1 *n* (*for floor*) moppu モップ
2 *v/t floor* moppu de fuku モップ
でふく; *eyes, face* nuguu ぬぐう

♦**mop up** *spillage* ... o fuku ...を
ふく; *gravy* ... ni tsukeru ...につけ
る; MIL ... o sōtō suru ...を掃討す
る

mope fusagikomu ふさぎ込む

moral 1 *adj dilemma, standards*
dōtokuteki (na) 道徳的(な);
support, victory seishinteki (na)
精神的(な); *person* seigikan no
tsuyoi 正義感の強い; *behavior*
tadashii 正しい **2** *n* (*of story*)
kyōkun 教訓; **~s** dōtoku 道徳

morale shiki 士気

morality dōtoku 道徳

morbid byōteki (na) 病的(な)

more 1 *adj* motto ōku (no) もっと多
く(の); **some ~ tea?** kōcha no
okawari wa 紅茶のおかわりは;
are there any ~ questions?
shitsumon wa mada arimasu ka?
質問はまだありますか; **there is no
~ money/coffee** okane/kōhī wa
mō arimasen お金/コーヒーはも
うありません; **a few ~ days/
weeks** ato sūjitsu/sūshūkan あと

数日/数週間; **~ and ~ students /
companies** masumasu ōku no
gakusei/kigyō ますます多くの学
生/企業; **~ and ~ time** masumasu
nagai jikan ますます長い時間
2 adv motto もっと; **~ important**
motto daiji (na) もっと大事(な); **~
and ~** masumasu ますます; **~ or
less** daitai だいたい; **once** ~ mō
ichido もう一度; **~ than** ...以上; **I
don't live there any** ~ mō soko ni
wa sunde imasen もうそこには住
んでいません **3** pron: **do you want
some** ~? mō sukoshi ikaga desu
ka もう少しいかがですか; **a little** ~
mō sukoshi もう少し

moreover sara ni さらに

morgue shitai-hokanjo 死体保管所

morning asa 朝; **in the** ~ asa ni 朝
に; (tomorrow) ashita no asa ni あ
したの朝に; **this** ~ kesa けさ;
tomorrow ~ ashita no asa あした
の朝; **good** ~ ohayō gozaimasu お
はようございます

moron manuke まぬけ

morose kimuzukashii 気難しい

morphine moruhine モルヒネ

morsel: **a ~ of** hitokuchi no... ひと
口の...

mortal 1 adj itsuka shinu koto ni
natte iru いつか死ぬことになって
いる; blow chimeiteki (na) 致命的
(な); **~ enemy** fugutaiten no teki
不倶戴天の敵 **2** n ningen 人間

mortality shinu unmei 死ぬ運命;
(death rate) shibōritsu 死亡率

mortar¹ MIL hakugekihō 迫撃砲

mortar² (cement) morutaru モルタ
ル

mortgage 1 n jūtaku-rōn 住宅ロー
ン **2** v/t teitō ni irete shakkin o
suru 抵当に入れて借金をする

mortician sōgi-ya 葬儀屋

mortuary reianshitsu 霊安室

mosaic mozaiku モザイク

Moscow Mosukuwa モスクワ

mosquito ka 蚊

mosquito coil katorisenkō 蚊取り線
香

mosquito net kaya 蚊帳

moss koke こけ

mossy koke de ōwareta こけでおお
われた

most 1 adj taitei (no) たいてい(の);
he won the ~ votes kare ga
mottomo ōku no tōhyō o eta 彼が
もっとも多くの投票を得た **2** adv
(very) taihen たいへん; **the ~
beautiful/interesting** mottomo
utsukushii/omoshiroi 最も美し
い/おもしろい; **that's the one I
like** ~ watashi ga ichiban suki na
no wa sore desu 私が一番好きなの
はそれです; **~ of all** nani yori mo
何よりも **3** pron hotondo ほとんど;
at (the) ~ seizei せいぜい; **make
the ~ of** ...o dekiru dake katsuyō
suru ...をできるだけ活用する; **~ of
her novels** kanojo no shōsetsu no
hotondo 彼女の小説のほとんど; **~
of the time** taitei たいてい

mostly (mainly) omo ni おもに;
(generally) futsū wa 普通は

motel mōteru モーテル

moth ga 蛾

mother 1 n okāsan お母さん;
(talking to outsiders about one's
own ~) haha 母; **become a ~**
hahaoya ni naru 母親になる **2** v/t
(look after like a mother) ...no
sewa o yaku ...の世話をやく;
(pamper) amayakasu 甘やかす

motherboard COMPUT mazābōdo マ
ザーボード; **motherhood** hahaoya
de aru koto 母親であること;
mother-in-law (talking to outsiders
about one's own ~) giri no haha, 義
理のお母さん; (talking to outsiders
about one's own ~) giri no haha, 義
理の母, shūtome しゅうとめ

motherly boseiteki na 母性的(な)

mother-of-pearl shinjubo 真珠母;
Mother's Day Haha no hi 母の日;
mother tongue bokokugo 母国語

motif (design) moyō 模様

motion 1 n ugoki 動き; (of car, ship)
yure yure 揺れ; (proposal) dōgi 動議;
set things in ~ jikkō suru 実行す
る **2** v/t: **he ~ed me forward** kare
wa watashi ni mae e deru yōni
aizu shita 彼は私に前へ出るように
合図した

motionless ugokanai 動かない

motivate yaruki ni saseru やる気に
させる

motivation dōki 動機

motive dōki 動機

motor mōtā モーター; (*of car*) enjin
エンジン

motorbike ōtobai オートバイ;
motorboat mōtābōto モーター
ボート; **motorcade** jidōsha no
gyōretsu 自動車の行列;
motorcycle ōtobai オートバイ;
motorcyclist raidā ライダー;
motor home kyanpingu-kā キャン
ピングカー

motorist doraibā ドライバー

motorscooter sukūtā スクーター

motor vehicle jidōsharyō 自動車両

motto mottō モットー, zayū no mei
座右の銘

mound (*hillock*) oka 丘; (*in
baseball*) maundo マウンド; (*pile*)
yama 山

mount 1 *n* (*mountain*) ... san ...山;
(*horse*) jōyōba 乗用馬 2 *v/t steps*
noboru 上る; *horse, bicycle* ... ni
noru ...に乗る; *campaign* hajimeru
始める; *photo* suetsukeru 据え付け
る 3 *v/i* (*increase*) masu 増す

◆**mount up** tamaru たまる

mountain yama 山

mountain bike mauntenbaiku マウ
ンテンバイク

mountaineer tozan-ka 登山家

mountaineering tozan 登山

mountainous yama no ōi 山の多い

mourn 1 *v/t death* nageki-
kanashimu 嘆き悲しむ 2 *v/i*: **- for**
... no shi o nageki-kanashimu ...
の死を嘆き悲しむ

mourner chōmonkyaku 弔問客

mournful *person* kanashimi ni
shizunda 悲しみに沈んだ; *song*
kanashige (na) 悲しげ(な)

mourning mo 喪; **be in -** mochū de
aru 喪中である; **wear -** mofuku o
kiru 喪服を着る

mouse nezumi ねずみ; COMPUT
mausu マウス

mouse mat COMPUT mausupaddo
マウスパッド

mouth *n* kuchi 口; (*of river*) kakō 河

口

mouthful (*of food*) hitokuchibun 一
口ぶん

mouthorgan hāmonika ハーモニカ;
mouthpiece (*of instrument*)
mausupīsu マウスピース;
(*spokesperson*) supōkusuman ス
ポークスマン; **mouthwash** mausu-
wosshu マウスウォッシュ;
mouthwatering yodare no desō
(na) よだれの出そう(な)

move 1 *n* (*in chess, checkers: of
piece*) te 手; (*turn to play*) ban 番;
(*step, action*) ugoki 動き; (*change
of house*) hikkoshi 引っ越し; **get a
- on!** isoide 急いで; **don't make a
-!** ugokuna 動くな 2 *v/t object*
ugokasu 動かす; *obstacle* dokasu
どかす; (*transfer*) idō saseru 移動
させる; (*emotionally*) kandō
saseru 感動させる 3 *v/i* ugoku 動
く; (*of traffic*) nagareru 流れる;
(*transfer*) idō suru 移動する; **- to
another school** tenkō suru 転校す
る; **- house** hikkoshi suru 引っ越
しする

◆**move around** (*in room*)
ugokimawaru 動き回る; (*from
place to place*) hinpan ni hikkosu
頻繁に引っ越す

◆**move away** tachisaru 立ち去る;
(*move house*) hikkoshite iku 引っ
越して行く

◆**move in** hikkoshite kuru 引っ越し
て来る

◆**move on** (*to another town*)
tachisaru 立ち去る; (*to another
job / subject*) utsuru 移る

◆**move out** (*of house*) hikkosu
引っ越す; (*of area*) dete iku 出て行
く

◆**move up** (*in league*) shōkaku
suru 昇格する; (*in company*)
shōshin suru 昇進する; (*in school*)
shinkyū suru 進級する; (*make
room*) tsumeru 詰める

movement ugoki 動き;
(*organization*) undō 運動; (*of
planet, moon*) unkō 運行; MUS
gakushō 楽章

movers unsō-ya 運送屋

movie eiga 映画; **go to a ~ / the ~s** eiga ni iku 映画に行く; **Japanese ~** hōga 邦画; **Western ~** yōga 洋画

moviegoer eiga-fan 映画ファン

movie theater eigakan 映画館

moving (*which can move*) ugoku 動く; (*emotionally*) kandōteki (na) 感動的(な)

mow *grass* karu 刈る

♦ mow down (*kill*) nagitaoshite korosu なぎ倒して殺す

mower shibakariki 芝刈機

MP (= *Military Policeman*) kenpei 憲兵

mph (= *miles per hour*) jisoku ... mairu 時速...マイル

Mr ... san ... さん

Mrs ... san ... さん

Ms ... san ... さん

Mt Fuji Fuji-san 富士山

much 1 *adj* ōku (no) 多く(の); **he has as ~ chance as you** kare wa anata to onaji dake no chansu ga aru 彼はあなたと同じだけのチャンスがある; **she does not have ~ money** kanojo wa amari kane o motte inai 彼女はあまり金を持っていない **2** *adv* hijō ni 非常に, totemo とても; *better, higher, smaller* haruka ni はるかに; *very* ~ hontō ni 本当に; **as ~ as ... ... to** onaji dake ...と同じだけ; **as ... thought as ~** sonna koto da to omotte ita そんなことだと思っていた; **you talk too ~** anata wa shaberisugiru あなたはしゃべりすぎる; **you did too ~** yarisugi da やりすぎだ; **I don't like it / him** (*very*) ~ sore / kare wa amari suki de wa arimasen それ/彼はあまり好きではありません **3** *pron* takusan たくさん; **nothing ~** taishita koto ja nai たいしたことじゃない

muck doro 泥

mucus nen'eki 粘液

mud doro 泥

muddle 1 *n* (*mess*) gochagocha ごちゃごちゃの; (*confusion*) konran 混乱 **2** *v/t person* konran saseru 混乱させる; *facts* kondō suru 混同する

♦ muddle up *person* ... o konran saseru ...を混乱させる; *dates, papers etc* ... o gochagocha ni suru ...をごちゃごちゃにする

muddy doro darake (no) 泥だらけ(の)

muffin mafin マフィン

muffle hikuku suru 低くする

♦ muffle up *v/i* kikomu 着込む

muffler MOT mafurā マフラー

mug¹ *n* (*for tea, coffee*) magukappu マグカップ; F (*face*) tsura 面

mug² *v/t* (*attack*) osotte kane o ubau 襲って金を奪う

mugger gōtō 強盗

mugging gōtō 強盗

muggy mushiatsui 蒸し暑い

mulberry kuwa 桑

mule (*animal*) raba らば; (*slipper*) surippa スリッパ

♦ mull over ... ni tsuite jikkuri kangaeru ...についてじっくり考える

multi-journey ticket kaisūken 回数券

multilingual *person* sūkakokugo o hanaseru 数か国語を話せる; *country* sūkakokugo-heiyō (no) 数か国語併用(の)

multimedia *n* maruchi-media マルチメディア

multinational 1 *adj* takokuseki (no) 多国籍(の) **2** *n* COM takokuseki-kigyō 多国籍企業

multiple *adj* fukusū (no) 複数(の); *injuries* fukugō (no) 複合(の)

multiplication kakezan 掛け算

multiply 1 *v/t*: ~ **3 by 4** san ni yon o kakeru 3に4を掛ける; **3 multiplied by 4 is 12** san kakeru yon wa jūni 3掛ける4は12 **2** *v/i* fueru 増える; (*of animal, plant*) hanshoku suru 繁殖する

mumble 1 *n* butsubutsu iu koe ぶつぶつ言う声 **2** *v/t & v/i* butsubutsu iu ぶつぶつ言う

mumps otafukukaze おたふくかぜ

munch *v/t & v/i* kamishimete taberu かみしめて食べる

municipal (*of city*) shi (no) 市(の);

(*of town*) machi (no) 町(の); (*of local government*) chihō-jichitai (no) 地方自治体(の)

mural *n* hekiga 壁画

murder 1 *n* satsujin 殺人 **2** *v/t* satsugai suru 殺害する; *song* dainashi ni suru 台なしにする

murderer satsujin-hannin 殺人犯人

murderous *rage, look* hidoi ひどい

murmur 1 *n* tsubuyaki つぶやき **2** *v/t* tsubuyaku つぶやく

muscle kinniku 筋肉

muscular *pain, strain* kinniku (no) 筋肉(の); *person* kinniku-ryūryū (no) 筋肉隆々(の)

muse *v/i* monoomoi ni fukeru もの思いにふける

museum hakubutsukan 博物館; (*of art*) bijutsukan 美術館

mushroom 1 *n* kinoko きのこ; (*small white*) masshurūmu マッシュルーム **2** *v/i* kyūsoku ni seichō suru 急速に成長する

music ongaku 音楽; (*score*) gakufu 楽譜

musical 1 *adj* ongaku (no) 音楽(の); (*interested in music*) ongakuzuki (na) 音楽好き(な); (*talented*) onkan no yoi 音感のよい; *voice* mimi ni kokochi yoi 耳に心地よい **2** *n* myūjikaru ミュージカル

musical instrument gakki 楽器

musician (*classical*) ongakuka 音楽家; (*pop, jazz*) myūjishan ミュージシャン

mussel mūru-gai ムール貝

must ◊ (*necessity*) ...nakereba naranai ...なければならない; *I ~ be on time* watashi wa jikan o mamoranakereba naranai 私は時間を守らなければならない ◊ (*with negatives*) ...te wa naranai ...てはならない; *I ~ n't be late* chikoku shite wa naranai 遅刻してはならない ◊ (*probability*): *it ~ be about 6 o'clock* rokujigoro ni chigainai 6時ごろに違いない; *they ~ have arrived by now* karera wa mō tsuita ni chigainai 彼らはもう

着いたに違いない

mustache kuchihige 口ひげ

mustard masutādo マスタード; (*Japanese*) karashi からし

musty kabikusai かび臭い

mute *adj* (*dumb*) kuchi no kikenai 口のきけない

muted *color* yawarakai 柔らかい; *criticism* yokusei shita 抑制した

mutilate setsudan suru 切断する

mutiny 1 *n* hanran 反乱 **2** *v/i* hanran o okosu 反乱を起こす

mutter *v/t* & *v/i* tsubuyaku つぶやく

mutton hitsuji no niku 羊の肉

mutual sōgo (no) 相互(の); (*shared*) kyōtsū (no) 共通(の)

muzzle 1 *n* (*of animal*) hanazura 鼻づら; (*for dog*) kuchiwa 口輪 **2** *v/t dog* ... ni kuchiwa o tsukeru ...に口輪をつける; *~ the press* atsuryoku o kakete hōdō o fūjiru 圧力をかけて報道を封じる

my ◊ watashi no 私の; *~ ticket* watashi no kippu 私の切符 ◊ (*omission of possessive*): *I cut ~ finger* watashi wa yubi o kega shimashita 私は指をけがしました; *I forgot ~ key* watashi wa kagi o wasuremashita 私はかぎを忘れました

myself: *I hurt ~* watashi wa kega o shimashita 私はけがをしました; *I saw ~ in the mirror* watashi wa kagami de jibun o mimashita 私は鏡で自分を見ました; *by ~* (*without help*) jibun de jibun o 自分で自分で; (*alone*) hitori de ひとりで

mysterious (*unexplained*) fushigi (na) 不思議(な); (*enigmatic*) nazomeita なぞめいた

mysteriously fushigi na koto ni 不思議なことに

mystery nazo なぞ; (*story*) misuterī ミステリー

mystify kemuri ni maku 煙に巻く

myth shinwa 神話; *fig* henken 偏見

mythical shinwa (no) 神話(の); (*imaginary*) kakū (no) 架空(の)

mythology shinwa 神話

N

nab (*take for oneself*) tsukamu つか
む

nag 1 *v/i* (*of person*) kogoto o iu 小
言を言う **2** *v/t* (*tell off*) … ni
kogoto o iu …に小言を言う; **~ X to
do Y** X ni Y suru yō ni urusaku
segamu XにYするようにうるさく
せがむ

nagging *person* kuchiurusai うるさ
い; *doubt* taezu tsukimatou 絶え
ずつきまとう; *pain* shitsukoi しつ
こい

nail (*for wood*) kugi くぎ; (*on
finger*) tsume つめ

nail clippers tsume-kiri つめ切り;
nail file tsume-yasuri つめやすり;
nail polish manikyua マニキュア;
nail polish remover jokōeki 除光
液; **nail scissors** tsume-kiri-
basami つめ切りばさみ; **nail
varnish** manikyua マニキュア

naive sekenshirazu (na) 世間知ら
ず(な)

naked hadaka no 裸の; *invisible
to the ~ eye* nikugan de wa
mienai 肉眼では見えない

name 1 *n* namae 名前; (*family ~*)
myōji 名字, sei 姓; (*of movie*)
taitoru タイトル; *what's your ~?*
onamae o onegaishimasu お名前
をお願いします; *call X ~s* X ni
akutai o tsuku Xに悪態をつく;
make a ~ for oneself yūmei ni
naru 有名になる **2** *v/t* nazukeru 名
づける

♦**name for**: *name X for Y* Y no na
o totte X to nazukeru Yの名をとっ
てXと名づける

namely sunawachi すなわち

namesake dōmei no hito 同名の人

nametag nafuda 名札

nanny *n* uba 乳母

nap *n* utatane うたた寝; *have a ~*
utatane o suru うたた寝をする

nape: *~ of the neck* unaji うなじ

napkin (*table ~*) napukin ナプキン;
(*sanitary ~*) seiriyō napukin 生理
用ナプキン

narcotic *n* mayaku 麻薬

narcotics agent mayaku-sōsakan
麻薬捜査官

narrate narēshon o ireru ナレー
ションを入れる

narration narēshon ナレーション

narrative 1 *n* monogatari 物語
2 *adj* poem, style monogatari-
keishiki (no) 物語形式(の)

narrator narētā ナレーター

narrow street, bed, mind semai 狭い;
person, views kyōryō (na) 狭量
(な); victory kiwadoi きわどい

narrowly win karōjite かろうじて; ~
escape … o karōjite nogareru …
をかろうじて逃れる

narrow-minded kokoro no semai
心の狭い

nasal voice hana ni kakatta 鼻にか
かった

nasty person, thing to say iji no
warui 意地の悪い; smell, weather
iya (na) いや(な); cut, wound,
disease hidoi ひどい

nation kokka 国家

national 1 *adj* identity, security
kokka (no) 国家(の); airline
kokuyū (no) 国有(の); ~
boundaries kokkyō 国境 **2** *n*: *a
Japanese* ~ Nihon-jin 日本人

national anthem kokka 国歌;
national debt kokusai 国債;
National Foundation Day
Kenkoku-kinenbi 建国記念日

nationalism minzoku-shugi 民族主義

nationality kokuseki 国籍

nationalize kokuyūka suru 国有化す
る

national park kokuritsu-kōen 国立
公園

native 1 adj land, city umarekokyō (no) 生まれ故郷(の); people dochaku (no) 土着(の); plant gensan (no) 原産(の); ~ language bokokugo 母国語 **2** n (local) jimoto no hito 地元の人; (tribesman) genjūmin 原住民; a ~ of New York Nyū-Yōku umare no hito ニューヨーク生まれの人; she speaks Japanese like a ~ kanojo wa neitibu-supīka no yō ni Nihongo o hanasu 彼女はネイティブスピーカーのように日本語を話す

native country bokoku 母国

native speaker neitibu-supīka ネイティブスピーカー

NATO (= North Atlantic Treaty Organization) Natō ナトー

natural shizen (no) 自然(の); (obvious) tōzen (no) 当然(の); a ~ blonde umaretsuki no burondo 生まれつきのブロンド

natural gas tennen-gasu 天然ガス

naturalist hakubutsu-gakusha 博物学者

naturalize: become ~d kika suru 帰化する

naturally (of course) tōzen 当然; behave, speak shizen ni 自然に; (by nature) motomoto もともと

natural science shizen-kagaku 自然科学

natural scientist shizen-kagaku-sha 自然科学者

nature shizen 自然; (of person) seishitsu 性質; (of problem) honshitsu 本質

nature reserve shizen-hogo-kuiki 自然保護区域

naughty gyōgi no warui 行儀の悪い; photograph, word etc etchi (na) エッチ(な)

nausea hakike 吐き気

nauseate mukamuka saseru むかむかさせる

nauseating smell, taste mukatsuku yō (na) むかつくよう(な); person zotto suru hodo iya (na) ぞっとするほどいや(な)

nauseous: feel ~ hakike ga suru 吐き気がする

nautical umi (no) 海(の)

nautical mile kairi 海里

naval kaigun (no) 海軍(の)

naval base kaigun-kichi 海軍基地

navel heso へそ

navigable kōkō-kanō (na) 航行可能(な)

navigate v/i (in ship, airplane) kōkō suru 航行する; (in car) michiannai suru 道案内する; COMPUT ... ni iku ...に行く

navigation (of ship, plane) kōkō 航行; (in car) yūdō 誘導

navigator (on ship) kōkaishi 航海士; (in airplane) kōkūshi 航空士; (in car) nabigētā ナビゲーター

navy kaigun 海軍

navy blue 1 n kon'iro 紺色 **2** adj kon'iro (no) 紺色(の)

near 1 adv chikaku ni 近くに **2** prep ...no chikaku ni ...の近くに; ~ the bank ginkō no chikaku ni 銀行の近くに **3** adj chikai 近い; the ~est bus stop ichiban chikai basu-tei いちばん近いバス停; in the ~ future chikai shōrai 近い将来

nearby adv chikaku ni 近くに

nearly hotondo ほとんど◊ (negative consequences): he ~ got arrested kare wa ayauku taiho sareru tokoro datta 彼はあやうく逮捕されるところだった

near-sighted kinshi (no) 近視(の)

neat room, desk seiton sareta 整とんされた; person kichin to shita te ちんとした; whiskey sutorēto (no) ストレート(の); solution tekisetsu (na) 適切(な); F (terrific) suteki (na) すてき(な)

necessarily hitsuzenteki ni 必然的に; that doesn't ~ mean that ... kanarazushimo ... to iu wake de wa nai 必ずしも...という訳ではない

necessary hitsuyō (na) 必要(な); it is ~ to ... ... suru koto ga hitsuyō da ...することが必要だ

necessitate ... o hitsuyō to suru ...を必要とする

necessity hitsuyō 必要; (thing) hitsujuhin 必需品

neck kubi 首

necklace nekkkuresu ネックレス;
 neckline nekkurain ネックライン;
 necktie nekutai ネクタイ

née kyūsei 旧姓

need 1 *n* hitsuyō 必要; *if* ~ *be* moshi
hitsuyō nara もし必要なら; *in* ~
komatte 困って; *be in* ~ *of* ... o
hitsuyō to shite iru ...を必要として
いる; *there's no* ~ *to be rude/
upset* shitsurei ni suru/
torimidasu hitsuyō wa nai 失礼に
する/取り乱す必要はない **2** *v/t*
hitsuyō to suru 必要とする; *you* ~ *to
buy one* sore o kau hitsuyō ga
arimasu それを買う必要がありま
す; *you don't* ~ *to wait* anata wa
matanakute mo ii desu あなたは待
たなくてもいいです; *I* ~ *to talk to
you* anata ni hanashi ga arimasu あ
なたに話があります; *I say more?*
kore ijō iu hitsuyō ga arimasu ka こ
れ以上言う必要がありますか

needle (*for sewing, on scale*) hari
針; MED chūshabari 注射針

needlework nuimono 縫い物

needy mazushii 貧しい

negative 1 *adj* verb, sentence hitei
(no) 否定(の); *attitude, person*
shōkyokuteki (na) 消極的(な);
ELEC mainasu (no) マイナス(の)
 2 *n*: *answer in the* ~ nō to
kotaeru ノーと答える

neglect 1 *n* hōchi 放置; (*of duty*)
taiman 怠慢 **2** *v/t* garden
hottarakashi ni suru ほったらかし
にする; *one's health* mushi suru 無
視する; ~ *to do* ... shiwasureru ...
し忘れる

neglected garden hottarakashi ni
sareta ほったらかしにされた;
author wasurerareta 忘れられた;
feel ~ wasurerarete iru to kanjiru
忘れられていると感じる

negligence taiman 怠慢

negligent fuchūi (na) 不注意(な)

negligible quantity toru ni taranai
取るに足らない

negotiable salary, contract kōshō
no yochi no aru 交渉の余地のある

negotiate 1 *v/i* kōshō suru 交渉する
 2 *v/t* deal torikimeru 取り決める;

obstacles kirinukeru 切り抜ける;
curve tōrinukeru 通り抜ける

negotiation kōshō 交渉

negotiator kōshō-sha 交渉者

Negro *n* Kokujin 黒人

neigh *v/i* inanaku いななく

neighbor kinjo no hito 近所の人

neighborhood chiiki 地域; *in the* ~
of ... *fig* oyoso ... およそ...

neighboring rinsetsu shita 隣接し
た; ~ *countries* kinrin-shokoku 近
隣諸国

neighborly shinsetsu (na) 親切(な)

neither 1 *adj* dochira no ... mo ...
de nai どちらの...も...でない; ~
applicant is any good dochira no
shigan-sha mo tekisetsu de nai ど
ちらの志願者も適切でない **2** *pron*:
which do you want? – ~, *thanks*
dochira ga hoshii – warui ga
dochira mo hoshiku nai どちらが
欲しい – 悪いがどちらも欲しくな
い **3** *conj*: ~ *my mother nor my
father knew* haha mo chichi mo
shiranakatta 母も父も知らなかっ
た; *I told* ~ *my mother nor my
father* haha ni mo chichi ni mo
iwanakatta 母にも父にも言わな
かった **4** *adv*: ~ *do I* watashi mo
desu 私もです

neon light neon-tō ネオン灯

Nepal Nepāru ネパール

Nepalese 1 *adj* Nepāru (no) ネパー
ル (の) **2** *n* (*person*) Nepāru-jin
ネパール人

nephew oi おい

nerd F otaku オタク

nerve shinkei 神経; (*courage*) yūki
勇気; (*impudence*) zūzūshi-sa ずう
ずうしさ; *it's bad for my* ~*s* sore
wa watashi no shinkei ni kotaeru
それは私の神経にこたえる; *get on
X's* ~*s* X no shinkei ni sawaru X
の神経にさわる

nerve-racking iraira suru いらいら
する

nervous (*tense*) shinkeishitsu (na)
神経質(な); (*timid*) ki no chiisai 気
の小さい; *twitch* shinkei (no) 神経
(の); *be* ~ *about doing X* X suru
no o shinpai shite iru Xするのを心

配している

nervous breakdown noirōze ノイローゼ

nervousness shinkei-kabin 神経過敏

nervous wreck: be a ~ hidoku piripiri shite iru ひどくぴりぴりしている

nervy (*fresh*) zūzūshii ずうずうしい

nest *n* su 巣

nestle yorisou 寄り添う

net[1] *n* (*for fishing*) ami 網; (*for tennis*) netto ネット

net[2] *adj weight, amount* shōmi (no) 正味(の); **~ price** seika 正価

net curtain rēsu no kāten レースのカーテン

net profit junrieki 純利益

netsuke netsuke 根付け

nettle *n* irakusa いらくさ

network (*of contacts, cells*), COMPUT nettowāku ネットワーク

neurologist shinkeika-i 神経科医

neurosis shinkeishō 神経症

neurotic *adj* shinkei-kabin (no) 神経過敏(の)

neuter *v/t animal* kyosei suru 去勢する

neutral 1 *adj country* chūritsu (no) 中立(の); *color* chūkan (no) 中間(の) **2** *n* (*gear*) nyūtoraru ニュートラル; **in ~** nyūtoraru ni ニュートラルに

neutrality chūritsu 中立

neutralize chūwa suru 中和する

never ◊ (*future tense*) kesshite… nai 決して…ない; **I'll ~ say that again** sore o mō kesshite iwanai それをもう決して言わない ◊ (*past tense*) … koto ga nai … ことがない; **I've ~ been there** soko ni wa itta koto ga nai そこには行ったことがない ◊ (*in disbelief*) masaka まさか; **you're ~ going to believe this** kore wa masaka shinjirarenai darō これはまさか信じられないだろう; **you ~ promised, did you?** masaka yakusoku shinakatta darō ne まさか約束しなかっただろうね

never-ending hateshinai 果てしない

nevertheless sore ni mo

kakawarazu それにもかかわらず

new atarashii 新しい; **this system is still ~ to me** kono shisutemu ni wa mada narete inai このシステムにはまだ慣れていない; **I'm ~ to the job** watashi wa shigoto ni narete inai 私は仕事に慣れていない; **that's nothing ~** nani mo ima ni hajimatta koto ja nai 何も今に始まったことじゃない

newborn *adj* umaretate (no) 生まれたて(の)

newcomer (*to place*) shinzanmono 新参者; (*to company*) shinnyū-shain 新入社員

newly (*recently*) saikin 最近

newly-weds shinkon-kappuru 新婚カップル

new moon shingetsu 新月

news nyūsu ニュース; (*from friend, family*) tayori 便り; **that's ~ to me** sore wa watashi ni wa mattaku hatsumimi desu それは私にはまったく初耳です

news agency tsūshinsha 通信社; **newscast** TV nyūsu-hōsō ニュース放送; **newscaster** TV kyasutā キャスター; **news dealer** shinbun-zasshi-hanbaiten 新聞雑誌販売店; **news flash** nyūsu-sokuhō ニュース速報; **newspaper** shinbun 新聞; **newsreader** TV *etc* kyasutā キャスター; **news report** hōdō-kiji 報道記事; **newsstand** shinbun-uriba 新聞売り場; **newsvendor** shinbun'uri 新聞売り

New Year Shinnen 新年, Shōgatsu 正月; **Happy ~!** Akemashite omedetō gozaimasu 明けましておめでとうございます

New Year's Day Gantan 元旦, Ganjitsu 元日; **New Year's card** nengajō 年賀状; **New Year's Eve** Ōmisoka 大みそか

New York Nyū-Yōku ニューヨーク

New Zealand Nyū-Jīrando ニュージーランド

New Zealander Nyū-Jīrando-jin ニュージーランド人

next 1 *adj* (*in time, order*) tsugi (no) 次(の); (*in space*) tonari (no)

隣(の); ~ **week** raishū 来週; **the ~ week / month he came back again** sono yokushū / yokugetsu kare wa mata kaette kita その翌週/翌月彼はまた帰ってきた; **who's ~?** tsugi no kata dōzo 次の方どうぞ 2 *adv* tsugi ni 次に; ~ **to** (*beside*) ... no tonari ni ...の隣に; (*in comparison with*) hotondo ... to onaji ほとんど...と同じ

next-door 1 *adj* neighbor tonari (no) 隣(の) 2 *adv* live tonari ni 隣に

next of kin mottomo chikai shinzoku もっとも近い親族

nibble *v/t* kajiru かじる

nice *person* shinsetsu (na) 親切(な); *weather, smile* ii いい; *party, trip, vacation* tanoshii 楽しい; *hair, color* kirei (na) きれい(な); *meal, food* oishii おいしい; **be ~ to your little sister** imōto ni yasashiku shite agenasai 妹にやさしくしてあげなさい; **that's very ~ of you** shinsetsu ni shite kudasatte arigatō gozaimasu 親切にしてくださってありがとうございます

nicely *written, presented* umaku うまく; (*pleasantly*) kimochi yoku 気持ちよく

niceties *social ~* reigi 礼儀

niche (*in market*) nitchi ニッチ; (*suitable position*) tekisho 適所

nick *n* (*cut*) kireme 切れ目; **in the ~ of time** chōdo ii toki ni ちょうどいい時に

nickel nikkeru ニッケル; (*coin*) go-sento-kōka 五セント硬貨

nickname *n* nikkunēmu ニックネーム

niece mei めい

niggardly kechikechi shita けちけちした

night yoru 夜; (*in hotel*) ippaku 一泊; **11 o'clock at ~** yoru jūichiji 夜十一時; **travel by ~** yoru ni idō suru 夜に移動する; **during the ~** yoru ni 夜に; **stay the ~** tomaru 泊まる; **a room for two ~s** nihaku no yotei de hitoheya 二泊の予定で一部屋; **work ~s** yakin suru 夜勤す

る; **good ~** oyasumi nasai おやすみなさい; **in the middle of the ~** mayonaka ni 真夜中に

nightcap (*drink*) nezake 寝酒; **nightclub** naitokurabu ナイトクラブ; **nightdress** naitodoresu ナイトドレス; **nightfall: at ~** yūgure ni 夕暮れに; **night flight** yakan-furaito 夜間フライト; **nightgown** naitodoresu ナイトドレス

nightingale naichingēru ナイチンゲール

nightlife yoasobi 夜遊び

nightly 1 *adj* yogoto (no) 夜ごと(の) 2 *adv* yogoto ni 夜ごとに

nightmare akumu 悪夢

night porter yakan-furonto-gakari 夜間フロント係; **night school** yakan-gakkō 夜間学校; **night shift** yakan-kinmu 夜間勤務; **nightshirt** nemaki 寝巻き; **nightspot** naitosupotto ナイトスポット; **nighttime: at ~** yakan ni 夜間に

nimble subayai すばやい

nine kyū 九; (*with count word*) kokonotsu 九つ

nineteen jūkyū 十九

nineteenth dai-jūkyū (no) 第十九(の)

ninetieth dai-kyūjū (no) 第九十(の)

ninety kyūjū 九十

ninth 1 *adj* dai-kyū (no) 第九(の) 2 *n* (*of month*) kokonoka 九日

nip *n*: **give X a ~** (*pinch*) X o tsuneru Xをつねる; (*bite*) X ni kamitsuku Xにかみつく

nipple chikubi 乳首

nitrogen chisso 窒素

No¹ (*~ play*) Nō 能; ~ **comedy** kyōgen 狂言

no² 1 *adv* iie いいえ ◊ (*using 'yes', ie yes, that is right*): **you don't know the answer, do you? – ~, I don't** kotae ga wakaranai n deshō – hai wakarimasen 答えがわからないんでしょう – はい、わかりません 2 *adj* **there's ~ coffee / tea left** kōhī / kōcha wa sukoshi mo nokotte inai コーヒー/紅茶は少しも残っていない; **I have ~ family** watashi ni wa kazoku ga inai 私に

は家族がいない; **I'm ~ expert** watashi wa ekisupāto de wa nai 私はエキスパートではない; **~ smoking** kin'en 禁煙; **~ parking** chūsha-kinshi 駐車禁止

nobility kōki-sa 高貴さ

noble person kōki (na) 高貴(な); gesture rippa (na) 立派(な)

nobody dare mo ... (+ neg verb) だれも...; **~ knows** dare mo shiranai だれも知らない; **there was ~ at home** dare mo ie ni inakatta だれも家にいなかった

nod 1 n unazuki うなずき; **give a ~** (agreeing) unazuku うなずく; **she greeted me with a ~** kanojo wa watashi ni atama o sageta 彼女は私に頭を下げた 2 v/i (agreeing) unazuku うなずく; (in greeting) atama o sageru 頭を下げる

♦ **nod off** inemuri suru 居眠りする

no-hoper mikominashi 見込みなし

noise oto 音; (unpleasant) zatsuon 雑音

noisy yakamashii やかましい

nominal amount wazuka (na) わずか(な)

nominate (appoint) ninmei suru 任命する; **~ X for a post** X o shoku ni suisen suru Xを職に推薦する

nomination (appointing) ninmei 任命; (proposal) suisen 推薦

nominee kōho-sha 候補者

nonalcoholic arukōru o fukumanai アルコールを含まない

nonaligned chūritsu (no) 中立(の)

nonchalant heizen to shita 平然とした

noncommissioned officer kashikan 下士官

noncommittal aimai (na) あいまい(な)

nondescript arifureta ありふれた

none (people) ... no dare mo ...nai ...のだれも...ない; (things) ... no dore mo ...nai ...のどれも...ない; **~ of the students has left yet** gakusei wa dare mo satte inai 学生はだれも去っていない; **~ of the apartments is vacant** apāto wa dore mo aite inai アパートはどれ

も空いていない; **there are ~ left** hitotsu mo nokotte inai ひとつも残っていない; **there is ~ left** sukoshi mo nokotte inai 少しも残っていない

nonentity toru ni taranai hito 取るに足らない人

nonetheless sore demo nao それでもなお

nonexistent sonzai shinai 存在しない; **nonfiction** non-fikushon ノンフィクション; **non(in)flammable** funensei (no) 不燃性(の); **nonintervention** naisei-fukanshō 内政不干渉; **non-iron** shirt airon no iranai アイロンのいらない

no-no: **that's a ~** sore wa dame desu それはだめです

no-nonsense approach genjitsu-rosen (no) 現実路線(の)

nonpayment fubarai 不払い; **nonpolluting** kankyō o osen shinai 環境を汚染しない; **nonresident** n (in country) hi-kyojūsha 非居住者; (in hotel) shukuhaku shite inai hito 宿泊していない人; **nonreturnable** kaette konai 返ってこない

nonsense tawagoto たわごと; **don't talk ~** baka na koto o iu na ばかなことを言うな; **~, it's easy!** tondemonai, kantan da とんでもない、簡単だ

nonskid tires suberidome o shita 滑り止めをした; **nonslip** surface suberanai 滑らない; **nonsmoker** (person) tabako o suwanai hito たばこを吸わない人; **nonstandard** hyōjungai (no) 標準外(の); **nonstick** pans tefuron-kakō (no) テフロン加工(の); **nonstop** 1 adj flight, train chokkō (no) 直行(の); chatter taema nai 絶え間ない 2 adv travel chokkō de 直行で; chatter, argue taema naku 絶え間なく; **nonswimmer** kanazuchi かなづち; **nonunion** rōdō-kumiai ni zokusanai 労働組合に属さない; **nonviolence** hi-bōryoku 非暴力; **nonviolent** hi-bōryoku (no) 非暴力(の)

noodles menrui めん類; (thick,

white) udon うどん; (*brown*) soba そば; *Chinese ~* rāmen らーめん

nook sumi 隅

noon shōgo 正午; *at ~* shōgo ni 正午に

noose wanawa 輪縄

nor: *~ do I* watashi mo desu 私もです

norm (*of society etc*) kihan 規範

normal futsū (no) 普通(の); *~ temperature* (*of body*) heinetsu 平熱

normality seijō 正常

normalize *relationships* seijōka suru 正常化する

normally futsū wa 普通は; (*in a normal way*) seijō ni 正常に

north 1 *n* kita 北; *to the ~ of* ... no kita ni ...の北に **2** *adj* kita (no) 北(の) **3** *adv travel etc* kita no hō ni 北の方に; *~ of* ... no kita ni ...の北に

North America Kita-Amerika 北アメリカ; **North American 1** *adj* Kita-Amerika (no) 北アメリカ(の) **2** *n* Kita-Amerika-jin 北アメリカ人; **northeast** *n* hokutō 北東

northerly *adj* kita (no) 北(の)

northern kita (no) 北(の)

northerner hokubu-shusshin-sha 北部出身者

North Korea Kita-chōsen 北朝鮮, *fml* Chōsen-minshu-shugi-jinmin-kyōwakoku 朝鮮民主主義人民共和国; **North Korean 1** *adj* Kita-chōsen (no) 北朝鮮(の) **2** *n* Kita-chōsen-jin 北朝鮮人; **North Pole** Hokkyoku 北極; **North Vietnam** Kita-Betonamu 北ベトナム; **North Vietnamese 1** *adj* Kita-Betonamu (no) 北ベトナム(の) **2** *n* Kita-Betonamu-jin 北ベトナム人;

northward kita no hō e 北の方へ; **northwest** *n* hokusei 北西

Norway Noruwē ノルウェー

Norwegian 1 *adj* Noruwē (no) ノルウェー(の) **2** *n* (*person*) Noruwē-jin ノルウェー人; (*language*) Noruwē-go ノルウェー語

nose hana 鼻; *it was right under my ~!* watashi no me no mae de 私の目の前で

♦**nose around** kagimawaru かぎ回る

nosebleed hanaji 鼻血; *have a ~* hanaji ga deru 鼻血が出る

nostalgia kyōshū 郷愁

nostalgic natsukashii 懐かしい

nostril hana no ana 鼻の穴

nosy sensakuzuki (na) せんさく好き(な); *don't be ~* sensaku shinaide せんさくしないで

not (*with verbs*) ...nai ...ない; (*past tense*) ...nakatta ...なかった; *I am ~ finished* watashi wa owatte inai 私は終わっていない; *he didn't help* kare wa tetsudawanakatta 彼は手伝わなかった ◊ (*when using masu*) ...masen ...ません; *I don't know* wakarimasen わかりません; *I am ~ American* watashi wa Amerika-jin de wa arimasen 私はアメリカ人ではありません◊; *~ this one, that one* kore de wa nakute, sore desu これではなくて、それです; *~ now* ima wa dame desu 今はだめです; *~ there* soko wa dame desu そこはだめです; *~ like that* sō de wa naku そうではなく; *~ before Tuesday / next week* kayōbi / raishū ikō ni 火曜日/来週以降に; *~ for me, thanks* dōmo, demo watashi wa kekkō desu どうも、でも私は結構です; *~ a lot* (*degree*) anmari あんまり; (*quantity*) sukoshi dake 少しだけ

notable chūmoku ni atai suru 注目に値する

notary kōshōnin 公証人

notch *n* kizamime 刻み目

note *n* (*short letter*) mijikai tegami 短い手紙; MUS onpu 音符; (*memo to self*) memo メモ; (*comment on text*) chū 注; *take ~s* nōto o toru ノートをとる; *take ~ of* ... ni chūi suru ...に注意する

♦**note down** ... o kakitomeru ...を書き留める

notebook nōto ノート; COMPUT nōto-pasokon ノートパソコン

noted yūmei (na) 有名(な)

notepad memochō メモ帳

notepaper binsen 便せん

nothing nani mo ... (+ *neg verb*) 何も ...; *there is ~ left* nani mo nokotte inai 何も残っていない; *I've had ~ to eat all day* ichinichi-jū nani mo tabenakatta 一日中何も食べなかった; *~ but* tada ... dake ただ...だけ; *~ much* taishite nani mo 大して何も; *for ~* (*free*) tada de ただで; (*for no reason*) riyū mo naku 理由もなく; *I'd like ~ better* (*accepting invitation*) yorokonde 喜んで; *~ for me thanks* kekkō desu, dōmo 結構です、どうも

notice 1 *n* (*on bulletin board*) keiji 掲示; (*in street*) harigami はり紙; (*advance warning*) keikoku 警告; (*in newspaper*) kōkoku 公告; (*to leave job / house*) tsūkoku 通告; *at short ~* girigiri no tsūtatsu de ぎりぎりの通達で; *until further ~* otte tsūchi ga aru made 追って通知があるまで; *give X his / her ~* (*to quit job*) X ni kaiko-tsūkoku suru X に解雇通告する; *hand in one's ~* (*to employer*) jishoku-todoke o dasu 辞職届を出す; *four weeks'~* (*to employee*) yonshūkan no kaiko-tsūkoku 四週間の解雇通告; (*to employer*) yonshūkan no jishoku-todoke 四週間の辞職届; *take ~ of ...* ni chūi o harau ...に注意を払う; *take no ~ of ...* o mushi suru ...を無視する **2** *v/t* ... ni ki ga tsuku ...に気がつく

noticeable medatta 目立った

notify ... ni tsūchi suru ...に通知する

notion kangae 考え

notions komamono 小間物

notorious akumei no takai 悪名の高い

nougat nugā ヌガー

noun meishi 名詞

nourishing eiyō no aru 栄養のある

nourishment eiyō 栄養

novel *n* shōsetsu 小説

novelist shōsetsu-ka 小説家

novelty (*being novel*) meatarashisa 目新しさ; (*sth novel*) meatarashii mono 目新しいもの

November jūichigatsu 十一月

novice shoshin-sha 初心者

now ima 今; *~ and again, ~ and then* tokidoki 時々; *by ~* ima made ni 今までに; *from ~ on* ima kara 今から; *right ~* genzai 現在; *just ~* (*at this moment*) ima wa 今は; (*a little while ago*) sakki さっき; *~, ~!* (*warning*) korakora こらこら; *~, where did I put it?* sate, doko ni oitakke さて、どこに置いたっけ

nowadays konogoro wa このごろは

nowhere doko ni mo ... (+*neg verb*) どこにも...; *there is ~ to stay* doko ni mo tomaru tokoro ga nai どこにも泊まるところがない; *it's ~ near finished* sore wa mattaku owatte inai それはまったく終わっていない

nozzle nozuru ノズル

nuclear kaku (no) 核(の)

nuclear energy genshiryoku 原子力; **nuclear fission** kakubunretsu 核分裂; **nuclear-free zone** hikakuchitai 非核地帯; **nuclear physics** genshi-butsurigaku 原子物理学; **nuclear power** genshiryoku 原子力; **nuclear power station** genshiryoku-hatsudensho 原子力発電所; **nuclear reactor** genshiro 原子炉; **nuclear waste** kaku-haikibutsu 核廃棄物; **nuclear weapons** kaku-heiki 核兵器

nude 1 *adj* hadaka (no) 裸(の) **2** *n* (*painting*) nūdo ヌード; *in the ~* hadaka de 裸で

nudge *v/t* sotto tsuku そっと突く

nudist *n* nūdisuto ヌーディスト

nuisance (*person*) meiwaku na hito 迷惑な人; (*thing*) yakkai na mono やっかいな物; (*having to do something*) mendō 面倒; *make a ~ of oneself* hito ni meiwaku o kakeru 人に迷惑をかける; *what a ~!* komatta mono da 困ったものだ

nuke *v/t* kakuheiki o tsukatte kōgeki suru 核兵器を使って攻撃する

null and void mukō de 無効で

numb *arm, leg* shibireta しびれた; (*with cold*) kajikanda かじかんだ;

(*emotionally*) kankaku no nai 感覚のない

number 1 *n* (*figure*) sūji 数字; (*quantity*) kazu 数; (*of hotel room, house, phone ~ etc*) bangō 番号; *a ~ of* (*some*) ikuraka no... いくらかの...; (*quite a few*) kanari ... no かなり ... の... **2** *v/t* (*put a number on*) bangō o tsukeru 番号をつける

numeral sūji 数字

numerate sūji ni tsuyoi 数字に強い

numerous tasū (no) 多数(の)

nun shūdōjo 修道女, ama 尼

nurse kangofu 看護婦; (*male*) kangoshi 看護士

nursery (*school*) hoikuen 保育園; (*for plants*) naedoko 苗床

nursery rhyme dōyō 童謡; **nursery school** hoikuen 保育園; **nursery school teacher** hobo 保母

nursing kango 看護

nursing home (*for old people*) rōjin-hōmu 老人ホーム

nut konomi 木の実; (*for bolt*) natto ナット; *~s* F (*testicles*) kintama きんたま

nutcrackers kurumiwari くるみ割り

nutrient yōbun 養分

nutrition eiyō 栄養

nutritious eiyō no aru 栄養のある

nuts *adj* F (*crazy*) ki ga kurutte 気が狂って; *be ~ about* ... ni muchū de aru ...に夢中である

nutshell: *in a ~* yō suru ni 要するに

nutty *taste* nattsu no fūmi no suru ナッツの風味のする; F (*crazy*) ki no kurutta 気の狂った

nylon 1 *n* nairon ナイロン **2** *adj* nairon (no) ナイロン(の)

O

oak (*tree*) kashi かし; (*wood*) ōku-zai オーク材; *Japanese ~* nara なら

oar ōru オール

oasis oashisu オアシス; *fig* ikoi no basho 憩いの場所

oath LAW sensei 宣誓; (*swearword*) nonoshiri-kotoba ののしり言葉; *on ~* sensei shite 宣誓して

oatmeal ōtomīru オートミール

oats ōto-mugi オート麦

obedience fukujū 服従

obedient iu koto o kiku 言うことを聞く

obey *the law* ... ni shitagau ...に従う; *parents* ... no iu koto o kiku ...の言うことを聞く

obituary *n* shibō-kiji 死亡記事

object[1] *n* (*thing*) mono 物; (*aim*) mokuteki 目的; GRAM mokutekigo 目的語

object[2] *v/i* hantai suru 反対する

♦ **object to** ... ni hantai suru ...に反対する

objection igi 異議

objectionable (*unpleasant*) iya (na) いや(な)

objective 1 *adj* kyakkanteki (na) 客観的(な) **2** *n* mokuteki 目的

obligation gimu 義務; *be under an ~ to* ... ni giri ga aru ...に義理がある

obligatory gimu (no) 義務(の); *qualifications* hitsuyō (na) 必要(な)

oblige: *much ~d!* dōmo arigatō どうもありがとう

obliging shinsetsu (na) 親切(な)

oblique 1 *adj reference* tōmawashi (no) 遠回し(の) **2** *n* (*in punctuation*) shasen 斜線

obliterate *city* kanzen ni hakai suru 完全に破壊する; *memory* kanzen ni wasureru 完全に忘れる

oblivion bōkyaku 忘却; *fall into ~* sukkari wasurerareru すっかり忘

れられる

oblivious: *be ~ of* ... ni zenzen ki ga tsukanai ...に全然気がつかない

oblong *adj* chōhōkei (no) 長方形(の)

obnoxious ki ni sawaru 気にさわる

obscene waisetsu (na) わいせつ (な); *salary, poverty* monosugoi ものすごい

obscure (*hard to see*) usugurai 薄暗い; (*hard to understand*) wakarinikui わかりにくい; (*little known*) mumei (no) 無名(の)

observant chūibukai 注意深い

observation (*of stars etc*) kansatsu 観察; (*comment*) iken 意見

observatory kansokujo 観測所

observe *birds, wildlife* kansatsu suru 観察する; (*notice*) ... ni ki ga tsuku ...に気がつく

observer (*of human nature etc*) kansatsu-sha 観察者; (*at elections etc*) obuzābā オブザーバー

obsess: *be ~ed by/with* ... ni toritsukarete iru ...に取りつかれている

obsession (*with idea*) kyōhaku-kannen 強迫観念; (*with thing, person*) shūchaku 執着

obsessive *person* kodawaru こだわる; *behavior* toritsukareta yō (na) 取りつかれた(な)

obsolete sutareta すたれた

obstacle shōgaibutsu 障害物; (*to progress etc*) shōgai 障害

obstetrician sankai 産科医

obstinacy ganko 頑固

obstinate ganko (na) 頑固(な)

obstruct fusagu ふさぐ; *police* samatageru 妨げる

obstruction (*on road*) shōgaibutsu 障害物

obstructive *behavior, tactics* jama ni naru yō (na) じゃまになるような

obtain eru 得る

obtainable *products* te ni irerareru 手に入れられる

obvious akiraka (na) 明らか(な); (*not subtle*) akarasama (na) 明らさま(な)

obviously akiraka ni 明らかに; *~!* mochiron もちろん

occasion bāi 場合; (*event, ceremony*) gyōji 行事; (*opportunity*) kikai 機会

occasional tama ni たま(の); *I like the ~ whiskey* watashi wa tama ni uisukī o nomu no ga suki desu 私はたまにウイスキーを飲むのが好きです

occasionally tama ni たまに

occult 1 *adj* okaruto (no) オカルト (の) **2** *n*: *the ~* okarutizumu オカルティズム

occupant (*of vehicle*) jōkyaku 乗客

occupation (*job*) shokugyō 職業; (*of country*) senryō 占領

occupy *one's time, mind* toru 取る; *position in company* shimeru 占める; *country* senryō suru 占領する

occur okoru 起こる; *it ~red to me that* ... to iu kangae ga futo ukanda ...という考えがふと浮かんだ

occurrence dekigoto できごと

ocean umi 海

Oceania Oseania オセアニア

o'clock: *at five/six ~* go/roku-ji ni 五/六時に

October jūgatsu 十月

octopus tako たこ

odd (*strange*) hen (na) 変(な); (*not even*) kisū (no) 奇数(の); *the ~ one out* (*thing*) hoka to wa chigau mono 他とは違う物; (*person*) hoka to wa chigau hito 他とは違う人; *50 ~* gojū chotto 五十ちょっと

odds: *be at ~ with* (*with people*) ... to arasotte iru ...と争っている; (*with proposal*) ... to mujun suru ...と矛盾する

odds and ends garakuta がらくた; (*things to do*) komakai ten 細かい点

odometer sōkō-kyorikei 走行距離計

odor nioi におい

of (*possession*) ... no ...の; *the name ~ the hotel* hoteru no namae ホテルの名前; *the works ~ Dickens* Dikenzu no sakuhin ディケンズの作品; *five/ten minutes ~ twelve* jūniji gofun/juppun mae

十二時五分/十分前; *die ~ cancer/ a stroke* gan/shinzō-hossa de shinu がん/心臓発作で死ぬ; *~ the three this is ...* mittsu no uchi de kore ga ... desu 三つのうちでこれが...です

off 1 *prep* ... kara ...から; *~ the main road* (*away from*) ōdōri kara hanarete 大通りから離れて; (*leading off*) ōdōri kara haitta tokoro ni 大通りから入ったところに; *$20 ~ the price* nijū doru nedan kara waribiite 二十ドル値段から割り引いて; *he's ~ his food* kare wa shokuyoku ga nai 彼は食欲がない 2 *adv*: *be ~* (*of light*, TV) keshite aru 消してある; (*of machine*) tomatte iru 止まっている; (*of brake*) kakatte inai かかっていない; (*of lid, top*) shimete inai 閉めていない; (*not at work*) yasumi de aru 休みである; (*canceled*) chūshi ni naru 中止になる; *we're ~ tomorrow* (*leaving*) watashitachi wa ashita shuppatsu shimasu 私たちは明日出発します; *I'm ~ to New York* watashi wa Nyū-Yōku e ikimasu 私はニューヨークへ行きます; *with his pants/hat ~* zubon/bōshi o nuide ズボン/帽子を脱いで; *take a day ~* ichinichi yasumu 一日休む; *it's 3 miles ~* sore wa san mairu hanarete imasu それは三マイル離れています; *it's a long way ~* (*in distance*) sore wa tōi desu それは遠いです; (*in future*) sore wa saki no koto desu それは先のことです; *drive ~* kuruma de hashirisaru 車で走り去る; *walk ~* tachisaru 立ち去る 3 *adj*: *the ~ switch* suitchi スイッチ

offend *v/t* (*insult*) okoraseru 怒らせる

offender LAW hanzai-sha 犯罪者

offense LAW hanzai 犯罪

offensive 1 *adj behavior, remark* shitsurei (na) 失礼(な); *smell* iya (na) いや(な) 2 *n* MIL kōgeki 攻撃; *go onto the ~* kōgeki shihajimeru 攻撃し始める

offer 1 *n* teikyō 提供 2 *v/t* teikyō

suru 提供する; *~ X Y drink etc* X ni Y o susumeru XにYを勧める; *job* X ni Y o teikyō suru XにYを提供する

offhand *adj attitude* muzōsa (na) 無造作(な)

office (*building*) jimusho 事務所; (*room*) jimushitsu 事務室, ofisu オフィス; (*position*) shoku 職

office block ofisubiru オフィスビル

office hours kinmu-jikan 勤務時間; (*of doctor*) shinsatsu-jikan 診察時間

officer MIL shikan 士官; (*in police*) keisatsukan 警察官

official 1 *adj statement, visit* kōshiki (no) 公式(の); *organization* kōteki (na) 公的(な) 2 *n* kōmuin 公務員

officially (*strictly speaking*) omotemuki wa 表向きは

off-line *adj working, input* ofurainshiki (no) オフライン式(の); *go ~* rain o kiru ラインを切る

off-peak *rates, season* kansanki (no) 閑散期(の)

off-season 1 *adj rates* shīzun'ofu (no) シーズンオフ(の) 2 *n* shīzun'ofu シーズンオフ

offset *v/t losses* umeawaseru 埋め合わせる

offside 1 *adj dōro* no chūōgawa (no) 道路の中央側(の) 2 *adv* SP ofusaido (no) オフサイド(の)

offspring kodomo 子供

off-white *adj* ofuhowaito (no) オフホワイト(の)

often yoku よく

oil 1 *n* (*for machine*) sekiyu 石油; (*for food*) oiru オイル, abura 油; (*for skin*) oiru オイル 2 *v/t bearings* abura o sasu 油をさす

oil company sekiyu-gaisha 石油会社; **oil painting** aburae 油絵; **oil rig** kaijō-saiyu-kichi 海上採油基地; **oil tanker** sekiyu-tankā 石油タンカー; **oil well** yusei 油井

oily aburappoi 脂っぽい

ointment nankō 軟こう

ok *adv* (*as reply*) ōkē オーケー; *can I? – ~* ii desu ka – ii desu yo いい

ですか – いいですよ；*is it ~ with you if I go home?* ie ni kaette mo ii desu ka 家に帰ってもいいですか；*that's ~ by me* watashi wa kamaimasen 私はかまいません；*are you ~?* (*well, not hurt*) daijōbu desu ka 大丈夫ですか；*are you ~ for Friday?* kin'yōbi wa daijōbu desu ka 金曜日は大丈夫ですか；*he's ~* (*is a good guy*) kare wa ii hito desu 彼はいい人です；*is this bus ~ for …?* kono basu wa … e ikimasu ka このバスは…へ行きますか

Okinawa Okinawa 沖縄

old *person* toshi o totta 年をとった；*vehicle, building, joke* furui 古い；*custom* mukashi kara (no) 昔から(の)；(*previous*) mae (no) 前(の)；*~ man / woman / people* otoshiyori お年寄り；*how ~ is he?* kare wa ikutsu desu ka 彼はいくつですか；*he's getting ~* kare wa mō toshi desu 彼はもう年です

old age rōnen 老年

old-fashioned furui 古い；*pej* furukusai 古くさい

olive orību オリーブ

olive oil orību-oiru オリーブオイル

Olympic Games Orinpikku オリンピック

omelet omuretsu オムレツ

ominous fukitsu (na) 不吉(な)

omission (*in text, process*) shōryaku 省略；(*of person, name*) jogai 除外

omit *word, check* shōryaku suru 省略する；*person, name* jogai suru 除外する；*~ to do X* Xshiwasureru X し忘れる

on 1 *prep* (*with verbs of being*) … ni …に；(*with verbs of activity*) … de … で；*it's ~ the table* tēburu ni aru テーブルにある；*he wasn't ~ the bus* kare wa basu ni notte inakatta 彼はバスに乗っていなかった；*I traveled ~ the bus* watashi wa basu de itta 私はバスで行った；*I met him ~ the plane* watashi wa hikōki de kare ni atta 私は飛行機で彼に会った；*~ TV / the radio* terebi / rajio de

テレビ / ラジオで；*~ Sunday* nichiyōbi ni 日曜日に；*~ the 1st of …* … (no) tsuitachi ni …(の)一日に；*this is ~ me* (*I'm paying*) kore wa watashimochi desu これは私持ちです；*~ his arrival* kare wa tōchaku suru to kare wa tōchaku suru to 彼は到着すると **2** *adv*: *be ~* (*of light, TV, computer*) tsuite iru ついている；(*of brake*) kakatte iru かかっている；(*of lid, top*) shimatte iru 閉まっている；(*of TV program: being broadcast*) hōei sarete iru 放映されている；(*of meeting etc: be scheduled to happen*) yotei sarete iru 予定されている；*what's ~ tonight?* (*on TV etc*) konban wa nani o yatte imasu ka 今晩は何をやっていますか；(*what's planned?*) konban no yotei wa nan desu ka 今晩の予定は何ですか；*with his jacket ~* uwagi o kite 上着を着て；*with his hat ~* bōshi o kabutte 帽子をかぶって；*you're ~* (*I accept your offer etc*) ii desu yo いいですよ；*that's not ~* (*not allowed, not fair*) sonna baka na koto wa nai そんなばかなことはない；*~ you go* (*go ahead*) dōzo どうぞ；*~ and so on* nado など；*~ talk / walk ~* aruki / hanashi-tsuzukeru 歩き / 話し続ける；*and so ~* nado など；*~ and ~ talk etc* en'en to えんえんと **3** *adj*: *the ~ switch* suitchi スイッチ

once 1 *adv* (*one time*) ichido 一度；(*formerly*) katsute かつて；*~ again, ~ more* mō ichido もう一度；*at ~* (*immediately*) sugu ni すぐに；*all at ~* (*suddenly*) totsuzen 突然；(*together*) mattaku dōji ni まったく同時に；*~ upon a time there was…* (*person*) mukashi mukashi … ga imashita 昔々…がいました；(*thing*) mukashimukashi … ga arimashita 昔々…がありました **2** *conj* ittan いったん；*~ he has finished, he can leave* (*kare wa*) ittan owatte shimaeba kaereru (彼は)いったん終わってしまえば帰れる

one 1 *n* (*number*) ichi 一 **2** *adj* (*with things*) hitotsu (no) 一つ(の)；(*with people*) hitori (no) 一人(の)

3 *pron*: **would you like ~?** anata mo hoshii desu ka あなたも欲しいですか; **I have a larger ~** watashi wa ōki no o motte imasu 私は大きいのを持っています; **~ is bigger than the other** sore no hō ga mō ippō yori ōkii それの方がもう一方より大きい; **which ~?** dotchi どっち; (*person*) dare だれ; **~ by ~** (*things*) hitotsu zutsu 一つずつ; (*people*) hitori zutsu 一人ずつ; **~ another** otagai ni お互いに

4 *personal pron*: **what can ~ say?** nani ka iiyō ga arimasu ka 何か言いようがありますか; **~ should take care of oneself** hito wa jibun o taisetsu ni surubeki da 人は自分を大切にするべきだ

one-off *n* (*event*) ikkai kagiri no koto 一回限りのこと; (*person*) hoka ni rui no nai hito 他に類のない人; (*exception*) reigai 例外

one-parent family kataoya no katei 片親の家庭

oneself: **by ~** (*without help*) jibun-jishin de 自分自身で; (*alone*) hitori de ひとりで

one-sided ippōteki (na) 一方的(な); **one-way street** ippō-tsūkō 一方通行; **one-way ticket** katamichi-kippu 片道切符

onion tamanegi たまねぎ

on-line *adj* onrain (no) オンライン(の); **go ~ to** … ni setsuzoku suru …に接続する

on-line service COMPUT onrain-sābisu オンラインサービス

onlooker kenbutsunin 見物人

only 1 *adv* … dake …だけ; **he's 6** kare wa hon no rokusai desu 彼はほんの六歳です; **it's ~ one o'clock** mada ichiji desu まだ一時です; **not ~ X but also Y** tada X dake de naku Y mo mata ただXだけでなくYもまた; **~ just manage** karōjite かろうじて **2** *adj* yuiitsu (no) 唯一(の); **~ son** / **daughter** hitori-musuko / musume 一人息子/娘

onset (*of illness*) hatsubyō 発病; (*of winter*) hajimari 始まり

onside *adv* SP onsaido オンサイド

onto: **put X ~ Y** (*on top of*) X o Y no ue ni oku XをYの上におく

onward (*in space*) zenpō e 前方へ; (*in time*) saki e 先へ; **from … ~ …** ikō …以降

ooze 1 *v/i* (*of liquid, mud*) nijimideru にじみ出る **2** *v/t*: **he ~s charm** kare wa miryoku ni afurete iru 彼は魅力にあふれている

opaque futōmei (na) 不透明(な); **~ glass** kumori-garasu くもりガラス

OPEC (= **Organization of Petroleum Exporting Countries**) OPEC

open 1 *adj* door, window, aita 開いた; *computer file* hiraita 開いた; *shop* eigyōchū (no) 営業中(の); *flower* saita 咲いた; (*honest, frank*) sōchoku (na) 率直(な); *relationship* jiyū (na) 自由(な); *countryside* hirobiro to shita 広々とした; **in the ~ air** kogai de 戸外で; **~ 24 hours** nijūyojikan-eigyō 24時間営業; **~ all year round** nenjū-mukyū 年中無休 **2** *v/t* hiraku 開く; *door, shop, window, bottle* akeru 開ける; *meeting* kaishi suru 開始する **3** *v/i* (*of door, shop*) hiraku 開く; (*of flower*) saku 咲く

♦ **open up** *v/i* (*of person*) uchitokeru 打ち解ける

open-air *adj* meeting, concert kogai (no) 戸外(の); *pool* okugai (no) 屋外(の)

open-ended *contract etc* mukigen (no) 無期限(の)

opening (*in wall etc*) sukima すき間; (*of movie, novel etc*) bōtō 冒頭; (*job*) aki 空き

openly (*frankly*) sotchoku ni 率直に

open-minded kokoro no hiroi 心の広い; **open plan office** ōpun-puran-ofisu オープンプランオフィス; **open ticket** ōpun-chiketto オープンチケット

opera opera オペラ

opera glasses opera-gurasu オペラグラス; **opera house** opera-hausu オペラハウス; **opera singer** opera-kashu オペラ歌手

operate 1 *v/i* (*of company*) eigyō

suru 営業する; (*of airline*) unkō suru 運航する; (*of bus service*) unkō suru 運行する; (*of machine*) ugoku 動く; MED shujutsu suru 手術する **2** *v/t machine* sōsa suru 操作する

♦ **operate on** MED … ni shujutsu o suru …に手術をする

operating instructions shiyō-setsumei 使用説明; **operating room** MED shujutsu-shitsu 手術室; **operating system** COMPUT operētingu-shisutemu オペレーティングシステム

operation MED shujutsu 手術; (*of machine*) sōsa 操作; **~s** (*of company*) jigyō-katsudō 事業活動; **have an ~** MED shujutsu o ukeru 手術を受ける

operator TELEC operētā オペレーター; (*of machine*) unten-sha 運転者; (*tour* ~) ryokō-dairiten 旅行代理店

ophthalmologist gankai-i 眼科医

opinion iken 意見; *in my* ~ watashi no iken de wa 私の意見では

opponent aite 相手

opportunity kikai 機会

oppose … ni hantai suru …に反対する; **be ~d to** … ni hantai de aru …に反対である; **as ~d to** … to taishōteki ni …と対照的に

opposite 1 *adj side of road,* mukōgawa (no) 向こう側(の); *end of town, direction* hantai (no) 反対(の); *views, characters* seihantai (no) 正反対(の); *meaning* gyaku (no) 逆(の); **the ~ sex** isei 異性 **2** *n* gyaku 逆

opposition (*to plan*) hantai 反対; POL yatō 野党

oppress *the people* yokuatsu suru 抑圧する

oppressive *rule* asseiteki (na) 圧制的(な); *weather* uttōshii うっとうしい

optical illusion me no sakkaku 目の錯覚

optician megane-ya 眼鏡屋

optimism rakkanron 楽観論

optimist rakkanron-sha 楽観論者

optimistic rakkanteki (na) 楽観的(な)

optimum 1 *adj* saiteki (na) 最適(な) **2** *n* saiteki-jōken 最適条件

option sentaku 選択

optional *subject* jiyū-sentaku (no) 自由選択(の); *it's ~* sore wa sentaku dekiru 選択できる

optional extras opushon オプション

or … ka soretomo … ka …かそれとも…か; (*otherwise*) samonaito さもないと; *he can't hear ~ see* kare wa miru koto mo kiku koto mo dekinai 彼は見ることも聞くこともできない; ~ *else!* samonaito taihen da yo さもないと大変だよ

oral *exam* kōtō (no) 口頭(の); ~ *hygiene* kuchi (no) 口(の); ~ *sex* ōraru-sekkusu オーラルセックス

orange 1 *adj* (*color*) orenji-iro (no) オレンジ色(の) **2** *n* (*fruit*) orenji オレンジ; (*color*) orenji-iro オレンジ色

orange juice orenji-jūsu オレンジジュース

orator enzetsu-sha 演説者

orbit 1 *n* kidō 軌道; *send … into* ~ … o kidō ni noseru …を軌道に乗せる **2** *v/t the earth* kidō o egaite … o mawaru 軌道を描いて…を回る

orchard kajuen 果樹園

orchestra ōkesutora オーケストラ

orchid ran らん

ordeal shiren 試練

order 1 *n* (*command*) meirei 命令; (*sequence*) jun 順; (*orderliness: in society*) chitsujo 秩序; (*in one's life*) kiritsu 規律; (*for goods, in restaurant*) chūmon 注文; *in ~ to* … suru tame ni …するために; *out of* ~ (*not functioning*) koshōchū de 故障中で; (*not in sequence*) junjo ga kurutte 順序が狂って **2** *v/t* (*put in sequence, proper layout*) seiri suru 整理する; *goods, meal* chūmon suru 注文する; ~ *X to do Y* X ni Y suru yō ni meijiru X にYするように命じる **3** *v/i* (*in restaurant*) chūmon suru 注文する

orderly 1 *adj lifestyle* kiritsu-tadashii 規律正しい; *person*

kichōmen (na) きちょうめん(な)
2 n (in hospital) tsukisoi 付き添い

ordinary futsū (no) 普通(の)

ore kōseki 鉱石

organ ANAT kikan 器官 MUS orugan オルガン

organic food, farming munōyaku (no) 無農薬(の); ~ **fertilizer** yūki-hiryō 有機肥料

organism seibutsu 生物

organization soshikitai 組織体; (organizing) kōsei 構成; (of conference) junbi 準備

organize people, team soshiki suru 組織する; conference junbi suru 準備する; data keitōdateru 系統立てる; one's life totonoeru 整える

organizer (person) shusai-sha 主催者

orgasm ōgazumu オーガズム

Orient Tōyō 東洋

orient v/t hōkō ni mukeru 方向に向ける; ~ **oneself** hōkōzuke suru 方向付けする

Oriental 1 adj Tōyō (no) 東洋(の) **2** n Tōyō-jin 東洋人

origami origami 折り紙

origin kigen 起源; person of Japanese ~ Nikkei no hito 日系の人

original 1 adj (genuine) honmono (no) 本物(の); (not copied) dokuji (no) 独自(の); (first) moto (no) もと(の) **2** n (painting etc) orijinaru オリジナル

originality dokusōsei 独創性

originally motomoto もともと; (at first) hajime wa 始めは

originate 1 v/t scheme, idea hajimeru 始める **2** v/i: ~ **in** (of idea, belief) umareru 生まれる; (of family) shusshin de aru 出身である

originator (of scheme etc) kōan-sha 考案者; **he's not an ~** kare wa aideaman de wa nai 彼はアイデアマンではない

ornament n kazari 飾り

ornamental kazari (no) 飾り(の)

ornate style etc kotta 凝った

orphan n koji 孤児

orphanage yōgo-shisetsu 養護施設

orthopedic seikei-geka (no) 整形外科(の)

Osaka Ōsaka 大阪

ostentatious hade (na) 派手(な)

other 1 adj hoka (no) ほか(の); **the ~ day** (recently) senjitsu 先日; **every ~ day/person** ichinichi/hitori oki ni 一日/一人おきに **2** n: **the ~** (thing) hoka no mono ほかの物; (person) hoka no hito ほかの人; **the ~s** (things) mō ippō no mono もう一方の物; (people) mō ippō no hito もう一方の人

otherwise samonaito さもないと; (differently) chigau fū ni 違うふうに

otter kawauso かわうそ

ought: **I ~ to know** watashi shiru hitsuyō ga aru 私は知る必要がある; **you ~ to have done it** sore o yatte okubeki datta それをやっておくべきだった

ounce onsu オンス

our ◊ watashitachi no 私たちの; ~ **mother** watashitachi no haha 私たちの母 ◊ (omission of possessive): **we forgot ~ keys** watashitachi wa kagi o wasureta 私たちはかぎを忘れた

ours watashitachi no mono 私たちのもの

ourselves: **by ~** (without help) jibuntachi de 自分たちで; (alone) watashitachi dake de 私たちだけで

oust (from office) tsuihō suru 追放する

out: **be ~** (of light) kirete iru 切れている; (of fire) kiete iru 消えている; (of flower) saite iru 咲いている; (of sun) dete iru 出ている; (not at home) rusu de aru 留守である; (not in office) gaishutsuchū de aru 外出中である; (of calculations) machigatte iru 間違っている; (be published) shuppan sarete iru 出版されている; (of secret) bareru ばれる; (of scandal) hakkaku suru 発覚する; (no longer in competition) haitai suru 敗退する; (in baseball) auto de aru アウトである; (no longer in fashion) ryūkōokure de aru 流行遅れである; **~ here in Dallas** koko Darasu de wa ここダラスでは; **he's ~ in the garden** kare wa niwa ni dete imasu 彼は庭に出ています; (**get**) **~!** dete ike 出ていけ; (**get**) **~ of my room!** watashi no heya kara dete ike 私の部屋から出ていけ; **that's ~!** (out of the question) sore wa rongai da それは論外だ; **he's ~ to win** (fully intending to) kare wa katsu tsumori da 彼は勝つつもりだ

outboard motor sengai-enjin 船外エンジン

outbreak (of violence, war) boppatsu ぼっ発

outburst (emotional) bakuhatsu 爆発

outcast tsuihō sareta 追放された

outcome kekka 結果

outcry kōgi 抗議

outdated jidai-okure (no) 時代後れ(の)

outdo shinogu しのぐ

outdoor toilet, facilities okugai (no) 屋外(の); activities, life yagai (no) 野外(の)

outdoors adv soto ni 外に

outer wall etc sotogawa (no) 外側(の)

outer space uchū-kūkan 宇宙空間

outfit (clothes) hitosoroi no fuku ひとそろいの服; (company) kaisha 会社; (organization) soshiki 組織

outgoing personality gaikōteki (na) 外向的(な); **~ flight** shuppatsubin 出発便

outgrow old ideas … kara nukedasu …から抜け出す

outing (trip) ensoku 遠足

outlet (of pipe) hakeguchi はけ口; (for sales) hanbaiten 販売店; ELEC soketto ソケット

outline 1 n (of person, building etc) rinkaku 輪郭; (of plan, novel) aramashi あらまし **2** v/t plans etc aramashi o setsumei suru あらましを説明する

outlive … yori nagaiki o suru …より長生きをする

outlook (prospects) mitōshi 見通し

中心を離れた

outnumber … yori kazu de masaru …より数で勝る

out of ◊ (motion): **run ~ the house** ie kara hashiridasu 家から走り出す; **look ~ the window** mado kara soto o miru 窓から外を見る ◊ (position); **20 miles ~ Detroit** Detoroito kara nijūmairu no tokoro de デトロイトから二十マイルの所で ◊ (cause): **~ jealousy / curiosity** netami / kōkishin kara ねたみ/好奇心から ◊ (without): **we are ~ gas / beer** gasorin / bīru ga kireta ガソリン/ビールが切れた ◊ (from a group): **5 – 10** jūnin chū gonin 十人中五人 ◊ (not within range): **~ sight** mienai tokoro de 見えない所で ◊ (sheltered from): **keep ~ the sun** chokusha-nikkō o sakete 直射日光を避けて

out-of-date jidai-okure (no) 時代遅れ(の)

out-of-the-way (remote) henpi (na) へんぴ(な)

outperform … yori sugurete iru …より優れている

output 1 n (of factory) seisandaka 生産高; COMPUT autoputto アウトプット **2** v/t (produce) seisan suru 生産する; COMPUT: signal … o shutsuryoku suru …を出力する

outrage 1 n (feeling) ikidōri いきどおり; (act) bōryoku-kōi 暴力行為 **2** v/t person … o gekido saseru …を激怒させる; **I was ~d to hear …** … to kiite hara ga tatta …と聞いて腹が立った

outrageous acts yurushigatai 許しがたい; prices akireta あきれた

outright 1 adj winner kanzen (na) 完全(な) **2** adv win kanzen ni 完全に; kill tetteiteki ni 徹底的に

outrun (run faster than) … yori hayaku hashiru …より速く走る; (run for longer than) … yori tōku e hashiru …より遠くへ走る

outset hajime 初め; **from the ~** hajime kara 初めから

outside 1 adj surface, wall, lane

sotogawa (no) 外側(の) **2** *adv* sit soto ni 外に; *go* soto e 外へ **3** *prep* ... no soto de/ni ...の外で/に; (*apart from*) ... igai de wa ...以外では; **~ the USA** Amerika igai de wa アメリカ以外では **4** *n* (*of building, case etc*) sotogawa 外側; **at the ~** saikō de 最高で

outside broadcast chūkei-hōsō 中継放送

outsider bugai-sha 部外者, tanin 他人; (*in race, election*) kachime no nai hito 勝ち目のない人

outsize *adj clothing* tokudai (no) 特大(の)

outskirts kōgai 郊外

outspoken sotchoku (na) 率直(な)

outstanding kesshutsu shita 傑出した; FIN miharai (no) 未払い(の)

outward *adj appearance* hyōmenteki (na) 表面的(な); **~ journey** ōro 往路

outwardly gaikenjō wa 外見上は

outweigh ... yori masaru ...より勝る

outwit dashinuku 出し抜く

oval *adj* daenkei (no) だ円形(の)

ovary ransō 卵巣

oven ōbun オーブン

over 1 *prep* (*above*) ... no ue ni ...の上に; (*across*) ... no mukōgawa ni ...の向こう側に; (*more than*) ... yori ōku ...より多く; (*during*) ... no aida ni ...の間に; *travel all ~ Japan* Nihonjū o tabi suru 日本中を旅する; *you find them all ~ Japan* sore wa Nihonjū doko ni demo aru それは日本中どこにでもある; *let's talk ~ a meal / drink* shokuji shinagara / nominagara hanasō 食事しながら/飲みながら話そう; *we're ~ the worst* saiaku wa sugita 最悪は過ぎた; *she's ~ 40* kanojo wa yonjussai o koete iru 彼女は四十歳を越えている **2** *adv*: *be ~* (*finished*) owari de aru 終わりである; (*left*) amatte iru 余っている; *~ to you* (*your turn*) anata no ban desu あなたの番です; *~ in Europe* (*with verbs of being*) Yōroppa ni ヨーロッパに; (*with verbs of activity*) Yōroppa de

ヨーロッパに; *~ here* (*with verbs of being*) kochira ni こちらに; (*with verbs of activity*) kochira de こちらで; *it hurts all ~* karadajū itai desu 体中痛いです; *painted white all ~* ichimen shiro ni nurarete iru 一面白に塗られている; *it's all ~* kore de oshimai da これでおしまいだ; *~ and ~ again* nando mo nando mo 何度も何度も; *do X ~* (*again*) X kurikaesu Xを繰り返す

overall *adj length* zentai (no) 全体(の); *cost* zenbu (no) 全部(の)

overawe: *be ~d by* ... ni attō sareru ...に圧倒される

overboard: *man ~!* dare ka ochitazo だれか落ちたぞ; *go ~ for* ... ni do ga sugiru ...に度が過ぎる

overcast *day, sky* kumotta くもった

overcharge *v/t* jissai yori takaku seikyū suru 実際より高く請求する

overcoat ōbā オーバー

overcome *difficulties*... ni uchikatsu ...に打ち勝つ; *be ~ by emotion* kanjōteki ni mairu 感情的に参る

overcrowded chōman'in (no) 超満員(の)

overdo (*exaggerate*) yari-sugiru やりすぎる; (*in frying, grilling*) yaki-sugiru 焼きすぎる; *vegetables* ni-sugiru 煮すぎる; *you're ~ing things* kimi wa nan demo yari-sugiru 君は何でもやりすぎる

overdone *meat* yakisugita 焼きすぎた; *vegetables* nisugita 煮すぎた; **overdose** *n* (*of sleeping pills etc*) chishiryō 致死量; (*of illegal substance*) yarisugi やりすぎ; (*given by doctor*) kajō-tōyo 過剰投与; **overdraft** tōza-karikoshi 当座借越; *have an ~* (*authorized*) tōza-karikoshi ga mitomerarete iru 当座借越が認められている; *have an ~* (*unauthorized*) kōza ga karikoshi ni natte iru 口座が借り越しになっている; **overdraw** *account* karikosu 借り越す; *be $800 ~n* happyaku doru karikoshite iru 800ドル借り越している; **overdrive**

MOT ōbādoraibu オーバードライブ; **overdue** *apology, alteration* okureta 遅れた; **overestimate** kadai ni hyōka suru 過大に評価する; **overexpose** *photograph* roshutsu-kado ni suru 露出過度にする

overflow *v/i (of water)* afureru あふれる; *(of river)* hanran suru はんらんする

overgrown *garden* kusabōbō (no) 草ぼうぼう(の); **he's an ~ baby** kare wa sodachisugi no akanbō da 彼は育ちすぎの赤ん坊だ

overhaul *v/t engine* ōbāhōru suru オーバーホールする; *plans* minaosu 見直す

overhead 1 *adj railway* kōka (no) 高架(の); **~light** tenjō no denki 天井の電気 2 *n* FIN kansetsu-keihi 間接経費

overhear futo mimi ni suru ふと耳にする

overjoyed ōyorokobi (no) 大喜び(の)

overland 1 *adj route* rikuro (no) 陸路(の) 2 *adv travel* rikuro de 陸路で

overlap *v/i (of tiles, periods of time)* kasanaru 重なる; *(of theories)* kyōtsū suru bubun ga aru 共通する部分がある

overload *v/t vehicle* ... ni ni o tsumisugiru ...に荷を積みすぎる; ELEC ... ni fuka o kakesugiru ...に負荷をかけすぎる

overlook *(of building etc)* miorosu 見下ろす; *(not see: accidentally)* miotosu 見落とす; *(deliberately)* minogasu 見逃す

overly kado ni 過度に; **not ~ ...** amari ... de nai あまり...でない

overnight *adv* ippaku 一泊

overnight bag shōryokōyō no kaban 小旅行用のかばん

overpaid kyūryō ga shiharawaresugi (no) 給料が支払われすぎ(の)

overpass kōka-dōro 高架道路

overpower *v/t (physically)* oshitaosu 押し倒す

overpowering *smell* kyōretsu (na) 強烈(な); *sense of guilt* attōteki (na) 圧倒的(な)

overpriced ... ni takane o tsukesugiru ...に高値をつけすぎる

overrated kadai-hyōka sareta 過大評価された

overrule *decision* mukō ni suru 無効にする

overrun *country* shinryaku suru 侵略する; *time* chōka suru 超過する; **be ~ with** ... de ippai de aru ...でいっぱいである

overseas 1 *adv live* kaigai ni 海外に; *work* kaigai de 海外で; *travel* kaigai o 海外を 2 *adj travel* kaigai (no) 海外(の); *visitor* kaigai kara (no) 海外から(の)

oversee kantoku suru 監督する

oversight miotoshi 見落とし

oversleep nesugosu 寝過ごす

overtake *(in work, development)* ... o shinogu ...をしのぐ; *Br* MOT ... ni oitsuku ...に追いつく

overthrow *government* taosu 倒す

overtime 1 *n (in the evening)* zangyō 残業; *(on Sunday, holiday)* kyūjitsu-shukkin 休日出勤; SP enchōsen 延長戦 2 *adv (in the evening)* zangyō de 残業で; *(on Sunday, holiday)* kyūjitsu-shukkin de 休日出勤で

overture MUS jokyoku 序曲; **make ~s to** ... ni mōshiire o suru ...に申し入れをする

overturn 1 *v/t* hikkurikaesu ひっくり返す; *government* datō suru 打倒する 2 *v/i (of vehicle)* hikkurikaeru ひっくり返る

overweight futori-sugi (no) 太りすぎ(の)

overwhelm attō suru 圧倒する; **be ~ed by** *(very pleased: by response)* ... no mune ga ippai ni naru ...のために胸が一杯になる

overwork 1 *n* karō 過労; **death from ~** karōshi 過労死 2 *v/i* hataraki-sugiru 働きすぎる 3 *v/t employee* hatarakase-sugiru 働かせすぎる; *machine* tsukai-sugiru 使いすぎる

owe v/t ... ni shakkin o shite iru ... に借金をしている; ~ ... **$500** ... ni gohyaku doru karite iru ...に500ドル借りている; ~ ... **an apology** ... ni ayamaranakereba naranai ...に謝らなければならない; **how much do I ~ you?** ikura haraeba ii desu ka いくら払えばいいですか

owing to ... no tame ni ...のために

owl fukurō ふくろう

own[1] v/t shoyū suru 所有する

own[2] **1** adj jibun-jishin (no) 自分自身(の) **2** pron: **a car/an apartment of my** ~ jibun no kuruma/apāto 自分の車/アパート; **on my/his** ~ hitori de ひとりで

♦**own up** hakujō suru 白状する

owner shoyū-sha 所有者

ownership shoyū-ken 所有権

oxide sankabutsu 酸化物

oxygen sanso 酸素

oyster kaki かき

ozone ozon オゾン

ozone layer ozon-sō オゾン層

P

pace 1 n (step) ipo 一歩; (speed) pēsu ペース **2** v/i: aruku 歩く; ~ **up and down** urouro to arukimawaru うろうろと歩き回る

pacemaker MED, SP pēsumēkā ペースメーカー

Pacific: **the** ~ (**Ocean**) Taiheiyō 太平洋

Pacific Rim: **the** ~ kan-Taiheiyō 環太平洋; ~ **countries** kan-Taiheiyō-shokoku 環太平洋諸国

Pacific War (1941-45) Taiheiyō-sensō 太平洋戦争

pacifier oshaburi おしゃぶり

pacifism heiwa-shugi 平和主義

pacifist n heiwa-shugi-sha 平和主義者

pacify nadameru なだめる

pack 1 n (back~) bakku-pakku バックパック; (of sausages etc) pakku パック; (of cereal, cigarettes) hako 箱; (of candy) fukuro 袋; (of cards) hitokumi 一組 **2** v/t tsumeru 詰める; bag ... ni nimotsu o tsumeru ...に荷物を詰める **3** v/i nizukuri o suru 荷造りをする

package 1 n (parcel) kozutsumi 小包; (of offers etc) ikkatsu-keiyaku 一括契約 **2** v/t (in packs) hōsō suru 包装する; (for promotion) pakkēji suru パッケージする

package deal (for vacation) setto-hanbai セット販売

package tour pakku-ryokō パック旅行

packaging (of product) hōsō 包装; (of rock star etc) imēji イメージ

packed (crowded) komiatta 込み合った

packet kobukuro 小袋, pakku パック

pact kyōtei 協定

pad[1] **1** n (piece of cloth etc) paddo パッド; (for writing) binsen 便せん **2** v/t (with material) ... ni tsumemono o suru ...に詰めものをする; speech, report hikinobasu 引き延ばす

pad[2] v/i (move quietly) sotto aruku そっと歩く

padded jacket, shoulders kata-paddo no haitta 肩パッドの入った

padding (material) tsumemono 詰めもの; (in speech etc) yodan 余談

paddle[1] **1** n (for canoe) padoru パドル, kai かい **2** v/i (in canoe) kogu こぐ

paddle[2] v/i (in water) bachabacha oyogu ばちゃばちゃ泳ぐ

paddock (on farm) shōbokujō 小牧場; (at racetrack) padokku パドック

padlock 1 n nankinjō 南京錠 **2** v/t

gate ... ni nankinjō o kakeru ...に
南京錠をかける; **~ X to Y** X ni
kagi o kakete Y ni tomeru Xに鍵
をかけてYに止める

page¹ n pēji ページ; **~ number** pēji
ページ

page² v/t (call) yobidasu 呼び出す

pager pokettoberu ポケットベル

pagoda tō塔

paid employment: be in ~ shigoto o
motte iru 仕事を持っている

pail baketsu バケツ

pain itami 痛み; **be in ~** itami ga aru
痛みがある; **take ~s to ... ...** suru
no ni hone o oru ...するのに骨を折
る; **a ~ in the neck** F (person) iya
na yatsu いやなやつ

painful arm, leg etc itai 痛い;
(distressing) tsurai つらい;
(laborious) konnan (na) 困難(な)

painfully (extremely) hijō ni 非常に

painkiller itamidome 痛み止め

painless mutsū (no) 無痛(の); (not
problematic) tayasui たやすい

painstaking work hone o oreru 骨
の折れる; worker kinben (na) 勤勉
(な)

paint 1 n (for wall) penki ペンキ;
(for artist) enogu 絵の具 **2** v/t
wall etc ... ni penki o nuru ...にペ
ンキを塗る; picture kaku 描く **3** v/i
(as art form) e o kaku 絵を描く

paintbrush hake はけ; (of artist)
efude 絵筆

painter (decorator) penki-ya ペン
キ屋; (artist) ekaki 絵かき, gaka
画家

painting (picture) e 絵; (decorating)
penkinuri ペンキ塗り

paintwork tosō 塗装

pair (of animals, birds) tsugai つが
い; (of people) futarigumi 二人組;
SP pea ペア; (of objects) tsui 対; **a
~ of shoes / sandals** kutsu /
sandaru issoku 靴/サンダル一足;
a ~ of scissors hasami itchō はさ
み一丁; **a ~ of pants** zubon
itchaku ズボン一着

pajama jacket pajama no uwagi パ
ジャマの上着

pajama pants pajama no zubon パ

ジャマのズボン

pajamas pajama パジャマ

Pakistan Pakisutan パキスタン

Pakistani 1 adj Pakisutan (no) パキ
スタン(の) **2** n Pakisutan-jin パキ
スタン人

pal F tomodachi 友達; **hey ~, got a
light?** nē, matchi motte nai ねー、
マッチ持ってない

palace kyūden 宮殿

palate kōgai 口がい; fig mikaku 味覚

pale person aojiroi 青白い; **look ~**
kaoiro ga warui 顔色が悪い; **go ~**
aozameru 青ざめる; **~ pink / blue**
usui pinku-iro / burū うすいピンク
色/ブルー

pallet (for goods) nidai 荷台

pallor irojiro-sa 色白さ

palm¹ (of hand) tenohira 手のひら

palm² (tree) yashi やし

palpitations MED dōki 動き

paltry sum wazuka (na) わずか(な)

pamper amayakasu 甘やかす

pamphlet panfuretto パンフレット

pan 1 n furaipan フライパン **2** v/t F
(criticize) kokiorosu こきおろす

**♦pan out: let's wait and see how
things ~** chotto matte dō naru ka
mite miyo ちょっと待ってどうなる
か見てみよ

pancake hottokēki ホットケーキ

panda panda パンダ

pandemonium daikonran 大混乱

pane (of glass) madogarasu 窓ガラ
ス

panel (section) paneru パネル; **a ~
of experts** senmonka no ichidan
専門家の一団

paneling panerubari パネル張り

panhandle v/i F monogoi o suru 物
乞いをする

panic 1 n panikku パニック **2** v/i
(of person) awateru あわてる; (of
crowd) panikku-jōtai ni naru パ
ニック状態になる; **don't ~**
awateruna あわてるな

panic selling FIN rōbai uri ろうばい
売り

panic-stricken panikku-jōtai ni
natta パニック状態になった

panorama panorama パノラマ

panoramic panorama (no) パノラマ(の)

pansy (*flower*) panjī パンジー

pant *v/i* ikigire suru 息切れする

panties pantī パンティー

pants zubon ズボン; *a pair of ~* zubon itchaku ズボン一着

pantyhose pantīsutokkingu パンティーストッキング

paper 1 *n* (*material*) kami 紙; (*news~*) shinbun 新聞; (*wall~*) kabegami 壁紙; (*academic*) ronbun 論文; (*examination ~*) shiken 試験; *~s* (*documents*) shorui 書類; (*identity ~s*) mibun-shōmeisho 身分証明書; *a piece of ~* kamikire ichimai 紙切れ一枚; *Japanese ~* washi 和紙 2 *adj* kami (no) 紙(の) 3 *v/t walls* ... ni kabegami o haru ...に壁紙をはる

paperback pēpābakku ペーパーバック; **paper bag** kamibukuro 紙袋; **paper clip** kurippu クリップ; **paper cup** kamikoppu 紙コップ; **paperwork** shorui-jimu 書類事務

par (*in golf*) pā パー; *be on a ~ with* ... to dōto de aru ...と同等である; *feel below ~* itsumo no chōshi de nai いつもの調子でない

parachute 1 *n* parashūto パラシュート 2 *v/i* parashūto de oriru パラシュートで降りる 3 *v/t supplies* parashūto de otosu パラシュートで落とす

parade 1 *n* (*procession*) parēdo パレード 2 *v/i* (*to celebrate*) parēdo suru パレードする; (*to be noticed*) koremiyogashi ni aruku これみよがしに歩く; (*of soldiers*) kōshin suru 行進する 3 *v/t* misebirakasu 見せびらかす

paradise tengoku 天国; (*biblical*) Eden no sono エデンの園

paradox gyakusetsu 逆説, paradokkusu パラドックス

paradoxical gyakusetsuteki (na) 逆説的(な)

paradoxically gyakusetsuteki ni 逆説的に

paragraph danraku 段落

parallel 1 *n* (*line*) heikō 平行; (*of latitude*) isen 緯線; *fig* ruijiten 類似点; *do two things in ~* futatsu no koto o heiretsu shite okonau 二つのことを並列して行う 2 *adj line* heikō (no) 平行(の) 3 *v/t* (*match*) ... ni hitteki suru ...に匹敵する

paralysis mahi 麻ひ

paralyze mahi saseru 麻ひさせる; *fig* ... no kinō o mahi saseru ...の機能を麻ひさせる

paramedic iryō-hojoin 医療補助員

parameter seigen-han'i 制限範囲

paramilitary 1 *adj* jungunjiteki (na) 準軍事的(な) 2 *n* jungunji-soshiki no kōseiin 準軍事組織の構成員

paramount saikō (no) 最高(の); *be ~* mottomo jūyō de aru もっとも重要である

paranoia saigishin さいぎ心

paranoid *adj* kangurisugi (no) かんぐりすぎ(の)

paranoid *adj* kangurisugi (no) かんぐりすぎ(の)

paraphernalia mochimono 持ち物

paraphrase *v/t* iikaeru 言いかえる

paraplegic *n* kahanshin-mahi no hito 下半身麻ひの人

parasite kiseichū 寄生虫

parasol parasoru パラソル

paratrooper rakkasanhei 落下傘兵

parcel kozutsumi 小包

♦**parcel up** kozutsumi ni suru 小包にする

parch *v/t*: *be ~ed* (*of person*) nodo ga karakara de aru のどがからからである

pardon 1 *n* LAW onsha 恩赦; *I beg your ~?* (*what did you say?*) nan to osshaimashita ka 何とおっしゃいましたか; *I beg your ~* (*I'm sorry*) gomen nasai ごめんなさい 2 *v/t* yurusu 許す; LAW shamen suru 赦免する; *~ me?* nan to osshaimashita ka 何とおっしゃいましたか

pare (*peel*) ... no kawa o muku ...の皮をむく

parent oya 親; *~s* ryōshin 両親

parental oya (no) 親(の)

parent company oyagaisha 親会社

parent-teacher association pītēē

PTA

park¹ (*area*) kōen 公園

park² *v/t&v/i* MOT chūsha suru 駐車する

parka anorakku アノラック

parking MOT chūsha 駐車; *no ~* chūsha-kinshi 駐車禁止

parking brake saidoburēki サイドブレーキ; **parking garage** chūshajō 駐車場; **parking lot** chūshajō 駐車場; **parking meter** pākingu-mētā パーキングメーター; **parking place** chūsha-supēsu 駐車スペース; **parking ticket** chūsha-ihan no yobidashijō 駐車違反の呼び出し状

parliament gikai 議会

parliamentary gikai (no) 議会(の)

parole 1 *n* karishussho 仮出所; *be on ~* karishussho shite iru 仮出所している **2** *v/t* karishussho saseru 仮出所させる

parrot ōmu おうむ

parsley paseri パセリ

part 1 *n* (*portion*) ichibu 一部; (*section*) bu 部; (*area*) bubun 部分; (*of country*) chihō 地方; (*of machine*) buhin 部品; (*in play, movie*) yaku 役; MUS pāto パート; (*in hair*) wakeme 分け目; *take ~ in* … ni sanka suru …に参加する; *mix two ~s vinegar with three ~s oil* su ni, abura san no wariai de mazeru 酢2、油3の割合で混ぜる **2** *adv* (*partly*) ichibun wa 一部分は **3** *v/i* wakareru 別れる **4** *v/t* wakeru 分ける

♦**part with** tebanasu 手放す

part exchange shitadori 下取り; *take … in ~* … o shitadori suru …を下取りする

partial (*incomplete*) bubunteki (na) 部分的(な); *be ~ to* … ga suki de aru …が好きである

partially bubunteki ni 部分的に

participant sanka-sha 参加者

participate sanka suru 参加する; *~ in* … ni sanka suru …に参加する

participation sanka 参加

particle PHYS ryūshi 粒子; (*small amount*) kakera かけら

particular (*specific*) tokutei (no) 特定(の); (*special*) tokubetsu (no) 特別(の); (*fussy*) yakamashii やかましい; *in ~* toku ni 特に; *this ~ morning / case* sono asa/kono bāi ni kagitte その朝/この場合に限って; *for a ~ reason* toku ni riyū ga atte 特に理由があって

particularly toku ni 特に

parting (*of people*) wakare 別れ

partition 1 *n* (*screen*) majikiri 間仕切り; (*of country*) bunkatsu 分割 **2** *v/t country* bunkatsu suru 分割する

♦**partition off** … o shikiru …を仕切る

partly bubunteki ni 部分的に; *that's ~ the reason* sore mo riyū no hitotsu da それも理由の1つだ

partner COM kyōdō-keiei-sha 共同経営者; (*at work*) kumu aite 組む相手; (*husband, wife*) haigū-sha 配偶者; (*in long-term relationship*) koibito 恋人; (*in particular activity*) pātonā パートナー

partnership (*business*) kyōdō-keiei-jigyō 共同経営事業; (*relationship: in business*) kyōdō-keiei-sha 共同経営者; (*in dance, sport*) kyōryoku-kankei 協力関係; POL kyōryoku 協力

part of speech hinshi 品詞; **part owner** kyōdō-shoyū-sha 共同所有者; **part-time 1** *adj* pātotaimu (no) パートタイム(の), baito (no) バイト(の); *teacher* hijōkin (no) 非常勤(の) **2** *adv work* pātotaimu de パートタイムで

party 1 *n* (*celebration*) pātī パーティー; POL seitō 政党; (*group of people*) ichidan 一団; *be a ~ to* … ni kuwawaru …に加わる **2** *v/i* F omoikiri asobu 思い切り遊ぶ

pass 1 *n* (*for entry*) nyūjōken 入場券; (*permit*) tsūkōshō 通行証; (*membership card*) kaiinshō 会員証; (*for public transportation*) teikiken 定期券; SP pasu パス; (*in mountains*) tōge 峠; *make a ~ at* … ni mōshon o kakeru …にモーションをかける **2** *v/t* (*hand*) watasu 渡す; *salt* mawasu 回す; (*go past*) tōrisugiru 通り過ぎる; MOT oikosu 追い越す; (*go beyond*) koeru 越える; (*approve*) kaketsu suru 可決する; *new drug* ninka suru 認可する; SP pasu suru パスする; *~ an exam* shiken ni gōkaku suru 試験に合格する; *~ sentence* LAW hanketsu o kudasu 判決を下す; *~ the time* jikan o sugosu 時間を過ごす **3** *v/i* (*of time*) tatsu たつ; (*in exam*) ukaru 受かる; SP pasu suru パスする; (*go away*) kieru 消える

♦**pass around** ... o mawasu ...を回す

♦**pass away** (*die*) nakunaru 亡くなる

♦**pass by 1** *v/t* (*go past*) ... o tōrisugiru ...を通り過ぎる **2** *v/i* (*go past*) tōrisugiru 通り過ぎる

♦**pass on 1** *v/t information,* ... o tsutaeru ...を伝える; *book* ... o mawasu ...を回す; *costs, savings* ... o mawasu ...を回す **2** *v/i* (*die*) shinu 死ぬ

♦**pass out** (*faint*) ki o ushinau 気を失う

♦**pass through** *town* ... o tōrinukeru ...を通り抜ける

♦**pass up** *opportunity* ... o miokuru ...を見送る

passable *road* tsūkō-kanō (na) 通行可能(な); (*acceptable*) māmā (no) まあまあ(の)

passage (*corridor*) tsūro 通路; (*from poem, book*) issetsu 一節; (*of time*) keika 経過

passageway tsūro 通路

passenger jōkyaku 乗客

passenger seat joshuseki 助手席

passer-by tsūkōnin 通行人

passion jōnetsu 情熱; (*sexual desire*) jōyoku 情欲

passionate jōnetsuteki (na) 情熱的(な)

passive 1 *adj* ukemi (no) 受身(の) **2** *n* GRAM ukemi 受身; *in the ~* ukemi de 受身で

pass mark gōkakuten 合格点

passport pasupōto パスポート;

passport control (*arrivals*) nyūkoku-shinsa 入国審査; (*departures*) shukkoku-shinsa 出国審査; **password** pasuwādo パスワード

past 1 *adj* (*former*) izen (no) 以前(の); *the ~ few days* kono sūjitsu この数日; *that's all ~ now* sore wa mō owatta koto da それはもう終わったことだ **2** *n* kako 過去; *in the ~* kako ni 過去に **3** *prep* (*in time*) ... o sugite ...を過ぎて; (*in position*) ... o tōrisugite ...を通り過ぎて; *it's half ~ two* niji han desu 二時半です **4** *adv: run/walk ~* hashitte/aruite tōrisugiru 走って/歩いて通り過ぎる

paste 1 *n* (*adhesive*) nori のり **2** *v/t* (*stick*) nori de haru のりではる

pastel 1 *n* (*color*) pasuteru パステル **2** *adj* pasuteru-chō (no) パステル調(の)

pastime shumi 趣味

pastor bokushi 牧師

past participle kako-bunshi 過去分詞

pastrami pasutorami パストラミ

pastry (*for pie*) pai-kiji パイ生地; (*small cake*) pēsutorī ペーストリー

past tense kakokei 過去形

pasty *adj face* aojiroi 青白い

pat 1 *n: with a ~ of her hand* te o karuku tatakinagara 手を軽くたたきながら; *give ... a ~ on the back fig* ... o homeru ...を褒める **2** *v/t* karuku tataku 軽くたたく

patch 1 *n* (*on clothing*) tsugi つぎ; (*area*) ichibu 一部; *be not a ~ on* ... to wa kurabemono ni naranai ...とは比べものにならない; *go through a bad ~* junchō ni ikanai jiki ni naru 順調にいかない時期になる **2** *v/t clothing* ... ni tsugi o ateru ...につぎを当てる

♦**patch up** (*repair*) ... ni ōkyū no shochi o suru ...に応急の処置をする; *quarrel* nakanaori suru 仲直りする

patchwork 1 *n* (*needlework*) patchiwāku パッチワーク **2** *adj*

quilt patchiwāku de dekita パッチ
ワークでできた

patchy *fog* mura no aru むらのある;
work, performance fukanzen (na)
不完全(な)

patent 1 *adj* meihaku (na) 明白(な)
2 *n* (*for invention*) tokkyo 特許
3 *v/t invention* … no tokkyo o toru
…の特許を取る

patent leather enameru-gawa エナ
メル革

patently akiraka ni 明らかに

paternal *relative* chichikata (no) 父
方(の); *pride, love* chichioya (no)
父親(の)

paternalism kanshō 干渉

paternalistic kanshōgamashii 干渉
がましい

paternity chichioya de aru koto 父
親であること

path komichi 小道; (*to the front
door, also fig*) michi 道

pathetic aware (na) 哀れ(な); F
(*very bad*) nasakenai hodo heta
(na) 情けないほど下手(な)

pathological byōteki (na) 病的(な)

pathologist byōrigaku-sha 病理学者

pathology byōrigaku 病理学

patience nintai 忍耐

patient 1 *n* kanja 患者 **2** *adj*
gamanzuyoi 我慢強い; *just be ~!*
gaman shinasai 我慢しなさい

patiently gamanzuyoku 我慢強く

patio terasu テラス

patriot aikoku-sha 愛国者

patriotic aikokuteki (na) 愛国的(な)

patriotism aikoku-shin 愛国心

patrol 1 *n* junkai 巡回, patorōru パ
トロール; *be on ~* junkaichū de
aru 巡回中である **2** *v/t streets,
border* junkai suru 巡回する

patrol car patokā パトカー; **patrolman** junsa 巡査; **patrol wagon**
shūjin-gosō-sha 囚人護送車

patron (*of store, movie house*)
kokyaku 顧客; (*of artist, charity
etc*) kōen-sha 後援者

patronize (*be condescending to*) …
ni meuebutta taido o toru …に目
上ぶった態度を取る

patronizing meuebutta 目上ぶった

patter 1 *n* (*of rain etc*) parapara to
iu oto ぱらぱらという音; F (*of
salesman*) urikomi 売り込み **2** *v/i*
parapara to oto o tatete ochiru ぱ
らぱらと音を立てて落ちる

pattern *n* (*on fabric*) moyō 模様;
(*for knitting, sewing*) katagami 型
紙; (*model*) mihon 見本; (*in
behavior, events*) patān パターン

patterned moyōiri (no) 模様入り(の)

paunch taikobara 太鼓腹

pause 1 *n* ma 間 **2** *v/i* (*in speaking*)
ma o akeru 間をあける; (*in doing
sth*) chūdan suru 中断する **3** *v/t
tape* ichiji-teishi suru 一時停止す
る

pave hosō suru 舗装する; *~ the way
for* … e no michi o hiraku …への
道を開く

pavement (*roadway*) hosō 舗装; *Br
(sidewalk)* hodō 歩道

paving stone shikiishi 敷石

paw 1 *n* (*of animal*) ashi 足; F
(*hand*) te 手 **2** *v/t* F sawaru 触る

pawn¹ *n* (*in chess*) pōn ポーン; *fig*
tesaki 手先

pawn² *v/t* shichi ni ireru 質に入れる

pawnbroker shichi-ya 質屋

pawnshop shichi-ya 質屋

pay 1 *n* kyūryō 給料; *in the ~ of* …
ni yatowarete …に雇われて **2** *v/t
employee* … ni shiharau …に支払
う; *sum, bill* harau 払う; *~
attention* chūi o harau 注意を払う;
~ X a compliment X o homeru X
を褒める **3** *v/i* shiharai o suru 支
払いをする; (*be profitable*)
mōkaru もうかる; *it doesn't ~ to
…* … suru no wa wari ni awanai …
するのは割に合わない; *~ for
purchase* … no daikin o shiharau
…の代金を支払う; *you'll ~ for
this!* kitto kono mukui o ukeruzo
きっとこの報いを受けるぞ

♦**pay back** *person* … ni kane o
kaesu …に金を返す; *repay* … o
kaesu …を返す; (*get revenge on*) …
… ni shikaeshi o suru …に仕返し
をする

♦**pay in** (*to bank*) … o haraikomu
…を払い込む

♦ pay off 1 v/t *debt* … o sukkari hensai suru …をすっかり返済する; *corrupt official* … o baishū suru …を買収する **2** v/i (*be profitable*) hikiau 引き合う

♦ pay up sukkari harau すっかり払う

payable shiharaubeki 支払うべき

pay check kyūryō 給料

payday kyūryōbi 給料日

payee uketori-nin 受取人

pay envelope kyūryōbukuro 給料袋

payer shiharai-nin 支払い人

payment (*of bill*) shiharai 支払い; (*money*) shiharai-kingaku 支払い金額

pay phone kōshū-denwa 公衆電話

payroll (*money*) kyūryō-sōgaku 給料総額; (*employees*) jūgyōin-meibo 従業員名簿; **be on the ~** yatowarete iru 雇われている

PC (= *personal computer*) pasokon パソコン; (= *politically correct*) shakaiteki ni tadashii 社会的に正しい

pea endōmame えんどう豆

peace heiwa 平和; (*quietness*) shizuke-sa 静けさ; **~ of mind** kokoro no yasuragi 心の安らぎ

peaceable *person* odayaka (na) 穏やか(な)

Peace Corps Heiwa-butai 平和部隊

peaceful (*quiet*) shizuka (na) 静か(な); (*not violent*) heiwa (na) 平和(な)

peacefully heiwa ni 平和に; **sleep ~** anmin suru 安眠する

peach momo 桃

peacock kujaku くじゃく

peak 1 n (*of mountain*) chōjō 頂上; (*mountain*) mine 峰; *fig* pīku ピーク **2** v/i pīku ni tassuru ピークに達する

peak hours pīku-ji ピーク時

peanut pīnattsu ピーナッツ; **get paid ~s** F wazuka na kyūryō o uketoru わずかな給料を受け取る; **that's ~s to him** F hashitagane は した金

peanut butter pīnattsu-batā ピーナッツバター

pear (*oriental*) nashi なし; (*western*) seiyōnashi 西洋なし

pearl shinju 真珠

Pearl Harbor Shinjuwan 真珠湾

peasant nōmin 農民

pebble koishi 小石

pecan pekan ペカン

peck 1 n (*kiss*) karui kisu 軽いキス **2** v/t (*bite*) tsutsuku つつく; (*kiss*) … ni karuku kisu o suru …に軽くキスをする

peculiar (*strange*) myō (na) 妙(な); **~ to** … ni dokutoku (na) …に独特(な)

peculiarity (*strangeness*) kuse 癖; (*special feature*) tokuchō 特徴

pedal 1 n (*of bike*) pedaru ペダル **2** v/i (*turn ~s*) pedaru o fumu ペダルを踏む; (*cycle*) jitensha o kogu 自転車をこぐ

pedantic shakushi-jōgi (na) しゃくし定規(な)

pedestal (*for statue*) dai 台

pedestrian n hokō-sha 歩行者

pedestrian precinct sharyō-tachiiri-kinshi-kuiki 車両立ち入り禁止区域

pediatrician shōnikai 小児科医

pediatrics shōnika 小児科

pedicab rintaku 輪タク

pedigree 1 n (*of dog*) kettō 血統 **2** adj junketsu (no) 純血(の)

pee v/i F oshikko o suru おしっこをする

peek v/i nozomi suru のぞき見する

peel 1 n kawa 皮 **2** v/t *fruit, vegetables* … no kawa o muku …の皮をむく **3** v/i (*of nose, shoulders*) mukeru むける; (*of paint*) hageochiru はげ落ちる

peep → peek

peephole nozokiana のぞき穴

peer[1] n (*equal*) dōhai 同輩; (*in school*) dōkyūsei 同級生

peer[2] v/i jitto miru じっと見る; **~ through the mist** kiri o tōshite jitto miru 霧を通してじっと見る; **~ at** jitto miru じっと見る

peeved F okotta 怒った

peg n (*for hat, coat*) fukku フック;

(for tent) pegu ペグ; **off the ~** kisei (no) 既製(の)

pejorative keibetsuteki (na) 軽べつ的(な)

pellet chiisana tama 小さな玉; *(bullet)* sandan 散弾

pelt 1 *v/t*: **~ X with Y** X ni Y o nagetsukeru XにYを投げつける **2** *v/i*: **they ~ed along the road** zenryoku de hashiru 全力で走る; **it's ~ing down** ame ga hidoku futte iru 雨がひどく降っている

pelvis kotsuban 骨盤

pen¹ *n (ballpoint ~)* bōrupen ボールペン; *(fountain ~)* mannenhitsu 万年筆

pen² *(enclosure)* ori おり

pen³ → *penitentiary*

penalize *(punish)* shobatsu suru 処罰する; SP ... ni penarutī o kasuru ...にペナルティーを科する; *(disadvantage)* furi ni suru 不利にする

penalty *(punishment)* batsu 罰; *(fine)* bakkin 罰金; SP penarutī ペナルティー

penalty area SP penarutī-eria ペナルティーエリア

penalty clause iyaku-jōkō 違約条項

pencil enpitsu 鉛筆

pencil sharpener enpitsu-kezuri 鉛筆削り

pendant *(necklace)* pendanto ペンダント

pending 1 *prep* ... (suru) made ... (する)まで **2** *adj*: **be ~** *(awaiting a decision)* mikettei de aru 未決定である; LAW shinrichū de aru 審理中である; *(about to happen)* sashisematte iru 差し迫っている

penetrate *(of knife)* kantsū suru 貫通する; *(of water, smell)* ... ni shimikomu ...にしみ込む; *(of sun, light)* tōru 通る; *market* ... ni sannyū suru ...に参入する

penetrating *stare, sound* tsukisasu yō (na) 突き刺すよう(な); *analysis* surudoi 鋭い

penetration *(by enemy)* shinnyū 侵入; *(of market)* sannyū 参入

pen friend penfurendo ペンフレンド

penicillin penishirin ペニシリン

peninsula hantō 半島

penis penisu ペニス

penitence kōkai 後悔

penitent *adj* kōkai shite iru 後悔している

penitentiary keimusho 刑務所

pen name pennēmu ペンネーム

pennant penanto ペナント

penniless muichimon (no) 無一文(の)

pen pal penfurendo ペンフレンド

pension nenkin 年金

♦ pension off ... o oharaibako ni suru ...をお払い箱にする

pension fund nenkin-kikin 年金基金

pensive mono-omoi ni shizunda もの思いに沈んだ

Pentagon: **the ~** Amerika-kokubō-sōshō アメリカ国防総省

penthouse saijōkai no apāto 最上階のアパート

pent-up usseki shita うっ積した

penultimate saigo kara nibanme (no) 最後から二番目(の)

peony botan ぼたん

people hitobito 人々; *(inhabitants)* jūmin 住民; *(race, tribe)* minzoku 民族; **two ~** futari ふたり; **ten ~** jūnin 十人; **the ~** *(citizens)* shimin 市民; **the American ~** Amerika-kokumin アメリカ国民; **other ~** hoka no hito tachi 他の人たち; **~ say ...** ... to iu uwasa de aru ...といううわさである

pepper *(spice)* koshō こしょう; *(vegetable)* pīman ピーマン

peppermint *(candy)* minto-kyandī ミントキャンディー; *(flavoring)* pepāminto ペパーミント

pep talk: **give a ~** happa o kakeru 発破をかける

per ... ni tsuki ...につき

per annum ichinen ni tsuki 一年につき

perceive *(with senses)* chikaku suru 知覚する; *(view, interpret)* uketoru 受け取る

percent pāsento パーセント; **10 ~** juppāsento 十パーセント

percentage wariai 割合

perceptible ninshiki dekiru 認識できる

perceptibly ninshiki dekiru hodo ni 認識できるほどに

perception (*with senses*) chikaku 知覚; (*of situation*) ninshiki 認識; (*insight*) dōsatsuryoku 洞察力

perceptive *person, remark* surudoi 鋭い

perch 1 *n* (*for bird*) tomarigi 止り木 **2** *v/i* (*of bird*) tomaru 止まる; (*of person*) koshikakeru 腰掛ける

percolate *v/i* (*of coffee*) hairu はいる

percussion dagakki 打楽器

percussion instrument dagakki 打楽器

perfect 1 *n* GRAM kanryōkei 完了形 **2** *adj* (*flawless*) kanpeki (na) 完ぺき(な); (*ideal*) uttetsuke (no) うってつけ(の) **3** *v/t* kansei suru 完成する

perfection kanpeki 完ぺき; *to ~* kanpeki ni 完ぺきに

perfectionist *n* kanpeki-shugi-sha 完ぺき主義者

perfectly kanpeki ni 完ぺきに; (*totally*) mattaku 全く

perforated *line* mishinme (no) ミシン目(の)

perforations mishinme ミシン目

perform 1 *v/t* (*carry out*) okonau 行う; *play* jōen suru 上演する; *piece of music* ensō suru 演奏する **2** *v/i* (*of actor*) enzuru 演ずる; (*of theater group*) kōen suru 公演する; (*of musician*) ensō suru 演奏する; *~ well* (*of machine*) seinō ga yoi 性能がよい; *~ badly* (*of machine*) seinō ga warui 性能が悪い

performance (*by actor*) engi 演技; (*by theater company*) kōen 公演; (*by musician*) ensō 演奏; (*of employee, company etc*) seiseki 成績; (*by machine*) seinō 性能

performance car kōseinō-sha 高性能車

performer (*actor, dancer*) engi-sha 演技者; (*musician*) ensō-sha 演奏者

perfume kōsui 香水; (*of flower*) kaori 香り

perfunctory ii kagen (na) いい加減(な)

perhaps tabun たぶん; *you could ~ try...* ... o moshikashitara tameseru kamo ...をもしかしたら試せるかも

peril kiken 危険

perilous kiken (na) 危険(な)

perimeter shūi 周囲

perimeter fence bōgyo-fensu 防御フェンス

period (*time*) kikan 期間; (*menstruation*) seiri 生理; (*punctuation mark*) piriodo ピリオド; *I don't want to, ~!* sore wa iya nan desu, ijō それはいやなんです、以上

periodic shūkiteki (na) 周期的(な)

periodical *n* zasshi 雑誌

periodically teikiteki ni 定期的に

peripheral 1 *adj* (*not crucial*) samatsu (na) さ末(な) **2** *n* COMPUT shūhen-kiki 周辺機器

periphery shūhen 周辺

perish (*of rubber*) boroboro ni naru ぼろぼろになる; (*die*) shinu 死ぬ

perishable *food* kusariyasui 腐りやすい

perjure *~ oneself* gishō suru 偽証する

perjury gishō 偽証

perk *n* (*of job*) yakutoku 役得

♦perk up 1 *v/t* ... o genki-zukeru ...を元気づける **2** *v/i* genki ni naru 元気になる

perky (*cheerful*) akarui 明るい

perm 1 *n* pāma パーマ **2** *v/t* pāma o kakeru パーマをかける

permanent *adj* eikyūteki (na) 永久的(な); *~ employee* seishain 正社員; *~ job* teishoku 定職; *~ address* teijūsho 定住所

permanently eikyū ni 永久に

permissible yurusareru 許される

permission kyoka 許可

permissive amai 甘い

permit 1 *n* kyokashō 許可証 **2** *v/t* kyoka suru 許可する; *~ X to do Y* X ga Y suru no o kyoka suru Xが Yするのを許可する

perpendicular *adj* suichoku (no) 垂直(の)

perpetual (*permanent*) eikyūteki (na) 永久的(な); (*continual*) taema nai 絶え間ない

perpetually (*continually*) hikkirinashi ni ひっきりなしに

perpetuate eizoku saseru 永続させる

perplex nayamaseru 悩ませる

perplexed tomadotta とまどった

perplexity tomadoi とまどい

persecute (*oppress*) hakugai suru 迫害する; (*hound*) urusaku nayamasu うるさく悩ます

persecution hakugai 迫害

perseverance konki 根気

persevere ganbaru がんばる

persimmon kaki 柿

persist (*last*) tsuzuku 続く; (*keep on*) koshitsu suru 固執する; ~ *in doing X* Xshitsuzukeru Xし続ける

persistence (*perseverance*) konkizuyo-sa 根気強さ; (*continuation*) jizoku 持続

persistent nebarizuyoi 粘り強い; (*negative sense*) shitsukoi しつこい; *rain* itsu made mo tsuzuku いつまでも続く

persistently (*continually*) itsu mademo いつまでも

person hito 人; *in* ~ jibun de 自分で

personal *opinion, life* kojinteki (na) 個人的(な); *belongings, secretary* kojin (no) 個人(の); (*private*) shiteki (na) 私的(な); *don't make* ~ *remarks* hito o kizutsukeru koto wa iuna 人を傷つけることは言うな

personal assistant kojin-hisho 個人秘書; **personal computer** pā sonaru-konpyūtā パーソナルコンピューター; **personal hygiene** karada no eisei 体の衛生

personality jinkaku 人格; (*celebrity*) yūmeijin 有名人; *he has no* ~ kare wa kosei ga nai 彼は個性がない

personally (*for my part*) watashi to shite wa 私としては; (*in person*) jibun de 自分で; *don't take it* ~ ki

o waruku shinaide kudasai 気を悪くしないでください

personal pronoun ninshō-daimeishi 人称代名詞

personal stereo wōkuman ウォークマン®

personnel shokuin 職員; (*department*) jinjibu 人事部

personnel manager jinji-buchō 人事部長

perspiration hakkan 発汗

perspire ase o kaku 汗をかく

persuade settoku suru 説得する; ~ *X to do Y* X o settoku shite Y saseru Xを説得してYさせる

persuasion settoku 説得

persuasive settokuryoku no aru 説得力のある

pertinent tekisetsu (na) 適切(な)

perturb fuan ni saseru 不安にさせる

perturbing fuan (na) 不安(な)

pervasive *influence, ideas* hirogaru 広がる

perverse (*awkward*) tsumujimagari (no) つむじ曲り(の)

perversion (*sexual*) seiteki-tōsaku 性的倒錯

pervert *n* (*sexual*) hentai 変態

pessimism hikanron 悲観論

pessimist hikanron-sha 悲観論者

pessimistic hikanteki (na) 悲観的(な)

pest (*insect*) gaichū 害虫; (*animal*) gaijū 害獣; F (*person*) yakkaimono やっかいもの

pest control gaichū-kujo 害虫駆除

pester urusaku itte komaraseru うるさく言って困らせる; ~ *X to do Y* X ni Y suru yō ni segande komaraseru XにYするようにせがんで困らせる

pesticide satchūzai 殺虫剤

pet 1 *n* (*animal*) petto ペット; (*favorite*) okiniiri お気に入り **2** *adj* otokui (no) お得意(の) **3** *v/t animal* naderu なでる **4** *v/i* (*of couple*) pettingu suru ペッティングする

petal hanabira 花びら

♦**peter out** (*of path*) dandan nakunaru だんだんなくなる; (*of*

rain) shidai ni yamu しだいにやむ

petite kyasha (na) きゃしゃ(な)

petition *n* seigansho 請願書

petrified kyōfu ni karitaterareta 恐怖に駆り立てられた

petrify kyōfu ni karitateru 恐怖に駆り立てる

petrochemical *adj* sekiyu-kagaku (no) 石油化学(の)

petroleum sekiyu 石油

petty *person, behavior* kokoro no semai 心の狭い; *details, problem* toru ni taranai 取るに足らない

petty cash tōzayō genkin 当座用現金

petulant *person* okorippoi 怒りっぽい; *remark* okotta yō (na) 怒ったよう(な)

pew kyōkai no zaseki 教会の座席

pewter shirome しろめ

pharmaceutical seiyaku (no) 製薬 (の)

pharmaceuticals kusuri 薬

pharmacist (*in store*) yakuzaishi 薬剤師

pharmacy (*store*) yakkyoku 薬局

phase (*stage*) dankai 段階

♦ **phase in** ... o dankaiteki ni dōnyū suru ...を段階的に導入する

♦ **phase out** ... o dankaiteki ni haishi suru ...を段階的に廃止する

PhD (= *Doctor of Philosophy*) hakase-gō 博士号

pheasant kiji きじ

phenomenal odoroku hodo (no) 驚くほど(の)

phenomenally sugoku すごく

phenomenon genshō 現象

philanthropic nasakebukai 情け深い

philanthropist jizen-ka 慈善家

philanthropy jizen-jigyō 慈善事業

Philippines: *the* ~ Firipin-shotō フィリピン諸島

philistine *n* kyōyō no nai hito 教養のない人

philosopher tetsugaku-sha 哲学者

philosophical tetsugakuteki (na) 哲学的(な); *fig* reisei (na) 冷静(な)

philosophy tetsugaku 哲学; (*of life*) jinseikan 人生観

phobia kyōfushō 恐怖症

phone 1 *n* denwa 電話 **2** *v/t* ... ni denwa o kakeru ...に電話をかける **3** *v/i* denwa o suru 電話をする

phone book denwachō 電話帳; **phone booth** kōshū-denwa-bokkusu 公衆電話ボックス; **phone call** denwa 電話; **phone number** denwa-bangō 電話番号

phon(e)y *adj name, address* uso (no) うそ(の); *bill, accent* nise (no) 偽(の); *person* shin'yō dekinai 信用できない

photo *n* shashin 写真

photo album arubamu アルバム; **photocopier** kopī-ki コピー機; **photocopy 1** *n* kopī コピー **2** *v/t* kopī suru コピーする

photogenic shashin'utsuri no yoi 写真うつりのよい

photograph 1 *n* shashin 写真 **2** *v/t* ... no shashin o toru ...の写真をとる

photographer kameraman カメラマン

photography shashin-satsuei 写真撮影

phrase 1 *n* GRAM ku 句; (*what s.o. said*) kotoba 言葉; (*expression*) iikata 言い方 **2** *v/t* hyōgen suru 表現する

phrasebook kaiwa-hyōgenshū 会話表現集

physical 1 *adj* (*bodily*) shintaiteki (na) 身体的(な); *attraction, labor* nikutaiteki (na) 肉体的(な); **the ~ world** busshitsukai 物質界 **2** *n* MED kenkō-shindan 健康診断

physical handicap shintai-shōgai 身体障害

physically shintaiteki ni 身体的に, nikutaiteki ni 肉体的に

physician naikai 内科医

physicist butsuri-gakusha 物理学者

physics butsurigaku 物理学

physiotherapist butsuri-ryōhōshi 物理療法士

physiotherapy butsuri-ryōhō 物理療法

physique taikaku 体格

pianist pianisuto ピアニスト

piano piano ピアノ

pick 1 n: **take your ~** suki na no o erande kudasai 好きなのを選んでください **2** v/t (choose) erabu 選ぶ; flowers tsumu 摘む; fruit mogu もぐ; **~ one's nose** hanakuso o hojiru 鼻くそをほじる **3** v/i: **~ and choose** yorigonomi suru より好みする

♦**pick at**: **~ one's food** honno sukoshi shika tabenai ほんの少ししか食べない

♦**pick on** (treat unfairly) … o ijimeru …をいじめる; (select) … o erabidasu …を選び出す

♦**pick out** (identify) … o miwakeru …を見分ける

♦**pick up 1** v/t … o toriageru …を取り上げる; (from ground) … o hiroiageru …を拾い上げる; (collect: person) … o mukae ni iku …を迎えに行く; dry cleaning etc … o tori ni iku …を取りに行く; information … o atsumeru …を集める; (in car) … o noseru …を乗せる; (in sexual sense) … o hikkakeru …をひっかける; language, skill … o oboeru …を覚える; habit … o mi ni tsukeru …を身につける; illness … ni kakaru …にかかる; (buy) … o te ni ireru …を手に入れる; criminal … o taiho suru …を逮捕する **2** v/i (improve) yoku naru よくなる

picket 1 n (of strikers) pike ピケ **2** v/t kanshi suru 監視する

picket fence kuisaku くい柵

picket line pikerain ピケライン

pickle v/t suzuke ni suru 酢漬けにする

pickled plum umeboshi 梅干し

pickled vegetables (Japanese-style) tsukemono 漬物

pickles pikurusu ピクルス

pickpocket suri すり

pick-up (truck) kogata-torakku 小型トラック

picky F konomi no urusai 好みのうるさい

picnic 1 n pikunikku ピクニック **2** v/i pikunikku o suru ピクニックをする

picture 1 n e 絵; (photo) shashin 写真; **keep … in the ~** … ni jijō o shirasete oku …に事情を知らせておく **2** v/t sōzō suru 想像する

picture book ehon 絵本

picturesque e no yō ni utsukushii 絵のように美しい

pie pai パイ

piece (fragment) kakera かけら; (component) bubun 部分; (in board game) koma こま; **a ~ of pie / bread** hitokire no pai / pan 一切れのパイ／パン; **a ~ of string / ribbon** ippon no himo / ribon 一本のひも／リボン; **a ~ of advice / information** chotto shita adobaisu / jōhō ちょっとしたアドバイス／情報; **a ~ of music** ikkyoku no ongaku 一曲の音楽; **go to ~s** uchinomesareru 打ちのめされる; **take to ~s** barabara ni suru ばらばらにする

♦**piece together** broken plate … o tsunagiawaseru …をつなぎ合わせる; facts, evidence … o matomeageru …をまとめ上げる

piecemeal adv sukoshi zutsu 少しずつ

piecework n dekidakabarai no shigoto 出来高払いの仕事

pierce (penetrate) tsuranuku 貫く; (of bullet) kantsū suru 貫通する; ears … ni piasu o suru …にピアスをする

piercing noise mimi o tsunzaku 耳をつんざく; eyes sasu yō (na) 刺すよう(な); wind mi ni shimiru 身にしみる

pig (animal) buta 豚; (unpleasant person) butayarō 豚野郎

pigeon hato はと

pigheaded gōjō (na) 強情(な)

pigpen (also fig) buta-goya 豚小屋; **pigskin** buta-gawa 豚皮; **pigtail** osagegami おさげ髪

pile yama 山; **a ~ of work** yama hodo no shigoto 山ほどの仕事

♦**pile up 1** v/i (of work, bills) tamaru たまる **2** v/t … o tsumiageru …を積み上げる

piles MED ji ぢ

pile-up MOT tamatsuki-shōtotsu 玉突き衝突

pilfering kosodoro こそ泥

pilgrim junrei-sha 巡礼者

pilgrimage junrei 巡礼

pill kusuri 薬; **the ~** (contraceptive ~) piru ピル; **be on the ~** piru o nonde iru ピルを飲んでいる

pillar hashira 柱

pillion (of motor bike) kōbu-zaseki 後部座席

pillow n makura まくら

pillowcase makura-kabā まくらカバー

pilot 1 n (of airplane) pairotto パイロット **2** v/t airplane ... no pairotto o tsutomeru ...のパイロットを務める

pilot plant shiken-kōjō 試験工場

pilot scheme shikenteki na keikaku 試験的な計画

pimp n ponbiki ポン引き

pimple nikibi にきび

PIN (= personal identification number) anshō-bangō 暗証番号

pin 1 n (also in bowling) pin ピン; (for sewing) machibari 待ち針; (badge) burōchi ブローチ **2** v/t (hold down) osaetsukeru 押さえつける; (attach) pin de tomeru ピンで留める

♦ **pin down**: pin ... down to a date ... ni nichiji o yakusoku saseru ...に日時を約束させる

♦ **pin up** notice gabyō de tomeru 画びょうで留める

pinball (upright) pachinko パチンコ

pincers yattoko やっとこ

pinch 1 n: a ~ of salt shio hitotsumami 塩一つまみ; at a ~ masaka no toki ni wa まさかの時には **2** v/t tsuneru つねる **3** v/i (of shoes) shimetsukeru 締めつける

pine[1] n (tree) matsu 松

pine[2] v/i: ~ for koishigaru 恋しがる

pineapple painappuru パイナップル

ping 1 n chin to iu oto ちんという音 **2** v/i chin to iu oto ga suru ちんという音がする

ping-pong pinpon ピンポン

pink adj pinku-iro (no) ピンク色(の)

pinnacle fig zetchō 絶頂

pinpoint (identify) tsukitomeru つきとめる; (accurately describe) seikaku ni shimesu 正確に示す

pins and needles: have ~ shibireru しびれる

pinstripe adj pinsutoraipu ピンストライプ

pint painto パイント

pin-up (girl) pinnappu no moderu ピンナップのモデル

pioneer 1 n fig senku-sha 先駆者 **2** v/t ... no michi o hiraku ...の道をひらく

pioneering adj work senkuteki (na) 先駆的(な)

pious shinjinbukai 信心深い

pip n (of fruit) tane 種

pipe 1 n (for smoking, gas etc) paipu パイプ; **water ~** suidōkan 水道管 **2** v/t paipu de hakobu パイプで運ぶ

♦ **pipe down** damaru 黙る

piped music yūsen-ongaku-hōsō 有線音楽放送

pipeline yusōkan 輸送管; in the ~ shinkōchū de 進行中で

piping hot atsuatsu (no) 熱々(の)

pirate v/t software ... no kaizokuban o tsukuru ...の海賊版を作る

piss ∨ **1** v/i (urinate) shōben o suru 小便をする **2** n shōben 小便

pissed ∨ (annoyed) mutto shita むっとした; Br (drunk) yopparatta 酔っ払った

pistol pisutoru ピストル

piston pisuton ピストン

pit n (hole) ana 穴; (coal mine) tankō 炭坑; (in fruit) tane 種

pitch[1] n MUS chōshi 調子

pitch[2] 1 v/i (in baseball) tōkyū suru 投球する **2** v/t tent haru 張る; ball nageru 投げる

pitch black makkura (na) 真っ暗(な)

pitcher[1] (baseball) pitchā ピッチャー

pitcher[2] (container) mizusashi 水差し

piteous aware (na) 哀れ(な)

pitfall otoshiana 落し穴

pith (*of fruit*) nakakahi 中果皮

pitiful *sight* aware (na) 哀れ(な); *excuse etc* nasakenai 情けない

pitiless reikoku (na) 冷酷(な)

pittance suzume no namida すずめの涙

pity 1 *n* awaremi 哀れみ; *it's a ~ that* ... to wa zannen desu ...とは残念です; *what a ~!* zannen 残念; *take ~ on* kinodoku ni omou 気の毒に思う **2** *v/t person* kinodoku ni omou 気の毒に思う

pivot *v/i* kaiten suru 回転する

pizza piza ピザ

placard purakādo プラカード

place 1 *n* (*bar, restaurant*) mise 店; (*apartment, house*) uchi うち; (*in book*) yomikake no tokoro 読みかけの所; (*in race, competition*) jun'i 順位; (*seat*) seki 席; *at my / his ~* watashi/kare no uchi de 私/彼のうちで; *in ~ of* no kawari ni ...のかわりに; *feel out of ~* bachigai ni kanjiru 場違いに感じる; *take ~* okoru 起こる; (*of ceremony*) okonawareru 行われる; *in the first ~* (*firstly*) mazu daiichi ni まず第一に; (*in the beginning*) somosomo そもそも **2** *v/t* (*put*) oku 置く; (*identify*) ... ga dare ka omoidasu ...がだれか思い出す; *~ an order* chūmon suru 注文をする

place mat ranchonmatto ランチョンマット

placid ochitsuita 落ち着いた

plague 1 *n* ekibyō 疫病 **2** *v/t* (*bother*) nayamasu 悩ます

plaice karei かれい

plain[1] *n* heichi 平地

plain[2] 1 *adj* (*clear, obvious*) meihaku (na) 明白(な); (*not elaborate*) kanso (na) 簡素(な); (*not flavored*) fūmi no tsuite inai 風味のついていない; (*not pretty*) saenai さえない; (*not patterned*) muji (no) 無地(の); (*blunt*) sotchoku (na) 率直(な); *~ chocolate* burakku-chokorēto ブラックチョコレート **2** *adv* akiraka

ni 明らかに; *it's ~ crazy* mattaku dōka shite iru まったくどうかしている

plain clothes: *in ~* shifuku de 私服で

plainly (*clearly*) akiraka ni 明らかに; (*bluntly*) sotchoku ni 率直に; (*simply*) kanso ni 簡素に

plain-spoken sotchoku (na) 率直(な)

plaintiff genkoku 原告

plaintive kanashisō (na) 悲しそう(な)

plait 1 *n* (*in hair*) osagegami おさげ髪 **2** *v/t hair* amu 編む

plan 1 *n* (*project*) keikaku 計画; (*intention*) kangae 考え; (*drawing*) zumen 図面 **2** *v/t* (*prepare*) keikaku suru 計画する; (*design*) sekkei suru 設計する; *~ to do, ~ on doing* ... suru tsumori de aru ...するつもりである **3** *v/i* keikaku suru 計画する

plane[1] *n* (*airplane*) hikōki 飛行機

plane[2] (*tool*) kanna かんな

planet wakusei 惑星

plank (*of wood*) ita 板; *fig* (*of policy*) seitō-kōryō no shuyō-kōmoku 政党綱領の主要項目

planning keikaku 計画; *at the ~ stage* keikakuchū de 計画中で

plant[1] 1 *n* shokubutsu 植物 **2** *v/t* ueru 植える

plant[2] *n* (*factory*) kōjō 工場; (*equipment*) kikai-setsubi 機械設備

plantation purantēshon プランテーション

plaque (*on wall*) meiban 銘板; (*on teeth*) shikō 歯こう

plaster 1 *n* (*on wall, ceiling*) shikkui しっくい **2** *v/t wall, ceiling* ... ni shikkui o nuru ...にしっくいを塗る; *be ~ed with* (*with posters, notices*) ... ga betabeta hatte aru ...がべたべた張ってある; (*with make-up etc*) ... ga betabeta nutte aru ...がべたべた塗ってある

plaster cast gipusu ギプス

plastic 1 *n* purasuchikku プラスチック **2** *adj* purasuchikku-sei (no) プラスチック製(の)

plastic bag binīru-bukuro ビニール袋; **plastic money** kurejitto-kādo クレジットカード; **plastic surgeon** keisei-gekai 形成外科医; **plastic surgery** keisei-geka 形成外科; (*cosmetic*) seikei-shujutsu 整形手術

plate *n* sara 皿; (*of metal*) kinzokuban 金属板; (*license ~*) nanbā-purēto ナンバープレート

plateau kōgen 高原

platform (*stage*) endan 演壇; *fig* (*political*) kōryō 綱領; RAIL purattohōmu プラットホーム; **~ 6** roku-bansen 六番線

platform ticket nyūjōken 入場券

platinum 1 *n* purachina プラチナ **2** *adj* purachina-sei (no) プラチナ製(の)

platitude kimarimonku 決まり文句

platonic *relationship* puratonikku (na) プラトニック(な)

platoon (*of soldiers*) shōtai 小隊

platter (*for food*) ōzara 大皿

plausible *excuse* mottomorashii もっともらしい

play 1 *n* THEA geki 劇; (*on TV*) dorama ドラマ; (*of children*) asobi 遊び; TECH asobi あそび; SP purē プレー **2** *v/i* (*of children*) asobu 遊ぶ; (*of musician*) ensō suru 演奏する; (SP: *perform*) suru する; (SP: *take part*) shutsujō suru 出場する **3** *v/t* *musical instrument, music* hiku 弾く; *wind instrument* fuku 吹く; *game* suru する; *opponent ... to* shiai o suru ...と試合をする; (*perform*): *Macbeth etc*) jōen suru 上演する; *particular role* enjiru 演じる; *pirates, house ...* gokko o shite asobu ...ごっこをして遊ぶ; **~ a joke on** karakau からかう

♦ **play around** (*be unfaithful*) asobimawaru 遊びまわる; **~ with** ... o asobimawatte iru ...と遊びまわっている

♦ **play down** ... o karuku atsukau ...を軽く扱う

♦ **play up** (*of machine, tooth*) chōshi ga waruku naru 調子が悪くなる; (*of child*) atsukainikuku naru 扱

いにくくなる

playact (*pretend*) furi o suru ふりをする

playback saisei 再生

playboy purēbōi プレーボーイ

player SP senshu 選手; (*musician*) ensō-sha 演奏者; (*actor*) haiyū 俳優

playful *punch* honki de nai 本気でない; *person, dog* yōki (na) 陽気(な)

playground asobiba 遊び場

playing card toranpu トランプ

playing field undōjō 運動場

playwright geki-sakka 劇作家

plaza (*for shopping*) shoppingu-sentā ショッピングセンター

plea *n* tangan 嘆願

plead *v/i*: **~ for** tangan suru 嘆願する; **~ guilty** tsumi o mitomeru 罪を認める; **~ not guilty** muzai o shuchō suru 無罪を主張する; **~ with ...** ni kongan suru ...に懇願する

pleasant *weather* kimochi no yoi 気持ちのよい; *room, hotel* kaiteki (na) 快適(な); *person* kanji no ii 感じのいい; *meal* tanoshii 楽しい

please 1 *adv* dōzo どうぞ; **will you pass the salt ~** sumimasen ga, shio o totte itadakemasu ka すみませんが、塩をとっていただけますか; **close the door ~** doa o shimete kudasai ドアを閉めてください; **more tea? - yes,** ocha no okawari wa - hai, arigatō お茶のおかわりは-はい、ありがとう; **~ do** ē, dōzo ええ、どうぞ **2** *v/t* yorokobasu 喜ばす; **~ yourself** katte ni shinasai 勝手にしなさい

pleased yorokonda 喜んだ; **~ to meet you** hajimemashite はじめまして

pleasing *design, person* kanji no ii 感じのいい; *weather, sound* kokochiyoi 心地よい

pleasure (*happiness, satisfaction*) yorokobi 喜び; (*enjoyment*) tanoshimi 楽しみ; (*not business*) asobi 遊び; **it's a ~** (*you're welcome*) dō itashimashite どういたしまして; **with ~** yorokonde 喜

んで

pleat n (*in skirt*) purītsu プリーツ

pledge 1 n (*promise*) yakusoku 約束; (*security*) teitō 抵当 **2** v/t (*promise*) chikau 誓う

Pledge of Allegiance Chūsei no Chikai 忠誠の誓い

plentiful jūbun (na) 十分(な)

plenty: **~ of** (*a lot of*) takusan (no) たくさん(の); (*enough*) jūbun (na) 十分(な); **that's ~** jūbun desu 十分です; **there's ~ for everyone** minna no bun jūbun ni arimasu みんなの分十分にあります

pliable jūnan (na) 柔軟(な)

pliers penchi ペンチ; **a pair of ~** penchi itchō ペンチ一丁

plight kukyō 苦境

plod v/i (*walk*) tobotobo aruku とぼとぼ歩く

♦ **plod along** (*with a job*) kotsukotsu hataraku こつこつ働く

plodder (*at work*) jimichi na hito 地道人; (*at school*) gariben がり勉

plot¹ n (*land*) jisho 地所

plot² 1 n (*conspiracy*) inbō 陰謀; (*of novel*) suji 筋 **2** v/t&v/i takuramu たくらむ

plotter inbō-sha 陰謀者; COMPUT purottā プロッター

plow 1 n suki すき **2** v/t & v/i tagayasu 耕す

♦ **plow back** profits ... o saitōshi suru ...を再投資する

pluck v/t eyebrows nuku 抜く; chicken ... no hane o mushiru ...の羽をむしる

♦ **pluck up**: **~ courage** yūki o dasu 勇気を出す

plug 1 n (*for sink, bath*) sen 栓; (*electrical*) puragu プラグ; (*spark ~*) tenka-puragu 点火プラグ; (*for new book etc*) senden 宣伝 **2** v/t hole ... ni sen o suru ...に栓をする; new book etc senden suru 宣伝する

♦ **plug away** F kotsukotsu yaru こつこつやる

♦ **plug in** v/t puragu o sashikomu プラグを差し込む

plum 1 n puramu プラム; (*Japanese*) ume 梅 **2** adj F oishii おいしい

plumage tori no hane 鳥の羽

plumb adj suichoku 垂直(の)

plumber haikankō 配管工

plumbing (*pipes*) haikan 配管

plummet (*of airplane*) suichoku ni rakka suru 垂直に落下する; (*of prices*) kyūraku suru 急落する

plump adj person, hand potchari shita ぽっちゃりした; baby, chicken marumaru to futotta まるまると太った

♦ **plump for** ... o erabu ...を選ぶ

plunge 1 n tobikomi 飛び込み; (*in prices*) kyūraku 急落; **take the ~** omoikitte yatte miru 思い切ってやってみる **2** v/i tobikomu 飛び込む; (*of prices*) kyūraku suru 急落する **3** v/t hand tsukkomu 突っ込む; knife tsukisasu 突き刺す; **the city was ~d into darkness** totsuzen machijū ga makkura ni natta 突然街中が真っ暗になった; **the news ~d him into despair** sono nyūsu o kiite kare wa zetsubō ni ochiitta そのニュースを聞いて彼は絶望に陥った

plunging neckline munamoto no aita 胸元の開いた

plural 1 adj fukusū (no) 複数(の) **2** n fukusūkei 複数形

plus 1 prep: **2 ~ 2 is 4** ni tasu ni wa yon da 2足す2は4だ; **~ tax** zeikin o kuwaete 税金を加えて; **children ~ teachers** kodomotachi no hoka ni sensei 子供たちの他に先生 **2** adj ijō 以上; **$500 ~** gohyaku doru ijō 500ドル以上 **3** n (*symbol*) purasu プラス; (*advantage*) riten 利点 **4** conj (*moreover, in addition*) sore ni kuwaete それに加えて

plush gōka 豪華(な)

plywood beniya-ita ベニヤ板

p.m. gogo (no) 午後(の)

pneumatic kūki no haitta 空気の入った

pneumatic drill kūki-doriru 空気ドリル

pneumonia haien 肺炎

poach¹ v/t (*cook*) yuderu ゆでる

poach² 1 v/i (*for fish*) mitsuryō

poached egg otoshitamago 落し卵

P.O. Box shishobako 私書箱

pocket 1 n poketto ポケット; *line one's own ~* shifuku o koyasu 私腹をこやす; *be out of ~* son o suru 損をする **2** adj (*miniature*) kogata (no) 小型(の) **3** v/t (*steal*) chakufuku suru 着服する; (*put in ~*) poketto ni shimau ポケットにしまう

pocketbook (*purse*) handobaggu ハンドバッグ; (*billfold*) saifu 財布; (*book*) bunkobon 文庫本; **pocket calculator** dentaku 電卓; **pocketknife** pokettonaifu ポケットナイフ

podium endai 演台; MUS shikidai 指揮台

poem shi 詩

poet shijin 詩人

poetic shiteki (na) 詩的(な)

poetic justice inga-ōhō 因果応報

poetry shi 詩

poignant itamashii 痛ましい

point 1 n (*of pencil, knife*) saki 先; (*in competition, exam*) tensū 点数; (*purpose*) imi 意味; (*moment*) jiten 時点; (*in argument, discussion*) yōten 要点; (*in decimals*) ten 点; (*decimal ~*) shōsūten 少数点; *beside the ~* kentōchigai de 見当違いで; *be on the ~ of doing X* X suru tokoro de aru Xするところである; *get to the ~* hondai ni hairu 本題に入る; *there's no ~ in waiting / trying* matte ite mo / tsuzukete mo muimi da 待っていても/続けても無意味だ **2** v/i sasu 指す **3** v/t gun mukeru 向ける

♦**point at** (*with finger*) … o yubisasu …を指さす

♦**point out** *sights* … o sashishimesu …を指し示す; *advantages etc* … o shiteki suru …を指摘する

♦**point to** (*with finger*) … o sasu …を指す; *fig* (*indicate*) … o shimesu

…を示す

point-blank 1 adj *refusal* tantō-chokunyū (na) 単刀直入(な); *at ~ range* shikin-kyori de 至近距離で **2** adv *refuse, deny* kippari to きっぱりと

pointed *remark* shinratsu (na) しんらつ(な)

pointer (*for teacher*) sashibō 指し棒; (*hint*) jogen 助言; (*sign, indication*) shishin 指針

pointless muimi (na) 無意味(な); *it's ~ trying to persuade him* kare o settoku-shiyō to suru no wa muimi da 彼を説得しようとするのは無意味だ

point-of-sale hanbaiten 販売店; (*promotional material*) hanbaisokushin zairyō 販売促進材料

point of view kanten 観点

poise ochitsuki 落ち着き

poised *person* ochitsuita 落ち着いた

poison 1 n doku 毒 **2** v/t *person, animal* … ni doku o moru …に毒を盛る; *water, land* osen suru 汚染する; *relationship* dame ni suru だめにする

poisonous yūdoku (na) 有毒(な)

poke v/t (*prod*) tsutsuku つつく; (*stick*) tsukkomu 突っ込む; *~ fun at* … o karakau …をからかう; *~ one's nose into* … o sensaku suru …をせん索する; *~ one's head out of the window* mado no soto ni atama o tsukidasu 窓の外に頭を突き出す

♦**poke around** sagashimawaru 探し回る

poker (*card game*) pōkā ポーカー

poky (*cramped*) semakurushii 狭苦しい

Poland Pōrando ポーランド

polar (*Arctic*) hokkyoku (no) 北極(の); (*Antarctic*) nankyoku (no) 南極(の)

polar bear shirokuma 白くま

polarize v/t ryōkyokuka suru 両極化する

Pole Pōrando-jin ポーランド人

pole[1] (*of wood, metal*) bō 棒

pole² (*of earth*) kyoku 極

polevault n bōtakatobi 棒高跳び

police n keisatsu 警察

police box kōban 交番; **policeman** keikan 警官; **police state** keisatsu-kokka 警察国家; **police station** keisatsu-sho 警察署; **policewoman** fujin-keikan 婦人警官

policy¹ (*of government*) seisaku 政策; (*of company, individual*) hōshin 方針

policy² (*insurance* ~) hoken-shōken 保険証券

polio shōni-mahi 小児まひ

Polish 1 adj Pōrando (no) ポーランド(の) **2** n Pōrando-go ポーランド語

polish 1 n (*product*) tsuyadashi つや出し; (*nail* ~) manikyua マニキュア; **shoe** ~ kutsuzumi 靴墨 **2** v/t migaku 磨く; **speech** ... ni migaki o kakeru ...に磨きをかける

♦ **polish off** food ... o tairageru ...を平らげる

♦ **polish up** skill ... o fukushū suru ...を復習する; work ... no shiage o suru ...の仕上げをする

polished performance senren sareta 洗練された

polite reigi-tadashii 礼儀正しい

politely teinei ni ていねいに

politeness reigitadashi-sa 礼儀正しさ

political career seiji (no) 政治(の); consideration, problem seijiteki (na) 政治的(な); ~ **party** seitō 政党; ~ **correspondent** seijibu-kisha 政治部記者

politically correct shakaiteki ni tadashii 社会的に正しい

politician seijika 政治家

politics seiji 政治; **what are his ~?** kare no seiji ni kan suru kangaekata wa dō nan desu ka 彼の政治に関する考え方はどうなんですか

poll 1 n (*survey*) seron-chōsa 世論調査; **the** ~**s** (*election*) tōhyō 投票; **go to the** ~**s** tōhyō suru 投票する **2** v/t people ... no seron-chōsa o suru ...の世論調査をする; votes

kakutoku suru 獲得する

pollen kafun 花粉

pollen count kafunsū 花粉数

polling booth tōhyō-yōshi-kinyūjo 投票用紙記入所

pollster seron-chōsain 世論調査員

pollutant osen-busshitsu 汚染物質

pollute osen suru 汚染する

pollution osen 汚染

polo neck tātorunekku タートルネック

polo shirt poroshatsu ポロシャツ

polyester poriesuteru ポリエステル

polyethylene poriechiren ポリエチレン

polystyrene porisuchiren ポリスチレン

polyunsaturated tafuhōwa (no) 多不飽和(の)

pompous mottaibutta もったいぶった

pond ike 池

ponder v/i jukkō suru 熟考する

pony ponī ポニー

ponytail ponītēru ポニーテール

poodle pūdoru プードル

pool¹ (*swimming* ~) pūru プール; (*of water, blood*) tamari たまり

pool² (*game*) pūru プール

pool³ v/t resources mochiyoru 持ちよる

pool hall tamatsukijō 玉突き場

pool table pūru-dai プール台

pooped F hetoheto ni tsukareta へとへとに疲れた

poor 1 adj (*not wealthy*) mazushii 貧しい; (*not good*) heta (na) 下手 (な); (*unfortunate*) aware (na) 哀れ(な); **be in** ~ **health** kenkō ga sugurenai 健康がすぐれない; ~ **old Tony!** Tonī mo kinodoku ni トニーも気の毒に **2** n: **the** ~ mazushii hitobito 貧しい人々

poorly 1 adv heta ni 下手に **2** adj (*unwell*) kibun ga sugurenai 気分がすぐれない

pop¹ 1 n (*noise*) pon to iu oto ぽんという音 **2** v/i (*of balloon etc*) pon to iu oto o tateru ぽんという音を立てる **3** v/t cork pon to nuku ぽんと抜く; balloon pān to haretsu saseru ぱーんと破裂させる

pop² 1 n MUS poppusu ポップス
2 adj poppusu (no) ポップス(の)

pop³ (father) tōchan 父ちゃん

pop⁴ F (put) hyoi to ireru ひょいと
入れる

♦**pop up** v/i (appear) hyokkori
arawareru ひょっこり現われる

popcorn poppukōn ポップコーン

pope Rōma-hōō ローマ法王

poppy popī ポピー

Popsicle® aisukyandī アイスキャ
ンディー

pop song poppusu ポップス

popular ninki no aru 人気のある;
belief, support ippan (no) 一般(の)

popularity ninki 人気

populate shokumin suru 植民する

population jinkō 人口

porcelain 1 n jiki 磁器 2 adj jiki
(no) 磁器(の)

porch beranda ベランダ

porcupine yama-arashi やまあらし

pore (of skin) keana 毛穴

♦**pore over** designs, map ... o
jukkō suru ...を熟考する;
document ... o jukudoku suru ...を
熟読する

pork butaniku 豚肉

porn n poruno ポルノ

porn(o) adj poruno (no) ポルノ(の)

pornographic poruno (no) ポルノ
(の)

pornography poruno ポルノ

porous kyūsui shiyasui 吸水しやす
い

port¹ n (town) minatomachi 港町;
(area) minato 港

port² adj (left-hand) sagen (no) 左
げん(の)

portable 1 adj keitaiyō (no) 携帯用
(の) 2 n COMPUT rapputoppu ラッ
プトップ; (TV set) keitaiyō terebi
携帯用テレビ

porthole NAUT gensō げん窓

portion n bubun 部分; (of food)
ichininmae 1人前

portrait 1 n (painting, photograph)
shōzōga 肖像画; (depiction) byōsha
描写 2 adv print tatemuki 縦向き

portray (of artist) ... no shōzō o

egaku ...の肖像を描く; (of actor)
... no yaku o enjiru ...の役を演じ
る; (of author) egaku 描く

portrayal (by actor) engi 演技; (by
author) byōsha 描写

Portugal Porutogaru ポルトガル

Portuguese 1 adj Porutogaru (no)
ポルトガル(の) 2 n (person)
Porutogaru-jin ポルトガル人;
(language) Porutogaru-go ポルト
ガル語

pose 1 n (pretense) misekake 見せ
かけ 2 v/i (for artist,
photographer) pōzu o toru ポーズ
をとる; ~ as ... no furi o suru ...の
ふりをする 3 v/t: ~ a problem
mondai o umu 問題を生む

position 1 n (location) ichi 位置;
(stance) shisei 姿勢; (in race,
competition) jun'i 順位; (occupied
by soldiers) jinchi 陣地; (point of
view) iken 意見; (situation)
tachiba 立場; (job) shoku 職;
(status) chii 地位; fourth ~ (in
race) daiyon'i 第四位 2 v/t haichi
suru 配置する

positive attitude sekkyokuteki (na)
積極的(な); response maemuki
(na) 前向き(な); medical test yōsei
(no) 陽性(の); GRAM genkyū (no)
原級(の); ELEC purasu (no) プラス
(の); be ~ (sure) jishin ga aru 自
信がある; are you sure? - I'm ~
tashika desu ka - machigai
arimasen 確かですか - 間違いあり
ません

positively (decidedly) mattaku まっ
たく; (definitely) tashika ni 確かに

possess car, house shoyū suru 所有
する; sth that can be carried shoji
suru 所持する; skills ... ga aru ...
がある

possession (of car, house) shoyū 所
有; (of sth that can be carried)
shoji 所持; (thing owned)
shoyūbutsu 所有物; ~s shoyūbutsu
所有物

possessive person dokusen'yoku
no tsuyoi 独占欲の強い; GRAM
shoyūkaku (no) 所有格(の)

possibility kanōsei 可能性

possible kanō (na) 可能(な); *the quickest ~ route* saitan no michi 最短の道; *the highest ~ speed* saidaigen no supīdo 最大限のスピード; *the best ~ ...* dekirudake yoi ... できるだけよい...

possibly dekirudake できるだけ; (*perhaps*) osoraku おそらく; *that can't ~ be right* sore wa totemo tadashii to wa omoenai それはとても正しいとは思えない; *could you ~ tell me the time?* jikan o oshiete itadakemasen ka 時間を教えていただけませんか

post¹ 1 n (*of wood, metal*) hashira 柱 **2** v/t *notice* haru はる; *profits* kōhyō suru 公表する; *keep ~ed* (*informed*) ... ni shiraseru ...に知らせる

post² 1 n (*place of duty*) shoku 職; (*of soldier*) mochiba 持ち場 **2** v/t *soldier, employee* haizoku suru 配属する; *guards* haichi suru 配置する

postage yūsōryō 郵送料

postal yūbin (no) 郵便(の)

postcard hagaki はがき

postdate sakihizuke ni suru 先日付にする

poster posutā ポスター

posterior n F oshiri おしり

posterity kōsei 後世

postgraduate 1 n daigakuinsei 大学院生 **2** adj daigakuin (no) 大学院(の)

posthumous shigo (no) 死後(の)

posthumously shigo ni 死後に

posting (*assignment*) haizoku 配属

postmark keshiin 消印

postmortem kenshi 検死

post office yūbinkyoku 郵便局

postpone enki suru 延期する

postponement enki 延期

posture shisei 姿勢

postwar sengo (no) 戦後(の)

pot¹ (*for cooking in*) nabe なべ; (*for coffee, tea*) potto ポット; (*for plant*) uekibachi 植木鉢

pot² F (*marijuana*) marifana マリファナ

potato jagaimo じゃがいも

potato chips poteto-chippusu ポテトチップス

potent *medicine* kikime no aru 効き目のある

potential 1 adj kanō (na) 可能(な); *customer, problem* senzaiteki (na) 潜在的(な); *failure* okoriuru 起こりうる **2** n kanōsei 可能性

potentially senzaiteki ni 潜在的に

pothole (*in road*) ana 穴

potter n tōkō 陶工

pottery (*activity*) tōgei 陶芸; (*items*) tōki 陶器; (*place*) tōki-seizōjo 陶器製造所

potty n (*for baby*) omaru おまる

pouch (*bag*) pōchi ポーチ

poultry (*birds*) kakin 家きん; (*meat*) toriniku 鳥肉

pounce v/i (*of animal*) tobikakaru とびかかる; *fig* kyūshū suru 急襲する

pound¹ n (*weight*) pondo ポンド

pound² (*for strays*) ori おり; (*for cars*) kuruma-okiba 車置き場

pound³ v/i (*of heart*) dokidoki suru どきどきする; *~ on door, desk ...* o dondon tataku ...をどんどんたたく; *~ on the roof* (*of rain*) yane ni tatakitsukeru 屋根にたたきつける

pound sterling Igirisu-pondo イギリスポンド

pour 1 v/t *drink* tsugu つぐ; *oil, water* ireru 入れる **2** v/i: *it's ~ing* (*with rain*) doshaburi da どしゃ降りだ

♦ **pour out** *drink* ... o tsugu つぐ; *troubles* ... o buchimakeru ...をぶちまける

pout v/i fukureru 膨れる

poverty hinkon 貧困

poverty-stricken hijō ni binbō (na) 非常に貧乏(な)

powder 1 n kona 粉; (*for face*) oshiroi おしろい **2** v/t *face* ... ni oshiroi o nuru ...におしろいを塗る

powder room keshōshitsu 化粧室

power 1 n (*strength*) chikara 力; (*of engine*) shutsuryoku 出力; (*authority*) kenryoku 権力; (*of parliament*) kengen 権限; (*energy*) dōryoku 動力; (*electricity*) denryoku 電力; *atomic ~*

genshiryoku 原子力; *in ~* POL
seiken o nigitta 政権を握った; *fall
from ~* POL shikkyaku suru 失脚す
る 2 *v/t*: *be ~ed by* ... de ugoku ...
で動く

power cut teiden 停電

powerful *blow, drug* kyōryoku (na)
強力(な); *car, engine* bariki no aru
馬力のある; *man, union* yūryoku
(na) 有力(な)

powerless muryoku (na) 無力(な);
be ~ to ... ... suru chikara ga nai
...する力がない

power line densen 電線; **power
outage** teiden 停電; **power station**
hatsudensho 発電所; **power
steering** pawā-sutearingu パワー
ステアリング; **power unit** pawā-
yunitto パワーユニット

PR (= *public relations*) piiaru ピー
アール

practical *experience* jissaiteki (na)
実際的(な); *studies, work* jitchi
(no) 実地(の); *person* genjitsuteki
(na) 現実的(な); *color, knowledge*
jitsuyōteki (na) 実用的(な)

practical joke warufuzake 悪ふざけ

practically *behave, think*
genjitsuteki ni 現実的に; (*almost*)
jisshitsuteki ni 実質的に

practice 1 *n* (*not theory*) jissen 実
践; (*training*) renshū 練習;
(*rehearsal*) keiko けいこ;
(*custom*) shūkan 習慣; *in ~* (*in
reality*) jissai ni wa 実際には; *be
out of ~* renshū-busoku de aru 練
習不足である 2 *v/i* renshū suru 練
習する 3 *v/t* renshū suru 練習する;
~ law bengoshi o shite iru 弁護士
をしている; *~ medicine* isha o
shite iru 医者をしている

pragmatic jitsuyōteki (na) 実用的
(な)

pragmatism jitsuyō-shugi 実用主義

prairie sōgen 草原

praise 1 *n* shōsan 称賛 2 *v/t* shōsan
suru 称賛する

praiseworthy shōsan ni atai suru
称賛に値する

prank itazura いたずら

prattle *v/i* mudabanashi o suru むだ
話をする

pray inoru 祈る

prayer inori no kotoba 祈りの言葉;
(*praying*) inori 祈り

preach 1 *v/i* (*in church*) sekkyō o
suru 説教をする; (*moralize*)
osekkyō o suru お説教をする 2 *v/t*
sermon ... ni tsuite sekkyō o suru
...について説教をする

preacher sekkyōshi 説教師

precarious fuantei 不安定(な)

precariously fuantei ni 不安定に

precaution yōjin 用心; *take ~s* (*use
contraceptive*) hinin suru 避妊する

precautionary *measure* yōjin no
tame (no) 用心のため(の)

precede *v/t* (*in time*) ... yori saki ni
kuru ...より先に来る; (*go ahead
of*) ... yori saki ni iku ...より先に
行く

precedence: *take ~* yūsen sareru
優先される; *take ~ over ...* ...
yori yūsen suru ...より優先する

precedent senrei 先例

preceding mae (no) 前(の)

precinct (*district*) chiku 地区

precious kichō 貴重

precipitate *v/t crisis* hayameru 早
める

précis *n* yōyaku 要約

precise seikaku (na) 正確(な)

precisely seikaku ni 正確に; *~!*
sono tōri そのとおり

precision seikaku-sa 正確さ

precocious *child* sōjuku 早熟
(な)

preconceived: *~ idea* sennyūkan 先
入観

precondition zentei-jōken 前提条件

predator (*animal*) hoshoku-
dōbutsu 捕食動物

predecessor (*in job*) zennin-sha 前
任者; (*machine*) mae no mono 前の
もの

predestination unmei no yoteisetsu
運命の予定説

predicament kukyō 苦境

predict yogen suru 予言する

predictable yosō no tsuku 予想のつ
く

prediction yogen 予言

predominant *question, color* medatsu 目立つ; *mood* attōteki (na) 圧倒的(な)

predominantly attōteki ni attōteki ni 圧倒的に

predominate ... ga yūsei de aru ... が優勢である

prefabricated purehabu (no) プレハブ(の)

preface *n* jobun 序文

prefecture ken 県

prefer ... no hō o konomu ...のほうを好む; **~ X to Y** Y yori X no hō ga suki de aru X より Y よりX のほうが好きである; **~ to do** ... suru hō ga suki de aru ...するほうが好きである

preferable nozomashii 望ましい; **be ~ to** ... yori nozomashii ...より望ましい

preferably dekireba できれば

preference konomi 好み

preferential yūsen (no) 優先(の)

prefix settōji 接頭辞

pregnancy ninshin 妊娠

pregnant ninshin shite iru 妊娠している

prehistoric senshi-jidai (no) 先史時代(の)

prejudice 1 *n* henken 偏見 **2** *v/t person* ... ni henken o idakaseru ...に偏見を抱かせる; *chances* sokonau 損なう

prejudiced henken no aru 偏見のある

preliminary *adj* yobiteki (na) 予備的(な)

premarital konzen (no) 婚前(の)

premature *action, decision* hayamatta 早まった; *death, arrival* hayasugita 早過ぎた; **~ baby** mijukuji 未熟児

premeditated keikakuteki (na) 計画的(な)

premier *n* POL shushō 首相

première *n* (*of movie*) fūkiri 封切り; (*of play*) shonichi 初日

premises (*of business*) shikichi 敷地; (*of store*) mise 店

premium *n* (*in insurance*) hokenryō 保険料

premonition yokan 予感

prenatal shussan mae (no) 出産前

(の)

preoccupied uwa no sora (no) うわの空(の)

preparation (*act*) junbi 準備; *in ~ for* ... no junbi de ...の準備で; **~s** junbi 準備

prepare 1 *v/t* ... no junbi o suru ...の準備をする; **be ~d to do X** (*willing*) yorokonde X suru 喜んでX する **2** *v/i* junbi suru 準備する

preposition zenchishi 前置詞

preposterous tohō mo nai 途方もない

prerequisite hissu-jōken 必須条件

prescribe (*of doctor*) shohō suru 処方する

prescription MED shohōsen 処方せん

presence iru koto 居ること; *in the ~ of* ... no mae de ...の前で

presence of mind kiten 機転

present[1] **1** *adj* (*current*) genzai (no) 現在(の); **be ~** iru いる; (*at conference, meeting, in class*) shusseki shite iru 出席している **2** *n*: *the ~* genzai 現在; GRAM genzaikei 現在形; *at ~* ima no tokoro 今のところ

present[2] **1** *n* (*gift*) purezento プレゼント **2** *v/t award, bouquet* okuru 贈る; *program* teikyō suru 提供する; **~ X with Y, ~ Y to X** X ni Y o okuru XにYを贈る

presentation (*of new product*) shōkai 紹介, purezen プレゼン; (*of plan*) teiji 提示; (*of meal etc*) misekata 見せ方

present-day gendai (no) 現代(の)

presently (*at the moment*) ima no tokoro 今のところ; (*soon*) mamonaku まもなく

preservation hozon 保存

preservative *n* hozonzai 保存剤

preserve 1 *n* (*domain*) ryōiki 領域 **2** *v/t standards, peace etc* iji suru 維持する; *wood, building, food* hozon suru 保存する

preside *v/i* (*at meeting*) gichō o tsutomeru 議長を務める; **~ over** *meeting* ... no gichō o tsutomeru ...の議長を務める

presidency (*office of president*) daitōryō no chii 大統領の地位; (*term as president*) daitōryō no ninki 大統領の任期

president POL daitōryō 大統領; (*of company*) shachō 社長

presidential daitōryō (no) 大統領(の)

press 1 *n*: *the ~* shinbun-zasshi 新聞雑誌; (*journalists*) hōdōjin 報道陣 **2** *v/t button* osu 押す; (*urge*) sekasu せかす; *hand* nigirishimeru 握りしめる; *grapes* shiboru しぼる; *clothes* ... ni airon o kakeru ...にアイロンをかける **3** *v/i*: *~ for* segamu せがむ

press conference kisha-kaiken 記者会見

pressing *adj* kinkyū (no) 緊急(の)

pressure 1 *n* atsuryoku 圧力; (*of work, demands*) jūatsu 重圧; *be under ~* puresshā o kanjiru プレッシャーを感じる; *be under ~ to do* ... suru yō ni atsuryoku o kakerareru ...するように圧力をかけられる **2** *v/t* ... ni atsuryoku o kakeru ...に圧力をかける

prestige meisei 名声

prestigious *award* nadakai 名高い; *school* meimon (no) 名門(の)

presumably tabun 多分

presume ... to suitei suru ...と推定する; *~ to do* ... atsukamashiku mo ... suru 厚かましくも...する

presumption (*of innocence, guilt*) suitei 推定

presumptuous okogamashii おこがましい

pre-tax zeikomi (no) 税込み(の)

pretend 1 *v/t* ... no furi o suru ...のふりをする **2** *v/i* furi o suru ふりをする

pretense misekake 見せかけ

pretentious kidotta 気取った

pretext kōjitsu 口実

pretty 1 *adj woman, house* kirei (na) きれい(な); *child, doll* kawairashii かわいらしい **2** *adv* (*quite*) kanari かなり

prevail katsu 勝つ

prevailing *opinion* ippanteki (na) 一般的(な); *wind* yoku fuku よく吹く

prevent fusegu 防ぐ; *~ X (from) doing Y* X ga Y suru no o samatageru XがYするのを妨げる

prevention bōshi 防止

preventive yobō (no) 予防(の)

preview *n* (*of movie*) shishakai 試写会; (*trailer*) yokokuhen 予告編; (*of exhibition*) nairan 内覧

previous mae (no) 前(の)

previously mae ni 前に

prewar senzen (no) 戦前(の)

prey *n* emono 獲物

♦**prey on** ... o totte kuu ...を取って食う; *fig* (*of conman etc*) ... o kuimono ni suru ...を食い物にする

price 1 *n* nedan 値段 **2** *v/t* COM ... ni nedan o tsukeru ...に値段をつける

priceless hijō ni kichō (na) 非常に貴重(な)

price war nebiki-kyōsō 値引き競争

prick¹ 1 *n* (*pain*) chikutto suru itami チクッとする痛み **2** *v/t* (*jab*) sasu 刺す

prick² *n* ∨ (*penis*) chinpoko ちんぽこ; (*person*) iya na yatsu いやなやつ

♦**prick up**: *~ one's ears* (*of dog*) mimi o tateru 耳を立てる; (*of person*) mimi o sobadateru 耳をそば立てる

prickle (*on plant*) toge とげ

prickly *fabric, beard* chikuchiku suru ちくちくする; *plant* togedarake (no) とげだらけ(の)

pride 1 *n* (*in person, achievement*) jiman 自慢; (*self-respect*) jisonshin 自尊心, puraido プライド; (*arrogance*) unubore うぬぼれ **2** *v/t*: *~ oneself on* ... o hokori ni suru ...を誇りにする

priest (*Christian*) shisai 司祭; (*Buddhist*) sōryo 僧侶; (*Shinto*) kannushi 神主

primarily omo ni 主に

primary 1 *adj* shuyō (na) 主要(な) **2** *n* POL yobi-senkyo 予備選挙

prime: *be in one's ~* jinsei no sakari ni aru 人生の盛りにある **2** *adj example, reason* mottomo jūyō (na) もっとも重要(な); *of ~*

importance saijūyō (no) 最重要 (の)

prime minister sōri-daijin 総理大臣, shushō 首相

prime time TV gōruden-awā ゴールデンアワー

primitive *man, culture* genshi (no) 原始(の); *tool, conditions* genshiteki (na) 原始的(な)

prince ōji 王子

princess ōjo 王女

principal 1 *adj* shuyō (na) 主要(な) **2** *n* (*of school*) kōchō 校長

principally omo ni 主に

principle (*in moral sense*) shugi 主義; (*rule*) genri 原理; **on ~** shugi to shite 主義として; **in ~** gensokuteki ni wa 原則的には

print 1 *n* (*in book, newspaper etc*) insatsu sareta moji 印刷された文字; (*photograph*) purinto プリント; **out of ~** zeppan de 絶版で; **wood block ~** ukiyoe 浮世絵 **2** *v/t* insatsu suru 印刷する; (*using block capitals*) katsujitai de kaku 活字体で書く

♦ **print out** *text, file* purinto-auto suru プリントアウトする

printed matter insatsubutsu 印刷物

printer (*person*) insatsu-gyōsha 印刷業者; (*machine*) purintā プリンター

printing press insatsuki 印刷機

printout purinto-auto プリントアウト

prior 1 *adj engagement* saki (no) 先(の); *knowledge* jizen (no) 事前(の) **2** *prep*: **~ to** ... yori mae ni ... より前に

prioritize (*put in order of priority*) ... no yūsen-jun'i o kimeru ...の優先順位を決める; (*give priority to*) yūsen saseru 優先させる

priority (*sth urgent*) yūsen-jikō 優先事項; (*most important thing*) saijūyō-jikō 最重要事項; **have ~** yūsen suru 優先する

prison keimusho 刑務所

prisoner shūjin 囚人; **take ~** ... o horyo ni suru ...を捕虜にする

prisoner of war horyo 捕虜

privacy puraibashī プライバシー

private 1 *adj life, conversation* shiteki (na) 私的(な); *office* kojinyō (no) 個人用(の); *property* shiyū (no) 私有(の); *industry* minkan (no) 民間(の); *school* shiritsu (no) 私立(の); *place* hitome ni tsukanai 人目につかない; *thought* hisoka (na) 秘か(な); *person* uchiki (na) 内気(な); (*on letter*) shinten 親展; (*on door*) kankeisha-igai-tachiiri-kinshi 関係者以外立ち入り禁止; **~ room** koshitsu 個室; **~ patient** shihichiryō no kanja 私費治療の患者 **2** *n* MIL heisotsu 兵卒; **in ~** hito no inai tokoro de 人のいないところで

privately (*in private*) hito no inai tokoro de 人のいないところで; *funded, owned* shiteki ni 私的に; (*inwardly*) kojinteki ni 個人的に

private sector minkan-kigyō 民間企業

privilege (*special treatment*) tokken 特権; (*honor*) meiyo 名誉

privileged tokken no aru 特権のある; (*honored*) kōei (na) 光栄(な)

prize 1 *n* shō 賞 **2** *v/t* taisetsu ni suru 大切にする

prizewinner jushō-sha 受賞者

prizewinning jushō shita 受賞した

pro[1] *n*: **the ~s and cons** sanpiryōron 賛否両論

pro[2] (*professional*) puro プロ

pro[3]: **be ~ ...** (*in favor of*) ... sanseiha de aru ...賛成派である

probability mikomi 見込み

probable arisō (na) ありそう(な)

probably tabun たぶん

probation LAW shikkō-yūyo 執行猶予; **on ~** (*in job*) shiyōkikanchū de 試用期間中で

probation officer hogo-kansatsukan 保護観察官

probation period (*in job*) shiken-saiyō-kikan 試験採用期間

probe 1 *n* (*investigation*) chōsa 調査; MED saguribari 探り針; **space ~** uchū-tansaki 宇宙探査機 **2** *v/t* saguribari de saguru 探り針で探る; (*investigate*) chōsa suru 調査する

problem mondai 問題; *(trouble)* toraburu トラブル; *I don't want to be a ~* toraburu ni wa naritaku nai トラブルにはなりたくない; *no ~ ii desu yo* いいですよ

procedure tetsuzuki 手続き

proceed 1 *v/i (go: of people)* susumu 進む; *(of work etc)* shinkōsuru 進行する **2** *v/t: ~ to do X* X shihajimeru Xし始める

proceedings ichibu-shijū 一部始終

proceeds shūeki 収益

process 1 *n* katei 過程; *in the ~ (while doing it)* sono katei de その過程で **2** *v/t food, raw materials* kakō suru 加工する; *data* shori suru 処理する; *application etc* shinsa suru 審査する

procession gyōretsu 行列

processor COMPUT enzanshori-sōchi 演算処理装置

proclaim sengen suru 宣言する

prod 1 *n* hitotsuki ひと突き **2** *v/t* tsuku 突く

prodigy: *(child) ~* tensai 天才

produce 1 *n (fruit and vegetables)* seisanbutsu 生産物 **2** *v/t commodity* seisan suru 生産する; *(bring about)* motarasu もたらす; *(bring out)* toridasu 取り出す; *play, movie, TV program* seisaku suru 製作する

producer *(of commodity)* seisan-sha 生産者, seizō-gaisha 製造会社; *(country)* seisankoku 生産国; *(of play, movie, TV program)* purodyūsā プロデューサー

product seihin 製品; *(result)* kekka 結果

production seisan 生産; *(of machinery, automobiles)* seisaku 製作; *(of play, movie, TV program)* seisaku 制作

production capacity seisan-nōryoku 生産能力

production costs seisakuhi 製作費

productive seisanryoku no takai 生産力の高い; *meeting* seisanteki (na) 生産的(な)

productivity seisansei 生産性

profane *language* gehin (na) 下品 (な)

profess *(claim)* kōgen suru 公言する

profession shokugyō 職業

professional 1 *adj (not amateur)* puro (no) プロ(の); *advice, help* senmonka (no) 専門家(の); *piece of work* puro-nami (no) プロ並み(の); *turn ~* puro ni tenkō suru プロに転向する **2** *n (doctor, lawyer etc)* senmonshoku no hito 専門職の人; *(not an amateur)* puro プロ

professionally *play sport* puro to shite プロとして; *(well, skillfully)* takumi ni 巧みに

professor kyōju 教授

proficiency jukuren 熟練

proficient jukuren shita 熟練した

profile *(of face)* yokogao 横顔; *(description)* gaiyō 概要

profit 1 *n* rieki 利益 **2** *v/i: ~ by, ~ from* ... kara rieki o eru ...から利益を得る

profitability shūekisei 収益性

profitable mōke ni naru もうけになる

profit margin rizaya 利ざや

profound *thought* shin'en (na) 深遠 (な); *hatred* fukai 深い; *shock, effect* tsuyoi 強い

profoundly fukaku 深く; *shock* tsuyoku 強く

prognosis yochi 予知

program 1 *n* keikaku 計画; *(on radio, TV)* bangumi 番組; *(in theater, COMPUT)* puroguramu プログラム **2** *v/t* COMPUT ... ni puroguramu o ireru ...にプログラムを入れる

programmer COMPUT puroguramā プログラマー

progress 1 *n* shinpo 進歩; *make ~* shinpo suru 進歩する; *in ~* shinkōchū de 進行中で **2** *v/i (advance in time)* shinkō suru 進行する; *(move on)* susumu 進む; *(make progress; in lesson)* jōtatsu suru 上達する; *how is the work ~ing?* shigoto wa donna guai ni hakadotte imasu ka 仕事はどんな具合にはかどっていますか

progressive adj dankaiteki (na) 段階的(な); (enlightened) shinpoteki (na) 進歩的(な)

progressively dandan to だんだんと

prohibit kinshi suru 禁止する

prohibition kinshi 禁止; **Prohibition** Kinshuhō-jidai 禁酒法時代

prohibitive prices hōgai (na) 法外(な)

project[1] n (plan) keikaku 計画; EDU kenkyū-kadai 研究課題; (housing area) jūtaku-danchi 住宅団地

project[2] 1 v/t figures, sales yosō suru 予想する; movie eisha suru 映写する 2 v/i (stick out) tsukideru 突き出る

projection (forecast) mitsumori 見積もり

projector (for slides) eishaki 映写機

prolific writer, artist tasaku (na) 多作(な)

prolong enchō suru 延長する

prom (school dance) dansu-pātī ダンスパーティー

prominent nose takai 高い; chin tsukideta 突き出た; (significant) jūyō (na) 重要(な)

promiscuity dare to demo neru koto 誰とでも寝ること

promiscuous aite o erabanai 相手を選ばない

promise 1 n yakusoku 約束 2 v/t person ... ni yakusoku suru ...に約束する; ~ to ... ... to yakusoku suru ...と約束する; ~ X to Y Y ni X o yakusoku suru YにXを約束する 3 v/i yakusoku suru 約束する

promising zento-yūbō (na) 前途有望(な)

promote employee shōshin saseru 昇進させる; (encourage, foster) sokushin suru 促進する; COM senden suru 宣伝する

promoter (of sports event) shusai-sha 主催者

promotion (of employee) shōshin 昇進; (of scheme, idea) sokushin 促進; COM hanbai-sokushin 販売促進

prompt 1 adj person jikan o

mamoru 時間を守る; train teikoku kikkari (no) 定刻きっかり(の); (speedy) jinsoku (na) 迅速(な) 2 adv: at two o'clock ~ niji kikkari ni 二時きっかりに 3 v/t (cause) ... no kikkake to naru ...のきっかけとなる; actor ... ni serifu o tsukeru ...にせりふをつける; ~ X to do Y X ni Y saseru XにYさせる 4 n COMPUT puronputo プロンプト

promptly (on time) kikkari ni きっかりに; (immediately) sokuza ni 即座に

prone: be ~ to ... shigachi de aru ...しがちである

pronoun daimeishi 代名詞

pronounce word hatsuon suru 発音する; (declare) ... to sengen suru ...と宣言する

pronounced accent meihaku (na) 明白(な); views kakko to shita 確固とした

pronunciation hatsuon 発音

proof n shōko 証拠; (of book) kōseizuri 校正刷り

prop 1 v/t tatekakeru 立てかける 2 n (in theater) kodōgu 小道具

♦ **prop up** o sasaeru を支える

propaganda puropaganda プロパガンダ

propel suishin suru 推進する

propellant (in aerosol) kōatsu-gasu 高圧ガス

propeller sukuryū スクリュー

proper (real) chanto shita ちゃんとした; (correct) tadashii 正しい; (fitting) tekitō (na) 適当(な)

properly chanto ちゃんと

property shoyūbutsu 所有物; (land) tochi 土地

property developer tochi-kaihatsu-gyōsha 土地開発業者

prophecy yogen 予言

prophesy ... to yogen suru ...と予言する

proportion wariai 割合; (part, percentage) bubun 部分; ~s (dimensions) tsuriai つり合い

proportional hirei shita 比例した

proposal (suggestion) teian 提案; (of

marriage) puropōzu プロポーズ

propose 1 *v/t* (*suggest*) teian suru 提案する; (*plan*) keikaku suru 計画する 2 *v/i* (*to marry*) puropōzu suru プロポーズする

proposition 1 *n* teian 提案 2 *v/t woman* ... ni iiyoru ...に言い寄る

proprietor ōnā オーナー

proprietress josei-ōnā 女性オーナー

prose sanbun 散文

prosecute *v/t* LAW kiso suru 起訴する

prosecution LAW kiso 起訴; (*lawyers*) kensatsugawa 検察側

prosecutor → **public prosecutor**

prospect 1 *n* (*chance, likelihood*) nozomi 望み; (*thought of sth in the future*) mikomi 見込み; **~s** mitōshi 見通し 2 *v/i*: **~ for gold** ... o shikutsu suru ...を試掘する

prospective mikomi no aru 見込みのある

prosper han'ei suru 繁栄する

prosperity han'ei 繁栄

prosperous *person, business* seikō shita 成功した; *city, country* han'ei shita 繁栄した

prostitute *n* baishunfu 売春婦; *male* ~ danshō 男娼

prostitution baishun 売春

prostrate: **be ~ with grief** hitan ni kurete iru 悲嘆にくれている

protect hogo suru 保護する, mamoru 守る

protection hogo 保護

protection money mikajimeryō みかじめ料

protective *clothing, equipment* hogoyō (no) 保護用(の); *mother* sewazuki (no) 世話好き(の)

protein tanpakushitsu たんぱく質

protest 1 *n* kōgi 抗議; (*demonstration*) kōgi-shūkai 抗議集会 2 *v/t* ... to shuchō suru ...と主張する; (*object to*) ... ni hantai suru ...に反対する 3 *v/i* kōgi suru 抗議する

Protestant 1 *n* Purotesutanto プロテスタント 2 *adj* Purotesutanto (no) プロテスタント(の)

protester kōgi-sha 抗議者

protocol gaikō-girei 外交儀礼

prototype genkei 原型

protracted nagabiita 長引いた

protrude *v/i* tsukideru 突き出る

proud *owner, father* hokorashige (na) 誇らしげ(な); (*independent*) jisonshin no tsuyoi 自尊心の強い; (*arrogant*) unubore ga tsuyoi うぬぼれが強い; **be ~ of** ... o hokori ni omou ...を誇りに思う

proudly hokorashige ni 誇らしげに

prove shōmei suru 証明する

proverb kotowaza ことわざ

provide (*for society, school*) kyōkyū suru 供給する; (*for person*) ataeru 与える; **~ Y to X, ~ X with Y** X ni Y o ataeru XにYを与える; **~d** (*that*)... to iu jōken de ...という条件で

♦ **provide for** *family* ... o yashinau ...を養う; (*of law etc*) ... ni sonaeru ...に備える

province shū 州

provincial *city* chihō (no) 地方(の); *pej* shiya no semai 視野の狭い

provision (*supply*) kyōkyū 供給; (*of law, contract*) jōkō 条項

provisional jōkentsuki (no) 条件つき(の)

proviso jōken 条件

provocation chōhatsu 挑発

provocative chōhatsuteki (na) 挑発的(な)

provoke (*cause*) hikiokosu 引き起こす; (*annoy*) okoraseru 怒らせる

prow NAUT senshu 船首

prowess shuwan 手腕

prowl *v/i* urotsuku うろつく

prowler urotsuku hito うろつく人

proximity chika-sa 近さ

proxy (*authority*) inin 委任; (*person*) dairinin 代理人

prude kamatoto かまとと

prudence shinchō-sa 慎重さ

prudent shinchō (na) 慎重(な)

prudish kamatotobutta かまととぶった

prune¹ *n* purūn プルーン

prune² *v/t plant* sentei suru せん定する; *fig* kiritsumeru 切り詰める

pry sensaku suru せん索する

♦ **pry into** ... no koto o sensaku suru ...のことをせん索する

PS (= *postscript*) tsuishin 追伸

pseudonym pen-nēmu ペンネーム

psychiatric seishinka (no) 精神科 (の)

psychiatrist seishinkai 精神科医

psychiatry seishin-igaku 精神医学

psychic 1 *adj* chōnōryoku (no) 超能 力(の) **2** *n* chōnōryoku-sha 超能 力者

psychoanalysis seishin-bunseki 精 神分析

psychoanalyst seishin-bunsekii 精 神分析医

psychoanalyze ... no seishin-bunseki o suru ...の精神分析をする

psychological shinriteki (na) 心理 的(な); *research, study* shinrigakuteki (na) 心理学的(な)

psychologically shinriteki ni 心理的 に

psychologist shinri-gakusha 心理学 者

psychology shinrigaku 心理学

psychopath seishin-ijōsha 精神異 常者

pub pabu パブ; (*Japanese-style*) izakaya 居酒屋

puberty shishunki 思春期

pubic hair inmō 陰毛

public 1 *adj* (*in ~*) kōzen (no) 公然 (の); (*of the ~*) kokumin (no) 国民 (の); (*not private*) ōyake (no) 公 (の); (*for the ~*) kōkyō (no) 公共 (の); (*open to the ~*) kōkai (no) 公 開(の); *school, library* kōritsu (no) 公立(の); *~ bath* sentō 銭湯 **2** *n*: *the ~* ippan no hitobito 一般の 人々; *open to the ~* ippankōkai sarete iru 一般公開されている; *in ~* hitome de 人前で

publication (*of book, report*) shuppan 出版; (*by newspaper: of photographs*) kōhyō 公表; (*of story*) hōdō 報道; (*of ship, newspaper*) shuppanbutsu 出版物

publicity (*advertisements*) senden 宣伝; (*media attention*) chūmoku

注目; *it got a lot of ~* chūmoku o atsumeta 注目を集めた

publicize (*make known*) kōhyō suru 公表する; COM senden suru 宣伝す る

publicly kōzen to 公然と

public prosecutor kensatsukan 検 察官; **public relations** kōhō-katsudō 広報活動; **public school** kōritsu-gakkō 公立学校; **public sector** kōei-bumon 公営部門

publish shuppan suru 出版する

publisher (*company*) shuppan-sha 出版社; (*person*) hakkō-sha 発行者

publishing shuppan 出版

publishing company shuppan-sha 出版社

puddle *n* mizutamari 水たまり

puff 1 *n*: *a ~ of smoke* ippuku 一服; *a ~ of wind* ichijin no kaze 一陣の 風 **2** *v/i* (*pant*) aegu あえぐ

puffy *eyes* harebottai はれぼったい; *face* mukunda むくんだ

pull 1 *n* (*on rope*) hippari 引っ張り; F (*appeal*) miryoku 魅力; F (*influence*) eikyōryoku 影響力 **2** *v/t* hipparu 引っ張る; *tooth* hikinuku 引き抜く; *muscle* itameru 痛める **3** *v/i* hipparu 引っ張る

♦ **pull apart** ... o hikihanasu ...を引 き離す

♦ **pull away** *v/t* ... o hikihanasu ... を引き離す

♦ **pull down** (*lower*) ... o hikiorosu ...を引き下ろす; (*demolish*) ... o torikowasu ...を取り壊す

♦ **pull in** (*of bus, train*) tōchaku suru 到着する

♦ **pull off** *leaves* ... o mogitoru ...を もぎ取る; *clothes* ... o nugu ...を脱 ぐ; F (*succeed in*) ... o yaritogeru ...をやり遂げる

♦ **pull out 1** *v/t* ... o nuku ...を抜く; *troops* ... o tettai saseru ...を撤退 させる **2** *v/i* (*of an agreement, a competition*) te o hiku 手を引く; (*of troops*) tettai suru 撤退する; (*of ship*) shuppatsu suru 出発する

♦ **pull through** (*from an illness*) kaifuku suru 回復する

♦ **pull together 1** *v/i* (*cooperate*)

kyōryoku suru 協力する **2** *v/t*: **pull oneself together** ki o shizumeru 気を静める

♦ **pull up 1** *v/t* (*raise*) ... o hippariageru ...を引っ張り上げる; *plant, weeds* ... o hikinuku ...を引き抜く **2** *v/i* (*of car etc*) tomaru 止まる

pulley kassha 滑車

pulp (*of fruit*) kaniku 果肉; (*for paper-making*) parupu パルプ

pulpit sekkyōdan 説教壇

pulsate (*of blood*) myaku-utsu 脈打つ; (*of rhythm*) kodō suru 鼓動する

pulse myakuhaku 脈拍

pulverize funsai suru 粉砕する

pump 1 *n* ponpu ポンプ; (*gas ~*) kyūyu-ponpu 給油ポンプ **2** *v/t water* ponpu de okuru ポンプで送る; *air* ponpu de ireru ポンプで入れる

♦ **pump up** ponpu de kūki o ireru ポンプで空気を入れる

pumpkin kabocha かぼちゃ

pun dajare だじゃれ

punch 1 *n* (*blow*) panchi パンチ; (*tool*) ana-akeki 穴あけ機 **2** *v/t* (*with fist*) kobushi de naguru こぶしで殴る; *hole, ticket* akeru 開ける

punch line ochi 落ち

punctual jikan ni seikaku (na) 時間に正確(な)

punctuality jikan o mamoru koto 時間を守ること

punctually jikan dōri ni 時間どおりに

punctuate kutōten o utsu 句読点を打つ

punctuation kutōten no uchikata 句読点の打ち方

punctuation mark kutōten 句読点

puncture 1 *n* ana 穴 **2** *v/t* ... ni ana o akeru ...に穴を開ける

pungent shigekiteki (na) 刺激的(な)

punish *person* bassuru 罰する

punishing *schedule* kitsui きつい

punishment batsu 罰; LAW keibatsu 刑罰

puny *person* yaseppochi (no) やせっぽち(の)

pup (*young dog*) koinu 子犬

pupil¹ (*of eye*) dōkō どう孔

pupil² (*student*) seito 生徒; (*disciple*) deshi 弟子

puppet (*on strings*) ayatsuri-ningyō 操り人形; (*finger ~*) yubiningyō 指人形; *fig* kairai かいらい

puppet government kairai-seifu かいらい政府

puppy koinu 子犬

purchase¹ 1 *n* (*action*) kōnyū 購入; (*object*) kōnyūhin 購入品 **2** *v/t* kōnyū suru 購入する

purchase² (*grip*) tegakari 手がかり

purchaser kaite 買い手

pure *silk, gold* junsui (na) 純粋(な); *air, water, sound* sunda 澄んだ; (*morally*) junketsu (na) 純潔(な)

purely tan ni 単に

purge 1 *n* (*of political party*) shukusei 粛清 **2** *v/t* shukusei suru 粛清する

purify *water* jōka suru 浄化する

Puritan REL Seikyōto 清教徒

puritanical genkaku (na) 厳格(な)

purity junsui-sa 純粋さ; (*moral*) junketsu 純潔

purple *adj* murasaki (no) 紫(の)

Purple Heart MIL meiyo-senshō-kunshō 名誉戦傷勲章

purpose mokuteki 目的; **on ~** waza to わざと

purposeful danko to shita 断固とした

purposely waza to わざと

purr *v/i* (*of cat*) gorogoro to nodo o narasu ごろごろとのどを鳴らす

purse *n* (*pocketbook*) handobaggu ハンドバッグ

pursue *v/t person* tsuiseki suru 追跡する; *career, aim* tsuikyū suru 追求する; *course of action* tsuzukeru 続ける

pursuer tsuiseki-sha 追跡者

pursuit (*chase*) tsuiseki 追跡; (*of happiness etc*) tsuikyū 追求; (*pastime*) shumi 趣味; **those in ~** otte 追っ手

pus umi うみ

push 1 *n* (*shove*) hitooshi ひと押し **2** *v/t* (*shove*) osu 押す; (*pressure*) sekitateru せきたてる; *drugs* mitsubai suru 密売する; *be ~ed for ...* ga nakute komatte iru ...がなくて困っている; *be ~ing 40* yonjū ni chikazuku 四十に近づく 3 *v/i* osu 押す

♦ **push along** *cart etc* oshisusumu 押し進む

♦ **push away** ... o oshiyaru ...を押しやる

♦ **push off 1** *v/t lid* ... o oshiageru ...を押し上げる **2** *v/i* F (*leave*) saru 去る; *~!* itte shimae 行ってしまえ

♦ **push on** *v/i* (*continue*) saki e susumu 先へ進む

♦ **push up** *prices* ... o oshiageru ...を押し上げる

push-button oshi-botan 押しボタン

pusher (*of drugs*) mayaku-mitsubai-nin 麻薬密売人

push-up udetatefuse 腕立て伏せ

pushy gōin (na) 強引(な)

puss, pussy (*cat*) neko-chan 猫ちゃん

put (*place*) oku 置く; *question* dasu 出す; *~ the cost at ...* to hiyō o mitsumoru ...と費用を見積もる

♦ **put aside** *money* ... o totte oku ...を取っておく; *work* ... o chūdan suru ...を中断する

♦ **put away** (*in closet etc*) ... o shimau ...をしまう; (*in prison*) ... o keimusho ni ireru ...を刑務所に入れる; (*in mental home*) ... o seishin-byōin ni ireru ...を精神病院に入れる; (*consume*) ... o tairageru ...を平らげる; *money* ... o chokin suru ...を貯金する; *animal* ... o shimatsu suru ...を始末する

♦ **put back** (*replace*) ... o kaesu ...を返す

♦ **put by** *money* ... o tameru ...をためる

♦ **put down** ... o oku ...を置く; *deposit* ... o atamakin to shite harau ...を頭金として払う; *rebellion* ... o chin'atsu suru ...を鎮圧する; (*belittle*) ... o kenasu ...をけなす; (*in writing*) ... o kaku ...を書く; *put one's foot down* (*in car*) supīdo o dasu スピードを出す; (*be firm*) danko to shita taido o toru 断固とした態度を取る; *put X down to Y* (*attribute*) X o Y no sei to minasu XをYのせいとみなす

♦ **put forward** *idea etc* teian suru 提案する

♦ **put in** ... o ireru ...を入れる; *time* ... o tsugikomu ...をつぎ込む; *claim* ... o teishutsu suru ...を提出する

♦ **put in for** ... o shinsei suru ...を申請する

♦ **put off** *light, radio, TV* kesu 消す; (*postpone*) enki suru 延期する; (*deter*) omoi-todomaraseru 思いとどまらせる; (*repel*) fukai ni saseru 不快にさせる; *the experience put me off shellfish* sono keiken no sei de watashi wa kai ga iya ni natta その経験のせいで私は貝がいやになった

♦ **put on** *light, radio, TV* ... o tsukeru ...をつける; *tape, music, glasses, brake* ... o kakeru ...をかける; *jacket, shirt* ... o kiru ...を着る; *shoes, pants* ... o haku ...をはく; *gloves* ... o hameru ...をはめる; *hat* ... o kaburu ...をかぶる; *make-up* ... o suru ...をする; (*perform*) ... o jōen suru ...を上演する; (*assume*) ... no furi o suru ...のふりをする; *~ weight* futoru 太る; *she's just putting it on* kanojo wa tan ni furi o shite iru dake desu 彼女は単にふりをしているだけです

♦ **put out** *hand* ... o sashidasu ...を差し出す; *fire, light* ... o kesu ...を消す

♦ **put through** (*on phone*) ... o tsunagu ...をつなぐ

♦ **put together** (*assemble*) ... o kumitateru ...を組み立てる; (*organize*) ... o soshiki suru ...を組織する

♦ **put up** *v/t hand, hair, prices* ... o ageru ...を上げる; *person* ... o tomeru ...を泊める; (*erect*) ... o tateru ...を建てる; *poster, notice* ... o kakageru ...を掲げる; *money* ...

o teikyō suru ...を提供する; **~ up for sale** uri ni dasu 売りに出す
♦ **put up with** (*tolerate*) ... o gaman suru ...を我慢する
putty pate パテ
puzzle 1 *n* (*mystery*) nazo なぞ; (*game*) pazuru パズル; (*jigsaw ~*) jigusō-pazuru ジグソーパズル;

(*crossword ~*) kurosuwādo-pazuru クロスワードパズル **2** *v/t* komaraseru 困らせる
puzzling wake no wakaranai わけのわからない
PVC pori-enka-binīru ポリ塩化ビニール
pylon tettō 鉄塔

Q

quack¹ 1 *n* (*of duck*) gāgā naku koe がーがー鳴く声 **2** *v/i* gāgā naku がーがー鳴く
quack² F (*bad doctor*) yabuisha やぶ医者
quadrangle (*figure*) shikakkei 四角形; (*courtyard*) nakaniwa 中庭
quadruped yotsuashi (no) 四つ足(の)
quadruple *v/i* yonbai ni naru 四倍になる
quadruplets yotsugo 四つ子
quaint *cottage* kofū (na) 古風(な); *ideas etc* kimyō (na) 奇妙(な)
quake 1 *n* (*earthquake*) jishin 地震 **2** *v/i* (*of earth*) yureru 揺れる; (*with fear*) furueru 震える
qualification (*from university etc*) shikaku 資格; (*of remark etc*) jōken 条件; *have the right ~s for a job* shigoto ni tekishita shikaku o motte iru 仕事に適した資格を持っている
qualified *doctor, engineer etc* nintei sareta 認定された; (*restricted*) gentei sareta 限定された; *I am not ~ to judge* watashi ni handan suru shikaku wa nai 私に判断する資格はない
qualify **1** *v/t* (*of degree, course etc*) ... ni shikaku o ataeru ...に資格を与える; *remark etc* gentei suru 限定する **2** *v/i* (*get degree etc*) shikaku o toru 資格を取る; *our

team has qualified for the semifinal* watashitachi no chīmu wa junkesshō ni susunda 私達のチームは準決勝に進んだ; *that doesn't ~ as ...* sore wa ... to mitomerarenai それは...と認められない
quality shitsu 質; (*characteristic*) tokuchō 特徴
quality control (*activity*) hinshitsu-kanri 品質管理; (*department*) hinshitsu-kanribu 品質管理部
qualm gimon 疑問; *have no ~s about ...* ... ni taishite nani mo gimon o kanjinai ...に対して何も疑問を感じない
quantify ... o ryō de arawasu ...を量で表す
quantity ryō 量
quarantine *n* kakuri 隔離
quarrel 1 *n* kenka けんか **2** *v/i* kenka suru けんかする
quarrelsome kenkappayai けんかっぱやい
quarry (*for mining*) ishikiriba 石切り場
quart kuwōto クウォート
quarter 1 *n* yonbun no ichi 四分の一; (*25 cents*) nijūgo sento dama 25セント玉; (*part of town*) chiku 地区; *a ~ of an hour* jūgo fun 十五分; *a ~ of 5* go ji jūgo fun mae 五時十五分前; *~ after 5* go ji jūgo fun 五時十五分 **2** *v/t* yontōbun

suru 四等分する

quarterback SP kuwōtābakku ク
ウォーターバック; **quarterfinal**
junjun-kesshō 準々決勝;
quarterfinalist junjun-kesshō-
shutsujō-senshu 準々決勝出場選
手

quarterly 1 adj shihanki (no) 四半
期(の) **2** adv publish kikan de 季
刊で; pay shihanki goto ni 四半期
毎に

quarternote MUS shibu-onpu 四分音
符

quarters MIL heisha 兵舎

quartet MUS karutetto カルテット

quartz suishō 水晶

quaver 1 n (in voice) furuegoe 震
え声 **2** v/i (of voice) furueru 震え
る

queen joō 女王

queen bee joō-bachi 女王ばち

queer (peculiar) hen (na) 変(な)

quench flames kesu 消す; ~ one's
thirst nodo no kawaki o iyasu の
どの渇きをいやす

query 1 n shitsumon 質問 **2** v/t
(express doubt about) … ni
toitadasu …に問いただす; (check)
kiku 聞く; ~ X with Y Y ni X o
kiku YにXを聞く

question 1 n shitsumon 質問;
(matter) mondai 問題; in ~ (being
talked about) wadai (no) 話題(の);
(in doubt) mondai (no) 問題(の);
it's a ~ of money / time okane
no/jikan no mondai da お金の/時
間の問題だ; that's out of the ~
sore wa mondai-gai da それは問題
外だ **2** v/t person … ni shitsumon
suru …に質問する; LAW jinmon
suru 尋問する; (doubt) utagau 疑
う

questionable honesty utagawashii
疑わしい; figures, statement fushin
(na) 不審(な)

questioning look, tone
utagawashige (na) 疑わしげ(な)

question mark gimonfu 疑問符

questionnaire ankēto アンケート

quick hayai 速い; be ~! hayaku 早
く; let's have a ~ drink chotto

nomi ni ikō ちょっと飲みに行こう;
can I have a ~ look? chotto mite
mo ii desu ka ちょっと見てもいい
ですか; that was ~! hayakatta ne
早かったね

quicksand ryūsa 流砂; **quicksilver**
suigin 水銀; **quickwitted** kiten no
kiku 機転のきく

quiet voice, music engine shizuka
(na) 静か(な); life heion (na) 平穏
(な); town, street kansan to shita
閑散とした; person mono-shizuka
(na) 物静か(な); keep ~ about …
o damatte iru …を黙っている; ~!
shizuka ni 静かに

♦**quieten down 1** v/t children
shizuka ni saseru 静かにさせる
2 v/i (of children) shizuka ni naru
静かになる; (of situation)
osamaru 収まる

quilt (on bed) kakebuton 掛け布団

quinine kinīne キニーネ

quip 1 n jōdan 冗談 **2** v/i jōdan o iu
冗談を言う

quirky kimagure (na) 気まぐれ(な)

quit 1 v/t job yameru 辞める; ~
doing X X suru no o yameru Xす
るのを止める **2** v/i (leave job)
yameru 辞める; COMPUT owari ni
suru 終わりにする

quite (fairly) kanari かなり;
(completely) mattaku まったく;
not ~ ready mada junbi ga dekite
inai まだ準備ができていない; I
didn't ~ understand watashi wa
amari yoku wakaranakatta 私はあ
まりよく分からなかった; is that
right? - not ~ sore de ii – chotto
chigau それでいい-ちょっと違う;
~! sono tōri そのとおり; a lot
kanari かなり; it was ~ a surprise
sore wa kanari odoroki datta それ
はかなり驚きだった

quits: be ~ with … to aiko da …と
あいこだ

quiver v/i (of voice, hand) furueru
震える; (of leaf) yureru 揺れる

quiz 1 n kuizu クイズ **2** v/t
shitsumon suru 質問する

quiz program kuizu-bangumi クイ
ズ番組

quota wariate 割り当て

quotation (*from author*) in'yō 引用; (*price*) mitsumori 見積もり; **give X a ~ for Y** X ni Y no mitsumori o dasu XにYの見積もりを出す

quotation marks in'yōfu 引用符

quote 1 *n* (*from author*) in'yō 引用;

(*price*) mitsumori 見積もり; (*quotation mark*) in'yōfu 引用符 **2** *v/t text* inyō suru 引用する; *price* ... no mitsumori o dasu ...の見積もりを出す **3** *v/i*: **~ from an author** aru chosha kara in'yō suru ある著者から引用する

R

rabbit usagi うさぎ

rabies kyōkenbyō 狂犬病

raccoon araiguma あらいぐま; **~ dog** tanuki たぬき

race¹ *n* (*of people*) jinshu 人種

race² *1* *n* SP kyōsō 競走, rēsu レース; *fig* kyōsō 競争, rēsu レース; **the ~s** (*horse ~s*) keiba 競馬 *2* *v/i* (*run fast*) isoide iku 急いで行く; SP kyōgi ni deru 競技に出る; **he ~d through his meal/work** kare wa ōisogi de shokuji o shita/shigoto o shita 彼は大急ぎで食事をした/仕事をした *3* *v/t*: **I'll ~ you** anata to kyōsō suru あなたと競争する

racecourse keiba-jō 競馬場; **racehorse** kyōsō-ba 競走馬; **racetrack** (*for athletes*) torakku トラック; (*for cars*) sākitto サーキット

racial jinshu (no) 人種(の); **~ equality** jinshu-byōdō 人種平等

racing kyōsō 競争

racing car rēshingu-kā レーシングカー

racing driver rēsā レーサー

racism jinshu-sabetsu 人種差別

racist *1* *n* jinshu-sabetsu-shugi-sha 人種差別主義者 *2* *adj* jinshu-sabetsuteki (na) 人種差別的(な)

rack *1* *n* (*for parking bikes*) rakku ラック; (*for bags on train,*) tana 棚; (*for CDs*) tate 立て *2* *v/t*: **~ one's brains** chie o shiboru 知恵を絞る

racket¹ SP raketto ラケット

racket² (*noise*) sōon 騒音; (*criminal activity*) sagi 詐欺

radar rēdā レーダー

radiant *smile, appearance* kagayaku yō (na) 輝くよう(な)

radiate *v/i* (*of heat, light*) hōsha suru 放射する

radiation PHYS hōshanō 放射能

radiator rajiētā ラジエーター

radical *1* *adj* konponteki (na) 根本的(な); POL *views* kyūshinteki (na) 急進的(の); *person* kageki (na) 過激(な) *2* *n* POL kyūshin-ha 急進派

radicalism POL kyūshin-shugi 急進主義

radically konponteki ni 根本的に

radio rajio ラジオ; **on the ~** rajio de ラジオで; **by ~** musen de 無線で

radioactive hōsei (no) 放射性(の); **radioactivity** hōshanō 放射能; **radio alarm** mezamashi-rajio 目覚ましラジオ; **radio station** rajio-hōsōkyoku ラジオ放送局; **radiotherapy** hōshasen-ryōhō 放射線療法

radish hatsuka-daikon はつかだいこん

radius hankei 半径

raffle *n* kuji くじ

raft ikada いかだ

rafter hari はり

rag (*for cleaning etc*) zōkin ぞうきん; **~s** (*clothes*) boro ぼろ

rage *1* *n* gekido 激怒; **be in a ~** ikarikurutte iru 怒り狂っている; **all**

***the* ~** būmu (no) ブーム(の) **2** *v/i* (*of person*) ikarikuruu 怒り狂う; (*of storm*) arekuruu 荒れ狂う

ragged *clothes etc* boroboro (no) ぼろぼろ(の)

raid 1 *n* (*by troops, police*) shūgeki 襲撃; (*by robbers*) gōtō 強盗; FIN urikuzushi 売り崩し **2** *v/t* (*of troops, police*) shūgeki suru 襲撃する; (*of robbers*) gōtō ni hairu 強盗に入る

raider (*on bank etc*) gōtō 強盗

rail (*on track*) rēru レール; (*hand ~*) tesuri 手すり; (*for towel*) kake 掛け; **by ~** ressha de 列車で

railings (*around park etc*) saku さく

railroad tetsudō 鉄道

railroad station eki 駅

rain 1 *n* ame 雨; **in the ~** ame no naka de 雨の中で; **the ~s** uki 雨季 **2** *v/i* ame ga furu 雨が降る; **it's ~ing** ame ga futte iru 雨が降っている

rainbow niji にじ; **raincheck: can I take a ~ on that?** tsugi no kikai de ii kashira 次の機会でいいかしら; **raincoat** reinkōto レインコート; **raindrop** amadare 雨だれ; **rainfall** kōsuiryō 降水量; **rain forest** urin 雨林; **rainstorm** bōfū 暴風雨

rainy amemoyō 雨模様; **it's ~** amemoyō de aru 雨模様である

rainy season uki 雨季; (*in Japan*) tsuyu 梅雨

raise 1 *n* (*in salary*) shōkyū 昇給 **2** *v/t* *shelf etc* mochiageru 持ち上げる; *offer* ageru 上げる; *children* sodateru 育てる; *question* teiki suru 提起する; *money* atsumeru 集める

raisin hoshibudō 干しぶどう

rake *n* (*for garden*) kumade くま手

rally *n* (*meeting, reunion*) shūkai 集会; (*for cars, in tennis*) rarī ラリー

♦**rally around** *v/i* tasuke ni kuru 助けに来る **2** *v/t*: **~ X** X no tokoro ni tasuke ni kuru Xの所に助けに来る

RAM (= *random access memory*) ramu ラム

ram 1 *n* ohitsuji 雄ひつじ **2** *v/t* *ship, car* ... ni shōtotsu suru ...に

衝突する

ramble 1 *n* (*walk*) haikingu ハイキング **2** *v/i* (*walk*) haikingu suru ハイキングする; (*when speaking*) toritomenaku naru とりとめなくなる; (*talk incoherently*) toritome no nai hanashi o suru とりとめのない話をする

rambler (*walker*) haikā ハイカー

rambling 1 *n* (*walking*) haikingu ハイキング; (*in speech*) kanwa 閑話 **2** *adj* *speech* toritome no nai とりとめのない

ramp surōpu スロープ; (*for raising vehicle*) ranpu ランプ

rampage 1 *v/i* abaremawaru 暴れまわる **2** *n*: **go on the ~** abaremawatte iru 暴れまわっている

rampart jōheki 城壁

ramshackle gatagata (no) がたがた(の)

ranch daibokujō 大牧場

rancher bokujō-keiei-sha 牧場経営者

rancid kusatta 腐った

rancor urami うらみ

R & D (= *research and development*) kenkyū-kaihatsu 研究開発

random 1 *adj* teatari-shidai (no) 手当たり次第(の); (*in statistics*) COMPUT musakui (no) 無作為(の); **~ sample** musakui-chūshutsu 無作為抽出 **2** *n*: **at ~** teatari-shidai ni 手当たり次第に

range 1 *n* (*of products*) haba 幅; (*of voice*) seiiki 声域; (*of gun*) shatei-kyori 射程距離; (*of airplane*) kōzoku-kyori 航続距離; (*of mountains*) sanmyaku 山脈 **2** *v/i*: **~ from X to Y** X kara Y no han'i X からYの範囲 **ranger** (*forest ~*) shinrin-keibi-taiin 森林警備隊員

rank 1 *n* MIL kaikyū 階級; (*in society*) chii 地位; **the ~s** MIL heishi 兵士 **2** *v/t* ... ni kakuzuke suru ...に格付けする

♦**rank among** ... no uchi ni kazoerareru ...のうちに数えられる

ransack kumanaku sagasu くまな

く探す

ransom minoshirokin 身の代金;
hold ... to ~ ... o hitojichi ni shite
minoshirokin o yōkyū suru ...を人
質にして身の代金を要求する

rant: *~ and rave* ōgoe de
wamekichirasu 大声でわめきちら
す

rap 1 n (*at door etc*) tonton tataku
oto とんとんたたく音; MUS rappu
ラップ **2** v/t *table etc* tonton tataku
とんとんたたく

♦**rap at** *window etc* ... o tonton
tataku ...をとんとんたたく

rape 1 n gōkan 強かん **2** v/t gōkan
suru 強かんする

rape victim gōkan no higai-sha 強
かんの被害者

rapid hayai 速い

rapidity haya-sa 速さ

rapids kyūryū 急流

rapist gōkan-sha 強かん者

rapture uchōten 有頂天

rapturous nekkyōteki (na) 熱狂的
(な)

rare (*infrequent*) mare (na) まれ
(な); (*unusual*) mezurashii めずら
しい; *steak* rea レア

rarely metta ni...nai めったに...ない

rarity chinpin 珍品

rascal itazurakko いたずらっ子

rash[1] MED hasshin 発しん

rash[2] *action, behavior* keisotsu
(na) 軽率(な)

raspberry kiichigo 木いちご,
razuberī ラズベリー

rat n nezumi ねずみ

rate 1 n rēto レート; (*price*) ryōkin
料金; (*speed*) sokudo 速度; *~ of
interest* FIN rishi 利子; *at an
hourly ~ of* (*be paid at*)
jikankyū... de 時間給...で; *at this
~* (*at this speed*) kono sokudo de
この速度で; (*carrying on like this*)
kono chōshi de wa この調子では
2 v/t (*consider, rank*) hyōka suru
評価する

rather kanari かなり; (*polite
understatement*) sukoshi 少し; *I
would ~ stay here* watashi wa
dochiraka to iu to koko ni itai

desu 私はどちらかと言うとここに
いたいです; *or would you ~ ...?*
sō de nakereba mushiro ...shitai
desu ka そうでなければむしろ...し
たいですか

ration 1 n haikyū-bun 配給分 **2** v/t
supplies haikyū suru 配給する

rational *person* riseiteki (na) 理性
的(な); *method etc* gōriteki (na) 合
理的(な)

rationality gōrisei 合理性

rationalization (*of production etc*)
gōrika 合理化

rationalize 1 v/t *production* gōrika
suru 合理化する; *emotions, one's
actions etc* seitōka suru 正当化す
る **2** v/i seitōka suru 正当化する

rat race kyōsō-shakai 競争社会

rattle 1 n (*noise*) garagara to iu oto
がらがらという音; (*toy*) garagara
がらがら **2** v/t *chains etc* ... ni
garagara oto o tatesaseru ...にが
らがら音を立てさせる **3** v/i (*of
chains etc*) garagara oto ga suru
がらがら音がする; (*of crates*)
gatagata oto ga suru がたがた音が
する

♦**rattle off** *poem, list* ... o surasura
iu ...をすらすら言う

rattlesnake garagarahebi がらがら
へび

ravage: *~d by war* sensō de hakai
sareta 戦争で破壊された

rave v/i (*talk deliriously*) uwagoto
o iu うわ言を言う; (*talk wildly*)
wameku わめく; *~ about* (*enthuse*)
... o homesoyasu ...をほめそやす

raven watarigarasu わたりがらす

ravenous *appetite* harapeko (no)
腹ペコ(の)

rave review kōhyō 好評

ravine keikoku 渓谷

raving: *~ mad* kyōran shita 狂乱し
た

ravishing miwakuteki (na) 魅惑的
(な)

raw *meat, vegetable* nama (no) 生
(の); *sugar, iron* kakō shite inai 加
工していない

raw materials genryō 原料

ray kōsen 光線; *a ~ of hope*

hitosuji no kibō 一筋の希望

razor kamisori かみそり

razor blade kamisori no ha かみそりの刃

re COM ... ni kanshite ...に関して

reach 1 n: *within ~* te no todoku tokoro 手の届くところ; *out of ~* te no todokanai tokoro 手の届かないところ; *the bus station is within easy ~ of the house* basutei wa uchi no sugu chikaku ni arimasu バス停はうちのすぐ近くにあります **2** v/t *city etc* ... ni tsuku ...に着く; (*go as far as*) ... ni todoku ...に届く; *decision, agreement* ... ni tassuru ...に達する; (*contact*) ... ni renraku suru ...に連絡する

♦ **reach out** v/i ude o nobasu 腕を伸ばす

react hannō suru 反応する

reaction hannō 反応

reactionary 1 n POL handō-shugi-sha 反動主義者 **2** adj POL handōteki (na) 反動的(な)

reactor (*nuclear*) genshiro 原子炉

read 1 v/t yomu 読む; *diskette* yomitoru 読み取る **2** v/i yomu 読む; *~ to* ... ni yomikikaseru ...に読み聞かせる

♦ **read out** v/t (*aloud*) ...o rōdoku suru ...を朗読する

♦ **read up on** ... o tetteiteki ni kenkyū suru ...を徹底的に研究する

readable *handwriting* yomeru 読める; *book* yomaseru 読ませる

reader (*person*) dokusha 読者

readily *admit, agree* susunde 進んで

readiness: be in a state of ~ junbi ga totonotte iru 準備が整っている; *surprised at their ~ to agree* karera no susunde sansei suru taido ni odoroita 彼らの進んで賛成する態度に驚いた

reading (*activity*) dokusho 読書; (*from meter etc*) kiroku 記録

reading matter yomimono 読み物

readjust v/t *equipment, controls* chōsetsu suru 調節する **2** v/i (*to situation*) ... ni nareru ...に慣れる

read-only file COMPUT yomidashi-sen'yō-fairu 読み出し専用ファイル

read-only memory COMPUT yomidashi-sen'yō-memorī 読み出し専用メモリー

ready (*prepared*) junbi ga dekita 準備ができた; (*willing*) susunde... suru 進んで...する; *get (oneself) ~* junbi suru 準備する; *get X ~* X no junbi o suru Xの準備をする

ready-made *stew etc* dekiai (no) 出来合い(の); *solution* kisei (no) 既製(の)

ready-to-wear kiseifuku (no) 既製服(の)

real hontō (no) 本当(の); *gold, leather* honmono (no) 本物(の)

real estate fudōsan 不動産

real estate agent fudōsan-ya 不動産屋

realism genjitsu-shugi 現実主義

realist genjitsu-shugi-sha 現実主義者

realistic genjitsuteki (na) 現実的(な)

reality jijitsu 事実

realization jikkan 実感; (*of hopes, plan*) jitsugen 実現

realize v/t kizuku 気付く; *hopes, plan* jitsugen suru 実現する; FIN rieki o ageru 利益を上げる; *I ~ now that ...* watashi wa ima ... ni ki ga tsuita 私は今...に気が付いた

really hontō ni 本当に; *~?* hontō 本当; *not ~* (*not much*) anmari あんまり

real time COMPUT riarutaimu リアルタイム

real-time COMPUT riarutaimu (no) リアルタイム(の)

realtor fudōsan-ya 不動産屋

reap shūkaku suru 収穫する

reappear futatabi arawareru 再び現れる

rear 1 n kōbu 後部 **2** adj ushiro (no) 後ろ(の); *seats, wheels, lights* kōbu (no) 後部(の)

rearm v/t & v/i saigunbi suru 再軍備する

rearmost saikōbi (no) 最後尾(の)

rearrange *flowers, furniture* narabenaosu 並べ直す; *schedule* saichōsei suru 再調整する

rear-view mirror bakku-mirā バックミラー

reason 1 n (faculty) risei 理性; (cause) riyū 理由 **2** v/i: **~ with** ... o settoku suru ...を説得する

reasonable person, behavior funbetsu no aru 分別のある; price datō (na) 妥当(な); **a ~ number of people** māmā no ninzū まあまあの人数

reasonably act, behave jōshikiteki ni 常識的に; (quite) kanari かなり

reassure anshin saseru 安心させる

reassuring anshin saseru 安心させる

rebate (money back) haraimodoshi 払い戻し

rebel 1 n POL hangyaku-sha 反逆者; (against parents) hankō-bunshi 反抗分子; **~ troops** hanran-gun 反乱軍 **2** v/i POL hanran o okosu 反乱を起こす; (against parents) hankō suru 反抗する

rebellion POL hanran 反乱; (against parents) hankō 反抗

rebellious hankōteki (na) 反抗的(な)

rebound v/i (of ball etc) hanekaeru はね返る

rebuff n kyozetsu 拒絶

rebuild wall tatenaosu 建て直す; relationship tatenaosu 立て直す

rebuke v/t hinan suru 非難する

recall v/t ambassador yobimodosu 呼び戻す; (remember) omoidasu 思い出す

recapture MIL dakkan suru 奪還する; criminal saitaiho suru 再逮捕する; emotion torimodosu 取り戻す

receding hair hagete kite iru はげてきている

receipt (for money) ryōshū-sho 領収書, reshīto レシート; (for goods) juryō-sho 受領書; **acknowledge ~ of** ... o tashika ni uketorimashita koto o oshirase shimasu ...を確かに受け取りましたことをお知らせします; **~s** FIN shūnyū 収入

receive uketoru 受け取る

receiver (of letter) uketorinin 受取人; TELEC juwaki 受話器; RAD jushinki 受信機

receivership: **be in ~** kanzainin no kanrika ni aru 管財人の管理下にある

recent saikin (no) 最近(の)

recently saikin 最近

reception (in company) uketsuke 受付; (in hotel) furonto フロント; (formal party) resepushon レセプション; (welcome) kangei 歓迎; (for radio, phone) jushin 受信

reception desk (in company) uketsuke 受付; (in hotel) furonto フロント

receptionist (in company) uketsuke-gakari 受付係; (in hotel) furonto-gakari フロント係

receptive: **be ~ to** ... ni maemuki de aru ...に前向きである

recess (in wall etc) kubomi くぼみ; EDU yasumi-jikan 休み時間; (of Congress) kyūkai 休会

recession keiki-kōtai 景気後退

recharge battery jūden suru 充電する

recipe reshipi レシピ

recipient uketorinin 受取人

reciprocal sōgo (no) 相互(の)

recital MUS risaitaru リサイタル

recite poem anshō suru 暗唱する; details, facts rekkyo suru 列挙する

reckless mucha (na) 無茶(な)

reckon (think, consider) omou 思う

♦ **reckon with**: **have X to ~** X o kōryo ni ireru Xを考慮に入れる

reclaim land from sea umetateru 埋め立てる; lost items torimodosu 取り戻す

recline v/i motareru もたれる

recluse inton-sha 隠とん者

recognition (of state, s.o.'s achievements) shōnin 承認; (of person) ninshiki 認識; **changed beyond ~** miwake ga tsukanai hodo kawatta 見分けがつかないほど変わった

recognizable miwake ga tsuku 見分けがつく

recognize person, voice, tune ... ni oboe ga aru ...に覚えがある;

symptoms kakunin suru 確認する; POL: *state* shōnin suru 承認する; *it can be ~d by ...* ... de kakunin dekiru ...で確認できる

recollect omoidasu 思い出す

recollection omoide 思い出

recommend susumeru 勧める

recommendation suisen 推薦

reconcile *people* nakanaori saseru 仲直りさせる; *facts, differences* chōwa saseru 調和させる; *~ oneself to ...* ... o shikata ga nai to ukeireru ...をしかたがないと受け入れる; *be ~d (of two people)* nakanaori suru 仲直りする

reconciliation (*of people*) wakai 和解; (*of facts, differences*) chōwa 調和

recondition shūri suru 修理する

reconnaissance MIL teisatsu 偵察

reconsider *v/t & v/i* kangaenaosu 考え直す

reconstruct *city* saiken suru 再建する; *one's life* tatenaosu 立て直す; *crime* saigen suru 再現する

record 1 *n* MUS rekōdo レコード; SP *etc* saikō-kiroku 最高記録; (*written document, in database etc*) kiroku 記録; *~s* kiroku 記録; *say off the ~* ... o hikōshiki ni iu ...を非公式に言う; *have a criminal ~* zenka ga aru 前科がある; *have a good ~ for* ... ni yoi jisseki o agete iru ...に良い実績を上げている **2** *v/t* (*on tape etc*) rokuon suru 録音する; (*in writing*) kiroku suru 記録する

record-breaking kiroku-yaburi (no) 記録破り(の)

recorder MUS rikōdā リコーダー

record holder kiroku-hojisha 記録保持者

recording rokuon 録音

recording studio rokuon-sutajio 録音スタジオ

record player rekōdo-pureiyā レコードプレイヤー

recoup *losses* torimodosu 取り戻す

recover 1 *v/t sth lost, stolen* torimodosu 取り戻す; *composure* kaifuku suru 回復する **2** *v/i* (*from illness*) genki ni naru 元気になる

recovery (*of sth lost, stolen*) kaishū 回収; (*from illness*) kaifuku 回復; *he has made a good ~* kare wa sukkari kaifuku shita 彼はすっかり回復した

recreation goraku 娯楽

recruit 1 *n* MIL shinpei 新兵; (*to company*) shinnyū-shain 新入社員 **2** *v/t new staff* boshū suru 募集する

recruitment boshū 募集

recruitment drive boshū-katsudō 募集活動

rectangle chōhōkei 長方形

rectangular chōhōkei (no) 長方形(の)

recuperate kaifuku suru 回復する

recur kurikae sareru 繰り返される; (*of illness*) saihatsu suru 再発する

recurrent tabitabi okoru 度々起こる

recycle sairiyō suru 再利用する

recycling risaikuru リサイクル

red 1 *adj* akai 赤い **2** *n* aka 赤; *be in the ~* (*of person*) shakkin shite iru 借金している; ~ (*of account*) akaji de aru 赤字である

Red Cross Sekijūji 赤十字

redden *v/i* (*blush*) akaku naru 赤くなる

redecorate *v/t* kaisō suru 改装する

redeem *debt* shōkan suru 償還する; *sinners* sukuu 救う

redeeming: *~ feature* torie 取り柄

redevelop *part of town* saikaihatsu suru 再開発する

red-handed: *catch X ~* X o genkōhan de tsukamaeru Xを現行犯で捕まえる; **redhead** akage no hito 赤毛の人; **red-hot** sugoku atsui すごく熱い; **red light** (*at traffic light*) akashingō 赤信号; **red light district** akasen-chiku 赤線地区; **red meat** akami no niku 赤身の肉; **redneck** hoshu-ha rōdō-sha kaikyū no hakujin 保守派労働者階級の白人; **red pepper** tōgarashi とうがらし; **red tape** kanryō-shugi 官僚主義

reduce herasu 減らす; *speed, price* sageru 下げる; *size* chiisaku suru 小さくする

reduction genshō 減少; (*of price*)

nesage 値下げ

redundant (*unnecessary*) yobun (na) 余分(な)

reed BOT ashi あし

reef (*in sea*) anshō 暗礁

reef knot komamusubi こま結び

reek v/i niou 臭う; *~ of ...* ... no nioi ga punpun suru ...の臭いがぷんぷんする

reel n (*of film*) rīru リール; (*of thread*) maki 巻

refer v/t: *~ a decision / problem to ...* ... ni kettei / mondai o itaku suru ...に決定/問題を委託する

♦ **refer to** (*allude to*) ... o honomekasu ...をほのめかす; *dictionary etc* ... o sanshō suru ...を参照する

referee SP shinpan 審判; (*for job*) mimoto-hoshōnin 身元保証人

reference (*allusion*) genkyū 言及; (*for job*) suisenjō 推薦状; *with ~ to* ... ni kanshite ...に関して

reference book sankōtosho 参考図書

reference number shōkai-bangō 照会番号

referendum jūmin-tōhyō 住民投票

refill v/t tank ... ni hojū suru ...に補充する; glass ... ni mō ippai tsugu ...にもう一杯つぐ

refine oil, sugar seisei suru 精製する; technique senren suru 洗練する

refined manners senren sareta 洗練された

refinery seisei-jo 精製所

reflation rifureishon リフレーション

reflect 1 v/t light hansha suru 反射する; *be ~ed in ...* ... ni utsutte iru ...に映っている **2** v/i (*think*) yukkuri kangaeru ゆっくり考える

reflection hansha 反射; (*consideration*) jukkō 熟考

reflex (*in body*) hansha-nōryoku 反射能力

reflex reaction hansha-undō 反射運動

reform 1 n kaikaku 改革 **2** v/t kaikaku suru 改革する

refrain¹ v/i tsutsushimu 慎む; *please ~ from smoking* kitsuen wa goenryo kudasai 喫煙はご遠慮下さい

refrain² n (*in song etc*) kurikaeshi 繰り返し

refresh person genki-zukeru 元気づける; *feel ~ed* kibun ga sawayaka ni naru 気分がさわやかになる

refresher course kenshū-kai 研修会

refreshing drink sawayaka (na) さわやか(な); experience sugasugashii すがすがしい

refreshments keishoku 軽食

refrigerate reizō suru 冷蔵する

refrigerator reizōko 冷蔵庫

refuel 1 v/t airplane ... ni nenryō o hokyū suru ...に燃料を補給する **2** v/i (*of airplane*) nenryō no hokyū o ukeru 燃料の補給を受ける

refuge hinan-basho 避難場所; *take ~* (*from storm etc*) hinan suru 避難する

refugee nanmin 難民

refund 1 n haraimodoshi 払い戻し **2** v/t haraimodosu 払い戻す

refusal kyozetsu 拒絶

refuse gift kotowaru 断る; permission kyohi suru 拒否する; invitation jitai suru 辞退する; *~ to do X* X suru no o kotowaru Xするのを断る

regain control, the lead torimodosu 取り戻す

regard 1 n: *have great ~ for ...* o sonkei suru ...を尊敬する; *in this ~* kore ni kanshite これに関して; *with ~ to ...* ni kanshite ...に関して; (*kind*) *~s* keigu 敬具; *give my ~s to Yoko* Yōko san ni yoroshiku otsutae kudasai ようこさんによろしくお伝え下さい; *with no ~ for ...* ... ni okamainaku ...にお構いなく **2** v/t: *~ X as Y* X o Y to omou XをYと思う; *as ~s ...* ... ni kanshite wa ...に関しては

regarding ... ni kanshite wa ...に関しては

regardless kamawazu ni 構わずに; *~ of ...* ni mo kakawarazu ...にもかかわらず

regime (*government*) seiji-taisei 政治体制

regiment *n* rentai 連隊

region chiiki 地域; *in the ~ of* yaku ... 約...

regional chihō (no) 地方(の)

register 1 *n* tōrokubo 登録簿 **2** *v/t* *birth, death* todokederu 届け出る; *vehicle* tōroku suru 登録する; *letter* kakitome ni suru 書留めにする; *emotion* arawasu 表す; *send a letter ~ed* kakitome de okuru 書留で送る **3** *v/i* (*at university*) nyūgaku-tetsuzuki o suru 入学手続きをする; (*for a course*) jukōtetsuzuki o suru 受講手続きをする; (*with police*) tōroku suru 登録する

registered letter kakitome-shokan 書留書簡

registration (*vehicle number*) tōroku 登録; (*of birth, death*) todokede 届出; (*at university*) nyūgaku-tetsuzuki 入学手続; (*for course*) jukō-tetsuzuki 受講手続

regret 1 *v/t* kōkai suru 後悔する; *loss* kuyamu 悔やむ; *inconvenience* sumanai to omou すまないと思う **2** *n* kōkai 後悔

regrettable zannen (na) 残念(な)

regrettably zannen nagara 残念ながら

regular 1 *adj* teikiteki (na) 定期的 (な); *breathing* kisokuteki (na) 規則的(な); *pattern, shape* taishōteki (na) 対称的(な); (*normal, ordinary*) tsūjō (no) 通常(の) **2** *n* (*at bar etc*) jōren 常連

regulate *costs* kisei suru 規制する; *machine* chōsetsu suru 調節する

regulation (*rule*) kisoku 規則; (*of expenditure*) kisei 規制; (*of machine*) chōsetsu 調節

rehabilitate shakaifukki saseru 社会復帰させる

rehearsal rihāsaru リハーサル

rehearse 1 *v/t* ... no rihāsaru o suru ...のリハーサルをする **2** *v/i* rihāsaru o suru リハーサルをする

reign 1 *n* chisei 治世; *fig* shihai 支配 **2** *v/i* kunrin suru 君臨する; *fig*

reimburse haraimodosu 払い戻す; (*for damage*) benshō suru 弁償する

rein tazuna 手綱

reincarnation rinne 輪ね

reinforce *structure* hokyō suru 補強する; *army* kyōka suru 強化する; *beliefs* urazukeru 裏付ける

reinforced concrete tekkin-konkurīto 鉄筋コンクリート

reinforcements MIL engun 援軍

reinstate *person in office* fukki saseru 復帰させる; *paragraph etc* moto ni modosu 元に戻す

reject *v/t* kyozetsu suru 拒絶する; *applicant* fusaiyō ni suru 不採用にする; *goods* uketsukenai 受け付けない

rejection kyozetsu 拒絶; (*of applicant*) fusaiyō 不採用

relapse MED saihatsu 再発; *have a ~* saihatsu suru 再発する

relate 1 *v/t* *story* hanasu 話す; *~ X to Y* X to Y o musubitsukeru XとYを結び付ける **2** *v/i*: *~ to ...* (*be connected with*) ... ni kankei ga aru ...に関係がある; *he doesn't ~ to people* kare wa hito to shitashiku shinai 彼は人と親しくしない

related (*by family*) ketsuen-kankei (no) 血縁関係(の); *events, ideas etc* kankei ga aru 関係がある

relation (*in family*) shinseki 親せき; (*connection*) kankei 関係; *business / diplomatic ~s* shigoto / gaikō kankei 仕事/外交関係

relationship kankei 関係; (*sexual*) nikutai kankei 肉体関係

relative 1 *n* shinseki 親せき **2** *adj* sōtaiteki (na) 相対的(な); *X is ~ to Y* X wa Y ni yoru XはYによる

relatively hikakuteki 比較的

relax 1 *v/i* kutsurogu くつろぐ; *~!, don't get angry* ochitsuite okoranaide 落ち着いて 怒らないで **2** *v/t* *muscle* hogusu ほぐす; *pace of work* yurumeru 緩める

relaxation kibarashi 気晴らし

relay 1 *v/t* *message* tsutaeru 伝える;

radio, TV signals chūkei suru 中継する **2** *n*: ~ (*race*) rirē リレー

release 1 *n* (*from prison*) shakuhō 釈放; (*of CD etc*) hatsubai 発売 **2** *v/t prisoner* shakuhō suru 釈放する; *parking brake* hanasu 放す; *CD etc* hatsubai suru 発売する; *information* kōhyō suru 公表する; *movie* kōkai suru 公開する

relent taido ga nanka suru 態度が軟化する

relentless (*determined*) shūnen-bukai 執念深い; *rain etc* taema no nai 絶え間のない

relevance kanren 関連

relevant kanren suru 関連する; *is this ~ to our discussion?* kore wa watashitachi no giron ni tekisetsu na mono desu ka これは私達の議論に適切なものですか

reliability (*of person, machine*) shinraisei 信頼性; (*of information*) shinpyōsei 信ぴょう性

reliable *person, machine* shinrai dekiru 信頼できる; *information* shin'yō dekiru 信用できる

reliably kakujitsu ni 確実に; *I am ~ informed that ...* ... o tashika na suji kara kiita tokoro ni yoru to ... を確かな筋から聞いたところによると

reliance izon 依存; **~ on** ... o shin'yō suru ...を信用する

relic ibutsu 遺物

relief ando 安ど; (*in art*) ukibori 浮き彫り; *that's a ~* hotto shita ほっとした

relieve *pressure, pain* yawarageru 和らげる; (*take over from*) ... to kōtai suru ...と交替する; *be ~d* (*at news etc*) anshin suru 安心する

religion shūkyō 宗教

religious shūkyō (no) 宗教(の); *person* shinjinbukai 信心深い

religiously (*conscientiously*) kichin to きちんと

relish 1 *n* (*sauce*) tsukeawase 付け合わせ; (*pleasure*) tanoshimi 楽しみ **2** *v/t prospect* tanoshimu 楽しむ

relive *the past* tsuitaiken suru 追体験する

relocate *v/i* idō suru 移動する

reluctance ki ga susumanai koto 気が進まないこと

reluctant ki ga susumanai 気が進まない; *be ~ to do X* X suru koto ni ki ga susumanai Xすることに気が進まない

reluctantly iyaiya-nagara いやいやながら

♦ **rely on** (*depend on*) ... ni tayoru ...に頼る; (*count on*) shin'yō suru 信用する; *~ X to do Y* Y suru koto o X ni tayoru YすることをXに頼る

remain (*be left*) nokoru 残る; (*stay*) todomaru とどまる; *they ~ unconvinced* karera wa kakushin dekinai mama de iru 彼らは確信できないままでいる

remainder nokori 残り; MATH sa 差

remains (*of body*) itai 遺体

remand 1 *v/t*: *~ in custody* ... o kōchi suru ...を拘置する **2** *n*: *be on ~* kōchi-chū de aru 拘置中である

remark 1 *n* hatsugen 発言 **2** *v/t* ... to iu ...と言う

remarkable subarashii すばらしい

remarkably ijō ni 異常に

remarry *v/i* saikon suru 再婚する

remedy *n* MED, *fig* chiryōhō 治療法

remember 1 *v/t s.o., sth* omoidasu 思い出す; *I must ~ to do ...* ... suru no o oboete okanakereba naranai ...するのを覚えておかなければならない; *~ to lock the door* doa no kagi o kakeru no o wasurenai de ドアのかぎをかけるのを忘れないで; *~ me to her* kanojo ni yoroshiku otsutae kudasai 彼女によろしくお伝え下さい **2** *v/i*: *I don't ~* oboete inai 覚えていない

remind: *~ X to do Y* X ni Y o wasurenai yō ni chūi suru XにYを忘れないように注意する; *Tokyo ~s me of ...* Tōkyō wa watashi ni ... o omoidasaseru 東京は私に...を思い出させる; *you ~ me of your sister* anata o miru to onēsan o omoidasu あなたを見るとお姉さんを思い出す

reminder omoidasaseru mono 思い

出せる物; *letter* oboegaki 覚え書
き; COM saisokujō 催促状

reminisce omoidebanashi o suru 思
い出話をする

reminiscent: *be ~ of* ... o
omoidasaseru ...を思い出させる

remnant nokori 残り

remorse hageshii kōkai 激しい後悔

remorseless *person* reikoku (na)
冷酷(な); *pace, demands* yōsha nai
容赦ない

remote *village* henpi (na) へんぴ
(な); *possibility, connection*
kasuka (na) かすか(な); *(aloof)*
hanareta 離れた; *ancestor* tōi 遠い

remote access COMPUT rimōto-
akusesu リモートアクセス

remote control rimōto-kontorōru
リモートコントロール

remotely *related, connected* wazuka
ni わずかに; *just ~ possible*
wazuka ni kanōsei ga aru わずか
に可能性がある

removal jokyo 除去; MED setsujo 切
除

remove torinozoku 取り除く; MED
setsujo suru 切除する; *feet* dokeru
どける; *demonstrators* oiharau 追
い払う; *top, lid* toru 取る; *coat etc*
nugu 脱ぐ; *doubt, suspicion*
toriharau 取り払う

remuneration hōshū 報酬

remunerative wari no au 割の合う

rename atarashii namae o tsukeru
新しい名前をつける

render *service* suru する; *~ X
helpless / unconscious* X o
muryoku ni / kizetsu saseru Xを
無力に/気絶させる

rendering *(of music)* ensō 演奏

rendez-vous *(romantic)*
machiawase 待ち合わせ; MIL
shūketsu-chiten 集結地点

renew *contract, license* kōshin suru
更新する; *discussions* saikai suru
再開する

renewal *(of contract etc)* kōshin 更
新; *(of discussions)* saikai 再開

renounce *title, rights* hōki suru 放
棄する

renovate kaizō suru 改造する

renovation kaizō 改造

renown meisei 名声

renowned yūmei (na) 有名(な)

rent 1 *n* yachin 家賃; *for ~* kashiie
ari 貸し家あり **2** *v/t apartment, car*
kariru 借りる; *(~ out)* kasu 貸す

rental *(for apartment)* yachin 家賃;
(for TV etc) chintai-ryō 賃貸料

rental agreement chintai-
keiyakusho 賃貸契約書

rental car renta-kā レンタカー

rent-free *adv* chintairyō nashi de
賃貸料なしで

reopen 1 *v/t* saikai suru 再開する
2 *v/i (of theater etc)* saikai suru 再
開する

reorganization *(of business,
schedule)* saihensei 再編成; *(of
room)* moyōgae 模様替え

reorganize *business, schedule*
saihensei suru 再編成する; *room*
moyōgae suru 模様替えする

rep COM sērusuman セールスマン

repaint nurinaosu 塗り直す

repair 1 *v/t* shūri suru 修理する **2** *n*:
be in a good / bad state of ~ teire
ga ikitodoite iru/inai 手入れが行
き届いている/いない

repairman shūri-ya 修理屋

repatriate sōkan suru 送還する

repay *money* haraimodosu 払い戻
す; *person* ongaeshi o suru 恩返し
をする

repayment hensai 返済

repeal *v/t law* haishi suru 廃止する

repeat 1 *v/t sth said* kurikaeshite
iu 繰り返して言う; *performance,
experience* kurikaesu 繰り返す;
am I ~ing myself? mata onaji
koto itte imasu ka また同じことを
言っていますか **2** *v/i* kurikaeshite
iu 繰り返して言う; *I ~, do not
touch it* kurikaeshimasu, sore ni
sawaranaide 繰り返します、それ
に触らないで **3** *n* TV *etc* saihōsō 再
放送

repeat business COM tsuika no
torihiki 追加の取り引き

repeated saisan (no) 再三(の)

repeat order COM saichūmon 再注
文

repel v/t invaders, attack gekitai suru 撃退する; insects oiharau 追い払う; (disgust) mukatsukaseru むかつかせる

repellent 1 n (insect ~) mushiyoke 虫よけ **2** adj totemo iya (na) とてもいや(な)

repent kōkai suru 後悔する

repercussions eikyō 影響

repetition (of word, event etc) kurikaeshi 繰り返し; (repeating things) chōfuku 重複

repetitive style kudoi くどい; work kurikaeshi (no) 繰り返し(の)

replace (put back) moto ni modosu 元に戻す; (take the place of) ... ni kawaru ...に代わる

replacement (person: permanent) kōkei-sha 後継者; (person: temporary) kōtai-yōin 交代要員; (thing) daiyōhin 代用品

replacement part torikae-buhin 取替部品

replay 1 n (recording) saisei 再生; (game) saishiai 再試合 **2** v/t game ... no saishiai o suru ...の再試合をする

replica fukusei 複製, repurika レプリカ

reply 1 n henji 返事 **2** v/t ... to henji suru ...と返事する **3** v/i henji suru 返事する

report 1 n (account) hōkoku-sho 報告書; (by journalist) hōdō 報道 **2** v/t facts hōdō suru 報道する; (to authorities) hōkoku suru 報告する; ~ one's findings to X X ni ketsuron o hōkoku suru Xに結論を報告する; ~ X to the police keisatsu ni X no koto o tsūhō suru 警察にXのことを通報する; he is ~ed to be in Hong Kong kare wa Honkon ni iru to hōkoku sarete iru 彼は香港にいると報告されている **3** v/i (of journalist) hōkoku suru 報告する; (present oneself) shuttō suru 出頭する

♦**report to** (be accountable to) ...ga jōshi de aru ...が上司である

report card EDU tsūchi-hyō 通知票

reporter kisha 記者

repossess COM kaishū suru 回収する

reprehensible hinansubeki 非難すべき

represent (act for) ... no dairi o suru ...の代理をする; (stand for) ... no tenkei de aru ...の典型である; one's country etc daihyō suru 代表する; (of images in painting etc) hyōgen suru 表現する

representative 1 n dairi 代理; (of nation) daihyō 代表; COM sērusuman セールスマン; POL kain-giin 下院議員 **2** adj (typical) tenkeiteki (na) 典型的(な)

repress revolt yokuatsu suru 抑圧する; feelings, urges osaeru 抑える; laugh koraeru こらえる

repression POL dan'atsu 弾圧

repressive POL dan'atsuteki (na) 弾圧的(な)

reprieve 1 n LAW shikeishikkō-yūyo 死刑執行猶予; fig enki 延期 **2** v/t prisoner shikei-shikkō o yūyo suru 死刑執行を猶予する

reprimand v/t shisseki suru 叱責する

reprint 1 n zōsatsu 増刷 **2** v/t zōsatsu suru 増刷する

reprisal hōfuku 報復; take ~s hōfuku suru 報復する

reproach 1 n hinan 非難; be beyond ~ mōshibun no nai 申し分のない **2** v/t hinan suru 非難する

reproachful togameru yō (na) とがめるよう(な)

reproduce 1 v/t atmosphere, mood saigen suru 再現する; painting, document fukusei suru 複製する **2** v/i BIO hanshoku suru 繁殖する

reproduction BIO hanshoku 繁殖; (of sound, images) saisei 再生; (piece of furniture) fukusei 複製

reproductive BIO hanshoku (no) 繁殖(の)

reptile hachūrui は虫類

republic kyōwakoku 共和国

Republican 1 n Kyōwatōin 共和党員 **2** adj Kyōwatō (no) 共和党(の)

Republic of Korea Daikan-minkoku 大韓民国

repudiate (*deny*) hitei suru 否定する

repulsive ken'o subeki 嫌悪すべき

reputable hyōban no yoi 評判の良い

reputation hyōban 評判; *have a good/bad* ~ hyōban no yoi/warui 評判の良い/悪い

request 1 *n* yōsei 要請; (*on radio program*) rikuesuto リクエスト; *on* ~ irai shidai de 依頼次第で
2 *v/t* onegai suru お願いする

require (*need*) ...ga hitsuyō de aru が必要である; *it* ~*s care* sore wa taihen na chūi ga hitsuyō desu それは大変な注意が必要です; *as* ~*d by law* hōritsu ni yotte yōkyū sarete iru 法律によって要求されている

required hitsuyō (na) 必要(な)

requirement (*need*) yōkyū 要求; (*condition*) jōken 条件

reroute *airplane etc* ukai saseru う回させる

rerun *tape* saisei suru 再生する

rescue 1 *n* kyūjo 救助; *come to X's* ~ X o tasuke ni kuru Xを助けに来る **2** *v/t* kyūjo suru 救助する

rescue party kyūjo-tai 救助隊

research *n* kenkyū 研究
♦ **research into** ...ni tsuite kenkyū suru ...について研究する

research and development kenkyū-kaihatsu 研究開発

research assistant kenkyū-joshu 研究助手

researcher kenkyū-sha 研究者

research project kenkyū-purojekuto 研究プロジェクト

resemblance ruijiten 類似点

resemble ...ni nite iru ...に似ている

resent ...ni hara o tateru ...に腹を立てる

resentful okotte iru 怒っている

resentment urami 恨み

reservation (*of room, table*) yoyaku 予約; (*mental*) utagai 疑い; (*special area*) tokubetsu-horyūchi 特別保留地; *I have a* ~ yoyaku shite arimasu 予約してあります

reserve 1 *n* (*store*) bichiku 備蓄;

(*aloofness*) enryo 遠慮; SP hoketsu 補欠; ~*s* FIN junbikin 準備金; *keep X in* ~ X o totte oku Xを取っておく **2** *v/t seat, table* yoyaku suru 予約する; *judgment* horyū suru 保留する

reserved *person, manner* hikaeme (na) 控えめ(な); *table, seat* yoyaku (no) 予約(の)

reservoir chosuichi 貯水池

reside kyojū suru 居住する

residence (*house etc*) jūtaku 住宅; (*stay*) zaijū 在住

residence permit zairyū-kyoka 在留許可

resident 1 *n* kyojū-sha 居住者; (*in hotel*) shukuhaku-kyaku 宿泊客 **2** *adj manager etc* rejidento (no) レジデント(の)

residential district jūtakuchi 住宅地

residue zanryūbutsu 残留物

resign 1 *v/t position* jinin suru 辞任する; ~ *oneself to* akiramete ... o mitomeru あきらめて...を認める **2** *v/i* (*from job*) jinin suru 辞任する

resignation (*from job*) jinin 辞任; (*mental*) akirame あきらめ

resigned akirameta あきらめた; *we have become* ~ *to the fact that* ... watashitachi wa ... to iu jijitsu o akiramete mitometa 私達は...という事実をあきらめて認めた

resilient *personality* tachinaori no hayai 立ち直りの早い; *material* nagamochi suru 長持ちする

resin jushi 樹脂

resist 1 *v/t enemy, advances, new measures* teikō suru 抵抗する; *temptation* gaman suru 我慢する **2** *v/i* teikō suru 抵抗する

resistance teikō 抵抗; (*to disease, heat etc*) teikō-ryoku 抵抗力

resistant: ~ *to heat* tainetsu (no) 耐熱(の); ~ *to rust* taishoku (no) 耐食(の)

resolute danko to shita 断固とした

resolution (*decision*) ketsugi 決議; (*New Year* ~) kesshin 決心; (*determination*) kyōko na ishi 強固な意志; (*of problem*) kaiketsu 解決;

(*of image*) kaizō-ryoku 解像力

resolve *problem, mystery* kaiketsu suru 解決する; **~ to do X** Xshiyō to kesshin suru Xしようと決心する

resort 1 *n* (*place*) kōrakuchi 行楽地, rizōto リゾート; **as a last ~** saigo no shudan to shite 最後の手段として

resounding *success, victory* kanzen (na) 完全(な)

resource shigen 資源

resourceful rinki-ōhen (no) 臨機応変(の)

respect 1 *n* sonkei 尊敬; (*consideration*) sonchō 尊重; **show ~ to** ... ni keii o harau ...に敬意を払う; **with ~ to** ... ni kanshite ...に関しては; **in this / that ~** kore ni kanshite wa これに関しては; **in many ~s** iroiro na ten de 色々な点で; **pay one's last ~s to** ... no meifuku o inoru ...のめい福を祈る **2** *v/t person* sonkei suru 尊敬する; *opinion, privacy* sonchō suru 尊重する; *law* mamoru 守る

respectable rippa (na) 立派(な)

Respect-for-the-Aged Day Keirō no hi 敬老の日

respectful reigi-tadashii 礼儀正しい

respectfully teinei ni 丁寧に

respective sorezore (no) それぞれ(の)

respectively sorezore それぞれ

respiration kokyū 呼吸

respirator MED jinkōkokyū-sōchi 人工呼吸装置

respite kyūsoku 休息; **without ~** yasuminaku 休みなく

respond (*answer*) kotaeru 答える; (*react*) ōjiru 応じる; (*to treatment*) kōka o arawasu 効果を表す

response (*answer*) kotae 答え; (*reaction*) hannō 反応

responsibility sekinin 責任; (*duty*) gimu 義務; (*in job*) shokumu 職務; **a job with ~** sekinin no aru shigoto 責任のある仕事; **accept ~ for** sekinin o toru 責任を取る

responsible (*liable, for children,*

production etc) sekinin ga aru 責任がある; (*trustworthy*) shinrai dekiru 信頼できる; (*involving responsibility: job*) sekinin no omoi 責任の重い

responsive *audience, brakes* yoku hannō suru よく反応する

rest¹ 1 *n* yasumi 休み **2** *v/i* yasumu 休む; **~ on** (*be based on*) ... ni motozuku ...に基づく; (*lean against*) ... ni tatekakeru ...にたてかける; **it all ~s with him** kare no handan ni kakatte iru 彼の判断にかかっている **3** *v/t* (*lean, balance etc*) yorikakeru 寄り掛ける

rest²: the ~ nokori 残り

restaurant resutoran レストラン

restaurant car shokudōsha 食堂車

rest cure ansei 安静

rest home yōrōin 養老院

restless ochitsukanai 落ち着かない; **have a ~ night** nemurenai 眠れない

restoration (*of building*) shūfuku 修復; (*of health*) kaifuku 回復

restore *building etc* shūfuku suru 修復する; *health* kaifuku suru 回復する

restrain *dog, troops* seishi suru 制止する; *emotions* osaeru 抑える; **~ oneself** jibun o osaerarenai 自分を抑えられない

restraint (*moderation*) setsudo 節度

restrict seigen suru 制限する; **I'll ~ myself to ...** ... ni seigen suru ...に制限する

restricted *view* kagirareta 限られた

restricted area MIL tachiiri-kinshi no basho 立ち入り禁止の場所

restriction seigen 制限

rest room otearai お手洗

result *n* kekka 結果; (*of exam*) seiseki 成績; **as a ~ of this** kono kekka この結果

◆**result from** ... no kekka ...の結果

◆**result in** ... ni owaru ...に終わる

resume *v/t* ... ni modoru ...に戻る

résumé rirekisho 履歴書

resurface 1 *v/t roads* hosō shinaosu 舗装し直す **2** *v/i* (*of problems*) saifujō suru 再浮上する; (*of person*) saitōjō suru 再登場する

resurrection REL Kirisuto no fukkatsu キリストの復活

resuscitate ikikaeraseru 生き返らせる

retail 1 *adv* kourine de 小売値で **2** *v/i*: kouri sareru 小売りされる; **~ at ...** ... de kouri suru ...で小売りする

retailer kouri-gyōsha 小売業者

retail price kouri-kakaku 小売価格

retain tamotsu 保つ

retainer FIN komon-ryō 顧問料

retaliate hōfuku suru 報復する

retaliation hōfuku 報復

retarded chie-okure (no) 知恵遅れ(の)

retire *v/i* (*from work*) taishoku suru 退職する

retired taishoku shita 退職した

retirement taishoku 退職

retirement age teinen 定年

retiring hikkomijian (no) 引込み思案(の)

retort 1 *n* shippegaeshi しっぺ返し **2** *v/i* iikaesu 言い返す

retrace *footsteps* hikikaesu 引き返す

retract *v/t claws, undercarriage* hikkomeru 引っ込める; *statement* tekkai suru 撤回する

retreat 1 *v/i* MIL taikyaku suru 退却する; (*in discussion etc*) hikisagaru 引き下がる **2** *n* MIL taikyaku 退却; (*place*) kakurega 隠れ家

retrieve *sth lost* torimodosu 取り戻す; *larger object* kaishū suru 回収する; COMPUT kensaku suru 検索する

retriever (*dog*) retorībā レトリーバー

retroactive *law etc* sakanoboru さかのぼる

retrograde *move, decision* atomodori (no) 後戻り(の)

retrospect: *in ~* furikaette miru to 振り返ってみると

retrospective *n* kaiko 回顧

return 1 *n* (*coming back, going back*)

kikan 帰還; (*giving back*) henkyaku 返却; COMPUT, (*in tennis*) ritān リターン; *by ~* (*of post*) orikaeshi de 折り返しで; *~s* (*profit*) rieki 利益; *many happy ~s* (*of the day*) otanjōbi omedetō gozaimasu お誕生日おめでとうございます **2** *v/t* (*give back*) henkyaku suru 返却する; (*put back*) modosu 戻す; *favor, invitation* kaesu 返す **3** *v/i* (*go back, come back*) kaeru 帰る; (*of good times, doubt etc*) modoru 戻る

return flight kaeri no bin 帰りの便

return journey kaeri 帰り

reunification saitōitsu 再統一

reunion atsumari 集まり; EDU dōsōkai 同窓会

reunite *v/t old friends* saikai saseru 再会させる; *country* saitōgō suru 再統合する

reusable sairiyō dekiru 再利用できる

reuse sairiyō suru 再利用する

rev *n* kaiten 回転; *~s per minute* maifun-kaitensū 毎分回転数

♦ **rev up** *v/t engine* ... o fukasu ...をふかす

revaluation kiriage 切り上げ

reveal (*make visible*) miseru 見せる; (*make known*) akiraka ni suru 明らかにする; *feelings* shimesu 示す

revealing *remark* akiraka ni suru 明らかにする; *dress* hada o arawa ni suru 肌をあらわにする

revelation igai na hakken 意外な発見; (*scandalous*) bakuro 暴露

revenge fukushū 復しゅう; *take one's ~ on* ... ni fukushū suru ...に復しゅうする

revenue shūnyū 収入; (*of government*) sainyū 歳入

reverberate (*of sound*) hibiku 響く

Reverend: *the ~ John Smith* Jon Sumisu shi ジョンスミス師

reverent uyauyashii うやうやしい

reverse 1 *adj sequence* gyaku (no) 逆(の) **2** *n* (*opposite*) gyaku 逆; (*back*) ura 裏; MOT bakku バック **3** *v/t sequence* gyaku ni suru 逆にする; *vehicle* bakku saseru バック

させる; *decision* hikkurikaesu
ひっくり返す **4** *v/i* MOT bakku
suru バックする

review 1 *n* (*of book, movie*) hihyō
批評; (*of troops*) eppei 閲兵; (*of
situation etc*) saikentō 再検討
2 *v/t book, movie* hihyō suru 批評
する; *troops* eppei suru 閲兵する;
situation etc saikentō suru 再検討
する; EDU fukushū suru 復習する

reviewer (*of book, movie*) hyōron-
ka 評論家

revise *v/t text, figures* shūsei suru
修正する; *opinion* kaeru 変える

revision (*of text, figures*) shūsei 修
正; (*of opinion*) henkō 変更

revival (*of custom etc*) fukkatsu 復
活; (*of patient*) kaifuku 回復; THEA
ribaibaru リバイバル

revive 1 *v/t custom, old style etc*
fukkatsu saseru 復活させる;
patient ishiki o kaifuku saseru 意
識を回復させる; *economy* kaifuku
saseru 回復させる; THEA saijōen
suru 再上演する **2** *v/i* (*of business,
exchange rate etc*) kaifuku suru 回
復する; (*of patient*) ishiki o
torimodosu 意識をとりもどす

revoke *law, license* mukō ni suru 無
効にする

revolt 1 *n* hangyaku 反逆 **2** *v/i*
hangyaku suru 反逆する

revolting (*disgusting*)
mukatsukaseru むかつかせる

revolution POL *etc* kakumei 革命;
(*turn*) kaiten 回転

revolutionary 1 *n* POL kakumei-ka
革命家 **2** *adj spirit, forces* kakumei
(no) 革命(の); *ideas* kakumeiteki
(na) 革命的(な)

revolutionize kakumei o okosu 革命
を起こす

revolve *v/i* kaiten suru 回転する

revolver riborubā リボルバー

revolving door kaiten-doa 回転ドア

revue THEA rebyū レビュー

revulsion ken'o 嫌悪

reward 1 *n* (*financial*) shōkin 賞金;
(*benefit derived*) hōbi ほうび **2** *v/t*
(*financially*) shōkin o ataeru 賞金
を与える

rewarding tame ni naru ためになる

rewind *v/t film, tape* makimodosu 巻
き戻す

rewrite *v/t* kakinaosu 書き直す

rhetoric retorikku レトリック

rheumatism ryūmachi リューマチ

rhinoceros sai さい

rhubarb rūbābu ルバーブ

rhyme 1 *n* in 韻 **2** *v/i* in o fumu 韻を
踏む; **~ with ...** ... to in o fumu ...
と韻を踏む

rhythm rizumu リズム

rib *n* rokkotsu ろっ骨

ribbon ribon リボン

rice kome 米; (*cooked*) gohan ご飯

rice ball onigiri おにぎり; **rice bowl**
gohan-jawan ご飯茶碗; **rice
cooker** suihanki 炊飯器; **rice
cracker** senbei せんべい; **ricefield**
suiden 水田; **rice wine** sake 酒

rich 1 *adj* kanemochi (no) 金持ち
(の); *country* yutaka (na) 豊か
(な); *soil* hiyoku (na) 肥よく(な);
food kotteri shita こってりした
2 *n*: **the ~** kanemochi 金持

rid: **get ~ of** ... o torinozoku ...を取
り除く; *feeling, state of affairs* ...
kara nukedasu ...から抜け出す

ride 1 *n* (*on horse*) jōba 乗馬; (*in
vehicle*) doraibu ドライブ;
(*journey*) ryokō 旅行; **do you
want a ~ into town?** machi made
notte ikimasen ka 町まで乗って行
きませんか **2** *v/t horse, bike* ... ni
noru ...に乗る **3** *v/i* (*on horse*)
jōba o suru 乗馬をする; (*on bike*)
jitensha ni noru 自転車に乗る; (*in
vehicle*) kuruma ni noru 車に乗る

rider (*on horse*) kishu 騎手; (*on
bike*) norite 乗り手

ridge (*on earth*) une 畝; (*of
mountain*) one 尾根; (*of roof*)
teppen 天辺

ridicule 1 *n* azakeri あざけり **2** *v/t*
azakeru あざける

ridiculous bakageta ばかげた

ridiculously bakabakashii hodo ば
かばかしいほど

riding (*on horseback*) jōba 乗馬

rifle *n* raifuru ライフル

rift (*in earth*) kiretsu 亀裂; (*in party*

etc) tairitsu 対立

rig 1 *n* (*oil ~*) yusei-kussakusōchi 油井掘削装置; (*truck*) torakku トラック 2 *v/t* elections fuseisōsa suru 不正操作する

right 1 *adj* (*correct*) tadashii 正しい; (*morally*) seitō (na) 正当(な); (*fair, just*) tekisetsu (na) 適切(な); (*proper, appropriate*) tekitō (na) 適当(な); (*not left*) migi (no) 右(の); *be ~* (*be correct*) tadashii 正しい; (*of clock*) seikaku de aru 正確である; *that's ~!* sono tōri そのとおり; *put things ~* naosu 直す → *alright* 2 *adv* (*directly*) sugu すぐ; (*correctly*) tadashiku 正しく; (*completely*) sukkari すっかり; (*not left*) migi ni 右に; *~ now* (*immediately*) ima sugu ni 今すぐに; (*at the moment*) ima 今; *~ on time* chōdo no jikan ちょうどの時間 3 *n* (*civil, legal etc*) kenri 権利; (*not left*) migi 右; POL uha 右派; *on the ~* migi ni 右に; POL uha 右派(の); *turn to the ~, take a ~* migi ni magaru 右に曲がる; *be in the ~* tadashii 正しい; *know ~ from wrong* shinjitsu o shiru 真実を知る

right-angle chokkaku 直角; *at ~s to … …* to chokkaku ni …と直角に

rightful heir, owner etc seitō (na) 正当(な)

right-hand *adj* migi (no) 右(の); *on the ~ side* migigawa (no) 右側(の); **right-hand drive** MOT migi-handoru (no) 右ハンドル(の); **right-handed** migikiki (no) 右利き(の); **right-hand man** migiude 右腕; **right of way** (*in traffic*) yūsen-ken 優先権; (*across land*) tsūkō-ken 通行権; **right wing** 1 *n* POL uyoku 右翼; (*within party*) uha 右派; SP raito-uingu ライトウイング 2 *adj* POL uyoku (no) 右翼(の); (*within party*) uha (no) 右派(の); **right-wing extremism** POL kyokuu 極右; **right-winger** POL uyoku 右翼

rigid material katai 固い; principles kibishii 厳しい; attitude yūzū no kikanai 融通の利かない

rigor (*of discipline*) genkaku-sa 厳格さ; *the ~s of the winter* fuyu no kibishi-sa 冬の厳しさ

rigorous discipline genkaku (na) 厳格(な); tests, analysis genmitsu (na) 厳密(な)

rim (*of wheel*) rimu リム; (*of cup*) fuchi 縁; (*of eyeglasses*) furēmu フレーム

ring [1] (*circle*) wa 輪; (*on finger*) yubiwa 指輪; (*in boxing, at circus*) ringu リング

ring [2] 1 *n* (*of bell*) beru no naru oto ベルの鳴る音; (*of voice*) hibiki 響き 2 *v/t* bell narasu 鳴らす 3 *v/i* (*of bell*) naru 鳴る; *please ~ for attention* goyō no sai wa beru o narashite kudasai ご用の際はベルを鳴らして下さい

ringleader shubō-sha 首謀者

ring-pull puru-tabu プルタブ

rink rinku リンク

rinse 1 *n* (*for hair color*) hea-dai ヘアダイ 2 *v/t* clothes, dishes susugu すすぐ; hair rinsu suru リンスする

riot 1 *n* bōdō 暴動 2 *v/i* bōdō o okosu 暴動を起こす

rioter bōto 暴徒

riot police kidōtai 機動隊

rip 1 *n* (*in cloth etc*) sakeme 裂け目 2 *v/t* cloth etc saku 裂く; *~ open …* o yabutte akeru …を破って空ける

♦ **rip off** F (*cheat*) damasu だます; customers fukkakekeru 吹っかける

ripe fruit ureta 熟れた

ripen *v/i* (*of fruit*) juku suru 熟する

ripeness (*of fruit*) seijuku 成熟

rip-off *n* F sagi 詐欺

ripple (*on water*) sazanami さざ波

rise 1 *v/i* (*from chair etc*) tachiagaru 立ち上がる; (*of sun*) noboru 昇る; (*of rocket*) ririku suru 離陸する; (*of price, temperature, water level*) agaru 上がる 2 *n* (*in price, temperature, water level*) jōshō 上昇; (*in salary*) shōkyū 昇給

rising sun: *the land of the ~* hi izuru tokoro no kuni 日出ずる処の国

risk 1 *n* kiken 危険; *take a ~* kiken o okasu 危険を冒す **2** *v/t* kiken ni sarasu 危険にさらす; *reputation* kiken o okasu 危険を冒す; *let's ~ it* yatte miyō やってみよう

risky kiken (na) 危険(な)

ritual 1 *n* gishiki 儀式 **2** *adj* gishikiteki (na) 儀式的(な)

rival 1 *n* raibaru ライバル **2** *v/t* ... ni hitteki suru ...に匹敵する; *I can't ~ that* kore ni wa katenai これには勝てない

rivalry kyōsō 競争

river kawa 川

riverbed kawadoko 川床

riverside kawagishi 川岸

rivet 1 *n* ribetto リベット **2** *v/t* ribetto de tomeru リベットで留める; *~ X to Y* Y ni X o ribetto de tomeru Y に X をリベットで留める

road dōro 道路; *it's just down the ~* sugu soko desu すぐそこです

roadblock kenmon-sho 検問所; **road hog** ranbō na doraibā 乱暴なドライバー; **road holding** (*of vehicle*) sōkōanteisei 走行安定性; **road map** dōro-chizu 道路地図; **roadside**: *at the ~* dōrowaki ni道路脇に; **roadsign** dōro-hyōshiki 道路標識; **roadway** shadō 車道; **road works** dōro-kōji 道路工事; **roadworthy** seibi sareta 整備された

roam samayou さまよう

roar 1 *n* (*of traffic, engine*) gōon ごう音; (*of lion*) hoegoe ほえ声; (*of person: in anger*) wamekigoe わめき声 **2** *v/i* (*of engine*) gōon o tateru ごう音を立てる; (*of lion*) hoeru ほえる; (*of person: in anger*) wameku わめく; *~ with laughter* ōwarai suru 大笑いする

roast 1 *n* (*beef etc*) rōsuto ロースト **2** *v/t* yaku 焼く; *nuts, coffee* iru いる **3** *v/i* (*of food*) yakeru 焼ける; *we're ~ing* F sugoku atsui すごく暑い

roast beef rōsuto-bīfu ローストビーフ

roast pork rōsuto-pōku ローストポーク

rob *person, bank* ...kara ubau ...か

ら奪う; *I've been ~bed* watashi wa gōtō ni osowareta 私は強盗に襲われた

robber gōtō 強盗

robbery gōtō 強盗

robe (*of judge, priest*) shikifuku 式服; (*bath~*) basu-rōbu バスローブ

robin komadori こまどり

robot robotto ロボット

robust *person* takumashii たくましい; *economy* kenzen (na) 健全(な); *structure* ganjō (na) 頑丈(な)

rock 1 *n* ganseki 岩石; (*small*) ishi 石; MUS rokku ロック; *on the ~s drink* on za rokku オンザロック; *of marriage* hatan sunzen de 破たん寸前で **2** *v/t cradle* yuri ugokasu 揺り動かす; *baby* ayasu あやす; (*surprise*) dōyō saseru 動揺させる **3** *v/i* (*on chair*) yure ugoku 揺れ動く; (*of boat*) yureru 揺れる

rock bottom: *reach ~* donzoko ni ochiru どん底に落ちる

rock-bottom *prices* sokone (no) 底値(の)

rocket 1 *n* roketto ロケット **2** *v/i* (*of prices etc*) kyūjōshō suru 急上昇する

rocking chair yuriisu 揺りいす

rock 'n' roll rokkun-rōru ロックンロール

rock star rokku-stā ロックスター

rocky *beach, path* iwadarake (no) 岩だらけ(の)

rod bō 棒; (*for fishing*) tsuri-zao 釣ざお

rodent gesshirui げっ歯類

rogue akutō 悪党

role yakuwari 役割

role model risō no sugata 理想の姿

roll 1 *n* (*bread*) rōru-pan ロールパン; (*of film*) maki 巻き; (*of thunder*) todoroki とどろき; (*list, register*) meibo 名簿 **2** *v/i* (*of ball etc*) korogaru 転がる; (*of boat*) yureru 揺れる **3** *v/t*: *~ X into a ball* X o maite tama ni suru X を巻いて玉にする

♦**roll over 1** *v/i* negaeri o utsu 寝返りを打つ **2** *v/t person, object* ... o korogasu ...を転がす; (*renew*)

kōshin suru 更新する

♦ **roll up** 1 v/t sleeves … o makuru …をまくる 2 v/i F (arrive) arawareru 現れる

roll call tenko 点呼

roller (for hair) kārā カーラー

roller blade n rōrā-burēdo ローラーブレード; **roller coaster** jetto-kōsutā ジェットコースター; **roller skate** n rōrā-sukēto ローラースケート

rolling pin menbō めん棒

ROM (= **read only memory**) romu ロム

Roman Catholic 1 n Katorikku-shinja カトリック信者 2 adj Katorikku (no) カトリック(の)

Roman script Rōmaji ローマ字

romance (affair) ren'ai 恋愛; (novel) ren'ai-shōsetsu 恋愛小説; (movie) ren'ai-eiga 恋愛映画

romantic romanchikku (na) ロマンチック(な)

roof yane 屋根

roof rack MOT rūfu-rēru ルーフレール

room heya 部屋; (space) basho 場所; (scope) yochi 余地; **there's no ~ for …** … no basho ga nai …の場所がない; **Japanese-style ~** washitsu 和室

room clerk furonto フロント; **roommate** rūmu-mēto ルームメート; **room service** rūmu-sābisu ルームサービス

roomy house etc hirobiro to shita 広々とした; clothes yuttari shita ゆったりした

root ne 根; (of word) gokan 語幹; (of problem) kongen 根源; **~s** (of person) rūtsu ルーツ

♦ **root out** (get rid of) … o nekosogi ni suru …を根こそぎにする; (find) … o sagashidasu …を捜し出す

rope rōpu ロープ

♦ **rope off** … o rōpu de shikiru …をロープで仕切る

rose BOT bara ばら

rostrum endan 演壇

rosy cheeks akai 赤い; future akarui 明るい; color barairo (no) ばら色

(の)

rot 1 n (in wood) fuhai 腐敗; (in teeth) mushiba 虫歯 2 v/i (of food, wood) kusaru 腐る; (of teeth) mushiba ni naru 虫歯になる

rotate v/i kaiten suru 回転する

rotation kaiten 回転; **do X in ~** X o kōtai de suru Xを交替でする

rotten food, wood etc kusatta 腐った; trick, thing to do hiretsu (na) 卑劣(な); weather, luck hidoi ひどい

rough 1 adj surface zarazara shita ざらざらした; hands, skin, crossing, seas areta 荒れた; voice shagareta しゃがれた; (violent) ranbō (na) 乱暴(な); (approximate) daitai だいたい; town, area chian no warui 治安の悪い; **~ draft** shitagaki 下書き 2 adv: **sleep ~** nojuku suru 野宿する 3 n (in golf) rafu ラフ 4 v/t: **~ it** genshiteki na seikatsu o suru 原始的な生活をする

roughage (in food) sen'i 繊維

roughly (approximately) daitai だいたい

roulette rūretto ルーレット

round 1 adj marui 丸い; **in ~ figures** daitai だいたい 2 n (of mailman etc) junkai 巡回; (of toast) hitokire 一切れ; (of drinks) kai 回; (of competition) kaisen 回戦; (in boxing match) raundo ラウンド 3 v/t the corner magaru 曲がる 4 adv & prep → **around**

♦ **round off** edges … o maruku suru …を丸くする; meeting, evening … o oeru …を終える

♦ **round up** figure … o kiriageru …を切り上げる; suspects, criminals … o kenkyo suru …を検挙する

roundabout adj way of saying sth tōmawashi (no) 遠回し(の); route tōmawari (no) 遠回り(の); **round trip** ōfuku 往復; **round trip ticket** ōfuku-kippu 往復切符

round-up (of cattle) kakiatsumeru koto かき集めること; (of suspects, criminals) kenkyo 検挙; (of news) matome まとめ

rouse (*from sleep*) okosu 起こす; (*interest, emotions*) hikiokosu 引き起こす

rousing *speech etc* nekkyōteki (na) 熱狂的(な)

route rūto ルート; (*walking*) tōrimichi 通り道

routine 1 *adj* (*customary*) nichijō (no) 日常(の); (*predictable*) okimari (no) お決まり(の) **2** *n* (*habitual behavior*) shūkan 習慣; (*set sequence of events*) itsumo no tejun いつもの手順; *as a matter of ~* okimari no shigoto お決まりの仕事

row[1] (*line*) retsu 列; *5 days in a ~* itsuka renzoku de 五日連続で

row[2] **1** *v/t boat* kogu こぐ **2** *v/i* bōto o kogu ボートをこぐ

rowboat bōto ボート

rowdy ranbō (na) 乱暴(な); *party* sōzō shii 騒々しい

row house terasu-hausu テラスハウス

royalty ōzoku 王族; (*on book etc*) inzei 印税

rub *v/t* kosuru こする

♦ **rub down** (*to clean*) kosutte migaku こすって磨く

♦ **rub off 1** *v/t dirt* ... o kosuritoru ...をこすり取る; *paint etc* hagasu はがす **2** *v/i*: *it rubs off on you* anata ni utsuru あなたにうつる

rubber 1 *n* (*material*) gomu ゴム **2** *adj* gomu (no) ゴム(の)

rubble gareki がれき

ruby (*jewel*) rubī ルビー

rucksack ryukku sakku リュックサック

rudder kaji かじ

ruddy *complexion* kesshoku no yoi 血色の良い

rude *person* burei (na) 無礼(な); *behavior, language* gehin (na) 下品(な); *it is ~ to ...* ... suru no wa burei de aru ...するのは無礼である; *I didn't mean to be ~* burei na mane o suru tsumori de wa nakatta 無礼なまねをするつもりではなかった

rudeness burei 無礼

rudimentary *skills* shohoteki (na) 初歩的(な); *knowledge* kisoteki (na) 基礎的(な)

rudiments kiso 基礎

ruffian gorotsuki ごろつき

ruffle 1 *n* (*on dress*) hidakazari ひだ飾り **2** *v/t hair, clothes* midasu 乱す; *person* dōyō saseru 動揺させる; *get ~d* dōyō suru 動揺する

rug shikimono 敷き物; (*blanket*) hizakake ひざ掛け

rugged *scenery, cliffs* kewashii 険しい; *face* hori no fukai 彫りの深い; *resistance* ganken (na) 頑健(な)

ruin 1 *n* hakai 破壊; *~s iseki* 遺跡; *in ~s city, building*) kōhai shite 荒廃して; *plans, marriage* dame ni natte だめになって **2** *v/t plans, birthday, vacation* dame ni suru だめにする; *plans* kowasu 壊す; *reputation* kegasu 汚す; *be ~ed* (*financially*) hasan suru 破産する

rule 1 *n* (*of club, game*) kisoku 規則, rūru ルール; (*of monarch*) tōchi 統治; (*for measuring*) monosashi 物差し; *as a ~* gaishite 概して **2** *v/t country* shihai suru 支配する; *the judge ~d that ...* saibankan ga ... to saitei suru 裁判官が...と裁定する **3** *v/i* (*of monarch*) tōchi suru 統治する

♦ **rule out** ... o jogai suru ...を除外する

ruler (*for measuring*) monosashi 物差し; (*of state*) shihai-sha 支配者

ruling 1 *n* kettei 決定 **2** *adj*: *~ party* yotō 与党

rum (*drink*) ramu-shu ラム酒

rumble *v/i* (*of stomach*) gorogoro naru ゴロゴロ鳴る; (*of train in tunnel*) gōon o hibikasete hashiru ごう音を響かせて走る

♦ **rummage around** hikkurikaeshite sagasu ひっくり返して探す

rummage sale garakuta-ichi がらくた市

rumor 1 *n* uwasa うわさ **2** *v/t*: *it is ~ed that ...* ... to iu uwasa da ...と言ううわさだ

rump (*of animal*) shiri しり

rumple *clothes, paper* kushakusha ni suru くしゃくしゃにする

rumpsteak ranpusutēki ランプステーキ

run 1 *n* (*on foot*) kakeashi 駆け足; (*in pantyhose*) densen 伝線; (THEA: *of play*) renzoku-kōen 連続公演; **go for a ~** jogingu suru ジョギングする; **make a ~ for it** (*run away*) nigeru 逃げる; **a criminal on the ~** tōsōchū no hannin 逃走中の犯人; **in the short ~** mesaki no koto to shite kangaeru to 目先の事として考えると; **in the long ~** nagai me de miru to 長い目で見ると; **a ~ on the dollar** doru no kaininki shūchū ドルの買い人気集中 **2** *v/i* (*of person, animal*) hashiru 走る; (*of river, paint, make-up*) nagareru 流れる; (*of trains etc*) unkō suru 運行する; (*of nose*) hanamizu ga tareru 鼻水が垂れる; (*of faucet*) deru 出る; (*of play*) renzoku-kōen suru 連続公演する; (*of engine, machine*) sadō suru 作動する; (*of software*) tsukaeru 使える; (*in election*) shutsuba suru 出馬する; **~ for President** daitōryō-sen ni shutsuba suru 大統領選に出馬する **3** *v/t race* kyōgikai ni deru 競技会に出る; *3 miles etc* hashiru 走る; *business, hotel, project etc* keiei suru 経営する; *software* sadō suru 作動する; *car* tsukau 使う; **would you like me to ~ you to the station?** eki made okurimashō ka 駅まで送りましょうか; **he ran his eye down the page** kare wa pēji ni me o hashiraseta 彼はページに目を走らせた

♦ **run across** (*meet*) ... ni dekuwasu ...に出くわす; (*find*) ... o gūzen mitsukeru ...を偶然見つける

♦ **run away** nigeru 逃げる

♦ **run down 1** *v/t* (*by car*) ... o hiku ...をひく; (*criticize*) ... o kenasu ...をけなす; *stocks* ... o herasu ...を減らす **2** *v/i* (*of battery*) kireru 切れる

♦ **run into** (*meet*) ... ni dekuwasu ...に出くわす; *difficulties* ... ni butsukaru ...にぶつかる

♦ **run off 1** *v/i* nigedasu 逃げ出す **2** *v/t* (*print*) ... o insatsu suru ...を印刷する

♦ **run out** (*of contract*) kireru 切れる; (*of supplies*) nakunaru なくなる; **time is running out** jikangire ni natte kita 時間切れになってきた

♦ **run out of** *patience* ... ga nakunaru ...がなくなる; *supplies* ... ga kireru ...が切れる; **I ran out of gas** gasuketsu ni narimashita ガス欠になりました

♦ **run over 1** *v/t* (*in car*) ... o hiku ...をひく; **can we ~ the details again?** mō ichido shōsai ni me o tōshite ii desu ka もう一度詳細に目を通していいですか **2** *v/i* (*of water etc*) ... ga afureru ...があふれる

♦ **run through** (*rehearse, go over*) rihāsaru o suru リハーサルをする; *details* tōsu 通す

♦ **run up** *v/t debts, bill* ... ga kasamu ...がかさむ; *clothes* ... o isoide tsukuru ...を急いで作る

run-down *person* hetoheto (no) へとへと(の); *area, building* sabirete iru さびれている

rung (*of ladder*) dan 段

runner (*athlete*) sōsha 走者

runner-up ni chaku no hito 二着の人

running 1 *n* SP kyōsō 競走; (*jogging*) jogingu ジョギング; (*of business*) keiei 経営 **2** *adj*: **for two days ~** futsuka-kan renzoku 二日間連続

running water (*supply*) suidōsui 水道水

runny *liquid* mizuppoi 水っぽい; *egg* yurui 緩い; *nose* tareru 垂れる

run-up SP josō 助走; **in the ~ to** ... e no junbi-kikan de ...への準備期間で

runway kassōro 滑走路

rupture 1 *n* (*in pipe*) haretsu 破裂; (*in relations*) ketsuretsu 決裂; MED herunia ヘルニア **2** *v/i* (*of pipe etc*) haretsu suru 破裂する

rural inaka (no) 田舎(の); *economy* chihō (no) 地方(の)

rush 1 *n* ōisogi 大急ぎ; **do X in a ~** X o

ōisogi de suru Xを大急ぎでする;*be in a ~* isoide iru 急いでいる;*what's the big ~?* dōshite sonna ni isoide iru no desu ka どうしてそんなに急いでいるのですか **2** *v/t person* isogaseru 急がせる; *meal* isoide tabesaseru 急いで食べさせる;*~ X to the hospital* X o ōisogi de byōin ni tsurete itta Xを大急ぎで病院に連れていった **3** *v/i* isogu 急ぐ

rush hour rasshu-awā ラッシュアワー

Russia Roshia ロシア

Russian 1 *adj* Roshia (no) ロシア(の) **2** *n* Roshia-jin ロシア人; *(language)* Roshia-go ロシア語

Russo-Japanese War *(1904-05)* Nichiro-sensō 日露戦争

rust 1 *n* sabi さび **2** *v/i* sabiru さびる

rustle *v/i (of silk)* sarasara to naru さらさらと鳴る; *(of leaves)* kasakasa to naru かさかさと鳴る

♦ **rustle up** F *meal* ... o tebayaku ryōri suru ...を手早く料理する

rust-proof *adj* sabinai さびない

rust remover sabitorizai さび取り剤

rusty sabita さびた; *French, math etc* ...ga dame ni natta ...がだめになった;*I'm a little ~* sukoshi dame ni natte imasu すこしだめになっています

rut *(in road)* wadachi わだち; *be in a ~* kata ni hamaru 型にはまる

ruthless reikoku (na) 冷酷(な)

ruthlessness reikoku 冷酷

rye raimugi ライ麦

rye bread raimugi-pan ライ麦パン

S

sabbatical *n (of academic)* kenkyū-kyūka 研究休暇

sabotage 1 *n* hakai-kōsaku 破壊工作 **2** *v/t* hakai suru 破壊する

saccharin *n* sakkarin サッカリン

sachet *(of shampoo, cream etc)* ko-bukuro 小袋

sack *n* ō-bukuro 大袋

sacred shinsei (na) 神聖(な)

sacrifice 1 *n (act)* gisei 犠牲; *(person, animal sacrificed)* ikenie いけにえ; *make ~s fig* gisei o harau 犠牲をはらう **2** *v/t* ikenie to shite sasageru いけにえとして捧げる; *freedom etc* gisei ni suru 犠牲にする

sad kanashii 悲しい; *face* kanashisō (na) 悲しそう(な)

saddle *n* kura くら

sadism sadizumu サディズム

sadist sadisuto サディスト

sadistic kagyakuteki (na) 加虐的(な)

sadly *look, sing etc* kanashi-sō ni 悲しそうに; *(regrettably)* zannen na koto ni 残念なことに

sadness kanashimi 悲しみ

safe 1 *adj (not dangerous)* anzen (na) 安全(な); *(not in danger)* buji (na) 無事(な); *investment, prediction* kakujitsu (na) 確実(な) **2** *n* kinko 金庫

safeguard 1 *n* anzen-taisaku 安全対策; *as a ~ against* ... ni taisuru anzen-taisaku to shite ...に対する安全対策として **2** *v/t* hogo suru 保護する

safekeeping: *give X to Y for ~* Y ni X o hokan shite morau yō ni azukeru YにXを保管してもらうように預ける

safely *arrive* buji ni 無事に; *drive* anzen ni 安全に; *assume* machigainaku 間違いなく; *they will be ~ looked after* karera wa machigainaku sewa o shite

moraemasu 彼らは間違いなく世話
をしてもらえます

safety anzen 安全; (*of investment*)
anzensei 安全性; *be in ~* buji de
aru 無事である; *reach ~* anzen na
tokoro ni tadori-tsuku 安全なとこ
ろにたどりつく

safety-conscious anzen-ishiki ni
takai 安全意識の高い; **safety first**
anzen-daiichi (no) 安全第一(の);
safety pin anzen-pin 安全ピン

sag 1 *n* (*in ceiling etc*) tawami たわ
み **2** *v/i* (*of ceiling, rope*) tarumu
たるむ; (*of output, tempo*) naka-
darumi suru 中だるみする

sage (*herb*) sēji セージ

sail 1 *n* ho 帆; (*trip*) kōkai 航海; *go
for a ~* sēringu ni iku セーリング
に行く **2** *v/t yacht* sēringu suru
セーリングする **3** *v/i* sēringu suru
セーリングする; (*depart*) shukkō
suru 出港する

sailboard 1 *n* sāfu-bōdo サーフボー
ド **2** *v/i* windo-sāfin o suru ウィン
ドサーフィンをする

sailboarding windosāfin ウィンド
サーフィン

sailboat yotto ヨット

sailing SP sēringu セーリング

sailing ship hansen 帆船

sailor (*in the navy*) suihei 水兵; SP
yottoman ヨットマン; *be a good/
bad ~* funayoi shinai/suru hito 船
酔いしない/する人

saint seijin 聖人

sake: *for my/your ~*
watashi/anata no tame ni 私/あな
たのために; *for the ~ of* ... no
tame ni ...のために

sake sake 酒; *sweet ~* amazake 甘
酒; *cold ~* hiya 冷や; *hot ~* atsukan
熱かん

sake cup choko ちょこ

sake flask tokkuri とっくり

salad sarada サラダ

salad dressing doresshingu ドレッ
シング

salary kyūryō 給料

salary scale kyūryō-taikei 給料体系

sale hanbai 販売; (*reduced prices*)
tokubai 特売, sēru セール; *for ~*

(*sign*) urimono 売り物; *be on ~*
hanbai sarete iru 販売されている;
(*at reduced prices*) yasuuri sarete
iru 安売りされている

sales (*department*) eigyō-bu 営業部

sales clerk ten'in 店員; **sales
figures** uriagedaka 売上高;
salesman sērusuman セールスマ
ン; **sales manager** eigyō-kachō
営業課長; **sales meeting** hanbai-
kaigi 販売会議

saliva daeki だ液

salmon sake さけ

saloon (*bar*) bā バー

salt shio 塩

saltcellar shioire 塩入れ

salty shiokarai 塩辛い

salutary *experience* yūeki (na) 有益
(な)

salute 1 *n* MIL keirei 敬礼; *take the ~*
keirei o ukeru 敬礼を受ける **2** *v/t*
... ni aisatsu suru ...にあいさつする
3 *v/i* aisatsu suru あいさつする

salvage *v/t* sukuidasu 救い出す

salvation tamashii no kyūsai 魂の救
済

Salvation Army Kyūseigun 救世軍

same 1 *adj* onaji 同じ **2** *pron*: *the ~*
(*things*) onaji mono 同じ物;
(*abstracts*) onaji koto 同じこと;
Happy New Year – the ~ to you
Akemashite omedetō gozaimasu
– kochira koso Akemashite
omedetō gozaimasu 明けましてお
めでとうございます―こちらこ
そ、明けましておめでとうござい
ます; *he's not the ~ any more*
kare wa mō moto no kare de wa
nai 彼はもう元の彼ではない; *but
all the ~, it does seem strange*
tonikaku hen da とにかく変だ; *but
I still love her all the ~* yappari
kanjo o aishite iru やっぱり彼女を
愛している; *men are all the ~*
otoko wa mina nitari yottari de
aru 男は皆似たり寄ったりである;
it's all the ~ to me watashi wa
nan demo kamaimasen 私は何でも
かまいません **3** *adv*: *look/sound
the ~* onaji ni mieru/kikoeru 同
じに見える/聞こえる

sample n mihon 見本, sanpuru サンプル

Samurai Samurai 侍; **~ sword** katana 刀

sanction 1 n (approval) ninka 認可; (penalty) seisai 制裁 **2** v/t (approve) ninka suru 認可する

sanctity shinsei-sa 神聖さ

sanctuary REL seiiki 聖域; (for animals) hogo-kuiki 保護区域

sand 1 n suna 砂 **2** v/t (with sandpaper) ... ni yasuri o kakeru ...にやすりをかける

sandal sandaru サンダル; **Japanese ~** zōri ぞうり

sandbag suna-bukuro 砂袋

sand dune sakyū 砂丘

sander (tool) kenmaki 研磨機

sandpaper 1 n kami-yasuri 紙やすり **2** v/t kami-yasuri de migaku 紙やすりで磨く; **sandpit** sunaba 砂場; **sandstone** sagan 砂岩

sandwich 1 n sandoitchi サンドイッチ **2** v/t: **be ~ed between two ...** no aida ni hasamarete iru ...の間に挟まれている

sandy beach, soil suna (no) 砂(の); hair sunairo (no) 砂色(の)

sane shōki (na) 正気(の)

sanitarium ryōyō-sho 療養所

sanitary conditions, installations eiseiteki (na) 衛生的(な)

sanitary napkin seiriyō napukin 生理用ナプキン

sanitation (sanitary installations) eisei-setsubi 衛生設備; (removal of waste) gesui-setsubi 下水設備

sanitation department eiseikyoku 衛生局

sanity shōki 正気

Santa Claus Santa-kurōsu サンタクロース

sap 1 n (in tree) jueki 樹液 **2** v/t s.o.'s energy yowaraseru 弱らせる

sapphire n (jewel) safaia サファイア

sarcasm hiniku 皮肉

sarcastic iyami (na) 嫌み(な)

sardine iwashi いわし

sash (on dress, uniform) kazariobi 飾り帯; (in window) sasshi サッシ

sashimi sashimi さしみ

Satan Maō 魔王

satellite (natural) eisei 衛星; (man-made) jinkō-eisei 人工衛星

satellite dish parabora-antena パラボラアンテナ

satellite TV eisei-terebi 衛星テレビ

satin saten サテン

satire fūshi 風刺

satirical fūshiteki (na) 風刺的(な)

satirist fūshi-sakka 風刺作家

satisfaction manzoku 満足; **get ~ out of ...** ni manzoku o miidasu ...に満足を見出す; **a feeling of ~** manzoku-kan 満足感; **is that to your ~?** oki ni meshimashita deshō ka お気に召しましたでしょうか

satisfactory manzoku no iku 満足のいく; (just good enough) nami (no) 並み(の); **this is not ~** kore de wa manzoku dekinai これでは満足できない

satisfy customers manzoku saseru 満足させる; needs ... ni ōjiru ...に応じる; conditions, hunger, desires mitasu 満たす; **I am satisfied** (had enough to eat) manpuku desu 満腹です; **I am satisfied that** (convinced) watashi wa ... to kakushin shite iru 私は...と確信している; **I hope you're satisfied!** kore de manzoku shita deshō これで満足したでしょう

Saturday doyōbi 土曜日

sauce sōsu ソース

saucepan katate-nabe 片手なべ

saucer ukezara 受け皿

saucy person namaiki (na) 生意気(な); dress shareta しゃれた

Saudi Arabia Sauji-Arabia サウジアラビア

Saudi (Arabian) **1** adj Sauji-Arabia (no) サウジアラビア(の) **2** n (person) Sauji-Arabia-jin サウジアラビア人

sauna sauna サウナ

saunter nonbiri to aruku のんびりと歩く

sausage sōsēji ソーセージ

savage 1 adj animal dōmō (na) どう猛(な); attack zannin (na) 残忍

(な); *criticism* zankoku (na) 残酷
(な) **2** *n* yaban-jin 野蛮人
save 1 *v/t* (*rescue*) sukuu 救う;
money tameru ためる; *time*
setsuyaku suru 節約する; (*collect*)
totte oku 取っておく; COMPUT
hozon suru 保存する; *goal* fusegu
防ぐ; *you could ~ yourself a lot of
effort* anata no tema ga unto
habukeru あなたの手間がうんと省
ける **2** *v/i* (*put money aside*)
chokin suru 貯金する; (*in soccer*)
tokuten o fusegu 得点を防ぐ; (*in
baseball*) sēbu suru セーブする
3 *n* SP sēbu セーブ
♦ **save up for** ... no tame ni chokin
suru ...のために貯金する
saving (*amount saved*) setsuyaku
節約; (*activity*) chochiku 貯蓄
savings chokin 貯金
savings account futsū-yokin-kōza
普通預金口座
savings bank futsū-ginkō 普通銀行
savior REL kyūseishu 救世主;
(*Christian*) Kirisuto キリスト
savor *v/t* ajiwau 味わう
savory *adj* (*salty*) shioaji (no) 塩
味(の); (*spicy*) piritto shita ぴりっ
とした
saw *n* (*tool*) nokogiri のこぎり
♦ **saw off** nokogiri de kiriotosu の
こぎりで切り落とす
sawdust ogakuzu おがくず
saxophone sakusofōn サクソフォーン
say 1 *v/t* iu 言う; *can I ~
something?* hitokoto iwasete
moraemasu ka 一言言わせてもら
えますか; *that is to ~* tsumari つま
り; *what do you ~ to that?* anata
wa dō omoimasu ka あなたはどう
思いますか **2** *n*: *have one's ~*
iibun ga aru 言い分がある
saying kotowaza ことわざ
scab (*on cut*) kasabuta かさぶた
scaffolding ashiba 足場
scald *v/t* yakedo saseru やけどさせ
る
scale¹ (*on fish*) uroko うろこ
scale² **1** *n* (*size*) kibo 規模; (*on
thermometer etc*) memori 目盛り;

(*of map*) shukushaku 縮尺; MUS
onkai 音階; *on a larger / smaller ~*
dai kibo / shō kibo ni 大規模/小規
模に **2** *v/t cliffs etc* noboru 登る
scale drawing shukuzu 縮図
scales hakari はかり; (*for person*)
taijūkei 体重計
scalp *n* atamo no kawa 頭の皮
scalpel mesu メス
scalper shitsukoku kan'yū suru
hito しつこく勧誘する人
scam F sagi 詐欺
scan 1 *v/t horizon* miwatasu 見渡す;
page ... ni zatto me o tōsu ...にざっ
と目を通す; MED sukyan o kakeru
スキャンをかける; COMPUT
sukyanā o kakete sagasu スキャ
ナーをかけて探す **2** *n* MED sukyan
スキャン
♦ **scan in** COMPUT sukyanā de
yomikomu スキャナーで読み込む
scandal sukyandaru スキャンダル
scandalous tondemonai とんでもな
い
scanner MED sukyan スキャン;
COMPUT sukyanā スキャナー
scantily: ~ *clad* hotondo nani mo
kite inai ほとんど何も着ていない
scanty *clothes* hada o roshutsu
shita 肌を露出した
scapegoat migawari 身代わり
scar 1 *n* kizuato 傷跡 **2** *v/t* ... ni
kizuato o nokosu ...に傷跡を残す
scarce (*in short supply*) fujūbun
(na) 不十分(な); *make oneself ~*
(*go away*) tachisaru 立ち去る;
(*stay away*) hikkonde iru 引っ込
んでいる
scarcely hotondo...nai ほとんど...
ない; *I ~ know her* watashi wa
hotondo kanojo o shiranai 私はほ
とんど彼女を知らない
scarcity fusoku 不足
scare 1 *v/t* kowagaraseru 怖がらせ
る; *be ~d of* ... o kowagaru ...を怖
がる **2** *n* (*alarm*) kyōfu 恐怖;
(*panic*) panikku パニック; *give ...
a ~* ... o bikkuri saseru ...をびっく
りさせる
♦ **scare away** ... o odoshite
oiharau ...を脅して追い払う

scarecrow kakashi かかし

scaremonger dema o tobasu hito デマを飛ばす人

scarf (around neck) mafurā マフラー; (over head) sukāfu スカーフ

scarlet adj hiro (no) ひ色(の)

scarlet fever shōkōnetsu しょう紅熱

scary music, movie kowai 怖い

scathing tsuretsu (na) 痛烈(な)

scatter 1 v/t leaflets, baramaku ばらまく; seeds maku まく; be ~ed all over the room heyajū ni chirakatte iru 部屋中にちらかっている 2 v/i (of crowd etc) chirijiri ni naru ちりぢりになる

scatterbrained chūi-sanman (na) 注意散漫(な)

scattered family, villages tenzai shite iru 点在している; ~ showers niwaka-ame にわか雨

scenario sujigaki 筋書き; (of movie) shinario シナリオ

scene THEA ba 場; (view, sight) jōkyō 情況; (of accident, crime etc) genba 現場; (of novel, movie) butai 舞台; (argument) ōsawagi 大騒ぎ; make a ~ sōdō / o okosu 騒動を起こす; ~s THEA haikei 背景; jazz / rock ~ jazu / rokku no bun'ya ジャズ/ロックの分野; behind the ~s butaiura de 舞台裏で; fig kage de 陰で

scenery keshiki 景色; THEA butai-sōchi 舞台装置

scent n (smell) kaori 香り; (perfume) kōsui 香水; (of animal) shūseki 臭跡

schedule 1 n (of events, work) sukejūru スケジュール; (for trains etc) jikoku-hyō 時刻表; (of lessons) jikan-wari 時間割; be on ~ (of work, workers, etc) yotei dōri de aru 予定どおりである; (of train etc) teikoku dōri de aru 定刻通りである; be behind ~ (of work, workers, train etc) yotei yori okureru 予定より遅れる 2 v/t (put on schedule) yotei suru 予定する; it's ~d for completion next month raigetsu ni kansei ga yotei sarete imasu 来月

に完成が予定されています

scheduled flight teikibin 定期便

scheme 1 n keikaku 計画; (plot) takurami たくらみ 2 v/i (plot) takuramu たくらむ

scheming adj haraguroi 腹黒い

schizophrenia seishin-bunretsushō 精神分裂症

schizophrenic 1 n seishin-bunretsushō-kanja 精神分裂症患者 2 adj seishin-bunretsushō (no) 精神分裂症(の)

scholar gakusha 学者

scholarship (scholarly work) gakumon 学問; (financial award) shōgakukin 奨学金

school gakkō 学校; (university) daigaku 大学

schoolbag gakusei-kaban 学生かばん; **schoolboy** danshi-seito 男子生徒; **schoolchildren** seito 生徒; **school days** gakusei-jidai 学生時代; **schoolgirl** joshi-seito 女子生徒; **schoolteacher** sensei 先生

sciatica zakotsu-shinkeitsū 座骨神経痛

science kagaku 科学

science fiction SF

scientific kagakuteki (na) 科学的(な)

scientist kagaku-sha 科学者

scissors hasami はさみ

scoff[1] v/t (eat fast) gatsugatsu taberu がつがつ食べる; (eat all of) tairageru 平らげる

scoff[2] v/i azawarau あざ笑う

♦**scoff at** ... o azawarau ...をあざ笑う

scold v/t shikaru しかる

scoop 1 n (for ice cream) sābā サーバー; (for mud) sukoppu スコップ; (story) sukūpu スクープ 2 v/t (pick up) sukui ageru すくい上げる

♦**scoop up** ... o hiroi ageru ...を拾い上げる

scooter sukūtā スクーター

scope han'i 範囲; (opportunity) yochi 余地; (freedom) jiyū 自由

scorch v/t kogasu 焦がす

scorching hot yaketsuku yō ni atsui 焼けつくように暑い

score 1 *n* SP tokuten 得点; (*written music*) gakufu 楽譜; (*of movie etc*) sukoa スコア; **what's the ~?** tokuten wa dō natte imasu ka 得点はどうなっていますか; **have a ~ to settle with** ... ni urami o harasu ...に恨みを晴らす **2** *v/t goal, point* tokuten suru 得点する; (*cut: line*) kirime o tsukeru 切り目をつける **3** *v/i* tokuten suru 得点する; (*keep the ~*) kiroku suru 記録する; **that's where he ~s** soko ga kare no tsuyomi da そこが彼の強みだ

scorer (*of goal, point*) tokuten-sha 得点者; (*scorekeeper*) kiroku-gakari 記録係

scorn 1 *n* keibetsu 軽べつ; **pour ~ on** ... o keibetsu suru ...を軽べつする **2** *v/t idea, suggestion* hanetsukeru はねつける

scornful keibetsu shita 軽べつした

Scot Sukottorando-jin スコットランド人

Scotch (*whiskey*) Sukotchi uisukī スコッチウイスキー

Scotland Sukottorando スコットランド

Scottish Sukottorando (no) スコットランド(の)

scot-free: **get off ~** buji ni nigeru 無事に逃げる

scoundrel akutō 悪党

scour¹ (*search*) sagashimawaru 捜しまわる

scour² *pans* goshigoshi arau ごしごし洗う

scout *n* (*boy ~*) bōi sukauto ボーイスカウト

scowl 1 *n* shikamettsura しかめっ面 **2** *v/i* kao o shikameru 顔をしかめる

scram F sassa to useru さっさと失せる; **~!** sassa to usero さっさと失せろ

scramble 1 *n* (*rush*) awatadashi-sa 慌ただしさ **2** *v/t message* hachō o kaeru 波長を変える **3** *v/i* (*climb*) saki o arasotte yojinoboru 先を争ってよじ登る; **he ~d to his feet** kare wa kyū ni tachiagatta 彼は急に立ち上がった

scrambled eggs sukuranburu eggu スクランブルエッグ

scrap 1 *n* (*metal*) kuzu くず; (*fight*) kenka けんか; (*little bit*) sukoshi 少し **2** *v/t plan, paragraph etc* yameru やめる

scrapbook sukurappu bukku スクラップブック

scrape 1 *n* (*on paint etc*) kosuru koto こすること **2** *v/t paint, one's arm etc* kosuru こする; *vegetables* muku むく; **~ a living** nantoka seikatsu suru 何とか生活する

♦**scrape through** (*in exam*) nantoka pasu suru 何とかパスする

scrap heap gomi no yama ごみの山; **good for the ~** suteru shikanai 捨てるしかない

scrap metal kuzutetsu くず鉄

scrappy *work* zatsu (na) 雑(な)

scratch 1 *n* (*mark*) hikkakikizu 引っかき傷; **have a ~** (*to stop itching*) kaku かく; **start from ~** zero kara hajimeru ゼロから始める; **not up to ~** jūbun de nai 充分でない **2** *v/t* (*mark: skin, paint*) hikkaku 引っかく; (*because of itch*) kaku かく **3** *v/i* (*of cat, nails*) hikkaku 引っかく

scrawl 1 *n* nagurigaki なぐり書き **2** *v/t* nagurigaki suru なぐり書きする

scream 1 *n* himei 悲鳴 **2** *v/i* himei o ageru 悲鳴をあげる

screech 1 *n* (*of tires*) kī to naru oto キーとなる音; (*scream*) kanakirigoe 金切り声 **2** *v/i* (*of tires*) kī to oto o tateru キーと音を立てる; (*scream*) kanakirigoe o ageru 金切り声をあげる

screen 1 *n* (*in room, hospital*) tsuitate ついたて; (*decorative*) byōbu 屏風; (*protective*) maku 幕; (*in movie theater*) sukurīn スクリーン; COMPUT gamen 画面; **on the ~** (*in movies*) eiga ni deru 映画に出る; **on (the) ~** COMPUT gamen ni deru 画面に出る **2** *v/t* (*protect, hide*) ōikakusu 覆い隠す; *movie* eisha suru 映写する; (*for security reasons*) shinsa suru 審査する

screenplay eiga no shinario 映画の

シナリオ; **screen saver** COMPUT
sukurīn sēbā スクリーンセーバー;
screen test ōdishon オーディショ
ン

screw 1 n neji ねじ; V (sex) sekkusu
セックス **2** v/t neji de tomeru ねじ
で留める; V sekkusu suru セックス
する; F (cheat) damasu だます; **~ X
to Y** X o Y ni neji de tomeru X を Y に
ねじで留める

♦ **screw up 1** v/t eyes … o
shikameru …をしかめる; piece of
paper … o marumeru …を丸める;
F (make a mess of) … o dainashi
ni suru …を台無しにする **2** v/i F
(make a bad mistake) dame ni
suru だめにする

screwdriver doraibā ドライバー
screwed up F (psychologically)
dame ni naru だめになる
screw top neji buta ねじぶた
scribble 1 n hashirigaki 走り書き
2 v/t (write quickly) hashirigaki
suru 走り書きする **3** v/i rakugaki
suru 落書きする
script (for play etc) kyakuhon 脚本;
(form of writing) moji 文字
Scripture: the (Holy) ~s Seisho 聖
書
scriptwriter kyakuhon-ka 脚本家
scroll n (manuscript) makimono 巻
き物; hanging ~ kakejiku 掛け軸
♦ **scroll down** v/i COMPUT sukurōru
suru スクロールする
♦ **scroll up** v/i COMPUT sukurōru
suru スクロールする
scrounger takari たかり
scrub v/t floor, hands goshigoshi
arau ごしごし洗う
scrubbing brush (for floor)
burashi ブラシ
scruffy misuborashii みすぼらしい
♦ **scrunch up** plastic cup etc … o
baritto tsubusu …をばりっとつぶ
す
scruples ryōshin no togame 良心の
とがめ; have no ~ about doing X
nan no tamerai mo naku X suru 何
のためらいもなく X する
scrupulous (with moral principles)
seijitsu (na) 誠実(な); (thorough)

kichōmen (na) きちょうめん(な);
attention to detail menmitsu (na)
綿密(な)
scrutinize (examine) menmitsu ni
shiraberu 綿密に調べる
scrutiny menmitsu na chōsa 綿密な
調査; come under ~ kanshi sarete
iru 監視されている
scuba diving sukyūba daibingu ス
キューバダイビング
scuffle n rantō 乱闘
sculptor chōkoku-ka 彫刻家
sculpture n chōkoku 彫刻
scum ukikasu 浮きかす; pej
(people) kasu かす
scythe n kusakarigama 草刈りがま
sea umi 海; by the ~ kaigan 海岸
sea bass suzuki すずき; **sea bream**
tai たい; **Sea Day** Umi no hi 海の
日; **seafaring** nation kaiyō (no) 海
洋(の); **seafood** gyokairui 魚介類,
shīfūdo シーフード; **seafront**
kaigandōri 海岸通り; **seagoing**
vessel en'yō-kōkaiyō (no) 遠洋航
海用(の); **seagull** kamome かもめ
seal[1] n (animal) azarashi あざらし
seal[2] **1** n (on document) inshō 印章;
TECH fū 封 **2** v/t container mippei
suru 密閉する
♦ **seal off** area … o fūsa suru …を封
鎖する
sea level: above ~ kaibatsu 海抜 ;
below ~ kaimenka 海面下
seam n (on garment) nuime 縫い目;
(of ore) hakusō 薄層
seaman sen'in 船員
Sea of Japan nihonkai 日本海; **Sea
of Okhotsk** Ohōtsuku-kai オホー
ツク海; **seaport** minatomachi 港町;
sea power (nation) kaigun no
chikara 海軍の力
search 1 n chōsa 調査; (for
happiness) tsuikyū 追求; COMPUT
kensaku 検索 **2** v/t city, files
sagasu 捜す
♦ **search for** … o sagasu …を捜す
searching adj look, question
surudoi 鋭い
searchlight sāchiraito サーチライ
ト; **search party** sōsaku-tai 捜索
隊; **search warrant**

katakusōsaku-reijō 家宅捜索令状

seasick funayoi (no) 船酔い(の);
get ~ funayoi suru 船酔いする;
seaside umibe 海辺; *at the ~*
umibe de 海辺で; *go to the ~*
umibe ni iku 海辺に行く; **seaside
resort** umibe no kōrakuchi 海辺の
行楽地

season n (winter etc) kisetsu 季節;
(for tourism etc) shīzun シーズン

seasoned wood kansō shita 乾燥し
た; traveler etc keiken yutaka (na)
経験豊か(な)

seasoning chōmiryō 調味料

season ticket (for bus etc) teikiken
定期券; (for football, opera)
shīzun chiketto シーズンチケット

seat 1 n zaseki 座席; (of pants)
shiri しり; *please take a ~*
osuwari kudasai お座り下さい
2 v/t (have seating for) seki ga
aru 席がある; *please remain ~ed*
seki ni tsuita mama de ite kudasai
席に着いたままでいてください

seat belt shīto-beruto シートベルト

sea urchin uni うに

seaweed kaisō 海草; (dried to eat)
nori のり

secluded hitozato hanareta 人里離
れた

seclusion kakuri 隔離

second 1 n (of time) byō 秒; (of
month) futsuka 二日; *just a ~* chotto
matte kudasai ちょっと待って下さ
い 2 adj dai-ni (no) 第二 (の); *~
biggest* nibanme ni ōkii 二番目に
大きい 3 adv nibanme ni 二番目
に; *come in* nii de 二位で 4 v/t
motion shiji suru 支持する

secondary nijiteki (na) 二次的(な);
of ~ importance amari jūyō de
nai あまり重要でない

secondary education chūtō-kyōiku
中等教育

second best adj nibanme ni yoi 二
番目によい; **second class** adj
ticket nitō 二等; **second gear** MOT
sekando セカンド; **second hand**
(on clock) byōshin 秒針;
secondhand 1 adj chūko (no) 中
古(の) 2 adv buy chūko de 中古で

secondly daini ni 第二に

second-rate niryū (no) 二流(の)

second thoughts: *I've had ~* ki ga
kawatta 気が変わった

secrecy himitsu ni suru koto 秘密に
すること; *the X51 was developed
in great ~* ekkusu gojūichi wa
himitsuri no uchi ni kaihatsu
sareta X51は秘密裏のうちに開発
された

secret 1 n himitsu 秘密; *do X in ~*
hisoka ni X suru ひそかにXする
2 adj passage himitsu (no) 秘密
(の); work kimitsu 機密

secret agent supai スパイ

secretarial job hisho (no) 秘書(の)

secretary hisho 秘書; POL daijin 大
臣

Secretary of State Kokumu-
chōkan 国務長官

secrete (give off) bunpitsu suru 分
泌する; (hide away) kossori
kakusu こっそり隠す

secretion (of liquid) bunpitsu 分泌;
(liquid secreted) bunpitsu-butsu
分泌物; (hiding) intoku 隠匿

secretive himitsushugi (no) 秘密主
義(の)

secretly naimitsu de 内密で

secret police himitsu keisatsu 秘密
警察

secret service himitsu-chōhōkikan
秘密諜報機関

sect shūha 宗派

section bubun 部分; (of book, text)
shō 章; (of company, department)
...bu ...部

sector (of city) kuiki 区域; (of
society) bumon 部門; (of diskette,
lung) bubun 部分

secular sezoku (no) 世俗(の)

secure 1 adj shelf etc kotei sareta
固定された; job, feeling antei shita
安定した 2 v/t shelf kotei suru 固
定する; help kakuho suru 確保する

security (in job) hoshō 保証;
(guarantee) tanpo 担保; (at airport etc) keibi 警備; (department)
keibi-bumon 警備部門; (of beliefs
etc) kakushin 確信; **securities** FIN
yūka-shōken 有価証券; **securities**

market FIN shōken-shijō 証券市場
security alert (*state*) keikai-taisei
警戒態勢; (*warning*) keikai-keihō
警戒警報; **security check**
sekyuritī-chekku セキュリティー
チェック; **security-conscious**
keibi-ishiki no takai 警備意識の高
い; **security forces** bōeigun 防衛
軍; **security guard** keibiin 警備員;
security risk (*person*) kiken-
jinbutsu 危険人物
sedan MOT sedan セダン
sedative *n* chinseizai 鎮静剤
sediment chindenbutsu 沈殿物
seduce yūwaku suru 誘惑する
seduction (*sexual*) yūwaku 誘惑
seductive *dress* miwakuteki (na) 魅
惑的(な); *offer* miryokuteki (na)
魅力的(な)
see miru 見る; (*understand*) wakaru
わかる; *I* ~ wakarimashita わかり
ました; *can I* ~ *the manager?*
manējā ni aemasu ka マネー
ジャーに会えますか; *you should* ~
a doctor isha ni itta hō ga ii desu
医者に行ったほうがいいです; ~
home ... o ie made okuru ...を家
まで送る; *I'll* ~ *you to the door*
genkan made okurimasu 玄関まで
送ります; ~ *you!* mata ne またね
♦ **see about** (*attend to*) ... o
torihakarau ...を取り計らう
♦ **see off** (*at airport etc*) ... o okuru
...を送る; (*chase away*) ... o
oiharau ...を追い払う
♦ **see to**: ~ *it that X gets done* X
ga okonawareru yō ni ki o tsukeru
Xが行われるように気をつける
seed tane 種; (*in tennis*) shīdo シー
ド; *go to* ~ (*of person, district*)
sakari o sugiru 盛りを過ぎる
seedling nae 苗
seedy *bar, district* misuborashii み
すぼらしい
seeing (that) ... de aru kara ...であ
るから
seeing eye dog mōdōken 盲導犬
seek 1 *v/t employment* sagasu 捜す;
truth motomeru もとめる **2** *v/i*
sagasu 捜す
seem ... no yō ni mieru ...のように

見える; *it* ~*s that ...* ... no yō ni
omowareru ...のように思われる
seemingly mita tokoro de wa 見たと
ころでは
seep (*of liquid*) shimideru 染み出る
♦ **seep out** (*of liquid*) sukoshi zutsu
deru 少しずつ出る
seesaw shīsō シーソー
see-through *dress, material* shīsurū
(no) シースルー(の)
segment ichibu 一部; (*of orange*)
fukuro 袋
segmented bundan sareta 分断され
た
segregate bunri suru 分離する
segregation sabetsu 差別
seismology jishin-gaku 地震学
seize tsukamu つかむ; *opportunity*
toraeru とらえる; (*of customs,
police etc*) ōshū suru 押収する
♦ **seize up** (*of engine*) ugokanaku
naru 動かなくなる
seizure MED hossa 発作; (*of drugs
etc*) ōshū 押収
seldom metta ni nai めったにない
select 1 *v/t* erabidasu 選び出す
2 *adj* (*exclusive*) erabareta 選ば
れた
selection (*choosing*) sentaku 選択;
(*that / those chosen*) senbatsu 選抜;
(*assortment*) korekushon コレク
ション
selection process senbatsu-hōhō
選抜方法
selective sentaku suru chikara no
aru 選択する力のある
self jiko 自己
self-addressed envelope jibun ate
no fūtō 自分あての封筒; **self-
assured** jishin no aru 自信のある;
self-catering apartment jisuiyō no
apāto 自炊用のアパート; **self-
centered** jiko-chūshin (no) 自己中
心(の); **self-confessed** jinin suru
自認する; **self-confidence** jishin 自
信; **self-confident** jishin no aru 自信
のある; **self-conscious** uchiki (na)
内気(な); **self-contained** *apartment*
setsubi-kanbi (no) 設備完備(の);
self-control jisei 自制; **self-
defense** jiko-bōei 自己防衛; **self-**

discipline jiko-kisei 自己規制; **self-doubt** jiko-fushin 自己不信; **self-employed** jieigyō (no) 自営業(の); **self-evident** jimei (no) 自明(の); **self-interest** riko-shugi 利己主義

selfish wagamama (na) わがまま(な)

selfless muyoku (no) 無欲(の)

self-made man tatakiage no hito たたき上げの人; **self-possessed** ochitsuita 落ち着いた; **self-reliant** jiritsu shita 自立した; **self-respect** jisonshin 自尊心; **self-righteous** pej hitoriyogari (no) 独りよがり(の); **self-satisfied** pej jiko-manzoku (no) 自己満足(の); **self-service** adj serufu-sābisu (no) セルフサービス(の)

sell 1 v/t uru 売る; **you have to ~ yourself** jibun o urikomanakute wa narimasen 自分を売り込まなくてはなりません **2** v/i (of products) uru 売る

seller urite 売り手

selling n COM eigyō 営業

selling point COM sērusu pointo セールスポイント

semen seieki 精液

semester gakki 学期

semi (truck) torērā トレーラー

semicircle han'en 半円; **semicircular** han'en (no) 半円(の); **semiconductor** ELEC handōtai 半導体; **semifinal** junkesshō 準決勝

seminar semina セミナー

semiskilled adj hanjukuren (no) 半熟練(の)

senate jōin 上院

senator jōin-giin 上院議員

send v/t okuru 送る; **~ X to Y** thing X o Y ni okuru X を Y に送る; person X o Y no tokoro e ikaseru X を Y のところへ行かせる; **~ her my best wishes** kanojo ni yoroshiku itte oite kudasai 彼女によろしく言ってください

♦ **send back** … o hensō suru …を返送する; food in restaurant … o kaesu …を返す

♦ **send for** doctor, help … o yobu yō ni tanomu …を呼ぶように頼む

♦ **send in** troops … o haken suru …を派遣する; next interviewee … o tōsu …を通す; application form … o teishutsu suru …を提出する

♦ **send off** letter etc … o hassō suru …を発送する

♦ **send up** (mock) … o karakau …をからかう

sender (of letter) sashidashi-nin 差出人

senile mōroku shita もうろくした

senility mōroku もうろく

senior (older) nenchō (no) 年長(の); (in rank) jōi (no) 上位(の); **be ~ to** (in rank) … yori jōi (no) …より上位(の)

senior citizen kōrei-sha 高齢者

sensation (feeling) kankaku 感覚; (surprise event) sensēshon センセーション; (s.o./sth very good) daininki 大人気

sensational news, discovery sensēshonaru (na) センセーショナル(な); (very good) subarashii 素晴らしい

sense 1 n (meaning) imi 意味; (purpose, point) ito 意図; (common ~) jōshiki 常識; (of sight, smell etc) kankaku 感覚; (feeling) kanji 感じ; **in a ~** aru imi de wa ある意味では; **talk ~, man!** majime ni shite yo まじめにしてよ; **it doesn't make ~** imi ga wakarimasen 意味がわかりません; **there's no ~ in trying / waiting** shite mo / matte mo muda desu しても/待っても無駄です **2** v/t s.o.'s presence kanjiru 感じる

senseless (pointless) muimi (na) 無意味(な)

sensible person, decision jōshiki no aru 常識のある; advice kenmei (na) 賢明(な)

sensitive skin binkan (na) 敏感(な); person shinkeishitsu (na) 神経質(な)

sensitivity (of skin, person) binkan-sa 敏感さ

sensual kannōteki (na) 官能的(な)

sensuality kōshoku 好色

sensuous kansei ni uttaeru 感性に訴える

sentence 1 *n* GRAM bun 文; LAW senkoku 宣告 **2** *v/t* LAW hanketsu o senkoku suru 判決を宣告する

sentiment (*sentimentality*) kanshō 感傷; (*opinion*) iken 意見

sentimental kanshōteki (na) 感傷的 (な)

sentimentality kanshō 感傷

sentry mihari 見張り

separate 1 *adj* wakeru 分ける; **keep X ~ from Y** X to Y o wakeru X と Y を分ける **2** *v/t* wakeru 分ける; *people* hikihanasu 引き離す; **~ X from Y** X o Y to kubetsu suru X を Y と区別する **3** *v/i* (*of couple*) bekkyo suru 別居する

separated *couple* bekkyo shita 別居 した

separately betsubetsu ni 別々に

separation bunri 分離; (*of couple*) bekkyo 別居

September kugatsu 九月

septic kansen shita 感染した; **go ~** (*of wound*) kansen suru 感染する

sequel tsuzuki 続き

sequence *n* renzoku 連続; **in ~** junban ni 順番に; **out of ~** barabara ni ばらばらに; **the ~ of events** ichiren no dekigoto 一連の 出来事

serene odayaka (na) 穏やか(な)

sergeant (*army*) gunsō 軍曹; (*police*) junsa-buchō 巡査部長

serial *n* rensai 連載

serialize (*on TV, radio*) tsuzukimono toshite hōsō suru 続 き物として放送する; (*in magazine, newspaper*) rensai suru 連載する

serial killer renzoku-satsujinhan 連 続殺人犯; **serial number** seizō bangō 製造番号; **serial port** COMPUT shiriaru pōto シリアル ポート

series (*of numbers, events*) renzoku 連続

serious *situation, damage* jūdai (na) 重大(な); *illness* omoi 重い; (*person: earnest*) majime (na) ま じめ(な); *company* katai 堅い; **I'm ~** watashi wa honki desu 私は本気 です; **listen, this is ~** nē, kore wa

jūdai desu ねー、これは重大です; **we'd better take a ~ look at it** shinken ni mita hō ga ii desu 真剣 に見たほうがいいです

seriously *injured* hidoku ひどく; *understaffed* shinkoku ni 深刻に; **~ intend to ...** honki de...shiyō to 本 気で...しようと; **~? hontō 本当!; take X ~** X o majime ni uketomeru X を まじめに受けとめる

sermon sekkyō 説教

servant shiyōnin 使用人

serve 1 *n* (*in tennis*) sābu サーブ **2** *v/t food, meal* dasu 出す; *customer ...* no yō o ukagau ... の 用をうかがう; *one's country, the people ...* ni tsukaeru ...に仕える; **it ~s you / him right** jigō-jitoku no jigyō jitoku da 自業自得だ **3** *v/i* (*give out food*) shokuji o dasu 食事を出す; (*as politician etc*) tsutomeru 勤める; (*in tennis*) sābu suru サーブする

♦ **serve up** *meal* ... o dasu ...を出す

server SP, COMPUT sābā サーバー

service 1 *n* (*to customers*) sābisu サービス; (*for vehicle, machine*) tenken-shūri 点検修理; (*in tennis*) sābisu サービス; **the ~s** heieki 兵 役 **2** *v/t vehicle, machine* tenken-shūri suru 点検修理する

service area sābisu-eria サービス エリア; **service charge** (*in restaurant, club*) sābisu-ryō サー ビス料; **service industry** sābisu-sangyō サービス産業; **serviceman** MIL gunjin 軍人; **service provider** COMPUT purobaidā プロバイダー; **service sector** sābisu-sangyō サービス産業; **service station** gasorin sutando ガソリンスタンド

session kaigi 会議; (*with analyst, consultant etc*) sōdan 相談; (*of aerobics etc*) sesshon セッション

set 1 *n* (*of tools, books etc*) isshiki 一 式; (*group of people*) nakama 仲間; MATH shūgō 集合; THEA: *scenery* setto セット; (*where a movie is made*) satsuei-genba 撮影現場; (*in tennis*) setto セット; *television* ~ terebi-juzōki テレビ受像機 **2** *v/t* (*place*) oku 置く; *movie, novel etc* settei suru 設定する; *date, time, limit* sadameru 定める; *mechanism* chōsei suru 調整する; *alarm clock, broken limb* awaseru 合わせる; *jewel* hamekomarete iru はめこまれている; *(for exam) text, book* totonoeru 整える; ~ **the table** shokutaku no yōi o suru 食卓の用意をする; ~ **a task for** shigoto o... ni ataeru 仕事を...に与える **3** *v/i (of sun)* shizumu 沈む; *(of glue)* katamaru 固まる **4** *adj* views, ideas kata ni hamatta 型にはまった; **be dead ~ on** ...ni kataku kesshin suru ...に堅く決心する; **be very ~ in one's ways** kata ni hamatte iru 型にはまっている; ~ **book/reading** *(in course)* shitei-tosho 指定図書; ~ **meal** teishoku 定食

♦ **set apart**: **set X apart from Y** X o Y to kubetsu suru X とY を区別する

♦ **set aside** *(for future use)* ... o totte oku ...を取っておく

♦ **set back** *(in plans etc)* ... o okuraseru ...を遅らせる; **it set me back $400** yonhyaku doru kakaru 四百ドルかかる

♦ **set off 1** *v/i (on journey)* shuppatsu suru 出発する **2** *v/t explosion, chain reaction* ... o hikiokosu ...を引き起こす

♦ **set out 1** *v/i (on journey)* shuppatsu suru 出発する; ~ **to do X** *(intend)* X shiyō to kokoromiru X しようと試みる **2** *v/t proposal* ... o setsumei suru ...を説明する; *goods* ... o naraberu ...を並べる

♦ **set to** *(start)* torikakaru 取りかかる

♦ **set up 1** *v/t company* ... o setsuritsu suru ...を設立する; *system* ... o tachiageru ...を立ち上げる; *equipment, machine* ... o junbi suru ...を準備する; *market stall* ... o setchi suru ...を設置する; F *(frame)* ... o wana ni kakeru ...をわなにかける **2** *v/i (in business)* kaigyō suru 開業する

setback kōtai 後退

setting *(of novel etc)* settei 設定; *(of house)* kankyō 環境

settle 1 *v/i (of bird)* tomaru とまる; *(of liquid)* shizumeru すませる; *(of dust)* shizumeru 静める; *(to live)* ochitsuku 落ち着く **2** *v/t* dispute, argument kaiketsu suru 決着をつける; *issue, uncertainty* kaiketsu suru 解決する; *s.o.'s debts* harau 払う; *check* seisan suru 清算する; **that ~s it!** sore de kimari それで決まり

♦ **settle down** *v/i (stop being noisy)* shizumaru 静まる; *(stop wild living)* teijū suru 定住する; *(in an area)* ochitsuku 落ち着く

♦ **settle for** *(take, accept)* ... de te o utsu ...で手を打つ

settlement *(of claim, debt)* kessai 決済; *(of dispute)* ketchaku 決着; *(payment)* shiharai 支払; *(of building)* chinka 沈下

settler kaitaku-imin 開拓移民

set-up *(structure)* soshiki 組織; *(relationship)* kankei 関係; F *(frame-up)* wana わな

seven nana 七

seventeen jūnana 十七

seventeenth dai jūnana (no) 第十七 (の)

seventh 1 *adj* dai nana (no) 第七 (の) **2** *n (of month)* nanoka 七日

seventieth dai-nanajū (no) 第七十 (の)

seventy nanajū 七十

sever *arm, cable etc* setsudan suru 切断する; *relations* tatsu 絶つ

several 1 *adj* ikutsu ka (no) 幾つか (の); *people* ikunin ka (no) 幾人か (の) **2** *pron* ikutsu ka 幾つか

severe *penalty, winter* kibishii 厳しい; *teacher* genkaku (na) 厳格(な); ~ **illness** taibyō 大病

severely *punish* kibishiku 厳しく; *speak, stare* hageshiku 激しく; *injured, disrupted* hidoku ひどく

severity *(of illness, penalty)* shinkoku-sa 深刻さ; *(of look, winter etc)* kibishi-sa 厳しさ

sew 1 *v/t* nuu 縫う **2** *v/i* nuimono o suru 縫い物をする

♦ **sew on** ... o nuitsukeru ...を縫いつける

sewage gesui 下水

sewage plant gesuishorijō 下水処理場

sewer gesuidō 下水道

sewing (*skill*) saihō 裁縫; (*that being sewn*) nuimono 縫い物

sewing machine mishin ミシン

sex (*act*) sekkusu セックス; (*gender*) seibetsu 性別; **have ~ with** sekkusu o suru セックスをする

sexual seiteki (na) 性的(な)

sexual harrassment sekuhara セクハラ; **sexual intercourse** seikō 性交

sexually transmitted disease seikō-kansen byō 性交感染病

sexy sekushī (na) セクシー(な)

shabby *coat etc* yoreyore (no) よれよれ(の); *treatment* hiretsu (na) 卑劣(な)

shack hottate goya 掘っ建て小屋

shade 1 *n* hikage 日陰; (*for lamp*) kasa かさ; (*of color*) iroai 色合い; (*on window*) buraindo ブラインド; **in the ~** hikage ni 日陰に **2** *v/t* (*from sun, light*) kage ni suru 陰にする

shadow *n* kage 陰

shady *spot* hikage (no) 日陰(の); *character, dealings* ikagawashii いかがわしい

shaft (*of axle*) kaitenjiku 回転軸; (*of mine*) tatekō 縦杭

shaggy *hair, dog* mojamoja (no) もじゃもじゃ(の)

shake 1 *n* furu koto 振ること; **give X a good ~** X o hageshiku yusaburu Xを激しく揺さぶる **2** *v/t* furu 振る; **~ hands** akushu suru 握手する; **~ hands with** ... to akushu suru ...と握手する; **~ one's head** kubi o furu 首を振る **3** *v/i* (*of hands, voice*) furueru 震える; (*of building*) yureru 揺れる

shaken (*emotionally*) dōyō suru 動揺する

shake-up saihensei 再編成

shaky *table etc* gatagata (no) がたがた(の); (*after illness, shock*) furafura (no) ふらふら(の); *grasp of sth, grammar etc* ayashii 怪しい

shall: **I ~ do my best** besuto o tsukushimasu ベストをつくします; **~ we go now?** ikimashō ka 行きましょうか

shallow *water* asai 浅い; *person* asahaka (na) 浅はか(な)

shame 1 *n* haji 恥; **bring ~ on** ... no kao ni doro o nuru ...の顔に泥を塗る; **what a ~!** zannen da 残念だ; **~ on you!** haji o shire 恥を知れ **2** *v/t* hazukashimeru 辱める; **~ X into doing Y** X o hajirasete Y saseru Xを恥じ入らせてYさせる

shameful hazubeki 恥ずべき

shameless hajishirazu (no) 恥知らず(の)

shampoo 1 *n* shanpū シャンプー; **a ~ and set** shanpū to setto シャンプーとセット **2** *v/t* shanpū suru シャンプーする

shape 1 *n* katachi 形 **2** *v/t clay* katachizukuru 形づくる; *s.o.'s life* hōkōzukeru 方向づける; *the future* kettei suru 決定する

shapeless *dress etc* kakkō warui 格好悪い

shapely *figure* sutairu no ii スタイルのいい

share 1 *n* wakemae 分け前; FIN kabu 株; **do one's ~ of the work** jibun no buntan no shigoto o suru 自分の分担の仕事をする **2** *v/t* wakeru 分ける; *room, bed* kyōyō suru 共用する; *s.o.'s feelings, opinions* wakachiau 分かち合う **3** *v/i* buntan suru 分担する; **do you mind sharing with Patrick?** (*bed, room, table*) Patorikku to issho demo kamaimasen ka パトリックと一緒でもかまいませんか

♦ **share out** bunpai 分配

shareholder kabunushi 株主

shark same さめ

sharp 1 *adj knife* surudoi 鋭い; *mind* rikō (na) 利口(な); *pain* hageshii 激しい; *taste* piritto shita ピリッとした **2** *adv* MUS han'on takaku 半音高く; **at 3 o'clock ~** chōdo ちょうど

sharpen *knife* togu 研ぐ; *skills* surudoku suru 鋭くする

shatter 1 v/t glass konagona ni waru 粉々に割る; illusions dainashi ni suru 台無しにする **2** v/i (of glass) konagona ni wareru 粉々に割れる

shattered F (exhausted) totemo tsukareta とても疲れた; (very upset) gakkuri kita がっくりきた

shattering news, experience shokkingu (na) ショッキング(な); effect bikkuri saseru びっくりさせる

shave 1 v/t & v/i soru そる **2** n higesori ひげそり; have a ~ hige o soru ひげをそる; that was a close ~ kan'ippatsu no tokoro deshita 間一髪のところでした

♦ **shave off** beard soriotosu そりおとす; bit of wood kiriotosu 切り落とす

shaven head sotta そった

shaver (electric) denki-kamisori 電気かみそり

shaving brush higesoriyō burashi ひげそり用ぶらし

shaving soap higesoriyō kurīmu ひげそり用クリーム

shawl shōru ショール

she n kanojo 彼女; she's a doctor kanojo wa isha desu 彼女は医者です ◊ (omission of pronoun): who is ~? - is my daughter are wa dare desu ka – musume desu あれは誰ですか – 娘です

shears hasami はさみ

sheath n (for knife) saya さや; (contraceptive) kondōmu コンドーム

shed¹ v/t blood, tears nagasu 流す; leaves otosu 落とす; ~ light on fig hikari o sosogu 光を注ぐ

shed² n koya 小屋

sheep hitsuji 羊

sheepdog bokuyōken 牧羊犬

sheepish hazukashisō (na) 恥ずかしそう(な)

sheepskin adj hitsuji no kegawa 羊の毛皮

sheer adj madness, luxury mattaku (no) 全く(の); drop, cliffs kiritatta 切り立った

sheet (for bed) shītsu シーツ; a ~ of paper / glass ichimai no kami / garasu 一枚の紙／ガラス

shelf tana 棚; **shelves** tana 棚

shell 1 n (of mussel etc) kaigara 貝殻; (of egg) kara 殻; (of tortoise) kōra 甲羅; MIL bakuhatsubutsu 爆発物; come out of one's ~ fig jibun no kara o yaburu 自分の殻を破る **2** v/t peas muku むく; MIL hōgeki suru 砲撃する

shellfire hōgeki 砲撃; come under ~ hōgeki sareru 砲撃される

shellfish kōkakurui 甲殻類

shelter 1 n (refuge) hinan-sho 避難所; (construction) amayadori no basho 雨宿りの場所 **2** v/i (from rain, bombing etc) hinan suru 避難する **3** v/t (protect) mamoru 守る

sheltered place mamorarete iru 守られている; lead a ~ life seken no aranami kara mamorareta seikatsu o okuru 世間の荒波から守られた生活を送る

sherry sherī-shu シェリー酒

shiatsu shiatsu 指圧

shield 1 n tate 盾; (sports trophy) tategata-torofī 盾型トロフィー; TECH shīrudo シールド **2** v/t (protect) hogo suru 保護する

shift 1 n (in attitude, thinking) henka 変化; (switchover) tenkan 転換; (in direction of wind etc) henka 変化; (period of work) kōtai 交替 **2** v/t (move) ugokasu 動かす; stains etc torinozoku 取り除く; ~ the emphasis onto kyōchō suru tokoro o ... ni kaeru 強調するところを…に変える **3** v/i (move) ugoku 動く; (in attitude, opinion) kawaru 変わる; (of wind) hōkō ga kawaru 方向が変わる; that's ~ing! F sore wa hayai それは速い

shift key COMPUT shifuto kī シフトキー

shift work kōtaisei no shigoto 交替制の仕事

shifty pej zurui ずるい

shifty-looking pej ayashige na kaotsuki (no) 怪しげな顔つき(の)

Shikoku Shikoku 四国

shimmer v/i chirachira hikaru ちらちら光る

shin n mukōzune 向うずね

shine 1 v/i (of sun, moon) kagayaku 輝く; (of shoes etc) hikaru 光る; fig (of student etc) sugureru 優れる **2** v/t flashlight etc terasu 照らす

shingle (on beach) jari 砂利

shingles MED obijō-hōshin 帯状疱疹

Shinto Shintō 神道

Shinto altar kamidana 神棚

Shinto priest kannushi 神主

ship 1 n fune 船 **2** v/t (send) okuru 送る; (send by sea) funabin de okuru 船便で送る

shipment (consignment) kamotsu-yusō 貨物輸送

shipowner senshu 船主

shipping (sea traffic) senpaku 船舶; (sending) hassō 発送; (sending by sea) funabin 船便

shipping company unsōgyō 運送業

shipshape adj seizen to shita 整然とした; **shipwreck 1** n nanpa 難破 **2** v/t nanpa suru 難破する; **be ~ed** nanpa shita 難破した; **shipyard** zōsen-sho 造船所

shirk kaihi suru 回避する

shirt shatsu シャツ; **in his ~ sleeves** uwagi nashi de 上着なしで

shit F **1** n kuso くそ; (bad quality goods, work) garakuta がらくた; **I need a ~** unko shitai うんこしたい **2** v/i daiben o suru 大便をする **3** interj kuso' くそっ

shitty F hidoi ひどい

shiver v/i furueru 震える

shock 1 n shokku ショック; ELEC dengeki 電撃; **be in ~** MED shokku jōtai ni aru ショック状態にある **2** v/t shokku o ataeru ショックを与える; **be ~ed by** bikkuri saserareru びっくりさせられる

shock absorber MOT kanshōki 緩衝器

shocking behavior, poverty shōgekiteki (na) 衝撃的(な); F (very bad) hidoi ひどい

shoddy goods mikake daoshi (no) 見かけ倒し(の); behavior keibetsu

subeki 軽べつすべき

shoe kutsu 靴

shoelace kutsu-himo 靴ひも;
shoestore kutsu-ya 靴屋;
shoestring: do X on a ~ shōgaku-shikin de X suru 小額資金でXする

Shogun Shōgun 将軍

Shogunate Bakufu 幕府

♦**shoo away** shitto itte oiharau しっと言って追い払う

shoot 1 n BOT shinme 新芽 **2** v/t utsu 撃つ; (and kill) uchikorosu 撃ち殺す; movie satsuei suru 撮影する; **~ X in the leg** X no ashi o utsu Xの足を撃つ

♦**shoot down** airplane uchiotosu 撃ち落とす; suggestion hanetsukeru はねつける

♦**shoot off** (rush off) tobidasu 飛び出す

♦**shoot up** (of prices) kyūjōshō suru 急上昇する; (of children) kyū ni seichō suru 急に成長する; (of new suburbs etc) kyū ni hatten suru 急に発展する

shooting star nagare-boshi 流れ星

shop 1 n mise 店; **talk ~** shigoto no hanashi o suru 仕事の話をする **2** v/i kaimono o suru 買い物をする; **go ~ping** kaimono ni iku 買い物に行く

shopkeeper tenshu 店主

shoplifter manbiki 万引き

shopper kaimono-kyaku 買い物客

shopping (activity) kaimono 買い物; (items) katta shinamono 買った品物; **do one's ~** ... ga kaimono o suru ...が買い物をする

shopping mall shoppingu-sentā ショッピングセンター

shop steward rōdōkumiai-daihyōiin 労働組合代表委員

shore kishi 岸; **on ~** riku de 陸で

short 1 adj (in height) se no hikui 背の低い; road, distance, time mijikai 短い; **be ~ of** ... ga tarinai ...が足りない **2** adv: **cut a vacation / meeting ~** kyūka / mītingu o mijikaku kiriageru 休暇／ミーティングを短く切り上げる; **stop a person ~** kyū ni tachidomaru 急に立ち止まる；**go ~ of** ...nashi de sumasu ...なしですます；**in ~** yō suru ni 要するに

shortage fusoku 不足

short circuit n shōto ショート；**shortcoming** ketten 欠点；**shortcut** chikamichi 近道

shorten v/t mijikaku suru 短くする

shortfall fusoku 不足；**shorthand** n sokki 速記；**shortlist** n (of candidates) saishū-kōho-sha 最終候補者；**short-lived** tsukanoma (no) つかの間(の)

shortly (soon) sugu ni すぐに；**~ before ten o'clock** jūji sukoshi mae ni 十時少し前に

shorts han-zubon 半ズボン；(underwear) pantsu パンツ

shortsighted kingan (no) 近眼(の)；fig kinshiganteki (na) 近視眼的(な)；**short-sleeved** hansode 半そで(の)；**short-staffed** hitode-busoku (no) 人手不足(の)；**short story** tanpen-shōsetsu 短編小説；**short-tempered** tanki (na) 短気(な)；**short-term** tankikan (no) 短期間(の)；**short time**: **be on ~** sōgyō-tanshuku suru 操業短縮する；**short wave** tanpa 短波

shot (from gun) hassha 発射；(photograph) shotto ショット；(injection) chūsha 注射；**be a good / poor ~** shageki no umai / heta na hito 射撃のうまい／下手な人；**like a ~ - accept, run off** teppōdama no yō ni 鉄砲弾のように

shotgun sandanjū 散弾銃

should ...subeki de aru ...すべきである；**what – I do?** dō shitara ii desu ka どうしたらいいですか；**you ~n't do that** sore o subeki de nai それをすべきでない；**that – be long enough** jūbun nagai to omoimasu 充分長いと思います；**you – have heard him!** kare no iu koto o kiite itara 彼の言うことを聞いていたら

shoulder n kata 肩

shoulder blade kenkōkotsu 肩甲骨

shout 1 n ōgoe 大声 2 v/i donaru 怒鳴る 3 v/t order ōgoe de iu 大声で言う

♦ **shout at** ... o donaru ...を怒鳴る

shouting n sakebigoe 叫び声

shove 1 n hitooshi ひと押し 2 v/t & v/i osu 押す

♦ **shove in** v/i (in line-up) tsukkomu 突っ込む

♦ **shove off** v/i F (go away) dete iku 出て行く

shovel n shaberu シャベル

show 1 n THEA, TV shō ショー；(display) hyōgen 表現；**on ~** (at exhibition) tenjichū 展示中；**it's all done for ~** zenbu misekake dake de aru 全部見せかけだけである 2 v/t passport, ticket miseru 見せる；interest, emotion arawasu 表す；(at exhibition) tenji suru 展示する；movie jōei suru 上映する；**~ X to Y** Y ni X o miseru YにXを見せる 3 v/i (be visible) mieru 見える；(of movie) jōei sareru 上映される；**does it ~?** wakaru わかる

♦ **show off 1** v/t skills ... o miseru ...を見せる 2 v/i pej misebirakasu 見せびらかす

♦ **show up 1** v/t faults etc ... o abaku ...を暴く；**don't show me up in public** mina no mae de haji o kakasenaide 皆の前で恥をかかせないで 2 v/i (arrive) arawareru 現れる；(be visible) mieru 見える

show business geinōkai 芸能界

showdown taiketsu 対決

shower 1 n (of rain) niwaka-ame にわか雨；(to wash) shawā シャワー；**take a ~** shawā o abiru シャワーを浴びる 3 v/t: **~ X with compliments / praise** X o homechigiru Xをほめちぎる

shower cap shawā-kyappu シャワーキャップ；**shower curtain** shawā-kāten シャワーカーテン；**showerproof** adj bōsui (no) 防水(の)

show jumping shōgaihietsu 障害飛越

show-off unubore-ya うぬぼれや

showroom shōrūmu ショールーム；**in ~ condition** hotondo shinpin no jōtai de ほとんど新品の状態で

showy *jacket, behavior* hade (na) 派手(な)

shred 1 *n (of paper etc)* danpen 断片; *(of evidence etc)* kirehashi 切れ端 **2** *v/t paper* shureddā ni kakeru シュレッダーにかける; *(in cooking)* mijingiri ni suru みじん切りにする

shredder shureddā シュレッダー

shrewd nukeme no nai 抜け目のない

shriek 1 *n* himei 悲鳴 **2** *v/i* himei o ageru 悲鳴をあげる

shrimp ebi えび

shrine jinja 神社

shrink *v/i (of material)* chijimu 縮む; *(of support etc)* heru 減る

shrink-wrap rappu de tsutsumu ラップで包む

shrink-wrapping *(process)* rappu-hōsō ラップ包装; *(material)* rappu ラップ

shrivel *(of skin)* shiwa ga yoru しわがよる; *(of material)* chijimu 縮む

shrub kanboku かん木

shrubbery uekomi 植え込み

shrug 1 *n* kata o sukumeru koto 肩をすくめること **2** *v/t & v/i*: ~ **(one's shoulders)** kata o sukumeru 肩をすくめる

shudder 1 *n (of fear, disgust)* miburui 身震い; *(of earth etc)* yure 揺れ **2** *v/i (with fear, disgust)* furueru 震える; *(of earth, building)* yureru 揺れる

shuffle 1 *v/t cards* kiru 切る **2** *v/i (in walking)* ashi o hikizutte aruku 足を引きずって歩く

shun sakeru さける

shut 1 *v/t* shimeru 閉める **2** *v/i* shimaru 閉まる; **they were ~** shimatte iru 閉まっている

♦ **shut down 1** *v/t business* ... o heisa suru ...を閉鎖する; *computer* ... o shūryō suru ...を終了する **2** *v/i (of business)* heisa ni naru 閉鎖になる; *(of computer)* shūryō suru 終了する

♦ **shut up** *v/i (be quiet)* damaru 黙る; **~!** damare 黙れ

shutter *(on window, PHOT)* shattā シャッター

shuttle *v/i* ōfuku suru 往復する

shuttlebus shatoru-basu シャトルバス; **shuttlecock** SP shatoru シャトル; **shuttle service** orikaeshi-unten 折返し運転

shy hazukashigari (no) 恥ずかしがり(の)

shyness uchiki 内気

Siamese twins shamu-sōseiji シャム双生児

sick byōki (no) 病気(の); *sense of humor* burakku yūmoa ブラックユーモア; *society* kusatta 腐った; **I'm going to be ~** hakisō desu 吐きそうです; **be ~ of** *(fed up with)* ... ni unzari suru ...にうんざりする

sicken 1 *v/t (disgust)* mukatsukaseru むかつかせる **2** *v/i* byōki ni naru 病気になる; **be ~ing for** ... no shōjō o shimesu ...の症状を示す

sickening fukai (na) 不快(な)

sickle kama かま

sick leave byōketsu 病欠; **be on ~** byōketsuchū (no) 病欠中(の)

sickly *person* byōjaku (na) 病弱(な); *color* aojiroi 青白い

sickness byōki 病気

side *n (of box, house)* sokumen 側面; *(of room, field)* gawa 側; *(of mountain)* sanpuku 山腹; *(of person)* waki わき; SP chīmu チーム; **take ~s** *(favor one side)* mikata o suru 味方をする; **take ~s with** ... o shiji suru ...を支持する; **I'm on your ~** watashi wa anata no mikata desu 私はあなたの味方です; **~ by ~** narande 並んで; **at the ~ of the road** rokata ni 路肩に; **on the big/small ~** sukoshi ōkii/chiisai 少し大きい/小さい

♦ **side with** ... no mikata o suru ...の味方をする

sideboard shokkidana 食器棚; **side dish** tsukeawase 付け合わせ; **side effect** fukusayō 副作用; **sidelight** MOT saidoraito サイドライト; **sideline 1** *n* fukugyō 副業 **2** *v/t*: **feel ~d** hazusareta ki ga suru はずされた気がする; **side street** wakimichi 脇道

わき道; **sidetrack**: *get ~ed*
yokomichi ni soreru 横道にそれる;
sidewalk hodō 歩道; **sidewalk café**
kafeterasu カフェテラス; **side-
ways** *adv* yokomuki ni 横向きに

siege hōi 包囲; *lay ~ to* … o hōi-
kōgeki suru …を包囲攻撃する

sieve *n* furui ふるい

sift *v/t corn, ore* furui ni kakeru ふ
るいにかける; *data* genmitsu ni
shiraberu 厳密に調べる

♦ **sift through** *data* … o genmitsu ni
shiraberu …を厳密に調べる

sigh 1 *n* tameiki ため息; *heave a ~
of relief* hotto tameiki o tsuku
ほっとため息をつく **2** *v/i* tameiki
o tsuku ため息をつく

sight *n* kōkei 光景; (*power of
seeing*) shiryoku 視力; *~s* (*of city*)
keshiki 景色; *catch ~ of* … o
mitsukeru …を見つける; *know by
~* mishitte iru 見知っている; *within
~* mieru tokoro ni 見えるところ
に; *out of ~* mienai tokoro ni 見え
ないところに; *what a ~ you are!*
kimi wa mirareta mono de wa nai
yo きみは見られた物ではないよ;
lose ~ of objective etc … o
miushinau …を見失う

sightseeing kankō 観光; *go ~* kankō
ni dekakeru 観光に出かける

sightseeing tour kankō-ryokō 観光
旅行

sightseer kankō-kyaku 観光客

sign 1 *n* (*indication*) chōkō 兆候;
(*road ~*) hyōshiki 標識; (*on shop,
building*) hyōji 表示; *it's a ~ of
the times* jidai no nagare desu 時
代の流れです **2** *v/t document* … ni
shomei suru …に署名する **3** *v/i*
shomei suru 署名する

♦ **sign up** *v/i* (*for course*) jukō-
tetsuzuki o suru 受講手続きをする

signal 1 *n* aizu 合図, RAIL shingō 信
号; *be sending out all the
right/wrong ~s* tadashii/
machigatta shingō o okuru 正し
い/間違った信号を送る **2** *v/i* (*of
driver*) aizu suru 合図する

signatory shomei-sha 署名者; (*to
treaty*) chōin-sha 調印者

signature shomei 署名

signature tune tēma-ongaku テーマ
音楽

signature seal inkan 印鑑

significance igi 意義

significant *event etc* jūyō (na) 重要
(な); (*large*) kanari (no) かなり
(の)

signify imi suru 意味する

sign language shuwa 手話

signpost annai-hyōshiki 案内標識

silence 1 *n* (*of place*) seijaku 静寂;
(*of person*) chinmoku 沈黙; *in ~
work, march* mugon de 無言で; *~!*
shizuka ni 静かに **2** *v/t*
damaraseru 黙らせる

silencer (*on gun*) shōon sōchi 消音
装置

silent shizuka (na) 静か(な); *movie*
musei (no) 無声(の); *stay ~* (*not
comment*) genkyū shinai 言及しな
い

silent partner tōshi suru dake no
shain 投資するだけの社員

silhouette *n* shiruetto シルエット

silicon shirikon シリコン

silicon chip shirikon chippu シリコ
ンチップ

silicone shirikon シリコン

silk 1 *n* kinu 絹 **2** *adj* shirt etc kinu
(no) 絹(の)

silly baka (na) ばか(な)

silver 1 *n* gin 銀 **2** *adj* ring gin (no)
銀(の); *hair* ginpatsu (no) 銀髪
(の)

silver medal gin medaru 銀メダル

silver-plated gin mekki (no) 銀めっ
き(の)

similar ruiji shita 類似した

similarity ruiji 類似

simmer *v/i* (*in cooking*) torobi de
torotoro niru とろ火でとろとろ煮
る; (*with rage*) bakuhatsu sunzen
de aru 爆発寸前である

♦ **simmer down** shizumaru 静まる

simple (*easy*) kantan (na) 簡単(な);
(*not very bright*) tanjun (na) 単純
(な)

simplicity kantan-sa 簡単さ

simplify kantan ni suru 簡単にする

simplistic kantan ni shita 簡単にした

simply (*absolutely*) mattaku 全く; (*in a simple way*) tan ni 単に; *it's ~ the best* sore wa mattaku saikō desu それは全く最高です

simulate shimyurēto suru シミュレートする

simultaneous dōji (no) 同時(の)

simultaneously dōji ni 同時に

sin 1 *n* tsumi 罪 **2** *v/i* tsumi o okasu 罪を犯す

since 1 *prep* irai 以来; *~ last week* senshū irai 先週以来 **2** *adv* sore irai それ以来; *I haven't seen him ~* sore irai kare ni atte imasen それ以来彼に会っていません **3** *conj* (*expressions of time*) ...shite irai ...して以来; (*seeing that*) ...dakara ...だから; *~ you left* anata ga satte irai あなたが去って以来; *~ you don't like it* anata wa sore ga kirai dakara あなたはそれが嫌いだから

sincere seijitsu (na) 誠実(な)

sincerely seijitsu ni 誠実に; *hope ~* kokoro kara 心から

sincerity seijitsu-sa 誠実さ

sinful tsumibukai 罪深い

sing *v/t & v/i* utau 歌う

Singapore Shingapōru シンガポール

Singaporean 1 *adj* Shingapōru (no) シンガポール (の) **2** *n* (*person*) Shingapōru-jin シンガポール人

singe *v/t* kogasu 焦がす

singer kashu 歌手

single 1 *n* (*sole*) hitotsu dake (no) 一つだけ(の); (*not double*) hitoe no 一重(の); (*not married*) dokushin (no) 独身(の); *there wasn't a ~ person there* soko ni wa dare mo inakatta そこには誰も居なかった; *in ~ file* ichiretsu-jūtai de 一列縦隊で **2** *n* MUS shinguru-ban シングル盤; *~s* (*in tennis*) shingurusu シングルス

♦ **single out** (*choose*) ... o erabu ... を選ぶ; (*distinguish*) kubetsu suru 区別する

single-breasted shinguru (no) シングル(の); **single-handed 1** *adj* dokuryoku (no) 独力(の) **2** *adv* dokuryoku de 独力で; **single-**

minded hitamuki (na) ひたむき (な); **single mother** shinguru-mazā シングルマザー; **single parent** kataoya (no) 片親(の); **single parent family** (*father only*) fushi katei 父子家庭; (*mother only*) boshi katei 母子家庭

singular GRAM **1** *adj* tansū (no) 単数(の) **2** *n* tansūkei 単数形; *in the ~* tansūkei (no) 単数形(の)

sinister ayashige (na) 怪しげ(な)

sink 1 *n* nagashi 流し **2** *v/i* (*of ship, object, sun*) shizumu 沈む; (*of interest rates, pressure etc*) ochikomu 落ち込む; *he sank onto the bed* kare wa beddo ni taorekonda 彼はベッドに倒れ込んだ **3** *v/t ship* shizumeru 沈める; *funds* tsugikomu つぎ込む

♦ **sink in** *v/i* (*of liquid*) shimikomu 染み込む; *it still hasn't really sunk in* mada jūbun ni rikai shite inai まだ充分に理解していない

sinner zainin 罪人

Sino-Japanese War (*1894-95*) Nisshin-sensō 日清戦争

sinusitis MED jōmyaku-dōen 静脈洞炎

sip 1 *n* hitokuchi 一口 **2** *v/t* sukoshi zutsu nomu 少しずつ飲む

sir (*to teacher*) sensei 先生; (*to customer*) okyaku-san お客さん; *excuse me, ~* chotto sumimasen ちょっとすみません

siren sairen サイレン

sirloin sāroin サーロイン

sister (*own, elder*) ane 姉; (*s.o. else's, elder*) onēsan お姉さん; (*own, younger*) imōto 妹; (*s.o. else's, younger*) imōtosan 妹さん; *~s* shimai 姉妹

sister-in-law (*older*) giri no onēsan 義理のお姉さん; (*younger*) giri no imōto 義理の妹; (*s.o. else's*) giri no imōtosan 義理の妹さん; (*talking to outsiders about one's own ~*) giri no ane 義理の姉

sit 1 *v/i* suwaru 座る **2** *v/t exam* ukeru 受ける

♦ **sit down** suwaru 座る

♦ **sit up** (*in bed*) okinaoru 起き直る;

(*straighten back*) kichin to suwaru きちんと座る; (*wait up*) okite iru 起きている

sitcom renzoku hōmu komedī 連続ホームコメディー

site 1 *n* basho 場所 **2** *v/t new offices etc* ... no yōchi o sadameru ...の用地を定める

sitting (*of committee, court*) kaikichū 会期中; (*for artist*) sesshon セッション; (*for meals*) shokuji-jikan 食事時間

sitting room ribingu-rūmu リビングルーム

situated: **be ~** ichi shite iru 位置している

situation jōsei 情勢; (*of building etc*) ritchi-jōken 立地条件

six roku 六

sixteen jūroku 十六

sixteenth dai-jūroku (no) 第十六(の)

sixth 1 *adj* dai-roku (no) 第六(の) **2** *n* (*of month*) muika 六日

sixtieth dai-rokujū (no) 第六十(の)

sixty rokujū 六十

size ōki-sa 大きさ; (*of jacket, shoes*) saizu サイズ

♦ **size up** ... o hyōka suru ...を評価する

sizeable kanari ōki (na) かなり大き(な)

sizzle shūshū oto o tateru シュウシュウ音をたてる

skate 1 *n* sukēto スケート **2** *v/i* sukēto o suru スケートをする

skateboard *n* sukēto-bōdo スケートボード

skater sukētā スケーター

skating sukēto スケート

skeleton gaikotsu がい骨

skeleton key masutā-kī マスターキー

skeptic utagaibukai hito 疑い深い人

skeptical kaigiteki na 懐疑的(な)

skepticism gimon 疑問

sketch 1 *n* suketchi スケッチ; THEA shōhin 小品 **2** *v/t* shasei suru 写生する

sketchbook suketchi bukku スケッチブック

sketchy ōzappa (na) 大雑把(な)

ski 1 *n* sukī スキー **2** *v/i* sukī o suru スキーをする

skid 1 *n* surippu スリップ **2** *v/i* surippu suru スリップする

skier sukīyā スキーヤー

skiing sukī スキー

ski lift sukī-rifuto スキーリフト

skill gijutsu 技術

skilled jukuren (no) 熟練(の)

skilled worker jukuren-kō 熟練工

skillful jōzu (na) 上手(な)

skim *surface* hyōmen o kasumete tobu 表面をかすめて飛ぶ

♦ **skim off** *the best* ... o erabitoru ...を選び取る

♦ **skim through** *text* zatto me o tōsu ざっと目を通す

skimmed milk sukimu miruku スキムミルク

skimpy *account etc* fujūbun (na) 不十分(な); *little dress* mijikasugiru 短すぎる

skin 1 *n* hifu 皮膚 **2** *v/t* kawa o hagu 皮をはぐ

skin diving sukin daibingu スキンダイビング

skinny yaseta やせた

skin-tight karada ni pittari (no) 体にぴったり(の)

skip 1 *n* (*little jump*) sukippu スキップ **2** *v/i* sukippu suru スキップする **3** *v/t* (*omit*) tobasu 飛ばす

ski pole sukī stokku スキーストック

skipper NAUT senchō 船長; (*of team*) kyaputen キャプテン

skirt *n* sukāto スカート

ski run gerende ゲレンデ

ski tow sukītō スキートー

skull zugaikotsu 頭がい骨

sky sora 空

skylark hibari ひばり; **skylight** tenmado 天窓; **skyline** sukairain スカイライン; **skyscraper** chōkosō-biru 超高層ビル

slab (*of stone*) sekiban 石版; (*of cake etc*) atsugiri 厚切り

slack *rope* yurui ゆるい; *discipline* tarunda たるんだ; *person* iikagen (na) いい加減(な); *work* fuchūi (na) 不注意(な); *period* kakki no

nai 活気のない
slacken v/t rope yurumeru 緩める; pace otosu 落とす
♦ **slacken off** v/i (of trading) heru 減る; (of pace) ochiru 落ちる
slacks surakkusu スラックス
slam 1 v/t (blow) hirateuchi 平手打ち
batan to shimeru バタンと閉める **2** v/i (of door etc) batan to shimaru バタンと閉まる
♦ **slam down** ... o gachan to oku ...
をガチャンと置く
slander 1 n waruguchi 悪口 **2** v/t chūshō suru 中傷する
slang surangu スラング; (of a specific group) ingo 隠語
slant 1 v/i katamuku 傾く **2** n keisha 傾斜; (given to a story) mikata 見方
slanting naname (no) 斜め(の); eyes tsuriagatta つり上がった
slap 1 n (blow) hirateuchi 平手打ち **2** v/t pishatto utsu ピシャッと打つ
slash 1 n (cut) kirikizu 切り傷; (in punctuation) surasshu スラッシュ **2** v/t skin etc satto kiru さっと切る; prices, costs kirisageru 切り下げる; ~ **one's wrists** tekubi o kiru 手首を切る
slate n surēto スレート
slaughter 1 n (of animals) tosatsu と殺; (of people) gyakusatsu 虐殺 **2** v/t animal tosatsu suru と殺する; people gyakusatsu suru 虐殺する
slave n dorei 奴隷
slay korosu 殺す
slaying (murder) satsujin 殺人
sleazy bar, character misuborashii みすぼらしい
sled(ge) n sori そり
sledge hammer hanmā ハンマー
sleep 1 n nemuru 眠る; **go to ~** neru 寝る; **I need a good ~** watashi ni wa tappuri no suimin ga hitsuyō desu 私にはたっぷりの睡眠が必要です; **I couldn't get to ~** nemurenakatta 眠れなかった **2** v/i nemuru 眠る
♦ **sleep on** ... o yukkuri kangaeru ...をゆっくり考える
♦ **sleep with** (have sex with) ... to sekkusu o suru ...とセックスをす

る
sleeping bag nebukuro 寝袋;
sleeping car shindai-sha 寝台車;
sleeping pill suimin'yaku 睡眠薬
sleepless night nemurenai 眠れない
sleepwalker muyūbyō-sha 夢遊病者
sleepy yawn nemui 眠い; town kakki no nai 活気のない; **I'm ~** watashi wa nemui 私は眠い
sleet n mizore みぞれ
sleeve (of jacket etc) sode そで
sleeveless sodenashi (no) そでなし(の)
sleight of hand kōmyō na hayawaza 巧妙なはやわざ
slender figure, arms hossori shita ほっそりした; chance, income, margin wazuka (na) わずか(な)
slice 1 n hitokire ひときれ; fig (of profits etc) wakemae 分け前 **2** v/t loaf etc usuku kiru 薄く切る
sliced bread usugiri no pan 薄切りのパン
slick 1 adj performance subarashii 素晴らしい; pej (cunning) kuchi no umai 口のうまい **2** n (of oil) yumaku 油膜
slide 1 n (for kids) suberidai 滑り台; PHOT suraido スライド **2** v/i suberu 滑る; (of exchange rate etc) genshō suru 減少する **3** v/t suberaseru 滑らせる
sliding door hikido 引き戸; (room partition in Japan) fusuma ふすま; (made of paper) shōji しょうじ
slight 1 adj wazuka (na) わずか(な); person, figure kyasha (na) きゃしゃ(な); **have a ~ headache** sukoshi zutsū ga suru 少し頭痛がする; **not in the ~est** sukoshi mo...nai 少しも...ない (insult) bujoku 侮辱
slightly sukoshi 少し
slim 1 adj hossori shita ほっそりした; chance wazuka (na) わずか(な) **2** v/i daietto suru ダイエットする
slime nurunuru shita mono ぬるぬるした物
slimy liquid nebaneba shita ねばねばした; person pekopeko shita ペ

こべこした

sling 1 n (for arm) sankaku-kin 三
角巾 **2** v/t (throw) hōru ほうる
slip 1 n (on ice etc) surippu スリッ
プ; (mistake) machigai 間違い; **a ~
of paper** ichimai no kamikire 一
枚の紙切れ; **a ~ of the tongue**
ukkari iu うっかり言う; **give ...
the ~** ... o maku ...をまく **2** v/i (on
ice etc) suberu 滑る; (decline: of
quality etc) teika suru 低下する;
he ~ped out of the room kare wa
kossori heya kara dete itta 彼は
こっそり部屋から出ていった **3** v/t
(put) suberikomaseru 滑り込ませ
る; **he ~ped it into his briefcase**
(kare wa sore o) burīfukēsu ni
suberikomaseta (彼はそれを)ブ
リーフケースに滑り込ませた

♦ **slip away** (of time) suguiru 過ぎる;
(of opportunity) kiesaru 消え去る;
(die) shizuka ni iki o hikitoru 静か
に息を引き取る

♦ **slip off** v/t coat ... o nugu ...を脱
ぐ

♦ **slip out** v/i (go out) nukedasu 抜
け出す

♦ **slip up** v/i (make mistake)
machigau 間違う

slipped disc tsuikanban herunia つ
い間板ヘルニア

slipper heyabaki 部屋ばき

slippery suberiyasui 滑りやすい

slipshod zonzai (na) ぞんざい(な)

slit 1 n (tear) sakeme 裂け目; (hole)
sukima すき間; (in skirt) suritto ス
リット **2** v/t kirihiraku 切り開く

slither v/i zuruzuru suberu ずるず
る滑る

slobber v/i yodare o tarasu よだれ
を垂らす

slogan surōgan スローガン

slop v/t kobosu こぼす

slope 1 n katamuki 傾き; (of
mountain) sanpuku 山腹; **be built
on a ~** shamen ni taterarete iru
斜面に建てられている **2** v/i
naname ni naru 斜めになる; **the
road ~s down to the sea** dōro wa
umi no hō e kudarizaka ni natte
iru 道路は海の方へ下り坂になって

sloppy work, editing zusan (na) ず
さん(な); (in dressing) darashinai
だらしない; (too sentimental)
kanshōteki (na) 感傷的な

sloshed F (drunk) yopparatta 酔っ
払った

slot n tōnyūguchi 投入口; (in
schedule) jikantai 時間帯

♦ **slot in 1** v/t ... o hamekomu ...を
はめ込む **2** v/i hairu 入る

slot machine (for vending)
jidōhanbai-ki 自動販売機; (for
gambling) surotto mashin スロッ
トマシン

slouch v/i maekagami ni naru 前か
がみになる

slovenly darashinai だらしない

slow osoi 遅い; **be ~** (of clock)
okurete iru 遅れている

♦ **slow down 1** v/t ... o okuraseru
...を遅らせる; traffic supīdo o
otosaseru スピードを落とさせる
2 v/i osoku naru 遅くなる; **the
doctor told her to ~** oisha-san ni
kanojo ni yukkuri suru yō ni itta
お医者さんは彼女にゆっくりする
ように言った

slowdown (in production) gensan
減産

slow motion: **in ~** surō mōshon de
スローモーションで

slug n (animal) namekuji なめくじ

sluggish kanman (na) 緩慢(な)

slum n suramugai スラム街

slump 1 n (in trade) fukeiki 不景気
2 v/i (economically) bōraku suru
暴落する; (collapse: of person)
dosun to taoreru ドスンと倒れる

slur 1 n (on s.o.'s character) chūshō
中傷 **2** v/t words mogomogo iu も
ごもご言う

slurred speech fumeiryō (na) 不明
りょう(な)

slush n handoke no yuki 半解けの
雪; pej (sentiment) kanshōteki na
hanashi 感傷的な話

slush fund fusei-shikin 不正資金

slut darashinai onna だらしない女

sly zurui ずるい; **on the ~** kossori
to こっそりと

smack 1 *n* hirateuchi 平手打ち
2 *v/t child* pishatto utsu ピシャッ
と打つ; *bottom* butsu ぶつ

small 1 *adj* chiisai 小さい **2** *n*: *the ~
of the back* koshi no kubireta
bubun 腰のくびれた部分

small change kozeni 小銭; **small
hours** yonaka 夜中; **smallpox**
tennentō 天然痘; **small print** saiji-
bubun 細字部分; **small talk**
sekenbanashi 世間話

smart 1 *adj* (*elegant*) iki (na) いき
(な); (*intelligent*) atama ga ii 頭が
いい; *pace* hayai 速い; *get ~ with
...* ni taishite namaiki ni naru ...に
対して生意気になる **2** *v/i* (*hurt*)
uzuku うずく

smart card sumāto kādo スマート
カード

♦ **smarten up** *v/t* ... o kogirei ni
suru ...をこぎれいにする

smash 1 *n* (*noise*) gachan to iu oto
ガチャンという音; (*car crash*)
shōtotsu 衝突; (*in tennis*)
sumasshu スマッシュ **2** *v/t*
(*break*) mechamecha ni kowasu め
ちゃめちゃに壊す; (*hit*) kyōda
suru 強打する; *~ to pieces ...* o
konagona ni suru ...を粉々にする
3 *v/i* (*break*) konagona ni naru
粉々になる; *the driver ~ed into ...*
untenshu wa ... ni tsukkon de itta
運転手は...に突っ込んでいった

smash hit F dai hitto 大ヒット

smashing F subarashii 素晴らしい

smattering: *I have a ~ of Chinese*
watashi wa Chūgoku-go o sukoshi
kajitta 私は中国語を少しかじった

smear 1 *n* (*of ink etc*) shimi 染み;
MED tofu-kensa 塗布検査; (*on
character*) chūshō 中傷 **2** *v/t paint
etc ...* ni nuritsukeru ...に塗り付け
る; *character* chūshō suru 中傷する

smear campaign chūshō gassen 中
傷合戦

smell 1 *n* (*of ink etc*) shimi 染み; *it has no ~*
nioi ga shinai においがしない;
sense of ~ shūkaku 臭覚 **2** *v/t*
nioi ga suru においがする **3** *v/i*
(*unpleasantly*) niou におう;
(*sniff*) nioi o kagu においをかぐ;

what does it ~ of? nan no nioi ga
shimasu ka 何のにおいがしますか;
you ~ of beer bīru no nioi ga suru
ビールのにおいがする

smelly kusai くさい

smile 1 *n* hohoemi ほほ笑み **2** *v/i*
hohoemu ほほ笑む

♦ **smile at** ... ni hohoemu ...にほほ
笑む

smirk 1 *n* niyaniya-warai にやにや
笑い **2** *v/i* niyaniya-warau にやに
や笑う

smog sumoggu スモッグ

smoke 1 *n* kemuri 煙; *have a ~*
tabako o suu たばこを吸う **2** *v/t
cigarettes* suu 吸う; *bacon* ibusu い
ぶす **3** *v/i* tabako o suu たばこを吸
う; *I don't ~* watashi wa tabako o
suwanai 私はたばこを吸わない

smoker (*person*) kitsuen-ka 喫煙家

smoking kitsuen 喫煙; *no ~* kin'en
禁煙

smoking compartment RAIL
kitsuen-sha 喫煙車

smoky *room, air* kemui 煙い

smolder (*also fig*) kusuburu くすぶ
る

smooth 1 *adj surface, skin, sea*
nameraka (na) なめらか(な); *ride*
shizuka (na) 静か(な); *transition*
junchō (na) 順調(な); *pej: person*
oseji no umai お世辞のうまい **2** *v/t
hair* nadetsukeru なでつける

♦ **smooth down** (*with sandpaper
etc*) nameraka ni suru なめらかに
する

♦ **smooth out** *paper, cloth ...* o
nobasu ...をのばす

♦ **smooth over**: *smooth things
over* kaiketsu suru 解決する

smother *flames ...* ni ...o kabusete
kesu ...に...をかぶせて消す;
person chissoku saseru 窒息させ
る; *~ with kisses ...* ni kisu o
abiseru ...にキスを浴びせる

smudge 1 *n* shimi 染み **2** *v/t* yogosu
汚す

smug hitoriyogari (no) 独りよがり
(の)

smuggle *v/t* mitsuyu suru 密輸する

smuggler mitsuyu-gyōsha 密輸業者

smuggling mitsuyu 密輸

smutty *joke, sense of humor* waisetsu (na) わいせつ(な)

snack *n* keishoku 軽食

snack bar keishokudō 軽食堂

snag (*problem*) shōgai 障害

snail katatsumuri かたつむり

snake *n* hebi 蛇

snap 1 *n* patan to iu oto パタンという音; PHOT sunappu shashin スナップ写真 **2** *v/t* (*break*) pokin to oru ぽきんと折る; (*say sharply*) kamitsuku かみつく **3** *v/i* (*break*) pokin to oreru ぽきんと折れる **4** *adj decision* kyū (na) 急(な)

♦ **snap up** *bargain* ... o tobitsuite kau ...を飛びついて買う

snappy *person, mood* kamitsukisō (na) かみつきそう(な); *decision, response* hayai 速い; (*elegant*) shareta しゃれた

snapshot snappu shashin スナップ写真

snarl 1 *n* (*of dog*) unari うなり **2** *v/i* ha o mukidashite unaru 歯をむき出してうなる

snatch 1 *v/t* (*steal*) hittakuru ひったくる; (*kidnap*) yūkai suru 誘拐する **2** *v/i* hittakuru ひったくる

snazzy iki (na) 粋(な)

sneak 1 *v/t* (*remove, steal*) kossori toru こっそりとる; ~ *a glance at* ... o nusumimi ru ...を盗み見る **2** *v/i*: ~ *into the room / out of the room* kossori heya ni hairu / heya o deru こっそり部屋に入る/部屋を出る

sneakers sunīkā スニーカー

sneaking: *have a ~ suspicion that* ... ... o hisoka ni utagatte iru ...をひそかに疑っている

sneaky F (*crafty*) inken (na) 陰険(な)

sneer 1 *n* reishō 冷笑 **2** *v/i* azawarau あざ笑う

sneeze 1 *n* kushami くしゃみ **2** *v/i* kushami o suru くしゃみをする

sniff *v/t* (*to clear nose*) hana o susuru はなをすする; (*of dog*) kunkun kagu くんくんかぐ **2** *v/t* (*smell*) nioi o kagu においをかぐ

sniper sogekihei 狙撃兵

snitch F **1** *n* (*telltale*) tsugeguchi-ya 告げ口屋 **2** *v/i* tsugeguchi suru 告げ口する

snob kidori-ya 気取り屋

snobbish kidotta 気取った

snooker biriyādo ビリヤード

♦ **snoop around** hisoka ni nozokimawaru ひそかにのぞき回る

snooty gōman (na) ごう慢(な)

snooze 1 *n* inemuri 居眠り; *have a* ~ inemuri suru 居眠りする **2** *v/i* inemuri suru 居眠りする

snore *v/i* ibiki o kaku いびきをかく

snoring *n* ibiki いびき

snorkel shunkeru シュノーケル

snort *v/i* (*of bull, horse*) hana o narasu 鼻を鳴らす; (*of person: disdainfully*) fun to hana o narasu ふんと鼻を鳴らす

snout (*of pig, dog*) hana 鼻

snow 1 *n* yuki 雪 **2** *v/i* yuki ga furu 雪が降る

♦ **snow under**: *be snowed under with* ... ... de totemo isogashii ...でとても忙しい

snowball yukidama 雪玉; **snowbound** yuki ni tojikomerareta 雪に閉じ込められた; **snow chains** MOT chēn チェーン; **snowdrift** yuki no fukidamari 雪の吹きだまり; **snowdrop** matsuyukisō まつゆきそう; **snowflake** yuki no hitohira 雪のひとひら; **snowman** yukidaruma 雪だるま; **snowplow** josetsuki 除雪機; **snowstorm** fubuki 吹雪

snowy *weather* yuki no ōi 雪の多い; *roads, hills* yuki no tsumotta 雪の積もった

snub 1 *n* bujoku 侮辱 **2** *v/t* bujoku suru 侮辱する

snub-nosed shishibana (no) しし鼻(の)

snug atatakaku kokochi yoi 暖かく心地よい; (*tight-fitting*) pittari atta ぴったり合った

♦ **snuggle down** kokochi yoku yokotawaru 心地よく横たわる

♦ **snuggle up to** ... ni yorisou ...に

寄り添う

so 1 *adv*: ~ *hot*/*cold* totemo atsui/samui ここはとても暑い/寒い; *not* ~ *much* amari あまり; ~ *much better*/*easier* zutto yoi/kantan na ずっと良い/簡単な; *eat*/*drink* ~ *much* takusan tabeta/nonda たくさん食べた/飲んだ; ~ *many ...* takusan ...たくさん...; ~ *am I*/*do I* watashi mo sō desu わたしもそうです; ~ *is she*/*does she* kanojo mo sō desu 彼女もそうです; *and* ~ *on* ... nado ...など 2 *pron*: *I hope* ~ sō kibō shimasu そう希望します; *I think* ~ sō omoimasu そう思います; *you didn't tell me* – *I did* ~ watashi ni iwanakatta deshō – watashi wa sō iimashita 私に言わなかったでしょう私はそういいました; *50 or* ~ daitai gojussai 大体五十歳 3 *conj* (*for that reason*) sono kekka その結果; (*in order that*) node ので; *and* ~ *I missed the train* sō iu wake de densha ni noriokuremashita そういう訳で電車に乗り遅れました; ~ (*that*) *I can come too* ...nanode watashi mo koraremasu ...なので私も来られます; ~ *what?* sore de それで

soak *v/t* (*steep*) tsukeru つける; (*of water, rain*) nurasu ぬらす

♦**soak up** *liquid* ... o kyūshū suru ...を吸収する

soaked bishonure ni natta びしょぬれになった

so-and-so F (*unknown person*) daresore 誰それ; (*annoying person*) aitsu あいつ

soap *n* (*for washing*) sekken 石けん

soap (*opera*) renzoku merodorama 連続メロドラマ

soapy *water* sekken darake (no) 石けんだらけ(の)

soar (*of rocket etc*) maiagaru 舞い上がる; (*of prices*) kyūjōshō suru 急上昇する

sob 1 *n* susurinaki すすり泣き 2 *v/i* nakijakuru 泣きじゃくる

sober (*not drunk*) shirafu (no) しらふ(の); (*serious*) majime (na) まじめ(な)

♦**sober up** yoi ga sameru 酔いが覚める

so-called (*referred to as*) iwayuru いわゆる; (*incorrectly referred to as*) nabakari (no) 名ばかり(の)

soccer sakkā サッカー

sociable shakōteki (na) 社交的(な)

social *adj* shakai (no) 社会(の); (*recreational*) shakō (no) 社交(の)

socialism shakai-shugi 社会主義

socialist 1 *adj* shakai-shugi (no) 社会主義(の) 2 *n* shakai-shugisha 社会主義者

socialize tsukiau 付き合う

social work shakaifukushi-jigyō 社会福祉事業

social worker sōsharu-wākā ソーシャルワーカー

society shakai 社会; (*organization*) kyōkai 協会; (*informal club*) kurabu クラブ

sociology shakai-gaku 社会学

sock[1] kutsushita 靴下

sock[2] 1 *n* (*punch*) kyōda 強打 2 *v/t* (*punch*) kyōda suru 強打する

socket ELEC soketto ソケット; (*of arm*) kataguchi 肩口; (*of eye*) ganka 眼か

soda (~ *water*) sōda ソーダ; (*ice-cream* ~) kurīmu sōda クリームソーダ; (*soft drink*) saidā サイダー

sofa sofa ソファ

sofa-bed sofabeddo ソファベッド

soft yawarakai 柔らかい; (*lenient*) yasashii 優しい; *have a* ~ *spot for* ...ga daisuki da ...が大好きだ

soft drink seiryō-inryōsui 清涼飲料水

soften 1 *v/t* *position* nanka suru 軟化する; *impact, blow* yawarageru 和らげる 2 *v/i* (*of butter, ice cream*) yawarakaku naru 柔らかくなる

softly shizuka ni 静かに

software sofuto ソフト

soggy mizubitashi (no) 水浸し(の); *pastry* betobeto shita べとべとした

soil 1 *n* (*earth*) tsuchi 土 2 *v/t* yogosu 汚す

solar energy taiyō-enerugī 太陽エネルギー

solar panel taiyō-denchiban 太陽電池板

soldier gunjin 軍人

sole¹ *n* (*of foot*) ashi no ura 足の裏; (*of shoe*) kutsu no soko 靴の底

sole² *adj* yuiitsu (no) 唯一(の)

solely ...dake ...だけ

solemn (*serious*) genshuku (na) 厳粛(な); *promise* shinken (na) 真剣(な)

solid *adj* (*hard*) katai 固い; (*without holes*) sukima no nai すき間のない; *gold, silver* junsui (no) 純粋(の); (*sturdy*) ganjō (na) 頑丈(な); *evidence* kakko taru 確固たる; *support* shikkari shita しっかりした

solidarity kessoku 結束

solidify *v/i* katamaru 固まる

solitaire (*game*) hitori toranpu 一人トランプ

solitary *life* kodoku (na) 孤独(な); *walk* hitoridake (no) 一人だけ(の); (*single*) tatta hitori dake (no) たった一人だけ(の)

solitude kodoku 孤独

solo 1 *n* MUS dokusō 独奏 2 *adj* tandoku (no) 単独(の)

soloist sorisuto ソリスト

soluble *substance* tokeru 溶ける; *problem* kaiketsu dekiru 解決できる

solution kaitō 解答; (*mixture*) yōeki 溶液

solve toku 解く

solvent *adj* (*financially*) shiharai-nōryoku no aru 支払能力のある

somber *dark* kurai 暗い; (*serious*) shinkoku (na) 深刻(な)

some 1 *adj* (*with countable nouns*) ikutsuka (no) 幾つか(の), sukoshi 少し; (*with uncountable nouns*) ikuraka (no) 幾らか(の), sukoshi 少し; ~ *people say that* ... ... to itteru hito mo imasu ...と言ってる人も居ます; *would you like* ~ *water / cookies?* (sukoshi) mizu/ kukkī wa ikaga desu ka (少し)水は/クッキーはいかがですか; ~ *woman I met on the train* densha de atta aru onna 電車で会ったある

女 2 *pron* (*for countable nouns*) ikutsuka (no) 幾つか(の), sukoshi 少し; (*for uncountable nouns*) ikuraka (no) 幾らか(の), sukoshi 少し; ~ *of my relatives think* ... ... to omotte iru shinseki mo imasu ...と思っている親戚もいます; ~ *of the group* gurūpu no nanninka グループの何人か; *would you like* ~? sukoshi ikaga 少しいかが; *give me* ~ sukoshi kudasai 少し下さい 3 *adv* (*a bit*) sukoshi 少し; *we'll have to wait* ~ sukoshi matanakereba narimasen 少し待たなければなりません

somebody dareka 誰か

someday itsu no hi ka いつの日か

somehow (*by one means or another*) nantoka shite 何とかして; (*for some unknown reason*) nazeka なぜか

someone → **somebody**

someplace → **somewhere**

somersault 1 *n* tonbogaeri とんぼ返り 2 *v/i* tonbogaeri suru とんぼ返りする

something nanika 何か; *would you like* ~ *to drink / eat?* nanika nomimasen ka/tabemasen ka 何か飲みませんか/食べませんか; *is* ~ *wrong?* nanika okashii desu ka 何かおかしいですか

sometime sono uchi そのうち; ~ *last year* kyonen no itsuka 去年のいつか

sometimes tokidoki 時々

somewhere 1 *adv* (*with verbs of being*) dokoka de どこかで; (*with verbs of activity*) dokoka ni どこかに 2 *pron* dokoka どこか

son musuko 息子

song uta 歌

songwriter sakushi-ka 作詞家

son-in-law giri no musuko 義理の息子

son of a bitch ∨ kono yarō この野郎

soon (*in a short time*) mō sugu もうすぐ; (*a short time after*) sugu ni すぐに; *how* ~ *can you be ready to leave?* dono kurai de deru junbi ga dekimasu ka どのくらい

で出る準備ができますか; *it's too ~ to say...* ... を判断するには早すぎる; *as ~ as* ... すると早く; *as ~ as possible* dekiru dake hayaku できるだけ早く; *~er or later* itsuka wa いつかは; *the ~er the better* hayakereba hayai hodo ii 早ければ早いほどいい

soot susu すす

soothe *person* nagusameru なぐさめる; *pain* yawarageru やわらげる

sophisticated *person, tastes* senren sareta 洗練された; *machine* kōdo (na) 高度(な)

sophomore ninensei 二年生

soprano *n* soprano ソプラノ

sordid *affair, business* kitanai 汚い

sore 1 *adj* (*painful*) itai 痛い; F (*angry*) kizutsuku 傷つく; *is it ~?* itai desu ka 痛いですか **2** *n* kizuguchi 傷口

sorrow *n* kanashimi 悲しみ

sorry *sight* sabishisō (na) さびしそう(な); *day* kanashii 悲しい; (*I'm*) *~!* (*apologizing*) sumimasen すみません; *I'm ~* (*regretting*) sumimasen ga すみませんが; *I'm ~ but I can't help* mōshiwake arimasen ga tetsudaemasen 申し訳ありませんが手伝えません*I won't be ~ to leave here* koko o saru no wa zannen dewa nai ここを去るのは残念ではない*I feel ~ for her* kanojo ni dōjō suru 彼女に同情する

sort 1 *n* shurui 種類; *~ of ...* chotto... ちょっと...; *is it finished? - ~ of* F owarimashita ka – daitai 終わりましたか – だいたい **2** *v/t* bunrui suru 分類する; COMPUT sōto suru ソートする

♦ **sort out** *papers* ... o seiri suru ... を整理する; *problem* kaiketsu suru 解決する

so-so *adv* māmā まあまあ

soul REL tamashii 魂; *fig* (*of nation etc*) seishin 精神; (*character*) kyarakutā キャラクター; (*person*) hito 人

sound¹ 1 *adj* (*sensible*) kenjitsu (na) 堅実(な); (*healthy*) kenzen (na) 健全(な) **2** *adv*: *~ asleep* gussuri nemutte ぐっすり眠って

sound² 1 *n* oto 音; (*noise*) sawagi 騒ぎ **2** *v/t* (*pronounce*) hatsuon suru 発音する; MED chōshin suru 聴診する; *~ one's horn* kurakushon o narasu クラクションを鳴らす **3** *v/i*: *that ~s interesting* sore wa omoshiro-sō da それはおもしろそうだ; *that ~s like a good idea* ii aidea no yō da いいアイデアのようだ; *she ~ed happy* kanojo wa shiawase-sō datta 彼女は幸せそうだった

soundly *sleep* gussuri ぐっすり; *beaten* koppidoku こっぴどく

soundproof *adj* bōon (no) 防音(の)

soundtrack saundotrakku サウンドトラック

soup sūpu スープ; *clear ~* sumashijiru すまし汁

soup bowl sūpu-zara スープ皿

sour *adj* *apple, orange* suppai 酸っぱい; *milk* suppaku natta 酸っぱくなった; *expression, comment* ijiwaru (na) 意地悪(な)

source *n* minamoto 源; (*of river*) suigenchi 水源地; (*person*) jōhōgen 情報源

south 1 *adj* minami (no) 南(の) **2** *n* minami 南; (*of country*) nanbu 南部; *to the ~ of ...* ... no minami ni ...の南に **3** *adv* minami ni 南に

South Africa Minami-Afurika 南アフリカ; **South African 1** *adj* Minami-Afurika (no) 南アフリカ(の) **2** *n* Minami-Afurika-jin 南アフリカ人; **South America** Nanbei 南米; **South American 1** *adj* Nanbei (no) 南米(の) **2** *n* Nanbei-jin 南米人; **southeast 1** *n* nantō 南東 **2** *adj* nantō (no) 南東(の) **3** *adv* nantō ni 南東に; *it's ~ of ...* ... no nantō desu ...の南東です; **Southeast Asia** Tōnan Ajia 東南アジア; **Southeast Asian** *adj* Tōnan Ajia (no) 東南アジア(の); **southeastern** nantōbu (no) 南東部(の)

southerly adj minami kara (no) 南から(の)

southern nanbu (no) 南部(の)

South Korea Kankoku 韓国; **South Korean 1** adj Kankoku (no) 韓国(の) **2** n Kankoku-jin 韓国人

southward adv nanpō e 南方へ

southwest 1 n nansei 南西 **2** adj nansei (no) 南西(の) **3** adv nansei ni 南西に; **it's ~ of ...** ... no nansei desu ...の南西です

southwestern nanseibu (no) 南西部(の)

souvenir o-miyage おみやげ

sovereign adj state dokuritsu shita 独立した

sovereignty (of state) shuken 主権

Soviet Union Sobieto-renpō ソビエト連邦

sow¹ n (pig) mesubuta 雌豚

sow² v/t seeds maku まく

soy bean daizu 大豆

soy sauce shōyu しょうゆ

space n (outer ~) uchū-kūkan 宇宙空間; (area) yohaku 余白; (room) basho 場所

♦**space out** kankaku o oku 間隔を置く

spacebar COMPUT supēsu-bā スペースバー; **spaceship** uchū-sen 宇宙船; **space shuttle** supēsu-shatoru スペースシャトル; **space station** uchū-sutēshon 宇宙ステーション; **spacesuit** uchū-fuku 宇宙服

spacious hirobiro to shita 広々とした

spade sukoppu スコップ; **~s** (in cards) supēdo スペード

Spain Supein スペイン

span v/t ... ni oyobu ...に及ぶ; (of bridge) ... ni kakatte iru ...かかっている

Spaniard Supein-jin スペイン人

Spanish 1 adj Supein (no) スペイン(の) **2** n (language) Supein-go スペイン語

spank ... no shiri o tataku ...のしりをたたく

spare 1 v/t time, money ataeru 与える; (do without) ...nashi de

sumasu ...なしで済ます; **can you ~ me 5 minutes** watashi ni gofun kurenai 私に五分くれない; **can you ~ me $50?** gojū doru kashite kurenai 五十ドル貸してくれない; **can you ~ the time?** jikan o tsukureru 時間をつくれる; **there are 5 to ~** yobun ni goko arimasu 余分に五個あります **2** adj yobi (no) 予備(の) **3** n (part) kōkan-buhin 交換部品

spare ribs supearibu スペアリブ; **spare room** yobi no heya 予備の部屋; **spare time** yoka 余暇; **spare tire, spare wheel** supea taiya スペアタイヤ

spark n hibana 火花

sparkle v/i kagayaku 輝く

sparkling wine happō-wain 発泡ワイン

spark plug tenka-puragu 点火プラグ

sparrow suzume すずめ

sparse vegetation tenzai suru 点在する

sparsely: **~ populated** jinkō-mitsudo no hikui 人口密度の低い

spatter v/t mud, paint ... ni hanekakeru ...にはねかける

speak 1 v/i hanasu 話す; (make a speech) enzetsu suru 演説する; **we're not ~ing (to each other)** watashitachi wa (otagai ni) kuchi o kiiteinai 私達は(お互いに)口をきいていない; **can I ~ to Charles – ~ing** Chārusu-san wa irasshaimasu ka – watashi desu チャールスさんはいらっしゃいますか – 私です **2** v/t foreign language hanasu 話す; **~ one's mind** jibun no kangae o hakkiri iu 自分の考えをはっきり言う

♦**speak for** ... o daiben suru ...を代弁する

♦**speak out** sotchoku ni iken o noberu 率直に意見を述べる

♦**speak up** (speak louder) ōki na koe de hanasu 大きな声で話す

speaker (at conference) enzetsu-sha 演説者; (orator) yūben-ka 雄弁家; (of sound system) supīkā ス

ピーカー

spearmint supeaminto スペアミント

special tokubetsu (na) 特別(な)

specialist senmon-ka 専門家; MED senmon-i 専門医

♦ **specialize in** ... o senmon ni suru ...を専門にする; *subject* ... o senkō suru ...を専攻する

specially → *especially*

specialty tokushoku 特色; (*food*) jiman-ryōri 自慢料理

species shu 種

specific tokutei (no) 特定(の)

specifically toku ni 特に

specifications (*of machine etc*) shiyō 仕様

specify shitei suru 指定する; *details* meisai ni shirusu 明細に記す

specimen (*sample*) mihon 見本; MED hyōhon 標本

speck (*of dust, soot*) tsubu 粒

spectacle (*impressive sight*) supekutakuru スペクタクル

spectacular adj *profit, success* gekiteki (na) 劇的(な); *view, building* gōka (na) 豪華(な)

spectator kankyaku 観客

spectator sport miru supōtsu 見るスポーツ

spectrum fig han'i 範囲

speculate v/i okusoku suru 憶測する; FIN tōki suru 投機する

speculation okusoku 憶測; FIN tōki 投機

speculator FIN tōki-ka 投機家

speech (*address*) supīchi スピーチ; (*in play*) serifu せりふ; (*ability to speak*) hanasu nōryoku 話す能力; (*way of speaking*) hanashikata 話し方

speechless koe mo denai 声も出ない

speech defect gengo-shōgai 言語障害; **speech therapist** gengo-ryōhōshi 言語療法士; **speech writer** supīchi-raitā スピーチライター

speed 1 n haya-sa 速さ; (*of car, plane etc*) supīdo スピード; **at a ~ of 150 mph** maiji hyakugojū

mairu no hayasa de 毎時百五十マイルの速さで **2** v/i isogu 急ぐ; (*drive too quickly*) ihan-sokudo de hashiru 違反速度で走る

♦ **speed by** sugisaru 過ぎ去る

♦ **speed up 1** v/i supīdo ga agaru スピードが上がる **2** v/t ... no supīdo o ageru ...のスピードを上げる

speedboat mōtābōto モーターボート

speedily subayaku 素早く

speeding n supīdo-ihan スピード違反

speeding fine supīdo-ihan no bakkin スピード違反の罰金

speed limit seigen-sokudo 制限速度

speedometer sokudo-kei 速度計

speedy hayai 速い

spell¹ v/t & v/i tsuzuru つづる

spell² n (*period of time*) sukoshi no aida 少しの間; *I'll take a ~ at the wheel* kōtai shite watashi ga unten shimasu 交替して私が運転します

spellbound miserareta 魅せられた;

spellcheck COMPUT superu-chekku スペルチェック; *do a ~ on* ... ... ni superu-chekku o kakeru ...にスペルチェックをかける;

spellchecker COMPUT superu-chekkā スペルチェッカー

spelling tsuzuri つづり, superingu スペリング

spend *money* tsukau 使う; *time* sugosu 過ごす; *don't ~ too much time on it* sore ni jikan o kakesuginai de それに時間をかけ過ぎないで

spendthrift n pej rōhi-ka 浪費家

sperm seishi 精子; (*semen*) seieki 精液

sperm bank seishi-ginkō 精子銀行

sphere kyū 球; fig (*field*) bun'ya 分野; *~ of influence* eikyō no oyobu han'i 影響の及ぶ範囲

spice n (*seasoning*) kōshinryō 香辛料

spicy *food* kōshinryō no kiita 香辛料の利いた

spider kumo くも

spiderweb kumo no su くもの巣

spike n (of railings) kugi くぎ; (of plant) toge とげ; (on shoe) supaiku スパイク; (of animal) hari 針

spill 1 v/t kobosu こぼす 2 v/i koboreru こぼれる

spin¹ 1 n (turn) kaiten 回転 2 v/t kaiten saseru 回転させる 3 v/i (of wheel) kaiten suru 回転する; **my head is ~ning** kurakura suru くらくらする

spin² v/t wool, cotton tsumugu 紡ぐ; web su o tsukuru 巣をつくる

♦**spin around** (of person, car) kaiten suru 回転する

♦**spin out** ... o hikinobasu ...を引き延ばす

spinach hōrensō ほうれん草

spinal sebone (no) 背骨(の)

spinal column sebone 背骨

spin doctor supōkusuman スポークスマン; **spin-dry** v/t dassui suru 脱水する; **spin-dryer** dassui-ki 脱水機

spine (of person, animal) sebone 背骨; (of book) se 背; (on plant) toge とげ; (on hedgehog) hari 針

spineless fig ikuji no nai 意気地のない

spin-off fukusanbutsu 副産物

spiral 1 n rasenkei ら旋形 2 v/i (rise quickly) kyūjōshō suru 急上昇する

spiral staircase rasen kaidan ら旋階段

spire sentō せん塔

spirit n (as opposed to body) seishin 精神; (of dead person) rei 霊; (energy) katsuryoku 活力; (courage) kiryoku 気力; (attitude) keikō 傾向; **we did it in a ~ of cooperation** watashitachi wa kyōryoku no seishin de sore o shimashita 私達は協力の精神でそれをしました

spirited (energetic) seiryokuteki (na) 精力的(な)

spirit level suijunki 水準器

spirits¹ (alcohol) jōryūshu 蒸留酒

spirits² (morale) shiki 士気; **be in good / poor ~** kibun wa jōjō de

aru / saiaku de aru 気分は上々である/最悪である

spiritual adj reiteki (na) 霊的(な)

spiritualism kōreisetsu 降霊説

spiritualist n kōreijutsu-sha 降霊術者

spit v/i (of person) tsuba o haku つばを吐く; **it's ~ting with rain** ame ga shitoshito futte iru 雨がしとしとと降っている

♦**spit out** food etc ... o hakidasu ...を吐き出す

spite n akui 悪意; **in ~ of** ... ni mo kakawarazu ...にもかかわらず

spiteful ijiwaru (na) 意地悪(な)

spitting image: **be the ~ of** ... ni sokkuri de aru ...にそっくりである

splash 1 n (noise) zabun to iu oto ザブンという音; (small amount: of liquid, of color) sukoshi (no) 少し(の) 2 v/t person mizu o tobichirasu 水を飛び散らす; water, mud hanekakeru 跳ねかける 3 v/i mizu o haneru 水を跳ねる; (of water) tobichiru 飛び散る

♦**splash down** (of spacecraft) chakusui suru 着水する

♦**splash out** taikin o tsukau 大金を使う

splendid gōka (na) 豪華(な)

splendor gōka-sa 豪華さ

splint n MED fukuboku 副木

splinter 1 n (of wood, bone) hahen 破片, toge とげ 2 v/i kudakeru 砕ける

splinter group bunretsu gurūpu 分裂グループ

split 1 n (in material) sakeme 裂け目; (in wood) wareme 割れ目; (disagreement) bunretsu 分裂; (division, share) bunpai 分配 2 v/t (damage) saku 裂く; logs waru 割る; (cause disagreement) bunretsu saseru 分裂させる; (divide) wakeru 分ける 3 v/i (tear) sakeru 裂ける; (of wood etc) wareru 割れる; (disagree) bunretsu suru 分裂する

♦**split up** v/i (of couple) wakareru 別れる

split personality PSYCH nijū-jinkaku 二重人格

splitting *adj*: **~ headache** atama ga wareső na zutsū 頭が割れそうな頭痛

spoil *v/t* dame ni suru だめにする; *child* amakasu 甘やかす

spoilsport F za o shirakesaseru hito 座を白けさせる人

spoilt *adj child* amayaka sareta 甘やかされた; **be ~ for choice** erabu no ni komaru 選ぶのに困る

spoke *(of wheel)* supôku スポーク

spokesman supôkusu-man スポークスマン

spokesperson supôkusu-pâson スポークスパーソン

spokeswoman josei-supôkusuman 女性スポークスマン

sponge *n* suponji スポンジ

♦sponge off F ... ni takaru ...にたかる

sponger F takari たかり

sponsor 1 *n (for immigration, membership)* hoshōnin 保証人; *(of radio, TV program, event)* suponsā スポンサー **2** *v/t (for immigration, membership)* hoshōnin to naru 保証人となる; *program, event* suponsā ni naru スポンサーになる

sponsorship kōen 後援

spontaneous jihatsuteki (na) 自発的(な)

spooky F obake no deső (na) お化けの出そう(な)

spool *n (for thread)* itomaki 糸巻き; *(for film)* rīru リール

spoon *n* supūn スプーン

spoonfeed *fig* amayakasu 甘やかす

spoonful supūn-ippai スプーン一杯

sporadic barabara (no) バラバラ(の)

sport *n* supôtsu スポーツ

sporting *event* supôtsu (no) スポーツ(の); *(fair)* kōhei (na) 公平(な); *(generous)* kimae ga ii 気前がいい; **a ~ gesture** kōhei na kōi 公平な行為

sportscar supôtsu-kā スポーツカー; **sportscoat** supôtsu-jaketto スポーツジャケット; **Sports Day** Taiiku no hi 体育の日; **sports**

journalist supôtsu-kisha スポーツ記者; **sportsman** supôtsu-man スポーツマン; **sports news** supôtsu-nyūsu スポーツニュース; **sports page** supôtsu-ran スポーツ欄; **sportswoman** supôtsu-ūman スポーツウーマン

sporty *person* supôtsu-zuki (na) スポーツ好き(な); *clothes* supôtī (na) スポーティー(な)

spot[1] *(pimple)* nikibi にきび; *(caused by measles etc)* dekimono できもの; *(part of pattern)* mizutama 水玉

spot[2] *(place)* basho 場所; **on the ~** *(in the place in question)* genba de 現場で; *(immediately)* sono ba de その場で; **put X on the ~** X o komaraseru Xを困らせる

spot[3] *v/t (notice, identify)* mitsukeru 見つける

spot check nukitori-kensa 抜き取り検査; **carry out spot checks** *(of customs, police)* nukiuchi-kensa o suru 抜き打ち検査をする

spotless seiketsu (na) 清潔(な)

spotlight *n* supottoraito スポットライト

spotted *fabric* mizutama moyō (no) 水玉模様(の)

spotty *(with pimples)* nikibidarake (no) にきびだらけ(の)

spouse *fml* haigū-sha 配偶者

spout 1 *n* sosogiguchi 注ぎ口 **2** *v/i (of liquid)* hotobashiru ほとばしる

sprain 1 *n* nenza ねんざ **2** *v/t* nenza suru ねんざする

sprawl *v/i (lying)* nesoberu ねそべる; *(sittin)* darashinaku suwaru だらしなく座る; *(of city)* zatsuzen to shita basho 雑然とした場所; **send ~ing** ... o jimen ni tatakinomesu ...を地面に叩きのめす

sprawling *city* mukeikaku ni hirogatta 無計画に広がった

spray 1 *n (of water)* shibuki しぶき; *(paint, for hair)* supurē スプレー **2** *v/t* furikakeru ふりかける; **~ X with Y** X ni Y o furikakeru XにYをふりかける

spraygun fukitsuke-ki 吹き付け機

spread 1 n (*of disease, religion etc*) hirogari 広がり; F (*big meal*) gochisō ごちそう **2** v/t (*lay*) hirogeru 広げる; *butter, jam* nuru 塗る; *news, rumor, disease* hiromeru 広める; *arms, legs* nobasu 伸ばす **3** v/i hiromaru 広まる; (*of butter*) nuru 塗る

spreadsheet COMPUT supureddoshīto スプレッドシート

spree: *go* (*out*) *on a* ~ F bakasawagi suru ばか騒ぎする; *go on a shopping* ~ shōdōgai o suru 衝動買いをする

sprightly kakushaku to shita かくしゃくとした

spring[1] n (*season*) haru 春

spring[2] n (*device*) bane ばね

spring[3] **1** n (*jump*) chōyaku 跳躍; (*stream*) izumi 泉 **2** v/i tobiagaru 飛び上がる; ~ *from* ...kara kite iru ...からきている

springboard tobiita 飛び板; **spring chicken**: *she's no* ~ F kanojo wa mō wakaku wa nai 彼女はもう若くはない; **spring-cleaning** ōsōji 大掃除; **springtime** shunki 春期; **Spring Equinox Day** Shunbun no hi 春分の日

springy *mattress, ground* danryokusei no aru 弾力性のある; *walk* keikai (na) 軽快(な)

sprinkle v/t furikakeru ふりかける; ~ *X with Y* X ni Y o furikakeru X にYをふりかける

sprinkler supurinkurā スプリンクラー

sprint 1 n zenryoku-shissō 全力疾走; SP tankyori-kyōsō 短距離競走 **2** v/i zensokuryoku de hashiru 全速力で走る

sprinter SP tankyori-senshu 短距離選手

sprout 1 v/i (*of seed*) hatsuga suru 発芽する **2** n: me 芽; (*Brussels*) ~*s* mekyabetsu 芽キャベツ

spruce *adj* kogirei (na) こぎれい(な)

spur n fig shigeki 刺激; *on the* ~ *of the moment* shōdōteki ni 衝動的に

♦**spur on** (*encourage*) ... e to

karitateru ...へとかりたてる

spurt 1 n (*in race*) supāto スパート; *put on a* ~ rasuto-supāto o kakeru ラストスパートをかける **2** v/i (*of liquid*) fukidasu 噴き出す

spy 1 n supai スパイ **2** v/i supai o suru スパイをする **3** v/t me ni suru 目にする

♦**spy on** ... o saguru ...をさぐる

squabble 1 n kenka けんか **2** v/i kenka suru けんかする

squalid fuketsu (na) 不潔(な)

squalor fuketsu-sa 不潔さ

squander *money* rōhi suru 浪費する

square 1 *adj* (*in shape*) seihōkei (no) 正方形(の); ~ *mile* / *yard* heihō mairu / yādo 平方マイル / ヤード **2** n (*shape*) seihōkei 正方形; (*in town*) hiroba 広場; (*in board game*) masu ます; MATH nijō 二乗; *we're back to* ~ *one* furidashi ni modoru 振り出しに戻る

square root heihōkon 平方根

squash[1] n (*vegetable*) urirui うり類

squash[2] n (*game*) sukasshu スカッシュ

squash[3] v/t (*crush*) tsubureru つぶれる

squat 1 *adj* (*in shape*) zunguri shita ずんぐりした **2** v/i (*sit*) shagamu しゃがむ; (*illegally*) fuhō-kyojū suru 不法居住する

squatter fuhōkyojū-sha 不法居住者

squeak 1 n (*of mouse*) chūchū naku koe チューチュー鳴く声; (*of hinge*) kīkī kishimu oto キーキーきしむ音 **2** v/i (*of mouse*) chūchū naku チューチュー鳴く; (*of hinge, shoes*) kīkī naru キーキー鳴る

squeal 1 n kanakirigoe 金切り声; (*of brakes*) kī to kishimu oto キーときしむ音 **2** v/i kanakirigoe o ageru 金切り声をあげる; (*of brakes*) kishimu きしむ

squeamish sugu ni kimochi ga waruku naru すぐに気持ちが悪くなる

squeeze 1 n: *he gave her hand a* ~ kare wa kanojo no te o gyutto nigirishimeta 彼は彼女の手をぎゅっと握り締めた **2** v/t (*press*)

gyutto nigirishimeru ぎゅっと握
り締める; (*remove juice from*)
gyutto shiboru ぎゅっと絞る

♦ **squeeze in** 1 *v/i* (*to a car etc*)
tsumekomareru 詰め込まれる
2 *v/t* ... o oshikomu ...を押し込む

♦ **squeeze up** *v/i* (*to make space*)
tsumeru 詰める

squid ika いか

squint *n* shashi 斜視

squirm (*wriggle*) karada o
kuneraseru 体をくねらせる; (*in
embarrassment*) mojimoji suru も
じもじする

squirrel *n* risu りす

squirt 1 *v/t* fukikakeru 噴きかける
2 *n* F (*pej*) namaiki na yatsu 生意
気なやつ

stab 1 *n*: **have a ~ at** F ... o chotto
yatte miru ...をちょっとやってみ
る 2 *v/t* person sasu 刺す

stability *n* antei 安定

stabilize 1 *v/t* prices, currency, boat
etc antei saseru 安定させる 2 *v/i*
(*of prices etc*) antei suru 安定する

stable[1] *n* (*for horses*) umagoya 馬
小屋

stable[2] *adj* antei shita 安定した

stack 1 *n* (*pile*) yama 山; (*smoke~*)
entotsu 煙突 2 *v/t* tsumikasaneru
積み重ねる

stadium kyōgijō 競技場, sutajiamu
スタジアム

staff *n* (*employees*) shain 社員;
(*teachers, in government office*)
shokuin 職員

staffer shain 社員; (*in government
office*) shokuin 職員

staffroom (*in school*) shokuin-
shitsu 職員室

stage[1] (*in life, project etc*) dankai
段階; (*of journey*) kōtei 行程

stage[2] 1 *n* THEA butai 舞台; **go on
the ~** yakusha ni naru 役者になる
2 *v/t* play jōen suru 上演する;
demonstration, strike okonau 行う

stage door gakuya-guchi 楽屋口

stagger 1 *v/i* yoromeku よろめく
2 *v/t* (*amaze*) bikkuri suru びっく
りする; coffee breaks etc zurasu ず
らす

staggering shinjirarenai 信じられ
ない

stagnant water yodonda よどんだ;
economy teitai shita 停滞した

stagnate (*of person, mind*) dareru
だれる

stag party sutaggu-pātī スタッグ
パーティー

stain 1 *n* (*dirty mark*) shimi 染み;
(*for wood*) chakushokuzai 着色剤
2 *v/t* (*dirty*) yogosu 汚す; wood
chakushoku suru 着色する 3 *v/i*
(*of wine etc*) shimi ni naru 染みに
なる; (*of fabric*) yogoreru 汚れる

stained-glass window sutendo-
gurasu no mado ステンドグラスの
窓

stainless steel 1 *n* sutenresu ステ
ンレス 2 *adj* sutenresu (no) ステ
ンレス(の)

stain remover shiminuki 染み抜き

stair dan 段; **the ~s** kaidan 階段

staircase kaidan 階段

stake 1 *n* (*of wood*) kui くい; (*when
gambling*) kakekin 賭け金;
(*investment*) tōshi 投資; **be at ~**
kiken ni sarasarete iru 危険にさ
らされている 2 *v/t* tree kui de
sasaeru くいで支える; money
kakeru 賭ける; person enjo suru
援助する

stale bread furuku natta 古くなっ
た; air yodonda よどんだ; news
furukusai 古くさい

stalemate (*in chess*) tezumari 手詰
まり; fig kōchaku-jōtai こう着状態

stalk[1] *n* (*of plant*) kuki 茎; (*of fruit*)
e 柄

stalk[2] *v/t* (*follow*) ou 追う; person
tsukimatou つきまとう

stalker (*of person*) sutōkā ストー
カー

stall[1] *n* (*at market*) yatai 屋台; (*for
cow, horse*) kachikugoya no heya
家畜小屋の部屋

stall[2] 1 *v/i* (*of plane, engine*) enjin
ga tomaru エンジンが止まる; (*of
vehicle*) ensuto suru エンスト する;
(*play for time*) jikankasegi suru
時間稼ぎする 2 *v/t* engine tomeru
止める; s.o. hikitomeru 引き止める

stallion taneuma 種馬

stalwart adj shikkari shita しっかりした

stamina sutamina スタミナ

stammer 1 n domori どもり **2** v/i domoru どもる

stamp¹ 1 n (for letter) kitte 切手; (device) kokuin 刻印; (mark made with device) sutanpu スタンプ **2** v/t document, passport sutanpu o osu スタンプを押す

stamp² v/t: ~ one's feet ashi o fumitsukeru 足を踏みつける

◆**stamp out** (eradicate) ... o konzetsu suru ...を根絶する

stampede n (of cattle) shūdan-bōsō 集団暴走; (of people) sattō 殺到

stance (position) shisei 姿勢

stand 1 n (at exhibition) sutando スタンド; (witness ~) shōnin-seki 証人席; (support, base) dai 台; take the ~ LAW shōgen suru 証言する **2** v/i (be situated: of person) tatte iru 立っている; (of object) oite aru 置いてある; (of building) tatte iru 建っている; (as opposed to sit) tatsu 立つ; (rise) tachiagaru 立ち上がる; ~ still jitto shite iru じっとしている; where do I ~ with you? watashi wa anata ni totte nani na no desu ka 私はあなたにとって何なのですか **3** v/t (tolerate) gaman suru 我慢する; (put) oku 置く; you don't ~ a chance anata ni wa chansu ga arimasen あなたにはチャンスがありません; ~ one's ground ato e hikanai 後へ引かない

◆**stand back** sagaru 下がる

◆**stand by 1** v/i (not take action) bōkan suru 傍観する; (be ready) taiki suru 待機する **2** v/t person shiji suru 支持する; decision koshu suru 固守する

◆**stand down** (withdraw) mi o hiku 身を引く

◆**stand for** (tolerate) ... o gaman suru ...を我慢する; (represent) ... no ryaku de aru ...の略である

◆**stand in for** ... no dairi o suru ...の代理をする

◆**stand out** medatsu 目立つ

◆**stand up 1** v/i tachiagaru 立ち上がる **2** v/t F ... ni machibōke o kuwasu ...に待ちぼうけを食わす

◆**stand up for** ... o mamoru ...を守る

◆**stand up to** ... ni tachimukau ...に立ち向かう

standard 1 adj (usual) tsūrei no 通例(の) **2** n (level of excellence) suijun 水準; (expectation) kijun 基準; TECH kikaku 規格; be up to ~ kijun ni tassuru 基準に達する; not be up to ~ hyōjun ika de aru 標準以下である

standardize v/t kikakuka suru 規格化する

standard of living seikatsu-suijun 生活水準

standby: on ~ (for flight) kyanseru machi (no) キャンセル待ち(の)

standby passenger kyanseru machi no kyaku キャンセル待ちの客

standing n (in society etc) chii 地位; (repute) hyōban 評判; a musician/politician of some ~ chii no aru ongakuka/seijika 地位のある音楽家/政治家

standing order Br jidō-furikae 自動振替

standing room (in theater) tachimiseki 立ち見席; (in bus) tachiseki 立ち席

standoffish yosoyososhii よそよそしい; **standpoint** kanten 観点; **standstill**: be at a ~ teishi shite iru 停止している; bring to a ~ tomaru 止まる

staple¹ n (foodstuff) shuyō-shokuryōhin 主要食料品

staple² n (fastener) hotchikisu no hari ホッチキスの針 **2** v/t tomeru とめる

staple diet shushoku 主食

staple gun sutēpuru-gan ステープルガン

stapler hotchikisu ホッチキス®

star 1 n (in sky) hoshi 星; fig sutā スター **2** v/t (of movie) shuen saseru 主演させる **3** v/i (in movie) shuen suru 主演する

starboard adj ugen (no) 右げん(の)

stare 1 n gyōshi 凝視 **2** v/i jitto mitsumeru じっと見つめる; **~ at ...** o niramu ...をにらむ

starfish hitode ひとで

stark 1 adj landscape kōryō to shita 荒涼とした; reminder, contrast etc akarasama (na) 明らさま(な) **2** adv: **~ naked** maruhadaka de 丸裸で

starling mukudori むくどり

Stars and Stripes Seijōki 星条旗

start 1 n hajimari 始まり; **get off to a good/bad ~** (in race, marriage, career) kōchō na/fuchō na sutāto o kiru 好調な/不調なスタートをきる; **from the ~** hajime kara はじめから; **well, it's a ~!** sā, kore ga shuppatsuten desu さあ、これが出発点です **2** v/i hajimaru 始まる; (of engine, car) shidō suru 始動する; **~ing from tomorrow** ashita kara hajimaru 明日から始まる **3** v/t hajimeru 始める; engine, car shidō suru 始動する; business sōritsu suru 創立する; **~ to do X** X o hajimeru Xを始める

starter (part of meal) zensai 前菜; (of car etc) sutātā スターター

starting point (for walk etc) shuppatsu-chiten 出発地点; (for discussion, thesis) kiten 起点

starting salary hajime no kyūryō 初めの給料

startle odorokasu 驚かす

startling odoroku yō (na) 驚くよう(な)

starvation kiga 飢餓

starve v/i ueru 飢える; **~ to death** uejini suru 飢え死にする; **I'm starving** onaka ga pekopeko desu おなかがペコペコです

state¹ 1 n (of car, house etc) jōtai 状態; (part of country) shū 州; (country) kokka 国家; **the States** Beikoku 米国 **2** adj capital etc shū (no) 州(の); banquet etc kōshiki (no) 公式(の)

state² v/t noberu 述べる

State Department Kokumushō 国務省

statement (to police) chinjutsu 陳述; (announcement) seimei 声明; (bank ~) kōzashūshi-hōkokusho 口座収支報告書; **make a ~** chinjutsu o suru 陳述をする; (of government) seimei o happyō suru 声明を発表する

state of emergency kinkyū-jitai 緊急事態

state-of-the-art adj saishin-gijutsu (no) 最新技術(の)

statesman ōmono seijika 大物政治家

state trooper shū-keisatsukan 州警察官

state visit kōshiki-hōmon 公式訪問

static (electricity) seidenki 静電気

station 1 n RAIL eki 駅; RAD, TV channeru チャンネル **2** v/t guard etc haichi suru 配置する; **be ~ed at** (of soldier) ... ni chūton shite iru ...に駐屯している

stationary tomatte iru 止まっている

stationery bunbōgu 文房具

stationery store bunbōgu-ten 文房具店

station wagon wagon-sha ワゴン車

statistical tōkeijō (no) 統計上(の)

statistically tōkeijō 統計上

statistics (science) tōkei-gaku 統計学; (figures) tōkei 統計

statue zō 像

Statue of Liberty Jiyū no Megamizō 自由の女神像

status (position) chii 地位; (class) mibun 身分

status symbol suteitasu-shinboru ステイタスシンボル

statute hōritsu 法律

staunch adj chūjitsu (na) 忠実(な)

stay 1 n taizai 滞在 **2** v/i (in a place) taizai suru 滞在する; (in a condition) ... no mama de iru ...のままでいる; **I don't want to ~ at home all day** ichinichijū ie ni itaku nai 一日中家にいたくない; **~ in a hotel** hoteru ni tomaru ホテルに泊まる; **~ right there!** soko o ugokanaide そこを動かないで; **~ put** todomaru とどまる

♦ **stay away** chikazukanai 近づか

ない

♦**stay away from** ... o sakeru ...を避ける

♦**stay behind** inokoru 居残る

♦**stay up** (*not go to bed*) okite iru 起きている

steadily *improve etc* chakuchaku to 着々と

steady 1 *adj* (*not shaking*) shikkari shita しっかりした; (*regular*) antei shita 安定した; (*continuous*) chakujitsu (na) 着実(な) **2** *adv*: *be going* ~ majime ni tsukiau まじめに付き合う; *~ on!* ochitsuite 落ち着いて **3** *v/t* antei saseru 安定させる

steak sutēki ステーキ

steal 1 *v/t money etc* nusumu 盗む **2** *v/i* (*be a thief*) nusumi o suru 盗みをする; (*move quietly*) kossori iku こっそり行く

stealthy hisoka (na) ひそか(な)

steam 1 *n* suijōki 水蒸気 **2** *v/t food* musu 蒸す

♦**steam up 1** *v/i* (*of window*) jōki de kumoru 蒸気で曇る **2** *v/t*: *be steamed up* F punpun okoru プンプン怒る

steamer (*for cooking*) mushiki 蒸し器

steam iron suchīmu-airon スチームアイロン

steel 1 *n* kōtetsu 鋼鉄 **2** *adj* kōtetsusei (no) 鋼鉄製(の)

steep[1] *adj hill etc* kewashii 険しい; F *prices* mechakucha takai めちゃくちゃ高い

steep[2] *v/t* (*soak*) hitasu 浸す

steeplechase (*in athletics*) shōgaibutsu-sō 障害物走

steer[1] *n* (*animal*) kyosei sareta koushi 去勢された子牛

steer[2] *v/t car, boat* unten suru 運転する; *person* ... ni michibiku ...に導く; *conversation* ... ni mukeru ...に向ける

steering MOT sutearingu ステアリング

steering wheel handoru ハンドル

stem[1] *n* (*of plant*) miki 幹; (*of pipe*) jiku 軸; (*of word*) gokan 語幹

♦**stem from** ... ni kiin suru ...に起因する

stem[2] *v/t* (*block*) tomeru 止める

stemware ashitsuki-gurasu 足付きグラス

stench akushū 悪臭

step 1 *n* (*pace*) ippo 一歩; (*stair*) dan 段; (*measure*) kōdō 行動; *~ by ~* sukoshi zutsu 少しずつ **2** *v/i* fumiireru 踏み入れる

♦**step down** (*from post etc*) jinin suru 辞任する

♦**step out** *v/i* (*go out for a short time*) chotto deru ちょっと出る

♦**step up** *v/t* (*increase*) ... o suteppu-appu suru ...をステップアップする

stepbrother (*son of stepfather*) ifu kyōdai 異父兄弟; (*son of stepmother*) ibo kyōdai 異母兄弟; **stepdaughter** mama-musume まま娘; **stepfather** mama-chichi まま父; **stepladder** kyatatsu 脚立; **stepmother** mama-haha まま母

stepping stone tobiishi 飛び石; *fig* fumidai 踏み台

stepsister (*daughter of stepfather*) ifu-shimai 異父姉妹; (*daughter of stepmother*) ibo-shimai 異母姉妹

stepson mama-musuko まま息子

stereo *n* suterero ステレオ

stereotype *n* koteigainen 固定概念, sutereotaipu ステレオタイプ

sterile *woman, man* funin (no) 不妊(の); MED sakkin shita 殺菌した

sterilize *woman* hinin-shujutsu o suru 避妊手術をする; *equipment* sakkin suru 殺菌する

sterling *n* FIN Eikoku-tsūka 英国通貨

stern *adj* kibishii 厳しい

steroids suteroido ステロイド

stethoscope chōshinki 聴診器

Stetson® sutettoson ステットソン

stevedore kōwan-rōdōsha 港湾労働者

stew *n* shichū シチュー

steward (*on plane, ship*) suchuwādo スチュワード

stewardess (*on plane, ship*) suchuwādesu スチュワーデス

stick[1] *n* (*wood*) bōkire 棒切れ; (*of*

policeman) konbō こん棒; (*walking ~*) sutekki ステッキ; *the ~s* F inaka 田舎

stick² 1 *v/t* (*with adhesive*) haritsukeru はり付ける; F (*put*) tsukkomu 突っ込む 2 *v/i* (*jam*) ugokanaku naru 動かなくなる; (*adhere*) hittsuku 引っ付く

◆**stick around** F kono hen de urouro suru この辺でうろうろする

◆**stick by** F ... o misutenai ...を見捨てない

◆**stick out** *v/i* (*protrude*) tsukideru 突き出る; (*be noticeable*) medatsu 目立つ

◆**stick to** (*of sth sticky*) ... ni hittsuku ...に引っ付く; F *path, advice* ... kara hanarenai ...から離れない; F (*when following s.o.*) ... ni haritsuku ...に張り付く

◆**stick together** F kuttsuite iru くっ付いている

◆**stick up** *poster* ... o haritsukeru ...をはり付ける

◆**stick up for** F ... o aku made mamoru ...をあくまで守る

sticker sutekkā ステッカー

sticking plaster bansōkō ばんそうこう

stick-in-the-mud: *he's such a ~!* kare wa hontō ni hoshuteki da na 彼は本当に保守的だな

sticky *hands, surface* betobeto shita べとべとした; *label* nori no tsuita のりの付いた

stiff 1 *adj brush, leather* katai 堅い; *muscle, body* kowabatta こわばった; *mixture, paste* katai 固い; (*in manner*) katakurushii 堅苦しい; *drink* tsuyoi 強い; *competition, fine* kibishii 厳しい 2 *adv*: *be scared ~* F totemo bikkuri suru とてもびっくりする; *be bored ~* F totemo taikutsu suru とても退屈する

stiffen *v/i* kowabaru こわばる

◆**stiffen up** (*of muscle*) kataku naru 堅くなる

stifle *v/t yawn, laugh* osaeru 抑える; *criticism, debate* yokuatsu suru 抑圧する

stifling ikigurushii 息苦しい

stigma omei 汚名

stilettos (*shoes*) haihīru ハイヒール

still¹ 1 *adj* shizuka (na) 静か(な) 2 *adv* ugokanai de 動かないで; *keep ~!* ugokanai de 動かないで; *stand ~!* sono mama tatte ite そのまま立っていて

still² *adv* (*yet*) mada まだ; (*nevertheless*) sore demo それでも; *do you ~ want it?* mada sore ga hoshii desu ka まだそれが欲しいですか; *she ~ hasn't finished* kanojo wa mada owatte imasen 彼女はまだ終わっていません; *she might ~ come* kanojo wa mada kuru kamo shiremasen 彼女はまだ来るかもしれません; *they are ~ my parents* karera wa sore demo watashi no oya desu 彼らはそれでも私の親です; *~ more* sara ni さらに

stillborn: *be ~* shizan shita 死産した

stilted katakurushii 堅苦しい

stimulant kakuseizai 覚せい剤

stimulate *person* kōfun saseru 興奮させる; *growth, demand* shigeki suru 刺激する

stimulating shigekiteki (na) 刺激的(な)

stimulation shigeki 刺激

stimulus (*incentive*) shigeki 刺激

sting 1 *n* (*from bee, jellyfish*) mushisasare 虫刺され; *I felt a ~ on my elbow* watashi wa hiji ga mushi ni sasareta no o kanjimashita 私はひじが虫に刺されたのを感じました 2 *v/t* (*of bee, jellyfish*) sasu 刺す 3 *v/i* (*of eyes*) hirihiri suru ひりひりする; (*of scratch*) shimiru しみる

stinging *remark, criticism* gusatto kuru ぐさっとくる

stingy F kechi (na) けち(な)

stink 1 *n* akushū 悪臭; F (*fuss*) monchaku もん着; *make a ~* F monchaku o okosu もん着を起こす 2 *v/i* niou 臭う; F (*be very bad*) hidoi ひどい

stint *n* ninki 任期; *do one's ~ in the army* rikugun de ninki o tsutomeru 陸軍で任期を勤める

♦ **stint on** ... o kechiru ...をけちる

stipulate jōken to suru 条件とする

stipulation jōken 条件

stir 1 *n*: *cause a ~* sawagi o okosu 騒ぎを起こす **2** *v/t soup etc* kakimazeru かき混ぜる **3** *v/i* (*of sleeping person*) miugoki suru 身動きする

♦ **stir up** *crowd* hikiokosu 引き起こす; *bad memories* kokoro o kakimidasu 心をかき乱す

stir-crazy: *be ~* F ikarete ita いかれていた

stir-fry *v/t* tsuyobi de itameru 強火でいためる

stirring *music, speech* kandōteki (na) 感動的(な)

stitch 1 *n* (*in sewing*) hitohari 一針; (*in knitting*) hitoami 一編み; *~es* MED hōgō 縫合; *she needed six ~es* kanojo wa rokuhari mo nuwanakereba narimasen deshita 彼女は六針も縫わなければなりませんでした; *take the ~es out* basshi suru 抜糸する; *have a ~* wakibara ga itamu わき腹が痛む **2** *v/t* (*sew*) nuu 縫う

♦ **stitch up** *wound* ... o hōgō suru ...を縫合する

stitching (*stitches*) nuime 縫い目

stock 1 *n* (*reserves*) shigen 資源; (*COM: in store*) shōhin 商品; (*animals*) kachikurui 家畜類; FIN kabushiki 株式; (*of food*) chōzōhin 貯蔵品; *be in / out of ~* zaiko ga aru / nai 在庫がある/ない; *take ~* kentō suru 検討する **2** *v/t* COM mise ni oku 店に置く

♦ **stock up on** ... o kaidame suru ...を買いだめする

stockbroker kabushiki-nakagai-nin 株式仲買人; **stock exchange** shōken-torihiki-sho 証券取引所; **stockholder** kabunushi 株主

stocking sutokkingu ストッキング

stock market kabushiki-shijō 株式市場; **stockmarket crash** kabushiki-shijō no bōraku 株式市場の暴落; **stockpile 1** *n* (*of food, weapons*) bichiku 備蓄 **2** *v/t* bichiku suru 備蓄する;

stockroom chozō-shitsu 貯蔵室;

stocktaking tanaoroshi 棚卸し

stocky gasshiri shita がっしりした

stock-still: *stand ~* jitto shite じっとして

stodgy *food* kotteri shita こってりした

stomach 1 *n* (*inside*) i 胃; (*abdomen*) onaka おなか **2** *v/t* (*tolerate*) gaman suru 我慢する

stomach-ache fukutsū 腹痛

stone *n* (*material*) ishi 石; (*pebble*) koishi 小石; (*precious ~*) hōseki 宝石

stoned F (*on drugs*) itte shimatte iru いってしまっている

stone-deaf mattaku mimi no kikoenai まったく耳の聞こえない

stonewall *v/i* iinogare suru 言い逃れする

stony *ground, path* ishi darake (no) 石だらけ(の)

stool (*seat*) sutsūru スツール

stoop[1] 1 *n*: *have a ~* nekoze de aru 猫背である; *walk with a ~* maekagami ni natte aruku 前かがみになって歩く **2** *v/i* (*bend down*) kagamu かがむ; (*have bent back*) koshi ga magaru 腰が曲がる

stoop[2] *n* (*porch*) pōchi ポーチ

stop 1 *n* (*for train*) eki 駅; (*for bus*) teiryūjo 停留所; *come to a ~* tomaru 止まる; *put a ~ to* ... o yamesaseru ...をやめさせる **2** *v/t* (*put an end to, prevent*) yamesaseru やめさせる; (*cease*) yameru やめる; *person on street, car, bus, train* tomeru 止める; ~ *talking immediately!* ima sugu oshaberi o yamenasai! 今すぐおしゃべりをやめなさい; *I ~ped her from leaving* watashi wa kanojo ga saru no o yamesasemashita 私は彼女が去るのをやめさせました; *it has ~ped raining* ame ga yande imasu 雨がやんでいます; ~ *a check* kogitte no shiharai o teishi suru 小切手の支払いを停止する **3** *v/i* (*come to a halt*) tomaru 止まる; (*of rain, snow*) yamu やむ

♦ **stop by** (*visit*) yoru 寄る

♦ **stop off** yoru 寄る

♦ **stop over** tachiyoru 立ち寄る

♦ **stop up** *sink* tsumaru 詰まる

stopgap sonobashinogi その場しのぎ; **stoplight** (*traffic light*) teishishingō 停止信号; (*brake light*) burēki-ranpu ブレーキランプ; **stopover** (*in air travel*) tochū-kōki 途中降機

stopper (*for bath, bottle*) sen 栓

stopping: *no* ~ teisha-kinshi 停車禁止

stop sign ichijiteishi-hyōshiki 一時停止標識

stopwatch sutoppu-wotchi ストップウォッチ

storage hokan 保管; *put in* ~ ...o hokan shite morau ...を保管してもらう; *be in* ~ hokan sarete iru 保管されている

storage capacity COMPUT kioku-yōryō 記憶容量

storage space oshiire 押し入れ

store 1 *n* mise 店; (*stock*) takuwae 蓄え; (*storehouse*) sōko 倉庫 2 *v/t* shimau しまう; COMPUT hozon suru 保存する

storefront tentō 店頭; **storehouse** sōko 倉庫; **storekeeper** shōten-shu 商店主; **storeroom** sōko 倉庫; **store window** shō-windō ショーウィンドウ

storm *n* arashi あらし

storm drain haisuikō 排水溝; **storm window** bōfūyō-mado 防風用窓; **storm warning** bōfu-keihō 暴風警報

stormy *weather* aremoyō (no) 荒れ模様(の); *relationship* hageshii 激しい

story[1] (*tale*) monogatari 物語; (*account*) hanashi 話; (*newspaper article*) kiji 記事; F (*lie*) tsukuri-banashi 作り話

story[2] (*of building*) kai 階

stout *adj person* futotta 太った; *boots* ganjō (na) 頑丈(な)

stove (*for cooking*) renji レンジ; (*for heating*) sutōbu ストーブ

stow shimau しまう

♦ **stow away** *v/i* mikkō suru 密航する

stowaway mikkō-sha 密航者

straight 1 *adj line, hair, back* massugu (na) まっすぐ(な); (*honest, direct*) shōjiki (na) 正直(な); (*not criminal*) matomo (na) まとも(な); *whiskey etc* sutorēto (no) ストレート(の); (*tidy*) kichin to shita きちんとした; (*conservative*) majime (na) まじめ(な); (*not homosexual*) dōseiai de wa nai 同性愛でない; *be a* ~ *A student* yūshū na gakusei de aru 優秀な学生である 2 *adv* (*in a straight line*) massugu ni まっすぐに; (*directly, immediately*) sugu ni すぐに; (*clearly*) chanto ちゃんと; *stand up* ~! massugu tatte まっすぐ立って; *look X* ~ *in the eye* X no me o massugu mitsumeru Xの目をまっすぐ見つめる; *go* ~ F (*of criminal*) katagi ni naru 堅気になる; *give it to me* ~ F hakkiri itte kure はっきりいってくれ; *be* ~ *ahead* massugu mae ni aru まっすぐ前にある; *drive* ~ *on* massugu iku まっすぐ行く; ~ *ahead look* massugu miru まっすぐ見る; *carry* ~ *on* (*of driver etc*) sonomama massugu iku そのままっすぐ行く; ~ *away*, ~ *off* sugu ni すぐに; ~ *out* sotchoku ni 率直に; ~ *up* (*without ice*) kōri nashi de 氷なしで

straighten *v/t* massugu ni suru まっすぐにする

♦ **straighten out** 1 *v/t situation* ...o kaiketsu suru ...を解決する 2 *v/i* (*of road*) massugu ni naru まっすぐになる

♦ **straighten up** *v/i* nobi o suru 伸びをする

straightforward (*honest, direct*) shōjiki (na) 正直(な); (*simple*) tanjun (na) 単純(な)

strain[1] 1 *n* (*on rope*) hari 張り; (*on engine, heart, person*) futan 負担 2 *v/t* (*injure*) itameru 痛める; *finances, budget* futan o kakeru 負担をかける

strain[2] *v/t vegetables* mizuke o kiru 水気を切る; *oil, fat etc* kosu こす

strainer (*for vegetables*) koshiki こ
し器; *tea* ~ chakoshi 茶こし

strait kaikyō 海峡

straitlaced genkaku (na) 厳格(な)

strand¹ *n* (*of hair, wool*) ippon 一本

strand² *v/t* zashō saseru 座礁させ
る; *be ~ed* ashidome sareru 足留
めされる

strange (*odd*) hen (na) 変(な);
(*unknown, foreign*) shiranai 知ら
ない

strangely (*oddly*) hen ni 変に; ~
enough kimyō na koto ni 奇妙なこ
とに

stranger (*person you don't know*)
mishiranu hito 見知らぬ人; *I'm a
~ here myself* watashi wa koko
de wa yosomono desu 私はここで
はよそ者です

strangle shimekorosu 絞め殺す

strap *n* (*of purse, dress*) katahimo
肩ひも; (*of watch*) bando バンド;
(*of shoe*) sutorappu ストラップ

♦ **strap in** ... no shītoberuto o
shimeru ...のシートベルトを締め
る

strapless katahimo nashi (no) 肩ひ
も無し(の)

strategic senryakuteki (na) 戦略的
(な)

strategy senryaku 戦略

straw¹ (*for drink*) mugiwara 麦わら; *that's the
last ~!* mō gaman dekinai もう我
慢できない

straw² (*for drink*) sutorō ストロー

strawberry ichigo いちご

stray 1 *adj animal* hagureta はぐれ
た; *bullet* nagareta 流れた **2** *n*
(*dog*) nora-inu 野良犬; (*cat*) nora-
neko 野良猫 **3** *v/i* (*of animal*)
hagureru はぐれる; (*of child*)
mayou 迷う; *fig* (*of eyes, thoughts*)
soreru それる

streak (*of dirt, paint*) suji 筋; *he's
got a mean ~* kare ni wa sukoshi
ijiwaru na tokoro ga arimasu 彼に
は少し意地悪なところがあります
2 *v/i* (*move quickly*) subayaku
hashiru 素早く走る **3** *v/t: be ~ed
with* ... de shima ni natte iru ...で
しまになっている

stream 1 *n* ogawa 小川; *a ~ of* (*of
people, complaints*) ichiren no ...
一連の...; *come on ~*
kadōshihajimeru 稼動し始める
2 *v/i* (*of people*) zokuzoku to dete
kuru 続々と出てくる; *sunlight ~ed
into the room* hizashi ga heya ni
sashikondekita 日差しが部屋に差
し込んできた

streamer kami-tēpu 紙テープ

streamline *v/t fig* gōrika suru 合理
化する

streamlined *car, plane* ryūsenkei
(no) 流線形(の); *fig: organization*
gōrika sareta 合理化された

street tōri 通り

streetcar romen-densha 路面電車;
streetlight gaitō 街灯; **streetpeople** hōmuresu ホームレス;
streetwalker baishunfu 売春婦;
streetwise *adj* jijotsū (no) 事情通
(の)

strength tsuyo-sa 強さ; (*of emotion,
friendship, currency, physical ~*)
chikara 力; (*strong point*) tsuyomi
強み; (*of organization*) seiryoku
勢力

strengthen 1 *v/t* tsuyoku suru 強く
する **2** *v/i* tsuyoku naru 強くなる

strenuous hageshii 激しい; *effort*
nesshin (na) 熱心(な)

stress 1 *n* (*emphasis*) jūten 重点;
(*on syllable*) kyōsei 強勢;
(*tension*) sutoresu ストレス; *be
under* ~ sutoresu no aru ストレス
のある **2** *v/t syllable* kyōsei o oku
強勢を置く; *importance etc* kyōchō
suru 強調する; *I must ~ that ...*
watashi wa ... o kyōchō shinakute
wa narimasen 私は...を強調しなく
てはなりません

stressed out F sutoresu ga tamatte
iru ストレスがたまっている

stressful sutoresu no ōi ストレスの
多い

stretch 1 *n* (*of land, water*)
hirogari 広がり; *at a ~* (*nonstop*)
ikki ni 一気に **2** *adj fabric*
shinshukusei no aru 伸縮性のある
3 *v/t material* nobasu 伸ばす;
income yarikuri suru やりくりす

る；F *rules* mageru 曲げる；*he ~ed out his hand* kare wa te o nobashita 彼は手を伸ばした；*a job that ~es me* watashi o nobashite kureru shigoto 私を伸ばしてくれる仕事 **4** *v/i* (*to relax muscles*) nobi o suru 伸びをする；(*to reach sth*) karada o nobasu 体を伸ばす；(*extend*) hirogaru 広がる；(*of fabric*) nobiru 伸びる；*~ from X to Y* (*extend*) X kara Y e nobite iru XからYへ伸びている

stretcher tanka 担架

strict *person* kibishii 厳しい；*instructions, rules* genmitsu (na) 厳密(な)

strictly kibishiku 厳しく；*it is ~ forbidden* sore wa kibishiku kinjirarete imasu それは厳しく禁じられています

stride 1 *n* ōmata 大また；*take X in one's ~* X o nannaku ukeireru X を難なく受け入れる **2** *v/i* ōmata de aruku 大またで歩く

strident kandakai 甲高い；*fig: demands* shitsukoi しつこい

strike 1 *n* (*of workers*) sutoraiki ストライキ；(*in baseball, bowling*) sutoraiku ストライク；(*of oil*) hakken 発見；*be on ~* sutoraikichū de aru ストライキ中である；*go on ~* sutoraiki ni hairu ストライキに入る **2** *v/i* (*of workers*) sutoraiki o suru ストライキをする；(*of disaster*) osou 襲う；(*of clock*) utsu 打つ **3** *v/t* (*hit*) utsu 打つ；(*of disaster, illness*) osou 襲う；*match* tsukeru つける；(*of idea, thought*) kokoro ni ukabu 心に浮かぶ；*oil* hakken suru 発見する；*she struck me as being ...* kanojo wa ... de aru to iu kanji o ataeta 彼女は...で あるという感じを与えた

♦**strike out** *v/t* (*delete*) ... ni sen o hiite kesu ...に線を引いて消す

strikebreaker sutoyaburi スト破り

striker (*person on strike*) sutoraiki-sankasha ストライキ参加者

striking (*marked*) medatsu 目立って；(*eye-catching*) kiwadatte 際

string *n* (*cord*) himo ひも；(*of violin, cello etc*) gen 弦；(*of tennis racket*) gatto ガット；*~s* (*musicians*) gengakki-sōsha 弦楽器奏者；*pull ~s* ito o hiku 糸を引く；*a ~ of* (*series*) ichiren no ... 一連の...

♦**string along 1** *v/i* tsuite iku ついて行く **2** *v/t*: *string X along* X o damasu Xをだます

♦**string up** F ... o shibarikubi ni suru ...を縛り首にする

stringed instrument gengakki 弦楽器

stringent kibishii 厳しい

string player gengakki-sōsha 弦楽器奏者

strip 1 *n* (*comic ~*) koma-manga コマ漫画；*a ~ of land* hosonagai tochi 細長い土地；*a ~ of cloth* hosonagai ippen no nunokire 細長い一片の布切れ **2** *v/t* (*remove*) hagasu はがす；(*undress*) hadaka ni suru 裸にする；*~ X of Y* X kara Y o toriageru XからYを取り上げる **3** *v/i* (*undress*) hadaka ni naru 裸になる

strip club sutorippu-goya ストリップ小屋

stripe shima しま；(*indicating rank*) sodeshō そで章

striped shimamoyō (no) しま模様 (の)

stripper sutorippā ストリッパー

strip show sutorippu-shō ストリップショー

striptease sutorippu-shō ストリップショー

strive 1 *v/t*: *~ to do X* Xshiyō to doryoku suru Xしようと努力する **2** *v/i*: *~ for* ... no tame ni doryoku suru ...のために努力する

stroke 1 *n* MED nōshukketsu 脳出血；(*in writing*) kaku 画；(*in Chinese characters*) kakusū 画数；(*style of swimming*) eihō 泳法；*~ of luck* omoigakenai kōun 思いがけない幸運；*she never does a ~* (*of work*) kanojo wa zenzen (shigoto) o shinai 彼女は全然(仕

事)をしない **2** v/t naderu なでる

stroll 1 n sanpo 散歩 **2** v/i yukkuri aruku ゆっくり歩く

stroller (for baby) isugata-bebīkā いす型ベビーカー

strong currency, smell, person, wind, alcohol tsuyoi 強い; structure ganjō (na) 頑丈(な); candidate yūryoku (na) 有力(な); support kyōryoku (na) 強力(な); tea, coffee, taste koi 濃い; views, objections kyōko (na) 強固(な)

stronghold fig kyoten 拠点

strongly tsuyoku 強く

strong-minded danko to shita 断固 とした

strong-willed ishi no tsuyoi 意志の 強い

structural kōzōteki (na) 構造的 (な); ~ **engineering** kōzō-kōgaku 構造工学

structure 1 n (sth built) kōzō 構造; (mode of construction) kōsei 構成 **2** v/t kōsei suru 構成する

struggle 1 n (fight) arasoi 争い; (hard time) kutō 苦闘 **2** v/i (with person) arasou 争う; (have a hard time) kurō suru 苦労する **3** v/t: ~ **to do X** X ni kutō suru X に苦闘する

strum kakinarasu かき鳴らす

strut v/i kidotte aruku 気取って歩く

stub 1 n (of cigarette) suigara 吸い 殻; (of check, ticket) hanken 半券 **2** v/t: ~ **one's toe** tsumasaki o butsukeru つま先をぶつける

♦**stub out** tabako o momikesu たば こをもみ消す

stubble (of beard) bushōhige 無精 ひげ

stubborn ganko (na) 頑固(な); defense kyōko (na) 強固(な)

stubby mijikakute futoi 短くて太い

stuck: be ~ **on** F … ni noboseru … にのぼせる

stuck-up F kōmanchiki (na) 高慢ち き(な)

student (at high school) seito 生徒; (at university) gakusei 学生

student nurse minarai-kangofu 見 習い看護婦

student teacher kyōiku-jisshūsei

教育実習生

studio (of artist, sculptor) atorie ア トリエ; (recording ~, TV ~) sutajio スタジオ; (film ~) satsuei-sho 撮 影所; (apartment) wanrūmu-manshon ワンルームマンション

studious benkyōzuki (na) 勉強好き (な)

study 1 n (room) shosai 書斎; (learning) benkyō 勉強; (investigation) kenkyū 研究 **2** v/t (at school, university) benkyō suru 勉強する; (observe) kansatsu suru 観察する; (examine) shiraberu 調べる **3** v/i benkyō suru 勉強する

stuff 1 n (things, belongings) mono 物 **2** v/t turkey tsumemono o suru 詰め物をする; ~ **X into Y** X o Y ni oshikomu X を Y に押し込む

stuffed toy nuigurumi ぬいぐるみ

stuffing (for turkey, in chair, toy) tsumemono 詰め物

stuffy room mutto shita むっとした; person furukusai 古くさい

stumble v/i tsumazuku つまずく

stumble across … o gūzen mitsukeru …を偶然見つける

stumble over tsumazuite kokeru つ まずいてこける; words tsumaru つ まる

stumbling block shōgai 障害

stump 1 n (of tree) kirikabu 切り株 **2** v/t (of question) heikō saseru 閉 口させる

♦**stump up** F kane o dasu 金を出す

stun (of blow) kizetsu saseru 気絶 させる; (of news) shokku o ataeru ショックを与える

stunning (amazing) bikkuri saseru びっくりさせる; (very beautiful) utsukushii 美しい

stunt n (for publicity) senden-kōi 宣伝行為; (in movie) sutanto スタ ント

stuntman sutantoman スタントマン

stupefy bōtto saseru ぼーっとさせ る

stupendous namihazureta 並外れた

stupid baka (na) ばか(な)

stupidity oroka-sa 愚かさ

stupor ishikimōrō 意識もうろう

sturdy jōbu (na) 丈夫(な)

stutter v/i domoru どもる

style n (method, manner) yōshiki 様式; (fashion) ryūkō 流行; (elegance) yūga-sa 優雅さ, sutairu スタイル; ~ of writing buntai 文体; go out of ~ ryūkōokure ni naru 流行遅れになる

stylish jōhin (na) 上品(な)

stylist sutairisuto スタイリスト

subcommittee shō-iinkai 小委員会

subcompact (car) junkogata-jidōsha 準小型自動車

subconscious: the ~ (mind) senzai-ishiki 潜在意識

subcontract v/t shitauke saseru 下請けさせる

subcontractor shitauke-gaisha 下請け会社

subdivide v/t saibunkatsu suru 再分割する

subdued shizuka (na) 静か(な); light, color yawarakai 柔らかい

subheading komidashi 小見出し

subject 1 n (of country) kokumin 国民; (topic) shudai 主題; (branch of learning) kamoku 科目; GRAM shugo 主語; change the ~ wadai o kaeru 話題を変える **2** adj: be ~ to ... suru keikō ga aru ...する傾向がある; ~ to availability ticket kūseki-jōkyō ni yorimasu 空席状況によります; product kazu ni kagiri ga arimasu 数に限りがあります **3** v/t ... ni sarasu ...にさらす; ~ X to torture X o gōmon ni kakeru Xを拷問にかける

subjective shukanteki (na) 主観的(な)

sublet v/t matagashi suru 又貸しする

submachine gun kei-kikanjū 軽機関銃

submarine sensuikan 潜水艦

submerge 1 v/t ... o shizumeru ... を沈める **2** v/i (of submarine) sensui suru 潜水する

submission (surrender) kōfuku 降伏; (to committee etc) hōkoku 報告

submissive jūjun (na) 従順(な)

submit v/t plan, proposal teishutsu suru 提出する

subordinate 1 adj hojoteki (na) 補助的(な) **2** n buka 部下

subpoena 1 n shōkan-jō 召喚状 **2** v/t person shōkan suru 召喚する

♦**subscribe to** magazine etc ... o teiki-kōdoku suru ...を定期購読する; theory ... ni dōi suru ...に同意する

subscriber (to magazine) teiki-kōdoku-sha 定期購読者

subscription kōbai-keiyaku 購買契約

subsequent sono ato (no) その後(の)

subsequently sono ato その後

subside (of flood waters) hiku ひく; (of winds) yamu やむ; (of building) chinka suru 沈下する; (of panic) osamaru 収まる

subsidiary n kogaisha 子会社

subsidize joseikin o ataeru 助成金を与える

subsidy joseikin 助成金

♦**subsist on** ... de ikinagaraeru ...で生きながらえる

subsistence farmer jikyū-jisoku no nōka 自給自足の農家

subsistence level saitei-seikatsusuijun 最低生活水準

substance (matter) busshitsu 物質

substandard hyōjun-ika (no) 標準以下(の)

substantial sōtō (na) 相当(な); meal tappuri shita たっぷりした

substantially (considerably) kanari (no) かなり(の); (in essence) jisshitsuteki ni 実質的に

substantiate shōmei suru 証明する

substantive jisshitsuteki (na) 実質的(な)

substitute 1 n (for person) dairi 代理; (for commodity) daiyōhin 代用品; SP hoketsu 補欠 **2** v/t: ~ X for Y Y no kawari ni X o tsukau Yの代わりにXを使う **3** v/i: ~ for ... no kawari o suru ...の代わりをする

substitution (act) okikae 置き換え; make a ~ SP senshu-kōtai o suru 選手交代をする

subtitle 1 n jimaku 字幕 **2** v/t movie

jimaku o tsukeru 字幕をつける

subtle bimyō (na) 微妙(な); *person* kōmyō (na) 巧妙(な)

subtract v/t *number* hiku 引く; ~ *X from Y* Y kara X o hiku YからXを引く

suburb kōgai 郊外; *the* ~s kōgai 郊外

suburban kōgai (no) 郊外(の); *attitudes, lifestyle* inaka kusai 田舎くさい

subversive 1 adj hakaiteki (na) 破壊的(な) **2** n hakai-bunshi 破壊分子

subway chikatetsu 地下鉄

subzero adj reika (no) 零下(の)

succeed 1 v/i seikō suru 成功する; (*of emperor, in office*) keishō suru 継承する; ~ *in doing X* X suru koto ni seikō suru Xすることに成功する **2** v/t (*come after*) ... no ato o tsugu ...の後を継ぐ; (*in office*) kōnin suru 後任する

succeeding sono ato (no) その後(の)

success seikō 成功; *be a* ~ seikō suru 成功する

successful seikō shita 成功した

successfully umaku うまく

succession (*sequence*) renzoku 連続; (*in office*) ōi-keishō 王位継承; *in* ~ renzoku shite 連続して

successive renzoku shite 連続して; ~ *managers have tried to* ... manējātachi wa aitsuide ... o tameshitemita マネージャー達は相次いで...を試してみた

successor kōnin-sha 後任者

succinct kanketsu (na) 簡潔(な)

succulent *meat, fruit* shiru ga ōkute oishii 汁が多くておいしい

succumb (*give in*) taerarenai 耐えられない; ~ *to temptation* yūwaku ni makeru 誘惑に負ける

such 1 adj: ~ *a* (*so much of a*) sonna そんな; *it was* ~ *a surprise!* sore wa hontō ni odoroki datta それは本当に驚きだった; *he gave me* ~ *a fright* kare wa watashi o hontō ni bikkuri saseta 彼はわたしを本当にびっくりさせた; ~ *as*

... no yō na ...のような; *there is no* ~ *word as ...* ... no yō na kotoba wa sonzai shinai ...のような言葉は存在しない **2** adv totemo とても; ~ *a nice day* totemo otenki no ii hi とてもお天気のいい日; *and, as* ~, *she deserves ...* sorenari ni kanojo wa ... ni atai suru それなりに彼女は...に値する; *the job as* ~ *is not interesting* shigoto jitai wa omoshiroku nai 仕事自体はおもしろくない

suck *candy* nameru なめる; ~ *one's thumb* oyayubi o suu 親指を吸う; ~ *X from Y* Y kara X o suitoru YからXを吸い取る

♦ **suck up 1** v/t ... o kyūshū suru ... を吸収する **2** v/i: ~ *to* goma o suru ごまをする

sucker F (*person*) kamo かも; F (*lollipop*) bōtsuki-kyandē 棒付きキャンデー

suction kyūin 吸引

sudden totsuzen (no) 突然(の); *all of a* ~ totsuzen 突然

suddenly totsuzen 突然

suds (*soap* ~) sekken no awa 石けんの泡

sue v/t ... o kiso suru ... を起訴する

suede n suēdo スエード

suffer 1 v/i (*be in pain*) kurushimu 苦しむ; (*deteriorate*) akka suru 悪化する; *be* ~*ing from* ... de kurushinde iru ...で苦しんでいる **2** v/t *loss* kōmuru 被る; *setback* kurushimu 苦しむ

suffering n kurushimi 苦しみ

sufficient jūbun (na) 十分(な)

sufficiently jūbun ni 十分に

suffocate 1 v/i chissoku suru 窒息する **2** v/t chissoku saseru 窒息させる

suffocation chissoku 窒息

sugar 1 n satō 砂糖 **2** v/t ... ni satō o ireru ...に砂糖を入れる

sugar bowl satō ire 砂糖入れ

sugar cane satō kibi 砂糖きび

suggest v/t (*propose*) teian suru 提案する; (*imply*) shisa suru 示唆する; *I* ~ *that we stop now* ima yame masen ka 今止めませんか

suggestion (*proposal*) teian 提案; (*implication*) shisa 示唆

suicide jisatsu 自殺; **commit ~** jisatsu suru 自殺する

suit 1 *n* (*for men*) sebiro 背広, sūtsu スーツ; (*for women*) sūtsu スーツ; (*in cards*) kumifuda 組札 **2** *v/t* (*of clothes, color*) … ni niau …に似合う; **~ yourself!** katte ni shiro 勝手にしろ; **be ~ed for** … ni teki shite iru …に適している

suitable tekitō (na) 適当(な); *time* tsugō no ii 都合のいい

suitcase sūtsukēsu スーツケース

suite (*of rooms*) suīto-rūmu スイートルーム; (*furniture*) kagu-isshiki 家具一式; MUS kumikyoku 組曲

sukiyaki sukiyaki すきやき

sulfur iō 硫黄

sulk *v/i* suneru すねる

sulky suneta すねた

sullen suneta すねた

sultry *climate* mushiatsui 蒸し暑い; (*sexually*) kannōteki (na) 官能的(な)

sum (*total*) gōkei 合計; (*amount*) kingaku 金額; (*in arithmetic*) keisan-mondai 計算問題; **a large ~ of money** tagaku no kane 多額の金; **~ insured** hoshō sareta kingaku 保証された金額; **the ~ total of his efforts** kare no doryoku no subete 彼の努力のすべ

♦ **sum up** *v/t* (*summarize*) … o yōyaku suru …を要約する; (*assess*) … o hyōka suru …を評価する **2** *v/i* LAW baishin ni saiban no yōten o setsumei suru 陪審に裁判の要点を説明する

summarize *v/t* yōyaku suru 要約する

summary *n* yōyaku 要約

summer natsu 夏

summit (*of mountain*) chōjō 頂上; *fig* chōten 頂点; POL shunō-kaigi 首脳会議, samitto サミット

summon *staff, ministers* yobu 呼ぶ; *meeting* shōshū suru 招集する

♦ **summon up** *strength* … o furuitataseru …を奮い立たせる

summons LAW shuttō-meirei 出頭命令

sumo sumō 相撲

sumo wrestler sumō tori 相撲取り

sump (*for oil*) aburadame 油だめ

sun taiyō 太陽; **in the ~** hinata 日なた; **out of the ~** hikage 日陰; **he has had too much ~** kare wa nikkō ni atarisugita 彼は日光に当たりすぎた

sunbathe nikkōyoku suru 日光浴する; **sunblock** hiyake-dome 日焼け止め; **sunburn** hiyake 日焼け; **sunburnt** hidoku hi ni yaketa ひどく日に焼けた

Sunday nichiyōbi 日曜日

sundial hidokei 日時計

sundries zakka 雑貨; (*expenses*) zappi 雑費

sunglasses sangurasu サングラス

sunken *cheeks* yasekoketa やせこけた

sunny *day* hareta 晴れた; *disposition* kaikatsu (na) 快活(な); **it's ~** yoku harete imasu よく晴れています

sunrise hinode 日の出; **sunset** nichibotsu 日没; **sunshade** hiyoke 日よけ; (*parasol*) higasa 日傘; **sunshine** nikkō 日光; **sunstroke** nisshabyō 日射病; **suntan** hiyake 日焼け; **get a ~** hiyake suru 日焼けする

super *adj* F sugoi すごい **2** *n* (*janitor*) kanrinin 管理人

superb subarashii 素晴らしい

superficial *comments, analysis* hyōmenteki (na) 表面的(な); *person* usupperai 薄っぺらい; *wounds* asai 浅い

superfluous yokei (na) 余計(な)

superhuman *efforts* chōjinteki (na) 超人的(な)

superintendent (*of apartment block*) kanrinin 管理人

superior 1 *adj* (*better*) yori sugureta よりすぐれた; *pej*: *attitude* gōman (na) ごう慢(な) **2** *n* (*in organization*) jōshi 上司; (*in society*) meue no hito 目上の人

supermarket sūpāmāketto スー

パーマーケット; **supernatural
1** *adj powers* chōshizen (no) 超自
然(の) **2** *n:* **the ~** chōshizen-
genshō 超自然現象; **superpower**
POL chōtaikoku 超大国;
supersonic chōonsoku (no) 超音
速(の)

superstition meishin 迷信

superstitious *person* meishin-bukai
迷信深い

supervise kantoku suru 監督する

supervisor (*at work*) kantoku 監督

supper yūshoku 夕食

supple jūnan (na) 柔軟(な)

supplement (*payment*) hosoku-
ryōkin 補足料金

supplier COM nōnyū-gyōsha 納入業
者

supply 1 *n* kyōkyū 供給; **~ and
demand** juyō to kyōkyū 需要と供
給; **supplies** (*food*) chozōhin 貯蔵
品; (*materials*) zaikohin 在庫品
2 *v/t goods* kyōkyū suru 供給する;
~ X with Y X ni Y o kyōkyū suru X
にYを供給する; **be supplied with**
...ga sōbi sarete iru ...が装備され
ている

support 1 *n* (*for structure*) shichū
支柱; (*backing*) shien 支援 **2** *v/t
building, structure* sasaeru 支える;
(*financially*) yashinau 養う;
(*back*) shiji suru 支持する

supporter shiji-sha 支持者; (*fan*)
fan ファン

supportive kyōryokuteki (na) 協力
的(な)

suppose (*imagine*) ...da to omou ...
だと思う; **I ~ so** sō deshō ne そう
でしょうね; **be ~d to ...** (*be meant
to*) ... suru hazu ni natte iru ...す
るはずになっている; (*be said to
be*) ... to iwarete iru ...と言われて
いる; **you are not ~d to ...** (*not
allowed to*) ...shite wa ikenai koto
ni natte iru ...してはいけない事に
なっている

suppository MED zayaku 座薬

suppress *rebellion* chin'atsu suru
鎮圧する; *feelings* osaeru 抑える

suppression (*of rebellion*)
chin'atsu 鎮圧; (*of feelings*)

yokusei 抑制

supremacy yūsei 優勢

supreme *effort, courage* saikō (no)
最高(の); **~ commander** saikō-
shireikan 最高司令官

Supreme Court Saikō-saibansho
最高裁判所

surcharge *n* tsuika-ryōkin 追加料金

sure 1 *adj* kakujitsu (na) 確実(な);
I'm ~ hontō desu 本当です; **I'm
not ~** yoku wakarimasen よくわか
りません; **be ~ about** ... wa
tashika de aru ...は確かである;
make ~ that ... ...を気をつける **2** *adv* tashika ni
確かに; **~ enough** an no jō 案の定;
it ~ is hot today F kyō wa hontō ni
atsui desu 今日はほんとうに暑い
です; **~!** mochiron もちろん

surely (*in negative sentence*)
masaka まさか; (*in affirmative
sentence*) kitto きっと; (*gladly*)
mochiron もちろん

surf 1 *n* (*on sea*) uchiyoseru nami
打ち寄せる波 **2** *v/t:* **~ the Net**
netto sāfin o suru ネットサーフィ
ンをする

surface 1 *n* (*of table, object*)
hyōmen 表面; (*of water*) suimen 水
面; **on the ~** *fig* hyōmenjō wa 表面
上は **2** *v/i* (*of swimmer, submarine*)
suimen ni fujō suru 水面に浮上す
る; (*appear*) sugata o arawasu 姿
を表す

surface mail futsū-yūbin 普通郵便

surfboard sāfu-bōdo サーフボード

surfer (*on sea*) sāfā サーファー

surfing sāfin サーフィン

surge *n* (*in current, demand,
growth*) kyūzō 急増; (*of interest
etc*) takamari 高まり

♦ **surge forward** (*of crowd*) tosshin
suru 突進する

surgeon geka-i 外科医

surgery geka 外科; **undergo ~**
geka-shujutsu o ukeru 外科手術を
受ける

surgical gekateki (na) 外科的(な)

surly buaisō (na) 無愛想(な)

surmount *v/t difficulties* norikoeru
乗り越える

surname myōji 名字
surpass koeru 越える
surplus 1 *n* yojō 余剰 **2** *adj* yojō (no) 余剰(の)
surprise 1 *n* odoroki 驚き; *it'll come as no ~ to hear that...* ... o kiite mo odorokanai ...を聞いても驚かない **2** *v/t* odorokasu 驚かす; *be ~d* odoroita yō da 驚いたようだ
surprising odoroku beki 驚くべき; *it is not ~ that he left the firm* kare ga kaisha o yameta no wa igai de wa nakatta 彼が会社を辞めたのは意外ではなかった
suprisingly odoroku hodo 驚く程
surrender 1 *v/i (of army)* kōfuku suru 降伏する **2** *v/t weapons etc* hikiwatasu 引き渡す **3** *n* kōfuku 降伏; *(of weapons etc)* hikiwatashi 引き渡し
surrogate mother dairibo 代理母
surround 1 *v/t* kakomu 囲む; *be ~ed by ...* ... ni kakomarete iru ...に囲まれている **2** *n (of picture etc)* fuchi 縁
surrounding *adj* shūi (no) 周囲(の)
surroundings kankyō 環境
survey 1 *n (of literature etc)* gaisetsu 概説; *(of consumer habits etc)* chōsa 調査; *(of building)* sokuryō 測量 **2** *v/t (look at)* miwatasu 見渡す; *building* sokuryō suru 測量する
surveyor sokuryō-gishi 測量技師
survival seizon 生存
survive 1 *v/i (of species)* ikinokoru 生き残る; *(of patient)* tasukaru 助かる; *how are you? - surviving* dō - nantoka yatte iru yo どう-何とかやっているよ; *his two surviving daughters* kare no ikinokotta futari no musumetachi 彼の生き残った二人の娘達 **2** *v/t accident, operation* ikinobiru 生き延びる; *(outlive)* ...yori nagaiki suru ...より長生きする
survivor seizon-sha 生存者; *he's a ~ fig* kare wa fujimi da 彼は不死身だ
susceptible *(emotionally)* eikyō o ukeyasui 影響を受けやすい; *be ~ to the cold / heat* samusa / atsusa ni binkan de aru 寒さ/暑さに敏感である

sushi sushi すし
suspect 1 *n* yōgi-sha 容疑者 **2** *v/t person* utagau 疑う; *(suppose)* ...to omou ...と思う
suspected *murderer* utagai o kakerarete iru 疑いをかけられている; *cause, heart attack etc* utagai no aru 疑いのある
suspend *(hang)* tsurusu つるす; *(from office, duties)* teishoku-shobun ni suru 停職処分にする
suspenders *(for pants)* sasupendā サスペンダー
suspense sasupensu サスペンス
suspension *(in vehicle)* sasupenshon サスペンション; *(from duty)* teishoku 停職
suspension bridge tsuribashi つり橋
suspicion utagai 疑い
suspicious *(causing suspicion)* ayashii 怪しい; *(feeling suspicion)* utagai-bukai 疑い深い; *be ~ of ...* ... o utagatte iru ...を疑っている
sustain iji suru 維持する
swab *n* shōdokumen 消毒綿
swagger: *walk with a ~* ibatte aruku 威張って歩く
swallow¹ *v/t & v/i* nomikomu 飲み込む
swallow² *n (bird)* tsubame つばめ
swamp 1 *n* numachi 沼地 **2** *v/t: be ~ed with* ... de ippai ni naru ...で一杯になる
swampy jimejime shita じめじめした
swan hakuchō 白鳥
swap 1 *v/t: ~ X for Y* X to Y o kōkan suru XとYを交換する **2** *v/i* kōkan suru 交換する
swarm 1 *n (of bees)* mure 群れ **2** *v/i (of ants, tourists etc)* muragaru 群がる; *the town was ~ing with* machi wa... de ippai de aru 町は...で一杯である
swarthy asaguroi 浅黒い
swat *v/t insect, fly* tataku たたく
sway 1 *n (influence, power)* shihai 支配 **2** *v/i* yureru 揺れる

swear v/i (*use swearword*) akutai o tsuku 悪態をつく; (*promise*) chikau 誓う; LAW sensei suru 宣誓する; **~ at** ... o nonoshiru ...をののしる

♦ **swear in** *witnesses etc* sensei-shūnin suru 宣誓就任する

swearword akutai 悪態

sweat 1 n ase 汗; *covered in ~* asebisshori ni naru 汗びっしょりになる 2 v/i ase o kaku 汗をかく

sweater sētā セーター

sweatshirt torēnā トレーナー

sweaty *hands, smell* asebanda 汗ばんだ

Swede Suwēden-jin スウェーデン人

Sweden Suwēden スウェーデン

Swedish 1 adj Suwēden (no) スウェーデン(の) 2 n Suwēden-go スウェーデン語

sweep 1 v/t *floor, leaves* haku 掃く 2 n (*long curve*) ōki na kābu 大きなカーブ

♦ **sweep up** v/t *mess* ... o hakiyoseru ...を掃き寄せる

sweeping adj *generalization, statement* jippahitokarage (no) 十把一からげ(の); *changes* zenmenteki (na) 全面的(な)

sweet adj *taste, tea* amai 甘い; F (*kind*) shinsetsu (na) 親切(な); F (*cute*) kawaii かわいい

sweet and sour adj amazuppai 甘酸っぱい

sweetcorn tōmorokoshi とうもろこし

sweeten v/t *drink, food* amaku suru 甘くする

sweetener (*for drink*) kanmiryō 甘味料

sweetheart koibito 恋人

sweet potato satsuma-imo さつま芋

swell 1 v/i (*of limb*) hareru 腫れる 2 adj F (*good*) suteki (na) 素敵(な) 3 n (*of sea*) uneri うねり

swelling n MED hare 腫れ

sweltering udaru yō (na) うだるよう(な)

swerve v/i (*of driver, car*) soreru それる

swift adj hayai 速い

swim 1 v/i oyogu 泳ぐ; **go ~ming** oyogi ni iku 泳ぎに行く; **my head is ~ming** atama ga mawatte iru 頭が回っている 2 n suiei 水泳; **go for a ~** oyogi ni iku 泳ぎに行く

swimmer oyogu hito 泳ぐ人; **she's a good ~** kanojo wa oyogu no ga umai 彼女は泳ぐのがうまい

swimming suiei 水泳

swimming pool pūru プール

swimsuit mizugi 水着

swindle 1 n sagi 詐欺 2 v/t damashitoru だまし取る; **~ X out of Y** Y kara X o damashitoru YからXをだまし取る

swine F (*person*) iya na yatsu いやなやつ

swing 1 n yure 揺れ; (*for child*) buranko ブランコ; **~ to the Democrats** Minshutō ni katamuku 民主党に傾く 2 v/t furu 振る 3 v/i yureru 揺れる; (*turn*) muki ga kawaru 向きが変わる; (*of public opinion etc*) kawaru 変わる

swing-door jizai-doa 自在ドア

Swiss 1 adj Suisu (no) スイス(の) 2 n (*person*) Suisu-jin スイス人

switch 1 n (*for light*) suitchi スイッチ; (*change*) tenkan 転換 2 v/t (*change*) kirikaeru 切り替える; (*swap*) torikaeru 取り替える 3 v/i (*change*) kirikaeru 切り替える

♦ **switch off** v/t *lights, TV* ... o kesu ...を消す; *engine, PC* ... o kiru ...を切る

♦ **switch on** v/t *lights, TV* ... o tsukeru ...をつける; *PC* ... no suitchi o ireru ...のスイッチを入れる; *engine* ... o kakeru ...をかける

switchboard kōkandai 交換台

switchover (*to new system*) kirikaeru 切り替える

Switzerland Suisu スイス

swivel v/i mawaru 回る

swollen hareta 腫れた; *stomach* fukureta 膨れた

swoop v/i (*of bird*) maioriru 舞い下りる

♦ **swoop down on** *prey* ... ni tobikakaru ...に飛びかかる

♦ **swoop on** (*of police etc*) ... o teire

suru …を手入れする
sword katana 刀
swordfish kajiki かじき
sycamore kaede かえで
syllable onsetsu 音節
syllabus kōgi-gaiyō 講義概要
symbol (*character*) kigō 記号; (*in poetry etc*) shōchō 象徴
symbolic shōchōteki (na) 象徴的 (な)
symbolism shōchōteki-imi 象徴的な意味
symbolize shōchō suru 象徴する
symmetric(al) taishōteki (na) 対称的 (な)
symmetry taishō 対称
sympathetic (*showing pity*) dōjōteki (na) 同情的(な); (*understanding*) kōiteki (na) 好意的(な); *be ~ toward a person / an idea* hito ni / kangae ni kōiteki de aru 人に/考えに好意的である
♦ **sympathize with** *person* … ni dōjō suru …に同情する; *views* … ni kyōkan suru …に共感する
sympathizer POL shien-sha 支援者
sympathy (*pity*) dōjō 同情; (*understanding*) kyōkan 共感
symphony kōkyōkyoku 交響曲

symptom MED shōjō 症状; *fig* kizashi 兆し
symptomatic: *be ~ of* MED … no shōjō ga aru …の症状がある; *fig* … no kizashi ga aru …の兆しがある
synchronize *watches* jikan o awaseru 時間を合わせる; *operations* dōji ni ugokasu 同時に動かす
synonym dōigo 同意語
syntax tōgoron 統語論
synthetic gōsei (no) 合成(の)
syphilis baidoku 梅毒
syringe chūshaki 注射器
syrup shiroppu シロップ
system soshiki 組織; (*method*) hōhō 方法; (*of grammar, categorization etc*) taikei 体系; (*computer*) shisutemu システム; *the braking / digestive ~* burēki / shōkaki keitō ブレーキ/消化器系統
systematic *approach* soshikiteki (na) 組織的(な)
systematically *analyze, study* keitōteki ni 系統的に; *destroy* tetteiteki ni 徹底的に
systems analyst COMPUT shisutemu-anarisuto システムアナリスト

T

tab *n* (*for pulling*) tsumami つまみ; (*in text*) tabu タブ; *~ up the tab* kanjō o harau 勘定を払う
table *n* shokutaku 食卓, tēburu テーブル; (*of figures*) hyō 表
tablecloth fukin ふきん
tablespoon tēburu-supūn テーブルスプーン; (*measure*) ōsaji 大さじ
tablet MED jōzai 錠剤
table tennis takkyū 卓球
tabloid *n* (*newspaper*) taburoido タブロイド
taboo *adj* tabū (no) タブー(の)

tacit anmoku (no) 暗黙(の)
tack 1 *n* (*nail*) byō びょう **2** *v/t* (*sew*) byō de tomeru びょうで留める **3** *v/i* (*of yacht*) magiru 間切る
tackle 1 *n* (*equipment*) yōgu 用具; (*for fishing*) tsuri-dōgu 釣り道具; SP takkuru タックル **2** *v/t* SP takkuru suru タックルする; *problem* torikumu 取り組む; *intruder* tobikakaru 飛びかかる
tacky *paint, glue* betobeto shita べとべとした; (*cheap, poor quality*) yasuppoi 安っぽい; *behavior*

kokoro no semai 心の狭い

tact kiten 気転

tactful josainai 如才ない

tactical sakuryaku ni tomu 策略に富む

tactics sakusen 作戦

tactless kiten no kikanai 気転の利かない

tadpole otamajakushi おたまじゃくし

tag (*label*) fuda 札

tail *n* shippo 尻尾

tail light bitō 尾灯

tailor yōfuku-ya 洋服屋

tailor-made *suit* shitate (no) 仕立て(の); *solution* mokuteki ni au yō ni tsukutta 目的に合うようにつくった

tail wind oikaze 追い風

Taiwan Taiwan 台湾

Taiwanese 1 *adj* Taiwan (no) 台湾(の) **2** *n* Taiwan-jin 台湾人; (*dialect*) Taiwan-go 台湾語

take *v/t* (*remove*) toru 取る; (*steal*) nusumu 盗む; (*transport, accompany*) tsurete iku 連れて行く; (*accept: money, gift*) uketoru 受け取る; *credit cards* tsukau 使う; (*study: math, French*) toru 取る; *photograph, photocopy* toru 撮る; *exam, degree* ukeru 受ける; *shower* abiru 浴びる; *stroll* sanpo suru 散歩する; *s.o.'s temperature* hakaru 計る; (*endure*) gaman suru 我慢する; (*require*) hitsuyō to suru 必要とする; (*time*) kakaru かかる; *how long does it ~?* dorekurai kakarimasu ka どれくらいかかりますか; *I'll ~ it* (*when shopping*) kaimasu 買います

♦ **take after** ... ni nite iru ...に似ている

♦ **take away** *pain* ... o torinozoku ...を取り除く; *object* ... o katazukeru ...を片づける; MATH ... o hiku ...を引く; *take X away from Y* X kara Y o toriageru XからYを取り上げる

♦ **take back** (*return: object*) ... o kaesu ...を返す; *person* ... o okuru ...を送る; *husband etc* ... o

ukeireru ...を受け入れる; *that takes me back* sore ga omoidasaseru それが思い出させる

♦ **take down** (*from shelf*) ... o motte kuru ...を持ってくる; *scaffolding* ... o hazusu ...をはずす; *pants* ... o nugu ...を脱ぐ; (*write down*) ... o kakitomeru ...を書き留める

♦ **take in** (*indoors*) ... o toriireru ...を取り入れる; (*give accommodation*) ... o tomeru ...を泊める; (*make narrower*) ... o tsumeru ...をつめる; (*deceive*) ... o damasu ...をだます; (*include*) ... o fukumu ...を含む

♦ **take off 1** *v/t clothes, hat* ... o nugu ...を脱ぐ; *10% etc* ... o toru ...を取る; (*mimic*) ... no mane suru ...の真似する; *can you take a bit off here?* (*to barber*) konohen o chotto katto shite moraemasen ka この辺をちょっとカットしてもらえませんか; *take a day / week off* ichinichi / isshūkan yasumi o toru 一日／一週間休みをとる **2** *v/i* (*of airplane*) ririku suru 離陸する; (*become popular*) ninki ga deru 人気が出る

♦ **take on** *job* ... o toru ...を取る; *staff* ... o yatou ...を雇う

♦ **take out** (*from bag, pocket*) ... o toridasu ...を取り出す; *stain* ... o torinozoku ...を取り除く; *appendix, tonsils, word from text* ... o toru ...を取る; *tooth* ... o nuku ...を抜く; *money from bank* ... o hikidasu ...を引き出す; (*to dinner etc*) ... o shokuji ni tsurete iku ...を食事に連れて行く; (*romantically*) ... o dēto ni tsurete iku ...をデートに連れて行く; *dog* ... o sanpo ni tsurete iku ...を散歩に連れて行く; *insurance policy* ... ni kanyū suru ...に加入する; *take it out on* ... ni ataru ...にあたる

♦ **take over 1** *v/t company etc* ... o nottoru ...を乗っ取る; *tourists ~ the town* ... o kankōkyaku ga machi o senryō suru ...を観光客が

町を占領する **2** v/i (*of new management etc*) hikitsugu 引き継ぐ; (*do sth in s.o.'s place*) kōtai suru 交代する

♦ **take to** (*like*) suki ni naru 好きになる; (*form habit of*) suru yō ni naru するようになる

♦ **take up** *carpet etc* ... o hagasu ...をはがす; (*carry up*) ... o motte iku ...を持って行く; *dress etc* ... o mijikaku suru ...を短くする; *judo, Spanish* ... o narai hajimeru ...を習い始める; *offer* ... o ukeru ...を受ける; *new job, hobby* ... o hajimeru ...を始める; *space, time* ... o shimeru ...を占める; *I'll take you up on your offer* anata no mōshide o ukeireru あなたの申し出を受け入れる

take-home pay tedori-kyūryō 手取り給料; **takeoff** (*of airplane*) ririku 離陸; (*impersonation*) mane 真似; **takeover** COM baishū suru 買収する; **takeover bid** kabushiki-kōkai-kaitsuke 株式公開買い付け

takings uriage 売り上げ

talcum powder tarukamu-paudā タルカムパウダー

tale monogatari 物語

talent sainō 才能

talented sainō ga aru 才能がある

talk 1 v/i (*like*) hanasu 話す; *can I ~ to ...?* ...san to hanasemasu ka ...さんと話せますか; *I'll ~ to him about it* watashi ga kare ni hanashite okimasu 私が彼に話しておきます **2** v/t *English etc* hanasu 話す; *business, politics* hanashiau 話し合う; *~ X into Y* X ni Y o settoku suru XにYを説得する **3** n (*conversation*) kaiwa 会話; (*lecture*) kōgi 講義; *he's all ~* pej kare wa kuchisaki dake no hito desu 彼は口先だけの人です

♦ **talk over** ... o hanashiau ...を話し合う

talkative oshaberi (na) おしゃべり (な)

talk show tōku-shō トークショー

tall takai 高い; *person* se ga takai 背が高い

tall order muzukashii yōkyū 難しい要求

tall story mayutsuba-mono まゆつばもの

tame *animal* kainarasareta 飼い慣らされた; *joke etc* tsumaranai つまらない

♦ **tamper with** ijiru いじる

tampon tanpon タンポン

tan 1 n (*from sun*) hiyake 日焼け; (*color*) shakudōiro 赤銅色 **2** v/i (*in sun*) hi ni yakeru 日に焼ける **3** v/t *leather* kawa o namesu 皮をなめす

tandem (*bike*) futarinori no jitensha 二人乗りの自転車

tangerine mikan みかん

tangle n motsure もつれ

♦ **tangle up**: *get tangled up* (*of string etc*) motsureru もつれる

tango n tango タンゴ

tank tanku タンク; MOT tankusha タンク車; MIL sensha 戦車; (*for skin diver*) sanso-bonbe 酸素ボンベ

tanker (*ship*) tankā タンカー; (*truck*) tanku rōrī タンクローリー

tanned hi ni yaketa 日に焼けた

tantalizing jirashita じらした

tantamount: *be ~ to* ... to onaji de aru ...と同じである

tantrum kanshaku かんしゃく

tap 1 n jaguchi 蛇口 **2** v/t (*knock*) karuku utsu 軽く打つ; *phone* tōchō suru 盗聴する

♦ **tap into** *resources* ... o riyō suru ...を利用する

tap dance n tappu-dansu タップダンス

tape 1 n (*for recording*) kasetto-tēpu カセットテープ; (*sticky*) setchaku-tēpu 接着テープ **2** v/t *conversation etc* rokuon suru 録音する; (*with sticky ~*) hittsukeru 引っつける

tape deck tēpu-dekki テープデッキ; **tape drive** COMPUT tēpu-doraibu テープドライブ; **tape measure** makijaku 巻尺

taper v/i shidai ni hosoku naru 次第に細くなる

♦ **taper off** (*of production, figures*)

shidai ni heru 次第に減る

tape recorder tēpu-rekōdā テープ
レコーダー

tape recording tēpu-rokuon テープ
録音

tapestry tapesutorī タペストリー

tar n tāru タール

tardy osoi 遅い

target 1 n (in shooting) mato 的;
(for sales, production) mokuhyō
目標 **2** v/t market mato ni suru 的
にする

target date mokuhyō-kijitsu 目標期
日; **target group** COM taishō-
gurūpu 対象グループ; **target
market** taishō-shijō 対象市場

tariff (price) ryōkinhyō 料金表;
(tax) kanzei 関税

tarmac (at airport) kūkō-epuron
空港エプロン

tarnish v/t metal ... no kōtaku o
kumoraseru ...の光沢を曇らせる;
reputation ... o kegasu ...を汚す

tarpaulin bōsui-shīto 防水シート

tart n taruto タルト

task shigoto 仕事

task force tokubetsu-taisakuhonbu
特別対策本部; MIL kidō-butai 機動
部隊

tassel fusa 房

taste 1 n (sense) mikaku 味覚; (of
food etc) aji 味; (in clothes art etc)
konomi 好み; **he has no ~** kare
wa sensu ga nai 彼はセンスがない
2 v/t food ajimi suru 味見する;
freedom etc ajiwau 味わう

tasteful shumi no yoi 趣味のよい

tasteless food mazui まずい;
remark taikutsu (na) 退屈(な)

tasty oishii おいしい

tatami mat tatami たたみ

team chīmu チーム

tattered boroboro ni natta ぼろぼろ
になった

tatters: in ~ clothes boroboro ni
natte ぼろぼろになって;
reputation, career zutazuta ni
natte ずたずたになって

tattoo n irezumi いれずみ

taunt 1 n azakeri あざけり **2** v/t
azakeru あざける

taut pin to hatta ぴんと張った

tax 1 n zeikin 税金; **before ~**
zeikomi 税込み; **after ~** zeibikigo
税引き後 **2** v/t people, product
kazei suru 課税する

taxation (act) kazei 課税; (taxes)
zeikin 税金

tax code takkusu-kōdo タックス
コード; **tax-deductible** shotoku
kara kōjo sareru 所得から控除され
る; **tax-free** menzei (no) 免税(の)

taxi takushī タクシー

taxidriver takushī-untenshu タク
シー運転手

taxi rank takushī-noriba タクシー
乗り場

tax payer nōzei-sha 納税者

tax return (form) kakutei-
shinkokusho 確定申告書

tea (drink) cha 茶; (meal) gogo no
ocha 午後のお茶; **Japanese ~**
ocha お茶; **green ~** ryokucha 緑茶

teabag tībaggu ティーバッグ

tea ceremony sadō 茶道

teach 1 v/t person, subject oshieru
教える; **~ X to do Y** X ni Y o
oshieru XにYを教える **2** v/i
kyōshi o suru 教師をする

teacher kyōshi 教師, sensei 先生

teacher training kyōin-kenshū 教員
研修

teaching (profession) kyōshoku 教
職

teaching aid hojo-kyōzai 補助教材

teaching assistant joshu 助手

tea cloth fukin ふきん; **teacup**
kōcha-jawan 紅茶茶碗; (for green
tea) yunomi ゆのみ; **tea drinker**
kōcha o konomu hito 紅茶を好む人

teak chīku チーク

tea leaves cha no ha 茶の葉

team chīmu チーム

team spirit danketsushin 団結心

teamster trakku no untenshu ト
ラックの運転手

teamwork chīmuwāku チームワーク

teapot tīpotto ティーポット

tear¹ 1 n (in cloth etc) sakeme 裂け
目 **2** v/t paper, cloth hikisaku 引き
裂く; **be torn between two
alternatives** itabasami ni naru 板
ばさみになる **3** v/i (run fast)

mōretsu na ikioi de hashiru 猛烈な勢いで走る; (*drive fast*) mōretsu na ikioi de unten suru 猛烈な勢いで運転する

♦ **tear up** *paper* ... o yaburu ...を破る; *agreement* ... o haki suru ...を破棄する

tear² (*in eye*) namida 涙; *be in ~s* namida ni kureru 涙にくれる

teardrop namida no hitoshizuku 涙のひとしずく

tearful namida de ippai (no) 涙でいっぱい(の)

tear gas sairui-gasu 催涙ガス

tearoom tīrūmu ティールーム

tease *v/t* ijimeru いじめる

tea service, tea set tīsetto ティーセット

teaspoon tīspūn ティースプーン

teat chikubi 乳首

tea towel fukin ふきん

technical senmonteki (na) 専門的(な)

technicality (*technical nature*) senmonteki-jikō 専門的事項; LAW hōritsujō no tetsuzuki 法律上の手続き; *that's just a ~* komakai koto 細かい事

technically (*strictly speaking*) genmitsu ni wa 厳密には; *written* kami no ue de wa ue de wa 紙の上では

technician gishi 技師

technique gijutsu 技術

technological kagaku-gijutsu (no) 科学技術(の)

technology kagaku-gijutsu 科学技術

technophobia kagaku-gijutsu-kyōfushō 科学技術恐怖症

tedious taikutsu (na) 退屈(な)

tee *n* (*in golf*) tī ティー

teem: *be ~ing with rain* doshaburi de aru 土砂降りである; *be ~ing with tourists / ants* ryokō-sha / ari de ippai de aru 旅行者/ありで一杯である

teenage *fashions* tīn'eijā (no) ティーンエイジャー(の); *~ boy / girl* jūdai no shōnen / shōjo 十代の少年/少女

teenager tīn'eijā ティーンエイ

ジャー

teens: *be in one's ~* jūdai de aru 十代である; *reach one's ~* jūdai ni naru 十代になる

telecommunications denki-tsūshin 電気通信

telegram denpō 電報

telegraph pole denshinbashira 電信柱

telepathic terepashī (no) テレパシー(の); *you must be ~!* anata wa terepashī ga aru ni chigainai あなたはテレパシーがあるに違いない

telepathy terepashī テレパシー

telephone 1 *n* denwa 電話; *be on the ~* (*be speaking*) hanashichū de aru 話中である; (*have a phone*) denwa o hiite iru 電話をひいている **2** *v/t person* ... ni denwa o kakeru ...に電話をかける **3** *v/i* denwa suru 電話する

telephone booth kōshū-denwa bokkusu 公衆電話ボックス; **telephone call** denwa 電話; **telephone directory** denwachō 電話帳; **telephone exchange** denwa-kōkanshitsu 電話交換室; **telephone number** denwa-bangō 電話番号

telephoto lens bōen-renzu 望遠レンズ

telesales denwa-sērusu 電話セールス

telescope bōenkyō 望遠鏡

televise terebi-hōsō suru テレビ放送する

television terebi-hōsō テレビ放送; (*set*) terebi テレビ; *what's on ~ tonight?* konban terebi de nani o yatte imasu ka 今晩テレビで何をやっていますか; *watch ~* terebi o miru テレビを見る

television program terebi-bangumi テレビ番組; **television set** terebi テレビ; **television studio** sutajio スタジオ

tell 1 *v/t story* hanasu 話す; *lie* tsuku つく; *the difference* wakaru わかる; *~ X Y* X ni Yo iu XにYを言う; *don't ~ Mom* okāsan ni wa iu na お母さんに

は言うな; **could you ~ me the way to ...?** ... e no michi o oshiete itadakemasu ka ...への道を教えていただけますか; **~ X to do Y** X ni Y suru yō ni iu XにYするように言う; **you're ~ing me!** sono tōri da その通りだ **2** v/i (have effect) kikime ga aru 効き目がある; **the heat is ~ing on him** atsusa ga kare no mi ni kotaeru 暑さが彼の身にこたえる; **time will ~** jikan ga oshiete kureru 時間が教えてくれる

♦ **tell off** (reprimand) ... o shikaru ...をしかる

teller (in bank) madoguchi 窓口

telltale 1 adj signs kakushikirenai 隠しきれない **2** n tsugeguchi suru hito 告げ口する人

temp 1 n (employee) rinji-shokuin 臨時職員, haken 派遣 **2** v/i rinji-yatoi de hataraku 臨時雇いで働く

temper (bad ~) kigen 機嫌; **be in a ~** fukigen de aru 不機嫌である; **keep one's ~** heisei o tamotsu 平静を保つ; **lose one's ~** hara o tateru 腹を立てる

temperament kishitsu 気質

temperamental (moody) kimagure (na) 気まぐれ(な)

temperature ondo 温度; (fever) netsu 熱; **have a ~** netsu ga aru 熱がある

temple[1] REL shinden 神殿; (Japanese) tera 寺

temple[2] ANAT komekami こめかみ

tempo tenpo テンポ

temporarily ichijiteki ni 一時的に

temporary ichiji (no) 一時(の)

tempt yūwaku suru 誘惑する

temptation yūwaku 誘惑

tempting offer, invitation miwakuteki (na) 魅力的(な); food oishisō (na) おいしそう(な)

tempura tenpura てんぷら

ten jū 十

tenacious tsuyoi 強い

tenant shakuchi-nin 借地人

tend[1] v/t (look after) ... no sewa o suru ...の世話をする

tend[2]: **~ to do X** X suru keikō ga aru Xする傾向がある; **~ toward ...**

ni narigachi de aru ...になりがちである

tendency keikō 傾向

tender[1] adj (sore) itai 痛い; (affectionate) yasashii 優しい; steak yawarakai 柔らかい

tender[2] n COM nyūsatsu 入札

tenderness (soreness) itami 痛み; (of kiss etc) yasashi-sa 優しさ; (of steak) yawaraka-sa 柔らかさ

tendon ken 腱

tennis tenisu テニス

tennis ball tenisu-bōru テニスボール; **tennis court** tenisu-kōto テニスコート; **tennis player** tenisu-pureiyā テニスプレイヤー; **tennis racket** tenisu-raketto テニスラケット

tenor n MUS tenōru テノール

tense[1] n GRAM jisei 時制

tense[2] adj muscle pin to hatta ピンと張った; voice, person kinchō shita 緊張した; moment haritsumeta 張り詰めた

♦ **tense up** v/i (of muscles) haru 張る; (of person) kinchō suru 緊張する

tension (of rope) hariguai 張りぐあい; (in atmosphere, voice) kinchō 緊張; (in movie, novel) kinpaku 緊迫

tent tento テント

tentacle shokushu 触手

tentative shikenteki (na) 試験的(な); smile tameraigachi (na) ためらいがち(な)

tenterhooks: be on ~ yakimoki shite iru やきもきしている

tenth 1 adj dai-jū (no) 第十(の) **2** n (of month) tōka 十日

tepid water namanurui なまぬるい; reaction netsui no nai 熱意のない

term (period of time) kikan 期間; (condition) jōken 条件; (word) yōgo 用語; **be on good/bad ~s with ...** to ii/warui kankei de aru ...といい/悪い関係である; **in the long ~** nagai me de mireba 長い目で見れば; **in the short ~** mesaki wa 目先は; **come to ~s with ...** o ukeireru ...を受け入れる

terminal 1 n (at airport) tāminaru ターミナル; (for buses) basu-tā

minaru バスターミナル; (for containers) **kontena** コンテナ; ELEC **tanshi** 端子; COMPUT **tanmatsu** 端末 **2** adj illness **makki (no)** 末期(の)

terminally: ~ ill **makki no byōki** 末期の病気

terminate 1 v/t contract **owaraseru** 終わらせる; pregnancy **chūzetsu suru** 中絶する **2** v/i **owaru** 終わる

termination (of contract) **shūryō** 終了; (of pregnancy) **chūzetsu** 中絶

terminology **senmon-yōgo** 専門用語

terminus (for buses, trains) **tā minaru** ターミナル

terrace (on hillside) **dandan-batake** 段々畑; (patio) **terasu** テラス

terra cotta **terakotta** テラコッタ

terrain **chikei** 地形

terrestrial 1 n **chikyūjō no seibutsu** 地球上の生物 **2** adj: ~ television **chijōha-terebi** 地上波テレビ

terrible **hidoi** ひどい

terribly (very) **totemo** とても

terrific **sugoi** すごい

terrifically (very) **sugoku** すごく

terrify **totemo kowagaraseru** とても怖がらせる; be terrified **kyōfu ni karareru** 恐怖にかられる

terrifying **osoroshii** 恐ろしい

territorial **ryōdo (no)** 領土(の)

territorial waters **ryōkai** 領海

territory **ryōdo** 領土; fig **ryōiki** 領域

terror **kyōfu** 恐怖

terrorism **tero** テロ

terrorist **terorisuto** テロリスト

terrorist organization **tero-soshiki** テロ組織

terrorize **obiesaseru** おびえさせる

test 1 n **shiken** 試験, **tesuto** テスト **2** v/t **tamesu** 試す

testament (to s.o.) **shōko** 証拠; Old / New Testament REL **Kyū / Shin'yaku Seisho** 旧/新約聖書

testicle **kōgan** こう丸

testify v/i LAW **shōgen suru** 証言する

testimonial n **suisenjō** 推薦状

test tube **shikenkan** 試験管

test-tube baby **shikenkan-bebī** 試験管ベビー

testy **tanki (na)** 短気(な)

tetanus **hashōfū** 破傷風

tether v/t horse **tsunagu** つなぐ **2** n **tsunagi-zuna** つなぎ綱; be at the end of one's ~ **genkai ni tasshite iru** 限界に達している

text **honbun** 本文

textbook **kyōkasho** 教科書

textile **orimono** 織物

texture **tezawari** 手触り; (of food) **shitazawari** 舌触り

Thai 1 adj **Tai (no)** タイ(の) **2** n (person) **Tai-jin** タイ人; (language) **Tai-go** タイ語

Thailand **Tai** タイ

than …yori …より; bigger / faster ~ me **watashi yori ōkii / hayai** 私より大きい/速い; more ~ 50 **gojū yori takusan** 五十よりたくさん

thank v/t … ni kansha suru …に感謝する; ~ you **arigatō gozaimasu** ありがとうございます; no ~ you **kekkō desu** 結構です

thanks **kansha** 感謝; ~! **arigatō** ありがとう; ~ to … no okage de …のおかげで

thankful **kansha shite iru** 感謝している

thankfully **kansha shite** 感謝して; (luckily) **arigatai koto ni** ありがたいことに

thankless task **wari ni awanai** 割に合わない

Thanksgiving (Day) **Kanshasai** 感謝祭

that 1 adj (further away from both speaker and listener) **ano** あの; (nearer to listener, previously known to listener) **sono** その; ~ one wa **are** は あれ; sore それ **2** pron ◊ (further away from both speaker and listener) **are** あれ; (nearer to listener, previously known to listener) **sore** それ; what's ~? (pointing at sth) **are / sore wa nan desu ka** あれ/それは何ですか; who's ~? (pointing at photo) **ano hito / sono hito wa dare desu ka** あの人/その人はだれですか; (when there's a noise outside) **dochirasama desu ka** どちら様ですか; ~'s mine **are / sore wa**

watashi no desu あれ/それは私のです; **~'s very kind** sore wa shinsetsu desu ne それは親切ですね; **the** (*relative*): **the person/car ~ you saw** anata ga mita hito/kuruma あなたが見た人/車 **3** *conj*: **I think ~ ...** watashi wa ... to omou 私は...と思う **4** *adv* (*so*) sore hodo それ程; **~ big** sore hodo ōkii それ程大きい

thaw *v/i* (*of snow*) tokeru 溶ける; (*of frozen food*) kaitō suru 解凍する

the ◊ (*no equivalent in Japanese*): **~ border** kokkyō 国境 ◊ (*identifying or with previous reference*) sono その; **~ doctor who treated me** watashi no chiryō shita sono isha 私を治療したその医者; **is that ~ ring he gave you?** sono yubiwa ga kare kara moratta mono nano その指輪が彼からもらったものなの; **~ blue bag is mine** sono aoi kaban wa watashi no desu その青いかばんは私のです◊; **~ sooner ~ better** hayakereba hayai hodo ii 速ければ速いほどいい

theater gekijō 劇場

theatrical engeki (no) 演劇(の); (*overdone*) wazatorashii わざとらしい

theft nusumi 盗み

their ◊ karera no 彼らの; (*of female subjects also*) kanojora no 彼女らの; (*of inanimate objects*) sorera no それらの ◊ (*omission of possessive*): **they forgot ~ keys** karera wa kagi o wasureta 彼らはかぎを忘れた; (*his or her*): **somebody has left ~ bag here** dare ka ga kaban o koko ni wasurete iru 誰かがここにかばんを忘れている

theirs karera no mono 彼らのもの; (*of female subjects also*) kanojora no mono 彼女らのもの; **a friend of ~** karera no tomodachi no hitori 彼らの友達の一人

them ◊ **who do you mean? - ~** dare no koto o itteru no - karera 誰のことを言ってるの-彼ら; **without ~** (*people*) karera nashi

de 彼らなしで; (*things*) sorera nashi de それらなしで◊ (*direct object*) karera o 彼らを; (*female also*) kanojora o 彼女らを; (*things*) sorera o それらを; **do you know ~?** karera o shitte imasu ka 彼らを知っていますか◊ (*indirect object*) karera ni 彼らに; (*female also*) kanojora ni 彼女らに; (*things*) sorera ni それらに; **I sent it to ~** karera ni sore o okutta 彼らにそれを送った◊ (*him or her*): **if a person asks for help, you should help ~** moshi dare ka ga tasuke o motomete itara, tasukete ageru beki da もし誰かが助けを求めていたら、助けてあげるべきだ

theme tēma テーマ

theme park tēma-yūenchi テーマ遊園地

theme song tēma-songu テーマソング

themselves: **they hurt ~** (*male*) karera wa kega o shita 彼らはけがをした; (*female also*) kanojora wa kega o shita 彼女らはけがをした; **they saw ~ in the mirror** karera wa jibuntachi no kagami de mita 彼らは自分達を鏡でみた; **what do they think ~?** karera wa dō kangaete iru no 彼らはどう考えているの; **but the boxes ~ have no value** sono hako wa sore dake dewa kachi ga nai その箱はそれだけでは価値がない; **by ~** (*alone*) jibuntachi dake de 自分達だけで; (*without help*) jibuntachi de 自分達で

then (*at that time*) sono tōji その当時; (*after that*) sorekara それから; (*deducing*) sorenara それなら; **by ~** soremade ni それまでに

theology shingaku 神学

theoretical rironteki (na) 理論的(な)

theory riron 理論; **in ~** rironteki ni wa 理論的には

therapeutic chiryōhō (no) 治療法(の)

therapist serapisuto セラピスト

therapy serapī セラピー

there (*with verbs of being*) asoko ni あそこに; (*with verbs of activity*) asoko de あそこで; **I used to live ~** watashi wa izen asoko ni sunde ita 私は以前あそこに住んでいた; **I used to work ~** watashi wa izen asoko de hataraite ita 私は以前あそこで働いていた; **over-/down-** asoko あそこ; **~ is/are** (*of person, animal*) … ga iru …がいる; (*polite*) … ga imasu …がいます; (*of things*) … ga aru …がある; (*polite*) … ga arimasu …があります; **is/are ~ …?** (*of person, animal*) … ga imasu ka …がいますか; (*of things*) … ga arimasu ka …がありますか; **~ is/are not** (*of person, animal*) …ga inai …がいない; (*polite*) … ga imasen …がいません; **~** (*of things*) …ga nai …がない; (*polite*) … ga arimasen …がありません; **~ you are** (*giving sth*) hai dōzo はいどうぞ; (*finding sth*) hora ほら; (*completing sth*) hai dekimashita はいできました; **~ and back** ōfuku 往復; **~ he is!** imashita いました; **~, ~** nēnē ねーねー

thereabouts sono kurai そのくらい

therefore shitagatte 従って

thermometer (*for room*) ondokei 温度計; MED taionkei 体温計

thermos flask mahōbin 魔法瓶

thermostat sāmosutatto サーモスタット

these 1 *adj* kono この **2** *pron* kore これ

thesis ronbun 論文

they karera 彼ら; (*female also*) kanojora 彼女ら; (*things*) sorera それら; **~ are American** karera wa Amerika-jin desu 彼らはアメリカ人です ◊ (*omission of pronoun*): **where are ~? ~ have left** karera wa doko desu ka – mō ikimashita 彼らはどこですか – もう行きました ◊ (*he or she*): **if anyone looks at this, ~ will see that …** moshi dareka ga kore o mitara … to wakaru darō もし誰かがこれをみたら…とわかるだろう; **if somebody thinks ~ know the answer** moshi

dareka ga seikai o shitte iru to omottara もし誰かが正解を知っていると思ったら ◊ (*impersonal*): **~ say that …** … to iwarete iru … と言われている; **~ are going to change the law** tōkyoku wa hōritsu o kaeru tsumori desu 当局は法律を変えるつもりです

thick *hair* ōi 多い; *soup, fog* koi 濃い; *wall, book* atsui 厚い; (*stupid*) nibui 鈍い

thicken *sauce* koku suru 濃くする

thickset zunguri shita ずんぐりした

thickskinned donkan (na) 鈍感(な)

thief dorobō 泥棒

thigh momo もも

thimble yubinuki 指貫

thin *hair, soup, coat* usui 薄い; *person, line* hosoi 細い

thing mono 物; (*abstract*) koto 事; **~s** (*belongings*) mochimono 持物; **how are ~s?** chōshi wa dō desu ka 調子はどうですか; **good ~ you told me** itte kurete tasukarimashita 言ってくれて助かりました; **what a ~ to do/say!** nante koto o shita no/itta no なんてことをした の/言った の

thingumajig F nantoka iu mono 何とかいうもの

think kangaeru 考える, omou 思う; **I ~ so** sō omoimasu そう思います; **I don't ~ so** sōda to wa omoimasen そうだとは思いません; **I ~ so too** watashi mo sō omoimasu 私もそう思います; **what do you ~?** dō omoimasu ka どう思いますか; **what do you ~ of it?** sore o dō omoimasu ka それをどう思いますか; **I can't ~ of anything more** kore ijō kangaeraremasen これ以上考えられません; **~ hard!** yoku kangaenasai よく考えなさい; **I'm ~ing about emigrating** ijū shiyō ka to omotte imasu 移住しようかと思っています

♦ **think over** … o yoku kangaeru …をよく考える

♦ **think through** … o shinchō ni kangaeru …を慎重に考える

♦ **think up** *plan* … o kangaedasu …

を考え出す

third 1 adj dai san (no) 第三(の) **2** n dai san banme 第三番目; (of month) mikka 三日; (in race) san'i 三位; (fraction) sanbun no ichi 三分の一

thirdly dai san ni 第三に

third-party insurance songaibaishō-hoken 損害賠償保険; **third-rate** sanryū (no) 三流(の); **Third World** Daisan-sekai 第三世界

thirst nodo no kawaki 喉の渇き

thirsty: I'm ~ nodo ga kawaite iru 喉が渇いている; it's ~ work nodo no kawaku shigoto da のどの渇く仕事だ

thirteen jūsan 十三

thirteenth dai-jūsan (no) 第十三(の)

thirtieth dai-san jū (no) 第三十(の)

thirty sanjū 三十

this 1 adj kono この; ~ one kore これ **2** pron kore これ; ~ is good kore wa ii これはいい; ~ is... (introducing) kochira wa ... san desu こちらは...さんです; TELEC ... to mōshimasu ga ...と申しますが **3** adv koregrai これぐらい; ~ big koregurai ōkii これぐらい大きい

thorn toge とげ

thorough search tetteiteki (na) 徹底的(な); knowledge kanzen (na) 完全(な); person tettei shite iru 徹底している

thoroughbred (horse) sarabureddo サラブレッド

those 1 adj (further away from both speaker and listener) ano あの; (nearer to listener, previously known to listener) sono その **2** pron (further away from both speaker and listener) are あれ; (nearer to listener, previously known to listener) sore それ

though 1 conj (although) keredomo けれども; ~ it might fail shippai suru kamo shirenai ga 失敗するかもしれないが; as ~ ...no yō ni ...のように **2** adv demo でも; it's not finished ~ owatte inai

keredo 終わっていないけれど

thought (single) kangae 考え; (collective) shisō 思想

thoughtful kangaekonda 考え込んだ; (considerate) omoiyari no aru 思いやりのある

thoughtless keisotsu (na) 軽率(な)

thousand sen 千; ten ~ man 万; ~s of tasū no... 多数の...

thousandth dai-issen (no) 第一千(の)

thrash v/t utsu 打つ; SP uchimakasu 打ち負かす

♦ **thrash around** (with arms etc) furimawasu 振り回す

♦ **thrash out** solution ... o dakai suru ...を打開する

thrashing ōda 殴打

thread 1 n ito 糸; (of screw) nejiyama ネジ山 **2** v/t needle ... ni ito o tōsu ...に糸を通す; beads tōsu 通す

threadbare surikireta すりきれた

threat kyōhaku 脅迫; (to national security, environment) kyōi 脅威

threaten kyōhaku suru 脅迫する; national security, environment obiyakasu 脅かす

threatening gesture, tone osoroshii 恐ろしい; ~ sky aresō na sora 荒れそうな空

three san 三; (with countword) mittsu 三つ

three-quarters n yonbun no san 四分の三

thresh corn dakkoku suru 脱穀する

threshold (of house) shikii 敷居; (limit) genkai 限界; (of new age) sakaime 境目; on the ~ of ... no iriguchi ni ...の入り口に; I have a low pain ~ watashi no itami ni tai suru genkai wa hikui 私の痛みに対する限界は低い

thrift ken'yaku 倹約

thrifty shisso (na) 質素(な)

thrill 1 n suriru スリル **2** v/t: be ~ed wakuwaku suru わくわくする

thriller surirā-mono スリラー物

thrilling wakuwaku saseru わくわくさせる

thrive (of plant) sodatsu 育つ; (of

firm, economy) sakaeru 栄える

throat nodo のど

throat lozenges nodo-ame のどあめ

throb 1 *n* (*of heart*) kodō 鼓動; (*of music*) rizumu リズム **2** *v/i* (*of heart*) kodō suru 鼓動する; (*of music*) rizumu o utsu リズムを打つ

thrombosis kessenshō 血栓症

throne ōza 王座

throttle 1 *n* (*on motorbike, boat*) surottoru スロットル **2** *v/t* (*strangle*) ... no nodo o shimeru ...ののどを絞める

♦ **throttle back** *v/i* gensoku suru 減速する

through 1 *prep* ◊ (*across*) yokogitte 横切って; **go ~ the city** machi o tōri nukeru 町を通り抜ける ◊ (*with time*): **~ the winter / summer** fuyu / natsu jū 冬/夏中; **Monday ~ Friday** getsuyōbi kara kin'yōbi made 月曜日から金曜日まで ◊ (*by means of*) ... o tōshite ...を通して; **arranged ~ him** kare o tōshite tehai shita 彼を通して手配した **2** *adv*: **wet ~** bishonure de びしょぬれで; **watch a movie ~** eiga o saigo made miru 映画を最後まで見る; **read a book ~** hon o yomitōsu 本を読み通す **3** *adj*: **be ~** (*of couple*) owaru 終わる; (*have arrived: of news etc*) todoku 届く; **you're ~** TELEC tsunagarimashita つながりました; **I'm ~ with him** kare to wa owatta 彼とは終わった; **give me the paper back when you're ~ with it** yomiowattara shinbun o kaeshite kudasai 読み終わったら新聞を返してください

through flight chokkō-bin 直行便

throughout 1 *prep*: **~ the day** shūjitsu 終日; **~ the night** shūya 終夜; **~ one's life** shōgai o tsūjite 生涯を通じて; **~ the war** sensō no aidajū 戦争の間中; **~ the book** hon no hajime kara owari made 本の初めから終わりまで **2** *adv* (*in all parts*) zenbu 全部

through train chokkō-ressha 直行列車

throw 1 *v/t* nageru 投げる; (*of*

horse) furiotosu 振り落とす; (*disconcert*) konran saseru 混乱させる; *party* hiraku 開く **2** *n* nage 投げ

♦ **throw away** ... o suteru ...を捨てる

♦ **throw out** *old things* ... o suteru ...を捨てる; *drunk, husband* ... o oidasu ...を追い出す; *plan* ... o kyakka suru ...を却下する

♦ **throw up 1** *v/t ball* ... o nageru ...を投げる; **~ one's hands** odoroku 驚く **2** *v/i* (*vomit*) haku 吐く

throw-away *remark* sarigenai さりげない; (*disposable*) tsukaisute (no) 使い捨て(の)

throw-in SP surō in スローイン

thru → **through**

thrush (*bird*) tsugumi つぐみ

thrust *v/t* (*push hard*) tsuyoku osu 強く押す; **~ X into Y's hands** X o Y no te ni oshitsukeru XをYの手に押しつける; **~ one's way through the crowd** hitogomi o oshiwakete susumu 人込みを押し分けて進む

thud *n* dosun to ochiru oto ドスンと落ちる音

thug yakuza やくざ

thumb 1 *n* oyayubi 親指 **2** *v/t*: **~ a ride** hitchi-haiku suru ヒッチハイクする

thumbtack gabyō 画びょう

thump 1 *n* (*blow*) naguru koto 殴ること; (*noise*) gotsun to iu oto ゴツンという音 **2** *v/t person* naguru 殴る; **~ one's fist on the table** kobushi de tēburu tataku こぶしでテーブルをたたく **3** *v/i* (*of heart*) shinzō gadokidoki suru 心臓がドキドキする; **~ on the door** doa o dondon tataku ドアをドンドンたたく

thunder *n* kaminari 雷

thunderstorm raiu 雷雨

thundery *weather* kaminari no kisō (na) 雷のきそう(な)

Thursday mokuyōbi 木曜日

thus (*in this way*) kōshite こうして; (*as a consequence*) shitagatte 従って

thwart dame ni suru だめにする
thyroid (gland) kōjōsen 甲状腺
Tibet Chibetto チベット
Tibetan 1 *adj* Chibetto (no) チベット(の) **2** *n* (*person*) Chibetto-jin チベット人; (*language*) Chibetto-go チベット語
tick 1 *n* (*of clock*) kachikachi naru oto カチカチなる音; (*checkmark*) chekku no shirushi チェックの印 **2** *v/i* (*of clock*) kachikachi naru カチカチなる
♦**tick off** ... o shikaru ...をしかる
ticket kippu 切符
ticket barrier kaisatsu-guchi 改札口; **ticket collector** kaisatsu-gakari 改札係; **ticket inspector** shashō 車掌; **ticket machine** kippu-hanbaiki 切符販売機; **ticket office** (*at station*, THEA) kippu-uriba 切符売場
tickle 1 *v/t* kusuguru くすぐる **2** *v/i* (*of material*) chikuchiku suru チクチクする; (*of person*) kusuguttai くすぐったい
ticklish *person* kusuguttagari (no) くすぐったがり(の)
tidal wave tsunami 津波
tide shio 潮の干満; **high** ~ manchō 満潮; **low** ~ kanchō 干潮; **the** ~ **is in/out** manchō/kanchō da 満潮/干潮だ
tidy *person, habits* kichin to shita きちんとした; *room, house* kogirei (na) こぎれい(な)
♦**tidy up 1** *v/t room, shelves* ... o katazukeru ...を片付ける; **tidy oneself up** kichin to suru きちんとする **2** *v/i* katazukeru 片付ける
tie 1 *n* (*necktie*) nekutai ネクタイ; (SP: *even result*) hikiwake 引き分け; **he doesn't have any** ~**s** kare ni wa nani mo sokubaku suru mono ga nai 彼には何も束縛するものがない **2** *v/t knot* musubu 結ぶ; *hands* tsunagu つなぐ **3** *v/i* SP dōten ni naru 同点になる
♦**tie down** (*with rope*) ... o shibaritsukeru ...を縛り付ける; (*restrict*) ... o kōsoku suru ...を拘束する
♦**tie up** *person* ... o shibaru ...を縛

る; *laces, hair* ... o musubu ...を結ぶ; *boat* ... o tsunagu ...をつなぐ; **I'm tied up tomorrow** ashita wa isogashii 明日は忙しい
tier (*of hierarchy*) sō 層; (*in stadium*) dan 段
tiger tora トラ
tight 1 *adj clothes* kitsui きつい; *security* kibishii 厳しい; (*hard to move*) katai 堅い; (*properly shut*) kichin to shimatte iru きちんと閉まっている; (*not leaving much time*) kitsui きつい; F (*drunk*) dekiagatte iru 出来上がっている **2** *adv hold* shikkari しっかり; *shut* kichin to きちんと
tighten *screw* kataku shimeru 堅く絞める; *control, security* kibishiku suru 厳しくする; ~ **one's grip on** ... o shikkari nigiru ...をしっかり握る
♦**tighten up** *v/i* (*in discipline, security*) kibishiku naru 厳しくなる
tight-fisted kechi (na) けち(な)
tightrope tsuna-watari no tsuna 綱渡りの綱
tile tairu タイル
till[1] → **until**
till[2] (*cash register*) reji レジ
till[3] *v/t soil* tagayasu 耕す
tilt 1 *v/t katamukeru* 傾ける **2** *v/i* katamuku 傾く
timber zaimoku 材木
time jikan 時間; (*occasion*) kai 回; ~ **is up** jikangire de aru 時間切れである; **for the ~ being** ima no tokoro 今のところ; **have a good** ~ tanoshimu 楽しむ; **have a good** ~! tanoshinde ne 楽しんでね; **what's the ~?, what** ~ **is it?** ima nanji desu ka 今何時ですか; **the first** ~ hajimete 初めて; **four ~s** yon kai 四回; ~ **and again** nankai mo 何回も; **all the** ~ zutto ずっと; **they came in two/three at a** ~ karera wa futari/sannin zutsu haitte kita 彼らは二人/三人ずつ入って来た; **at the same** ~ *speak, reply etc* dōji ni 同時に; (*however*) shikashi しかし; **be in** ~ ma ni au 間に合う;

on ~ jikan dōri 時間どおり; **in no ~** sugu ni すぐに

time bomb jigen bakudan 時限爆弾; **time clock** (*in factory*) taimu-rekōdā タイムレコーダー; **time-consuming** jikan no kakaru 時間のかかる; **timelag** jikan no zure 時間のずれ; **time limit** shimekiri 締め切り

timely taimingu ga ii タイミングがいい

time out SP taimu-auto タイムアウト

timer taimā タイマー

timesaving *n* jikan no setsuyaku 時間の節約; **timescale** (*of project*) nagare 流れ; **time switch** taimā タイマー; **timetable** (*for trains*) jikokuhyō 時刻表; (*at school*) jikanwari 時間割; **timewarp** wāpu ワープ; **time zone** jikantai 時間帯

timid okubyō(na) 憶病(な)

timing (*choosing a time*) taimingu タイミング; (*of actor, dancer*) ma no torikata 間の取り方

tin (*metal*) suzu すず

tinfoil hoiru ホイル

tinge: a ~ of red akamigakatta iro 赤みがかった色; **a ~ of sadness** monoganashi-sa もの悲しさ

tingle *v/i* hirihiri itamu ひりひり痛む

♦ **tinker with** ... o ijiru ...をいじる

tinkle *n* (*of bell*) rinrin to naru oto リンリンと鳴る音

tinsel mōru モール

tint 1 *n* (*of color*) iroai 色合い; (*in hair*) kezome 毛染め **2** *v/t hair* kami o someru 髪を染める

tinted *glasses* iro no tsuita 色のついた; *paper* irotsuki (no) 色つき(の)

tiny totemo chiisai とても小さい

tip¹ *n* (*of stick, finger*) saki 先; (*of mountain*) chōjō 頂上; (*of cigarette*) sentan 先端

tip² *n* **1** (*piece of advice*) mimiyori no jōhō 耳寄りの情報; (*money*) chippu チップ **2** *v/t waiter etc* chippu o watasu チップを渡す

♦ **tip off** ... o naihō suru ...を内報する

♦ **tip over** *glass, liquid* ... o hikkurikaesu ...をひっくりかえす;

he tipped water all over me kare wa watashi ni mizu o kakemashita 彼はわたしに水をかけました

tipped *cigarettes* firutā no tsuita フィルターのついた

tippy-toe: on ~ tsumasakidachi de つま先立ちで

tipsy chotto yopparatta ちょっと酔っ払った

tire¹ *n* taiya タイヤ

tire² **1** *v/t* tsukare saseru 疲れさせる **2** *v/i* tsukareru 疲れる; **he never ~s of it** kare wa zenzen sore ni akinai 彼は全然それにあきない

tired tsukareta 疲れた; **be ~ of** ... ni unzari shita ...にうんざりした

tireless *efforts* fudan (no) 不断(の)

tiresome taikutsu (na) 退屈(な)

tiring tsukareru 疲れる

tissue ANAT soshiki 組織; (*handkerchief*) orimono 織物

tissue paper tisshu pēpā ティッシュペーパー

tit¹ (*bird*) shijūkara しじゅうから

tit²: ~ for tat shippegaeshi しっぺ返し

tit³ ∨ (*breast*) chibusa 乳房

title *n* (*of book*) katagaki 肩書き; LAW kenri 権利

titter *v/i* kusukusu warau くすくす笑う

to 1 *prep:* **~ Japan** Nihon e 日本へ; **~ Chicago** Shikago e シカゴへ; **go ~ my place** watashi no uchi ni iku 私の家に行く; **walk ~ the station** eki made aruku 駅まで歩く; **~ the north / south of** ... no kita / minami e ...の北/南へ; **give X ~ Y** Xo Yni ageru XをYにあげる; **from Monday ~ Wednesday** getsuyōbi kara suiyōbi made 月曜日から水曜日まで; **from 10 ~ 15 people** jūnin kara jūgonin made 十人から十五人まで **2** (*with verbs*) ... suru koto ...すること; **~ speak** hanasu koto 話すこと; **~ shout** sakebu koto 叫ぶこと; **learn ~ drive** unten o narau 運転を習う; **it's nice ~ eat** oishii desu おいしいです; **too heavy ~ carry** omosugite motenai 重過ぎて持てない; **~**

honest with you ... shōjiki ni iu
to 正直に言うと **3** *adv*: **~ and fro**
ittari kitari 行ったり来たり
toad hikigaeru ひきがえる
toadstool doku kinoko 毒きのこ
toast 1 *n* tōsuto トースト; (*when
drinking*) kanpai 乾杯; **propose a
~ to** ... ni kanpai ...に乾杯 **2** *v/t*
(*when drinking*) kanpai suru 乾杯
する
tobacco tabako タバコ
toboggan *n* sori そり
today kyō 今日
toddle (*of child*) yochiyochi aruku
よちよち歩く
toddler yochiyochi aruki no yōji よ
ちよち歩きの幼児
toe 1 *n* ashi no yubi 足の指; (*of
shoe*) tsumasaki つま先 **2** *v/t*: **~
the line** kitaidōri ni furumau 期待
どうりに振る舞う
toffee kyandī キャンディ
tofu tōfu とうふ
together issho ni 一緒に; (*at the
same time*) dōji ni 同時に
toil *n* kurō 苦労
toilet toire トイレ; **go to the ~** toire
ni iku トイレに行く
toilet paper toiretto pēpā トイレッ
トペーパー
toiletries senmen yōgu 洗面用具
token (*sign*) shirushi しるし; (*gift
~*) shōhinken 商品券
Tokyo Tōkyō 東京
tolerable *pain etc* gaman dekiru 我
慢できる; (*quite good*) kanari yoi
かなりよい
tolerance kan'yō 寛容
tolerant kan'yō (na) 寛容(な)
tolerate *noise, person* kyoyō suru
許容する; **I won't ~ it!** gaman
dekinai 我慢できない
toll[1] *v/i* (*of bell*) naru 鳴る
toll[2] (*deaths*) gisei-sha no kazu 犠牲
者の数
toll[3] (*for bridge, road*) tsūkō-ryō 通
行料; TELEC chōkyori-tsūwaryō 長
距離通話料
toll booth ryōkin-sho 料金所; **toll-
free** TELEC furī-daiaru フリーダイ
アル; **toll road** yūryō-dōro 有料道路

tomato tomato トマト
tomato ketchup tomato-kechappu
トマトケチャップ
tomb haka 墓
tomboy otenba おてんば
tombstone hakaishi 墓石
tomcat osuneko おす猫
tomorrow ashita 明日; **the day after
~** asatte あさって; **~ morning**
ashita no asa 明日の朝; **tomorrow ~**
ashita no yoru 明日の夜
ton ton トン
tone (*of color*) nōtan 濃淡; (*of
musical instrument*) neiro 音色;
(*of conversation etc*) chōshi 調子;
(*of neighborhood*) fun'iki 雰囲気;
~ of voice kuchō 口調
♦**tone down** *demands, criticism*
yawarageru 和らげる
toner tonā トナー
tongs (*for sugar*) satō-basami 砂糖
ばさみ; (*for ice*) kōri-basami 氷ば
さみ; (*for fire*) hi-basami 火ばさ
み; (*for hair*) kote こて
tongue *n* shita 舌
tonic MED kyōsōzai 強壮剤
tonic (**water**) tonikku wōtā トニッ
クウォーター
tonight konban 今晩
tonsillitis hentōsen-en 扁桃腺炎
tonsils hentōsen 扁桃腺
too (*also*) ...mo mata ...もまた;
(*excessively*) ...sugiru ...すぎる;
me ~ watashi mo 私も; **~ big / hot**
ōki-sugiru / atsu-sugiru 大きすぎ
る / 熱すぎる; **~ much rice** gohan
ga ō-sugiru ごはんが多すぎる; **eat
~ much** tabe-sugiru 食べ過ぎる
tool dōgu 道具
tooth ha 歯
toothache haita 歯痛
toothbrush ha-burashi 歯ブラシ
toothless hanashi (no) 歯なし(の)
toothpaste ha-migaki 歯磨き
toothpick tsumayōji つまようじ
top 1 *n* (*of mountain, tree*) sentan
先端; (*upper part*) ue 上; (*lid: of
bottle etc, pen*) futa ふた; (*of the
class, league*) ichiban 一番;
(*clothing*) uwagi 上着; (MOT: *gear*)
toppu gia トップギア; **on ~ of** ...

no ue ni ...の上に; **at the ~ of ...**
no ichiban ni ...の一番に; **at the ~
of the tree** kozue ni こずえに; **at
the ~ of the mountain** chōjō ni 頂
上に; **get to the ~** (of company
etc) toppu ni noboritsumeru トッ
プにのぼりつめる; **be over the ~**
(exaggerated) yari-sugiru やりす
ぎる **2** adj branches saikō (no) 最
高(の); floor saijōkai 最上階;
management, official saikō-kanbu
最高幹部; player sugureta senshu
優れた選手; speed, note saikō 最高
3 v/t ... no ue o ōu ...の上をおおう;
~ped with cream ue ni kurīmu de
kazatta 上にクリームで飾った

♦ **top up** glass, tank ... o ue ni
tsugitasu ...を上につぎたす

top hat shiruku hatto シルクハット;
topheavy atamadekkachi (no) 頭
でっかち(の); **top knot**
chonnmage ちょんまげ

topic wadai 話題

topical wadai (no) 話題(の)

topless adj toppuresu (no) トップ
レス(の)

topmost branches, floor ichiban ue
(no) 一番上(の)

topping (on pizza) toppingu トッピ
ング

topple 1 v/i kuzureochiru 崩れ落ち
る **2** v/t government taosu 倒す

top secret adj saikō-kimitsu (no)
最高機密(の)

topsy-turvy adj (in disorder)
sakasama (no) 逆さま(の); world
konran-jōtai (no) 混乱状態(の)

torch (with flame) taimatsu たいまつ

torment 1 n kurushimi 苦しみ **2** v/t
person, animal itametsukeru 痛め
つける; ~ed by doubt utagai ni
nayamasareta 疑いに悩まされた

tornado tatsumaki 竜巻

torrent gekiryū 激流; (of abuse,
words) renpatsu 連発; ~ of lava
yōganryū 溶岩流

torrential doshaburi (no) 土砂降り
(の)

tortoise kame かめ

torture 1 n gōmon 拷問 **2** v/t gōmon
ni kakeru 拷問にかける

toss 1 v/t ball nageru 投げる; rider
furiotosu 振り落とす; salad
kakimazeru かき混ぜる; ~ a coin
koin o nagete kimeru コインを投
げて決める **2** v/i: ~ and turn
negaeri o utsu 寝返りをうつ

total 1 n gōkei 合計 **2** adj sum,
amount gōkei (no) 合計(の);
disaster, idiot hidoi ひどい;
stranger mattaku (no) まったく
(の) **3** v/t F car mechamecha (no)
めちゃめちゃ(の)

totalitarian zentai-shugi (no) 全体
主義(の)

totally mattaku まったく

tote bag ōgata no tesage baggu 大
型の手提げバッグ

totter (of person) yoromeku よろめ
く

touch 1 n (act of touching)
tezawari 手ざわり; (sense)
kanshoku 感触; (little bit) sukoshi
少し; SP tatchi タッチ; **lose ~ with**
... to renraku ga todaeru ...と連絡
が途絶える; **keep in ~ with** ... to
renraku shite iru ...と連絡してい
る; **we kept in ~** yaritori o
tsuzukeru やりとりを続ける; **be
out of ~** ... to sesshoku o ushinau
...の感触を失う **2** v/t sawaru 触る;
(emotionally) kandō saseru 感動
させる **3** v/i sawaru 触る; (of two
lines etc) sesshoku suru 接触する

♦ **touch down** v/i (of airplane)
chakuriku suru 着陸する; SP
tatchidaun suru タッチダウンする

♦ **touch on** (mention) ... ni chotto
furete oku ...にちょっと触れておく

♦ **touch up** photo ... o shūsei suru
...を修正する

touchdown (of airplane) chakuriku
着陸; SP tatchidaun タッチダウン

touching adj mune o utsu 胸をうつ

touchline SP saidorain サイドライン

touchy person shinkeishitsu (na)
神経質(な)

tough person ki no tsuyoi 気の強い;
meat katai 固い; question, exam
muzukashii 難しい; material
tsuyoi 強い; punishment omoi 重い

tough guy tafu gai タフガイ

tour 1 *n* ryokō 旅行 **2** *v/t area* ryokō suru 旅行する

tourism kankō jigyō 観光事業

tourist kankōkyaku 観光客

tourist (information) office kankō annaisho 観光案内所

tournament tōnamento トーナメント

tour operator ryokō-gaisha 旅行会社

tousled *hair* midareta 乱れた

tow 1 *v/t car, boat* hipparu 引っ張る **2** *n: give X a ~* X o ken'in suru X をけん引する

♦**tow away** *car* ken'in sarete motte ikareru けん引されて持っていかれる

toward *prep* ... no hō e ...の方へ

towel taoru タオル

tower *n* tō 塔

town machi 町

town council chōgikai 町議会; **town councilor** chōgikai-giin 町議会議員; **town hall** shiyakusho 市役所

towrope ken'in-rōpu けん引ロープ

toxic yūdoku (na) 有毒(な)

toy omocha おもちゃ

♦**toy with** *object* ... o ijikuru ...をいじくる; *idea* ... o chotto kangaete iru ...をちょっと考えている

trace 1 *n* (*of substance*) ato 跡 **2** *v/t* (*find*) sagashidasu 捜し出す; *footsteps* shiraberu 調べる; (*draw*) utsusu 写す

track *n* (*path*) komichi 小道; (*for racing*) kōsu コース; RAIL tetsudō senro 鉄道線路; **~ 10** RAIL jū-bansen 十番線; **keep ~ of** ... o kiroku suru ...を記録する

♦**track down** ... o mitsukedasu ...を見つけ出す

tracksuit suwetto sūtsu スウェットスーツ

tractor torakutā トラクター

trade 1 *n* (*commerce*) bōeki 貿易; (*profession, craft*) shokugyō 職業 **2** *v/i* (*do business*) torihiki suru 取り引きする; **~ in** ... o atsukau ...を扱う **3** *v/t* (*exchange*) kōkan suru 交換する; **~ X for Y** X o Y to kōkan suru XをYと交換する

♦**trade in** *v/t* (*when buying*) ... o shitadori suru ...を下取りする

trade fair mihon'ichi 見本市; **trademark** tōroku-shōhyō 登録商標; **trade mission** bōeki-shisetsudan 貿易使節団

trader FIN torēdā トレーダー

trade secret kigyō-himitsu 企業秘密

tradesman (*plumber etc*) shokunin 職人

trade(s) union rōdō-kumiai 労働組合

tradition dentō 伝統, iitsutae 言い伝え

traditional dentōteki (na) 伝統的(な)

traditionally dentōteki ni 伝統的に

traffic *n* (*on roads*) kōtsū 交通; (*at airport*) ōrai 往来; (*in drugs*) mitsubaibai 密売買

♦**traffic in** *drugs* ... o mitsubaibai suru ...を密売買する

traffic circle rōtarī ロータリー; **traffic cop** F kōtsū-keisatsukan 交通警察官; **traffic island** anzenchitai 安全地帯; **traffic jam** kōtsū-jūtai 交通渋滞; **traffic light** shingō 信号; **traffic police** kōtsū-keisatsu 交通警察; **traffic sign** kōtsū-hyōshiki 交通標識; **traffic warden** kōtsū-kanshiin 交通監視員

tragedy higeki 悲劇

tragic higeki (no) 悲劇(の)

trail 1 *n* (*path*) michi 道; (*of blood*) ato 跡 **2** *v/t* (*follow*) ato o tsukeru 跡をつける; (*tow*) hipparu 引っぱる **3** *v/i* (*lag behind*) okure o toru 後れを取る

trailer (*pulled by vehicle*) torērā トレーラー; (*mobile home*) torērā hausu トレーラーハウス; (*of movie*) yokokuhen 予告編

train¹ *n* ressha 列車; **go by ~** ressha de iku 列車で行く

train² 1 *v/t team, athlete* kitaeru 鍛える; *employee* kyōiku suru 教育する; *dog* chōkyō suru 調教する **2** *v/i* (*of team, athlete*) kitaeru 鍛える; (*of teacher etc*) kenshū suru 研修する

trainee kenshūsei 研修生

trainer SP torēnā トレーナー; (of dog) chōkyō-shi 調教師

trainers Br (shoes) sunīkā スニーカー

training (of staff) kenshū 研修; SP renshū 練習; **be in ~** SP renshū o tsunde iru 練習を積んでいる; **be out of ~** SP renshū-busoku de aru 練習不足である

training course kenshū kōsu 研修コース

training scheme renshū-keikaku 練習計画

train station eki 駅

trait tokushoku 特色

traitor hangyaku-sha 反逆者

tramp v/i omoi ashidori de aruku 重い足取りで歩く

trample v/t fumitsukeru 踏みつける; **be ~d to death** fumikorosareru 踏み殺される; **be ~d underfoot** fumikorosare-sōni naru 踏み殺されそうになる

♦ **trample on** person, object ... o fumitsukeru ...を踏みつける

trampoline toranporin トランポリン

trance yume-utsutsu 夢うつつ; **go into a ~** kōkotsu-jōtai ni naru こうこつ状態になる

tranquil shizuka (na) 静か(な)

tranquility seijaku 静寂

tranquilizer seishin-anteizai 精神安定剤

transact deal, business okonau 行う

transaction torihiki 取引

transatlantic Taiseiyō ōdan (no) 大西洋横断(の)

transcendental chōshizenteki (na) 超自然的(な)

transcript (of meeting, trial) kiroku-bunsho 記録文書

transfer 1 v/t idō saseru 移動させる 2 v/i (switch) kirikaeru 切り替える; (in travel) idō suru 移動する 3 n idō 移動; (in travel) norikae 乗り換え; (of money) sōkin 送金

transferable ticket jōto dekiru 譲渡できる

transform v/t henkei saseru 変形させる

transformation henkei 変形

transformer ELEC hen'atsuki 変圧器

transfusion yuketsu 輸血

transistor toranjisutā トランジスター; (radio) rajio ラジオ

transit: **in ~** goods, passengers idōchū (no) 移動中(の)

transition utsurikawari 移り変わり

transitional katoki (no) 過渡期(の)

transit lounge norikae-kyakuyō-raunji 乗り換え客用ラウンジ

translate hon'yaku suru 翻訳する

translation hon'yaku 翻訳

translator hon'yaku-sha 翻訳者

transliterate on'yaku suru 音訳する

transmission (of program) dentatsu 伝達; (of disease) densen 伝染; MOT hensokuki 変速機

transmit program okuru 送る; disease utsusu うつす

transmitter RAD, TV sōshinki 送信機

transpacific Taiheiyō-ōdan (no) 太平洋横断(の)

transparent tōmei (no) 透明(の); (obvious) miesuita 見え透いた

transplant MED 1 v/t ishoku suru 移植する 2 n ishoku 移植

transport 1 v/t yusō suru 輸送する 2 n yusō 輸送

transportation yusō-kikan 輸送機関; **means of ~** kōtsū-kikan 交通機関; **public ~** kōkyō-kōtsūkikan 公共交通機関; **Department of Transportation** Un'yushō 運輸省

transvestite fukusōtōsaku-sha 服装倒錯者

trap 1 n (for animal) wana わな; (question, set-up etc) sakuryaku 策略; **set a ~ for** ... o wana ni kakeru ...をわなにかける 2 v/t animal ... ni wana o shikakeru ...にわなをしかける; person wana ni kakeru わなにかける; **be ~ped** (by enemy, etc) hamatta ni matta はまったにまった; **be ~ped by the flames** honō ni torikomareta 炎にとりこまれた

trapdoor otoshido 落とし戸

trapeze kūchū-buranko 空中ブランコ

trappings (of power) tokuten 特典

trash (garbage) kuzu くず; (poor

product) garakuta がらくた; (*book, movie*) dasaku 駄作; **he's ~** kare wa kudaranai hito da 彼はくだらない人だ

trashcan kuzuire くず入れ

trashy *goods* kudaranai くだらない

traumatic shōgekiteki (na) 衝撃的 (な)

travel 1 *n* ryokō 旅行; **~s** ryokō-chū 旅行中 **2** *v/i* ryokō suru 旅行する; (*to work*) tsūkin suru 通勤する; **~ by boat/train** fune/densha de iku 船/電車で行く **3** *v/t*: **I ~ 15 miles by car every day** mainichi jūgo mairu kuruma de hashiru 毎日15 マイル車で走る

travel agency ryokō-sha 旅行社

travel bag ryokō-kaban 旅行かばん

traveler ryokō-sha 旅行者

traveler's check toraberāzu-chekku トラベラーズチェック

travel expenses shutchō-ryohi 出張旅費; **travel insurance** ryokō-hoken 旅行保険; **travelsick** norimonoyoi shita 乗り物酔いした

trawler torōru-sen トロール船

tray (*for food etc*) bon 盆; (*to go in oven*) ōbun-zara オーブン皿; (*in printer, copier*) torei トレイ

treacherous *person* fuseijitsu (na) 不誠実(な); *current, road* kiken (na) 危険(な)

treachery uragiri 裏切り

tread 1 *n* ashioto 足音; (*of tire*) toreddo トレッド **2** *v/i* aruku 歩く ♦ **tread on** *s.o.'s foot* ... o fumu ... を踏む

treason hangyakuzai 反逆罪

treasure 1 *n* takara 宝; **he is a ~** kare wa subarashii hito da 彼はすばらしい人だ **2** *v/t* *gift etc* taisetsu ni suru 大切にする

treasurer kaikei-gakari 会計係

Treasury Department Ōkura-shō 大蔵省

treat 1 *n* tanoshimi 楽しみ; **it was a real ~** totemo tanoshikatta desu とても楽しかったです; **I have a ~ for you** anata o yorokobasu mono ga arimasu あなたを喜ばすものがあります; **it's my ~** (*I'm paying*) watashi no ogori desu 私のおごりです **2** *v/t* *materials* shori suru 処理する; *illness* chiryō suru 治療する; (*behave toward*) atsukau 扱う; **~ X to Y** X ni Y o ogoru XにYをおごる

treatment (*of materials*) toriatsukai 取り扱い; (*of illness*) chiryō 治療; (*of people*) taigū 待遇

treaty jōyaku 条約; **the Japan-US Security Treaty** Nichibeianzen-hoshōjōyaku 日米安全保障条約

treble¹ (*singer*) bōi-sopurano ボーイソプラノ

treble² *adv*: **~ the price** nedan ga sanbai ni naru 値段が三倍になる **2** *v/i* sanbai ni naru 三倍になる

tree ki 木

tremble furueru 震える; (*of building*) yureru 揺れる

tremendous (*very good*) subarashii すばらしい; (*enormous*) monosugoi ものすごい

tremendously hijō ni 非常に

tremor (*of earth*) shindō 震動

trench zangō ざんごう

trend keikō 傾向; (*fashion*) ryūkō 流行

trendy hayari (no) はやり(の)

trespass ... ni fuhō-shinnyū suru ...に不法侵入する; **no ~ing** tachiiri-kinshi 立ち入り禁止 ♦ **trespass on** *land* ... ni fuhō-shinnyū suru ...に不法侵入する; *privacy* ... o shingai suru ...を侵害する

trespasser fuhō-shinnyū-sha 不法侵入者

trial LAW saiban 裁判; (*of equipment*) tesuto テスト; **on ~** LAW saiban ni kakerarete 裁判にかけられて; **have on ~** *equipment* ... o tameshite miru ...を試してみる

trial period (*for employee*) shiyō-kikan 試用期間; (*for equipment*) tesuto-kikan テスト期間

triangle sankakkei 三角形

triangular sankaku (no) 三角(の)

tribe shuzoku 種族

tribunal shingi-iinkai 審議委員会

tributary shiryū 支流

trick 1 *n* (*to deceive*) keiryaku 計略; (*knack*) kotsu こつ; *play a ~ on* … o damasu …をだます **2** *v/t* damasu だます; *~ X into doing Y* X o damashite Y saseru Xをだまして Yさせる

trickery keiryaku 計略

trickle *v/i* sukoshi zutsu nagareru 少しずつ流れる

trickster sagishi 詐欺師

tricky (*difficult*) yayakoshii ややこ しい

tricycle sanrinsha 三輪車

trifle (*triviality*) sasai na koto ささ いなこと

trifling kudaranai くだらない

trigger *n* hikigane 引き金
♦ **trigger off** … no hikigane ni naru …の引き金になる

trim 1 *adj* (*neat*) teire sareta 手入れ された; (*figure*) hikishimatta 引き締 まった **2** *v/t hair, hedge* kirisoroeru 切りそろえる; *budget, costs* kiritsumeru 切り詰める; (*decorate: dress*) kazaru 飾る **3** *n* (*light cut*) karikomi 刈り込み; *just a ~, please* (*to hairdresser*) soroete kudasai そ ろえてください; *in good ~* chōshi no ii 調子のいい

trimming (*on clothes*) kazari 飾り; *with all the ~s dish* tsukeawase zenbu to tsuke-awase 全部と; *fig* fuzokuhin zenbu to 付属品全部と

trinket sōshingu 装身具

trio MUS sanjūsō 三重奏

trip 1 *n* (*journey*) ryokō 旅行 **2** *v/i* (*stumble*) tsumazuku つまずく **3** *v/t* (*make fall*) … no ashi o sukuu …の足をすくう
♦ **trip up 1** *v/t* (*make fall*) … no ashi o sukuu …の足をすくう; (*cause to go wrong*) … o konran saseru …を混乱させる **2** *v/i* (*stumble*) ashi o sukuwareru 足を すくわれる; (*make a mistake*) hema o suru へまをする

tripe ushi no i 牛の胃

triple → **treble**[2]

triplets mitsugo 三つ子

tripod PHOT sankyaku 三脚

trite arifureta ありふれた

triumph *n* shōri 勝利

trivial sasai (na) ささい(な)

triviality heibon 平凡

trombone toronbōn トロンボーン

troops guntai 軍隊

trophy torofī トロフィー

tropic kaikisen 回帰線

tropical nettai (no) 熱帯(の)

tropics nettaichihō 熱帯地方

trot *v/i* hayaashi de kakeru 速足で かける

trouble 1 *n* (*difficulties*) kurō 苦労; (*disease*) byōki 病気; (*inconvenience*) mendō 面倒; (*quarrel*) sawagi 騒ぎ; (*armed conflict*) funsō 紛争; *go to a lot of ~ to do X* X suru no ni hone o oru Xす るのに骨を折る; *no ~!* daijōbu 大丈 夫; *get into ~* mendō na koto ni naru 面倒なことになる **2** *v/t* (*worry*) nayamaseru 悩ませる; (*bother, disturb*) meiwaku o kakeru 迷惑を かける; (*of back, liver etc*) chōshi o waruku suru 調子を悪くする

trouble-free koshō no nai 故障のな い; **troublemaker** toraburu-mēkā トラブルメーカー; **troubleshooter** (*mediator*) chōteinin 調停人; **troubleshooting** mondai-kaiketsu 問題解決

troublesome mendō (na) 面倒(な)

trousers *Br* zubon ズボン

trout masu ます

truce kyūsen 休戦

truck torakku トラック

truck driver torakku no untenshu トラックの運転手; **truck farm** shijōmuke-yasaien 市場向け野菜 園; **truck farmer** shijōmuke-yasai saibai-gyōsha 市場向け野菜栽培業 者; **truck stop** keishokudō 軽食堂

trudge 1 *v/i* tobotobo aruku とぼとぼ ぼ歩く **2** *n* omoi ashidori 重い足取 り

true *story, friend* hontō (no) 本当 (の); *come ~* (*of hopes, dream*) genjitsu ni naru 現実になる

truly hontō ni 本当に; *Yours ~* keigu 敬具

trumpet *n* toranpetto トランペット

trunk (*of tree*) miki 幹; (*of body*) dō

胴; (*of elephant*) hana 鼻; (*container, of car*) toranku トランク

trust 1 *n* shinrai 信用; FIN shintaku 信託 **2** *v/t* shin'yō suru 信用する; *I ~ you* anata o shin'yō suru あなたを信用する

trusted shin'yō sareta 信用された

trustee jutaku-sha 受託者

trustful, trusting shin'yō shiyasui 信用しやすい

trustworthy ate ni naru 当てになる

truth shinjitsu 真実; *the eternal ~s of …* … no eien no shinri …の永遠の真理

truthful seijitsu (na) 誠実(な)

try 1 *v/t* tamesu 試す; LAW saiban suru 裁判する; *~ to do X* X shiyō to suru X しようとする **2** *v/i* tamesu 試す; *you must ~ harder* motto ganbaranakereba narimasen もっとがんばらなければなりません **3** *n* kokoromi 試み; *can I have a ~?* (*of food*) tabete mite mo ii desu ka 食べてみてもいいですか; (*at doing sth*) tameshitemite mo ii desu ka 試してみてもいいですか

♦**try on** *clothes* … o shichaku suru …を試着する

♦**try out** *machine, method* … o tameshitemiru …を試してみる

trying (*annoying*) tsurai つらい

T-shirt tī-shatsu ティーシャツ

tsunami tsunami 津波

tub (*bath*) furo-oke 風呂おけ; (*of liquid*) kame かめ; (*for yoghurt, ice cream*) iremono 入れ物

tubby *adj* zunguri shita ずんぐりした

tube (*pipe*) kuda 管, chikatetsu 地下鉄; (*of toothpaste, ointment*) chūbu チューブ

tubeless *tire* chūburesu taiya チューブレスタイヤ

tuberculosis kekkaku 結核

tuck 1 *n* (*in dress*) hida ひだ **2** *v/t* (*put*) shimaikomu しまい込む

♦**tuck away** (*put away*) … o shimaikomu …をしまい込む; (*eat*) … o kakikomu …をかき込む

♦**tuck in 1** *v/t children* … o kurumu

…をくるむ; *sheets* … o hasami komu …を挟み込む **2** *v/i*: *~!* tappuri tabenasai たっぷり食べなさい

♦**tuck up** *sleeves etc* … o makuru …をまくる; *tuck X up in bed* X o nekasu X を寝かす

Tuesday kayōbi 火曜日

tuft taba 束

tug 1 *n* NAUT tagubōto タグボート; *I felt a ~ at my sleeve* sode o hippareru no o kanjita そでを引っ張られるのを感じた **2** *v/t* (*pull*) hipparu 引っ張る

tuition: *private ~* katei-kyōshi 家庭教師

tulip chūrippu チューリップ

tumble *v/i* taoreru 倒れる

tumbledown tsuburesō (na) つぶれそう(な)

tumbler (*for drink*) gurasu グラス; (*in circus*) karuwaza-shi 軽業師

tummy onaka おなか

tummy ache onakaita おなか痛

tumor shuyō しゅよう

tumult sōdō 騒動

tumultuous sōzōshii 騒々しい

tuna maguro まぐろ; (*canned*) tsuna ツナ

tune 1 *n* merodī メロディー; *in ~* chōshi ga atte iru 調子が合っている; *out of ~* chōshi ga hazurete iru 調子がはずれている **2** *v/t instrument* chōritsu suru 調律する

♦**tune in** *v/i* RAD, TV channeru o awaseru チャンネルをあわせる

♦**tune in to** *v/t* RAD, TV … ni channeru o awaseru …にチャンネルをあわせる

♦**tune up 1** *v/i* (*of orchestra*) chōshi o awaseru 調子を合わせる **2** *v/t engine* … o chōsei suru …を調整する

tuneful merodī no utsukushii メロディーの美しい

tuner (*hi-fi*) chūnā チューナー

tunic EDU chunikku チュニック

tunnel *n* tonneru トンネル

turbine tābin タービン

turbot ōhirame 大ひらめ

turbulence (*in air travel*) rankiryū

乱気流

turbulent areru 荒れる
turf shiba 芝
Turk Toruko-jin トルコ人
Turkey Toruko トルコ
turkey shichimenchō 七面鳥
Turkish 1 adj Toruko (no) トルコ(の)
2 n (language) Toruko-go トルコ語
turmoil konran 混乱
turn 1 n (rotation) kaiten 回転; (in road) kābu カーブ; (in vaudeville) dashimono 出し物; **take a ~s doing X** kōtai de X o suru 交替でXをする; **it's my ~** watashi no junban desu 私の順番です; **it's not your ~ yet** mada anata no junban ja nai まだあなたの順番じゃない; **take a ~ at the wheel** sukoshi unten suru 少し運転する; **do X a good ~** X no tame ni naru koto o suru Xのためになることをする **2** v/t wheel kaiten saseru 回転させる; corner magaru 曲がる; **~ one's back on** ... ni se o mukeru ...に背を向ける **3** v/i (of driver, car) magaru 曲がる; (of wheel) kaiten suru 回転する; **~ right/left here** koko de migi/hidari ni magatte ここで右/左に曲がって; **it has ~ed sour/cold** suppaku/samuku naru すっぱく/寒くなる; **he has ~ed 40** kare wa yonjūdai ni natte iru 彼は四十代になっている
♦ **turn around 1** v/t object ... o hōkō-tenkan suru ...を方向転換する; company kōten saseru 好転させる; (COM: deal with) taisho suru 対処する **2** v/i (of person) furikaeru 振り返る; (of car) muki o kaeru 向きを変える
♦ **turn away 1** v/t (send away) ... o oiharau ...を追い払う **2** v/i (walk away) muki o kaete tachisaru 向きを変えて立ち去る; (look away) kao o somukeru 顔を背ける
♦ **turn back 1** v/t edges, sheets ... o orikaesu ...を折り返す **2** v/i (in walking, procedure) hikikaesu 引き返す
♦ **turn down** v/t offer, invitation ... o kotowaru ...を断る; volume, TV o chiisaku suru ...を小さくする;

heating ... o yowaku suru ...を弱くする; edge, collar ... o orikaesu ...を折り返す
♦ **turn in 1** v/i (go to bed) neru 寝る **2** v/t (to police) mikkoku suru 密告する
♦ **turn off 1** v/t radio, TV etc ... o kesu ...を消す; faucet, heater, engine ... o tomeru ...を止める; F (sexually) ... o unzarisaseru ...をうんざりさせる **2** v/i (of car, driver) waki e hairu わきへ入る; (of machine) kieru 消える
♦ **turn on 1** v/t radio, TV, engine etc ... o tsukeru ...をつける; faucet, heater ... o ireru ...をいれる; F (sexually) ... o kōfun saseru ...を興奮させる **2** v/i (of machine) tsuku つく
♦ **turn out 1** v/t lights ... o kesu ...を消す **2** v/i: as it turned out kekkyoku no tokoro 結局のところ
♦ **turn over 1** v/i (in bed) negaeri o utsu 寝返りをうつ; (of vehicle) hikkuri kaeru ひっくり返る **2** v/t (put upside down) tenpuku saseru 転覆させる; page mekuru めくる; FIN shōbai o suru 商売をする
♦ **turn up 1** v/t collar ... o orikaesu ...を折り返す; volume ... o ageru ...をあげる; heating ... o tsuyoku suru ...を強くする **2** v/i (arrive) arawareru 現れる
turning magarikado 曲がり角
turning point fushime 節目
turnip kabu かぶ
turnout (of people) shussekiritsu 出席率; **turnover** FIN uriage 売り上げ; **turnpike** yūryō-kōsokudōro 有料高速道路; **turnstile** kaitenshiki kido 回転式木戸; **turntable** (of record player) kaitenban 回転盤
turquoise adj aomidoriiro (no) 青緑色(の)
turret (of castle) shōtō 小塔; (of tank) jūza 銃座
turtle kame かめ
turtleneck (sweater) tātorunekku タートルネック
tusk kiba きば
tutor 1 v/t oshieru 教える **2** n

(*private*) ~ katei-kyōshi 家庭教師
tuxedo takishīdo タキシード
TV terebi テレビ; *be on* ~ terebi de yatte iru テレビでやっている; ~ *program* terebi bangumi テレビ番組
twang 1 n: *the ~ of his accent* hana ni kakatta akusento 鼻にかかたアクセント **2** v/t *guitar string* bün to narasu ブーンと鳴らす
tweezers pinsetto ピンセット
twelfth dai-jūni (no) 第十二(の)
twelve jūni 十二
twentieth 1 adj dai-nijū (no) 第二十(の) **2** n (*of month*) hatsuka 二十日
twenty nijū 二十
twice nikai 二回; ~ *as much* nibai 二倍
twiddle ijiru いじる; ~ *one's thumbs* yubi o moteasobu 指をもてあそぶ
twig n koeda 小枝
twilight tasogare たそがれ
twin futago 双子
twin beds tsuin-beddo ツインベッド
twinge (*of pain*) uzuki うずき
twinkle v/i (*of stars*) kirakira hikaru キラキラ光る; (*of eyes*) kagayaku 輝く
twin town shimai-toshi 姉妹都市
twirl 1 v/t kurukuru mawasu くるくる回す **2** n (*of cream etc*) uzumaki kazari うずまき飾り
twist 1 v/t nejiru ねじる; ~ *one's ankle* nenza suru ねんざする **2** v/i (*of road, river*) magarikuneru 曲がりくねる **3** n (*in rope*) nejire ねじれ; (*in road*) kābu カーブ; (*in plot, story*) hineri ひねり

twisty *road* magarikunetta 曲がりくねった
twit F bakamitai ばかみたい
twitch 1 n (*nervous*) keiren けいれん **2** v/i (*jerk*) keiren suru けいれんする
twitter v/i (*of birds*) saezuru さえずる
two ni 二; (*with count word*) futatsu 二つ; *the ~ of them* sono futatsu その二つ
two-faced uraomote no aru 裏表のある
two-way traffic taimen-kōtsū (no) 対面交通(の)
tycoon ōmono 大物
type 1 n (*sort*) taipu タイプ; *what ~ of...?* donna taipu no... どんなタイプの... **2** v/i (*use a keyboard*) taipu o utsu タイプを打つ **3** v/t (*with a typewriter*) taipu suru タイプする
typewriter taipu-raitā タイプライター
typhoid (fever) chō-chifusu 腸チフス
typhoon taifū 台風
typhus chifusu チフス
typical tenketeki (na) 典型的(な); *that's ~ of you / him!* anatarashii / karerashii あなたらしい / 彼らしい
typically gaishite 概して; ~ *American* tenketeki na Amerika-jin 典型的なアメリカ人
typist taipisuto タイピスト
tyrannical bōkun (no) 暴君(の)
tyrannize shiitageru 虐げる
tyranny assei 圧制
tyrant bōkun 暴君

U

ugly minikui 醜い
UK (= *United Kingdom*) Eikoku 英国

ulcer kaiyō かいよう
ultimate (*best, definitive*) kyūkyoku (no) 究極(の); (*final*) saishū (no)

最終(の); (*fundamental*)
konponteki (na) 根本的(な)
ultimately (*in the end*) kekkyoku 結局
ultimatum saigotsūchō 最後通ちょう
ultrasound MED chōonpa 超音波
ultraviolet *adj* shigaisen (no) 紫外線(の)
umbilical cord heso no o へその緒
umbrella kasa 傘
umpire *n* shinpan 審判
umpteen: *I have told you ~ times* F nankai mo itta deshō 何回も言ったでしょう
UN (= *United Nations*) Kokuren 国連
unable: *be ~ to do X* X suru koto ga dekinai …することができない
unacceptable mitomerarenai 認められない; *it is ~ that* … wa mitomerarenai …は認められない
unaccountable setsumei dekinai 説明できない
unaccustomed: *be ~ to* … ni narete inai …に慣れていない
unadulterated (*absolute*) mattaku (no) 全く(の)
un-American Amerika-jin rashikunai アメリカ人らしくない
unanimous *verdict* manjō-itchi (no) 満場一致(の); *be ~ on* … ni zenkai itchi de aru …に全会一致である
unanimously manjō-itchi de 満場一致で
unapproachable *person* chikazukinikui 近づきにくい
unarmed *person* busō shite inai 武装していない; *~ combat* buki o tsukawanai bujutsu 武器を使わない武術
unassuming kidoranai 気取らない
unattached (*without a partner*) tsukiatte iru hito no inai 付き合っている人のいない
unattended hottarakashi (no) ほったらかし(の); *leave ~* … o hottarakashi ni suru …をほったらかしにする
unauthorized mukyoka (no) 無許可(の); (*lacking official approval*)

muninka (no) 無認可(の)
unavoidable sakerarenai 避けられない
unavoidably: *be ~ detained* hikitomerareru no o sakerarenakatta 引き止められるのを避けられなかった
unaware: *be ~ of* … ni ki ga tsukanai …に気が付かない
unawares: *catch X ~* X ni fuiuchi o kuwaseru X に不意打ちを食わせる
unbalanced katayotta 偏った; *design* baransu no warui バランスの悪い; PSYCH kurutta 狂った
unbearable taerarenai 耐えられない; *person* gaman dekinai 我慢できない
unbeatable *team, quality* subarashii 素晴らしい
unbeaten *team* muteki (no) 無敵(の)
unbeknownst: *~ to* … ni kizukarezu ni …に気付かれずに
unbelievable shinjirarenai 信じられない; F *heat, value* sugoi すごい; *he's ~* F (*very good / bad*) kare wa tondemonai 彼はとんでもない
unbias(s)ed kōsei (na) 公正(な)
unblock *pipe* tsumari o torinozoku 詰まりを取り除く
unborn onaka no naka (no) お腹の中(の)
unbreakable *plates* kowarenai 壊れない; *world record* yaburu koto no dekinai 破ることのできない
unbutton botan o hazusu ボタンをはずす
uncalled-for yokei (na) 余計(な)
uncanny bukimi (na) 不気味(な); *knack* hitonami-hazureta 人並みはずれた
unceasing taemanai 絶え間ない
uncertain *future, origins* hakkiri shinai はっきりしない; *weather* fuantei (na) 不安定(な); *be ~ about* … ni tsuite hakkiri wakaranai …についてはっきりわからない
uncertainty (*of the future*) fukakujitsu 不確実; *there is still ~ about* … ni wa mada fukakujitsu

na tokoro ga aru ...にはまだ不確
実なところがある

unchecked: *let X go* ~ X o chekku
shinaide sumasu Xをチェックしな
いですます

uncle oji おじ; (*s.o. else's*) ojisan お
じさん

uncomfortable *chair* kokochi-warui
心地悪い; *sitting position*
ochitsukanai 落ち着かない; *feel* ~
about ... o fuan ni kanjiru ...を不
安に感じる; *I feel* ~ *with him* kare
to iru to kizumari de aru 彼といる
と気詰まりである

uncommon mezurashii 珍しい; *it's*
not ~ mezurashiku nai 珍しくない

uncompromising dakyō shinai 妥協
しない

unconcerned kanshin no nai 関心の
ない; *be* ~ *about* ... o ki ni
shiteinai ...を気にしていない

unconditional mujōken (no) 無条件
(の)

unconscious MED ishikifumei (no)
意識不明(の); PSYCH muishiki (no)
無意識(の); *knock* ~ shisshin
saseru 失神させる; *be* ~ *of* (*not*
aware) ... ni ki ga tsukanai ...に気
が付かない

uncontrollable *anger, desire*
osaerarenai 抑えられない;
children te ni oenai 手に負えない

unconventional kata ni hamaranai
型にはまらない

uncooperative hikyōryokuteki
(na) 非協力的(な)

uncork *bottle* ... no koruku-sen o
nuku ...のコルク栓を抜く

uncover (*remove cover from*) ... no
ōi o toru ...の覆いを取る; *plot*
bakuro suru 暴露する; *ancient*
remains hakkutsu suru 発掘する

undamaged higai o ukete inai 被害
を受けていない

undaunted: *carry on* ~ kujikenaide
tsuzukeru くじけないで続ける

undecided kimatte inai 決まってい
ない; *be* ~ *about* ... ni tsuite mada
kimete inai ...についてまだ決めて
いない

undeniable hitei dekinai 否定でき

undeniably tashika ni 確かに

under 1 *prep* ... no shita ni ...の下
に; (*less than*) ...miman de ...未満
で; *it is* ~ *review / investigation*
sore wa minaoshi-chū / chōsa-chū
de aru それは見直し中/調査中で
ある **2** *adv* (*anesthetized*)
muishiki-jōtai ni 無意識状態に

underage *drinking etc* miseinen
(no) 未成年(の); *be* ~ miseinen de
aru 未成年である

underarm *adv throw* jakushita nage
(no) 下手投げ(の)

undercarriage chakuriku-sōchi 着
陸装置

undercover *adj agent* naimitsu
(no) 内密(の)

undercut *v/t* COM ...yori yasui ne
de uru ...より安い値で売る

underdog jakusha 弱者

underdone *meat* namayake (no) 生
焼け(の)

underestimate *v/t person, skills,*
task mikubiru 見くびる

underexposed PHOT roshutsu-
busoku (no) 露出不足(の)

underfed eiyōbusoku (no) 栄養不足
(の)

undergo *surgery, treatment* ukeru
受ける; *experience* keiken suru 経
験する

underground 1 *adj passage etc*
chika (no) 地下(の); POL:
resistance, newpaper etc
chikasoshiki (no) 地下組織(の)
2 *adv work* chika de 地下で; *go* ~
POL chika ni moguru 地下にもぐる

undergrowth shitabae 下生え

underhand *adj* (*devious*) fusei (na)
不正(な)

underlie *v/t* (*form basis of*) ... no
kiso ni natte iru ...の基礎になって
いる

underline *v/t text* kasen o hiku 下線
を引く

underlying *causes, problems*
kihonteki (na) 基本的(な)

undermine *s.o.'s position*
yowameru 弱める; *theory*
yurugasu 揺るがす

underneath 1 *prep* ... no shita ni ... の下に **2** *adv* shita ni 下に

underpants pantsu パンツ

underpass (*for pedestrians*) chikadō 地下道

underprivileged megumarenai 恵まれない

underrate *v/t* mikubiru 見くびる

undershirt hadagi 肌着

undersized *person* kogara (no) 小柄(の)

underskirt pechikōto ペチコート

understaffed hitodebusoku (no) 人手不足(の)

understand 1 *v/t* rikai suru 理解する; **I ~ that you** anata wa ... da to kiite imasu あなたは...だと聞いています; **they are understood to be in Canada** karera wa Kanada ni iru to omowarete iru 彼らはカナダにいると思われている **2** *v/i* wakaranai わからない

understandable rikai dekiru 理解できる

understandably: **they were ~ annoyed** karera ga mutto shita no wa tōzen da 彼らがむっとしたのは当然だ

understanding 1 *adj person* omoiyari no aru 思いやりのある **2** *n* (*of problem, situation*) rikai 理解; (*agreement*) gōi 合意; **on the ~ that** ... no jōken de ...の条件で

understatement hikaeme na hyōgen 控えめな表現

undertake *task* hikiukeru 引き受ける; **~ to do X** (*agree to*) X o suru koto o hikiukeru Xをすることを引き受ける

undertaking (*enterprise*) jigyō 事業; (*promise*) yakusoku 約束

undervalue *v/t* kashō-hyōka suru 過小評価する

underwear shitagi 下着

underweight *adj* taijū-fusoku (no) 体重不足(の)

underworld (*criminal*) ankokugai 暗黒街; (*in mythology*) ano yo あの世

underwrite *v/t* FIN ... no hoken o hikiukeru ...の保険を引き受ける

undeserved *praise* fusōō (na) 不相応(な); *blame* futō (na) 不当(な)

undesirable konomashiku nai 好ましくない; **~ elements** konomashiku nai renchū 好ましくない連中

undisputed *champion, leader* monku nashi (no) 文句無し(の)

undo *parcel, envelop* akeru 開ける; *wrapping, shoelaces* hodoku ほどく; *buttons* hazusu はずす; *shirt* nugu 脱ぐ; *s.o. else's work* muda ni suru 無駄にする

undoubtedly utagau yochi naku 疑う余地なく

undreamt-of *riches* yume ni mo omowanai 夢にも思わない

undress 1 *v/t* ifuku o nugaseru 衣服を脱がせる; **get ~ed** ifuku o nugu 衣服を脱ぐ **2** *v/i* ifuku o nugu 衣服を脱ぐ

undue (*excessive*) yokei (na) 余計(な)

unduly futō ni 不当に

unearth *ancient remains* hakkutsu suru 発掘する; *fig* (*find*) hakken suru 発見する; *secret* abaku 暴く

unearthly: **at this ~ hour** tondemonai jikan ni とんでもない時間に

uneasy *relationship, peace* fuantei (na) 不安定(な); **feel ~ about** ... o fuan ni kanjiru ...を不安に感じる

uneatable taberarenai 食べられない

uneconomic fukeizai (na) 不経済

uneducated mugaku (no) 無学(の)

unemployed shitsugyō shita 失業した; **the ~** shitsugyō-sha 失業者

unemployment shitsugyō 失業

unending hateshinai 果てしない

unequal fubyōdō (na) 不平等(な); **be ~ to the task** sono shigoto ni wa taerarenai その仕事には耐えられない

unerring *judgment, instinct* kakujitsu (na) 確実(な)

uneven *quality* fuzoroi (no) 不ぞろい(の); *surface, ground* dekoboko (no) でこぼこ(の)

unevenly *distributed, applied* fukisoku ni 不規則に; **~ matched** tsuriatte inai 釣り合っていない

uneventful tanchō (na) 単調(な)

unexpected omoigakenai 思いがけない

unexpectedly fui ni 不意に

unfair futō (na) 不当(な)

unfaithful *husband, wife* uwaki (na) 浮気(な); **be ~ to** ... ni taishite fuseijitsu de aru ...に対して不誠実である

unfamiliar shiranai 知らない; **be ~ with** ... o yoku shiranai ...を良く知らない

unfasten *belt* hazusu はずす

unfavorable *report, conditions* yoku nai 良くない; *review* hihanteki (na) 批判的(な)

unfeeling *person* reikoku (na) 冷酷(な)

unfinished mikansei (no) 未完成(の); **leave ~** ... o tochū de hotte oku ...を途中でほっておく

unfit (*physically*) undōbusoku (no) 運動不足(の); (*morally*) ... ni fumuki (na) ...に不向き(な); **be ~ to eat/drink** nomu/taberu no ni tekishite inai 飲む/食べるのに適していない

unfix *part* torihazusu 取り外す

unflappable heizen to shita 平然とした

unfold 1 *v/t sheets* hirogeru 広げる; *letter* hiraku 開く; *one's arms* hodoku ほどく **2** *v/i (of story etc)* tenkai suru 展開する; (*of view*) hirogaru 広がる

unforeseen omoigakenai 思いがけない

unforgettable wasurerarenai 忘れられない

unforgivable yurusenai 許せない; **that was ~ of you** sore wa yurusenai それは許せない

unfortunate (*wretched*) aware (na) 哀れ(な); (*unlucky*) fukō (na) 不幸(な); *choice of words* mazui まずい; **that's ~ for you** sore wa zannen da それは残念だ

unfortunately zannen nagara 残念ながら

unfounded konkyo no nai 根拠のない

unfriendly fushinsetsu (na) 不親切(な); *software* tsukai nikui 使いにくい

unfurnished kagutsuki de nai 家具付きでない

ungodly: **at this ~ hour** tondemonai jikan ni とんでもない時間に

ungrateful onshirazu (no) 恩知らず(の)

unhappiness fukō 不幸

unhappy fukō (na) 不幸(な); *customers etc* fuman (na) 不満(な); **be ~ with an explanation** setsumei ni fuman ga aru 説明に不満がある

unharmed buji (na) 無事(な)

unhealthy *person* fukenkō (na) 不健康(な); *food, conditions* kenkō ni warui 健康に悪い; *atmosphere, economy* fukenzen (na) 不健全(な)

unheard-of (*shocking*) zendaimimon (no) 前代未聞(の); (*unknown*) shirarete inai 知られていない

unhurt buji (na) 無事(な)

unhygienic hieiseiteki (na) 非衛生的(な)

unification tōitsu 統一

uniform 1 *n* seifuku 制服; (*SP*) yunifōmu ユニフォーム **2** *adj* ittei (no) 一定(の)

unify tōitsu suru 統一する

unilateral ippōteki (na) 一方的(な)

unimaginable sōzō dekinai 想像できない

unimaginative sōzōteki de nai 創造的でない; (*boring*) taikutsu (na) 退屈(な)

unimportant jūyō de nai 重要でない

uninhabitable hito ga sumenai 人が住めない

uninhabited mujin (no) 無人(の)

uninjured kizutsuite inai 傷ついていない

unintelligible rikai dekinai 理解できない

unintentional koi de nai 故意でない

unintentionally muishiki ni 無意識に

uninteresting tsumaranai つまらない

uninterrupted *sleep, two hours' work* togirenai 途切れない

union POL rengō 連合; (*labor ~*) rōdō-kumiai 労働組合

unique dokutoku (no) 独特(の);F (*very good*) yunīku (na) ユニーク(な); *with his own ~ humor* kare dokutoku no yūmoa 彼独特のユーモア

unit (*of measurement*) tan'i 単位; (*section: of machine, structure*) yunitto ユニット; (*part with separate function*) buhin 部品; (*department*) bu 部; MIL butai 部隊

unit cost COM tanka 単価

unite 1 *v/t* hitotsu ni suru 一つにする; *country* ketsugō suru 結合する **2** *v/i* danketsu suru 団結する

united hitotsu ni natta 一つになった; *effort* danketsu shita 団結した

United Kingdom Rengō-ōkoku 連合王国

United Nations 1 *n* Kokusai-rengō 国際連合 **2** *adj* Kokuren (no) 国連の

United States (of America) (Amerika) Gasshūkoku (アメリカ)合衆国

unity kessoku 結束; (*harmony*) chōwa 調和

universal fuhenteki (na) 普遍的(な)

universally fuhenteki ni 普遍的に

universe uchū 宇宙

university daigaku 大学; *he is at ~* kare wa daigakusei desu 彼は大学生です

unjust futō (na) 不当(な)

unkempt *appearance* darashi no nai だらしのない; *hair* mojamoja (no) もじゃもじゃ(の)

unkind fushinsetsu (na) 不親切(な)

unknown 1 *adj* shirarete inai 知られていない **2** *n: a journey into the ~* michi no sekai e no tabi 未知の世界への旅

unleaded *adj* muen (no) 無鉛の

unless: *don't say anything ~ you're sure* moshi tashika de nakereba nanimo iu na もし確か

でなければ何も言うな; *~ he pays us tomorrow...* moshi kare ga ashita harawanai nara... もし彼が明日払わないなら...

unlike *prep* ... to chigatte ...と違って; *it's ~ him to drink so much* sonna ni takusan nomu nante kare rashikunai そんなにたくさん飲むなんて彼らしくない; *the photograph was completely ~ her* shashin wa kanojo to zenzen nite inai 写真は彼女と全然似ていない

unlikely arisō mo nai ありそうもない; *he is ~ to win* kare wa kachisō de nai 彼は勝ちそうでない; *it is ~ that* ... to iu koto wa arisō mo nai ...ということはありそうもない

unlimited museigen (no) 無制限(の)

unlisted: *be ~* denwachō ni dete inai 電話帳に出ていない

unlock kagi o akeru 鍵を開ける

unluckily un no warui koto ni 運の悪い事に

unlucky *day, choice* fuun (na) 不運(な); *number* engi no warui 縁起の悪い; *person* fukō (na) 不幸(な); *that was so ~ for you!* sore wa un ga warukatta ne それは運が悪かったね

unmade-up *face* suppin (no) 素っぴん(の)

unmanned *spacecraft* mujin (no) 無人(の)

unmarried mikon (no) 未婚(の)

unmistakable machigaeyō no nai 間違えようのない

unmoved (*emotionally*) kokoro o ugokasarenai 心を動かされない

unmusical *person* ongakuteki de nai 音楽的でない; *sounds* mimizawari (na) 耳障り(な)

unnatural fushizen (na) 不自然(な); *it's not ~ to be annoyed* mutto shite tōzen de aru むっとして当然である

unnecessary fuhitsuyō (na) 不必要(な)

unnerving ki o sogu-yō (na) 気をそ
ぐよう(な)

unnoticed: *it went ~* miotosarete
ita 見落とされていた

unobtainable *goods* te ni ireru koto
no dekinai 手に入れる事のできな
い; *the number is ~* TELEC kono
bangō wa genzai tsukawarete
orimasen この番号は現在使われて
おりません

unobtrusive *person* hikaeme (na)
控えめ(な); *thing* medatanai 目立
たない

unoccupied *building, house* hito no
sunde inai 人の住んでいない;
person burabura shite iru ぶらぶ
らしている; *~ post* ketsuin 欠員; *~
room* akibeya 空き部屋

unofficial kōhyō sarete inai 公表さ
れていない; *strike, action* kōnin
sarete inai 公認されていない

unofficially hikōshiki ni wa 非公式
には

unpack 1 *v/t* ... no nakami o
dashite katazukeru ...の中身を出
して片づける **2** *v/i* nimotsu o
dashite katazukeru 荷物を出して
片づける

unpaid *work* mukyū (no) 無給(の);
invoice miharai (no) 未払い(の)

unpleasant fuyukai (na) 不愉快
(な); *he was very ~ to her* kare
wa kanojo ni totemo burei datta
彼は彼女にとても無礼だった

unplug *v/t* TV, *computer* konsento o
nuku コンセントを抜く

unpopular *person* ninki no nai 人気
のない; *decision* fuhyō (no) 不評
(の)

unprecedented zenrei no nai 前例
のない; *it was ~ for a woman to
...* josei ga ... suru no wa zendaimimon datta 女性が...するのは前
代未聞だった

unpredictable yosō dekinai 予想で
きない

unprincipled sessō no nai 節操のな
い

unpretentious *person, style,*
hikaeme (na) 控えめ(な); *hotel*
hade de nai 派手でない

unproductive *meeting, discussion*
hiseisanteki (na) 非生産的(な);
soil minori no nai 実りのない

unprofessional *person, behavior*
shokugyōrinri ni hansuru 職業倫
理に反する; *workmanship* shirōto
(no) 素人(の)

unprofitable rieki no nai 利益のない

unpronounceable hatsuon shinikui
発音しにくい

unprotected *borders* bōbi nashi
(no) 防備なし(の); *machine* kabā
nashi (no) カバーなし(の); *~ sex*
kondōmu nashi no sekkusu コン
ドームなしのセックス

unprovoked *attack* seitō na riyū no
nai 正当な理由のない

unqualified *worker, doctor etc*
shikaku no nai 資格のない

unquestionably (*without doubt*)
utagai mo naku 疑いもなく

unquestioning *attitude, loyalty*
utagawanai 疑わない

unravel *v/t* *string, knitting* hogusu
ほぐす; *mystery, complexities*
kaimei suru 解明する

unreadable *book* yominikui 読みに
くい

unreal (*not matching reality*)
higenjitsuteki (na) 非現実的(な);
(*that doesn't actually exist*) kakū
(no) 架空(の); *this is ~!* F
shinjirarenai 信じられない

unrealistic higenjitsuteki (na) 非現
実的(な)

unreasonable *person* riseiteki de
nai 理性的でない; *demand,
expectation* futō (na) 不当(な)

unrelated *issues* kankei no nai 関係
のない; *people* shinzoku de nai 親
族でない

unrelenting yōsha nai 容赦ない

unreliable *person* shinrai dekinai
信頼できない; *car, machine* ate ni
naranai 当てにならない

unrest fuan 不安

unrestrained *emotions* yokusei
sarenai 抑制されない

unroadworthy rojō-shiyō ni
tekishite inai 路上使用に適してい
ない

unroll v/t carpet, scroll hirogeru 広げる

unruly te ni oenai 手に負えない

unsafe kiken (na) 危険(な); **~ to drink / eat** nomu / taberu no ni tekishite inai 飲む/食べるのに適していない

unsanitary conditions, drains hieiseiteki (na) 非衛生的(な)

unsatisfactory fumanzoku (na) 不満足(な)

unsavory person, reputation konomashikunai 好ましくない; district ikagawashii いかがわしい

unscathed person mukizu (no) 無傷(の); thing songai o ukete inai 損害を受けていない

unscrew ... no neji o nuku ...のネジを抜く; top nejitte akeru ねじって開ける

unscrupulous akutoku 悪徳

unselfish omoiyari no aru 思いやりのある

unsettled issue mikettei (no) 未決定(の); weather, stock market kawariyasui 変わりやすい; lifestyle ochitsukanai 落ち着かない; bills miharai (no) 未払い(の)

unshaven bushōhige (no) 無精ひげ(の)

unsightly minikui 醜い

unskilled mijuku (na) 未熟(な)

unsociable buaisō (na) 無愛想(な)

unsophisticated person, beliefs senren sarete inai 洗練されていない; equipment tanjun (na) 単純(な)

unstable person jōcho-fuantei (na) 情緒不安定(な); structure, region, economy fuantei (na) 不安定(な)

unsteady (on one's feet) furafura shita ふらふらした; ladder guragura shita ぐらぐらした

unstinting: she was ~ in her efforts kanojo wa oshiminai doryoku o shita 彼女は惜しみない努力をした; she was ~ in her generosity kanojo wa oshiminai yasashi-sa o ataeta 彼女は惜しみない優しさを与えた

unstuck: come ~ (of notice etc) hagareru はがれる; F (of plan etc)

dame ni naru だめになる

unsuccessful writer etc urete inai 売れていない; candidate rakusen shita 落選した; party tsumaranai つまらない; attempt shippai shita 失敗した; he tried but was ~ kare wa yatte mita ga shippai datta 彼はやってみたが失敗だった

unsuccessfully try, apply shippai shite 失敗して

unsuitable futekitō (na) 不適当(な); clothes bachigai (no) 場違い(の)

unsuspecting kizuite inai 気付いていない

unswerving loyalty, devotion kakko to shita 確固とした

unthinkable kangaerarenai 考えられない

untidy room, desk, chirakatta 散らかった; hair, appearance darashinai だらしない

untie knot, laces hodoku ほどく; prisoner nawa o toku 縄を解く

until 1 prep ...made ...まで; **from Monday ~ Friday** getsuyōbi kara kin'yōbi made 月曜日から金曜日まで; I can wait ~ tomorrow ashita made matemasu 明日まで待てます; not ~ Friday kin'yōbi made wa dame da 金曜日まではだめだ; it won't be finished ~ July shichigatsu made wa owaranai deshō 7月までは終わらないでしょう **2** conj ...suru made ...するまで; can you wait ~ I'm ready? watashi no junbi ga dekiru made matte kureru 私の準備ができるまで待ってくれる; they won't do anything ~ you say so karera wa anata ga sō iu made nani mo shinai de shō 彼らはあなたがそう言うまで何もしないでしょう

untimely ori no warui 折りの悪い; ~ death hayajini 早死に

untiring efforts tayumanu たゆまぬ

untold riches, suffering hakarishirenai はかりしれない; story akiraka ni sarete inai 明らかにされていない

untranslatable hon'yaku dekinai 翻

訳できない

untrue uso (no) うそ(の)

unused[1] *goods* mishiyō (no) 未使用 (の)

unused[2]: *be ~ to...* ... ni narete inai ...に慣れていない; *be ~ to doing X* X suru koto ni narete inai Xする ことに慣れていない

unusual (*rare*) mezurashii 珍しい; (*strange*) kawatta 変わった

unusually mezurashiku 珍しく; *it is ~ cold for the time of year* kono jiki ni shite wa hijō ni samui この 時期にしては非常に寒い

unveil *memorial etc* ... no jomakushiki o okonau ...の除幕式 を行う

unwell kibun ga warui 気分が悪い

unwilling: *be ~ to do X* X suru no o iyagatte iru Xするのを嫌がってい る

unwind 1 *v/t tape* hodoku ほどく **2** *v/i* (*of tape*) hodokeru ほどける; (*of story*) hakkiri suru はっきりす る; (*relax*) kutsurogu くつろぐ

unwise asahaka (na) 浅はか(な)

unwrap *v/t gift* akeru 開ける

unwritten: *~ rule* fubunritsu 不文律

unzip *v/t dress etc* fasunā o sageru ファスナーを下げる;COMPUT asshuku fairu o kaitō suru 圧縮 ファイルを解凍する

up 1 *adv* ue e 上へ; *~ in the sky* sora no ue ni 空の上に; *~ on the roof* yane no ue ni 屋根の上に; *~ here/there* kono/ano ue この/あ の上を; *be ~* (*out of bed*) okite iru; (*of sun*) nobotte iru 昇っている; (*be built*) tatte iru ; (*of shelves*) sonaetsukerarete iru 備え付けら れている; (*of prices, temperature*) agatte iru ; (*have expired*) kigen ga kirete iru 期限が切れている; *your time is ~* jikan-gire desu 時 間切れです; *what's ~?* nani ka atta 何かあった; *~ to the year 1989* sen kyūhyaku hachijūkyū nen made 千九百八十九年まで; *he came ~ to me* kare ga watashi no tokoro ni yatte kita 彼が私のとこ ろにやって来た; *what are you ~*

to these days? saikin dō shite iru 最近どうしている; *what are those kids ~ to?* ano kodomotachi wa nani yatte irun darō あの子供たち は何やっているんだろう; *be ~ to something* (*bad*) nani ka takurande iru 何かたくらんでいる; *I don't feel ~ to it* watashi wa sore ni tsuite ikenai to omoimasu 私はそれについていけないと思い ます; *it's ~ to you* anata shidai desu あなた次第です; *it is ~ to them to solve it* karera no sekinin de kaiketsu suru koto desu 彼らの責任で解決することで す; *be ~ and about* (*after illness*) okireru yō ni naru narareru yō ni naる 2 *prep* ue ni 上に; *further ~ the mountain* yama no ue no hō ni 山の上の方に; *he climbed ~ a tree* kare wa ki ni nobotta 彼は木に 登った; *they ran ~ the street* tōrizoi ni hashitta 通り沿いに走っ た; *the water goes ~ this pipe* mizu wa kono paipu o agatte iku 水はこのパイプを上がっていく; *we traveled ~ to Sendai* watashitachi wa Sendai e ryokō shita 私達は仙 台へ旅行した 3 *n*: *~s and downs* ukishizumi 浮き沈み

upbringing shitsuke しつけ

upcoming *adj* (*forthcoming*) mamonaku yatte kuru まもなく やって来る

update 1 *v/t file, records* kōshin suru 更新する; *~ X on Y* Y no saishinjōhō o X ni shiraseru Yの 最新情報をXに知らせる 2 *n* (*of files, records*) kōshin 更新; (*software version*) saishinban 最 新版; *can you give me an ~ on the situation?* saishin no jōkyō o oshiete kuremasu ka 最新の状況 を教えてくれます

upgrade 1 *v/t computer, product etc* hinshitsu o takameru 品質を高める; (*replace with new versions*) gurēdo appu suru グレードアップする; *ticket* kakuage suru 格上げする

upheaval (*emotional*) dōyō 動揺; (*physical*) hendō 変動; (*political,* social) dōran 動乱

uphill 1 adv walk ue no hō e 上のほ
うへ **2** adj struggle taihen (na) 大
変(な)

uphold traditions, rights mamoru 守
る; (vindicate) mitomeru 認める

upholstery (covering) isu ni hatta
kiji いすに張った生地; (padding)
isu ni tsukau tsumemono いすに使
う詰め物

upkeep n (of buildings, parks etc)
iji-kanri 維持管理

upload v/t COMPUT sābā ni dēta o
okuru サーバーにデータを送る

upmarket adj restaurant, hotel
kōshotoku-sō (no) 高所得層(の)

upon → **on**

upper part of sth jōbu (no) 上部
(の); stretches of a river jōryū
(no) 上流(の)

upper atmosphere taikiken no
saijōsō 大気圏の最上層; **upper-
class** jōryū-kaikyū (no) 上流階級
(の); **upper classes** jōryū-kaikyū
上流階級; **upper deck** uekanban
上甲板

upright 1 adj citizen shōjiki (na) 正
直(な) **2** adv sit massugu ni 真っす
ぐに

upright (piano) tate piano たてピア
ノ

uprising bōdō 暴動

uproar (loud noise) ōsawagi 大騒
ぎ; (protest) kōgi 抗議

upset 1 v/t drink, glass
hikkurikaesu ひっくり返す;
(emotionally) kanashimaseru 悲
しませる **2** adj (emotionally)
kanashimu 悲しむ; **get ~ about** ...
de kanashimu ...で悲しむ; **have
an ~ stomach** onaka o kowashite
iru おなかをこわしている

upsetting tsurai つらい

upshot (result) kekka 結果

upside down adv sakasama ni 逆さ
まに; **turn ~** box etc ... o sakasama
ni suru ...を逆さまにする

upstairs 1 adv ue no kai ni 上の階
に; **he went ~** kare wa nikai ni itta
彼は二階に行った **2** adj room ue
no kai (no) 上の階(の)

upstart n nariagari 成り上がり

upstream adv jōryū ni 上流に

uptight F (nervous) piripiri shita ぴ
りぴりした; (inhibited)
katakurushii 堅苦しい

up-to-date information saishin
(no) 最新(の); fashions saishin-
ryūkō (no) 最新流行(の)

upturn (in economy) kōten 好転

upward adv fly, move uemuki ni 上
向きに; **~ of 10,000** ichiman o
koeta 一万を超えた

uranium uraniumu ウラニウム

urban toshi (no) 都市(の)

urbanization toshika 都市化

urchin gaki がき; **street ~** furōji 浮
浪児

urge 1 n shōdō 衝動 **2** v/t: **~ X to do
Y** X ni Y suru yō ni susumeru Xに
Yするように勧める

♦ **urge on** ... o hagemasu ...を励ます

urgency kinkyūsei 緊急性

urgent job, letter kinkyū (na) 緊急
(な); **be in ~ need of** ... no
hitsuyō ni semararete iru ...の必
要に迫られている; **is it ~?** kinkyū
no yō desu ka 緊急の用ですか

urinate hainyō suru 排尿する

urine nyō 尿

urn tsubo つぼ

US (= **United States**) Gasshūkoku
合衆国

us ◊ **who's that? – it's ~** dare desu
ka - watashitachi desu 誰です か –
私達です; **that's for ~** sore wa
watashitachi no tame desu それは
私達のためです ◊ (direct object)
watashitachi o 私達を; **they helped
~** karera wa watashitachi o
tasuketa 彼らは私達を助けた ◊
(indirect object) watashitachi ni
私達に; **can you fax it to ~?**
watashitachi ni fakkusu shite
moraemasu ka 私達にファックス
してもらえますか

USA (= **United States of
America**) Amerika-gasshūkoku
アメリカ合衆国

usable shiyō dekiru 使用できる

usage (linguistic) kan'yō 慣用

use 1 v/t tool, word tsukau 使う;

skills, knowledge katsuyō suru 活用する; *s.o.'s car* kariru 借りる; *a lot of gas* shōhi suru 消費する; *pej person* riyō suru 利用する; *I could ~ a drink* F nomitai 飲みたい **2** *n* shiyō 使用; *be of great ~ to* ... no totemo yaku ni tatsu ...のとても役に立つ; *be of no ~ to* ... no zenzen yaku ni tatanai ...の全然役に立たない; *is that of any ~?* nanika no yaku ni tatsu 何かの役に立つ; *it's no ~* muda desu 無駄です; *it's no ~ trying/waiting* yatte mo muda desu/matte mo muda desu やっても無駄です/待っても無駄です

♦ **use up** ... o tsukaihatasu ...を使い果たす

used[1] *car etc* chūko (no) 中古(の)

used[2]: *be ~ to* ... ni narete iru ...に慣れている; *get ~ to* ... ni narete kuru ...に慣れてくる; *be ~ to doing X* X suru no ni narete iru ...するのに慣れている; *get ~ to doing X* X suru no ni narete kuru Xするのに慣れてくる

used[3]: *I ~ to like/know him* izen kare o suki datta/shitte ita 以前彼を好きだった/知っていた; *I don't work there now, but I ~ to* ima soko de wa hataraite inai, shikashi izen wa hataraite ita 今そこでは働いていないしかし、以前は働いていた

useful yaku ni tatsu 役に立つ

usefulness jitsuyōsei 実用性

useless *information* yaku ni tatanai 役に立たない; F *person* yakutatazu (no) 役立たず(の); *machine, computer* tsukaenai 使えない; *it's ~ trying* yattemo muda de aru やっても無駄である

user *(of product)* shiyō-sha 使用者

user-friendly tsukaiyasui 使いやすい

usher *n* annaigakari 案内係

♦ **usher in** *new era* ... no sakigake to naru ...の先駆けとなる

usual itsumo (no) いつも(の); *(customary)* futsū (no) 普通(の); *as ~* itsumo no yō ni いつもの様に; *the ~, please* itsumo no kudasai いつもの下さい

usually futsū wa 普通は

utensil yōgu 用具; *kitchen ~* daidokoro-yōhin 台所用品

uterus shikyū 子宮

utility *(usefulness)* jitsuyōsei 実用性; *public utilities* kōkyō-jigyō 公共事業

utilize riyō suru 利用する

utmost 1 *adj caution, difficulty* saidai (no) 最大(の); *tact, skill* saikō (no) 最高(の) **2** *n: do one's ~* saizen o tsukusu 最善を尽くす

utter 1 *adj* kanzen (na) 完全(な) **2** *v/t sound* hassuru 発する

utterly mattaku 全く

U-turn yū-tān Uターン; *(in policy)* hyakuhachijūdo no hōkō-tenkan 百八十度の方向転換

V

vacant *building* aite iru 空いている; *position* ketsuin ni natte iru 欠員になっている; *look, expression* utsuro (na) うつろ(な)

vacate *room* akeru 空ける

vacation *n* kyūka 休暇; *be on ~* kyūkachū de aru 休暇中である; *go*

to ... *on ~* ... de kyūka o sugosu ...で休暇を過ごす

vacationer kōrakukyaku 行楽客

vaccinate ... ni yobō-sesshu o suru ...に予防接種をする; *be ~d against* ... ... ni tai suru yobō-sesshu o ukete iru ...に対する予防

接種を受けている
vaccination wakuchin-sesshu ワクチン接種
vaccine wakuchin ワクチン
vacuum 1 *n* PHYS shinkū 真空; *fig (in one's life)* kūhaku 空白 **2** *v/t floors* sōjiki o kakeru 掃除機をかける
vacuum cleaner denki-sōjiki 電気掃除機; **vacuum flask** mahōbin 魔法瓶; **vacuum-packed** shinkū-pakku (no) 真空パック(の)
vagina chitsu 膣
vaginal chitsu (no) 膣(の)
vague *answer, wording* aimai (na) あいまい(な); *feeling, resemblance* hakkiri shinai はっきりしない; *taste of sth* honoka (na) ほのか(な); *he was very ~ about it* kare wa sore ni tsuite zenzen hakkiri shite inai 彼はそれについて全然はっきりしていない
vaguely *answer* bakuzen to 漠然と; *(slightly)* nantonaku 何となく; *possible* tabun たぶん
vain 1 *adj person* unubore iru うぬぼれている; *hope* muda (na) 無駄(な) **2** *n*: *in ~* munashiku むなしく; *their efforts were in ~* karera no doryoku wa muda datta 彼等の努力は無駄だった
valet *(person)* meshitsukai 召し使い
valet service *(for clothes)* kurīningu sābisu クリーニングサービス; *(for cars)* kuruma no sensha sābisu 車の洗車サービス
valiant yūkan (na) 勇敢(な)
valid *passport, document* yūkō (na) 有効(な); *reason, argument* datō (na) 妥当(な)
validate *(with official stamp)* yūkō ni suru 有効にする; *(back up)* shōmei suru 証明する
validity *(of reason, argument)* datōsei 妥当性; *(of ticket, document)* yūkōsei 有効性
valley tani 谷
valuable 1 *adj help, advice* kichō (na) 貴重(な); *jewel* kōka (na) 高価(な) **2** *n*: *~s* kichōhin 貴重品

valuation *(estimate)* kachi 価値; *(value as calculated by expert)* hyōka 評価; *at his ~* kare no hyōka de wa 彼の評価では
value 1 *n* kachi 価値; *(expressed in monetary terms)* kakaku 価格; *be good ~* kachi ga aru 価値がある; *get ~ for money* kane ni miau mono o eru 金に見合うものを得る; *rise / fall in ~* kachi ga agaru / sagaru 価値が上がる/下がる **2** *v/t s.o.'s friendship, one's freedom* sonchō suru 尊重する; *I ~ your advice* anata no jogen o sonchō shimasu あなたの助言を尊重します; *have an object ~d* kachi no mitsumori o suru 価値の見積もりをする
valve barubu バルブ; *(in heart)* ben 弁
van ban バン
vandal kokoronai hakai-sha 心無い破壊者
vandalism hakai-kōdō 破壊行動
vandalize hakai suru 破壊する
vanilla 1 *n* banira バニラ **2** *adj* banira (no) バニラ(の)
vanish kieru 消える
vanity *(of person)* kyoeishin 虚栄心; *(of hopes)* munashi-sa むなしさ
vanity case keshō-pōchi 化粧ポーチ
vantage point *(on hill etc)* kansatsuten 観察点
vapor jōki 蒸気
vaporize *v/t (of bomb)* jōhatsu saseru 蒸発させる
vapor trail hikōki-gumo 飛行機雲
variable 1 *adj amount* sadamaranai 定まらない; *moods, weather* kawariyasui 変わりやすい **2** *n* MATH, COMPUT hensū 変数
variation henka 変化
varicose vein jōmyakuryū 静脈瘤
varied *quality* samazama (na) 様々(な); *range* iroiro (na) 色々(な); *diet* katayoranai 偏らない
variety henka 変化; *(type)* shurui 種類; *a ~ of things to do* suru koto ga iroiro aru する事が色々ある
various *(several)* samazama (na) 様々(な); *(different)* iroiro (na)

色々(な)

varnish 1 n (for wood) nisu ニス; (for nails) manikyua マニキュア **2** v/t wood ... ni nisu o nuru ...にニスを塗る; nails ... ni manikyua suru ...にマニキュアする

vary 1 v/i henka suru 変化する; it varies sono toki ni yotte chigau その時によって違う **2** v/t henka o tsukeru 変化をつける

vase kabin 花瓶

vast desert, city kōdai (na) 広大(な); collection bōdai (na) 膨大(な); knowledge, sum of money bakudai (na) ばく大(な)

vaudeville baraetī-shō バラエティーショー

vault¹ n (in roof) marutenjō 丸天井; ~s (for wine) chika-chozōshitsu 地下貯蔵室; (of bank) kinkoshitsu 金庫室

vault² **1** n SP chōba 跳馬 **2** v/t fence etc tobikoeru 飛び越える

VCR (= video cassette recorder) bideo ビデオ

veal koushiniku 子牛肉

vegan 1 n kanzen-saishokushugi-sha 完全菜食主義者 **2** adj kanzen-saishokushugi (no) 完全菜食主義(の)

vegetable yasai 野菜

vegetarian 1 n saishoku-shugisha 菜食主義者 **2** adj saishoku-shugi (no) 菜食主義(の)

vehicle kuruma 車; (for information etc) shudan 手段

veil 1 n bēru ベール **2** v/t bēru de ōu ベールで覆う

vein ANAT jōmyaku 静脈

Velcro® n berukuro ベルクロ

velocity sokudo 速度

velvet n berubetto ベルベット

vending machine jidō-hanbaiki 自動販売機

vendor LAW urite 売り手

veneer (on wood) keshōbari 化粧張り; (of politeness etc) misekake 見せかけ

venereal disease seibyō 性病

venetian blind itasudare 板すだれ

vengeance fukushū 復しゅう; with

venison shikaniku しか肉

venom (of snake) doku 毒

vent n (for air) tsūkikō 通気孔; give ~ to feelings, emotions ... o hakidasu ...を吐き出す

ventilate room, building ... no kanki o suru ...の換気をする

ventilation kanki 換気

ventilation shaft kankikō 換気孔

ventilator kanki-sōchi 換気装置

ventriloquist fukuwajutsu-shi 腹話術師

venture 1 n (undertaking) benchā-jigyō ベンチャー事業; COM tōki 投機 **2** v/i omoikitte... suru 思い切って...する

venue kaisaichi 開催地

veranda pōchi ポーチ; (in Japanese houses) engawa 縁側

verb dōshi 動詞

verdict LAW hyōketsu 評決; (opinion, judgment) iken 意見

verge n (of road) rokata 路肩; be on the ~ of ruin, collapse ... no sunzen de aru ...の寸前である; of tears ima ni mo...shisō de aru 今にも...しそうである

♦verge on ...dōzen de aru ...同然である

verification shōmei 証明; (confirmation) kakunin 確認

verify (check out) shōmei suru 証明する; (confirm) kakunin suru 確認する

vermin (animals) gaijū 害獣; (fleas, lice) gaichū 害虫

vermouth berumotto ベルモット

vernacular n hanashi-kotoba 話し言葉

versatile person tasai (no) 多才(の); machine, tool tsukaimichi no ōi 使い道の多い

versatility (of person) tasai 多才; (of machine, tool) bannō 万能

verse (poetry) shi 詩; (part of poem, song) setsu 節

versed: be well ~ in ... ni kuwashii ...に詳しい

version kata 型; (of book, report) ban 版; (of events) setsumei 説明

versus SP, LAW tai 対

vertebra sekitsuikotsu せきつい骨

vertebrate n sekitsui-dōbutsu せきつい動物

vertical suichoku (no) 垂直(の)

vertigo memai めまい

very 1 adv totemo とても; was it cold? – not ~ samukatta – anmari 寒かった - あんまり; the ~ best saikō (no) 最高(の) **2** adj chōdo ちょうど; in the ~ act genkōhan de 現行犯で; that's the ~ thing I need kore ga masa ni watashi ga hitsuyō to shite iru mono desu これがまさに私が必要としている物です; the ~ thought of ... o kangaeta dake de ...を考えただけで; right at the ~ top / bottom sono ichiban ue / shita その一番上/下

vessel NAUT fune 船

vest besuto ベスト

vestige (of previous civilization etc) keiseki 形跡; (of truth) kakera かけら

vet[1] (for animals) jūi 獣医

vet[2] v/t applicants etc shinsa suru 審査する

veteran 1 n (of war) taieki-gunjin 退役軍人; (old hand) beteran ベテラン **2** adj (old) beteran (no) ベテラン(の); (experienced) rōren (na) 老練(な)

veterinarian jūi 獣医

veto 1 n kyohiken 拒否権 **2** v/t ... ni kyohiken o kōshi suru ...に拒否権を行使する

vexed (worried) komatta 困った; the ~ question of ... ... no yakkai na mondai ...のやっかいな問題

via keiyu de 経由で

viable life form seichō dekiru 成長できる; company ikinokoresō (na) 生き残れそう(な); alternative, plan jikkō kanō (na) 実行可能(な)

vibrate v/i shindō suru 振動する

vibration shindō 振動

vice akutoku 悪徳; the problem of ~ akugyō 悪行

vice president (of company) fuku-shachō 副社長; (senior executive) baisu-purejidento バイスプレジデ

ント; POL fuku-daitōryō 副大統領

vice squad fūzokuhanzai-torishimarihan 風俗犯罪取り締まり班

vice versa gyaku no bāi mo onaji 逆の場合も同じ

vicinity kinjo 近所; in the ~ of the church etc ... no kinjo ni ...の近所に; $500 etc oyoso ... およそ...

vicious dog dōmō (na) どう猛(な); attack, temper, criticism zankoku (na) 残酷(な)

victim gisei-sha 犠牲者

victimize gisei ni suru 犠牲にする

victor shōri-sha 勝利者

victorious shōri o eta 勝利を得た

victory shōri 勝利; win a ~ over ... ... ni katsu ...に勝つ

video 1 n bideo ビデオ; have X on ~ X o bideo ni totte aru Xをビデオにとってある **2** v/t bideo ni rokuga suru ビデオに録画する

video camera bideo-kamera ビデオカメラ; **video cassette** bideo-tēpu ビデオテープ; **video conference** TELEC terebi-kaigi テレビ会議; **video game** terebi-gēmu テレビゲーム; **videophone** terebi-denwa テレビ電話; **video recorder** bideo-tēpu-rekōdā ビデオテープレコーダー; **video recording** bideo-rokuga ビデオ録画; **videotape** bideo-tēpu ビデオテープ

Vietnam Betonamu ベトナム

Vietnamese 1 adj Betonamu (no) ベトナム(の) **2** n Betonamu-jin ベトナム人; (language) Betonamu-go ベトナム語

view 1 n keshiki 景色; (of situation) iken 意見; in ~ of ... ... o kangaeru to ...を考えると; be on ~ (of paintings) tenjichū de aru 展示中である; with a ~ to ... ... suru tsumori de ...するつもりで **2** v/t & v/i miru 見る

viewer TV shichō-sha 視聴者

viewfinder PHOT faindā ファインダー

viewpoint mikata 見方; (place) kansatsu-chiten 観察地点

vigor (energy) genki 元気

vigorous *person*, kappatsu (na) 活発(な); *shake* ikioi no aru 勢いのある; *denial* tsuyoi 強い

vile *smell* hidoi ひどい; *thing to do* geretsu (na) 下劣(な)

village mura 村

villager murabito 村人

villain akunin 悪人

vindicate (*show to be correct*) ... no tadashi-sa o shōmei suru ...の正しさを証明する; (*show to be innocent*) ... no keppaku o shōmei suru ...の潔白を証明する; *I feel ~d* watashi wa seitōsei o mitomerareta to kanjita 私は正当性を認められたと感じた

vindictive fukushūshin ni moeta 復しゅう心に燃えた

vine budō no ki ぶどうの木

vinegar su 酢

vineyard budōen ぶどう園

vintage 1 *n* (*of wine*) budō-shūkakunen ぶどう収穫年 **2** *adj* (*classic*) tenkeiteki (na) 典型的(な)

violate *rules, treaty* ihan suru 違反する; *sanctity* kegasu 汚す

violation (*of rules, treaty*) ihan 違反; (*of sanctity*) bōtoku 冒とく; *traffic ~* kōtsū-ihan 交通違反

violence (*of person, movie*) bōryoku 暴力; (*of emotion, reaction*) hageshi-sa 激しさ; (*of gale*) mōi 猛威; *outbreak of ~* hanran no boppatsu 反乱のぼっ発

violent *person, movie* bōryokuteki (na) 暴力的(な); *emotion, reaction, storm* hageshii 激しい; *have a ~ temper* hageshii kishō de aru 激しい気性である

violently *react* hageshiku 激しく; *object* hidoku ひどく; *fall ~ in love with* hageshiku ... ni koi o suru 激しく...に恋をする

violet (*color*) murasakiiro 紫色; (*plant*) sumire すみれ

violin baiorin バイオリン

violinist baiorin-sōsha バイオリン奏者

VIP (= *very important person*) yōjin 要人, VIP ブイアイピー

viral uirusu (no) ウイルス(の)

virgin (*male*) dōtei 童貞; (*female*) shojo 処女

virginity (*male*) dōtei 童貞; (*female*) shojo 処女; *lose his ~* dōtei o ushinau 童貞を失う; *lose her ~* shojo o ushinau 処女を失う

virile *man* otokorashii 男らしい; *prose* chikarazuyoi 力強い

virility otokorashi-sa 男らしさ; (*sexually*) seiteki-nōryoku 性的能力

virtual jijitsujō (no) 事実上(の)

virtually jisshitsuteki ni wa 実質的には

virtual reality kasō-genjitsu 仮想現実

virtue bitoku 美徳; *in ~ of* ... de aru koto de ...であることで

virtuoso MUS meijin 名人

virtuous kōketsu (na) 高潔(な)

virulent *disease* akusei (no) 悪性(の)

virus MED, COMPUT uirusu ウイルス

visa sashō 査証, biza ビザ

visibility shikai 視界

visible *object, anger* me ni mieru 目に見える; *difference* akiraka (na) 明らか(な); *not ~ to the naked eye* nikugan de wa mienai 肉眼では見えない

visibly *different* me ni miete 目にみえて; *he was ~ moved* kare wa akiraka ni kandō shite ita 彼は明らかに感動していた

vision (*eyesight*) shiryoku 視力; (*foresight, of a new world*) bijon ビジョン; REL *etc* maboroshi 幻

visit 1 *n* (*to person*) hōmon 訪問; (*to place, country, city*) kenbutsu 見物; *pay a ~ to the doctor / dentist* isha / haisha ni iku 医者/歯医者に行く; *pay X a ~* X o tazuneru Xを訪ねる **2** *v/t person* hōmon suru 訪問する; *place, country, city* tazuneru 訪ねる; *doctor, dentist* ... ni iku ...に行く

visiting card meishi 名刺

visiting hours (*at hospital*) menkai-jikan 面会時間

visitor (*guest*) kyaku 客; (*to museum etc*) nyūkan-sha 入館者;

(*tourist*) kankōkyaku 観光客

visor (*of helmet*) men 面; (*of cap*) tsuba つば

visual shikakuteki (na) 視覚的(な)

visual aid shikaku-kyōzai 視覚教材

visual display unit monitā モニター

visualize sōzō suru 想像する

visually shikakuteki ni 視覚的に

visually impaired me no fujiyū (na) 目の不自由(な)

vital (*essential*) jūyō (na) 重要(な); *it is ~ that ...* ... suru koto wa jūyō da ...することは重要だ

vitality (*of person*) genki 元気; (*of city*) kakki 活気

vitally: *~ important* kiwamete jūyō (na) 極めて重要(な)

vital organs seimei-iji ni hitsuyō na kikan 生命維持に必要な器官

vital statistics (*of woman*) surī-saizu スリーサイズ

vitamin bitamin ビタミン

vitamin pill bitamin-zai ビタミン剤

vivacious kappatsu (na) 活発(な)

vivacity kaikatsu 快活

vivid *color* azayaka (na) 鮮やか(な); *memory* hakkiri shita はっきりした; *imagination* kappatsu (na) 活発(な)

V-neck bui-nekku ブイネック

vocabulary goi 語い; (*list of words*) yōgoshū 用語集

vocal koe (no) 声(の); (*expressing opinions*) hakkiri mono o iu はっきり物を言う

vocal cords seitai 声帯

vocal group MUS bando バンド

vocalist MUS bōkaru ボーカル

vocation (*calling*) tenshoku 天職; (*profession*) shokugyō 職業; *have a ~ for ...* ... ni shimeikan o motsu ...に使命感を持つ

vocational *guidance* shokugyō (no) 職業(の)

vodka wokka ウォッカ

vogue ryūkō 流行; *be in ~* ninki ga aru 人気がある

voice 1 *n* koe 声 2 *v/t opinions* hyōmei suru 表明する

voicemail rusuban-denwa sābisu 留守番電話サービス

void 1 *n* (*space*) uchū-kūkan 宇宙空間; *fig* (*emptiness*) kūkyo 空虚 2 *adj:* *~ of ...* ...ga nai ...がない

volatile *personality* kimagure (na) 気まぐれ(な)

volcano kazan 火山

volley *n* (*in tennis*) borē ボレー; *a ~ of gunfire* issei-shageki 一斉射撃

volleyball barēbōru バレーボール

volt boruto ボルト

voltage den'atsu 電圧

volume (*of container*) yōseki 容積; (*of liquid*) yōryō 容量; (*of work, business, etc*) ryō 量; (*of book*) satsu 冊, kan 巻; (*of radio etc*) boryūmu ボリューム

volume control boryūmu-chōsetsu ボリューム調節

voluntary *adj helper* jihatsuteki (na) 自発的(な); *work* borantia (no) ボランティア(の)

volunteer 1 *n* borantia ボランティア; MIL shigan-sha 志願者 2 *v/i* jihatsuteki ni... suru 自発的に...する

voluptuous kannōteki (na) 官能的(の)

vomit 1 *n* hedo ヘど 2 *v/i* haku 吐く
♦ **vomit up** ... o haku ...を吐く

voracious *appetite* ōsei (no) 旺盛(の)

vote 1 *n* tōhyō 投票; (*process*) hyōketsu 票決; (*votes cast*) tōhyōsū 投票数; *have the ~* tōhyōken o motsu 投票権を持つ 2 *v/i* POL tōhyō suru 投票する; *~ for/against ...* ... ni sansei/hantai no tōhyō o suru ...に賛成/反対の投票をする 3 *v/t:* *they ~ him President* karera wa tōhyō de kare o daitōryō ni kimeta 彼等は投票で彼を大統領に決めた; *they ~d to stay behind* karera wa nokoru koto ni tōhyō de kimeta 彼らは残ることに投票で決めた
♦ **vote in** *member* ... ni senshutsu sareru ...に選出される
♦ **vote on** *issue* ... ni tsuite tōhyō suru ...について投票する
♦ **vote out** (*of office*) tōhyō de

tsuihō suru 投票で追放する

voter (*entitled to vote*) yūken-sha 有権者; (*who votes*) tōhyō-sha 投票者

voting POL tōhyō 投票

voting booth tohyōyoshi-kinyūsho 投票用紙記入所

♦ **vouch for** ... o hoshō suru ...を保証する

voucher (*for gas*) kūpon クーポン; (*for food*) shokken 食券; (*gift ~*) shōhinken 商品券

vow 1 *n* chikai 誓い **2** *v/t*: **~ to do X** X suru to chikau Xすると誓う

vowel boin 母音

voyage (*by sea*) funatabi 船旅; (*in space*) uchū-ryokō 宇宙旅行

vulgar *person, language* gehin (na) 下品(な)

vulnerable (*to attack*) kōgeki sareyasui 攻撃されやすい; (*to criticism etc*) kizutsukiyasui 傷つきやすい

vulture hagetaka はげたか

W

wad *n* (*of paper*) taba 束; (*of absorbent cotton*) katamari 固まり; **a ~ of $100 bills** hyaku doru satsu no taba 百ドル札の束

waddle *v/i* (*of baby, duck*) yochiyochi aruku よちよち歩く; (*of person*) yotayota aruku よたよた歩く

♦ **wade across** mizu no naka o aruite wataru 水の中を歩いて渡る

♦ **wade through** *book* ... o kurō shite yomu ...を苦労して読む

wafer (*cookie*) uehāsu ウエハース

waffle[1] *n* (*to eat*) waffuru ワッフル

waffle[2] *v/i* tsumaranai hanashi o suru つまらない話をする

wag 1 *v/t* *tail, finger* furu 振る **2** *v/i* (*of tail*) yureru 揺れる

wage[1] *v/t* *war* okonau 行う

wage[2] *n* kyūryō 給料

wage earner chingin-rōdō-sha 賃金労働者

waggle *v/t* *hips, tail* furu 振る; *ears, eyebrows* ugokasu 動かす; *loose screw, tooth etc* guragura ugokasu ぐらぐら動かす

wagon: **be on the ~** F sake o tatte iru 酒を断っている

wail 1 *n* (*of person, baby*) nakigoe 泣き声; (*of siren*) unari うなり **2** *v/i*

(*of person, baby*) nakisakebu 泣き叫ぶ; (*of siren*) unaru うなる

waist koshi 腰, uesuto ウエスト

waistcoat *Br* besuto ベスト

waistline dōmawari 胴回り; (*of clothes*) uesuto ウエスト

wait 1 *n*: **have a long ~** nagaku matasareru 長く待たせる **2** *v/i* matsu 待つ; **we'll ~ until he's ready** kare no junbi ga dekiru made machimasu 彼の準備ができるまで待ちます **2** *v/t* *meal* matsu 待つ; **~ table** ueitā/ueitoresu o suru ウエイター/ウエイトレスをする

♦ **wait for** ... o matsu ...を待つ; **~ me!** matte 待って

♦ **wait on** *person* ... ni kyūji suru ...に給仕する

♦ **wait up** nenaide matsu 寝ないで待つ

waiter ueitā ウエイター; **~!** sumimasen すみません

waiting *n* matsu koto 待つこと; **no sign** teisha-kinshi no hyōji 停車禁止の表示

waiting list junban-machi no meibo 順番待ちの名簿

waiting room machiaishitsu 待合室

waitress ueitoresu ウエイトレス

wake[1]: **~ (up) 1** *v/i* me ga sameru

目が覚める **2** *v/t* okosu 起こす

wake² (*of ship*) kōseki 航跡; **in the ~ of** … ni hikitsuzuite …に引き続いて; **follow in the ~ of** … ni hikitsuzuite kuru …に引き続いて来る

wake-up call mōningu-kōru モーニングコール

walk 1 *n* toho 徒歩; (*path*) hodō 歩道; **it's a long / short ~ to the office** kaisha made chotto aruku / aruite sugu da 会社までちょっと歩く/歩いてすぐだ; **go for a ~** sanpo ni iku 散歩に行く; (*as opposed to taking the car / bus etc*) aruite iku 歩いていく; (*hike*) haikingu suru ハイキングする **3** *v/t dog* sanpo ni tsurete iku 散歩に連れて行く; **~ the streets** (*walk around*) arukimawaru 歩き回る

♦ **walk out** (*of spouse, from room etc*) dete iku 出て行く; (*go on strike*) sutoraiki suru ストライキする

♦ **walk out on** *spouse* … o misuteru …を見捨てる

walker (*hiker*) yamaaruki no hito 山歩きの人; (*for baby, old person*) hokōki 歩行器; **be a slow / fast ~** aruku no ga osoi / hayai 歩くのが遅い/速い

walkie-talkie toranshībā トランシーバー

walk-in closet ōkii kurōzetto 大きいクローゼット

walking (*as opposed to driving*) aruki 歩き; (*hiking*) haikingu ハイキング; **be within ~ distance** aruite ikeru kyori ni aru 歩いて行ける距離にある

walking stick sutekki ステッキ

walking tour toho-ryokō 徒歩旅行

Walkman® wōkuman ウォークマン; **walkout** (*strike*) sutoraiki ストライキ; **walkover** (*easy win*) rakushō 楽勝; **walk-up** *n* erebētā no nai apā to エレベーターのないアパート

wall (*also fig*) kabe 壁; **go to the ~** (*of company*) tōsan suru 倒産する

wallet satsuire 札入れ

wallop F **1** *n* (*blow*) panchi パンチ

2 *v/t* butsu ぶつ; *opponent* uchinomesu 打ちのめす

wallpaper 1 *n* kabegami 壁紙 **2** *v/t* … ni kabegami o haru …に壁紙をはる

Wall Street Wōru-gai ウォール街

wall-to-wall carpet shikikomi kā petto 敷込みカーペット

walnut kurumi クルミ

waltz *n* warutsu ワルツ

wan *face* aozameta 青ざめた

wand mahō no tsue 魔法のつえ

wander *v/i* (*roam*) buratsuku ぶらつく; (*stray*) mayou 迷う; (*of attention*) yokomichi ni soreru 横道にそれる

♦ **wander around** burabura suru ぶらぶらする

wane *v/i* (*of interest*) usureru 薄れる; (*of moon*) kakeru 欠ける

wangle *v/t* F umai guai ni te ni ireru うまい具合に手に入れる

want 1 *n*: **for ~ of** …ga nai node …がないので **2** *v/t* …ga hoshii …が欲しい; (*need*) …ga hitsuyō de aru …が必要である; **~ to do X** X ga shitai Xがしたい; **I ~ to stay here** watashi wa koko ni itai desu 私はここにいたいです; **do you ~ to come too? – no, I don't ~ to** anata mo kitai – iie, watashi wa ikitaku nai あなたも来たい–いいえ、私は行きたくない; **you can have whatever you ~** anata no suki na mono nandemo totte kudasai あなたの好きなもの何でも取ってください; **it's not what I ~ed** sore wa watashi no hoshikatta mono de wa nai それは私の欲しかった物ではない; **she ~s you to go back** kanojo wa anata ni modotte hoshii 彼女はあなたに戻って欲しい; **he ~s a haircut** kare wa katto ni iku beki desu 彼はカットに行くべきです **3** *v/i*: **~ for nothing** nani mo fujiyū shite inai 何も不自由していない

want ad kyūjin-kōkoku 求人広告

wanted (*by police*) shimei-tehai chū (no) 指名手配中(の)

wanting: be ~ in … ni kakete iru …

に欠けている

wanton *adj* akui no aru 悪意のある

war *n* sensō 戦争; **be at ~** sensōchū de aru 戦争中である; **~ criminal** senpan 戦犯

warble *v/i* (*of bird*) saezuru さえずる

ward *n* (*in hospital*) byōtō 病棟; (*child*) hikōken-nin 被後見人

♦ **ward off** ... o kawasu ...をかわす

warden (*of prison*) shochō 所長

wardrobe (*for clothes*) yōfuku-dansu 洋服ダンス; (*clothes*) yōfuku-isshiki 洋服一式

warehouse sōko 倉庫

warfare sensō 戦争

warhead dantō 弾頭

warily yōjin bukaku 用心深く

warm *adj* atatakai 暖かい; *welcome, smile* kokoro kara (no) 心から(の)

♦ **warm up 1** *v/t* ... o atatameru ... を暖める **2** *v/i* atatamaru 暖まる; (*of athlete etc*) wōmuappu suru ウォームアップする

warmhearted kokoro no atatakai 心の温かい

warmly *dressed* atatakaku 暖かく; *welcome, smile* kokoro kara 心から

warmth atataka-sa 暖かさ; (*of welcome, smile*) atatakami 温かみ

warn keikoku suru 警告する

warning *n* keikoku 警告; **without ~** yokoku nashi ni 予告なしに

warp 1 *v/t* wood hizumaseru ひずませる; *character* yugameru ゆがめる **2** *v/i* (*of wood*) yugamu ゆがむ

warped *fig* hinekureta ひねくれた

warplane gun'yōki 軍用機

warrant 1 *n* reijō 令状 **2** *v/t* (*deserve, call for*) ... ni atai suru ...に値する

warranty hoshō 保証; **be under ~** hoshō-kikanchū de aru 保証期間中である

warrior senshi 戦士

warship gunkan 軍艦

wart ibo いぼ

wartime senji 戦時

wary yōjin-bukai 用心深い; **be ~ of** ... ni yōjin suru ...に用心する

wash 1 *n*: **have a ~** arau 洗う; *that*

jacket/shirt needs a ~ sono jaketto wa/sono shatsu wa arau beki da そのジャケットは/そのシャツは洗うべきだ; *clothes* sentaku suru 洗濯する **3** *v/i* senmen suru 洗面する

♦ **wash up** *v/i* (*wash one's hands and face*) senmen suru 洗面する

washable sentaku dekiru 洗濯できる

washbasin, washbowl senmenki 洗面器

washcloth hando-taoru ハンドタオル

washed out tsukarekitta 疲れ切った

washer (*for faucet etc*) zagane 座金; → *washing machine*

washing sentakumono 洗濯物; *do the ~* sentaku o suru 洗濯をする

washing machine sentakuki 洗濯機

Washington (*city*) Washinton ワシントン

washroom otearai お手洗い

wasp (*insect*) hachi はち

waste 1 *n* rōhi 浪費; (*from industrial process*) haikibutsu 廃棄物; **it's a ~ of time/money** jikan/okane no mudazukai da 時間/お金の無駄使いだ **2** *adj* fuyō (no) 不用(の) **3** *v/t* mudazukai suru 無駄使いする

♦ **waste away** yaseotoroeru やせ衰える

wasteful fukeizai (na) 不経済(な)

wasteland arechi 荒れ地; **waste-paper** kamikuzu 紙くず; **waste-paper basket** kuzukago くずかご; **waste product** haikibutsu 廃棄物

watch 1 *n* (*timepiece*) udedokei 腕時計; **keep ~** mihari o suru 見張りをする **2** *v/t* movie, TV miru 見る; (*look after*) ... ni ki o tsukeru ...に気をつける **3** *v/i* miru 見る

♦ **watch for** ... o matte iru ...を待っている

♦ **watch out** ki o tsukeru 気を付ける; **~!** ki o tsukete 気を付けて

♦ **watch out for** ... ni ki o tsukeru ...に気を付ける

watchdog kanshi-iinkai 監視委員会

watchful chūi-bukai 注意深い

watchmaker tokei-ya 時計屋

water 1 *n* mizu 水; **~s** NAUT ryōkai 領海 **2** *v/t plant* mizu o yaru 水をやる **3** *v/i* (*of eyes*) namida ga deru 涙が出る; **my mouth is ~ing** yodare ga dete iru よだれが出ている

♦ **water down** *drink* mizu de usumeru 水で薄める

watercolor (*painting*) suisaiga 水彩画; (*paint*) suisai-enogu 水彩絵の具; **watercress** kureson クレソン; **waterfall** taki 滝

watering can jōro じょうろ

water level suii 水位; **water lily** suiren スイレン; **waterline** (*on ship*) kissuisen 喫水線; **waterlogged** shinsui shita 浸水した; **watermark** sukashi 透かし; **watermelon** suika スイカ; **water polo** suikyū 水球; **waterproof** *adj* bōsui (no) 防水(の); **waterside** *n* mizube (no) 水辺(の); **at the ~** mizube ni/de 水辺に/で; **waterskiing** suijō-sukī 水上スキー; **watertight** *compartment* mizu o tōsanai 水を通さない; **waterway** suiro 水路; **waterwings** ukiwa 浮き輪

watery mizuppoi 水っぽい

watt watto ワット

wave¹ *n* (*in sea*) nami 波

wave² *1 n* (*of hand*): **with a ~ of his hand** kare wa te o futte 彼は手を振って **2** *v/i* (*with hand*) te o furu 手を振る; **~ to** ... ni te o furu ...に手を振る **3** *v/t flag etc* furu 振る

wavelength RAD shūhasū 周波数; **be on the same ~** *fig* hachō ga au 波長が合う

waver yuragu 揺らぐ

wavy *line* kunekune shita くねくねした; *hair* uēbu no kakatta ウエーブのかかった

wax *n* (*for floor, furniture*) wakkusu ワックス; (*in ear*) mimiaka 耳あか

way 1 *n* (*method, manner*) hōhō 方法; (*route*) iku michi 行く道; **this ~** (*like this*) kono yarikata このやり方; (*in this direction*) kono hōkō

この方向; **please come this ~** kochira e dōzo こちらへどうぞ; **by the ~** (*incidentally*) tokoro de ところで; **by ~ of** (*via*) ...keiyu de ...経由で; (*in the form of*) ... to shite ...として; **in a ~** (*in certain respects*) aru imi de wa ある意味では; **be under ~** shinkōchū de aru 進行中である; **give ~** MOT shinro yuzure 進路譲れ; (*collapse*) kuzureru 崩れる; **give ~ to** (*be replaced by*) ... ni totte kawaru ...に取って代わる; **have one's (own) ~** omoidōri ni suru 思い通りにする; **OK, we'll do it your ~** wakatta anata no omoidōri ni shimashō 分かったあなたの思い通りにしましょう; **lead the ~** sentō ni tatte iku 先頭に立っていく; **lose one's ~** mayou 迷う; **be in the ~** jama ni naru 邪魔になる; **it's on the ~ to the station** sore wa eki ni iku tochū ni aru それは駅に行く途中にある; **I was on my ~ to the station** eki ni iku tochū deshita 駅に行く途中でした; **no ~!** jōdan ja nai 冗談じゃない; **there's no ~ he can do it** kare ni wa zettai dekinai 彼には絶対できない **2** *adv* F (*much*) suggoku すっごく; **it's ~ too soon to decide** kimeru no ni wa hayasugiru 決めるのには早過ぎる; **they are ~ behind with their work** karera wa suggoku okurete iru 彼等の仕事はすっごく遅れている

way in iriguchi 入り口; **way of life** seikatsu-yōshiki 生活様式; **way out** deguchi 出口; *fig* kaiketsuhō 解決法

we watashitachi 私達, wareware 我々; **~ are Americans / students** watashitachi wa Amerika-jin / gakusei desu 私達はアメリカ人/学生です ◊ (*omission of pronoun*): **~ don't know** shirimasen 知りません

weak yowai 弱い; *tea, coffee* usui 薄い; *currency* yasui 安い; (*morally*) ishi ga yowai 意志が弱い

weaken 1 *v/t* yowaku suru 弱くする

2 *v/i* yowaku naru 弱くなる; (*of health*) otoroeru 衰える; (*morally*) yowaki ni naru 弱気になる

weakling kyojaku 虚弱; (*morally*) yowamushi 弱虫

weakness jakuten 弱点; **have a ~ for** (*liking*) ... ni me ga nai ...に目がない

wealth zaisan 財産, tomi 富; **a ~ of** hōfu na ... 豊富な...

wealthy yūfuku (na) 裕福(な)

weapon buki 武器

wear 1 *n*: **the engine has had a lot of ~ and tear** enjin ga sukkari itande iru エンジンがすっかり痛んでいる; **clothes for everyday ~** heifuku 平服 **2** *v/t shirt, dress, suit raincoat, special clothing* kiru 着る; *hat* kaburu かぶる; *shoes, socks, skirt, pants, pantyhose* haku はく; *necktie* shimeru 締める; *brassiere* tsukeru つける; *gloves, ring* hameru はめる; *make-up* suru する; *glasses* kakeru かける; (*damage*) tsukai-furusu 使い古す; **what was he ~ing?** kare wa nani o kite ita no 彼は何を着ていたの **3** *v/i* (*of carpet, fabric: wear out*) surikireru 擦り切れる; (*last*) motsu もつ

♦ **wear away 1** *v/i* suriheru 擦り減る **2** *v/t* ... o suriherasu ...を擦り減らす

♦ **wear off** (*of effect, feeling*) kieru 消える

♦ **wear out 1** *v/t* (*tire*) ... o tsukare saseru ...を疲れさせる; *shoes* ... o suriherasu ...を擦り減らす **2** *v/i* (*of shoes, carpet*) suriheru 擦り減る

wearing (*tiring*) tsukareru 疲れる

weary tsukarehateta 疲れ果てた

weather 1 *n* tenki 天気; **be feeling under the ~** kibun ga warui 気分が悪い **2** *v/t crisis* norikiru 乗り切る

weather-beaten fū ni sarasareta 風雨にさらされた; **weather chart** tenkizu 天気図; **weather forecast** tenki-yohō 天気予報; **weatherman** tenki-yohō-gakari 天気予報係

weave 1 *v/t cloth* oru 織る; *basket* amu 編む **2** *v/i* (*move*) nū yō ni susumu 縫うように進む

Web¹: the ~ webu ウェブ

web² (*of spider*) kumo no su くもの巣

webbed feet mizukakino aru ashi 水かきのある足

web page webu-pēji ウェブページ

web site webu-saito ウェブサイト

wedding kekkonshiki 結婚式

wedding anniversary kekkon-kinenbi 結婚記念日; **wedding cake** uedingu-kēki ウエディングケーキ; **wedding day** kekkon no hi 結婚の日; **wedding dress** uedingu-doresu ウエディングドレス; **wedding ring** kekkon-yubiwa 結婚指輪

wedge *n* (*to hold sth in place*) kusabi くさび; (*of cheese etc*) hitokire 一切れ

Wednesday suiyōbi 水曜日

weed 1 *n* zassō 雑草 **2** *v/t* kusatori o suru 草取りをする

♦ **weed out** ... o torinozoku ...を取り除く

weed-killer josōzai 除草剤

week shū 週; (*duration*) shūkan 週間; **a ~ tomorrow** raishū no ashita 来週の明日

weekday heijitsu 平日, uīkudē ウイークデー

weekend shūmatsu 週末, uīkuendo ウイークエンド; **on the ~** shūmatsu ni 週末に

weekly 1 *adj* maishū (no) 毎週(の) **2** *n* (*magazine*) shūkan 週刊 **3** *adv* maishū 毎週

weep shikushiku naku しくしく泣く

weigh¹ 1 *v/t* omo-sa o hakaru 重さを量る **2** *v/i* omo-sa ga ... de aru 重さが...である; **how much does the bag ~?** kaban no omo-sa wa ikura desu ka かばんの重さはいくらですか; **how much do you ~?** taijū wa dono kurai arimasu ka 体重はどのくらいありますか

weigh²: ~ anchor ikari o ageru いかりを上げる

♦ **weigh down**: **be weighed down**

with … no omomi de shizumu …の重みで沈む; *with worries* … de ki o omoku saseru …で気を重くさせる

♦ **weigh up** (*assess*) … o hyōka suru …を評価する

weight (*of person*) taijū 体重; (*of object*) omo-sa 重さ

weightlessness mujūryoku 無重力

weightlifter jūryōage-senshu 重量挙げ選手

weightlifting jūryōage 重量挙げ

weir seki せき

weird hen (na) 変(な)

weirdo *n* F hen na hito 変な人

welcome 1 *adj* kangei subeki 歓迎すべき; *you're ~!* dō itashimashite どういたしました; *you're ~ to try some* dōzo tameshite mite kudasai どうぞ試してみてください **2** *n also fig* kangei 歓迎 **3** *v/t guests* kangei suru 歓迎する; *decision etc* ureshiku omou うれしく思う

weld *v/t* yōsetsu suru 溶接する

welder yōsetsu-kō 溶接工

welfare shiawase 幸せ; (*financial assistance*) fukushi 福祉; *be on ~* seikatsu-hogo o ukete iru 生活保護を受けている

welfare check seikatsu-hogo no kogitte 生活保護の小切手; **welfare state** fukushi-kokka 福祉国家; **welfare work** fukushi-jigyō 福祉事業; **welfare worker** sōsharu-wākā ソーシャルワーカー

well¹ *n* (*for water*) ido 井戸; *oil ~* yusei 油井

well² 1 *adv* yoku よく; *as ~* (*too*) … mo …も; *as ~ as* (*in addition to*) … no hoka ni …のほかに; (*do sth*) … to onaji gurai …と同じぐらい; *it's just as ~ you told me* anata ga itte kurete yokatta あなたが言ってくれてよかった; *very ~* (*acknowledging an order*) hai wakarimashita はい わかりました; (*reluctant acceptance*) yoku wakarimashita よくわかりました; *~, ~!* (*surprise*) ē' エーッ; *~ …* (*uncertainty, thinking*) ētto … えーっと… **2** *adj* *be ~* genki de aru 元気である; *feel ~* kibun ga ii

気分がいい; *get ~ soon!* hayaku yoku natte 早く良くなって

well-balanced *person* jōshiki no aru 常識のある; *meal, diet* baransu no toreta バランスの取れた; **well-behaved** gyōgi no ii 行儀のいい; **well-being** kōfuku 幸福; **well-done** *meat* shikkari yaketa しっかり焼けた; **well-dressed** minari no yoi 身なりの良い; **well-earned** jibun de hataraite eta 自分で働いて得た; **well-known** yūmei (na) 有名(な); **well-made** yoku dekita 良く出来た; **well-mannered** reigi tadashii 礼儀正しい; **well-off** yūfuku (na) 裕福(な); **well-read** hakushiki (no) 博識(の); **well-timed** taimingu no ii タイミングのいい; **well-to-do** yūfuku (na) 裕福(な); **well-worn** tsukai furushita 使い古した

west 1 *n* nishi 西; *the West* (*nations*) Nishigawa-shokoku 西側諸国; (*part of a country*) seibu 西部 **2** *adj* nishi (no) 西(の) **3** *adv* nishi e 西へ; *~ of* … no nishi no hō ni …の西の方に

West Coast (*of USA*) Nishikaigan 西海岸

westerly nishitori (no) 西寄り(の)

western 1 *adj* nishi (no) 西(の); *Western* Nishigawa (no) 西側(の) **2** *n* (*movie*) seibugeki 西部劇

Westerner Seiyōjin 西洋人

westernized seiyōka 西洋化

westward nishi e 西へ

wet *adj* nureta ぬれた; (*rainy*) ame no ōi 雨の多い; *"~ paint"* penki-nuritate ペンキ塗りたて; *be ~ through* bishonure ni naru びしょぬれになる

whack F **1** *n* (*blow*) kyōda 強打 **2** *v/t* hippataku 引っぱたく

whale kujira 鯨

whaling hogei 捕鯨

wharf *n* hatoba 波止場

what 1 *pron* ◊ (*interrogative*) nani 何; *~ is that?* sore wa nan desu ka それは何ですか; *~ is it?* (*~ do you want?*) nannano 何なの; *~!* (*astonishment*) nani' 何; *~ about* *some dinner?* yūshoku ni shimasen ka 夕食にしませんか; ~ *about heading home?* ie ni kaerimasen ka 家に帰りませんか; ~ *for?* (*why?*) dōshite どうして; *so ~?* sore de それで ◊ (*relative*): *I don't know ~ you're talking about* anata ga nani o itte iru no ka wakarimasen あなたが何を言っているのか分かりません; *take ~ you need* hitsuyō na mono o totte kudasai 必要なものを取って下さい; *this is ~ I wanted* kore ga watashi no hoshikatta mono desu これが私の欲しかったものです 2 *adj* dono どの; ~ *university are you at?* dono daigaku ni itte iru no どの大学に行っているの; ~ *experience have you had?* don na keiken ga arimasu ka どんな経験がありますか; ~ *color is the car?* kuruma wa nani iro desu ka 車は何色ですか; ~ *a beautiful girl!* nante kirei na onna no ko darō 何てきれいな女の子だろう

whatever 1 *pron* nan demo 何でも; (*regardless of what*) … ni kakawarazu …にかかわらず; ~ *people say* hito no iukoto ni kakawarazu 人の言うことにかかわらず 2 *adj* donna… demo どんな…でも; *you have no reason ~ to worry* anata wa mattaku shinpai suru hitsuyō wa arimasen あなたはまったく心配する必要はありません

wheat komugi 小麦

wheedle: ~ *X out of Y* kuchiguruma ni nosete Y kara X o damashitoru 口車に乗せてYからXをだましとる

wheel 1 *n* sharin 車輪; (*steering ~*) handoru ハンドル 2 *v/t bicycle* osu 押す 3 *v/i* (*of birds*) senkai suru 旋回する

♦ **wheel around** kyū ni mukinaoru 急に向き直る

wheelbarrow teoshi-guruma 手押し車; **wheelchair** kurumaisu 車いす; **wheel clamp** ihan-chūsha no sharindome 違反駐車の車輪止め

wheeze *v/i* zeizei iu ゼイゼイ言う

when 1 *adv* itsu いつ; ~ *is breakfast?* asagohan wa itsu desu ka 朝ご飯はいつですか 2 *conj* toki 時; *I was a child* watashi ga kodomo datta toki 私が子供だった時; ~ *I've finished* watashi ga owattara 私が終わったら; *it was the year ~* … no toshi datta …の年だった; *on the day ~ he was born* kare ga umareta hi ni 彼が生まれた日に

whenever (*any time*) … suru toki wa itsu demo …する時はいつでも; (*each time*) … suru tabi ni …する度に; *call me ~ you like* itsu demo denwa shite いつでも電話して

where 1 *adv* doko ni どこに; ~ *do you come from?* anata wa doko no shusshin desu ka あなたはどこの出身ですか 2 *conj*: *the hotel ~ the Beatles stayed* Bītoruzu ga tomatta hoteru ビートルズが泊まったホテル; *this is ~ I used to live* koko wa watashi ga izen sunde ita tokoro desu ここは私が以前住んでいた所です

whereabouts 1 *n* ibasho 居場所 2 *adv* dono atari ni どの辺りに; ~ *did you lose it?* dono atari de nakushita no desu ka どの辺りでなくしたのですか

whereas … ga が; ~ *he thought …, the others …* kare wa … to kangaeta ga, hoka no hitotachi wa 彼は…と考えたが、他の人達は

wherever 1 *conj* doko ni …shite mo どこに…しても; *sit ~ you like* doko de mo suki na tokoro ni suwatte kudasai どこでも好きな所に座って下さい 2 *adv* ittai doko ni 一体どこに; ~ *can he be?* kare wa ittai doko ni iru no 彼は一体どこにいるの

whet *appetite* sosoru そそる

whether …ka dō ka …かどうか; ~ *you approve or not* anata ga mitomete mo mitomenakute mo あなたが認めても認めなくても

which 1 *adj* dono どの, dochira (no) どちら(の); (*referring to people*) dono hito どの人; ~ *one is yours?*

dochira ga anata no desu ka どちらがあなたのですか; ~ **student would you select?** dono gakusei o erabimasu ka どの学生を選びますか 2 pron ◊ (interrogative) dore どれ; (referring to people) dono hito どの人; ~ **do you like best?** dore ga ichiban suki desu ka どれが一番好きですか; **take one, it doesn't matter** ~ dore de mo ii kara totte kudasai どれでもいいから取って下さい ◊ (relative): **the house,** ~ **was designed by XYZ** XYZ no dezain shita ie XYZのデザインした家; **the chair on** ~ **I'm sitting** watashi ga suwatte iru isu 私が座っているいす

whichever 1 adj: ~ **style you choose** anata ga dono sutairu o erabu ni shite mo あなたがどのスタイルを選ぶにしても; **choose** ~ **color you like** suki na iro o dore demo erabe 好きな色をどれでも選んで 2 pron dore demo どれでも

whiff (smell) kasuka na kaori かすかな香り

while 1 conj ... suru aida ...する間; (although) ... suru ni mo kakawarazu ...するにもかかわらず; (whereas) ... de aru no ni ...であるのに 2 n: **a long** ~ nagai aida 長い間; **for a** ~ shibaraku no aida しばらくの間; **I haven't seen you for a** ~ hisashiburi desu 久しぶりです; **I'll wait a** ~ **longer** mō sukoshi machimashō もう少し待ちましょう

♦ **while away** burabura sugosu ぶらぶら過ごす

whim kimagure 気まぐれ

whimper 1 n kawaisō na nakigoe かわいそうな泣き声 2 v/i kawaisō na nakigoe o dasu かわいそうな泣き声をだす

whine v/i (of dog) kunkun naku くんくん泣く; F (complain) nakigoto o iu 泣き言を言う

whip 1 n muchi むち 2 v/t (beat) muchiutsu むち打つ; (cream) awadateru 泡立てる; F (defeat) uchimakasu 打ち負かす

♦ **whip out** F (take out) ...o satto toridasu ...をさっと取り出す

♦ **whip up** (arouse) ... o aoru ...をあおる

whipping (beating) muchiuchi むち打ち; F (defeat) haiboku 敗北

whirl 1 n: **my mind is in a** ~ kōfun shite atama ga mawatte iru 興奮して頭が回っている 2 v/i kurukuru mawaru くるくる回る; (of leaves) uzumaku 渦巻く

whirlpool (in river) uzumaki 渦巻; (for relaxation) jakūji ジャクージ

whirlwind tsumujikaze つむじ風

whirr v/i unaru うなる

whisk 1 n (kitchen utensil) awadateki 泡立て器 2 v/t eggs awadateru 泡立てる

♦ **whisk away** ... o subayaku katazukeru ...を素早く片付ける

whiskers (of man, animal) hige ひげ

whiskey uisukī ウイスキー; ~ **and soda** haibōru ハイボール; ~ **and water** mizuwari 水割り

whisper 1 n sasayaki ささやき 2 v/t & v/i sasayaku ささやく

whistle 1 n (sound) kuchibue 口笛; (device) fue 笛 2 v/i kuchibue o fuku 口笛をふく; (of wind) pyūtto naru ピューっーっと鳴る 3 v/t kuchibue de fuku 口笛で吹く

white 1 n (color) shiro 白; (of egg) shiromi 白身; (person) hakujin 白人 2 adj shiroi 白い; (pale) aojiroi 青白い; person hakujin (no) 白人(の)

white-collar worker howaito-karā no sararīman ホワイトカラーのサラリーマン; **White House** Howaito-hausu ホワイトハウス; **white lie** tsumi no nai uso 罪のないうそ; **white meat** shiromi no niku 白身の肉; **white-out** (for text) shūseieki 修正液; **whitewash** n suisei-hakushoku-toryō 水性白色塗料; fig gomakashi ごまかし; **white wine** shiro wain 白ワイン

whittle wood kezuru 削る

♦ **whittle down** ... o herasu ...を減らす

whizz: **be a** ~ **at** F ... no tensai de

aru ...の天才である

♦**whizz past** (*of time, car*) byūn to tōrisugiru ビューンと通り過ぎる

whizzkid F tensai 天才

who ◊ (*interrogative*) dare 誰; **~'s that guy?** ano hito wa dare desu ka あの人は誰ですか ◊(*relative*): **the woman ~ saved the boy** otoko no ko o tasuketa fujin 男の子を助けた婦人; **I don't know ~ to believe** dare o shinjireba ii ka wakaranai 誰を信じればいいか分からない

whoever dare demo 誰でも; **~ can that be?** ittai dare darō 一体誰だろう

whole 1 *adj* zentai (no) 全体(の); **the ~ town/country** machi-zentai/kuni-zentai 町全体/国全体; **the ~ night** yorujū 夜中; **it's a ~ lot easier/better** zutto kantan da/zutto ii ずっと簡単だ/ずっといい **2** *n* zentai 全体; **the ~ of the United States** Amerika zentai アメリカ全体; **on the ~** zentai to shite 全体として

whole-hearted kokoro kara (no) 心から(の); **wholesale 1** *adj* oroshi (no) 卸(の); *fig* musabetsu (no) 無差別(の) **2** *adv* oroshi de 卸で; **wholesaler** ton'ya 問屋; **wholesome** kenkō ni yoi 健康に良い; *fig* kenzen (na) 健全(な)

wholly kanzen ni 完全に

whom *fml* dare o/ni 誰を/に

whooping cough hyakunichizeki 百日ぜき

whore *n* baita 売女

whose 1 *pron* ◊ (*interrogative*) dare no mono 誰の物; **~ is this?** kore wa dare no mono desu ka これは誰の物ですか ◊ (*relative*): **a man ~ wife has left him** tsuma ni suterareta otoko 妻に捨てられた男; **a country ~ economy is booming** keizai ga kakkizuite iru kuni 経済が活気付いている国 **2** *adj* dare (no) 誰(の); **~ bike is that?** kore wa dare no jitensha desu ka これは誰の自転車ですか

why dōshite どうして, naze なぜ; **~**

do you ask? naze kikun desu ka なぜ聞くんですか; **~ not?** dōshite iya na no どうしていやなの; (*agreeing to suggestion*) ii kangae da いい考えだ; **~ don't you come?** (*suggesting*) kimasen ka 来ませんか; **I don't know ~ I said that** dōshite sonna koto o itta no ka wakarimasen どうしてそんな事を言ったのかわかりません; **that's ~** dakara だから

wick shin しん

wicked (*evil*) jaaku (na) 邪悪(な); (*mischievous*) ijiwaru (na) 意地悪(な)

wicker tōami とう編み

wicker chair tō no isu とうのいす

wicket (*in station, bank etc*) madoguchi 窓口

wide *adj* hiroi 広い; *experience* hōfu (na) 豊富(な); **be 12 foot ~** haba jūni fīto de aru 幅十二フィートである

wide-awake sukkari me ga sameta すっかり目が覚めた

wide-angle lens kōkaku-renzu 広角レンズ

widely *used, known* hiroku 広く

widen 1 *v/t* hiroku suru 広くする **2** *v/i* hiroku naru 広くなる

wide-open hiroku hiraita 広く開いた

widespread hirogatta 広がった

widow mibōjin 未亡人

widower otokoyamome 男やもめ

width hiro-sa 広さ

wield *weapon, power* furimawasu 振りまわす

wife tsuma 妻; (*talking to outsiders about one's own ~ also*) kanai 家内; (*s.o. else's*) okusan 奥さん

wig katsura かつら

wiggle *v/t hips* kunerasu くねらす; *loose screw etc* guragura ugokasu ぐらぐら動かす

wild 1 *adj animal, flowers* yasei (no) 野生(の); *land, sea* areta 荒れた; *teenager* ranbō (na) 乱暴(な); *party* ōsawagi (no) 大騒ぎ(の); *scheme* toppi (na) 突飛(な); *applause* kōfun shita 興奮した; **be**

~ about ... (*enthusiastic*) ... ni muchū de aru ...に夢中である; **go ~** kyōki suru 狂喜する; (*become angry*) gekido suru 激怒する; **run ~** (*of children*) katte kimama o suru 勝手気ままをする; (*of plants*) nobihōdai ni suru 伸び放題にする **2** *n*: **the ~s** kōya 荒野

wilderness mikaichi 未開地

wildfire: **spread like ~** matataku ma ni hirogaru 瞬く間に広がる; **wildgoose chase** mudaashi 無駄足; **wildlife** yasei-dōbutsu 野生動物

will[1] *n* LAW yuigon 遺言

will[2] *n* (~*power*) ishi 意志

will[3]: **I ~ let you know tomorrow** ashita shirasemasu 明日知らせます; **~ you be there too?** anata mo iku no あなたも行くの; **I won't be back until late** osoku narimasu 遅くなります; **you ~ call me, won't you?** denwa shite kureru yo ne 電話をしてくれますよね; **I'll pay for this – no, I ~** watashi ga koko wa haraimasu – iie watashi ga harai masu 私がここは払います–いいえ私が払います; **the car won't start** kuruma ga ugokanai 車が動かない; **~ you tell her that ...?** kanojo ni ... to itte kureru 彼女に...と言ってくれる; **~ you have some more tea?** mō sukoshi ocha wa ikaga desu ka もう少しお茶はいかがですか; **~ you stop that!** yamenasai 止めなさい

willful *person* wagamama (na) わがまま(な); *action* koi (no) 故意(の)

willing *worker, attitude* iyoku no aru 意欲のある; **be ~ to do X** kokoroyoku X suru 快くXする

willingly (*with pleasure*) yorokonde 喜んで; (*readily*) susunde 進んで

willingness (*of worker*) iyoku 意欲; **his ~ to help** kare no susunde tetsudaō to iu kimochi 彼の進んで手伝おうという気持ち

willow yanagi 柳

willpower ishi no chikara 意志の力

willy-nilly (*at random*) nariyuki-makase ni 成り行きまかせに

wilt *v/i* (*of plant*) shioreru しおれる

wily zurugashikoi ずる賢い

wimp F yowamushi 弱虫

win 1 *n* shōri 勝利 **2** *v/t* ... ni katsu ...に勝つ; (*lottery, money, prize* ateru 当てる; **~ an election** tōsen suru 当選する **3** *v/i* katsu 勝つ

wince *v/i* kao ga kowabaru 顔がこわばる

winch *n* uinchi ウインチ

wind[1] *n* kaze 風; (*flatulence*) gasu ガス; **get ~ of ...** o kagitsukeru ... をかぎつける **2** *v/t*: **be ~ed** iki ga kireru 息が切れる

wind[2] **1** *v/i* (*of path, river*) magaru 曲がる; (*of ivy*) karamitsuku 絡み付く **2** *v/t* karamaseru 絡ませる; *scarf* makitsuku 巻き付ける

♦ **wind down 1** *v/i* (*of party etc*) ochitsuku 落ち着く **2** *v/t* car window ... o akeru ...を空ける; business ... o shukushō suru ...を縮小する

♦ **wind up 1** *v/t* clock ... o neji o maku ...をネジを巻く; car window ... o shimeru ...を閉める; speech, presentation ... o shimekukuru ...を締めくくる; affairs ... o oeru ...を終える; company ... o tatamu ...を畳む **2** *v/i* (*finish*) owaru 終わる; **~ in the hospital** byōin ni iku koto ni naru 病院に行くことになる

windfall tanabota 棚ぼた

winding magarikunetta 曲がりくねった

wind instrument kangakki 管楽器

windmill fūsha 風車

window mado 窓; **in the ~** (*of store*) shōuindō ni ショーウインドーに

windowpane madogarasu 窓ガラス; **window-shop**: **go ~ping** uindō-shoppingu suru ウインドーショッピングする; **windowsill** mado no shitawaku 窓の下枠

windshield furontogarasu フロントガラス; **windshield wiper** waipā ワイパー; **windsurfer** sāfā サーファー; (*board*) sāfu-bōdo サーフボード; **windsurfing** uindosāfin ウインドサーフィン

windy *weather, day* kaze no tsuyoi 風の強い; **it's getting ~** kaze ga

tsuyoku natte kita 風が強くなって
きた

wine wain ワイン

wine list wainrisuto ワインリスト

wing n hane 羽; (of plane) tsubasa
翼; SP uingu ウイング

wink 1 n uinku ウインク **2** v/i (of
person) uinku suru ウインクする;
~ at ... ni uinku suru ...にウインク
する

winner (of race) shō-sha 勝者; (of
prize) jushō-sha 受賞者; (of
election, lottery) tōsen-sha 当選者

winning adj katta 勝った; number
atatta 当たった

winning post kesshōten 決勝点

winnings shōkin 賞金

winter n fuyu 冬

winter sports uintā-supōtsu ウイン
タースポーツ

wintry fuyurashii 冬らしい

wipe v/t fuku ふく; eyes, feet nuguu
ぬぐう; tape kesu 消す

♦ **wipe out** (kill, destroy) ... o
zenmetsu saseru ...を全滅させる;
debt ... o hensai suru ...を返済する

wire harigane 針金; ELEC densen 電
線

wireless n rajio ラジオ

wire netting kanaami 金網

wiring ELEC denki-haisen 電気配線

wiry person sujibatta 筋張った

wisdom (of person) chie 知恵; (of
action) kenmei-sa 賢明さ

wisdom tooth oyashirazu 親知らず

wise kashikoi 賢い

wisecrack n iyami 嫌み

wise guy pej shittakaburi-ya 知っ
たかぶり屋

wisely act kenmei ni 賢明に

wish 1 n nozomi 望み; best ~es
omedetō おめでとう **2** v/t nozomu
望む; I ~ that ... ...sureba ii no ni
to omou ...すればいいのにと思う;
~ X well X no kōun o inoru X の幸
運を祈る; I ~ed him good luck
kare no kōun o inoru to iimashita
彼の幸運を祈ると言いました

♦ **wish for** ... o nozomu ...を望む

wishful thinking kibōteki-kansoku
希望的観測

wishy-washy person yūjū-fudan
(no) 優柔不断(の); color usui 薄い

wisteria fuji 藤

wistful zannen sō (na) 残念そう(な)

wit (humor) yūmoa ユーモア;
(person) yūmoa no aru hito ユー
モアのある人; be at one's ~s' end
dō sureba ii ka wakaranakunaru
どうすればいいかわからなくなる

witch majo 魔女

with ◊ (accompanied by) ... to ...と;
she came ~ her little sister
kanojo wa imōto to kita 彼女は妹
と来た; a treaty ~ Japan Nihon to
no jōyaku 日本との条約; are you ~
me? (do you understand?)
wakarimasu ka 分かりますか; ~ no
money kane nashi de 金なしで ◊
(proximity) ... to issho ni ...と一
緒に; I live ~ my aunt watashi wa
oba to issho ni sunde iru 私はおば
と一緒に住んでいる ◊ (agency) ...
de ...で; stabbed ~ a knife naifu
de sashita ナイフで刺した;
decorated ~ flowers hana de
kazatta 花で飾った ◊ (cause)
kyōfu de furueta 恐怖で震えた;
shivering ~ fear ◊ (possession)
no ...の; the house ~ the red door
akai doa no uchi 赤いドアの家; a
girl ~ brown eyes chairo no me
no onna no ko 茶色の目の女の子;
we need someone ~ experience
watashitachi wa dareka keiken no
aru hito ga hitsuyō desu 私達は誰
か経験のある人が必要です ◊; ~ a
smile / ~ a wave hohoende / te o
futte ほほ笑んで/手を振って ◊; be
angry ~ X X ni hara o tatete iru X
に腹をたてている

withdraw 1 v/t complaint,
application torikesu 取り消す;
money from bank hikidasu 引き出
す; troops tettai saseru 撤退させる
2 v/i (of competitor) mi o hiku 身
を引く; (of troops) tettai suru 撤退
する

withdrawal (of complaint,
application) torikeshi 取り消し;
(of money) hikidashi 引き出し; (of
troops) tettai 撤退; (from drugs)

shiyō-chūshi 使用中止

withdrawal symptoms kindan-shōjō 禁断症状

withdrawn *adj person* hikkomigachi (na) 引っ込みがち (な)

wither kareru 枯れる

withhold *consent, payment* horyū suru 保留する; *information, name* kakusu 隠す

within *prep* (*inside*) … no naka de …の中で; (*in expressions of time*) …inai de …以内で; (*in expressions of distance*) … no han'inai de …の範囲内で; **we kept ~ the budget** watashitachi wa yosan nai ni osamemashita 私達は予算内に収めました; *~ my power* watashi no chikara no oyobu han'i de 私の力の及ぶ範囲で; *~ reach* te no todoku tokoro ni 手の届くところに

without …nashi de …なしで; *~ looking* / *~ asking* nani mo minaide / nani mo shitsumon shinaide 何も見ないで/何も質問しないで

withstand …ni taeru …に耐える

witness 1 *n* (*at trial*) shōnin 証人; (*of accident, crime*) mokugeki-sha 目撃者; (*to signature*) hoshō-nin 保証人 **2** *v/t accident, crime* mokugeki suru 目撃する; *signature* hoshō-nin toshite sain suru 保証人としてサインする

witness stand shōninseki 証人席

witticism jōdan 冗談

witty yūmoa no aru ユーモアのある

wobble *table* fuantei (na) 不安定 (な); *voice* furueru 震える

wobbly *table* fuantei (na) 不安定 (な); *voice* furueru 震える

wolf 1 *n* (*animal*) ōkami おおかみ; *fig* (*womanizer*) onnatarashi 女たらし **2** *v/t*: *~* (*down*) gatsugatsu taberu がつがつ食べる

wolf whistle *n josei ni mukete dansei ga narasu kuchibue* 女性に向けて男性がならす口笛

woman josei 女性

woman doctor joi 女医

womanizer onnatarashi 女たらし

womanly onna-rashii 女らしい

woman priest josei-shisai 女性司祭

womb shikyū 子宮

women's lib ūman ribu ウーマンリブ

women's libber ūman ribu no katsudōka ウーマンリブの活動家

wonder 1 *n* (*amazement*) odoroki 驚き; *no ~!* tōzen da 当然だ; *it's a ~ that* … wa odoroki da …は驚きだ **2** *v/i* … no koto o kangaeru …の事を考える **3** *v/t*: *I ~ why she said that* naze kanojo ga sō itta no ka na to omou なぜ彼女がそういったのかなと思う; *I ~ what he's like* kare wa donna hito kashira 彼はどんな人かしら; *I ~ if you could help* tetsudatte kudasaimasen ka 手伝って下さいませんか

wonderful subarashii 素晴らしい

wood mokuzai 木材; (*forest*) hayashi 林

wooded ki de ōwareta 木で覆われた

wooden (*made of wood*) mokusei (no) 木製(の)

woodpecker kitsutsuki きつつき; **woodwind** MUS mokkan-gakki pāto 木管楽器パート; **woodwork** (*wooden parts*) mokuzōbu 木造部; (*activity*) mokkō-zaiku 木工細工

wool keito 毛糸

woolen 1 *adj* ūru (no) ウール(の) **2** *n* ūru ウール

word 1 *n* ◊ (*unit of language*) tango 単語; *this is a new ~* kore wa atarashii tango desu これは新しい単語です ◊ (*with a number, in linguistics*) go 語; *500 ~s* gohyaku-go 500語 ◊ (*way of expressing sth*) kotoba 言葉; *there is no ~ for it in* … … go niwa sono kotoba wa nai …語にはその言葉はない; *a polite ~ for* … … no teinei na kotoba …のていねいな言葉 ◊ (*news*) shirase 知らせ; *is there any ~ from* …? …kara nani ka shirase ga atta …から何か知らせがあった; ◊ (*promise*) yakusoku 約束; *you have my ~* yakusoku shimasu 約束します◊ (*of song*): *~s* kashi 歌詞◊ (*expressions*): **have ~s** (*argue*) kuchigenka suru 口げんかする; *have a ~ with* ... to hanasu ...と話す **2** *v/t article, letter* kotoba o erabu 言葉を選ぶ

wording iimawashi 言い回し

word processing wāpuro de no bunsho-sakusei ワープロでの文書作成

word processor (*software*) wāpuro ワープロ

work 1 *n* shigoto 仕事; (*of art, literature*) sakuhin 作品; *be out of ~* shitsugyō shite iru 失業している; *be at ~* shigotochū de aru 仕事中である; *I go to ~ by bus* basu de tsūkin suru バスで通勤する **2** *v/i* (*of person*) hataraku 働く; (*study*) benkyō suru 勉強する; (*of machine*) ugoku 動く; (*succeed*) kiku 効く; *what are you ~ing on?* ima nani ni torikunde imasu ka 今何に取り組んでいますか; *I used to ~ with him* watashi wa izen kare to hataraite imashita 私は以前彼と働いていました; *how does it ~?* (*of device*) dō iu fū ni ugoku no desu ka どういう風に動くのですか **3** *v/t employee* hatarakaseru 働かせる; *student* benkyō saseru 勉強させる; *machine* ugokasu 動かす

♦ **work off** *bad mood, anger* ... no uppun o harasu ...のうっぷんを晴らす; *flab* ... o herasu ...を減らす

♦ **work out 1** *v/t problem* ... o kaiketsu suru ...を解決する; *solution* ... o mitsukeru ...を見つける **2** *v/i* (*at gym*) torēningu suru トレーニングする; (*of relationship etc*) umaku iku うまく行く

♦ **work out to** (*add up to*) ... ni naru ...になる

♦ **work up** *enthusiasm* ... o hikiokosu ...を引き起こす; *appetite* ... o okosaseru ...を起こさせる; *get worked up* (*angry*) ki ga tatsu 気が立つ; (*nervous*) iraira suru いらいらする

workable *solution* jikkō dekiru 実行できる

workaholic *n* shigoto-chūdoku 仕事中毒

worker rōdō-sha 労働者; (*in office*) sararīman サラリーマン; *she's a good ~* (*of student*) kanojo wa yoku benkyō suru 彼女はよく勉強する

work day (*hours of work*) shūgyō-jikan 就業時間; (*not a holiday*) kinmubi 勤務日; **workforce** rōdōryoku 労働力; **work hours** kinmu-jikan 勤務時間

working class rōdōsha-kaikyū 労働者階級; **working-class** rōdōsha-kaikyū (no) 労働者階級(の); **working knowledge** kiso-chishiki 基礎知識

workload shigotoryō 仕事量; **workman** shokunin 職人; **work-manlike** takumi (na) 巧み(な); **workmanship** dekibae 出来栄え; **work of art** geijutsu-sakuhin 芸術作品; **workout** torēningu トレーニング; **work permit** rōdō-biza 労働ビザ; **workshop** sagyōba 作業場; (*seminar*) wāku-shoppu ワークショップ; **work station** wāku-sutēshon ワークステーション

world sekai 世界; *the ~ of computers / the theater* konpyūtā / engeki no sekai コンピューター/演劇の世界; *out of this ~* F tobikiri (no) とびきり(の)

worldly sezokuteki (na) 世俗的(な); *person* sesai ni taketa 世才にたけた; *~ goods* zaisan 財産

world power sekaiteki-kyōkoku 世界的強国

world war sekaitaisen 世界大戦

worldwide 1 *adj* sekaiteki (na) 世界的(な) **2** *adv* sekaijū ni 世界中に

worm *n* mimizu みみず

worn-out *shoes, carpet, part* tsukaifurushita 使い古した; *person* hetoheto ni naru へとへとになる

worried shinpaisō (na) 心配そう(な)

worry 1 *n* shinpai 心配 **2** *v/t* shinpai saseru 心配させる; (*upset*) ... ga ki ni naru ...が気になる **3** *v/i* shinpai suru 心配する; *it will* *be alright, don't ~!* daijōbu dakara shinpai shinaide 大丈夫だから心配しないで

worrying shinpai (na) 心配(な)

worse 1 *adj* sara ni warui 更に悪い **2** *adv* sara ni waruku 更に悪く

worsen *v/i* akka suru 悪化する

worship 1 *n* sūhai 崇拝 **2** *v/t* sūhai suru 崇拝する; *fig* netsuai suru 熱愛する

worst 1 *adj* saiaku (no) 最悪(の) **2** *adv* mottomo hidoku 最もひどく **3** *n: the ~* saiaku no jitai 最悪の事態; *the ~ of the bad weather* akutenkō no saiaku no bubun 悪天候の最悪の部分; *if the ~ comes to ~* saiaku no bāi ni wa 最悪の場合には

worth *adj: $20 ~ of gas* nijū doru bun no gasorin 二十ドル分のガソリン; *be ~ (in monetary terms)* ... no kachi ga aru ...の価値がある; *be ~ reading / seeing* yomu / miru kachi ga aru 読む/見る価値がある; *be ~ it* yaru kachi ga aru やる価値がある

worthless *object* kachi ga nai 価値がない; *person* yakutatazu (no) 役立たず(の)

worthwhile *cause* tame ni naru ためになる; *be ~ (beneficial, useful)* yaku ni tatsu 役に立つ; *(worth the effort, worth doing)* ... suru kachi ga aru ...する価値がある

worthy ... ni fusawashii ...にふさわしい; *cause* ... ni atai suru ...に値する; *be ~ of (deserve)* ... ni atai suru ...に値する

would: *I ~ help if I could* dekireba tetsudaimasu できれば手伝います; *I said that I ~ go* watashi wa iku to iimashita 私は行くと言いました; *I told him I ~ not leave unless ....* kare ni... de nakereba dete ikanai to iimashita 彼に...でなければ出て行かないと言いました; *~ you like to go to the movies?* eiga ni ikimasen ka 映画に行きませんか; *~ you mind if I smoked?* tabako o sutte mo ii desu ka タバコをすってもいいですか; *~ you tell*

her that ...? ... to kanojo ni tsutaete moraemasu ka ...と彼女に伝えてもらえますか; *~ you close the door?* doa o shimete moraemasu ka ドアを締めてもらえますか; *I ~ not have been so angry if ...* moshi ... nara watashi wa sonna ni okoranakatta deshō もし...なら私はそんなに怒らなかったでしょう

wound 1 *n* kizu 傷 **2** *v/t (with weapon,)* ... ni kizu o owaseru ...に傷を負わせる; *(with remark)* kizutsukeru 傷つける

wow *interj* wā' わー

wrap *v/t* *parcel, gift* tsutsumu 包む; *(wind, cover)* maku 巻く

♦ **wrap up** *v/i (against the cold)* atatakai fukusō o suru 暖かい服装をする

wrapper *(on candy etc)* tsutsumi 包み; *(of book)* kabā カバー

wrapping hōsō-zairyō 包装材料

wrapping paper hōsōshi 包装紙

wreath hanawa 花輪

wreck 1 *n* zangai 残がい; *(of ship)* nanpasen 難破船; *be a nervous ~* shinkei ga maitte iru 神経が参っている **2** *v/t* *ship* nanpa saseru 難破させる; *car, plans, career, marriage* dainashi ni suru 台無しにする

wreckage *(of car, plane)* zangai 残がい

wrecker rekkā-sha レッカー車

wrecking company jikosha-toriatsukai-gyōsha 事故車取扱業者

wrench 1 *n (tool)* supana スパナ; *(injury)* nenza ねんざ **2** *v/t (injure)* nenza suru ねんざする; *(pull)* mogitoru もぎ取る

wrestle ... to kakutō suru ...と格闘する

♦ **wrestle with** *problems* ... ni torikumu ...に取り組む

wrestler resurā レスラー

wrestling resuringu レスリング

wrestling contest resuringu no shiai レスリングの試合

wriggle *v/i (squirm)* kunekune suru

くねくねする; (*along the ground*) hau はう
♦ **wriggle out of** ... o kirinukeru ... を切り抜ける
♦ **wring out** *v/t cloth* ... o shiboru ... を絞る
wrinkle 1 *n* shiwa しわ **2** *v/t clothes* shiwa o yoseru しわを寄せる **3** *v/i* (*of clothes*) shiwa ga yoru しわが寄る
wrist tekubi 手首
wristwatch udedokei 腕時計
write 1 *v/t* kaku 書く; *check* kiru 切る **2** *v/i* ji o kaku 字を書く; (*of author*) hon o kaku 本を書く; (*send a letter*) tegami o kaku 手紙を書く
♦ **write down** ... o kakitomeru ... を書き留める
♦ **write off** *debt* ... o chōkeshi ni suru ... を帳消しにする; *car* ... o shūri-fukanō ni suru ... を修理不可能にする
writer sakka 作家; (*of a document etc*) kaki 書き手
write-up hihyō 批評
writhe *v/i* mimodae suru 身もだえ

writing (*as career*) chojutsugyō 著述業; (*hand-~*) hisseki 筆跡; (*words*) bunshō 文章; (*script*) moji 文字; **in ~** shomen de 書面で
writing paper binsen 便せん
wrong 1 *adj* machigatta 間違った; (*morally*) yokunai 良くない; **be ~** (*of person, answer, clock*) machigatte iru 間違っている; (*morally*) yoku nai koto da 良くないことだ; **what's ~?** dōshita no どうしたの; **there is something ~ with the car** kono kuruma wa dokoka okashii この車はどこかおかしい **2** *adv* machigatte 間違って; **go ~** (*of person*) machigau 間違う; (*of marriage, plan etc*) umaku ikanai うまくいかない **3** *n* fusei 不正; **be in the ~** machigatte iru 間違っている
wrongful futō (na) 不当(な)
wrongly machigatte 間違って
wrong number bangō-machigai 番号間違い
wry hinikuppoi 皮肉っぽい

X

xenophobia gaikokujin-girai 外国人嫌い
X-ray 1 *n* ekkusu-sen X線; (*picture*) rentogen-shashin レントゲン **2** *v/t* ... no rentogen-shashin o toru ...のレントゲン写真を撮る

Y

yacht yotto ヨット
yachting yotto-asobi ヨット遊び
yachtsman yottonori ヨット乗り
Yank *n* F yankī ヤンキー

yank *v/t* hipparu 引っ張る
yap *v/i* (*of dog*) kyankyan hoeru きゃんきゃんほえる; F (*talk a lot*) pechakucha shaberu ぺちゃくちゃ

しゃべる

yard[1] (*of prison, institution etc*) kōnai 構内; (*behind house*) uraniwa 裏庭; (*for storage*) okiba 置き場

yard[2] (*measurement*) yādo ヤード

yardstick handan no shakudo 判断の尺度

yarn n (*thread*) ito 糸; F (*story*) horabanashi ほら話

yawn 1 n akubi あくび **2** v/i akubi suru あくびする

year toshi 年; (*with count word*) nen 年; *two/three ~s* ni/san nen 二/三年; *for ~s* nannen mo 何年も; *this ~* kotoshi 今年; *next ~* rainen 来年; *last ~* kyonen 去年; *12 ~s old* jūni-sai 十二歳

yearly 1 adj salary ichinenkan (no) 1年間(の); event, result maitoshi (no) 毎年(の) **2** adv maitoshi 毎年

yearn v/i setsubō suru 切望する
♦**yearn for** ... ni akogareru ...にあこがれる

yearning n akogare あこがれ

yeast īsuto イースト

yell 1 n sakebigoe 叫び声 **2** v/i sakebu 叫ぶ **3** v/t ... to sakebu ...と叫ぶ

yellow 1 n kiiro 黄色 **2** adj kiiro (no) 黄色(の)

yellow pages ierōpēji イエローページ

yelp 1 n himei 悲鳴 **2** v/i himei o ageru 悲鳴をあげる

yen FIN en 円

yes hai はい; *John! – ~?* Jon – nani ジョン - なに; ◊ (*using 'no', ie no, that is not right*): *you don't know the answer, do you? – oh –, I do* kotae ga wakaranai deshō-iie wakarimasu 答えがわからないんでしょう-いいえ、わかります

yesman pej iesuman イエスマン

yesterday kinō 昨日; *the day before ~* ototoi おととい

yet adv kore made de これまでで; *as ~* mada まだ; *have you finished ~?* mō owarimashita ka もう終わりましたか; *he hasn't*

arrived ~ mada kare wa kite imasen まだ彼は来ていません; *is he here ~? – not ~* mō kare wa kimashita ka – mada desu もう彼はきましたか - まだです; *~ bigger/longer* sara ni ōkiku/nagaku さらに大きく/長く **2** conj soredemo それでも; *~ I'm not sure* soredemo yoku wakarimasen それでもよくわかりません

yield 1 n (*from fields*) shūkaku 収穫; (*from investment*) rieki 利益 **2** v/t fruit, interest motarasu もたらす **3** v/i (*give way*) yuzuru 譲る

yoghurt yōguruto ヨーグルト

Yokohama Yokohama 横浜

yolk kimi 黄身

you ◊ (*singular: polite*) anata あなた; (*familiar*) kimi きみ; (*plural: polite*) anatatachi あなたたち; (*familiar*) kimitachi きみたち; *~ are very kind* anata wa totemo shinsetsu da あなたはとても親切だ; *he knows ~* kare wa anata o shitte imasu 彼はあなたを知っています; *I told ~ you before* anata ni mae ni hanashimashita あなたに前に話しました ◊ (*omission of pronoun*): *are ~ sure?* honto ほんと ◊ (*impersonal*): *~ never know* dō naru ka wakarimasen ne どうなるかわかりませんね; *it's good for ~* tame ni naru ためになる

young wakai 若い

youngster wakamono 若者

your ◊ (*singular: polite*) anata no あなたの; (*familiar*) kimi no きみの; (*plural: polite*) anatatachi no あなたたちの; (*familiar*) kimitachi no きみたちの ◊ (*omission of possessive*): *did you bring ~ passport?* pasupōto motte kimashita ka パスポート持ってきましたか

yours (*singular: polite*) anata no mono あなたのもの; (*familiar*) kimi no mono きみのもの; (*plural: polite*) anatatachi no mono あなたたちのもの; (*familiar*) kimitachi no mono きみたちのもの; *a friend* of ~ anata no tomodachi no hitori あなたの友達の一人; **Yours ...** (*at end of letter*) keigu 敬具

yourself: **did you hurt ~?** (*polite*) anata wa kega o shimashita ka あなたはけがをしましたか; (*familiar*) kimi wa kega o shita no きみはけがをしたの; **did you see ~ in the mirror?** anata wa jibun de kagami o mimashita ka あなたは自分で鏡を見ましたか; **by ~** (*alone*) hitori de ひとりで; (*without help*) jibun de 自分で

yourselves: **did you hurt ~?** (*polite*) anatatachi wa kega o

shimashita ka あなた達はけがをしましたか; (*familiar*) kimitachi wa kega o shita no きみ達はけがをしたの; **did you see ~ in the mirror?** anatatachi wa jibun de kagami o mimashita ka あなた達は自分で鏡を見ましたか; **by ~** (*alone*) anatatachi dake de あなた達だけで; (*without help*) jibuntachi de 自分達で

youth (*young man*) seinen 青年; (*young people*) seishōnen 青少年

youthful wakawakashii 若々しい

youth hostel yūsu-hosuteru ユースホステル

Z

zap *v/t* COMPUT (*delete*) sakujo suru 削除する; F (*kill*) korosu 殺す; F (*hit*) naguru なぐる

♦ **zap along** F (*move fast*) subayaku ugokimawaru すばやく動き回る

zapped F (*exhausted*) kutakuta (no) くたくた(の)

zappy F *car*, *pace* kibikibi shita きびきびした; (*lively*) ikiiki shita いきいきした; (*energetic*) seiryokuteki (na) 精力的(な)

zeal netsujō 熱情

zebra shimauma しまうま

Zen Zen 禅

Zen Buddhism Zenshū 禅宗

zero zero ゼロ; **10 below ~** reika jūdo 零下10度

zero growth zero-seichō ゼロ成長

♦ **zero in on** (*identify*) ... ni shūchū suru ...に集中する

zest (*zeal*) netsui 熱意

zigzag 1 *n* jiguzagu ジグザグ **2** *v/i* jiguzagu ni susumu ジグザグに進む

zilch F nani mo 何も

zinc aen 亜鉛

♦ **zip up** *v/t dress*, *jacket* ... no fasunā o shimeru ...のファスナーを締める; COMPUT asshuku suru 圧縮する

zip code yūbin-bangō 郵便番号

zipper fasunā ファスナー

zodiac kōdōtai 黄道帯; **signs of the ~** seiza 星座

zombie F (*barely human person*) zonbi ゾンビ; **feel like a ~** (*exhausted*) hetoheto ni tsukarete iru へとへとに疲れている

zone chitai 地帯

zoo dōbutsuen 動物園

zoological dōbutsugaku (no) 動物学(の)

zoology dōbutsugaku 動物学

zoom F (*move fast*) mōsupīdo de susumu 猛スピードで進む

♦ **zoom in on** PHOT ... o kurōzu-appu suru ...をクローズアップする

zoom lens zūmu-renzu ズームレンズ

Numbers and Dates

0	**zero, rei**	ゼロ, 零
1	**ichi**	一
2	**ni**	二
3	**san**	三
4	**yon, shi**	四
5	**go**	五
6	**roku**	六
7	**nana, shichi**	七
8	**hachi**	八
9	**kyū**	九
10	**jū**	十
11	**jū-ichi**	十一
12	**jū-ni**	十二
13	**jū-san**	十三
20	**ni-jū**	二十
21	**ni-jū-ichi**	二十一
30	**san-jū**	三十
35	**san-jū-go**	三十五
40	**yon-jū**	四十
50	**go-jū**	五十
60	**roku-jū**	六十
70	**nana-jū**	七十
80	**hachi-jū**	八十
90	**kyū-jū**	九十
100	**hyaku**	百
101	**hyaku-ichi**	百一
200	**ni-hyaku**	二百
300	**san-byaku**	三百
400	**yon-hyaku**	四百
500	**go-hyaku**	五百
600	**rop-pyaku**	六百
700	**nana-hyaku**	七百
800	**hap-pyaku**	八百
900	**kyū-hyaku**	九百
1,000	**sen**	千
2,000	**ni-sen**	二千
3,000	**san-zen**	三千
4,000	**yon-sen**	四千
5,000	**go-sen**	五千
6,000	**roku-sen**	六千
7,000	**nana-sen**	七千
8,000	**hass-sen**	八千
9,000	**kyū-sen**	九千
10,000	**ichi-man**	一万
20,000	**ni-man**	二万
100,000	**jū-man**	十万
1,000,000	**hyaku-man**	百万
2,000,000	**ni-hyaku-man**	二百万

10,000,000	**sen-man**	千万
100,000,000	**ichi-oku**	一億

Ordinal numbers

Ordinal numbers are formed by putting **dai** in front of the cardinal numbers:

1st	**dai-ichi**	第一
2nd	**dai-ni**	第二
3rd	**dai-san**	第三

Dates

1st	**tsuitachi**	一日
2nd	**futsuka**	二日
3rd	**mikka**	三日
4th	**yokka**	四日
5th	**itsuka**	五日
6th	**muika**	六日
7th	**nanoka**	七日
8th	**yōka**	八日
9th	**kokonoka**	九日
10th	**tōka**	十日
11th	**jū-ichi-nichi**	十一日
12th	**jū-ni-nichi**	十二日
13th	**jū-san-nichi**	十三日
14th	**jū-yokka**	十四日
15th	**jū-go-nichi**	十五日
16th	**jū-roku-nichi**	十六日
17th	**jū-nana-nichi**	十七日
18th	**jū-hachi-nichi**	十八日
19th	**jū-ku-nichi**	十九日
20th	**hatsuka**	二十日
21st	**ni-jū-ichi-nichi**	二十一日
22nd	**ni-jū-ni-nichi**	二十二日
23rd	**ni-jū-san-nichi**	二十三日
24th	**ni-jū-yokka**	二十四日
25th	**ni-jū-go-nichi**	二十五日
26th	**ni-jū-roku-nichi**	二十六日
27th	**ni-jū-nana-nichi**	二十七日
28th	**ni-jū-hachi-nichi**	二十八日
29th	**ni-jū-ku-nichi**	二十九日
30th	**san-jū-nichi**	三十日
31st	**san-jū-ichi-nichi**	三十一日